Lecture Notes in Computer Science   9841

Commenced Publication in 1973
Founding and Former Series Editors:
Gerhard Goos, Juris Hartmanis, and Jan van Leeuwen

More information about this series at http://www.springer.com/series/7410

Vassilis Zikas · Roberto De Prisco (Eds.)

Security and Cryptography for Networks

10th International Conference, SCN 2016
Amalfi, Italy, August 31 – September 2, 2016
Proceedings

 Springer

Editors
Vassilis Zikas
Rensselaer Polytechnic Institute
Troy, NY
USA

Roberto De Prisco
University of Salerno
Fisciano
Italy

ISSN 0302-9743   ISSN 1611-3349   (electronic)
Lecture Notes in Computer Science
ISBN 978-3-319-44617-2   ISBN 978-3-319-44618-9   (eBook)
DOI 10.1007/978-3-319-44618-9

Library of Congress Control Number: 2016947481

LNCS Sublibrary: SL4 – Security and Cryptology

Preface

The 10th Conference on Security and Cryptography for Networks (SCN 2016) was held in Amalfi, Italy, from August 31 to September 2, 2016. The conference has traditionally been held in Amalfi, with the exception of the fifth edition that was held in the nearby Maiori. The first three editions of the conference were held in 1996, 1999, and 2002. Since 2002, the conference has been held biannually.

Modern communication is achieved mostly through the use of computer networks. Computer networks bring many advantages, such as easy access to information and fast communication. However guaranteeing security of distributed transactions is a challenging task. The SCN conference is an international meeting whose goal is to bring together researchers, practitioners, and developers interested in the security of communication networks, in order to foster cooperation, facilitate exchange of ideas, and disseminate research results.

The conference received 67 submissions in a broad range of cryptography and security areas. The Program Committee has selected, among the many high-quality submissions, 30 technical papers for publication in these proceedings. The selection took into account quality, originality, and relevance to the conference's scope. In addition, this year we received a crypto-lyrics paper titled "Zero-Knowledge Made Easy So It Won't Make You Dizzy" that the Program Committee found to be of great quality and therefore decided to grant it a special slot in the proceedings. It is our hope that this can motivate more of these high-quality creative and entertaining types of submissions in the future.

The international Program Committee (PC) consisted of 32 members who are top experts in the conference fields. At least three PC members reviewed each submitted paper, while submissions co-authored by a PC member were subjected to the more stringent evaluation of four PC members. In addition to the PC members, many external reviewers joined the review process in their particular areas of expertise. We were fortunate to have this knowledgeable and energetic team of experts, and are deeply grateful to all of them for their hard and thorough work, which included a very active discussion phase. Special thanks to Jeremiah Blocki, Alessandra Scafuro, Susumu Kiyoshima, Dimitris Papadopoulos, Juan Garay, and Sanjam Garg, for their extra work as shepherds.

The program was further enriched by the invited talks of Aggelos Kiayias (University of Edinburgh, UK) and Rafael Pass (Cornell University and Cornell NYC Tech, USA).

SCN 2016 was organized in cooperation with the International Association for Cryptologic Research (IACR). The paper submission, review, and discussion processes were effectively and efficiently made possible by the IACR Web-Submission-and-Review software, written by Shai Halevi. Many thanks to Shai for his assistance with the system's various features and constant availability.

We thank all the authors who submitted papers to this conference, the Organizing Committee members, colleagues, and student helpers for their valuable time and effort, and all the conference attendees who made this event truly intellectually stimulating through their active participation.

We finally thank the Dipartimento di Informatica of the Università degli Studi di Salerno, InfoCert, and the Università degli Studi di Salerno for their financial support.

September 2016   Vassilis Zikas
                                                                Roberto De Prisco

SCN 2016

The 10th Conference on
Security and Cryptography for Networks

Amalfi, Italy
August 31 to September 2, 2016

Organized by
Dipartimento di Informatica
Università di Salerno

In Cooperation with
The International Association for Cryptologic Research (IACR)

Program Chair

Vassilis Zikas   Rensselaer Polytechnic Institute (RPI), USA

General Chair

Roberto De Prisco   Università di Salerno, Italy

Organizing Committee

Carlo Blundo   Università di Salerno, Italy
Aniello Castiglione   Università di Salerno, Italy
Luigi Catuogno   Università di Salerno, Italy
Paolo D'Arco   Università di Salerno, Italy

Steering Committee

Alfredo De Santis   Università di Salerno, Italy
Ueli Maurer   ETH Zürich, Switzerland
Rafail Ostrovsky   University of California - Los Angeles, USA
Giuseppe Persiano   Università di Salerno, Italy
Jacques Stern   ENS, France
Douglas Stinson   University of Waterloo, Canada
Gene Tsudik   University of California - Irvine, USA
Moti Yung   Snapchat and Columbia University, USA

Program Committee

Divesh Aggarwal   EPFL, Switzerland
Shweta Agrawal   Indian Institute of Technology, India
Joël Alwen   IST, Austria

External Reviewers

Eyal Kushilevitz
Kim Laine
Joshua Lampkins
Adeline Langlois
Enrique Larraia
Tancrede Lepoint
Satyanarayana Lokam
Bernardo Machado David
Rusydi Makarim
Antonio Marcedone
Nico Marcel Döttling
Alexander May
Sebastian Meiser
Peihan Miao
Sonia Mihaela Bogos
Katerina Mitrokotsa
Pratyay Mukherjee

Kartik Nayak
Dimitris Papadopoulos
Kostas Papagiannopoulos
Alain Passelgue
Antigoni Polychroniadou
Ishaan Preet Singh
Srinivasan Raghuraman
Somindu Ramanna
Kim Ramchen
Vanishree Rao
Tom Ristenpart
Abhi shelat
Katerina Samari
Daniel Slamanig
Nigel Smart
Pratik Soni
Akshayaram Srinivasan

Douglas Stebila
Bjoern Tackmann
Qiang Tang
Alin Tomescu
Roberto Trifiletti
Daniel Tschudi
Daniele Venturi
Frederik Vercauteren
Ivan Visconti
Michael Walter
Xiao Wang
Udi Weinsberg
Sophia Yabukov
Yupeng Zhang
Joe Zimmerman

Sponsoring Institutions

Dipartimento di Informatica, Università di Salerno, Italy

InfoCert, Rome, Italy

Università di Salerno, Italy

Abstracts of Invited Talks

Foundations of Blockchain Protocols

Aggelos Kiayias

School of Informatics, University of Edinburgh, 10 Crichton St.,
Edinburgh EH8 6AB, UK
Aggelos.Kiayias@ed.ac.uk

Abstract. The bitcoin system is a remarkable solution. But to what problem? The rise of bitcoin and other cryptocurrencies puts forth a wealth of interesting questions in distributed systems and cryptography that relate to building decentralized systems. We initiate a formal investigation of this class of protocols and of their basic properties.

The core of the bitcoin protocol can be abstracted in a simple algorithmic form that has been termed the bitcoin backbone in [1]. This work also provided a synchronous model for the analysis of the protocol. This algorithmic abstraction and modeling enabled the expression of simple provable properties about the blockchain data structure maintained by the protocol called chain quality, common prefix and chain growth. In this model, the concept of a robust transaction ledger can also be defined and analyzed as captured by its two basic properties, persistence and liveness. Given the above we show how a robust transaction ledger can be reduced to a blockchain protocol that satisfies these simple properties, cf. [2]. Alternative proof strategies are possible and will be also examined.

Given our formal definition of the robust transaction ledger problem, one can ask next whether the bitcoin backbone is the optimal solution. One important aspect of efficiency is the overhead to confirm transactions in the presence of an adversary, cf. [3], which is intimately related to the liveness of the ledger. Alternative designs such as GHOST used in the Ethereum system, are possible and will be analyzed and compared within the model with respect to their security and efficiency characteristics.

Finally, the relation of a robust transaction ledger to the consensus problem will be also examined and we will consider a number of model extensions that include rational players and dynamically changing user sets.

References

1. Garay, J.A., Kiayias, A., Leonardos, N.: The Bitcoin backbone protocol: analysis and applications. In: Oswald, E., Fischlin, M. (eds.) EUROCRYPT 2015. LNCS, vol. 9057, pp. 281–310. Springer, Berlin

A. Kiayias—Most of the work reported performed while at the National and Kapodistrian University of Athens. Research was supported by ERC project CODAMODA # 259152.

2. Kiayias, A., Panagiotakos, G.: Speed-Security Tradeoffs in Blockchain Protocols. IACR Cryptology ePrint Archive 2015: 1019 (2015)
3. Kiayias, A., Panagiotakos, G.: On Trees, Chains and Fast Transactions in the Blockchain. IACR Cryptology ePrint Archive 2016: 545 (2016)

Cryptography and Game Theory

Rafael Pass

Cornell Tech, New York, USA
rafael@cs.cornell.edu

Abstract. Cryptographic notions of knowledge consider the knowledge obtained, or possessed, by *computationally-bounded* agents under *adversarial* conditions. In this talk, we will survey some recent cryptographically-inspired approaches for reasoning about agents in the context of game-theory and mechanism design (where agents typically are modelled as computationally *unbounded*).

R. Pass—Supported in part by NSF Award CNS-1217821, NSF Award TWC-1561209, AFOSR Award FA9550-15-1-0262, a Microsoft Faculty Fellowship, and a Google Faculty Research Award.

Contents

Encryption

Memory Protection

Multi-party Computation

Zero-Knowledge Proofs

Efficient Protocols

Outsourcing Computation

Digital Signatures

Cryptanalysis

Two-party Computation

Secret Sharing

Obfuscation

Encryption

A Tag Based Encoding:
An Efficient Encoding for Predicate Encryption in Prime Order Groups

Jongkil Kim[1][⊠], Willy Susilo[1], Fuchun Guo[1], and Man Ho Au[2]

[1] Centre of Computer and Information Security Research,
School of Computing and Information Technology, University of Wollongong,
Wollongong, Australia
{jk057,wsusilo,fuchun}@uow.edu.au
[2] The Hong Kong Polytechnic University, Hung Hom, Hong Kong
csallen@comp.polyu.edu.hk

Abstract. We introduce a *tag based encoding*, a new generic framework for modular design of Predicate Encryption (PE) schemes in prime order groups. Our framework is equipped with a compiler which is adaptively secure in prime order groups under the standard Decisional Linear Assumption (DLIN). Compared with prior encoding frameworks in prime order groups which require multiple group elements to interpret a tuple of an encoding in a real scheme, our framework has a distinctive feature which is that each element of an encoding can be represented with only a group element and an integer. This difference allows us to construct a more efficient encryption scheme. In the current literature, the most efficient compiler was proposed by Chen, Gay and Wee (CGW) in Eurocrypt'15. It features one tuple of an encoding into two group elements under the Symmetric External Diffie-Hellman assumption (SXDH). Compared with their compiler, our encoding construction saves the size of either private keys or ciphertexts up-to 25 % and reduces decryption time and the size of public key up-to 50 % in 128 security level. Several new schemes such as inner product encryption with short keys, dual spatial encryption with short keys and hierarchical identity based encryption with short ciphertexts are also introduced as instances of our encoding.

Keywords: Encodings · Prime order groups · Inner product encryption · Spatial encryption · Predicate encryption

1 Introduction

Predicate Encryption (PE) is a public key cryptographic system supporting a fine-grained access control. PE schemes have been proposed to support various types of predicates, but many of them share similar features in their constructions and security proofs. Two independent works [2,30] have been presented by observing the coupling of PE. They formalized common features of PE schemes in

© Springer International Publishing Switzerland 2016
V. Zikas and R. De Prisco (Eds.): SCN 2016, LNCS 9841, pp. 3–22, 2016.
DOI: 10.1007/978-3-319-44618-9_1

composite order groups by encoding predicate parts of the schemes. Those encoding frameworks provide a new direction of proving security since one can show security of a PE scheme by only proving that an encoding satisfies the syntax required in the framework. Therefore, the encoding frameworks provide a new insight of properties leading to adaptive security.

Despite the advantage, the usage of encoding frameworks [2,30] were limited since they were introduced only in composite order groups. It is well known that composite order groups significantly harm the efficiency of encryption systems [13,14,21]. According to Guillevic [14], to achieve 128 bits security level, the minimum group orders for prime order and composite order bilinear group are 256 and 2,644 bits, resp. Moreover, a pairing computation in composite order groups is about 254 times slower than that of prime order bilinear groups. Hence, constructing adaptively secure PE schemes in prime order groups is desirable to ensure that they are adoptable in practice.

Recently, Chen, Gay and Wee (CGW) presented a dual system attribute based encryption [8] which can be considered as a new compiler in prime order groups for the predicate encoding [30]. They introduced compilers in prime order groups by adopting Dual System Groups (DSG) [9]. In the most efficient compiler of theirs, one composite order group element [30] is represented by two prime order elements. Independently, Attrapadung [3] and Agrawal and Chase [1] also proposed other compilers in prime order groups, but they showed similar results from an efficiency perspective[1]. All existing compilers show a similar behavior from an efficiency perspective. Specifically, the number of parameters and computation of the resulting scheme in the prime order group is always bounded below by a multiplicative factor, say n, of their counterparts in the composite order groups. The best compiler achieves a factor of $n = 2$ under SXDH assumption in [1,8]. Moreover, in [1,3,8] $n = 3$ is achieved under the DLIN assumption which is weaker than the SXDH assumption. This appears to be the lower bound of the techniques of dual system groups with orthogonal vectors since the size of vectors must be at least 2 to "simulate" the properties of a composite order group. Therefore, it remains an interesting research problem to achieve PE schemes in prime order groups without using vector properties since it may imply more efficient schemes.

1.1　Our Contribution

We introduce a *tag based encoding*, a new generic framework for PE schemes in prime order groups. Compared with prior encoding frameworks in prime order groups, our framework improves the efficiency of prior encodings when the size of an encoding scheme is large. Our encoding framework does not use DPVS, DSG or composite order groups. Instead, we utilize *tag*s to construct adaptively secure

---

[1] Attrapadung's compiler [3] needs three group elements for a tuple of an encoding under the DLIN assumption. Agrawal and Chase's compiler [1] requires two group elements under the SXDH assumption and three group elements under the DLIN assumption.

Predicates and functions	Encodings	Compiler	Schemes
$(x, y) \in \mathcal{X} \times \mathcal{Y}$	$\mathbf{kE}(x, \cdot)$	Setup KeyGen	PE
$R : \mathcal{X} \times \mathcal{Y} \to \{0, 1\}$ $\longrightarrow$	$\mathbf{cE}(y, \cdot)$ $\longrightarrow$	Encryption $\longrightarrow$ Decryption	(IBE, HIBE, IPE, ...)

Fig. 1. Encoding frameworks for PE

Table 1. An efficiency comparison between our and CGW's compilers [8].

	Assump.	PK	SK	CT
CGW [8]	SXDH	$(2\ell+3)|G_1| + |G_T|$	$2(m_k+1)|G_2|$	$2(m_c+1)|G_1| + |G_T|$
	DLIN	$(6\ell+8)|G_1| + 2|G_T|$	$3(m_k+1)|G_2|$	$3(m_c+1)|G_1| + |G_T|$
Ours	DLIN	$(\ell+11)|G_1| + |G_T|$	$(m_k+7)|G_2| + m_k|\mathbb{Z}_p|$	$(m_c+8)|G_1| + m_c|\mathbb{Z}_p| + |G_T|$

	Assump.	PK (by bits)	SK (by bits)	CT (by bits)	Decryption
CGW [8]	SXDH	$3840 + 512\,\ell$	$1024 + 1024\,m_k$	$3584 + 512\,m_c$	$4P + 2\,\ell\,E$
	DLIN	$8192 + 1536\,\ell$	$1536 + 1536\,m_k$	$3840 + 768\,m_c$	$6P + 3\,\ell\,E$
Ours	DLIN	$5888 + 256\,\ell$	$3584 + 768\,m_k$	$5120 + 512 m_c$	$8P + \ell\,E$

ℓ: a predicate size (the size of common values in an encoding),
m_k and m_c: the size of encoding schemes used for keys and ciphertexts,
For 128 bits security level [14], we use $|G_1| = |\mathbb{Z}_p| = 256$ bits, $|G_2| = 512$ bits, $|G_T| = 3072$ bits.

PE schemes. We observe common properties of PE schemes as other encoding frameworks, but generalize them as a new encoding framework using *tag*. The generic construction of our encoding is adaptively secure under the Decisional Linear assumption.

Tag Based Encoding. We introduce a *tag based encoding*. For a predicate R with input domains $\mathcal{X}$ and $\mathcal{Y}$, $R : \mathcal{X} \times \mathcal{Y} \to \{0, 1\}$, a tag based encoding for R comprises two algorithms, namely, $\mathbf{kE}$ and $\mathbf{cE}$, together with a field $\mathbb{Z}_p^\ell$ where p is a prime number and ℓ is a value allocated for each function R such as the size of predicate vectors for Inner Product Encryption. We let $\mathbf{kE}(x, \mathbf{h})$ and $\mathbf{cE}(y, \mathbf{h})$ denote the outputs of $\mathbf{kE}$ taking as inputs $x \in \mathcal{X}$ and $\mathbf{h} \in \mathbb{Z}_p^\ell$ and $\mathbf{cE}$ taking as inputs $y \in \mathcal{Y}$ and $\mathbf{h} \in \mathbb{Z}_p^\ell$, respectively. The tag based encoding must satisfy three essential properties, namely Reconstruction, Linearity and $\mathbf{h}$-hiding. Instances of our encoding are interpreted as PE schemes via our constructions. These constructions are often called compilers since they compile encodings to form PE schemes (Fig. 1).

An Improved Efficiency. Prior to our work, the most efficient compiler in prime order groups was proposed by Chen et al. [8], which is subsequently referred as CGW in this work. The compiler was proposed for the predicate encoding [30]. Multiple compilers under the generalized k-linear assumption [12] were also included in the CGW's framework. The number of group elements that a compiler in the CGW's framework uses to represent a tuple of an encoding (e.g. **kE** and **cE**) depends on computational assumptions of which the compiler is based on. More concretely, each tuple of an encoding scheme is represented by $k+1$ group elements in private keys and ciphertexts. Also, $k(k+1)$ elements are required for each coordinate of **h** in public keys where **h** is a shared input of **kE** and **cE**. The most efficient compiler is under the SXDH assumption (i.e. when k is equal to 1). Two group elements are used for a tuple of an encoding in this compiler. Other encoding frameworks [1,3] were also proposed independently, but they are similar to the CGW's framework from the efficiency perspective. Hence, without losing generality, we compare our compiler with CGW's compiler to highlight our contribution.

In our compiler, only one group element is required for each entity of **h** in public keys. Hence, if the size of **h** is large, our compiler reduces the size of public key to 50 % compared with the CGW's compiler. Also, it reduces decryption time by 50 % under the same condition. For the other parameters such as private keys and ciphertexts, our compiler needs a group element and an integer for one tuple of an encoding scheme. The size of the integer in our compiler is the same as the group order of the underlying bilinear group. In other words, it is as small as the size of a group element of G_1 but much less than that of G_2 due to embedding degree of asymmetric bilinear maps. Thus, our compiler reduces the size of either private keys or ciphertexts depending on where G_2 is used for. For example, in 128 bits security level, G_2 requires at least 512 bits. It is twice of the size of $\mathbb{Z}_p$ [14]. It means that only 768 bits are required to represent a tuple in our compiler. This outperforms CGW's approach which requires 1024 bits for a tuple. Therefore, our compiler saves the size of private keys or ciphertexts by 25 % compared to their compiler under the SXDH assumption when the size of an encoding is large.

Moreover, the CGW's framework is also realized under the weaker assumption, namely the DLIN assumption, in comparison to ours[2]. It should be noted that in this setting, 6 group elements are required for public keys for their compiler. It implies that our compiler outperforms their compiler as well in this setting. More concretely, under the same assumption at a 128 bits security level, our compiler saves 83 % in a public key, 50 % in private keys, 33 % in ciphertexts and 66 % in decryption time if the size of encodings and their shared input is large. We provide Table 1 for the details. To compare the efficiency in practice, we compare our inner product encryption with short keys and public attribute inner product encryption to those of other encodings. The instance of Public Attribute Inner Product Encryption (PAIPE) which is taken from [4] is introduced in the full version of this paper. It should be noted that encodings for our IPE schemes are slightly different from those of CGW [8] and Wee [30]. Our instances require one or two fewer elements.

---

[2] The DLIN assumption with asymmetric bilinear maps can be featured in various forms since it expanded from the DLIN assumption originally equipped with symmetric pairing. The DLIN assumption of the CGW's compiler is slightly different from our assumption. In particular, it has two fewer group elements in G_2.

Table 2. Efficiency comparison of inner product encryption (IPE) between encodings.

Scheme	Assumption	PK	SK	CT	Decryption
Wee [30]	SDs	$\ell\|G_N\| + \|G_{N,T}\|$	$2\|G_N\|$	$(\ell+1)\|G_N\| + \|G_{N,T}\|$	$2P + \ell E$
CGW [8]	SXDH	$(2\ell+4)\|G_1\| + \|G_T\|$	$4\|G_2\|$	$2(\ell+1)\|G_1\| + \|G_T\|$	$4P + 2\ell E$
	DLIN	$(6\ell+8)\|G_1\| + 2\|G_T\|$	$6\|G_2\|$	$3(\ell+1)\|G_1\| + \|G_T\|$	$6P + 3\ell E$
Ours	DLIN	$(11+\ell)\|G_1\| + \|G_T\|$	$8\|G_2\| + \|\mathbb{Z}_p\|$	$(7+\ell)\|G_1\| + (\ell-1)\|\mathbb{Z}_p\| + \|G_T\|$	$8P + \ell E$

ℓ: the size of a predicate vector (the length of common parameter in the encoding),
P: Pairing computation, E: Exponentiations over a group element,
G_N and $G_{N,T}$: group elements of a composite order N,
G_1, G_2 and G_T: Group elements of order p of $e : G_1 \times G_2 \to G_T$

Table 3. Efficiency comparison of public attribute IPE between encodings.

Scheme	Assumption	PK	SK	CT	Decryption
CGW [8]	SXDH	$(2\ell+4)\|G_1\| + \|G_T\|$	$(2\ell+4)\|G_2\|$	$4\|G_1\| + \|G_T\|$	$4P + 2\ell E$
	DLIN	$(6\ell+8)\|G_1\| + 2\|G_T\|$	$(3\ell+6)\|G_2\|$	$6\|G_1\| + \|G_T\|$	$6P + 3\ell E$
Ours, AL [4]	DLIN	$(11+\ell)\|G_1\| + \|G_T\|$	$(6+\ell)\|G_2\|$ $+ (\ell-1)\|\mathbb{Z}_p\|$	$9\|G_1\| + \|\mathbb{Z}_p\| + \|G_T\|$	$8P + \ell E$

ℓ: the size of a predicate vector (the length of common parameter in the encoding),
P: Pairing computation, E: Exponentiation over a group element,
G_1, G_2 and G_T: Group elements of order p of $e : G_1 \times G_2 \to G_T$

A Compiler with Symmetric Bilinear Maps. We also provide a new compiler with symmetric bilinear maps in the full version of this paper. Prior to our works, with symmetric bilinear maps, all encodings [2,8,30] are secure only in composite order groups. It is because all prior encodings [1,3,8] in prime order groups are based on dual system groups [9] which requires asymmetric pairings to feature different properties of left-hand groups and right-hand groups in pairings. To the best of our knowledge, our construction is *the only compiler* that provides adaptive security for encodings with symmetric pairings in prime order groups. This gives our framework an additional flexibility when the encryption scheme is implemented under a special requirement of the pairing type (Tables 2 and 3).

New Schemes. We introduce a number of new schemes as instances, namely: Inner Product Encryption with short keys, Dual Spatial Encryption with short keys and Hierarchical Identity Based Encryption with short ciphertexts. Particularly, dual spatial encryption is a new primitive. It is a symmetric conversion of a spatial encryption [15]. In this primitive, an affine space and an affine vector are taken to generate ciphertexts and keys, respectively. Moreover, in the full version of this paper, we describe as encodings a number of existing schemes such as IBE [29], (Public Attribute) Inner Product Encryption [4], Spatial Encryption and Doubly Spatial Encryption [7] to show the versatility of our framework.

1.2 Our Technique

Our encoding framework generalizes Waters' dual system encryption methodology [29] which is widely used to analyze PE schemes. In Waters' dual system encryption, private keys and ciphertexts are changed into auxiliary types, namely semi-functional keys and semi-functional ciphertexts in the security analysis. After converting all keys and the challenge ciphertext to semi-functional type, proving security becomes much easier in their methodology since semi-functional keys cannot decrypt semi-functional ciphertexts. Prior encodings [2,30] in composite order groups and their compilers [1,3,8] in prime order groups also generalized and utilized the dual system encryption methodology. The most distinctive feature of our encoding compared to theirs is our compiler. Our compiler is constructed for tag based compiler by utilizing and expanding Waters' IBE [29]. Therefore, our compiler is adaptively secure in prime order groups under the standard DLIN assumption (which is the same as Water's IBE).

The critical part of the dual system encryption is proving semi-functional key invariance. In this proof, it is shown that a normal key and a semi-functional key are indistinguishable when the challenge ciphertext is already fixed as semi-functional. Therefore, the key becomes a valid key into an invalid key against the challenge ciphertext since the semi-functional challenge ciphertext can be decrypted only by a normal key. In Waters' IBE, tags are used to hide the type of the challenge key against not only the adversary but also the simulator. The simulator can try to distinguish the type of the challenge key by generating a valid semi-functional ciphertext to be decrypted only if the key is normal. This trial must be hindered in the analysis. Tags take an important role to restrict the simulator's trial. In Waters' IBE, tags in the challenge key and the challenge ciphertext are enforced to share the same values. In particular, they become $h_1 \cdot ID_{key} + h_2$ and $h_1 \cdot ID_{ct} + h_2$ where h_1 and h_2 are values which are initially information theoretically hidden to the adversary. Therefore, if the simulator generates a ciphertext to test the challenge key, the simulator can only simulate the challenge key with the same tag as the ciphertext, such that the self-decryption cannot be used to distinguish the challenge key because decryption requires two distinct tags. At the same time, since the values of h_1 and h_2 are hidden to the adversary, the correlation between tags in the challenge ciphertext and the challenge key is also hidden since they are pairwise independent. In other words, tags are randomly distributed to the adversary.

In our framework, tags have structures. We reveal the structures of tags, but they take as inputs random values (e.g. h_1 and h_2 in Waters' IBE). In more detail, in our compiler, tags are constructed by the encodings $\mathbf{kE}$ and $\mathbf{cE}$ but take random inputs instead of public parameters. Formally, tags in our compiler are generated as $\mathbf{kE}(x, \mathbf{h'})$ and $\mathbf{cE}(y, \mathbf{h''})$ where x and y are predicates and $\mathbf{h'}$ and $\mathbf{h''}$ are random values. Therefore, our tags are not random but they retain structures. This approach is actually beneficial for our encoding since we describe tags more formally, but it still works for the dual system encryption methodology. Particularly, in the key invariance proof, those tags must share the same random values (i.e. $\mathbf{h'} = \mathbf{h''}$). This enforces the simulator's trial to fail as in the Waters' IBE system during the decryption process. Also, sharing inputs of encodings can be hidden by utilizing the independence argument such as pairwise independence for IBE. Requiring independence between tags may be a bit more strict than the similar property of the previous encodings. For example, we do not know how linear secret sharing scheme [6] can be utilized into our encoding, but it provides efficiency benefits for PE and still flexible to capture a number of PE schemes.

Duality. Another distinct feature of our encodings is that required properties for **kE** and **cE** are identical. This is useful since without any conversion technique or efficiency loss, one encoding scheme realizes two encryption schemes; one scheme uses **kE** for a key and **cE** for a ciphertext and the other scheme uses **cE** for a key and **kE** for a ciphertext. The previous encodings require a new variable incurring efficiency loss for symmetric conversion [5]. We introduce several new schemes as instances of our encoding. Some of them are generated as the symmetric conversions of existing schemes (e.g. Dual spatial encryption as the symmetric conversion of spatial encryption [7]).

2 Related Works

Dual system encryption [29] provides a break-through technique of proving the security of PE. It implements auxiliary types of keys and ciphertexts, namely semi-functional keys and semi-functional ciphertexts, appearing only in the security proof. Subsequently, it shows that a security game consisting of semi-functional keys and semi-functional ciphertexts is indistinguishable from the original security game. Since semi-functional keys cannot decrypt semi-functional ciphertexts, the security proof for the transformed game becomes much easier than that of the original game. Waters showed that dual system encryption is a powerful tool in public key encryptions and signatures by introducing a number of adaptive encryption schemes.

Several encryption systems [4,7,11] have been introduced in prime order groups under standard assumption. In particular, all of them share similar constructions and security proofs. Interestingly, their techniques are quite different from those of dual system groups. They are more similar to Waters' IBE [29], but provide different predicates for their own purposes. Compared with similar constructions in composite order groups [4,17,30], they are considered to be efficient and secure since they are constructed in prime order groups and their security depends only on standard assumption.

Encoding frameworks [2,30] well formalize the core properties that the dual system encryption requires. The frameworks consist of syntax and a compiler of encodings. PE schemes were simply written by encoding instances in the frameworks. Then, the compiler is applied to instances of encodings to result in encryption schemes. Those outputs are also adaptively secure since the adaptive security of the compiler is already proved using properties defined in the syntax. Initially, they [2,30] were suggested only in composite order groups. Several techniques [13,16,18,21,28] to convert encryption systems in composite order to those in prime order have also been proposed. Nevertheless, the techniques in [13,16,28] are not applicable to dual system encryption since they do not hide parameters. It means that it is not applicable to encoding frameworks.

Dual Pairing Vector Spaces (DPVS) [22–24] have been widely used as a tool that overcomes the inefficiency of composite order groups. In DPVS, core properties which are accomplished by subgroups of composite order groups for adaptive security are featured by orthogonal vectors in prime order groups. DPVS has been used not only to achieve PE schemes directly [19,22,23,25], but also to convert schemes from composite order groups to prime order groups [8,18,21]. Lewko and Waters suggest a generic technique in [18] to transform a construction in composite order groups into prime order groups by utilizing DPVS, but it still incurs a loss in efficiency caused by the size of vectors. The technique suggested by [18] requires the size of vectors to increase linearly with a size of predicates when DPVS is used to convert a PE scheme in composite order groups into prime order groups.

Recently, adaptively secure IPE which has a good efficiency was introduced from Ramanna [26]. It is adaptively secure with a short ciphertext in prime order groups. Interestingly, their construction also uses tags as ours although their scheme is not a generic construction as ours. Also, their scheme has shorter fixed parameters in both keys and ciphertexts compared to our general construction, but their scheme relies on the SXDH assumption which is stronger than DLIN assumption in our construction. Therefore, one may think that their scheme is a trade-off between security and efficiency compared to IPE scheme in our works.

There exist variants of Waters' IBE from Ramanna et al. [27] and Lewko and Waters [20]. Since our encoding framework generalize Water's IBE, These variants may be also applicable to our generic construction. Using those variants one may achieve PE schemes which have fewer fixed elements in keys and ciphertexts, but under stronger assumptions as those in Ramanna [26].

3   Background

3.1   Bilinear Maps

We let G_1, G_2 and G_T denote three multiplicative cyclic groups of prime order p. Also, we let g_1 and g_2 be generators of G_1 and G_2, resp., and e be a bilinear map, $e : G_1 \times G_2 \to G_T$. The bilinear map e has the following properties:

1. Bilinearity: for all $u \in G_1, v \in G_2$ and $a, b \in \mathbb{Z}_p$, we have $e(u^a, v^b) = e(u, v)^{ab}$.
2. Non-degeneracy: $e(g_1, g_2) \neq 1$.

We say that G_1 and G_2 are bilinear groups if the group operation in G_1 and G_2 and the bilinear map $e : G_1 \times G_2 \to G_T$ are efficiently computable. If $G_1 \neq G_2$, the map e is an asymmetric bilinear map. Otherwise, we can simply denote G_1 and G_2 as G and call $e : G \times G \to G_T$ a symmetric bilinear map.

3.2   Complexity Assumptions

We expand both the DLIN and the DBDH into asymmetric bilinear maps. Hence, we let G_1, G_2, and G_T be prime order groups of order p such that $e : G_1 \times G_2 \to$

G_T where e is an asymmetric bilinear map. We use subscripts to denote the type of groups. For example, g_1 denotes a generator of G_1, and g_2 denotes a generator of G_2.

(Asymmetric) Decisional Bilinear Diffie-Hellman ($DBDH$) Assumption. Let g_1 and g_2 be a generator of G_1 and of G_2, respectively. Let c_1, c_2 and c_3 be selected randomly from $\mathbb{Z}_p$. Given $\{g_1, g_1^{c_2}, g_1^{c_3} \in G_1, g_2, g_2^{c_1}, g_2^{c_2} \in G_2, T \in G_T\}$, there is no PPT algorithm that can distinguish whether T is $e(g_1, g_2)^{c_1 c_2 c_3}$ or a random from G_T with a non-negligible advantage.

(Asymmetric) Decisional Linear ($DLIN$) Assumption. Let g_1 and g_2 be random generators of G_1 and G_2, respectively. Let y_f, y_ν, c_1, c_2 be selected randomly from $\mathbb{Z}_p$ set $f_1 = g_1^{y_f}, \nu_1 = g_1^{y_\nu}, f_2 = g_2^{y_f}$ and $\nu_2 = g_2^{y_\nu}$. Given $\{g_1, f_1, \nu_1, g_1^{c_1}, f_1^{c_2}, T \in G_1, g_2, f_2, \nu_2 \in G_2\}$, there is no PPT algorithm can distinguish whether T is $\nu_1^{c_1+c_2}$ or a random from G_1 with a non-negligible advantage.

It is worth noting that (Asymmetric) DBDH assumption also reduced to (Asymmetric) DLIN assumption.

Proposition 1. *Suppose that there exists an algorithm $\mathcal{A}$ which breaking (Asymmetric) DBDH with non-negligible advantage ϵ. Then, we can build an algorithm $\mathcal{B}$ which breaks (Asymmetric) DLIN assumption with advantage ϵ.*

Proof. $\mathcal{B}$ takes $\{g_1, f_1, \nu_1, g_1^{c_1}, f_1^{c_2}, T, g_2, f_2, \nu_2\}$ as an instance from *(Asymmetric) DLIN* assumption. $\mathcal{B}$ will simulate *(Asymmetric) DBDH* from the instance using $\mathcal{A}$ who breaks *(Asymmetric) DLIN* assumption with non-negligible advantage.

If $\mathcal{A}$ requests a instance of *(Asymmetric) DBDH* $\{\tilde{g}_1, \tilde{g}_1^{\tilde{c}_2}, \tilde{g}_1^{\tilde{c}_3}, \tilde{g}_2, \tilde{g}_2^{\tilde{c}_1}, \tilde{g}_2^{\tilde{c}_2}, \tilde{T}\}$ to break *(Asymmetric) DLIN*, the algorithm sets

$$\tilde{g}_1 = g_1, \tilde{g}_1^{\tilde{c}_2} = f_1, \tilde{g}_1^{\tilde{c}_3} = g_1^{\tilde{c}_1}, \tilde{g}_2 = g_2, \tilde{g}_2^{\tilde{c}_1} = \nu_2, \tilde{g}_2^{\tilde{c}_2} = f_2, \tilde{T} = e(T, f_2)/e(f_1^{c_2}, \nu_2).$$

This implicitly sets $\tilde{c}_1 = y_\nu, \tilde{c}_2 = y_f$ and $\tilde{c}_3 = c_1$ where y_ν and y_f are the discrete logarithms of ν_1 and f_1 to the base g_1 modulo p, respectively. If T is $\nu_1^{c_1+c_2}$, then $\tilde{T} = e(T, f_2)/e(f_1^{c_2}, \nu_2) = e(\nu_1, f_2)^{c_1} = e(\tilde{g}_1^{\tilde{c}_1}, \tilde{g}_2^{\tilde{c}_2})^{\tilde{c}_3} = e(\tilde{g}_1, \tilde{g}_2)^{\tilde{c}_1 \tilde{c}_2 \tilde{c}_3}$. Otherwise, if T is a random element from G_1, $\tilde{T}$ is randomized by T.

3.3 Predicate Encryption

PE definition and its adaptive security are adopted from [2,30].

Definition of Predicate Encryption. For a predicate $R : \mathcal{X} \times \mathcal{Y} \to \{0, 1\}$, our PE consists of Setup, Encrypt, KeyGen and Decrypt as follows:

Setup$(1^\lambda, \ell) \to (PK, MSK)$: takes as input a security parameter 1^λ and an integer ℓ allocated to a predicate. The output is a public parameter PK and a master secret key MSK.

KeyGen$(x, MSK, PK) \to SK$: takes as input a predicate $x \in \mathcal{X}$, a master secret key MSK and a public parameter PK. The output is a private key SK.

Encrypt$(y, M, PK) \to CT$: takes as input a description $y \in \mathcal{Y}$, a public parameter PK and a plaintext M. The output is a ciphertext CT.

Decrypt$(x, y, SK, CT) \to M$: takes as input a secret key SK for x and a ciphertext CT for y. If $R(x, y) = 1$, the output is M. Otherwise, $\perp$.

Correctness. For all $M, x \in \mathcal{X}, y \in \mathcal{Y}$ such that $R(x, y) = 1$, if SK is the output of KeyGen(x, MSK, PK) and CT is the output of Encrypt(y, M, PK) where PK and MSK are the outputs of Setup$(1^\lambda, \ell)$, then Decrypt(x, y, SK, CT) outputs M.

Definition of Adaptive Security of Predicate Encryption [2]. With q_t private key queries where q_t is polynomial, a PE scheme for a predicate R is adaptively secure if there is no PPT adversary $\mathcal{A}$ which has a non-negligible advantage in the game between $\mathcal{A}$ and the challenger $\mathcal{C}$ defined below.

Setup: The challenger runs Setup$(1^\lambda, \ell)$ to create (PK, MSK). PK is sent to $\mathcal{A}$.

Phase 1: The adversary requests a private key for $x_i \in \mathcal{X}$ for $i \in [1, q_1]$. For each x_i, the challenger returns SK_i created by running KeyGen(x_i, MSK, PK).

Challenge: When the adversary requests the challenge ciphertext for $y \in \mathcal{Y}$ such that $R(x_i, y) = 0 \ \forall i \in [1, q_1]$, and submits equal-length messages M_0 and M_1, the challenger randomly selects b from $\{0, 1\}$ and returns the challenge ciphertext CT created by running Encrypt(y, M_b, PK).

Phase 2: This is identical to Phase 1 except the additional restriction that $x_i \in \mathcal{X}$ for $i \in [q_1 + 1, q_t]$ such that $R(x_i, y) = 0; \forall i \in [q_1 + 1, q_t]$.

Guess: The adversary outputs $b' \in \{0, 1\}$. If $b = b'$, then the adversary wins.

We define the advantage of the adversary against a predicate encryption as

$$Adv_{\mathcal{A}}^{PE}(\lambda) := |\Pr[b = b'] - 1/2|.$$

3.4 Notations

Throughout the paper, we use bold font to denote vectors. Furthermore, vector exponentiations of group elements imply vector group elements. For example, we let $\mathbf{a} = (a_1, a_2)$ where $\mathbf{a} = (a_1, a_2) \in \mathbb{Z}_p^2$. For a group element g, $g^{\mathbf{a}}$ is equal to (g^{a_1}, g^{a_2}). In addition, multiplication of vectors in exponents implies component-wise product of two vectors. For example, $g^{\mathbf{ab}}$ is equal to $(g^{a_1 b_1}, g^{a_2 b_2})$ where $\mathbf{b} = (b_1, b_2) \in \mathbb{Z}_p^2$. Similarly, a scalar exponentiation to a vector of group elements means a scalar multiplication to a vector in exponent. For example, $(g^{(a_1, a_2)})^r = (g^{(ra_1, ra_2)})$ where $r \in \mathbb{Z}_p$. Also, a multiplication of vector groups implies an addition of vectors in their exponents (e.g. $g^{\mathbf{a}} g^{\mathbf{b}} = g^{\mathbf{a+b}}$). It should be noted that this multiplication is possible only if $|\mathbf{a}| = |\mathbf{b}|$. When it comes to a pairing operation, a pairing with vectors implies multiple pairing computations, that is, $e(g, g^{\mathbf{a}})$ requires two pairing computations $e(g, g^{a_1})e(g, g^{a_2})$ where $\mathbf{a} = (a_1, a_2) \in \mathbb{Z}_p^2$, but the same result is achieved only by one pairing since $e(g, g^{a_1} g^{a_2}) = e(g, g^{a_1})e(g, g^{a_2})$.

4   Tag Based Encoding

For a predicate $R : \mathcal{X} \times \mathcal{Y} \to \{0, 1\}$, tag based encoding $\mathbf{TE}(R)$ is a tuple of $(\ell, \mathbf{kE}, \mathbf{cE})$. In an encoding $(\ell, \mathbf{kE}, \mathbf{cE})$, ℓ is an integer allocated for a predicate R (e.g. the size of a universe of attributes in ABE, the dimension of an affine space in spatial encryption) and used to generate common parameter $\mathbf{h} \in \mathbb{Z}_p^\ell$. Also, $\mathbf{kE}(x, \mathbf{h})$ and $\mathbf{cE}(y, \mathbf{h})$ are two deterministic algorithms which take as inputs $x \in \mathcal{X}$ and $y \in \mathcal{Y}$, resp. together with $\mathbf{h}$.

We let ℓ_k and ℓ_c denote the sizes of $\mathbf{kE}(x, \mathbf{h})$ and $\mathbf{cE}(y, \mathbf{h})$ (i.e. $\ell_k = |\mathbf{kE}(x, \mathbf{h})|$ and $\ell_c = |\mathbf{cE}(y, \mathbf{h}')|$), resp. Then, tag based encodings satisfy following properties:

Property 1. (Reconstruction) For all (x, y) such that $R(x, y) = 1$, there exists an efficient algorithm to compute non-zero vectors $\mathbf{m}_x \in \mathbb{Z}_p^{\ell_k}$ and $\mathbf{m}_y \in \mathbb{Z}_p^{\ell_c}$ such that

$$\mathbf{m}_x \mathbf{kE}(x, \mathbf{h}) = \mathbf{m}_y \mathbf{cE}(y, \mathbf{h}), \quad \forall \mathbf{h} \in \mathbb{Z}_p^\ell.$$

Property 2. (*Linearity*) For all $(x, y, \mathbf{h}', \mathbf{h}'') \in \mathcal{X} \times \mathcal{Y} \times \mathbb{Z}_p^\ell \times \mathbb{Z}_p^\ell$,

$$\mathbf{kE}(x, \mathbf{h}') + \mathbf{kE}(x, \mathbf{h}'') = \mathbf{kE}(x, \mathbf{h}' + \mathbf{h}'') \text{ and}$$

$$\mathbf{cE}(y, \mathbf{h}') + \mathbf{cE}(y, \mathbf{h}'') = \mathbf{cE}(y, \mathbf{h}' + \mathbf{h}'').$$

Property 3. (h-*hiding*) For all $(x, y) \in \mathcal{X} \times \mathcal{Y}$ such that $R(x, y) = 0$,

$$(x, y, \mathbf{kE}(x, \mathbf{h}), \mathbf{cE}(y, \mathbf{h})) \text{ and } (x, y, \mathbf{kE}(x, \mathbf{h}), \mathbf{cE}(y, \mathbf{h}'))$$

are statistically indistinguishable where $\mathbf{h}$ and $\mathbf{h}'$ are randomly selected from $\mathbb{Z}_p^\ell$.

Remark 1. *Reconstruction* is necessary for the correctness of our construction. In our construction, $\mathbf{kE}(x, \mathbf{h})$ and $\mathbf{cE}(y, \mathbf{h})$ cancel each other out. Hence, the property implies that there exists an efficient algorithm to make both tuples identical.

An Example of Tag Based Encodings. We provide a simple IBE scheme as an instance of our encoding from Waters' IBE [29]. This encoding results in an adaptively secure IBE scheme via our compiler introduced in the next section. Let $\mathcal{X} = \mathcal{Y} := \mathbb{Z}_p$. For all $ID \in \mathcal{X}$ and $ID' \in \mathcal{Y}$, $R(ID, ID') = 1$ iff $ID = ID'$.

- $\ell = 2$ and $\mathbf{h} = (y_u, y_h) \in \mathbb{Z}_p^2$
- $\mathbf{kE}(ID, (y_u, y_h)) := (y_u ID + y_h) \in \mathbb{Z}_p$
- $\mathbf{cE}(ID', (y_u, y_h)) := (y_u ID' + y_h) \in \mathbb{Z}_p$
- **Reconstruction:** This is an exact cancellation. Therefore, $\mathbf{m}_x = \mathbf{m}_y = 1$.
- **Linearity:** For all $\mathbf{h}' = (y_u', y_h')$,

$$\mathbf{kE}(ID, (y_u', y_h')) + \mathbf{kE}(ID, (\tilde{y}_u, \tilde{y}_h)) = y_u' ID + y_h' + \tilde{y}_u ID + \tilde{y}_h$$
$$= \mathbf{kE}(ID, (y_u' + \tilde{y}_u, y_h' + \tilde{y}_h))$$

The linearity of $\mathbf{cE}(ID', (y_u', y_h'))$ is identical showed with $\mathbf{kE}(ID, (y_u', y_h'))$.

- **h-hiding:** Given an instance $(ID, ID', \mathbf{kE}(ID, (y_u, y_h)), \mathbf{cE}(ID', (y_u, y_h)))$, because $\mathbf{kE}$ and $\mathbf{cE}$ are pairwise independence functions and the values of y_u and y_h are hidden. If $ID \neq ID'$, they do not correlate to each other. Therefore, sharing y_u and y_h between $\mathbf{kE}$ and $\mathbf{cE}$ are statistically hidden.

5   Our Compiler

Our compiler is similar to those of Waters' IBE [29]. The main differences between Waters' IBE and ours are the way of generating tags in KeyGen and Encrypt and the types of bilinear maps which are equipped with. In particular, tags in our construction have structures although tags of Waters' IBE are created randomly.

5.1   The Construction

For a tag based encoding $\mathbf{TE}(R)$ for a predicate R where $R : \mathcal{X} \times \mathcal{Y} \to \{0,1\}$, with ℓ which is an integer to associated with R, $\mathbf{PE}_A(\mathbf{TE}(R))$ is constructed as follows.

- Setup(1^λ, ℓ): The algorithm takes ℓ of the encoding as an input. Then, it randomly generates three groups G_1, G_2 and G_T from $\mathcal{G}(\lambda, p)$. Next, it generates $g_1 \in G_1$ and $g_2 \in G_2$ and exponents α, y_u, y_v, y'_v, y_w, a_1, a_2, b, h_1, $\ldots$, $h_\ell \in \mathbb{Z}_p$. Let $\tau_1 = g_1^{y_u + a_1 \cdot y_v}$, $\tau'_1 = g_1^{y_u + a_2 \cdot y'_v}$ and $\mathbf{h} = (h_1, ..., h_\ell)$. The MSK consists of $(g_2, g_2^\alpha, g_2^{\alpha \cdot a_1}, g_2^b, u_2 = g_2^{y_u}, v_2 = g_2^{y_v}, v'_2 = g_2^{y'_v}, w_2 = g_2^{y_w}, g_2^{\mathbf{h}})$. It publishes the public parameters PK as follows

$$g_1, g_1^b, g_1^{a_1}, g_1^{a_2}, g_1^{b \cdot a_1}, g_1^{b \cdot a_2}, \tau_1, \tau'_1, \tau_1^b, {\tau'_1}^b, w_1 = g_1^{y_w}, g_1^{\mathbf{h}}, e(g_1, g_2)^{\alpha \cdot a_1 \cdot b}$$

- Keygen(MSK, PK, x): The algorithm chooses randomly $r_1, r_2, z_1, z_2, h'_1, ..., h'_\ell \in \mathbb{Z}_p$ and sets $r = r_1 + r_2$ and $\mathbf{Tag}_k = \mathbf{kE}(x, \mathbf{h}')$ where $\mathbf{h}'$ is equal to $(h'_1, ..., h'_\ell)$. Then, it sets

$$D_1 = g_2^{\alpha \cdot a_1} u_2^r, D_2 = g_2^{-\alpha} v_2^r g_2^{z_1}, D_3 = (g_2^b)^{-z_1}, D_4 = {v'_2}^r g_2^{z_2}, D_5 = (g_2^b)^{-z_2},$$

$$D_6 = (g_2^b)^{r_2}, D_7 = g_2^{r_1}, \mathbf{K} = (g_2^{\mathbf{kE}(x, \mathbf{h})} w_2^{\mathbf{Tag}_k})^{r_1}.$$

It outputs $SK = (D_1, ..., D_7, \mathbf{K}, \mathbf{Tag}_k)$.

- Encrypt(PK, M, y): The algorithm randomly selects s_1, s_2, t, $h''_1, ..., h''_\ell \in \mathbb{Z}_p$ and set $s = s_1 + s_2$, and $\mathbf{Tag}_c = \mathbf{cE}(y, \mathbf{h}'')$ where $\mathbf{h}''$ is equal to $(h''_1, ..., h''_\ell)$. It sets

$$C = M \cdot (e(g_1, g_2)^{\alpha a_1 \cdot b})^{s_2}, C_1 = (g_1^b)^s, C_2 = (g_1^{b \cdot a_1})^{s_1}, C_3 = (g_1^{a_1})^{s_1},$$

$$C_4 = (g_1^{b \cdot a_2})^{s_2}, C_5 = (g_1^{a_2})^{s_2}, C_6 = \tau_1^{s_1} {\tau'_1}^{s_2}, C_7 = (\tau_1^b)^{s_1} ({\tau'_1}^b)^{s_2} w_1^{-t},$$

$$C_8 = g_1^t, \mathbf{E} = (g_1^{\mathbf{cE}(y, \mathbf{h})} w_1^{\mathbf{Tag}_c})^t.$$

It outputs $CT = (C, C_1, ..., C_8, \mathbf{E}, \mathbf{Tag}_c)$.[3]

---

[3] Linearity of $\mathbf{kE}(x, \mathbf{h})$ and $\mathbf{cE}(x, \mathbf{h})$ implies that $\mathbf{kE}$ and $\mathbf{cE}$ are linear functions over $\mathbf{h}$ when x and y are given. Therefore, $g^{\mathbf{kE}(x, \mathbf{h})}$ and $g^{\mathbf{cE}(y, \mathbf{h})}$ can be efficiently computed from $g^{\mathbf{h}}$ if x and y are given.

- Decrypt(x, y, SK, CT, PK): First, the algorithm calculates

$$A_1 = e(C_1, D_1)e(C_2, D_2)e(C_3, D_3)e(C_4, D_4)e(C_5, D_5),$$

$$A_2 = e(C_6, D_6)e(C_7, D_7).$$

Since $R(x, y) = 1$, there exist reconstruction vectors $\mathbf{m}_x$ and $\mathbf{m}_y$ s.t. $\mathbf{m}_x \mathbf{kE}(x, \mathbf{h}) = \mathbf{m}_y \mathbf{cE}(y, \mathbf{h})$ (by Property 1). If $\mathbf{m}_x \mathbf{Tag}_k - \mathbf{m}_y \mathbf{Tag}_c$ is 0, it aborts. Otherwise,

$$A_3 = e(C_8, \mathbf{K}^{\mathbf{m}_x})/e(\mathbf{E}^{\mathbf{m}_y}, D_7) = e(g_1, g_2)^{y_w r_1 t(\mathbf{m}_x \mathbf{Tag}_k - \mathbf{m}_y \mathbf{Tag}_c)}.$$

Therefore, $M = C \cdot A_2/(A_1 \cdot A_3^{1/(\mathbf{m}_x \mathbf{Tag}_k - \mathbf{m}_y \mathbf{Tag}_c)})$.

Correctness. Calculating A_1/A_2 is trivial and can be found in [29]. We only point out that $A_1/A_2 = e(g_1, g_2)^{\alpha a_1 \cdot b s_2} e(g_1, w_2)^{-r_1 t}$. For $\mathbf{m}_x$ and $\mathbf{m}_y$ such that $\mathbf{m}_x \mathbf{kE}(x, \mathbf{h}) = \mathbf{m}_y \mathbf{cE}(y, \mathbf{h})$, the correctness of A_3 is calculated as follows

$$
\begin{aligned}
A_3 &= \frac{e(C_8, \mathbf{K}^{\mathbf{m}_x})}{e(\mathbf{E}^{\mathbf{m}_y}, D_7)} = \frac{e(g_1^t, (g_2^{\mathbf{kE}(x,\mathbf{h})} w_2^{\mathbf{Tag}_k})^{r_1 \cdot \mathbf{m}_x})}{e((g_1^{\mathbf{cE}(y,\mathbf{h})} w_1^{\mathbf{Tag}_c})^{t \cdot \mathbf{m}_y}, g_2^{r_1})} \\
&= \frac{e(g_1, g_2)^{r_1 \cdot t \cdot \mathbf{m}_x \mathbf{kE}(x,\mathbf{h})} e(g_1, w_2)^{r_1 \cdot t \cdot \mathbf{m}_x \mathbf{Tag}_k}}{e(g_1, g_2)^{r_1 \cdot t \cdot \mathbf{m}_y \cdot \mathbf{cE}(y,\mathbf{h})} e(g_1, w_2)^{r_1 \cdot t \cdot \mathbf{m}_y \cdot \mathbf{Tag}_c}} \\
&= e(g_1, w_2)^{r_1 t \cdot (\mathbf{m}_x \mathbf{Tag}_k - \mathbf{m}_y \mathbf{Tag}_c)}.
\end{aligned}
$$

Therefore, $M = C \cdot A_2/(A_1 \cdot A_3^{1/(\mathbf{m}_x \mathbf{Tag}_k - \mathbf{m}_y \mathbf{Tag}_c)})$.

Remark 2. Alternatively, to reduce the number of pairing computations, we sets $\mathbf{m'}_x = \mathbf{m}_x/(\mathbf{m}_x \mathbf{Tag}_k - \mathbf{m}_y \mathbf{Tag}_c)$ and $\mathbf{m'}_y = \mathbf{m}_y/(\mathbf{m}_x \mathbf{Tag}_k - \mathbf{m}_y \mathbf{Tag}_c)$.

Then, the decryption can be done by calculating

$$A_1' := e(C_1, D_1)e(C_2, D_2)e(C_3, D_3)e(C_4, D_4)e(C_5, D_5)/e(C_6, D_6),$$

$$A_2' := e(C_8, \mathbf{K}^{\mathbf{m'}_x/a_1})/e(\tilde{\mathbf{E}}, D_7).$$

where $\tilde{\mathbf{E}} := (C_7, \mathbf{E}^{\mathbf{m'}_y})$. Finally, M is retrieved since $M = C/(A_1' \cdot A_2')$.

Theorem 1. *Suppose there exists a tag based encoding* **TE**, *then our* $\mathbf{PE}_A(\mathbf{TE})$ *is adaptively secure under the* (Asymmetric) DLIN *assumption.*

Proof. This is proved by Lemmas 1 to 3.

6 Security Analysis

Semi-functional Ciphertext. By running Encrypt algorithm for a message M and an input y, the algorithm generates a normal ciphertext $CT = (C', C_1', ..., C_8', \mathbf{E}', \mathbf{Tag}_c')$. Then, it randomly selects $\kappa \in \mathbb{Z}_p$ and sets

$$C = C', \quad C_1 = C_1', \quad C_2 = C_2', \quad C_3 = C_3', \quad C_4 = C_4' g_1^{ba_2\kappa},$$

$$C_5 = C_5' g_1^{a_2\kappa}, \quad C_6 = C_6' v_1'^{a_2\kappa}, \quad C_7 = C_7' v_1'^{a_2 b\kappa}, \quad C_8 = C_8', \quad \mathbf{E} = \mathbf{E}', \quad \mathbf{Tag}_c = \mathbf{Tag}_c'.$$

Semi-functional Key. The algorithm generates a normal key $SK = (D_1', ..., D_7', \mathbf{K}', \mathbf{Tag}_k')$ by running Keygen algorithm for an input x. Then, it sets

$$D_1 = D_1' g_2^{-a_1a_2\gamma}, \quad D_2 = D_2' g_2^{a_2\gamma}, \quad D_3 = D_3', \quad D_4 = D_4' g_2^{a_1\gamma}$$

$$D_5 = D_5', \quad D_6 = D_6', \quad D_7 = D_7', \quad \mathbf{K} = \mathbf{K}', \quad \mathbf{Tag}_k = \mathbf{Tag}_k'.$$

It should be noted that $e(g_1, g_2)^{a_1a_2b\kappa\gamma}$ will be added to the message to be encrypted if the semi-functional key is used to decrypt the semi-functional ciphertext.

Security Games.

Game$_{real}$: This game is a real game. It is identical to the adaptive security model.
Game$_i$: This game is identical to Game$_{real}$ except the challenge ciphertext and the first i keys. In this game, the challenge ciphertext and the first i keys are semi-functional.
Game$_{final}$: This game is identical to Game$_{q_t}$ except the challenge ciphertext where q_t is the total number of key queries. In this game, the challenge ciphertext is still semi-functional, but it is an encryption of a random message.

First, we prove that Game$_{real}$ and Game$_0$ are indistinguishable (*semi-functional ciphertext invariance*) in Lemma 1. Then, we show that Game$_{k-1}$ is also indistinguishable from Game$_k$ (*semi-functional key invariance*) in Lemma 2. Finally, in Lemma 3, we prove the invariance between Game$_{q_t}$ and Game$_{final}$ (*semi-functional security*). This completes the security analysis since no attacker has a non-negligible advantage in Game$_{final}$. Lemmas 1 and 3 are provided in the full version of this paper.

Lemma 2 (Semi-functional Key Invariance). *Suppose that there exists an algorithm $\mathcal{A}$ which distinguishes Game$_{k-1}$ and Game$_k$ with a non-negligible advantage ϵ. Then, we can build an algorithm $\mathcal{B}$ which breaks (Asymmetric) DLIN assumption with ϵ.*

Proof. G_1 and G_2 of (Asymmetric) DLIN are reversed. Therefore, $\mathcal{B}$ takes $\{g_1, f_1, \nu_1, g_2, f_2, \nu_2, g_2^{c_1}, f_2^{c_2}, T\}$ as an instance from *(Asymmetric) DLIN* assumption. Depending on the value of T, $\mathcal{B}$ will simulate Game$_{k-1}$ or Game$_k$ to take an advantage from $\mathcal{A}$ which can distinguish. It should be noted that T is in G_2 in the reversed assumption.

Setup. $\mathcal{B}$ chooses $\alpha, a_1, a_2, y_v, y'_v, y_w, h'_1, ...h'_\ell, \tilde{h}_1, ...\tilde{h}_\ell$, randomly from $\mathbb{Z}_p$. It sets

$$e(g_1, g_2)^{\alpha \cdot a_1 b} = e(f_1, g_2)^{\alpha \cdot a_1}, g_1 = g_1, g_1^b = f_1, g_1^{b \cdot a_1} = f_1^{a_1}, g_1^{b \cdot a_2} = f_1^{a_2},$$

$$u_1 = \nu_1^{-a_1 a_2}, v_1 = \nu_1^{a_2} \cdot g_1^{y_v}, v'_1 = \nu_1^{a_1} \cdot g_1^{y'_v}, \tau_1 = u_1 v_1^{a_1} = g_1^{y_v a_1}, \tau'_1 = u_1 v_1'^{a_2} = g_1^{y'_v a_2},$$

$$\tau_1^b = f_1^{y_{v_1} a_1}, \tau_1'^b = f_1^{y'_v a_2}, w_1 = f_1 g_1^{y_w}, \{g_1^{h_i} = f_1^{-h'_i} g_1^{\tilde{h}_i}; \forall i \in [1, \ell]\}$$

Then, it publishes the public parameters

$$g_1, g_1^b, g_1^{a_1}, g_1^{a_2}, g_1^{b \cdot a_1}, g_1^{b \cdot a_2}, \tau_1, \tau'_1, \tau_1^b, \tau_1'^b, w_1, g_1^{\mathbf{h}}, e(g_1, g_2)^{\alpha \cdot a_1 \cdot b}$$

where $\mathbf{h} = (h_1, ..., h_\ell)$. $\mathcal{B}$ sets $MSK = \{g_2, g_2^\alpha, g_2^{\alpha \cdot a_1}, g_2^b = f_2, u_2 = \nu_2^{-a_1 a_2}, v_2 = \nu_2^{a_2} g_2^{y_v}, v'_2 = \nu_2^{a_1} g_2^{y'_v}, w_2 = f_2 g_2^{y_w}, \{g_2^{h_i} = f_2^{-h'_i} g_2^{\tilde{h}_i}; \forall i \in [1, \ell]\}\}$.

In the setting, $\mathbf{h}$ is implicitly set by $\tilde{\mathbf{h}} - y_f \mathbf{h}'$ where $\mathbf{h}' = (h'_1, ...h'_\ell)$ and $\tilde{\mathbf{h}} = (\tilde{h}_1, ...\tilde{h}_\ell)$ if we write $f_1 = g_1^{y_f}$. $\mathcal{B}$ calculates $g_1^{\mathbf{h}}$ because it knows $g_1, f_1, \tilde{\mathbf{h}}, \mathbf{h}'$. It should be noted that the values of $\{h'_i; \forall i \in [1, \ell]\}$ are not revealed. It means that they are initially information theoretically hidden because, for all $i \in [1, \ell]$, $\tilde{h}_i$ is uniquely added where h'_i appears.

Phase I and II. For the first $k - 1$ semi-functional keys, $\mathcal{B}$ generates a normal key and selects γ randomly from $\mathbb{Z}_p$. It then adds semi-functional parts to the normal key. This is possible because $\mathcal{B}$ knows a_1, a_2 and MSK. Similarly, for the rest keys except k^{th} key ($i > k$), $\mathcal{B}$ can generate normal keys using the key generation algorithm, **KeyGen**, for the same reason.

For the kth key, $\mathcal{B}$ sets $\mathbf{Tag}'_k = \mathbf{kE}(x, \mathbf{h}')$. Then, with $\mathbf{Tag}'_k$, it generates a normal key $SK' = (D'_1, ..., D'_7, \mathbf{K}', \mathbf{Tag}'_k)$ using the key generation algorithm. Then, it reuses $\mathbf{Tag}'_k$ in the kth key (i.e. $\mathbf{Tag}_k = \mathbf{Tag}'_k$) and sets the other elements as follows

$$D_1 = D'_1 T^{-a_1 a_2}, D_2 = D'_2 T^{a_2} (g_2^{c_1})^{y_v}, D_3 = D'_3 (f_2^{c_2})^{y_v}, D_4 = D'_4 T^{a_1} (g_2^{c_1})^{y'_v},$$

$$D_5 = D'_5 (f_2^{c_2})^{y'_v}, D_6 = D'_6 f_2^{c_2}, D_7 = D'_7 (g_2^{c_1}), \mathbf{K} = \mathbf{K}' (g_2^{c_1})^{\mathbf{kE}(x, \tilde{\mathbf{h}} + y_w \mathbf{h}')}.$$

We let r'_1, r'_2, z'_1, z'_2 denote the random exponents of SK'. Then, it implicitly sets $z_1 = z'_1 - y_v c_2$ and $z_2 = z'_2 - y'_v c_2$. Also, by *linearity* property,

$$g_2^{\mathbf{kE}(x, \mathbf{h})} = g_2^{\mathbf{kE}(x, -y_f \mathbf{h}' + \tilde{\mathbf{h}})} = g_2^{\mathbf{kE}(x, -y_f \mathbf{h}')} g_2^{\mathbf{kE}(x, \tilde{\mathbf{h}})} = f_2^{-\mathbf{kE}(x, \mathbf{h}')} g_2^{\mathbf{kE}(x, \tilde{\mathbf{h}})}$$

Therefore, the value of $\mathbf{K}'$ can be represented as follows:

$$\mathbf{K}' = (f_2^{-\mathbf{kE}(x, \mathbf{h}')} g_2^{\mathbf{kE}(x, \tilde{\mathbf{h}})} (f_2 g_2^{y_w})^{\mathbf{kE}(x, \mathbf{h}')})^{r'_1} = (g_2^{\mathbf{kE}(x, \tilde{\mathbf{h}} + y_w \mathbf{h}')})^{r'_1}.$$

This implies that $\mathbf{K} = \mathbf{K}' (g_2^{c_1})^{\mathbf{kE}(x, \tilde{\mathbf{h}} + y_w \mathbf{h}')} = (g_2^{\mathbf{kE}(x, \tilde{\mathbf{h}} + y_w \mathbf{h}')})^{r'_1 + c_1}$.

If T is equal to $\nu_2^{c_1 + c_2}$, then the kth key is a normal key with $r_1 = r'_1 + c_1$ and $r_2 = r'_2 + c_2$. Otherwise, if T is $\nu_2^{c_1 + c_2} g_2^\gamma$, which means a random group element, then, the kth key is a properly distributed semi-functional key.

Challenge Ciphertext. When the adversary requests the challenge ciphertext for y^* with messages M_0, M_1, $\mathcal{B}$ randomly selects β from $\{0, 1\}$. With $\mathbf{Tag}'_c = \mathbf{cE}(y^*, \mathbf{h}')$, $\mathcal{B}$ runs the encryption algorithm to generate a normal ciphertext $CT' = (C', C'_1, ..., C'_8, \mathbf{E}', \mathbf{Tag}'_c)$ for y^* and M_β. We let s'_1, s'_2, t' denote the random exponents of CT'. To make the semi-functional challenge ciphertext, it randomly selects $\kappa \in \mathbb{Z}_p$ and sets $C = C', C_1 = C'_1, C_2 = C'_2, C_3 = C'_3$. Additionally, it sets

$$C_4 = C'_4 f_1^{a_2 \cdot \kappa}, \quad C_5 = C'_5 \cdot g_1^{a_2 \cdot \kappa}, \quad C_6 = C'_6 \cdot v_1'^{a_2 \kappa}, \quad C_7 = C'_7 \cdot f_1^{y'_v \cdot \kappa \cdot a_2} v_1^{-a_1 \cdot \kappa \cdot y_w \cdot a_2}$$

$$C_8 = g_1^{t'} \cdot v_1^{a_1 a_2 \kappa}, \quad \mathbf{E} = \mathbf{E}' \cdot (v_1^{\mathbf{cE}(y^*, \tilde{\mathbf{h}} + y_w \mathbf{h}')})^{a_1 a_2 \kappa}, \quad \mathbf{Tag}_c = \mathbf{Tag}'_c$$

This implicitly sets $g_1^t = g_1^{t'} \cdot v_1^{a_1 a_2 \kappa}$. Also, $v_1^{a_1 a_2 b \kappa}$ of $v_1'^{a_2 b \kappa}$ is cancelled out by w_1^{-t} in C_7.

The fact that $\mathbf{Tag}_c$ and $\mathbf{Tag}_k$ share the same vector $\mathbf{h}'$ is hidden to the adversary by h-*hiding* property since $R(x, y^*) = 0$. Therefore, $\mathbf{Tag}_c$ with correlated $\mathbf{h}'$ can be switched to $\mathbf{Tag}_c$ with a random vector from $\mathbb{Z}^\ell$. Also, $\mathbf{E}$ is valid since

$$\mathbf{E}' = (f_1^{-\mathbf{cE}(y^*, \mathbf{h}')} g_1^{\mathbf{cE}(y^*, \tilde{\mathbf{h}})} (f_1 g_1^{y_w})^{\mathbf{cE}(y^*, \mathbf{h}')})^{t'} = (g_1^{\mathbf{cE}(y^*, \tilde{\mathbf{h}} + y_w \mathbf{h}')})^{t'}.$$

The second equality of the above equation holds by *linearity* property.

$\mathcal{B}$ cannot test whether the kth key is normal or semi-functional by creating a ciphertext which can be decrypted only by a normal key because $\mathbf{Tag}_k$ and $\mathbf{Tag}_c$ share $\mathbf{h}'$. It means that $\mathbf{m}_x \mathbf{Tag}_k - \mathbf{m}_{y^*} \mathbf{Tag}_c$ is equal to 0 if the simulator creates a semi-functional ciphertext such that $R(x, y) = 1$. Hence, the decryption algorithm will abort.

7   New Schemes

We provide instances for our encoding to achieve new PE schemes. The instances of Inner Product Encryption (IPE) with short keys, Dual Spatial Encryption (Dual SE) with short keys and HIBE with short ciphertexts will be presented. Inner Product Encryption (IPE) with short keys and Dual Spatial Encryption (Dual SE) are new instances. HIBE with short ciphertexts is also found in [10, 30], but applying this instance to our compilers results in new schemes both in asymmetric and symmetric bilinear maps. It should be noted that security analysis of each scheme is replaced by showing that the corresponding instance satisfies the properties that tag based encoding requires.

Inner Product Encryption with Short Keys. Let define $\mathcal{X} = \mathcal{Y} := \mathbb{Z}_p^\ell$. For all, $\mathbf{x} \in \mathcal{X}$ and $\mathbf{y} \in \mathcal{Y}$, $R(x, y) = 1$ iff $\langle \mathbf{x}, \mathbf{y} \rangle = 0$.

- ℓ is the size of a predicate and $\mathbf{h} \in \mathbb{Z}_p^\ell$.
- $\mathbf{kE}(\mathbf{x}, \mathbf{h}) := \langle \mathbf{h}, \mathbf{x} \rangle \in \mathbb{Z}_p$
- $\mathbf{cE}(\mathbf{y}, \mathbf{h}) := (-h_1(y_2/y_1) + h_2, ..., -h_1(y_\ell/y_1) + h_\ell) \in \mathbb{Z}_p^{\ell-1}$
- **Reconstruction:** $\mathbf{m}_x = 1$ and $\mathbf{m}_y = (x_2, ..., x_\ell)$.

- **Linearity:** Firstly, the linearity of $\mathbf{kE}$ holds trivially since $\langle \mathbf{h}, \mathbf{x} \rangle + \langle \mathbf{h'}, \mathbf{x} \rangle = \langle \mathbf{h+h'}, \mathbf{x} \rangle$. Also, $\mathbf{cE}(\mathbf{y}, \mathbf{h}) + \mathbf{cE}(\mathbf{y}, \mathbf{h'}) = \mathbf{cE}(\mathbf{y}, \mathbf{h+h'})$ since, for all $i \in [1, \ell-1]$, $-h_1(y_{i+1}/y_1) + h_{i+1} - h'_1(y_{i+1}/y_1) + h'_{i+1} = -(h_1+h'_1)(y_{i+1}/y_1) + h_{i+1} + h'_{i+1}$.
- **h-hiding:** In the following equation, the first $\ell - 1$ coordinates of the right hand vector in the above equation are independent from the last coordinate by ℓ-*wise independence* [4]. Hence, sharing $\mathbf{h}$ between $\mathbf{kE}, \mathbf{cE}$ is hidden to the adversary.

$$\begin{pmatrix} -y_2/y_1 & 1 & & \\ \vdots & & \ddots & \\ -y_\ell/y_1 & & & 1 \\ x_1 & x_2 & x_3 \cdots & x_\ell \end{pmatrix} \begin{pmatrix} h_1 \\ \vdots \\ h_{\ell-1} \\ h_\ell \end{pmatrix} = \begin{pmatrix} -h_1(y_2/y_1) + h_2 \\ \vdots \\ -h_1(y_\ell/y_1) + h_\ell \\ \langle \mathbf{h}, \mathbf{x} \rangle \end{pmatrix}$$

Dual Spatial Encryption with Short Keys. For a matrix $M \in \mathbb{Z}_p^{(\ell-1) \times d}$ and a vector $\mathbf{c} \in \mathbb{Z}_p^{\ell-1}$, it defines the affine space $\mathrm{Aff}(M, \mathbf{c}) = \{M\mathbf{w} + \mathbf{c} | \mathbf{w} \in \mathbb{Z}_p^d\}$. Then, $R(\mathbf{x}, \mathrm{Aff}(M, \mathbf{c})) = 1$ iff there exists $\mathbf{w} \in \mathbb{Z}_p^d$ such that $M\mathbf{w} + \mathbf{c} = \mathbf{x}$.

- ℓ is the number of rows of an affine matrix $(+1)$ and $\mathbf{h} = (u_0, \mathbf{u}) \in \mathbb{Z}_p^\ell$.
- $\mathbf{kE}(\mathbf{x}, \mathbf{h}) := u_0 + \mathbf{x}^\mathsf{T}\mathbf{u} \in \mathbb{Z}_p$.
- $\mathbf{cE}(\mathrm{Aff}(M, \mathbf{c}), \mathbf{h}) := (u_0 + \mathbf{c}^\mathsf{T}\mathbf{u}, M^\mathsf{T}\mathbf{u}) \in \mathbb{Z}_p^{d+1}$
- **Reconstruction:** $\mathbf{m}_x = 1$ and $\mathbf{m}_y = (1, \tilde{\mathbf{w}}^\mathsf{T})$ where $\tilde{\mathbf{w}} \in \mathbb{Z}_p^d$ s.t. $M\tilde{\mathbf{w}} + \mathbf{c} = \mathbf{x}$.
- **Linearity:** All coordinates of $\mathbf{kE}(\mathbf{x}, \mathbf{h})$ and $\mathbf{cE}(\mathrm{Aff}(M, \mathbf{c}), \mathbf{h})$ are linear over $\mathbf{h}$.
- **h-hiding:** In the following equation, for $\mathbf{x} \in \mathcal{X}$, there is no $\mathbf{w}$ such that $M\mathbf{w} + \mathbf{c} = \mathbf{y}$ since $R(\mathbf{x}, \mathrm{Aff}(M, \mathbf{c})) = 0$. Hence, the last row of the matrix on the left is linearly independent from the other rows. Hence, it is hidden that they share u_0 and $\mathbf{u}$.

$$\begin{pmatrix} 1 & \mathbf{c}^\mathsf{T} \\ 0 & M^\mathsf{T} \\ 1 & \mathbf{x}^\mathsf{T} \end{pmatrix} \begin{pmatrix} u_0 \\ \mathbf{u} \end{pmatrix} = \begin{pmatrix} u_0 + \mathbf{c}^\mathsf{T}\mathbf{u} \\ M^\mathsf{T}\mathbf{u} \\ u_0 + \mathbf{x}^\mathsf{T}\mathbf{u} \end{pmatrix}$$

HIBE with Short Ciphertexts [10, 30]. For a vector $\mathbf{ID}_d := (id_1, ..., id_d) \in \mathbb{Z}_p^d$ and a vector $\mathbf{ID'}_{d'} := (id'_1, ..., id'_{d'}) \in \mathbb{Z}_p^{d'}$, $R(\mathbf{ID}_d, \mathbf{ID'}_{d'}) = 1$ iff $d \le d'$ and $id_i = id'_i \ \forall i \in [1, d]$.

- ℓ is the maximum depth of an identity $(+1)$ and $\mathbf{h} = (h_0, ..., h_\ell) \in \mathbb{Z}_p^\ell$.
- $\mathbf{kE}(\mathbf{ID}_d, \mathbf{h}) := (h_0 + h_1(id_1) + ... + h_d(id_d), h_{d+1}, ..., h_\ell) \in \mathbb{Z}_p^{\ell-d}$
- $\mathbf{cE}(\mathbf{ID'}_{d'}, \mathbf{h}) := h_0 + h_1(id'_1) + ... + h_{d'}(id'_{d'}) \in \mathbb{Z}_p$
- **Reconstruction:** $\mathbf{m}_x = (1, id'_{d+1}, ..., id'_{d'}, 0, ..., 0) \in \mathbb{Z}_p^{\ell-d}$ and $\mathbf{m}_y = 1$.
- **Linearity:** All coordinates of $\mathbf{kE}(\mathbf{ID}_d, \mathbf{h})$ and $\mathbf{cE}(\mathbf{ID'}_d, \mathbf{h})$ are linear over $\mathbf{h}$.
- **h-hiding:** In the following equation, the first $\ell - d + 1$ rows are linearly independent with the last row of matrix on the left since $id_d \ne id'_d$ and $h_0, ..., h_\ell$ appear at most twice. Therefore, the sharing $\mathbf{h}$ between the first

$\ell + 1$ coordinates of the vector of the right hand of the equation with the last coordinate of the vector is hidden.

$$\begin{pmatrix} 1 \ id_1 \cdots id_d & & & \\ & 1 & & \\ & & \ddots & \\ & & & 1 \\ 1 \ id'_1 \cdots id'_d \cdots id'_{d'} & & & \end{pmatrix} \begin{pmatrix} h_0 \\ \vdots \\ h_{\ell-1} \\ h_\ell \end{pmatrix} = \begin{pmatrix} h_0 + h_1(id_1) + \ldots + h_d(id_d) \\ h_{d+1} \\ \vdots \\ h_\ell \\ h_0 + h_1(id'_1) + \ldots + h_{d'}(id'_{d'}) \end{pmatrix}$$

8   Conclusion

In this paper, we proposed a new encoding framework for PE schemes. Our framework provides an encryption scheme having a better efficiency when the size of their encoding is large compared with prior encoding frameworks. We provided two generic constructions for our framework as compilers of encodings. They are adaptively secure under the standard assumption. Consequently, we showed that our encoding is versatile by proposing a number of new instances that are applicable to our encodings.

References

1. Agrawal, S., Chase, M.: A study of pair encodings: predicate encryption in prime order groups. In: Kushilevitz, E., et al. (eds.) TCC 2016-A. LNCS, vol. 9563, pp. 259–288. Springer, Heidelberg (2016). doi:10.1007/978-3-662-49099-0_10
2. Attrapadung, N.: Dual system encryption via doubly selective security: framework, fully secure functional encryption for regular languages, and more. In: Nguyen, P.Q., Oswald, E. (eds.) EUROCRYPT 2014. LNCS, vol. 8441, pp. 557–577. Springer, Heidelberg (2014)
3. Attrapadung, N.: Dual system encryption framework in prime-order groups. IACR Cryptology ePrint Archive, 2015:390 (2015)
4. Attrapadung, N., Libert, B.: Functional encryption for public-attribute inner products: achieving constant-size ciphertexts with adaptive security or support for negation. J. Math. Cryptol. 5(2), 115–158 (2012)
5. Attrapadung, N., Yamada, S.: Duality in ABE: converting attribute based encryption for dual predicate and dual policy via computational encodings. In: Nyberg, K. (ed.) CT-RSA 2015. LNCS, vol. 9048, pp. 87–105. Springer, Heidelberg (2015)
6. Beimel, A.: Secure schemes for secret sharing and key distribution. Ph.D. thesis, Israel Institute of Technology, Technion, Haifa, Israel (1996)
7. Chen, C., Zhang, Z., Feng, D.: Fully secure doubly-spatial encryption under simple assumptions. In: Takagi, T., Wang, G., Qin, Z., Jiang, S., Yu, Y. (eds.) ProvSec 2012. LNCS, vol. 7496, pp. 253–263. Springer, Heidelberg (2012)
8. Chen, J., Gay, R., Wee, H.: Improved dual system ABE in prime-order groups via predicate encodings. In: Oswald, E., Fischlin, M. (eds.) EUROCRYPT 2015. LNCS, vol. 9057, pp. 595–624. Springer, Heidelberg (2015)
9. Chen, J., Wee, H.: Fully, (almost) tightly secure IBE and dual system groups. In: Canetti, R., Garay, J.A. (eds.) CRYPTO 2013, Part II. LNCS, vol. 8043, pp. 435–460. Springer, Heidelberg (2013)

10. Chen, J., Wee, H.: Dual system groups and its applications - compact HIBE and more. IACR Cryptology ePrint Archive, 2014:265 (2014)
11. Datta, P., Dutta, R., Mukhopadhyay, S.: Fully secure self-updatable encryption in prime order bilinear groups. In: Chow, S.S.M., Camenisch, J., Hui, L.C.K., Yiu, S.M. (eds.) ISC 2014. LNCS, vol. 8783, pp. 1–18. Springer, Heidelberg (2014)
12. Escala, A., Herold, G., Kiltz, E., Ràfols, C., Villar, J.: An algebraic framework for Diffie-Hellman assumptions. In: Canetti, R., Garay, J.A. (eds.) CRYPTO 2013, Part II. LNCS, vol. 8043, pp. 129–147. Springer, Heidelberg (2013)
13. Freeman, D.M.: Converting pairing-based cryptosystems from composite-order groups to prime-order groups. In: Gilbert, H. (ed.) EUROCRYPT 2010. LNCS, vol. 6110, pp. 44–61. Springer, Heidelberg (2010)
14. Guillevic, A.: Comparing the pairing efficiency over composite-order and prime-order elliptic curves. In: Jacobson, M., Locasto, M., Mohassel, P., Safavi-Naini, R. (eds.) ACNS 2013. LNCS, vol. 7954, pp. 357–372. Springer, Heidelberg (2013)
15. Hamburg, M.: Spatial encryption. IACR Cryptology ePrint Archive, 2011:389 (2011)
16. Herold, G., Hesse, J., Hofheinz, D., Ràfols, C., Rupp, A.: Polynomial spaces: a new framework for composite-to-prime-order transformations. In: Garay, J.A., Gennaro, R. (eds.) CRYPTO 2014, Part I. LNCS, vol. 8616, pp. 261–279. Springer, Heidelberg (2014)
17. Lee, K., Choi, S.G., Lee, D.H., Park, J.H., Yung, M.: Self-updatable encryption: time constrained access control with hidden attributes and better efficiency. In: Sako, K., Sarkar, P. (eds.) ASIACRYPT 2013, Part I. LNCS, vol. 8269, pp. 235–254. Springer, Heidelberg (2013)
18. Lewko, A.: Tools for simulating features of composite order bilinear groups in the prime order setting. In: Pointcheval, D., Johansson, T. (eds.) EUROCRYPT 2012. LNCS, vol. 7237, pp. 318–335. Springer, Heidelberg (2012)
19. Lewko, A., Okamoto, T., Sahai, A., Takashima, K., Waters, B.: Fully secure functional encryption: attribute-based encryption and (hierarchical) inner product encryption. In: Gilbert, H. (ed.) EUROCRYPT 2010. LNCS, vol. 6110, pp. 62–91. Springer, Heidelberg (2010)
20. Lewko, A.B., Waters, B.: New techniques for dual system encryption and fully secure HIBE with short ciphertexts. In: IACR Cryptology ePrint Archive, 2009:482 (2009)
21. Lewko, A., Waters, B.: New proof methods for attribute-based encryption: achieving full security through selective techniques. In: Safavi-Naini, R., Canetti, R. (eds.) CRYPTO 2012. LNCS, vol. 7417, pp. 180–198. Springer, Heidelberg (2012)
22. Okamoto, T., Takashima, K.: Hierarchical predicate encryption for inner-products. In: Matsui, M. (ed.) ASIACRYPT 2009. LNCS, vol. 5912, pp. 214–231. Springer, Heidelberg (2009)
23. Okamoto, T., Takashima, K.: Fully secure functional encryption with general relations from the decisional linear assumption. In: Rabin, T. (ed.) CRYPTO 2010. LNCS, vol. 6223, pp. 191–208. Springer, Heidelberg (2010)
24. Okamoto, T., Takashima, K.: Achieving short ciphertexts or short secret-keys for adaptively secure general inner-product encryption. In: Lin, D., Tsudik, G., Wang, X. (eds.) CANS 2011. LNCS, vol. 7092, pp. 138–159. Springer, Heidelberg (2011)
25. Okamoto, T., Takashima, K.: Fully secure unbounded inner-product and attribute-based encryption. In: Wang, X., Sako, K. (eds.) ASIACRYPT 2012. LNCS, vol. 7658, pp. 349–366. Springer, Heidelberg (2012)

26. Ramanna, S.C.: More efficient constructions for inner-product encryption. In: Manulis, M., Sadeghi, A.-R., Schneider, S. (eds.) ACNS 2016. LNCS, vol. 9696, pp. 231–248. Springer, Heidelberg (2016). doi:10.1007/978-3-319-39555-5_13
27. Ramanna, S.C., Chatterjee, S., Sarkar, P.: Variants of waters' dual system primitives using asymmetric pairings. In: Fischlin, M., Buchmann, J., Manulis, M. (eds.) PKC 2012. LNCS, vol. 7293, pp. 298–315. Springer, Heidelberg (2012)
28. Seo, J.H.: On the (Im)possibility of projecting property in prime-order setting. In: Wang, X., Sako, K. (eds.) ASIACRYPT 2012. LNCS, vol. 7658, pp. 61–79. Springer, Heidelberg (2012)
29. Waters, B.: Dual system encryption: realizing fully secure IBE and HIBE under simple assumptions. In: Halevi, S. (ed.) CRYPTO 2009. LNCS, vol. 5677, pp. 619–636. Springer, Heidelberg (2009)
30. Wee, H.: Dual system encryption via predicate encodings. In: Lindell, Y. (ed.) TCC 2014. LNCS, vol. 8349, pp. 616–637. Springer, Heidelberg (2014)

Non-zero Inner Product Encryption with Short Ciphertexts and Private Keys

Jie Chen[1,2]($\boxtimes$), Benoît Libert[1]($\boxtimes$), and Somindu C. Ramanna[1]($\boxtimes$)

[1] Laboratoire LIP, École Normale Supérieure de Lyon, Lyon, France
{benoit.libert,somindu.ramanna}@ens-lyon.fr
[2] East China Normal University, Shanghai, China
s080001@e.ntu.edu.sg

Abstract. We describe two constructions of non-zero inner product encryption (NIPE) systems in the public index setting, both having ciphertexts and secret keys of constant size. Both schemes are obtained by tweaking the Boneh-Gentry-Waters broadcast encryption system (Crypto 2005) and are proved selectively secure under previously considered assumptions in groups with a bilinear map. Our first realization builds on prime-order bilinear groups and is proved secure under the Decisional Bilinear Diffie-Hellman Exponent assumption, which is parameterized by the length n of vectors over which the inner product is defined. By moving to composite order bilinear groups, we are able to obtain security under static subgroup decision assumptions following the Déjà Q framework of Chase and Meiklejohn (Eurocrypt 2014) and its extension by Wee (TCC 2016). Our schemes are the first NIPE systems to achieve such parameters, even in the selective security setting. Moreover, they are the first proposals to feature optimally short private keys, which only consist of *one* group element. Our prime-order-group realization is also the first one with a deterministic key generation mechanism.

Keywords: Functional encryption · Non-zero inner products · (Identity-based) revocation

1 Introduction

Attribute-based encryption (ABE) [20,35] allows fine-grained access control to encrypted data. In an ABE system, a ciphertext has an associated attribute x and a secret key for a user associated to some attribute y can successfully decrypt iff some relation R on x, y holds true i.e., $R(x, y) = 1$. An ABE scheme is said to be secure if a collusion attack by a group of users does not compromise the security of a ciphertext they are not allowed to decrypt. In this work, we consider attributes belonging to some inner product space V and the relation is given by $R(x, y) = 1$ iff $\langle x, y \rangle \neq 0$, for $x, y \in V$. Such an ABE (referred to as non-zero inner product encryption scheme or NIPE) is known to imply identity-based revocation, an important cryptographic primitive in its own right.

© Springer International Publishing Switzerland 2016
V. Zikas and R. De Prisco (Eds.): SCN 2016, LNCS 9841, pp. 23–41, 2016.
DOI: 10.1007/978-3-319-44618-9_2

Identity-based revocation (IBR) allows a sender to encrypt and broadcast a message to a number of identities, given a set of revoked users $\mathcal{R}$, so that only secret keys associated with identities outside of $\mathcal{R}$ can decrypt the message. NIPE systems are known to imply IBR – the attribute associated with the ciphertext (of length n) is nothing but the vector of coefficients of the polynomial $p_{\mathcal{R}}(Z) = \prod_{\mathsf{id}_i \in \mathcal{R}}(Z - \mathsf{id}_i)$ where $|\mathcal{R}| \leq n$ and the secret key for an identity id corresponds to the vector $(1, \mathsf{id}, \ldots, \mathsf{id}^n)$. The inner product is non-zero if and only if $p_{\mathcal{R}}(\mathsf{id}) \neq 0$ or equivalently $\mathsf{id} \notin \mathcal{R}$, in which case decryption succeeds.

In this paper, our main goal is to design NIPE (and thus revocation) schemes that simultaneously provide short ciphertexts and private keys. We will also seek to prove security under well-studied hardness assumptions.

Our Contribution. We first present a NIPE system employing prime-order bilinear groups where ciphertexts *and* secret keys *both* have constant[1] size. Our scheme is the first one where both sizes can be constant. Indeed, all earlier realizations [4,5,34] providing $O(1)$-size ciphertexts (resp. $O(1)$-size private keys) indeed required $O(n)$ group elements in private keys (resp. in ciphertexts), where n denotes the dimension of the inner product space which is fixed at setup time. Even in the selective model [4,5], all previous constructions thus had linear complexities in the size of ciphertexts or private keys.

The scheme is also the first NIPE realization to feature optimally short private keys – which only consist of one group element – via a deterministic private key extraction algorithm. In particular, our NIPE scheme implies the first (identity-based) revocation system that simultaneously provides $O(1)$-size ciphertexts and private keys. It thus performs in the same way as the Boneh-Gentry-Waters (BGW) broadcast encryption [12] system and relies on the same assumption. Like earlier NIPE proposals, our scheme requires $O(n)$ group elements in the public parameters. In the revocation setting, this translates into a linear public key size in the maximal number of revoked users per ciphertext, which is on par with solutions [29,38] based on the Naor-Pinkas technique [29].

The security of our scheme is proved against selective adversaries under the n-Decisional Bilinear Diffie-Hellman (n-DBDHE) assumption, the strength of which depends on the dimension n of handled vectors. While relying on such a parameterized assumption is certainly a caveat [17], our scheme can be modified so as to dispense with variable-size assumptions.

Our second contribution is a NIPE system based on composite order pairing groups with security under constant-size subgroup decision assumptions. The proof follows the Déjà Q framework of [16,40]. Even in the restrictive selective model of security, our scheme is the first one to achieve constant size ciphertexts and keys under static assumptions.

---

[1] One may object saying the linear-length vector x still has to be appended to the ciphertext. Nevertheless, in many applications the description of x can be very short. For example, in an ordinary (i.e., non-identity-based) broadcast encryption scheme for n users, x is uniquely determined by the n-bit word that specifies which users are in the revoked set. In this case, our ciphertexts reduce the communication overhead from $O(n\lambda)$ to $O(n + \lambda)$ bits if λ is the security parameter.

In the context of revocation, not only do we provide the first identity-based revocation systems with constant-size ciphertexts and keys, but we also give a solution based on fairly well-studied subgroup assumptions in composite order groups. It remains a challenging open problem (at least without using a complexity leveraging argument [8] entailing an exponential security loss) to achieve similar efficiency tradeoffs while proving security against adaptive adversaries.

Outline of the Constructions and Proofs. We begin with the first construction based on an asymmetric prime-order pairing $e : \mathbb{G} \times \hat{\mathbb{G}} \rightarrow \mathbb{G}_T$ with group order p. The public key consists of $g^{\alpha^i}, \hat{g}^{\alpha^i}$ for $i \in [1, 2n] \setminus \{n+1\}$ along with g^γ where g and α, γ are sampled at random from $\mathbb{G}$ and $\mathbb{Z}_p$, respectively. In addition the element $e(g, \hat{g})^{\alpha^{n+1}}$ is provided. A ciphertext for an attribute vector $\boldsymbol{x} \in \mathbb{Z}_p^n$ and message m consists of $(m \cdot e(g, \hat{g})^{\alpha^{n+1}s}, g^s, (v \cdot g^{\sum_{i=1}^{n} \alpha^i x_i})^s)$. Secret key associated with a vector $\boldsymbol{y}$ is computed deterministically as $\hat{g}^{\gamma \sum_{i=1}^{n} \alpha^{n-i+1} y_i}$. The structure is reminiscent of the Boneh-Gentry-Waters broadcast encryption scheme [12]. The proof of security is a reduction from the hardness of the n-DBDHE problem – an instance consists of $g^{\alpha^i}, \hat{g}^{\alpha^i}$ for $i \in [1, 2n] \setminus \{n + 1\}, g^s \in \mathbb{G}, T \in \mathbb{G}_T$ and asks to decide whether $T = e(g, \hat{g})^{\alpha^{n+1}s}$ or $T \xleftarrow{R} \mathbb{G}_T$. The attacker declares a target vector $\boldsymbol{x}^*$ which is used to program $\gamma = \sum_{i=1}^{n} \alpha^i x_i^*$. For any $\boldsymbol{y} \in \mathbb{Z}_p^n$ with $\langle \boldsymbol{x}^*, \boldsymbol{y} \rangle = 0$, secret key $d_{\boldsymbol{y}}$ can be simulated using the elements provided in the instance because for $d_{\boldsymbol{y}}$, the coefficient of α^{n+1} in the exponent of $\hat{g}$ would be $\langle \boldsymbol{x}^*, \boldsymbol{y} \rangle = 0$. The attacker then provides two messages m_0, m_1 to which the challenger responds with the ciphertext $(m_\beta \cdot T, g^s, (v \cdot g^{\sum_{i=1}^{n} \alpha^i x_i})^s)$ for a randomly chosen bit β. An adversary's ability to determine whether the message encrypted in the challenge ciphertext is real or random can be leveraged to solve the given instance of the decision problem.

We then consider a variant in the setting of a composite-order symmetric pairing $e : \mathbb{G} \times \mathbb{G} \rightarrow \mathbb{G}_T$ of common group order $N = p_1 p_2 p_3$, similar to Wee's composite-order variant [40] of the broadcast encryption in [12]. (Let $\mathbb{G}_q$ denote the subgroup of $\mathbb{G}$ of order q where q would be of the form $p_1^{e_1} p_2^{e_2} p_3^{e_3}$ for $e_1, e_2, e_3 \in \{0, 1\}$). The public key is composed of $v = g^\gamma, (g^{\alpha^i})_{i=1}^n, U_j = u^{\alpha^j}, j \in [1, 2n] \setminus \{n+1\}$ for some $g, u \xleftarrow{R} \mathbb{G}$ and $\alpha, \gamma \in \mathbb{Z}_N$ along with a pairwise-independent hash function $\mathsf{H} : \mathbb{G}_T \rightarrow \{0, 1\}^\lambda$. Decryption key for a vector $\boldsymbol{y}$ is defined as $u^{\gamma \sum_{i=1}^{n} \alpha^{n-i+1} y_i}$ and the ciphertext for attribute $\boldsymbol{x}$ and message M is defined as $(M \oplus \mathsf{H}(e(g, u)^{\alpha^{n+1}s}), g^s, (v \cdot g^{\sum_{i=1}^{n} \alpha^i x_i})^s)$. In addition, the parameters U_j and secret keys are randomized with $\mathbb{G}_{p_3}$-components. The security is reduced to two standard subgroup decision assumptions, denoted $(p_1 \rightarrow p_1 p_2)$ and $(p_1 p_3 \rightarrow p_1 p_2 p_3)$, where $(q_1 \rightarrow q_2)$ subgroup decision problem asks to distinguish between random elements of $\mathbb{G}_{q_1}$ from random elements of $\mathbb{G}_{q_2}$. The reduction gradually adds $\mathbb{G}_{p_2}$-components to the challenge ciphertext as well as elements $(U_j)_{j=1}^{2n}$ so that at the end, each U_j has in its exponent a pseudorandom function $RF : [1, 2n] \rightarrow \mathbb{Z}_{p_2}$ evaluated at j. The element $v = g^\gamma$ is programmed based on the challenge attribute $\boldsymbol{x}^*$ in a manner similar to the reduction in the prime-order case. Additionally, this ensures that the challenge ciphertext components are independent of $\alpha \bmod p_2$. Given this and the fact that keys are generated only for vectors $\boldsymbol{y}$ with $\langle \boldsymbol{x}^*, \boldsymbol{y} \rangle = 0$, α^{n+1} does not appear in the exponent of u in any of the keys. On the other hand, the message is masked by the hash of an element of $\mathbb{G}_T$ determined by $RF(n+1)$. Since all information provided to the attacker is independent of $RF(n+1)$, we use the left over hash lemma to argue that the mask on the message is uniformly distributed and hence statistically hides the message from the attacker.

Related Work. The inner product functionality was first considered by Katz et al. [22] in the design of predicate encryption systems (i.e., ABE schemes in the private index setting). Their construction [22] initiated a large body of work [2,24,30–34,36] which considered hierarchical extensions [30,33], additional properties in the secret-key setting [36] and adaptively secure realizations [24,31–34].

In the public-index setting, inner products also proved useful [4] to build adaptively secure identity-based broadcast encryption (IBBE) and revocation schemes with short ciphertexts under simple assumptions. The first construction of non-zero IPE appeared in [4] with security in the *co-selective* model under the Decision Linear [9] and Decisional Bilinear Diffie-Hellman assumptions. Co-selective security requires an adversary to commit to the attributes corresponding to private key queries before seeing the public parameters of the scheme, as opposed to target attribute set in the selective model. It is slightly stronger than the selective model but weaker than the adaptive model. The scheme has constant-size ciphertexts whereas its public parameters and keys are of size linear in n. More efficient realizations (but with asymptotically similar parameters) were put forth by Attrapadung *et al.* [5] and Yamada *et al.* [41] under the n-DBDHE assumption. While some of the NIPE constructions of [5,41] have exactly the same ciphertext length (resp. private key length) as our scheme, they require $O(n)$-size private keys (resp. $O(n)$-size ciphertexts). We thus prove security under the same assumption as [5,41] with only one group element per private key and 3 group elements per ciphertext.

The first adaptively secure NIPE scheme was proposed in [34] with $O(n)$ group elements in the public parameters and either $O(1)$-size ciphertexts or $O(1)$-size keys with a security reduction to the Decision Linear assumption. A more efficient construction was provided in [15] via an instantiation of predicate encodings [39] in prime-order groups. On the other hand, either ciphertexts or secret keys had size linear in n. Previously known constructions did not consider simultaneously achieving constant size ciphertexts and secret keys.

More recently, Abdalla *et al.* [1] suggested a different inner product functionality which evaluates linear functions of encrypted data (i.e., their inner product with a vector associated with the private key), instead of only testing if they evaluate to 0 as in [22,24,31–34]. Under simple assumptions, they obtained practical solutions based on the standard Decision Diffie-Hellman and Learning-With-Errors assumptions. Their results were extended to handle adaptive adversaries [3] and function-privacy in the secret-key setting [6].

In the context of IBBE scheme, Delerablée [18] suggested a selectively secure construction with constant-size ciphertexts and private keys based on strong q-type assumptions. Her construction actually remains the most efficient IBBE in the literature to date. The IBR system implied by our first NIPE construction can be seen as the revocation analogue of Delerablée's IBBE as it simultaneously provides $O(1)$-size ciphertexts and keys (the public parameters also have linear length in the maximal number of receivers per ciphertext in [18]). Unlike our IBR system, however, [18] is not known to have a counterpart based on simple assumptions in composite order groups. In the identity-based revocation setting, the constructions of Lewko et al. [23] feature constant-size private keys and public parameters, but their ciphertext size is linear in the number of revoked users. While their first construction has very short private keys and public parameters (made of 3 and 4 group elements, respectively), its underlying complexity assumption is very *ad hoc* and even stronger than n-DBDHE.

The Déjà Q framework, introduced by Chase and Meiklejohn [16], allows reducing well-studied fixed-size assumptions, such as the Subgroup Decision assumption [11] to some families of parameterized assumptions in composite-order groups. As a result, some well-known constructions such as Dodis-Yampolskiy PRF [19] and Boneh-Boyen signatures [7], when instantiated in composite order groups, could be shown secure under subgroup decision assumptions. Wee [40] further advanced the framework to cover certain encryption primitives as well, in addition to removing the restriction to work with asymmetric composite order groups. The primitives include adaptively secure identity-based encryption and selectively secure broadcast encryption. Recently, Libert *et al.* [26] applied Wee's framework to obtain functional commitment schemes for linear functions and accumulators from simple assumptions.

2 Background

2.1 Bilinear Maps and Complexity Assumptions

ASSUMPTIONS IN PRIME ORDER GROUPS. Let $(\mathbb{G}, \hat{\mathbb{G}}, \mathbb{G}_T)$ be groups of prime order p with a bilinear map $e : \mathbb{G} \times \hat{\mathbb{G}} \to \mathbb{G}_T$. We rely on a parameterized assumption introduced by Boneh et al. [12]. While this assumption was defined using symmetric pairings [10,12], we consider a natural extension to asymmetric pairings, which will enable our most efficient construction.

Definition 1. *Let $(\mathbb{G}, \hat{\mathbb{G}}, \mathbb{G}_T)$ be bilinear groups of prime order p. The n-Decision Bilinear Diffie-Hellman Exponent (n-DBDHE) problem is, given a tuple $(g, g^\alpha, g^{(\alpha^2)}, \ldots, g^{(\alpha^n)}, g^{(\alpha^{n+2})}, \ldots, g^{(\alpha^{2n})}, h, \hat{g}, \hat{g}^\alpha, \hat{g}^{(\alpha^2)}, \ldots, \hat{g}^{(\alpha^n)}, \hat{g}^{(\alpha^{n+2})}, T)$ where $g, h \xleftarrow{R} \mathbb{G}$, $\hat{g} \xleftarrow{R} \hat{\mathbb{G}}$, $\alpha \xleftarrow{R} \mathbb{Z}_p$ and $T \in_R \mathbb{G}_T$, to decide if $T = e(h, \hat{g})^{(\alpha^{n+1})}$ or if T is a random element of $\mathbb{G}_T$.*

ASSUMPTIONS IN COMPOSITE ORDER GROUPS. We use groups $(\mathbb{G}, \mathbb{G}_T)$ of composite order $N = p_1 p_2 p_3$ endowed with an efficiently computable map (a.k.a. pairing) $e : \mathbb{G} \times \mathbb{G} \to \mathbb{G}_T$ such that: (1) $e(g^a, h^b) = e(g, h)^{ab}$ for any $(g, h) \in \mathbb{G} \times \mathbb{G}$ and $a, b \in \mathbb{Z}$; (2) if $e(g, h) = 1_{\mathbb{G}_T}$ for each $h \in \mathbb{G}$, then $g = 1_{\mathbb{G}}$. An important property of composite order groups is that pairing two elements of order p_i and p_j, with $i \neq j$, always gives the identity element $1_{\mathbb{G}_T}$.

In the following, for each $i \in \{1, 2, 3\}$, we denote by $\mathbb{G}_{p_i}$ the subgroup of order p_i. For all distinct $i, j \in \{1, 2, 3\}$, we call $\mathbb{G}_{p_i p_j}$ the subgroup of order $p_i p_j$. In this setting, we rely on the following assumptions introduced in [25].

Assumption 1. Given a description of $(\mathbb{G}, \mathbb{G}_T, e)$ as well as $g \xleftarrow{R} \mathbb{G}_{p_1}, g_3 \xleftarrow{R} \mathbb{G}_{p_3}$ and $T \in \mathbb{G}$, it is infeasible to efficiently decide if $T \in \mathbb{G}_{p_1 p_2}$ or $T \in \mathbb{G}_{p_1}$.

Assumption 2. Let $g, X_1 \xleftarrow{R} \mathbb{G}_{p_1}, X_2, Y_2 \xleftarrow{R} \mathbb{G}_{p_2}, g_3, Y_3 \xleftarrow{R} \mathbb{G}_{p_3}$. Given a description of $(\mathbb{G}, \mathbb{G}_T, e)$, a set of group elements $(g, X_1 X_2, g_3, Y_2 Y_3)$ and T, it is hard to decide if $T \in_R \mathbb{G}_{p_1 p_3}$ or $T \in_R \mathbb{G}$.

These assumptions are non-interactive and falsifiable [28]. Moreover, in both of them, the number of input elements is constant (*i.e.*, independent of the number of adversarial queries).

2.2 Non-zero Inner Product Encryption (IPE)

Definition 2 (NIPE). *Let V denote an inner product space of dimension n and $\mathcal{M}$ denote the message space. A non-zero inner product encryption (NIPE) scheme for inner products over V, is defined by four probabilistic algorithms – Setup, Encrypt, KeyGen and Decrypt.*

Setup(λ, n): *Takes as input a security parameter λ and the dimension of V. It outputs the public parameters mpk and the master secret msk.*

KeyGen($msk, \boldsymbol{y}$): *On input a vector $\boldsymbol{y} \in V$ and the master secret msk; this algorithm outputs a secret key $d_{\boldsymbol{y}}$ for $\boldsymbol{y}$.*

Encrypt($mpk, m, \boldsymbol{x}$): *Takes as input a message m and an attribute vector $\boldsymbol{x} \in V$ and outputs a ciphertext $\mathcal{C}$.*

Decrypt($mpk, \mathcal{C}, d_{\boldsymbol{y}}$): *If $\langle \boldsymbol{x}, \boldsymbol{y} \rangle \neq 0$, this algorithm returns the message m and $\perp$ otherwise.*

Correctness. A NIPE scheme satisfies the correctness condition if for all vectors $\boldsymbol{x}, \boldsymbol{y} \in V$ with $\langle \boldsymbol{x}, \boldsymbol{y} \rangle \neq 0$ and for any message $m \in \mathcal{M}$, any keys $(\mathsf{mpk}, \mathsf{msk}) \leftarrow \mathsf{Setup}(\lambda, n)$, $d_{\boldsymbol{y}} \leftarrow \mathsf{KeyGen}(\mathsf{msk}, \boldsymbol{y})$ and any ciphertext $\mathcal{C} \leftarrow \mathsf{Encrypt}(\mathsf{mpk}, m, \boldsymbol{x})$, then $\Pr[m = \mathsf{Decrypt}(\mathsf{mpk}, \mathcal{C}, d_{\boldsymbol{y}})] = 1$.

Definition 3 (Selective Security). *Selective security of a non-zero inner product encryption scheme is formalized in terms of the following game between an adversary $\mathcal{A}$ and a challenger.*

Initialization: *The adversary $\mathcal{A}$ declares a challenge vector $\boldsymbol{x}^\star$.*

Setup: *The challenger runs the Setup algorithm of the NIPE and gives the public parameters to the adversary $\mathcal{A}$.*

Key Extraction Phase 1: *The adversary makes a number of key extraction queries adaptively. For a query on a vector $\boldsymbol{y}$ with the restriction that $\langle \boldsymbol{x}^\star, \boldsymbol{y} \rangle = 0$, the challenger responds with a key $d_{\boldsymbol{y}}$.*

Challenge: *The adversary $\mathcal{A}$ provides two equal-length messages M_0, M_1. The challenger chooses a bit β uniformly at random from $\{0, 1\}$, encrypts M_β to $\boldsymbol{x}^\star$ and returns the resulting ciphertext $C^\star$ to $\mathcal{A}$.*

Key Extraction Phase 2: *$\mathcal{A}$ makes more key extraction queries under the same restriction that it can only query keys for vectors $\boldsymbol{y}$ with $\langle \boldsymbol{x}^\star, \boldsymbol{y} \rangle = 0$.*

Guess: *$\mathcal{A}$ outputs a bit β'.*

If $\beta = \beta'$, then $\mathcal{A}$ wins the game. The advantage of $\mathcal{A}$ in winning the above game is defined as

$$Adv_{\text{NIPE},\mathcal{A}}(\lambda) = \left| \Pr[\beta = \beta'] - \frac{1}{2} \right|.$$

The NIPE scheme is said to be secure if every PPT adversary has negligible advantage in winning the above game.

3   A Construction for Non-zero Inner Products with Constant-Size Ciphertexts and Private Keys

Our scheme builds on the Boneh-Gentry-Waters broadcast encryption [12] and inherits its efficiency. In particular, the public parameters are exactly those of the BGW construction. In order to adapt it in the context of non-zero inner product encryption, we extend earlier observations which leveraged the BGW technique in the design of accumulators [13] and vector commitments [21, 27].

It was shown in [21] that a public key of the form

$$\{(g_i = g^{(\alpha^i)}, \hat{g}_i = \hat{g}^{(\alpha^i)})\}_{i \in [1,2n] \setminus \{n+1\}}$$

allows committing to a vector $\boldsymbol{x} = (x_1, \ldots, x_n)$ in such a way that the commitment string $C = g^\gamma \cdot \prod_{j=1}^n g_j^{x_j}$ makes it possible to convincingly reveal the partial information $z = \langle \boldsymbol{x}, \boldsymbol{y} \rangle$ about the committed message $\boldsymbol{x}$. Namely, a single group element

$$W_z = \prod_{i=1, i \neq j}^n (\hat{g}_{n+1-i}^\gamma \prod_{j=1}^n \hat{g}_{n+1+j-i}^{x_j})^{y_i} \in \hat{\mathbb{G}} \tag{1}$$

can serve as a witness that $z = \langle \boldsymbol{x}, \boldsymbol{y} \rangle$, for public $\boldsymbol{x} \in \mathbb{Z}_p^n$ and $z \in \mathbb{Z}_p$, and the verifier accepts (z, W_z) if and only if the following relation holds:

$$e(C, \prod_{j=1}^n \hat{g}_{n+1-j}^{y_j}) = e(g_1, \hat{g}_n)^z \cdot e(g, W_z) \tag{2}$$

The binding property of the commitment scheme relies on the fact that neither $g_{n+1} = g^{(\alpha^{n+1})}$ nor $\hat{g}_{n+1} = \hat{g}^{(\alpha^{n+1})}$ is publicly available.

Our non-zero IPE scheme proceeds by randomizing both members of (2) – by raising them to a random power $s \in \mathbb{Z}_p$ – so that the randomized C can be embedded in the ciphertext (together with g^s) while W_z serves as a decryption token. The decryption operation then computes $e(g_1, \hat{g}_n)^{s \cdot \langle \boldsymbol{x}, \boldsymbol{y} \rangle}$, which uncovers $e(g_1, \hat{g}_n)^s$ whenever $\langle \boldsymbol{x}, \boldsymbol{y} \rangle \neq 0$.

Our ciphertexts are of the form $\left(M \cdot e(g_1, \hat{g}_n)^s, g^s, (g^\gamma \cdot \prod_{j=1}^n g_j^{x_j})^s \right)$ and the challenge is thus to associate each vector $\boldsymbol{y} \in \mathbb{Z}_p$ with a short private key $d_{\boldsymbol{y}}$ so as to enable decryption. To achieve this, we observe that (1) can be re-written

$$W_z = (\prod_{i=1}^n \hat{g}_{n+1-i}^{y_i})^\gamma \cdot \prod_{i=1, i \neq j}^n \prod_{j=1}^n \hat{g}_{n+1+j-i}^{x_j y_i} \in \hat{\mathbb{G}},$$

where the second term is publicly computable as it does not depend on $\hat{g}_{n+1} = \hat{g}^{(\alpha^{n+1})}$. This implies that, if $\gamma \in \mathbb{Z}_p$ is the master secret key, the private key for a vector $\boldsymbol{y}$ can only consist of a single group element $d_{\boldsymbol{y}} = (\prod_{j=1}^n \hat{g}_{n+1-j}^{y_j})^\gamma \in \hat{\mathbb{G}}$.

Somewhat surprisingly, private keys are generated in a deterministic manner and, at first glance, their shape seems at odds with the collusion-resistance requirement: if $d_{\boldsymbol{y}_1}$ is a private key for $\boldsymbol{y}_1 \in \mathbb{Z}_p$ and $d_{\boldsymbol{y}_2}$ is a private key for $\boldsymbol{y}_2 \in \mathbb{Z}_p$, the product $d_{\boldsymbol{y}_1} \cdot d_{\boldsymbol{y}_2}$ is a valid private key for $\boldsymbol{y}_1 + \boldsymbol{y}_2$. However, this does not affect the functionality since any ciphertext that neither $d_{\boldsymbol{y}_1}$ nor $d_{\boldsymbol{y}_2}$ can decrypt must be labeled with a vector $\boldsymbol{x}$ such that $\langle \boldsymbol{x}, \boldsymbol{y}_1 \rangle = \langle \boldsymbol{x}, \boldsymbol{y}_2 \rangle = 0$, which implies $\langle \boldsymbol{x}, \boldsymbol{y}_1 + \boldsymbol{y}_2 \rangle = 0$. Said otherwise, combining several keys that cannot decrypt a given ciphertext only yields another key that remains unable to decrypt.

Setup(λ, n): Choose bilinear groups $(\mathbb{G}, \hat{\mathbb{G}}, \mathbb{G}_T)$ of prime order $p > 2^\lambda$ and define the bilinear map e. Choose $g \xleftarrow{R} \mathbb{G}$, $\hat{g} \xleftarrow{R} \hat{\mathbb{G}}$, $\alpha, \gamma \xleftarrow{R} \mathbb{Z}_p$ at random in order to define $v = g^\gamma \in \mathbb{G}$ and

$$\begin{aligned} g_1 &= g^\alpha, & \cdots & & g_n &= g^{(\alpha^n)} \\ g_{n+2} &= g^{(\alpha^{n+2})}, & \cdots & & g_{2n} &= g^{(\alpha^{2n})} \end{aligned}$$

and

$$\begin{aligned} \hat{g}_1 &= \hat{g}^\alpha, & \cdots & & \hat{g}_n &= \hat{g}^{(\alpha^n)} \\ \hat{g}_{n+2} &= \hat{g}^{(\alpha^{n+2})}, & \cdots & & \hat{g}_{2n} &= \hat{g}^{(\alpha^{2n})} \end{aligned}$$

Define the master public key to consist of

$$\mathsf{mpk} := \left((\mathbb{G}, \hat{\mathbb{G}}, \mathbb{G}_T, e), \ g, \ \hat{g}, \ v, \ \{(g_j, \hat{g}_j)\}_{j \in [1, 2n] \setminus \{n+1\}} \right).$$

The master secret key is $\mathsf{msk} := \gamma$.

KeyGen$(\mathsf{msk}, \boldsymbol{y})$: To generate a key for the vector $\boldsymbol{y} = (y_1, \ldots, y_n) \in \mathbb{Z}_p^n$, compute and output $d_{\boldsymbol{y}} = \left(\prod_{i=1}^n \hat{g}_{n+1-i}^{y_i} \right)^\gamma \in \hat{\mathbb{G}}$.

Encrypt$(\mathsf{mpk}, \boldsymbol{x}, M)$: To encrypt $M \in \mathbb{G}_T$ under $\boldsymbol{x} = (x_1, \ldots, x_n) \in \mathbb{Z}_p^n$, choose $s \xleftarrow{R} \mathbb{Z}_p$ in order to compute and output

$$\mathcal{C} = (C_0, C_1, C_2) = \left(M \cdot e(g_1, \hat{g}_n)^s, \ g^s, \ (v \cdot \prod_{j=1}^n g_j^{x_j})^s \right).$$

Decrypt(mpk, $\mathcal{C}$, $\boldsymbol{x}$, $d_{\boldsymbol{y}}$, $\boldsymbol{y}$): Given a ciphertext $\mathcal{C}$ labeled with $\boldsymbol{x} = (x_1, \ldots, x_n) \in \mathbb{Z}_p^n$ and a private key $d_{\boldsymbol{y}}$ associated with the vector $\boldsymbol{y} = (y_1, \ldots, y_n) \in \mathbb{Z}_p^n$, return $\perp$ if $\langle \boldsymbol{x}, \boldsymbol{y} \rangle = 0$. Otherwise, conduct the following steps.

1. Compute

$$\hat{A}_i = \prod_{j=1, j \neq i}^{n} \hat{g}_{n+1+j-i}^{x_j} \qquad \forall i \in \{1, \ldots, n\}. \tag{3}$$

2. Compute and output

$$M = C_0 \cdot \left(\frac{e(C_1, d_{\boldsymbol{y}} \cdot \prod_{i=1}^{n} \hat{A}_i^{y_i})}{e(C_2, \prod_{i=1}^{n} \hat{g}_{n+1-i}^{y_i})} \right)^{1/\langle \boldsymbol{x}, \boldsymbol{y} \rangle}. \tag{4}$$

The correctness of the scheme is easily verified by observing that

$$\frac{e\big(g, (\prod_{i=1}^{n} \hat{g}_{n+1-i}^{y_i})^\gamma \cdot \prod_{i=1}^{n} \prod_{j=1, j \neq i}^{n} \hat{g}_{n+1-i+j}^{x_j y_i}\big)}{e\big(g^\gamma \cdot \prod_{j=1}^{n} g_j^{x_j}, \prod_{i=1}^{n} \hat{g}_{n+1-i}^{y_i}\big)}$$

$$= \frac{e\big(g, (\prod_{i=1}^{n} \hat{g}_{n+1-i}^{y_i})^\gamma \cdot \prod_{i=1}^{n} \prod_{j=1, j \neq i}^{n} \hat{g}_{n+1-i+j}^{x_j y_i}\big)}{e\big(g^\gamma \cdot \prod_{j=1}^{n} \hat{g}_{n+1-i}^{y_i}\big) \cdot e\big(g, \prod_{i=1}^{n} \prod_{j=1}^{n} g_{n+1-i+j}^{x_j y_i}\big)} = e(g, \hat{g}_{n+1})^{-\sum_{i=1}^{n} x_i y_i}. \tag{5}$$

By raising both members of (5) to the power $s \in \mathbb{Z}_p$ and using (3), we obtain the equality

$$e(C_1, d_{\boldsymbol{y}} \cdot \prod_{i=1}^{n} \hat{A}_i^{y_i}) / e(C_2, \prod_{i=1}^{n} \hat{g}_{n+1-i}^{y_i}) = e(g_1, \hat{g}_n)^{-s \cdot \langle \boldsymbol{x}, \boldsymbol{y} \rangle},$$

which explains why M can be computed as per (4) whenever $\langle \boldsymbol{x}, \boldsymbol{y} \rangle \neq 0$.

From an efficiency point of view, the receiver has to compute a product of only two pairings (which is faster than two individual pairing evaluations) while the encryption and decryption algorithms both require at most $O(n)$ exponentiations. Indeed, the value $d_{\boldsymbol{y}} \cdot \prod_{i=1}^{n} \hat{A}_i^{y_i}$ is computable via a multi-exponentiation involving $2n - 1$ base elements (rather than n^2 in a naive computation).

Theorem 1. *The scheme is selectively secure under the n-DBDHE assumption.*

Proof. Towards a contradiction, let $\mathcal{A}$ be a PPT adversary with non-negligible advantage ε in the selective security game. We build a reduction algorithm that takes as input $((\mathbb{G}, \hat{\mathbb{G}}, \mathbb{G}_T, e), g, h, \{(g_i, \hat{g}_i) = (g^{(\alpha^i)}, \hat{g}^{(\alpha^i)})\}_{i \in [1,2n] \setminus \{n+1\}}, T)$ and uses $\mathcal{A}$ to decide if $T = e(h, \hat{g})^{(\alpha^{n+1})}$ or $T \in_R \mathbb{G}_T$.

The adversary $\mathcal{A}$ first chooses a target vector $\boldsymbol{x}^\star = (x_1^\star, \ldots, x_n^\star) \in \mathbb{Z}_p^n$. To construct the master public key mpk, $\mathcal{B}$ chooses $\tilde{\gamma} \xleftarrow{R} \mathbb{Z}_p$ and computes

$$v = g^{\tilde{\gamma}} \cdot \prod_{j=1}^{n} g_j^{-x_j^\star} \in \mathbb{G},$$

which implicitly defines the master secret key msk to be $\gamma = \tilde{\gamma} - \sum_{j=1}^{n} x_j \cdot \alpha^j$. The adversary $\mathcal{A}$ is run on input of

$$\mathsf{mpk} := \Big(g, \ \hat{g}, \ v, \ \{(g_i, \hat{g}_i) = (g^{(\alpha^i)}, \hat{g}^{(\alpha^i)})\}_{i \in [1,2n] \setminus \{n+1\}} \Big).$$

Observe that mpk is distributed as in the real scheme as v is uniformly distributed over $\mathbb{G}$. At any time, $\mathcal{A}$ can request a private key $d_{\boldsymbol{y}}$ for any vector $\boldsymbol{y} \in \mathbb{Z}_p^N$ such that $\langle \boldsymbol{x}, \boldsymbol{y} \rangle = 0$. To generate the private key $d_{\boldsymbol{y}} = (\prod_{i=1}^{n} \hat{g}_{n+1-i}^{y_i})^{\gamma} \in \hat{\mathbb{G}}$, algorithm $\mathcal{B}$ can exploit the fact that, in the product,

$$\Big(\sum_{i=1}^{n} y_i \cdot \alpha^{n+1-i} \Big) \cdot \Big(\sum_{j=1}^{n} x_j^{\star} \cdot \alpha^j \Big) = \sum_{i=1}^{n} \sum_{j=1}^{n} x_j^{\star} \cdot y_i \cdot \alpha^{n+1-i+j},$$

the coefficient of α^{n+1} is exactly $\langle \boldsymbol{x}^{\star}, \boldsymbol{y} \rangle$, which must be zero in any legal private key query $\boldsymbol{y} \in \mathbb{Z}_p^n$. Specifically, $\mathcal{B}$ can compute

$$d_{\boldsymbol{y}} = (\prod_{i=1}^{n} \hat{g}_{n+1-i}^{y_i})^{\tilde{\gamma}} / \prod_{i=1}^{n} \prod_{j=1, j \neq i}^{n} \hat{g}_{n+1-i+j}^{x_j^{\star} \cdot y_i}. \tag{6}$$

For any vector $\boldsymbol{y} \in \mathbb{Z}_p^n$ such that $\langle \boldsymbol{x}^{\star}, \boldsymbol{y} \rangle = 0$, $\mathcal{B}$ can thus compute the private key $d_{\boldsymbol{y}}$ as per (6).

In the challenge phase, $\mathcal{A}$ chooses messages $M_0, M_1 \in \mathbb{G}_T$ and expects to receive an encryption of one of these. At this point, $\mathcal{B}$ flips a fair coin $\beta \xleftarrow{R} \{0, 1\}$ and computes

$$\mathcal{C} = (C_0, C_1, C_2) = \big(M_{\beta} \cdot T, \ h, \ h^{\tilde{\gamma}} \big),$$

which is returned as a challenge to $\mathcal{B}$. It is easy to see that, if $T = e(h, \hat{g})^{(\alpha^{n+1})}$, then $\mathcal{C}$ is a valid encryption of M_{β} for the vector $\boldsymbol{x}^{\star} = (x_1^{\star}, \dots, x_n^{\star})$ and the encryption exponent $s = \log_g(h)$. In contrast, if $T \in_R \mathbb{G}_T$, the ciphertext carries no information about $\beta \in \{0, 1\}$.

When $\mathcal{A}$ halts, it outputs a bit $\beta' \in \{0, 1\}$. If $\beta' = \beta$, the reduction $\mathcal{B}$ outputs 1 (meaning that $T = e(h, \hat{g})^{(\alpha^{n+1})}$). Otherwise, it outputs 0. $\square$

4   NIPE from Constant-Size Subgroup Assumptions

In this section, we present a non-zero inner-product encryption (NIPE) scheme based on composite order pairings $e : \mathbb{G} \times \mathbb{G} \to \mathbb{G}_T$ of common group order $N = p_1 p_2 p_3$, with security under the subgroup decision assumptions. For inner products over length-n vectors in $\mathbb{Z}_N$, the public parameter size is linear in n while ciphertexts and keys have constant size (independent of n). The resulting scheme is the first to achieve such parameters with selective security under constant size assumptions.

Similar to the prime-order case, it seems possible to derive this construction from a functional commitment scheme for linear functions [26] by randomizing commitments and the verification equation. However, the transformation is not generic. A commitment C to $\boldsymbol{x} \in \mathbb{Z}_N^n$ in [26] is computed as $C = g^\gamma \cdot g^{\sum_{i=1}^n \alpha^i \cdot x_i}$. Elements $\left(g^\gamma, \{g^{\alpha^i}\}_{i=1}^n\right)$ are made available in the public parameters along with elements $U_j = u^{\alpha^j} \cdot R_{3,j}$ for $j \in [1, 2n] \setminus \{n+1\}$ with $R_{3,j}$ being randomly distributed in $\mathbb{G}_{p_3}$. The U_j's allow creating a short witness W_z for the statement $z = \langle \boldsymbol{x}, \boldsymbol{y} \rangle$ (for some $\boldsymbol{y} \in \mathbb{Z}_N^n$) using the secret random exponent γ.

$$W_z = \prod_{i=1}^n W_i^{y_i}, \quad \text{where} \quad W_i = U_{n-i+1}^\gamma \prod_{j=1, j\neq i}^n U_{n+1+j-i}.$$

Consolidating all the terms that depend on γ into $W_{z,1}$, write $W_z = W_{z,1} \cdot W_{z,2}$. More precisely, we have

$$W_{z,1} = \prod_{i=1}^n U_{n-i+1}^\gamma \quad \text{and} \quad W_{z,2} = \prod_{i=1}^n \left(\prod_{j=1, j\neq i}^n U_{n+1+j-i}\right)^{y_i}.$$

Observe that the computation of $W_{z,2}$ is solely based on information available in the public parameters and $W_{z,1}$ is independent of $\boldsymbol{x}$. One can verify the validity of the witness W_z by simply checking whether the following equation holds.

$$e(C, \prod_{i=1}^n U_i^{y_i}) = e(g^\alpha, U_n)^z \cdot e(g, W_z).$$

Randomizing both sides of the above equation with $s \in \mathbb{Z}_N$ in the exponent leads us to the non-zero IPE. Namely, a ciphertext for a vector $\boldsymbol{x}$ and a message $M \in \{0,1\}^\lambda$ would consist of C^s, g^s and $M \oplus \mathsf{H}\left(e(g^\alpha, U_n)^s\right)$, where $\mathsf{H} : \mathbb{G}_T \to \{0,1\}^\lambda$ is a pairwise-independent hash function. The decryption key for a vector $\boldsymbol{y}$ is nothing but $W_{z,1}$. For a valid key, the fact that $z = \langle \boldsymbol{x}, \boldsymbol{y} \rangle \neq 0$ enables us to recover the blinding factor on the message from $e(g^\alpha, U_n)^{zs}$.

Setup(λ, n): Takes as input n, the dimension of the inner product space. Choose bilinear groups $(\mathbb{G}, \mathbb{G}_T)$ of composite order $N = p_1 p_2 p_3$, where $p_i > 2^{l(\lambda)}$ for each $i \in \{1, 2, 3\}$, for a suitable polynomial $l : \mathbb{N} \to \mathbb{N}$. Define the bilinear map $e : \mathbb{G} \times \mathbb{G} \to \mathbb{G}_T$. We consider inner products defined over $\mathbb{Z}_N^n$. Choose $g, u \xleftarrow{R} \mathbb{G}_{p_1}$, $R_3 \xleftarrow{R} \mathbb{G}_{p_3}$ and $\alpha, \gamma \xleftarrow{R} \mathbb{Z}_N$ at random in order to define

$$G_1 = g^\alpha, \qquad G_2 = g^{(\alpha^2)}, \qquad \dots \qquad , G_n = g^{(\alpha^n)}$$

and

$$U_1 = u^\alpha \cdot R_{3,1}, \qquad U_2 = u^{(\alpha^2)} \cdot R_{3,2}, \qquad \dots \qquad , U_n = u^{(\alpha^n)} \cdot R_{3,n}$$
$$U_{n+2} = u^{(\alpha^{n+2})} \cdot R_{3,n+2}, \qquad \dots \qquad , U_{2n} = u^{(\alpha^{2n})} \cdot R_{3,2n},$$

where $R_{3,j} \xleftarrow{R} \mathbb{G}_{p_3}$ for each $j \in [1, 2n]\setminus\{n+1\}$. Define the public parameters to consist of

$$\mathsf{mpk} := \Big((\mathbb{G}, \mathbb{G}_T, e), g, \ g^\gamma, \ \{G_j\}_{j=1}^n, \ \{U_j\}_{j \in [1,2n] \setminus \{n+1\}}, \ \mathsf{H} \Big),$$

where $\mathsf{H} : \mathbb{G}_T \to \{0,1\}^\lambda$ is a pairwise-independent hash function. The master secret key is given by $\mathsf{msk} := (u, R_3, \gamma, \alpha)$.

Encrypt$(\mathsf{mpk}, M, \boldsymbol{x} = (x_1, \ldots, x_n))$: To encrypt $M \in \{0,1\}^\lambda$ under $\boldsymbol{x} \in \mathbb{Z}_N^n$, choose $s \xleftarrow{R} \mathbb{Z}_N$ and define the ciphertext $\mathcal{C}$ to consist of three components – one from $\mathbb{G}_T$ and two from $\mathbb{G}$ given by

$$C_0 = M \oplus \mathsf{H}(e(g,u)^{\alpha^{n+1} s}), \qquad C_1 = g^s, \qquad C_2 = g^{s \cdot (\gamma + \sum_{i=1}^n \alpha^i \cdot x_i)},$$

where C_0 and C_2 are computed as $M \oplus \mathsf{H}\big(e(G_1, U_n)^s\big)$ and $(g^\gamma \cdot \prod_{i=1}^n G_i^{x_i})^s$ respectively. The algorithm outputs $\mathcal{C} = (C_0, C_1, C_2)$.

KeyGen$(\mathsf{msk}, \boldsymbol{y})$: The secret key for $\boldsymbol{y} = (y_1, \ldots, y_n) \in \mathbb{Z}_N^n$ is given by

$$d_{\boldsymbol{y}} = \left(\prod_{i=1}^n u^{\alpha^i \cdot y_i} \right)^\gamma \cdot X_3,$$

where $X_3 \xleftarrow{R} \mathbb{G}_{p_3}$ is sampled using R_3.

Decrypt$(\mathcal{C}, \boldsymbol{x}, \boldsymbol{y}, d_{\boldsymbol{y}})$: Let $z = \langle \boldsymbol{x}, \boldsymbol{y} \rangle \bmod N$. If $z \neq 0$ the algorithm computes $A_i = \prod_{j=1, j \neq i}^n U_{n+1+j-i}^{x_j}$ for all $i \in [1,n]$, and recovers $M \in \{0,1\}^\lambda$ as

$$M = C_0 \oplus \mathsf{H} \left(\left(\frac{e(C_1, d_{\boldsymbol{y}} \cdot \prod_{i=1}^n A_i^{y_i})}{e(C_2, \prod_{i=1}^n U_{n-i+1}^{y_i})} \right)^{1/z} \right).$$

Correctness. Correctness follows from the observation that

$$e(C_2, U_{n-i+1}) = e \left(g^{s \cdot (\gamma + \sum_{i=1}^n \alpha^i x_i)}, u^{(\alpha^{n-i+1})} \cdot R_{3,n+2} \right)$$

$$= e \left(g^\gamma \cdot \prod_{i=1}^n g^{\alpha^i \cdot x_i}, u^{(\alpha^{n-i+1})} \right)^s$$

$$= e(g,u)^{\alpha^{n+1} \cdot s \cdot x_i} \cdot e \left(g, u_{n-i+1}^\gamma \cdot \prod_{j=1, j \neq i}^n u^{\alpha^{n+1+j-i} \cdot x_j} \right)^s$$

$$= e(g,u)^{\alpha^{n+1} \cdot s \cdot x_i} \cdot e \left(g, u_{n-i+1}^\gamma \cdot A_i \right)^s.$$

Raising both sides of the above equality to y_i and taking a product over all $i \in [1,n]$ gives us

$$e \left(C_2, \prod_{i=1}^n U_{n-i+1}^{y_i} \right) = \prod_{i=1}^n e(g,u)^{\alpha^{n+1} \cdot s \cdot x_i \cdot y_i} \cdot \prod_{i=1}^n e \left(g, u^{(\alpha^{n-i+1}) \cdot \gamma} \cdot A_i \right)^{s \cdot y_i}$$

$$= e(g,u)^{\alpha^{n+1} \cdot s \cdot \langle \boldsymbol{x}, \boldsymbol{y} \rangle} \cdot e \left(g^s, \prod_{i=1}^n u^{(\alpha^{n-i+1}) \cdot \gamma \cdot y_i} \cdot A_i^{y_i} \right)$$

$$= e(g,u)^{\alpha^{n+1} \cdot s \cdot z} \cdot e \left(C_1, d_{\boldsymbol{y}} \cdot \prod_{i=1}^n A_i^{y_i} \right),$$

as required. Note that in the last step, we replaced $\prod_{i=1}^{n} u^{(\alpha^{n-i+1}) \cdot \gamma \cdot y_i}$ by d_y as the $\mathbb{G}_{p_3}$ component vanishes upon pairing.

Theorem 2. *The NIPE construction is selectively secure if Assumption 1 and Assumption 2 hold.*

Proof. The proof relies on a series of modifications to the distribution of public parameters. To define these alternative distributions, we use a family of functions

$$\{F_k : [1, 2n] \to \mathbb{Z}_{p_2}\}_{k=0}^{2n}$$

such that for all $j \in [1, 2n]$,

$$F_k(j) = \begin{cases} 0 & \text{if } k = 0 \\ \sum_{i=1}^{k} r_j \cdot \alpha_i^j \bmod p_2 & \text{if } k \in [1, 2n] \end{cases}$$

where $r_1, \ldots, r_{2n}, \alpha_1, \ldots, \alpha_{2n}$ are randomly distributed in $\mathbb{Z}_{p_2}$. The modified distributions are defined on the parameters $\{U_j\}_{j=1}^{2n}$.

Type k parameters $(0 \leq k \leq 2n)$: are parameters where elements $\{U_i\}_{i \in [1, 2n]}$ have a $\mathbb{G}_{p_2}$ component determined by the function $F_k(.)$: namely,

$$U_i = u^{(\alpha^i)} \cdot g_2^{F_k(i)} \cdot R_{3,i} \qquad \forall i \in [1, 2n].$$

The proof proceeds through a sequence of $2n + 4$ games denoted G_0, G_1, G_2, $G_{3,1}, \ldots, G_{3,2n}, G_4$ as defined below. Let $\text{win}_\square$ denote the event that the adversary $\mathcal{A}$ wins in game $G_\square$.

Game G_0: is the real attack game (described in Sect. 2.2).

Game G_1: This game is similar to G_0 except for the following changes. At the beginning of the game, the challenger chooses $\tilde{\gamma} \xleftarrow{R} \mathbb{Z}_N$ and sets $\gamma = \tilde{\gamma} - \sum_{i=1}^{n} \alpha^i x_i^\star$ where $\boldsymbol{x}^\star = (x_1^\star, \ldots, x_n^\star)$ is the challenge vector. The public parameter g^γ is generated as $g^{\tilde{\gamma}} \cdot \prod_{i=1}^{n} G_i^{-x_i^\star}$. The challenge ciphertext is computed as:

$$C_1 \xleftarrow{R} \mathbb{G}_{p_1}, \qquad C_2 = C_1^{\tilde{\gamma}}, \qquad C_0 = M_\beta \oplus \mathsf{H}\big(e(C_1, U_{n+1})\big).$$

Since γ is known to the challenger, secret key queries can be answered by running the KeyGen algorithm. The change is only conceptual and hence $\Pr[\text{win}_0] = \Pr[\text{win}_1]$.

Game G_2: In this game, we start modifying the distribution of the challenge ciphertext. Namely, the challenger now picks C_1 uniformly at random in $\mathbb{G}_{p_1 p_2}$ instead of $\mathbb{G}_{p_1}$. The adversary's ability to distinguish between games G_1 and G_2 can be leveraged to break Assumption 1 as formalized in the following lemma.

Lemma 1. *If Assumption 1 holds, then $|\Pr[\text{win}_1] - \Pr[\text{win}_2]|$ is negligible.*

Game $G_{3,k}$ for $k = 1, \ldots, 2n$: We let game $G_{3,0}$ be identical to G_2 for notational convenience. In game $G_{3,k}$ the adversary is given Type k parameters. We argue that the adversary can detect this change with negligible probability if Assumption 2 holds.

Lemma 2. *If Assumption 2 holds, then* $| \Pr[\text{win}_{3,k-1}] - \Pr[\text{win}_{3,k}]|$ *is negligible for each $k \in [1, 2n]$.*

In game $G_{3,2n}$ the parameters U_j have their $\mathbb{G}_{p_2}$ components defined by $F_{2n}(j)$, which is a $2n$-wise independent function from $[1, 2n]$ to $\mathbb{Z}_{p_2}$. The adversary's view thus remains identical if we replace the function F_{2n} by a truly random function $RF : [1, 2n] \to \mathbb{Z}_{p_2}$ which allows defining the $\mathbb{G}_{p_2}$ component of U_j as $g_2^{RF(j)}$ for each $j \in [1, 2n]$.

Game G_4: This game is identical to game $G_{3,2n}$ with the difference that, in the challenge ciphertext, C_0 is chosen as a random string in $\{0,1\}^\lambda$. We argue that any legitimate adversary's view remains statistically close to that of game $G_{3,2n}$. To see this, we first note that the $\mathbb{G}_{p_2}$ components of the secret keys contain linear combinations of $RF(j)$ in the exponent excluding $RF(n+1)$. Indeed, recall that the adversary can only make private key queries on vectors $\boldsymbol{y}$ such that $\langle \boldsymbol{y}, \boldsymbol{x}^\star \rangle = 0$. Programming γ as $\gamma = \tilde{\gamma} - \sum_{i=1}^n \alpha^i \cdot x_i^\star$ requires the creation of a $\mathbb{G}_{p_1}$ component with the exponent

$$\left(\sum_{i=1}^n y_i \cdot \alpha^{n-i+1} \right) \cdot \left(\tilde{\gamma} - \sum_{i=1}^n \alpha^i \cdot x_i^\star \right),$$

in order to generate a secret key for $\boldsymbol{y}$. Note that the coefficient of α^{n+1} is $\langle \boldsymbol{y}, \boldsymbol{x}^\star \rangle$ which is 0 for all legal private key queries. Hence, the private key $d_{\boldsymbol{y}}$ can be computed without using U_{n+1}, ensuring that $RF(n+1)$ remains completely independent of any information revealed to $\mathcal{A}$. As a result, the distribution of

$$\mathsf{H}\big(e(C_1, U_{n+1})\big) = \mathsf{H}\big(e(C_1, u^{\alpha^{n+1}}) \cdot e(C_1, g_2^{RF(n+1)})\big)$$

is statistically uniform over $\{0,1\}^\lambda$ as long as C_1 as a non-trivial $\mathbb{G}_{p_2}$ component (which occurs with probability $1 - 1/p_2$). This follows from the fact that, if $e(C_1, g_2) \neq 1_{\mathbb{G}_T}$, the $\mathbb{G}_{p_2}$ component of $e(C_1, g_2^{RF(n+1)})$ has $\log(p_2)$ bits of min-entropy. Since $\mathsf{H} : \mathbb{G}_T \to \{0,1\}^\lambda$ is a pairwise-independent hash function, the Leftover Hash Lemma ensures that, conditionally on the adversary's view, the distribution of $\mathsf{H}\big(e(C_1, u^{\alpha^{n+1}}) \cdot e(C_1, g_2^{RF(n+1)})\big)$ is within distance $2^{-\lambda}$ from the uniform distribution over $\{0,1\}^\lambda$. This implies that $| \Pr[\text{win}_{3,2n}] - \Pr[\text{win}_4]| \leq 1/p_2 + 1/2^\lambda$, which is statistically negligible as claimed. Since $\beta \in \{0,1\}$ is perfectly hidden from the adversary in G_4, we have $\Pr[\text{win}_4] = 1/2$.

Combining the above, we find

$$\mathsf{Adv}_{\text{NIPE},\mathcal{A}}(\lambda) = |\Pr[\text{win}_0] - \Pr[\text{win}_4]| \leq \mathsf{Adv}_{\mathcal{G},\mathcal{B}}^1(\lambda) + 2n \cdot \mathsf{Adv}_{\mathcal{G},\mathcal{B}}^2(\lambda) + \frac{1}{p_2} + \frac{1}{2^\lambda}$$

which is negligible in the security parameter λ provided Assumption 1 and Assumption 2 both hold in $(\mathbb{G}, \mathbb{G}_T)$. $\qquad\square$

Proof (of Lemma 1). Let (g, g_3, T) be an instance of Assumption 1. We show how $\mathcal{B}$ simulates the different stages of the security game.

Initialize: $\mathcal{A}$ commits to the challenge vector $\boldsymbol{x}^\star = (x_1^\star, \ldots, x_n^\star)$.

Setup: Pick $u \xleftarrow{R} \mathbb{G}_{p_1}$, $\alpha \xleftarrow{R} \mathbb{Z}_N$ and compute $G_j = g^{\alpha^j}$ for $j = 1, \ldots, n$, $U_j = u^{\alpha^j} \cdot R_{3,j}$ for $j \in [1, 2n]$ where $R_{3,j}$'s are sampled from $\mathbb{G}_{p_3}$ using g_3. Choose $\tilde{\gamma} \xleftarrow{R} \mathbb{Z}_N$ and set $\gamma = \tilde{\gamma} - \sum_{i=1}^{n} \alpha^i \cdot x_i^\star$. The adversary is given the following public parameters

$$\mathsf{mpk} := \left(g, \ g^\gamma, \ \{G_j\}_{j=1}^n, \ \{U_j\}_{j \in [1,2n] \setminus \{n+1\}}, \ \mathsf{H} \right).$$

Key Extraction: Upon a query on vector $\boldsymbol{y} \in \mathbb{Z}_N^n$, the adversary is given $d_{\boldsymbol{y}} = \left(u^{\sum_{i=1}^{n} \alpha^{n-i+1} \cdot y_i} \right)^\gamma \cdot X_3$, where $X_3 \xleftarrow{R} \mathbb{G}_{p_3}$.

Challenge: $\mathcal{A}$ provides two messages M_0, M_1. $\mathcal{B}$ picks $\beta \xleftarrow{R} \{0,1\}$ and computes the ciphertext $C^\star = (C_0, C_1, C_2)$, where,

$$C_1 = T, \qquad C_2 = T^{\tilde{\gamma}}, \qquad C_0 = M_\beta \oplus \mathsf{H}\big(e(C_1, U_{n+1})\big).$$

Guess: $\mathcal{A}$ returns a bit β'. $\mathcal{B}$ returns 1 if $\beta = \beta'$ and 0 otherwise.

If $T \xleftarrow{R} \mathbb{G}_{p_1}$, then $C^\star$ is distributed as in G_1. Otherwise, $T \xleftarrow{R} \mathbb{G}_{p_1 p_3}$ and $\mathcal{B}$ simulates G_2. We have

$$
\begin{aligned}
|\Pr[\mathsf{win}_1] - \Pr[\mathsf{win}_2]| &= |\Pr[\beta = \beta' | T \xleftarrow{R} \mathbb{G}_{p_1}] - \Pr[\beta = \beta' | T \xleftarrow{R} \mathbb{G}_{p_1 p_2}]| \\
&= |\Pr[\mathcal{B} \text{ returns } 1 | T \xleftarrow{R} \mathbb{G}_{p_1}] - \Pr[\mathcal{B} \text{ returns } 1 | T \xleftarrow{R} \mathbb{G}_{p_1 p_2}]| \\
&= \mathsf{Adv}_{\mathcal{G},\mathcal{B}}^1(\lambda) ,
\end{aligned}
$$

which is negligible under Assumption 1. $\qquad\square$

Proof (of Lemma 2). Using $\mathcal{A}$ show how to construct an algorithm $\mathcal{B}$ that breaks Assumption 2. $\mathcal{B}$ receives an instance $(g, X_1 X_2, g_3, Y_2 Y_3, T)$ of the problem and simulates the game as follows. Suppose that $T = u \cdot g_2^{r_2} \cdot g_3^{r_3}$ where either $r_2 = 0$ or $r_2 \xleftarrow{R} \mathbb{Z}_{p_2}$.

Initialize: $\mathcal{A}$ commits to the challenge vector $\boldsymbol{x}^\star = (x_1^\star, \ldots, x_n^\star)$.

Setup: Pick $\alpha \xleftarrow{R} \mathbb{Z}_N$, $r_1', \ldots, r_{k-1}' \xleftarrow{R} \mathbb{Z}_N$ and compute $G_j = g^{\alpha^j}$ for $j = 1, \ldots, n$ and

$$U_j = T^{\alpha^j} \cdot (Y_2 Y_3)^{\sum_{i=1}^{k-1} r_i' \cdot \alpha_i^j} \cdot R_{3,j}'$$

for $j \in [1, 2n]$ where $R_{3,j}' \xleftarrow{R} \mathbb{G}_{p_3}$. Choose $\tilde{\gamma} \xleftarrow{R} \mathbb{Z}_N$ and set $\gamma = \tilde{\gamma} - \sum_{i=1}^{n} \alpha^i x_i^\star$. The adversary is given the following public parameters

$$\mathsf{mpk} := \left(g, \ g^\gamma, \ \{G_j\}_{j=1}^n, \ \{U_j\}_{j \in [1,2n] \setminus \{n+1\}}, \ \mathsf{H} \right).$$

Key Extraction: Upon a query on vector $\boldsymbol{y} \in \mathbb{Z}_N^n$, the adversary is given $d_{\boldsymbol{y}} = \left(\prod_{i=1}^n U_{n-i+1}^{y_i}\right)^\gamma \cdot X_3'$, where $X_3' \xleftarrow{R} \mathbb{G}_{p_3}$.

Challenge: $\mathcal{A}$ provides two messages M_0, M_1. $\mathcal{B}$ picks $\beta \xleftarrow{R} \{0,1\}$ and computes the ciphertext $\mathcal{C}^* = (C_0, C_1, C_2)$, where,

$$C_1 = X_1 X_2, \qquad C_2 = (X_1 X_2)^{\tilde{\gamma}}, \qquad C_0 = M_\beta \oplus \mathsf{H}\big(e(C_1, U_{n+1})\big).$$

Guess: $\mathcal{A}$ returns a bit β'. $\mathcal{B}$ returns 1 if $\beta = \beta'$ and 0 otherwise.

If $r_2 = 0$, then the parameters have the Type $k - 1$ distribution. Otherwise, $r_2 \xleftarrow{R} \mathbb{Z}_{p_2}$ and the parameters have the Type k distribution for reasons explained next. The $\mathbb{G}_{p_2}$-components of U_j (for $j \in [1, 2n]$) would be given by

$$g_2^{r_2 \cdot \alpha^j} \cdot Y_2^{\sum_{i=1}^{k-1} r_i \cdot \alpha_i^j}. \tag{7}$$

All the information provided to $\mathcal{A}$ is independent of $\alpha \bmod p_2$ (by the Chinese Remainder Theorem) and hence we can substitute $\alpha \bmod p_2$ with a uniformly random $\alpha_k \in \mathbb{Z}_{p_2}$. The $\mathbb{G}_{p_2}$ component of U_j in (7) can thus be replaced by

$$g_2^{\sum_{i=1}^k r_i \cdot \alpha_i^j}.$$

as required. Moreover, the $\mathbb{G}_{p_3}$ component of U_j is uniformly distributed since we randomize it by $R'_{3,j}$. We thus have

$$|\Pr[\mathsf{win}_{3,k-1}] - \Pr[\mathsf{win}_{3,k}]| \leq \mathsf{Adv}^2_{\mathcal{G},\mathcal{B}}(\lambda),$$

which is negligible under Assumption 2. $\qquad\qquad\qquad\qquad\qquad\qquad\qquad \Box$

Acknowledgements. The authors were funded by the "Programme Avenir Lyon Saint-Etienne de l'Université de Lyon" in the framework of the programme "Investissements d'Avenir" (ANR-11-IDEX-0007). Jie Chen was also supported in part by the National Natural Science Foundation of China (Grant No. 61472142).

References

1. Abdalla, M., Bourse, F., De Caro, A., Pointcheval, D.: Simple functional encryption schemes for inner products. In: Katz, J. (ed.) PKC 2015. LNCS, vol. 9020, pp. 733–751. Springer, Heidelberg (2015)
2. Agrawal, S., Freeman, D.M., Vaikuntanathan, V.: Functional encryption for inner product predicates from learning with errors. In: Lee, D.H., Wang, X. (eds.) ASIACRYPT 2011. LNCS, vol. 7073, pp. 21–40. Springer, Heidelberg (2011)
3. Agrawal, S., Libert, B., Stehlé, D.: Fully secure functional encryption for inner products, from standard assumptions. In: Robshaw, M., Katz, J. (eds.) CRYPTO 2016. LNCS, vol. 9816, pp. 333–362. Springer, Heidelberg (2016). doi:10.1007/978-3-662-53015-3_12. Cryptology ePrint Archive: Report 2015/608
4. Attrapadung, N., Libert, B.: Functional encryption for inner product: achieving constant-size ciphertexts with adaptive security or support for negation. In: Nguyen, P.Q., Pointcheval, D. (eds.) PKC 2010. LNCS, vol. 6056, pp. 384–402. Springer, Heidelberg (2010)

5. Attrapadung, N., Libert, B., de Panafieu, E.: Expressive key-policy attribute-based encryption with constant-size ciphertexts. In: Catalano, D., Fazio, N., Gennaro, R., Nicolosi, A. (eds.) PKC 2011. LNCS, vol. 6571, pp. 90–108. Springer, Heidelberg (2011)
6. Bishop, A., Jain, A., Kowalczyk, L.: Function-hiding inner product encryption. In: Iwata, T., et al. (eds.) ASIACRYPT 2015. LNCS, vol. 9452, pp. 470–491. Springer, Heidelberg (2015). doi:10.1007/978-3-662-48797-6_20
7. Boneh, D., Boyen, X.: Short signatures without random oracles. In: Cachin, C., Camenisch, J.L. (eds.) EUROCRYPT 2004. LNCS, vol. 3027, pp. 56–73. Springer, Heidelberg (2004)
8. Boneh, D., Boyen, X.: Efficient selective-ID secure identity-based encryption without random oracles. In: Cachin, C., Camenisch, J.L. (eds.) EUROCRYPT 2004. LNCS, vol. 3027, pp. 223–238. Springer, Heidelberg (2004)
9. Boneh, D., Boyen, X., Shacham, H.: Short group signatures. In: Franklin, M. (ed.) CRYPTO 2004. LNCS, vol. 3152, pp. 41–55. Springer, Heidelberg (2004)
10. Boneh, D., Boyen, X., Goh, E.-J.: Hierarchical identity based encryption with constant size ciphertext. In: Cramer, R. (ed.) EUROCRYPT 2005. LNCS, vol. 3494, pp. 440–456. Springer, Heidelberg (2005)
11. Boneh, D., Goh, E.-J., Nissim, K.: Evaluating 2-DNF formulas on ciphertexts. In: Kilian, J. (ed.) TCC 2005. LNCS, vol. 3378, pp. 325–341. Springer, Heidelberg (2005)
12. Boneh, D., Gentry, C., Waters, B.: Collusion resistant broadcast encryption with short ciphertexts and private keys. In: Shoup, V. (ed.) CRYPTO 2005. LNCS, vol. 3621, pp. 258–275. Springer, Heidelberg (2005)
13. Camenisch, J., Kohlweiss, M., Soriente, C.: An accumulator based on Bilinear maps and efficient revocation for anonymous credentials. In: Jarecki, S., Tsudik, G. (eds.) PKC 2009. LNCS, vol. 5443, pp. 481–500. Springer, Heidelberg (2009)
14. Catalano, D., Fiore, D.: Concise vector commitments and their applications to zero-knowledge elementary databases. In: Cryptology ePrint Archive: Report 2011/495 (2011)
15. Chen, J., Gay, R., Wee, H.: Improved dual system ABE in prime-order groups via predicate encodings. In: Oswald, E., Fischlin, M. (eds.) EUROCRYPT 2015. LNCS, vol. 9057, pp. 595–624. Springer, Heidelberg (2015)
16. Chase, M., Meiklejohn, S.: Déjà Q: using dual systems to revisit q-type assumptions. In: Nguyen, P.Q., Oswald, E. (eds.) EUROCRYPT 2014. LNCS, vol. 8441, pp. 622–639. Springer, Heidelberg (2014)
17. Cheon, J.H.: Security analysis of the strong Diffie-Hellman problem. In: Vaudenay, S. (ed.) EUROCRYPT 2006. LNCS, vol. 4004, pp. 1–11. Springer, Heidelberg (2006)
18. Delerablée, C.: Identity-based broadcast encryption with constant size ciphertexts and private keys. In: Kurosawa, K. (ed.) ASIACRYPT 2007. LNCS, vol. 4833, pp. 200–215. Springer, Heidelberg (2007)
19. Dodis, Y., Yampolskiy, A.: A verifiable random function with short proofs and keys. In: Vaudenay, S. (ed.) PKC 2005. LNCS, vol. 3386, pp. 416–431. Springer, Heidelberg (2005)
20. Goyal, V., Pandey, O., Sahai, A., Waters, B.: Attribute-based encryption for fine-grained access control of encrypted data. In: ACM CCS 2006, pp. 89–98 (2006)
21. Izabachène, M., Libert, B., Vergnaud, D.: Block-wise P-signatures and non-interactive anonymous credentials with efficient attributes. In: Chen, L. (ed.) IMACC 2011. LNCS, vol. 7089, pp. 431–450. Springer, Heidelberg (2011)

22. Katz, J., Sahai, A., Waters, B.: Predicate encryption supporting disjunctions, polynomial equations, and inner products. In: Smart, N.P. (ed.) EUROCRYPT 2008. LNCS, vol. 4965, pp. 146–162. Springer, Heidelberg (2008)
23. Lewko, A., Sahai, A., Waters, B.: Revocation systems with very small private keys. In: IEEE Symposium on Security and Privacy 2010, pp. 273–285. IEEE Computer Society (2010)
24. Lewko, A., Okamoto, T., Sahai, A., Takashima, K., Waters, B.: Fully secure functional encryption: attribute-based encryption and (Hierarchical) inner product encryption. In: Gilbert, H. (ed.) EUROCRYPT 2010. LNCS, vol. 6110, pp. 62–91. Springer, Heidelberg (2010)
25. Lewko, A., Waters, B.: New techniques for dual system encryption and fully secure HIBE with short ciphertexts. In: Micciancio, D. (ed.) TCC 2010. LNCS, vol. 5978, pp. 455–479. Springer, Heidelberg (2010)
26. Libert, B., Ramanna, S.C., Yung, M.: Functional commitment schemes: from polynomial commitments to pairing-based accumulators from simple assumptions. In: ICALP 2016 (2016, to appear)
27. Libert, B., Yung, M.: Concise mercurial vector commitments and independent zero-knowledge sets with short proofs. In: Micciancio, D. (ed.) TCC 2010. LNCS, vol. 5978, pp. 499–517. Springer, Heidelberg (2010)
28. Naor, M.: On cryptographic assumptions and challenges. In: Boneh, D. (ed.) CRYPTO 2003. LNCS, vol. 2729, pp. 96–109. Springer, Heidelberg (2003)
29. Naor, M., Pinkas, B.: Efficient trace and revoke schemes. In: Frankel, Y. (ed.) FC 2000. LNCS, vol. 1962, pp. 1–20. Springer, Heidelberg (2001)
30. Okamoto, T., Takashima, K.: Hierarchical predicate encryption for inner-products. In: Matsui, M. (ed.) ASIACRYPT 2009. LNCS, vol. 5912, pp. 214–231. Springer, Heidelberg (2009)
31. Okamoto, T., Takashima, K.: Fully secure functional encryption with general relations from the decisional linear assumption. In: Rabin, T. (ed.) CRYPTO 2010. LNCS, vol. 6223, pp. 191–208. Springer, Heidelberg (2010)
32. Okamoto, T., Takashima, K.: Adaptively attribute-hiding (Hierarchical) inner product encryption. In: Pointcheval, D., Johansson, T. (eds.) EUROCRYPT 2012. LNCS, vol. 7237, pp. 591–608. Springer, Heidelberg (2012)
33. Okamoto, T., Takashima, K.: Fully secure unbounded inner-product and attribute-based encryption. In: Wang, X., Sako, K. (eds.) ASIACRYPT 2012. LNCS, vol. 7658, pp. 349–366. Springer, Heidelberg (2012)
34. Okamoto, T., Takashima, K.: Achieving short ciphertexts or short secret-keys for adaptively secure general inner-product encryption. Des. Codes Crypt. **77**(2–3), 725–771 (2015)
35. Sahai, A., Waters, B.: Fuzzy identity-based encryption. In: Cramer, R. (ed.) EUROCRYPT 2005. LNCS, vol. 3494, pp. 457–473. Springer, Heidelberg (2005)
36. Shen, E., Shi, E., Waters, B.: Predicate privacy in encryption systems. In: Reingold, O. (ed.) TCC 2009. LNCS, vol. 5444, pp. 457–473. Springer, Heidelberg (2009)
37. Waters, B.: Dual system encryption: realizing fully secure IBE and HIBE under simple assumptions. In: Halevi, S. (ed.) CRYPTO 2009. LNCS, vol. 5677, pp. 619–636. Springer, Heidelberg (2009)
38. Wee, H.: Threshold and revocation cryptosystems via extractable hash proofs. In: Paterson, K.G. (ed.) EUROCRYPT 2011. LNCS, vol. 6632, pp. 589–609. Springer, Heidelberg (2011)
39. Wee, H.: Dual system encryption via predicate encodings. In: Lindell, Y. (ed.) TCC 2014. LNCS, vol. 8349, pp. 616–637. Springer, Heidelberg (2014)

40. Wee, H.: Déjà Q: encore! Un Petit IBE. In: Kushilevitz, E., et al. (eds.) TCC 2016-A. LNCS, vol. 9563, pp. 237–258. Springer, Heidelberg (2016). doi:10.1007/978-3-662-49099-0_9
41. Yamada, S., Attrapadung, N., Hanaoka, G., Kunihiro, N.: A framework and compact constructions for non-monotonic attribute-based encryption. In: Krawczyk, H. (ed.) PKC 2014. LNCS, vol. 8383, pp. 275–292. Springer, Heidelberg (2014)

Attribute-Based Encryption for Range Attributes

Nuttapong Attrapadung[1](✉), Goichiro Hanaoka[1], Kazuto Ogawa[2],
Go Ohtake[2], Hajime Watanabe[1], and Shota Yamada[1]

[1] National Institute of Advanced Industrial Science and Technology (AIST),
Tokyo, Japan
{n.attrapadung,hanaoka-goichiro,h-watanabe,yamada-shota}@aist.go.jp
[2] Japan Broadcasting Corporation (NHK), Tokyo, Japan
{ogawa.k-cm,ohtake.g-fw}@nhk.or.jp

Abstract. Attribute-Based Encryption (ABE) is an advanced form
of public-key encryption where access control mechanisms based on
attributes and policies are possible. In conventional ABE, attributes are
specified as *strings*. However, there are certain applications where it is
useful to specify attributes as *numerical values* and consider a predicate
that determines if a certain *numerical range* would include a certain
value. Examples of these types of attributes include time, position coordinate, person's age, rank, identity, and so on. In this paper, we introduce ABE for boolean formulae over Range Membership (ABE-RM).
We show generic methods to convert conventional ABE to ABE-RM.
Our generic conversions are efficient as they introduce only logarithmic
overheads (in key and ciphertext sizes), as opposed to trivial methods,
which would pose linear overheads. By applying our conversion to previous ABE schemes, we obtain new efficient and expressive ABE-RM
schemes. Previous works that considered ABE with range attributes are
specific and can only deal with either a single relation of range membership (Paterson and Quaglia at SCN 2010, and Kasamatsu *et al.* at SCN
2012), or limited classes of policies, namely, only AND-gates of range
attributes (Shi *et al.* at IEEE S&P 2007, and some subsequent work).
Our schemes are generic and can deal with expressive boolean formulae.

1 Introduction

Attribute-Based Encryption (ABE) is an advanced form of public-key encryption
where access control mechanisms based on attributes and policies are possible.
ABE is typically categorized into two types: key-policy (KP) or ciphertext-policy
(CP). In KP-ABE [22], a secret key associated with a policy is distributed to
each user and data is encrypted with a set of attributes. In CP-ABE [14], a
secret key associated with a set of attributes is distributed to each user, and
data is encrypted with a policy. The decryption should be possible iff the set of
attributes satisfies the policy. ABE can be used in a variety of situations, such
as file-sharing and content distribution, where there are many users who decrypt
one ciphertext.

© Springer International Publishing Switzerland 2016
V. Zikas and R. De Prisco (Eds.): SCN 2016, LNCS 9841, pp. 42–61, 2016.
DOI: 10.1007/978-3-319-44618-9_3

In conventional ABE, attributes are specified as *strings*. However, there are certain applications where it is useful to specify attributes as *numerical values* and consider a predicate that determines if a certain *numerical range* would include a certain value. Examples of these types of attributes include time, position coordinate, person's age, rank, identity, and so on. We consider the following KP-ABE system for paid-content distribution as an example application. An encrypted content is associated with an assignment of attributes, such as ('genre' = *music*), ('day' = 20160515), ('hour' = 22), among others attributes (such as title, language, and so on). In such a system, many attributes are numerical data, and hence it is useful to allow users to specify ranges of attribute values. For example, a user may subscribe to the system with a policy:

$$\Big(('genre' = sport \vee 'genre' = music) \wedge 'day' \in [20160501, 20160525]\Big)$$
$$\vee\, 'hour' \in [0,6]. \quad (1)$$

To enforce this access control policy, we can use conventional ABE in a trivial manner by specifying ranges as disjunctions of values in the ranges. In our example, this will be

$$\Big(('genre' = sport \vee 'genre' = music) \wedge ('day' = 20160501 \vee \cdots$$
$$\vee\, 'day' = 20160525)\Big) \vee 'hour' = 0 \vee \cdots \vee 'hour' = 6. \quad (2)$$

However, this would result in a very large size of policy, more precisely, the size expansion overhead of linear complexity would be required, and hence resulting in inefficient systems. More importantly, it cannot deal with ranges of exponential size (in the security parameter).

Previous ABE schemes that can deal with range attributes and have sub-linear complexity have been proposed; however, they can deal with only limited classes of policies (over these range attributes), namely, only single range membership relation [24,34], or policies with only AND gates [20,25,36]. To the best of our knowledge, constructing ABE for range attributes with sub-linear complexity that can deal with expressive policies has remained an open problem.

1.1   Our Contributions

In this paper, we affirmatively solve the above problem by proposing *ABE over Ranges Membership* (ABE-RM). Our schemes have sub-linear complexity as the overheads regarding ranges for key and ciphertext sizes are $O(\log n)$, where n denotes the maximum size of ranges. Hence, they can deal with n of exponential size. They can deal with expressive policies, namely, the class of span programs, which is known to imply any boolean formulae [12,22]. Our result is generic as we show a generic conversion from any ABE for span programs to ABE-RM. This is in contrast with previous ABE for range attributes [20,24,25,34,36], which are specific constructions (besides being able to deal with only limited classes, as mentioned above). We compare these ABE schemes for ranges in Table 1.

Table 1. Comparison among all available (non-trivial) ABE for ranges

Scheme	Allowed policies	Type (in our terminology)
PQ10 [34], KME+12 [24]	no conjunction allowed	CP-ABE Type 1
SBC+07 [36], GMW15 [20]	only AND	KP-ABE Type 1
KMHI12 [25]	only AND	CP-ABE Type 1
This work	any Boolean formula	KP-ABE, CP-ABE, Type 1,2

Our conversions work for both KP-ABE and CP-ABE. Moreover, for the sake of generality, we further consider two types of ABE-RM, regarding where ranges are specified. The first type is when ranges are specified in (literals of) policies, while values to be checked if it is in ranges is specified in attribute sets. This corresponds to the example above. The second type is vice versa: a point is specified in policies while a range is specified in attribute sets.[1]

Our Approach. In order to achieve sub-linear complexity, we use the classical segment tree method [13]. This method allows us to represent any range by a set of size $O(\log n)$ and any value by also a set of size $O(\log n)$, and has the following useful property: a value is in a range if and only if their corresponding representation sets are intersected. Therefore, our goal of constructing ABE-RM reduces to construct ABE that can deal with set intersection in each of literals in a policy. We call this intermediate scheme as *ABE for Set Intersection* (ABE-SI). Intuitively, taking the above example (KP-ABE Type 1) for concreteness, we consider a policy of which one of its literal is of the form: ('day' $\cap S_{[20160501,20160525]} \neq \emptyset$), while an assignment of attributes is of the form: ('day' $= T_{20160515}$), where S_R, T_x are the representation sets for a range R and a value x via the segment tree method, respectively. However, again, conventional ABE does not directly deal with set intersections in the first place. To this end, our idea to implement ABE-SI is to treat each element in the representation sets S_R, T_x as separate attributes. But a problem arises again as we cannot simply let the attribute assignment contain distinct specifications of the same attribute, namely, we cannot define assignment ('day' $= y$), ('day' $= y'$) for some value $y \neq y'$, as it contradicts each other. Nevertheless, this can be simply solved by hashing $H($'day'$, y)$ and treat it as an attribute. Intuitively, a literal in a policy then becomes: $\bigvee_{w \in S_{[20160501,20160525]}} H($'day'$, w)$, while an attribute set becomes: $\{ H($'day'$, y) \mid y \in T_{20160515} \}$, and we can use conventional ABE for them. This causes a linear expansion as in the trivial scheme; however, now we have $|S_R|, |T_x|$ bounded by $O(\log n)$ thanks to the segment tree method, hence the resulting scheme is efficient.[2]

---

[1] For example, an attribute set may look like: ('genre' $=$ *music*), ('day' $=$ [20160501, 20160525]), ('hour' $=$ [0, 6]), while a policy may look like: (('genre' $=$ *sport* $\vee$ 'genre' $=$ *music*) $\wedge$ 20160515 $\in$ 'day') $\vee$ 22 $\in$ 'hour'.

[2] Although we explain our idea via ABE for Boolean formula here, for generality we will work on ABE for span programs in the main body, which is well-known to imply the former.

Our Alternative Approach. Our above approach requires expansions in both policies and attribute sets, resulting in possible expansion in both keys and ciphertexts. We propose an alternative way for constructing ABE-SI that requires an expansion for only policies. Hence, it has an advantage in that ciphertext sizes will be preserved in the KP case (and key sizes in the CP case). This conversion, however, has to start from more expressive ABE called KP-DSE (Key-policy over Doubly Spatial Encryption), introduced in [2]. Roughly speaking, KP-DSE allows to specify an affine space as an attribute, and a literal evaluates to true if the affine spaces are intersected. (See more details in Sect. 2.2.) We first identify that the set membership relation can be embedded in the affine space intersection. We then embed the whole representation set T_x at once using one affine space, and hence need not expand T_x as in the previous method.

Outline of the Paper. After preliminaries in Sect. 2, we provide the definitions of ABE-RM, ABE-SI in Sect. 3. Our conversions are given in Sect. 4, as outlined in Fig. 1. Efficiency comparisons are given in Sect. 5. Some extensions (see below) are briefly described in Sect. 6, where the details are deferred to the full version [7].

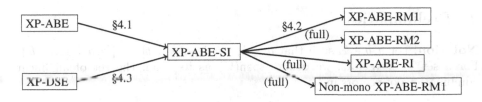

Fig. 1. Our conversions. XP stands for either KP or CP.

Extensions. Beside range membership, we also consider *ABE over Range Intersection* (ABE-RI). We show how this can be converted from ABE-SI in Sect. 6. Also, in the main body, for simplicity we consider policies being monotone span programs, which is known to imply monotone Boolean formulae. We describe how to extend this to non-monotone span programs, which can deal with the range non-membership relation, in Sect. 6. The details are given in the full version.

1.2 Related Work

The concept of ABE was first proposed by Sahai and Waters [37] in the context of fuzzy IBE, which consider threshold access structures. Goyal et al. [22] proposed the first KP-ABE for monotone Boolean formulae, and monotone span programs (the latter in the equivalent terminology of linear secret sharing). The two predicates are related via the result of Beimel [12]. Bethencourt et al. proposed the first CP-ABE. Subsequently, many ABE schemes featuring better efficiency, more expressive policy, or improved security, are proposed in [1–6,9,11,19,21,23,27–33,35,38–40], to name just a few.

ABE for Range. There have been several studies on ABE for ranges. Shi et al. [36] proposed a predicate encryption scheme where a coordinate point is associated to a ciphertext and a multi-dimensional range is associated to a key, and the decryption works if the point is in the range. In our terminology, it is KP-ABE-RM of Type 1 supporting AND-gates, albeit with an additional feature called attribute-hiding. Paterson and Quaglia [34] proposed the concept of time-specific encryption (TSE) and showed efficient constructions, which were later improved by [24]. In TSE, a ciphertext can be decrypted only when the time associated with a secret key is within the time interval specified in the encryption algorithm. TSE can be viewed as CP-ABE-RM Type 1, albeit with no conjunction allowed in a policy. Kasamatsu et al. [25] later improved it to support AND-gates. Gay et al. [20] recently described a lattice-based variant of the Shi et al. scheme.

In the original CP-ABE paper [14] by Bethencourt et al., an example of CP-ABE for ranges was already sketched (See Sect. 4.3 in [14]). Their idea was to represent a range as a policy of some pre-defined attributes using AND, OR. However, the method of representing range was not described in general. Contrastingly, we describe a general method for converting ABE to ABE-RM.

2 Preliminaries

Notation. For $a, b \in \mathbb{Z}$ such that $a \leq b$, we denote $[a, b] := \{ a, a+1, \ldots, b \}$. For a set V of vectors, we denote $\mathsf{span}(V)$ as its span: the set of all linear combinations of vectors in V.

2.1 Definitions for General ABE

Predicate Family. Let $R = \{ R_\kappa : \mathbb{X}_\kappa \times \mathbb{Y}_\kappa \to \{0, 1\} \mid \kappa \in \mathcal{K} \}$ be a predicate family where $\mathbb{X}_\kappa$ and $\mathbb{Y}_\kappa$ denote "key attribute" and "ciphertext attribute" spaces. The index κ or "parameter" denotes a list of some parameters such as the universes of attributes, and/or bounds on some quantities, hence its domain $\mathcal{K}$ will depend on that predicate. We will often omit κ when the context is clear.

General ABE Syntax. Let $\mathcal{M}$ be a message space. An ABE scheme[3] for predicate family R is defined by the following algorithms:

- $\mathsf{Setup}(1^\lambda, \kappa) \to (\mathsf{PK}, \mathsf{MSK})$: takes as input a security parameter 1^λ and a parameter κ of predicate family R, and outputs a master public key PK and a master secret key MSK.
- $\mathsf{Encrypt}(Y, M, \mathsf{PK}) \to \mathsf{CT}$: takes as input a ciphertext attribute $Y \in \mathbb{Y}_\kappa$, a message $M \in \mathcal{M}$, and public key PK. It outputs a ciphertext CT. We assume that Y is implicit in CT.
- $\mathsf{KeyGen}(X, \mathsf{MSK}, \mathsf{PK}) \to \mathsf{SK}$: takes as input a key attribute $X \in \mathbb{X}_\kappa$ and the master key MSK. It outputs a secret key SK.

---

[3] It is also called public-index predicate encryption, classified in the definition of Functional Encryption [18].

- Decrypt(CT, SK) → M: given a ciphertext CT with its attribute Y and the decryption key SK with its attribute X, it outputs a message M or $\perp$.

Correctness. Consider all parameters κ, all $M \in \mathcal{M}$, $X \in \mathbb{X}_\kappa$, $Y \in \mathbb{Y}_\kappa$ such that $R_\kappa(X, Y) = 1$. If Encrypt(Y, M, PK) → CT and KeyGen(X, MSK, PK) → SK where (PK, MSK) is generated from Setup(1^λ, κ), then Decrypt(CT, SK) → M.

Security. The standard notion for ABE is called full security. We refer its definition to the full version, as we do not work directly on it but rather use the embedding lemma for implications (Lemma 1).

Duality of ABE. For a predicate $R : \mathbb{X} \times \mathbb{Y} \to \{0, 1\}$, we define its dual as $\bar{R} : \mathbb{Y} \times \mathbb{X} \to \{0, 1\}$ by setting $\bar{R}(Y, X) = R(X, Y)$. In particular, if R is considered as key-policy type, then its dual, $\bar{R}$, is the corresponding ciphertext-policy type. Hence, wlog, throughout the paper, we will give the definitions of predicates for only the KP type.

2.2 Definitions for Some Previous Predicates

ABE for Monotone Span Program. We recapture the predicate definition for KP-ABE for monotone span program [22]. If not stated otherwise, we will refer to ABE for monotone span program as "normal ABE" throughout the paper. It is well known that such an ABE scheme implies ABE for monotone Boolean formulae [12, 22] (*cf.* see a concise explanation in Sect. C of [29]).

- **Parameter.** It is specified by a positive integer N (which specifies $\mathbb{Z}_N$) and an attribute universe $\mathcal{U}$. If $\mathcal{U} = \{0, 1\}^*$, or equivalently[4] $|\mathcal{U}|$ is super-polynomial size in λ, then it is called large universe [22, 35]; otherwise, it is called small universe. Some schemes also require optional parameters $\bar{m}, \bar{k}, \bar{\ell}$ that specify maximum bounds for $m, k, |S|$ described below.
- **Key Attribute.** It is specified by a pair $\mathbb{A} = (A, \pi)$ where A is a matrix in $\mathbb{Z}_N^{m \times k}$ for some $m, k \in \mathbb{N}$, and π is a row labelling map $\pi : [1, m] \to \mathcal{U}$. The pair $\mathbb{A}$ is also called a monotone span program (over $\mathcal{U}$).
- **Ciphertext Attribute.** It is specified by an attribute set $S \subseteq \mathcal{U}$.
- **Evaluation.** For a set $S \subseteq \mathcal{U}$, let $\mathbb{A}|_S$ be the sub-matrix of A that takes all the rows j such that $\pi(j) \in S$. We say that (A, π) accepts S if the fixed vector $\mathbf{1} := (1, 0, \ldots, 0)$ is in the row span of $\mathbb{A}|_S$. Denote A_i as the row i of A. That is, we define

$$R^{\mathsf{KP\text{-}ABE}}((A, \pi), S) = 1 \iff \mathbf{1} \in \mathsf{span}\{A_i \mid \pi(i) \in S\}. \tag{3}$$

We will also present an implication of ABE for ranges from a primitive called KP-DSE [2]. We briefly review it here, starting from the notion for affine spaces.

Notion for Affine Spaces. Let $N, d, w \in \mathbb{N}$ where $0 \leq w \leq d$. Let $t^\top$ be a vertical vector in $\mathbb{Z}_N^d$. Let $M \in \mathbb{Z}_N^{d \times w}$ be a matrix whose columns are all

---

[4] The latter implies the former via applying any collision-resistant hash $H : \{0, 1\}^* \to \mathcal{U}$, as done in [15, 22].

linearly independent. An affine space in $\mathbb{Z}_N^d$ specified by a pair (t, M) is defined as $t^\top + \mathsf{cspan}(M)$, where $\mathsf{cspan}()$ denotes the column span; more precisely, it is

$$t^\top + \mathsf{cspan}(M) = \{\, t^\top + Mv^\top \mid v \in \mathbb{Z}_N^w \,\}.$$

We also define $\mathsf{AffSp}(\mathbb{Z}_N^d)$ as the set of all affine spaces in $\mathbb{Z}_N^d$.

Key-Policy over Doubly Spatial Encryption (KP-DSE). The predicate is defined as follows.

- **Parameter.** It is specified by $(N, d) \in \mathbb{N}^2$. Optionally, we can specify some bounds $\bar{m}, \bar{k}, \bar{\ell}$ for $m, k, |T|$ described below.
- **Key Attribute.** It is specified by $\mathbb{A} = (A, \pi)$ where A is a matrix in $\mathbb{Z}_N^{m \times k}$ for some $m, k \in \mathbb{N}$, and π is a labelling that maps each row in $[1, m]$ to an affine space in $\mathbb{Z}_N^d$.
- **Ciphertext Attribute.** It is specified by a set T of affine spaces in $\mathbb{Z}_N^d$.
- **Evaluation.** Let $\mathbb{A}|_T$ be the sub-matrix of A that takes all the rows i such that there exists an affine space $Y \in T$ that intersects with the affine space $\pi(i)$. We say that (A, π) accepts S if the fixed vector $\mathbf{1} := (1, 0, \ldots, 0)$ is in the row span of $\mathbb{A}|_T$. That is,

$$R^{\mathsf{KP\text{-}DSE}}((A, \pi), T) = 1 \iff \mathbf{1} \in \mathsf{span}\{\, A_i \mid \exists Y \in T \text{ s.t. } \pi(i) \cap Y \neq \emptyset \,\}.$$

2.3 Embedding Lemma

The following useful lemma from [5,17] describes a sufficient criterion for implication from ABE for a given predicate to ABE for another predicate. The lemma considers two arbitrary predicate families: $R_\kappa^{\mathsf{F}} : \mathbb{X}_\kappa \times \mathbb{Y}_\kappa \to \{0, 1\}$, and $R_{\kappa'}^{\mathsf{F'}} : \mathbb{X}'_{\kappa'} \times \mathbb{Y}'_{\kappa'} \to \{0, 1\}$, which are parametrized by $\kappa \in \mathcal{K}$ and $\kappa' \in \mathcal{K}'$ respectively. Suppose that there exists three efficient mappings

$$f_\mathsf{p} : \mathcal{K}' \to \mathcal{K} \qquad f_\mathsf{e} : \mathbb{X}'_{\kappa'} \to \mathbb{X}_{f_\mathsf{p}(\kappa')} \qquad f_\mathsf{k} : \mathbb{Y}'_{\kappa'} \to \mathbb{Y}_{f_\mathsf{p}(\kappa')}$$

which map parameters, ciphertext attributes, and key attributes, respectively, such that for all $X' \in \mathbb{X}'_{\kappa'}, Y' \in \mathbb{Y}'_{\kappa'}$, we have the "embedding" relation:

$$R_{\kappa'}^{\mathsf{F'}}(X', Y') = 1 \quad \Leftrightarrow \quad R_{f_\mathsf{p}(\kappa')}^{\mathsf{F}}(f_\mathsf{e}(X'), f_\mathsf{k}(Y')) = 1. \tag{4}$$

We can then construct an ABE scheme Π' for predicate $R_{\kappa'}^{\mathsf{F'}}$ from an ABE scheme Π for predicate R_κ^{F} by setting $\Pi'.\mathsf{Setup}(1^\lambda, \kappa') = \Pi.\mathsf{Setup}(1^\lambda, f_\mathsf{p}(\kappa'))$ and

$$\Pi'.\mathsf{Encrypt}(\mathsf{PK}, M, X') \quad = \Pi.\mathsf{Encrypt}(\mathsf{PK}, M, f_\mathsf{e}(X')),$$
$$\Pi'.\mathsf{KeyGen}(\mathsf{MSK}, \mathsf{PK}, Y') \quad = \Pi.\mathsf{KeyGen}(\mathsf{MSK}, \mathsf{PK}, f_\mathsf{k}(Y')),$$

and $\Pi'.\mathsf{Decrypt}(\mathsf{CT}_{X'}, \mathsf{SK}_{Y'}) = \Pi.\mathsf{Decrypt}(\mathsf{CT}_{f_\mathsf{e}(X')}, \mathsf{SK}_{f_\mathsf{k}(Y')})$.

Lemma 1 (Embedding Lemma [5,17]). *If Π is correct and secure, then so is Π'. This holds for both the cases of selective security and full security.*

Remark 1. We observe that the embedding relation (4) between R^{F} and $R^{\mathsf{F}'}$ via maps $(f_{\mathsf{p}}, f_{\mathsf{c}}, f_{\mathsf{k}})$ is equivalent to that between their respective duals, *i.e.*, $\overline{R^{\mathsf{F}}}$ and $\overline{R^{\mathsf{F}'}}$, via maps $(f_{\mathsf{p}}, f_{\mathsf{k}}, f_{\mathsf{c}})$. (That is, we swap maps for key and ciphertext attributes for its dual predicate.) This observation ensures that it is sufficient to prove the embedding relation only for the KP case, so that the embedding relation for its dual, the CP case, will be automatically obtained. *Wlog, we will deal with only the KP case throughout the paper.*

2.4 Efficient Encoding for Range Membership

We use the classical *segment tree method*, rooted back in 1977 [13], that allows us to express ranges efficiently.[5] It was first applied to the context of ABE by Shi *et al.* [36] (where an ABE scheme for AND gates was presented). We first describe some notations. Let $\mathbb{T}_n$ be the complete binary tree that has leaves corresponding to each index in $[1, n]$. Let $\mathbb{S}_n$ be the set of all nodes in $\mathbb{T}_n$ that are labeled in a systematic way. Let $\mathcal{D}_n := \{ [u, v] \mid 1 \leq u \leq v \leq n \}$. For a node $w \in \mathbb{S}_n$, let parent(w) denote its parent node in $\mathbb{T}_n$. Consider node $w, y, z \in \mathbb{S}_n$; z is an *ancestor* of w if z is on the path from w to the root (including w); y is a *descendant* of w if y is on a path from w moving away from the root (including w). For any range $R \in \mathcal{D}_n$, a node $w \in \mathbb{S}_n$ is called a *cover node* of R, and we write $w \in \text{cover}(R)$, if all the leaves that are descendants of w are in R. Let $2^{\mathbb{S}_n}$ be the collection of all subsets of $\mathbb{S}_n$. We define two encoding functions:

- **Range Encoding** rangeEnc$: \mathcal{D}_n \to 2^{\mathbb{S}_n}$. For $R \in \mathcal{D}_n$, define

$$\text{rangeEnc}(R) := \{ w \in \mathbb{S}_n \mid w \in \text{cover}(R), \quad \text{parent}(w) \notin \text{cover}(R) \}.$$

- **Point Encoding** pointEnc$: [1, n] \to 2^{\mathbb{S}_n}$. For $x \in [1, n]$, define pointEnc(x) as the set of all ancestors of x in $\mathbb{T}_n$.

Lemma 2 [13,36]. *For $x \in [1, n]$, $R \in \mathcal{D}_n$,*

$$|\text{rangeEnc}(R) \cap \text{pointEnc}(x)| = \begin{cases} 1 & \text{if } x \in R \\ 0 & \text{if } x \notin R \end{cases}.$$

Furthermore, there exists an efficient algorithm which takes x, R where $x \in R$ as input and outputs the intersection node $z \in \text{rangeEnc}(R) \cap \text{pointEnc}(x)$.

Lemma 3 [13,36]. *For any $R \in \mathcal{D}_n$, we have $|\text{rangeEnc}(R)| \leq 2 \log n - 2$. For any $x \in [1, n]$, we have $|\text{pointEnc}(x)| = \log n + 1$.*

Figures 2 and 3 illustrate examples when $n = 8$. Since $6 \in [2, 8]$, we have that rangeEnc$([2, 8]) \cap$ pointEnc(6) is not empty: the node number 14 is in the intersection.

---

[5] We remark that our segment *tree* method here should not be confused with another completely different *tree*-based method for the original ABE of Goyal *et al.* [22], which was used for expressing boolean formulae.

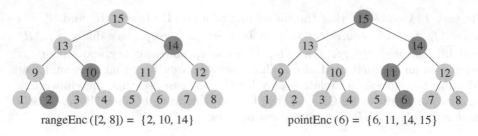

rangeEnc ([2, 8]) = {2, 10, 14}   pointEnc (6) = {6, 11, 14, 15}

Fig. 2. Example of range encoding   **Fig. 3.** Example of point encoding

3 Definitions for New Predicates

KP-ABE for Monotone Span Program over Set Intersection (ABE-SI).
Let $\mathcal{A}$ be the universe of attribute *names*. For each attribute name $a \in \mathcal{A}$, let $\mathcal{U}_a$
be the universe of attribute *values* that can be associated to the attribute name a.
Let the collection of all *name-value* pairs be $\mathcal{X} := \{\,(a,x) \mid a \in \mathcal{A}, x \in \mathcal{U}_a\,\}$.

We will also associate a set of values to attribute where we bound its size
to a parameter t. We call a pair of an attribute name and a set of its val-
ues a *name-set pair*: it is of the form (a, S), where $a \in \mathcal{A}$ and $S \in \binom{\mathcal{U}_a}{\leq t} :=$
$\{\, U \mid U \subseteq \mathcal{U}_a, |U| \leq t\,\}$. The collection $\mathcal{P}$ (resp., $\mathcal{P}_a$) of all name-set pairs (resp.,
of all name-set pairs with attribute name a) is denoted by

$$\mathcal{P} := \left\{ (a, S) \,\middle|\, a \in \mathcal{A}, S \in \binom{\mathcal{U}_a}{\leq t} \right\}, \qquad \mathcal{P}_a := \left\{ (a, S) \,\middle|\, S \in \binom{\mathcal{U}_a}{\leq t} \right\}.$$

- **Parameter.** It is specified by an integer N, the collection $\mathcal{X}$ of all name-value
  pairs, and the bound t. Optionally, we can specify some bounds $\bar{m}, \bar{k}, \bar{\ell}$ for
  $m, k, |T|$ described below.
- **Key Attribute.** It is specified by a monotone span program $\mathbb{A} = (A, \pi)$ where
  A is a matrix in $\mathbb{Z}_N^{m \times k}$ for some $m, k \in \mathbb{N}$, and π is a map $\pi : [1, m] \to \mathcal{P}$. We
  write $\pi(i) = (\pi_{\mathsf{name}}(i), \pi_{\mathsf{set}}(i))$.
- **Ciphertext Attribute.** It is specified by a set of name-set pairs with all
  distinct names: it is of the form $T = \{\,(a_i, S_i) \in \mathcal{P}_{a_i} \mid i \in [1, \ell]\,\}$ for some
  $\ell \in \mathbb{N}$ and distinct $a_1, \dots, a_\ell \in \mathcal{A}$.
- **Evaluation.** We say that (A, π) accepts T if $\mathbf{1} := (1, 0, \dots, 0)$ is in the row
  span of a submatrix $\mathbb{A}|_T$ of A, where $\mathbb{A}|_T$ is formed by taking all the rows i
  as follows. Parse the name-set pair $\pi(i) = (a, S)$. Then, find a pair $(a, \tilde{S})$ in T
  such that $S \cap \tilde{S} \neq \emptyset$. If a pair exists, we include the row i to $\mathbb{A}|_T$. That is,

$$R^{\mathsf{KP\text{-}ABE\text{-}SI}}((A, \pi), T) = 1 \quad \Longleftrightarrow$$

$$\mathbf{1} \in \mathsf{span}\left\{ A_i \,\middle|\, \exists(\pi_{\mathsf{name}}(i), \tilde{S}) \in T \text{ s.t. } \pi_{\mathsf{set}}(i) \cap \tilde{S} \neq \emptyset \right\}.$$

KP-ABE for Monotone Span Program over Range Membership (ABE-RM). Let $\mathcal{A}$ be the universe of attribute names. For each $a \in \mathcal{A}$, let

$\min_a, \max_a \in \mathbb{Z}$ specify the minimum and maximum values that can be associated to the attribute name a. Its range universe is thus $\mathcal{W}_a :=$ $\{ [u, v] \mid \min_a \leq u \leq v \leq \max_a \}$. The collection $\mathcal{R}$ of all *name-range* pairs and the collection $\mathcal{V}$ of all *name-value* pairs are

$$\mathcal{R} := \{ (a, R) \mid a \in \mathcal{A}, R \in \mathcal{W}_a \}, \quad \mathcal{V} := \{ (a, x) \mid a \in \mathcal{A}, x \in [\min_a, \max_a] \}$$

respectively. Let $\mathcal{R}_a := \{ (a, R) \mid R \in \mathcal{W}_a \}$; $\mathcal{V}_a := \{ (a, x) \mid x \in [\min_a, \max_a] \}$.

For simplicity and wlog, we assume $\min_a = 1$ for all $a \in \mathcal{A}$ (this can be done by simply offsetting all the values).

We can define two types of ABE-RM. For the first type, we have ranges specified in a policy (for a key attribute), while points (values) are specified in an attribute set (for a ciphertext attribute). For the second type, the roles of ranges and values are swapped. We describe the details of the first type here and defer the second one, which can be defined analogously, to the full version.

(KP-ABE-RM Type 1: Range at Policy, Value at Attribute)

- **Parameter.** It is specified by an integer N, and the collection $\mathcal{V}$ of all name-value pairs. Optionally, as usual, we can specify some bounds $\bar{m}, \bar{k}, \bar{\ell}$ for $m, k, |T|$ described below.
- **Key Attribute.** It is specified by a monotone span program $\mathbb{A} = (A, \pi)$ where A is a matrix in $\mathbb{Z}_N^{m \times k}$ for some $m, k \in \mathbb{N}$, and π is a map $\pi : [1, m] \to \mathcal{R}$. We write $\pi(i) = (\pi_{\mathsf{name}}(i), \pi_{\mathsf{range}}(i))$.
- **Ciphertext Attribute.** It is specified by a set of name-value pairs with all distinct names: it is of the form $T = \{ (a_i, x_i) \in \mathcal{V}_{a_i} \mid i \in [1, \ell] \}$ for some $\ell \in \mathbb{N}$ and distinct $a_1, \ldots, a_\ell \in \mathcal{A}$.
- **Evaluation.** We say that (A, π) accepts T if $\mathbf{1} := (1, 0, \ldots, 0)$ is in the row span of a submatrix $\mathbb{A}|_T$ of A, where $\mathbb{A}|_T$ is formed by taking all the rows i as follows. Parse the name-range pair $\pi(i) = (a, R)$. Then, find a pair (a, x) in T such that $x \in R$. If such a pair exists, we include the row i to $\mathbb{A}|_T$. That is,

$$R^{\mathsf{KP\text{-}ABE\text{-}RM1}}((A, \pi), T) = 1 \iff$$
$$\mathbf{1} \in \mathsf{span}\{ A_i \mid \exists(\pi_{\mathsf{name}}(i), x) \in T \text{ s.t. } x \in \pi_{\mathsf{range}}(i) \}.$$

4   Generic Constructions

4.1   From ABE to ABE-SI

In this section, we show that normal KP-ABE implies KP-ABE-SI. The conversion is as follows.

- **Mapping Parameters.** For the name-value universe $\mathcal{X}$ of KP-ABE-SI, let $\mathcal{U}$ be a universe of KP-ABE such that there exists an efficiently computable injective function $H : \mathcal{X} \to \mathcal{U}$. We map $f_{\mathsf{p}} : (N, \mathcal{X}, t, \bar{m}, \bar{k}, \bar{\ell}) \mapsto (N, \mathcal{U}, \bar{m}', \bar{k}', \bar{\ell}')$, where we defer how to determine them below.

- **Mapping Key Attributes.** Consider a monotone span program $\mathbb{A} = (A, \pi)$ for KP-ABE-SI, where $A \in \mathbb{Z}_N^{m \times k}$ and $\pi : [1, m] \to \mathcal{P}$. We map

$$f_k : \quad \mathbb{A} = (A, \pi) \quad \mapsto \quad \mathbb{A}' = (A', \pi')$$

where A' is a matrix in $\mathbb{Z}_N^{m' \times k}$ and π' is a map $\pi' : [1, m'] \to \mathcal{U}$, defined as follows.

   1. For each $i \in [1, m]$, parse the name-set pair $\pi(i) = (\pi_{\mathsf{name}}(i), \pi_{\mathsf{set}}(i))$, and parse the set $\pi_{\mathsf{set}}(i) = \{x_{i,1}, \dots, x_{i,k_i}\}$ in some lexicographical order, where we denote $k_i := |\pi_{\mathsf{set}}(i)|$.
   2. We index the rows of A' by a pair of indexes (i, j), ranging as

$$(1, 1), \dots, (1, k_1), \dots, (m, 1), \dots, (m, k_m).$$

   Hence, the number of rows of A' is $m' = k_1 + \cdots + k_m$ and the row index (i, j) corresponds to the row number $\mathrm{num}(i, j) := k_1 + \cdots + k_{i-1} + j$.
   3. For each $i \in [1, m]$, and each $j \in [1, k_i]$, we define

$$A'_{\mathrm{num}(i,j)} = A_i, \qquad \pi'\big(\mathrm{num}(i,j)\big) = H\big(\pi_{\mathsf{name}}(i), x_{i,j}\big). \qquad (5)$$

   In particular, we define the row $\mathrm{num}(i, j)$ of A' to be simply A_i, the same for all $j \in [1, k_i]$.[6]
- **Mapping Ciphertext Attributes.** Consider a set of name-set pairs for KP-ABE-SI, $T = \{\, (a_z, S_z) \in \mathcal{P}_{a_z} \mid z \in [1, \ell] \,\}$. We map

$$f_c : \quad T = \{\, (a_z, S_z) \in \mathcal{P}_{a_z} \mid z \in [1, \ell] \,\} \quad \mapsto \quad S' = \{\, H(a_z, x) \mid z \in [1, \ell], x \in S_z \,\}. \qquad (6)$$

Justifying Parameters. We now justify how to relate parameters $\mathcal{U}, \bar{m}', \bar{k}', \bar{\ell}'$ of ABE, so that constructing ABE-SI with parameters $\mathcal{X}, t, \bar{m}, \bar{k}, \bar{\ell}$ from such ABE is possible.

- If we allow $\mathcal{U} = \{0, 1\}^*$ (large-universe ABE), then we can deal with any $\mathcal{X}$, since for any $\mathcal{X}$ we have that an injective function $H : \mathcal{X} \to \mathcal{U}$ trivially exists.
- If we allow only polynomial-size $\mathcal{U}$ (small-universe ABE), then we also require $\mathcal{A}$ (the attribute name universe), $\mathcal{U}_a$ for each $a \in \mathcal{A}$ (the attribute value universe) to be polynomial-size, so that $|\mathcal{X}|$, which is at most $|\mathcal{A}| \cdot \max_{a \in \mathcal{A}} |\mathcal{U}_a|$ by definition, is polynomial-size. We then pick $\mathcal{U}$ of exactly this size, so that an injective function $H : \mathcal{X} \to \mathcal{U}$ trivially exists.

---

[6] Intuitively, making a copy of A_i to all the rows with indexes from $(i, 1)$ to (i, k_i) corresponds to implementing the OR literal, namely, $\bigvee_w H(\text{`day'}, w)$ as in our example in Sect. 1.1. This is since any row from $(i, 1)$ to (i, k_i) will contribute the same vector A_i in the span when we evaluate the span program, as in Eq. (3). In other words, any of attributes in these rows acts the same when evaluating the policy: this exactly represents the OR functionality.

- By inspection, the bounds $\bar{m}', \bar{k}', \bar{\ell}'$ of ABE relate to the bounds $t, \bar{m}, \bar{k}, \bar{\ell}$ of ABE-SI as follows.

$$\bar{m}' \geq t\bar{m}, \qquad\qquad \bar{k}' \geq \bar{k}, \qquad\qquad \bar{\ell}' \geq t\bar{\ell}, \qquad (7)$$

Indeed, if we allow ABE with unbounded parameters in either $\bar{m}', \bar{k}', \bar{\ell}'$, then the corresponding parameters of ABE-SI on the right hand-side of the inequalities do not have to be bounded.

Implication. We now show the following lemma for the above conversion. The implication from KP-ABE to KP-ABE-SI will then follow from the embedding lemma.

Lemma 4. *For any monotone span program* $\mathbb{A} = (A, \pi)$ *and a set of name-set pairs* T *for KP-ABE-SI, we have*

$$R_\kappa^{KP\text{-}ABE\text{-}SI}(\mathbb{A}, T) = 1 \quad \Longleftrightarrow \quad R_{f_p(\kappa)}^{KP\text{-}ABE}(f_k(\mathbb{A}), f_c(T)) = 1.$$

Proof. Consider the submatrices that define evaluations in KP-ABE-SI and KP-ABE:

$$\mathbb{A}|_T = \left\{ A_i \mid \exists (\pi_{\mathsf{name}}(i), \tilde{S}) \in T \text{ s.t. } \pi_{\mathsf{set}}(i) \cap \tilde{S} \neq \emptyset \right\}, \quad \mathbb{A}'|_{S'} = \{ A'_\iota \mid \pi'(\iota) \in S' \}$$

respectively, where here we set $(A', \pi') = f_k(A, \pi)$ and $S' = f_c(T)$ from the conversion. To prove the statement of the theorem, it suffices to prove that: $\mathbb{A}|_T = \mathbb{A}'|_{S'}$.

Forward Direction (Proving $\mathbb{A}|_T \subseteq \mathbb{A}'|_{S'}$). Suppose $A_i \in \mathbb{A}|_T$. Hence, there exists $(\pi_{\mathsf{name}}(i), \tilde{S}) \in T$ such that $\pi_{\mathsf{set}}(i) \cap \tilde{S} \neq \emptyset$. Let $z^\star$ be the index of such a name-set pair in T, and let $x_{i,j^\star}$ be an element in the latter intersection; namely, we have $(\pi_{\mathsf{name}}(i), \tilde{S}) = (a_{z^\star}, S_{z^\star})$ and $x_{i,j^\star} \in \pi_{\mathsf{set}}(i) \cap \tilde{S}$. We then consider the row $\iota^\star := \mathrm{num}(i, j^\star)$ of A'. By Eq. (5), we have $A'_{\iota^\star} = A_i$ and $\pi'(\iota^\star) = H(\pi_{\mathsf{name}}(i), x_{i,j^\star}) = H(a_{z^\star}, x_{i,j^\star})$. But since $x_{i,j^\star} \in \tilde{S} = S_{z^\star}$, and from Eq. (6) we have that $\pi'(\iota^\star) \in S'$. Hence, from the definition of $\mathbb{A}'|_{S'}$, we have $A'_{\iota^\star} = A_i \in \mathbb{A}'|_{S'}$. This concludes the proof for the forward part.

Backward Direction (Proving $\mathbb{A}'|_{S'} \subseteq \mathbb{A}|_T$). Suppose $A'_\iota \in \mathbb{A}'|_{S'}$. Hence, $\pi'(\iota) \in S'$. Parse i, j such that $\mathrm{num}(i, j) = \iota$ (this is uniquely determined since num is bijective). By Eq. (5), we have $A'_\iota = A_i$ and $\pi'(\iota) = H(\pi_{\mathsf{name}}(i), x_{i,j})$. From $\pi'(\iota) \in S'$, together with the fact that H is injective, and Eq. (6), we have that there exists $z^\star \in [1, \ell]$ where $\pi_{\mathsf{name}}(i) = a_{z^\star}, x_{i,j} \in S_{z^\star}$, and $(a_{z^\star}, S_{z^\star}) \in T$. Since $x_{i,j} \in \pi_{\mathsf{set}}(i)$ by notation, we have $x_{i,j} \in \pi_{\mathsf{set}}(i) \cap S_{z^\star}$. In other words, there exists $(\pi_{\mathsf{name}}(i), S_{z^\star}) \in T$ where $\pi_{\mathsf{set}}(i) \cap S_{z^\star} \neq \emptyset$. But this is exactly the condition in defining $A_i \in \mathbb{A}|_T$. Thus, $A_i = A'_\iota \in \mathbb{A}|_T$. This concludes the proof. $\quad\square$

4.2   From ABE-SI to ABE-RM1

In this section, we show that KP-ABE-SI implies KP-ABE-RM. We will show the conversion for ABE-RM Type 1 here and defer that of Type 2, which can be described analogously, to the full version. The ABE-SI-to-ABE-RM1 conversion is as follows.

- **Mapping Parameters.** We map parameters of ABE-RM to those of ABE-SI via $f_{\mathsf{p}} : (N, \mathcal{V}, \bar{m}, \bar{k}, \bar{\ell}) \mapsto (N, \mathcal{X}, t, \bar{m}, \bar{k}, \bar{\ell})$, defined as follows. Parse the name universe $\mathcal{A}$ from the name-value universe $\mathcal{V}$. For each $a \in \mathcal{A}$, parse $\max_a$ also from $\mathcal{V}$.[7] Let n_a be a power of 2 such that $n_a/2 < \max_a \le n_a$, so that the complete binary tree with n_a leaves, namely, $\mathbb{T}_{n_a}$, can contain $[1, \max_a]$ as its leaves. We set $\mathcal{U}_a$ (for ABE-SI) as the set of all nodes in the tree, namely, $\mathbb{S}_{n_a}$. Note that $\mathcal{A}$ and $\{\mathcal{U}_a\}_{a \in \mathcal{A}}$ completely defines the name-value universe $\mathcal{X}$ of ABE-SI. We justify t later below.
- **Mapping Key Attributes.** Consider a monotone span program $\mathbb{A} = (A, \pi)$ for KP-ABE-RM1, where $A \in \mathbb{Z}_N^{m \times k}$ and $\pi : [1, m] \to \mathcal{R}$. Recall that $\pi(i)$ is a name-range pair, where we write $\pi(i) = (\pi_{\mathsf{name}}(i), \pi_{\mathsf{range}}(i))$. We map

$$f_{\mathsf{k}} : \mathbb{A} = (A, \pi) \mapsto \mathbb{A}' = (A, \pi')$$

where we define $\pi' : [1, m] \to \mathcal{P}$ which maps

$$\pi' : i \mapsto \big(\pi_{\mathsf{name}}(i), \mathsf{rangeEnc}(\pi_{\mathsf{range}}(i))\big), \tag{8}$$

where, here, $\mathsf{rangeEnc} : \mathcal{D}_{n_a} \to 2^{\mathbb{S}_{n_a}}$ is the range encoding in the tree $\mathbb{T}_{n_a}$, where $a = \pi_{\mathsf{name}}(i)$.
- **Mapping Ciphertext Attributes.** Consider a set of name-value pairs for KP-ABE-RM1, $T = \{ (a_z, x_z) \in \mathcal{V}_{a_z} \mid z \in [1, \ell] \}$. We map

$$f_{\mathsf{c}} : T = \{ (a_z, x_z) \in \mathcal{V}_{a_z} \mid z \in [1, \ell] \} \mapsto$$
$$T' = \{ (a_z, \mathsf{pointEnc}(x_z)) \in \mathcal{P}_{a_z} \mid z \in [1, \ell] \}. \tag{9}$$

where, here, $\mathsf{pointEnc} : [1, n_{a_z}] \to 2^{\mathbb{S}_{n_{a_z}}}$ is the point encoding in the tree $\mathbb{T}_{n_{a_z}}$.

Justifying Parameter. We require t to be at least the maximum size of the sets in any name-set pairs appearing in either key or ciphertext attributes. That is, let $n := \max_{a \in \mathcal{A}} n_a$, we require

$$t \ge \max \{ 2 \log n - 2, \ \log n + 1 \}, \tag{10}$$

since, from Lemma 3, the maximum size of $\mathsf{rangeEnc}(R)$ for any range R in the tree $\mathbb{T}_n$ is $2 \log n - 2$, and the size of $\mathsf{pointEnc}(x)$ for any leaf x is always $\log n + 1$.

Implication. We now show the following lemma for the above conversion. The implication from KP-ABE-SI to KP-ABE-RM will then follow from the embedding lemma.

Lemma 5. *For any monotone span program $\mathbb{A} = (A, \pi)$ and a set of name-value pairs T for KP-ABE-RM1, we have*

$$R_\kappa^{\mathit{KP\text{-}ABE\text{-}RM1}}(\mathbb{A}, T) = 1 \quad \Longleftrightarrow \quad R_{f_{\mathsf{p}}(\kappa)}^{\mathit{KP\text{-}ABE\text{-}SI}}(f_{\mathsf{k}}(\mathbb{A}), f_{\mathsf{c}}(T)) = 1.$$

---

[7] Recall that on the other hand, for simplicity and wlog, we let $\min_a = 1$.

Proof. Consider the submatrices that define evaluations in KP-ABE-RM and KP-ABE-SI:

$$\mathbb{A}|_T = \left\{ A_i \mid \exists (\pi_{\mathsf{name}}(i), x) \in T \text{ s.t. } x \in \pi_{\mathsf{range}}(i) \right\},$$

$$\mathbb{A}'|_{T'} = \left\{ A_i \mid \exists (\pi'_{\mathsf{name}}(i), \tilde{S}) \in T' \text{ s.t. } \pi'_{\mathsf{set}}(i) \cap \tilde{S} \neq \emptyset \right\},$$

respectively, where here we set $(A, \pi') = f_{\mathsf{k}}(A, \pi)$ and $T' = f_{\mathsf{c}}(T)$ from the conversion. To prove the statement of the theorem, it suffices to prove that: $\mathbb{A}|_T = \mathbb{A}'|_{T'}$. But this holds since

$$\mathbb{A}|_T = \{ A_i \mid \exists (\pi_{\mathsf{name}}(i), x) \in T \text{ s.t. } x \in \pi_{\mathsf{range}}(i) \}$$

$$= \{ A_i \mid \exists (\pi_{\mathsf{name}}(i), x) \in T \text{ s.t. } \mathsf{rangeEnc}(\pi_{\mathsf{range}}(i)) \cap \mathsf{pointEnc}(x) \neq \emptyset \} \quad (11)$$

$$= \{ A_i \mid \exists (\pi_{\mathsf{name}}(i), \mathsf{pointEnc}(x)) \in T'$$
$$\text{s.t. } \mathsf{rangeEnc}(\pi_{\mathsf{range}}(i)) \cap \mathsf{pointEnc}(x) \neq \emptyset \} \quad (12)$$

$$= \left\{ A_i \mid \exists (\pi_{\mathsf{name}}(i), \tilde{S}) \in T' \text{ s.t. } \mathsf{rangeEnc}(\pi_{\mathsf{range}}(i)) \cap \tilde{S} \neq \emptyset \right\} \quad (13)$$

$$= \left\{ A_i \mid \exists (\pi'_{\mathsf{name}}(i), \tilde{S}) \in T' \text{ s.t. } \pi'_{\mathsf{set}}(i) \cap \tilde{S} \neq \emptyset \right\} = \mathbb{A}'|_{T'}, \quad (14)$$

where Eq. (11) holds due to the property of the Range/Point Encodings (Lemma 2), while Eq. (12) is from the definition of T' (Eq. (9)), Eq. (13) is simply a renaming of variable $\mathsf{pointEnc}(x)$ as $\tilde{S}$, and Eq. (14) is due to the definition of π' (Eq. (8)).

4.3 From KP-DSE to ABE-SI

In this section, we show that KP-DSE implies KP-ABE-SI. We will use the following value/set encodings as building blocks. They are also implicitly used previously in [2].

- **Value Encoding** $\mathsf{valueEnc} : \mathbb{Z}_N \to \mathsf{AffSp}(\mathbb{Z}_N^{t+1})$. For a value $x \in \mathbb{Z}_N$, define

$$\mathsf{valueEnc}(x) := \mathsf{cspan} \begin{pmatrix} -x & -x^2 & \cdots & -x^t \\ 1 & & & \\ & 1 & & \\ & & \ddots & \\ & & & 1 \end{pmatrix}.$$

- **Set Encoding** $\mathsf{setEnc} : \binom{\mathbb{Z}_N}{\leq t} \to \mathsf{AffSp}(\mathbb{Z}_N^{t+1})$. For a set $S \subseteq \mathbb{Z}_N$ of size at most t, define $\mathsf{setEnc}(S)$ as a 0-dimensional affine space (an affine space with only one fixed point) as

$$\mathsf{setEnc}(S) := \left\{ (c_0, c_1, \dots, c_t)^\top \right\},$$

where c_ι is the coefficient of z^ι in a polynomial $p_S(z) := \prod_{y \in S}(z - y) = c_0 + c_1 z + \cdots + c_t z^t$.

Lemma 6. *We have* $x \in S \iff \mathsf{setEnc}(S) \cap \mathsf{valueEnc}(x) \neq \emptyset$.

The proof for this lemma is deferred to the full version. We are ready to describe the conversion.

- **Mapping Parameters.** For the name-value universe $\mathcal{X}$ of KP-ABE-SI, let $H : \mathcal{X} \to \mathbb{Z}_N$ be an efficiently computable injective function. We map $f_{\mathsf{p}} :$ $(N, \mathcal{X}, t, \bar{m}, \bar{k}, \bar{\ell}) \mapsto (N, t+1, \bar{m}', \bar{k}', \bar{\ell}')$. That is, we set $d = t+1$ for KP-DSE. The remaining parameters will be specified later below.
- **Mapping Key Attributes.** Consider a monotone span program $\mathbb{A} = (A, \pi)$ for KP-ABE-SI, where $A \in \mathbb{Z}_N^{m \times k}$ and $\pi : [1, m] \to \mathcal{P}$. We map

$$f_{\mathsf{k}} : \mathbb{A} = (A, \pi) \ \mapsto \ \mathbb{A}' = (A', \pi')$$

where $A' \in \mathbb{Z}_N^{m' \times k}$ and π' that maps each row in $[1, m']$ to an affine space in $\mathbb{Z}_N^{t+1}$ are defined as follows. We proceed to define the row number $\mathrm{num}(i, j)$ in exactly the same way as Procedure 1,2 in Mapping key attributes in Sect. 4.1. Then, for $i \in [1, m]$, $j \in [1, k_i]$, we define

$$A'_{\mathrm{num}(i,j)} = A_i, \qquad \pi'\big(\mathrm{num}(i,j)\big) = \mathsf{valueEnc}\Big(H\big(\pi_{\mathsf{name}}(i), x_{i,j}\big)\Big). \qquad (15)$$

- **Mapping Ciphertext Attributes.** Consider a set of name-set pairs for KP-ABE-SI, $T = \{ (a_z, S_z) \in \mathcal{P}_{a_z} \mid z \in [1, \ell] \}$. Let $S'_z := \{ H(a_z, x) \mid x \in S_z \}$, for $z \in [1, \ell]$. We map

$$f_{\mathsf{c}} : T = \{ (a_1, S_1), \ldots, (a_\ell, S_\ell) \} \ \mapsto \ T' = \{ \mathsf{setEnc}(S'_1), \ldots, \mathsf{setEnc}(S'_\ell) \}. \qquad (16)$$

Justifying Parameters. By inspection, the remaining bounds $\bar{m}', \bar{k}', \bar{\ell}'$ of KP-DSE can be related to the bounds $t, \bar{m}, \bar{k}, \bar{\ell}$ of ABE-SI as follows.

$$\bar{m}' \geq t\bar{m}, \qquad\qquad \bar{k}' \geq \bar{k}, \qquad\qquad \bar{\ell}' \geq \bar{\ell}. \qquad (17)$$

In particular, if we allow ABE with unbounded parameters in either $\bar{m}', \bar{k}', \bar{\ell}'$, the corresponding parameters of ABE-SI on the right hand-side of the above inequalities do not have to be bounded.

Lemma 7. *For any monotone span program $\mathbb{A} = (A, \pi)$ and a set of name-set pairs T for KP-ABE-SI, we have*

$$R_\kappa^{\mathsf{KP\text{-}ABE\text{-}SI}}(\mathbb{A}, T) = 1 \quad \Longleftrightarrow \quad R_{f_{\mathsf{p}}(\kappa)}^{\mathsf{KP\text{-}DSE}}(f_{\mathsf{k}}(\mathbb{A}), f_{\mathsf{c}}(T)) = 1.$$

The proof, deferred to the full version, proceeds similarly to that of Lemma 4 (converting ABE to ABE-SI). Intuitively, this is since we replace values and sets via their value/set encodings, but their relation is still preserved via Lemma 6.

5   Instantiations and Performances

In this section, we describe the performances of new ABE-RM schemes obtained via applying our generic constructions to existing schemes in the literature.

Schemes via the ABE-to-ABE-RM Conversion (Sects. 4.1 + 4.2). We first give a general observation for the performance of the converted ABE-RM scheme compared to its original ABE scheme as follows. Assume that the sizes $(|\mathsf{PK}|, |\mathsf{C}|, |\mathsf{SK}|)$ of an ABE scheme can be written as a function $F(|\mathcal{A}|, m, \bar{m}, k, \bar{k}, \ell, \bar{\ell})$, where we recall that m, k are the sizes of a monotone span program, ℓ is the size of an attribute set, and the barred elements are their allowed maximums, *if any*. Then, the converted ABE-RM with maximum range size n has the sizes

$$(|\mathsf{PK}|, |\mathsf{C}|, |\mathsf{SK}|) = F\Big(|\mathcal{A}|n, O(m \log n), O(\bar{m} \log n), k, \bar{k}, O(\ell \log n), O(\bar{\ell} \log n)\Big).$$

This can be seen by inspection from our generic conversions and the range/point encoding; particularly, they follow from Eqs. (7) and (10). Our conversion introduces only $O(\log n)$ factor, compared to the factor $O(n)$ for the trivial scheme.

By applying the above observation to ABE schemes in the literature, we show the performances of their ABE-RM counterparts obtained via our conversions in Tables 2 and 3 for key-policy and ciphertext-policy variants, respectively. We compare them to trivial ABE-RM schemes obtained from ABE via the trivial conversion as explained in Sect. 1. As expected, almost all the ABE-RM schemes obtained from our conversions require only $O(\log n)$ overhead (for both key and ciphertext sizes). Only the two resulting KP-ABE-RM schemes with $O(1)$-size ciphertext require $O(\log^2 n)$ overhead (only for key sizes), and only the resulting CP-ABE-RM scheme with $O(1)$-size key requires $O(\log^2 n)$ overhead (only for ciphertext sizes). In contrast, the ABE-RM schemes obtained from the trivial conversion requires $O(n)$ overhead in either the key or ciphertext sizes (in some case, also the public key sizes), depending on its type of ABE-RM being type 1 or 2, respectively.

Schemes via the KP-DSE-to-ABE-RM Conversion (Sects. 4.3 + 4.2). Let $F'(d, m, \bar{m}, k, \bar{k}, \ell, \bar{\ell})$ be the size function analogously to F in the above discussion, albeit here we consider KP-DSE schemes and have the first input as d (the full dimension of affine spaces). From Eqs. (17) and (10), we have that the ABE-RM scheme via this conversion has the sizes

$$(|\mathsf{PK}|, |\mathsf{C}|, |\mathsf{SK}|) = F'\Big(O(\log n), O(m \log n), O(\bar{m} \log n), k, \bar{k}, \ell, \bar{\ell}\Big),$$

where we notice that there is no overhead expansion for $\ell, \bar{\ell}$. We then apply the conversion to available KP-DSE of [2,3] and CP-DSE of [3,4] and obtain the efficiency shown in the last line of Tables 2 and 3, respectively. The resulting KP-ABE-RM has key size $O(m \log^2 n)$ due to the fact that the KP-DSE of [2,3] requires $d = O(\log n)$ group elements per each affine space (and there are $m' = O(m \log n)$ spaces) in a key. In contrast, the ciphertext size is only $O(\ell)$, which is independent of n. This is since the KP-DSE of [2,3] requires $O(1)$ group elements per each affine space (and there are ℓ spaces) in a ciphertext. The case for CP-ABE-RM, constructed from CP-DSE of [3,4], is analogous.

Table 2. Instantiations and performances of KP-ABE-RM schemes

Scheme	Type	$|PK|$	$|C|$	$|SK|$	Security	Assumption
GPSW [22] + trivial	1	$O(\bar{\ell})$	$O(\ell)$	$O(mn)$	Selective	DBDH
GPSW [22] + trivial	2	$O(\bar{\ell}n)$	$O(\ell n)$	$O(m)$	Selective	DBDH
GPSW [22] + our Sects. 4.1 and 4.2	1, 2	$O(\bar{\ell}\log n)$	$O(\ell \log n)$	$O(m \log n)$	Selective	DBDH
LOSTW [27] + trivial	1	$O(|\mathcal{A}|n)$	$O(\ell)$	$O(mn)$	Full	Subgrp-Deci.
LOSTW [27] + trivial	2	$O(|\mathcal{A}|n)$	$O(\ell n)$	$O(m)$	Full	Subgrp-Deci.
LOSTW [27] + our Sects. 4.1 and 4.2	1, 2	$O(|\mathcal{A}|n)$	$O(\ell \log n)$	$O(m \log n)$	Full	Subgrp-Deci.
ALP [11] + trivial	1	$O(\bar{\ell})$	$O(1)$	$O(m\bar{\ell}n)$	Selective	DBDHE
ALP [11] + trivial	2	$O(\bar{\ell}n)$	$O(1)$	$O(m\bar{\ell}n)$	Selective	DBDHE
ALP [11] + our Sects. 4.1 and 4.2	1,2	$O(\bar{\ell}\log n)$	$O(1)$	$O(m\bar{\ell}\log^2 n)$	Selective	DBDHE
Att1 [2,3] + trivial	1	$O(\bar{\ell})$	$O(1)$	$O(m\bar{\ell}n)$	Full	EDHE-3,4
Att1 [2,3] + trivial	2	$O(\bar{\ell}n)$	$O(1)$	$O(m\bar{\ell}n)$	Full	EDHE-3,4
Att1 [2] + our Sects. 4.1 and 4.2	1, 2	$O(\bar{\ell}\log n)$	$O(1)$	$O(m\bar{\ell}\log^2 n)$	Full	EDHE-3,4
RW [35] + trivial	1	$O(1)$	$O(\ell)$	$O(mn)$	Selective	RW-2
RW [35] + trivial	2	$O(1)$	$O(\ell n)$	$O(m)$	Selective	RW-2
RW [35] + our Sects. 4.1 and 4.2	1, 2	$O(1)$	$O(\ell \log n)$	$O(m \log n)$	Selective	RW-2
Att2 [2,3] + trivial	1	$O(1)$	$O(\ell)$	$O(mn)$	Full	EDHE-3,4
Att2 [2,3] + trivial	2	$O(1)$	$O(\ell n)$	$O(m)$	Full	EDHE-3,4
Att2 [2,3] + our Sects. 4.1 and 4.2	1, 2	$O(1)$	$O(\ell \log n)$	$O(m \log n)$	Full	EDHE-3,4
Att3 [2,3] + our Sects. 4.3 and 4.2	1, 2	$O(\log n)$	$O(\ell)$	$O(m \log^2 n)$	Full	EDHE-3,4

Table 3. Instantiations and performances of CP-ABE-RM schemes

Scheme	Type	$|PK|$	$|C|$	$|SK|$	Security	Assumption
BSW [14] + trivial	1	$O(1)$	$O(mn)$	$O(\ell)$	Selective	Generic group
BSW [14] + trivial	2	$O(1)$	$O(m)$	$O(\ell n)$	Selective	Generic group
BSW[14] + our Sects. 4.1 and 4.2	1,2	$O(1)$	$O(m \log n)$	$O(\ell \log n)$	Selective	Generic group
Wat [38] + trivial	1	$O(|\mathcal{A}|n)$	$O(mn)$	$O(\ell)$	Selective	Para-DBDHE
Wat [38] + trivial	2	$O(|\mathcal{A}|n)$	$O(m)$	$O(\ell n)$	Selective	Para-DBDHE
Wat [38] + our Sects. 4.1 and 4.2	1,2	$O(|\mathcal{A}|n)$	$O(m \log n)$	$O(\ell \log n)$	Selective	Para-DBDHE
RW [35] + trivial	1	$O(1)$	$O(mn)$	$O(\ell)$	Selective	RW-1
RW [35] + trivial	2	$O(1)$	$O(m)$	$O(\ell n)$	Selective	RW-1
RW [35] + our Sects. 4.1 and 4.2	1, 2	$O(1)$	$O(m \log n)$	$O(\ell \log n)$	Selective	RW-1
LOSTW [27] + trivial	1	$O(|\mathcal{A}|n)$	$O(mn)$	$O(\ell)$	Full	Subgrp-Deci.
LOSTW [27] + trivial	2	$O(|\mathcal{A}|n)$	$O(m)$	$O(\ell n)$	Full	Subgrp-Deci.
LOSTW [27] + our Sects. 4.1 and 4.2	1, 2	$O(|\mathcal{A}|n)$	$O(m \log n)$	$O(\ell \log n)$	Full	Subgrp-Deci.
AY1 [3,4] + trivial	1	$O(\bar{\ell})$	$O(m\bar{\ell}n)$	$O(1)$	Full	EDHE-3,4
AY1 [3,4] + trivial	2	$O(\bar{\ell}n)$	$O(m\bar{\ell}n)$	$O(1)$	Full	EDHE-3,4
AY1 [3,4] + our Sects. 4.1 and 4.2	1, 2	$O(\bar{\ell}\log n)$	$O(m\bar{\ell}\log^2 n)$	$O(1)$	Full	EDHE-3,4
AY2 [3,4] + trivial	1	$O(1)$	$O(mn)$	$O(\ell)$	Full	EDHE-3,4
AY2 [3,4] + trivial	2	$O(1)$	$O(m)$	$O(\ell n)$	Full	EDHE-3,4
AY2 [3,4] + our Sects. 4.1 and 4.2	1, 2	$O(1)$	$O(m \log n)$	$O(\ell \log n)$	Full	EDHE-3,4
AY3 [3,4] + our Sects. 4.3 and 4.2	1, 2	$O(\log n)$	$O(m \log^2 n)$	$O(\ell)$	Full	EDHE-3,4

6   Extensions

ABE over Range Intersection (ABE-RI). We can define a useful extension called *ABE over Range Intersection* (ABE-RI). It is defined in exactly the same manner as ABE over Set Intersection (ABE-SI) except that all the attribute value sets will be confined to only ranges. The predicate evaluation amounts to see if ranges are intersected. We give its definition in the full version. We illustrate its application as follows. We can use policies with ranges as in Sect. 1. Now, not only the policy for user but also the content attribute can be specified with ranges; for example, a content with attributes such as ('genre' $= music$), ('day' $= [20160517, 20160529]$), ('hour' $= [22, 23]$). The key for the policy (1) mentioned in Sect. 1 can be used to decrypt this content in the ABE-RI system since the ranges for attribute 'day' are intersected (and the rest is satisfied).

We can construct ABE-RI from ABE-RM as follows. Consider two ranges $[u, v]$ and $[c, d]$. We observe that they intersect if and only if $c \in [u, v]$, $d \in [u, v]$, or $u \in [c, d]$. In other words, range intersection can be expressed as a disjunction of three instances of range membership. The full construction will use ABE-SI (instead of using ABE-RM directly), and is deferred to the full version.

ABE for Non-monotone Span Programs over Range Membership. Our scheme can be extended to also deal with range non-membership relations. This is captured as Non-monotonic ABE-RM, where we deferred its definition to the full version. Intuitively, we implement non-monotonic ABE-RM simply by observing that $x \notin [u, v]$ if and only if $x \in [1, u - 1]$ or $x \in [v + 1, n]$. Hence, it can be expressed as a disjunction of two instances of range membership. The full construction will use ABE-SI (instead of using ABE-RM directly), and is deferred to the full version.

References

1. Agrawal, S., Chase, M.: A study of pair encodings: predicate encryption in prime order groups. In: Kushilevitz, E., et al. (eds.) TCC 2016-A. LNCS, vol. 9563, pp. 259–288. Springer, Heidelberg (2016). doi:10.1007/978-3-662-49099-0_10
2. Attrapadung, N.: Dual system encryption via doubly selective security: framework, fully secure functional encryption for regular languages, and more. In: Nguyen, P.Q., Oswald, E. (eds.) EUROCRYPT 2014. LNCS, vol. 8441, pp. 557–577. Springer, Heidelberg (2014)
3. Attrapadung, N.: Dual system encryption framework in prime-order groups. IACR Cryptology ePrint Archive, 2015:390 (2015)
4. Attrapadung, N., Yamada, S.: Duality in ABE: converting attribute based encryption for dual predicate and dual policy via computational encodings. In: Nyberg, K. (ed.) CT-RSA 2015. LNCS, vol. 9048, pp. 87–105. Springer, Heidelberg (2015)
5. Attrapadung, N., Hanaoka, G., Yamada, S.: Conversions among several classes of predicate encryption and applications to ABE with various compactness trade-offs. In: Iwata, T., et al. (eds.) ASIACRYPT 2015. LNCS, vol. 9452, pp. 574–601. Springer, Heidelberg (2015). doi:10.1007/978-3-662-48797-6_24
6. Attrapadung, N., Hanaoka, G., Matsumoto, T., Teruya, T., Yamada, S.: Attribute based encryption with direct efficiency tradeoff. In: Manulis, M., Sadeghi, A.-R., Schneider, S. (eds.) ACNS 2016. LNCS, vol. 9696, pp. 249–266. Springer, Heidelberg (2016). doi:10.1007/978-3-319-39555-5_14
7. Attrapadung, N., Hanaoka, G., Ogawa, K., Ohtake, G., Watanabe, H., Yamada, S.: Attribute-based encryption for range attributes. Full version of this paper, to be posted on IACR Cryptology ePrint Archive (2016)

8. Attrapadung, N., Herranz, J., Laguillaumie, F., Libert, B., Panafieu, E., Rafols, C.: Attribute-based encryption schemes with constant-size ciphertexts. Theor. Comput. Sci. **422**, 15–38 (2012)
9. Attrapadung, N., Imai, H.: Dual-policy attribute based encryption. In: Abdalla, M., Pointcheval, D., Fouque, P.-A., Vergnaud, D. (eds.) ACNS 2009. LNCS, vol. 5536, pp. 168–185. Springer, Heidelberg (2009)
10. Attrapadung, N., Libert, B.: Functional encryption for inner product: achieving constant-size ciphertexts with adaptive security or support for negation. In: Nguyen, P.Q., Pointcheval, D. (eds.) PKC 2010. LNCS, vol. 6056, pp. 384–402. Springer, Heidelberg (2010)
11. Attrapadung, N., Libert, B., de Panafieu, E.: Expressive key-policy attribute-based encryption with constant-size ciphertexts. In: Catalano, D., Fazio, N., Gennaro, R., Nicolosi, A. (eds.) PKC 2011. LNCS, vol. 6571, pp. 90–108. Springer, Heidelberg (2011)
12. Beimel, A.: Secure schemes for secret sharing and key distribution. Ph.D. thesis, Israel Institute of Technology, Technion, Haifa, Israel (1996)
13. Bentley, J.L.: Solutions to Klee's rectangle problems'. Technical report, Carnegie-Mellon University (1977)
14. Bethencourt, J., Sahai, A., Waters, B.: Ciphertext-policy attribute-based encryption. In: Proceedings of 2007 IEEE Symposium on Security and Privacy, pp. 321–334 (2007)
15. Boneh, D., Franklin, M.: Identity-based encryption from the weil pairing. In: Kilian, J. (ed.) CRYPTO 2001. LNCS, vol. 2139, pp. 213–229. Springer, Heidelberg (2001)
16. Boneh, D., Gentry, C., Waters, B.: Collusion resistant broadcast encryption with short ciphertexts and private keys. In: Shoup, V. (ed.) CRYPTO 2005. LNCS, vol. 3621, pp. 258–275. Springer, Heidelberg (2005)
17. Boneh, D., Hamburg, M.: Generalized identity based and broadcast encryption schemes. In: Pieprzyk, J. (ed.) ASIACRYPT 2008. LNCS, vol. 5350, pp. 455–470. Springer, Heidelberg (2008)
18. Boneh, D., Sahai, A., Waters, B.: Functional encryption: definitions and challenges. In: Ishai, Y. (ed.) TCC 2011. LNCS, vol. 6597, pp. 253–273. Springer, Heidelberg (2011)
19. Chen, J., Gay, R., Wee, H.: Improved dual system ABE in prime-order groups via predicate encodings. In: Oswald, E., Fischlin, M. (eds.) EUROCRYPT 2015. LNCS, vol. 9057, pp. 595–624. Springer, Heidelberg (2015)
20. Gay, R., Méaux, P., Wee, H.: Predicate encryption for multi-dimensional range queries from lattices. In: Katz, J. (ed.) PKC 2015. LNCS, vol. 9020, pp. 752–776. Springer, Heidelberg (2015)
21. Goyal, V., Jain, A., Pandey, O., Sahai, A.: Bounded ciphertext policy attribute based encryption. In: Aceto, L., Damgård, I., Goldberg, L.A., Halldórsson, M.M., Ingólfsdóttir, A., Walukiewicz, I. (eds.) ICALP 2008, Part II. LNCS, vol. 5126, pp. 579–591. Springer, Heidelberg (2008)
22. Goyal, V., Pandey, O., Sahai, A., Waters, B.: Attribute-based encryption for fine-grained access control of encrypted data. In: Proceedings of ACM-CCS 2006, pp. 89–98 (2006)
23. Hohenberger, S., Waters, B.: Attribute-based encryption with fast decryption. In: Hanaoka, G., Kurosawa, K. (eds.) PKC 2013. LNCS, vol. 7778, pp. 162–179. Springer, Heidelberg (2013)

24. Kasamatsu, K., Matsuda, T., Emura, K., Attrapadung, N., Hanaoka, G., Imai, H.: Time-specific encryption from forward-secure encryption. In: Visconti, I., De Prisco, R. (eds.) SCN 2012. LNCS, vol. 7485, pp. 184–204. Springer, Heidelberg (2012)

25. Kasamatsu, K., Matsuda, T., Hanaoka, G., Imai, H.: Ciphertext policy multi-dimensional range encryption. In: Kwon, T., Lee, M.-K., Kwon, D. (eds.) ICISC 2012. LNCS, vol. 7839, pp. 247–261. Springer, Heidelberg (2013)

26. Katz, J., Sahai, A., Waters, B.: Predicate encryption supporting disjunctions, polynomial equations, and inner products. In: Smart, N.P. (ed.) EUROCRYPT 2008. LNCS, vol. 4965, pp. 146–162. Springer, Heidelberg (2008)

27. Lewko, A., Okamoto, T., Sahai, A., Takashima, K., Waters, B.: Fully secure functional encryption: attribute-based encryption and (hierarchical) inner product encryption. In: Gilbert, H. (ed.) EUROCRYPT 2010. LNCS, vol. 6110, pp. 62–91. Springer, Heidelberg (2010)

28. Lewko, A., Sahai, A., Waters, B.: Revocation systems with very small private keys. In: Proceedings of IEEE Symposium on Security and Privacy, pp. 273–285 (2010)

29. Lewko, A., Waters, B.: Decentralizing attribute-based encryption. In: Paterson, K.G. (ed.) EUROCRYPT 2011. LNCS, vol. 6632, pp. 568–588. Springer, Heidelberg (2011)

30. Lewko, A., Waters, B.: New proof methods for attribute-based encryption: achieving full security through selective techniques. In: Safavi-Naini, R., Canetti, R. (eds.) CRYPTO 2012. LNCS, vol. 7417, pp. 180–198. Springer, Heidelberg (2012)

31. Ostrovsky, R., Sahai, A., Waters, B.: Attribute-based encryption with non-monotonic access structures. In: Proceedings of ACM-CCS 2007, pp. 195–203 (2007)

32. Okamoto, T., Takashima, K.: Fully secure functional encryption with general relations from the decisional linear assumption. In: Rabin, T. (ed.) CRYPTO 2010. LNCS, vol. 6223, pp. 191–208. Springer, Heidelberg (2010)

33. Okamoto, T., Takashima, K.: Fully secure unbounded inner-product and attribute-based encryption. In: Wang, X., Sako, K. (eds.) ASIACRYPT 2012. LNCS, vol. 7658, pp. 349–366. Springer, Heidelberg (2012)

34. Paterson, K.G., Quaglia, E.A.: Time-specific encryption. In: Garay, J.A., De Prisco, R. (eds.) SCN 2010. LNCS, vol. 6280, pp. 1–16. Springer, Heidelberg (2010)

35. Rouselakis, Y., Waters, B.: Practical constructions and new proof methods for large universe attribute-based encryption. In: Proceedings of ACM-CCS 2013, pp. 463–474 (2013)

36. Shi, E., Bethencourt, J., Chan, H., Song, D., Perrig, A.: Multi-dimensional range query over encrypted data. In: Proceedings of 2007 IEEE Symposium on Security and Privacy, pp. 350–364 (2007)

37. Sahai, A., Waters, B.: Fuzzy identity-based encryption. In: Cramer, R. (ed.) EUROCRYPT 2005. LNCS, vol. 3494, pp. 457–473. Springer, Heidelberg (2005)

38. Waters, B.: Ciphertext-policy attribute-based encryption: an expressive, efficient, and provably secure realization. In: Catalano, D., Fazio, N., Gennaro, R., Nicolosi, A. (eds.) PKC 2011. LNCS, vol. 6571, pp. 53–70. Springer, Heidelberg (2011)

39. Wee, H.: Dual system encryption via predicate encodings. In: Lindell, Y. (ed.) TCC 2014. LNCS, vol. 8349, pp. 616–637. Springer, Heidelberg (2014)

40. Yamada, S., Attrapadung, N., Hanaoka, G., Kunihiro, N.: A framework and compact constructions for non-monotonic attribute-based encryption. In: Krawczyk, H. (ed.) PKC 2014. LNCS, vol. 8383, pp. 275–292. Springer, Heidelberg (2014)

Naor-Yung Paradigm with Shared Randomness and Applications

Silvio Biagioni[1]([✉]), Daniel Masny[2], and Daniele Venturi[3]

[1] Department of Information Engineering, Sapienza University of Rome,
Rome, Italy
sil.biagioni@yahoo.it
[2] Horst-Görtz Institute for IT Security, Ruhr-Universität Bochum,
Bochum, Germany
[3] Department of Information Engineering and Computer Science,
University of Trento, Trento, Italy

Abstract. The Naor-Yung paradigm (Naor and Yung, STOC '90) allows to generically boost security under chosen-plaintext attacks (CPA) to security against chosen-ciphertext attacks (CCA) for public-key encryption (PKE) schemes. The main idea is to encrypt the plaintext twice (under independent public keys), and to append a non-interactive zero-knowledge (NIZK) proof that the two ciphertexts indeed encrypt the same message. Later work by Camenisch, Chandran, and Shoup (Eurocrypt '09) and Naor and Segev (Crypto '09 and SIAM J. Comput. '12) established that the very same techniques can also be used in the settings of key-dependent message (KDM) and key-leakage attacks (respectively).

In this paper we study the conditions under which the two ciphertexts in the Naor-Yung construction can share the same random coins. We find that this is possible, provided that the underlying PKE scheme meets an additional simple property. The motivation for re-using the same random coins is that this allows to design much more efficient NIZK proofs. We showcase such an improvement in the random oracle model, under standard complexity assumptions including Decisional Diffie-Hellman, Quadratic Residuosity, and Subset Sum. The length of the resulting ciphertexts is reduced by 50 %, yielding truly efficient PKE schemes achieving CCA security under KDM and key-leakage attacks.

As an additional contribution, we design the first PKE scheme whose CPA security under KDM attacks can be directly reduced to (low-density instances of) the Subset Sum assumption. The scheme supports key-dependent messages computed via any affine function of the secret key.

1 Introduction

Forty years ago, in their seminal paper [25], Diffie and Hellman put forward the concept of public-key cryptography. Since then, the field has experienced huge advances, making public-key encryption (PKE) one of the most fundamental and deployed cryptographic applications. Intuitively, PKE allows a sender to encrypt

© Springer International Publishing Switzerland 2016
V. Zikas and R. De Prisco (Eds.): SCN 2016, LNCS 9841, pp. 62–80, 2016.
DOI: 10.1007/978-3-319-44618-9_4

a message under a receiver's public key; the receiver, holding the corresponding secret key, is the only one able to decrypt the resulting ciphertext and thus recover the transmitted message. In order for the above idea to work we need a mechanism to certify users' public keys, which is typically achieved using digital signatures within a public-key infrastructure.

1.1 Motivation

It is of fundamental importance to understand what type of security properties a PKE scheme should satisfy, in order to be used effectively in applications. The most basic requirement is to say that it should be unfeasible to recover the plaintext behind a given ciphertext. This is, however, not sufficient in many applications, as it does not exclude, e.g., the possibility that one is able to recover partial information on the encrypted message.

Seminal work on the subject [38,47,60] established the equivalence of different formulations leading to the following minimal requirement: No efficient adversary, given a target public key, should be able to distinguish the encryption of two chosen messages. This notion is often known under the name of indistinguishability under *chosen-plaintext* attacks (CPA), and it is by far the most basic security requirement a PKE scheme should meet. Yet, CPA security is insufficient in many applications. For instance, in some case, we might require ciphertexts to be non-malleable, meaning that it should be hard, given a cipher-text encrypting some message, to create a valid ciphertext encrypting a related message; *non-malleable* PKE [8,21,27,52] is important in many contexts, e.g., for online auctions.

The de-facto standard notion of security for PKE is called indistinguishability under *chosen-ciphertext* attacks (CCA) which requires that CPA security should hold even in the presence of decryption queries (i.e., the adversary is allowed to ask for the decryption of arbitrary messages but the challenge ciphertext). It is important to note that CCA security is not a theoretical concern, as emphasized by the celebrated Bleichenbacher attack on PKCS #1 [14]. However, there are specific settings in which even CCA security is not enough. We review two such settings below.

KDM Attacks. An adversary might be able to see ciphertexts encrypting messages related to the secret key. This is the case, e.g., in disk encryption software (including Windows Vista's BitLocker utility) and in certain anonymous credential systems [20], or could be due to careless key management. Such key-dependent message (KDM) attacks are captured within the notions of CPA/CCA security by requiring that encryptions of messages depending on the secret key (via adversarial functions) are indistinguishable from encryptions of a fixed string [13,20].

Several PKE schemes with CPA/CCA-KDM security exist, under different complexity assumptions including Learning with Errors [6,18], Decisional Diffie-Hellman [15,18,40,59], Quadratic Residuosity [17,40,59], and Learning Parity with Noise [28].

Key-Leakage Attacks. An adversary might be able to learn partial information on the secret key by means of so-called side-channel attacks, exploiting physical phenomena such as timing [44], power consumption [45], and electronic emission [53]. Such bounded key-leakage attacks are captured within the notions of CPA/CCA security by empowering the adversary with access to a so-called Λ-leakage oracle: Upon input an efficiently computable function, the oracle returns the result of the function applied to the secret key, for a total of at most Λ bits.

Several PKE schemes with CPA/CCA security under bounded key-leakage attacks exist, under different complexity assumptions including Learning with Errors [1], Decisional Diffie-Hellman [26,48,49], and Quadratic Residuosity [17].

1.2   Our Contributions

The Naor-Yung paradigm is a method to generically transform a CPA-secure PKE scheme into a CCA-secure one, in a non-black-box way. Specifically, to encrypt a given message m, one samples two independent public keys pk and pk' for the underlying CPA-secure PKE, encrypts the message m twice yielding ciphertexts c and c' (the first one under pk and the second one under pk'), and finally gives a non-interactive proof π that the ciphertexts indeed encrypt the same message. One can show that if the non-interactive proof satisfies zero-knowledge, and moreover it is simulation-sound [57], the resulting PKE meets CCA security.

Later work by Camenisch et al. [19], and by Naor and Segev [48,49], showed that the original Naor-Yung paradigm also works in the more generic settings of KDM attacks and key-leakage attacks. However, the resulting PKE scheme is not very efficient in the standard model due to the cost of simulation-sound non-interactive zero-knowledge (NIZK) proof systems. The efficiency of the Naor-Yung paradigm is very competitive, instead, in the random oracle model of Bellare and Rogaway [9], where each party (including the adversary) is given access to a random hash function. As proven by Faust *et al.* [33], the Fiat-Shamir heuristic [35] is sufficient for instantiating the NIZK in the Naor-Yung construction (in the ROM), leading the most efficient instantiations of PKE schemes with CCA security under KDM and key-leakage attacks known today.

A Twist of Naor-Yung. In this work we analyze a slight modification of the original Naor-Yung paradigm. The main idea is to have the two ciphertexts c and c' share the same random coins. As we will see, this allows for a substantial efficiency improvement in the design of the NIZK, yielding beyond state-of-the-art PKE schemes with CCA security under KDM and key-leakage attacks (in the ROM).

Our analysis (see Sect. 3) shows that the above idea indeed works, provided that the underlying CPA-secure PKE scheme meets an additional property that we dub "randomness fusion": Given two ciphertexts c and c' of messages m and m' respectively (computed under independent public keys pk and pk') it is possible to re-randomize (c, c') into a new pair $(\tilde{c}, \tilde{c}')$ such that the distribution of $(\tilde{c}, \tilde{c}')$ is statistically close to the distribution of $(\hat{c}, \hat{c}')$ where $(\hat{c}, \hat{c}')$ are computed using the normal encryption with the same (uniform) randomness r^*.

A similar requirement has been put forward by Bellare *et al.* [7] in their study of randomness re-use in multi-recipient PKE. Our requirement is however weaker than the one in [7], and, as we show, it is sufficient for our application.

KDM Security from Subset Sum. As a contribution of independent interest, in Sect. 4, we design the first PKE scheme whose KDM-CPA security can be based directly on low-density instances of the Subset Sum problem. Such an assumption is particularly interesting given its robustness to quantum attacks [12]. The set of supported KDM functions consists of all possible (efficiently computable) affine modifications of the secret key; a result of Applebaum [5] allows to generically boost this form of KDM security to security against all functions that can be computed in some fixed polynomial time.

Our construction borrows ideas from [6], that we needed to carefully adapt to the case of Subset Sum. The PKE scheme we design can be effectively used in our framework (as we argue below), yielding a truly efficient PKE scheme with CCA-KDM security from the Subset Sum assumption (in the ROM).

Comparison. Finally, we instantiate our twist of the Naor-Yung construction under three complexity assumptions: Decisional Diffie-Hellman, Quadratic Residuosity, and Subset Sum. As our analysis shows (see Sect. 5), ciphertexts computed via our approach are shorter by a factor of roughly 50 % compared to those one would obtain via the original Naor-Yung paradigm.

The reason behind such an efficiency improvement is best understood using an example. Consider the ElGamal PKE scheme [30], whose CPA-security can be based on the Decisional Diffie-Hellman assumption. A public key consists of a single element h, within a cyclic group $\mathbb{G}$ of prime order q (with generator g); an encryption of $m \in \mathbb{G}$ under h equals $c := (c_1, c_2) = (g^r, h^r \cdot m)$, for uniform randomness $r \in \mathbb{Z}_q$. The PKE scheme is easily seen to meet the randomness fusion property.[1]

When using the above PKE scheme in the original Naor-Yung construction one samples two independent public keys $h, h' \in \mathbb{G}$, and computes a "double encryption" of message m by defining $c := (c_1, c_2) = (g^r, h^r \cdot m)$ and $c' := (c'_1, c'_2) = (g^{r'}, (h')^{r'} \cdot m)$, for independent randomness $r, r' \in \mathbb{Z}_q$. Finally, one needs to compute a (simulation-sound) NIZK proof π for the fact that c and c' are well-distributed ciphertexts encrypting the same messages; this is equivalent to showing knowledge of r, r' such that $c_1 = g^r$, $c'_1 = g^{r'}$, and $c_2/c'_2 = h^r/(h')^{r'}$. We refer to the pair $x := (r, r')$ as the witness, and to $y := (h, (c_1, c_2), h', (c'_1, c'_2))$ as the statement to be proven.

The standard way to compute π (in the ROM) is by applying the Fiat-Shamir heuristic [35] to a so-called Sigma-protocol for the above considered language.[2] In the case of ElGamal (see [33, Section 5]) $\pi := (\alpha, \gamma)$, where $\alpha := (\alpha_1, \alpha_2, \alpha_3) =$

---

[1] In fact, it satisfies the reproducibility test of Bellare *et al.* [7] which implies the randomness fusion property.

[2] A Sigma-protocol is a public-coin interactive protocol consisting of three messages (α, β, γ), satisfying certain properties; see Sect. 5 for a more precise definition.

$(g^s, g^{s'}, h^s \cdot (h')^{s'})$ and $\gamma := (\gamma_1, \gamma_2) = (s - \beta r, s' + \beta r')$, with random $s, s' \in \mathbb{Z}_q$ and β implicitly defined as $\beta := H(y\|\alpha)$ through the application of the random oracle H.

This way, a ciphertext consists of 9 group elements. Using our twist of the Naor-Yung construction one can completely drop α_2 and γ_2, thus saving 3 group elements (note that $c_1 = c_1'$). Hence, a ciphertext consists of 6 group elements yielding a 33 % gain in ciphertext size. While the above instantiation is not interesting on its own right (as one can obtain CCA security in the standard model under the same complexity assumption, with even shorter ciphertexts [22]) it contains the crux of our method, and moreover it constitutes the base for understanding our concrete instantiations in Sect. 5.

1.3   Related Work

The first PKE scheme with CPA security directly based on Subset Sum has been constructed by Lyubashevsky et al. [46]; their work has recently been extended to the setting of CCA security by Faust et al. [34]. Subset Sum also found application in the context of outsourced pattern matching [32].

While we focused on public-key encryption, KDM security can also be defined in the secret-key setting. See, among others, [6,13]. Sometimes KDM security is defined in a multi-key variant, where there are polynomially many public/secret key pairs and the key-dependent message is chosen as a function of all the keys. Although our twist of the Naor-Yung paradigm works even in the multi-user setting, our Subset Sum based PKE scheme is only proven secure in the single-key setting.

Many definitions for security under key-leakage attacks exist in the literature, beyond the setting of bounded leakage considered in this paper. We refer the reader directly to the literature (e.g., [3,58]) for a more in-depth discussion on the relevance of each definition. We also dispose of many leakage-resilient primitives beyond public-key encryption, see, among many others, [2,16,24,29,31,42,51].

Rackoff and Simon [54] considered a variation of the Naor-Yung paradigm in which the sender encrypts the message only once, and then it proves in zero-knowledge that it knows the plaintext corresponding to the transmitted cipher-text. In order for this to work, the NIZK proof system needs to satisfy a stronger version of soundness known as simulation extractability. Unfortunately, this par-adigm does not lead to very efficient instantiations in the ROM due to the fact that Fiat-Shamir NIZK are not known to be simulation extractable. (See [10,11] for negative indications on this matter.) An alternative (always in the ROM) is to use Fischlin's transformation [36], but the price to instantiate the NIZK might be higher [23].

An alternative construction to generically boost CPA security to CCA security for PKE in the random oracle model is due to Fujisaki and Okamoto [37]. The security of this construction under KDM attacks has been recently analyzed in [43].

2   Preliminaries

2.1   Notation

We write $\lambda \in \mathbb{N}$ for the security parameter. We say that a function ν is negligible in λ, if it is asymptotically smaller than the inverse of any polynomial in λ, i.e. $\nu(\lambda) = \lambda^{-\omega(1)}$. An algorithm A is probabilistic polynomial-time (PPT) if A is randomized, and for any input $x, r \in \{0, 1\}^*$ the computation of $\mathsf{A}(x; r)$ (i.e., A with input x and random coins r) terminates in at most $\text{poly}(|x|)$ steps. When the coins are left implicit, we write $y \leftarrow_{\$} \mathsf{A}(x)$ to denote the output of $\mathsf{A}(x; r)$ with uniform randomness. If $\mathcal{X}$ is a set, then $x \leftarrow_{\$} \mathcal{X}$ denotes that x is sampled uniformly at random from $\mathcal{X}$.

For a distribution $\mathbf{D}$, we denote with $x \leftarrow_{\$} \mathbf{D}$ that x is sampled according to the distribution $\mathbf{D}$. For two distributions $\mathbf{D}$ and $\mathbf{D}'$ over a shared domain $\mathcal{D}$ we write $\mathbf{D}(x)$ for the probability assigned to $x \in \mathcal{D}$ and $\Delta(\mathbf{D}, \mathbf{D}') := \frac{1}{2} \sum_{x \in \mathcal{D}} |\mathbf{D}(x) - \mathbf{D}'(x)|$ for the statistical distance between $\mathbf{D}$ and $\mathbf{D}'$. Whenever the statistical distance is negligible, we write $\mathbf{D} \approx_s \mathbf{D}'$. Similarly, given two ensembles $\mathbf{X} = \{X_\lambda\}_{\lambda \in \mathbb{N}}$ and $\mathbf{Y} = \{Y_\lambda\}_{\lambda \in \mathbb{N}}$, we write $\mathbf{X} \approx_c \mathbf{Y}$ to denote that the two ensembles are computationally indistinguishable.

Vectors and matrices are denoted in boldface. For two vectors $\mathbf{u}, \mathbf{v}$, with $\mathbf{u} = (u_1, \ldots, u_n)$ and $\mathbf{v} = (v_1, \ldots, v_n)$, the inner product between $\mathbf{u}$ and $\mathbf{v}$ is defined as $\langle \mathbf{u}, \mathbf{v} \rangle := \sum_{i=1}^{n} u_i \cdot v_i$. We represent elements in $\mathbb{Z}_p$ as values in the range $[-(p-1)/2, (p-1)/2]$, where $p > 2$ is a prime number. The absolute value of $v \in \mathbb{Z}_p$, denoted $|v|$, is the absolute value of the corresponding value in $[-(p-1)/2, (p-1)/2]$, and the infinity norm of a vector $\mathbf{v} := (v_1, \ldots, v_n) \in \mathbb{Z}_p^n$ is $\|\mathbf{v}\|_\infty := \max_{i \in [n]} |v_i|$. We will also use the following rounding functions: $\lfloor \cdot \rceil : \mathbb{R} \to \mathbb{Z}$ which maps a real number to its closest integer, $\lfloor \cdot \rfloor : \mathbb{R} \to \mathbb{Z}$ which maps a real number to its closest smaller integer, and $\lceil \cdot \rceil : \mathbb{R} \to \mathbb{Z}$ which maps a real number to its closest larger integer. For any $q, p \in \mathbb{N}$, we denote by $\lfloor x \rceil_p : \mathbb{Z}_q \to \mathbb{Z}_p$ the rounding function $\lfloor x \rceil_p := \lfloor \frac{p}{q} \cdot x \rceil$; in case $\mathbf{v}$ is a vector, we write $\lfloor \mathbf{v} \rceil_p$ for the application of $\lfloor \cdot \rceil_p$ component wise.

2.2   Public-Key Encryption

A Public-Key Encryption (PKE) scheme is a tuple of algorithms $\Pi = (\mathsf{Gen}, \mathsf{Enc}, \mathsf{Dec})$ defined as follows. (1) Algorithm Gen takes as input the security parameter and outputs a public/secret key pair (pk, sk); for a given value of the security parameter $\lambda \in \mathbb{N}$, the set of all secret keys is denoted by $\mathcal{SK}_\lambda$ and the set of all public keys by $\mathcal{PK}_\lambda$. (2) The randomized algorithm Enc takes as input the public key pk, a message $m \in \mathcal{M}$, and implicit randomness $r \in \mathcal{R}$, and outputs a ciphertext $c = \mathsf{Enc}(pk, m; r)$; the set of all ciphertexts is denoted by $\mathcal{C}$ and we sometimes write $\mu \in \mathbb{N}$ for the bit-length of a plaintext $m \in \mathcal{M}$. (3) The deterministic algorithm Dec takes as input the secret key sk and a ciphertext $c \in \mathcal{C}$ and outputs $m = \mathsf{Dec}(sk, c)$ which is either equal to some message $m \in \mathcal{M}$ or to an error symbol $\bot$.

Experiment $\mathbf{Exp}_{\Pi,\mathsf{A}}^{\mathrm{kdm\text{-}cca}}(\lambda,\mathcal{F})$:	Oracle $\mathcal{O}_{sk,b}^{\mathrm{kdm}}(f)$:	Oracle $\mathcal{O}_{sk}^{\mathrm{dec}}(c)$:
$(pk,sk) \leftarrow_\$ \mathsf{Gen}(1^\lambda);\ b \leftarrow_\$ \{0,1\}$	If $b=0$	Return $\mathsf{Dec}(sk,c)$
$\mathcal{Q}_{\mathrm{dec}}, \mathcal{Q}_{\mathrm{kdm}} \leftarrow \emptyset$	$\quad$ Return $c \leftarrow_\$ \mathsf{Enc}(pk,0^\mu)$	$\mathcal{Q}_{\mathrm{dec}} \leftarrow \mathcal{Q}_{\mathrm{dec}} \cup \{c\}$
$b' \leftarrow \mathsf{A}^{\mathcal{O}_{sk}^{\mathrm{dec}}(\cdot),\mathcal{O}_{sk,b}^{\mathrm{kdm}}(\cdot)}(pk)$	Else	
Return $(b'=b) \wedge (\mathcal{Q}_{\mathrm{dec}} \cap \mathcal{Q}_{\mathrm{kdm}} = \emptyset)$	$\quad$ Return $c \leftarrow_\$ \mathsf{Enc}(pk,f(sk))$	
	$\mathcal{Q}_{\mathrm{kdm}} \leftarrow \mathcal{Q}_{\mathrm{kdm}} \cup \{c\}$	

Fig. 1. Experiment defining KDM security of a PKE scheme.

Correctness. We say that Π satisfies *correctness* if for all $(pk,sk) \leftarrow_\$ \mathsf{Gen}(1^\lambda)$ there exists a negligible function $\nu : \mathbb{N} \to [0,1]$ such that that $\mathbb{P}[\mathsf{Dec}(sk, \mathsf{Enc}(pk, m)) = m] \geq 1 - \nu(\lambda)$ (where the randomness is taken over the internal coin tosses of algorithm Enc).

KDM Security. We now turn to defining key-dependent message (KDM) security for PKE, both in the case of chosen-plaintext attacks (CPA) and chosen-ciphertext attacks (CCA).

Definition 1 (KDM security). *Let $\Pi = (\mathsf{Gen}, \mathsf{Enc}, \mathsf{Dec})$ be a PKE scheme with message space $\mathcal{M}$ and secret-key space $\mathcal{SK}_\lambda$ (for security parameter $\lambda \in \mathbb{N}$), and let $\mathcal{F} : \mathcal{SK}_\lambda \to \mathcal{M}$ be a set of efficiently computable functions. We say that Π has $\mathcal{F}$-key-dependent message security under chosen-ciphertext attacks ($\mathcal{F}$-KDM-CCA for short), if for all PPT adversaries A there exists a negligible function $\nu : \mathbb{N} \to [0,1]$ such that*

$$\left| \mathbb{P}\left[\mathbf{Exp}_{\Pi,\mathsf{A}}^{\mathrm{kdm\text{-}cca}}(\lambda,\mathcal{F}) = 1 \right] - \frac{1}{2} \right| \leq \nu(\lambda),$$

where the experiment $\mathbf{Exp}_{\Pi,\mathsf{A}}^{\mathrm{kdm\text{-}cca}}(\lambda,\mathcal{F})$ is defined in Fig. 1.

Moreover, we say that Π has $\mathcal{F}$-KDM-CPA security if the above holds for all PPT adversaries that are not allowed any query to oracle $\mathcal{O}_{sk}^{\mathrm{dec}}(\cdot)$; in this case we denote by $\mathbf{Exp}_{\Pi,\mathsf{A}}^{\mathrm{kdm\text{-}cpa}}(\lambda,\mathcal{F})$ the corresponding experiment.

We remark that $\mathcal{F}$-KDM-CPA security implies standard CPA security by considering the set $\mathcal{F}$ of all constant functions that output a given (hard-coded) plaintext in the message space, i.e. $\mathcal{F}_{\mathrm{msg}} := \{f_m : f_m(\cdot) = m\}_{m \in \mathcal{M}}$.

2.3 Non-Interactive Zero-Knowledge

A *decision problem* related to a language $L \subseteq \{0,1\}^*$ requires to determine if a given string y is in L or not. We can associate to any NP-language L a polynomial-time recognizable relation $R \subseteq \{0,1\}^* \times \{0,1\}^*$ defining L itself, i.e. $L = \{y : \exists x \text{ s.t. } (y,x) \in R\}$ for $|x| \leq \mathrm{poly}(|y|)$. The string x is called a *witness* for membership of $y \in L$.

Let L be an NP-language. We now recall the definition of a non-interactive zero-knowledge (NIZK) argument system for L, in the random oracle model (ROM). Let H be a hash function (modeled as a random oracle). A non-interactive argument system for L is a pair of PPT algorithms $(\mathsf{P}^H, \mathsf{V}^H)$ specified as follows. (1) Algorithm P^H takes as input a pair (y, x) such that $(y, x) \in R$, and returns a proof π. (2) Algorithm V^H takes as input a pair (y, π) and returns a decision bit. We write P^H, V^H, to specify that both algorithms are allowed random oracle queries.

By correctness, we mean that $\mathsf{V}^H(y, \pi) = 1$ whenever $\pi \leftarrow_\$ \mathsf{P}^H(y, x)$ and $(y, x) \in R$ Below we define two further properties of non-interactive arguments, namely zero-knowledge and simulation soundness. The definitions are taken from [33].

Zero-Knowledge. The zero-knowledge property captures the intuition that a non-interactive proof π for a given statement y does not reveal anything beyond the fact that $y \in L$. This intuition is formalized by the existence of an efficient simulator S that is able to simulate π without knowing a witness. The simulator is allowed to fully control the random oracle, as we make explicit in the definition below.

Definition 2 (NIZK). *Let L be an NP-language, and let H be a hash function (modeled as a random oracle). Denote by $\mathsf{S}_1, \mathsf{S}_2$ the oracles such that $\mathsf{S}_1(\cdot)$ returns the first output of $(h, \tau) \leftarrow_\$ \mathsf{S}(1, \tau, \cdot)$ and $\mathsf{S}_2(y, x)$ returns the first output of $(\pi, \tau) \leftarrow_\$ \mathsf{S}(2, \tau, y)$ if $(y, x) \in R$. We say that $(\mathsf{P}^H, \mathsf{V}^H)$ is a NIZK for L in the random oracle model, if there exists a PPT simulator S such that for all PPT distinguishers D there is a negligible function $\nu : \mathbb{N} \to [0, 1]$ for which*

$$\left| \mathbb{P}\left[\mathsf{D}^{H(\cdot), \mathsf{P}^H(\cdot, \cdot)}(1^\lambda) = 1 \right] - \mathbb{P}\left[\mathsf{D}^{\mathsf{S}_1(\cdot), \mathsf{S}_2(\cdot, \cdot)}(1^\lambda) = 1 \right] \right| \leq \nu(\lambda),$$

where both oracles P and S_2 return $\bot$ in case $(y, x) \notin R$.

Simulation Soundness. The simulation soundness property captures the intuition that it should be hard to find an accepting proof π for a false statement $y \notin L$, even after seeing polynomially many simulated proofs of possibly false statements.

Definition 3 (Simulation soundness). *Let L be an NP-language, and let H be a hash function (modeled as a random oracle). Consider a NIZK $(\mathsf{P}^H, \mathsf{V}^H)$ for L, with zero-knowledge simulator S. Denote by $\mathsf{S}_1, \mathsf{S}_2'$ the oracles such that $\mathsf{S}_1(\cdot)$ returns the first output of $(h, \tau) \leftarrow_\$ \mathsf{S}(1, \tau, \cdot)$ and $\mathsf{S}_2'(y)$ returns the first output of $(\pi, \tau) \leftarrow_\$ \mathsf{S}(2, \tau, y)$. We say that $(\mathsf{P}^H, \mathsf{V}^H)$ is simulation sound in the random oracle model, if for all PPT adversaries A there is a negligible function $\nu : \mathbb{N} \to [0, 1]$ such that*

$$\mathbb{P}\left[\mathsf{V}^{\mathsf{S}_1}(y^*, \pi^*) = 1 \wedge y^* \notin L \wedge (y^*, \pi^*) \notin \mathcal{Q} : (y^*, \pi^*) \leftarrow_\$ \mathsf{A}^{\mathsf{S}_1(\cdot), \mathsf{S}_2'(\cdot)}(1^\lambda) \right] \leq \nu(\lambda),$$

where $\mathcal{Q}$ contains the list of pairs (y_i, π_i) such that y_i was asked to S_2' yielding answer π_i.

3   Naor-Yung Paradigm with Shared Randomness

We start by describing a twist of the Naor-Yung paradigm, in Sect. 3.1, where the same random string is used to generate both ciphertexts in the Naor-Yung construction. Then, in Sect. 3.2, we put forward a simple property of a PKE scheme which will be useful for proving security of the modified Naor-Yung paradigm. Our main theorem, and its proof, can be found in Sect. 3.3. Finally, Sect. 3.4 discusses a few generalizations of our result.

3.1   A Twist of Naor-Yung

The original Naor-Yung paradigm combines two CPA-secure PKE schemes Π and Π' into a new PKE scheme Π^* that achieves CCA security [50]. A ciphertext in Π^* consists of two independent encryptions of the same message (using fresh randomness), together with a non-interactive proof that the two ciphertexts indeed encrypt the same message. This paradigm was later extended to the setting of KDM security by Camenisch et al. [19], and to the setting of key-leakage by Naor and Segev [48,49].

Below, we present a twist of the Naor-Yung construction in which the two encryptions share the same random coins. As we will see in the sequel (cf. Sect. 5) this allows for significant efficiency improvements in the size of the resulting non-interactive proofs. Although our construction works for any pair of PKE schemes with shared message and randomness space, for simplicity we consider the special case in which $\Pi' = \Pi$.

Let $\Pi = (\mathsf{Gen}, \mathsf{Enc}, \mathsf{Dec})$ be a PKE scheme with message space $\mathcal{M}$ and randomness space $\mathcal{R}$, and let let $(\mathsf{P}^H, \mathsf{V}^H)$ be a NIZK in the ROM for the following NP-language

$$L_{\mathrm{NY}}^{\Pi} := \left\{ (pk, pk', c, c') : \exists m, r^* \text{ s.t. } \begin{array}{l} c = \mathsf{Enc}(pk, m; r^*) \\ c' = \mathsf{Enc}(pk', m; r^*) \end{array} \right\}. \tag{1}$$

The modified PKE scheme $\Pi^* = (\mathsf{Gen}^*, \mathsf{Enc}^*, \mathsf{Dec}^*)$ is described in Fig. 2.

3.2   Randomness Fusion

We now put forward a simple property of a PKE scheme Π which will be useful for proving security of the modified Naor-Yung construction. Informally, the property says that given two ciphertexts c and c' of messages m and m' respectively (computed under independent public keys pk and pk') it is possible to re-randomize (c, c') into a new pair $(\tilde{c}, \tilde{c}')$ such that the distribution of $(\tilde{c}, \tilde{c}')$ is statistically close to the distribution of $(\hat{c}, \hat{c}')$ where $(\hat{c}, \hat{c}')$ are computed using Enc with the same (uniform) random input r^*.

Definition 4 (Randomness fusion). *Let $\Pi = (\mathsf{Gen}, \mathsf{Enc}, \mathsf{Dec})$ be a PKE scheme. There exists a PPT algorithm Rand such that for all $m, m' \in \mathcal{M}$ it holds*

Naor-Yung Paradigm with Shared Randomness

Consider the following PKE scheme $\Pi^* = (\mathsf{Gen}^*, \mathsf{Enc}^*, \mathsf{Dec}^*)$ based on an auxiliary PKE scheme $\Pi = (\mathsf{Gen}, \mathsf{Enc}, \mathsf{Dec})$ and on a non-interactive argument system for the language L_{NY}^{Π} of Eq. (1).

Key generation: Given as input the security parameter λ, algorithm Gen^* runs Gen twice obtaining $(pk, sk) \leftarrow_{\$} \mathsf{Gen}(1^\lambda)$ and $(pk', sk') \leftarrow_{\$} \mathsf{Gen}(1^\lambda)$. Hence, it outputs $pk^* = (pk, pk')$ and $sk^* = sk$ (the key sk' is erased).

Encryption: Given as input a message $m \in \mathcal{M}$, algorithm Enc^* samples random coins $r^* \leftarrow_{\$} \mathcal{R}$, computes $c = \mathsf{Enc}(pk, m; r^*)$ and $c' = \mathsf{Enc}(pk', m; r^*)$, and obtains a proof $\pi \leftarrow_{\$} \mathsf{P}^H((pk, pk', c, c'), (m, r^*))$ for membership of $(pk, pk', c, c') \in L_{\mathsf{NY}}^{\Pi}$. Hence, it outputs the ciphertext $c^* = (c, c', \pi)$.

Decryption: Given as input a ciphertext $c^* = (c, c', \pi)$, algorithm Dec^* first runs $\mathsf{V}^H((pk, pk', c, c'), \pi)$; if the output is zero Dec^* outputs $\bot$ and stops. Otherwise, it outputs the same as $\mathsf{Dec}(sk, c)$.

Fig. 2. Modified Naor-Yung construction

that $\mathbf{D}_{m,m'} \approx_s \tilde{\mathbf{D}}_{m,m'}$, where the distributions $\mathbf{D}_{m,m'}$ and $\tilde{\mathbf{D}}_{m,m'}$ are defined as follows:

$$\mathbf{D}_{m,m'} := \left\{ (\hat{c}, \hat{c}') : \begin{array}{c} (pk, sk) \leftarrow_{\$} \mathsf{Gen}(1^\lambda); (pk', sk') \leftarrow_{\$} \mathsf{Gen}(1^\lambda); r^* \leftarrow_{\$} \mathcal{R} \\ \hat{c} = \mathsf{Enc}(pk, m; r^*); \hat{c}' = \mathsf{Enc}(pk', m'; r^*) \end{array} \right\} \quad (2)$$

$$\tilde{\mathbf{D}}_{m,m'} := \left\{ (\tilde{c}, \tilde{c}') : \begin{array}{c} (pk, sk) \leftarrow_{\$} \mathsf{Gen}(1^\lambda); (pk', sk') \leftarrow_{\$} \mathsf{Gen}(1^\lambda) \\ r, r' \leftarrow_{\$} \mathcal{R}; c = \mathsf{Enc}(pk, m; r); c' = \mathsf{Enc}(pk', m'; r') \\ \mathsf{aux} := (pk, pk', sk', r', m') \\ (\tilde{c}, \tilde{c}') \leftarrow_{\$} \mathsf{Rand}((c, c'), \mathsf{aux}) \end{array} \right\} . \quad (3)$$

Alternative Formulations. A particular case is the one where the distribution of ciphertexts using independent randomness or shared randomness are directly statistically close. Such a requirement is more stringent, and can be cast in Definition 4 by requiring that Rand simply outputs the pair (c, c').

Yet another variation of the above property has been considered by Bellare *et al.* [7] in their study of randomness re-use in multi-recipient PKE. The reproducibility test of [7] can be cast in Definition 4 by requiring that $\mathbf{D}_{m,m'}$ and $\tilde{\mathbf{D}}_{m,m'}$ are identically distributed, and moreover Rand can produce the pair $(\tilde{c}, \tilde{c}')$ without knowing the randomness r' (corresponding to ciphertext c').

Our choice to go for the formulation above is due to the fact that Definition 4 is a weaker requirement, yet it is sufficient to prove security of our twist of the Naor-Yung paradigm.

3.3   Main Theorem

We now turn to state our main theorem, which quantifies the security of our twist of the Naor-Yung paradigm. The proof can be found in the full version.

Theorem 1 (Main theorem, KDM security). *Let Π be a PKE scheme satisfying $\mathcal{F}$-KDM-CPA security and with the randomness fusion property (cf. Definition 4), and let $(\mathsf{P}^H, \mathsf{V}^H)$ be a simulation-sound NIZK for the language L_{NY}^{Π} of Eq. (1). Then, the PKE scheme Π^* described in Fig. 2 satisfies $\mathcal{F}$-KDM-CCA security in the random oracle model.*

3.4 Extensions

We mention two generalizations of Theorem 1, beyond the setting of key-dependent message security considered in this section.

First, it is easy to see that Theorem 1 holds also if we start with a CPA-secure PKE scheme; in this case, of course, we simply obtain a PKE scheme satisfying CCA security. Second, it is possible to show that a similar result as the one in Theorem 1 applies to the setting of bounded key-leakage attacks (see, e.g., [26,48]). Informally a PKE scheme is CPA-secure under Λ-key-leakage attacks if it remains CPA-secure even given Λ bits of (adaptive) leakage on the secret key. CCA security under Λ-key-leakage attacks is defined similarly, but now the adversary can additionally ask for decryption queries.

As proven in [33,48] the classical Naor-Yung paradigm allows to boost CPA security under Λ-key-leakage attacks to CCA security under Λ-key-leakage attacks. A similar result holds for our twist of the Naor-Yung construction, assuming the underlying PKE scheme meets the randomness fusion property. As the security proof under key-dependent message and key-leakage attacks are very similar, we omit the proof for the leakage case here.

4   KDM Security from Subset Sum

We start by recalling the Subset Sum assumption in Sect. 4.1. Our new Subset-Sum based PKE scheme is described in Sect. 4.2, and its correctness and security are showed in Sects. 4.3 and 4.4, respectively.

4.1   The Subset Sum Problem

In its simplest form, the *search* version of the Subset Sum problem—denoted $\mathrm{SS}(n, q)$ and parametrized by values $n(\lambda), q(\lambda) \in \mathbb{N}$—asks to compute a secret vector $\mathbf{s}$ given $(\mathbf{a}, t)$ such that $t := \langle \mathbf{a}, \mathbf{s} \rangle \bmod q$, where both $\mathbf{a} \in \mathbb{Z}_q^n$ and $\mathbf{s} \in \{0, 1\}^n$ are randomly chosen. The decisional version of the problem, instead, asks to distinguish $(\mathbf{a}, t)$ from $(\mathbf{a}, u)$ where u is uniform in $\mathbb{Z}_q$. The equivalence between the search and the decisional version of the Subset Sum problem has been established in a seminal paper by Impagliazzo and Naor [41].

Below, we recall a variant of the Subset Sum problem which was considered for the first time by Lyubashevsky et al. [46]. Here the modulus q is a power of an odd number; in our case we will set $q := p^m$, for some $m \in \mathbb{N}$. Such a variant of the problem helps interpreting the Subset Sum problem as an instance of the Learning with Errors [55,56] (LWE) problem with "deterministic noise", as we recall below.

Definition 5 (Subset Sum assumption). *For security parameter* $\lambda \in \mathbb{N}$, *and parameters* $n(\lambda)$, $p(\lambda)$, $m(\lambda) \in \mathbb{N}$, *consider the following distribution* $\mathbf{D}_{\mathsf{SS}}(\lambda, n, p, m)$:

- *Sample* $\mathbf{A} \leftarrow_{\$} \mathbb{Z}_p^{m \times n}$ *and* $\mathbf{s} \leftarrow_{\$} \{0, 1\}^n$.
- *Parse* $\mathbf{A} := (a_{1,1}, \ldots, a_{m,n})$, $\mathbf{s} := (s_1, \ldots, s_n)$, *compute* $\mathbf{A} \cdot \mathbf{s} \in \mathbb{Z}_p^n$, *and let* $e_1(\mathbf{A}, \mathbf{s}) := 0$. *For all* $j \in [m]$, $j \neq 1$, *compute*

$$e_j(\mathbf{A}, \mathbf{s}) := \left\lfloor \frac{e_{j-1}(\mathbf{A}, \mathbf{s}) + \sum_{i=1}^n a_{j-1,i}}{p} \right\rfloor \bmod p.$$

- *Set* $\mathbf{e}(\mathbf{A}, \mathbf{s}) := (e_m(\mathbf{A}, \mathbf{s}), \ldots, e_1(\mathbf{A}, \mathbf{s}))^{\mathsf{T}}$ *and* $\mathbf{t} := \mathbf{A} \cdot \mathbf{s} + \mathbf{e}(\mathbf{A}, \mathbf{s})$. *Output* $(\mathbf{A}, \mathbf{t}, \mathbf{s})$.

We say that the decisional Subset Sum assumption $\mathsf{SS}(n, p^m)$ *holds, if for all PPT distinguishers* D *there exists a negligible function* $\nu : \mathbb{N} \to [0, 1]$ *such that*

$$\big| \mathbb{P}\left[\mathsf{D}(\mathbf{A}, \mathbf{t}) = 1 : (\mathbf{A}, \mathbf{t}, \mathbf{s}) \leftarrow_{\$} \mathbf{D}_{\mathsf{SS}}(\lambda, n, p, m) \right]$$
$$- \mathbb{P}\left[\mathsf{D}(\mathbf{A}, \mathbf{u}) = 1 : (\mathbf{A}, \mathbf{u}) \leftarrow_{\$} \mathbb{Z}_p^{m \times n} \times \mathbb{Z}_p^m \right] \big| \leq \nu(\lambda).$$

Once again, it can be shown that the above decisional version of Subset Sum is equivalent to the search version (i.e., to finding $\mathbf{s}$). In fact, [46] showed that the representation $(\mathbf{A}, \mathbf{t}) \in \mathbb{Z}_p^{m \times n} \times \mathbb{Z}_p^m$ of Subset Sum is equivalent to the original representation $(\mathbf{a}, t) \in \mathbb{Z}_q^n \times \mathbb{Z}_q$, whenever $q = p^m$ and $p \geq 2\sqrt{n} \log n + 3$. In particular, given $\mathbf{a} := (a_1, \ldots, a_n)$ and $\mathbf{s} := (s_1, \ldots, s_n)$, the matrix $\mathbf{A} := (a_{1,1}, \ldots, a_{m,n})$ can be defined as follows. For $i \in [n]$ and $j \in [m]$, let $a_{j,i} := \lfloor \frac{a_i}{p^{j-1}} \rfloor \bmod p$, and interpret the vector $\mathbf{e}(\mathbf{A}, \mathbf{s})$ as the vector of carries in the computation of $t := \sum_{i=1}^n s_i \cdot a_i \bmod p^m$. This way, the value t directly corresponds to

$$\left(\sum_{i=1}^n s_i \begin{pmatrix} a_{m,i} \\ \vdots \\ a_{1,i} \end{pmatrix} \right) + \begin{pmatrix} e_m(\mathbf{A}, \mathbf{s}) \\ \vdots \\ e_0(\mathbf{A}, \mathbf{s}) \end{pmatrix} = \mathbf{t},$$

as desired.

Therefore, Subset Sum can be seen as LWE with deterministic noise $\mathbf{e}(\mathbf{A}, \mathbf{s})$ which only depends on $\mathbf{A}$ and $\mathbf{s}$. An important difference between Subset Sum and LWE is that for LWE the value m can be arbitrarily large as long as it remains polynomial. Instead, for Subset Sum the density $\delta := n/\log q = n/(m \log p)$ decreases with the size of m; this implies that Subset Sum can be solved efficiently for $m \approx n^2$. However, the problem is considered to be hard whenever $\delta \in O(1/\log n)$.

The following lemma, which can be easily derived from [46, Lemma 3.4], states that the deterministic noise $\mathbf{e}(\mathbf{A}, \mathbf{s})$ is small, and additionally it remains small when multiplied by a matrix $\mathbf{R}$ with components of bounded size.

Lemma 1 [46] *For security parameter* $\lambda \in \mathbb{N}$, *and parameters* $n(\lambda)$, $p(\lambda)$, $m(\lambda)$, $\ell(\lambda) \in \mathbb{N}$, *let* $\ell, m \in \mathrm{poly}(\lambda)$ *and* p *be a prime such that* $p \geq 2\sqrt{n} \log n + 3$.

Let $(\mathbf{A}, \mathbf{t}, \mathbf{s}) \leftarrow_{\$} \mathbf{D}_{SS}(\lambda, n, p, m)$ and $\mathbf{R} \leftarrow_{\$} [-\lfloor\sqrt{p}/2\rfloor, \lfloor\sqrt{p}/2\rfloor]^{\ell \times m}$. There exist negligible functions $\nu, \nu' : \mathbb{N} \to [0, 1]$ such that

$$\mathbb{P}\left[\|\mathbf{e}(\mathbf{A}, \mathbf{s})\|_\infty < \sqrt{n}\log n + 1\right] \geq 1 - \nu(\lambda)$$

$$\mathbb{P}\left[\|\mathbf{R} \cdot \mathbf{e}(\mathbf{A}, \mathbf{s})\|_\infty < \sqrt{pmn}\log^2 n + n\sqrt{p}\right] \geq 1 - \nu'(\lambda). \qquad (4)$$

Leftover Hash Lemma. Let $\mathcal{H} := \{h : \mathcal{D} \to \mathcal{I}\}$ be a family of hash functions with domain $\mathcal{D}$ and image $\mathcal{I}$. Recall that $\mathcal{H}$ is called *universal* if for any $x \in \mathcal{D}$ and $x' \in \mathcal{D}$ the following holds:

$$\mathbb{P}_{h \leftarrow_{\$} \mathcal{H}} [h(x) = h(x')] = \frac{1}{|\mathcal{I}|}.$$

The celebrated leftover hash lemma [4,39] states that, over the random choice of $h \leftarrow_{\$} \mathcal{H}$, $x \leftarrow_{\$} \mathcal{D}$, and $u \leftarrow_{\$} \mathcal{I}$, the statistical distance between $(h, h(x))$ and (h, u) is smaller than $1/2\sqrt{|\mathcal{I}|/|\mathcal{D}|}$.

It is easy to show that matrices in $\mathbb{Z}_p^{m \times n}$ are a family of universal hash functions for prime p and any domain $\mathcal{D} \subseteq \mathbb{Z}_p^m$. As a consequence, we obtain the following lemma which will be important for showing security of our PKE scheme.

Lemma 2. *For prime p and values $n, m, \ell \in \mathbb{N}$, let $\mathbf{A} \leftarrow_{\$} \mathbb{Z}_p^{m \times n}$, $\mathbf{u}_1, \mathbf{u}_2 \leftarrow_{\$} \mathbb{Z}_p^m$, $\mathbf{R} \leftarrow_{\$} [-\lfloor\sqrt{p}/2\rfloor, \lfloor\sqrt{p}/2\rfloor]^{\ell \times m}$, and $\mathbf{B} \leftarrow_{\$} \mathbb{Z}_p^{\ell \times (n+2)}$. Then,*

$$\Delta\left((\mathbf{A}, \mathbf{u}_1, \mathbf{u}_2, \mathbf{R}\mathbf{A}, \mathbf{R}\mathbf{u}_1, \mathbf{R}\mathbf{u}_2); (\mathbf{A}, \mathbf{u}_1, \mathbf{u}_2, \mathbf{B})\right) \leq \frac{\ell}{2} \sqrt[4]{2^{2(n+2)\log p - m\log(p-2)}}.$$

Proof. Since $\mathcal{H} := \mathbb{Z}_p^{m \times n}$ is a family of universal hash functions with $\mathcal{D} := [-\lfloor\sqrt{p}/2\rfloor, \lfloor\sqrt{p}/2\rfloor]^{\ell \times m}$ and $\mathcal{I} := \mathbb{Z}_p^m$, the statement follows directly by the leftover hash lemma and the triangle inequality (via a standard hybrid argument).

4.2 Scheme Description

We now describe a PKE scheme $\Pi = (\mathsf{Gen}, \mathsf{Enc}, \mathsf{Dec})$, with message space $\mathcal{M} = \{0, 1\}^\ell$ for an arbitrary polynomial $\ell(\cdot)$. The scheme depends on the Subset Sum distribution of Definition 5, with parameters $n, p, m \in \mathbb{N}$.

Key Generation: Upon input the security parameter $\lambda \in \mathbb{N}$, the randomized key generation algorithm Gen samples $(\mathbf{A}, \mathbf{t}, \mathbf{s}) \leftarrow_{\$} \mathbf{D}_{SS}(\lambda, n, p, m)$ and defines $pk := (\mathbf{A}, \mathbf{t})$ and $sk := \mathbf{s}$.

Encryption: Upon input a plaintext $M \in \{0, 1\}^\ell$ and the public key $pk := (\mathbf{A}, \mathbf{t})$, the randomized encryption algorithm Enc picks a random matrix $\mathbf{R} \leftarrow_{\$} [-\lfloor\sqrt{p}/2\rfloor, \lfloor\sqrt{p}/2\rfloor]^{\ell \times m}$ and returns $C := (\mathbf{A}', \mathbf{t}' + \mathbf{m} \cdot \lfloor\frac{p}{2}\rfloor)$ such that $\mathbf{A}' := \mathbf{R} \cdot \mathbf{A}$, $\mathbf{t}' := \mathbf{R} \cdot \mathbf{t}$, and $\mathbf{m} \in \mathbb{Z}_2^\ell$ is the vector representation of the plaintext $M \in \{0, 1\}^\ell$.

Decryption: Upon input the secret key $sk := \mathbf{s}$ and a ciphertext $C := (\mathbf{C}_1, \mathbf{c}_2)$, the deterministic decryption algorithm Dec returns $\lfloor\mathbf{c}_2 - \mathbf{C}_1 \cdot \mathbf{s}\rceil_2 \in \{0, 1\}^\ell$.

4.3 Proof of Correctness

The theorem below states that the above defined PKE scheme meets the correctness requirement, i.e. decryption of honestly computed ciphertexts yields the corresponding plaintext. The proof can be found in the full version.

Theorem 2 (Correctness of PKE scheme). *Let $n, p, q \in \mathbb{N}$ be parameters such that p is a prime, $p \geq 25mn \log^4 n$, $n \geq 10$, $m \in \Theta(n)$, and $\ell \in O(n^k)$ for some constant $k \in \mathbb{N}$. Then, the PKE scheme of Sect. 4.2 satisfies correctness.*

Further, correctness holds for ciphertexts of the form $C := (\mathbf{A}', \mathbf{t}' + \mathbf{m} \circ \lfloor \boldsymbol{\xi}/2 \rfloor)$, for any vector $\boldsymbol{\xi} \in [p - n - 1, p]^\ell$, and where $\circ$ denotes the Hadamard product.

4.4 Proof of Security

We now prove that our PKE scheme satisfies a form of KDM security, as formalized in the theorem below. The set of manipulations tolerated by the scheme consists of the set of all affine functions of the form

$$\mathcal{F}_{\mathrm{aff}} := \{f :\ f(\mathbf{s}) := \mathbf{F} \cdot \mathbf{s} + \mathbf{f}\}_{\mathbf{F} \in \mathbb{Z}_2^{\ell \times n}, \mathbf{f} \in \mathbb{Z}_2^\ell}.$$

We remark that a generic amplification theorem by Applebaum [5] allows to boost $\mathcal{F}_{\mathrm{aff}}$-KDM-CPA security to $\mathcal{G}$-KDM-CPA security, where $\mathcal{G}$ consists of the family of functions that can computed in some fixed polynomial time (or the set of all polynomial-size circuits whose size grows with their input and output lengths via a fixed polynomial rate).

For technical reasons, we need that when encrypting a function of the secret key, the ciphertext has a slightly different form. Namely, $\mathbf{c}_2' := \mathbf{t}' + (\mathbf{F} \cdot \lfloor \frac{p}{2} \rfloor) \cdot \mathbf{s} + \lfloor \frac{p}{2} \rfloor \cdot \mathbf{f}$ instead of $\mathbf{c}_2 := \mathbf{t}' + (\mathbf{F} \cdot \mathbf{s} + \mathbf{f}) \lfloor \frac{p}{2} \rfloor$. This can be easily done by the encryption algorithm whenever $\mathbf{F}$, $\mathbf{f}$ and $\mathbf{s}$ is known. Furthermore, $\mathbf{c}_2'$ and $\mathbf{c}_2$ decrypt to the same value. This can be seen by noticing that $\lfloor \frac{p}{2} \rfloor = \frac{p-1}{2}$, the multiplication with $\mathbf{s}$ and addition with $\mathbf{f}$ is for each component the sum of at most $n + 1$ values $\frac{p-1}{2}$ modulo p, and hence $\mathbf{c}_2'$ is a ciphertext of the form $\mathbf{c}_2' = \mathbf{t}' + \lfloor \frac{p}{2} \rfloor \circ \mathbf{m}$ for some $\boldsymbol{\xi} \in [p - n - 1, p]^\ell$ (cf. Theorem 2).

The reason for this obstacle is that we need to map the function f, which lives in $\mathbb{Z}_2$, into $\mathbb{Z}_p$. Since p is prime, it does not have a subgroup of size 2 to which we could map the components of $\mathbf{F}$ and $\mathbf{f}$. Therefore we need to map them to either $\frac{p-1}{2}$ (when 1) or to 0 (when 0). Since we do not map them to a subgroup, the output of f will also not be in a subgroup, but within range $[p - n - 1, p]$ (when 1) or $[-n - 1, 0]$ (when 0). One could resolve this obstacle by choosing p even, but then the leftover-hash lemma does only apply for a matrix $\mathbf{R}$ with components in $\{0, 1\}$, such that m needs to be larger. This would decrease the density of the underlying Subset Sum instance to $1/\log^2(n)$. Therefore, we prefer our approach.

We obtain the following result, whose proof appears in the full version.

Theorem 3 (KDM security of PKE scheme). *Let $n, p, q \in \mathbb{N}$ be parameters such that p is a prime, $p \geq 25mn \log^4 n$, $m \in \Theta(n)$, and $\ell \in O(n^k)$ for some* *constant $k \in \mathbb{N}$. If the $\mathrm{SS}(n, p^m)$ assumption holds (achieved with density $\delta \in \Theta(1/\log n)$), then the PKE scheme Π from Sect. 4.2 satisfies $\mathcal{F}_{\mathrm{aff}}$-KDM-CPA security.*

5   Concrete Instantiations and Comparisons

As shown in [33], a large class of Sigma-protocols yields a simulation-sound NIZK in the random oracle model through the Fiat-Shamir heuristic [35]. Hence, in order to instantiate our twist of the Naor-Yung paradigm it suffices to take any PKE scheme satisfying the randomness fusion property, together with a Sigma-protocol for the language defined in Eq. (1).

Table 1 compares two instantiations of our scheme w.r.t. the original Naor-Yung paradigm, based on two different complexity assumptions: Decisional Diffie-Hellman (DDH) and Quadratic Residuosity (QR). We make the comparison for both cases of CCA security under key-dependent message and key-leakage attacks. For space reasons, the description of the corresponding PKE schemes and Sigma-protocols are deferred to the full version, where we additionally describe an instantiation based on Subset Sum using our PKE scheme from Sect. 4.

Table 1. Comparing two instantiations of our twist of the Naor-Yung paradigm under the DDH and QR assumptions. KDM and LKG stand for CCA security under key-dependent message and key-leakage attacks, respectively. The third and forth columns contain the ciphertext size expressed in group elements or exponents, for the standard Naor-Yung construction and our modified version (respectively). All instantiations are in the random oracle model.

PKE scheme	Security	Standard NY	Ours	Assumption
BHHO08 [15]	KDM/LKG	$4\ell + 5$	$2\ell + 4$	DDH
BG10 [17]	KDM/LKG	$4\ell + 5$	$2\ell + 4$	QR

6   Conclusion and Open Problems

We have studied a twist of the classical Naor-Yung paradigm [50] to boost CPA security to CCA security, both under key-dependent message and key-leakage attacks. The twist consists in having the two ciphertexts in the Naor-Yung PKE scheme share the same randomness.

In order to prove security, we require the underlying CPA-secure PKE scheme to satisfy an additional property. The main benefit of our approach is that one can instantiate the NIZK in the Naor-Yung PKE more efficiently, as we have explored in the random oracle model. We have also constructed a new PKE scheme with KDM-CPA security under the Subset Sum assumption, and showed that such a scheme can be used within our paradigm.

Open problems include to construct a PKE scheme with CPA security under key-leakage attacks directly based on Subset Sum, or alternatively to show that our construction additionally satisfies this property.[3] Also, it would be interesting to analyze KDM security of our scheme with multiple keys, and to construct a PKE scheme with KDM-CCA security directly based on the Subset Sum assumption in the standard model, without relying on NIZK.

References

1. Akavia, A., Goldwasser, S., Vaikuntanathan, V.: Simultaneous hardcore bits and cryptography against memory attacks. In: Reingold, O. (ed.) TCC 2009. LNCS, vol. 5444, pp. 474–495. Springer, Heidelberg (2009)
2. Alwen, J., Dodis, Y., Wichs, D.: Leakage-resilient public-key cryptography in the bounded-retrieval model. In: Halevi, S. (ed.) CRYPTO 2009. LNCS, vol. 5677, pp. 36–54. Springer, Heidelberg (2009)
3. Alwen, J., Dodis, Y., Wichs, D.: Survey: leakage resilience and the bounded retrieval model. In: Kurosawa, K. (ed.) ICITS 2009. LNCS, vol. 5973, pp. 1–18. Springer, Heidelberg (2010)
4. Alwen, J., Peikert, C.: Generating shorter bases for hard random lattices. Theor. Comput. Syst. **48**(3), 535–553 (2011)
5. Applebaum, B.: Key-dependent message security: generic amplification and completeness. J. Cryptol. **27**(3), 429–451 (2014)
6. Applebaum, B., Cash, D., Peikert, C., Sahai, A.: Fast cryptographic primitives and circular-secure encryption based on hard learning problems. In: Halevi, S. (ed.) CRYPTO 2009. LNCS, vol. 5677, pp. 595–618. Springer, Heidelberg (2009)
7. Bellare, M., Boldyreva, A., Staddon, J.: Randomness re-use in multi-recipient encryption schemeas. In: PKC, pp. 85–99 (2003)
8. Bellare, M., Desai, A., Pointcheval, D., Rogaway, P.: Relations among notions of security for public-key encryption schemes. In: Krawczyk, H. (ed.) CRYPTO 1998. LNCS, vol. 1462, pp. 26–45. Springer, Heidelberg (1998)
9. Bellare, M., Rogaway, P.: Random oracles are practical: a paradigm for designing efficient protocols. In: ACM CCS, pp. 62–73 (1993)
10. Bernhard, D., Fischlin, M., Warinschi, B.: Adaptive proofs of knowledge in the random oracle model. In: Katz, J. (ed.) PKC 2015. LNCS, vol. 9020, pp. 629–649. Springer, Heidelberg (2015)
11. Bernhard, D., Fischlin, M., Warinschi, B.: On the hardness of proving CCA-security of signed ElGamal. In: Cheng, C.-M., Chung, K.-M., Persiano, G., Yang, B.-Y. (eds.) PKC 2016. LNCS, vol. 9614, pp. 47–69. Springer, Heidelberg (2016)
12. Bernstein, D.J., Jeffery, S., Lange, T., Meurer, A.: Quantum algorithms for the subset-sum problem. In: Gaborit, P. (ed.) PQCrypto 2013. LNCS, vol. 7932, pp. 16–33. Springer, Heidelberg (2013)
13. Black, J., Rogaway, P., Shrimpton, T.: Encryption-scheme security in the presence of key-dependent messages. In: Nyberg, K., Heys, H. (eds.) SAC 2002. LNCS, vol. 2595, pp. 62–75. Springer, Heidelberg (2002)
14. Bleichenbacher, D.: Chosen ciphertext attacks against protocols based on the RSA encryption standard PKCS #1. In: Krawczyk, H. (ed.) CRYPTO 1998. LNCS, vol. 1462, pp. 1–12. Springer, Heidelberg (1998)

---

[3] The PKE scheme of [46] only achieves a weak for of leakage resilience, where the leakage cannot depend on the public key.

15. Boneh, D., Halevi, S., Hamburg, M., Ostrovsky, R.: Circular-secure encryption from decision Diffie-Hellman. In: Wagner, D. (ed.) CRYPTO 2008. LNCS, vol. 5157, pp. 108–125. Springer, Heidelberg (2008)
16. Boyle, E., Segev, G., Wichs, D.: Fully leakage-resilient signatures. J. Cryptol. **26**(3), 513–558 (2013)
17. Brakerski, Z., Goldwasser, S.: Circular and leakage resilient public-key encryption under subgroup indistinguishability. Cryptology ePrint Archive, Report 2010/226 (2010)
18. Brakerski, Z., Goldwasser, S., Kalai, Y.T.: Black-box circular-secure encryption beyond affine functions. In: Ishai, Y. (ed.) TCC 2011. LNCS, vol. 6597, pp. 201–218. Springer, Heidelberg (2011)
19. Camenisch, J., Chandran, N., Shoup, V.: A public key encryption scheme secure against key dependent chosen plaintext and adaptive chosen ciphertext attacks. In: Joux, A. (ed.) EUROCRYPT 2009. LNCS, vol. 5479, pp. 351–368. Springer, Heidelberg (2009)
20. Camenisch, J.L., Lysyanskaya, A.: An efficient system for non-transferable anonymous credentials with optional anonymity revocation. In: Pfitzmann, B. (ed.) EUROCRYPT 2001. LNCS, vol. 2045, pp. 93–118. Springer, Heidelberg (2001)
21. Coretti, S., Dodis, Y., Tackmann, B., Venturi, D.: Non-malleable encryption: simpler, shorter, stronger. In: Kushilevitz, E., et al. (eds.) TCC 2016-A. LNCS, vol. 9562, pp. 306–335. Springer, Heidelberg (2016). doi:10.1007/978-3-662-49096-9_13
22. Cramer, R., Shoup, V.: A practical public key cryptosystem provably secure against adaptive chosen ciphertext attack. In: Krawczyk, H. (ed.) CRYPTO 1998. LNCS, vol. 1462, pp. 13–25. Springer, Heidelberg (1998)
23. Dagdelen, Ö., Venturi, D.: A second look at Fischlin's transformation. In: Pointcheval, D., Vergnaud, D. (eds.) AFRICACRYPT 2014. LNCS, vol. 8469, pp. 356–376. Springer, Heidelberg (2014)
24. Davì, F., Dziembowski, S., Venturi, D.: Leakage-resilient storage. In: Garay, J.A., De Prisco, R. (eds.) SCN 2010. LNCS, vol. 6280, pp. 121–137. Springer, Heidelberg (2010)
25. Diffie, W., Hellman, M.E.: New directions in cryptography. IEEE Trans. Inf. Theor. **22**(6), 644–654 (1976)
26. Dodis, Y., Haralambiev, K., López-Alt, A., Wichs, D.: Efficient public-key cryptography in the presence of key leakage. In: Abe, M. (ed.) ASIACRYPT 2010. LNCS, vol. 6477, pp. 613–631. Springer, Heidelberg (2010)
27. Dolev, D., Dwork, C., Naor, M.: Non-malleable cryptography (extended abstract). In: ACM STOC, pp. 542–552 (1991)
28. Döttling, N.: Low noise LPN: KDM secure public key encryption and sample amplification. In: Katz, J. (ed.) PKC 2015. LNCS, vol. 9020, pp. 604–626. Springer, Heidelberg (2015)
29. Dziembowski, S., Pietrzak, K.: Leakage-resilient cryptography. In: IEEE FOCS, pp. 293–302 (2008)
30. ElGamal, T.: A public key cryptosystem and a signature scheme based on discrete logarithms. IEEE Trans. Inf. Theor. **31**(4), 469–472 (1985)
31. Faonio, A., Nielsen, J.B., Venturi, D.: Mind your coins: fully leakage-resilient signatures with graceful degradation. In: Halldórsson, M.M., Iwama, K., Kobayashi, N., Speckmann, B. (eds.) ICALP 2015. LNCS, vol. 9134, pp. 456–468. Springer, Heidelberg (2015)
32. Faust, S., Hazay, C., Venturi, D.: Outsourced pattern matching. In: Fomin, F.V., Freivalds, R., Kwiatkowska, M., Peleg, D. (eds.) ICALP 2013, Part II. LNCS, vol. 7966, pp. 545–556. Springer, Heidelberg (2013)

33. Faust, S., Kohlweiss, M., Marson, G.A., Venturi, D.: On the non-malleability of the Fiat-Shamir transform. In: Galbraith, S., Nandi, M. (eds.) INDOCRYPT 2012. LNCS, vol. 7668, pp. 60–79. Springer, Heidelberg (2012)

34. Faust, S., Masny, D., Venturi, D.: Chosen-ciphertext security from subset sum. In: Cheng, C.-M., Chung, K.-M., Persiano, G., Yang, B.-Y. (eds.) PKC 2016. LNCS, vol. 9614, pp. 35–46. Springer, Heidelberg (2016)

35. Fiat, A., Shamir, A.: How to prove yourself: practical solutions to identification and signature problems. In: Odlyzko, A.M. (ed.) CRYPTO 1986. LNCS, vol. 263, pp. 186–194. Springer, Heidelberg (1987)

36. Fischlin, M.: Communication-efficient non-interactive proofs of knowledge with online extractors. In: Shoup, V. (ed.) CRYPTO 2005. LNCS, vol. 3621, pp. 152–168. Springer, Heidelberg (2005)

37. Fujisaki, E., Okamoto, T.: How to enhance the security of public-key encryption at minimum cost. In: Fujisaki, E., Okamoto, T. (eds.) PKC 1999. LNCS, vol. 1560, pp. 53–68. Springer, Heidelberg (1999)

38. Goldwasser, S., Micali, S.: Probabilistic encryption. J. Comput. Syst. Sci. 28(2), 270–299 (1984)

39. Håstad, J., Impagliazzo, R., Levin, L.A., Luby, M.: A pseudorandom generator from any one-way function. SIAM J. Comput. 28(4), 1364–1396 (1999)

40. Hofheinz, D.: Circular chosen-ciphertext security with compact ciphertexts. In: Johansson, T., Nguyen, P.Q. (eds.) EUROCRYPT 2013. LNCS, vol. 7881, pp. 520–536. Springer, Heidelberg (2013)

41. Impagliazzo, R., Naor, M.: Efficient cryptographic schemes provably as secure as subset sum. J. Cryptol. 9(4), 199–216 (1996)

42. Katz, J., Vaikuntanathan, V.: Signature schemes with bounded leakage resilience. In: Matsui, M. (ed.) ASIACRYPT 2009. LNCS, vol. 5912, pp. 703–720. Springer, Heidelberg (2009)

43. Kitagawa, F., Matsuda, T., Hanaoka, G., Tanaka, K.: On the key dependent message security of the Fujisaki-Okamoto constructions. In: Cheng, C.-M., Chung, K.-M., Persiano, G., Yang, B.-Y. (eds.) PKC 2016. LNCS, vol. 9614, pp. 99–129. Springer, Heidelberg (2016)

44. Kocher, P.C.: Timing attacks on implementations of Diffie-Hellman, RSA, DSS, and other systems. In: Koblitz, N. (ed.) CRYPTO 1996. LNCS, vol. 1109, pp. 104–113. Springer, Heidelberg (1996)

45. Kocher, P.C., Jaffe, J., Jun, B.: Differential power analysis. In: Wiener, M. (ed.) CRYPTO 1999. LNCS, vol. 1666, pp. 388–397. Springer, Heidelberg (1999)

46. Lyubashevsky, V., Palacio, A., Segev, G.: Public-key cryptographic primitives provably as secure as subset sum. In: Micciancio, D. (ed.) TCC 2010. LNCS, vol. 5978, pp. 382–400. Springer, Heidelberg (2010)

47. Micali, S., Rackoff, C., Sloan, B.: The notion of security for probabilistic cryptosystems. SIAM J. Comput. 17(2), 412–426 (1988)

48. Naor, M., Segev, G.: Public-key cryptosystems resilient to key leakage. In: Halevi, S. (ed.) CRYPTO 2009. LNCS, vol. 5677, pp. 18–35. Springer, Heidelberg (2009)

49. Naor, M., Segev, G.: Public-key cryptosystems resilient to key leakage. SIAM J. Comput. 41(4), 772–814 (2012)

50. Naor, M., Yung, M.: Public-key cryptosystems provably secure against chosen ciphertext attacks. In: ACM STOC, pp. 427–437 (1990)

51. Nielsen, J.B., Venturi, D., Zottarel, A.: Leakage-resilient signatures with graceful degradation. In: Krawczyk, H. (ed.) PKC 2014. LNCS, vol. 8383, pp. 362–379. Springer, Heidelberg (2014)

52. Pass, R., Shelat, A., Vaikuntanathan, V.: Relations among notions of non-malleability for encryption. In: Kurosawa, K. (ed.) ASIACRYPT 2007. LNCS, vol. 4833, pp. 519–535. Springer, Heidelberg (2007)
53. Quisquater, J., Samyde, D.: Electromagnetic analysis (EMA): measures and counter-measures for smart cards. In: Attali, I., Jensen, T. (eds.) E-smart 2001. LNCS, vol. 2140, pp. 200–210. Springer, Heidelberg (2001)
54. Rackoff, C., Simon, D.R.: Non-interactive zero-knowledge proof of knowledge and chosen ciphertext attack. In: Feigenbaum, J. (ed.) CRYPTO 1991. LNCS, vol. 576, pp. 433–444. Springer, Heidelberg (1992)
55. Regev, O.: On lattices, learning with errors, random linear codes, and cryptography. In: ACM STOC, pp. 84–93 (2005)
56. Regev, O.: On lattices, learning with errors, random linear codes, and cryptography. J. ACM **56**(6), 1–40 (2009)
57. Sahai, A.: Non-malleable non-interactive zero knowledge and adaptive chosen-ciphertext security. In: IEEE FOCS, pp. 543–553 (1999)
58. Standaert, F., Pereira, O., Yu, Y., Quisquater, J., Yung, M., Oswald, E.: Leakage resilient cryptography in practice. In: Sadeghi, A.-R., Naccache, D. (eds.) Towards Hardware-Intrinsic Security - Foundations and Practice, pp. 99–134. Springer, Heidelberg (2010)
59. Wee, H.: KDM-security via homomorphic smooth projective hashing. In: Cheng, C.-M., Chung, K.-M., Persiano, G., Yang, B.-Y. (eds.) PKC 2016. LNCS, vol. 9615, pp. 159–179. Springer, Heidelberg (2016)
60. Yao, A.C.: Theory and applications of trapdoor functions (extended abstract). In: IEEE FOCS, pp. 80–91 (1982)

Memory Protection

Provably-Secure Remote Memory Attestation for Heap Overflow Protection

Alexandra Boldyreva[1(✉)], Taesoo Kim[1], Richard Lipton[1],
and Bogdan Warinschi[2]

[1] Georgia Institute of Technology, Atlanta, USA
sasha@gatech.edu
[2] University of Bristol, Bristol, UK

Abstract. Memory corruption attacks may lead to complete takeover of systems. There are numerous works offering protection mechanisms for this important problem. But the security guarantees that are offered by most works are only heuristic and, furthermore, most solutions are designed for protecting the local memory. In this paper we initiate the study of *provably secure* remote memory attestation; we concentrate on provably detecting heap-based overflow attacks and consider the setting where we aim to protect the memory in a remote system. We present two protocols offering various efficiency and security trade-offs (but all solutions are efficient enough for practical use as our implementation shows) that detect the presence of injected malicious code or data in remotely-stored heap memory. While our solutions offer protection only against a specific class of attacks, our novel formalization of threat models is general enough to cover a wide range of attacks and settings.

1 Introduction

Memory corruption attacks are among the most common techniques used to take control of arbitrary programs. These attacks allow an adversary to exploit running programs either by injecting their own code or diverting program's execution, often giving the adversary complete control over the compromised program. While this class of exploits is classically embodied in the buffer overflow attack, many other instantiations exist, including use-after-free vulnerabilities and heap overflow. The latter is the focus of our work. Without question, this problem is of great importance and has been extensively studied by the security community.

Existing solutions (such as Stack and heap canaries [14,17,19,31] or address space layout randomization (ASLR) [27,37], etc.) vary greatly in terms of security guarantees, performance, utilized resources (software or hardware-based), etc. While these techniques are implemented and deployed in many systems to prevent a number of attacks in practice, their constructions are only appropriate in the context of local systems: for example, an authority checking the integrity of heap canaries, has to monitor every single step of the program's execution. However, this requirement is making the existing heap-based protection schemes

© Springer International Publishing Switzerland 2016
V. Zikas and R. De Prisco (Eds.): SCN 2016, LNCS 9841, pp. 83–103, 2016.
DOI: 10.1007/978-3-319-44618-9_5

hardly applicable to remote memory attestation where the authority might reside outside of a local machine. For example, a straight-forward construction to keep track of all locations of heap canaries and validate their integrity upon request not only incurs noticeable performance overheads, but also requires a trusted communication channel between the program and a remote verifier.

More critically, none of the prior works targeting heap overflow attacks provided provable security guarantees. Without a clear adversarial model it is hard to judge the scope of the protection, and often the attackers, who are getting more and more sophisticated, are still able to bypass many such mitigation techniques.

Proving that a given protocol can resist all possible attacks within a certain well-defined class is the gold standard in modern cryptography. However, protocols that are provably secure are rather rarely used in real systems either because they commonly target extremely strong security definitions and hence are too slow for practical use, or they rely on impractical assumptions about attackers. Our work tries to bridge this gap in the context of remote attestation by designing practical protocols with provable security guarantees against realistic threats and satisfying practical system requirements. Our treatment utilizes the formal provable-security approach of modern cryptography that works hand in hand with applied systems expertise.

In this paper, we realized our theoretical findings as a working prototype system that can mitigate, (still limited), heap overflow attacks in applications running remotely outside of user's local computer. Although the current implementation therefore focuses on protecting user's programs running on the cloud environment or firmware running outside of the main CPU, the proposed security model is general enough to be useful for future works addressing other classes of adversaries. We now discuss our focus and contributions in more detail.

OUR FOCUS. Our focus is on the *remote* verification setting, motivated by the widespread use of cloud computing. In our setting, two entities participate in the protocol; a program that is potentially vulnerable, and a remote verifier who attests the state of the program's memory (e.g., heap). This setting is particularly useful for verifying the integrity of software that is deployed and runs outside of a local machine: a deployed program on the cloud is one example, and a firmware running outside of the main CPU is another example. Note that if the cloud is completely untrusted, we cannot guarantee security without relying on secure hardware (and our focus is software-based solution only). Hence we need to trust the cloud to a certain degree, but at the same time we want to avoid changing the operating system there. Since we do not trust the program which is potentially malicious, we create another entity, a wrapper, that is not directly affected by the program, unless an adversary bypasses the protection boundary provided by an operating system.

In practice, system software (e.g., browser or operating system) is vulnerable to memory corruptions because it heavily relies on unsafe low-level programming languages like C for either performance or compatibility reasons. As we mentioned, we do not attempt to prevent entire classes of memory corruption attacks (e.g., use-after-free or bad-casting) nor exploitation techniques (e.g., return-oriented programming (ROP)) with one system. We only consider one particular type of memory corruption attack that overwrites a consecutive region of memory (e.g., buffer) to compromise a control-sensitive data structure (e.g., function pointer or virtual function table). However, we believe such memory corruptions are still very common (e.g., the recent GHOST vulnerability in GLibc [4]), and become more important in the cloud setting where we have to rely on the cloud provider.

Within this scope, our goal is to find solutions that (1) provide provable security guarantees and (2) are practically efficient.

RMA SECURITY DEFINITION. Providing security guarantees is not possible without having a well-defined security model. We start with defining a *remote memory attestation (RMA)* protocol, whose goal is protecting the integrity of a program's data memory (e.g., heap). It is basically an interactive challenge-response protocol between a prover and a verifier, which is initialized by a setup algorithm that embeds a secret known to the verifier into a program's memory. The goal of the verifier is to detect memory corruptions.

Next we propose the first security model for RMA protocols. The definition is one of our main contributions. Our model captures various adversarial capabilities (what attackers know and can do), reflecting real security threats. We assume that an attacker can have some a-priori knowledge of the memory's contents (e.g., binary itself) and can learn parts of it, adaptively, over time.

Since we target a setting where the communication between the prover and the verifier is over untrusted channels, we let the adversary observe the legitimate communication between the prover and the verifier. Moreover, we let it impersonate either party and assume it can modify or substitute their messages with those of its choice. To model malicious writes to the memory we allow the attacker to tamper the memory. The goal of the attacker is to make the verifier accept at a point where the memory is corrupted.

We note that on the one hand no security may be possible if an attacker's queries are unrestricted and on the other we would like to avoid hardwiring in the model a particular set of restrictions on these queries. Accordingly we state security with respect to abstract classes of functions that model the read and write capabilities of the attackers. This allows us to keep the definition very general. We leave it for the theorem statements that state the security of particular protocols to specify these classes, and thus define the scope of attacks the protocol defends against.

To prevent against the aforementioned GHOST attack [4] where a read (e.g., information leak) follows by write to the same location and leaves the key intact, any solution in our setting needs to perform a periodic key refresh. Our protocol definition and the security model take this into account. But of course, we do not guarantee security if the attack happens within a refresh time window. This is a common caveat with preventing timing attacks.

An RMA protocol proven to satisfy our security definition for specific read and write capabilities classes would guaranty security against *any* efficient attacker with such practical restrictions, under reasonable computational assumptions. This is in contrast to previous schemes, which were only argued to protect against certain specific attacks, informally.

PROVABLY-SECURE RMA CONSTRUCTIONS. The idea underlying our solutions is simple and resembles the one behind stack or heap canaries. We embed secrets throughout the memory and, for attestation, we verify that they are intact. This is similar to how canaries are used, but for the setting where the verifier is remote the ideas need to be adapted. A simple but illustrative example is the protocol where the prover simply sends to the verifier the hash of all of the (concatenated) canaries. Here, the attacker can replay this value after modifying the memory. The following discussion illustrates further potential weaknesses of this protocol uncovered when trying to derive provable security guarantees.

For clarity, instead of calling the secrets canaries, let us refer to the secrets we embed in the memory as shares, i.e., we split a secret into multiple shares and spread them out in memory. For now, let's assume for simplicity that the shares are embedded at equal intervals. Then an adversary who injects malicious code, and hence writes a string that is at least one-block long, will over-write at least one share, even if it knows the shares' locations. Verification just checks whether the original secret can be reconstructed and used in a simple challenge-response protocol that prevents re-plays. For example, the verifier could send a random challenge, and the prover would reply with the hash of the reconstructed secret and the challenge. Note that the prover will run in a totally separate memory space so the secrecy of the reconstructed key at time of verification is not an issue.

We note that our solution does not readily apply for the stack because the stack doesn't have explicit unit or boundaries to statically place secret shares), unlike the heap that has a unit (a page) of allocation that makes the key placement efficient and easy.

The standard security of an n-out-of-n secret sharing scheme ensures that unless the attacker reads all memory (and in this case no security can be ensured anyway), the key is information-theoretically hidden. However, the adversary could read and then tamper the memory while leaving the share intact. To mitigate this, the periodic updates could re-randomize all shares, while keeping the same secret. The size of the blocks and the frequency of the updates are the parameters that particular applications could choose for the required tradeoff between security and efficiency. In the ideal setting, we would refresh the shares whenever the leakage of a share happens. However, since the occurrence of such events is not always clear, the alternative solution of refreshing "often" enough may lead to unreasonable overheads. In our current implementation, we keep the frequency of updates a parameter and developers can simply incorporate timing that reflect realistic assumptions on the adversary in our implementation.

Although the solution approach seems simple and sound, it turns out that assessing its security and practicality raises numerous subtleties and complications, both from the systems and cryptographic points of view. For example, our system can not fix the size of memory object, which naturally underutilizes the memory space (e.g., de-fragmentation). In our system, we support various memory slots for allocation, from the smallest 8 byte objects incrementally to over 100 MB, depending on the user's configuration.

The obvious choice for producing the secrets to be embedded in the memory is to use an n-out-of-n secret sharing scheme as a building block for our constructions. It turns out however, that the standard security of secret sharing schemes is not sufficient to guarantee the security of the protocol. First, we have to extend the security definition to take into account key updates. The attacker should be able to access the whole memory as long as it does not do it in between consecutive updates. The extended notion is known as proactive secret sharing [20]. Also, for the proof we need the additional properties that modifying at least one share implies changing a secret, and one extra property we discuss later. Fortunately, all these properties are satisfied by a simple XOR-based secret sharing scheme.

We show that combing the simple XOR-based secret sharing scheme (or any generic secret sharing scheme with some extra properties we define) and the hash-based challenge-response protocol yields a secure and efficient RMA protocol, for attackers with restricted, but quite reasonable abilities to read and tamper the memory. The proof we provide relies on the random oracle (RO) model [8]. Since the RO is unsound [12] for security-critical applications it may be desirable to have protocols which provably provide guarantees in the standard (RO devoid) model.

An intuitively appealing solution is to employ some symmetric-key identification protocol, e.g., replying with a message authentication code (MAC) of the random challenge, where the MAC is keyed with the reconstructed secret. However, given the capabilities that we ascribe to realistic adversaries, a formal proof would require a MAC secure in the presence of some leakage on and tampering of the secret key. The latter property is also known as security against related key attacks (RKA) [6]. Unfortunately, there are no suitable leakage and tamper-resilient MACs for a wide class of leakage and tampering functions, as the existing solutions, e.g. [5,10], only address specific algebraic classes of tampering functions and are rather inefficient.

Perhaps unexpectedly, we consider a challenge response protocol based on a public key encryption scheme – the verifier sends a random challenge and expects an encryption of the challenge together with the (reconstructed) secret. This solution requires that the public key of the verifier is stored so that it is accessible by the prover, and cannot be tampered (otherwise we would need a public-key scheme secure with respect to related public key attacks, and similarly to the symmetric setting, there are no provably secure schemes wrt this property, except for few works addressing a narrow class of tamper functions [7,38]).

To ensure non-malleability of the public key, our system separates the memory space of a potentially malicious program from its prover (e.g., different processes), and store its public key in the prover's memory space. Since the verification procedure is unidirectional (e.g., a prover accesses the program's memory), our system can guarantee the non-malleability of the public key in practice (e.g., unless no remote memory overwriting or privilege escalation). This level of security is afforded by deployed computational platforms (e.g. MMU commodity processors).

It is natural to expect some form of non-malleability from the encryption scheme. Otherwise, the attacker could modify a legitimate response for one challenge into another valid one for the same key and a new challenge. An IND-CCA secure encryption such as Cramer Shoup [15] could work for us. We note however that IND-CCA secure is an overkill for our application since we do not need to protect against arbitrary maulings of the ciphertext; instead, the attacker only needs to produce a valid ciphertext for a particular message, known to the verifier. We show that an encryption scheme secure against a weaker notion of plaintext-checking attacks [32] is sufficient for us. Accordingly, we use the "Short" Cramer-Shoup (SCS) scheme proposed and analyzed very recently by Abdalla et al. [1]. This allows us to save communication one group element compared to regular Cramer Shoup. We discuss that one can optimize further and save an additional group element in the communication by slightly increasing computation.

IMPLEMENTATION RESULTS. To demonstrate the feasibility of RMA, we implemented a prototype system that supports arbitrary programs without any modification (e.g., tested with popular software with a large codebase, such as Firefox, Thunderbird and SPEC Benchmark). Our evaluation shows that the prototype incurs very small performance overheads and detects heap-based memory corruptions with the remote verifier.

In a bit more detail, we implemented both, the hash- and encryption-based, protocols. Interestingly, both protocols showed similar performance, despite the latter one relying on public key operations, which are much slower than a hash computation. This is because the significant part of the performance overhead comes from the implementation of the custom memory allocator, side-effects of memory fragmentation and network bandwidth, which all make the differences in times of crypto operations insignificant.

RELATED WORK. The works that is perhaps closest in spirit and application domain to ours is by Francillon et al. [18] who address the problem of remote device attestation. Their approach is also based on provable security, but consider a significantly weaker model where the adversary not tamper or read parts of the internal memory of the device. These are key features of the adversary that we aim to defend against.

Canaries are random values placed throughout a stack or heap, which are later checked by the kernel. Canary-based protection has been adopted to prevent stack smashing [2]: e.g., ProPolice [17], StackGuard [14], StackGhost [19]. Similarly, canaries (or guard as a general form) have been used for heap protection, in particular metadata of heap [33,39] (e.g., double free): HeapShield [9] or AddressSanitizer [34]. These solutions do not immediately work in our setting. This is mainly because all canaries need to be sent and checked by the remote verifier without leaking or without being compromised by an adversary. While heavy solutions like employing secure channels (e.g. TLS) would help mitigate this problem, the resulting system would need to transfer large quantities of data, making it unsuitable for practical use.

Our solutions could be viewed as a novel variant of "compact" cryptographic canaries, suitable for remote setting and providing provable security guarantees under precisely defined threat models.

Software-based attestation has been explored in various contexts: peripheral firmware [16,23,25], embedded devices [13,24,36], or legacy software [35]. That line of work, which falls under the generic idea of *software based attestation* is different from ours in two main differences. First, the setting of firmware attestation uses a different adversarial model. There, an adversary aims to tamper with the firmware on a peripheral and still wants to convince an external verifier that the firmware has not been tampered with. In its attack, the adversary has complete access to the device prior to the execution of the attestation protocol; the protocol is executed however without adversarial interference. Our model considers an adversary who can glean only partial information on the state of the memory prior to its attack, but who acts as man-in-the-middle during the attestation protocol.

Challenge-response protocols are natural solutions in both situations. Since we aim for solutions that admit rigorous security proofs we rely on primitives with cryptographic guarantees. In contrast due to constraints imposed by the application domain solutions employed peripheral attestation cannot afford to rely on cryptographic primitives. Instead, constructions employ carefully crafted check-sum functions where unforgeability *heuristically* relies on timing assumptions and lack of storage space on the device. Jacobsson and Johansson [22] show that such assumptions can be grounded in the assumptions that RAM access is faster than access to the secondary storage [22]. Our work is similar in its goals with that of Armknecht et al. [3] who provide formal foundations for the area of software attestation.

More recently, a handful of hardware-based (e.g., coprocessor or trusted chip) attestation has been proposed as well: Flicker [29] and TrustVisor [28] using TPM, and Haven using Intel SGX [21,30]. Our work differs in that we do not explicitly rely on hardware assumptions and provides provable security guarantee.

Finally, a recent paper [26] addresses the problem of a virus detection from a provable security perspective. The authors introduce the virus detection scheme primitive that can be used to check if computer program has been infected with a virus injecting malicious code. They describe a compiler, which outputs a protected version of the program that can run natively on the same machine. The verification is triggered by an external verifier. Even though the considered problems and the basic idea of spreading the secret shares are similar, the treatment and the results in [26] are quite different from ours. The major difference is that the attacker in the security model of [26] is not allowed to learn any partial information about the secret shares. Our security definition, in turn, does take partial leakage of the secret into account. Their security definition, however, allows the attacker to learn the contents of the registers during the attack. This is not a threat in our setting since the computations happen within the trusted wrapper.

Also, their solutions do not rely on the PKI, which is a plus. The other important difference is that the proposal in [26] is mostly of theoretical interest (as they rely on leakage-resilient encryption for which there are no efficient implementations), while our solution is quite efficient. The work [26] has additional results about protection against tiny overwrites but that requires CPU modifications.

2   Notation

$X \xleftarrow{\$} S$ denotes that X is selected uniformly at random from S. If A is a randomized algorithm, then the notation $X \xleftarrow{\$} A$ denotes that X is assigned the outcome of the experiment of running A, possibly on some inputs. If A is deterministic, we drop the dollar sign above the arrow. If X, Y are strings, then $X\|Y$ denotes the concatenation of X and Y. We write $L :: a$ for the list obtained by appending a to the list L and $L[i, \ldots, j]$ for the sublist of L between indexes i and j. We write id for the identity function (the domain is usually clear from the context) and write $\mathcal{U}_S$ for the uniform distribution on set S. If n is an integer we write $[n]$ for the set $1, 2, \ldots, n$. For an integer k, and a bit b, b^k denotes the string consisting of k consecutive "b" bits.

3   Remote Memory Attestation

SYNTAX. We start with defining the abstract functionality of *remote memory attestation (RMA)* protocol.

Definition 1 (RMA Protocol). *A remote memory attestation protocol is defined by a tuple of algorithms* (SS, Init, (MA, MV), Update, Extract) *where:*

- *The setup algorithm* SS *takes as input a security parameter 1^κ and outputs a pair of public/secret keys (pk, sk). (SS is run by the verifier.) This output is optional.*
- *The initialization algorithm* Init *takes as input a bitstring M (representing the memory to be protected), a public key pk and the secret key sk and outputs a bitstring M_s (that represents the protected memory), and a bitstring s (secret information that one can use to certify the state of the memory).*
- *The pair of interactive algorithms* (MA, MV), *run by the prover and verifier resp., form the attestation protocol. Algorithm* MA *takes as inputs the public key pk and a bitstring M_s and the verifier takes as inputs the secret key sk and secret s. The verifier outputs a bit, where 1 indicates acceptance, and 0 – rejection.*
- *The update algorithm* Update *takes as input a bitstring M_s and outputs a bitstring M_s' (this is a "refreshed" protected memory). It can be ran by the prover at any point in the execution.*
- *The* Extract *algorithm takes as input a bitstring M_s (representing a protected memory) and outputs a bitstring M (represented the real memory protected in M_s) and secret s. This is used in the analysis mostly, but also models how the OS can read the memory.*

The correctness condition requires that for every (pk, sk) output by SS, every $M \in \{0,1\}^*$, and every (M_s, s) output by Init(M, pk, sk), the second party in (MA(pk, M_s), MV(sk, s)) returns 1 with probability 1. Also, Extract$(M_s) = (M, s')$ for some s' with probability 1. These conditions should hold even for an arbitrary number of runs of Update protocol.

In practice the remote verifier initializes the wrapper with the secret before being sent to the cloud. The wrapper later acts as the local prover to the remote verifier. In practice the wrapper is a separate process that gets memory access via *ptrace* mechanism.

RMA SECURITY. We now formally define the security model for an RMA protocol, which is part of our main contributions.

We consider an attacker who can read the public key (if any), and can observe the interactions between the prover and the verifier. The attacker works in two stages. In the first stage of its attack, it can read arbitrary parts of the memory and can over-write a part of the memory by injecting data of its choosing. In this phase, the adversary can observe and interfere with the interaction between the prover and the verifier. This is captured by giving the adversary access to the oracles that execute the interactive RMA protocol; in particular, the adversary can chose to observe a legitimate execution of the protocol by simply forwarding the answers of one oracle to the other. Of course, the adversary can choose to manipulate the conversation, or even supply inputs of its own choosing. We only model a single session of the protocol as we do not expect parallel sessions to be run in practice. Also, at any point, the attacker can request that the shares of the secret get updated. In the second stage the adversary specifies how it wants to alter the memory (where and what data it wants to over-write). The memory is modified, one extra update is performed, and then the attacker can continue its actions allowed in the first stage, with the exception that it is not given the ability to read the memory anymore, and this is the reason we consider two stages of the attacker. This captures the fact noted in the Introduction, that security is only possible if the memory update procedure is performed in between the read and write, which can be arbitrary and thus leave the secret intact (by reading and over-writing it).

We say that the adversary wins if it makes the verifier accept in the second stage, despite the memory being modified by the attacker. This captures the idea that the verifier does not notice that the memory has been corrupted.

We observe that it is necessary to restrict the adversary's abilities, for a couple of reasons. First, as we mentioned in the Introduction, no security may be possible if an attacker's queries are unrestricted. For instance, the adversary may read the whole memory in between the secret updates or it could read a block and immediately over-write it maintaining intact the associated secret share. Moreover, note that an adversary who can over-write memory bit by bit, could eventually learn the whole secret by fixing each bit for both possible values, one by one and then observing the outcome of the interaction between the prover and the verifier. In short, no security is possible if we do not impose (reasonable) restrictions on the adversary.

Second, it seems unlikely that a unique solution suffices to protect against a wide class of attacks and that different solutions would work for different applications and classes of attacks. Yet, we would want to avoid providing a diffrent security definition for each individual scenario.

Accordingly, we state security with respect to abstract classes of functions that parametrize the read and write queries that model the legitimate read and tamper requests the attacker can do. This allows our definition to be quite general; we leave it to the theorem statements for particular protocols and applications to specify these classes and hence clarify the scope of attacks the protocol prevents against.

$$\text{Exp}_{A,\Pi}^{\text{rma-}(\mathcal{L},\mathcal{T})}:$$

$(pk, sk) \leftarrow \text{SS}$

$M \leftarrow A(pk)$

$(M_s, s) \leftarrow \text{Init}(M, pk, sk)$

$g' \leftarrow A^{\text{Read}(\cdot),\text{Tamper}(\cdot),\text{MA}(pk,M_s),\text{MV}(sk,s),\text{Update}}$

If $g \notin \mathcal{T}$ return $\perp$

$M_s \leftarrow \text{Update}(M_s)$

$M_s \leftarrow g'(M_s)$

$A^{\text{Tamper}(\cdot),\text{MA}(pk,M_s),\text{MV}(sk,s)}$

Output 1 iff MV accepts in the 2nd stage

and at that point the first part of $\text{Extract}(M_s)$ is not M.

Oracle Read(f):

if $f \notin \mathcal{L}$ return $\perp$

otherwise return $f(M_s)$

Oracle Tamper(g):

if $g \notin \mathcal{T}$ return $\perp$

$M_s \leftarrow g(M_s)$

Fig. 1. Game defining the security of the memory attestation scheme $\Pi = (\text{SS}, \text{Init}, (\text{MA}, \text{MV}), \text{Update}, \text{Extract})$.

Definition 2 (RMA Scheme Security). *Let* $\mathcal{L}$ *and* $\mathcal{T}$ *be two classes of* leakage *and* tampering *functions. Consider an RMA protocol* $\Pi = (\text{SS}, \text{Init}, (\text{MA}, \text{MV}), \text{Update}, \text{Extract})$. *We define its security via the experiment* $\text{Exp}_{A,\Pi}^{\text{rma-}(\mathcal{L},\mathcal{T})}$ *involving the adversary A which we present in Fig. 1.*

We call Π *secure wrt* $\mathcal{L}$ *and* $\mathcal{T}$ *if for every (possibly restricted) efficient adversary A the probability that* $\text{Exp}_{A,\Pi}^{\text{rma-}(\mathcal{L},\mathcal{T})}$ *returns 1 is negligible in the security parameter.*

The design of the above model is influenced directly by studying the practical threats. In particular, reading memory to leak information has been a prerequisite pretty much to all attacks from ten years back. Taking the man-in-the-middle attacks into account is motivated by the observation that even though we trust the cloud provider, we do not necessarily trust the path between the provider and the client, e.g., when using a cafe's WiFi. We demand that the secure attestation be done without employing secure channels.

REMARK. Turns out that the practical classes of read and write functions may not describe the necessary restrictions by themselves. Thus one can further restrict the adversaries, but again, this is done in the security statements. For instance, security of our constructions will tolerate any attacker who can read all but one "block" of the memory and can over-write any arbitrary part of the memory as long as that part is longer than some minimum number of bits.

4 Building Blocks

REFRESHABLE SECRET SHARING SCHEME. Our schemes rely on an n-out-of-n secret sharing scheme where one needs all of the shares to reconstruct the secret; any subset of $n-1$ shares is independent from the secret. In addition to the standard property, we also require that it is possible to refresh shares in such a way that all subsets of $n-1$ shares, each obtained in between updates, are independent of the secret. This property is known as proactive secret sharing [20]. In addition, we require two more security properties which we describe later in this section.

Syntax. We first provide the syntax of the secret sharing schemes that we consider.

Definition 3. *A refreshable n-out-of-n secret sharing scheme is defined by algorithms* (KS, KR, SU) *for sharing and reconstructing a secret, and for refreshing the shares[1]. For simplicity we assume that the domain of secrets is $\{0,1\}^\kappa$ (where κ is the security parameter). The sharing algorithm KS takes a secret s and outputs a set $(s_1, s_2, \ldots, s_n)$ of shares[2]. The reconstruction algorithm KR takes as input a set of shares $s_1, s_2, \ldots, s_n$ and returns a secret s. The update algorithm SU takes as input a set of shares $(s_1, s_2, \ldots, s_n)$ and returns the updated set $(s'_1, s'_2, \ldots, s'_n)$, a new re-sharing of the same secret.*

For correctness we demand that for any $s \in \{0,1\}^\kappa$ and any $(s_1, s_2, \ldots, s_n)$ obtained via $(s_1, s_2, \ldots, s_n) \xleftarrow{\$} \mathsf{KS}(s)$ it holds that $\mathsf{KR}((s_1, s_2, \ldots, s_n)) = s$ and $\mathsf{KR}(\mathsf{SU}^i((s_1, s_2, \ldots, s_n)) = s$ with probability 1 for any integer $i \geq 1$, where $\mathsf{SU}^i((s_1, s_2, \ldots, s_n))$ denotes i consecutive invocations of SU as $\mathsf{SU}(\mathsf{SU}(\ldots \mathsf{SU}((s_1, s_2, \ldots, s_n)) \ldots))$.

Security. We require that the secret sharing scheme that we use satisfies three security properties.

SECRET PRIVACY. The most basic one, secret privacy for refreshable secret sharing scheme (aka proactive secret sharing) guarantees that $n-1$ shares do not give the adversary any information about the secret, and this holds even for

---

[1] We use the mnemonics KS, KR to indicate that we think of the secret as being some cryptographic key.

[2] We do not use the set notation for simplicity.

an arbitrary number of updates to each set of shares. The formal definition is in
the full version [11].

OBLIVIOUS RECONSTRUCTION. We also require that the scheme enjoys *oblivious
reconstruction*. Intuitively, this demands that given an adversary who can read
and replace some of the shares, it is possible to determine at any point if the
value encoded in the shares is the same as the original value or not. This property
is related but is different from Verifiable Secret Sharing: the ability to tell that
the shares are consistent with some secret does not necessarily mean that one
can tell if transforming a set of shares to another (valid) one has changed or not
the underlying secret.

More formally, fix a secret $s \in \{0,1\}^\kappa$ and let $(s_1, s_2, \ldots, s_n) \xleftarrow{\$} \mathsf{KS}(s)$. Con-
sider an adversary who can intermitently issue two types of querries. On a query
$i \in \{1, \ldots, n\}$ the adversary receives s_i; on a query $(i, v) \in (\{1, 2, \ldots, n\} \times \{0,1\}^\kappa$
the value of s_i is set to v.

We require that there exists a "secret changed?" algorithm SC, formalized
in Fig. 2, which given the queries made by A and the answers it receives can
efficiently decide (with overwhelming probability) if the value of the secret that
is encoded is equal to the value of the original secret.

$\mathbf{Exp}_{A,\Pi}^{\mathrm{rec}}$:

$s \xleftarrow{\$} A; L \leftarrow [\,]$

$\{s_1, s_2, \ldots, s_n\} \leftarrow \mathsf{KS}(s)$

$A^{\mathsf{ShareInfo}(\cdot)}$

$b \leftarrow SC(L)$

$s' \leftarrow \mathsf{KR}(s_1, s_2, \ldots, s_n)$

return 1 iff

$(b = 1 \text{ and } s = s')$ or $(b = 0 \text{ and } s \neq s')$

Oracle ShareInfo($\cdot$):

On input $i \in \{1, \ldots, n\}$

$L \leftarrow L :: (i, s_i)$

return s_i

On input $(i, v) \in \{1, 2, \ldots, n\} \times \{0,1\}^\kappa$

$L \leftarrow L :: (i, v)$

$s_i \leftarrow v$

Fig. 2. Experiment defining the oblivious reconstruction property for secret sharing.

SHARE UNPREDICTABILITY. This property demands that for any secret (chosen
by the adversary) and any sharing of the secret, following an Update an adversary
cannot tamper (in any meaningful way) with any of the resulting fresh shares
in a way that does not alter the secret. This intuition is formalized using the
game $\mathbf{Exp}_{A,\Pi}^{\mathrm{unpred}}$ in Fig. 3. First,the experiment samples a random secret. After
the adversary learns some (but not all) of the shares, the shares are refreshed,
and the adversary needs to tamper with at least one share. The adversary wins
if the secret that is shared stayed unchanged through the process. We say that
Π satisfies share unpredictability if for any adversary which calls the Read oracle
at most $n - 1$ times and the Tamper oracle at least once, the probability that
the experiment returns 1 is negligible.

$$\begin{array}{|ll|}
\hline
\textbf{Exp}_{A,\Pi}^{\text{unpred}}: & \\
s \leftarrow \{0,1\}^\kappa & \textbf{Oracle Read}(i) \\
A^{\text{Read}(\cdot)} & \\
 & \text{return } s_i \\
(s_1, s_2, \ldots, s_n) \leftarrow \text{SU}(s_1, s_2, \ldots, s_n) & \textbf{Oracle Tamper}(i,v) \\
A^{\text{Tamper}(\cdot)} & \\
 & s_i \leftarrow v \\
\text{return } s \stackrel{?}{=} \text{KS}(s_1, s_2, \ldots, s_n) & \\
\hline
\end{array}$$

Fig. 3. Game defining share unpredictability for for secret sharing. We demand that A queries his Tamper at least once.

Secure Construction. Here we present a very simple n-out-of-n refreshable secret-sharing scheme with oblivious reconstructability and argue its security.

Construction 41 (Refreshable Secret Sharing). We define the scheme (KS, KR, SU) as follows.

- KS takes secret $s \in \{0,1\}^\kappa$, picks $s_i \stackrel{\$}{\leftarrow} \{0,1\}^\kappa$ for $1 \le i \le n-1$, computes $s_n \leftarrow s \oplus s_1 \oplus \ldots \oplus s_{n-1}$
- KR on input $(s_1, \ldots, s_n)$ returns $s_1 \oplus \ldots \oplus s_n$
- SU takes $(s_1, \ldots, s_n)$ and for $1 \le i \le n-1$, computes $r_i \stackrel{\$}{\leftarrow} \{0,1\}^\kappa$, $s_i \stackrel{\$}{\leftarrow} s_i \oplus r_i$. Finally, $s_n \leftarrow s_n \oplus r_1 \oplus \ldots \oplus r_{n-1}$, and SU returns $(s_1, \ldots, s_n)$.

It is immediate to see that the above scheme is correct. The following theorem states (information-theoretic) security. The proof is in the full version [11].

Theorem 1. *The scheme of Construction 41 is a refreshable secret sharing scheme with secret privacy, oblivious reconstructability and share unpredictability.*

IND-PCA SECURE ENCRYPTION. Our second construction uses a (labeled) encryption scheme that satisfies indistinguishability under plaintext-checking attacks (IND-PCA) [32]. One concrete scheme which satisfies IND-PCA security is the "Short" Cramer-Shoup (SCS) scheme proposed by Abdalla et al. [1]. We recall the primitive and the scheme in the full version [11]. The following result about IND-PCA security of the SCS scheme is by Abdalla et al. [1].

Theorem 2. *Under the DDH assumption on $\mathbb{G}$ and assuming that H is a target collision resistant hash function, the SCS scheme by Abdalla et al. [1] is IND-PCA.*

5   RMA Constructions

We are now ready to present two constructions of an RMA protocol for a limited, but quite practical class of attacks. The first construction combines a secret sharing scheme with a hash function, and does not rely on public key cryptography. The scheme is quite efficient and is secure in the random oracle model; the second construction uses a public key encryption scheme secure under plaintext checking attacks.

Both construction share the same underlying idea. A secret is shared and the resulting shares are placed in the memory. In our construction we assume that shares are at equal distance – other options are possible provided that this placement ensures that tampering with the memory (using the tampering functions provided to the RMA adversary) does tamper with these protective shares. The attestation protocol is challenge response: the verifier selects a random nonce and sends it to the prover. Upon receiving the nonce, the prover collects the shares, reconstructs the secret and uses it in a cryptographic operation; the verifier then confirms that the secret used is the same that he holds.

In the first scheme, which we present below, the prover hashes the secret together with the nonce and sends it to the verifier who checks consistency with his locally stored secret by and the nonce he has sent.

5.1   Hash-Based RMA

Construction 51 (Hash-Based RMA). Fix a refreshable n-out-of-n secret sharing scheme $SSh = (\mathsf{KS}, \mathsf{KR}, \mathsf{SU})$. Let Divide be any function that on input a bitstring of size greater than n breaks M into n consecutive substrings $(M_1, \ldots, M_n)$. Let $H : \{0,1\}^* \to \{0,1\}^h$ be a hash function. These scheme does not use asymmetric keys for the parties so below we omit them from the description of the algorithms. We define the RMA protocol hash2rma(H) by the algorithms $(\mathsf{SS}, \mathsf{Init}, (\mathsf{MA}, \mathsf{MV}), \mathsf{Update}, \mathsf{Extract})$ below:

- $\mathsf{SS}(1^k)$ returns ϵ.
- Init on input M does
    - $s \xleftarrow{\$} \{0,1\}^\kappa$
    - $(s_1, \ldots, s_n) \leftarrow \mathsf{KS}(n, s)$
    - $(M_1, \ldots, M_n) \leftarrow \mathsf{Divide}(M)$
    - Return $(M_1\|s_1\| \ldots \|M_n\|s_n, s)$.
- Extract on input M_s parses M_s as $M_1\|s_1\| \ldots \|M_n\|s_n$, runs $s \leftarrow \mathsf{KR}(s_1, \ldots, s_n)$ and returns (M, s).
- MV on input s picks $l \xleftarrow{\$} \{0,1\}^{l(\kappa)}$ and sends l to MA
- MA on input M_s gets l from MV, calculates $(M, s) \leftarrow \mathsf{Extract}(M_s)$, and sends back $t = H(s\|l)$.
- MV gets t from MA returns the result of the comparison $t = H(s\|l)$.
- Update on input M_s M_s as $M_1\|s_1\| \ldots \|M_n\|s_n$ and returns $\mathsf{SU}(s_1, \ldots, s_n)$.

The following theorem states the security guarantees the above construction provides – the details of the proof are in the full version of the paper [11].

Theorem 3. *Let $SSh = (\mathsf{KS}, \mathsf{KR}, \mathsf{SU})$ be an n-out-of-n refreshable secret sharing scheme. Let Divide be any function that on input a bitstring M, which for simplicity we assume is nm bits, breaks M into n consecutive substrings $(M_1, \ldots, M_n)$. Let hash2rma(H) $= (\mathsf{SS}, \mathsf{Init}, (\mathsf{MA}, \mathsf{MV}), \mathsf{Update}, \mathsf{Extract})$ be the hash-based RMA protocol as per Construction 51.*

Let $\mathcal{L}$ be the class of functions that on inputs integers a, b such that $1 \leq a < b \leq m$, returns $M_s[a \ldots b]$. Let $\mathcal{T}$ be the class of functions that on inputs an index $1 \leq i \leq n$ and bitstring c of size $m + k$ returns M_s with its ith block changed to c.

Let us call the adversary restricted if during all its queries to Read and Tamper oracles between the Update queries, there is a substring of M_s of length at least n, which has not been read, i.e., not returned by Read.

Then if SSh has secret privacy, oblivious reconstructability and share unpredictability then hash2rma(H) is secure wrt $\mathcal{L}$ and $\mathcal{T}$ and the adversaries restricted as above, in the random oracle model.

We remark that while our protocol descriptions and treatment assume that the shares are embedded into the memory over equal intervals for simplicity, our implementations use blocks of increasing size, for systems functionality purposes. Our security analyses still apply though. This is because it is clear how the read and tamper queries correspond to reading and tampering the shares, and in addition, any tampering query to a memory part that has not been read must change the secret.

We justify the restrictions in the security statement from the systems point of view. We require that an attacker does not read the whole memory. This is reasonable, as reading incorrect memory address results in segmentation fault (e.g., termination of the process). Given that 64-bit address of modern processors, it's unlikely that attackers infer the whole memory space.

Since our threat model is not arbitrary memory write, rather a consecutive memory overrun like buffer overflow, it is natural to assume in this threat model an attacker needs to over-write the boundary between the blocks.

Given that the memory randomization is a common defense (outside of our model though), attackers should correctly identify the location of shares to over-write (which is randomized), hence we do not model completely arbitrary writes.

5.2 Encryption-Based RMA

The construction is based on a similar idea as that underlying the hash-based RMA protocol above. The difference is in the attestation and verification algorithms. Instead of the hash, the prover computes and sends the encryption of the secret currently encoded in the memory with the nonce sent by the verifier as label.

Construction 52 (Encryption-Based RMA). Let $SSh = (\mathsf{KS}, \mathsf{KR}, \mathsf{SU})$ and Divide be as in Construction 51. Let $\Pi = (\mathcal{KeyGen}, \mathcal{Enc}, \mathcal{Dec})$ be a labeled asymmetric encryption scheme. The RMA scheme enc2rma(Π) is defined by

- $\mathsf{SS}(1^\kappa)$ runs $(pk, sk) \xleftarrow{\$} \mathcal{KeyGen}(1^\kappa)$ and returns (pk, sk)
- Init is as in Construction 51.
- Extract on input M_s parses M_s as $M_1\|s_1\|\ldots\|M_n\|s_n$, runs $s \leftarrow \mathsf{KR}(s_1, \ldots, s_n)$ and returns (M, s).
- MV on input s picks $l \xleftarrow{\$} \{0, 1\}^{l(\kappa)}$ and sends l to MA

- MA on input M_s gets l from MV and does
  - $(M, s_1, \ldots, s_n) \leftarrow \text{Extract}(M_s)$,
  - $C \xleftarrow{\$} \mathcal{E}nc^l(s)$ and
  - send C to the verifier.
- MV on input C calculates $s' \leftarrow \mathcal{D}ec^l(C)$ and returns the result of $s \overset{?}{=} s'$.
- The Update algorithm is as in Construction 51.

The intuition behind security of the construction is as follows. The prover sends the encrypted secret (for some label chosen by the verifier) to the verifier; the goal of the adversary is to (eventually) create a *new* ciphertext of *the same* secret under a new label received from the verifier. If this is possible, a plaintext-checking oracle would allow to distinguish such an encryption from the encryption of a different secret. The following proposition establishes the security of the above construction. The proof is in [11].

Theorem 4. *If SSh is a refreshable secret sharing scheme with secret privacy, oblivious reconstructability and share unpredictability and $\Pi = (\mathcal{K}ey\mathcal{G}en, \mathcal{E}nc, \mathcal{D}ec)$ is an IND-PCA secure then $\text{enc2rma}(\Pi)$ defined by Construction 52 is a secure RMA scheme with respect to $\mathcal{L}$, $\mathcal{T}$ and any efficient but restricted adversary defined in Theorem 3.*

OPTIMIZATION. The above theorem establishes that we can instantiate an RMA scheme using the SCS scheme that we presented in Sect. 4. It turns out that we can further optimize the communication complexity of that protocol (where each interaction requires the prover to send three group elements) by observing that the verifier already has the plaintext that the ciphertext it receives should contain. In this case, the prover does not have to send the second component of the ciphertext (as this component can actually be recomputed by the verifier using its secret key). For completeness, we give below the relevant algorithms of the optimized scheme.

Construction 53 (SCS-Based RMA).

- $\text{SS}(1^\kappa)$ obtains $\mathbb{G}$ and $(h, c, d), (x, a, b, a', b')$ by running $\mathcal{K}ey\mathcal{G}en_{\text{SCS}}(1^\kappa)$.
- MV on input s picks $l \xleftarrow{\$} \{0, 1\}^{l(\kappa)}$ and sends l to MA
- MA on input M_s and (h, c, d) gets l from MV, obtains the shares of the secret via $(M, s_1, \ldots, s_n) \leftarrow \text{Extract}(M_s)$, and samples random coins $r \in [\|\mathbb{G}\|]$ and computes $(u = g^r, e = h^r \cdot m, v = (c \cdot d^\alpha)^r)$, where $\alpha = H(l, u, e)$. It sends (u, v) to the server.
- MV on input its secret key (x, a, b, a', b') the challenge l and secret s operates as follows on input (u, v) from the prover and returns the result of the comparison $v = u^{a + \alpha a'} \cdot (u^x)^{b + \alpha b'}$, where $\alpha = H(l, u, u^x \cdot s)$.

The following security statement follows directly from Theorems 4 and 2.

Theorem 5. *If SSh is a refreshable secret sharing scheme with secret privacy, oblivious reconstructability and share unpredictability, and $\Pi =$*

($\mathcal{KeyGen}, \mathcal{Enc}, \mathcal{Dec}$) *is as per Construction 52 then the RMA protocol defined by Construction 53 is a secure RMA scheme with respect to* $\mathcal{L}$, $\mathcal{T}$ *and any efficient but restricted adversary defined in Theorem 3, assuming the DDH problem is hard in the underlying group and the hash is target collision-resistant.*

6 Implementation and Evaluation

Our prototype can seamlessly enable the remote memory attestation in any applications that are using standard libraries. At runtime, the prototype implementation interposes all memory allocations (`malloc()`) and deallocations (`free()`) by incorporating LD_PRELOAD when the application starts executing. Before the application runs, our custom runtime pre-allocates memory regions with varying sizes, and carefully insert key shares between the memory objects.

Specifically, we provide a simple wrapper program (called *prover*) which end users use to perform all these operations. When requested, the prover launches the program, and then inserts our custom library for memory allocations of the target application. Before the program starts, the prover pre-allocates a list of chunked memory, starting from 8 bytes object to a few mega bytes (128 MB by default) incrementally. In our current prototype, we pre-allocate N blocks (configurable, 10 by default) per size (e.g., N 8-byte blocks up to 128 MB).

For attestation, the prover initiates the secrets with the public key provided, performs the memory attestation of the program it launched, and communicates with the remote verifier. To access the memory of a remote program, it attaches to the program via `ptrace` interface in UNIX-like operating system, and runs the protocol.

We evaluate a prototype of RMA in three aspects: (1) runtime overheads of computation-oriented tasks such as SPEC benchmark; (2) worst case overheads (e.g., launching an application) that end-user might be facing when using RMA; (3) break-down of performance overheads and data transferred on the course of remote attestation by using our prototype. We performed all experiments with the prototype implementation of the encryption-based RMA. As we mentioned in the Introduction, this protocol is not as efficient (in terms of crypto operations) as the hash-based one, but it provides stronger security (no reliance on the

Component	Lines of code
Verifier	298 lines of C
Prover	638 lines of C
Memory allocator	343 lines of C
Total	1,279 lines of code

Fig. 4. The complexity of RMA in terms of lines of code of each components, including verifier, launcher and memory allocator.

random oracle model), and performs equally well in the presence of system-dependent overheads.

MICRO-BENCHMARK. We evaluate a prototype of RMA by running the standard SPEC CPU2006 integer benchmark suite. All benchmarks were run on Intel Xeon CPU E7-4820 @2.00 GHz machine with 128 GB RAM, and the baseline benchmark ran with standard libraries provided by Ubuntu 15.04 with Linux 3.19.0-16. As shown in Fig. 5, due to the simplicity of the implementation, RMA incurs negligible performance overheads to SPEC benchmark programs: 3.1 % on average, ranging from 0.0 % to 4.8 % depending on a SEPC benchmark program. During the experiments, we found out that the significant part of performance overheads comes from the implementation of the custom memory allocator and the side-effects of memory fragmentation, thereby diluting the overheads related to crypto operations. We believe that different types of applications requiring frequent validation or updates of share keys might need better optimization of crypto-related software stack. It is worth noting that our prototype never focuses on optimization in any sort (e.g., using a coarse-grained, global lock to support multi-threading) and the overall performance can be dramatically improved if necessary.

Programs	Baseline (s)	RMA (s)	Overhead (%)
400.perlbench	545	566	3.9%
401.bzip2	749	770	2.8%
403.gcc	521	537	3.1%
429.mcf	385	395	2.6%
445.gobmk	691	691	0.0%
456.hmmer	638	665	4.2%
458.sjeng	779	805	3.3%
462.libquantu	1,453	1,514	4.2%
464.h264ref	917	950	3.6%
471.omnetpp	540	547	1.3%
473.astar	606	635	4.8%
483.xalancbmk	361	373	3.3%

Fig. 5. Runtime overheads of SPEC benchmark programs with RMA.

MACRO-BENCHMARK. To measure performance overhands that end-user might be encountering when using RMA, we construct a macro-benchmark with three applications for four different tasks; launching a web browser (Firefox), an email client (Thunderbird), compressing and decompressing files (Tar). All experiments were conducted on a laptop running Ubuntu 12.04 with standard glibc library (Ubuntu/Linaro 4.6.3-1ubuntu5), and we measured each benchmark ten times, we provide the summary in [11]. i Note that launching application is the worst-case scenario to RMA because it has to allocate memory space at program's startup and initiate all key shares before executing the program. According to our benchmark, it incurs acceptable performance overheads even in the worst-cast construction, but we believe the latency that users actually feel is minimal: 0.023 s in Firefox and 0.199 s in Thunderbird.

PERFORMANCE BREAK-DOWN. We also measured how long it takes to proceed each stage of the RMA protocol with our prototype implementation. We measured the amount of data that needs to be transferred as well. In short, it is feasible to implement the proposed RMA protocol in practice: our unoptimized system incurs negligible performance overheads (the details are in [11]) and the amount of messages between the prover and the verifier is minimal (e.g., 12 bytes up to 396 bytes). According to our evaluation, we believe our RMA protocol can be utilized in an efficient manner in practice.

Acknowledgements. The first author was supported in part by the NSF award CNS-1422794. The fourth author was supported in part by European Union Seventh Framework Programme (FP7/2007–2013) grant agreement 609611 (PRACTICE). We thank Sangmin Lee for great help with implementations. We thank Tom Conte and Milos Prvulovic for useful discussions and Rafail Ostrovsky and Vassilis Zikas for clarifications on [26].

References

1. Abdalla, M., Benhamouda, F., Pointcheval, D.: Public-key encryption indistinguishable under plaintext-checkable attacks. In: Katz, J. (ed.) PKC 2015. LNCS, vol. 9020, pp. 332–352. Springer, Heidelberg (2015)
2. One, A.: Smashing the stack for fun and profit. Phrack **7**(49), 14–16 (1996)
3. Armknecht, F., Sadeghi, A.-R., Schulz, S., Wachsmann, C.: A security framework for the analysis and design of software attestation. In: Proceedings of 2013 ACM SIGSAC Conference on Computer & Communications Security, pp. 1–12. ACM (2013)
4. Barnett, R.: GHOST gethostbyname() heap overflow in glibc (CVE-2015-0235). https://www.trustwave.com/Resources/SpiderLabs-Blog/GHOST-gethostbyname ()-heap-overflow-in-glibc-(CVE-2015-0235)
5. Bellare, M., Cash, D., Miller, R.: Cryptography secure against related-key attacks and tampering. In: Lee, D.H., Wang, X. (eds.) ASIACRYPT 2011. LNCS, vol. 7073, pp. 486–503. Springer, Heidelberg (2011)
6. Bellare, M., Kohno, T.: A theoretical treatment of related-key attacks: RKA-PRPs, RKA-PRFs, and applications. In: Biham, E. (ed.) EUROCRYPT 2003. LNCS, vol. 2656, pp. 491–506. Springer, Heidelberg (2003)
7. Bellare, M., Paterson, K.G., Thomson, S.: RKA security beyond the linear barrier: IBE, encryption and signatures. In: Wang, X., Sako, K. (eds.) ASIACRYPT 2012. LNCS, vol. 7658, pp. 331–348. Springer, Heidelberg (2012)
8. Bellare, M., Rogaway, P.: Random oracles are practical: a paradigm for designing efficient protocols. In: Proceedings of 1st ACM Conference on Computer and Communications Security, pp. 62–73. ACM (1993)

9. Berger, E.D.: HeapShield: library-based heap overflow protection for free. University of Massachusetts Amherst, TR 06–28 (2006)
10. Bhattacharyya, R., Roy, A.: Secure message authentication against related-key attack. In: Moriai, S. (ed.) FSE 2013. LNCS, vol. 8424, pp. 305–324. Springer, Heidelberg (2014)
11. Boldyreva, A., Kim, T., Lipton, R., Warinschi, B.: Provably-secure remote memory attestation to prevent heap overflow attacks. Cryptology ePrint Archive, Report 2015/729 (2015). Full version of this paper http://eprint.iacr.org/2015/729
12. Canetti, R., Goldreich, O., Halevi, S.: The random oracle methodology, revisited. J. ACM (JACM) 51(4), 557–594 (2004)
13. Castelluccia, C., Francillon, A., Perito, D., Soriente, C.: On the difficulty of software-based attestation of embedded devices. In: Proceedings of 16th ACM Conference on Computer and Communications Security, CCS 2009 (2009)
14. Cowan, C., Pu, C., Maier, D., Hintony, H., Walpole, J., Bakke, P., Beattie, S., Grier, A., Wagle, P., Zhang, Q.: StackGuard: automatic adaptive detection and prevention of buffer-overflow attacks. In: Proceedings of 7th Conference on USENIX Security Symposium, SSYM 1998, vol. 7 (1998)
15. Cramer, R., Shoup, V.: A practical public key cryptosystem provably secure against adaptive chosen ciphertext attack. In: Krawczyk, H. (ed.) CRYPTO 1998. LNCS, vol. 1462, pp. 13–25. Springer, Heidelberg (1998)
16. Duflot, L., Perez, Y.-A., Morin, B.: What if you can't trust your network card? In: Sommer, R., Balzarotti, D., Maier, G. (eds.) RAID 2011. LNCS, vol. 6961, pp. 378–397. Springer, Heidelberg (2011)
17. Etoh, H.: GCC extension for protecting applications from stack-smashing attacks (ProPolice) (2003). http://www.trl.ibm.com/projects/security/ssp/
18. Francillon, A., Nguyen, Q., Rasmussen, K.B., Tsudik, G.: A minimalist approach to remote attestation. In: Design, Automation and Test in Europe Conference and Exhibition, DATE 2014, pp. 1–6 (2014)
19. Frantzen, M., Shuey, M.: StackGhost: hardware facilitated stack protection. In: Proceedings of 10th Usenix Security Symposium, pp. 55–66 (2001)
20. Herzberg, A., Jarecki, S., Krawczyk, H., Yung, M.: Proactive secret sharing or: how to cope with perpetual leakage. In: Coppersmith, D. (ed.) CRYPTO 1995. LNCS, vol. 963, pp. 339–352. Springer, Heidelberg (1995)
21. Hoekstra, M., Lal, R., Pappachan, P., Phegade, V., Del Cuvillo, J.: Using innovative instructions to create trustworthy software solutions. In: Proceedings of 2nd International Workshop on Hardware and Architectural Support for Security and Privacy (HASP) (2013)
22. Jakobsson, M., Johansson, K.-A.: Practical and secure software-based attestation. In: 2011 Workshop on Lightweight Security and Privacy: Devices, Protocols and Applications (LightSec), pp. 1–9. IEEE (2011)
23. Kovah, X., Kallenberg, C., Weathers, C., Herzog, A., Albin, M., Butterworth, J.: New results for timing-based attestation. In: 2012 IEEE Symposium on Security and Privacy (SP), pp. 239–253. IEEE (2012)
24. Li, Y., McCune, J.M., Perrig, A.: SBAP: software-based attestation for peripherals. In: Acquisti, A., Smith, S.W., Sadeghi, A.-R. (eds.) TRUST 2010. LNCS, vol. 6101, pp. 16–29. Springer, Heidelberg (2010)
25. Li, Y., McCune, J.M., Perrig, A.: Viper: verifying the integrity of peripherals' firmware. In: Proceedings of 18th ACM Conference on Computer and Communications Security, pp. 3–16. ACM (2011)

26. Lipton, R.J., Ostrovsky, R., Zikas, V.: Provable virus detection: using the uncertainty principle to protect against Malware. Cryptology ePrint Archive, Report 2015/728 (2015). http://eprint.iacr.org/
27. Lu, K., Song, C., Lee, B., Chung, S.P., Kim, T., Lee, W.: ASLR-guard: stopping address space leakage for code reuse attacks. In: Proceedings of 22nd ACM SIGSAC Conference on Computer and Communications Security, CCS 2015 (2015)
28. McCune, J.M., Li, Y., Qu, N., Zhou, Z., Datta, A., Gligor, V., Perrig, A.: Trustvisor: efficient TCB reduction and attestation. In: Proceedings of 2010 IEEE Symposium on Security and Privacy, SP 2010, pp. 143–158 (2010)
29. McCune, J.M., Parno, B.J., Perrig, A., Reiter, M.K., Isozaki, H.: Flicker: An execution infrastructure for TCB minimization. In: Proceedings of 3rd ACM SIGOPS/EuroSys European Conference on Computer Systems 2008, Eurosys 2008 (2008)
30. McKeen, F., Alexandrovich, I., Berenzon, A., Rozas, C.V., Shafi, H., Shanbhogue, V., Savagaonkar, U.R.: Innovative instructions and software model for isolated execution. In: Proceedings of 2nd International Workshop on Hardware and Architectural Support for Security and Privacy (HASP) (2013)
31. Nikiforakis, N., Piessens, F., Joosen, W.: HeapSentry: kernel-assisted protection against heap overflows. In: Rieck, K., Stewin, P., Seifert, J.-P. (eds.) DIMVA 2013. LNCS, vol. 7967, pp. 177–196. Springer, Heidelberg (2013)
32. Okamoto, T., Pointcheval, D.: REACT: rapid enhanced-security asymmetric cryptosystem transform. In: Naccache, D. (ed.) CT-RSA 2001. LNCS, vol. 2020, pp. 159–175. Springer, Heidelberg (2001)
33. Robertson, W., Kruegel, C., Mutz, D., Valeur, F.: Run-time detection of heap-based overflows. In: Proceedings of 17th USENIX Conference on System Administration, LISA 2003 (2003)
34. Serebryany, K., Bruening, D., Potapenko, A., Vyukov, D.: AddressSanitizer: a fast address sanity checker. In: Proceedings of 2012 USENIX Conference on Annual Technical Conference, USENIX ATC 2012 (2012)
35. Seshadri, A., Luk, M., Shi, E., Perrig, A., van Doorn, L., Khosla, P.: Pioneer: verifying code integrity and enforcing untampered code execution on legacy systems. In: Proceedings of 20th ACM Symposium on Operating Systems Principles, SOSP 2005 (2005)
36. Seshadri, A., Perrig, A., Van Doorn, L., Khosla, P.: SWATT: software-based attestation for embedded devices. In: 2004 IEEE Symposium on Security and Privacy, Proceedings, pp. 272–282. IEEE (2004)
37. Shacham, H., Page, M., Pfaff, B., Goh, E.-J., Modadugu, N., Boneh, D.: On the effectiveness of address-space randomization. In: Proceedings of 11th ACM Conference on Computer and Communications Security, CCS 2004 (2004)
38. Wee, H.: Public key encryption against related key attacks. In: Public Key Cryptography - PKC 2012–15th International Conference on Practice and Theory in Public Key Cryptography Proceedings, pp. 262–279 (2012)
39. Younan, Y., Joosen, W., Piessens, F.: Efficient protection against heap-based buffer overflows without resorting to magic. In: Ning, P., Qing, S., Li, N. (eds.) ICICS 2006. LNCS, vol. 4307, pp. 379–398. Springer, Heidelberg (2006)

Memory Erasability Amplification

Jan Camenisch[1]([⊠]), Robert R. Enderlein[1,2]([⊠]), and Ueli Maurer[2]([⊠])

[1] IBM Research - Zurich, Rueschlikon, Switzerland
jca@zurich.ibm.com, scn2016@e7n.ch
[2] Department of Computer Science, ETH Zürich, Zurich, Switzerland
maurer@inf.ethz.ch

Abstract. Erasable memory is an important resource for designing practical cryptographic protocols that are secure against adaptive attacks. Many practical memory devices such as solid state drives, hard disks, or file systems are not perfectly erasable because a deletion operation leaves traces of the deleted data in the system. A number of methods for constructing a large erasable memory from a small one, e.g., using encryption, have been proposed. Despite the importance of erasable memory in cryptography, no formal model has been proposed that allows one to formally analyse such memory constructions or cryptographic protocols relying on erasable memory.

The contribution of this paper is three-fold. First, we provide a formal model of erasable memory. A memory device allows a user to store, retrieve, and delete data, and it is characterised by a leakage function defining the extent to which erased data is still accessible to an adversary.

Second, we investigate how the erasability of such memories can be amplified. We provide a number of constructions of memories with strong erasability guarantees from memories with weaker guarantees. One of these constructions of perfectly erasable memories from imperfectly erasable ones can be considered as the prototypical application of Canetti et al.'s All-or-Nothing Transform (AoNT). Motivated by this construction, we propose some new and better AoNTs that are either perfectly or computationally secure. These AoNTs are of possible independent interest.

Third, we show (in the constructive cryptography framework) how the construction of erasable memory and its use in cryptographic protocols (for example to achieve adaptive security) can naturally be composed to obtain provable security of the overall protocol.

Keywords: Secure memory erasure · Secure deletion · Adaptive corruption · Constructive cryptography · All-or-nothing-transforms (AoNT)

The first and second author were supported by the European Commission through the Seventh Framework Programme under the ERC grant #321310 (PERCY) and the third author was supported by the Zurich Information Security & Privacy Center (ZISC).

V. Zikas and R. De Prisco (Eds.): SCN 2016, LNCS 9841, pp. 104–125, 2016.
DOI: 10.1007/978-3-319-44618-9_6

1 Introduction

Persistent and erasable memory is a crucial ingredient of many practical cryptographic protocols that are secure against adaptive adversaries. However, for storage devices such as solid state disks, hard disks, and tapes it is rather difficult to truly erase information written on them. Therefore, constructions have been proposed that use a small amount of memory that is easier to erase (or at least harder for an attacker to tap into), such as smart cards and processor registers, to store a cryptographic key, and then to encrypt the data to be stored so that it no longer matters whether or not the ciphertext can be erased [9,11,17–21]. This approach is sometimes referred to as crypto paging. Surprisingly, no formal model of erasable memory has been proposed to date, despite of the importance of erasable memory for cryptographic protocol design and the cryptographic constructions for it.

1.1 Contributions of This Paper

In this paper we rectify this and first model erasable memory as a general resource in the constructive cryptography framework [14,15]. Our memory resource defines how a user, an adversary, and the environment can interact with the resource and to what extent stored data can be erased. In particular, different memory resources are characterized by what information about the stored data an adversary will be able to obtain when the environment allows it access to the memory resource. As we discuss, this allows one to model many different types of memory such as hard disks, solid state drives, RAM, and smart cards. Next, we study different constructions of erasable memory from one with weaker erasability properties or, in other words, constructions that amplify erasability. These constructions also show how memory resources can be used in protocol design and analysis. We then study the approach of crypto paging in our setting, i.e., constructions of a large erasable memory from a small one and a non-erasable memory. As it turns out, achieving the strongest possible type of erasable memory with this approach requires non-committing encryption and hence is only possible in the random oracle model (or requires additional communication between sender and receiver, which is not applicable here). We also show what kind of erasable memory can be achieved with this approach in the standard model.

One of our memory constructions employs All-or-Nothing Transforms (AoNT) [3] to obtain a perfectly erasable memory from one that leaks a constant fraction of the erased data. Motivated by this protocol, we study AoNTs and propose several new transforms that enjoy better parameters than previously known ones, a result that may be of independent interest. For example, we improve the standard construction of a perfectly-secure AoNT from a Linear Block Code (LBC), by observing that an LBC with a large minimum distance does not yield an AoNT with optimal privacy threshold. We propose the metric of *ramp minimum distance* and show that LBCs optimized for this metric yield perfectly secure AoNTs with better parameters than what can be achieved with the standard construction. We further propose a computationally secure AoNT that operates over a large alphabet (large enough for one symbol to encode a cryptographic key) and that is optimal: the encoded data is just one symbol longer than the original data, and the transform is secure even if all but one of the symbols of the encoded data leak. We show that such an AoNT can be realized from a pseudo-random generator (PRG) with some specific properties.

1.2 Related Work

In most security frameworks, unlimited and perfectly erasable memory is available to protocols as part of the framework, with the exception of protocols that are proven to be adaptively secure in the non-erasure model, where no erasable memory is available. However, as mentioned already, no security framework explicitly models memory and consequently security proofs treat the adversary's access to the memory of a compromised party informally only. The only exception to this is the work by Canetti et al. and Lim [4,13], who model memory as special tapes of the parties' Turing machines and define how an adversary can access these special tapes. This very specific modelling therefore changes the machine model underlying the UC framework.

Hazay et al. [10] follow a different approach. They introduce the concept of *adaptive security with partial erasures*, where security holds if at least one party of a given protocol can successfully erase. Their model requires a special protocol design and has some restrictions regarding composition.

Both these approaches are rather limited. Indeed, if one wanted to consider different types of memory, one would have to change the modelling framework each time and potentially have to prove all composition theorems all over again. Moreover, these approaches do not allow one to analyse protocols that construct one type of memory from another type of memory, as we do in this paper. Indeed, one cannot analyse the security of protocols such as Yee's crypto-paging technique [20,21] and the constructions of Di Crescenzo et al. [6]. In contrast, we model memory as a resource (or ideal functionality) *within* the security framework (the constructive cryptography framework in our case) and thus do not suffer from these limitations.

2 Preliminaries

This section defines the notation used throughout this paper, presents the constructive cryptography model, and recalls various cryptographic building blocks and their security properties.

2.1 Notation

Let $GF(q)$ denote the Galois field of q elements, where q is a prime power. If u is a vector or a list, let u_i or $u[i]$ denote the ith element of u. If $u = (u_1, \ldots, u_n)$ and $v = (v_1, \ldots, v_m)$ are lists, then (u, e) denotes the list $(u_1, \ldots, u_n, e)$ and (u, v)

denotes the list $(u_1, \ldots, u_n, v_1, \ldots, v_n)$; we write $e \in u$ to denote $(\exists i : e = u_i)$; we write $v = (u, \cdot)$ to denote that $(\forall i \in \{1, \ldots, n\} : u_i = v_i)$. If L is a set of positive integers, let $[u]_L$ denote the subvector of u taken at all positions in L. If S is a set, then 2^S denotes the powerset of S (the set of all subsets of S). Let I_r denote the identity matrix of size $r \times r$, and let 0 denote the zero matrix of appropriate size.

If A is a deterministic polynomial-time algorithm, then $y \leftarrow A(x)$ denotes the assignment of variable y to the output of $A(x)$. If A is a probabilistic polynomial-time (PPT) algorithm, then $y \xleftarrow{\$} A(x)$ denotes the assignment of y to the output of $A(x)$ when run with fresh random coins on input x. For a set $\mathbb{A}$: $x \xleftarrow{\$} \mathbb{A}$ denotes the assignment of x to a value chosen uniformly at random from $\mathbb{A}$. For a distribution $A(x)$, we denote the ensemble $\{A(x)\}_{x \in \{1^\eta | \eta \in \mathbb{N}, \eta > \eta_0\}}$ by the shorthand $\{A\}_{1^\eta}$.

Throughout this paper we denote the security parameter by $\eta \in \mathbb{N}$. Let 1^η denote the string consisting of η ones. Unless otherwise noted, all algorithms in this paper are PPT and take 1^η as extra (often implicit) input.

2.2 Constructive Cryptography

We present our results in the Constructive Cryptography framework [14, 15]. The framework argues about *resources* and how to securely construct a resource from other resources using a protocol which consists of a set of *converters*. Resources and converters are systems that have a set of interfaces. Resources have an interface for each party considered (e.g., *Alice*), one for the adversary (the *Eve* interface), and one for the distinguisher (the *World* interface). The latter is an example of what Gaži et al. [8] introduce as a free interface and allows one to model the influence of the distinguisher (environment) on a resource, e.g., to define when a memory becomes readable by the adversary or to model adaptive adversarial behaviour. Converters have only two interfaces, an *inner interface* that connects to a party interface of a resource and an *outer interface* to which a party can connect. A *simulator* is a converter that attaches to the adversary interface of a resource. In this paper we consider only resources that have a single party interface, i.e., *Alice*. The *security* condition of Constructive Cryptography is as follows (we do not consider the *availability* condition in this paper) [15].

Definition 2.1. *A protocol (converter) π constructs resource S from resource R with respect to simulator σ, within ϵ, denoted*

$$R \xrightarrow{\pi, \sigma, \epsilon} S,$$

if for all distinguishers D we have $\Delta^D(\pi^{Alice}R, \sigma^{Eve}S) \leq \epsilon(D)$, where Δ^D is the advantage of D in distinguishing the two systems [15].

The distinguisher D is a system itself and has access to all external interfaces of the composition of the resources and converters (cf. Fig. 1). With $\pi^{Alice}R$ we denote the system obtained by attaching the inner interface of π to the interface *Alice* of resource R, and likewise for σ^{Eve}. In this definition, ϵ is a function mapping distinguishers to positive real numbers. Informally, computational security corresponds to π and σ being efficiently implementable and $\epsilon(D)$ being negligible for all efficiently implementable D. Constructions are composable, i.e., if $R \xrightarrow{\pi_1,\sigma_1,\epsilon_1} S$ and $S \xrightarrow{\pi_2,\sigma_2,\epsilon_2} T$, then $R \xrightarrow{\pi_2\pi_1,\sigma_1\sigma_2,\epsilon_2+\epsilon_1} T$.

2.3 Cryptographic Building Blocks

For our constructions, we require pseudo-random generators and exposure-resilient functions, the definitions of which we recall here for convenience.

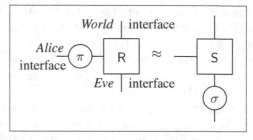

Definition 2.2. *An ℓ-pseudo-random generator (PRG), i.e., prg : $\{0,1\}^\eta \mapsto \{0,1\}^{\ell(\eta)}$, is secure if these ensembles are computationally indistinguishable: $\{b\}_{1^\eta}$ for $b \xleftarrow{\$} \{0,1\}^{\ell(\eta)}$; and $\{prg(a)\}_{1^\eta}$ for $a \xleftarrow{\$} \{0,1\}^\eta$* [12].

Definition 2.3. *A d-exposure-resilient function (ERF) erf : $\Phi^n \mapsto \Phi^k$, also denoted (Φ, n, d, k)-ERF, is ϵ-secure if for any set $L \subset \{1,\dots n\}$ of size at most d,*

Fig. 1. The constructive statement for a resource with interfaces *Alice*, *Eve*, and *World*. Protocol π constructs S from R if there is a simulator σ such that R with π attached to its *Alice*-interface is indistinguishable from the resource S with σ attached to its *Eve*-interface (cf. Defintion 2.1).

these distributions are ϵ-indistinguishable: $([b]_L, x_0)$ for $b \xleftarrow{\$} \Phi^n, x_0 \leftarrow erf(b)$; and $([b]_L, x_1)$ for $b \xleftarrow{\$} \Phi^n, x_1 \xleftarrow{\$} \Phi^k$ [3].

2.4 All-or-Nothing Transform (AoNT)

An all-or-nothing transform (AoNT) [3] is similar to a secret-sharing scheme that requires all shares in order to reconstruct the secret. It consists of two algorithms aenc and adec.

Definition 2.4. *A d-AoNT with aenc : $\Phi^k \xmapsto{\$} \Phi^n$ and adec : $\Phi^n \mapsto \Phi^k$, also denoted (Φ, n, d, k)-AoNT, is ϵ-secure if: (Completeness) For all messages $a \in \Phi^k$, $a = adec(aenc(a))$. (Privacy) For any set $L \subset \{1,\dots n\}$ of size at most d, and for any two messages $a_0, a_1 \in \Phi^k$ the following two distributions are ϵ-indistinguishable: $(a_0, a_1, [aenc(a_0)]_L)$ and $(a_0, a_1, [aenc(a_1)]_L)$* [3].

Computational Security. In the context of computational security, the two functions aenc and adec take as additional input a (usually implicit) security parameter; Φ, n, k, and d may depend on that security parameter. For the privacy condition, it is required that the *ensembles* $\{(a_0, a_1, [aenc(1^\eta, a_0)]_L)\}_{1^\eta}$ and $\{(a_0, a_1, [aenc(1^\eta, a_1)]_L)\}_{1^\eta}$ be indistinguishable. In the sequel we also denote such computationally secure AoNTs as (Φ, n, d, k)-AoNTs, where the security parameter is implicit.

AoNT with Public Part. A $(\Phi, n + \nu, d, k)$-AoNT has a ν-public part, if in the privacy condition above the last ν symbols of $\mathsf{aenc}(\boldsymbol{a})$ are output in addition to $[\mathsf{aenc}(\boldsymbol{a})]_L$.

Realization from a Secret Sharing Scheme. It is easy to realize a perfect (Φ, n, d, k)-AoNT from any secret sharing scheme over alphabet Φ that outputs m shares, has a reconstruction threshold of n, a privacy threshold of d, and that encodes messages of size k shares, by simply ignoring all shares after the first n ones. This technique also works in the statistical and computational case.

Realization from an ERF. It is easy to realize an ϵ-secure $(\Phi, n + k, d, k)$-AoNT with a k-public part from any ϵ-secure (Φ, n, d, k)-ERF: $\mathsf{aenc}(\boldsymbol{a}) \overset{\$}{\mapsto} \boldsymbol{b} || (\mathsf{erf}(\boldsymbol{b}) + \boldsymbol{a})$ where $\boldsymbol{b} \overset{\$}{\leftarrow} \Phi^n$; and $\mathsf{adec}(\boldsymbol{b} || \boldsymbol{x}) \mapsto \boldsymbol{x} - \mathsf{erf}(\boldsymbol{b})$ [3]. This technique also works in the computational case.

3 Modelling Imperfectly Erasable Memory

We now present our erasable memory resource. Recall that we aim to model memory that is used for persistent storage (such as hard disks, solid state drives, RAM, and smart cards), and not processor registers that store temporary values during computations. To this end, we define how the resource behaves upon inputs on the user (Alice), the adversary, and the world interfaces. It allows a user *Alice* to store a single data item *once*, retrieve it (many times), and erase it. The adversary can get access to the data only if such access is enabled on the *World*-interface. That is, the data stored is not initially available to her. Then, once access is enabled via a *weaken* input on the *World*-interface, the adversary can either *read* the data item stored (if the user has not yet deleted it) or *leak* the data, meaning that she will obtain as answer a function of the once stored data. This function determines the information that is still *leaked* although the data has been deleted. The adversary can influence the leakage by providing an additional input to the function (e.g., specify some bits that are leaked).

In reality, there might be many different reason why an adversary gains access to the contents of a memory. This might be because the memory device is lost, the adversary controlling some malware on the computer that uses the memory, or the adversary running a cache-timing attack [1] on the computer, etc. Offering a *World*-interface via which it is determined what access is given to the adversary by the memory resource, models any such event. The UC and GNUC frameworks use a similar mechanism for corrupting parties, except that they (ab)use the party interfaces to do so. In UC, it is the adversary who corrupts and the environment is informed of the corruption through the party interfaces. In GNUC, the environment corrupts parties and the adversary is informed thereof.

There seem to be two natural extensions to our erasable memory resource which for simplicity we chose not to consider. First, we assume that inputs at the *World*-interface do not impact the user's ability to access the data, which might often not be the case. Although this would not be hard to model, it is not

---

The resource $\mathsf{M}\langle \Sigma, \psi, \rho, \kappa \rangle$:

Internal state and initial values: DATA $= \bot$, LDAT $= \bot$, HIST $= ()$.

Behavior:

- *Alice*(store, $\mu \in \Sigma$): if DATA $= \bot$: DATA $\leftarrow \mu$; LDAT $\overset{\$}{\leftarrow} \psi(\mu)$; *Alice* $\leftarrow ()$.
- *Alice*(retrieve): if "e" $\notin$ HIST: *Alice* $\leftarrow$ DATA.
- *Alice*(erase): if "e" $\notin$ HIST $\wedge$ DATA $\neq \bot$: HIST $\leftarrow$ (HIST, "e"); *Alice* $\leftarrow ()$.

- *Eve*(gethist): *Eve* $\leftarrow$ HIST.
- *Eve*(read): if ρ(HIST): *Eve* $\leftarrow$ DATA.
- *Eve*(leak, ξ): if κ(HIST, ξ): HIST $\leftarrow$ (HIST, "l"$\|\xi$); *Eve* $\leftarrow \xi$(LDAT).

- *World*(weaken, w): if ("w"$\|w$) $\notin$ HIST: HIST $\leftarrow$ (HIST, "w"$\|w$); *World* $\leftarrow ()$.

Fig. 2. The general (imperfectly) erasable memory resource $\mathsf{M}\langle \cdot \rangle$.

important for the scope of this paper. Second, the user cannot change the stored data or store many different data items. Again, while it would not be hard to extend the resource to allow for that, we choose not to do that for simplicity. Also, this is not a serious restrictions as such requirements can also be addressed by using several instances of our memory resources.

3.1 Specification of the General Imperfectly Erasable Memory Resource $\mathsf{M}\langle \cdot \rangle$

We now present our formal specification of the general resource for imperfectly erasable memory $\mathsf{M}\langle \Sigma, \psi, \rho, \kappa \rangle$ that is given in Fig. 2 and then discuss in the next subsection a few instantiations of this general resource that match different types of memory. The resource maintains three variables DATA, LDAT, and HIST. The first one stores the data provided by the user, the second the data that can potentially be leaked to the adversary, and the third one logs the history of events, namely the erasure event, the parameter of each call on the *World* interface, and the input arguments of each successful leakage query. The resource is parametrized by an alphabet Σ, a conditional probability distribution ψ, and two predicates ρ and κ. The alphabet Σ is the set of possible values that can be stored. The conditional distribution ψ operates on the data and determines what information could potentially leak to the adversary by outputting LDAT. This models the extent to which the resource is able to erase the data. The predicate ρ takes as input the history of the resource and determines whether or not the adversary is allowed to read the memory. Finally, the predicate κ takes as input the history of the resource and the deterministic function ξ submitted by the adversary and determines whether or not the adversary obtains the leakage ξ(LDAT).

Most of the commands that can be submitted to the resource and its behaviour should now be clear from Fig. 2, however, a few details merit explanation. First, the data that is potentially leaked, LDAT, is determined using ψ already when the data is stored in the resource. This is without loss of generalty but is here useful because, depending on the predicate κ, the adversary may query the resource multiple times with the `leak` command and the answers to these commands need to be consistent. Second, when the adversary queries the resource with a leak command, she can input a parameter ξ that may influence the leakage she obtains. This models the process of an adversary reading the erased data from a memory device, e.g., an adversary might try to read the data bit by bit, each time influencing the remaining bits in the memory. Third, the adversary is allowed to obtain the history from the resource at any time. This is necessary so that a simulator has enough information to properly simulate a construction. Finally, the *World*-interface accepts any value w for an external event, because these depend on the particular resource that is modelled and possibly on how it is constructed. This will become clear later when we discuss constructions of one type of memory from other types in Sect. 4.

3.2 Instantiations of $M\langle \Sigma, \psi, \rho, \kappa \rangle$

We now describe special cases of the $M\langle \Sigma, \psi, \rho, \kappa \rangle$ resource that correspond to memory devices appearing in the real world. We start by describing non-erasable memory, i.e., memory that becomes readable by the adversary once access is enabled by the *World*-interface. This models what happens in a typical file system: files that are unlinked are not actually erased and can often be completely recovered with specialized tools (at least until the blocks are re-used). We then describe perfectly erasable memory. Such a memory could be implemented by specialized hardware, such as smartcards, but often will have only limited capacity. Large perfectly erasable memories are often not directly available in reality. We are thus interested in the construction of such memories from resources with lesser guarantees. Each of the latter can be influenced through *World*-events separately, hence we will describe both a variant of the perfectly erasable memory that accepts a single type of *World*-event (easier to describe) and a variant that accepts an arbitrary number of events. Finally we describe imperfectly erasable memories, i.e., memories with security guarantees between the two extremes just discussed. Such memories leak partial information if the adversary is granted access by *World after* an erasure. In reality, often not all the data is actually removed during an erasure: on magnetic storage, overwritten data can still be partially recovered with specialized equipment [9]. Similarly, often parts of the data were copied to a different medium (swap space, backup, file system journal, etc.) before the erasure and the copies were not fully erased themselves. One can thus easily imagine that the adversary can deduce a constant number of bits that were stored, or obtains a noisy version of the data that was stored. For simplicity, we consider imperfectly erasable memories which ignore the parameter of `weaken` (only a single *World*-event can be modelled), and only leak once (no adaptive leakage). We now describe these categories of memory in detail. Table 1 provides an overview of these and further specialization of them that we consider in the following sections.

Table 1. Different specializations of $M\langle\Sigma,\psi,\rho,\kappa\rangle$ that allow one to erase data.

Perfectly erasable memory	Influence of the *World* interface
$PM\langle\Sigma\rangle$	single world event makes memory readable by adversary
$PMW\langle\Sigma\rangle$	multiple world events are modelled
$PMWa\langle\Sigma\rangle$	specific version of $PMW\langle\Sigma\rangle$ (Fig. 4)
$PMWb\langle\Sigma\rangle$	specific version of $PMW\langle\Sigma\rangle$ (Fig. 4)
$PMWc\langle\Sigma\rangle$	specific version of $PMW\langle\Sigma\rangle$ (Fig. 4)
Imperfectly erasable memory	Information adversary obtains on deleted data
$IM\langle\Sigma,\psi,\Xi\rangle$	reveals $\xi(\text{LDAT})$ if $\Xi(\xi)=1$
$IMD\langle\Phi,n,d\rangle$	reveals d symbols to adversary
$IMDP\langle\Phi,s_1,s_2,d\rangle$	reveals d symbols of first part, all symbols of second part
$IMI\langle\Phi,n,d\rangle$	each symbol revealed independently with probability p
$IMN\langle\Phi,n,d\rangle$	reveals through noisy channel
$IML\langle\Sigma,v\rangle$	reveals through a length shrinking function
$IMLP\langle\Phi,n,a+k,v\rangle$	reveals a length shrinking function on first part, full second part

Non-erasable Memory. To model non-erasable memory, we let ρ return true if weaken was called irrespective of erase. (In fact, the erase command could be dropped entirely.) The memory does not leak, hence κ always returns false and ψ is irrelevant. The only relevant parameter is the alphabet Σ and thus we denote this resource by $NM\langle\Sigma\rangle$.

Perfectly Erasable Memory. To model perfectly erasable memory, we let ρ return true only if weaken was called (perhaps multiple times with specific parameters) before erase was called.[1] This memory does not leak, hence κ always returns false and ψ is irrelevant. We describe two versions of the resource: $PM\langle\Sigma\rangle$ fixes ρ to return true if weaken appears in the history earlier than or without erase, hence only a single *World*-event can be modelled. $PMW\langle\Sigma,\rho\rangle$ lets one specify a custom ρ, allowing the modelling of many *World*-events. Figure 4 in the next section shows examples of ρ in the case where there are two relevant *World*-events.

---

[1] In this paper, we chose to consider monotone ρ's. We chose to model the memory resource in such a way that it only responds on the same interface it was activated, hence it is not possible for the adversary to be notified of an event that causes the memory to become readable. To simplify the modelling of simulators, we consider the adversary to be eager and trying to read the memory as soon as possible and then placing the resulting data in an "intermediate buffer" that can then be collected through the *Eve*-interface at a later point.

Imperfectly Erasable Memory. To model imperfectly erasable memory, we fix ρ and split κ into two predicates, a fixed predicate that checks only the history and a freely specifiable predicate Ξ that checks only the adversary's choice ξ. The other parameters Σ and ψ can be freely specified. We denote this resource by $\mathsf{IM}\langle\Sigma, \psi, \Xi\rangle$. We consider only resources allowing for a single *World*-event. The predicate ρ returns true only if the first recorded event in the history is a `weaken` command (as opposed to an `erase` command). The fixed predicate returns true if the first two recorded events in the history are an `erase` command followed by a `weaken` command (if `weaken` was called first, the adversary should call `read` and not `leak`), and no `leak` query succeeded previously. Thus, we consider only resources allowing for a single *World*-event. The predicate κ returns true if the fixed predicate does so and Ξ accepts ξ. In the next section, when we discuss erasability amplification, we further specialize this resource.

4   Constructing Better Memory Resources

In this section we consider constructions of memory resources with stronger security properties from memory resources with weaker ones. We start by showing how to use our memory resources in protocol constructions and then explain the issues that arise when doing so. Thereafter, we describe several specializations of the imperfectly erasable memory resource $\mathsf{IM}\langle\cdot\rangle$ presented in the previous section and then show how to construct memory resources with stronger properties from ones with weaker properties. For example, we show how to construct perfectly erasable memories from memories that leak a certain number of bits. Finally, we consider the construction of a large perfectly erasable memory from a small one plus a large non-erasable memory.

4.1   Admissible Converters for Constructions Using Erasable Memory

As stated previously, one of our reasons to model memory is to be able to analyse cryptographic protocols where the adversary at some point obtains access to the memory. This means that one needs to restrict converters to use only our memory resources for storage. Assuming that an adversary in a real environment may typically not be able to get access to processor registers, we still allow a converter to store temporary values locally and use a memory resource only for persistent storage. Let us now formalize the distinction between persistent and temporary storage and the restrictions we put on converters.

The computation done by a converter is divided in *computation phases*. A phase starts when a converter is activated outside of a computation phase. Informally, a phase ends as soon as the converter responds to that activation or makes a request that is not guaranteed to be answered immediately, i.e., where there is a chance that the adversary is activated before the request completes. For example, a computation phase ends if the converter makes a request that goes over an unreliable communication network, but does not end if the converter asks to store or retrieve data from a memory resource.

In this paper, all our resources always respond on the same interface they were activated. It is then easy to define a computation phase of a converter: the phase starts as soon as the converter's outer interface is activated, and stops as soon as the converter writes on its outer interface. That is, activations of the inner interface do not interrupt the phase. However, in a more general setting, resources may respond on a different interface than the one they were activated on, and thereby activate a different party or the adversary. The definition of computation phase of converters must therefore be adjusted to take this into account.

State that is discarded at the end of a computation phase is *temporary*. State that must persist between two or more computation phases is *persistent*. (Converters must keep all persistent state in memory resources.) This distinction ensures that whenever the adversary has control, the entire internal state of a protocol is inside memory resources, and thus subject to attack.

Discussion. Other models, notably Canetti et al. and Lim [4,13], also make a distinction between storage needed during computation and persistent storage. However they do it in a way that does not cleanly separate the various layers of abstraction: they assume the existence of a constant number of "processor registers" that are perfectly erasable and place no restriction on the amount of time that data can remain in such a register. For example, their model therefore does not exclude reserving a part of the CPU registers to permanently store a cryptographic key, and use a crypto paging technique [20,21] to have as much (computationally secure) perfectly erasable memory as required. Thus, to ensure a meaningful analysis, a similar restriction would have to be used in their approach.

4.2   Memory Erasability Amplification

We now describe several variants of imperfectly erasable memory that are relevant for practice, namely memory that leaks a constant number of bits, memory that leaks bits with a certain probability, memory that leaks a noisy version of the data, and memory that leaks the output of a length-shrinking function of the data. We then show how to construct memories which leak less information from each of these variants, in other words, we show how to amplify the erasability of each variant.

4.2.1   Amplifying Memory Leaking Exactly d Symbols

On many file systems, unlinked files are not necessarily immediately erased in their entirety. For instance, on most SSDs, deleted data persists until the flash translation layer flashes the corresponding erase block. Furthermore, data may survive erasure if it was copied to another medium, such as a cache, the swap space or backups. An adversary could therefore potentially recover parts of data that were believed to be erased. In full generality, the adversary may not obtain the entire data but still have an influence on which parts of the data she obtains in an attack, e.g., because she can steal just one backup tape, because of the cost of the attack or time constrains forcing her to choose the most juicy parts of the data, or because the adversary could influence the system beforehand to some degree and ensure that the parts of the data she is interested in were backed-up/swapped/cached.

To model such a scenario, we define the memory resource $\mathsf{IMD}\langle \Phi, n, d \rangle$ storing n symbols of an alphabet Φ, and where the adversary can obtain exactly d symbols of his choice when the memory leaks. This resource is a specialization of $\mathsf{IM}\langle \Sigma, \psi, \Xi \rangle$, where $\Sigma = \Phi^n$, ψ is the identity function, and Ξ accepts any function that reads at most d symbols from LDAT.

In a real setting, and depending on the nature of the attack, the adversary may obtain less than d symbols or might not have full control over which symbols she obtains. A memory resource in such a setting can be perfectly constructed from $\mathsf{IMD}\langle \Phi, n, d \rangle$ with the identity converter. (A memory resource where the adversary can obtain more than d symbols with a small probability ϵ can also be constructed from $\mathsf{IMD}\langle \Phi, n, d \rangle$, albeit with an error probability equal to ϵ; see, e.g., Sect. 4.2.2.)

The converter I2P shown in Fig. 3 constructs $\mathsf{PM}\langle \Phi^k \rangle$ from $\mathsf{IMD}\langle \Phi, n, d \rangle$. This converter is parametrized by an AoNT (cf. Sect. 2.4). In a nutshell, I2P just applies the AoNT encoding algorithm $\mathsf{aenc}(\cdot)$ to the incoming data before storing it in $\mathsf{IMD}\langle\cdot\rangle$; and decodes the encoded data stored in $\mathsf{IMD}\langle\cdot\rangle$ using $\mathsf{adec}(\cdot)$ before outputting it. The erasure command is transmitted to $\mathsf{IMD}\langle\cdot\rangle$ directly. The privacy property of the AoNT guarantees that if the adversary obtains d symbols of the encoded data, she obtains no meaningful information about the original data. Thus, we obtain the following theorem.

The converter I2P$\langle \Phi, k, \mathsf{aenc}, \mathsf{adec} \rangle$:

Behavior:
- *Outer*($\mathtt{store}, \mu \in \Phi^k$): *Inner* $\xleftarrow{\$}$ ($\mathtt{store}, \mathsf{aenc}(\mu)$). *Inner* $\rightarrow$ (). *Outer* $\leftarrow$ ().
- *Outer*($\mathtt{retrieve}$): *Inner* $\leftarrow$ ($\mathtt{retrieve}$). *Inner* $\rightarrow \phi$.
    If $\phi \neq$ (): *Outer* $\leftarrow \mathsf{adec}(\phi)$. Else: *Outer* $\leftarrow$ ().
- *Outer*($\mathtt{erase}$): *Inner* $\leftarrow$ ($\mathtt{erase}$). *Inner* $\rightarrow$ (). *Outer* $\leftarrow$ ().

Fig. 3. The converter I2P constructing $\mathsf{PM}\langle \Phi^k \rangle$ from $\mathsf{IMD}\langle \Phi, n, d \rangle$. The converter is parametrized by a (Φ, n, d, k)-AoNT ($\mathsf{aenc}, \mathsf{adec}$).

Theorem 4.1. *If* ($\mathsf{aenc}, \mathsf{adec}$) *is an ϵ-secure (Φ, n, d, k)-AoNT, then*
$$\mathsf{IMD}\langle \Phi, n, d \rangle \xrightarrow{\pi, \sigma, \epsilon} \mathsf{PM}\langle \Phi^k \rangle,$$
where $\pi = $ I2P$\langle \Phi, k, \mathsf{aenc}, \mathsf{adec} \rangle$ and σ is the simulator provided in the proof.

The proof this theorem is found in the full version of this paper. A similar theorem can be stated for the computational case.

Multi-part Leakage. It is sometimes the case that the memory is segmented into multiple independent parts, e.g., over two different file systems on different partitions of the same physical disc and that each part reacts differently to an attack.

We define a multi-part memory resource $\mathsf{IMDP}\langle\Phi, s_1, s_2, d\rangle$ storing data in $\Phi^{s_1+s_2}$. The memory is divided in two parts, the first part consisting of the first s_1 symbols and the second of the other s_2 symbols. The first part of the memory leaks similarly to $\mathsf{IMD}\langle\Phi, s_1, d\rangle$, while the second one leaks the entire data. When attacking the memory, the adversary must submit the choice of leakage for the first part *before* obtaining the leakage of the second part. We get the following theorem, the proof of which is similar to the one of Theorem 4.1 and is omitted.

Theorem 4.2. *If* (aenc, adec) *is an ϵ-secure $(\Phi, n + \nu, d, k)$-AoNT with public part ν, then*

$$\mathsf{IMDP}\langle\Phi, n, \nu, d\rangle \xrightarrow{\ \pi,\sigma,\epsilon\ } \mathsf{PM}\langle\Phi^k\rangle,$$

where $\pi = \mathsf{I2P}\langle\Phi, k, \mathsf{aenc}, \mathsf{adec}\rangle$ and σ is the simulator provided in the proof.

A similar theorem can be stated for the computational case.

Choice of Alphabet. The most suitable choice of Φ depends on the application. Possible values are $\mathrm{GF}(2)$ when bits can be leaked independently, e.g., because the adversary must read them one by one from the surface of a disc; $\mathrm{GF}(2^{512\cdot 8})$ to $\mathrm{GF}(2^{4096\cdot 8})$ when the smallest leakable unit is a file system block; or even $\mathrm{GF}(2^{128\cdot 1024\cdot 8})$ to $\mathrm{GF}(2^{8192\cdot 1024\cdot 8})$ when the smallest leakable unit is an erase blocks of an SSD. In the latter two cases, it is also possible to design the system in such a way that only parts of a block are written to before proceeding with the next one, thereby reducing the alphabet size and limiting the amount of exposure per leaked block.

4.2.2   Amplifying Memory Leaking Symbols with Probability p

Above, we modelled an adversary who chooses which symbols leak from the imperfect memory. In practice, the adversary may not have this much power: for example, some parts of a deleted file might still be present in the journal, but the adversary has no control over which ones. To model this, let us now consider an adversary who obtains each symbol of the data uniformly and independently at random with a certain probability p during a leakage. We denote a memory with such a behaviour by $\mathsf{IMI}\langle\Phi, n, d\rangle$. This resource is a specialization of $\mathsf{IM}\langle\Sigma, \psi, \Xi\rangle$ where $\Sigma = \Phi^n$, ψ acts like an erasure channel with erasure probability $(1 - p)$ (i.e., each symbol of the data is transmitted correctly with probability p and otherwise is replaced with "$\perp$"), and Ξ accepts only the identity function.

One can treat $\mathsf{IMI}\langle\cdot\rangle$ similarly to $\mathsf{IMD}\langle\cdot\rangle$ in constructions with just a small statistical error, as the following observation shows. Constructing $\mathsf{PM}\langle\Phi^k\rangle$ from $\mathsf{IMI}\langle\Phi, n, p\rangle$ directly without first constructing $\mathsf{IMD}\langle\Phi, n, d\rangle$ might be more efficient (better parameters, less statistical error), but such a direct construction is out of the scope of this paper. The proof of the following observation is found in the full version of this paper.

Observation 4.3. *For all* $(n,d) \in \mathbb{N}^2$, $p \in [0,1]$, *and fields* Φ *we have that* $\mathsf{IMI}\langle\Phi,n,p\rangle \xrightarrow{id,\sigma,\epsilon} \mathsf{IMD}\langle\Phi,n,d\rangle$, *where* id *is the identity converter,* σ *is the simulator provided in the proof, and* $\epsilon = (1 - \mathrm{BinomialCDF}(d;n,p)) = \sum_{i=d+1}^{n} \binom{n}{i} p^i \cdot (1-p)^{n-i}$.

4.2.3 Amplifying Memory with Noisy Leakage

Another possible setting is that the data is written to and erased from magnetic storage, and the adversary, who has physical access to the storage medium, must make an educated guess for each bit of the data [9]. One can model this as if the data was transmitted through a noisy binary symmetric channel. We denote such a memory by $\mathsf{IMN}\langle\Phi,n,d\rangle$. This resource is a specialization of $\mathsf{IM}\langle\Sigma,\psi,\Xi\rangle$ where $\Sigma = \Phi^n$, ψ acts like a noisy $|\Phi|$-ary channel with crossover probability $(1-p)/|\Phi|$ (i.e., each symbol of the data is transmitted correctly with probability p and otherwise is replaced with a symbol drawn uniformly at random from Φ), and Ξ accepts only the identity function.

Observation 4.4. *For all* $(n,d) \in \mathbb{N}^2$, $p \in [0,1]$, *and fields* Φ *we have that* $\mathsf{IMN}\langle\Phi,n,p\rangle \xrightarrow{\pi,\sigma,0} \mathsf{IMI}\langle\Phi,n,p\rangle$, *where* $\pi = $ id *is the identity converter and* σ *is the simulator that replaces all erased symbols in the leakage by random symbols.*

4.2.4 Amplifying Memory with Limited Leakage Output Domain

Another possible setting is that the adversary does not obtain individual symbols of the data but rather a function of the data. For example, with a cache-timing attack [1], she might deduce some information about the data without recovering it completely. In general, one can consider an adversary that obtains any *length-shrinking* function of the contents of the memory. We denote such a memory by $\mathsf{IML}\langle\Sigma,v\rangle$. This resource is a specialization of $\mathsf{IM}\langle\Sigma,\psi,\Xi\rangle$, where ψ is the identity function and Ξ accepts only functions that have at most v different output values.

For any non-trivial parameters, it is not possible to construct a perfectly erasable memory from $\mathsf{IML}\langle\cdot\rangle$, because the adversary can submit a leakage function $\xi \in \Xi$ that runs the decoding logic of the converter. The reason for this is as follows. Let $v \geq 2$, $|\Sigma'| \geq 2$, $|\Sigma| \geq 2$, and let π be a converter that constructs $\mathsf{PM}\langle\Sigma'\rangle$ from $\mathsf{IML}\langle\Sigma,v\rangle$. We now show that this construction has a statistical error of at least $\frac{1}{2}$. The distinguisher chooses two distinct messages $a_0, a_1 \in \Sigma'$, flips a coin $b \xleftarrow{\$} \{0,1\}$, and stores a_b. He then makes the memory weak by setting the relevant flags on the *World*-interface and submits a leakage function ξ that returns 0 iff a_0 was encoded in $\mathsf{IML}\langle\cdot\rangle$ by using the decoding logic of π—recall that the distinguisher may depend on π. The distinguisher then outputs 1 iff ξ outputs b. No simulator will be able to properly simulate that scenario with probability more than $\frac{1}{2}$ as it does not know if the distinguisher stored a_0 or a_1.

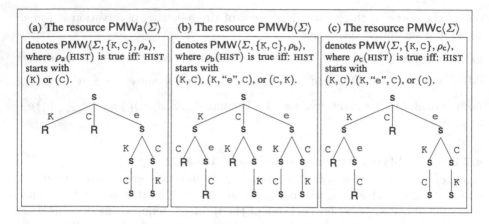

Fig. 4. Several variants of a perfectly erasable memory resource with two *World*-flags. The prefix decision trees visualize whether the adversary has read access to the memory depending on the event history HIST. A branch labelled "e" represents an erasure event, and branches labelled "K" (key) or "C" (ciphertext) represent the setting of the corresponding flags on the *World*-interface. An "R" node means that the memory is readable (and allows the adversary to collect the data at any time from then on), and an "s" (secure) node means that it does not.

The converter XPM⟨ℓ, prg⟩:

Behavior:
- *Outer*(store, $\mu \in$ GF($2^{\ell(\eta)}$)): $sk \xleftarrow{\$}$ GF(2^η). $\delta \leftarrow$ prg(sk) $+ \mu$. *Inner* ← (PM, store, sk).
  Inner → (). *Inner* ← (NM, store, δ). *Inner* → (). *Outer* ← ().
- *Outer*(retrieve): upon error in the following, abort with *Outer* ← ().
  Inner ← (PM, retrieve). *Inner* → $sk \in$ GF(2^η).
  Inner ← (NM, retrieve). *Inner* → δ. $\mu \leftarrow \delta -$ prg(sk). *Outer* ← μ.
- *Outer*(erase): *Inner* ← (PM, erase); *Inner* → (). *Outer* ← ().

Fig. 5. The converter XPM constructing a large perfectly erasable memory PMWa⟨GF($2^{\ell(\eta)}$)⟩ or PMWc⟨GF($2^{\ell(\eta)}$)⟩ using a small perfectly erasable memory PM⟨GF(2^η)⟩ and a large non-erasable memory NM⟨GF($2^{\ell(\eta)}$)⟩. The converter is parametrized by an ℓ-PRG prg, and the implicit security parameter η.

However, one can obtain a meaningful construction by starting from a memory resource with multi-part leakage. Let IMLP⟨Φ, s_1, s_2, v⟩ be analogous to IMDP⟨Φ, s_1, s_2, d⟩ defined previously, except that the first part leaks similarly to IML⟨Φ^{s_1}, v⟩. Here it is crucial to note that the function ξ submitted by the adversary can read only the first part of the memory. In particular, given a universal hash function h : $\Phi^a \times \Phi^n \mapsto \Phi^k$, one can construct the resource PM⟨Φ^k⟩ from IMLP⟨$\Phi, n, a + k, v$⟩, by using I2P with an AoNT obtained from a universal hash function (see full paper for details). The construction is $(2v2^{(k-n)/2})$-secure [3,5]. This construction is essentially the one proposed by Canetti et al. [4] and Lim [13].

4.3 Constructing a Large Perfectly Erasable Memory from a Small One

We now discuss how a small perfectly erasable memory can be used together with a large, possibly non-erasable memory to construct a large perfectly erasable memory. The basic idea underlying this construction is that of Yee et al.'s crypto paging [20,21]: one stores a cryptographic key in the small perfectly erasable memory, encrypts the data with that key, and stores the resulting ciphertext in the large, possibly non-erasable memory. The resulting resource $\mathsf{PMWa}\langle\mathrm{GF}(2^{\ell(\eta)})\rangle$ will allow the adversary to read the stored data if the resource is weakened by the environment before the user erases the key. The specification of this resource is given in Fig. 4a and the protocol XPM for the construction is provided in Fig. 5.

The resource just constructed allows the adversary to read the stored data if either the small erasable or the large non-erasable memory become weak before the user erases the key. Thus, this resource is weaker than what one would expect, i.e., it should be the case that the adversary can only read the data if $both$ underlying resources become weak before the user erases the key. The corresponding resource $\mathsf{PMWb}\langle\mathrm{GF}(2^{\ell(\eta)})\rangle$ is depicted in Fig. 4b. Unfortunately, the realization of this resource would require a non-committing and non-interactive encryption scheme, which can only be constructed in the random oracle model but not in the standard model.

However, it is possible to construct the somewhat better resource $\mathsf{PMWc}\langle\mathrm{GF}(2^{\ell(\eta)})\rangle$, shown in Fig. 4c. Here the adversary can read the stored data if the memory storing the ciphertext becomes weak before the user calls delete. It is not hard to see that $\mathsf{PMWc}\langle\mathrm{GF}(2^{\ell(\eta)})\rangle$ implies $\mathsf{PMWa}\langle\mathrm{GF}(2^{\ell(\eta)})\rangle$, essentially the simulator attached to the Eve interface of $\mathsf{PMWa}\langle\mathrm{GF}(2^{\ell(\eta)})\rangle$ has to hold back the leaked data until the non-erasable memory becomes leakable. In summary, we get the following theorem, the proof of which is found in the full paper.

Theorem 4.5. *If* prg *is a secure ℓ-PRG, then*

$$[\mathsf{PM}\langle\mathrm{GF}(2^\eta)\rangle, \mathsf{NM}\langle\mathrm{GF}(2^{\ell(\eta)})\rangle] \xrightarrow{\pi,\sigma,\epsilon} \mathsf{PMWc}\langle\mathrm{GF}(2^{\ell(\eta)})\rangle,$$

where $\pi = \mathsf{XPM}\langle\ell,\mathsf{prg}\rangle$, σ *is given in the full version, and* ϵ *is a negligible function.*

As stated above, XPM also constructs $\mathsf{PMWa}\langle\mathrm{GF}(2^{\ell(\eta)})\rangle$ from the same resources. Furthermore, in the random oracle model, a protocol that is identical to XPM except that calls to prg are replaced by calls to the random oracle, constructs $\mathsf{PMWb}\langle\mathrm{GF}(2^{\ell(\eta)})\rangle$ from the same resources.

Let us discuss our the memory resources just discussed in light of some secure memory constructions in the literature. As mentioned, Yee et al. introduce crypto paging [20,21] to let a secure co-processor encrypt its virtual memory before paging it out to its host's physical memory or hard disk. Translated to our setting, this means that the non-erasable memory is weak from the beginning. Therefore, to get meaningful guarantees, only the resource $\mathsf{PMWb}\langle \mathrm{GF}(2^{\ell(n)})\rangle$ can be used in their setting, the other two would allow the adversary to always read the data. Thus, to realize their system, Yee et al. require a non-committing and non-interactive encryption scheme (and hence random oracles).

Di Crescenzo et al. [6] consider a memory resource that allows one to update the stored data such that when the resource becomes weak the adversary can only read the data stored last. They then provide a construction for a large such resource from a small one and a large non-erasable memory. Again they assume that for both resources the data can be updated and that the non-erasable one leaks all data ever stored in it. None of our resources does allow for such updates but, as already discussed, resources that allow this can be constructed by using several of our respective resources in parallel. Thus, their security definition and construction can be indeed modelled and analysed with the memory resources we define, however, doing this is out of scope of this extended abstract.

5   New Realizations of All-or-Nothing Transforms

In Sect. 4 we saw the importance of AoNTs for constructing perfectly erasable memory from certain types of imperfectly erasable ones. In this section we present several novel AoNTs. We start by showing the dual of the I2P protocol: any protocol that constructs $\mathsf{PM}\langle \Phi^k \rangle$ from $\mathsf{IMD}\langle \Phi, n, d \rangle$ can be used to realize a (Φ, n, k, d)-AoNT. We then present a perfect AoNT with better parameters than what is found in the literature, based on the novel concept of *ramp minimum distance* of a matrix. We then show that one can combine several AoNTs to achieve an AoNT over a small field but with a large message space and a good privacy threshold d. Finally, we provide a computationally-secure AoNT over a large field that has a very large privacy threshold.

5.1   AoNT from a Protocol that Constructs $\mathsf{PM}\langle \Phi^k \rangle$ from $\mathsf{IMD}\langle \Phi, n, d \rangle$

Sect. 4.2.1 described the protocol I2P, parametrized by an AoNT, that constructs a perfectly erasable memory $\mathsf{PM}\langle \Phi^k \rangle$ from an imperfectly erasable one $\mathsf{IMD}\langle \Phi, n, d \rangle$. As the following theorem states, any protocol π (not necessarily one based on an AoNT) that constructs $\mathsf{PM}\langle \Phi^k \rangle$ from $\mathsf{IMD}\langle \Phi, n, d \rangle$ can be used to construct an AoNT using the algorithm C2A (given in Fig. 6), albeit one where adec is a probabilistic algorithm and where decoding might fail with a small probability.

Theorem 5.1. *If (π, σ, ϵ) are such that $\mathsf{IMD}\langle \Phi, n, d \rangle \xrightarrow{\pi, \sigma, \epsilon} \mathsf{PM}\langle \Phi^k \rangle$, then the algorithm $\mathsf{C2A}\langle \Phi, n, k, \pi \rangle$ is a 6ϵ-secure (Φ, n, d, k)-AoNT with a probabilistic* adec *and where decoding may fail with probability less than 2ϵ.*

The proof of this theorem is found in the full version of this paper. One can make an analogous statement in the computational case.

The algorithm C2A$\langle \Phi, n, k, \pi \rangle$:

Behavior:

- aenc($\mu \in \Phi^k$): $\pi.Outer \leftarrow$ (store, μ).
    While true:
        If $\pi.Inner \rightarrow$ (store, $\phi \in \Phi^n$): return ϕ.
        Else if anything is sent by $\pi.Inner$: $\pi.Inner \leftarrow$ ().
        Else: abort by returning $\bot$.

- adec($\phi \in \Phi^n$): $\pi.Outer \leftarrow$ (retrieve).
    While true:
        If $\pi.Inner \rightarrow$ (retrieve): $\pi.Inner \leftarrow \phi$.
        Else if $\pi.Outer \rightarrow \mu \in \Phi^k$: return μ.
        Else if $\pi.Inner \rightarrow$ (erase): abort by returning $\bot$.
        Else if anything is sent by $\pi.Inner$: $\pi.Inner \leftarrow$ ().
        Else: abort by returning $\bot$.

Fig. 6. The algorithm C2A that realizes a (Φ, n, d, k)-AoNT from a converter π, where π constructs $\mathsf{PM}\langle \Phi^k \rangle$ from $\mathsf{IMD}\langle \Phi, n, d \rangle$.

5.2 Perfectly Secure AoNT Based on Matrices with Ramp Minimum Distance

This subsection shows how one can improve the standard realization of AoNTs based on linear block codes of Canetti et al. [3] by using our novel concept of *ramp minimum distance*.

The Standard Realization. Let G be the $k \times n$ generator matrix with elements in $\mathrm{GF}(q)$ of a linear block code with minimum distance d. The encoding function of the perfectly secure $(\mathrm{GF}(q), (n + k), d, k)$-AoNT is as follows:

$$\mathsf{aenc}(a \in \mathrm{GF}(q)^k) : b \xleftarrow{\$} \mathrm{GF}(q)^n; y \leftarrow \begin{bmatrix} I_n & 0 \\ G & I_k \end{bmatrix} \begin{bmatrix} b \\ a \end{bmatrix}; \text{ return } y.$$

Further details are given in the full paper.

Let us now show how to use the concept of ramp minimal distance to construct better AoNTs.

Definition 5.2. *A $k \times n$ matrix G with elements in $\mathrm{GF}(q)$ has* ramp minimum distance d *if for every $r \in \{1, \ldots, k\}$, every $r \times (n - (d - r))$ submatrix of G has rank r.*

Note that the concept of (regular) minimum distance comes from coding theory, and requires that all $k \times (n - (d - 1))$ sub-matrices of G have rank k (which is equivalent to saying that for every $r \in \{1, \ldots, k\}$, all $r \times (n - (d - 1))$ sub-matrices of G have rank r), where G is the generator matrix of a linear block code. A matrix with minimum distance d also has a *ramp* minimum distance d (the converse is obviously not true).

Now for the generator matrix with ramp minimum distance, we can construct an AoNT and thus obtain the following theorem, the proof of which is found in the full version of this paper.

Theorem 5.3. *The standard realization of an AoNT (sketched above and detailed in the full paper), parametrized by a $k \times n$ matrix $\boldsymbol{G}$ with elements in $\mathrm{GF}(q)$ with ramp (instead of regular) minimum distance d, is a perfectly secure $(\mathrm{GF}(q), (n + k), d, k)$-AoNT.*

It remains to find a matrix with a desired ramp minimum distance. One way is to chose a random matrix, as shown by the following theorem that we prove in the full paper.

Theorem 5.4. *For all $(n, k, d) \in \mathbb{N}^3$, and all prime powers q, a $k \times n$ matrix where all elements were chosen independently and uniformly at random over $\mathrm{GF}(q)$, has ramp minimum distance d with probability at least*

$$1 - \sum_{i=1}^{k} \binom{k}{i} (q-1)^i q^{\left(H_q\left(\frac{d-i}{n}\right)-1\right)n},$$

where $H_q(x) := \begin{cases} 0 \text{ if } x = 0 \text{ or } x = 1; \\ x \log_q(q-1) - x \log_q(x) - (1-x) \log_q(1-x) \text{ if } 0 < x < 1. \end{cases}$

Unfortunately, we do not know of any efficient method to check whether a random matrix has a given ramp minimum distance. For practical parameters, however, it is feasible to generate and test such matrices with small values of k and d (e.g., less than 20).

Better AoNTs Using our Realization. Given a fixed size, it is sometimes possible to find matrices with a given ramp minimum distance but no matrix with the same (regular) minimum distance. Hence AoNTs based on matrices with a ramp minimum distance can achieve better parameters than previously known realizations. We now illustrate this fact with a numerical example. Let us determine the best message length k that a perfect AoNT with fixed parameters $n = 30$, $d = 12$, and $q = 2$ can achieve with both our realization and the standard realization. Both realizations will require a matrix with $(30 - k)$ rows and (ramp or regular, respectively) minimum distance $d = 12$. First, observe that there exists a 6×24 matrix over $\mathrm{GF}(2)$ with ramp minimum distance 12 (see the full paper). Hence using our realization, we can achieve $k = 6$. Plotkin [16] showed that a binary code with block length $2d$ and distance d can have at most $4d$ codewords. Hence there cannot exist a 6×24 matrix with (regular) minimum distance $d = 12$ (as it would generate a code with $2^6 = 64$ codewords, which is more than $4d = 48$). The best AoNT one can hope for using the standard realization thus has $k = 5$.

Statistical Security. Theorem 5.4 stated that by choosing a random generator matrix, one can achieve a certain ramp minimum distance with a certain probability $(1 - \epsilon)$. If one uses our realization, but without checking that the matrix actually has the required ramp minimum distance, then the resulting AoNT will be perfectly secure with probability $(1 - \epsilon)$. (Note that this is different from saying that the AoNT is ϵ-secure, as the randomness used to generate the AoNT is not part of the distinguishing experiment.) In practice, one can make ϵ very small, e.g., $\epsilon < 2^{-\eta}$, and it might be acceptable to chose a random matrix and not check its properties to realize an AoNT.

5.3 Realizing a Perfectly Secure AoNT over a Small Field by Combining AoNTs

Designing perfectly-secure AoNTs over very small fields, e.g., $GF(2)$, is hard. The previous realization does not scale well to large message lengths k and large privacy thresholds d; and realizations based on Shamir's secret sharing scheme are always over large fields—using such a $(GF(2^a), n, d, k)$-AoNT unmodified over $GF(2)$ instead would result in a $(GF(2), an, d, ak)$-AoNT with a poor privacy threshold d. The leakage of any $GF(2)$ element means that the entire original $GF(2^a)$ element is compromised. We now show how to combine the two approaches to realize a perfectly secure AoNT over a small field but with large k and d.

Our realization requires two AoNTs, a "fine-grained" one and a "coarse-grained" one, operating over a small field S and a large field L, respectively. We require that the number of elements of L be a power of that of S and that $k^s = \log(|L|)/\log(|S|)$ be true. We need to interpret a string of $k^\ell k^s$ elements from S as a string of k^ℓ elements of L, an operation we denote by $S \triangleright L$. The converse operation is denoted $L \triangleright S$.

The encoding function of our combined AoNT then works as follows. One first applies the coarse-grained AoNT to the whole data vector and then applies the fine-grained AoNT to each element of the result:

$$\mathsf{aenc}(\boldsymbol{a} \in S^{k^s k^\ell}):$$

$$\boldsymbol{x} \overset{\$}{\leftarrow} \mathsf{aenc}^\ell(S \triangleright L(\boldsymbol{a})); \forall j \in \{1, \ldots, n^\ell\} : \boldsymbol{b}[j] \overset{\$}{\leftarrow} \mathsf{aenc}^s(L \triangleright S(\boldsymbol{x}[j])); \text{ return } \boldsymbol{b}.$$

It's easy to see how the decoding function adec of the combined AoNT works and it is thus omitted. We have the following theorem, the proof of which is found in the full version of this paper.

Theorem 5.5. *Given a perfectly secure* (S, n^s, d^s, k^s)*-AoNT* $(\mathsf{aenc}^s, \mathsf{adec}^s)$ *and a perfectly secure* $(L, n^\ell, d^\ell, k^\ell)$*-AoNT* $(\mathsf{aenc}^\ell, \mathsf{adec}^\ell)$ *such that* $k^s = \log(|L|)/\log(|S|)$*, the AoNT* $(\mathsf{aenc}, \mathsf{adec})$ *described above is a perfectly secure* $(S, n^s n^\ell, (d^s + 1)(d^\ell + 1) - 1, k^s k^\ell)$*-AoNT.*

Numerical Example. Let us suppose that we are interested in a perfect AoNT that operates over $S = GF(2)$ and that can store a cryptographic key of size $k = 256$ bits using at most $n = 8192$ bits (a kilobyte) of memory.

If we use a $(GF(2^{10}), 819, 793, 26)$-AoNT built according to Franklin and Yung [7] unmodified over the field $GF(2)$, we get a $(GF(2), 8190, 793, 260)$-AoNT. This AoNT has a privacy threshold d of only 793 bits.

By combining a $(GF(2), 32, 11, 8)$-AoNT (which can be found by exhaustive search) with a $(GF(2^8), 255, 223, 32)$-AoNT built according to Franklin and Yung [7], one gets a $(GF(2), 8160, 2687, 256)$-AoNT. This AoNT has a much better privacy threshold d of 2687, i.e., 2687 arbitrary bits may leak to the adversary.

5.4 Computationally Secure AoNT over a Large Field from a PRG

We now present a realization of a computationally secure AoNTs over a large field $GF(2^\eta)$, where η is the security parameter. Our realization is optimal in the sense that it achieves both an optimal message length $k = n - 1$ (thus an optimal rate $(n-1)/n$) and an optimal privacy threshold $d = n - 1$. That is, the AoNT needs just a single additional element to encode a message and remains private even if the adversary obtains all but any one element.

Definition 5.6. *An ℓ-PRG where the output length is a multiple of the input length, i.e., $\mathsf{prg} : GF(2^\eta) \mapsto GF(2^\eta)^{\ell(\eta)/\eta}$, is KD-secure, if for all $i = 1, \ldots, \ell(\eta)/\eta$, these ensembles are computationally indistinguishable:*

- $\{(x_1, \ldots, x_{i-1}, x'_i, x_{i+1}, \ldots, x_{\ell(\eta)/\eta})\}_{1^\eta}$ *where $sk \xleftarrow{\$} GF(2^\eta)$, $\boldsymbol{x} \leftarrow \mathsf{prg}(sk)$, and $x'_i \leftarrow x_i + sk$.*
- $\{\boldsymbol{x}\}_{1^\eta}$ *where $\boldsymbol{x} \xleftarrow{\$} GF(2^\eta)^{\ell(\eta)/\eta}$.*

Note that this property is somewhat reminiscent of the KDM-CCA2 security of encryption functions [2].

Our realization, somewhat reminiscent of the OAEP realization of Canetti et al. [3], is as follows:

$$\mathsf{aenc}(\boldsymbol{m} \in GF(2^\eta)^{\ell(\eta)/\eta}) : \quad sk \xleftarrow{\$} GF(2^\eta); \boldsymbol{x} \leftarrow \mathsf{prg}(sk); \boldsymbol{y} \leftarrow \boldsymbol{x} + \boldsymbol{m};$$
$$\text{return } \boldsymbol{y} \| \left(sk + \sum_{i=1}^{\ell(\eta)/\eta} y_i \right).$$

$$\mathsf{adec}(\boldsymbol{y} \| z) : \qquad\qquad \text{return } \boldsymbol{y} - \mathsf{prg}\left(z - \sum_{i=1}^{\ell(\eta)/\eta} y_i \right).$$

Theorem 5.7. *Given an ℓ-PRG that is both secure and KD-secure, the realization above yields a secure $(GF(2^\eta), 1 + \ell(\eta)/\eta, \ell(\eta)/\eta, \ell(\eta)/\eta)$-AoNT.*

The proof of this theorem is found in the full version of this paper. There we further observe that Canetti et al.'s [3] computationally-secure AoNT built by combining an exposure resilient function (ERF) with a pseudo-random generator (PRG) can have an essentially arbitrarily high message length k and message rate k/n, but cannot achieve a very high privacy threshold d.

References

1. Bernstein, D.J.: Cache-timing attacks on AES. Manuscript, April 2005. https://cr.yp.to/antiforgery/cachetiming-20050414.pdf

2. Camenisch, J., Chandran, N., Shoup, V.: A public key encryption scheme secure against key dependent chosen plaintext and adaptive chosen ciphertext attacks. In: Joux, A. (ed.) EUROCRYPT 2009. LNCS, vol. 5479, pp. 351–368. Springer, Heidelberg (2009)
3. Canetti, R., Dodis, Y., Halevi, S., Kushilevitz, E., Sahai, A.: Exposure-resilient functions and all-or-nothing transforms. In: Preneel, B. (ed.) EUROCRYPT 2000. LNCS, vol. 1807, pp. 453–469. Springer, Heidelberg (2000)
4. Canetti, R., Eiger, D., Goldwasser, S., Lim, D.-Y.: How to protect yourself without perfect shredding. In: Aceto, L., Damgård, I., Goldberg, L.A., Halldórsson, M.M., Ingólfsdóttir, A., Walukiewicz, I. (eds.) ICALP 2008, Part II. LNCS, vol. 5126, pp. 511–523. Springer, Heidelberg (2008)
5. Canetti, R., Eiger, D., Goldwasser, S., Lim, D.-Y.: How to protect yourself without perfect shredding. Cryptology ePrint Archive, Report 2008/291 (2008)
6. Di Crescenzo, G., Ferguson, N., Impagliazzo, R., Jakobsson, M.: How to forget a secret. In: Meinel, C., Tison, S. (eds.) STACS 1999. LNCS, vol. 1563, pp. 500–509. Springer, Heidelberg (1999)
7. Franklin, M.K., Yung, M.: Communication complexity of secure computation (extended abstract). In: 24th ACM STOC, pp. 699–710. ACM Press, May 1992
8. Gaži, P., Maurer, U., Tackmann, B.: Manuscript. (available from the authors)
9. Gutmann, P.: Secure deletion of data from magnetic and solid-state memory. In: Proceedings of the Sixth USENIX Security Symposium, vol. 14, San Jose, CA (1996)
10. Hazay, C., Lindell, Y., Patra, A.: Adaptively secure computation with partial erasures. Cryptology ePrint Archive, Report 2015/450 (2015)
11. Jarecki, S., Lysyanskaya, A.: Adaptively secure threshold cryptography: introducing concurrency, removing erasures (extended abstract). In: Preneel, B. (ed.) EUROCRYPT 2000. LNCS, vol. 1807, pp. 221–242. Springer, Heidelberg (2000)
12. Katz, J., Lindell, Y.: Introduction to Modern Cryptography. CRC Press, Boca Raton (2015)
13. Lim, D.-Y.: The paradigm of partial erasures. Ph.D. thesis, Massachusetts Institute of Technology (2008)
14. Maurer, U.: Constructive cryptography – a new paradigm for security definitions and proofs. In: Mödersheim, S., Palamidessi, C. (eds.) TOSCA 2011. LNCS, vol. 6993, pp. 33–56. Springer, Heidelberg (2012)
15. Maurer, U., Renner, R.: Abstract cryptography. In: ICS 2011, pp. 1–21. Tsinghua University Press, January 2011
16. Plotkin, M.: Binary codes with specified minimum distance. IRE Trans. Inf. Theor. 6(4), 445–450 (1960)
17. Reardon, J., Basin, D.A., Capkun, S.: SoK: secure data deletion. In: 2013 IEEE Symposium on Security and Privacy, pp. 301–315. IEEE Computer Society Press, May 2013
18. Reardon, J., Capkun, S., Basin, D.: Data node encrypted file system: efficient secure deletion for flashmemory. In: Proceedings of the 21st USENIX Conference on Security Symposium, pp. 17–17. USENIX Association (2012)
19. Reardon, J., Ritzdorf, H., Basin, D.A., Capkun, S.: Secure data deletion from persistent media. In: ACM CCS 2013, pp. 271–284. ACM Press, November 2013
20. Yee, B.: Using secure coprocessors. Ph.D. thesis, CMU (1994)
21. Yee, B., Tygar, J.D.: Secure coprocessors in electronic commerce applications. In: Proceedings of The First USENIX Workshop on Electronic Commerce, New York (1995)

Multi-party Computation

On Adaptively Secure Multiparty Computation with a Short CRS

Ran Cohen[1]([✉]) and Chris Peikert[2]

[1] Department of Computer Science, Bar-Ilan University, Ramat Gan, Israel
cohenrb@cs.biu.ac.il
[2] Computer Science and Engineering, University of Michigan, Ann Arbor, USA
cpeikert@umich.edu

Abstract. In the setting of multiparty computation, a set of mutually distrusting parties wish to securely compute a joint function of their private inputs. A protocol is *adaptively secure* if honest parties might get corrupted *after* the protocol has started. Recently (TCC 2015) three constant-round adaptively secure protocols were presented [10,11,15]. All three constructions assume that the parties have access to a *common reference string* (CRS) whose size depends on the function to compute, even when facing semi-honest adversaries. It is unknown whether constant-round adaptively secure protocols exist, without assuming access to such a CRS.

In this work, we study adaptively secure protocols which only rely on a short CRS that is independent on the function to compute.

- First, we raise a subtle issue relating to the usage of *non-interactive non-committing encryption* within security proofs in the UC framework, and explain how to overcome it. We demonstrate the problem in the security proof of the adaptively secure oblivious-transfer protocol from [8] and provide a complete proof of this protocol.
- Next, we consider the two-party setting where one of the parties has a polynomial-size input domain, yet the other has no constraints on its input. We show that assuming the existence of adaptively secure oblivious transfer, every deterministic functionality can be computed with adaptive security in a constant number of rounds.
- Finally, we present a new primitive called *non-committing indistinguishability obfuscation*, and show that this primitive is *complete* for constructing adaptively secure protocols with round complexity independent of the function.

R. Cohen—Work supported by the European Research Council under the ERC consolidators grant agreement n. 615172 (HIPS), by a grant from the Israel Ministry of Science, Technology and Space (grant 3-10883) and by the National Cyber Bureau of Israel.

C. Peikert—This material is based upon work supported by the National Science Foundation under CAREER Award CCF-1054495 and CNS-1606362, the Alfred P. Sloan Foundation, and by a Google Research Award. The views expressed are those of the authors and do not necessarily reflect the official policy or position of the National Science Foundation, the Sloan Foundation, or Google.

© Springer International Publishing Switzerland 2016
V. Zikas and R. De Prisco (Eds.): SCN 2016, LNCS 9841, pp. 129–146, 2016.
DOI: 10.1007/978-3-319-44618-9_7

1   Introduction

1.1   Background

In the setting of *secure multiparty computation*, a set of mutually distrusting parties wish to jointly compute a function on their private inputs in a secure manner. Loosely speaking, the security requirements ensure that even if a subset of dishonest parties collude, nothing is learned from the protocol other than the output (*privacy*), and the output is distributed according to the prescribed functionality (*correctness*). This threat is normally modeled by a central adversarial entity, that might corrupt a subset of the parties and control them. A protocol is considered secure if whatever an adversary can achieve when attacking an execution of the protocol, can be emulated in an ideal world, where an incorruptible trusted party helps the parties to compute the function.

Initial constructions of secure protocols were designed under the assumption that the adversary is *static*, meaning that the set of corrupted parties is determined prior to the beginning of the protocol's execution [20,31]. Starting from the work of Beaver and Haber [2] and of Canetti et al. [7], protocols that remain secure facing *adaptive* adversaries were considered. In this setting, the adversary can decide which parties to corrupt during the course of the protocol and based on its dynamic view. Adaptive security forms a greater challenge compare to static security, in particular because the adversary can corrupt honest parties *after* the protocol has completed. Furthermore, it can corrupt *all* the parties, thus learning all the randomness that was used in the protocol.[1]

The first adaptively secure protocol, which remains secure facing an arbitrary number of corrupted parties, was presented by Canetti et al.[8]. They showed that under some standard cryptographic assumptions, any *adaptively well-formed* functionality[2] can be securely computed facing adaptive malicious adversaries. This result follows the GMW paradigm [20], and consists of two stages: First, a protocol secure against adaptive semi-honest adversaries was constructed. This protocol is secure in the plain model, where no setup assumptions are needed; however, the number of communication rounds in this protocol depends on the circuit-depth of the underlying functionality. In the second stage, the protocol was compiled into a protocol secure against adaptive malicious adversaries; the semi-honest to malicious compiler, presented in [8], maintains the round complexity, and is secure assuming that all parties have access to a *common reference string* (CRS).[3]

Recently, three adaptively secure protocols that run in a constant number of rounds were independently presented by Canetti et al. [10], Dachman-

---

[1] In this work we do not assume the existence *secure erasures*, meaning that we do not rely on the ability of an honest party to erase specific parts of its memory.

[2] An adaptively well-formed functionality is a functionality that reveals its random input in case all parties are corrupted [8].

[3] Since the protocol of [8] is designed in the UC framework of Canetti [5], security against malicious adversaries requires some form of a trusted-setup assumption, see [6,9,27].

Soled et al. [11] and Garg and Polychroniadou [15]. All three protocols are designed in the CRS model and share the idea of embedding inside the CRS an obfuscated program that receives the circuit to compute as one of its input variables. It follows that the *size* of the CRS depends of the *size* of the circuit, and moreover, the CRS is needed even when considering merely semi-honest adversaries. Dachman-Soled et al. [11] and Garg and Polychroniadou [15] raised the question of whether these requirements are necessary.

1.2   Our Contribution

In this work we consider *adaptive security with a short CRS*. By this we mean two security notions: adaptive security facing semi-honest adversaries in the plain model (i.e., without a CRS) and adaptive security facing malicious adversaries in the CRS model, where the CRS does not depend on the *size* of the circuit to compute.

Non-interactive Non-committing Encryption in the UC Framework. A non-interactive non-committing encryption scheme is a public-key encryption scheme augmented with the ability to generate a fake public key and a fake ciphertext that can later be explained as an encryption of any message. This primitive serves as a building block for several cryptographic constructions, e.g., instantiating adaptively secure communication channels [7], adaptively secure oblivious transfer (OT) [8] and leakage-resilient protocols [3].

Although (interactive) non-committing encryption (NCE) was introduced well before the standard security models for adaptive security have been formalized, mainly the *sequential-composition* framework of [4] and the *universal-composability (UC) framework* of [5], it has been a folklore belief that non-interactive NCE is secure in these frameworks. We revisit the security of non-interactive NCE and show that although it is straightforward to prove the security in the framework of sequential composition, it is not as obvious in the UC framework. The reason lies in a subtle difference between the two frameworks: in the framework of [4], all the parties are initialized with their inputs *prior* to the beginning of the protocol, whereas in the UC framework, the environment can adaptively provide inputs to the parties *after* the protocol has started.

This may lead to the following attack. The environment first activates the receiver that generates a public key. This is simulated by generating the (fake) non-committing public key and ciphertext. Next, the adversary corrupts the receiver and learns its random coins (before the sender has been activated with input). At this point, the simulator must explain the key generation *before* the plaintext has been determined. Finally, the environment activates the sender with a random message. The problem is that once the random coins for the key generation have been fixed, the ciphertext becomes committing, and with a non-negligible probability will fail to decrypt to the random plaintext.

Not realizing these subtleties may lead to incomplete security proofs when using non-interactive NCE as a building block for protocols in the UC framework. We show that the simulator can in fact cater for such form of attacks, without any adjustments to the protocols, by carefully combining between non-committing ciphertexts and committing ciphertexts during the simulation. We thus prove that the definition of non-interactive NCE is valid in the UC framework. We further show that the proof of security of the adaptively secure OT in Canetti et al. [8] is incomplete and explain how to rectify it. We emphasize that the results in [8] are valid, and merely the proof is incomplete.

Functionalities with One-Sided Polynomial-Size Domain. We next consider deterministic two-party functionalities $f(x_1, x_2)$, where the input domain of P_1, denoted D_1, is of polynomial-size. We observe that in this situation, P_2 can locally compute f on its input x_2 and *every* possible input of P_1 and obtain all possible outputs. All that P_1 needs to do now is to select the output corresponding to its input x_1. Therefore, the computation of such functionalities boils down to the ability to compute 1-out-of-$|D_1|$ adaptively secure oblivious transfer. Using the adaptively secure OT from [8], we conclude that for every such functionality there exists a three-message protocol that is secure in the presence of adaptive semi-honest adversaries. Security against malicious adversaries follows using the CLOS compiler.

This result can be interpreted in two ways. On the one hand, it shows that restricting the domain of one of the parties yields a constant-round adaptively secure protocol. On the other hand, it shows that in order to try and prove a lower bound for constant-round adaptively secure protocols in general, one must consider either functionalities with super-polynomial input domains, or probabilistic functionalities.

Non-committing Indistinguishability Obfuscation. An indistinguishability obfuscator $i\mathcal{O}$ [1] is a machine that given a circuit, creates an "unintelligible" version of it, while maintaining its functionality. "Unintelligible" means, in this case, that given two circuits of the same length that compute exactly the same function, it is infeasible to distinguish between an obfuscation of the first circuit from an obfuscation of the second. This primitive has been shown to be useful for a vast amount of applications, and recently led to a construction of constant-round adaptively secure protocols in the CRS model [10,11,15].

All three protocols [10,11,15] share a clever idea of embedding an obfuscated program inside the CRS, such that a certain amount of the randomness that is used in the execution of the protocol is kept hidden, even if all parties are eventually corrupted. In this section we explore a different approach to this problem, inspired by the concept of NCE. We present an adaptive analogue for $i\mathcal{O}$ called *non-committing indistinguishability obfuscator*, which essentially allows the simulator to produce an obfuscated circuit for some circuit class, and later, given any circuit in the class, produce appropriate random coins explaining the obfuscation process. We then show that assuming the existence of non-committing $i\mathcal{O}$, every adaptively well-formed functionality can be computed with adaptive security and round complexity that is independent of the functionality.

We emphasize that currently we do not know how to construct non-committing $i\mathcal{O}$, or even if such a construction is possible. Rather, this result serves as a reduction from the problem of constructing adaptively secure protocols with round complexity independent of the function to the problem of constructing non-committing $i\mathcal{O}$. We note that the cryptographic literature has previously considered several complete primitives that *cannot* be instantiated in the plain model, e.g., "simultaneous broadcast" which is complete for partial fairness [24] and "fair reconstruction" which is complete for complete fairness [21]. In contrast, no such lower bound is known for the complete primitive presented in this work. We leave it as an interesting open question to determine whether non-committing $i\mathcal{O}$ can be instantiated in the plain model under standard assumptions or not.

By a non-committing indistinguishability obfuscator for some class of equivalent circuits (i.e., circuits that compute the same function), we mean an $i\mathcal{O}$ scheme for this class, augmented with a simulation algorithm that generates an obfuscated circuit $\tilde{C}$, such that later, given any circuit C from the class, it is possible to generate random coins that explain the obfuscated circuit $\tilde{C}$ as an obfuscation of the circuit C. It is not hard to see that if non-committing $i\mathcal{O}$ schemes exist in general, then the polynomial hierarchy collapses (see Sect. 5). In order to overcome this barrier, we consider a limited set of circuit classes, which turns out to be sufficient for our needs. In particular, we consider classes of equivalent "constant circuits", i.e., all circuits in the class are of the same size, receive no input and output the same value.

We next explain how to use non-committing $i\mathcal{O}$ in order to construct a protocol for any two-party functionality f, where the round complexity depends on the obfuscator rather than on f (this idea extends in a straightforward way to the multiparty setting). First, the parties use any adaptively secure protocol, e.g., the protocol from [8], to compute an intermediate functionality that given the parties' inputs and a circuit to compute f, hard-wires the input values to the input wires of the circuit. This way the intermediate functionality generates a "constant circuit" computing the desired output. Next, the intermediate functionality obfuscates this "constant circuit" using random coins provided by the parties and outputs to each party an obfuscated constant circuit. Finally, each party locally computes the output of the obfuscated constant circuit.

The underlying idea is that upon the first corruption request, the ideal-process adversary learns both the input and the output of the corrupted party, and so can prepare a simulated obfuscated constant circuit that outputs the correct value. Upon the second corruption request, the ideal-process adversary learns the input of the second party and can prepare the constant circuit as generated by the intermediate functionality. Using the non-committing properties of the obfuscation, the random coins explaining the obfuscated circuit can be computed at this point, and so the ideal-process adversary can correctly adjust the random coins that are used for the obfuscation.

1.3   Additional Related Work

Constant-round protocols that are secure facing adaptive adversaries corrupting an arbitrary number of parties that rely on a short CRS are not known to exist in general. Nonetheless, positive results have been achieved in weaker models.

In a model where the CRS can depend on the function, Canetti et al. [10], Dachman-Soled et al. [11] and Garg and Polychroniadou [15] have independently presented constant-round protocols that are adaptively secure facing an arbitrary number of corrupted parties. Garg and Sahai [16] showed that in the plain model (without assuming a CRS) constant-round protocols that are adaptively secure facing malicious adversaries, cannot be proven secure using a black-box simulator. The authors further showed that using non-black-box techniques, there exists a constant-round adaptively secure multiparty protocol, resilient to corruptions of all but one of the parties.

In case the adaptive adversary cannot corrupt all the parties, i.e., at least one party remains honest, there exist several constant-round protocols. Katz and Ostrovsky [25] showed that any statically secure constant-round two-party protocol can be transformed into an adaptive protocol with a single corruption by wrapping the communication with non-committing encryption. Hazay and Patra [22] achieved better efficiency using one-sided secure primitives. In the multiparty case, Damgård and Ishai [12] constructed a constant-round adaptively secure protocol assuming an honest majority. Compiling this protocol with the IPS compiler from Ishai et al. [23] yields a constant-round adaptively secure protocol that tolerates corruptions of all but one of the parties. Damgård et al. [14] used equivocal FHE to get better concrete constants for the round complexity.

Assuming the existence of secure erasures, Lindell [28] constructed a constant-round protocol that UC-realizes any two-party functionality facing adaptive semi-honest adversaries.

Organization of the Paper

In Sect. 2 we discuss the subtleties relating to non-interactive NCE and in Sect. 3, the implications to the security proof of the adaptive OT protocol from [8]. In Sect. 4 we construct a constant-round two-party protocol for one-sided polynomial-size domain. In Sect. 5 we define the notion of non-committing $i\mathcal{O}$ and show that this is a complete primitive for adaptively secure protocols with round complexity independent of the function.

2   Universally Composable Non-Interactive NCE

Non-committing encryption (NCE) is a cryptographic tool, used mainly for constructing adaptively secure multiparty protocols. This notion was first introduced by Canetti et al. [7] as an analogue in the adaptive setting to the instantiation of statically secure communication channels (using "standard" public-key encryption schemes). Since the introduction of NCE, further applications have been based on this primitive, for example, adaptively secure oblivious transfer [8] and leakage-resilient protocols [3].

When constructing adaptively secure protocols, two security models are normally considered: the framework of [4] which provides *sequential composition* and the *universal-composability (UC) framework* of [5]. The definition of NCE has evolved over the years, starting from a multiparty protocol instantiating the *secure message transmission* functionality and stabilizing on a non-interactive definition, which is an extension of standard public-key encryption schemes. Although it is fairly easy to verify that the various definitions are equivalent in the framework of [4], certain subtleties arise when considering non-interactive NCE in the UC framework. Not realizing these subtleties may lead to incomplete security proofs when using non-interactive NCE as a building block for UC-secure protocols. In this section, we prove that the definition of non-interactive NCE is valid in the UC framework.

2.1   Non-Committing Encryption

Canetti et al. [7] introduced the notion of NCE as an analogue to the way that public-key encryption is used to instantiate secure channels in the static setting. That is, NCE is defined as a multiparty protocol realizing the n-party functionality $f_{\mathsf{SMT}}(\mu, \lambda, \ldots, \lambda) = (\lambda, \mu, \lambda, \ldots, \lambda),$[4] for $\mu \in \{0,1\}^*$, that is secure in the presence of adaptive semi-honest adversaries that can corrupt a subset of the parties. The authors constructed an n-party protocol that is an $(n-1)$-resilient NCE scheme assuming the existence of a common-domain trapdoor system, and observed that basing the protocol on specific number-theoretic assumptions, such as RSA or CDH, yields two-party protocols of two rounds.

The definition above encounters several weaknesses. It considers a multiparty protocol in order to compute essentially a functionality involving two parties. In addition, the definition allows a subset of the parties to remain uncorrupted, which is undesirable in order to achieve composition of protocols in the adaptive setting. Furthermore, the adversary is limited to be semi-honest, and finally, the security model of [7] is somewhat weak as it does not even allow for sequential composition. Following these observations, Damgård and Nielsen [13] introduced a stronger definition of NCE as a two-party protocol for the two-party secure message transmission functionality f_{SMT}, in the presence of adaptive malicious adversaries, in the framework of Canetti [4].

Definition 1 (Strong NCE). *A strong non-committing encryption is a two-party protocol that securely computes the two-party functionality $f_{\mathsf{SMT}}(\mu, \lambda) = (\lambda, \mu)$, for $\mu \in \{0,1\}^*$, in the presence of adaptive malicious adversaries that can corrupt an arbitrary number of parties.*

The definition above does not require non-interactiveness, and indeed the authors proposed an interactive strong NCE protocol, assuming the existence of simulatable public-key encryption schemes.

---

[4] The input of P_1 is μ, the output of P_2 is μ, and all other parties have no input nor output.

Non-interactive NCE can be defined by extending Definition 1 and requiring that the protocol will consist of 2 rounds. However, proving that a protocol is adaptively secure is quite a tedious task. A simpler definition that captures the non-interactive property of non-committing encryption is given by Canetti et al. [8]. According to this definition, an NCE scheme is a public-key encryption scheme in which public keys and ciphertexts can be simulated and later be explained for any message.

Definition 2 (Non-interactive NCE). *A non-interactive non-committing (bit) encryption scheme consists of four algorithms* (Gen, Enc, Dec, Sim) *such that the following properties hold:*

- *The triplet* (Gen, Enc, Dec) *forms a public-key encryption scheme.*
- *Sim is a simulation algorithm that on input* 1^κ, *outputs* $(pk, c, \rho_G^0, \rho_E^0, \rho_G^1, \rho_E^1)$, *such that for any* $\mu \in \{0,1\}$ *the following distributions are computationally indistinguishable:*
    - *the joint view of an honest sender and an honest receiver in a normal encryption of* μ

$$\{(pk, c, r_G, r_E) \mid (sk, pk) = \text{Gen}(1^\kappa; r_G), c = \text{Enc}(pk, \mu; r_E)\},$$

    - *the simulated view of an encryption of* μ

$$\{(pk, c, \rho_G^\mu, \rho_E^\mu) \mid (pk, c, \rho_G^0, \rho_E^0, \rho_G^1, \rho_E^1) \leftarrow \text{Sim}(1^\kappa)\}.$$

It is easy to verify that in the framework of [4], non-interactive NCE as in Defnition 2 implies strong NCE. This follows since upon a corruption of either party, the simulator learns the message μ and can provide the appropriate randomness.

2.2 Non-Interactive NCE in the UC Framework

The definition of strong NCE can be easily adjusted to the UC framework, by considering protocols that UC-realize the secure message transmission ideal functionality $\mathcal{F}_{\text{SMT}}^l$ (see the full version). It is also not hard to see that the (interactive) protocol presented in [13] is UC-secure. However, when trying to use non-interactive NCE in the UC framework, things are not as immediate. Consider the standard protocol for realizing $\mathcal{F}_{\text{SMT}}^l$ using non-interactive NCE, as presented in Protocol 1.

The difficulty arises from a subtle difference between the framework of [4] and the UC framework. In the former, the parties are set with their inputs *before* the protocol begins, whereas in the later, the environment can adaptively set the inputs of the parties, meaning that parties may be set with inputs *after* the protocol has started. This may lead into a potential attack on Protocol 1 in the UC framework. The environment first activates the receiver P_2 (without input). The adversary waits for the public key pk to be sent from P_2 to P_1, and corrupts P_2 after it is sent. At this point, the internal state of P_2, which consists of the random coins r_G, used to generate (sk, pk), is revealed to the adversary which

---

Protocol 1 (Non-Interactive NCE).

Let (Gen, Enc, Dec, Sim) be a non-interactive NCE scheme.

- Upon the first activation with sid, the receiver P_2 computes $(sk, pk) \leftarrow$ Gen(1^κ) and sends (sid, pk) to P_1.
- Upon receiving (send, sid, μ) from $\mathcal{Z}$ and having received (sid, pk) from P_2, party P_1 encrypts the message $c \leftarrow \text{Enc}_{pk}(\mu)$ and sends (sid, c) to P_2.
- Having received (sid, c) from P_1, party P_2 decrypts $\mu' = \text{Dec}_{sk}(c)$ and outputs (sent, sid, μ').

The secure message transmission protocol

can pass it to the environment. Next, the environment activates the sender P_1 with a uniformly chosen bit $\mu \in_R \{0, 1\}$, and the protocol resumes: P_1 encrypts $c \leftarrow \text{Enc}_{pk}(\mu)$ and sends the ciphertext c to P_2. Once the adversary receives c, it sends it to the environment. The environment now has possession of r_G and c, and can verify that c decrypts to μ.

The ideal-process adversary cannot use committing public key and ciphertext, generated by Gen and Enc, during the simulation, since he must be able to explain the transcript upon a late corruption of the parties (after the bit μ has been provided by the environment). However, if the ideal-process adversary simulates this scenario using non-committing public key and ciphertext, generated as $(pk, c, \rho_G^0, \rho_E^0, \rho_G^1, \rho_E^1) \leftarrow \text{Sim}(1^\kappa)$, it needs to guess whether to reveal ρ_G^0 or ρ_G^1 as the random coins of P_1 upon the first corruption, and the ciphertext c will fail to decrypt to μ with probability $1/2$.

Fortunately, there is a solution to this issue. The key observation is that although for any simulated public key pk there exists a ciphertext c such that the pair (pk, c) is equivocal, the public key pk can still be used to encrypt other messages, albeit in a committing way. Therefore, if the ideal-process adversary $\mathcal{S}$ generates $(pk, c, \rho_G^0, \rho_E^0, \rho_G^1, \rho_E^1) \leftarrow \text{Sim}(1^\kappa)$ and receives a corruption request of the receiver P_2 after the first message pk has been simulated and before the sender P_1 has been activated with an input, $\mathcal{S}$ can choose the random coins for P_2 arbitrarily between ρ_G^0 and ρ_G^1. Say $\mathcal{S}$ sets ρ_G^0 as the random coins, this means that c is now a committing encryption of 0, however, it will no longer be used. Next, once the environment activates P_1 with some bit μ, $\mathcal{S}$ receives μ from $\mathcal{F}_{\text{SMT}}^l$ and can use the public key pk with fresh random coins r_E in order to encrypt μ as $c' = \text{Enc}_{pk}(\mu; r_E)$. The second message is now simulated using c' rather than c. Upon a late corruption of P_1, $\mathcal{S}$ sets the random coins to be r_E. Indistinguishability from the view of $\mathcal{A}$ in the real execution follows since otherwise the simulated public key generated using Sim can be distinguished from a public key generated using Gen.

Theorem 2. *If* (Gen, Enc, Dec, Sim) *is a non-interactive non-committing encryption scheme then Protocol 1 UC-realizes* $\mathcal{F}_{\text{SMT}}^l$, *in the presence of adaptive malicious adversaries.*

The proof of Theorem 2 can be found in the full version of this paper.

3   Proof of the Adaptively Secure OT from CLOS

In this section we show that the proof of security of the adaptively secure OT in [8] (see also Lindell [27]) is incomplete and explain how to rectify it. We emphasize that the results in [8] are valid, and merely the proof is incomplete.

Canetti et al. [8] used an augmented version of non-interactive NCE in order to construct a protocol instantiating the adaptively secure 1-out-of-ℓ oblivious-transfer functionality $\mathcal{F}_{OT}^\ell$ (see the full version). They considered a non-interactive NCE scheme with the additional algorithm OGen which allows to obliviously sample public keys without knowing their secret keys.

Definition 3 (Augmented Non-interactive NCE). *An* augmented non-interactive non-committing encryption scheme *is a non-interactive NCE scheme* (Gen, Enc, Dec, Sim) *augmented with an oblivious-sampling algorithm for public keys* $pk \leftarrow \text{OGen}(1^\kappa)$. *We require that the distribution of a public key generated by* Gen *is computationally indistinguishable from a public key generated by* OGen, *i.e.,*

$$\{pk \mid (sk, pk) \leftarrow \text{Gen}(1^\kappa)\} \stackrel{c}{\equiv} \{pk \mid pk \leftarrow \text{OGen}(1^\kappa)\}.$$

Furthermore, the algorithm OGen *has invertible sampling, meaning that there exists an algorithm* I_{OGen} *such that the following distributions are computationally indistinguishable*

$$\{(1^\kappa, pk, r) \mid pk = \text{OGen}(1^\kappa; r)\} \stackrel{c}{\equiv} \{(1^\kappa, pk, I_{\text{OGen}}(1^\kappa, pk)) \mid (sk, pk) \leftarrow \text{Gen}(1^\kappa)\}.$$

Protocol 3 describes the adaptive OT protocol from [8]. The idea behind this construction is for the receiver to generate ℓ public keys such that it knows the secret key only to the ith one. The sender encrypts every message using the corresponding public key and sends all the ciphertexts to the receiver. The receiver can decrypt only the ith ciphertext and thus obtain only x_i.

Protocol 3 (Adaptive OT).

Let (Gen, OGen, Enc, Dec, Sim) be a augmented non-interactive NCE scheme.

- Given input (receiver, sid, i), the receiver R computes $(sk, pk_i) \leftarrow \text{Gen}(1^\kappa)$ and runs $\ell - 1$ times $pk_j \leftarrow \text{OGen}(1^\kappa)$ for $j \in [\ell] \setminus \{i\}$. Then R sends (sid, $pk_1, \ldots, pk_\ell$) to T.
- Given input (sender, sid, $x_1, \ldots, x_\ell$), and having received (sid, $pk_1, \ldots, pk_\ell$) from R, sender T computes $c_j \leftarrow \text{Enc}_{pk_j}(x_j)$ for $j \in [\ell]$, and sends (sid, $c_1, \ldots, c_\ell$) to R.
- Having received (sid, $c_1, \ldots, c_\ell$) from T, receiver R computes $x_i = \text{Dec}_{sk}(c_i)$ and outputs (sid, x_i).

The adaptive, semi-honest oblivious transfer protocol [8]

Canetti et al. [8, Claim 4.2] proved that assuming (Gen, OGen, Enc, Dec, Sim) is an augmented non-interactive NCE scheme, then Protocol 3 UC-realizes $\mathcal{F}_{OT}^\ell$

in the presence of adaptive semi-honest adversaries. The idea behind the proof is for S to produce a non-committing transcript, i.e., for every $j \in [\ell]$, to generate $(pk_j, c_j, \rho^0_{G,j}, \rho^0_{E,j}, \rho^1_{G,j}, \rho^1_{E,j}) \leftarrow \mathsf{Sim}(1^\kappa)$. Next, the first message is simulated as $(\mathsf{sid}, pk_1, \ldots, pk_\ell)$ whereas the second message is simulated as $(\mathsf{sid}, c_1, \ldots, c_\ell)$. Upon a corruption of the ideal sender, S learns its input $(\mathsf{sender}, \mathsf{sid}, x_1, \ldots, x_\ell)$ and sets the virtual sender's random coins to be $(\rho^{x_1}_{E,1}, \ldots, \rho^{x_\ell}_{E,\ell})$. Upon a corruption of the ideal receiver, S learns its input $(\mathsf{receiver}, \mathsf{sid}, i)$ and output (sid, x_i) and for every $j \in [\ell] \setminus \{i\}$ it computes the invertible sampling $\rho^j_G \leftarrow I_{\mathsf{OGen}}(1^\kappa, pk_j)$, denotes $\rho^i_G = \rho^{x_i}_G$ and finally sets the virtual receiver's random coins to be $(\rho^1_G, \ldots, \rho^\ell_G)$.

However, during the security proof of the protocol, it is assumed that upon a corruption of the ideal receiver, the ideal-process adversary knows its output x_i and so can denote $\rho^i_G = \rho^{x_i}_G$. As we discussed, although valid in the framework of [4], such an assumption cannot be made in the UC framework. Hence, the security proof should be adjusted to cater for the corruption strategy in which the environment activates the receiver and the adversary corrupts the receiver *immediately after* the first message is sent from R to T and *before* the sender is activated with its input.

Proposition 1. *If* $(\mathsf{Gen}, \mathsf{OGen}, \mathsf{Enc}, \mathsf{Dec}, \mathsf{Sim})$ *is an augmented non-interactive non-committing encryption scheme then Protocol 3 UC-realizes* $\mathcal{F}^\ell_{\mathsf{OT}}$, *in the presence of adaptive semi-honest adversaries.*

The proof of Proposition 1 can be found in the full version of this paper. We note that adding initialization messages, such that a party sends OK once it is activated and the protocol begins only after both parties have been initialized, does not solve the problem. Consider an environment that activates the receiver R with input; R then sends OK to the sender. Next, the adversary corrupts R (before the sender is activated with input). The random tape of R should contain now the key generation random coins that will be used to generate (sk, pk_i) using Gen and pk_j using OGen for $j \in [\ell] \setminus \{i\}$. This means that although the message $(\mathsf{sid}, pk_1, \ldots, pk_\ell)$ has not been transmitted, it is essentially determined because the random coins that will generate it have been fixed.

4 Functionalities with One-Sided Poly-Size Domain

In this section, we focus on two-party deterministic functionalities for which the size of the input domain of one of the parties is polynomial in the security parameter, there are no restrictions on the input domain of the other party. More specifically, we consider functionalities of the form

$$f \colon D_1 \times \{0,1\}^{l_2} \to \{0,1\}^{m_1} \times \{0,1\}^{m_2},$$

where $D_1 \subseteq \{0,1\}^{l_1}$ and $|D_1| = O(\mathrm{poly}(\kappa))$.[5] The reason we consider D_1 to be a subset of $\{0,1\}^{l_1}$, rather than requiring that $l_1 = O(\log(\mathrm{poly}(\kappa)))$, is that we do

---

[5] The idea of using OT over domain which is of polynomial size first appeared in Poupard and Stern [30].

not limit the functionality to receive short inputs. The input of P_1 may consists of l_1 bits, however there are polynomially many inputs.

In this situation, since P_2 knows the input domain of P_1, it can locally compute all possible values $(y_x^1, y_x^2) = f(x, x_2)$, for every $x \in D_1$. P_1 should retrieve only $y_{x_1}^1$, i.e., the output corresponding to its input x_1. This is exactly the requirement of oblivious transfer, therefore using adaptively secure OT, P_1 obtains $y_{x_1}^1$ and nothing else whereas P_2 does not learn anything about x_1.

If P_2 also receives an output, then it may learn something about P_1's input, in particular, P_2 learns that the input of P_1 lies in the preimage of its output $y_{x_1}^2$ under the function $f_2(\cdot, x_2)$. However, this is valid in the setting of secure function evaluation, because this information is leaked from the output of the functionality, and therefore can also be learned in the ideal process. In order for P_2 to get its output $y_{x_1}^2$ without revealing it to P_1, P_2 masks every output it computes with a random string u. Now, during the OT, P_1 receives $y_{x_1}^2 \oplus u$ in addition to $y_{x_1}^1$ and returns it to P_2 that can remove the mask.

Protocol 4 (Computing $\mathcal{F}_{\mathsf{SFE}}^f$ in the $\mathcal{F}_{\mathsf{OT}}^\ell$-hybrid model).
Common input: A description of a two-party function $f \colon D_1 \times \{0,1\}^{l_2} \to \{0,1\}^{m_1} \times \{0,1\}^{m_2}$ and of the domain D_1 of P_1.

- Upon receiving $(\mathsf{input}, \mathsf{sid}, x_1)$ from $\mathcal{Z}$, party P_1 sends $(\mathsf{receiver}, \mathsf{sid}, x_1)$ to $\mathcal{F}_{\mathsf{OT}}^\ell$.
- Upon receiving $(\mathsf{input}, \mathsf{sid}, x_2)$ from $\mathcal{Z}$, party P_2 operates as follows:
    1. Sample a random string $u \in \{0,1\}^{m_2}$.
    2. For every $x \in D_1$, compute $(y_x^1, y_x^2) = f(x, x_2)$.
    3. Denote by Y the ordered tuple $(y_x^1, y_x^2 \oplus u)$ for every $x \in D_1$.
    4. Send to $\mathcal{F}_{\mathsf{OT}}^\ell$ the message $(\mathsf{sender}, \mathsf{sid}, Y)$.
- Upon receiving $(\mathsf{sid}, (w_1, w_2))$ from $\mathcal{F}_{\mathsf{OT}}^\ell$, party P_1 sends (sid, w_2) to P_2 and outputs $(\mathsf{output}, \mathsf{sid}, w_1)$.
- Upon receiving (sid, w_2) from P_1, party P_2 outputs $(\mathsf{output}, \mathsf{sid}, w_2 \oplus u)$.

The adaptive, semi-honest two-party protocol computing $\mathcal{F}_{\mathsf{SFE}}^f$

Theorem 5. *Let f be a deterministic two-party functionality where the cardinality of the domain of P_1 is polynomial in the security parameter. Then Protocol 4 UC-realizes $\mathcal{F}_{\mathsf{SFE}}^f$ in the $\mathcal{F}_{\mathsf{OT}}^\ell$-hybrid model in the presence of adaptive semi-honest adversaries.*

The proof of Theorem 5 can be found in the full version of this paper.

Using the adaptively secure OT presented in [8] (see Sect. 3) and using the composition theorem from [5], we obtain the following corollary:

Corollary 1. *Assuming the existence of augmented non-interactive NCE schemes, every deterministic two-party functionality, for which the cardinality of the domain of P_1 is polynomial in the security parameter, can be securely UC-realized, in the presence of adaptive semi-honest adversaries using a three-message protocol.*

We note that this approach does not extend to probabilistic functionalities. The reason is that if P_2 locally computes f, then it must know the random coins used in the computation. However, this information is not available to the ideal-process adversary if only P_2 is corrupted. Alternatively, when using the standard transformation from a randomized functionality into a deterministic one, by computing $g((x_1, r_1), (x_2, r_2)) = f(x_1, x_2; r_1 \oplus r_2)$, the input domain of P_1 is no longer polynomial.

Another important corollary from Theorem 5 is that in order to prove impossibility of constant-round adaptively secure two-party protocols, one must consider either functionalities where both parties have super-polynomial domains, or probabilistic functionalities.

5   Non-Committing Indistinguishability Obfuscation

An *indistinguishability obfuscator* [1,17] for a circuit class $\{\mathcal{C}_\kappa\}$ is a PPT machine $i\mathcal{O}$ satisfying the following conditions:

Correctness: For every κ and every $C \in \mathcal{C}_\kappa$, it holds that C and $i\mathcal{O}(C)$ compute the same function.

Polynomial slowdown: There is a polynomial p such that for all $C \in \mathcal{C}_\kappa$, $|i\mathcal{O}(1^\kappa, C)| \leq p(\kappa) \cdot |C|$.

Indistinguishability: For any sequence $\{C_{\kappa,0}, C_{\kappa,1}, \mathsf{aux}_\kappa\}_\kappa$, where $C_{\kappa,0}, C_{\kappa,1} \in \mathcal{C}_\kappa$, $|C_{\kappa,0}| = |C_{\kappa,1}|$ and $C_{\kappa,0}, C_{\kappa,1}$ compute the same function, and for any non-uniform PPT distinguisher $\mathcal{D}$, there exists a negligible function negl such that:

$$|\Pr\left[\mathcal{D}\left(i\mathcal{O}\left(1^\kappa, C_{\kappa,0}\right), \mathsf{aux}_\kappa\right) = 1\right] - \Pr\left[\mathcal{D}\left(i\mathcal{O}\left(1^\kappa, C_{\kappa,1}\right), \mathsf{aux}_\kappa\right) = 1\right]| \leq \mathrm{negl}(\kappa).$$

Indistinguishability obfuscation has recently led to a construction of a two-round statically secure protocol [18] and to constant-round adaptively secure protocols in the CRS model [10,11,15]. We consider an adaptive analogue for $i\mathcal{O}$ called *non-committing indistinguishability obfuscation* and show that this primitive is *complete* for constructing adaptively secure protocols with round complexity that is independent of the function to compute. We emphasize that currently we do not know how to construct non-committing indistinguishability obfuscation, and that this result serves as a reduction from the problem of constructing adaptively secure protocols with round complexity independent of the function to the problem of constructing non-committing $i\mathcal{O}$.

Given a circuit class consisting of circuits that compute the same function, we would like to have an indistinguishability obfuscator $i\mathcal{O}$ augmented with a simulation algorithm Sim_1 that outputs a "canonical" obfuscated circuit and some state s, such that later, given any circuit from the class and the state, a second algorithm Sim_2 can explain the randomness for the obfuscation algorithm to generate the canonical circuit as an obfuscation of this circuit. We note that such a notion of non-committing $i\mathcal{O}$ is unlikely to exists in general, since this will provide an efficient solution to the *circuit equivalence problem*, which is co-NP complete, and so will imply a collapse of the polynomial hierarchy. Given two circuits C_0, C_1, if and only if the circuits are equivalent, then there exists a non-committing $i\mathcal{O}$ for this family and it is possible to first compute $(\tilde{C}, s) \leftarrow \mathsf{Sim}_1(1^\kappa)$ and later explain $\tilde{C}$ both as $r_0 \leftarrow \mathsf{Sim}_2(s, C_0)$ and as $r_1 \leftarrow \mathsf{Sim}_2(s, C_1)$.

We overcome this difficulty by considering equivalent circuits that do not receive any input, i.e., a family of constant circuits that produce the same output. The circuit equivalence problem is easy in this scenario since one simply runs both circuits and compares the outputs. More specifically, consider a circuit C computing a function f and an input vector $\boldsymbol{x}$. We hard-wire to each input wire (i.e., to each *input terminal* in the terminology of Goldreich [19]) the corresponding input value. This yields a circuit that computes the constant function $f_{\boldsymbol{x}} = f(\boldsymbol{x})$. We say that a circuit is a *constant circuit* if all its input wires have hard-wired values (an so it computes a constant function).

Definition 4. *A non-committing indistinguishability obfuscator scheme for a circuit class $\{\mathcal{C}_\kappa\}$, consisting of constant circuits, is a triplet of PPT algorithms $\Pi = (i\mathcal{O}, \mathsf{Sim}_1, \mathsf{Sim}_2)$ such that:*

- *$i\mathcal{O}$ is an indistinguishability obfuscator for $\{\mathcal{C}_\kappa\}$.*
- *Upon receiving 1^κ, an integer m and a value y, Sim_1 outputs a constant circuit $\tilde{C}$ (of size m and output y) and a state s.*
- *Upon receiving a circuit $C \in \mathcal{C}_\kappa$ and a state s, Sim_2 outputs a string r.*
- *For any non-uniform PPT $\mathcal{D}$ and for large enough $\kappa \in \mathbb{N}$, it holds that:*

$$\Pr\left[\mathrm{EXPT}_{\Pi,\mathcal{D}}^{\mathrm{REAL}}(\kappa) = 1\right] - \Pr\left[\mathrm{EXPT}_{\Pi,\mathcal{D}}^{\mathrm{IDEAL}}(\kappa) = 1\right] \leq \mathsf{negl}(\kappa),$$

where the experiments $\mathrm{EXPT}_{\Pi,\mathcal{D}}^{\mathrm{REAL}}$ and $\mathrm{EXPT}_{\Pi,\mathcal{D}}^{\mathrm{IDEAL}}$ are defined below, and the probability is over the random coins of the experiments and of $\mathcal{D}$.

Experiment $\mathrm{EXPT}_{\Pi,\mathcal{D}}^{\mathrm{REAL}}(\kappa)$	Experiment $\mathrm{EXPT}_{\Pi,\mathcal{D}}^{\mathrm{IDEAL}}(\kappa)$
	Send 1^κ to $\mathcal{D}$ and get back a circuit $C \in \mathcal{C}_\kappa$.
Send 1^κ to $\mathcal{D}$ and get back a circuit $C \in \mathcal{C}_\kappa$	Run the circuit C and compute the output y.
Sample a uniformly distributed string r	Compute $(\tilde{C}, s) \leftarrow \mathsf{Sim}_1(1^\kappa, |C|, y)$.
Compute $\tilde{C} = i\mathcal{O}(1^\kappa, C; r)$	Compute $r \leftarrow \mathsf{Sim}_2(s, C)$.
Send $(\tilde{C}, r)$ to $\mathcal{D}$ and get back a bit b	Send $(\tilde{C}, r)$ to $\mathcal{D}$ and get back a bit b.
Return b	Return b

For our usage, we require that the depth of the circuit representing the obfuscator $i\mathcal{O}$ is independent of the depth of the (input variable) circuit C. This requirement is motivated by the construction of Garg et al. [17] for "standard" $i\mathcal{O}$, which satisfies this property.

We note that the technique of Katz et al. [26] does not seem to rule out non-committing $i\mathcal{O}$ for constant circuits, since the function that can be computed using the simulator is fixed in advance. Likewise, the technique of Nielsen [29] does not seem to work, since the number of constant circuits that can be explained is bounded in advance.

5.1 Adaptively Secure Protocol with Round Complexity Independent of f

We define the protocol in a hybrid model where the parties have access to an ideal obfuscate-circuit-with-input functionality $\mathcal{F}_{\mathsf{OCWI}}^C$. For simplicity we present the protocol for public-output deterministic functionalities, and the extension to private-output randomized functionalities follows using standard techniques. $\mathcal{F}_{\mathsf{OCWI}}^C$ is parametrized by a circuit C, each party sends its input to $\mathcal{F}_{\mathsf{OCWI}}^C$, which hard-wires the inputs to the circuit, obfuscates it and returns the obfuscated circuit to the parties. Each party sends an additional random string that is used as a share of the random coins for the obfuscation. The obfuscate-circuit-with-input functionality is described in Fig. 1.

Functionality $\mathcal{F}_{\mathsf{OCWI}}^C$

The functionality $\mathcal{F}_{\mathsf{OCWI}}^C$ proceeds as follows, interacting with parties $P_1, \ldots, P_n$ and an adversary $\mathcal{S}$, and parametrized by a circuit C and a non-committing $i\mathcal{O}$ scheme for constant circuits. For every party P_i initialize values $x_i \leftarrow \bot$ and $r_i \leftarrow 0$.

- Upon receiving $(\mathsf{ocwi\text{-}input}, \mathsf{sid}, (x, r))$ from P_i, set $x_i \leftarrow x$ and $r_i \leftarrow r$ and send a message $(\mathsf{ocwi\text{-}input}, \mathsf{sid}, P_i)$ to $\mathcal{S}$.
- Upon receiving $(\mathsf{ocwi\text{-}output}, \mathsf{sid})$ from P_i, do:
  1. If $x_i = \bot$ for some honest party P_i, return $\bot$.
  2. If the circuit $\tilde{C}$ has not been set yet:
     (a) Prepare the circuit C_1 by hard-wiring the values $x_1, \ldots, x_n$ to C.
     (b) Obfuscate the circuit C_1 as $\tilde{C} = i\mathcal{O}(1^\kappa, C_1; r_1 \oplus \ldots \oplus r_n)$.
  3. Send to P_i the obfuscated circuit $(\mathsf{ocwi\text{-}output}, \mathsf{sid}, \tilde{C})$.

Fig. 1. The obfuscate-circuit-with-input functionality

Based on the properties of non-committing $i\mathcal{O}$, the depth of a circuit computing $\mathcal{F}_{\mathsf{OCWI}}^C$ depends only on the depth of the obfuscator $i\mathcal{O}$ and not the depth of C.

Protocol 6 (Computing $\mathcal{F}_{\mathsf{SFE}}^f$ in the $\mathcal{F}_{\mathsf{OCWI}}^C$-hybrid model).
Common input: an n-party functionality $f \colon (\{0,1\}^*)^n \to (\{0,1\}^*)^n$ and a circuit C computing f.

- Upon receiving $(\mathsf{input}, \mathsf{sid}, x_i)$ from $\mathcal{Z}$, party P_i samples a random string $r_i \in_R \{0,1\}^*$ and sends $(\mathsf{ocwi\text{-}input}, \mathsf{sid}, (x_i, r_i))$ to $\mathcal{F}_{\mathsf{OCWI}}^C$.
- Upon receiving $(\mathsf{ocwi\text{-}output}, \mathsf{sid}, \tilde{C})$ from $\mathcal{F}_{\mathsf{OCWI}}^C$, P_i runs the circuit $\tilde{C}$, receives an output y and outputs $(\mathsf{output}, \mathsf{sid}, y)$.

The adaptive, semi-honest multiparty protocol computing $\mathcal{F}_{\mathsf{SFE}}^f$

Theorem 7. *Let f be an n-party functionality and let C be a circuit computing f. If $\Pi = (i\mathcal{O}, \mathsf{Sim}_1, \mathsf{Sim}_2)$ is a non-committing $i\mathcal{O}$ scheme for constant circuits, then Protocol 6 UC-realizes $\mathcal{F}^f_{\mathsf{SFE}}$ in the $\mathcal{F}^C_{\mathsf{OCWI}}$-hybrid model, in the presence of adaptive semi-honest adversaries.*

The proof of Theorem 7 can be found in the full version of this paper.

When instantiating the ideal functionality $\mathcal{F}^C_{\mathsf{OCWI}}$ using the protocol from Canetti et al. [8], the round complexity depends on the circuit representing $\mathcal{F}^C_{\mathsf{OCWI}}$, which is independent from the depth of f. Hence, using the composition theorem from Canetti [5] we conclude with the following corollary.

Corollary 2. *Assume that enhanced trapdoor permutations, augmented non-committing encryption and non-committing $i\mathcal{O}$ scheme for constant circuits exist. Then for any adaptively well-formed multiparty functionality f, there exists a protocol that UC-realizes $\mathcal{F}^f_{\mathsf{SFE}}$ in the presence of adaptive semi-honest adversaries, with round complexity that is independent of f.*

Acknowledgements. We would like to thank Yehuda Lindell for helpful discussions on the topic and to the anonymous referees for pointing to the work of [30] regarding OT over polynomial-size domain and for pointing out a problem in an earlier version of Definition 4.

References

1. Barak, B., Goldreich, O., Impagliazzo, R., Rudich, S., Sahai, A., Vadhan, S.P., Yang, K.: On the (im)possibility of obfuscating programs. In: Kilian, J. (ed.) CRYPTO 2001. LNCS, vol. 2139, pp. 1–18. Springer, Heidelberg (2001)
2. Beaver, D., Haber, S.: Cryptographic protocols provably secure against dynamic adversaries. In: Rueppel, R.A. (ed.) EUROCRYPT 1992. LNCS, vol. 658, pp. 307–323. Springer, Heidelberg (1993)
3. Bitansky, N., Canetti, R., Halevi, S.: Leakage-tolerant interactive protocols. In: Cramer, R. (ed.) TCC 2012. LNCS, vol. 7194, pp. 266–284. Springer, Heidelberg (2012)
4. Canetti, R.: Security and composition of multiparty cryptographic protocols. J. Cryptology **13**(1), 143–202 (2000)
5. Canetti, R.: Universally composable security: a new paradigm for cryptographi cprotocols. In: Proceedings of the 42nd Annual Symposium on Foundations of Computer Science (FOCS), pp. 136–145 (2001)
6. Canetti, R., Fischlin, M.: Universally composable commitments. In: Kilian, J. (ed.) CRYPTO 2001. LNCS, vol. 2139, pp. 19–40. Springer, Heidelberg (2001)
7. Canetti, R., Feige, U., Goldreich, O., Naor, M.: Adaptively secure multi-party computation. In: Proceedings of the 28th Annual ACM Symposium on Theory of Computing (STOC), pp. 639–648 (1996)
8. Canetti, R., Lindell, Y., Ostrovsky, R., Sahai, A.: Universally composable two-party and multi-party secure computation. In: Proceedings of the 34th Annual ACM Symposium on Theory of Computing (STOC), pp. 494–503 (2002)
9. Canetti, R., Kushilevitz, E., Lindell, Y.: On the limitations of universally composable two-party computation without set-up assumptions. J. Cryptology **19**(2), 135–167 (2006)

10. Canetti, R., Goldwasser, S., Poburinnaya, O.: Adaptively secure two-party computation from indistinguishability obfuscation. In: Dodis, Y., Nielsen, J.B. (eds.) TCC 2015, Part II. LNCS, vol. 9015, pp. 557–585. Springer, Heidelberg (2015)
11. Dachman-Soled, D., Katz, J., Rao, V.: Adaptively secure, universally composable, multiparty computation in constant rounds. In: Dodis, Y., Nielsen, J.B. (eds.) TCC 2015, Part II. LNCS, vol. 9015, pp. 586–613. Springer, Heidelberg (2015)
12. Damgård, I.B., Ishai, Y.: Constant-round multiparty computation using a black-box pseudorandom generator. In: Shoup, V. (ed.) CRYPTO 2005. LNCS, vol. 3621, pp. 378–394. Springer, Heidelberg (2005)
13. Damgård, I.B., Nielsen, J.B.: Improved non-committing encryption schemes based on a general complexity assumption. In: Bellare, M. (ed.) CRYPTO 2000. LNCS, vol. 1880, pp. 432–450. Springer, Heidelberg (2000)
14. Damgård, I., Polychroniadou, A., Rao, V.: Adaptively secure multi-party computation from LWE (via equivocal FHE). In: Cheng, C.-M., Chung, K.-M., Persiano, G., Yang, B.-Y. (eds.) PKC 2016. LNCS, vol. 9615, pp. 208–233. Springer, Heidelberg (2016). doi:10.1007/978-3-662-49387-8_9
15. Garg, S., Polychroniadou, A.: Two-round adaptively secure MPC from indistinguishability obfuscation. In: Dodis, Y., Nielsen, J.B. (eds.) TCC 2015, Part II. LNCS, vol. 9015, pp. 614–637. Springer, Heidelberg (2015)
16. Garg, S., Sahai, A.: Adaptively secure multi-party computation with dishonest majority. In: Safavi-Naini, R., Canetti, R. (eds.) CRYPTO 2012. LNCS, vol. 7417, pp. 105–123. Springer, Heidelberg (2012)
17. Garg, S., Gentry, C., Halevi, S., Raykova, M., Sahai, A., Waters, B.: Candidate indistinguishability obfuscation and functional encryption for all circuits. In: Proceedings of the 54th Annual Symposium on Foundations of Computer Science (FOCS), pp. 40–49 (2013)
18. Garg, S., Gentry, C., Halevi, S., Raykova, M.: Two-round secure MPC from indistinguishability obfuscation. In: Lindell, Y. (ed.) TCC 2014. LNCS, vol. 8349, pp. 74–94. Springer, Heidelberg (2014)
19. Goldreich, O.: Computational Complexity - A Conceptual Perspective. Cambridge University Press, Cambridge (2008). ISBN 978-0-521-88473-0
20. Goldreich, O., Micali, S., Wigderson, A.: How to play any mental game or a completeness theorem for protocols with honest majority. In: Proceedings of the 19th Annual ACM Symposium on Theory of Computing (STOC), pp. 218–229 (1987)
21. Gordon, D., Ishai, Y., Moran, T., Ostrovsky, R., Sahai, A.: On complete primitives for fairness. In: Micciancio, D. (ed.) TCC 2010. LNCS, vol. 5978, pp. 91–108. Springer, Heidelberg (2010)
22. Hazay, C., Patra, A.: One-sided adaptively secure two-party computation. In: Lindell, Y. (ed.) TCC 2014. LNCS, vol. 8349, pp. 368–393. Springer, Heidelberg (2014)
23. Ishai, Y., Prabhakaran, M., Sahai, A.: Founding cryptography on oblivious transfer – efficiently. In: Wagner, D. (ed.) CRYPTO 2008. LNCS, vol. 5157, pp. 572–591. Springer, Heidelberg (2008)
24. Katz, J.: On achieving the "best of both worlds" in secure multiparty computation. In: Proceedings of the 39th Annual ACM Symposium on Theory of Computing (STOC), pp. 11–20 (2007)
25. Katz, J., Ostrovsky, R.: Round-optimal secure two-party computation. In: Franklin, M. (ed.) CRYPTO 2004. LNCS, vol. 3152, pp. 335–354. Springer, Heidelberg (2004)

26. Katz, J., Thiruvengadam, A., Zhou, H.-S.: Feasibility and infeasibility of adaptively secure fully homomorphic encryption. In: Kurosawa, K., Hanaoka, G. (eds.) PKC 2013. LNCS, vol. 7778, pp. 14–31. Springer, Heidelberg (2013)
27. Lindell, Y.: Composition of Secure Multi-Party Protocols. LNCS, vol. 2815. Springer, Heidelberg (2003)
28. Lindell, A.Y.: Adaptively secure two-party computation with erasures. In: Fischlin, M. (ed.) CT-RSA 2009. LNCS, vol. 5473, pp. 117–132. Springer, Heidelberg (2009)
29. Nielsen, J.B.: Separating random oracle proofs from complexity theoretic proofs: the non-committing encryption case. In: Yung, M. (ed.) CRYPTO 2002. LNCS, vol. 2442, pp. 111–126. Springer, Heidelberg (2002)
30. Poupard, G., Stern, J.: Generation of shared RSA keys by two parties. In: Ohta, K., Pei, D. (eds.) ASIACRYPT 1998. LNCS, vol. 1514, pp. 11–24. Springer, Heidelberg (1998)
31. Yao, A.: Protocols for secure computations (extended abstract). In: Proceedings of the 23rd Annual Symposium on Foundations of Computer Science (FOCS), pp. 160–164 (1982)

Linear Overhead Optimally-Resilient Robust MPC Using Preprocessing

Ashish Choudhury[1], Emmanuela Orsini[2], Arpita Patra[3], and Nigel P. Smart[2(✉)]

[1] International Institute of Information Technology, Bangalore, India
ashish.choudhury@iiitb.ac.in
[2] Department of Computer Science, University of Bristol, Bristol, UK
Emmanuela.Orsini@bristol.ac.uk, nigel@cs.bris.ac.uk
[3] Department of Computer Science and Automation, Indian Institute of Science, Bangalore, India
arpita@csa.iisc.ernet.in

Abstract. We present a new technique for robust secret reconstruction with $\mathcal{O}(n)$ communication complexity. By applying this technique, we achieve $\mathcal{O}(n)$ communication complexity per multiplication for a wide class of robust practical Multi-Party Computation (MPC) protocols. In particular our technique applies to robust threshold computationally secure protocols in the case of $t < n/2$ in the pre-processing model. Previously in the pre-processing model, $\mathcal{O}(n)$ communication complexity per multiplication was only known in the case of computationally secure non-robust protocols in the dishonest majority setting (i.e. with $t < n$) and in the case of perfectly-secure robust protocols with $t < n/3$. A similar protocol was sketched by Damgård and Nielsen, but no details were given to enable an estimate of the communication complexity. Surprisingly our robust reconstruction protocol applies for both the synchronous and asynchronous settings.

1 Introduction

Secure MPC is a fundamental problem in secure distributed computing [8,14,27,33]. An MPC protocol allows a set of n mutually distrusting parties with private inputs to securely compute a joint function of their inputs, even if t out of the n parties are corrupted. Determining the communication complexity of MPC in terms of n, is a task which is both interesting from a theoretical and a practical standpoint. It is a folklore belief that the complexity should be essentially $\mathcal{O}(n)$ per multiplication in the computation. However, "most" *robust* secret-sharing based MPC protocols which are practical have complexity $\mathcal{O}(n^2)$.

To understand the problem notice that apart from the protocols for entering parties inputs and determining parties outputs, the main communication task in secret-sharing based MPC protocols is the evaluation of the multiplication gates (we assume a standard arithmetic circuit representation of the function to be computed for purely expository reasons, in practice other representations

© Springer International Publishing Switzerland 2016
V. Zikas and R. De Prisco (Eds.): SCN 2016, LNCS 9841, pp. 147–168, 2016.
DOI: 10.1007/978-3-319-44618-9_8

may be better). If we consider the classic information-theoretic passively secure sub-protocol for multiplication gates when $t < n/2$ (locally multiply the shares, reshare and then recombine) we require $\mathcal{O}(n^2)$ messages per multiplication gate [8,26]. This is because each party needs to send the shares representing its local multiplication to every other party, thus requiring $\mathcal{O}(n^2)$ messages, and hence $\mathcal{O}(n^2)$ bits if we only look at complexity depending on n.

Even if we look at such protocols in the pre-processing model, where the so-called "Beaver multiplication triples" are produced in an offline phase [4], and we are primarily concerned about the communication complexity of the online phase, a similar situation occurs. In such protocols, see for example [19], the standard multiplication sub-protocol is for each party to broadcast a masking of their shares of the gate input values to every other party. This again has $\mathcal{O}(n^2)$ communication complexity.

In the SPDZ protocol [22], for the case of *non-robust*[1] maliciously secure MPC (with abort) in the dishonest majority setting (i.e. with $t < n$), an online communication complexity of $\mathcal{O}(n)$ was achieved. This is attained by replacing the broadcast communication of the previous method with the following trick. For each multiplication gate one party is designated as the "reconstructor". The broadcast round is then replaced by each party sending their masked values to the reconstructor, who then reconstructs the value and then sends it to each party. This requires exactly $2 \cdot n$ messages being sent, and is hence $\mathcal{O}(n)$. However, this protocol is only relevant in the dishonest majority setting as any dishonest behaviour of any party is subsequently detected via the SPDZ MAC-checking procedure, in which case the protocol aborts. Our goal is to achieve such a result for robust protocols in the *pre-processing model*.

Related Work: With $t < n/3$, information-theoretically secure an online protocols with $\mathcal{O}(n)$ communication per multiplication are presented in [21]. There the basic idea is a new method of reconstructing a batch of $\Theta(n)$ secret-shared values with $\mathcal{O}(n^2)$ communication complexity, thus providing a linear overhead. However, the method is tailor-made only for $t < n/3$ (as it is based on the error-correcting capability of the Reed-Solomon (RS) codes) and will not work with $t < n/2$. Hence with $t < n/2$ in the computational setting, a new technique to obtain $\mathcal{O}(n)$ *online complexity* is needed. In [21] a similar protocol in the pre-processing model is also sketched, which uses the designatred reconstructor idea (similar to the idea used in SPDZ, discussed above). The protocol is only sketched, and appears to require $O(t)$ rounds to identify the faulty shares; as opposed to our method which requires no additional rounds.

In [28], a computationally-secure MPC protocol with $t < n/2$ and communication complexity $\mathcal{O}(n)$ per multiplication is presented. The protocol is not designed in the pre-processing model, but rather in the player-elimination framework, where the circuit is divided into segments and each segment is evaluated "optimistically", assuming no fault will occur. At the end of the segment evaluation, a detection

---

[1] An MPC protocol is called robust if the honest parties obtain the correct output at the end of the protocol irrespective of the behaviour of the corrupted parties, otherwise it is called non-robust.

protocol is executed to identify whether the segment is evaluated correctly and if any inconsistency is detected, then a fault-localization protocol is executed. The fault-localization process identifies a pair of parties, with at least one of them being corrupted. The pair is then neglected for the rest of the protocol execution and the procedure is repeated. There are several drawbacks of this protocol. The protocol cannot be adapted to the pre-processing model; so the benefits provided by the pre-processing based MPC protocols (namely efficiently generating circuit-independent raw materials for several instances of the computation in parallel) cannot be obtained. The protocol also makes expensive use of zero-knowledge (ZK) machinery throughout the protocol and it does not seem to be adaptable to the asynchronous setting with $\mathcal{O}(n)$ communication complexity. Our techniques on the other hand are focused on efficient protocols in the pre-processing model. For example we use ZK tools only in the offline phase, and our online methods are easily applicable to the asynchronous communication setting[2], which models real-world networks like the Internet more appropriately than the synchronous communication setting.

In [9], an information-theoretically secure MPC protocol in the pre-processing model with $t < n/2$ and $\mathcal{O}(n)$ communication complexity per multiplication is presented. Both the offline and online phase of [9] are designed in the dispute control framework [5], which is a generalisation of the player-elimination technique and so like other papers in the same framework it is not known if the protocol can be made to work in the more practical asynchronous communication setting. Moreover since their online phase protocol is in the dispute control framework, it requires $\mathcal{O}(n^2 + \mathcal{D})$ rounds of interaction in the online phase, where $\mathcal{D}$ is the multiplicative depth of the circuit. This is unlike other MPC protocols in the pre-processing model whose online phase requires only $\mathcal{O}(\mathcal{D})$ rounds of interaction [6,10,21,22]. Our technique for the online phase protocol does not deploy any player-elimination/dispute-control techniques and so requires fewer rounds than [9]. And our online phase can be executed even in the asynchronous setting with $t < n/2$ and $\mathcal{O}(n)$ communication complexity. Imagine a scenario involving a large number of parties, participating from various parts of the globe. Clearly (an asynchronous) online protocol with less number of communication rounds is desirable here and so our online phase protocol will fit the bill appropriately. In the non-preprocessing model, information-theoretically secure MPC protocols with "near linear" amortized communication complexity but *non-optimal resilience* are presented in [3,20,25]. Namely the overall communication complexity of these protocols are $\mathcal{O}(\text{polylog}(n, C) \cdot C)$, where C is the circuit size. While the protocol of [20] is perfectly-secure and can tolerate upto $t < (1/3 - \epsilon) \cdot n$ corruptions where $0 < \epsilon < 1/3$, the protocols in [3,25] are statistical with resilience $t < (1/2 - \epsilon) \cdot n$ where $0 < \epsilon < 1/2$. The central idea in these protocols is to take advantage of the non-optimal resilience by deploying packed secret-sharing, where "several" values are secret shared simultaneously

---

[2] We stress that we are interested only in the online complexity. Unlike our online phase, our offline phase protocol cannot be executed in a completely asynchronous setting with $t < n/2$.

via a single sharing instance. None of the protocols are known to work in asynchronous settings and all of them heavily rely on the fact that there are more honest parties than just $1/2$ (making them non-optimal in terms of resilience).

Finally we note that an asynchronous MPC protocol with $t < n/3$ and $\mathcal{O}(n)$ communication complexity in the pre-processing model is presented in [17]. However the online phase protocol of [17] is based on the $\mathcal{O}(n)$ reconstruction method of [6,21] with $t < n/3$ and hence cannot be adapted to the $t < n/2$ setting.

Our Contribution: We present a computationally-secure method to obtain $\mathcal{O}(n)$ communication complexity for the online phase of robust MPC protocols with $t < n/2$. We are focused on protocols which could be practically relevant, so we are interested in suitable modifications of protocols such as VIFF [19], BDOZ [10] and SPDZ [22]. Our main contribution is a trick to robustly reconstruct a secret with an amortized communication complexity of $\mathcal{O}(n)$ messages. Assuming our arithmetic circuit is suitably wide, this implies an $\mathcal{O}(n)$ online phase when combined with the standard method for evaluating multiplication gates based on pre-processed Beaver triples.

To produce this sub-protocol we utilize the error-correcting capability of the underlying secret-sharing scheme when error positions are already known. To detect the error positions we apply the pair-wise BDOZ MACs from [10]. The overall sub-protocol is highly efficient and can be utilized in practical MPC protocols. Interestingly our reconstruction protocol also works in the asynchronous setting. Thus we obtain a practical optimization in both synchronous and asynchronous setting.

Before proceeding we pause to examine the communication complexity of the offline phase of protocols such as SPDZ. It is obvious that in the case of a computationally secure offline phase one can easily adapt the somewhat homomorphic encryption (SHE) based offline phase of SPDZ to the case of Shamir secret sharing when $t < n/2$. In addition one can adapt it to generate SPDZ or BDOZ style MACs. And this is what we exactly do to implement our offline phase in the synchronous setting. In [22] the offline communication complexity is given as $\mathcal{O}(n^2/s)$ in terms of the number of messages sent, where s is the "packing" parameter of the SHE scheme. As shown in the full version of [23], assuming a cyclotomic polynomial is selected which splits completely modulo the plaintext modulus p, the packing parameter grows very slowly in terms of the number of parties (for all practical purposes it does not increase at all). In addition since s is in the many thousands, for all practical purposes the communication complexity of the offline phase is $\mathcal{O}(n)$ in terms of the number of messages. However, each message is $\mathcal{O}(s)$ and so the bit communication complexity is still $\mathcal{O}(n^2)$.

As our online phase also works in the asynchronous setting, we explore how the offline phase, and the interaction between the offline and online phases can be done asynchronously. For this we follow the VIFF framework [19], which implements the offline phase asynchronously with $t < n/3$ via the pseudo-random secret sharing, assuming a single synchronization point between the offline and online phases. Following the same approach, we show how the interaction between our offline and online phase can be handled asynchronously with $t < n/2$. However we require an additional technicality for $t < n/2$ to deal with the issue of agreement among the parties at the end of asynchronous offline phase. Specifically, we either require "few" synchronous rounds or a non-equivocation mechanism at the end of offline phase to ensure agreement among the parties. We stress that once this is done then the online phase protocol can be executed in a completely asynchronous fashion with $t < n/2$.

2 Preliminaries

We assume a set of parties $\mathcal{P} = \{P_1, \ldots, P_n\}$, connected by pair-wise authentic channels, and a centralized static, active PPT adversary $\mathcal{A}$ who can corrupt any $t < n/2$ parties. For simplicity we assume $n = 2t + 1$, so that $t = \Theta(n)$. The functionality that the parties wish to compute is represented by an arithmetic circuit over a finite field $\mathbb{F}$, where $|\mathbb{F}| > n$. We denote by μ and κ the statistical and cryptographic security parameter respectively. A negligible function in κ (μ) will be denoted by $\mathsf{negl}(\kappa)$ ($\mathsf{negl}(\mu)$), while $\mathsf{negl}(\kappa, \mu)$ denotes a function which is negligible in both κ and μ. We use both information-theoretic and public-key cryptographic primitives in our protocols. The security of the information theoretic primitives are parameterised with μ, while that of cryptographic primitives are parameterised with κ. We assume $\mathbb{F} = \mathrm{GF}(p)$, where p is a prime with $p \approx 2^{\mu}$, to ensure that the statistical security of our protocol holds with all but $\mathsf{negl}(\mu)$ probability. Each element of $\mathbb{F}$ can be represented by μ bits. For vectors $A = (a_1, \ldots, a_m)$ and $B = (b_1, \ldots, b_m)$, $A \otimes B$ denotes the value $\sum_{i=1}^{m} a_i b_i$. The ith element in a vector A is denoted as $A[i]$ and (i, j)th element in a matrix A as $A[i, j]$.

2.1 Communication Settings

In this paper we consider two communication settings. The first setting is the popular and simple, but less practical, synchronous channel setting, where the channels are synchronous and there is a strict upper bound on the message delays. All the parties in this setting are assumed to be synchronized via a global clock. Any protocol in this setting operates as a sequence of rounds, where in every round: A party first performs some computation, then they send messages to the others parties over the pair-wise channels and broadcast any message which need to be broadcast; this stage is followed by receiving both the messages sent to the party by the other parties over the pair-wise channels and the messages broadcast by the other parties. Since the system is synchronous, any (honest) party need not have to wait endlessly for any message in any round. Thus the standard behaviour is to assume that if a party does not receive a value which it is supposed to receive or instead it receives a "syntactically incorrect" value, then the party simply substitutes a default value (instead of waiting endlessly) and proceeds further to the next round.

The other communication setting is the more involved, but more practical, asynchronous setting; here the channels are asynchronous and messages can be arbitrarily (but finitely) delayed. The only guarantee here is that the messages sent by the honest parties will eventually reach their destinations. The order of the message delivery is decided by a *scheduler*. To model the worst case scenario, we assume that the scheduler is under the control of the adversary. The scheduler can only schedule the messages exchanged between the honest parties, without having access to the "contents" of these messages. As in [7,12], we consider a protocol execution in this setting as a sequence of *atomic steps*, where a single party is *active* in each step. A party is activated when it receives a message. On receiving a message, it performs an internal computation and then possibly sends messages on its outgoing channels. The order of the atomic steps are controlled by the scheduler. At the beginning of the computation, each party will be in a special *start* state. A party is said to *terminate/complete* the computation if it reaches a *halt* state, after which it does not perform any further computation. A protocol execution is said to be complete if all the honest parties terminate the computation.

It is easy to see that the asynchronous setting models real-world networks like the Internet (where there can be arbitrary message delays) more appropriately than the synchronous setting. Unfortunately, designing protocol in the asynchronous setting is complicated and this stems from the fact that we cannot distinguish between a corrupted sender (who does not send any messages) and a slow but honest sender (whose messages are arbitrarily delayed). Due to this the following unavoidable but inherent phenomenon is always present in any asynchronous protocol: at any stage of the protocol, no (honest) party can afford to receive communication from *all* the n parties, as this may turn out to require an endless wait. So as soon as the party hears from $n - t$ parties, it has to proceed to the next stage; but in this process, communication from t potentially honest parties may get ignored.

2.2   Primitives

Linearly-Homomorphic Encryption Scheme (HE). We assume an IND-CPA secure linearly-homomorphic public-key encryption scheme set-up for every $P_i \in \mathcal{P}$ with message space $\mathbb{F}$; a possible instantiation could be the BGV scheme [11]. Under this set-up, P_i will own a secret decryption key $\mathbf{dk}^{(i)}$ and the corresponding encryption key $\mathbf{pk}^{(i)}$ will be publicly known. Given $\mathbf{pk}^{(i)}$, a plaintext x and a randomness r, anyone can compute a ciphertext $\mathsf{HE.c}(x) \stackrel{def}{=} \mathsf{HE.Enc}_{\mathbf{pk}^{(i)}}(x, r)$ of x for P_i, using the encryption algorithm $\mathsf{HE.Enc}$, where the size of $\mathsf{HE.c}(x)$ is $\mathcal{O}(\kappa)$ bits. Given a ciphertext $\mathsf{HE.c}(x) = \mathsf{HE.Enc}_{\mathbf{pk}^{(i)}}(x, \star)$ and the decryption key $\mathbf{dk}^{(i)}$, P_i can recover the plaintext $x = \mathsf{HE.Dec}_{\mathbf{dk}^{(i)}}(\mathbf{c}_x)$ using the decryption algorithm $\mathsf{HE.Dec}$. The encryption scheme is assumed to be *linearly homomorphic*: given two ciphertexts $\mathsf{HE.c}(x) = \mathsf{HE.Enc}_{\mathbf{pk}^{(i)}}(x, \star)$ and $\mathsf{HE.c}(y) = \mathsf{HE.Enc}_{\mathbf{pk}^{(i)}}(y, \star)$, there exists an operation, say $\oplus$, such that $\mathsf{HE.c}(x) \oplus \mathsf{HE.c}(y) = \mathsf{HE.Enc}_{\mathbf{pk}^{(i)}}(x + y, \star)$. Moreover, given a ciphertext $\mathsf{HE.c}(x) = \mathsf{HE.Enc}_{\mathbf{pk}^{(i)}}(x, \star)$ and a public constant c, there exists some operation, say $\odot$, such that $c \odot \mathsf{HE.c}(x) = \mathsf{HE.Enc}_{\mathbf{pk}^{(i)}}(c \cdot x, \star)$.

Information-Theoretic MACs: We will use information-theoretically secure MAC, similar to the one used in [10]. Here a random pair $\mathsf{K} = (\alpha, \beta) \in \mathbb{F}^2$ is selected as the MAC key and the MAC tag on a value $a \in \mathbb{F}$, under the key K is defined as $\mathsf{MAC}_\mathsf{K}(a) \stackrel{def}{=} \alpha \cdot a + \beta$. The MACs will be used as follows: a party P_i will hold some value a and a MAC tag $\mathsf{MAC}_\mathsf{K}(a)$, while party P_j will hold the MAC key K. Later when P_i wants to disclose a to P_j, it sends a along with $\mathsf{MAC}_\mathsf{K}(a)$; P_j verifies if a is consistent with the MAC tag with respect to its key K. A *corrupted* party P_i on holding the MAC tag on a message gets one point on the straight-line $y = \alpha x + \beta$ and it leaves one degree of freedom on the polynomial. Therefore even a computationally unbounded P_i cannot recover K completely. So a corrupted P_i cannot reveal an incorrect value $a' \neq a$ to an honest P_j without getting caught, except with probability $\frac{1}{|\mathbb{F}|} \approx 2^{-\mu} = \mathsf{negl}(\mu)$, which is the probability of guessing a second point on the straight-line. We call two MAC keys $\mathsf{K} = (\alpha, \beta)$ and $\mathsf{K}' = (\alpha', \beta')$ *consistent* if $\alpha = \alpha'$. Given two consistent MAC keys $\mathsf{K} = (\alpha, \beta)$ and $\mathsf{K}' = (\alpha, \beta')$ and a public constant c, we define the following operations on MAC keys:

$$\mathsf{K} + \mathsf{K}' \stackrel{def}{=} (\alpha, \beta + \beta'), \quad \mathsf{K} + c \stackrel{def}{=} (\alpha, \beta + \alpha c) \quad \text{and} \quad c \cdot \mathsf{K} \stackrel{def}{=} (\alpha, c \cdot \beta).$$

Given two consistent MAC keys K, K' and a value c, the following *linearity* properties hold for the MAC:

– **Addition:**

$$\mathsf{MAC}_\mathsf{K}(a) + \mathsf{MAC}_{\mathsf{K}'}(b) = \mathsf{MAC}_{\mathsf{K}+\mathsf{K}'}(a + b).$$

– **Addition/Subtraction by a Constant:**

$$\mathsf{MAC}_{\mathsf{K}-c}(a + c) = \mathsf{MAC}_\mathsf{K}(a) \quad \text{and} \quad \mathsf{MAC}_{\mathsf{K}+c}(a - c) = \mathsf{MAC}_\mathsf{K}(a).$$

– **Multiplication by a constant:**

$$c \cdot \mathsf{MAC}_\mathsf{K}(a) = \mathsf{MAC}_{c \cdot \mathsf{K}}(c \cdot a).$$

2.3 The Various Sharings

We define following two types of secret sharing.

Definition 1 ([·]-sharing). *We say a value $s \in \mathbb{F}$ is [·]-shared among $\mathcal{P}$ if there exists a polynomial $p(\cdot)$ of degree at most t with $p(0) = s$ and every (honest) party $P_i \in \mathcal{P}$ holds a share $s_i \stackrel{def}{=} p(i)$ of s. We denote by $[s]$ the vector of shares of s corresponding to the (honest) parties in $\mathcal{P}$. That is, $[s] = \{s_i\}_{i=1}^n$.*

Definition 2 (⟨·⟩-sharing). *We say that a value $s \in \mathbb{F}$ is ⟨·⟩-shared among $\mathcal{P}$ if s is [·]-shared among $\mathcal{P}$ and every (honest) party P_i holds a MAC tag on its share s_i for a key K_{ji} held by every P_j. That is, the following holds for every pair of (honest) parties $P_i, P_j \in \mathcal{P}$: party P_i holds MAC tag $\mathsf{MAC}_{\mathsf{K}_{ji}}(s_i)$ for a MAC key K_{ji} held by P_j. We denote by ⟨s⟩ the vector of such shares, MAC keys and MAC tags of s corresponding to the (honest) parties in $\mathcal{P}$. That is, $\langle s \rangle = \{ s_i, \{\mathsf{MAC}_{\mathsf{K}_{ji}}(s_i), \mathsf{K}_{ij}\}_{j=1}^n \}_{i=1}^n.$*

While most of our computations are done over values that are $\langle \cdot \rangle$-shared, our efficient public reconstruction protocol for $\langle \cdot \rangle$-shared values will additionally require a tweaked version of $\langle \cdot \rangle$-sharing, where there exists some designated party, say P_j; and the parties hold the shares and the MAC tags in an encrypted form under the public key $\mathbf{pk}^{(j)}$ of an HE scheme, where P_j knows the corresponding secret key $\mathbf{dk}^{(j)}$. We stress that the shares and MAC tags will not be available in clear. More formally:

Definition 3 ($\langle\langle\langle\cdot\rangle\rangle\rangle_j$-sharing). *Let $s \in \mathbb{F}$ and $[s] = \{s_i\}_{i=1}^n$ be the vector of shares corresponding to an $[\cdot]$-sharing of s. We say that s is $\langle\langle\langle\cdot\rangle\rangle\rangle_j$-shared among $\mathcal{P}$ with respect to a designated party P_j, if every (honest) party P_i holds an encrypted share $\mathsf{HE.c}(s_i)$ and encrypted MAC tag $\mathsf{HE.c}(\mathsf{MAC}_{\mathsf{K}_{ji}}(s_i))$ under the public key $\mathbf{pk}^{(j)}$, such that P_j holds the MAC keys K_{ji} and the secret key $\mathbf{dk}^{(j)}$. We denote by $\langle\langle s \rangle\rangle_j$ the vector of encrypted shares and encrypted MAC tags corresponding to the (honest) parties in $\mathcal{P}$, along with the MAC keys and the secret key of P_j. That is, $\langle\langle s \rangle\rangle_j = \left\{ \{\mathsf{HE.c}(s_i), \mathsf{HE.c}(\mathsf{MAC}_{\mathsf{K}_{ji}}(s_i))\}_{i=1}^n, \{\mathsf{K}_{ji}\}_{i=1}^n, \mathbf{dk}^{(j)} \right\}$.*

Private Reconstruction of $\langle \cdot \rangle$ and $\langle\langle\langle\cdot\rangle\rangle\rangle$-shared Value Towards a Designated Party. Note that with $n = 2t + 1$, a $[\cdot]$-shared value cannot be robustly reconstructed towards a designated party just by sending the shares, as we cannot do error-correction. However, we can robustly reconstruct a $\langle \cdot \rangle$-sharing towards a designated party, say P_j, by asking the parties to send their shares, along with MAC tags to P_j, who then identifies the correct shares with high probability and reconstructs the secret. A similar idea can be used to reconstruct an $\langle\langle s \rangle\rangle_j$-sharing towards P_j. Now the parties send encrypted shares and MAC tags to P_j, who decrypts them before doing the verification. We call the

---

Protocol RecPrv($\langle s \rangle, P_j$)

- Every party $P_i \in \mathcal{P}$ sends its share s_i and the MAC tag $\mathsf{MAC}_{\mathsf{K}_{ji}}(s_i)$ to the party P_j.
- Party P_j on receiving the share s_i' and the MAC tag $\mathsf{MAC}'_{\mathsf{K}_{ji}}(s_i)$ from P_i computes
  $\mathsf{MAC}_{\mathsf{K}_{ji}}(s_i')$ and verifies if $\mathsf{MAC}_{\mathsf{K}_{ji}}(s_i') \overset{?}{=} \mathsf{MAC}'_{\mathsf{K}_{ji}}(s_i)$.
- If the verification passes then P_j considers s_i' as a valid share.
- Once $t + 1$ valid shares are obtained, using them P_j interpolates the sharing polynomial and outputs its constant term as s.

Protocol RecPrvEnc($\langle\langle s \rangle\rangle_j$)

- Every party $P_i \in \mathcal{P}$ sends $\mathsf{HE.c}(s_i)$ and $\mathsf{HE.c}(\mathsf{MAC}_{\mathsf{K}_{ji}}(s_i))$ to the party P_j.
- Party P_j, on receiving these values, computes $s_i' = \mathsf{HE.Dec}_{\mathbf{dk}^{(j)}}(\mathsf{HE.c}(s_i))$ and $\mathsf{MAC}'_{\mathsf{K}_{ji}}(s_i) = \mathsf{HE.Dec}_{\mathbf{dk}^{(j)}}(\mathsf{HE.c}(\mathsf{MAC}_{\mathsf{K}_{ji}}(s_i)))$. The rest of the steps are the same as for RecPrv($\star, P_j$).

Fig. 1. Protocols for reconstructing a $\langle \cdot \rangle$-sharing and $\langle\langle\langle\cdot\rangle\rangle\rangle$-sharing towards a designated party

resultant protocols $\mathsf{RecPrv}(\langle s \rangle, P_j)$ and $\mathsf{RecPrvEnc}(\langle\langle s \rangle\rangle_j)$ respectively, which are presented in Fig. 1. We stress that while $\langle s \rangle$ can be reconstructed towards *any* P_j, $\langle\langle s \rangle\rangle_j$ can be reconstructed only towards P_j, as P_j alone holds the secret key $\mathbf{dk}^{(j)}$ that is required to decrypt the shares and the MAC tags.

It is easy to see that if P_j is honest, then P_j correctly reconstructs the shared value in protocol RecPrv as well as in $\mathsf{RecPrvEnc}$, except with probability at most $\frac{t}{|\mathbb{F}|} \approx \mathsf{negl}(\mu)$. While protocol RecPrv has communication complexity $\mathcal{O}(\mu \cdot n)$ bits, protocol $\mathsf{RecPrvEnc}$ has communication complexity $\mathcal{O}(\kappa \cdot n)$ bits. Also note that both the protocols will work in the asynchronous setting. We argue this for RecPrv (the same argument will work for $\mathsf{RecPrvEnc}$). The party P_j will eventually receive the shares of s from at least $n-t = t+1$ honest parties, with correct MACs. These $t+1$ shares are enough for the robust reconstruction of s. So we state the following lemma for RecPrv. Similar statements hold for protocol $\mathsf{RecPrvEnc}$. Thus we have the following Lemmas.

Lemma 1. *Let s be $\langle\cdot\rangle$-shared among the parties $\mathcal{P}$. Let P_j be a specific party. Protocol RecPrv achieves the following in the synchronous communication setting:*

– *Correctness: Except with probability $\mathsf{negl}(\mu)$, an honest P_j reconstructs s.*
– *Communication Complexity: The communication complexity is $\mathcal{O}(\mu \cdot n)$ bits.*

Lemma 2. *Let s be $\langle\cdot\rangle$-shared among the parties $\mathcal{P}$. Let P_j be a specific party. Protocol RecPrv achieves the following in the asynchronous communication setting:*

– *Correctness & Communication Complexity: Same as in Lemma 1.*
– *Termination: If every honest party participates in RecPrv, then an honest P_j will eventually terminate.*

Linearity of Various Sharings. All of the previously defined secret sharings are linear, which for ease of exposition we shall now overview. We first define what is meant by key consistent sharings.

Definition 4 (Key-Consistent $\langle\cdot\rangle$ and $\langle\langle\cdot\rangle\rangle_j$ Sharings). *Two $\langle\cdot\rangle$-sharings $\langle a \rangle$ and $\langle b \rangle$ are said to be key-consistent if every (honest) P_i holds consistent MAC keys for every P_j across both the sharings.*

Sharings $\langle\langle a \rangle\rangle_j$ and $\langle\langle b \rangle\rangle_j$ with respect to a designated P_j are called key-consistent if P_j holds consistent MAC keys for every P_i across both the sharings, and the encryptions are under the same public key of P_j.

Linearity of $[\cdot]$-sharings: Given $[a] = \{a_i\}_{i=1}^n$ and $[b] = \{b_i\}_{i=1}^n$ and a public constant c, we have:

– *Addition:* To compute $[a+b]$, every party P_i needs to locally compute $a_i + b_i$,

$$[a] + [b] = [a+b] = \{a_i + b_i\}_{i=1}^n .$$

- *Addition by a Public Constant*: To compute $[c + a]$, every party P_i needs to locally compute $c + a_i$,

$$c + [a] = [c + a] = \{c + a_i\}_{i=1}^{n}.$$

- *Multiplication by a Public Constant*: To compute $[c \cdot a]$, every party P_i needs to locally compute $c \cdot a_i$,

$$c \cdot [a] = [c \cdot a] = \{c \cdot a_i\}_{i=1}^{n}.$$

<u>*Linearity of $\langle \cdot \rangle$-sharing*:</u> Given $\langle a \rangle = \left\{ a_i, \{\mathsf{MAC}_{\mathsf{K}_{ji}}(a_i), \mathsf{K}_{ij}\}_{j=1}^{n} \right\}_{i=1}^{n}$, and $\langle b \rangle = \left\{ b_i, \{\mathsf{MAC}_{\mathsf{K}'_{ji}}(b_i), \mathsf{K}'_{ij}\}_{j=1}^{n} \right\}_{i=1}^{n}$ that are key-consistent and a publicly-known constant c, we have:

- *Addition*: To compute $\langle a + b \rangle$, every party P_i needs to locally compute $a_i + b_i$, $\{\mathsf{MAC}_{\mathsf{K}_{ji}}(a_i) + \mathsf{MAC}_{\mathsf{K}'_{ji}}(b_i)\}_{j=1}^{n}$ and $\{\mathsf{K}_{ij} + \mathsf{K}'_{ij}\}_{j=1}^{n}$,

$$\langle a \rangle + \langle b \rangle = \langle a + b \rangle = \left\{ a_i + b_i, \{\mathsf{MAC}_{\mathsf{K}_{ji} + \mathsf{K}'_{ji}}(a_i + b_i), \mathsf{K}_{ij} + \mathsf{K}'_{ij}\}_{j=1}^{n} \right\}_{i=1}^{n}.$$

- *Addition by a Public Constant*: To compute $\langle c + a \rangle$, every party P_i needs to locally compute $c + a_i$, In addition recall that $\mathsf{MAC}_{\mathsf{K}_{ji} - c}(a_i + c) = \mathsf{MAC}_{\mathsf{K}_{ji}}(a_i)$. Hence we assign $\mathsf{MAC}_{\mathsf{K}_{ji}}(a_i)$ to $\mathsf{MAC}_{\mathsf{K}_{ji} - c}(a_i + c)$ and compute $\{\mathsf{K}_{ij} - c\}_{j=1}^{n}$.

$$c + \langle a \rangle = \langle c + a \rangle = \left\{ c + a_i, \{\mathsf{MAC}_{\mathsf{K}_{ji} - c}(a_i + c), \mathsf{K}_{ij} - c\}_{j=1}^{n} \right\}_{i=1}^{n}.$$

- *Multiplication by a Public Constant*: To compute $\langle c \cdot a \rangle$, every party P_i needs to locally compute $c \cdot a_i$, $\{c \cdot \mathsf{MAC}._{\mathsf{K}_{ji}}(a_i)\}_{j=1}^{n}$ and $\{c \cdot \mathsf{K}_{ij}\}_{j=1}^{n}$,

$$c \cdot \langle a \rangle = \langle c \cdot a \rangle = \left\{ c \cdot a_i, \{\mathsf{MAC}_{c \cdot \mathsf{K}_{ji}}(c \cdot a_i), c \cdot \mathsf{K}_{ij}\}_{j=1}^{n} \right\}_{i=1}^{n}.$$

<u>*Linearity of $\langle\langle \cdot \rangle\rangle_j$-sharings*:</u> Given $\langle\langle a \rangle\rangle_j = \left\{ \{\mathsf{HE.c}(a_i), \mathsf{HE.c}(\mathsf{MAC}_{\mathsf{K}_{ji}}(a_i)), \}_{i=1}^{n}, \{\mathsf{K}_{ji}\}_{i=1}^{n}, \mathbf{dk}^{(j)} \right\}$ and $\langle\langle b \rangle\rangle_j = \left\{ \{\mathsf{HE.c}(b_i), \mathsf{HE.c}(\mathsf{MAC}_{\mathsf{K}_{ji}}(b_i))\}_{i=1}^{n}, \{\mathsf{K}'_{ji}\}_{i=1}^{n}, \mathbf{dk}^{(j)} \right\}$ that are key-consistent we can add the sharings via the operation

$$\langle\langle a \rangle\rangle_j + \langle\langle b \rangle\rangle_j = \langle\langle a + b \rangle\rangle_j$$
$$= \left\{ \{\mathsf{HE.c}(a_i + b_i), \mathsf{HE.c}(\mathsf{MAC}_{\mathsf{K}_{ji} + \mathsf{K}'_{ji}}(a_i + b_i))\}_{i=1}^{n}, \right.$$
$$\left. \{\mathsf{K}_{ji} + \mathsf{K}'_{ji}\}_{i=1}^{n}, \mathbf{dk}^{(j)} \right\}$$

So to compute $\langle\langle a + b \rangle\rangle_j$, every party $P_i \in \mathcal{P}$ needs to locally compute the values $\mathsf{HE.c}(a_i) \oplus \mathsf{HE.c}(b_i)$ and $\mathsf{HE.c}(\mathsf{MAC}_{\mathsf{K}_{ji}}(a_i)) \oplus \mathsf{HE.c}(\mathsf{MAC}_{\mathsf{K}'_{ji}}(b_i))$, while party P_j needs to compute $\{\mathsf{K}_{ji} + \mathsf{K}'_{ji}\}_{i=1}^{n}$.

Generating $\langle\langle\cdot\rangle\rangle_j$-sharing from $\langle\cdot\rangle$-sharing. In our efficient protocol for public reconstruction of $\langle\cdot\rangle$-shared values, we come across the situation where there exists: a value r known only to a designated party P_j, a publicly known encryption $\mathsf{HE.c}(r)$ of r, under the public key $\mathbf{pk}^{(j)}$, and a $\langle\cdot\rangle$-sharing $\langle a\rangle = \{a_i, \{\mathsf{MAC}_{\mathsf{K}_{ji}}(a_i), \mathsf{K}_{ij}\}_{j=1}^n\}_{i=1}^n$. Given the above, the parties need to compute a $\langle\langle\cdot\rangle\rangle_j$ sharing:

$$\langle\langle r \cdot a\rangle\rangle_j = \Big\{\{\mathsf{HE.c}(r \cdot a_i), \mathsf{HE.c}(\mathsf{MAC}_{r \cdot \mathsf{K}_{ji}}(r \cdot a_i))\}_{i=1}^n, \{r \cdot \mathsf{K}_{ji}\}_{i=1}^n, \mathbf{dk}^{(j)}\Big\}$$

of $r \cdot a$. Computing the above needs only local computation by the parties. Specifically, each party $P_i \in \mathcal{P}$ locally computes the values $\mathsf{HE.c}(r \cdot a_i) = a_i \odot \mathsf{HE.c}(r)$ and

$$\mathsf{HE.c}(\mathsf{MAC}_{r \cdot \mathsf{K}_{ji}}(r \cdot a_i)) = \mathsf{HE.c}(r \cdot \mathsf{MAC}_{\mathsf{K}_{ji}}(a_i)) = \mathsf{MAC}_{\mathsf{K}_{ji}}(a_i) \odot \mathsf{HE.c}(r),$$

since $r \cdot \mathsf{MAC}_{\mathsf{K}_{ji}}(a_i) = \mathsf{MAC}_{r \cdot \mathsf{K}_{ji}}(a_i \cdot r)$. Finally party P_j locally computes $\{r \cdot \mathsf{K}_{ji}\}_{i=1}^n$.

3 Public Reconstruction of $\langle\cdot\rangle$-sharings with a Linear Overhead

We present a new protocol to publicly reconstruct $n(t+1)\frac{\kappa}{\mu} = \Theta(\frac{n^2\kappa}{\mu})$ $\langle\cdot\rangle$-shared values with communication complexity $\mathcal{O}(\kappa \cdot n^3)$ bits. So the amortized communication overhead for public reconstruction of one $\langle\cdot\rangle$-shared value is linear in n i.e. $\mathcal{O}(\mu \cdot n)$ bits. For a better understanding of the ideas used in the protocol, we first present a protocol RecPubSimple to publicly reconstruct $n(t+1)$ $\langle\cdot\rangle$-shared values with communication complexity $\mathcal{O}(\kappa \cdot n^3)$ bits. We will then extend this protocol for $n(t+1)\frac{\kappa}{\mu}$ secrets while retaining the same communication complexity; the resulting protocol is called RecPub.

Let $\{\langle a^{(i,j)}\rangle\}_{i=1,j=1}^{n,t+1}$ be the $\langle\cdot\rangle$-sharings, which need to be publicly reconstructed. The naive way of achieving the task is to run $\Theta(n^3)$ instances of RecPrv, where $\Theta(n^2)$ instances are run to reconstruct all the values to a single party. This method has communication complexity $\mathcal{O}(\kappa \cdot n^4)$ bits and thus has a quadratic overhead. Our approach outperforms the naive method, and works for both synchronous as well as asynchronous setting; for simplicity we first explain the protocol assuming a synchronous setting.

Let A be an $n \times (t+1)$ matrix, with (i,j)th element as $a^{(i,j)}$. Let $A_i(x)$ be a polynomial of degree t defined over the values in the ith row of A; i.e. $A_i(x) \stackrel{def}{=} A[i,1] + A[i,2]x + \ldots, A[i,t+1]x^t$. Let B denote an $n \times n$ matrix and $B[i,j] \stackrel{def}{=} A_i(j)$, for $i,j \in \{1,\ldots,n\}$. Clearly A can be recovered given any $t+1$ columns of B. We explain below how to reconstruct at least $t+1$ columns of B to all the parties with communication complexity $\mathcal{O}(\kappa \cdot n^3)$ bits. In what follows, we denote ith row and column of A as A_i and A^i respectively, with a similar notation used for the rows and columns of B.

Since B_i is linearly dependent on A_i, given $\langle \cdot \rangle$-sharing of A_i, it requires only local computation to generate $\langle \cdot \rangle$-sharings of the elements in B_i. Specifically, $\langle B[i,j] \rangle = \langle A[i,1] \rangle + \langle A[i,2] \rangle \cdot j + \ldots + \langle A[i,t+1] \rangle \cdot j^t$. Then we reconstruct the elements of A to all the parties in two steps. First B^i is reconstructed towards P_i using n instances of RecPrv with an overall cost $\mathcal{O}(\mu \cdot n^3)$ bits. Next each party P_i sends B^i to all the parties, requiring $\mathcal{O}(\mu \cdot n^3)$ bits of communication. If every P_i behaves honestly then every party would possess B at the end of the second step. However a corrupted P_i may not send the correct B^i. So what we need is a mechanism that allows an honest party to detect if a corrupted party P_i has sent an incorrect B^i. Detecting is enough, since every (honest) party is guaranteed to receive correctly the B^i columns from $t + 1$ honest parties. Recall that $t + 1$ correct columns of B are enough to reconstruct A.

After P_i reconstructs B^i, and before it sends the same to party P_j, we allow P_j to obtain a random linear combination of the elements in B^i (via interaction) in a way that the linear combiners are known to no one other than P_j. Later, when P_i sends B^i to P_j, party P_j can verify if the B^i received from P_i is correct or not by comparing the linear combination of the elements of the received B^i with the linear combination that it obtained before. It is crucial to pick the linear combiners randomly and keep them secret, otherwise P_i can cheat with an incorrect B^i without being detected by an honest P_j. In our method, the random combiners for an honest P_j are never leaked to anyone and this allows P_j to reuse them in a latter instance of the public reconstruction protocol. Specifically, we assume the following *one time setup* for RecPubSimple (which can be done beforehand in the offline phase of the main MPC protocol). Every party P_j holds a secret key $\mathbf{dk}^{(j)}$ for the linearly-homomorphic encryption scheme HE and the corresponding public key $\mathbf{pk}^{(j)}$ is publicly available. In addition, P_j holds a vector R^j of n random combiners and the encryptions $\mathsf{HE.c}(R^j[1]), \ldots, \mathsf{HE.c}(R^j[n])$ of the values in R^j under P_j's public key $\mathbf{pk}^{(j)}$ are available publicly. The above setup can be created once and for all, and can be reused across multiple instances of RecPubSimple.

Given the above random combiners in an encrypted form, party P_j can obtain the linear combination $c^{(i,j)} \overset{def}{=} \sum_{l=1}^{n} B^i[l] R^j[l]$ of the elements of B^i as follows. First note that the parties hold $\langle \cdot \rangle$-sharing of the elements of B^i. If the linear combiners were publicly known, then the parties could compute $\langle c^{(i,j)} \rangle = \sum_{l=1}^{n} R^j[l] \langle B^i[l] \rangle$ and reconstruct $c^{(i,j)}$ to party P_j using RecPrv. However since we do *not* want to disclose the combiners, the above task is performed in an encrypted form, which is doable since the combiners are encrypted under the linearly-homomorphic PKE. Specifically, given encryptions $\mathsf{HE.c}(R^j[l])$ under $\mathbf{pk}^{(j)}$ and sharings $\langle B^i[l] \rangle$, the parties first generate $\langle\langle R^j[l] \cdot B^i[l] \rangle\rangle_j$ for every P_j (recall that it requires only local computation). Next the parties linearly combine the sharings $\langle\langle R^j[l] \cdot B^i[l] \rangle\rangle_j$ for $l = 1, \ldots, n$ to obtain $\langle\langle c^{(i,j)} \rangle\rangle_j$, which is then reconstructed towards party P_j using an instance of RecPrvEnc. In total n^2 such instances need to be executed, costing $\mathcal{O}(\kappa \cdot n^3)$ bits. Protocol RecPubSimple is presented in Fig. 2.

Protocol RecPubSimple($\{\langle a^{(i,j)}\rangle\}_{i=1,j=1}^{n,t+1}$)

Each $P_j \in \mathcal{P}$ holds R^j and the encryptions $\mathsf{HE.c}(R^j[1]), \ldots, \mathsf{HE.c}(R^j[n])$, under P_j's public key $\mathbf{pk}^{(j)}$, are publicly known. Let A be the matrix of size $n \times (t+1)$, with (i,j)th entry as $a^{(i,j)}$, for $i \in \{1, \ldots, n\}$ and $j \in \{1, \ldots, t+1\}$. We denote the ith row and column of A as A_i and A^i respectively. Let $A_i(x) \overset{def}{=} a^{(i,1)} + \ldots + a^{(i,t+1)}x^t$ for $i \in \{1, \ldots, n\}$. Let B be the matrix of size $n \times n$, with the (i,j)th entry as $B[i,j] \overset{def}{=} A_i(j)$ for $i, j \in \{1, \ldots, n\}$. We denote the ith row and column of B as B_i and B^i respectively. The parties do the following to reconstruct A:

- **Computing $\langle \cdot \rangle$-sharing of every element of** B: For $i, j \in \{1, \ldots, n\}$, the parties compute $\langle B[i,j]\rangle = \langle A[i,1]\rangle + j \cdot \langle A[i,1]\rangle + \ldots + j^t \cdot \langle A[i,t+1]\rangle$.
- **Reconstructing** B^i **towards** P_i: For $i \in \{1, \ldots, n\}$, the parties execute $\mathsf{RecPrv}(\langle B[1,i]\rangle, P_i), \ldots, \mathsf{RecPrv}(\langle B[n,i]\rangle, P_i)$ to enable P_i robustly reconstruct B^i.
- **Reconstructing** $B^i \otimes R^j$ **towards** P_j: Corresponding to each $P_i \in \mathcal{P}$, the parties execute the following steps, to enable each $P_j \in \mathcal{P}$ to obtain the random linear combination $c^{(i,j)} \overset{def}{=} B^i \otimes R^j$:
  - The parties first compute $\langle\langle R^j[l] \cdot B^i[l]\rangle\rangle_j$ from $\mathsf{HE.c}(R^j[l])$ and $\langle B^i[l]\rangle$ for $l \in \{1, \ldots, n\}$ and then compute $\langle\langle c^{(i,j)}\rangle\rangle_j = \sum_{l=1}^{n}\langle\langle R^j[l] \cdot B^i[l]\rangle\rangle_j$.
  - The parties execute $\mathsf{RecPrvEnc}(\langle\langle c^{(i,j)}\rangle\rangle_j)$ to reconstruct $c^{(i,j)}$ towards P_j.
- **Sending** B^i **to all:** Each $P_i \in \mathcal{P}$ sends B^i to every $P_j \in \mathcal{P}$. Each P_j then reconstructs A as follows:
  - On receiving $\bar{B}^i$ from P_i, compute $c'^{(i,j)} = \bar{B}^i \otimes R^j$ and check if $c^{(i,j)} \overset{?}{=} c'^{(i,j)}$. If the test passes then P_j considers $\bar{B}^i$ as the valid i^{th} column of the matrix B.
  - Once $t+1$ valid columns of B are obtained by P_j, it then reconstructs A.

Fig. 2. Robustly reconstructing $\langle \cdot \rangle$-shared values with $\mathcal{O}(\kappa \cdot n)$ communication complexity

The correctness and communication complexity of the protocol are stated in Lemma 3, which follows in a straight forward fashion from the protocol description and the detailed protocol overview. The security of the protocol will be proven, in the full version, in conjunction with the online phase of our MPC protocol.

Lemma 3. *Let $\{\langle a^{(i,j)}\rangle\}_{i=1,j=1}^{n,t+1}$ be a set of $n(t+1)$ shared values which need to be publicly reconstructed by the parties. Then given a setup $(\mathbf{pk}^{(1)}, \mathbf{dk}^{(1)}), \ldots, (\mathbf{pk}^{(n)}, \mathbf{dk}^{(n)})$ for the linearly-homomorphic encryption scheme HE for the n parties and encryptions $\mathsf{HE.c}(R^j[1]), \ldots, \mathsf{HE.c}(R^j[n])$ of n random values in R^j on the behalf of each party $P_j \in \mathcal{P}$, with only P_j knowing the random values, protocol $\mathsf{RecPubSimple}$ achieves the following in the synchronous communication setting:*

- *Correctness: Except with probability $\mathsf{negl}(\kappa, \mu)$, every honest party reconstructs $\{a^{(i,j)}\}_{i=1,j=1}^{n,t+1}$.*
- *Communication Complexity: The communication complexity is $\mathcal{O}(\kappa \cdot n^3)$ bits.*

From $\mathcal{O}(\kappa \cdot n)$ to $\mathcal{O}(\mu \cdot n)$ Amortized Cost of Reconstruction. We note that the amortized complexity of reconstructing one secret via RecPubSimple is $\mathcal{O}(\kappa \cdot n)$, where κ is the cryptographic security parameter. To improve the amortized cost to $\mathcal{O}(\mu \cdot n)$, we make the following observation on the communication in RecPubSimple. There is a scope to amortize part of the communication to reconstruct more than $n(t + 1)$ secrets. This leads to a trick that brings down the amortized communication complexity per secret to $\mathcal{O}(\mu \cdot n)$ bits. We call our new protocol RecPub. which starts with $\frac{\kappa}{\mu}$ batches of secrets where each batch consists of $n(t + 1)$ secrets. For each batch, RecPub executes exactly the same steps as done in RecPubSimple except for the step involving the reconstruction of $B^i \otimes R^j$. RecPub keeps the communication cost of this step unperturbed by taking a random linear combination of $\frac{\kappa}{\mu} B^i$ columns together. Therefore RecPub still needs private reconstruction of $n^2 \langle\langle \cdot \rangle\rangle_j$-shared values and a communication of $\mathcal{O}(\kappa \cdot n^3)$ bits for this step. For the rest of the steps, the communication complexity of RecPub will be $\frac{\kappa}{\mu}$ times the communication complexity of the same steps in RecPubSimple. Since RecPubSimple requires $\mathcal{O}(\mu \cdot n^3)$ bits of communication for the rest of the steps, the communication complexity of RecPub will turn out to be $\mathcal{O}(\kappa \cdot n^3)$ bits of communication overall. Since the number reconstructed secrets are $n(t + 1)\frac{\kappa}{\mu}$, RecPub offers an amortized cost of $\mathcal{O}(\mu \cdot n)$ bits per secret. The formal specification of protocol RecPub is in Fig. 3.

We note that RecPub takes random linear combination of $\frac{\kappa n}{\mu}$ values. So the one time set up has to be enhanced where every P_j now holds $\frac{\kappa n}{\mu}$ random combiners, and the encryptions of them are available in public. Namely R^j is a vector of $\kappa n / \mu$ random values and the encryptions $\mathsf{HE.c}(R^j[1]), \ldots, \mathsf{HE.c}(R^j[\kappa n/\mu])$ done under P_j's public key $\mathbf{pk}^{(j)}$ are available publicly. We thus have the following Lemma.

Lemma 4. *Let* $\{\langle a^{(i,j,k)} \rangle\}_{i=1,j=1,k=1}^{n,t+1,\kappa/\mu}$ *be a set of* $n(t + 1)\frac{\kappa}{\mu}$ *shared values which need to be publicly reconstructed by the parties. Then given a setup* $(\mathbf{pk}^{(1)}, \mathbf{dk}^{(1)}), \ldots, (\mathbf{pk}^{(n)}, \mathbf{dk}^{(n)})$ *for the linearly-homomorphic encryption scheme* HE *for the* n *parties and encryptions* $\mathsf{HE.c}(R^j[1]), \ldots, \mathsf{HE.c}(R^j[\kappa n/\mu])$ *of* $\kappa n / \mu$ *random values in* R^j *on the behalf of each party* $P_j \in \mathcal{P}$, *with only* P_j *knowing the random values, protocol* RecPub *achieves the following in the synchronous communication setting:*

- *Correctness: Except with probability* $\mathsf{negl}(\kappa, \mu)$, *every honest party reconstructs* $\{a^{(i,j,k)}\}_{i=1,j=1,k=1}^{n,t+1,\kappa/\mu}$.
- *Communication Complexity: The communication complexity is* $\mathcal{O}(\kappa \cdot n^3)$ *bits.*

Protocol RecPubSimple and RecPub in the Asynchronous Setting: Consider the protocol RecPubSimple, and note that the steps involving interaction among the parties are during the instances of RecPrv and RecPrvEnc. All the remaining steps involve only local computation by the parties. As the instances of RecPrv and RecPrvEnc eventually terminate for each honest party, it follows

---

Protocol RecPub($\{\langle a^{(i,j,k)}\rangle\}_{i=1,j=1,k=1}^{n,t+1,\kappa/\mu}$)

Each $P_j \in \mathcal{P}$ holds $R^j = (R^j[1], \ldots, R^j[\kappa n/\mu])$ and the encryptions $\mathsf{HE.c}(R^j[1]), \ldots,$ $\mathsf{HE.c}(R^j[\kappa n/\mu])$, under P_j's public key $\mathbf{pk}^{(j)}$, are publicly known. For a k that varies over $1, \ldots, \kappa/\mu$, the set of secrets $\{a^{(i,j,k)}\}_{i=1,j=1}^{n,t+1}$ is denoted as the kth batch of secrets. Let $\mathcal{A}^{(k)}$ be the matrix of size $n \times (t+1)$ consisting of the kth batch i.e., the (i,j)th entry of $\mathcal{A}^{(k)}$ is $a^{(i,j,k)}$, for $i \in \{1, \ldots, n\}$ and $j \in \{1, \ldots, t+1\}$. We denote the ith row and column of $\mathcal{A}^{(k)}$ as $\mathcal{A}_i^{(k)}$ and $\mathcal{A}^{(k)i}$ respectively. We define $\mathcal{A}_i^{(k)}(x) \stackrel{def}{=} \mathcal{A}^{(k)}[i,1] + \mathcal{A}^{(k)}[i,2] \cdot x + \ldots + \mathcal{A}^{(k)}[i,t+1] \cdot x^t$ for $i \in \{1, \ldots, n\}$. Let $\mathcal{B}^{(k)}$ be the matrix of size $n \times n$, with the (i,j)th entry as $\mathcal{B}^{(k)}[i,j] \stackrel{def}{=} \mathcal{A}_i^{(k)}(j)$ for $i,j \in \{1, \ldots, n\}$. We denote the ith row and column of $\mathcal{B}^{(k)}$ as $\mathcal{B}_i^{(k)}$ and $\mathcal{B}^{(k)i}$ respectively. We denote the concatenation of the ith column of all the $\mathcal{B}^{(k)}$s as B^i i.e. $B^i = \left[(\mathcal{B}^{(1)i})^{tr}, \ldots, (\mathcal{B}^{(\frac{\kappa}{\mu})i})^{tr}\right]$ where $(\cdot)^{tr}$ denotes vector transpose. The parties do the following to reconstruct $\mathcal{A}^{(1)}, \ldots, \mathcal{A}^{(\frac{\kappa}{\mu})}$:

- **Computing $\langle \cdot \rangle$-sharing of elements of $\mathcal{B}^{(k)}$ for $k = 1, \ldots, \kappa/\mu$:** Same as in RecPubSimple.
- **Reconstructing $\mathcal{B}^{(k)i}$ towards P_i for $k = 1, \ldots, \kappa/\mu$:** Same as in RecPubSimple. Party P_i holds B^i at the end of this step.
- **Reconstructing $B^i \otimes R^j$ towards P_j:** Corresponding to each $P_i \in \mathcal{P}$, the parties execute the following steps, to enable each $P_j \in \mathcal{P}$ to obtain the random linear combination $c^{(i,j)} \stackrel{def}{=} B^i \otimes R^j = \sum_{l=1}^{\kappa n/\mu} R^j[l] B^i[l]$.
  - The parties first compute $\langle\langle R^j[l] B^i[l]\rangle\rangle_j$ from $\mathsf{HE.c}(R^j[l])$ and $\langle B^i[l]\rangle$ for $l \in \{1, \ldots, \frac{\kappa n}{\mu}\}$ and then compute $\langle\langle c^{(i,j)}\rangle\rangle_j = \sum_{l=1}^{\frac{\kappa n}{\mu}}\langle\langle R^j[l] B^i[l]\rangle\rangle_j$.
  - The parties execute $\mathsf{RecPrvEnc}(\langle\langle c^{(i,j)}\rangle\rangle_j)$ to reconstruct $c^{(i,j)}$ towards P_j.
- **Sending B^i to all:** Every party $P_i \in \mathcal{P}$ sends B^i to every party $P_j \in \mathcal{P}$. Each party P_j then reconstructs $\mathcal{A}^{(1)}, \ldots, \mathcal{A}^{(\frac{\kappa}{\mu})}$ as follows:
  - On receiving $\bar{B}^i$ from P_i, compute $c'^{(i,j)} = \bar{B}^i \otimes R^j$ and check if $c^{(i,j)} \stackrel{?}{=} c'^{(i,j)}$. If the test passes then P_j interprets $\bar{B}^i$ as $\left[(\mathcal{B}^{(1)i})^{tr}, \ldots, (\mathcal{B}^{(\frac{\kappa}{\mu})i})^{tr}\right]$ and considers $\mathcal{B}^{(k)i}$ as the valid i^{th} column of the matrix $\mathcal{B}^{(k)}$ for $k = 1, \ldots, \kappa/\mu$.
  - For $k = 1, \ldots, \kappa/\mu$, once $t+1$ valid columns of $\mathcal{B}^{(k)}$ are obtained by P_j, it then reconstructs $\mathcal{A}^{(k)}$.

Fig. 3. Robustly reconstructing $\langle \cdot \rangle$-shared values with $\mathcal{O}(\mu \cdot n)$ communication complexity

that RecPubSimple eventually terminates for each honest party in the asynchronous setting. Similar arguments hold for RecPub, so we get the following lemma.

Lemma 5. *Protocol* RecPub *achieves the following in the asynchronous communication setting:*

- *Correctness & Communication Complexity: Same as in Lemma 4*
- *Termination: Every honest party eventually terminates the protocol.*

4   Linear Overhead Online Phase Protocol

Let $f : \mathbb{F}^n \to \mathbb{F}$ be a publicly known function over $\mathbb{F}$, represented as an arithmetic circuit C over $\mathbb{F}$, consisting of M multiplication gates. Then using our efficient reconstruction protocol RecPub enables one to securely realize the standard ideal functionality $\mathcal{F}_f$ (see Fig. 4 for an explicit functionality) for the MPC evaluation of the circuit C, in the $\mathcal{F}_{\text{PREP}}$-hybrid model, with communication complexity $\mathcal{O}(\mu \cdot (n \cdot M + n^2))$ bits, thus providing a linear overhead per multiplication gate. More specifically, assume that the parties have access to an ideal pre-processing and input processing functionality $\mathcal{F}_{\text{PREP}}$, which creates the following *one-time* setup: **(i)** Every P_j holds a secret key $\mathbf{dk}^{(j)}$ for the linearly-homomorphic encryption scheme HE and the corresponding public key $\mathbf{pk}^{(j)}$ is available publicly. In addition, each P_j holds n random combiners $R^{(j)} = (r^{(j,1)}, \ldots, r^{(j,n)})$ and the encryptions $\text{HE.c}(r^{(j,1)}), \ldots, \text{HE.c}(r^{(j,n)})$ of these values under P_j's public key are publicly available. **(ii)** Each P_i holds α_{ij}, the α-component of all its keys for party P_j (recall that for key-consistent sharings every P_i has to use the same α-component for all its keys corresponding to P_j). The above setup can be reused across multiple instances of Π_{ONLINE} and can be created once and for all. In addition to the one-time setup, the functionality also creates at least M random $\langle \cdot \rangle$-shared multiplications triples (these are not reusable and have to be created afresh for every execution of Π_{ONLINE}) and $\langle \cdot \rangle$-shared inputs of the parties. Functionality $\mathcal{F}_{\text{PREP}}$ is presented in Fig. 5. In $\mathcal{F}_{\text{PREP}}$, the ideal adversary specifies all the data that the corrupted parties would like to hold as part of the various sharings generated by the functionality. Namely it specifies the shares, MAC keys and MAC tags. The functionality then completes the sharings while keeping them consistent with the data specified by the adversary.

Using $\mathcal{F}_{\text{PREP}}$ we design a protocol Π_{ONLINE} (see Fig. 6) which realizes $\mathcal{F}_f$ in the synchronous setting and provides *universal composability* (UC) security [10,13,16,22]. The protocol is based on the standard Beaver's idea of securely evaluating the circuit in a shared fashion using pre-processed shared random multiplication triples [4] and shared inputs. Namely, the parties evaluate the circuit C in a $\langle \cdot \rangle$-shared fashion by maintaining the following invariant for each gate in the circuit. Given a $\langle \cdot \rangle$-sharing of the inputs of the gate, the parties generate an $\langle \cdot \rangle$-sharing of the output of the gate. Maintaining the invariant for

---

Functionality $\mathcal{F}_f$

$\mathcal{F}_f$ interacts with the parties $P_1, \ldots, P_n$ and the adversary $\mathcal{S}$ and is parametrized by an n-input function $f : \mathbb{F}^n \to \mathbb{F}$ represented as an arithmetic circuit C.

- Upon receiving $(i, x^{(i)})$ from every party $P_i \in \mathcal{P}$ where $x^{(i)} \in \mathbb{F}$, the functionality computes $y = C(x^{(1)}, \ldots, x^{(n)})$, sends y to all the parties and the adversary $\mathcal{S}$ and halts. Here C denotes the arithmetic circuit over $\mathbb{F}$ representing f.

Fig. 4. The ideal functionality for computing a given function

---

Functionality $\mathcal{F}_{\mathbf{PREP}}$

The functionality interacts with the parties in $\mathcal{P}$ and the adversary $\mathcal{S}$ as follows. Let $\mathcal{C} \subset \mathcal{P}$ be the set of corrupted parties.

- **Setup Generation:** On input Setup from the parties in $\mathcal{P}$, the functionality does the following:
  - It creates n public key, secret key pairs $\{\mathbf{pk}^{(i)}, \mathbf{dk}^{(i)}\}_{i=1}^{n}$ of the linearly-homomorphic encryption scheme HE,
  - For each P_i, it selects $\frac{\kappa n}{\mu}$ random values $R^i = (r^{(i,1)}, \ldots, r^{(i,\frac{\kappa n}{\mu})})$, computes $\mathsf{HE.c}(r^{(i,1)}), \ldots, \mathsf{HE.c}(r^{(i,\frac{\kappa n}{\mu})})$ under $\mathbf{pk}^{(i)}$,
  - To party P_i it sends

$$\left(\mathbf{dk}^{(i)}, (r^{(i,1)}, \ldots, r^{(i,\frac{\kappa n}{\mu})}), \{\mathbf{pk}^{(j)}\}_{j=1}^{n}, \{\mathsf{HE.c}(r^{(j,1)}), \ldots, \mathsf{HE.c}(r^{(j,\frac{\kappa n}{\mu})})\}_{j=1}^{n} \right).$$

  - On the behalf of each honest $P_i \in \mathcal{P} \setminus \mathcal{C}$, it selects n random values $\{\alpha_{ij}\}_{j=1}^{n}$, where the jth value is designated to be used in the MAC key for party P_j. On the behalf of each corrupted party $P_i \in \mathcal{C}$, it receives from $\mathcal{S}$ the α_{ij} values that P_i wants to use in the MAC keys corresponding to the honest party P_j. On receiving, the functionality stores these values.
- **Triple Sharings:** On input Triples from all the parties in $\mathcal{P}$, the functionality generates $\langle \cdot \rangle$-sharing of χ random multiplication triples in parallel. To generate one such sharing $(\langle a \rangle, \langle b \rangle, \langle c \rangle)$, it does the following:
  - It randomly selects a, b and computes $c = ab$. It then runs 'Single $\langle \cdot \rangle$-sharing Generation' (see below) for a, b and c.
- **Input Sharings:** On input $(x^{(i)}, i, \mathsf{Input})$ from party P_i and (i, Input) from the remaining parties, the functionality runs 'Single $\langle \cdot \rangle$-sharing Generation' (given below) for $x^{(i)}$.

Single $\langle \cdot \rangle$-sharing Generation: The functionality does the following to generate $\langle s \rangle$-sharing for a given value s:

- On receiving the shares $\{s_i\}_{P_i \in \mathcal{C}}$ from $\mathcal{S}$ on the behalf of the corrupted parties, it selects a polynomial $S(\cdot)$ of degree at most t, such that $S(0) = s$ and $S(i) = s_i$ for each $P_i \in \mathcal{C}$. For $P_i \notin \mathcal{P} \setminus \mathcal{C}$, it computes $s_i = S(i)$.
- On receiving $\{\beta_{ij}\}_{P_i \in \mathcal{C}, \, P_j \notin \mathcal{C}}$ from $\mathcal{S}$, the second components of the MAC key that $P_i \in \mathcal{C}$ will have for an honest party P_j, it sets $\mathsf{K}_{ij} = (\alpha_{ij}, \beta_{ij})$ where α_{ij} was specified by $\mathcal{S}$ in 'Setup generation' stage. It computes the MAC tag $\mathsf{MAC}_{\mathsf{K}_{ij}}(s_j)$ of s_j for every honest P_j corresponding to the key of every corrupted P_i.
- On receiving MAC tags $\{\mathsf{MAC}_{ij}\}_{P_i \in \mathcal{C}, \, P_j \notin \mathcal{C}}$ that the corrupted parties would like to have on their shares s_i corresponding to the MAC key of honest P_j, it fixes the key of P_j corresponding to P_i as $\mathsf{K}_{ji} = (\alpha_{ji}, \beta_{ji})$ where $\beta_{ji} = \mathsf{MAC}_{ij} - \alpha_{ji} \cdot s_i$ and α_{ji} was selected by the functionality in 'Setup generation' stage.
- For every pair of honest parties (P_j, P_k), it chooses the key of P_j as $\mathsf{K}_{jk} = (\alpha_{jk}, \beta_{jk})$ where α_{jk} is taken from 'setup generation phase' and β_{jk} is chosen randomly. It then computes the corresponding MAC tag of P_k as $\mathsf{MAC}_{\mathsf{K}_{jk}}(s_k)$.
- It sends $\{s_j, \{\mathsf{MAC}_{\mathsf{K}_{kj}}, \mathsf{K}_{jk}\}_{k=1}^{n}\}$ to honest party P_j (no need to send anything to corrupted parties as $\mathcal{S}$ has the data of the corrupted parties already).

Fig. 5. Ideal functionality for setup generation, offline pre-processing and input processing

---

Protocol Π_{ONLINE}

Every party $P_i \in \mathcal{P}$ interact with $\mathcal{F}_{\text{PREP}}$ with input Setup, Triples and $(x^{(i)}, i, \text{Input})$ and receives $\mathbf{dk}^{(i)}$, $\{\mathbf{pk}^{(j)}\}_{j=1}^{n}$, $R^i = (r^{(i,1)}, \ldots, r^{(i, \frac{\kappa n}{\mu})})$, $\{\text{HE.c}(r^{(j,1)}), \ldots, \text{HE.c}(r^{(j, \frac{\kappa n}{\mu})})\}_{j=1}^{n}$, its information for multiplication triples $\{(\langle a^{(l)}\rangle, \langle b^{(l)}\rangle, \langle c^{(l)}\rangle)\}_{l=1}^{M}$ and its information for inputs $\{\langle x^{(j)}\rangle\}_{j=1}^{n}$. The honest parties associate the sharing $(\langle a^{(l)}\rangle, \langle b^{(l)}\rangle, \langle c^{(l)}\rangle)$ with the lth multiplication gate for $l \in \{1, \ldots, M\}$ and evaluate each gate in the circuit as follows:

- **Linear Gates**: using the linearity property of $\langle \cdot \rangle$-sharing, the parties apply the linear function associated with the gate on the corresponding $\langle \cdot \rangle$-shared gate inputs to obtain an $\langle \cdot \rangle$-sharing of the gate output.
- **Multiplication Gates**: M multiplication gates as grouped as a batch of $n \cdot (t + 1) \cdot \frac{\kappa}{\mu}$. We explain the evaluation for one batch. Let the inputs to the ith batch be $\{(\langle p^{(l)}\rangle, \langle q^{(l)}\rangle)\}_{l=1}^{n \cdot (t+1) \cdot \frac{\kappa}{\mu}}$ and let $\{(\langle a^{(l)}\rangle, \langle b^{(l)}\rangle, \langle c^{(l)}\rangle)\}_{l=1}^{n \cdot (t+1) \cdot \frac{\kappa}{\mu}}$ be the corresponding associated multiplication triples. To compute $\langle p^{(l)} \cdot q^{(l)} \rangle$, the parties do the following:
  - Locally compute $\langle d^{(l)}\rangle = \langle p^{(l)}\rangle - \langle a^{(l)}\rangle = \langle p^{(l)} - a^{(l)}\rangle$ and $\langle e^{(l)}\rangle = \langle q^{(l)}\rangle - \langle b^{(l)}\rangle_t = \langle q^{(l)} - b^{(l)}\rangle$.
  - Publicly reconstruct the values $\{d^{(l)}\}_{l=1}^{n \cdot (t+1) \cdot \frac{\kappa}{\mu}}$ and $\{e^{(l)}\}_{l=1}^{n \cdot (t+1) \cdot \frac{\kappa}{\mu}}$ using two instances of RecPub.
  - On reconstructing $d^{(l)}, e^{(l)}$, the parties set $\langle p^{(l)} \cdot q^l \rangle = d^{(l)} \cdot e^{(l)} + d^{(l)} \cdot \langle b^{(l)}\rangle + e^{(l)} \cdot \langle a^{(l)}\rangle + \langle c^{(l)}\rangle$.
- **Output Gate**: Let $\langle y \rangle$ be the sharing of the output gate. The parties execute RecPrv($\langle y \rangle, P_i$) for every $P_i \in \mathcal{P}$, robustly reconstruct y and terminate.

Fig. 6. Realizing $\mathcal{F}_f$ with a linear overhead in $\mathcal{F}_{\text{PREP}}$-hybrid model for the synchronous setting

linear gates requires only local computation, thanks to the linearity property of the $\langle \cdot \rangle$-sharing. For multiplication gates, the parties deploy a shared multiplication triple received from $\mathcal{F}_{\text{PREP}}$ and evaluate the multiplication gate by using Beaver's trick. Specifically, let $\langle p \rangle, \langle q \rangle$ be the sharing corresponding to the inputs of a multiplication gate and let $(\langle a \rangle, \langle b \rangle, \langle c \rangle)$ be the shared random multiplication triple obtained from $\mathcal{F}_{\text{PREP}}$, which is associated with this multiplication gate. To compute an $\langle \cdot \rangle$-sharing of the gate output $p \cdot q$, we note that

$$p \cdot q = (p - a + a) \cdot (q - b + b) = d \cdot e + d \cdot b + e \cdot a + c, \text{ where } d \overset{def}{=} p - a \text{ and } e \overset{def}{=} q - b.$$

So if d and e are publicly known then $\langle p \cdot q \rangle = d \cdot e + d \cdot \langle b \rangle + e \cdot \langle a \rangle + \langle c \rangle$ holds. To make d and e public, the parties first locally compute $\langle d \rangle = \langle p \rangle - \langle a \rangle$ and $\langle e \rangle = \langle q \rangle - \langle b \rangle$ and publicly reconstruct these sharings. Note that even though d and e are made public, the privacy of the gate inputs p and q is preserved, as a and b are random and private. Finally once the parties have the sharing $\langle y \rangle$ for the circuit output, it is publicly reconstructed to enable every party obtain the function output.

To achieve the linear overhead in Π_{ONLINE}, we require that the circuit is "wide" in the sense that at every level there are at least $n(t + 1)\frac{\kappa}{\mu}$ independent multiplication gates that can be evaluated in parallel. This is to ensure that we can use our linear-overhead reconstruction protocol RecPub. We note that similar restrictions are used in some of the previous MPC protocols to achieve a linear overhead in the online phase. For example, [6,15,21] requires $\Theta(n)$ independent multiplication gates at each level to ensure that they can use their linear-overhead reconstruction protocol to evaluate these gates. In practice many functions have such a level of parallel multiplication gates when expressed in arithmetic circuit format, and practical systems use algorithms to maximise the level of such parallelism in their execution, see e.g. [32].

The properties of Π_{ONLINE} are stated in Theorem 1, which is proved in the full version. In the protocol, $2M$ $\langle\cdot\rangle$-shared values are publicly reconstructed via RecPub while evaluating the multiplication gates. Assuming that the M multiplication gates can be divided into blocks of $n(t+1)\frac{\kappa}{\mu}$ independent multiplication gates, evaluating the same will cost $\mathcal{O}(\kappa n^3 \cdot \frac{\mu M}{n(t+1)\kappa}) = \mathcal{O}(\mu \cdot n \cdot M)$ bits. The only steps in Π_{ONLINE} which require interaction among the parties are during the instances of the reconstruction protocols, which eventually terminate for the honest parties. Hence we get Theorem 2 for the asynchronous setting.

Theorem 1. *Protocol Π_{ONLINE} UC-securely realizes the functionality $\mathcal{F}_f$ in the $\mathcal{F}_{\text{PREP}}$-hybrid model in the synchronous setting. The protocol has communication complexity $\mathcal{O}(\mu \cdot (n \cdot M + n^2))$ bits.*

Theorem 2. *Protocol Π_{ONLINE} UC-securely realizes the functionality $\mathcal{F}_f$ in the $\mathcal{F}_{\text{PREP}}$-hybrid model in the asynchronous setting. The protocol has communication complexity $\mathcal{O}(\mu \cdot (n \cdot M + n^2))$ bits.*

5   The Various Secure Realizations of $\mathcal{F}_{\text{PREP}}$

Securely Realizing $\mathcal{F}_{\text{PREP}}$ in the Synchronous Setting. In the full version, we present a protocol Π_{PREP} which realizes $\mathcal{F}_{\text{PREP}}$ in the synchronous setting and achieves UC security. The protocol is a straight forward adaptation of the offline phase protocol of [10,22] to deal with Shamir sharing, instead of additive sharing.

Securely Realizing $\mathcal{F}_{\text{PREP}}$ with Abort in the Partial Synchronous Setting. Any secure realization of $\mathcal{F}_{\text{PREP}}$ has to ensure that all the honest parties have an *agreement* on the final outcome, which is impossible in the asynchronous setting with $t < n/2$ [29,30]. Another difficulty in realizing $\mathcal{F}_{\text{PREP}}$ in an asynchronous setting is that it is possible to ensure input provision from only $n - t$ parties to avoid endless wait. For $n = 2t + 1$ this implies that there may be only one honest input provider. This may not be acceptable for most practical applications of MPC. To get rid of the latter difficulty, [19] introduced the following variant of the traditional asynchronous communication setting, which we refer as *partial asynchronous setting*:

- The protocols in the partial asynchronous setting have one *synchronization* point. Specifically, there exists a certain well defined time-out and the assumption is that all the messages sent by the honest parties before the deadline will reach to their destinations within this deadline.
- Any protocol executed in the partial asynchronous setting need not always terminate and provide output to all the honest parties. Thus the adversary may cause the protocol to fail. However it is required that the protocol up to the synchronization point does not release any new information to the adversary.

In the full version we examine how to make Π_{PREP} work in the partial asynchronous setting. We present two solutions; the first which allows some synchronous rounds after the synchronization point, and one which uses a non-equivocation mechanism (which can be implemented using a trusted hardware module).

Acknowledgements. This work has been supported in part by ERC Advanced Grant ERC-2010-AdG-267188-CRIPTO, by EPSRC via grants EP/I03126X and EP/M016803, by DARPA and the US Navy under contract #N66001-15-C-4070, and by the Infosys Foundation.

References

1. Asharov, G., Jain, A., López-Alt, A., Tromer, E., Vaikuntanathan, V., Wichs, D.: Multiparty computation with low communication, computation and interaction via threshold FHE. In: Pointcheval, D., Johansson, T. (eds.) EUROCRYPT 2012. LNCS, vol. 7237, pp. 483–501. Springer, Heidelberg (2012)
2. Backes, M., Bendun, F., Choudhury, A., Kate, A.: Asynchronous MPC with a strict honest majority using non-equivocation. In: Halldórsson, M.M., Dolev, S. (eds.) PODC, pp. 10–19. ACM (2014)
3. Baron, J., J., Defrawy, J., Lampkins, J., Ostrovsky, R.: How to withstand mobile virus attacks, revisited. In: Halldórsson, M.M., Dolev, S. (eds.) PODC, pp. 293–302. ACM (2014)
4. Beaver, D.: Efficient multiparty protocols using circuit randomization. In: Feigenbaum, J. (ed.) CRYPTO 1991. LNCS, vol. 576, pp. 420–432. Springer, Heidelberg (1992)
5. Beerliová-Trubíniová, Z., Hirt, M.: Efficient multi-party computation with dispute control. In: Halevi, S., Rabin, T. (eds.) TCC 2006. LNCS, vol. 3876, pp. 305–328. Springer, Heidelberg (2006)
6. Beerliová-Trubíniová, Z., Hirt, M.: Perfectly-secure MPC with linear communication complexity. In: Canetti, R. (ed.) TCC 2008. LNCS, vol. 4948, pp. 213–230. Springer, Heidelberg (2008)
7. Ben-Or, M., Canetti, R., Goldreich, O.: Asynchronous secure computation. In: Kosaraju, S.R., Johnson, D.S., Aggarwal, A. (eds) STOC, pp. 52–61. ACM (1993)
8. Ben-Or, M., Goldwasser, S., Wigderson, A.: Completeness theorems for non-cryptographic fault-tolerant distributed computation (extended abstract). In: Simon, J. (ed.) STOC, pp. 1–10. ACM (1988)
9. Ben-Sasson, E., Fehr, S., Ostrovsky, R.: Near-linear unconditionally-secure multiparty computation with a dishonest minority. In: Safavi-Naini, R., Canetti, R. (eds.) CRYPTO 2012. LNCS, vol. 7417, pp. 663–680. Springer, Heidelberg (2012)

10. Bendlin, R., Damgård, I., Orlandi, C., Zakarias, S.: Semi-homomorphic encryption and multiparty computation. In: Paterson, K.G. (ed.) EUROCRYPT 2011. LNCS, vol. 6632, pp. 169–188. Springer, Heidelberg (2011)
11. Brakerski, Z., Gentry, C., Vaikuntanathan, V.: (Leveled) fully homomorphic encryption without bootstrapping. TOCT **6**(3), 13:1–13:36 (2014)
12. Canetti, R.: Studies in secure multiparty computation and applications. Ph.D. thesis, Weizmann Institute, Israel (1995)
13. Canetti, R.: Security and composition of multiparty cryptographic protocols. J. Cryptol. **13**(1), 143–202 (2000)
14. Chaum, D., Crépeau, C., Damgård, I.: Multiparty unconditionally secure protocols (extended abstract). In: STOC, pp. 11–19. ACM (1988)
15. Choudhury, A., Hirt, M., Patra, A.: Asynchronous multiparty computation with linear communication complexity. In: Afek, Y. (ed.) DISC 2013. LNCS, vol. 8205, pp. 388–402. Springer, Heidelberg (2013)
16. Choudhury, A., Loftus, J., Orsini, E., Patra, A., Smart, N.P.: Between a rock and a hard place: interpolating between MPC and FHE. In: Sako, K., Sarkar, P. (eds.) ASIACRYPT 2013, Part II. LNCS, vol. 8270, pp. 221–240. Springer, Heidelberg (2013)
17. Choudhury, A., Patra, A.: Optimally resilient asynchronous MPC with linear communication complexity. In: Das, S.K., Krishnaswamy, D., Karkar, S., Korman, A., Kumar, M., Portmann, M., Sastry, S. (eds.) ICDCN, pp. 5:1–5:10. ACM (2015)
18. Clement, A., Junqueira, F., Kate, A., Rodrigues, R.: On the (limited) power of non-equivocation. In: Kowalski, D., Panconesi, A. (eds.) PODC, pp. 301–308. ACM (2012)
19. Damgård, I., Geisler, M., Krøigaard, M., Nielsen, J.B.: Asynchronous multiparty computation: theory and implementation. In: Jarecki, S., Tsudik, G. (eds.) PKC, pp. 160–179 (2009)
20. Damgård, I., Ishai, Y., Krøigaard, M.: Perfectly secure multiparty computation and the computational overhead of cryptography. In: Gilbert, H. (ed.) EUROCRYPT 2010. LNCS, vol. 6110, pp. 445–465. Springer, Heidelberg (2010)
21. Damgård, I.B., Nielsen, J.B.: Scalable and unconditionally secure multiparty computation. In: Menezes, A. (ed.) CRYPTO 2007. LNCS, vol. 4622, pp. 572–590. Springer, Heidelberg (2007)
22. Damgård, I., Pastro, V., Smart, N., Zakarias, S.: Multiparty computation from somewhat homomorphic encryption. In: Safavi-Naini, R., Canetti, R. (eds.) CRYPTO 2012. LNCS, vol. 7417, pp. 643–662. Springer, Heidelberg (2012)
23. Damgård, I., Keller, M., Larraia, E., Pastro, V., Scholl, P., Smart, N.P.: Practical covertly secure MPC for dishonest majority – or: breaking the SPDZ limits. In: Crampton, J., Jajodia, S., Mayes, K. (eds.) ESORICS 2013. LNCS, vol. 8134, pp. 1–18. Springer, Heidelberg (2013)
24. Fitzi, M., Hirt, M.: Optimally efficient multi-valued Byzantine agreement. In: Ruppert, E., Malkhi, D. (eds.) PODC, pp. 163–168. ACM Press (2006)
25. Genkin, D., Ishai, Y., Polychroniadou, A.: Efficient multi-party computation: from passive to active security via secure SIMD circuits. In: Gennaro, R., Robshaw, M. (eds.) CRYPTO 2015. LNCS, vol. 9216, pp. 721–741. Springer, Heidelberg (2015)
26. Gennaro, R., Rabin, M.O., Rabin, T.: Simplified VSS and fact-track multiparty computations with applications to threshold cryptography. In: Coan, B.A., Afek, Y. (eds.) PODC, pp. 101–111. ACM (1998)
27. Goldreich, O., Micali, S., Wigderson, A.: How to play any mental game or a completeness theorem for protocols with honest majority. In: STOC, pp. 218–229. ACM (1987)

28. Hirt, M., Nielsen, J.B.: Robust multiparty computation with linear communication complexity. In: Dwork, C. (ed.) CRYPTO 2006. LNCS, vol. 4117, pp. 463–482. Springer, Heidelberg (2006)
29. Hirt, M., Nielsen, J.B., Przydatek, B.: Cryptographic asynchronous multi-party computation with optimal resilience (extended abstract). In: Cramer, R. (ed.) EUROCRYPT 2005. LNCS, vol. 3494, pp. 322–340. Springer, Heidelberg (2005)
30. Hirt, M., Nielsen, J.B., Przydatek, B.: Asynchronous multi-party computation with quadratic communication. In: Aceto, L., Damgård, I., Goldberg, L.A., Halldórsson, M.M., Ingólfsdóttir, A., Walukiewicz, I. (eds.) ICALP 2008, Part II. LNCS, vol. 5126, pp. 473–485. Springer, Heidelberg (2008)
31. Katz, J., Koo, C.-Y.: On expected constant-round protocols for Byzantine agreement. In: Dwork, C. (ed.) CRYPTO 2006. LNCS, vol. 4117, pp. 445–462. Springer, Heidelberg (2006)
32. Keller, M., Scholl, P., Smart, N.P.: An architecture for practical actively secure MPC with dishonest majority. In: Sadeghi, A.-R., Gligor, V.D., Yung, M. (eds.) ACM CCS 2013, pp. 549–560. ACM (2013)
33. Yao, A.C.: Protocols for secure computations (extended abstract). In: FOCS, pp. 160–164. IEEE Computer Society (1982)

High-Precision Secure Computation of Satellite Collision Probabilities

Brett Hemenway[1], Steve Lu[2(✉)], Rafail Ostrovsky[3], and William Welser IV[4]

[1] University of Pennsylvania, Philadelphia, USA
fbrett@cis.upenn.edu
[2] Stealth Software Technologies, Inc., Los Angeles, USA
steve@stealthsoftwareinc.com
[3] University of California, Los Angeles, USA
rafail@cs.ucla.edu
[4] RAND Corporation, Santa Monica, USA
bwelser@rand.org

Abstract. The costs of designing, building, launching and maintaining satellites make satellite operators extremely motivated to protect their on-orbit assets. Unfortunately, privacy concerns present a serious barrier to coordination between different operators. One obstacle to improving safety arises because operators view the trajectories of their satellites as private, and refuse to share this private information with other operators. Without data-sharing, preventing collisions between satellites becomes a challenging task. A 2014 report from the RAND Corporation proposed using cryptographic tools from the domain of secure Multiparty Computation (MPC) to allow satellite operators to calculate collision probabilities (conjunction analyses) without sharing private information about the trajectories of their satellites.

In this work, we report on the design and implementation of a new MPC framework for high-precision arithmetic on real-valued variables in a two-party setting where, unlike previous works, there is no honest majority, and where the players are not assumed to be semi-honest. We show how to apply this new solution in the domain of securely computing conjunction analyses. Our solution integrates the integer-based Goldreich-Micali-Wigderson (GMW) protocol and Garbled Circuits (GC). We prove security of our protocol in the two party, semi-honest setting, assuming only the existence of one-way functions and Oblivious Transfer (the OT-hybrid model). The protocol allows a pair of satellite operators to compute the probability that their satellites will collide without sharing their underlying private orbital information. Techniques developed in this paper would potentially have a wide impact on general secure numerical analysis computations. We also show how to strengthen our construction with standard arithmetic message-authentication-codes (MACs) to enforce honest behavior beyond the semi-honest setting.

B. Hemenway—Work done while consulting for RAND Corporation.
R. Ostrovsky—Work done while consulting for Stealth Software Technologies, Inc.

© Springer International Publishing Switzerland 2016
V. Zikas and R. De Prisco (Eds.): SCN 2016, LNCS 9841, pp. 169–187, 2016.
DOI: 10.1007/978-3-319-44618-9_9

Computing a conjunction analysis requires numerically estimating a complex triple integral to a high degree of precision. The complexity of the calculation, and the possibility of numeric instability presents many challenges for MPC protocols which typically model calculations as simple (integer) arithmetic or binary circuits. Our secure numerical integration routines are extremely stable and efficient, and our secure conjunction analysis protocol takes only a few minutes to run on a commodity laptop.

The full version appears in [HLOW16].

1   Introduction

There are currently more than 1300 active satellites orbiting the earth [UCS15], and this number is growing rapidly. Technological improvements have drastically reduced the barriers to building, launching and maintaining satellites in orbit, and consequently the number of different governments and private corporations maintaining active satellites is growing at an increasing rate (see Fig. 1). As the number of satellites and operators grows, the problem of coordinating operations between the different operators becomes more challenging.

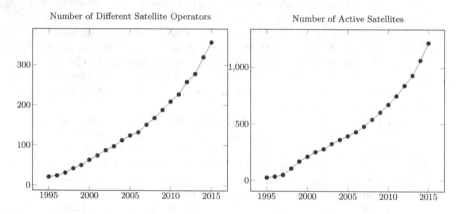

Fig. 1. The number of distinct satellite operators is increasing dramatically. In January 1995 there were only 21 different operators, while in January 2015 there were 357 according to the Union of Concerned Scientists [UCS15]. During the same time frame, the number of active satellites increased from 24 to over 1200.

In February 2009 the telecommunication satellite Iridium-33 collided with the Russian Kosmos 2251 in Low Earth Orbit (LEO). Their relative velocity was over 20,000 miles per hour, and both satellites were instantly destroyed and more than 1000 debris chunks over 4 in. in diameter were created [VO09].

Preventing future collisions requires coordination between a growing number of satellite operators. Unfortunately, privacy concerns present a barrier to cooperation, and in fact satellite operators view the precise trajectories of their on-orbit assets as private information. The Space Surveillance Network (SSN) managed by U.S. Strategic Command (USSTRATCOM) currently tracks more than 20,000 orbital objects with diameters greater than 10 cm. These tracking data, obtained by ground-based telescopes, are a valuable source of information, but they are too low-fidelity to calculate the probability that two active satellites will collide. Calculating collision probabilities (termed a "conjunction analyses") requires high-fidelity data from the satellites' on-board instrumentation – and these high-fidelity data are only available to the satellite's operator.

Thus we are in a situation where satellite operators want to keep their high-fidelity orbital information private, yet these are exactly the data needed to compute conjunction analyses and prevent further collisions. To overcome this obstacle, some operators have contracted the services of a trusted outside party (e.g. Analytical Graphics, Inc.). Operators then share their private data with the trusted party, the trusted party performs the conjunction analyses, and issues warnings if the collision probability exceeds a given threshold.

Trusted third parties do not provide a perfect solution, however, as many stakeholders cannot agree on a single trusted party, and even when such a mutually trusted party can be found, they can command a high price for their services. Secure multiparty computation (MPC) provides a cryptographic alternative to a trusted third party. Using MPC to securely compute satellite conjunction analyses was first proposed as a potential solution by Hemenway, Welser and Baiocchi [HWIB14]. Following that proposal, the problem of securely computing conjunction analyses was incorporated into DARPA's PROCEED program as a potential use-case for MPC technology, and received further media attention [HW15]. A three-party honest-majority protocol that could securely perform conjunction analyses was investigated in [KW14a].

Although MPC provides a general framework for computing arbitrary functions securely, efficiency is a primary concern. The four main approaches to MPC use Fully Homomorphic Encryption (FHE) [Gen09, BV11, LTV12], the GMW Protocol [GMW87], the information-theoretic BGW protocol [BGW88] or Garbled Circuits (GC) [Yao82, Yao86]. All four methods begin by converting the function of interest into a circuit (either Boolean or arithmetic) and then evaluating the circuit gate-by-gate.[1] This approach yields polynomial-time algorithms, but without heavy optimizations, these protocols are not practical for any but the simplest calculations. Indeed, one of the primary technical challenges in this area is to design protocols that are efficient enough to be used in practice. Several works in the past [FSW03, CS10, ABZS13, KW14b, PS15] have looked at optimizing MPC for real-valued computations, both for fixed and floating point, though these operate in the honest majority setting, which is a major barrier in the two-party setting for when two satellite operators only want to talk to each other.

---

[1] An alternative approach using Garbled RAM [LO13, GHL+14] avoids the problem of converting the calculation to a circuit. Practical implementations of GRAM is an interesting area to be explored.

1.1   Our Results

In this paper we describe a new design and implementation of a secure two-party computation framework for high-precision arithmetic of real-valued functions that go beyond standard floating point levels of accuracy. As an application, we show that it allows two satellite operators to perform a conjunction analysis securely without the need to share their private orbital information with each other or any outside party. From a theoretical standpoint, our solution is provably secure in the OT-hybrid model assuming only the existence of one-way functions.

Our main contribution is an efficient construction of a new scheme that can securely evaluate complex numerical calculations, in particular, the numerical integration of calculating the probability of collision in a conjunction analysis computation via "dynamic" fixed-point integer calculations. Our new scheme extends the integer-arithmetic GMW protocol [GMW87] and Garbled Circuits [Yao82, Yao86], and we show how to do it securely in the two-party setting where there is no honest majority. This scheme can evaluate not only arithmetic gates $(+, \times)$, but also augmented functionality gates which include comparison (which will be optimized as a less-than-zero gate), shift-by-constant, which then allows us to perform higher order functions such as integer division, square root, exp, erf, and numerical integration. As part of our new construction, we also introduce several optimizations and secure computation tools along the way, which may be of independent interest. Furthermore, our framework is sufficiently general that it could be of interest to other domains that require the secure computation of numerical analysis. Finally, we provide an extension to the scheme by deploying the arithmetic MAC technique of BeDOZa [BDOZ11] and SPDZ [DPSZ12] to provide security guarantees against a larger class of adversaries.

2   Background

2.1   Secure Computation

We use the standard real/ideal paradigm for defining security of a Multiparty Computation (MPC) protocol. We let $\stackrel{comp}{\approx}$ denote computational indistinguishability of probability distributions, i.e., no PPT algorithm can distinguish them with non-negligible probability.

Definition 1. *We say that a (two party) protocol π securely computes (in the semi-honest model) a deterministic functionality $\mathcal{F}$ if for every PPT algorithm A there is a PPT algorithm Sim such that* $\text{IDEAL}_{Sim}^{\mathcal{F}} \stackrel{comp}{\approx} \text{REAL}_{A}^{\pi}$ *,where* $\text{IDEAL}_{Sim}^{\mathcal{F}}$ *is the probability distribution of the output of the simulator Sim interacting with the ideal functionality (i.e., Sim gets the input and output of the corrupted party) and REAL_{A}^{π} is the probability distribution of the view (protocol messages and internal randomness) of the corrupted party A during the execution of the real protocol.*

Garbled Circuits. Garbled Circuits (GC) were originally proposed by Andrew Yao in oral presentations [Yao82, Yao86]. The first formal proof of security for Yao's GC protocol was given by Lindell and Pinkas [LP09], and later formalized as a standalone cryptographic primitive by Bellare, Hoang and Rogaway [BHR12a, BHR12b].

Although there have been many improvements and variants on Yao's original idea for garbled circuits, the important features of GC-based MPC protocols are: (1) the protocol can be done in two rounds of communication, independent of the size of the circuit. (2) Each garbled gate is encrypted using a symmetric-key cryptosystem (e.g. AES) so evaluating the garbled circuit requires roughly a number of AES operations proportional to the size of the circuit. (3) Transferring the input tokens requires OT, a public-key operation, and the size of this public-key computation is roughly proportional to the size of the secret inputs. We refer the reader to the full version for a more detaile exposition [HLOW16].

Secret-Sharing Based Protocols. Secret-sharing based protocols were first introduced by works of GMW [GMW87], or BGW [BGW88] and CCD [CCD88]. Although these three protocols are all based on secret-shared computations, each uses different mechanisms and has different security models (honest vs. no honest majority, the existence of Oblivious Transfer, etc.). In these protocols, each player begins by secret-sharing [Sha79] her private inputs among all the players. The players then engage in a protocol to compute the given circuit, gate-by-gate, on the shares. The GMW protocol requires OT for each multiplication gate, while the BGW protocol is information-theoretic and computing each gate requires only linear algebra (along with the assumption that a strict majority of players are honest). The important features of secret-sharing based protocols are: (1) the round complexity of the protocol is proportional to the depth of the circuit. (2) The GMW protocol requires a number of OTs roughly proportional to the number of multiplication gates in the circuit.

There have been many practical implementations of GMW-based MPC protocols including VIFF [DGKN09], TinyOT [NNOB12] and Wysteria [RHH14]. The Sharemind platform [BLW08] provides a general-purpose platform for secure computation based on the BGW protocol. The Sharemind platform has been used to perform conjunction analyses [KW14a]. A more detailed comparison of our work with the Sharemind implementation can be found in Sect. 6.2.

Archer et al. provide a survey on the state of practical MPC protocols [ABPP15].

Online/Offline Model of Secure Computation. Our construction works in the online/offline model of computation, and we briefly review the model here. The idea behind the online/offline model is that certain amounts of cryptographic material can be computed *independently* of the input, such that it can be stored and then recalled during the live computation when the inputs are available. To improve efficiency, we split our secure computation into two phases: the offline phase where input-independent data is precomputed and the online phase where input-dependent computations occur. Early research in this area was done by Beaver [Bea95, Bea97], and the power of this model continues to be demonstrated in works such as Ishai et al. [IKM+13] and have found use in implementations as well [BDOZ11, DPSZ12]

The offline phase may involve communication between the parties – as long as that communication is independent of their private inputs. In some situations, we can use the aid of an *offline dealer* that only participates during the offline phase and contributes no inputs nor receives any outputs during the online phase, but instead distributes correlated randomness to the parties. Secondly, we can talk about two kinds of pre-computed data: those that remain persistent across multiple online invocations (e.g. public keys and parameters being sent in advance), and those that are used and consumed (e.g. one-time pads being sent in advance). Then, during the online phase, cryptographic material from the offline phase is used in conjunction with the inputs in order to do the live computation. We will see many instantiations of this in the forthcoming sections.

2.2 Oblivious Transfer

Oblivious transfer (OT) is a cryptographic primitive introduced by Rabin [Rab05], and we use the 1-out-of-2 variant introduced by Even-Goldreich-Lempel [EGL82]. In this variant, a Sender holds two string values x_0 and x_1 and the Receiver holds a choice bit b. The Receiver should get x_b without learning anything about x_{1-b} and without the Sender learning anything about b. This can be viewed as a secure protocol for the functionality $\mathsf{OT}((x_0, x_1); b) = (\bot; x_b)$, where $\bot$ denotes the empty message. We write OT_m to indicate that the strings x_0 and x_1 are of length m. Oblivious transfer can be implemented under a variety of standard assumptions (cf. Goldreich's book [Gol01, Gol04] for details).

2.3 Shared Arithmetic Triples (Oblivious Linear-Function Evaluation)

Oblivious linear function evaluation is a natural extension of OT, where one party (e.g. the Sender) holding two values $a, b \in \mathbb{F}$ and another party (e.g. the Receiver) holding some value $x \in \mathbb{F}$. The goal is to have the Receiver get $ax + b$ without learning a, b and without the Sender learning x.

We consider two alternative, equivalent functionalities: one of shared-input-shared-output multiplication (SISO-M), and one of just shared-output multiplication (SO-M). Due to the symmetric nature of these notions, we refer to the two parties as Alice and Bob instead of the Sender and Receiver.

For SISO-M, Alice and Bob hold shares of two field elements, x, y and they would like to obtain shares of the product. In particular, Alice holds $x_0, y_0 \in \mathbb{F}$ and Bob holds $x_1, y_1 \in \mathbb{F}$ and the goal is to have Alice obtain a random $z_0 \in \mathbb{F}$ and Bob obtain z_1 such that $(z_0 + z_1) = (x_0 + x_1) \cdot (y_0 + y_1)$. Note that since each of the two outputs is uniformly distributed over the field, each party learns no additional information about the other party's input. In the shared-output version, Alice holds x, Bob holds y and they want to obtain z_0 and z_1 such that $(z_0 + z_1) = x \cdot y$.

2.4 Conjunction Analysis Calculations

Before we describe our secure conjunction analysis computation, we review the problem of computing it in the clear. Our secure computation solution is based on Alfano's method [Alf05].

Each satellite is modelled as a spherical object, and thus its dimensions are completely captured by a single parameter, its radius. Although the radius is not particularly sensitive, our solution will hide the radius as well the trajectory information. Each satellite operator's private input has four parts: **position: $\mathbf{p}_a, \mathbf{p}_b \in \mathbb{R}^3$, velocity: $\mathbf{v}_a, \mathbf{v}_b \in \mathbb{R}^3$, error: $\mathbf{C}_a, \mathbf{C}_b \in \mathbb{R}^{3 \times 3}$ and radius: $R_a, R_b \in \mathbb{R}$.**

Each satellite is assumed to deviate from its position, $\mathbf{p}$, and these deviations are assumed to be normally distributed with covariance matrix[2] $\mathbf{C}$. Thus each satellite's physical location is given by $\mathbf{p} + \mathcal{N}(\mathbf{C})$, These normal distributions are truncated at eight standard deviations [Alf07] resulting in a "density ellipsoid." Although each satellite is on an elliptical path, in any short time window, the satellite's trajectory is almost linear, and during the course of the conjunction analysis, the two satellites are assumed to have linear relative velocities. These simplifying assumptions were not introduced to facilitate a secure computation, but instead are all part of the routine (insecure) conjunction analyses being performed on a daily basis.

Because the positional errors on the two satellites are assumed to be independent, we can shift all the errors onto one body, and imagine a "hardbody" of radius $R_a + R_b$ passing through a density ellipsoid with covariance matrix $\mathbf{C}_a + \mathbf{C}_b$. This spherical hardbody traces a "collision tube" through the combined density ellipsoid, and the probability of collision is then simply the probability mass of the density ellipsoid within this collision tube (See Fig. 2).

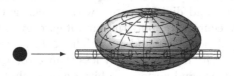

Fig. 2. The hardbody of radius $R_a + R_b$ traces out a collision tube through the combined density ellipsoid. The probability of collision is the probability mass of the density function inside the collision tube.

To simplify the calculation further, the three dimensional pdf is sliced, perpendicular to the relative velocity, at the point of nearest approach (where the density is largest). This defines the "encounter plane", and the cross-section of the ellipsoid in the encounter plane is a density ellipse.

Thus the final probability is calculated by integrating the two dimensional density ellipse in the region given by the cross-section of the hardbody. Given

---

[2] These covariance matrices are usually assumed to be diagonal, *i.e.*, the variances along the three principal axes are independent. This assumption does not significantly affect the computation.

the combined radius $R = R_a + R_b$, the center of the hardbody in the encounter plane, (x_m, y_m), and the lengths of the semi-principal axes (σ_x, σ_y) of the density ellipse, we calculate the probability of collision, p.

$$p = \frac{1}{2\pi\sigma_x\sigma_y} \int_{-R}^{R} \int_{-\sqrt{R^2-x^2}}^{\sqrt{R^2-x^2}} \exp\left[\frac{-1}{2}\left[\left(\frac{x-x_m}{\sigma_x}\right)^2 + \left(\frac{y-y_m}{\sigma_y}\right)^2\right]\right] dy dx \quad (1)$$

Changing variables, this becomes

$$p = \frac{3}{\sqrt{8\pi}\sigma_x} \int_{-R}^{R} \left[\mathrm{erf}\left(\frac{y_m + \sqrt{R^2-x^2}}{\sqrt{2}\sigma_y}\right) + \mathrm{erf}\left(\frac{-y_m + \sqrt{R^2-x^2}}{\sqrt{2}\sigma_y}\right)\right]$$
$$\exp\left(\frac{-(x+x_m)^2}{2\sigma_x^2}\right) dx \quad (2)$$

This integral does not have a closed form, and Alfano suggests approximating this integral using Simpson's Rule (*i.e.*, approximating the integral using arcs of parabola). A more thorough discussion of the mathematics involved is in the full version [HLOW16]. We also apply a change-of-variables $z = x/R$ so that the square root inside the integral and the limits of integration do not depend on inputs, which allows for greater flexibility in hardwiring constants into the circuit.

Pseudocode for the complete conjunction analysis calculation can also be found in [HLOW16].

3   Our Techniques

Our construction uses an "augmented" arithmetic circuit, consisting of (integer) addition, multiplication and division gates, with special gates for comparisons and bit-shifts, and we securely compute this circuit gate-by-gate. Our comparison and bit-shift gates are denoted < 0 and $>> c$. The < 0 gate takes a single integer as input and returns 1 if its input is strictly less than zero, and 0 otherwise. The $>> c$ gate takes an integer and performs a bitwise right-shift by a (fixed) public constant. A more thorough description of our circuit model can be found in the full version [HLOW16].

3.1   Combining GC with Arithmetic GMW

We compute (integer) addition and multiplications natively using GMW. To compute comparison and shift gates, we represent them as *Boolean* circuits and then evaluate them using GC. The GC must take two secret-inputs and compute a secret sharing of the output of the gate. Since the inputs are arithmetically secret shared, one must first convert them to bits before inputting them into the Boolean circuit that computes an augmented gate, and then convert them back into arithmetic shares. We explain how two parties can perform these computations in Algorithms 1 and 2. Share conversion of this nature has been investigated in previous works, e.g. Yu and Yang [YY12].

Algorithm 1. Share-converted Less-Than-Zero

1: **Hardwired:** A modulus $M = 2^m$
2: **Inputs:** Alice holds x_0, Bob holds x_1. Alice additionally provides a random R
3: $x \leftarrow x_0 + x_1 \pmod{M}$ using standard m-bit add-with-carry circuit
4: $b \leftarrow sgn(x)$
5: **Return:** $z_1 = b + R \pmod{M}$ to Bob. Alice sets $z_0 = -R \pmod{M}$ herself.

Algorithm 2. Share-converted shift-right-by-constant

1: **Hardwired:** A modulus $M = 2^m$ and a shift constant c.
2: **Inputs:** Alice holds x_0, Bob holds x_1. Alice additionally provides a random R
3: $x \leftarrow x_0 + x_1 \pmod{M}$ using standard m-bit add-with-carry circuit
4: $y \leftarrow x >> c$ by duplicating the sign bit wire and dropping c rightmost wires
5: **Return:** $z_1 = y + R \pmod{M}$ to Bob. Alice sets $z_0 = -R \pmod{M}$ herself.

Representing Mathematical Functions as Circuits: Evaluating the integral given in Eq. 2 requires division, $\exp(\cdot)$, $\sqrt{\cdot}$, and $\text{erf}(\cdot)$. We explain how we chose to implement these functions using our circuits.

Circuit Representation for Division: We implement integer division using repeated subtraction. Using known bounds on the inputs, we can track maximum and minimum values for each gate in the circuit, and using this (public) meta information, we can bound the number of subtractions necessary for each division in the circuit.

Circuit Representation for $\exp(\cdot)$: We represent the function $\exp(\cdot)$ using a degree-24 Taylor series. We hard-code the Taylor coefficients as constants in the circuit.

Circuit Representation for $\sqrt{\cdot}$: To approximate a square root, we use the iterative Babylonian Algorithm. Given an input S, and an initial estimate x_0, the Babylonian Algorithm computes

$$x_{n+1} = \frac{1}{2}\left(x_n + \frac{S}{x_n}\right)$$

For increased efficiency, we compute multiple steps at once, *i.e.*, computing x_{n+4} as a ratio of two degree 16 polynomials in S and x_0. For our calculations, we do 6 batches of degree 16 each to ensure a sufficient degree of accuracy.

Circuit Representation for $\text{erf}(\cdot)$: Taylor expansions of erf fare poorly outside of a very restricted domain (see the full version for more details [HLOW16]). Instead of the Taylor expansion, we approximate $\text{erf}(x)$ using a degree 96 rational function with uniform error bound of 10^{-7} across the entire range [AS65].

4 Main Construction

We now describe our main construction, which is the semi-honest two-party secure computation of the conjunction analysis functionality in the online/offline model. We let π_{CA} denote the protocol we are about to describe. We first describe how to precompute the cryptographic resources during the offline phase. In the offline preprocessing phase, we generate three cryptographic "resources" for later use.

4.1 Offline Phase

Pregenerated Random OTs. Our computation requires executing a huge number of OTs. Using a now standard trick due to Beaver [Bea95], we can generate random OTs during the precomputation phase and then later "consume" these random OTs during the online computation.

To pregenerate a random OT, the Sender holds *random* (r_0, r_1) and the Receiver holds a *random* bit z. After running OT on these random values, the Receiver gets r_z. We now describe how to use this random OT to perform an actual OT in the online phase.

Now suppose they want to run OT on actual inputs (s_0, s_1) for the Sender and b for the Receiver. To begin, the Receiver sends $w = z \oplus b$, then the Sender sends to the Receiver $(q_0, q_1) = (s_0 \oplus r_{0 \oplus w}, s_1 \oplus r_{1 \oplus w})$. Finally the Receiver outputs $t = q_b \oplus r_z$.

There are two methods by which the participants can generate the necessary random OT instances during the online phase. (1) The participants can generate a small number of OT instances and then use OT extension [IKNP03] to extend these to a huge number of OTs. (2) They can make use of a trusted dealer who simply provides correlated randomness to the two players, *i.e.*, the dealer will generate three random values (r_0, r_1, z) and provide r_0, r_1 to Alice and z, r_z to Bob.

Pregenerated Random Triples. Similar to OTs, for shared arithmetic triples, we can generate random arithmetic triples in the precomputation phase. We outline the technique on how to actually generate shared-output versions of these, which is due to the work of Ishai et al. [IPS09]. This technique works in batches of size t and makes use of OTs.

Suppose Alice holds $a_1, \ldots, a_t$ and Bob holds $b_1, \ldots, b_t$ and they want to compute shares of all $a_i \cdot b_i$. In other words, they want to compute a shared output multiplication. Let $k = 2t$ and $n = ck$ where c is a constant. Suppose we have t distinct evaluation points ζ_i and n distinct evaluation points θ_i, distinct from the ζs.

<u>Bob:</u> Let $B(x)$ be a random degree $k - 1$ polynomial such that $B(\zeta_i) = b_i$ for $i = 1 \ldots t$. Such a B can be found by interpolation. Sample the polynomial at the points θ_i to get $y_i = B(\theta_i)$ for $i = 1 \ldots n$. Sample $L \subset \{1, \ldots, n\}$ at random of size $t + k - 1$. Set $v_i = y_i$ if $i \in L$, and v_i to be random if $i \notin L$. Send the v_is to Alice.

Alice: Let $A(x)$ be the unique degree $t - 1$ polynomial such that $A(\zeta_i) = a_i$ for $i = 1 \ldots t$. Such an A can be found by interpolation. Let Alice choose $R(x)$, a random degree $t + k - 2$ polynomial. Compute $x_i = A(\theta_i)$ and $r_i = R(\theta_i)$ for $i = 1 \ldots n$. Set $w_i = x_i \cdot v_i - r_i$.

Alice and Bob: For each $i = 1 \ldots n$, Bob plays the role of the Receiver in an OT protocol with Alice, who plays the role of the Sender. Bob sets his bit b to be 1 if and only if $i \in L$, and Alice sets her messages $x_1 = w_i$ and x_0 to be random.

Bob: Bob sets Q to be the unique polynomial of degree $t + k - 2$ with $Q(\theta_i) = w_i$ for $i \in L$, again via interpolation. Bob sets $bob_i = Q(\zeta_i)$, Alice sets $alice_i = R(\zeta_i)$, for $i = 1 \ldots t$. These are the output shares $z_{0,i} = alice_i$ and $z_{1,i} = bob_i$ for Alice and Bob, respectively.

To see why this works, observe that $Q + R = A \cdot B$, and so $bob_i + alice_i = Q(\zeta_i) + R(\zeta_i) = A(\zeta_i) \cdot B(\zeta_i) = a_i \cdot b_i$.

To convert these into shared-input-shared-output triples, we proceed as follows: Suppose Alice holds x_0, y_0 and Bob holds x_1, y_1. They want to compute shares z_0 and z_1 of $(x_0 + x_1)(y_0 + y_1)$. This is just equal to $x_0 y_0 + x_0 y_1 + x_1 y_0 + x_1 y_1$. They can make two calls to the above protocol, once with x_0 and y_1 as inputs, and once with x_1 and y_0 as inputs, which allows us to get shares for the cross-terms $x_0 y_1$ and $x_1 y_0$.

Pregenerated Garbled Circuits. Our protocol will use garbled circuits to compute the shift and comparison gates on secret-shared values. Because the circuit garbling procedure is input-independent, we perform a small precomputation here where we generate all the Γ during this phase. Our garbled circuits implementation uses a fixed-key blockcipher (AES) as described in JustGarble [BHKR13], without any of the newer garbled circuit optimizations.

4.2 Online Phase

For the online phase, we use the arithmetic version of the Goldreich-Micali-Wigderson [GMW87] paradigm: each party secret shares his or her inputs, then performs gate-by-gate operations as described below. Alice and Bob's inputs are denoted X_0, Y_0 and X_1, Y_1 respectively.

- For every addition and subtraction gate, Alice and Bob respectively add or subtract their local shares $Z_0 = X_0 \pm Y_0$ and $Z_1 = X_1 \pm Y_1$.
- For every multiplication gate, Alice and Bob consume a shared triple to obtain a newly shared Z_0 and Z_1. We refer the reader to the full version [HLOW16] on how to perform this standard operation.
- For every shift gate, Alice and Bob's shares are X_0 and X_1 and they want to shift $(X_0 + X_1)$ by some publicly known amount N. This is accomplished using a (precomputed) garbled circuit computing Algorithm 2, where Alice sends Bob the garbled circuit and then Bob uses OT to obtain labels corresponding to his inputs.

- For every comparison gate (optimized as a less-than-zero gate), Alice has her share X_0 and Bob has his share X_1 and they want to see if $(X_0 + X_1)$ is positive or not. This is done via a circuit that computes Algorithm 1. We then use the garbled version of this circuit (that was precomputed earlier) to evaluate it where Alice sends Bob the garbled circuit and then Bob uses OT to obtain labels corresponding to his inputs.

Note that this process can be parallelized across an entire layer of the circuit, so that interaction occurs at each level of the arithmetic circuit rather than at each gate (excluding the free gates). In the end, the output values are shared as O_0 and O_1, whereupon Alice and Bob reveal to each other their shares to obtain the final output. We refer the reader to the full version for the proof [HLOW16]

5   Extending the Construction

In this section, we show how to extend our construction to provide security against semi-malicious adversaries. In the malicious security model, corrupted parties are allowed to deviate arbitrarily from the prescribed protocol, and the protocol is secure if nothing revealed beyond what is revealed by the output alone.

Our extended construction considers a slightly weaker model, where in the presence of malicious behavior, the honest party will detect such activity and will immediately abort the protocol. The event of abort reveals information about the honest player's decision to abort the protocol – but we allow this leakage.

The construction in this section achieves security against malicious adversaries *with correlated abort* (see e.g. [IKO+11]), *i.e.*, nothing is revealed except the output, unless in the case of an abort where nothing is learned except that an abort occurred.

In order to extend our solution from the semi-honest model to this stronger setting, we note that our shared triples generation is only secure in the semi-honest model, and thus in order to be able to now securely precompute triples we must resort to another technique. There are several works (e.g. [BDOZ11, DPSZ12] and their follow-up research) that focus on optimizing this offline construction, and our novel contribution is focused on the online phase. Therefore, we employ a secure two-party computation solution with an offline phase that assumes the assistance of a semi-trusted dealer.

We describe how to securely evaluate an arithmetic circuit $C(x, y) = C(x_1, \ldots, x_n, y_1, \ldots, y_n)$ containing $+, -, \times, < 0, >> c$ gates over the integers, where < 0 is the "less-than-zero" gate, and $>> c$ is the "arithmetic-shift-right-by-c" gate (we also include "constant" gates). In terms of representation, we bound the total number of bits of any intermediate value in the computation and choose a modulus N that is twice as large as the bound plus a security parameter, and use $[N/2, N/2)$ as the set of representatives for the integers modulo N. We henceforth take all arithmetic to be modulo N, where comparison to zero and shift still makes sense because we are taking the half-interval around zero representation.

Suppose Alice holds the inputs $x_1, \ldots, x_n$ and Bob holds the inputs $y_1, \ldots, y_n$. We will evaluate each gate individually, and thus evaluate the entire circuit by evaluating the "tree" of gates inductively (this is done in parallel to the furthest extent possible, we only wait if one gate depends on another gate). For addition, subtraction, multiplication, and constant gates, we employ an arithmetic MAC style strategy for evaluation (see, e.g. [BDOZ11]) which we describe here.

Let g be a gate, and let L and R be the left and right inputs, respectively, and let $O = g(L, R)$ be the output of the gate. Let $MAC_{\alpha, \beta}(x)$ be $\alpha x + \beta$. We inductively assume that the two inputs are shared and MACced in the following fashion:

- Alice and Bob each privately hold their own global MAC key, α_A and α_B, and they each hold a unique β for each wire in the circuit.
- Let $\beta_A^L, \beta_B^L, \beta_A^R, \beta_B^R$ denote the β for the left and right inputs, for Alice and Bob.
- Alice will then hold random shares x_L and x_R and Bob will hold random shares y_L and y_R subject to $x_L + y_L = L$ and $x_R + y_R = R$.
- Alice will hold $w_A^L = MAC_{\alpha_B, \beta_B^L}(x_L)$ and $w_A^R = MAC_{\alpha_B, \beta_B^R}(x_R)$.
- Bob will hold $w_B^L = MAC_{\alpha_A, \beta_A^L}(y_L)$ and $w_B^R = MAC_{\alpha_A, \beta_A^R}(y_R)$.
- **GOAL:** Obtain x_O, w_A^O, β_A^O for Alice and y_O, w_B^O, β_B^O for Bob such that the inductive invariants $x_O + y_O = O$, $w_A^O = MAC_{\alpha_B, \beta_B^O}(x_O)$, and $w_B^O = MAC_{\alpha_A, \beta_A^O}(y_O)$ hold.

For each gate type, we describe what is required as pregenerated content, and what is done online. As the first step to setup, the dealer generates α_A and α_B and sends them to Alice and Bob respectively.

CONSTANT GATES. For constant gates, if the constant is c, the dealer generates β_A, β_B at random, x at random, and sets $y = c - x$. It then computes $w_A = MAC_{\alpha_B, \beta_B}(x)$ and $w_B = MAC_{\alpha_A, \beta_A}(y)$. It sends x, w_A, β_A to Alice and y, w_B, β_B to Bob to store. During the online phase, Alice and Bob recall these values from storage when needed.

ADDITION AND SUBTRACTION GATES. For addition/subtraction gates, no pregeneration by the dealer is necessary. Indeed, Alice computes $\beta_A^O = \beta_A^L \pm \beta_A^R$, $w_A^O = w_A^L \pm w_A^R$, and $x_O = x_L + x_R$, and Bob performs the analogous computations. Then it is the case that the inductive invariant holds since: $x_O + y_O = x_L \pm x_R + y_L \pm y_R = (x_L + y_L) \pm (x_R + y_R) = L \pm R = O$, and $w_A^O = w_A^L \pm w_A^R = MAC_{\alpha_B, \beta_B^L}(x_L) \pm MAC_{\alpha_B, \beta_B^R}(x_R) = (\alpha_B \cdot x_L + \beta_B^L) \pm (\alpha_B \cdot x_R + \beta_B^R) = \alpha_B(x_L \pm x_R) + (\beta_B^L \pm \beta_B^R) = \alpha_B \cdot x_O + \beta_B^O = MAC_{\alpha_B, \beta_B^O}(x_O)$.

MULTIPLICATION GATES. For multiplication gates, the pregeneration consists of an authenticated "triple". The dealer generates two random numbers a, b and computes $c = a \cdot b$. The dealer then creates authenticated shares for each of these three values as follows. Randomly select $\beta_A^a, \beta_A^b, \beta_A^c, \beta_B^a, \beta_B^b, \beta_B^c$, and x_a, x_b, x_c at random, and set $y_a = a - x_a, y_b = b - x_b, y_c = c - x_c$. It then sets $w_A^a = MAC_{\alpha_B, \beta_B^a}(x_a), w_A^b = MAC_{\alpha_B, \beta_B^b}(x_b), w_A^c = MAC_{\alpha_B, \beta_B^c}(x_c)$ and

$w_B^a = MAC_{\alpha_A, \beta_A^a}(y_a), w_B^b = MAC_{\alpha_A, \beta_A^b}(y_b), w_B^c = MAC_{\alpha_A, \beta_A^c}(y_c)$. It sends $x_a, x_b, x_c, w_A^a, w_A^b, w_A^c, \beta_A^a, \beta_A^b, \beta_A^c$ to Alice, and $y_a, y_b, y_c, w_B^a, w_B^b, w_B^c, \beta_B^a, \beta_B^b, \beta_B^c$ to Bob.

During the online step, each party subtracts their a share from their left share (*i.e.*, subtracting w, x, β simultaneously), and the b share from their right share. The resulting differences, call them r and s are mutually revealed by sending each other the resulting MAC and value, and mutually verified. Then each computes their local result as the sum of their c share with the opened r times their right share, the opened s times their left share, and the opened value $r \cdot s$.

For the remaining two gate types, < 0 and $>> c$, we must take additional care because there are also MAC values attached to each wire, so simply running Algorithms 1 and 2 will not suffice. For example, if we are computing a < 0 gate, then we want to compute authenticated shares of $O = (L_A + L_B) < 0$, where O is 0 if it is false and 1 if it is true. The dealer will precompute both possible outputs: an authenticated sharing of 0 and of 1. However, in order to preserve privacy, we cannot reveal to either party which is the sharing of 0 and which is the sharing of 1, otherwise they would learn the output. Thus, we have a "flip" bit f, such that the output is flipped if f is 1. The parties share f: Alice holds f_A, Bob holds f_B such that $f = f_A \oplus f_B$. Thus, if we compute $((L_A + L_B) < 0) \oplus f_A \oplus f_B$ and reveal this Boolean result to both parties, it properly indexes which authenticated share they should each use, and will be a correct sharing of O with a MAC.

We model $LTZ = ((L_A + L_B) < 0) \oplus f_A \oplus f_B$ as a Boolean circuit: the addition is done via a straightforward adder-with-carry circuit, the comparison just looks at the sign bit, and it finishes with two XOR gates. In order to securely evaluate it, we use the garbled circuit methodology with precomputation. Additional details may be found in the full version [HLOW16]

For shift-by-constant gates, there are multiple output bits, and we treat each bit individually and reconstruct the output via the standard bits-to-integer $\sum a_i 2^i$ transformation, performed on the authenticated shares.

6   Benchmarks

6.1   Internal Testing and Benchmarks

Our implementation takes 20 integer inputs, each representing real numbers as follows: an integer n represents the real number $\frac{n}{2^{20}}$. These 20 inputs correspond to the satellite trajectories of Party 1 and Party 2, namely the vectors for position (x_i, y_i, z_i), velocity $(v_{x_i}, v_{y_i}, v_{z_i})$, error $(\sigma_{x_i}, \sigma_{y_i}, \sigma_{z_i})$, and a radius R_i for $i = 1, 2$. The output is a single integer representing the probability of collision in the same format. After significant optimization, the final circuit contained 2.67×10^5 gates.

Bounds and Error Tolerance. The goal of a conjunction analysis calculation is to facilitate decision-making and improve space situational awareness. Because our system is providing a numerical approximation to an integral without a closed form, it is important to ensure that the approximations provide sufficient accuracy to inform decision making. The probability region between 10^{-1} and 10^{-7} is called the "operational decision region," [Alf07], and it is most important to maximize the (relative) accuracy for probabilities within this region. A longer discussion about this can be found in [HLOW16].

Internally, we evaluated the circuit on 2000 test cases and obtained the following error bounds, when compared to a Maple implementation of [Alf07]:

Across all tests		In Operational Decision Region	
Absolute error $\|approx - true\|$	Relative error $\|\frac{approx-true}{true}\|$	Absolute error $\|approx - true\|$	Relative error $\|\frac{approx-true}{true}\|$
Min 9.000×10^{-10}	1.240×10^{-8}	Min 9.000×10^{-10}	2.190×10^{-6}
Max 8.512×10^{-4}	19 (see remark)	Max 9.608×10^{-5}	2.543×10^{-3}
Avg 7.027×10^{-5}	9.623×10^{-3}	Avg 5.759×10^{-7}	1.208×10^{-5}

Remark: In all cases where the relative error was extremely large, the true probabilities were extremely close to zero, and the large relative error would not impact decision making, e.g. cases where the "true" probability was 10^{-15}, and we estimated $2 \cdot 10^{-14}$.

Benchmarks. We benchmarked our system on a virtual machine running 64bit CentOS 6.4. The machine had 8 GB of RAM, 4 processors, and 100 GB of hard disk space. We tested both pregeneration time and online run time between two parties for a single conjunction, as well as disk space used. We present the average runtime over 2000 tests as well as bounds on the maximum and minimum times.

Pregeneration Time	
real	1m30s ± 15s
user	38s ± 15s
sys	27s ± 25s

Online Time	
real	5m2s ± 15s
user	4m59s ± 15s
sys	15s ± 10s

6.2   Comparison with the Sharemind Implementation [KW14a]

Secure computation of conjunction analyses was one of the target use-cases for MPC in DARPA's PROCEED program, and consequently it has been used as a benchmark for other secure computation systems. Our implementation was done in parallel with that of Kamm and Willemson [KW14a], but the design and goals of these projects are fundamentally different. In short, we focused on building a two-party protocol that was custom-tailored to the problem of securely computing conjunction analyses, while Kamm and Willemson focused on building an IEEE 754 floating point library for the three-party Sharemind system, and used the conjunction analysis application to exhibit the capabilities of their general platform. Additional discussion can be found in the full version [HLOW16].

7   Conclusion

In this work, we described the design and implementation of a custom secure computation protocol to compute the probability of satellite collisions. The underlying collision probability calculation requires numerically estimating a complicated integral – something that was, until recently, beyond the reach of secure computation techniques. We envision that our techniques can extend to other areas that require secure numerical computations as well. In order to improve efficiency, we custom built and optimized an augmented arithmetic circuit to estimate the collision probabilities. We constructed a secure computation protocol then used a combination of GMW and garbled circuits to evaluate these augmented circuits. Our secure computation works in the offline/online model, where during the offline phase the parties work to generate a large amount of correlated randomness in the form of OTs and shared arithmetic triples. Later, in the online phase, this correlated randomness is consumed to facilitate the secure computation. Because of the sheer quantity of correlated randomness needed, the limiting factor in our computation was disk I/O.

This work provides positive evidence for the fact that MPC technology is now capable of evaluating very complex functions securely and efficiently.

Acknowledgements. This work was supported in part by the DARPA. The U.S. Government is authorized to reproduce and distribute reprints for Governmental purposes notwithstanding any copyright annotation therein. Disclaimer: The views and conclusions contained herein are those of the authors and should not be interpreted as necessarily representing the official policies or endorsement, either expressed or implied, of DARPA, or the U.S. Government.

References

[ABPP15]   Archer, D.W., Bogdanov, D., Pinkas, B., Pullonen, P.: Maturity and Performance of Programmable Secure Computation (2015). https://eprint.iacr.org/2015/1039

[ABZS13]   Aliasgari, M., Blanton, M., Zhang, Y., Steele, A.: Secure computation on floating point numbers. In: NDSS 2013 (2013)

[Alf05]   Alfano, S.: A numerical implementation of spherical object collision probability. J. Astronaut. Sci. **53**(1), 103–109 (2005)

[Alf07]   Alfano, S.: Review of conjunction probability methods for short-term encounters. In: Proceedings of the AAS/AIAA Space Flight Mechanics Meeting, PART 1, vol. 127, pp. 719–746, February 2007

[AS65]   Abramowitz, M., Stegun, I.A. (eds.): Handbook of Mathematical Functions with Formulas, Graphs, and Mathematical Tables. Dover, New York (1965)

[BDOZ11]   Bendlin, R., Damgård, I., Orlandi, C., Zakarias, S.: Semi-homomorphic encryption and multiparty computation. In: Paterson, K.G. (ed.) EUROCRYPT 2011. LNCS, vol. 6632, pp. 169–188. Springer, Heidelberg (2011)

[Bea95]   Beaver, D.: Precomputing oblivious transfer. In: Coppersmith, D. (ed.) CRYPTO 1995. LNCS, vol. 963, pp. 97–109. Springer, Heidelberg (1995)

[Bea97]   Beaver, D.: Commodity-based cryptography (extended abstract). In: STOC 1997, pp. 446–455 (1997)

[BGW88]   Ben-Or, M., Goldwasser, S., Wigderson, A.: Completeness theorems for non-cryptographic fault-tolerant distributed computation (extended abstract). In: STOC 1988, pp. 1–10 (1988)

[BHKR13] Bellare, M., Hoang, V.T., Keelveedhi, S., Rogaway, P.: Efficient garbling from a fixed-key blockcipher. In: IEEE Symposium on Security and Privacy, SP 2013, pp. 478–492 (2013)

[BHR12a] Bellare, M., Hoang, V.T., Rogaway, P.: Adaptively secure garbling with applications to one-time programs and secure outsourcing. In: Wang, X., Sako, K. (eds.) ASIACRYPT 2012. LNCS, vol. 7658, pp. 134–153. Springer, Heidelberg (2012)

[BHR12b] Bellare, M., Hoang, V.T., Rogaway, P.: Foundations of garbled circuits. In: CCS 2012, pp. 784–796 (2012)

[BLW08]   Bogdanov, D., Laur, S., Willemson, J.: Sharemind: a framework for fast privacy-preserving computations. In: Jajodia, S., Lopez, J. (eds.) ESORICS 2008. LNCS, vol. 5283, pp. 192–206. Springer, Heidelberg (2008)

[BV11]   Brakerski, Z., Vaikuntanathan, V.: Efficient fully homomorphic encryption from (standard) LWE. In: FOCS 2011, pp. 97–106 (2011)

[CCD88]   Chaum, D., Crépeau, C., Damgård, I.B.: Multiparty unconditionally secure protocols. In: Pomerance, C. (ed.) CRYPTO 1987. LNCS, vol. 293, pp. 462–462. Springer, Heidelberg (1988)

[CS10]   Catrina, O., Saxena, A.: Secure computation with fixed-point numbers. In: Sion, R. (ed.) FC 2010. LNCS, vol. 6052, pp. 35–50. Springer, Heidelberg (2010)

[DGKN09] Damgård, I., Geisler, M., Krøigaard, M., Nielsen, J.B.: Asynchronous multiparty computation: theory and implementation. In: Jarecki, S., Tsudik, G. (eds.) PKC 2009. LNCS, vol. 5443, pp. 160–179. Springer, Heidelberg (2009)

[DPSZ12] Damgård, I., Pastro, V., Smart, N., Zakarias, S.: Multiparty computation from somewhat homomorphic encryption. In: Safavi-Naini, R., Canetti, R. (eds.) CRYPTO 2012. LNCS, vol. 7417, pp. 643–662. Springer, Heidelberg (2012)

[EGL82]   Even, S., Goldreich, O., Lempel, A.: A randomized protocol for signing contracts. In: Chaum, D., Rivest, R.L., Sherman, A.T. (eds.) CRYPTO 1982, pp. 205–210. Springer, New York (1982)

[FSW03]   Fouque, P.-A., Stern, J., Wackers, J.-G.: Cryptocomputing with rationals. In: Blaze, M. (ed.) FC 2002. LNCS, vol. 2357, pp. 136–146. Springer, Heidelberg (2003)

[Gen09]   Gentry, C.: Fully homomorphic encryption using ideal lattices. In: STOC 2009, pp. 169–178 (2009)

[GHL+14] Gentry, C., Halevi, S., Lu, S., Ostrovsky, R., Raykova, M., Wichs, D.: Garbled RAM revisited. In: Nguyen, P.Q., Oswald, E. (eds.) EUROCRYPT 2014. LNCS, vol. 8441, pp. 405–422. Springer, Heidelberg (2014)

[GMW87]   Goldreich, O., Micali, S., Wigderson, A.: How to play any mental game or a completeness theorem for protocols with honest majority. In: STOC 1987, pp. 218–229 (1987)

[Gol01]   Goldreich, O.: Foundations of Cryptography: Basic Tools. Cambridge University Press, Cambridge (2001)

[Gol04]   Goldreich, O.: Foundations of Cryptography: Basic Applications, vol. 2. Cambridge University Press, Cambridge (2004)

[HLOW16] Hemenway, B., Steve, L., Ostrovsky, R., William Welser, I.V.: High-precision secure computation of satellite collision probabilities. Cryptology ePrint Archive, Report 2016/319 (2016). http://eprint.iacr.org/2016/319

[HW15] Hemenway, B., Welser, W.: Cryptographers could prevent satellite collisions. Scientific American, 28–29 February 2015

[HWIB14] Hemenway, B., William Welser, I.V., Baiocchi, D.: Achieving higher-fidelity conjunction analyses using cryptography to improve information sharing. Technical report, RAND Corporation (2014)

[IKM+13] Ishai, Y., Kushilevitz, E., Meldgaard, S., Orlandi, C., Paskin-Cherniavsky, A.: On the power of correlated randomness in secure computation. In: Sahai, A. (ed.) TCC 2013. LNCS, vol. 7785, pp. 600–620. Springer, Heidelberg (2013)

[IKNP03] Ishai, Y., Kilian, J., Nissim, K., Petrank, E.: Extending oblivious transfers efficiently. In: Boneh, D. (ed.) CRYPTO 2003. LNCS, vol. 2729, pp. 145–161. Springer, Heidelberg (2003)

[IKO+11] Ishai, Y., Kushilevitz, E., Ostrovsky, R., Prabhakaran, M., Sahai, A.: Efficient non-interactive secure computation. In: Paterson, K.G. (ed.) EUROCRYPT 2011. LNCS, vol. 6632, pp. 406–425. Springer, Heidelberg (2011)

[IPS09] Ishai, Y., Prabhakaran, M., Sahai, A.: Secure arithmetic computation with no honest majority. In: Reingold, O. (ed.) TCC 2009. LNCS, vol. 5444, pp. 294–314. Springer, Heidelberg (2009)

[KW14a] Kamm, L., Willemson, J.: Secure floating point arithmetic and private satellite collision analysis. Int. J. Inf. Secur. **14**, 1–18 (2014)

[KW14b] Krips, T., Willemson, J.: Hybrid model of fixed and floating point numbers in secure multiparty computations. In: Chow, S.S.M., Camenisch, J., Hui, L.C.K., Yiu, S.M. (eds.) ISC 2014. LNCS, vol. 8783, pp. 179–197. Springer, Heidelberg (2014)

[LO13] Lu, S., Ostrovsky, R.: How to garble RAM programs? In: Johansson, T., Nguyen, P.Q. (eds.) EUROCRYPT 2013. LNCS, vol. 7881, pp. 719–734. Springer, Heidelberg (2013)

[LP09] Lindell, Y., Pinkas, B.: A proof of security of Yao's protocol for two-party computation. J. Cryptol. **22**(2), 161–188 (2009)

[LTV12] López-Alt, A., Tromer, E., Vaikuntanathan, V.: On-the-fly multiparty computation on the cloud via multikey fully homomorphic encryption. In: STOC 2012, pp. 1219–1234 (2012)

[NNOB12] Nielsen, J.B., Nordholt, P.S., Orlandi, C., Burra, S.S.: A new approach to practical active-secure two-party computation. In: Safavi-Naini, R., Canetti, R. (eds.) CRYPTO 2012. LNCS, vol. 7417, pp. 681–700. Springer, Heidelberg (2012)

[PS15] Pullonen, P., Siim, S.: Combining secret sharing and garbled circuits for efficient private IEEE 754 floating-point computations. In: FCS 2015, pp. 172–183 (2015)

[Rab05] Rabin, M.O.: How to exchange secrets with oblivious transfer. Cryptology ePrint Archive, Report 2005/187 (2005). http://eprint.iacr.org/2005/187

[RHH14] Rastogi, A., Hammer, M.A., Hicks, M.: Wysteria: a programming language for generic, mixed-mode multiparty computations. In: IEEE Symposium on Security and Privacy, pp. 655–670 (2014)

[Sha79] Shamir, A.: How to share a secret. Commun. Assoc. Comput. Mach. **22**(11), 612–613 (1979)

[UCS15] Union of concerned scientists (2015). http://www.ucsusa.org/. Accessed 11 Sept 2015

[VO09]   Associated Press Veronika Oleksyn: What a mess! experts ponder space junk problem. USA Today, February 2009

[Yao82]   Yao, A.C.-C.: Protocols for secure computations (extended abstract). In: FOCS 1982, pp. 160–164 (1982)

[Yao86]   Yao, A.C.-C.: How to generate and exchange secrets (extended abstract). In: FOCS 1986, pp. 162–167 (1986)

[YY12]   Yu, C.-H., Yang, B.-Y.: Probabilistically correct secure arithmetic computation for modular conversion, zero test, comparison, MOD and exponentiation. In: Visconti, I., De Prisco, R. (eds.) SCN 2012. LNCS, vol. 7485, pp. 426–444. Springer, Heidelberg (2012)

Zero-Knowledge Proofs

Zero-Knowledge Made Easy so It Won't Make You Dizzy

(A Tale of Transaction Put in Verse About an Illicit Kind of Commerce)

Trotta Gnam[✉]

Carpe Diem Consulting, Irvine, CA, USA
trotta.gnam@gmail.com

Abstract. For any research paper, as all the authors know
An abstract is required to keep the proper flow
An abstract is a lure that must be appetizing
It's typically stuffed with shameless aggrandizing
Which brings us to the subject of our seminal result
Its impact on the Zeitgeist will alter the Gestalt
This noble work is prompted by dominance of prose
The reason crypto papers make readers comatose
This paper makes an effort to change the status quo
By showing that crypto poetry is another way to go

Keywords: Fiat-Shamir · Crypto humor · Crypto poetry · Zero Knowledge · Crypto education · Crypto lyrics

1 Introduction

Whoever reads these lines shall have no fear
This rhyming opus will explain Fiat-Shamir [1]
The tricky concept known as Zero Knowledge [2]
Will be as easy to digest as oatmeal porridge
So, now read on and keep one thing in mind
That tortured rhymes are difficult to find

2 Setup and Preliminaries

Computed safely, back in ancient times
Is number $\mathcal{N}$ – a product of two primes
Its murky origin is subject to debate
Let's just assume that it was not the NSA
To make the protocol description very clear
All computations are mod $\mathcal{N}$ in Fiat-Shamir

Translated from the Slobonian by G. Tsudik, gts@ics.uci.edu.

V. Zikas and R. De Prisco (Eds.): SCN 2016, LNCS 9841, pp. 191–197, 2016.
DOI: 10.1007/978-3-319-44618-9_10

2.1   The Cast

The protocol involves a dweeb, called Bob
A lazy, nerdy and socially-awkward slob
Like many of his bored and geeky kind
Bob smokes a lot of weed to numb his mind

His dealer, Alice, is crafty trailer trash
Who offers pot, ecstasy, and high-grade hash
Like any merchant wanting customers' respect
She has integrity and stature to protect
For each transaction, Alice wants her client
To be completely Fiat-Shamir-compliant

2.2   Assumptions

To circumvent some simple online dangers
Suppose that Bob and Alice aren't strangers
Thus, we assume that $\mathcal{I}$ – Bob's ID string
Already hangs on Alice's public-key ring
Meanwhile, its secret square root, called $\mathcal{S}$
Bob had tattooed on his right foot, no less
NOTE: Due to consuming large quantities of pot
Bob's long-term memory is unfortunately shot

3   Interaction

Round 1:

The online phase begins with round one
When Bob's supply of cannabis is gone
Sneezing and coughing like a decrepit car
Bob generates a random number we'll call $\mathcal{R}$
Squaring it mod $\mathcal{N}$, yields a value $\mathcal{X}$
Which he then sends to Alice all in hex

Round 2:

Having received and stored $\mathcal{X}$, she is content
Since there is merchandise for her to vend
Next, from her private random numbers pit
Alice selects a brand new challenge bit
It is referred to as $\mathcal{C}$ from here on
She quickly forwards it to Bob over the phone

Round 3:

In round three, Bob readies his reply
Of course, it must on challenge C rely
Accordingly, it's $\mathcal{R}$ if C is zero,
Else, $\mathcal{R}$ times $\mathcal{S}$ is sent by our hero

For C of zero, Alice squares the reply and checks
Whether it matches Bob's prior commitment $\mathcal{X}$
She otherwise compares $\mathcal{X}$ times $\mathcal{I}$
With square mod $\mathcal{N}$ of Bob's previous reply

Should she encounter any kind of error
Alice drops everything and runs away in terror
For this behavior, there is a solid reason:
She simply doesn't want to land in prison

Back for more:

Assuming all goes well, it should be clear
That much remains to do in Fiat-Shamir
Though it is fast, simple, and discrete
There is a **50-50** chance that Bob can cheat
Thus, online phase must be re-run $\mathcal{K}$ times
Because of difficulty of coming up with rhymes

4   Epilog

Once the transaction is finally complete
Both parties hurry to get off the street
The dealer Alice now proactively decides
That time is right to re-stock the merchandise
Eager to sample freshly purchased hash
Bob rushes home while clutching his new stash

5   Security Proof (Sketch)

This is a mere sketch, no need to get excited
A real proof, as usual, will never be provided
As for security, there is but one direction
It's plainly evident by cursory inspection

■

6   Related Work

While feeling pride and yet not seeking fame
Having explored the literature, we claim
That this attempt at crypto-poetry is **first**
Which might result in stirring up a hornet's nest
Thus triggering a crypto-lyrical tsunami
Which sadly rhymes only with pastrami

7   Future Work

Before tapping this poem with a verbal cork
We summarize directions for the future work
Our research isn't finished and much is left to do
For instance, proving theorems completely in haiku
Devising crypto-protocols for alpine cows to yodel
That are proven secure in the standard crypto model
How to take advantage of symmetric-crypto tricks
To build one-way functions that spit out limericks
How to create lyrics, music and dance moves
That praise the shapely beauty of elliptic curves [3]
These are just examples and challenges abound
For any eager student open problems can be found

8   Conclusions

This paper demonstrated with obvious finesse
The awesome teaching power of pithy crypto-verse
Our research took advantage of a lucky trick
By picking Fiat-Shamir as its guinea pig

In sheer simplicity this method has no peer
Even a total idiot can comprehend Fiat-Shamir
To understand it, there's no need to go to college
Its only purpose is advancing Zero Knowledge

We've reached the end and it's time for a beer
Let's drink at least $\mathcal{K}$ rounds, as in Fiat-Shamir [1]
And if we drink too much and feel a bit delirious
Everyone we meet should be honest-but-curious

9   Disclaimer and Acknowledgments

Despite severe pressure from his poetic muse
The author of this poem doesn't advocate drug use
This literary effort was made possible in part
By generous funding from Endowment for the Art
We finally acknowledge, with self-important flair
Helpful comments by reviewers and the Program Chair

Appendix A: A Poetical Revenge on Diffie-Hellman Key Exchange

1. Introduction and Motivation

Teaching cryptography can be so boring
That one can hear students snoring
To verify this claim and see
Try introducing them to public key

Before we delve into this lecture
We need to first make a conjecture
Perhaps the boredom is caused
By dominance of sleep-inducing prose
We thus attempt to keep the audience alert
By rhymes to which we protocols convert

We start with Diffie-Hellman protocol [4]
Which is by far the simplest one of all
In this description, it isn't very terse
Since it's presented entirely in verse
NOTE: As we forward bravely plow
The rhyming tempo changes now

2. The Protocol

$\boxed{Setup}$

Before our Earth was ever trod
A large prime **p** was picked by God[1]
NOTE: In the protocol you'll see
All computations are mod **p**
Then, a generator **g** was chosen
And thereafter both were frozen

---

[1] And if you're a godless atheist
Assume that **p** was picked by NIST

Alice – one of fairer sex
Computes **g** to random X
Bob – a sketchy kind of guy
Raises **g** to chosen Y

Clock synchronization loose
They exchange the residues
Not to spoil all the fun ...
But, that's the end of round one

Alice, with her secret, next
Raises $\mathbf{g}^Y$ to the X
Feeling just a little high
Bob computes $\mathbf{g}^X$ to the Y
Now for both the time is ripe
To bootstrap a secure pipe

3. Correctness

To see that Diffie-Hellman works
Even between two total dorks
Consider that both Bob and Alice
Wind up computing equal values

4. Security

The Good News

A passive eavesdropper can see
How they obtain the shared key
But even best computing toys
Can't help distinguish it from noise

The Bad News

Alas this claim's no longer true
When adversary changes hue
When Eve adopts an active role
We're left with a broken protocol
She distracts Alice by playing fiddle
While fooling Bob with man-in-the-middle

References

1. Fiat, A., Shamir, A.: How to prove yourself: practical solutions to identification and signature problems. In: Odlyzko, A.M. (ed.) CRYPTO 1986. LNCS, vol. 263, pp. 186–194. Springer, Heidelberg (1987)
2. Quisquater, J.-J., Guillou, L.C., Berson, T.A.: How to explain zero-knowledge protocols to your children. In: Brassard, G. (ed.) CRYPTO 1989. LNCS, vol. 435, pp. 628–631. Springer, Heidelberg (1990)
3. Tate, J.: The Arithmetic of Elliptic Curves. Inventiones Math. **23**(3-4), 179–206 (1974)
4. Diffie, W., Hellman, M.: New directions in cryptography. IEEE Trans. Inf. Theor. **22**(6), 644–654 (1976)

Fiat–Shamir for Highly Sound Protocols
Is Instantiable

Arno Mittelbach[1] and Daniele Venturi[2(✉)]

[1] Cryptoplexity, Technische Universität Darmstadt, Darmstadt, Germany
[2] Department of Information Engineering and Computer Science,
University of Trento, Trento, Italy
daniele.venturi@unitn.it

Abstract. The Fiat–Shamir (FS) transformation (Fiat and Shamir, Crypto '86) is a popular paradigm for constructing very efficient non-interactive zero-knowledge (NIZK) arguments and signature schemes using a hash function, starting from any three-move interactive protocol satisfying certain properties. Despite its wide-spread applicability both in theory and in practice, the known positive results for proving security of the FS paradigm are in the random oracle model, i.e., they assume that the hash function is modelled as an external random function accessible to all parties. On the other hand, a sequence of negative results shows that for certain classes of interactive protocols, the FS transform cannot be instantiated in the standard model.

We initiate the study of complementary positive results, namely, studying classes of interactive protocols where the FS transform *does* have standard-model instantiations. In particular, we show that for a class of "highly sound" protocols that we define, instantiating the FS transform via a q-wise independent hash function yields NIZK arguments and secure signature schemes. For NIZK, we obtain a weaker "q-bounded" zero-knowledge flavor where the simulator works for all adversaries asking an a-priori bounded number of queries q; for signatures, we obtain the weaker notion of random-message unforgeability against q-bounded random message attacks.

Our main idea is that when the protocol is highly sound, then instead of using random-oracle programming, one can use complexity leveraging. The question is whether such highly sound protocols exist and if so, which protocols lie in this class. We answer this question in the affirmative in the common reference string (CRS) model and under strong assumptions. Namely, assuming indistinguishability obfuscation and puncturable pseudorandom functions we construct a compiler that transforms any 3-move interactive protocol with instance-independent commitments and simulators (a property satisfied by the Lapidot-Shamir protocol, Crypto '90) into a compiled protocol in the CRS model that is highly sound. We also present a second compiler, in order to be able to start from a larger class of protocols, which only requires instance-independent commitments (a property for example satisfied by the classical protocol for quadratic residuosity due to Blum, Crypto '81). For the second compiler we require dual-mode commitments.

We hope that our work inspires more research on classes of (efficient) 3-move protocols where Fiat–Shamir is (efficiently) instantiable.

© Springer International Publishing Switzerland 2016
V. Zikas and R. De Prisco (Eds.): SCN 2016, LNCS 9841, pp. 198–215, 2016.
DOI: 10.1007/978-3-319-44618-9_11

1 Introduction

The Fiat–Shamir (FS) transformation [26] is a popular[1] technique to build efficient non-interactive zero-knowledge (NIZK) arguments and signature schemes, starting from three-round *public-coin* (3PC) protocols satisfying certain properties. In a 3PC protocol the prover starts by sending a commitment α, to which the verifier replies with a challenge β drawn at random from some space $\mathcal{B}$; finally the prover sends a reply γ and the verifier's verdict is computed as a predicate of the transcript (α, β, γ).

1.1 Fiat–Shamir NIZK and Signatures

We briefly review both the main applications of the FS transform below.

- **NIZK.** A NIZK is a non-interactive protocol in which the prover—holding a witness w for membership of a statement x in some *NP*-language L—can convince the verifier—holding just x—that $x \in L$, by sending a single message π. NIZK should satisfy three properties. First, *completeness* says that an honest prover holding a valid witness (almost) always convinces an honest verifier. Second, *soundness* says that a malicious prover should not be able to convince the honest verifier into accepting a *false* statement, i.e. a statement $x \notin L$; we speak of *arguments* (resp., *proofs*) when the soundness requirement holds for all computationally bounded (resp., computationally unbounded) provers. Third, *zero-knowledge* requires that a proof does not reveal anything about the witness beyond the validity of the statement being proven.

    Apart from being a fascinating topic, NIZK have been demonstrated to be extremely useful for cryptographic applications (see, e.g., [11,12,22,24,28, 36]). NIZK require a setup assumption, typically in the form of a common reference string (CRS).

    Starting with a 3PC protocol, the FS transform makes it a NIZK by having the prover compute the verifier's challenge as a hash of the commitment α via some hash function H (with "hash key" hk); this results in a single message $\pi = (\alpha, \beta, \gamma)$, where $\beta = \mathsf{H}(\mathsf{hk}, \alpha)$, that is sent from the prover to the verifier.[2] (The description of the hash function, i.e. key hk, is included as part of the CRS.)

- **Signatures.** Digital signatures are among the most important and well-studied cryptographic tools. Signature schemes allow a signer (holding a public/secret key pair (pk, sk)) to generate a signature σ on a message m, in such a way that anyone possessing the public key pk can verify the validity of (m, σ). Signatures must be unforgeable, meaning that it should be hard to forge a signature on a "fresh" chosen message (even after seeing polynomially many signatures on possibly chosen messages).

---

[1] There are over 3.000 Google-Scholar-known citations to [26], as we type.

[2] The value β is typically omitted from the proof, as the verifier can compute it by itself.

Starting with a 3PC protocol, the FS transform makes it a signature by having the signer compute the verifier's challenge as a hash of the commitment α, concatenated with the message m, via some hash function H (with "hash key" hk); this results in a signature $\sigma = (\alpha, \beta, \gamma)$, where $\beta = \mathsf{H}(\mathsf{hk}, \alpha\|m)$.

1.2 Positive and Negative Results

We refer to the non-interactive system obtained by applying the FS transform to a 3PC protocol (i.e., a NIZK or a signature scheme) as the *FS collapse*. A fundamental question in cryptography is to understand what properties the initial 3PC protocol and the hash function should satisfy in order for the FS collapse to be a NIZK argument or a secure signature scheme. This question has been studied extensively in the literature; we briefly review the current state of affairs below.

Positive Results. All security proofs for the FS transform follow the random oracle methodology (ROM) of Bellare and Rogaway [4], i.e., they assume that the function H behaves like an external random function accessible to all parties (including the adversary). In particular, a series of papers [1,26,40,42] establishes that the FS transform yields a secure signature scheme in the ROM provided that the starting 3PC is a passively secure identification scheme. The first definition of NIZK in the ROM dates back to [4] (where a particular protocol was analyzed); in general, it is well known that, always in the ROM, the FS transform yields a NIZK satisfying sophisticated properties such as simulation-soundness [25] and simulation-extractability [6].

Barak *et al.* [3] put forward a new hash function property (called entropy preservation[3]) that allows to prove soundness of the FS collapse without random oracles; their result requires that the starting 3PC protocol is statistically sound, i.e. it is a *proof*. Dodis *et al.* [21] show that such hash functions exist if a conjecture on the existence of certain "condensers for leaky sources" turns out to be true. Canetti *et al.* [13] study the correlation intractability of obfuscated pseudorandom functions and show a close connection between entropy preservation and correlation intractability, but it remains open whether their construction achieves entropy preservation or, in fact, whether entropy-preserving hash functions exist in the standard model. A negative indication to this question was recently presented by Bitansky *et al.* [7] who show that entropy-preservation security cannot be proven via a black-box reduction to a *cryptographic game*.

Negative Results. It is often difficult to interpret what a proof in the ROM means in the standard model. This is not only because concrete hash functions seem far from behaving like random oracles, but stems from the fact that there exist cryptographic schemes that can be proven secure in the ROM, but are *always* insecure in the standard model [14].

---

[3] Entropy preservation roughly says that for all efficient adversaries that get a uniformly random hash key hk and produce a correlated value α, the conditional Shannon entropy of $\beta = \mathsf{H}(\mathsf{hk}, \alpha)$ given α, but not hk, is sufficiently large.

The FS transformation is not an exception in this respect. In their study of "magic functions", Dwork et al. [23] establish that whenever the initial 3PC protocol satisfies the zero-knowledge property, its FS collapse can never be (computationally) sound for any implementation of the hash function. Goldwasser and Kalai [29], building on previous work of Barak [2], construct a specially-crafted 3PC *argument* for which the FS transform yields an insecure signature scheme for any standard model implementation of the hash function.

Bitansky et al. [8] and Dachman-Soled et al. [18] (see also [7]) show an unprovability result that also covers 3PC *proofs*. More in detail, [8] shows that the FS transform cannot always preserve soundness when starting with a 3PC proof, under a black-box reduction to any falsifiable assumption (even ones with an inefficient challenger). [18] shows a similar black-box separation (although only for assumptions with an efficient challenger) for any concrete proof that is honest-verifier zero-knowledge against sub-exponential size distinguishers. In a related paper, Goyal et al. [30] obtain a negative result for non-interactive information-theoretically secure witness indistinguishable arguments.

1.3 Our Contributions

The negative results show that, for certain classes of interactive protocols, the FS transform cannot be instantiated in the standard model. We initiate the study of complementary positive results, namely, studying classes of interactive protocols where the FS transform *does* have a standard-model instantiation. We show that for a class of "highly sound" protocols that we define, instantiating the FS transform via a q-wise independent hash function yields both a NIZK argument in the CRS model and a secure signature scheme. In the case of NIZK, we get a weaker "q-bounded" zero-knowledge flavor where the simulator works for all adversaries asking an a-priori bounded number of queries q; in the case of signatures, we get the weaker notion of random-message unforgeability against q-bounded random message attacks, where the forger can observe signatures on random messages and has to produce a forgery on a fresh random message.

Very roughly, highly sound protocols are a special class of 3PC arguments and identification schemes satisfying three additional properties: (**P1**) The honest prover computes the commitment α independently of the instance being proven and of the corresponding witness; (**P2**) The soundness error of the protocol is tiny, in particular the ratio between the soundness error and the worst-case probability of guessing a given commitment is bounded-away from one; (**P3**) Honest conversations between the prover and the verifier on common input x can be simulated knowing just x, and moreover the simulator can fake α independently of x itself.

We are not aware of natural protocols that are directly highly sound according to our definition. (But we will later discuss that, e.g., the Lapidot-Shamir protocol [37] partially satisfies our requirements.) Hence, the question is whether such highly sound protocols exist and, if so, which languages and protocols lie in this class. We answer this question in the affirmative in the CRS model and under strong assumptions. Namely, assuming indistinguishability obfuscation, puncturable pseudorandom functions and equivocal commitments, we build a sequence of two compilers that transform any three-move interactive protocol with instance-independent commitments (i.e., property **P1**) into a compiled protocol in the CRS model that satisfies the required properties. Noteworthy, our compilers are language-independent, and we know that assuming one-way permutations three-move interactive protocols with instance-independent commitments exist for all of *NP*.

Our result avoids Dwork *et al.* [23], because we start from a protocol that is honest-verifier zero-knowledge rather than fully zero-knowledge. Note that our approach also circumvents the negative result of [8,30] as our technique applies only to a certain class of 3PC arguments. Furthermore, we circumvent the black-box impossibility result [18] by using complexity leveraging and sub-exponential security assumptions.

1.4   Perspective

The main contribution from our perspective is to initiate the study of restricted positive standard-model results for the FS transform. Namely, we show that for the class of highly sound protocols, the FS transform can be instantiated via a q-wise independent hash function (both for the case of NIZK and signatures). This is particularly interesting given the negative results in [7,23,29].

An important complementary question is, of course, to study the class of highly sound protocols. Under strong assumptions, our compilers show that highly sound protocols exist for all languages in *NP*. However, the compilers yield protocols in the CRS model and, at least for the case of NIZK, as we discuss now, one has to take care in interpreting positive results about the FS transform applied to 3PC protocols in the CRS model.

It is well known that in the CRS model one can obtain a NIZK both for *NP*-complete languages [10] and for specific languages [31]. Let L be a language. Given a standard 3PC protocol for proving membership of elements $x \in L$, and with transcripts (α, β, γ), consider the following dummy "compiler" for obtaining a 3PC protocol for L in the CRS model. The first message α^* and the second message β^* of the compiled protocol are equal to the empty string ε; the third message is a NIZK proof γ^* that $x \in L$. Note that the FS transform is easily seen to be secure (without random oracles) on such a dummy protocol, the reason for this being that α^* and β^* play no role at all in the obtained 3PC! Further note that this artificial "compiler" actually ignores the original protocol, and hence it does not rely on any of the security features of the underlying protocol. Regrettably, the above example does not shed any light on the security of the FS transform and when it applies.

In turn, our result for FS NIZK has two interesting features. First, our instantiation of the FS transform works even if the starting 3PC is in the standard model (provided that it satisfies **P1-P3**). Second, our CRS-based compiler is very different from the above dummy compiler in that we do not simply "throw away" the initial 3PC but instead rely on all of its properties in order to obtain a 3PC satisfying **P1-P3**.

We remark that the above limitation does not apply to our positive result for FS signatures, since assuming the initial 3PC protocol works in the CRS model does not directly yield a dummy "compiler" as the one discussed above.

1.5 Related Work

On Fiat–Shamir. It is worth mentioning that using indistinguishability obfuscation and puncturable PRFs one can directly obtain a NIZK for all *NP* as shown by Sahai and Waters [43]. However, our main focus is not on constructions of NIZK, rather we aim at providing a better understanding of what can be proved for the FS transform without relying on random oracles. In this respect, our result shares similarities to the standard-model instantiation of Full-Domain Hash given in [34].

In the case of NIZK, an alternative version of the FS transform is defined by having the prover hashing the statement x together with value α, in order to obtain the challenge β. The latter variant is sometimes called the *strong* FS transform (while the variant we analyze is known as the *weak* FS transform). Bernhard *et al.* [6] show that the weak FS transform might lead to problems in certain applications where the statement to be proven can be chosen adversarially (this is the case, e.g., in the Helios voting protocol). Unfortunately, it seems hard to use our proof techniques to prove zero-knowledge of the strong FS collapse, because the simulator for zero-knowledge does not know the x values in advance.

Our positive result for FS signatures shares some similarities with the work of Bellare and Shoup [5], showing that "actively secure" 3PC protocols yield a restricted type of secure signature schemes (so-called two-tier signatures) when instantiating the hash function in the FS transform via any collision-resistant hash function.

Compilers. Our approach of first compiling any "standard" 3PC protocol into one with additional properties that suffice for proving security of the FS transform is similar in spirit to the approach taken by Haitner [32] who shows how to transform any interactive argument into one for which parallel repetition decreases the soundness error at an exponential rate.

Lindell recently used a similar idea to first transform a 3PC into a new protocol in the CRS model, and then show that the resulting 3PC when transformed with (a slightly modified version of) Fiat–Shamir satisfies zero-knowledge in the standard model [38]. His approach was later improved in [17]. We note that the use of a CRS-enhanced interactive protocol is only implicit in Lindell's work as he directly analyzes the collapsed non-interactive version. On the downside, to prove soundness Lindell still requires (non-programmable) random oracles. We note that one of our compilers is essentially equivalent to the compiler used by Lindell. Before Lindell's work, interactive protocols in the CRS model have also been studied by Damgård who shows how to build 3-round concurrent zero-knowledge arguments for all *NP*-problems in the CRS model [20].

Alternative Transforms. Other FS-inspired transformations were considered in the literature. For instance Fischlin's transformation [27] (see also [19]) yields a simulation-sound NIZK argument with an online extractor; as mentioned above, Lindell [38] defines a twist of the FS transform that allows to prove zero-knowledge in the CRS model, and soundness in the non-programmable random oracle model. It is an interesting direction for future research to apply our techniques to analyze the above transformations without random oracles.

Concurrent Paper. Recently, in a concurrent and independent work, Kalai, Rothblum and Rothblum [35] showed a positive result for FS in the plain model, under complexity assumptions similar to ours. More in details, assuming sub-exponentially secure indistinguishability obfuscation, input-hiding obfuscation for the class of multi-bit point functions, and sub-exponentially secure one-way functions, [35] shows that, when starting with any 3PC *proof*, the FS transform yields a *two-round* computationally-sound interactive protocol.

On the positive side, their result applies to any 3PC proof (while ours only covers a very special class of 3PC arguments). On the negative side, their technique only yields a positive result for a two-round interactive variant of the FS transform (while our techniques apply to the full FS collapse, both for NIZK and for signatures).

1.6 Roadmap

Section 2 contains a detailed informal overview of our positive result for the case of FS NIZK; the corresponding formal definitions and proofs are deferred to the full version [39]. We present an overview of our compilers for obtaining highly sound protocols (in the CRS model) in Sect. 3; a more detailed treatment appears in the full paper [39], where we also explain how to adapt our techniques to the case of FS signatures.

2   FS NIZK

Fiat–Shamir Transform. The Fiat–Shamir (FS) transform [26] is a generic way to remove interaction from certain argument systems, using a hash function. For the rest of the paper, we consider only interactive arguments consisting of three messages—which we denote by (α, β, γ)—where the first message is sent by the prover. We also focus on so-called *public-coin* protocols where the verifier's message β is uniformly random over some space $\mathcal{B}$ (e.g., $\beta \in \{0,1\}^k$ for some $k \in \mathbb{N}$). We call this a 3PC argument system for short, and denote it by $\Pi = (\mathsf{K}, \mathsf{P}, \mathsf{V})$; here K generates a CRS crs,[4] whereas P and V correspond to prover and verifier algorithms.

---

[4] For standard-model 3PC arguments, the CRS contains the empty string ε. The reason for considering a CRS is that, looking ahead, our compilers yield highly sound protocols in the CRS model.

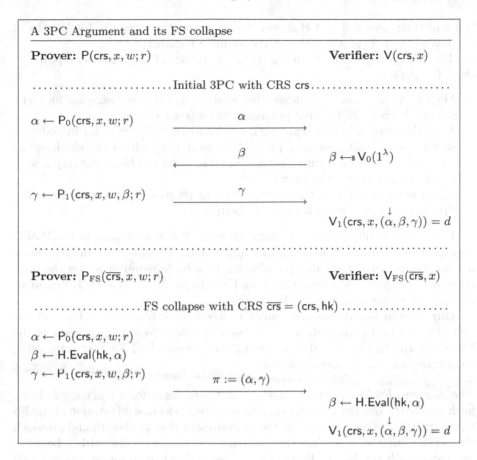

Fig. 1. Message flow of a typical 3PC argument system and its corresponding FS collapse.

For 3PC arguments we can think of the prover algorithm as being split into two sub-algorithms $P := (P_0, P_1)$, where P_0 takes as input a pair (x, w) and outputs the prover's first message α (the so-called commitment) and P_1 takes as input (x, w) as well as the verifier's challenge β to produce the prover's second message γ (the so-called response). In general P_0 and P_1 are allowed to share the same random tape, which we denote by $r \in \{0, 1\}^*$. In a similar fashion we can think of the verifier's algorithm as split into two sub-algorithms $V = (V_0, V_1)$, where V_0 outputs a uniformly random value $\beta \in \mathcal{B}$ and V_1 is deterministic and corresponds to the verifier's verdict (i.e., V_1 takes as input x and a transcript (α, β, γ) and returns a decision bit $d \in \{0, 1\}$).

The FS transform allows to remove interaction from any 3PC argument system for a polynomial-time computable relation R as specified below (see also Fig. 1). Let $\Pi = (K, P, V)$ be the initial 3PC argument system. Additionally, consider a family of hash functions H consisting of algorithms H.KGen, H.kl, H.Eval,

H.il and H.ol; here H.il and H.ol correspond, respectively, to the bit lengths of messages α and β (as a function of the security parameter λ).

The FS collapse of Π using H is a triple of algorithms $\overline{\Pi}_{FS,H} :=$ (K_{FS}, P_{FS}, V_{FS}):

- Algorithm K_{FS} takes as input the security parameter, samples $hk \leftarrow_\$ H.$ $KGen(1^\lambda)$, $crs \leftarrow_\$ K(1^\lambda)$, and publishes $\overline{crs} := (crs, hk)$.
- Algorithm P_{FS} takes as input $(\overline{crs}, x, w)$ and runs $P_0(crs, x, w)$ in order to obtain the commitment $\alpha \in \{0,1\}^{H.il(\lambda)}$; next P_{FS} defines the challenge as $\beta := H.Eval(hk, \alpha)$ and runs $P_1(crs, x, w, \beta)$ in order to obtain the response γ. Finally P_{FS} outputs $\pi := (\alpha, \gamma)$.
- Algorithm V_{FS} takes as input $(\overline{crs}, x, \pi)$ and returns 1 if and only if verifier $V_1(crs, x, (\alpha, \beta, \gamma)) = 1$ where $\beta = H.Eval(hk, \alpha)$.

Briefly, the result of Fiat and Shamir says that if Π is a (standard-model) 3PC argument satisfying completeness, computational soundness, and computational honest-verifier zero-knowledge (in addition to a basic requirement on the min-entropy of the prover's commitment), its FS collapse $\overline{\Pi}_{FS,H}$ is a NIZK argument system if H is modeled as a random oracle.

Our standard-model security proof proceeds in two modular steps. In the first step, we prove completeness and soundness of a "selective" variant of the FS transform; in the second step we analyze the standard FS transform using complexity leveraging. Details follow.

The Selective FS Transform. Consider a 3PC argument for a language L. For a hash family H, consider the following (interactive) selective adaptation of the FS transformation: The prover sends the commitment α as in the original protocol; the verifier, instead of sending the challenge $\beta \in \mathcal{B}$ directly, forwards a honestly generated hash key hk; finally the prover uses (hk, α) to compute $\beta = H(hk, \alpha)$ and then obtains the response γ as in the original 3PC argument.

In the full paper [39] we prove that if the starting 3PC protocol has instance-independent commitments, is complete and computationally sound, so is the one obtained by applying the selective FS transform. The idea is to use a "programmable" q-wise independent hash function (e.g., a random polynomial of degree $q - 1$ over a finite field) to "program" the hash function up-front; note that commitment α is computed before the hash key is generated and hence, we can embed the challenge value β into the hash function such that it maps α to β and reduce to the soundness of the underlying 3PC argument.

Complexity Leveraging. The second step in proving soundness of the FS collapse (we discuss zero-knowledge below) consists in applying complexity leveraging so that we can swap the order of α and β. Hence, this step can only be applied to protocols satisfying an additional property as we discuss next.

Let Π be the initial 3PC argument, and denote by $\overline{\Pi}$ its corresponding FS collapse. Given a malicious prover P^* breaking soundness of $\overline{\Pi}$, we construct a prover P attacking soundness of the selective FS transform as follows. P picks a random α from the space of all possible commitments, and forwards α to the verifier; after receiving the challenge hash key hk, prover P runs P* which outputs a proof (α^*, γ^*). Prover P simply hopes that $\alpha^* = \alpha$, in which case it forwards γ^* to the verifier (otherwise it aborts). It follows that if the selective FS has soundness roughly $s(\lambda)$ (for security parameter λ), the soundness of $\overline{\Pi}$ is roughly $s(\lambda)$ divided by the probability of guessing correctly the value α^* in the first step of the reduction.

Note that for the above argument to give a meaningful bound, we need that the soundness of $\overline{\Pi}$ is bounded away from one. This leads to the following (non-standard) requirement that the initial 3PC argument should satisfy.

P2: $\varrho(\lambda) := s(\lambda)/2^{-a(\lambda)} < 1$, where $s(\lambda)$ is the soundness error and $a(\lambda)$ is the maximum bit-length associated to the commitment α.

Zero-Knowledge. We assume that the initial 3PC is honest-verifier zero-knowledge (HVZK)—i.e., that it is zero-knowledge for honest verifiers. We need to show that $\overline{\Pi}$ satisfies zero-knowledge. Here, we require two additional properties as explained below; interactive protocols obeying the first property already appeared in the literature under the name of "input-delayed" protocols [15,16,33].

P1: The value α output by the prover is computed independently of the instance x being proven (and of the corresponding witness w).

P3: The value α output by the simulator is computed independently of the instance x being proven.

We now discuss the reduction for the zero-knowledge property and explain where **P1** and **P3** are used. We need to construct an efficient simulator that is able to simulate arguments for adaptively chosen (true) statements—without knowing a witness for such statements. The output of the simulator should result in a distribution that is computationally indistinguishable from the distribution generated by the real prover. The simulator gets extra power, as it can produce a "fake" CRS together with some trapdoor information tk (on which the simulator can rely) such that the "fake" CRS is indistinguishable from a real CRS.

In order to build some intuition, it is perhaps useful to recall the random-oracle-based proof for the zero-knowledge property of the FS transform. There, values α_i and β_i corresponding to the i-th adversarial query are computed by running the HVZK simulator and are later "matched" relying on the programmability of the random oracle. Roughly speaking, in our standard-model proof we take a similar approach, but we cannot use *adaptive* programming of the hash function. Instead, we rely on **P1** and **P3** to program the hash function in advance. More specifically, the trapdoor information will consist of q random tapes r_i (one for simulating each proof queried by the adversary) and the corresponding q challenges β_i (that can be pre-computed as a function of r_i, relying on **P1**). Since the challenges have the correct distribution, we can use the underlying HVZK simulator to simulate the proofs; here is where we need **P3**, as the simulator has to pre-compute the values α_i in order to embed the β_i values on the correct points.

A caveat is that our simulator needs to know the value of q in advance; for this reason we only get a weaker *bounded* flavor of the zero-knowledge property where there exists a "universal" simulator that works for all adversaries asking q queries, for some a-priori fixed value of q. Note, however, that the CRS—as it contains the description of a q-wise independent hash function—needs to grow with q, and hence bound q should be seen as a parameter of the construction rather than a parameter of the simulator.

It is an interesting open problem whether this limitation can be removed, thus proving that actually our transformation achieves unbounded zero-knowledge.

Putting it Together. We will call 3PC arguments satisfying properties **P1-P3** above (besides completeness and soundness) *highly sound* 3PC arguments. The theorem below summarizes the above discussion. Its proof is deferred to the full version [39].

Theorem 1. *Let $\Pi = (\mathsf{K}, \mathsf{P}, \mathsf{V})$ be a highly sound 3PC argument system for an NP language L, and H be a programmable q-wise independent hash function. Then, the FS collapse $\overline{\Pi}_{\mathsf{FS},\mathsf{H}}$ of Π using H yields a q-bounded NIZK argument system for L.*

3   Compilers

It remains to construct a highly sound 3PC argument, and to understand which languages admit such arguments. Unfortunately we do not know of a natural highly sound 3PC argument. However, we do know of protocols that partially satisfy our requirements. For instance the classical 3PC argument for quadratic residuosity due to Blum [9] satisfies **P1**, and moreover can be shown to achieve completeness, soundness, and HVZK, but it does not directly meet **P2** and **P3**. Another interesting example is given by the Lapidot-Shamir protocol for the NP-complete problem of graph Hamiltonicity [37] (see also [41, Appendix B]). Here, the prover's commitment consists of a (statistically binding) commitment to the adjacency matrix of a random k-vertex cycle, where k is the size of the Hamiltonian cycle.[5] Hence, the protocol clearly satisfies **P1**. Additionally the simulator fakes the prover's commitment by either committing to a random k-vertex cycle, or by committing to the empty graph. Hence, the protocol also satisfies **P3**. As a corollary, we know that assuming non-interactive statistically binding commitment schemes (which follow from one-way permutations [9]), for all languages in NP, there exist 3PC protocols that satisfy completeness, computational soundness, and HVZK, as well as **P1** and **P3**.

Motivated by the above examples, we turn to the question whether it is possible to compile a 3PC protocol (with completeness, soundness, and HVZK) satisfying either **P1** or **P1** and **P3**, into a highly sound argument. Our compilers

---

[5] Note that the value k can be included in the language, and thus considered as public.

rely on several cryptographic tools (including indistinguishability obfuscation, puncturable PRFs, complexity leveraging and equivocal commitment schemes), and yield a 3PC in the CRS model; note that this means that we obtain an interactive protocol with a CRS even if the original protocol was in the standard model. It is an intriguing open problem if a highly sound argument can be constructed in the standard model, or whether a CRS is, in fact, necessary.

3.1   First Compiler

We present a compiler that turns a 3PC argument (possibly in the CRS model) with instance-independent commitments and HVZK (i.e., properties **P1** and **P3**) into a 3PC argument which has the soundness-error-to-guessing ratio (i.e., property **P2**) needed for the complexity leveraging in our positive result for FS NIZK. The idea for the compiler is to provide a mechanism that allows to produce many challenges β given only a single commitment α. To this effect the CRS will contain two obfuscated circuits to help the prover and the verifier run the protocol. For obfuscation we use an indistinguishability obfuscator. The first circuit C_0 is used by the prover to generate a *pre-commitment* α^* which it sends over to the verifier. The verifier will then use the second circuit C_1 and run it on α^* to obtain multiple commitments. For this $C_1[k, \text{crs}]$ has a PRF key (for function F) and the crs for algorithm P_0 of the underlying protocol hardcoded, and computes ℓ commitments as follows:

$$\underline{C_1[k, \text{crs}](\alpha^*)}$$

for $i = 1, \ldots, \ell$ **do**
$\quad r^* \leftarrow \text{F.Eval}(k, \alpha^* + i)$
$\quad \alpha[i] \leftarrow \text{P}_0(\text{crs}; r^*)$
return α

Using C_1 the compiled verifier V^* can generate ℓ real commitments $\alpha[1]$ to $\alpha[\ell]$ given the single (short) pre-commitment α^*. The verifier will then run the underlying verifier V on all these commitments to receive $\beta_1, \ldots, \beta_\ell$ which it sends back to the prover.

In order to correctly continue the prover's computation (which was started on the verifier's side) the compiled prover P^* needs to somehow obtain the randomnesses r^* used within C_1. For this, we will build a backdoor into C_1 which allows to obtain the randomness r^* if one knows the randomness that was used to generate α^*. Once the prover has recovered randomnesses $r_1^*, \ldots, r_\ell^*$ it can run the underlying prover P on this randomness and the corresponding challenges β_i to get correct values γ_i which it sends back to the verifier. In a final step verifier V^* runs the original verifier on the implicit transcripts $(\alpha_i, \beta_i, \gamma_i)_{i=1,\ldots,\ell}$ and returns 1 if and only if the original verifier returns 1 on all the transcripts.

Compiler Description. Let $\Pi = (\mathsf{K}, \mathsf{P}, \mathsf{V})$ be a 3PC argument system where the prover generates instance-independent commitments and that satisfies instance-independent HVZK. Let rl denote an upper bound on the randomness used by the prover (i.e., $\mathsf{P}.\mathsf{rl}$) and HVZK simulator (i.e., $\mathcal{S}.\mathsf{rl}$). Let F_1 be a puncturable pseudorandom function which is length doubling. Let F_2 be a puncturable pseudorandom function with $\mathsf{F}_2.\mathsf{il} = \mathsf{F}_1.\mathsf{ol}$ and with $\mathsf{F}_2.\mathsf{ol} = \mathsf{rl}$. Let ℓ be a polynomial. We construct an argument system $\Pi^* = (\mathsf{K}^*, \mathsf{P}^*, \mathsf{V}^*)$ in the CRS model as follows. On input the security parameter K^* will construct an obfuscation of the following two circuits:

$\mathsf{K}^*(1^\lambda)$	$C_0[\mathsf{k}_1](\tau)$	$C_1[\mathsf{k}_1, \mathsf{k}_2, \ell, \mathsf{crs}](\alpha^*, \tau)$
$\mathsf{crs} \leftarrow_\$ \mathsf{K}(1^\lambda)$	$\alpha^* \leftarrow \mathsf{F}_1.\mathsf{Eval}(\mathsf{k}_1, \tau)$	**for** $i = 1, \ldots, \ell$ **do**
$\mathsf{k}_1 \leftarrow_\$ \mathsf{F}_1.\mathsf{KGen}(1^\lambda)$	**return** α^*	$\quad \mathbf{r}^*[i] \leftarrow \mathsf{F}_2.\mathsf{Eval}(\mathsf{k}_2, \alpha^* + i)$
$\mathsf{k}_2 \leftarrow_\$ \mathsf{F}_2.\mathsf{KGen}(1^\lambda)$		$\quad \mathsf{a}[i] \leftarrow \mathsf{P}_0(\mathsf{crs}; \mathbf{r}^*[i])$
$\overline{C}_0 \leftarrow_\$ \mathsf{iO}(C_0[\mathsf{k}_1])$		$\quad$ **if** $\alpha^* \neq \mathsf{F}_1.\mathsf{Eval}(\mathsf{k}_1, \tau)$ **then**
$\overline{C}_1 \leftarrow_\$ \mathsf{iO}(C_1[\mathsf{k}_1, \mathsf{k}_2, \ell, \mathsf{crs}])$		$\quad\quad \mathbf{r}^*[i] \leftarrow \perp$
$\overline{\mathsf{crs}} \leftarrow (\mathsf{crs}, \overline{C}_0, \overline{C}_1)$		**return** $(\mathsf{a}, \mathbf{r}^*)$
return $\overline{\mathsf{crs}}$		

Note that we assume that the underlying protocol is in the CRS model and has a setup algorithm K. If this is not the case one recovers the transformation for a 3PC in the standard model by assuming that K outputs the empty string ε. The compiled 3PC $\Pi^* = (\mathsf{K}^*, \mathsf{P}^*, \mathsf{V}^*)$ is then constructed as in Fig. 2.

Security Analysis. It remains to show that the compiled protocol is computationally sound, achieves (bounded) instance-independent HVZK, is complete, and that it has instance-independent commitments and a sufficient soundness-error-to-guessing ratio:

Theorem 2. *Let $\Pi = (\mathsf{K}, \mathsf{P}, \mathsf{V})$ be a 3PC argument system for a polynomial-time computable relation R such that Π is c-complete and s-sound and has instance-independent commitments and satisfies q-bounded instance-independent HVZK. Let iO be an indistinguishability obfuscator and F_1 and F_2 puncturable pseudorandom functions. Let ℓ be a polynomial. Then, in the CRS model, the compiled protocol $\Pi^* = (\mathsf{K}^*, \mathsf{P}^*, \mathsf{V}^*)$ is $(\ell \cdot c)$-complete, $(2 \cdot s^{-\ell} + 2^{\mathsf{F}_1.\mathsf{ol}(\lambda)} s^{-\ell})$-sound, has a worst-case collision probability of $2^{-\mathsf{F}_1.\mathsf{il}(\lambda)}$, and satisfies q/ℓ-bounded instance-independent HVZK. Furthermore the compiled protocol has instance-independent commitments.*

The proof to the above theorem appears in the full version [39].

3.2 Second Compiler

Next, we present a compiler that turns a 3PC protocol with HVZK and instance-independent commitments (i.e., property **P1**) into a 3PC protocol in the CRS

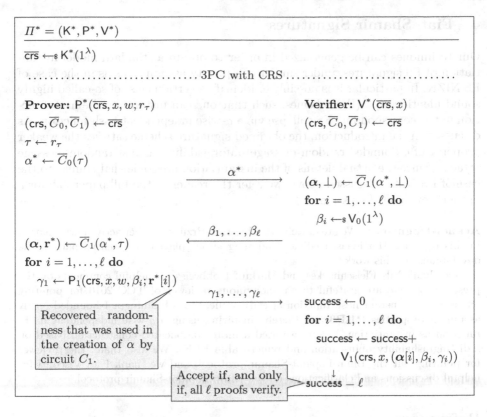

Fig. 2. The compiled protocol from Sect. 3.1 to turn a 3PC protocol into one that has a small soundness-error-to-guessing ratio (in the CRS model).

model that has instance-independent commitments *and* instance-independent simulators, that is, the HVZK simulator produces α and β independently of the instance (i.e., property **P3**).

The idea is inspired by Lindell's compiler [38]. Namely, we replace α by a commitment α^* to α where the deployed commitment scheme can come in one of two modes: if honestly generated the commitment will be *perfectly binding* thus allowing us to directly argue that the resulting compiled protocol retains soundness and completeness. On the other hand, the commitment scheme can be initialized to be *equivocal* (looking indistinguishably from the honest commitment setup) such that a simulator can open a commitment to arbitrary values. This way, the simulator can first commit to an arbitrary α^* and then, using the trapdoor in the CRS, it can open α^* to some arbitrary value α. In particular, in the reduction to the HVZK property, the verifier can choose α^* before knowing the statement that the simulator of the underlying protocol needs in order to produce α.

We refer the reader to the full paper [39] for a formal description of the above compiler, and for its security analysis.

4 Fiat–Shamir Signatures

Our techniques can be generalized in order to obtain a standard model instantiation of FS signatures, under similar complexity assumptions as in the case of FS NIZK. In particular it is possible to identify a certain class of so-called highly sound identification (ID) schemes, such that one can instantiate the hash function in the corresponding FS collapse via a q-wise independent hash function. As discussed in the introduction, the obtained signature scheme satisfies the weaker property of q-bounded random-message unforgeability against random-message attacks. Since the actual details of the instantiation are somewhat similar to the case of FS NIZK discussed above, we refer the reader to the full paper [39] for a more throughout discussion.

Acknowledgments. We are grateful to Christina Brzuska for her active participation in this research. Her ideas, feedback and suggestions played an essential part in the development of this work.

We thank Nils Fleischhacker and Markulf Kohlweiss for helpful comments on the presentation. We are grateful to an anonymous reviewer of TCC 2016 for pointing out that the constant hash function already suffices for obtaining a 1-bounded NIZK assuming properties **P1-P3** and thereby inspiring using a q-wise independent hash-function as instantiation. Before, we used a more complicated construction based on indistinguishability obfuscation and puncturable PRFs. We also thank the reviewer for pointing out the Blum-Lapidot-Shamir protocol, and we thank Ivan Visconti for helpful discussions and clarifications on the Blum-Lapidot-Shamir protocol.

References

1. Abdalla, M., An, J.H., Bellare, M., Namprempre, C.: From identification to signatures via the Fiat-Shamir transform: minimizing assumptions for security and forward-security. In: Knudsen, L.R. (ed.) EUROCRYPT 2002. LNCS, vol. 2332, pp. 418–433. Springer, Heidelberg (2002)
2. Barak, B.: How to go beyond the black-box simulation barrier. In: 42nd Annual Symposium on Foundations of Computer Science, 14–17 October 2001, pp. 106–115. IEEE Computer Society Press, Las Vegas (2001)
3. Barak, B., Lindell, Y., Vadhan, S.P.: Lower bounds for non-black-box zero knowledge. In: 44th Annual Symposium on Foundations of Computer Science, 11–14 October 2003, pp. 384–393. IEEE Computer Society Press, Cambridge (2003)
4. Bellare, M., Rogaway, P.: Random oracles are practical: a paradigm for designing efficient protocols. In: Ashby, V. (ed.) ACM CCS 93: 1st Conference on Computer and Communications Security, 3–5 November 1993, pp. 62–73. ACM Press, Fairfax (1993)
5. Bellare, M., Shoup, S.: Two-tier signatures, strongly unforgeable signatures, and Fiat-Shamir without random oracles. In: Okamoto, T., Wang, X. (eds.) PKC 2007. LNCS, vol. 4450, pp. 201–216. Springer, Heidelberg (2007)
6. Bernhard, D., Pereira, O., Warinschi, B.: How not to prove yourself: pitfalls of the Fiat-Shamir heuristic and applications to helios. In: Wang, X., Sako, K. (eds.) ASIACRYPT 2012. LNCS, vol. 7658, pp. 626–643. Springer, Heidelberg (2012)

7. Bitansky, N., Dachman-Soled, D., Garg, S., Jain, A., Kalai, Y.T., López-Alt, A., Wichs, D.: Why "Fiat-Shamir for proofs" lacks a proof. In: Sahai, A. (ed.) TCC 2013. LNCS, vol. 7785, pp. 182–201. Springer, Heidelberg (2013)
8. Bitansky, N., Garg, S., Wichs, D.: Why Fiat-Shamir for proofs lacks a proof. Cryptology ePrint Archive, Report 2012/705 (2012). http://eprint.iacr.org/2012/705
9. Blum, M.: Coin flipping by telephone. In: Gersho, A. (ed.) Advances in Cryptology - CRYPTO 1981. ECE Report 82–04, pp. 11–15. U.C. Santa Barbara, Department of Electrical and Computer Engineering, Santa Barbara, CA, USA (1981)
10. Blum, M., Feldman, P., Micali, S.: Non-interactive zero-knowledge and its applications (extended abstract). In: 20th Annual ACM Symposium on Theory of Computing, 2–4 May 1988, pp. 103–112. ACM Press, Chicago (1988)
11. Camenisch, J.L., Hohenberger, S., Lysyanskaya, A.: Compact e-cash. In: Cramer, R. (ed.) EUROCRYPT 2005. LNCS, vol. 3494, pp. 302–321. Springer, Heidelberg (2005)
12. Camenisch, J.L., Lysyanskaya, A.: Dynamic accumulators and application to efficient revocation of anonymous credentials. In: Yung, M. (ed.) CRYPTO 2002. LNCS, vol. 2442, pp. 61–76. Springer, Heidelberg (2002)
13. Canetti, R., Chen, Y., Reyzin, L.: On the correlation intractability of obfuscated pseudorandom functions. Cryptology ePrint Archive, Report 2015/334 (2015). http://eprint.iacr.org/
14. Canetti, R., Goldreich, O., Halevi, S.: The random oracle methodology, revisited (preliminary version). In: 30th Annual ACM Symposium on Theory of Computing, 23–26 May 1998, pp. 209–218. ACM Press, Dallas (1988)
15. Ciampi, M., Persiano, G., Scafuro, A., Siniscalchi, L., Visconti, I.: Improved OR-composition of sigma-protocols. In: Kushilevitz, E., et al. (eds.) TCC 2016-A. LNCS, vol. 9563, pp. 112–141. Springer, Heidelberg (2016). doi:10.1007/978-3-662-49099-0_5
16. Ciampi, M., Persiano, G., Scafuro, A., Siniscalchi, L., Visconti, I.: Online/offline or composition of sigma protocols. Cryptology ePrint Archive, Report 2016/175 (2016). http://eprint.iacr.org/
17. Ciampi, M., Persiano, G., Siniscalchi, L., Visconti, I.: A transform for NIZK almost as efficient and general as the Fiat-Shamir transform without programmable random oracles. In: Kushilevitz, E., et al. (eds.) TCC 2016-A. LNCS, vol. 9563, pp. 83–111. Springer, Heidelberg (2016). doi:10.1007/978-3-662-49099-0_4
18. Dachman-Soled, D., Jain, A., Kalai, Y.T., López-Alt, A.: On the (in)security of the Fiat-Shamir paradigm, revisited. IACR Cryptology ePrint Archive 2012, 706 (2012). http://eprint.iacr.org/2012/706
19. Dagdelen, Ö., Venturi, D.: A second look at Fischlin's transformation. In: Pointcheval, D., Vergnaud, D. (eds.) AFRICACRYPT 2014. LNCS, vol. 8469, pp. 356–376. Springer, Heidelberg (2014)
20. Damgård, I.B.: Efficient concurrent zero-knowledge in the auxiliary string model. In: Preneel, B. (ed.) EUROCRYPT 2000. LNCS, vol. 1807, pp. 418–430. Springer, Heidelberg (2000)
21. Dodis, Y., Ristenpart, T., Vadhan, S.: Randomness condensers for efficiently samplable, seed-dependent sources. In: Cramer, R. (ed.) TCC 2012. LNCS, vol. 7194, pp. 618–635. Springer, Heidelberg (2012)
22. Dolev, D., Dwork, C., Naor, M.: Non-malleable cryptography (extended abstract). In: 23rd Annual ACM Symposium on Theory of Computing, 6–8 May 1991, pp. 542–552. ACM Press, New Orleans (1991)

23. Dwork, C., Naor, M., Reingold, O., Stockmeyer, L.J.: Magic functions. In: 40th Annual Symposium on Foundations of Computer Science, 17–19 October 1999, pp. 523–534. IEEE Computer Society Press, New York (1999)

24. Elkind, E., Lipmaa, H.: Interleaving cryptography and mechanism design. In: Juels, A. (ed.) FC 2004. LNCS, vol. 3110, pp. 117–131. Springer, Heidelberg (2004)

25. Faust, S., Kohlweiss, M., Marson, G.A., Venturi, D.: On the non-malleability of the Fiat-Shamir transform. In: Galbraith, S., Nandi, M. (eds.) INDOCRYPT 2012. LNCS, vol. 7668, pp. 60–79. Springer, Heidelberg (2012)

26. Fiat, A., Shamir, A.: How to prove yourself: practical solutions to identification and signature problems. In: Odlyzko, A.M. (ed.) CRYPTO 1986. LNCS, vol. 263, pp. 186–194. Springer, Heidelberg (1987)

27. Fischlin, M.: Communication-efficient non-interactive proofs of knowledge with online extractors. In: Shoup, V. (ed.) CRYPTO 2005. LNCS, vol. 3621, pp. 152–168. Springer, Heidelberg (2005)

28. Goldreich, O., Micali, S., Wigderson, A.: How to play any mental game or a completeness theorem for protocols with honest majority. In: Aho, A. (ed.) 19th Annual ACM Symposium on Theory of Computing, 25–27 May 1987, pp. 218–229. ACM Press, New York City (1987)

29. Goldwasser, S., Kalai, Y.T.: On the (in)security of the Fiat-Shamir paradigm. In: 44th Annual Symposium on Foundations of Computer Science, 11–14 October 2003, pp. 102–115. IEEE Computer Society Press, Cambridge (2003)

30. Goyal, V., Ostrovsky, R., Scafuro, A., Visconti, I.: Black-box non-black-box zero knowledge. In: Shmoys, D.B. (ed.) 46th Annual ACM Symposium on Theory of Computing, May 31–June 3 2014, pp. 515–524. ACM Press, New York (2014)

31. Groth, J., Sahai, A.: Efficient non-interactive proof systems for bilinear groups. In: Smart, N.P. (ed.) EUROCRYPT 2008. LNCS, vol. 4965, pp. 415–432. Springer, Heidelberg (2008)

32. Haitner, I.: A parallel repetition theorem for any interactive argument. In: 50th Annual Symposium on Foundations of Computer Science, 25–27 October 2009, pp. 241–250. IEEE Computer Society Press, Atlanta (2009)

33. Hazay, C., Venkitasubramaniam, M.: On the power of secure two-party computation. Cryptology ePrint Archive, Report 2016/074 (2016). http://eprint.iacr.org/

34. Hohenberger, S., Sahai, A., Waters, B.: Replacing a random oracle: full domain hash from indistinguishability obfuscation. In: Nguyen, P.Q., Oswald, E. (eds.) EUROCRYPT 2014. LNCS, vol. 8441, pp. 201–220. Springer, Heidelberg (2014)

35. Kalai, Y.T., Rothblum, G.N., Rothblum, R.D.: From obfuscation to the security of Fiat-Shamir for proofs. Cryptology ePrint Archive, Report 2016/303 (2016). http://eprint.iacr.org/

36. Kiayias, A., Zacharias, T., Zhang, B.: End-to-end verifiable elections in the standard model. In: Oswald, E., Fischlin, M. (eds.) EUROCRYPT 2015. LNCS, vol. 9057, pp. 468–498. Springer, Heidelberg (2015)

37. Lapidot, D., Shamir, A.: Publicly verifiable non-interactive zero-knowledge proofs. In: Menezes, A., Vanstone, S.A. (eds.) CRYPTO 1990. LNCS, vol. 537, pp. 353–365. Springer, Heidelberg (1991)

38. Lindell, Y.: An efficient transform from sigma protocols to NIZK with a CRS and non-programmable random oracle. In: Dodis, Y., Nielsen, J.B. (eds.) TCC 2015, Part I. LNCS, vol. 9014, pp. 93–109. Springer, Heidelberg (2015)

39. Mittelbach, A., Venturi, D.: Fiat-Shamir for highly sound protocols is instantiable. IACR Cryptology ePrint Archive 2016, 313 (2016). http://eprint.iacr.org/2016/313

40. Okamoto, T.: Provably secure and practical identification schemes and correspond-
    ing signature schemes. In: Brickell, E.F. (ed.) CRYPTO 1992. LNCS, vol. 740, pp.
    31–53. Springer, Heidelberg (1993)
41. Ostrovsky, R., Visconti, I.: Simultaneous resettability from collision resistance.
    Electronic Colloquium on Computational Complexity (ECCC) 19, 164 (2012).
    http://eccc.hpi-web.de/report/2012/164
42. Pointcheval, D., Stern, J.: Security arguments for digital signatures and blind sig-
    natures. J. Cryptol. 13(3), 361–396 (2000)
43. Sahai, A., Waters, B.: How to use indistinguishability obfuscation: deniable encryp-
    tion, and more. In: Shmoys, D.B. (ed.) 46th Annual ACM Symposium on Theory
    of Computing, May 31–June 3 2014, pp. 475–484. ACM Press, New York (2014)

Verifiable Zero-Knowledge Order Queries and Updates for Fully Dynamic Lists and Trees

Esha Ghosh[1]([✉]), Michael T. Goodrich[2], Olga Ohrimenko[3], and Roberto Tamassia[1]

[1] Department Computer Science, Brown University, Providence, USA
{esha_ghosh,roberto_tamassia}@brown.edu
[2] Department Computer Science, University of California, Irvine, USA
goodrich@uci.edu
[3] Microsoft Research, Cambridge, UK
oohrim@microsoft.com

Abstract. We propose a three-party model for maintaining a dynamic data structure that supports verifiable and privacy-preserving (zero-knowledge) queries. We give efficient constructions supporting this model for order queries on data organized in lists, trees, and partially-ordered sets of bounded dimension.

1 Introduction

Cloud computing enables clients to outsource storage, computation, and services to online service providers, thus benefiting from scalability, availability, and usage-driven pricing. However, there are also some challenges that arise from cloud computing, such as the difficulty of maintaining assurances of data integrity and privacy as physical possession of data is delegated to a cloud storage provider. Thus, we are interested in the study of technical solutions that allow a cloud storage provider to prove the integrity of client data and the adherence to privacy policies concerning this data. Of course, in order for any such technical solution to be practically viable, the efficiency of such cloud-based integrity and privacy solutions should be a major factor in evaluating them.

The need for simultaneously providing efficiency, integrity, and privacy in cloud-based outsourced storage has motivated a considerable amount of recent research on a three-party model, where a *data owner* uploads a database to a *cloud server* so that a group of *clients* can interact with the server to execute queries on the outsourced database (e.g., see [14–16,21,22,29]). This approach has resulted in some interesting solutions, but most existing techniques appear to be limited to static datasets, where data is uploaded only once by the data owner and never updated, in spite of the fact that data changes over time in many practical applications. There is only a small amount of prior work that addresses integrity and privacy on dynamic outsourced data, and, to be best

---

Research supported in part by the U.S. National Science Foundation and by the Kanellakis Fellowship at Brown University.

V. Zikas and R. De Prisco (Eds.): SCN 2016, LNCS 9841, pp. 216–236, 2016.
DOI: 10.1007/978-3-319-44618-9_12

of our knowledge, all of this prior work considers only set membership and set algebra queries (e.g., see [7,13,25,33]).

In this paper, we provide a framework and formal security definitions for the problem of ensuring integrity and privacy in cloud services operating on dynamic data, with an efficient construction that can process a rich set of queries. The queries include membership and order queries on dynamic lists, trees, and partially-ordered sets of bounded dimension.

Our first main contribution is to formally define a model we call *dynamic privacy-preserving authenticated data structure* (DPPADS). In this model, a data *owner* outsources his data structure to a *server* who answers queries issued by *clients*. The owner can at any point update the data structure. The server answers queries in such a way that the clients (1) can verify the correctness of the answers but (2) do not learn anything about the data structure or the updates besides what can be inferred from the answers. In other words, the privacy property ensures that even a malicious client learns nothing about any update, unless she specifically queries for the updated item before and after the update. For example, consider the case when a new element, x, is inserted into a dataset. If a client queried for x before and after this update, she will *only* learn that x has been added to the database, but nothing else about the database.

The dynamic behavior of data structures raises challenges from a definitional point of view since an adversary (i.e., a malicious client) may choose update operations and later query the system to see their effect on nearby data, for example. Pöhls and Samelin [33] consider updates in the three-party model only for positive membership queries and their definition is specific to their data structure and cannot be easily generalized to support richer data structures and queries. Thus, we feel a richer framework, like DPPADS, is warranted.

Our DPPADS model strives to capture realistic uses of cloud services from the data owner's perspective. First, the owner's online presence is required only if he needs to update the data. Hence, clients' queries are performed solely by the server. Second, access control policies on the data can be seamlessly integrated with our model since integrity tokens sent to the clients to enable verification of query answers do not leak any information about the non-queried data.

Our second main contribution is to show how to efficiently instantiate DPPADS with membership and *order queries* on lists, trees, and partial orders of bounded dimension. Order queries are fundamental mechanisms for seeking relative order information about the elements of a partial order. In the simplest case, an order query for two elements, u and v, of a list L asks whether u precedes or follows v in L. Consider now an ordered tree, T, i.e., a rooted tree where a left-to-right ordering is defined among the descendants of each node. An order query on two nodes u and v, of T asks which one of the following relations holds: u is above v; u is below v; u is to the left of v; or u is to the right of v. The first two cases occur when one of u and v is a descendant of the other and the last two cases occur when u and v are in distinct subtrees of their least common ancestor. We note that none of the previous works supported dynamic behavior on such a rich set of structural data with integrity and privacy guarantees.

Our model implies that the client should be able to verify the data she queried with authentication tokens produced in part by the server (as the owner is not present in the query phase). Building constructions with such authentication tokens is challenging for several reasons. Beside being hard to forge, these tokens should bare no information about the rest of the data, not even the size of the data; only in this case we can protect privacy of non-queried data. Furthermore, dynamic datasets require corresponding updates to these tokens as a consequence. Hence, these tokens should be easily updatable.

Existing work comes short in achieving all of the requirements above at once. For example, commitments and zero-knowledge proofs [17] present a naive but unfortunately inefficient solution. In particular, a naive approach would require space and setup cost quadratic in the list/tree size and, hence, very inefficient. Though more efficient solutions exist [10, 14], they are set in the case where data does not change after the owner uploads it and they consider only sets and lists as underlying datasets. An attempt to cover dynamic datasets with integrity and privacy guarantees was made by Liskov [25] and Catalano and Fiore [7]. These constructions are set in a weaker privacy model which we elaborate further in Sect. 2. In fact, the authors comment on this limitation themselves: "Ideally, the adversary should learn nothing more than the values of elements for which a proof has been obtained (and possibly updated), and that updates have occurred. However, we have not been able to realize this full level of security, and instead offer a weaker but acceptable notion of security." [25] (We also note that the question of efficient constructions of zero-knowledge data structures more complex than sets is left open in [33]; we answer it affirmatively here.)

Due to these limitations, we take an algorithmic approach to this problem and identify efficient dynamic constructions for lists and trees. Then we integrate the lightweight cryptographic primitive developed in [14] with our algorithmic constructions in a novel way. But this alone was not sufficient to achieve our strong notion of privacy for updates that are influenced by a strong adversary. To this end, we have developed a technique of systematic, periodic re-randomization to achieve strong privacy guarantees. However, for some application, even this technique is not sufficient as the information that "an update has occurred" can itself be regarded as sensitive information. This leakage is out of the scope of the privacy definitions, but can be crucial for some applications from a practical point of view. We address this issue further and propose a technique that can be executed periodically in order to hide the existence of an update.

Our constructions strive to achieve good performance for all the three parties. In particular, all the parties run in *optimal time* except for a logarithmic (in the size of the source data structure) runtime overhead for the server. The client-server interaction consists of a single round: the client sends a query and the server returns the answer and the proof. The proof size and client verification time are proportional to the answer. The owner interacts with the server only when he needs to make an update to his data. We consider two types of owners: one that can keep a copy of the data structure (DPPADS) and one that prefers not to (due to limited storage resources) (SE-DPPADS). In the first case, the owner performs an update operation himself, in time linear in the size of a batch update. In the second case, he outsources the update operation to the server and later verifies it, incurring a logarithmic multiplicative cost in the size of the source data structure. In both cases, the owner performs constant-time updates, this time is amortized over the number of elements queried or updated since the last update. Our contributions can be summarized as follows:

- We formally define the DPPADS model for a dynamic privacy-preserving authenticated data structure that supports *zero-knowledge* proofs for queries and *zero-knowledge* updates (Sect. 3).
- We give an efficient construction of a DPPADS in the Random Oracle model for a list that supports order queries and updates (Sect. 4).
- We give an overview of a space-efficient variant of the DPPADS model in Sect. 4 and defer the detailed description to the technical report [12].
- We present an efficient extension of our DPPADS construction to trees and partial orders of bounded dimension (Sect. 5).

2 Related Work

We describe the related primitives and discuss how we compare with them. Detailed comparison of privacy properties and the asymptotic complexity of our constructions with the most efficient constructions in the literature is in Table 1.

Traditional authenticated data structures (ADS) [11,18,31,37] are often set in the three party model with a trusted owner, a *trusted* client and a malicious server; the owner outsources the data to the server and later the client interacts with the server to run queries on the data. The security requirement of such constructions is data authenticity for the client against the server. This integrity requirement is the same in our model. However, since the client is trusted, the strong privacy requirement of our model is usually violated by the ADS proofs. For example, Merkle Hash Tree (MHT) [26] reveals the number of elements in the dataset and the proof path in a MHT reveals order information.

Authenticity and privacy together were considered in the two-party model of *zero knowledge set* (ZKS) [8,10,24,27] introduced in [27] and later used in knowledge lists [14], statistically hiding sets [34] and consistent query protocols [30]. In this model a malicious prover commits to a database in the setup phase and later a malicious verifier queries it. The prover and the verifier are non-colluding. The prover may try to give answers inconsistent with the committed database, while the verifier may try to learn information beyond query answers. In this paper, we study a three-party model which can be seen as a relaxation of the ZKS model with similar privacy and integrity guarantees. That is, the committer is "honest" and the (malicious) prover is different from the committer. The three party model leads to efficiency enhancements since one can use primitives with a trapdoor (like bilinear aggregate signature in our case) as opposed to trapdoorless hash and commitments and generic zero-knowledge proofs. As a result, efficient constructions were proposed for positive membership queries [1,2,38], dictionary queries on sets [16,29], range queries [15], order queries and statistics on lists [6, 9, 14, 22, 23, 32, 35]. However, all of these models consider a *static* dataset. We enhance this three-party model to support a fully dynamic dataset and formalize the notion of privacy and integrity.

Updates in both of the above models have received only limited attention. The notion of updatable zero knowledge set was first proposed in [25]with two definitions: transparent and opaque. The transparent definition explicitly reveals that an update has occurred and the verifier can determine whether previously queried elements were updated. Constructions satisfying transparent updates are given in [7, 25]. Our zero-knowledge definition in Sect. 3 supports opaque updates in the three-party model, which is also satisfied by our constructions.

In the three-party model, updates on a set were considered in the recent work of [33]. This work supports privacy-preserving verification of positive membership only (i.e., a proof is returned only when the queried elements are members of the given set). Their formal definition for updates is based on an indistinguishability game and is specific to their data structure and cannot be easily extended to support richer data structures and queries. In comparison, we propose simulation based definition and our definition are not tailored to any specific data structure. Moreover, the construction of [33] supports only two update operations: addition of new elements and merge of two sets. Here, we consider operations on lists, trees and support addition, deletion and replace operations.

We compare privacy properties and the asymptotic complexity of our constructions with the static [14] and updatable [33] constructions in Table 1. We note that, the *static* construction for order queries in [14] was shown to outperform the existing static constructions of [6, 9, 20, 21, 32, 35, 36]. We show that the performance of our construction for queries is the same as that of [14]. Moreover, our list construction is the first to support fully dynamic zero-knowledge updates (inserts and deletes) and zero-knowledge queries (order and positive membership) with near optimal proof size and complexities for all three parties. In particular, the time and space complexities for setup and verification and space complexity of query phase are optimal.

Finally, we note that our work on privacy-preserving updates is not to be confused with *history independent data structures (HIDSs)* [28]. HIDS is concerned with the leakage one obtains when she looks at the *layout* of a data structure before and after a sequence of updates on it. In our model, the client (i.e., the adversary) obtains only some *content* of the data structure and not the layout. Furthermore, we require the client to be able to verify that query answers are correct and not leak any information about the rest of the content.

3   Dynamic Privacy Preserving Authenticated Data Structure (DPPADS)

An Abstract Data Type (ADT) is a data structure (DS) $\mathcal{D}$ with two types of operations defined on it: immutable operations $Q()$ and mutable operations $U()$. $Q(\mathcal{D}, \delta)$ takes as input a query δ on the elements of $\mathcal{D}$ and returns the answer

Table 1. Comparison of the efficiency of the dynamic operations of our construction with an existing updatable construction that supports privacy-preserving queries in the three party model. All the time and space complexities are asymptotic. Notation: n is the list size, m is the query size, L is the number of insertions/deletions in a batch, M is the number of distinct elements that have been queried since the last update (insertion/deletion), k is the security parameter. Wlog we assume list elements are k bit long. Following the standard convention, we omit a multiplicative factor of $O(k)$ for element size in every cell. Assumptions: Strong RSA Assumption (SRSA); Random Oracle Model (ROM); Division Intractible Hash Function (DIHF); n-Bilinear Diffie Hellman Inversion Assumption (nBDHI); (SE-)DPPAL/T denotes (space efficient) Dynamic Privacy Preserving Authenticated Lists and Trees. We use $\tilde{n}$ to denote $\min(m \log n, n)$.

	[14]	[33]	DPPAL/T	SE-DPPAL/T
Zero-knowledge update			✓	✓
Transparent update		✓	✓	✓
Owner's state size		n	n	1
Server storage size	n	n	n	n
Order query time	$\tilde{n}$		$\tilde{n}$	$\tilde{n}$
Order verification time	m		m	m
Positive membership query time	$\tilde{n}$	m	$\tilde{n}$	$\tilde{n}$
Positive membership verif. time	m	m	m	m
Proof size	m	m	m	m
Insertion time		L	$L + M$	$L \log n + M$
Deletion time			$L + M$	$L \log n + M$
Assumptions	ROM, nBDHI	DIHF, SRSA	ROM, nBDHI	ROM, nBDHI
Assumptions	ROM	DIHF	ROM	ROM
	nBDHI	SRSA	nBDHI	nBDHI

and it does not alter $\mathcal{D}$. $U(\mathcal{D}, u)$ takes as input an update request u (e.g., insert or delete), changes $\mathcal{D}$ accordingly, and outputs the modified data structure, $\mathcal{D}'$.

We present a three party model where a trusted owner generates an instantiation of an ADT, denoted as $(\mathcal{D}, Q, U)$, and outsources it to an untrusted server along with some auxiliary information. The owner also publicly releases a short digest of $\mathcal{D}$. The curious (potentially malicious) client(s) issues queries on the elements of $\mathcal{D}$ and gets answers and proofs from the server, where the proofs are zero-knowledge, i.e., they reveal nothing beyond the query answer. The client can use the proofs and the digest to verify query answers. Additionally, the owner can insert, delete or update elements in $\mathcal{D}$ and update the public digest and the auxiliary information that the server holds. (In this model the owner is required to keep a copy of $\mathcal{D}$ to perform updates, while in the space efficient version the owner keeps only a small digest.) We also require the updates to be zero-knowledge, i.e., an updated digest should be indistinguishable from a new digest generated for the unchanged $\mathcal{D}$.

Model. DPPADS is a tuple of six probabilistic polynomial time algorithms (KeyGen, Setup, UpdateOwner, UpdateServer, Query, Verify). We describe how these algorithms are used between the three parties and give their API.

The owner uses KeyGen to generate the necessary keys. He then runs Setup to prepare $\mathcal{D}_0$ for outsourcing it to the server and to compute digests for the client and the server. The owner can update his data structure and make corresponding changes to digests using UpdateOwner. Since the data structure and the digest of the server need to be updated on the server as well, the owner generates an update string that is enough for the server to make the update itself using UpdateServer. The client can query the data structure by sending queries to the server. For a query δ, the server runs Query and generates answer. Using its digest, it also prepares a proof of the answer. The client then uses Verify to verify the query answer against proof and the digest she has received from the owner after the last update.

$(\mathsf{sk}, \mathsf{pk}) \leftarrow \mathsf{KeyGen}(1^k)$ where 1^k is the security parameter. KeyGen outputs a secret key (for the owner) and the corresponding public key pk.

$(\mathsf{state}_O, \mathsf{digest}_C^0, \mathsf{digest}_S^0) \leftarrow \mathsf{Setup}(\mathsf{sk}, \mathsf{pk}, \mathcal{D}_0)$ where $\mathcal{D}_0$ is the initial data structure. Setup outputs the internal state information for the owner state_O, digests digest_C^0 and digest_S^0 for the client and the server, respectively.

$(\mathsf{state}_O, \mathsf{digest}_C^{t+1}, \mathsf{Upd}_{t+1}, \mathcal{D}_{t+1}, u_t) \leftarrow \mathsf{UpdateOwner}(\mathsf{sk}, \mathsf{state}_O, \mathsf{digest}_C^t, \mathsf{digest}_S^t, \mathcal{D}_t, u_t, \mathsf{SID}_t)$ where u_t is an update operation to be performed on $\mathcal{D}_t$. SID_t is a session information and is set to the output of a function f on the queries invoked since the last update (Setup is counted as the 0th update).

UpdateOwner returns the updated internal state information state_O, the updated public/client digest digest_C^{t+1}, update string Upd_{t+1} that is used to update digest_S^t and the updated $\mathcal{D}_{t+1} := U(\mathcal{D}_t, u_t)$.

$(\mathsf{digest}_S^{t+1}, \mathcal{D}_{t+1}) \leftarrow \mathsf{UpdateServer}(\mathsf{digest}_S^t, \mathsf{Upd}_{t+1}, \mathcal{D}_t, u_t)$ where Upd_{t+1} is used to update digest_S^t to digest_S^{t+1} and u_t is used to update $\mathcal{D}_t$ to $\mathcal{D}_{t+1}$.

$(\mathsf{answer}, \mathsf{proof}) \leftarrow \mathsf{Query}(\mathsf{digest}_S^t, \mathcal{D}_t, \delta)$ where δ is a query on elements of $\mathcal{D}_t$, answer is the query answer, and proof is the proof of the answer.

$b \leftarrow \mathsf{Verify}(\mathsf{pk}, \mathsf{digest}_C^t, \delta, \mathsf{answer}, \mathsf{proof})$ with input arguments are defined above. The output bit b is accept if answer $= Q(\mathcal{D}_t, \delta)$, and reject, otherwise.

Our model also supports the execution of a batch of updates as a single operation, which may be used to optimize overall performance (Sect. 4). We note that SID and f are introduced for efficiency reasons only. Intuitively, function f can be instantiated in a way that helps reduce the owner's work for maintaining zero-knowledge property of each update. We leave f to be defined by a particular instantiation. Once defined, f remains fixed for the instantiation. Since the function is public, anybody, who has access to the list of (authentic) queries performed since the last update, can compute it.

A DPPADS has three security properties: completeness, soundness and zero-knowledge.

Completeness dictates that if all three parties are honest, then for an instantiation of any ADT, the client will always accept an answer to her query from the server. Here, honest behavior implies that whenever the owner updates the data structure and its public digest, the server updates $\mathcal{D}$ and its digest accordingly and replies client's queries faithfully w.r.t. the latest data structure and digest.

Definition 1 (Completeness). *For an ADT $(\mathcal{D}_0, Q, U)$, any sequence of updates $u_0, u_1, \ldots, u_L$ on the data structure $\mathcal{D}_0$, and for all queries δ on $\mathcal{D}_L$:*

$$\Pr[(\mathsf{sk}, \mathsf{pk}) \leftarrow \mathsf{KeyGen}(1^k); (\mathsf{state}_O, \mathsf{digest}_C^0, \mathsf{digest}_S^0) \leftarrow \mathsf{Setup}(\mathsf{sk}, \mathsf{pk}, \mathcal{D}_0);$$
$$\big\{ (\mathsf{state}_O, \mathsf{digest}_C^{t+1}, \mathsf{Upd}_{t+1}, \mathcal{D}_{t+1}, u_t) \leftarrow$$
$$\mathsf{UpdateOwner}(\mathsf{sk}, \mathsf{state}_O, \mathsf{digest}_C^t, \mathsf{digest}_S^t, \mathcal{D}_t, u_t, \mathsf{SID}_t);$$
$$(\mathsf{digest}_S^{t+1}, \mathcal{D}_{t+1}) \leftarrow \mathsf{UpdateServer}(\mathsf{digest}_S^t, \mathsf{Upd}_{t+1}, \mathcal{D}_t, u_t); \big\}_{0 \le t \le L}$$
$$(\mathsf{answer}, \mathsf{proof}) \leftarrow \mathsf{Query}(\mathsf{digest}_S^L, \mathcal{D}_L, \delta):$$
$$\mathsf{Verify}(\mathsf{pk}, \mathsf{digest}_C^L, \delta, \mathsf{answer}, \mathsf{proof}) = \mathsf{accept} \wedge \mathsf{answer} = Q(\mathcal{D}_L, \delta)] = 1.$$

Soundness protects the client against a malicious server. This property ensures that if the server forges the answer to a client's query, then the client will accept the answer with at most negligible probability. The definition considers adversarial server that picks the data structure and adaptively requests updates. After seeing all the replies from the owner, it can pick any point of time (w.r.t. updates) to create a forgery.

Since, given the server digest, the server can compute answers to queries herself, it is superfluous to give Adv explicit access to Query algorithm.

Definition 2 (Soundness). *For all PPT adversaries Adv and for all possible valid queries δ on the data structure $\mathcal{D}_j$ of an ADT, there exists a negligible function $\nu(.)$ such that, the probability of winning the following game is negligible:*

Setup: *Adv receives pk where $(\mathsf{sk}, \mathsf{pk}) \leftarrow \mathsf{KeyGen}(1^k)$. Given pk, Adv picks an ADT of its choice, $(\mathcal{D}_0, Q, U)$ and receives the server digest digest_S^0 for $\mathcal{D}_0$, where $(\mathsf{state}_O, \mathsf{digest}_C^0, \mathsf{digest}_S^0) \leftarrow \mathsf{Setup}(\mathsf{sk}, \mathsf{pk}, \mathcal{D}_0)$.*

Query: *Adv adaptively chooses a series of updates $u_1, u_2, \ldots, u_L$ and corresponding SIDs, where $L = \mathsf{poly}(k)$. For every update request Adv receives an update string. Let $\mathcal{D}_{i+1}$ denote the state of the data structure after the (i)th update and Upd_{i+1} be the corresponding update string received by the adversary, i.e., $(\mathsf{state}_O, \mathsf{digest}_C^{i+1}, \mathsf{Upd}_{i+1}, \mathcal{D}_{i+1}, u_i) \leftarrow \mathsf{UpdateOwner}(\mathsf{sk}, \mathsf{state}_O, \mathsf{digest}_C^i, \mathsf{digest}_S^i, \mathcal{D}_i, u_i, \mathsf{SID}_i)$.*

Response: *Finally, Adv outputs $(\mathcal{D}_j, \delta, \mathsf{answer}, \mathsf{proof})$, $0 \le j \le L$, and wins the game if $\mathsf{answer} \ne Q(\mathcal{D}_j, \delta)$ and $\mathsf{Verify}(\mathsf{pk}, \mathsf{digest}_C^j, \delta, \mathsf{answer}, \mathsf{proof}) = \mathsf{accept}$.*

Zero-knowledge captures privacy guarantees about the data structure against a curious (malicious) client. Recall that the client receives a proof for every query answer. Periodically she also receives an updated digest, due to the owner making changes to $\mathcal{D}$. Informally, (1) the proofs should reveal nothing beyond the query answer, and (2) an updated digest should reveal nothing about update operations performed on $\mathcal{D}$. This security property guarantees that the client does not learn which elements were updated, unless she queries for an updated element (deleted or replaced), before and after the update.

Definition 3 (Zero-Knowledge). *Let* $\mathsf{Real}_{\mathcal{E},\mathsf{Adv}}$ *and* $\mathsf{Ideal}_{\mathcal{E},\mathsf{Adv},\mathsf{Sim}}$ *be defined as follows where, wlog the adversary is asks only for valid data and update queries.*[1]

$\mathsf{Real}_{\mathcal{E},\mathsf{Adv}}(1^k)$	$\mathsf{Ideal}_{\mathcal{E},\mathsf{Adv},\mathsf{Sim}}(1^k)$
The challenger, $\mathcal{C}$, runs $\mathsf{KeyGen}(1^k)$ to generate sk, pk, sends pk to Adv_1.	Sim_1 generates a public key, pk, sends it to Adv_1 and keeps a state, state_S.
Given pk, Adv_1 picks an ADT $(\mathcal{D}_0, Q, U)$ of its choice.	
Given $\mathcal{D}_0$, $\mathcal{C}$ runs $\mathsf{Setup}(\mathsf{sk}, \mathsf{pk}, \mathcal{D}_0)$ and sends digest_C^0 to Adv_1.	Sim_1 generates digest_C^0, sends it to Adv_1, updates state_S. (It is not given $\mathcal{D}_0$.)
With access to Adv_1's state, Adv_2 adaptively queries $\{q_1, q_2, \ldots, q_M\}$, $M = \mathsf{poly}(k)$:	
Let $\mathcal{D}_{t-1}$ denote the state of the data structure at the time of q_i.)	
On data query q_i:	
$\mathcal{C}$ runs Query algorithm for the query on $\mathcal{D}_{t-1}$ and the corresponding digest as its parameters. $\mathcal{C}$ returns answer and proof to Adv_2	Given the answer to the query, $Q(\mathcal{D}_{t-1}, q_i)$, and state_S, Sim_2 generates answer and proof, sends them to Adv_2 and updates its state.
On update query q_i:	
$\mathcal{C}$ runs UpdateOwner algorithm on q_i and returns the public digest digest_C^t.	Given state_S, Sim_2 returns updated digest digest_C^t and updates its state. (It is not given the update query q_i.)
Adv_2 outputs a bit b.	

A DPPADS $\mathcal{E}$ is zero-knowledge if there exists a PPT algorithm $\mathsf{Sim} = (\mathsf{Sim}_1, \mathsf{Sim}_2)$ *s.t. for all malicious stateful adversaries* $\mathsf{Adv} = (\mathsf{Adv}_1, \mathsf{Adv}_2)$ *there exists a negligible function $\nu(.)$ s.t.*

$$|\Pr[\mathsf{Real}_{\mathcal{E},\mathsf{Adv}}(1^k) = 1] - \Pr[\mathsf{Ideal}_{\mathcal{E},\mathsf{Adv},\mathsf{Sim}}(1^k) = 1]| \leq \nu(k).$$

We note that SID argument to UpdateOwner need not be used explicitly in the definition: Adv implicitly controls the input of f by choosing queries on $\mathcal{D}$ (recall that $\mathsf{SID} = f(\ldots)$), while the challenger and the simulator know all the queries and can compute f themselves.

Comparison with the update definitions of [7,25]**:** Liskov [25] introduced two notions of update (w.r.t. a zero-knowledge database): *Opaque:* an adversary should learn nothing more than the values of queried elements and the fact that an update has occurred. *Transparent:* in addition to what is revealed in the opaque update, an adversary learns the pseudonym of an updated key; pseudonyms are generated deterministically when keys are added to the database and do not change. The constructions in [25] and [7] achieve only the weaker

---

[1] This is not a limiting constraint, as we can easily force this behavior by checking if a query/update is valid in the Real game.

of the two, that is, they satisfy the transparent definition. Our zero-knowledge definition is close to the opaque definition where an updated client digest is indistinguishable from a fresh digest, and old proofs are not valid after an update.

4   Dynamic Privacy-Preserving Authenticated List

In this section we instantiate a DPPADS with a list (an ordered set of distinct elements) and refer to it as *dynamic privacy-preserving authenticated list*. We first describe the cryptographic primitives and assumptions that our construction relies on for security. We then explain how to maintain labeling of a dynamic list and how we use it to achieve efficient updates in our construction.

Preliminaries. Let $\mathcal{L}$ denote a list and Elements($\mathcal{L}$) denote the unordered set corresponding to $\mathcal{L}$. We refer to element's position in the list as it's rank. We define order queries on the elements of a list as δ. The query answer, answer, is the elements of δ rearranged according to their order in $\mathcal{L}$, i.e., answer $= \pi_{\mathcal{L}}(\delta)$. For example, with $\mathcal{L} = \{a, b, c, d, e\}$ and $\delta = (d, a, e)$, answer is $\{a, d, e\}$. An update operation on a list can be one of the following: linsertafter(x, y): insert element $x \notin \mathcal{L}$ after element $y \in \mathcal{L}$; ldelete(x): delete element x from $\mathcal{L}$; lreplace(x', x): replace element $x' \in \mathcal{L}$ with element $x \notin \mathcal{L}$.

Bilinear Maps: Let k be the security parameter, p be a large k-bit prime and $n =$ poly(k). G and G_1 are multiplicative groups of prime order p. A bilinear map $e : G \times G \to G_1$ is a map with properties: (1) $\forall u, v \in G$ and $\forall a, b \in \mathbb{Z}$, $e(u^a, v^b) = e(u, v)^{ab}$; (2) $e(g, g) \neq 1$ where g is a generator of G. As is standard, we assume that group action on G, G_1 and the bilinear map e can be computable in one unit time. We measure time complexity in terms of number of group actions.

Bilinear Aggregate Signature Scheme [5]: Given signatures $\sigma_1, \ldots, \sigma_n$ on *distinct* messages $M_1, \ldots, M_n$ from a user, it is possible to aggregate these signatures into a single short signature σ such that it (and the n messages) convince the verifier that the user indeed signed the n original messages. The scheme guarantees that σ is valid iff the aggregator used all σ_i's to construct it.

Hardness Assumption: Let p be a large k-bit prime where $k \in \mathbb{N}$ is a security parameter. Let $P \in \mathbb{N}$ be polynomial in k, $p = \text{poly}(k)$. Let $e : G \times G \to G_1$ be a bilinear map (as defined above) and g be a random generator of G. We denote a probabilistic polynomial time (PPT) adversary $\mathcal{A}$ as a probabilistic polynomial time Turing Machine running in time poly(k).

Definition 4 (*P*-Bilinear Diffie Hellman Inversion (*P*-BDHI) [4]). *Let s be a random element of $\mathbb{Z}_p^*$ and P be a positive integer. Then, for every PPT adversary $\mathcal{A}$ there exists a negligible function $\nu(.)$ such that: $Pr[s \xleftarrow{\$} \mathbb{Z}_p^*; y \leftarrow \mathcal{A}(\langle g, g^s, g^{s^2}, \ldots, g^{s^P} \rangle) : y = e(g, g)^{\frac{1}{s}}] \leq \nu(k)$.*

Online List Labeling (or File Maintenance) Problem [3,19,39]: In *online list labeling*, a mapping from a dynamic set of n elements is to be maintained to the integers in the universe $U = [1, N]$ such that the order of the elements respect the order of U. The integers, that the elements are mapped to, are called *tags*. The requirement of the mapping is to match the order of the tags with the order of the corresponding elements. Moreover, the mapping has to be maintained efficiently as the list changes.

We use the order data structure OD presented in [3] for online list labeling. We briefly describe OD and summarize its performance here. Let $U = [1, N]$ be the tag universe size and n be the number of elements in the dynamic set to be mapped to tags from U, where N is a function of n and is set to be a power of two. Then we consider a complete binary tree on the tags of U, where each leaf represents a tag form the universe. Note that, this binary tree is *implicit*, it is never explicitly constructed, but it is useful for the description and analysis.

At any state of the algorithm, n of the leaves are occupied, i.e., the tags used to label list elements. Each internal node encloses a (possible empty) sublist of the list, namely, the elements that have the tags corresponding to the leaves below that node. The *density* of a node is the fraction of its descendant leaves that are occupied. Then *overflow threshold* for the density of a node is defined as follows. Let α be a constant between 1 and 2. For a range of size 2^0 (leaf), the overflow threshold τ_0 is set to 1. Otherwise, for a range of size 2^i, $\tau_i = \frac{\tau_{i-1}}{\alpha} = \alpha^{-i}$. A range is in *overflow* if its density is above its overflow threshold. $\mathsf{OD}(n)$ supports the following operations:

insertafter(x, y): To insert an element x after y, do the following: (1) Examine the enclosing tag ranges of y. (2) Calculate the density of a tag range by traversing the elements within the tag range. (3) Relabel the smallest enclosing tag range that is not overflowing. (4) Return the relabeled tags and the tag of x.

delete(x): Delete x from the list and mark the corresponding tag as unoccupied.

tag(x): Return the tag of element x.

We note that the original list together with a sequence of updates on it deterministically define the tags of all elements in OD.

Complexity: Initially, we set $N = (2n)^{\frac{1}{1-\log\alpha}}$, $n_{\min} = n/2$ and $n_{\max} = 2n$, where n is the number of elements. As elements are inserted into or deleted from the list, the data structure can generate tags while $n_{\min} \leq n \leq n_{\max}$. If at any point, the current number of elements, n, falls below $n_{\min}$ or exceeds $n_{\max}$, the data structure is rebuilt for the new value of n and N is recomputed. Hence, the algorithm needs $\frac{\log n}{1-\log\alpha}$ bits to represent a tag. The rebuild introduces a constant amortized overhead (over the insert and delete operations). Hence, $\mathsf{OD}(n)$ uses $O(\log n)$ bits per tag and $O(n \log n)$ bits for storing all tags. $\mathsf{OD}(n)$ has $O(1)$ amortized insert and delete time, and $O(1)$ time for tag.

Dynamic Construction. Our construction of DPPAL uses as a starting point a static privacy-preserving authenticated list [14]. At a high level, the construction of PPAL works as follows: every element of the static list is associated with a member witness that encodes the rank of the element (using a component of the bilinear accumulator public key) "blinded" with randomness. Every pair of element and its member witness is signed by the owner and the signatures are aggregated using bilinear aggregate signature scheme (see above) to generate the public list digest. The client and the server receive the list digest, while the server also receives the signatures, member witnesses and the randomness used for blinding. Given a query from the client on a sublist of the source list, the server returns this sublist ordered as it is in the list with a corresponding proof of membership and order. The server proves membership of every element in the query using the homomorphic nature of bilinear aggregate signature, that is, without the owner's involvement. The server then uses the randomness and the bilinear accumulator public key to compute the order witness. The order witness encodes the distance between two elements, i.e., the difference between element ranks, without revealing anything about it.

Although this construction is efficient for static lists, data structures are often dynamic. The intuition behind our modifications is as follows. We first notice that the rank information of each element used in the construction of [14] can actually be replaced with *any tag* that respects the rank ordering. For example, let the rank of elements x and y be 5 and 6, respectively. We can replace this information with $\mathsf{tag}(x)$ and $\mathsf{tag}(y)$ as long as the following hold: 1) $\mathsf{tag}(x) < \mathsf{tag}(y)$ and 2) there is no other element in the list whose tag falls between $\mathsf{tag}(x)$ and $\mathsf{tag}(y)$. The tag generation algorithm of the order labeling data structure $\mathsf{OD}(n)$ has exactly this property: elements' tags respect the order of elements' ranks in the list. Hence, we use $\mathsf{OD}(n)$ to generate tags for the elements (instead of their ranks) to maintain list order. This enables efficient updates, albeit, in a non privacy-preserving way (e.g., information about ranks as well as which elements were updated is revealed). To this end, we develop a re-randomization method (explained in the subsequent *Update Phase*) to preserve privacy.

Our construction consists of instantiating the algorithms of DPPADS: Setup, UpdateOwner, UpdateServer, Query and Verify. We describe each algorithm in this section and give their pseudo-code in Algorithms 1–6. We use the following notation. $\mathcal{H} : \{0,1\}^* \to G$: cryptographic hash function that will be modeled as a random oracle in the security analysis; all arithmetic/group operations are performed mod p. System parameters are $(p, G, G_1, e, g, \mathcal{H})$, where p, G, G_1, e, g are defined in Sect. 4. $\mathcal{L}_0$ is the input list of size $n = \mathsf{poly}(\mathsf{k})$, where x_i's are distinct. $\mathsf{OD}(n)$ is used to generate the tags for the list elements and supports insertafter, delete, and tag operations.

KeyGen and Setup Phases: These algorithms proceed as follows. The owner randomly picks $s, v \in \mathbb{Z}_p^*$ and ω as part of his secret key sk and publishes $\mathsf{pk} = g^v$ as his public key as in [14]. But instead of using rank information, the owner inserts the elements of $\mathcal{L}_0$ in an empty order data structure $\mathsf{O} := \mathsf{OD}(n)$ respecting their order in $\mathcal{L}_0$ and generating tag for each element. Hence, the order induced by the tags of the elements is the list order. For every element $x_i \in \mathcal{L}_0$, the owner uses the following GenAuthTokens procedure: it generates fresh randomness r_i to blind $\mathsf{tag}(x_i)$; computes member witness $t_{x_i \in \mathcal{L}_0}$ as $g^{s^{\mathsf{tag}(x_i)} r_i}$ and its signature σ_{x_i}

Algorithm 1. $(\text{state}_O, \text{digest}_C^0, \text{digest}_S^0) \leftarrow$ **Setup**$(\text{sk}, \text{pk}, \mathcal{L}_0)$ where $\mathcal{L}_0 = \{x_1, \ldots, x_n\}$.

1: Set the internal state variable $\text{state}_O := \langle \mathcal{L}_0, \perp, \perp, \perp \rangle$. $\text{salt} \leftarrow (\mathcal{H}(\omega))^v$ where ω is a nonce in sk.
   % salt *is treated as a list identifier that protects against mix-and-match attacks and from*
   revealing that the queried elements represent the complete list.
2: % *Generate auxiliary data structure and authenticated information.*
   $(\sigma_{\mathcal{L}_0}, O, \Sigma_{\mathcal{L}_0}, \Omega_{\mathcal{L}_0}) \leftarrow \text{build}(\text{sk}, \text{state}_O, \mathcal{L}_0)$
3: $\text{state}_O := \langle \mathcal{L}_0, O, \forall x_i \in \mathcal{L}_0 : (t_{x_i \in \mathcal{L}_0}, \sigma_{x_i}, r_i) \rangle$ and $\text{digest}_C^0 := \sigma_{\mathcal{L}_0}$
4: $\text{digest}_S^0 := \langle \text{pk}, \sigma_{\mathcal{L}_0}, \langle g, g^s, g^{s^2}, \ldots, g^{s^n} \rangle, \Sigma_{\mathcal{L}_0}, \Omega_{\mathcal{L}_0} \rangle$
5: **return** $(\text{state}_O, \text{digest}_C^0, \text{digest}_S^0)$

---

as $\mathcal{H}(t_{x_i \in \mathcal{L}_t} || x_i)^v$. The owner then executes standard signature aggregation by multiplying element signatures into a list signature $\sigma_{\mathcal{L}_0}$. To preserve privacy of the size of the list, he further multiplies the list signature with $\text{salt} = (\mathcal{H}(\omega))^v$.

The owner sends $\sigma_{\mathcal{L}_0}$ to the client, as the client digest digest_C^0. To the server, he sends $\mathcal{L}_0$ and a digest digest_S^0 which contains the tag, the random value used for blinding, the member witness and the signature for every element in the list (we refer to these four units as *authentication units* of an element). He also sends $g^{s^0}, \ldots, g^{s^n}$, that help the server compute proofs for the client during the query phase. The owner saves $\mathcal{L}_0, O, \text{digest}_S^0$ in his state variable state_O, which he later uses to perform updates.

Update Phase: UpdateOwner (Algorithm 3) lets the owner perform update u_t on his outsourced data structure and propagate the update in the digests. For the actual update, the owner uses O to efficiently compute the new tag of an element and update the tags of the elements affected by the update. (We note this may include rebuild of O itself when the size of the list either falls below $n/2$ or grows above $2n$.) The owner then updates all the digests and authentication units that have to be updated due to the tag change. For the server, the owner computes the member witnesses and signatures since these operations rely on the secret keys. As we argue later, updating only elements whose tags have been modified due to the update is not sufficient to obtain zero-knowledge update. To this end, the owner has to also rerandomize any authentication units that were sent to the client. We elaborate on each step in the update below.

The update of authentication units depends on which one of the three update operations was performed on the list. If a new element x has been inserted in the list (i.e., linsertafter operation), then the owner recomputes all witnesses and signatures of elements in $\mathcal{Y}$ where $\mathcal{Y}$ is a set of elements whose tags were

---

Algorithm 2. $(\sigma_{\mathcal{L}_t}, O, \Sigma_{\mathcal{L}_t}, \Omega_{\mathcal{L}_t}) \leftarrow \text{build}(\text{sk}, \text{state}_O, \mathcal{L}_t)$ where sk contains v and ω and $\mathcal{L}_t = \{x_1, \ldots, x_{n'}\}$.

1: % *Build the order labeling data structure* O *to generate* $\text{tag}(x_i)$ $\forall x_i \in \mathcal{L}_t$.
   $O := \text{OD}(n')$ where $|\mathcal{L}_t| = n'$
2: **For every** $i < i \le n'$: $O.\text{insertafter}(x_{i-1}, x_i)$.
3: **For every** $x_i \in \mathcal{L}_t$: $r_i, t_{x_i \in \mathcal{L}_0}, \sigma_{x_i} \leftarrow \text{GenAuthTokens}(x_i)$
4: Compute list digest signature $\sigma_{\mathcal{L}_t} \leftarrow \text{salt} \times \prod_{x_i \in \mathcal{L}_t} \sigma_{x_i}$, where $\text{salt} = (\mathcal{H}(\omega))^v$.
5: $\Sigma_{\mathcal{L}_t} := \langle \forall x_i \in \mathcal{L}_t : (t_{x_i \in \mathcal{L}_t}, \sigma_{x_i}), \mathcal{H}(\omega) \rangle$ and $\Omega_{\mathcal{L}_t} := \langle \forall x_i \in \mathcal{L}_t : (r_i, \text{tag}(x_i)) \rangle$
6: **return** $(\sigma_{\mathcal{L}_t}, O, \Sigma_{\mathcal{L}_t}, \Omega_{\mathcal{L}_t})$

Algorithm 3. $(\text{state}_O, \text{digest}_C^{t+1}, \text{Upd}_{t+1}, \mathcal{L}_{t+1}, u_t) \leftarrow$ **UpdateOwner**$(\text{sk}, \text{state}_O,$ $\text{digest}_C^t, \text{digest}_S^t, \mathcal{L}_t, u_t, \text{SID}_t)$, where digest_C^t and digest_S^t are the client and the server digests corresponding to $\mathcal{L}_t$, respectively; $\mathcal{L}_t$ is the list after $(t-1)$th update, u_t is the update request (either linsertafter, ldelete or lreplace); and SID_t contains all the elements that were accessed by queries since update operation u_{t-1}.

```
1:  L_{t+1} := U(L_t, u_t)                                          % Update the list.
2:  If n/2 ≤ |L_{t+1}| ≤ 2n, then:
3:     Initialize Y := {}                                          % Elements to refresh.
4:     Initialize σ_tmp := 1                           % Accumulates changes to list signature.
5:     Initialize x_new := ⊥                                     % New element to add to list.
6:     If u_t = linsertafter(x, y):
7:        Y ← O.insertafter(x, y)              % Elements whose tags changed after insertion.
8:        x_new ← x
9:     Else if u_t = lreplace(x', x):                % Replace x' with x, where x ∉ L_t.
10:       Replace x' with x in O.
11:       σ_tmp ← σ_{x'}^{-1}                      % Remove a signature of the old element x'.
12:       x_new ← x
13:    Else if u_t = ldelete(z)                   % Delete z, its signature and auth. info.
14:       O.delete(z)
15:       σ_tmp ← σ_z^{-1}(g^{vr'}), where r' ←$ Z_p^*
16:       % Σ_Upd(+), Ω_Upd(+) contain information of elements to be added/replaced:
17:       Σ_Upd(+) := ⟨⟩ and Ω_Upd(+) := ⟨(r', ⊥)⟩
18:       % Σ_Upd(-), Ω_Upd(-) contain information of elements to be deleted:
19:       Σ_Upd(-) := ⟨(t_{z∈L_t}, σ_z)⟩ and Ω_Upd(-) := ⟨(r_z, tag(z))⟩.
20:    If x_new ≠ ⊥                                  % Generate auth. info. for new element.
21:       r ←$ Z_p^*
22:       Generate member witness t_{x_new∈L_{t+1}} ← (g^{s^{tag(x_new)}})^r.
23:       Compute signature σ_{x_new} ← H(t_{x_new∈L_{t+1}}||x_new)^v.
24:       σ_tmp ← σ_tmp σ_{x_new}                       % Add a signature of new element.
25:       Σ_Upd(+) := ⟨(t_{x_new∈L_{t+1}}, σ_{x_new})⟩ and Σ_Upd(-) := ⟨⟩.
26:       Ω_Upd(+) := ⟨(r_{x_new}, tag(x_new))⟩ and Ω_Upd(-) := ⟨⟩.
27:    (σ_refresh, ∀w ∈ SID_t ∪ Y : (r_w, σ_w)) ← refresh(sk, state_O, SID_t ∪ Y)
28:    Σ_Upd(+) := Σ_Upd(+) ∪ ⟨∀w ∈ SID_t ∪ Y : (t_{w∈L_{t+1}}, σ_w)⟩
29:    Ω_Upd(+) := Ω_Upd(+) ∪ ⟨∀w ∈ SID_t ∪ Y : (r_w, tag(w))⟩
30:    σ_{L_{t+1}} ← σ_{L_t} σ_tmp σ_refresh                      % Update signature.
31:    Upd_{t+1} := ⟨σ_{L_{t+1}}, ⊥, ⟨Σ_Upd(+), Σ_Upd(-)⟩, ⟨Ω_Upd(+), Ω_Upd(-)⟩⟩
32: Else:                                   % Update u_t significantly changed list size.
33:    (σ_{L_{t+1}}, O, Σ_{L_{t+1}}, Ω_{L_{t+1}}) ← build(sk, state_O, L_{t+1})   % Regenerate auth. info.
34:    Σ_Upd(+) := ⟨∀w ∈ L_{t+1} : (t_{w∈L_{t+1}}, σ_w)⟩ and Σ_Upd(-) = ⟨⟩.
35:    Ω_Upd(+) := ⟨∀w ∈ L_{t+1} : (r_i, tag(w_i))⟩ and Ω_Upd(-) = ⟨⟩.
36:    Upd_{t+1} := {σ_{L_{t+1}}, ⟨g, g^s, g^{s^2}, ..., g^{s^{n'}}⟩, ⟨Σ_Upd(+), Σ_Upd(-)⟩, ⟨Ω_Upd(+), Ω_Upd(-)⟩}.
37: digest_C^{t+1} := σ_{L_{t+1}}
38: state_O := ⟨L_{t+1}, O, ∀x_i ∈ L_{t+1} : (t_{x_i∈L_{t+1}}, σ_{x_i}, r_i)⟩
39: return (L_{t+1}, digest_C^{t+1}, u_t, Upd_{t+1}, state_O)
```

---

updated due to insertion (recall that $\mathcal{Y}$ is of amortized size $O(1)$). The owner also computes the member witness and a signature for the new x from scratch (called, x_{new} in the pseudo-code). Note that this step is equivalent to the steps in Setup for generating authentication units, only in this case it is for elements in $\mathcal{Y}$ and element x_{new} instead of the whole list. The owner then propagates these changes to the list digest signature $\sigma_{\mathcal{L}_t}$ as follows: (1) replaces signatures on the elements that have changed (i.e., elements in $\mathcal{Y}$); (2) adds a signature for x_{new}.

If an element x has been replaced with x' (i.e., lreplace operation), then the new member witness and signature is computed for x'. The owner propagates

---

Algorithm 4. $(\text{digest}_S^{t+1}, \mathcal{L}_{t+1}) \leftarrow \textbf{UpdateServer}(\text{digest}_S^t, \text{Upd}_{t+1}, \mathcal{L}_t, u_t)$, where u_t is an update to perform on $\mathcal{L}_t$ and Upd_{t+1} contains updates on authentication information generated by the owner.

1: Update the list: $\mathcal{L}_{t+1} := U(\mathcal{L}_t, u_t)$ where $|\mathcal{L}_{t+1}| = n'$.
2: Parse Upd_{t+1} as $\langle \sigma_{\mathcal{L}_{t+1}}, \mathcal{T}, \Sigma_{\text{Upd}}, \Omega_{\text{Upd}} \rangle$.
3: Compute $\Sigma_{\mathcal{L}_{t+1}}$: add/replace/delete elements from Σ_{Upd} in $\Sigma_{\mathcal{L}_t}$.
4: Compute $\Omega_{\mathcal{L}_{t+1}}$: add/replace/delete elements from Ω_{Upd} in $\Omega_{\mathcal{L}_t}$.
5: **If** $\mathcal{T} \neq \perp$: % u_t *caused regeneration of tags for all elements, hence authenticated information needs to be replaced with new one*
6:     $\text{digest}_S^{t+1} := \langle \text{pk}, \sigma_{\mathcal{L}_{t+1}}, \langle g, g^s, g^{s^2}, \ldots, g^{s^{n'}} \rangle, \Sigma_{\mathcal{L}_{t+1}}, \Sigma_{\mathcal{L}_{t+1}} \rangle$.
7: **Else**   % u_t *does not cause regeneration of tags for all elements*
8:     $\text{digest}_S^{t+1} := (\text{pk}, \sigma_{\mathcal{L}_{t+1}}, \langle g, g^s, g^{s^2}, \ldots, g^{s^n} \rangle, \Sigma_{\mathcal{L}_{t+1}}, \Omega_{\mathcal{L}_{t+1}})$ % *where* g^{s^i} *are from* digest_S^t
9: **return** $(\mathcal{L}_{t+1}, \text{digest}_S^{t+1})$

---

these change to the list digest signature $\sigma_{\mathcal{L}_t}$ as follows: (1) adds a signature for x'; (2) removes the signature of the old element x.

In case when element z is deleted, the owner removes the signature of the old element in the list digest signature $\sigma_{\mathcal{L}_t}$ and re-randomizes the list digest signature with fresh randomness r'. Notice that, in case of insert and replace operations, the list digest signature gets re-randomized implicitly, since the new membership witness gets refreshed with fresh randomness.

As described so far, UpdateOwner has a viable leakage channel. Recall that an update operation changes authentication units of elements in the update u_t and $\mathcal{Y}$. Hence, if the client accesses an element in $\mathcal{Y}$, before and after the update, she will notice that its authentication unit has changed and infer that a new element was inserted nearby. This violates the zero-knowledge property of DPPADS: the client should not learn information about updates to elements she did not query explicitly.

UpdateOwner achieves the zero-knowledge property as follows. We set f to be a function that takes client queries that have occurred since the last update and returns a set of elements accessed by them; recall that these are the elements whose authentication units are known to the client. Given these elements in UpdateOwner's input SID_t, the owner can recompute the member-witnesses of each of them using fresh randomness, update their signatures and the list digest with GenAuthTokens. We define a subroutine refresh which calls GenAuthTokens for each element in $\mathcal{Y}$ and SID_t, and returns σ_{refresh} which contains old signatures to be removed and new ones to be added to $\sigma_{\mathcal{L}_{t+1}}$. Since the member-witnesses and signatures of the elements in SID_t are changed independently of u_t, seeing refreshed units after the update reveals no information to the client. We define f this way for optimization. In a naive implementation, where f is defined as a constant function, or where SID_t is not used, the UpdateOwner algorithm has to randomize member-witnesses and signatures for *all* the list elements.

Finally, the owner updates state_O and sends u_t and authentication units (updated due to u_t and refresh) in Upd_{t+1} to the server and updated list digest $\sigma_{\mathcal{L}_{t+1}}$ to the client. The server runs UpdateServer (Algorithm 4) to

Algorithm 5. $(\text{answer}, \text{proof}) \leftarrow$ **Query**$(\text{digest}_S^t, \mathcal{L}_t, \delta)$, where $\delta = (z_1, \ldots, z_m)$, s.t. $z_i \in \mathcal{L}_t$, is the queried sublist and $\mathcal{L}_t$ is the most recent list.

1: $\text{answer} = \pi_{\mathcal{L}_t}(\delta) = \{y_1, \ldots, y_m\};$
2: $\text{proof} = \langle \Sigma_{\text{answer}}, \Omega_{\text{answer}} \rangle:$
3: $\quad \Sigma_{\text{answer}} := \langle \sigma_{\text{answer}}, T, \lambda_{\mathcal{L}'} \rangle$ where $\mathcal{L}' = \mathcal{L}_t \setminus \delta$ and:
4: $\quad\quad \sigma_{\text{answer}} \leftarrow \prod_{y_j \in \text{answer}} \sigma_{y_j}.$ % *Digest signature for the query elements.*
5: $\quad\quad T = (t_{y_1 \in \mathcal{L}_t}, \ldots, t_{y_m \in \mathcal{L}_t}).$ % *Member witnesses for query elements.*
6: $\quad\quad$ Let $\mathcal{S}$ be a set of random elements w/o tags, i.e., introduced in $\Omega_{\mathcal{L}_t}$ due to Idelete.
7: $\quad\quad$ The member verification unit: $\lambda_{\mathcal{L}'} \leftarrow \mathcal{H}(\omega) \times g^{\sum_{r \in \mathcal{S}} r} \times \prod_{x \in \mathcal{L}'} \mathcal{H}(t_{x \in \mathcal{L}_t} || x)$ where $\mathcal{H}(\omega)$ comes from $\text{digest}_S^t.$
8: $\quad\quad \Omega_{\text{answer}} = (t_{y_1 < y_2}, t_{y_2 < y_3}, \ldots, t_{y_{m-1} < y_m}):$
9: $\quad\quad\quad$ For every $j \in [1, m-1]$: Let $i' := \text{tag}(y_j)$ and $i'' := \text{tag}(y_{j+1})$, and $r' := \Omega_{\mathcal{L}}[i']^{-1}$ and $r'' := \Omega_{\mathcal{L}}[i'']$. Compute $t_{y_j < y_{j+1}} \leftarrow (g^{s^d})^{r'r''}$ where $d = |i' - i''|.$
10: **return** $(\text{answer}, \text{proof})$

Algorithm 6. $b \leftarrow$ **Verify**$(\text{pk}, \text{digest}_C^t, \delta, \text{answer}, \text{proof}).$

1: Compute $\xi \leftarrow \prod_{y_j \in \delta} \mathcal{H}(t_{y_j \in \mathcal{L}_t} || y_j)$

2: $e(\sigma_{\text{answer}}, g) \overset{?}{=} e(\xi, \text{pk})$ % *Verify* answer *digest is signed by the owner*
3: $e(\sigma_{\mathcal{L}_t}, g) \overset{?}{=} e(\sigma_{\text{answer}}, g) \times e(\lambda_{\mathcal{L}'}, \text{pk}).$ % *Verify* answer *is a part of the source list*
4: $\forall j \in [1, m-1]: e(t_{y_j \in \mathcal{L}_t}, t_{y_j < y_{j+1}}) \overset{?}{=} e(t_{y_{j+1} \in \mathcal{L}_t}, g).$ % *Verify the returned order*
5: If all equalities hold, then accept. Else reject.

---

propagate the update at its end. It uses u_t to update the list and Upd_{t+1} to add/substitute/remove authentication units in its digest.

Query Phase: The server has to perform two tasks when it receives query δ. It has to answer the query and compute the proof that the answer is correct. For the former step, it simply reorders the elements in δ according to their order in $\mathcal{L}_t$, sets answer to $\pi_{\mathcal{L}_t}(\delta)$. The latter step consists of proving that elements in answer are in $\mathcal{L}_t$ (i.e., membership) and that they are ordered correctly.

The detailed query phase is presented in Algorithm 5. In order to prove membership of every element in answer, the server uses its digest to obtain member witnesses $t_{y_j \in \mathcal{L}_t}$ and signatures σ_{y_j}, for each element $y_i \in \delta$, and includes them in the proof. It then proves that these y_is are indeed part of the source list $\mathcal{L}_t$ by computing the authentication digest for all elements not in the query. Let $\mathcal{L}' = \mathcal{L}_t \setminus \delta$. Then, computing the authentication digest, $\lambda_{\mathcal{L}'}$, is very similar to the computation of the list signature (i.e., client digest) by the owner albeit without using secret key v. That is, $\lambda_{\mathcal{L}'}$ is a product of hashed tags of elements in $\mathcal{L}'$ along with the hash of ω, given in the server digest.

The server proves the order condition as follows. For every pair of adjacent elements y_j, y_{j+1} in answer, the server computes an order witness $t_{y_j < y_{j+1}} := (g^{s^d})^{r''/r'}$, where $d = \text{tag}(y_{j+1}) - \text{tag}(y_j)$ and r' and r'' are randomness of y_j and y_{j+1} and g^{s^d} is part of server's digest. This part of the server digest, $t_{y_j < y_{j+1}}$, is used for verification in the equation $e(g^{\text{tag}(y_j)^{r'}}, t_{y_j < y_{j+1}}) = e(g^{\text{tag}(y_{j+1})^{r''}}, g).$

The above steps preserve privacy and integrity of the scheme. In particular, $t_{y_j \in \mathcal{L}_t}$'s do not reveal element ranks since the witnesses have blinded using secret randomness during the setup. Furthermore, it is hard for the server to compute an invalid order witnesses $t_{y_j < y_{j+1}}$ as this would require computing $(g^{s^{-d}})^{r''/r'}$. This, in turn is (almost) equivalent to computing an inverse in the exponent, violating the P-BDHI assumption as a result.

Verification Phase: Given (answer, proof), the client uses Verify (Algorithm 6) and her copy of the list digest signature to verify answer. She checks the membership of elements in answer by using the properties of bilinear aggregate signatures. In particular she can verify the relationship of $\mathcal{L}' = \mathcal{L}_t \setminus \delta$ by knowing elements in δ and their signatures, authentic list digest signature $\sigma_{\mathcal{L}_t}$ (received from the owner) and server computed authentication digest $\lambda_{\mathcal{L}'}$. We note that the client cannot tell if δ is the whole list or not, because of the blinding factor salt used in computing $\sigma_{\mathcal{L}_t}$. The client then uses bilinear map to verify order witnesses as it lets her verify algebraic properties of the exponents, i.e., that $d = \mathsf{tag}(y_{j+1}) - \mathsf{tag}(y_j)$ for $t_{y_j \in \mathcal{L}_t} = g^{r' s^{\mathsf{tag}(y_j)}}$ and $t_{y_{j+1} \in \mathcal{L}_t} = g^{r'' s^{\mathsf{tag}(y_{j+1})}}$.

Extensions: UpdateOwner can be easily generalized to *batch updates* for optimization. Our construction can also hide from the client the fact that *an update has happened* via periodic updates and refreshes. The details are in [12].

Efficiency: Our construction uses efficient cryptographic operations: multiplication and exponentiation in prime order groups, evaluation of a cryptographic hash function and bilinear map. As is standard, we assume they take constant time. Moreover, we use at most four of these operations per element. A member/order witness and a signature is a group element and is represented using $O(1)$ space (by standard convention, the word size is $\log(\mathsf{poly}(k))$ and k is the security parameter). Theorem 1 summarizes the security and performance.

Theorem 1. *The dynamic privacy-preserving authenticated list (DPPAL) construction of Sect. 4 satisfies the security properties of DPPADS including completeness, soundness (under the P-BDHI assumption [4]) and zero-knowledge in the random oracle model (inherited from [5]). The construction has the following performance, where n is the list size, m is the query size, L is the number of updates in a batch and M is the number of distinct elements that have been queried since the last update:*

- *The owner uses $O(n)$ time and space for setup, and keeps $O(n)$ state;*
- *In the update phase the owner sends a message of size $O(L+M)$ to the server and a message of size $O(1)$ to the client;*
- *The update phase requires $O(L+M)$ time for the owner and the server, or $O(1)$ amortized over the number of elements queried or updated since the last update;*
- *The server uses $O(n)$ space and performs the preprocessing in $O(n)$ time;*
- *The server computes the answer to a query and its proof in time $O(\min\{m \log n, n\})$;*
- *The proof size is $O(m)$;*
- *The client verifies the proof in $O(m)$ time and space.*

Space Efficient DPPADS: The model of Sect. 3 assumes the owner himself updates his data structure and sends information to the server to propagate the changes. So, the owner is required to keep the most recent version of $\mathcal{D}_t$ and any associated auxiliary information. He gets the advantage of remaining offline during the query phase and gets online only during an update. But this may not be ideal for an owner with small memory requirement. So we propose a model that is space efficient and relies on an authenticated data structure (ADS) protocol executed between the owner and the server and give an instantiation in [12]. We summarize the performance in Theorem 2 below.

Theorem 2. *The space efficient dynamic privacy-preserving authenticated list construction has the following performance, where n is the list size, L is the number of updates in a batch and M is the number of distinct elements that have been queried since the last update:*

- *The owner uses $O(n)$ time and space for setup, and keeps $O(1)$ state;*
- *The update phase requires one round of interaction between the owner and the server where they exchange a message of size $(L \log n + M)$;*
- *The update phase requires $O(L \log n + M)$ time for the owner and the server, or $O(\log n)$ amortized over the number of queried or updated elements.*

5 Dynamic Privacy-Preserving Authenticated Tree

We now propose a tree instantiation of DPPADS: a dynamic privacy-preserving tree (DPPAT) using a dynamic privacy-preserving authenticated list (Sect. 4). We only give the summary of the performance here, in Theorem 3, and defer the details of the construction to [12].

Order Queries: An *order query* on $\mathcal{T}$ is a pair of elements (x, y) from a tree $\mathcal{T}$. The corresponding answer is the pair rearranged according to their order in $\mathcal{T}$ along with a bit b indicating if the relation in ancestry or left-right (i.e., one node is to the left of the other with respect to their lowest common ancestor). For generality, the data structure also supports a *batch order query* where the returned answer is an *induced forest* of the queried elements.

DPPAT using DPPAL: A rooted tree $\mathcal{T}$ can be uniquely represented as two lists, L-Order$_\mathcal{T}$ and R-Order$_\mathcal{T}$, where the lists correspond to two different traversals of the tree constructed as follows. Both traversals start from the root, process each node they encounter, and recur on the subtrees of the current node. L-Order traverses subtrees left to right while R-Order traverses subtrees right to left. To construct a DPPAT, we construct two DPPAL's: on L-Order$_\mathcal{T}$ and R-Order$_\mathcal{T}$. DPPAT uses DPPAL to augment the answer with proofs of membership of x and y, and a proof of order. For a batch query of size m, the proof size is linear in the answer size, i.e., it is sufficient to prove $O(m)$ pairwise orders as we show in [12]. DPPAT can support all the dynamic operations, namely, link, cut and replace on $\mathcal{T}$ by making a *constant* number of update queries to the DPPALs of L-Order$_\mathcal{T}$ and R-Order$_\mathcal{T}$. We give the details in [12].

Theorem 3. *A dynamic privacy-preserving authenticated tree (DPPAT) can be implemented using a DPPAL. This scheme satisfies the security properties of a DPPADS: completeness, soundness and zero-knowledge. The runtime, space, and message size for every party is proportional to the corresponding runtime, space, and message size in the DPPAL scheme.*

Remark: The technique used for DPPAT can be further extended to d-dimensional Partial Orders (POs) for some constant d. The extension relies on the unique intersection of d total ordered lists of a PO. Hence, the dynamic privacy-preserving version can be implemented using d DPPALs (e.g., a tree is a special case of $d = 2$).

References

1. Ahn, J.H., Boneh, D., Camenisch, J., Hohenberger, S., Waters, B.: Computing on authenticated data. In: Cramer, R. (ed.) TCC 2012. LNCS, vol. 7194, pp. 1–20. Springer, Heidelberg (2012)
2. Attrapadung, N., Libert, B., Peters, T.: Computing on authenticated data: new privacy definitions and constructions. In: Wang, X., Sako, K. (eds.) ASIACRYPT 2012. LNCS, vol. 7658, pp. 367–385. Springer, Heidelberg (2012)
3. Bender, M.A., Cole, R., Demaine, E.D., Farach-Colton, M., Zito, J.: Two simplified algorithms for maintaining order in a list. In: Möhring, R.H., Raman, R. (eds.) ESA 2002. LNCS, vol. 2461, pp. 152–164. Springer, Heidelberg (2002)
4. Boneh, D., Boyen, X.: Efficient selective-ID secure identity-based encryption without random oracles. In: Cachin, C., Camenisch, J.L. (eds.) EUROCRYPT 2004. LNCS, vol. 3027, pp. 223–238. Springer, Heidelberg (2004)
5. Boneh, D., Gentry, C., Lynn, B., Shacham, H.: Aggregate and verifiably encrypted signatures from bilinear maps. In: Biham, Eli (ed.) EUROCRYPT 2003. LNCS, vol. 2656, pp. 416–432. Springer, Heidelberg (2003)
6. Brzuska, C., et al.: Redactable signatures for tree-structured data: definitions and constructions. In: Zhou, J., Yung, M. (eds.) ACNS 2010. LNCS, vol. 6123, pp. 87–104. Springer, Heidelberg (2010)
7. Catalano, D., Fiore, D.: Vector commitments and their applications. In: PKC (2013)
8. Catalano, D., Fiore, D., Messina, M.: Zero-knowledge sets with short proofs. In: Smart, N.P. (ed.) EUROCRYPT 2008. LNCS, vol. 4965, pp. 433–450. Springer, Heidelberg (2008)
9. Chang, E.-C., Lim, C.L., Xu, J.: Short redactable signatures using random trees. In: Fischlin, M. (ed.) CT-RSA 2009. LNCS, vol. 5473, pp. 133–147. Springer, Heidelberg (2009)
10. Chase, M., Healy, A., Lysyanskaya, A., Malkin, T., Reyzin, L.: Mercurial commitments with applications to zero-knowledge sets. In: Cramer, R. (ed.) EUROCRYPT 2005. LNCS, vol. 3494, pp. 422–439. Springer, Heidelberg (2005)
11. Devanbu, P.T., Gertz, M., Martel, C.U., Stubblebine, S.G.: Authentic third-party data publication. In: DBSec (2000)
12. Ghosh, E., Goodrich, M.T., Ohrimenko, O., Tamassia, R.: Fully-dynamic verifiable zero-knowledge order queries for network data. ePrint 2015/283 (2015)
13. Ghosh, E., Ohrimenko, O., Papadopoulos, D., Tamassia, R., Triandopoulos, N.: Zero-knowledge accumulators and set operations. ePrint 2015/404 (2015)

14. Ghosh, E., Ohrimenko, O., Tamassia, R.: Verifiable member and order queries on a list in zero-knowledge. In: ACNS (2015)

15. Ghosh, E., Ohrimenko, O., Tamassia, R.: Efficient verifiable range and closest point queries in zero-knowledge. PoPETs **2016**(4) (2016)

16. Goldberg, S., Naor, M., Papadopoulos, D., Reyzin, L., Vasant, S., Ziv, A.: NSEC5: provably preventing DNSSEC zone enumeration. In: NDSS (2015)

17. Goldreich, O.: The Foundations of Cryptography - Basic Applications, vol. 2. Cambridge University Press, Cambridge (2004)

18. Goodrich, M.T., Nguyen, D., Ohrimenko, O., Papamanthou, C., Tamassia, R., Triandopoulos, N., Lopes, C.V.: Efficient verification of web-content searching through authenticated web crawlers. PVLDB **5**(10), 920–931 (2012)

19. Itai, A., Konheim, A.G., Rodeh, M.: A sparse table implementation of priority queues. In: Even, S., Kariv, O. (eds.) Automata, Languages and Programming. LNCS, vol. 115, pp. 417–431. Springer, Heidelberg (1981)

20. Johnson, R., Molnar, D., Song, D., Wagner, D.: Homomorphic signature schemes. In: Preneel, B. (ed.) CT-RSA 2002. LNCS, vol. 2271, pp. 244–262. Springer, Heidelberg (2002)

21. Kundu, A., Atallah, M.J., Bertino, E.: Leakage-free redactable signatures. In: CODASPY (2012)

22. Kundu, A., Bertino, E.: Structural signatures for tree data structures. In: PVLDB (2008)

23. Kundu, A., Bertino, E.: Privacy-preserving authentication of trees and graphs. Int. J. Inf. Secur. **12**, 467–494 (2013)

24. Libert, B., Yung, M.: Concise mercurial vector commitments and independent zero-knowledge sets with short proofs. In: Micciancio, D. (ed.) TCC 2010. LNCS, vol. 5978, pp. 499–517. Springer, Heidelberg (2010)

25. Liskov, M.: Updatable zero-knowledge databases. In: Roy, B. (ed.) ASIACRYPT 2005. LNCS, vol. 3788, pp. 174–198. Springer, Heidelberg (2005)

26. Merkle, R.C.: A certified digital signature. In: Brassard, G. (ed.) CRYPTO 1989. LNCS, vol. 435, pp. 218–238. Springer, Heidelberg (1990)

27. Micali, S., Rabin, M.O., Kilian, J.: Zero-knowledge sets. In: FOCS (2003)

28. Naor, M., Teague, V.: Anti-presistence: history independent data structures. In: Proceedings on 33rd Annual ACM Symposium on Theory of Computing, 6–8 July 2001 (2001)

29. Naor, M., Ziv, A.: Primary-secondary-resolver membership proof systems. In: Dodis, Y., Nielsen, J.B. (eds.) TCC 2015, Part II. LNCS, vol. 9015, pp. 199–228. Springer, Heidelberg (2015)

30. Ostrovsky, R., Rackoff, C., Smith, A.: Efficient consistency proofs for generalized queries on a committed database. In: Díaz, J., Karhumäki, J., Lepistö, A., Sannella, D. (eds.) ICALP 2004. LNCS, vol. 3142, pp. 1041–1053. Springer, Heidelberg (2004)

31. Papadopoulos, D., Papamanthou, C., Tamassia, R., Triandopoulos, N.: Practical authenticated pattern matching with optimal proof size. PVLDB **8**(7), 750–761 (2015)

32. Poehls, H.C., Samelin, K., Posegga, J., De Meer, H.: Length-hiding redactable signatures from one-way accumulators in $O(n)$. Technical report MIP-1201, FIM. University of Passau (2012)

33. Pöhls, H.C., Samelin, K.: On updatable redactable signatures. In: Boureanu, I., Owesarski, P., Vaudenay, S. (eds.) ACNS 2014. LNCS, vol. 8479, pp. 457–475. Springer, Heidelberg (2014)

34. Prabhakaran, M., Xue, R.: Statistically hiding sets. In: Fischlin, M. (ed.) CT-RSA 2009. LNCS, vol. 5473, pp. 100–116. Springer, Heidelberg (2009)

35. Samelin, K., Pöhls, H.C., Bilzhause, A., Posegga, J., de Meer, H.: Redactable signatures for independent removal of structure and content. In: Ryan, M.D., Smyth, B., Wang, G. (eds.) ISPEC 2012. LNCS, vol. 7232, pp. 17–33. Springer, Heidelberg (2012)
36. Steinfeld, R., Bull, L., Zheng, Y.: Content extraction signatures. In: Kim, K. (ed.) ICISC 2001. LNCS, vol. 2288, pp. 285–304. Springer, Heidelberg (2002)
37. Tamassia, R.: Authenticated data structures. In: Di Battista, G., Zwick, U. (eds.) ESA 2003. LNCS, vol. 2832, pp. 2–5. Springer, Heidelberg (2003)
38. Wang, Z.: Improvement on Ahn et al.'s RSA P-homomorphic signature scheme. In: Keromytis, A.D., Di Pietro, R. (eds.) SecureComm 2012. LNICST, vol. 106, pp. 19–28. Springer, Heidelberg (2013)
39. Willard, D.E.: A density control algorithm for doing insertions and deletions in a sequentially ordered file in good worst-case time. Inf. Comput. **97**, 150–204 (1992)

On the Implausibility of Constant-Round Public-Coin Zero-Knowledge Proofs

Yi Deng[1]($\boxtimes$), Juan Garay[2], San Ling[3], Huaxiong Wang[3], and Moti Yung[4]

[1] SKLOIS, Institute of Information Engineering, Chinese Academy of Sciences,
Beijing, China
deng@iie.ac.cn
[2] Yahoo Research, Sunnyvale, USA
[3] Division of Mathematical Sciences, School of Physical and Mathematical Sciences,
Nanyang Technological University, Singapore, Singapore
[4] Snapchat and Columbia University, New York, USA

Abstract. We consider the problem of whether there exist non-trivial constant-round public-coin zero-knowledge (ZK) proofs. To date, in spite of high interest in the problem, there is no definite answer to the question. We focus on the type of ZK proofs that admit a universal simulator (which handles all malicious verifiers), and show a connection between the existence of such proof systems and a seemingly unrelated "program functionality distinguishing" problem: for a natural class of constant-round public-coin ZK proofs (which we call "canonical," since all known ZK protocols fall into this category), a session prefix output by the universal simulator can actually be used to distinguish a non-trivial property of the next-step functionality of the verifier's code.

Our result can be viewed as new evidence against the existence of constant-round public-coin ZK proofs, since the existence of such a proof system will bring about either one of the following: (1) a positive result for the above functionality-distinguishing problem, a typical goal in reverse-engineering attempts, commonly believed to be notoriously hard, or (2) a major paradigm shift in simulation strategies, beyond the only known (straight-line simulation) technique applicable to their argument counterpart, as we also argue. Note that the earlier negative evidence on constant-round public-coin ZK proofs is Barack, Lindell and Vadhan [FOCS 2003]'s result, which was based on the incomparable assumption of the existence of certain entropy-preserving hash functions, now known not to be achievable from standard assumptions via black-box reduction.

The core of our technical contribution is showing that there exists a single verifier step for constant-round public-coin ZK proofs whose functionality (rather than its code) is crucial for a successful simulation. This is proved by combining a careful analysis of the behavior of a set of verifiers in the above protocols and during simulation, with an improved structure-preserving version of the well-known Babai-Moran Speedup (de-randomization) Theorem, a key tool of independent interest.

The full version of this paper can be found at the *IACR Cryptology ePrint Archive* [12].

V. Zikas and R. De Prisco (Eds.): SCN 2016, LNCS 9841, pp. 237–253, 2016.
DOI: 10.1007/978-3-319-44618-9_13

1 Introduction

Goldwasser et al. [17] introduced the fascinating notion of a *zero-knowledge* (ZK) interactive proof, in which a party (called the prover) wishes to convince another party (called the verifier) of some statement, in such a way that the following two properties are satisfied: (1) zero knowledge— the prover does not leak any knowledge beyond the truth of the statement being proven, and (2) soundness— no cheating prover can convince the verifier of a false statement except with small probability. A vast amount of work ensued this pioneering result. Shortly after the introduction of a ZK proof et al. [3] defined a ZK proof system with relaxed soundness requirement, called a ZK *argument*, for which soundness is only required to hold against polynomial-time cheating provers.

The original ZK proof system for the quadratic residuosity problem presented in [17] is of a special form, in which the verifier simply sends independently random coins at each of his steps. Such a proof system is called a *public-coin* proof system, and has been found to be broadly applicable and versatile. Another notable feature of this type of proof systems is its round efficiency, as it consists of only 3 rounds, i.e., just 3 messages are exchanged in a session. This round efficiency, however, brings about a side effect of soundness error, which is too large to be used in cryptographic settings where typically a negligibly small such error is required. Indeed, there seems to be a tradeoff between round efficiency and soundness error for public-coin proof systems: we can achieve negligible soundness error by sequential repetition, but then the resulting system is no longer constant-round. This is in contrast with private-coin ZK proof systems, for which constant rounds and negligible soundness error can be achieved simultaneously.

In fact, whether constant-round public-coin ZK protocols (or even argument systems) with negligible soundness error exist for some non-trivial language was a long-standing open problem. In [16], Goldreich and Krawczyk showed that, for non-trivial languages, the zero knowledge property of such a proof system cannot be proven via black-box simulation. Black-box simulation was in fact the only known technique to demonstrate "zero-knowledgeness" for a long while, and hence the Goldreich-Krawczyk result was viewed as strong negative evidence against the existence of constant-round public-coin ZK proof systems.

A breakthrough result in 2001 changed the state of things. Indeed, in [2] Barak presented a non-black-box ZK argument in which the simulator makes use of the code of the malicious verifier in computing the prover messages (albeit without understanding it). Barak's construction follows the so-called "FLS paradigm" [13], which consists of two stages. In the first stage the prover sends a commitment c to a hash value of an arbitrary string, to which the verifier responds with a random string r; in the second stage, the prover proves using a witness indistinguishable (WI) universal argument that either the statement in question is true or c is a commitment to a hash value of some code Π, and, given input c, Π outputs r in some super-polynomial time. Note that this is a constant-round public-coin argument, and that its simulator does not "rewind" the malicious verifier (and it is hence called a *straight-line* simulator) and, furthermore, runs in strict polynomial time.

These features have been proved impossible to achieve when using black-box simulation [6,16].

Barak's argument system still left open the question whether non-trivial constant-round public-coin (non-black-box) ZK *proof* systems exist. At first sight, being able to extend his technique to a proof system seems challenging, mainly due to the fact that since a Turing machine or algorithm may have an arbitrarily long representation, a computationally unbounded prover may, after receiving the second verifier message r, be able to find a program Π (whose description may be different from the verifier's with which the prover is interacting) such that, $c = \mathrm{Com}(h(\Pi))$, and on input c, Π outputs r in the right amount of time.

In [8], Barak et al. showed further negative evidence for the above problem, by proving that if a certain class of entropy-preserving hash functions exist, then such a proof system cannot exist. Their formulation of entropy-preserving hash functions is mathematically simple, inspiring further research to base such hash functions on standard assumptions. Unfortunately, to our knowledge, we do not have a candidate for such functions thus far, and furthermore, as shown by Bitansky et al. [4], such functions *cannot* be based on any standard assumption via black-box reduction.

Our Results and Techniques. In this paper, we provide evidence of a different nature against the existence of constant-round public-coin ZK proof systems. We focus on the type of ZK proofs that admit a universal simulator, i.e., ZK proof systems for which there is a single simulator that can handle all malicious verifiers. (To our knowledge, all constructions of ZK proofs in the literature are of this type.)

We uncover an unexpected connection between the existence of such proof systems and a seemingly unrelated "program functionality distinguishing" problem: for a natural class of constant-round public-coin ZK proofs (which we call "canonical," as all known ZK protocols fall in this category), a universal simulator for such ZK proof system can actually be used to figure out some non-trivial property of a verifier's program functionality. (Since we will always be talking about distinguishing verifiers' programs, sometimes we will just refer to the problem as the "verifier distinguishing" problem). More specifically, we show that, given a constant-round public-coin ZK proof system $\langle P, V \rangle$, there exist a step index k and a set of polynomial number of verifiers that share the verifier next-message functions up to the $(k-1)$-th step but have distinct k-th next-message functions—say, t, for t a polynomial, and denoted by $(V_k^1, V_k^2, ..., V_k^t)$—such that for any polynomial-time constructible code V_k^* that is promised to have the same functionality as one of V_k^i's in the above set, the universal simulator, taking V_k^* as input, can generate a session prefix before the k-th verifier step that enables us to single out a V_k^j in the set which is functionally *different* from V_k^*.

In more detail, we construct a distinguishing algorithm U which, taking only $(V_k^1, V_k^2, ..., V_k^t)$ and the session prefix output by the simulator as input, is able to pin-point an element V_k^j in the set which behaves differently from V_k^*, with probability negligibly close to 1. This means that the universal simulator must have encoded some non-trivial property of V_k^*'s functionality in the session prefix prior to the verifier's k-th step, since otherwise if the session prefix is independent of V_k^*, the success probability of U will never exceed $1 - \frac{1}{t}$ (note that U does note take V_k^* as an input). In the case of private-coin ZK protocols, encoding the functionality of the next verifier step in a session prefix is typically done by having the simulator execute V_k^* first and then redo the prefix prior to the k-th verifier step such that it can now handle the challenge from V_k^*. It should be noted that, for constant-round protocols, such a rewinding strategy seems to work only for the cases where the functionality of V_k^* is bound to some of the verifier's previous steps, and this is not the case for public-coin protocols[1].

This is in a sharp contrast with Barak's public-coin argument system, in which the simulator does not need to "predict" the verifier's next-message functionality when computing a session prefix. Think of the first two steps in the simulation of Barak's argument, where the verifier sends a random hash function (h) and the prover replies with a commitment to a hash value of the *code* (instead of its functionality) of the next message function of the verifier's second step $(\mathrm{Com}(h(V_2^*)))$. Note that when the simulator computes this session prefix it does not need to figure out the functionality of V_2^*, and in fact the functionality of V_2^* is not bound to the history prefix $(h, \mathrm{Com}(h(V_2^*)))$. Indeed, when the commitment scheme $\mathrm{Com}(h(\cdot))$ is a perfectly hiding scheme (which is allowed in Barak's argument), the message $c = \mathrm{Com}(h(V_2^*))$ can be interpreted as a commitment to *any* code of any functionality, and thus it contains zero information about V_2^*'s functionality.

Thus, our result can be viewed as further evidence against the existence of constant-round public-coin ZK proof systems. On one hand, devising a rewinding technique (to figure out the next-step functionality of the verifier) that could be used in the simulation of such a public-coin proof appears to be fairly inconceivable, as in these proofs the message (challenge) from each step of the verifier is long and hard for a cheating prover to pass, and, intuitively, in this setting the rewinding behavior of a simulator (given the code of a malicious verifier) is akin to learning an arbitrarily complicated and obfuscated verifier's next-step function (which is, as a code, independent of any previous step functions) by just sampling a few input-output pairs of this function.

On the other hand, if such a proof does admit a straight-line simulator, then our "functionality distinguishing" result described above shows that one would be able to figure out some non-trivial functionality/property of V_k^* *without executing it* (since "straight-line" typically means that in producing the session prefix before the k-th verifier step, the simulator does not run V_k^*), a problem

---

[1] We note that the rewinding technique used for simulating the known public-coin protocols simply exploits the "guessing the next verifier's coins" strategy, and requires that the probability of a correct guess is very high. To meet such a requirement, the verifier's message has to be short, and as a consequence, the corresponding protocol either has large (non-negligible) soundness error, such as the original Blum's 3-round proof fro Graph Hamiltonicity [7], or is of super-constant number of rounds, such as the $\log^2 n$-fold sequential repetition of Blum's proof system.

commonly considered notoriously hard [20,21]. We note that exactly how hard the problem is in our concrete setting we leave as an interesting research question. (Indeed, although we do not give a definite answer to the question, we view our work as providing new negative evidence from a different angle and suggesting directions for further study towards that goal.)

One key tool in our reduction is an improved structure-preserving version of the well-known Babai-Moran Speedup (derandomization) Theorem [1,9,10], which is of independent interest. Essentially, our result says that for a constant-round public-coin interactive proof system in which the verifier sends m messages and each of the prover messages is of length p, if the cheating probability for an unbounded prover is ϵ, then there exist $(p/O(\log \frac{1}{\epsilon}))^m$ verifier random tapes such that the cheating probability for the unbounded prover over these tapes is bounded away from 1—and this holds even when the prover knows this small set of random tapes in advance. In contrast, in our setting the original Babai-Moran theorem would yield a much larger size (namely, $(O(p))^m$) of such set of verifier random tapes. In addition, we show that this result is tight with respect to round complexity, in the sense that there are public-coin proof systems with a super-constant number of rounds for which the prover's cheating probability is 1, over any polynomial number of verifier random tapes.

The way our derandomization lemma helps in the reduction to the verifier-distinguishing problem is as follows. Intuitively, for a proof system, it seems that there should be a verifier step k for which computing a session prefix prior to this step in the simulation requires the simulator to classify the codes of the "residual" verifiers according to their functionality, since by unconditional soundness a fixed session prefix can (even for an all powerful prover) make only a few (as opposed to all efficiently computable functions) of the residual verifiers accept. Derandomization allows us to focus on those few verifiers on which the cheating probability of an all powerful prover is still bounded away from 1, and then prove the existence of the above critical verifier step.

Related Work. As mentioned above, Barak et al. [8] conjectured the existence of certain entropy-preserving hash functions and proved that the conjecture's veracity would rule out the possibility of existence of constant-round public-coin ZK proof systems. Recent work by Bitansky *et al.* [4], however, showed that this conjecture cannot have a black-box reduction from any standard assumption.

A somewhat related problem to our functionality-distinguishing problem is program obfuscation, the theoretical study of which was initiated by Barak *et al.* [5]. At a high level, an obfuscator is an efficient compiler that takes a program as input and outputs an "unreadable" program with the same functionality as the input program. Hada [19], in particular, showed that the existence of a certain type of ZK protocol is tightly related to the existence of an obfuscator for some specific functionality. Unfortunately, for a large class of functionalities, it has been shown that obfuscators do not exist, and it is not clear whether the recent and exciting formulation and constructions of indistinguishability obfuscators (cf. [15] and numerous follow-ups) and "correlation intractable" hash functions [11] imply a negative answer to our problem.

Organization of the Paper. Preliminaries, notation and definitions that are used throughout the paper are presented in Sect. 2. Definitions of *canonical* ZK proofs, concrete examples, and the *verifier-distinguishing* problem are formulated in Sect. 3. The improved derandomization lemma is presented in Sect. 4, and the reduction of constant-round public-coin ZK proofs to the verifier-distinguishing problem, which makes use of it, in Sect. 5. Due to space limitations, comprehensive background definitions, illustrations, most of the detailed proofs, and complementary material, including a counterexample for superconstant-round proof systems, can be found in the full version of the paper [12].

2 Preliminaries

In this section we introduce relevant notation that will be used throughout the paper. Refer to the full version of the paper [12] for some more traditional definitions, such as negligible functions and interactive proofs, are given in

When referring to a Turing machine M, we will slightly abuse notation and use M to represent both its code and its functionality. Specifically, if we write $M \in \mathcal{G}$ for some set $\mathcal{G}$, we will mean that there is a Turing machine in $\mathcal{G}$ whose code is identical to the code of M; on the other hand, if we say that M^* is "functionally equivalent" to M (as defined below), both M^* and M will clearly refer to their functionality.

Definition 1. *For two deterministic (interactive) Turing machines M^1 and M^2, we say M^1 and M^2 have the same functionality, or are functionally equivalent if they compute the same collection of next-message functions. That is, for any input* hist, *the next message produced by M^1 is identical to the one produced by M^2—i.e., $M^1(\text{hist}) = M^2(\text{hist})$.*

We will use $M^1 \overset{f}{=} M^2$ as a shorthand for the above, and $M^1 \overset{f}{\neq} M^2$ as its negation.

Public-Coin Proof Systems and Verifier Decomposition. An interactive proof system is called *public-coin* if at every verifier step, the verifier sends only truly random messages.

We will use boldface lowercase letters to refer to the verifier's random tapes (e.g., $\mathbf{r}$), and italic for each verifier message (e.g., r). Thus, for a $2m$-round public-coin interactive proof system $\langle P, V \rangle$, we have $\mathbf{r} = [r_1, r_2, ..., r_m]$, where r_i is the i-th verifier message. We use superscripts to distinguish different verifier's random tapes; e.g., $\mathbf{r}^i$, $\mathbf{r}^j$, etc.

Given a random tape $\mathbf{r} = [r_1, r_2, ..., r_m]$, we can "decompose" the verifier $V(\mathbf{r})$ into a collection of next-message functions, $V = [V_1, V_2, ..., V_m]$, with each V_i being defined as:

$$r_i \text{ or } \bot \; \leftarrow \; V_i(\text{hist}, r_1, r_2, ..., r_i),$$

where hist refers to the current history up to the $(i-1)$-st prover step ; that is, given hist, $V_i(\text{hist}, r_1, r_2, ..., r_i)$ outputs r_i if hist is accepting, or aborts if not. Note that the next message function V_i needs the randomness $[r_1, r_2, ..., r_{i-1}]$ of previous verifier steps in order to check whether the current history is accepting or not.

We will sometimes abbreviate and use superscripts to distinguish verifiers running on different random tapes; that is, given two random tapes $\mathbf{r}^i = [r_1^i, r_2^i, ..., r_m^i]$ and $\mathbf{r}^j = [r_1^j, r_2^j, ..., r_m^j]$, we will use V^i and V^j as a shorthand for $V(\mathbf{r}^i)$ and $V(\mathbf{r}^j)$, respectively. Similarly, we will use V_k^i to denote the k-th next-message function of the verifier $V(\mathbf{r}^i)$.

Now, given a verifier $V^i = [V_1^i, ..., V_m^i]$, we will use $V_{[j,k]}^i$ to denote the partial verifier strategy starting with the j-th next message function and up to the k-th next message function. We will typically be concerned with the following partial strategies:

$$\text{prefix strategy: } V_{[1,k]}^i \triangleq [V_1^i, V_2^i, ..., V_k^i];$$

$$\text{suffix strategy: } V_{[k,m]}^i \triangleq [V_k^i, V_{k+1}^i, ..., V_m^i].$$

ZK Proofs with Universal Simulator. In the standard definition of zero knowledge proof, the simulation process for a malicious verifier V^* is typically as follows. The PPT simulator S, taking the common input x and V^*'s code as inputs, is to output a session transcript. S treats V^* as a subroutine, interacting (with possible "rewinds") with it *internally*, and outputting a view of V^* as the result of the interaction. Without loss of generality, one can think of the output of the simulator as the final (internal) interaction between $S(x, V^*)$ and V^*. In this paper, we wish to be able to obtain prover messages from S one by one, rather than obtaining the entire session transcript at once. For this purpose, we make the above (final) internal interaction "external," by casting the simulation process for a malicious verifier V^* as a real interaction between $S(x, V^*)$ (playing the role of the prover) and an external V^*, and whenever S wants to rewind V^*, it does it on its own copy of V^*. We denote this interaction by $(S(x, V^*) \Leftrightarrow V^*)$, and the view of V^* resulting from this interaction by $\{\text{View}_{V^*}^{S(x,V^*)}\}_{x \in L}$. (For brevity, we will sometimes drop x from the above notation.)

The following fact is easy to verify.

Fact 1. For any x and any V, V^* such that $V \overset{f}{=} V^*$, $(S(x, V^*) \Leftrightarrow V^*)$ generates the same session transcript as $(S(x, V^*) \Leftrightarrow V)$.

We conclude this section with the following definition of *ZK proof with universal simulator*, which differs from the standard ZK definition in the order of quantifiers ("$\exists S \forall V^*$" instead of "$\forall V^* \exists S$").[2]

Definition 2 (Zero-Knowledge Proofs with Universal Simulator). *An interactive proof system $\langle P, V \rangle$ for a language L is said to be* zero-knowledge with universal simulator *if there exists a probabilistic polynomial-time algorithm S*

---

[2] To our knowledge, all known ZK proofs admit a universal simulator, satisfying this stronger requirement.

such that for any probabilistic polynomial-time V^*, the distribution $\{\text{View}_{V^*}^P\}_{x \in L}$ is computationally indistinguishable from the distribution $\{\text{View}_{V^*}^{S(V^*)}\}_{x \in L}$.

3   Canonical ZK Proofs and the *Verifier-Distinguishing* Problem

In this paper we will focus on ZK proof systems with a certain property, which we call "canonical," since all known constructions (see below) fall in this category. We first give some intuition behind it. (To simplify notation, from here on we will drop the common input x from $(S(x, V^*) \Leftrightarrow V^*)$, and write the simulation simply as $(S(V^*) \Leftrightarrow V^*)$.) We observe that for many ZK protocols, if the simulation is formulated as an interaction between $S(V^*)$ and V^*, as in the previous section, then for a successful simulation to take place it is sufficient to feed S with only the *partial* code of V^*, rather than with its entire code. We elaborate on those systems in detail in Sect. 3.2.

3.1   Canonical ZK Proofs

We mentioned partial code of V^* above. The following definition about session prefixes of proof systems will become handy.

Definition 3 (*Good/Bad* Session Prefix). *Let $\langle P, V \rangle$ be a $2m$-round public-coin proof system for a language L, and let $\mathcal{V}_{[1,\ell]}$ denote the set of verifiers that share the same verifier prefix strategy $V_{[1,\ell]}$, for some $1 \leq \ell \leq m$. We call a session prefix $(r_1, p_1, ..., p_\ell)$ good with respect to $\mathcal{V}_{[1,\ell]}$ if there is a residual (unbounded) prover strategy with auxiliary input $\mathcal{V}_{[1,\ell]}$ which, based on this session prefix, can make a verifier randomly chosen from $\mathcal{V}_{[1,\ell]}$ accept with probability 1. Otherwise, we call the session prefix bad with respect to $\mathcal{V}_{[1,\ell]}$.*

We are now ready to define what we call *canonical* ZK proofs; these proofs are defined conditionally, predicated on the existence of a good prefix. Roughly speaking, the property states that if a simulator $S([V_{[1,k-1]}^*, V_k^*])$, taking the partial code $[V_{[1,k-1]}^*, V_k^*]$ as input, can generate a session prefix up to the $(k-1)$-th prover step that is good for verifiers with a k-th step function different from V_k^*, then S can do the same *without* being given verifier code V_k^*. Next, we present the definition of a canonical ZK proof system with an arbitrary (constant) number of rounds; in Sect. 3.2 we analyze concrete examples (e.g., 3-round proof systems).

Definition 4 (*Canonical* ZK Proofs). *Let $\langle P, V \rangle$ be a $2m$-round universally simulatable ZK proof system for a language L (Definition 2), S be the associated simulator and t be some polynomial. We call $\langle P, V \rangle$ canonical if for any common input x (not necessarily in L), every set $\mathcal{V}_{[1,k-1]}$ of verifiers that share prefix strategy $V_{[1,k-1]}$, $2 \leq k \leq m$ (as in Definition 3), but with t distinct k-th step strategies $V_k^1, V_k^2, ..., V_k^t$, the following holds.*

For any verifier code $V^*_{[1,k-1]}$ satisfying $V^*_{[1,k-1]} \stackrel{f}{=} V_{[1,k-1]}$, if, for some $1 \leq i \leq t$, there exists $V^*_k \stackrel{f}{=} V^i_k$ such that the session prefix $(r_1, p_1, ..., p_{k-1}) \leftarrow (S([V^*_{[1,k-1]}, V^*_k]) \Leftrightarrow [V^*_{[1,k-1]}, V^*_k])$ is good with respect to $\mathcal{V}_{[1,k-1]}$, then S, taking only $V^*_{[1,k-1]}$ as input, can also produce a session prefix (i.e., $(r_1, p'_1, ..., p'_{k-1}) \leftarrow (S(V^*_{[1,k-1]}) \Leftrightarrow V^*_{[1,k-1]}))$ which is good with respect to $\mathcal{V}_{[1,k-1]}$.

Remark 1. We stress that, for a zero knowledge proof, the canonical property above makes a demand on the simulator only when the condition of the "if" clause holds. We also note that the ability of the simulator $S([V^*_{[1,k-1]}, V^*_k])$ to produce a good session prefix may depend on the common input x (see the examples in the next section).[3]

3.2   Canonical ZK Proofs: Examples

To our knowledge, all constructions of ZK proofs satisfy Definition 4—cf. the FLS proof system [13] example at the beginning of the section, as well as those protocols that do not follow the FLS paradigm, such as, for example, Blum's 3-round ZK proof for Graph Hamiltonicity [7] (and its sequential repetition version), which we now analyze in more detail.

Blum's Graph Hamiltonicity ZK Proof. Consider Blum's 3-round ZK proof system for Graph Hamiltonicity (with soundness error $\frac{1}{2}$). In this case, we denote by V^1_1 and V^2_1 the verifiers that produce challenges 1 and 0, respectively[4]. Suppose that when the verifier sends challenge 1, the prover needs to reveal the isomorphism between the common input graph and the graph committed in the first prover message p_1. Note that when the simulator S takes any V^*_1 that is functionally equivalent to V^1_1, then it will simply choose an isomorphism and commit to a new graph isomorphic to the common input graph in the message p_1 (i.e., it acts as an honest prover in the first prover step). For this proof system, the "if" clause of Definition 4 holds depending on whether the common input graph is Hamiltonian or not:

– If the common input graph is Hamiltonian, then the "if" clause holds: Given a verifier code V^*_1 that is functionally equivalent to V^1_1 as input (i.e., $i = 1$ in Definition 4), $S(V^*_1)$ will generate a first prover message p_1, for which an unbounded prover can answer both challenges 1 and 0 (from V^1_1 and V^2_1, resp.), since the graph committed by $S(V^*_1)$ in p_1 is also Hamiltonian. In this case, the simulator S, without being given the code V^*_1, can also act as an honest prover in the first prover step and generate p_1 that will enable an unbounded

---

[3] Further, looking ahead, the only place where this property will be used is in the proof of our main theorem (step 3), where we fix a false statement x first and then discuss the properties of the simulator.

[4] To match our definition, we can think of these protocols as being of even number rounds by letting the verifier send a dummy message in the first step of the protocol, and denote by V^i_2 the challenge step of the verifier.

prover to answer both challenges 1 and 0^5—i.e., prefix p_1 is *good* with respect to the verifier set $\{V_1^1, V_1^2\}$.

– If the common input graph is not Hamiltonian, then the "if" clause does not hold: For $t \in \{1, 2\}$, given a verifier code V_1^* that is functionally equivalent to V_1^t as input, $S(V_1^*)$ will generate the first prover message p_1 for which an unbounded prover can only answer a challenge from V_1^t, since the graph committed in p_1 is either a graph isomorphic to the common input graph or a Hamiltonian graph (which is not isomorphic to the common input graph)— i.e., p_1 is *bad* with respect to the verifier set $\{V_1^1, V_1^2\}$.

In sum, Blum's 3-round ZK proof system for Graph Hamiltonicity is canonical according to Definition 4: whenever the definition's "if" clause is satisfied, i.e., the simulator $S(V_1^*)$ can generate p_1 that is good with respect to both verifier challenges, then S, without being given the code V_1^* as input, can also generate a good prefix p_1.

FLS-type ZK Proofs. The classical FLS-type ZK proofs [13] are also canonical. Recall how these proofs work. In the first stage, the verifier sends a perfectly hiding commitment c_1 to a random string, followed by a perfectly binding commitment c_2 to a random string from the prover, after which the verifier opens the commitment sent at its first step. In the second stage, the prover proves that the common input $x \in L$ or that the random string committed in c_1 matches the random string committed in c_2 via a Blum 3-round proof system as above (but with negligible soundness error). We view the two verifier steps in the first stage as a single step[6], and denote it by V_1, and denote by V_2 the verifier step in stage 2. We now analyze what happens at each step.

It is easy to verify that the second verifier step ($k = 2$) satisfies the definition, based on the following observation. Fix a code V_1^* of the first verifier step (recall that, by definition, we consider only the set of verifiers sharing the same first verifier step that is functionally equivalent to V_1^*). Observe that the simulator, given only a code V_1^* that is functionally equivalent to some V_1 as input, can generate a good first stage prefix (by rewinding the first stage verifier V_1^*) that will enable an unbounded prover answer any challenge from the second verifier step (since an unbounded prover can always recover the corresponding trapdoor from the transcript of the first stage and act as an honest prover to carry out the second stage in a straight-line fashion). I.e., the unbounded prover will, based on the first stage transcript output by $S(V_1^*)$, make a random verifier that share the same prefix V_1 accept.

For the first verifier step V_1, the "if" clause is satisfied depending on whether $x \in L$ or not:

– When $x \in L$, the "if" clause holds, since an unbounded prover can, based on any first stage transcript output by the simulator $S(V_1^*)$, make a random

---

[5] Recall that an honest prover can compute p_1 without knowledge of the corresponding witness.

[6] Note that the second verifier message is bound to the first verifier message c_1, and merging these two steps will simplify the analysis.

verifier (that may have a prefix functionally different from V_1^*) accept with probability 1 by finding the witness for $x \in L$ and acting as an honest prover in the second stage. In this case, the simulator S, without being given the code V_1^*, can also act as an honest prover in the first prover step and generate a random first stage transcript (which does not form a trapdoor), and based on this transcript, an unbounded prover can always find a witness for $x \in L$ to make a random verifier accept with probability 1.

– When $x \notin L$, the "if" clause does not hold: For every two different first verifier steps V_1^1, V_1^2, and every two different second verifier steps V_2^1, V_2^2 (that will output different challenges in Blum's protocol), where V_1^t ($t \in \{1,2\}$) commits to r_t and then opens the commitment, and V_2^b ($b \in \{1,2\}$) simply sends challenge e_b, the simulator S, given a code V_1^* that is functionally equivalent to V_1^i ($i \in \{1,2\}$) as input, will generate a first stage transcript for which an unbounded prover *cannot* make a random verifier from the set of four verifiers $\{V_1^t, V_2^b\}$ accept with probability 1, since for verifier prefix V_1^j different from V_1^i, the first stage transcript output by $S(V_1^*)$ will not form a valid trapdoor for the prover, and thus, if the random verifier is chosen from the verifier set $\{V_1^j, V_2^b\}$, based on this first stage transcript, an unbounded prover cannot make the random verifier accept with probability greater than $\frac{1}{2}$.

In sum, FLS-type ZK proofs are also canonical according to Definition 4: Whenever the "if" clause holds for a verifier step k, the simulator can generate a good prefix prior to the k-th verifier step without being given the code of this verifier step.

Barak's Argument System. Finally, one may wonder where Barak's argument system (not known to be a proof system) fits in all this. We view the first three messages in the system (the hash function selected by the verifier, the commitment computed by the prover, and the verifier's random challenge—recall the description in Sect. 1) as the first stage, and the remaining WIUA (Witness Indistinguishable Universal Argument) as the second stage. Thus, following the same reasoning as the one for the FLS-type ZK proofs above at the second ($k = 2$) verifier step, for every $k > 2$, the canonical property is satisfied at the k-th verifier step. However, for the second verifier step (at which the verifier outputs a random challenge), when $x \notin L$, we do not know if Definition 4's "if" clause holds.

Canonical ZK proofs are used in the next section to formulate the "verifier-distinguishing problem," to which the existence of constant-round public-coin ZK proofs is reduced.

3.3   The *Verifier-Distinguishing* Problem

In a nutshell, given a set of distinct verifier k-th next-message functions, the problem resides in constructing a distinguishing algorithm U which, given a session prefix (prior to the k-th verifier step) output by simulator S, such that for

any polynomial-time constructible program V_k^* that is promised to be functionally equivalent to one of the next-message functions, is able to discern one from
the set that is functionally *different* from V_k^*. Formally:

Definition 5 (The Verifier-Distinguishing Problem). *Let* $\langle P, V \rangle$ *be a*
2m-round canonical ZK proof system for a language L (Definition 4), S be its
simulator, p the length of each prover's message, and t a polynomial in the
security parameter n. Given are a set $\mathcal{V}_{[1,k-1]}$ of deterministic honest verifiers
that share the same prefix verifier $V_{[1,k-1]}$, but have t distinct k-th next-message
functions $V_k^1, V_k^2, ..., V_k^t$, denoted by set $\mathcal{V}_k$, and an auxiliary input aux[7]. The
verifier-distinguishing problem is to find a non-uniform algorithm U, running in
time $2^{O(p)}$, such that for every polynomial-time algorithm C, the following holds:

- *First, C picks a machine $V_k^i \in \mathcal{V}_k$ at random and outputs a polynomial-time*
  Turing machine V_k^* such that $V_k^* \overset{f}{=} V_k^i$.
- *Next, U, taking $(\mathcal{V}_{[1,k-1]}, \mathcal{V}_k)$ and a session prefix $(r_1, p_1, ..., p_{k-1})$ output by*
  $S(\mathsf{aux}, V_k^*)$, outputs $V_k^j \in \mathcal{V}_k$ such that $V_k^j \overset{f}{\neq} V_k^*$ with probability negligibly
  close to 1. I.e.,

$$\Pr\left[\begin{array}{l} V_k^* \leftarrow C(\mathcal{V}_k, i); \ (r_1, p_1, ..., p_{k-1}) \leftarrow S(\mathsf{aux}, V_k^*); \\ j \leftarrow U(\mathcal{V}_{[1,k-1]}, \mathcal{V}_k, r_1, p_1, ..., p_{k-1}) \end{array} : V_k^* \overset{f}{\neq} V_k^j \right] > 1 - \mathsf{neg}(n),$$

where the probability is taken over the random choice i and the randomness
used by C, U and S.

Remark 2. We now make a couple of remarks regarding Definition 5:

(a) By definition, a simulator for a ZK proof system needs to handle arbitrary
    verifiers. In our context we just deal with the arbitrary code of an *honest*
    verifier, which strengthens the result.
(b) We note that in the definition, algorithm U is not given V^*'s code as input.
    This means that if U is able to carry out its task, then the simulator must
    encode some non-trivial functionality of V_k^* in such a session prefix. As men-
    tioned before, this is in sharp contrast with known straight-line simulators
    such as Barak's, which are oblivious to the verifier's functionality in com-
    puting a session prefix. We elaborated on some of the difficulties in solving
    this problem in Sect. 1, overcoming which (if at all possible) would require a
    technical breakthrough in simulation techniques.

4   An Improved Derandomization Lemma for Interactive Proofs

In this section we prove a structure-preserving version of the well-known Babai-
Moran "Speedup Theorem" [1,9] with improved parameters for our application,

---

[7] This auxiliary input is given to S; in our main theorem (Theorem 2) it will be the
code of some verifier prefix strategy.

which we will then use in the proof of our main result (Theorem 2). Essentially, the result says that for any constant-round public-coin interactive proof system with small soundness error, there exists a polynomial set of random verifier tapes such that the cheating probability for the unbounded prover over these verifier tapes is bounded away from 1—and this holds even when the prover knows this small set of random tapes in advance.

We first recall the Babai-Moran theorem. Let $AM[k]$ denote the set of languages whose membership can be proved via a k-round public-coin proof system.

Theorem 1 ([9]). *For any polynomial $t(n)$, $AM[t + 1] = AM[t]$. In particular, for any constant k, $AM[k] = AM[2]$.*

For our application, we wish to de-randomize the verifier while keeping the original proof system structure intact (that is, without "collapsing" the round complexity). The $AM[k] = AM[2]$ proof—and its randomness-efficient variant in [10][8]—actually yield such a result: for any $2m$-round public-coin proof system with small soundness error ϵ, there exist $(O(p))^m$ verifier random tapes over which the cheating probability of an unbounded prover is still bounded away from 1, where p is the length of the prover's messages.

Next, we present an improvement to this result, in which the number of such verifier random tapes reduces to $(p/O(\log \frac{1}{\epsilon}))^m$. In addition, we show that this de-randomization lemma is essentially tight with respect to the round complexity, as there are super-constant-round public-coin proof systems for which the prover's cheating probability is 1, over any polynomial number of verifier random tapes.

Before stating the lemma, we introduce some additional notation:

- $V_{|(\mathbf{r}^1, \mathbf{r}^2 ..., \mathbf{r}^t)}$ denotes the honest verifier that is restricted to choose *uniformly at random* one of $\mathbf{r}^1, \mathbf{r}^2 ..., \mathbf{r}^t$ as its random tape, where t is a polynomial; we use $V_{|(\mathbf{r}^1, \mathbf{r}^2 ..., \mathbf{r}^t)}(\mathbf{r}^i)$ to denote the verifier that takes $\mathbf{r}^i$, $1 \leq i \leq t$, as its random tape.
- $P^*(\mathbf{r}^1, \mathbf{r}^2 ..., \mathbf{r}^t)$ denotes the unbounded *cheating* prover with auxiliary input $(\mathbf{r}^1, \mathbf{r}^2 ..., \mathbf{r}^t)$, indicating that it will interact with $V_{|(\mathbf{r}^1, \mathbf{r}^2 ..., \mathbf{r}^t)}$.

We now state the result formally. For simplicity, we assume that all the prover messages are of equal length.

Lemma 1. *Let m be a constant and $\langle P, V \rangle$ be a $2m$-round public-coin interactive proof system for language L with negligible soundness error ϵ. Let p*

---

[8] In [10], Bellare and Rompel present a randomness-efficient approach to transform $AM[k]$ into $AM[2]$: to halve the number of rounds of an Arthur-Merlin proof system, they introduce a so-called "oblivious sampler" and use a small amount of randomness to specify roughly $O(p)$ verifier messages in the original proof system. Their proof, however, yields almost the same result as the Speedup Theorem in our setting where we want to maintain the structure of the original proof system, and only care about the number of original verifier random tapes that are needed to make sure the resulting protocol after derandomization is still a proof system.

denote the length of the prover's messages. Then for every $x \notin L$, there exist $q = (p/O(\log\frac{1}{\epsilon}))^m$ different random tapes, $\mathbf{r}^1, \mathbf{r}^2, ...\mathbf{r}^q$, such that for every unbounded prover P,

$$\Pr[\langle P(\mathbf{r}^1, \mathbf{r}^2, ...\mathbf{r}^q), V_{|(\mathbf{r}^1, \mathbf{r}^2, ...\mathbf{r}^q)}\rangle(x) = 1] \leq 1 - \frac{1}{q}.$$

Here we present the intuition and basic inequalities that yield the proof for the case of a 3-round proof system[9] (similar ideas also appeared in [1,9]). Refer to the full version of the paper [12] for the full proof.

Let us consider a 3-round public-coin proof system $\langle P, V \rangle$ with negligible soundness error for some language L[10], in which the prover sends the first message p_1 and the last message p_2, and the verifier sends the second message $\mathbf{r}$ (its public coins). Without loss of generality, we assume $|p_1| = |p_2| = p$, and $|\mathbf{r}| = n$. We now prove that there exists a number p of verifier random tapes[11] $(\mathbf{r}^1, \mathbf{r}^2, ..., \mathbf{r}^p)$ over which the cheating probability is at most $1 - 1/p$.

For the sake of contradiction, assume that for some false statement $x \notin L$ there is an unbounded prover $P^\diamond$ such that for any p-tuple $(\mathbf{r}^1, \mathbf{r}^2, ..., \mathbf{r}^p)$, $P^\diamond(\mathbf{r}^1, \mathbf{r}^2, ..., \mathbf{r}^p)$ can cheat $V_{|(\mathbf{r}^1, \mathbf{r}^2, ...\mathbf{r}^p)}$ with probability 1. Now note that the number of such successful cheating provers is $\binom{2^n}{p}$, and that there are at most 2^p different first prover messages p_1. Thus, there is a number of at least $\binom{2^n}{p}/2^p$ $P^\diamond(\mathbf{r}^1, \mathbf{r}^2, ..., \mathbf{r}^p)$'s that produce the same first prover message, denote it p_1^*, for which if the verifier is using a random tape in any of the p-tuples

$$\{(\mathbf{r}^1, \mathbf{r}^2, ..., \mathbf{r}^p) : p_1^* \leftarrow P^\diamond(\mathbf{r}^1, \mathbf{r}^2, ..., \mathbf{r}^p)\},$$

we have an unbounded prover that can produce a second prover message p_2^* to make the verifier accept.

On the other hand, the number of p-tuple choices $(\mathbf{r}^1, \mathbf{r}^2, ..., \mathbf{r}^p)$ out of a $1/2e$ fraction of all possible verifier random tapes is at most $\binom{\frac{2^n}{2e}}{p}$. Since

$$\binom{\frac{2^n}{2e}}{p} < (\frac{2^n}{2p})^p < \frac{\binom{2^n}{p}}{2^p},$$

we have that the set $\{(\mathbf{r}^1, \mathbf{r}^2, ..., \mathbf{r}^p) : p_1^* \leftarrow P^\diamond(\mathbf{r}^1, \mathbf{r}^2, ..., \mathbf{r}^p)\}$ covers at least a $1/2e$ fraction of all possible verifier random tapes.

In sum, we are able conclude that there is an unbounded prover, which sends p_1^* as its first message, that can make the verifier accept the false statement with probability at least $1/2e$. This contradicts the negligible soundness error of $\langle P, V \rangle$.

---

[9] The basic reasoning here applies to a proof system of even number (4) of rounds as well, by having the verifier send a dummy message first.

[10] For example, the n-folded parallel version of Blum's 3-round proof for Graph Hamiltonicity [7], or the 3-round proof for Graph Isomorphism [18].

[11] For simplicity's sake, we do not optimize this parameter here.

5   Constant-Round Public-Coin Zero-Knowledge Proofs Imply Distinguishing Verifiers' Programs

We are now ready to present our main result, which exhibits a reduction from constant-round public-coin canonical ZK proofs to the functionality-distinguishing problem (Definition 5), a problem seemingly quite different in nature. We first fix some parameters and revisit notation:

- $\langle P, V \rangle$: A $2m$-round public-coin canonical ZK proof sytem for some constant m. We let n be the security parameter and p be the length of each prover's message.
- $\mathcal{V}_{[1,k-1]}$: A set of deterministic honest verifiers that share the same (honest) prefix verifier $V_{[1,k-1]}$, but have t *distinct* k-th step functions $V_k^1, V_k^2, ..., V_k^t$; $|\mathcal{V}_{[1,k-1]}| \leq q$, where t and q are polynomials (defined in Lemma 1)[12].
- $\mathcal{V}_k$: The set $\{V_k^1, V_k^2, ..., V_k^t\}$, as above.
- $V'_{[1,k-1]}$: The auxiliary input to S, which is the code of a prefix verifier such that $V'_{[1,k-1]} \stackrel{f}{=} V_{[1,k-1]}$. (When $k = 1$, it is set to the empty string.)

We now show that if $\langle P, V \rangle$ admits a universal simulator S, then there is an algorithm U, taking $\mathcal{V}_{[1,k-1]}$, $\mathcal{V}_k$ and a session prefix as inputs, which can solve the functionality-distinguishing problem (cf. Definition 5) with respect to verifier set $\mathcal{V}_k$. Formally:

Theorem 2. *Let $\langle P, V \rangle$ be a $2m$-round, public-coin canonical ZK proof system for a non-trivial language $L \notin \mathcal{BPP}$, and S be its universal simulator. Then, there exist an infinite set I, a sequence of false statements $x \notin L$ of length n for each $n \in I$, a constant k, $2 \leq k \leq m$, sets $\mathcal{V}_{[1,k-1]}$ and $\mathcal{V}_k$, a verifier code $V'_{[1,k-1]}$ as above, and an algorithm U, running in time $2^{O(p)}$, such that, for any polynomial-time algorithm C that on input $(\mathcal{V}_k, i)$, $1 \leq i \leq t$ outputs V_k^* satisfying $V_k^* \stackrel{f}{=} V_k^i \in \mathcal{V}_k$, the following holds:*

$$\Pr\left[\begin{array}{c} V_k^* \leftarrow C(\mathcal{V}_k, i); (r_1, p_1, ..., p_{k-1}) \leftarrow (S([V'_{[1,k-1]}, V_k^*]) \Leftrightarrow V'_{[1,k-1]}) \\ j \leftarrow U(\mathcal{V}_{[1,k-1]}, \mathcal{V}_k, r_1, p_1, ..., p_{k-1}) \end{array} : V_k^* \stackrel{f}{\neq} V_k^j \in \mathcal{V}_k \right]$$

$$> 1 - \mathsf{neg}(n),$$

where the probability is taken over the random choice i and the randomness used by C, U and S.

Here we give a high-level sketch of the proof, which mainly consists of three steps. The full proof of the theorem is given in [12].

---

[12]   At the k-th verifier step, the number of distinct next-message functions should in fact be t_k. For simplicity, we assume $t = t_k$ for all $1 \leq k \leq m$.

1. The first step is Lemma 1 from the previous section. Let $V^1, V^2, ..., V^q$ denote the q deterministic verifiers given by the lemma.
2. Next, we show that there exists a sequence of infinitely many false statements x such that for every verifier V^i, $1 \leq i \leq q$, and any polynomial-time constructible code V^* which is functionally equivalent to V^i, the session $(S(V^*) \Leftrightarrow V^*)$ (which, by Fact 1 is identical to $(S(V^*) \Leftrightarrow V^i)$) is accepting except with negligible probability.
3. For any false statement x in the above sequence, we prove that among these q verifiers, we can find (by using canonical property) a set of verifiers $\mathcal{V}_{[1,k-1]}$ that has the same prefix strategy $[V_1, V_2, ..., V_{k-1}]$ up to the $(k-1)$-th verifier step but "splits" at the k-th verifier step, and a code $V'_{[1,k-1]}$ that is functionally equivalent to $V_{[1,k-1]} = [V_1, V_2, ..., V_{k-1}]$, such that, for any polynomial-time constructible code V^*_k that is promised to be functionally equivalent to one of those V^i_k's (nodes) at level k, the following two conditions hold:
   - The session prefix $(r_1, p_1, ..., p_{k-1})$ produced by $(S([V'_{[1,k-1]}, V^*_k]) \Leftrightarrow V'_{[1,k-1]})$ (or equivalently, by $(S([V'_{[1,k-1]}, V^*_k]) \Leftrightarrow V_{[1,k-1]}))$ is *bad* with respect to $\mathcal{V}_{[1,k-1]}$.
   - However, the session prefix $(r_1, p_1, ..., p_{k-1})$ is *good* with respect to the set of verifiers that shares the same prefix strategy $[V_{[1,k-1]}, V^i_k]$

This enables us to construct an algorithm (running in time $2^{O(p)}$) that is able to "understand" the code V^*_k, by pin-pointing another verifier code, say, V^j_k, such that $V^j_k \overset{f}{\neq} V^*_k$.

6   Conclusions

A natural question which arises from our reduction is: How hard is the functionality-predicting problem (Definition 5)? As mentioned before, since our predicting algorithm U does not take the target code V^*_k as input, the simulator must encode some non-trivial functionality of V^*_k in the session prefix $(r_1, p_1, ..., p_{k-1})$. However, if the simulator runs in a straight-line manner such as Barak's [2], it does not execute V^*_k in computing the history prefix prior to the verifier's k-th step, and this means it is able to discern some non-trivial property of V^*_k's functionality and encode it in the session prefix $(r_1, p_1, ..., p_{k-1})$ without executing V^*_k, which seems to be highly unlikely (See, e.g., [20,21] for some general hardness results.) We leave the exact characterization of this problem's hardness as an interesting research question.

Since, as also argued in the introduction, rewinding seems to be out of the picture, this leads us to think of our main theorem as strong evidence against the existence of such proof systems, and safely conclude that constructing non-trivial constant-round public-coin ZK proofs (if they exist) requires a paradigm-shifting simulation technique.

Acknowledgements. The authors would like to thank Susumu Kiyoshima and Sanjam Garg for their valuable comments.

References

1. Babai, L.: Trading group theory for randomness. In: STOC, 1985, pp. 421–429 (1985)
2. Barak, B.: How to go beyond the black-box simulation barrier. In: FOCS 2001, pp. 106–115 (2001)
3. Brassard, G., Chaum, D., Crépeau, C.: Minimum disclosure proofs of knowledge. J. Comput. Syst. Sci. **37**(2), 156–189 (1988)
4. Bitansky, N., Dachman-Soled, D., Garg, S., Jain, A., Kalai, Y.T., López-Alt, A., Wichs, D.: Why "Fiat-Shamir for Proofs" lacks a proof. In: Sahai, A. (ed.) TCC 2013. LNCS, vol. 7785, pp. 182–201. Springer, Heidelberg (2013)
5. Barak, B., Goldreich, O., Impagliazzo, R., Rudich, S., Sahai, A., Vadhan, S.P., Yang, K.: On the (im)possibility of obfuscating programs. In: Kilian, J. (ed.) CRYPTO 2001. LNCS, vol. 2139, pp. 1–18. Springer, Heidelberg (2001)
6. Barak, B., Lindell, Y.: Strict polynomial-time in simulation and extraction.In: STOC, 2002, pp. 484–493 (2002)
7. Blum, M.: How to prove a theorem so no one else can claim it. In: Proceedings of the International Congress of Mathematicians, pp. 444–451 (1986)
8. Barak, B., Lindell, Y., Vadhan, S.P.: Lower bounds for non-black-box zero knowledge. In: FOCS 2003, pp. 384–393 (2003)
9. Babai, L., Moran, S.: Arthur-Merlin games: a randomized proof system, and a hierarchy of complexity classes. J. Comput. Syst. Sci. **36**(2), 254–276 (1988)
10. Bellare, M., Rompel, J.: Randomness-efficient oblivious sampling. In: FOCS 1994, pp. 276–287 (1994)
11. Canetti, R., Chen, Y., Reyzin, L.: On the correlation intractability of obfuscated pseudorandom functions. In: Kushilevitz, E., et al. (eds.) TCC 2016-A. LNCS, vol. 9562, pp. 389–415. Springer, Heidelberg (2016). doi:10.1007/978-3-662-49096-9_17
12. Deng, Y., Garay, J., Ling, S., Wang, H., Yung, M.: On the implausibility of constant-round public-coin zero-knowledge proofs. Cryptology ePrint Archive, Report 2012/508 (2012). http://eprint.iacr.org/2012/508
13. Feige, U., Lapidot, D., Shamir, A.: Multiple non-interactive zero knowledge proofs under general assumptions. SIAM J. Comput. **29**, 1–28 (1999)
14. Goldreich, O.: The Foundations of Cryptography, Volume 1, Basic Techniques Cambridge University Press (2001)
15. Garg, S., Gentry, C., Halevi, S., Raykova, M., Sahai, A., Waters, B.: Candidate indistinguishability obfuscation and functional encryption for all circuits. In: FOCS, pp. 40–49 (2013)
16. Goldreich, O., Krawczyk, H.: On the composition of zero-knowledge proof systems. SIAM J. Comput. **25**(1), 169–192 (1996)
17. Goldwasser, S., Micali, S., Rackoff, C.: The knowledge complexity of interactive proof systems. SIAM. J. Comput. **18**(1), 186–208 (1989)
18. Goldreich, O., Micali, S., Wigderson, A.: Proofs that yield nothing but their validity or all languages in NP have zero-knowledge proof systems. J. ACM **38**(3), 691–729 (1991)
19. Hada, S.: Zero-knowledge and code obfuscation. In: Okamoto, T. (ed.) ASIACRYPT 2000. LNCS, vol. 1976, pp. 443–457. Springer, Heidelberg (2000)
20. Landi, W.: Undecidability of static analysis. J. LOPLAS **1**(4), 323–337 (1992)
21. Ramalingam, G.: The undecidability of aliasing. ACM Trans. Program. Lang. Syst. **16**(5), 1467–1471 (1994)

Efficient Protocols

Critical Transitions

Improving Practical UC-Secure Commitments Based on the DDH Assumption

Eiichiro Fujisaki[✉]

NTT Secure Platform Laboratories, Tokyo, Japan
fujisaki.eiichiro@lab.ntt.co.jp

Abstract. At Eurocrypt 2011, Lindell presented practical static and adaptively UC-secure commitment schemes based on the DDH assumption. Later, Blazy et al. (at ACNS 2013) improved the efficiency of the Lindell's commitment schemes. In this paper, we present static and adaptively UC-secure commitment schemes based on the same assumption and further improve the communication and computational complexity, as well as the size of the common reference string.

1 Introduction

Universal composability (UC) framework [5] guarantees that if a protocol is proven secure in the UC framework, it remains secure even if it is run concurrently with arbitrary (even insecure) protocols. The UC framework allows one to divide the design of a large system into that of simpler sub-protocols, which provides the designer a fundamental benefit.

Commitment schemes are one of the most important tools in the cryptographic protocols. A commitment scheme consists of a two-phase protocol between two parties, a committer and a receiver. In the commit phase, a committer gives a receiver the digital equivalent of a *sealed envelope* containing value x. In the decommit phase, the committer reveals x in a way that the receiver can verify it. From the original concept, it is required that a committer cannot change the value inside the envelope (*binding property*), whereas the receiver can learn nothing about x (*hiding property*) unless the committer helps the receiver open the envelope. Commitment schemes that are secure in the UC framework were first presented by Canetti and Fischlin [6]. UC commitments are complete for constructing UC zero-knowledge protocols [6,13] and UC two-party and multiparty computation [7]. Informally, a UC commitment scheme maintains the above binding and hiding properties under *any concurrent composition with arbitrary protocols*. To achieve this, a UC commitment scheme requires *equivocability* and *extractability* at the same time. Since UC commitments cannot be realized without an additional set-up assumption [6], the common reference string (CRS) model is widely used.

Several UC commitment schemes in the CRS model have been proposed so far. After [6], Canetti et al. [7] constructed inefficient schemes from general assumptions. Damgård and Nielsen [13] proposed interactive schemes that are

© Springer International Publishing Switzerland 2016
V. Zikas and R. De Prisco (Eds.): SCN 2016, LNCS 9841, pp. 257–272, 2016.
DOI: 10.1007/978-3-319-44618-9_14

the first efficient UC-secure commitment schemes. Camenish and Shoup [4] also presented efficient interactive schemes. Although they are asymptotically efficient, their concrete instantiations are implemented on N^{d+1} modulus for RSA modulus N and $d \geq 1$, or $p^2 q$ modulus with primes, p and q.

In [24], Lindell presented the first practical UC commitment schemes based on an ordinary prime-order group. In practice, his constructions are much more efficient when implemented in elliptic curves whose security is equivalent to that of RSA modulus. He proposed two types of UC commitment schemes. One is *static* UC-secure and the other is *adaptively* UC-secure (with secure erasure). If an adversary should decide to corrupt parities only before a protocol starts, it is called *static* corruption. A corrupted party reveals its whole inner states to the adversary. A commitment scheme is called *static UC-secure* if it is UC-secure against static corruptions. On the other hand, if an adversary can decide to corrupt parties at any point in the executions of protocols, it is called *adaptive* corruption. A commitment scheme is called *adaptively UC-secure* if it is UC-secure against adaptive corruptions. Adaptive corruptions are more flexible and powerful attacks. Lindell's adaptively UC-secure commitment scheme assumes *secure erasure*, which means that parties can securely erase their unnecessary inner states that would have risks of their security at future corruptions. Lindell's static UC-secure commitment scheme has total communication complexity of 10 group elements plus 4 scalars, whereas his adaptively UC-secure one has that of 12 group elements plus 6 scalars. Shortly after, Fishlin et al. [15] transform Lindell's static UC-secure scheme into an non-interactive scheme adaptively UC-secure with erasure, by removing the interaction of the Sigma protocol using Groth-Sahai proofs [20]. Although their proposal is non-interactive, the communication and computational complexity is less efficient than [24], because it is implemented in symmetric bilinear groups and requires expensive pairing operations. We note that implementing it in asymmetric bilinear groups does not improve efficiency.

Blazy et al. [3] proposed the improvement of both Lindell's commitment schemes. Their static UC-secure commitment scheme has total communication complexity of 9 group elements plus 3 scalars. The commit phase is non-interactive and the decommit phase consists of 3 rounds (instead of 5 in Lindell's scheme). Their adaptively UC-secure commitment with secure erasure requires 10 group elements and 4 scalars. The commit phase has 3 rounds (instead of 5 in Lindell's scheme) and the decommit phase is non-interactive.

The static and adaptively UC-secure commitment schemes in [3,24] assume the DDH assumption and the existence of the collision resistant hash functions.

More on Related Works. The constructions of [12,17,26] are also asymptotically efficient. The constructions of [4,12,13,17,26] achieve adaptive UC-security without erasure in the CRS model. In [13], the CRS size grows linearly in the number of the parties. In [26], the CRS is one-time, i.e., one needs a new common-reference string for each execution of the commitment protocol. In the other works, the CRS is independent of the number of parties and re-usable. In addition, the work of [17] achieves non-interactiveness. The most efficient constructions of [12,17,26] are implemented on N^{d+1} modulus for RSA modulus N, which are less efficient than [3,24].

Recently, [8,9,11,16,19] have proposed UC commitment schemes in the UC oblivious transfer (OT) hybrid model. Their constructions are very useful when a huge number of UC commitments are required. Their common significant property is that the schemes are very fast except for the overhead of UC OT protocols. In addition, one can make the number of the execution of UC commitments independent of the number of the execution of OT protocols. However, the proposals are only *static* UC-secure.

Therefore, [3,24] are still the most efficient *adaptively* UC-secure commitment schemes.

Note. Lindell's adaptively UC-secure commitment scheme [24] contains a small bug. Blazy et al. [3] clarified and fixed it. See [3,18] for more details.

1.1 Our Contribution

In this paper we further improve the efficiency of Blazy et al. static and adaptively UC-secure schemes [3]. By observing the security proof in [3], we realize that:

- In the adaptive case, two trapdoor commitments can be reduced to one.
- It is an overkill to use an IND-CCA secure public-key encryption (PKE) scheme in both static and adaptive cases.

The first claim comes from a simple observation. The second claim derives from our main technical contribution. We claim that an IND-PCA secure PKE scheme suffices for the protocols. Here the IND-PCA security notion is formulated by Abdala et al. [1] as a variant of the OW-PCA security notion [27]. The IND-PCA security notion is defined as indistinguishability of PKE in the presence of the *plaintext checkable oracle*, and a short version of Cramer-Shoup cryptosystem [10] satisfies this security notion.

In the concrete instantiation, we present practical static and adaptively UC-secure commitment schemes under the same assumption as in [3,24]. Our *adaptively* UC-secure commitment scheme (with erasure) is more efficient than Blazy et al. *static* UC-secure one. Our statistic and adaptive schemes both have the total communication complexity of 7 group elements and 3 scalars with the computational complexity of 18 exponentiations.

In Table 1, we compare our proposals with the previous works. All schemes below are UC-secure commitment schemes assuming the DDH assumption on cyclic group $\mathbb{G}$ and the existence of the collision resistant hash functions. All adaptively UC-secure ones below assume secure erasure. κ denotes the security parameter. Let q be the order of $\mathbb{G}$. Then, $\log(q) = O(\kappa)$. $|\mathbb{G}|$ denotes the length of the description of an element in $\mathbb{G}$, which depends on the concrete instantiation, but is generally slightly bigger than $\log(q)$. If it is implemented in an elliptic curve, it is at least $|\mathbb{G}| \geq \log(q) + 1$. $T^{\mathsf{exp}}(\mathbb{G})$ denotes the computational cost of one exponentiation on $\mathbb{G}$.

Table 1. Comparison among the UC commitments based on the DDH assumption

Schemes	Public parameter	Communication complexity	Computational complexity	Rounds com/decom	Security
Lin11 [24, Sect. 3]	$7\|\mathbb{G}\|$	$10\|\mathbb{G}\| + 4\kappa$	$27T^{\mathsf{exp}}(\mathbb{G})$	1/4	Static
Lin11 [24, Sect. 4]	$8\|\mathbb{G}\|$	$12\|\mathbb{G}\| + 6\kappa$	$36T^{\mathsf{exp}}(\mathbb{G})$	5/1	Adaptive
BCPV13 [3, Sect. 5.1]	$7\|\mathbb{G}\|$	$9\|\mathbb{G}\| + 3\kappa$	$22T^{\mathsf{exp}}(\mathbb{G})$	1/3	Static
BCPV13 [3, Sect. 5.3]	$7\|\mathbb{G}\|$	$10\|\mathbb{G}\| + 4\kappa$	$26T^{\mathsf{exp}}(\mathbb{G})$	3/1	Adaptive
Ours (Sect. 4.2)	$5\|\mathbb{G}\|$	$7\|\mathbb{G}\| + 3\kappa$	$18T^{\mathsf{exp}}(\mathbb{G})$	1/3	Static
Ours (Sect. 4.1)	$5\|\mathbb{G}\|$	$7\|\mathbb{G}\| + 3\kappa$	$18T^{\mathsf{exp}}(\mathbb{G})$	3/1	Adaptive

2 Preliminaries

2.1 (Tag-Based) Public-Key Encryption

We recall a tag-based public-key encryption (Tag-PKE) scheme (or a PKE scheme supported with labels), following [22,25,31]. A Tag-PKE $\Pi = (\mathbf{K}, \mathbf{E}, \mathbf{D})$ consists of the following three algorithms. The key-generation algorithm $\mathbf{K}$ is a PPT algorithm that takes 1^κ and outputs a pair of public and secret keys, (pk, sk). The encryption algorithm $\mathbf{E}$ is a PPT algorithm that takes public key pk, tag $t \in \{0,1\}^\kappa$ and message $m \in \mathsf{MSP}^{\mathsf{enc}}$, draws string r uniformly from the coin space $\mathsf{COIN}^{\mathsf{enc}}$, and produces ciphertext (t, c) where $c = \mathbf{E}^t_{pk}(m; r)$. The decryption algorithm $\mathbf{D}$ is a DPT algorithm that takes sk and a presumable ciphertext (t, c) where $c \in \{0,1\}^*$, and returns message $m = \mathbf{D}^t_{sk}(c)$. We require that for every sufficiently large $\kappa \in \mathbb{N}$, it always holds that $\mathbf{D}^t_{sk}(\mathbf{E}^t_{pk}(m)) = m$, for every (pk, sk) generated by $\mathbf{K}(1^\kappa)$ and every $m \in \mathsf{MSP}^{\mathsf{enc}}$. We say that ciphertext (t, c) is **proper** if there exists $(m, r) \in \mathsf{MSP}^{\mathsf{enc}} \times \mathsf{COIN}^{\mathsf{enc}}$ such that $c = \mathbf{E}^t_{pk}(m; r)$.

To suit actual instantiations, we assume $\mathsf{MSP}^{\mathsf{enc}}$ and $\mathsf{COIN}^{\mathsf{enc}}$ are defined by pk.

IND-CCA. We recall CCA security for Tag-PKEs [25], also called *weak* CCA security in [22]. We define the advantage of $A = (A_1, A_2)$ for Π against indistinguishability against chosen ciphertext attacks (IND-CCA) as

$$\mathsf{Adv}^{\mathsf{cca}}_{\Pi,A}(\kappa) = \left| \Pr[\mathsf{Expt}^{\mathsf{cca}\text{-}0}_{\Pi,A}(\kappa) = 1] - \Pr[\mathsf{Expt}^{\mathsf{cca}\text{-}1}_{\Pi,A}(\kappa) = 1] \right|,$$

where experiment $\mathsf{Expt}^{\mathsf{cca}\text{-}b}_{\Pi,A}(\kappa)$ for $b \in \{0,1\}$ is defined in Fig. 1. The constraint of A in the experement is that A_2 is not allowed to submit $(t^*, \star)$ to $\mathbf{D}_{sk}(\cdot, \cdot)$ where t^* is the challenge tag. We say that Π is indistinguishable against chosen-ciphertext attacks (IND-CCA secure) if $\mathsf{Adv}^{\mathsf{cca}}_{\Pi,A}(\kappa) = \mathsf{negl}(\kappa)$ for every non-uniform PPT A.

We note that this security notion is weaker than the standard IND-CCA security notion [2,10,29] for PKE, because an adversary is not only prohibited from asking for the challenge ciphertext (t^*, c^*) but (t^*, c) with $c \neq c^*$.

IND-PCA. Recently, Abdalla et al. [1] proposed a security notion of indistinguishability against plaintext checkable attacks (IND-PCA) for PKE. This paper

$$
\begin{array}{|l|}
\hline
\mathsf{Expt}^{\mathsf{cca}\text{-}b}_{\Pi,A}(\kappa) \\
\quad (pk, sk) \leftarrow \mathbf{K}(1^\kappa); \quad (t^*, m_0, m_1, st) \leftarrow A_1^{\mathbf{D}_{sk}}(pk) \\
\quad c^* \leftarrow \mathbf{E}^{t^*}_{pk}(m_b); \quad b' \leftarrow A_2^{\mathbf{D}_{sk}}(st, (t^*, c^*)) \\
\quad \textbf{return bit } b'. \\
\hline
\end{array}
$$

Fig. 1. Experiment of $\mathsf{Expt}^{\mathsf{cca}\text{-}b}_{\Pi,A}$

utilizes a Tag-PKE variant. Let $\mathsf{Expt}^{\mathsf{pca}\text{-}b}_{\Pi,A}(\kappa)$ for $b \in \{0,1\}$ be the experiment as in Fig. 2. Here oracle O^{pca}_{sk} takes (t, m, c) and returns 1 if and only if c is a proper ciphertext of m on tag t. The constraint of A in the experiment is that A is not allowed to submit $(t^*, \star, \star)$ to $O^{\mathsf{pca}}_{sk}(\cdot, \cdot, \cdot)$ where t^* is the challenge tag. We define the advantage of A for Π against indistinguishability against the plaintext checkable attacks (IND-PCA) as

$$
\mathsf{Adv}^{\mathsf{pca}}_{\Pi,A}(\kappa) = \left| \Pr[\mathsf{Expt}^{\mathsf{pca}\text{-}0}_{\Pi,A}(\kappa) = 1] - \Pr[\mathsf{Expt}^{\mathsf{pca}\text{-}1}_{\Pi,A}(\kappa) = 1] \right|,
$$

We say that Π is indistinguishable against the plaintext checkable attacks (IND-PCA secure) if $\mathsf{Adv}^{\mathsf{pca}}_{\Pi,A}(\kappa) = \mathsf{negl}(\kappa)$ for every non-uniform PPT A.

$$
\begin{array}{|l|}
\hline
\mathsf{Expt}^{\mathsf{pca}\text{-}b}_{\Pi,A}(\kappa) \\
\quad (pk, sk) \leftarrow \mathbf{K}(1^\kappa); \quad (t^*, m_0, m_1, st) \leftarrow A_1^{O^{\mathsf{pca}}_{sk}}(pk) \\
\quad c^* \leftarrow \mathbf{E}^{t^*}_{pk}(m_b); \quad b' \leftarrow A_2^{O^{\mathsf{pca}}_{sk}}(st, (t^*, c^*)) \\
\quad \textbf{return bit } b'. \\
\hline
\end{array}
$$

Fig. 2. Experiment of $\mathsf{Expt}^{\mathsf{pca}\text{-}b}_{\Pi,A}$

2.2 Trapdoor Commitments

We define a trapdoor commitment scheme. Let $\mathsf{TCOM} = (\mathsf{Gen}^{\mathsf{tc}}, \mathsf{Com}^{\mathsf{tc}}, \mathsf{TCom}^{\mathsf{tc}}, \mathsf{TCol}^{\mathsf{tc}})$ be a tuple of the following four algorithms. $\mathsf{Gen}^{\mathsf{tc}}$ is a PPT algorithm takes as input security parameter κ and outputs a pair of public and trap-door keys (pk, tk). $\mathsf{Com}^{\mathsf{tc}}$ is a PPT algorithm takes as input pk and message $x \in \{0,1\}^{\lambda_m}$ committed to, chooses $r \leftarrow \mathsf{COIN}^{\mathsf{com}}$, and outputs a $\psi = \mathsf{Com}^{\mathsf{tc}}_{pk}(m; r)$. $\mathsf{TCom}^{\mathsf{tc}}$ is a PPT algorithm takes as input tk and outputs $(\psi, \chi) \leftarrow \mathsf{TCom}^{\mathsf{tc}}_{tk}(1^\kappa)$. $\mathsf{TCol}^{\mathsf{tc}}$ is a DPT algorithm that takes $(tk, \psi, \chi, \hat{x})$ where $\hat{x} \in \{0,1\}^{\lambda_m}$ and outputs $\hat{r} \in \mathsf{COIN}^{\mathsf{com}}$ such that $\psi = \mathsf{Com}^{\mathsf{tc}}_{pk}(\hat{x}; \hat{r})$.

We call TCOM is a trapdoor commitment scheme if the following two conditions hold.

Trapdoor Collision. For all pk generated by $\mathsf{Gen}^{\mathsf{tc}}(1^\kappa)$, and all $x \in \{0,1\}^{\lambda_m(\kappa)}$, the following ensembles are statistically indistinguishable in κ:

$$\left\{ (\psi, x, r) \mid r \leftarrow \mathsf{COIN}^{\mathsf{com}}; \psi = \mathsf{Com}^{\mathsf{tc}}_{pk}(x; r) \right\}_{\kappa \in \mathbb{N}, pk \in \mathsf{Gen}^{\mathsf{tc}}(1^\kappa), x \in \{0,1\}^{\lambda_m}}$$

$$\overset{\mathsf{s}}{\approx} \left\{ (\psi, x, r) \mid (\psi, \chi) \leftarrow \mathsf{TCom}^{\mathsf{tc}}_{tk}(1^\kappa); r = \mathsf{TCol}^{\mathsf{tc}}_{tk}(\psi, \chi, x) \right\}_{\kappa \in \mathbb{N}, pk \in \mathsf{Gen}^{\mathsf{tc}}(1^\kappa), x \in \{0,1\}^{\lambda_m}}.$$

Computational Binding. For all non-uniform PPT adversary A,

$$\Pr\left[\begin{array}{l} pk \leftarrow \mathsf{Gen}^{\mathsf{tc}}(1^\kappa); (x_1, x_2, r_1, r_2) \leftarrow A(pk): \\ \mathsf{Com}^{\mathsf{tc}}_{pk}(x_1; r_1) = \mathsf{Com}^{\mathsf{tc}}_{pk}(x_2; r_2) \wedge (x_1 \neq x_2) \end{array} \right] = \mathsf{negl}(\kappa).$$

2.3   Sigma Protocol

Let L be an NP language and R_L be the relation derived from L. Let $\Sigma = (\mathsf{P}^{\mathsf{com}}_\Sigma, \mathsf{P}^{\mathsf{ans}}_\Sigma, \mathsf{V}^{\mathsf{vrfy}}_\Sigma, \mathsf{simP}^{\mathsf{com}}_\Sigma)$ be a tuple of algorithms (associated with L) as follows:

- $\mathsf{P}^{\mathsf{com}}_\Sigma$ is a PPT algorithm that takes $(x, w) \in R_L$ and outputs $(\alpha, \xi) \leftarrow \mathsf{P}^{\mathsf{com}}_\Sigma(x, w)$. For simplicity, we assume that ξ is inner coins of $\mathsf{P}^{\mathsf{com}}_\Sigma$.
- $\mathsf{P}^{\mathsf{ans}}_\Sigma$ is a DPT algorithm that takes (x, w, ξ, β) and outputs $\gamma = \mathsf{P}^{\mathsf{ans}}_\Sigma(x, w, \xi, \beta)$ where $\beta \in \{0,1\}^{\lambda_{\mathsf{ch}}}$.
- $\mathsf{V}^{\mathsf{vrfy}}_\Sigma$ is a DPT algorithm that accepts or rejects $(x, \alpha, \beta, \gamma)$.
- $\mathsf{simP}^{\mathsf{com}}_\Sigma$ is a PPT algorithm that takes (x, β) and outputs $(\alpha, \beta, \gamma) \leftarrow \mathsf{simP}^{\mathsf{com}}_\Sigma(x, \beta)$.

Σ is called a Sigma protocol if it satisfies the following requirements:

Completeness: For every $(x, w) \in R_L$, every $(\alpha, \xi) \in \mathsf{P}^{\mathsf{com}}_\Sigma(x, w)$, and every $\beta \in \{0,1\}^{\lambda_{\mathsf{ch}}}$, it always holds that $\mathsf{V}^{\mathsf{vrfy}}_\Sigma(x, \alpha, \beta, \gamma) = 1$ where $\gamma = \mathsf{P}^{\mathsf{ans}}_\Sigma(x, w, \xi, \beta)$.

Special Soundness: If there are two different accepting conversations for the same α on x, i.e., (α, β, γ) and $(\alpha, \beta', \gamma')$, with $\beta \neq \beta'$, it must hold that $x \in L$ and there is an efficient extractor that takes (α, β, γ) and $(\alpha, \beta', \gamma')$ as input and outputs w such that $(x, w) \in R_L$. We call such a pair a *collision* on x. Special soundness implies that there is at most one e such that $\mathsf{V}^{\mathsf{vrfy}}_\Sigma(x, \alpha, \beta, \gamma) = 1$ for every $x \notin L$ and every α.

Honest-Verifier Statistical Zero-Knowledgeness (HVSZK): For all $(x, w) \in R_L$, and all $\beta \in \{0,1\}^{\lambda_{\mathsf{ch}}}$, the following ensembles are statistically indistinguishable in κ:

$$\{\mathsf{simP}^{\mathsf{com}}_\Sigma(x, \beta; r_\gamma)\}_{\kappa \in \mathbb{N}, (x,w) \in R_L, \beta \in \{0,1\}^{\lambda_{\mathsf{ch}}}}$$

$$\overset{\mathsf{s}}{\approx} \{(\mathsf{P}^{\mathsf{com}}_\Sigma(x, w; \xi)_1, \beta, \mathsf{P}^{\mathsf{ans}}_\Sigma(x, w, \xi, \beta))\}_{\kappa \in \mathbb{N}, (x,w) \in R_L, \beta \in \{0,1\}^{\lambda_{\mathsf{ch}}}},$$

where $\mathsf{P}^{\mathsf{com}}_\Sigma(x, w)_1$ denotes the first output of $\mathsf{P}^{\mathsf{com}}_\Sigma(x, w)$. Here the probability of the left-hand side is taken over random variable r_γ and the right-hand side is taken over random variable ξ.

3 Universal Composable Framework

The UC framework defines a non-uniform PPT environment machine $\mathcal{Z}$ that oversees the execution of a protocol in one of two worlds. In both worlds, there are an PPT adversary and honest parties (some of which may be corrupted by the adversary). In the *real world*, the real protocol is run among the parties with some possible attacks given by the real-world adversary. In the *ideal world*, there additionally exists a trusted uncorrupted party, *ideal functionality* $\mathcal{F}$, where the honest parties in the ideal world do not interact with each other and instead send their inputs to the ideal functionality $\mathcal{F}$, which carries out the computation of the protocol in the trusted manner and sends back to the outputs to each party. We say that protocol π UC-realizes ideal functionality $\mathcal{F}$ if there exists an ideal-world adversary (simulator) $\mathcal{S}$ such that no environment $\mathcal{Z}$ can distinguish the real world where it runs with the real adversary $\mathcal{A}$ from the ideal world where it runs with the ideal-world adversary (simulator) $\mathcal{S}$.

In both worlds, the environment adaptively chooses the inputs for the honest parties and receives the outputs that they get. The environment can control the adversary and order it to corrupt any honest party at the beginning of the execution of the protocol (**static corruption**) or at any timing during the execution of the protocol (**adaptive corruption**). When a honest party is corrupted, the adversary may read the inner state of the honest party and fully control it. In the ideal world, after a party is corrupted, the ideal-world adversary $\mathcal{S}$ may access to the ideal functionality as the party does. The environment can see the *inside* of the execution of the protocol – the actual interactions between the honest parties or between the honest parties and the adversary – via the adversary's view. Since there is no interaction between the honest parties or between the honest parties and the adversary in the ideal world, the ideal-world simulator has to simulate the real-world adversary's view as it comes from the inside of the protocol in the real world.

We consider a model with ideal authentication channels, and so the adversary is allowed to read the messages sent by uncorrupted honest party but cannot modify them. Our protocols are executed in the common reference string (CRS) model. This means that the protocol is run in a hybrid model where the parties have access to an ideal functionality $\mathcal{F}_{\mathsf{crs}}$ that chooses a CRS according to the prescribed distribution and hands it to any party that requests it. Our adaptively UC-secure protocol requires the **secure erasure** assumption that the honest parties can securely erase their unnecessary inner states, as with [3,24].

We denote by $\mathrm{IDEAL}_{\mathcal{F},\mathcal{S}^{\mathcal{A}},\mathcal{Z}}(\kappa, z)$ the output of the environment $\mathcal{Z}$ with input z after an ideal execution with the ideal adversary (simulator) $\mathcal{S}$ and functionality $\mathcal{F}$, with security parameter κ. We only consider black-box simulators $\mathcal{S}$ and denote the simulator by $\mathcal{S}^{\mathcal{A}}$, which means that it works with the adversary $\mathcal{A}$ attacking the real protocol. We denote by $\mathrm{HYBRID}_{\pi,\mathcal{A},\mathcal{Z}}^{\mathcal{F}_{\mathsf{crs}}}(\kappa, z)$ the output of the environment $\mathcal{Z}$ with input z after an execution of the protocol π in the $\mathcal{F}_{\mathsf{crs}}$ hybrid model (or in the real world in the CRS model). Informally, a protocol π **UC-realizes a functionality** $\mathcal{F}$ in the $\mathcal{F}_{\mathsf{crs}}$ hybrid model if there exists a PPT simulator $\mathcal{S}$ such that for every non-uniform PPT environment $\mathcal{Z}$ every PPT adversary $\mathcal{A}$, and every polynomial $p(\cdot)$, it holds that

$$\{\text{IDEAL}_{\mathcal{F},\mathcal{S}^{\mathcal{A}},\mathcal{Z}}(\kappa,z)\}_{\kappa\in\mathbb{N},z\in\{0,1\}^{p(\kappa)}} \overset{c}{\approx} \{\text{HYBRID}_{\pi,\mathcal{A},\mathcal{Z}}^{\mathcal{F}_{\text{crs}}}(\kappa,z)\}_{\kappa\in\mathbb{N},z\in\{0,1\}^{p(\kappa)}}.$$

The importance of the universal composability framework is that it satisfies a composition theorem that states that any protocol that is universally composable is secure when it runs concurrently with many other arbitrary protocols. For more details, see [5].

We consider UC commitment schemes that can be used repeatedly under a single common reference string (**re-usable common reference string**). The multi-commitment ideal functionality $\mathcal{F}_{\text{MCOM}}$ from [7] is the ideal functionality of such commitments. We formally provide it in Fig. 3.

Functionality $\mathcal{F}_{\text{MCOM}}$

$\mathcal{F}_{\text{MCOM}}$ proceeds as follows, running with parties, $P_1, \ldots, P_n$, and an adversary $\mathcal{S}$:

- **Commit phase:** Upon receiving input $(\texttt{commit}, \texttt{sid}, \texttt{ssid}, P_i, P_j, x)$ from P_i, proceed as follows: If a tuple $(\texttt{commit}, \texttt{sid}, \texttt{ssid}, \ldots)$ with the same $(\texttt{sid}, \texttt{ssid})$ was previously recorded, does nothing. Otherwise, record the tuple $(\texttt{sid}, \texttt{ssid}, P_i, P_j, x)$ and send $(\texttt{receipt}, \texttt{sid}, \texttt{ssid}, P_i, P_j)$ to P_j and $\mathcal{S}$.
- **Reveal phase:** Upon receiving input $(\texttt{open}, \texttt{sid}, \texttt{ssid})$ from P_i, proceed as follows: If a tuple $(\texttt{sid}, \texttt{ssid}, P_i, P_j, x)$ was previously recorded, then send $(\texttt{reveal}, \texttt{sid}, \texttt{ssid}, P_i, P_j, x)$ to P_j and $\mathcal{S}$. Otherwise, does nothing.

Fig. 3. The ideal multi-commitment functionality

4 Our Proposal

For the space limitation, we focus on the adaptively UC-secure case. The static case is just a simplified version of the adaptive case and hence the proof is omitted to avoid a redundant exposition.

4.1 Our Adaptively UC-Secure Commitment with Erasure

We start by explaining the basic idea of Lindell's scheme [24]. As mentioned before, UC commitments require *extractability* and *equivocability*. Therefore, it is natural to use a PKE scheme as an extractable commitment scheme in the CRS model, where the committer commits to a secret value by encrypting it using public-key pk put in the common reference string. In the simulation, the simulator can choose the public-key along with the corresponding secret-key and use it by extracting the committed value. However, UC commitments should be equivocable at the same time. So, it is not possible at the decommit phase to simply reveal the committed value and the randomness used to encrypt, because encryptions are perfectly binding. Therefore, the committer instead sends the committed value m and makes *a concurrent (straight-line) non-malleable zero-knowledge proof* such that CT is a proper ciphertext of m. The straight-line zero-knowledge simulation is needed, because in the UC setting, the rewinding simulation is not allowed. In addition, concurrent non-malleability is needed because the simulator makes a number of *fake* proofs (i.e., valid (simulated) proofs on false statements), but ensures that the adversary cannot produce any fake proof even after it sees many fake ones. To do so, Lindell utilized a dual mode encryption scheme, an IND-CCA secure PKE scheme, and a Sigma protocol. To make the scheme secure against the adaptive corruptions, he additionally used a trapdoor commitment scheme. It enables the committer to switch the order of messages in the proof and to run most of the proof in the commit phase. Then, the committer can erase the randomness used to encrypt before sending ciphertext CT, which makes the scheme adaptively UC-secure with erasure. Blazy et al. [3] showed that the dual mode encryption can be removed from the proofs in both static and adaptive cases. By this observation, they improved the number of the rounds from five to three at the commit phase in the adaptive case (resp. from four to three at the decommit phase in the static case). See Table 1.

Our starting point is the BCPV adaptively UC-secure commitment scheme. Before exposing the difference, we give the description of our adaptively UC-secure commitment scheme.

The Adaptively UC-Secure Commitment Scheme. Let $\Pi = (\mathbf{K}, \mathbf{E}, \mathbf{D})$ be a tag-based PKE scheme. Let $\Sigma = (\mathsf{P}_\Sigma^{\mathsf{com}}, \mathsf{P}_\Sigma^{\mathsf{ans}}, \mathsf{V}_\Sigma^{\mathsf{vrfy}}, \mathsf{simP}_\Sigma^{\mathsf{com}})$ be a Sigma protocol on a language such that

$$L = \{(\mathsf{pk}^{\mathsf{enc}}, m, t, \mathsf{CT}) \mid \exists w \in \mathsf{COIN}^{\mathsf{enc}} \text{ s.t. } \mathsf{CT} = \mathbf{E}_{\mathsf{pk}^{\mathsf{enc}}}^t(m; w)\}.$$

Let $\mathsf{TCOM} = (\mathsf{Gen}^{\mathsf{tc}}, \mathsf{Com}^{\mathsf{tc}}, \mathsf{TCom}^{\mathsf{tc}}, \mathsf{TCol}^{\mathsf{tc}})$ be a trap-door commitment scheme. Our adaptively UC-secure commitment scheme is constructed as follows.

Common Reference String. The trusted party computes $(\mathsf{pk}^{\mathsf{enc}}, \mathsf{sk}^{\mathsf{enc}}) \leftarrow \mathbf{K}(1^\kappa)$ and $(\mathsf{pk}^{\mathsf{tc}}, \mathsf{tk}^{\mathsf{tc}}) \leftarrow \mathsf{Gen}^{\mathsf{tc}}(1^\kappa)$. It chooses a collision-resistant hash $H \leftarrow \mathbb{H}$ such that $H : \{0,1\}^* \rightarrow \{0,1\}^{\lambda_m}$ and sets $\mathsf{crs} = (\mathsf{pk}^{\mathsf{enc}}, \mathsf{pk}^{\mathsf{tc}}, H)$.

The Commit Protocol.

1. Upon receiving $(\mathsf{commit}, \mathsf{sid}, \mathsf{ssid}, C, R, m)$ where $m \in \mathsf{MSP}_{\mathsf{pk}^{\mathsf{enc}}}$, committer C sets $t = (\mathsf{sid}, \mathsf{ssid}, C, R)$, chooses random $w \leftarrow \mathsf{COIN}_{\mathsf{pk}^{\mathsf{enc}}}$, and computes $\mathsf{CT} = \mathbf{E}_{\mathsf{pk}^{\mathsf{enc}}}(t, m; w)$.
2. Let $L = \{(\mathsf{pk}^{\mathsf{enc}}, m, t, \mathsf{CT}) \mid \exists w \in \mathsf{COIN}^{\mathsf{enc}} \text{ s.t. } \mathsf{CT} = \mathbf{E}_{\mathsf{pk}^{\mathsf{enc}}}(t, m; w)\}$. C computes $(\alpha, \xi) \leftarrow \mathsf{P}_\Sigma^{\mathsf{com}}(x, w)$ as the first message of Sigma protocol on $x = (\mathsf{pk}^{\mathsf{enc}}, m, t, \mathsf{CT})$.
3. C computes $\phi = H(t, x, \alpha)$ where $t = (\mathsf{sid}, \mathsf{ssid}, C, R)$.
4. C chooses random $r_{\mathsf{tc}} \leftarrow \mathsf{COIN}^{\mathsf{com}}$ and computes $\psi = \mathsf{Com}_{\mathsf{pk}^{\mathsf{tc}}}^{\mathsf{tc}}(\phi; r_{\mathsf{tc}})$.
5. C sends (t, ψ) to receiver R.

6. Receiver R checks $t = (\texttt{sid}, \texttt{ssid}, C, R)$. If there is nothing wrong, then it sends back $\beta \leftarrow \{0,1\}^{\lambda_{\text{ch}}}$.
7. C computes $\gamma = \mathsf{P}_\Sigma^{\text{ans}}(x, w, \xi, \beta)$.
8. C erases (w, ξ).
9. C sends CT to R.
10. R stores $(t, \mathsf{CT}, \psi, \beta)$ and outputs $(\texttt{receipt}, \texttt{sid}, \texttt{ssid}, C, R)$.

The Decommit Protocol.

1. Upon receiving $(\texttt{open}, \texttt{sid}, \texttt{ssid})$, committer C sends $(t, m, \alpha, \gamma, r_{\text{tc}})$ to receiver R where $t = (\texttt{sid}, \texttt{ssid}, C, R)$.
2. R computes $\phi = H(t, x, \alpha)$, where $x = (\mathsf{pk}^{\text{enc}}, m, t, \mathsf{CT})$, and verifies $\psi = \mathsf{Com}_{\mathsf{pk}^{\text{tc}}}^{\text{tc}}(\phi; r_{\text{tc}})$ and $\mathsf{V}_\Sigma^{\text{vrfy}}(x, (\alpha, \beta, \gamma)) = 1$. If all relations hold, R accepts and outputs $(\texttt{reveal}, \texttt{sid}, \texttt{ssid}, C, R, m)$.

Protocol Idea. The difference of our scheme from the BCPV scheme is the following two: Our scheme commits to ciphertext CT and the first message of the Sigma prorocol, denoted α, in the same *sealed envelope* ψ, whereas the BCPV scheme commits to CT and α in the distinct envelopes, ψ_1 and ψ_2, respectively. However, the committer can simply reveal CT (without any witness) at the commit phase and postpone to show the *witness* that ψ_1 really contains CT until the decommit phase. So, the two envelops can be unified. This is because in the ideal world, the value $\tilde{m}$ extracted by the simulator at the commit phase is revealed to the environment only when the corrupted committer (controlled by the adversary) successfully executes the decommit phase.

The second improvement comes from realizing that IND-PCA secure PKE [1] suffices, instead of IND-CCA secure PKE. We note that a simplified variant of Cramer-Shoup scheme, the Short Cramer-Shoup (SCS) scheme [1], is IND-PCA secure. The ciphertext of the SCS scheme consists of three group elements, instead of four. Hence, the first message of the Sigma protocol is also reduced to three group elements (instead of four).

We informally explain the reason that IND-PCA security suffices. In the ideal world, the simulator simulates an honest committer without knowing the committed *value* at the commit phase. In addition, when interacting with a corrupted committer as an honest receiver, the simulator must extract the committed value m' that the corrupted committer has committed to before the decommit phase. The extracted value $\tilde{m}'$ is revealed to the environment when the corrupted committer successfully executes the decommit phase. Therefore, if the extracted value is different from the value opened by the corrupted committer, the environment can distinguish the real world from the ideal world. By construction, at the decomit phase, a committer opens the committed value m' with the proof that CT is a proper ciphertext of m'. If it is a real proof, $\tilde{m}' = m'$ always holds. As long as the adversary only see the real proofs produced by the honest committer (or the simulator), the corrupted committer (controlled by the adversary) cannot make a fake proof (i.e., a "valid" proof on a false statement), because of the binding property of TCOM and the soundness property of the Sigma protocol. Hence, the valid proofs produced by the corrupted committer should be real. Thus, the extracted value $\widetilde{m}'$ should be the same as the opened value m'. This corresponds to Game 1. In Game 2, the simulator simulates the honest committer, by producing the simulated proofs on the *true* statements *that* $\mathsf{CT} = \mathbf{E}_{pk}(m)$ *is a proper ciphertext of m*. Still, the adversary cannot make a fake proof. This comes from the trapdoor collision property of TCOM and the HVSZK property of the Sigma protocol. Indeed, the simulated proofs on the true statements are statistically indistinguishable from the real proofs. In the next game, the simulator finally makes *fake* proofs when simulating the honest committer, i.e., simulated proofs on the *false* statements *that* $\mathsf{CT} = \mathbf{E}_{pk}(0)$ *is a proper ciphertext of m*. Here, to prove the environment's view is indistinguishable from that in the former game, the works of [3,24] rely on the power of IND-CCA secure PKE. However, *it is an overkill*. In Game 2, we know that the adversary cannot make a fake proof. Hence, if it can make a fake proof, it means that we are playing the latter game. To realize in which game we are playing, *we need the power of the PCA oracle*. We can then construct an IND-PCA adversary A whose advantage can be reduced to the probability of distinguishing these two games. If the adversary makes a fake proof, then A can see, with the power of the PCA oracle, that it is playing in the latter game. Then, it can halt and make a precise decision. If the adversary does not make fake proofs, then A can perfectly simulate either of two games according to which message, $\mathbf{E}_{pk}(m)$ or $\mathbf{E}_{pk}(0)$, is encrypted. We let A output the output of the environment. Then, if the difference of the environment's output in the two games is significant, the advantage of A in the IND-PCA game is also significant, which contradicts IND-PCA security.

We now state the main theorem.

Theorem 1. *Let* Π *be IND-PCA. Then, the above construction UC-securely realizes the* $\mathcal{F}_{\mathsf{MCOM}}$ *functionality in the* $\mathcal{F}_{\mathsf{CRS}}$-*hybrid model against the adaptive corruptions with secure erasure.*

Due to the space limitation, we provide the formal proof in the extended version [18].

4.2 Our Static UC-Secure Commitment

Our static UC-secure commitment scheme is constructed as follows.

Common Reference String. The trusted party computes $(\mathsf{pk}^{\mathsf{enc}}, \mathsf{sk}^{\mathsf{enc}}) \leftarrow \mathbf{K}(1^\kappa)$ and $(\mathsf{pk}^{\mathsf{tc}}, \mathsf{tk}^{\mathsf{tc}}) \leftarrow \mathsf{Gen}^{\mathsf{tc}}(1^\kappa)$. It chooses a collision-resistant hash $H \leftarrow \mathbb{H}$ such that $H : \{0,1\}^* \rightarrow \{0,1\}^{\lambda_m}$ and sets $\mathsf{crs} = (\mathsf{pk}^{\mathsf{enc}}, \mathsf{pk}^{\mathsf{tc}}, H)$.

The Commit Protocol.

1. Upon receiving $(\mathsf{commit}, \mathsf{sid}, \mathsf{ssid}, C, R, m)$ where $m \in \mathsf{MSP}_{\mathsf{pk}^{\mathsf{enc}}}$, committer C sets $t = (\mathsf{sid}, \mathsf{ssid}, C, R)$, chooses random $w \leftarrow \mathsf{COIN}_{\mathsf{pk}^{\mathsf{enc}}}$, and computes $\mathsf{CT} = \mathbf{E}_{\mathsf{pk}^{\mathsf{enc}}}(t, m; w)$.
2. C sends (t, CT) to receiver R.
3. R stores (t, CT) and outputs $(\mathsf{receipt}, t)$.

The Decommit Protocol.

1. Upon receiving $(\mathsf{open}, \mathsf{sid}, \mathsf{ssid})$, committer C sets $t = (\mathsf{sid}, \mathsf{ssid}, C, R)$, and computes $(\alpha, \xi) \leftarrow \mathsf{P}_\Sigma^{\mathsf{com}}(x, w)$ as the first message of Sigma protocol on $x = (\mathsf{pk}^{\mathsf{enc}}, m, t, \mathsf{CT})$ for $L = \{(\mathsf{pk}^{\mathsf{enc}}, m, t, \mathsf{CT}) \mid \exists w \in \mathsf{COIN}^{\mathsf{enc}} \text{ s.t. } \mathsf{CT} = \mathbf{E}_{\mathsf{pk}^{\mathsf{enc}}}(t, m; w)\}$.
2. C computes $\phi = H(t, x, \alpha)$ where $t = (\mathsf{sid}, \mathsf{ssid}, C, R)$.
3. C chooses random $r_{\mathsf{tc}} \leftarrow \mathsf{COIN}^{\mathsf{com}}$ and computes $\psi = \mathsf{Com}_{\mathsf{pk}^{\mathsf{tc}}}^{\mathsf{tc}}(\phi; r_{\mathsf{tc}})$.
4. C sends (t, ψ) to receiver R.
5. Receiver R checks $t = (\mathsf{sid}, \mathsf{ssid}, C, R)$. If there is nothing wrong, then it sends back $\beta \leftarrow \{0,1\}^{\lambda_{\mathsf{ch}}}$.
6. C computes $\gamma = \mathsf{P}_\Sigma^{\mathsf{ans}}(x, w, \xi, \beta)$.
7. Committer C sends $(t, m, \alpha, \gamma, r_{\mathsf{tc}})$ to receiver R where $t = (\mathsf{sid}, \mathsf{ssid}, C, R)$.
8. R computes $\phi = H(t, x, \alpha)$, where $x = (\mathsf{pk}^{\mathsf{enc}}, m, t, \mathsf{CT})$, and verifies $\psi = \mathsf{Com}_{\mathsf{pk}^{\mathsf{tc}}}^{\mathsf{tc}}(\phi; r_{\mathsf{tc}})$ and $\mathsf{V}_\Sigma^{\mathsf{vrfy}}(x, (\alpha, \beta, \gamma)) = 1$. If all relations hold, R accepts and outputs $(\mathsf{reveal}, \mathsf{sid}, \mathsf{ssid}, C, R, m)$.

Theorem 2. *Let* PKE *be IND-PCA. Then, the above construction UC-realizes the* $\mathcal{F}_{\mathsf{MCOM}}$ *functionality in the* $\mathcal{F}_{\mathsf{CRS}}$*-hybrid model against the static corruptions.*

The proof is omitted due to the similarity of the proof of Theorem 1.

4.3   Actual Instantiations

In the above constructions, we use the following building blocks.

The Short Cramer-Shoup (Tag-PKE) Scheme $\Pi^{\mathsf{pca}} = (\mathbf{K}, \mathbf{E}, \mathbf{D})$. This is a Tag-PKE variant of the short version of Cramer-Shoup (SCS) cryptosystem introduced in [1].

- $\mathbf{K}(1^\kappa, (\mathbb{G}, q))$: It picks up hash function $H' : \{0,1\}^* \to \mathbb{Z}/q\mathbb{Z}$ and a random generator g in $\mathbb{G}$. It picks up independent random elements $x_e, x_1, x_2, y_1, y_2 \leftarrow \mathbb{Z}/q\mathbb{Z}$ and computes $h = g^{x_e}$, $c = g^{x_1} h^{x_2}$, and $d = g^{y_1} h^{y_2}$. It finally outputs $(\mathsf{pk}^{\mathsf{enc}}, \mathsf{sk}^{\mathsf{enc}}) = ((\mathbb{G}, q, H', g, h, c, d), (x_e, x_1, x_2, y_1, y_2))$.
- $\mathbf{E}_{\mathsf{pk}^{\mathsf{enc}}}(t, m)$: To encrypt $m \in \mathbb{G}$ on tag $t \in \{0,1\}^\kappa$, it picks up random $w \leftarrow \mathsf{COIN}^{\mathsf{enc}}$, sets $\tau = H'(t, g^w)$, and outputs $\mathsf{CT} = (g^w, mh^w, (c^\tau d)^w)$.
- $\mathbf{D}_{\mathsf{sk}^{\mathsf{enc}}}(t, \mathsf{CT})$: It first parses $\mathsf{CT} = (C_1, C_2, C_3)$ and computes $m = C_2 C_1^{-x_e}$. It aborts if $C_3 = C_1^{\tau x_1 + y_1}(C_2/m)^{\tau x_2 + y_2}$ where $\tau = H(t, C_1)$; otherwise, it outputs m.

The SCS cryptosystem is proven (in [1]) IND-PCA secure if the DDH assumption holds and H' is a collision-resistant hash. The proof that the SCS Tag-PKE scheme is (the tag version of) IND-PCA secure defined in Sect. 2 is straightforward from the original proof in [1].

Pedersen Commitment $\mathsf{TCOM} = (\mathsf{Gen}^{\mathsf{tc}}, \mathsf{Com}^{\mathsf{tc}}, \mathsf{TCom}^{\mathsf{tc}}, \mathsf{TCol}^{\mathsf{tc}})$. The following is the description of Pedersen commitment scheme [28].

- $\mathsf{Gen}^{\mathsf{tc}}(1^\kappa, (\mathbb{G}, q, g))$: It picks up random $x_{\mathsf{tc}} \leftarrow \mathbb{Z}/q\mathbb{Z}$ and computes $\hat{h} = g^{x_{\mathsf{tc}}}$. It outputs $\mathsf{pk}^{\mathsf{tc}} = (\mathbb{G}, q, g, \hat{h})$ and $\mathsf{tk}^{\mathsf{tc}} = (\mathsf{pk}^{\mathsf{tc}}, x_{\mathsf{tc}})$.

- $\mathsf{Com}_{\mathsf{pk^{tc}}}^{\mathsf{tc}}(\phi)$: To commit to $\phi \in \{0,1\}^{\lambda_m}$, it picks up random $r_{\mathsf{tc}} \leftarrow \mathbb{Z}/q\mathbb{Z}$ and outputs $\psi = g^{r_{\mathsf{tc}}} \hat{h}^{\phi}$.
- $\mathsf{TCom}_{\mathsf{tk^{tc}}}^{\mathsf{tc}}(1^{\kappa})$: It picks up random $\xi \leftarrow \mathbb{Z}/q\mathbb{Z}$ and outputs $\psi = g^{\xi}$.
- $\mathsf{TCol}_{\mathsf{tk^{tc}}}^{\mathsf{tc}}(\xi, \hat{\phi})$: To open ψ to $\hat{\phi} \in \{0,1\}^{\lambda_m}$, it outputs $\hat{r}_{\mathsf{tc}} = \xi - \hat{\phi} \cdot x_{\mathsf{tc}} \mod q$. One can note that $\psi = g^{\hat{r}_{\mathsf{tc}}} \hat{h}^{\hat{\phi}}$.

The Pedersen commitment scheme holds the trapdoor collision property unconditionally and the computational binding property under the discrete log (DL) assumption on $\mathbb{G}$.

The Sigma Protocol on the Language Derived from the SCS Tag-PKE Scheme. Let

$$L^{\mathsf{enc}} = \{(\mathsf{pk}^{\mathsf{enc}}, m, t, \mathsf{CT}) \mid \exists w \text{ s.t. } C_1 = g^w, \ C_2 = m \cdot h^w, \text{ and } C_3 = (c^{\tau}d)^w\},$$

where $\tau = H'(t, C_1)$. Sigma protocol $\Sigma = (\mathsf{P}_{\Sigma}^{\mathsf{com}}, \mathsf{P}_{\Sigma}^{\mathsf{ans}}, \mathsf{V}_{\Sigma}^{\mathsf{vrfy}}, \mathsf{simP}_{\Sigma}^{\mathsf{com}})$ on L^{enc} is described as follows.

- $(\alpha, \xi) \leftarrow \mathsf{P}_{\Sigma}^{\mathsf{com}}(x, w)$, where $x = (\mathsf{pk}^{\mathsf{enc}}, m, \tau, \mathsf{CT})$ and $\alpha = (\alpha_1, \alpha_2, \alpha_3)$ such that $\xi \leftarrow \mathbb{Z}/q\mathbb{Z}$; $\alpha_1 = g^{\xi}$; $\alpha_2 = h^{\xi}$; and $\alpha_3 = (c^{\tau}d)^{\xi}$.
- $\gamma \leftarrow \mathsf{P}_{\Sigma}^{\mathsf{ans}}(x, w, \xi, \beta)$, where $\beta \in \{0,1\}^{\lambda_{\mathsf{ch}}}$ and $\gamma = \xi - \beta w \mod q$.
- $\mathsf{V}_{\Sigma}^{\mathsf{vrfy}}(x, (\alpha, \beta, \gamma)) = 1$ if and only if it holds that $\alpha_1 = g^{\gamma} C_1^{\beta}$, $\alpha_2 = h^{\gamma}(C_2/m)^{\beta}$, and $\alpha_3 = (c^{\tau}d)^{\gamma} C_3^{\beta}$.
- $(\alpha, \beta, \gamma) \leftarrow \mathsf{simP}_{\Sigma}^{\mathsf{com}}(x, \beta)$, where $\alpha = (\alpha_1, \alpha_2, \alpha_3)$ such that $\gamma \leftarrow \mathbb{Z}/q\mathbb{Z}$; $\alpha_1 = g^{\gamma} C_1^{\beta}$; $\alpha_2 = h^{\gamma}(C_2/m)^{\beta}$; $\alpha_3 = (c^{\tau}d)^{\gamma} C_3^{\beta}$.

Applied to Our Adaptively UC-Secure Commitment Scheme.

- Common Reference String: $\mathsf{crs} = (\mathbb{G}, q, H, H', g, h, c, d, \hat{h})$.
- The Commit phase:
  - Communication: $(\psi, \beta, \mathsf{CT}) \in \mathbb{G} \times \{0,1\}^{\lambda_{\mathsf{ch}}} \times \mathbb{G}^3$.
  - Committer's Computation: $w \leftarrow \mathbb{Z}/q\mathbb{Z}$; $\mathsf{CT} = (C_1, C_2, C_3) = (g^w, m \cdot h^w, (c^{\tau}d)^w)$ with $\tau = H'(t, C_1)$ for $t = (\mathsf{sid}, \mathsf{ssid}, C, R)$; $\xi \leftarrow \mathbb{Z}/q\mathbb{Z}$; $\alpha = (\alpha_1, \alpha_2, \alpha_3) = (g^{\xi}, h^{\xi}, (c^{\tau}d)^{\xi})$; $\gamma = \xi - \beta w \mod q$; $r_{\mathsf{tc}} \leftarrow \mathbb{Z}/q\mathbb{Z}$; $\psi = g^{\phi} \hat{h}^{r_{\mathsf{tc}}}$, where $\phi = H(t, x, \alpha)$ with $x = (\mathsf{pk}^{\mathsf{enc}}, m, t, \mathsf{CT})$.
  - Receiver's Computation: $\beta \leftarrow \{0,1\}^{\kappa}$.
- The Decommit phase:
  - Communication: $(m, \alpha, \gamma, r_{\mathsf{tc}})$ where $\alpha \in \mathbb{G}^3$ and $\gamma, r_{\mathsf{tc}} \in \mathbb{Z}/q\mathbb{Z}$.
  - Committer's Computation: None
  - Receiver's Computation: Verify $\psi = g^{\phi} \hat{h}^{r_{\mathsf{tc}}}$, $\alpha_1 = g^{\gamma} C_1^{\beta}$, $\alpha_2 = h^{\gamma}(C_3/m)^{\beta}$, and $\alpha_3 = (c^{\tau}d)^{\gamma} C_3^{\beta}$, where $\tau = H'(t, C_1)$ and $\phi = H(t, x, \alpha)$ with $t = (\mathsf{sid}, \mathsf{ssid}, C, R)$ and $x = (\mathsf{pk}^{\mathsf{enc}}, m, t, \mathsf{CT})$.

Applied to Our Static UC-Secure Commitment Scheme.

- Common Reference String: $\mathsf{crs} = (\mathbb{G}, q, H, H', g, h, c, d, \hat{h})$.
- The Commit phase:
  - Communication: $\mathsf{CT} \in \mathbb{G}$.
  - Committer's Computation: $w \leftarrow \mathbb{Z}/q\mathbb{Z}$; $\mathsf{CT} = (C_1, C_2, C_3) = (g^w, m \cdot h^w, (c^\tau d)^w)$ with $\tau = H'(t, C_1)$ for $t = (\mathsf{sid}, \mathsf{ssid}, C, R)$.
  - Receiver's Computation: None.
- The Decommit phase:
  - Communication: $(m, \psi, \alpha, \beta, \gamma, r_{\mathsf{tc}})$ where $\psi \in \mathbb{G}$, $\alpha \in \mathbb{G}^3$, $\beta \in \{0,1\}^{\lambda_{\mathsf{ch}}}$, and $\gamma, r_{\mathsf{tc}} \in \mathbb{Z}/q\mathbb{Z}$.
  - Committer's Computation: $\xi \leftarrow \mathbb{Z}/q\mathbb{Z}$; $\alpha = (\alpha_1, \alpha_2, \alpha_3) = (g^\xi, h^\xi, (c^\tau d)^\xi)$; $\gamma = \xi - \beta w \bmod q$; $r_{\mathsf{tc}} \leftarrow \mathbb{Z}/q\mathbb{Z}$; $\psi = g^\phi \hat{h}^{r_{\mathsf{tc}}}$, where $\phi = H(t, x, \alpha)$ with $x = (\mathsf{pk}^{\mathsf{enc}}, m, t, \mathsf{CT})$.
  - Receiver's Computation: $\beta \leftarrow \{0,1\}^\kappa$; Verify $\psi = g^\phi \hat{h}^{r_{\mathsf{tc}}}$, $\alpha_1 = g^\gamma C_1^\beta$, $\alpha_2 = h^\gamma (C_3/m)^\beta$, and $\alpha_3 = (c^\tau d)^\gamma C_3^\beta$, where $\tau = H'(t, C_1)$ and $\phi = H(t, x, \alpha)$ with $t = (\mathsf{sid}, \mathsf{ssid}, C, R)$ and $x = (\mathsf{pk}^{\mathsf{enc}}, m, t, \mathsf{CT})$.

Acknowledgments. We thank the members of public-key crypto study workshop at NTT and the anonymous reviewers of SCN 2016 for nice feedback in the early version of this work.

References

1. Abdalla, M., Benhamouda, F., Pointcheval, D.: Public-key encryption indistinguishable under plaintext-checkable attacks. In: Katz [21], pp. 332–352. See also http://eprint.iacr.org/2014/609
2. Bellare, M., Desai, A., Pointcheval, D., Rogaway, P.: Relations among notions of security for public-key encryption scheme. In: Krawczyk [23], pp. 26–45
3. Blazy, O., Chevalier, C., Pointcheval, D., Vergnaud, D.: Analysis and improvement of Lindell's UC-secure commitment schemes. In: Jacobson, M., Locasto, M., Mohassel, P., Safavi-Naini, R. (eds.) ACNS 2013. LNCS, vol. 7954, pp. 534–551. Springer, Heidelberg (2013)
4. Camenisch, J.L., Shoup, V.: Practical verifiable encryption and decryption of discrete logarithms. In: Boneh, D. (ed.) CRYPTO 2003. LNCS, vol. 2729, pp. 126–144. Springer, Heidelberg (2003)
5. Canetti, R.: Universally composable security: a new paradigm for cryptographic protocols. In: FOCS 2001, pp. 136–145. IEEE Computer Society (2001). The full version available at Cryptology ePrint Archive http://eprint.iacr.org/2000/067
6. Canetti, R., Fischlin, M.: Universally composable commitments. In: Kilian, J. (ed.) CRYPTO 2001. LNCS, vol. 2139, pp. 19–40. Springer, Heidelberg (2001)
7. Canetti, R., Lindell, Y., Ostrovsky, R., Sahai, A.: Universally composable two-party and multi-party secure computation. In: STOC 2002, pp. 494–503. ACM (2002). The full version is available at http://eprint.iacr.org/2002/140
8. Cascudo, I., Damgård, I., David, B., Döttling, N., Nielsen, J.B.: Rate-1, linear time and additively homomorphic UC commitments. IACR Cryptology ePrint Archive 2016:137 (2016)

9. Cascudo, I., Damgård, I., David, B.M., Giacomelli, I., Nielsen, J.B., Trifiletti, R.: Additively homomorphic UC commitments with optimal amortized overhead. In: Katz [21], pp. 495–515
10. Cramer, R., Shoup, V.: A practical public key cryptosystem provably secure against adaptive chosen ciphertext attack. In: Krawczyk [23], pp. 13–25
11. Damgård, I., David, B.M., Giacomelli, I., Nielsen, J.B.: Compact VSS and efficient homomorphic UC commitments. In: Sarkar and Iwata [30], pp. 213–232
12. Damgård, I., Groth, J.: Non-interactive and reusable non-malleable commitment schemes. In: STOC 2003, pp. 426–437. ACM (2003)
13. Damgård, I.B., Nielsen, J.B.: Perfect hiding and perfect binding universally composable commitment schemes with constant expansion factor. In: Yung, M. (ed.) CRYPTO 2002. LNCS, vol. 2442, pp. 581–596. Springer, Heidelberg (2002)
14. Feigenbaum, J. (ed.): CRYPTO 1991. LNCS, vol. 576. Springer, Heidelberg (1991)
15. Fischlin, M., Libert, B., Manulis, M.: Non-interactive and re-usable universally composable string commitments with adaptive security. In: Lee, D.H., Wang, X. (eds.) ASIACRYPT 2011. LNCS, vol. 7073, pp. 468–485. Springer, Heidelberg (2011)
16. Frederiksen, T.K., Jakobsen, T.P., Nielsen, J.B., Trifiletti, R.: On the complexity of additively homomorphic UC commitments. In: Kushilevitz, E., Malkin, T. (eds.) TCC 2016-A. LNCS, vol. 9562, pp. 542–565. Springer, Heidelberg (2016). doi:10.1007/978-3-662-49096-9_23
17. Fujisaki, E.: All-but-many encryption - a new framework for fully-equipped UC commitments. In: Sarkar and Iwata [30], pp. 426–447
18. Fujisaki, E.: Improving practical UC-secure commitments based on the DDH assumption. IACR Cryptology ePrint Archive 2016;656 (2016)
19. Garay, J.A., Ishai, Y., Kumaresan, R., Wee, H.: On the complexity of UC commitments. In: Nguyen, P.Q., Oswald, E. (eds.) EUROCRYPT 2014. LNCS, vol. 8441, pp. 677–694. Springer, Heidelberg (2014)
20. Groth, J., Sahai, A.: Efficient noninteractive proof systems for bilinear groups. SIAM J. Comput. 41(5), 1193–1232 (2012)
21. Katz, J. (ed.): PKC 2015. LNCS, vol. 9020. Springer, Heidelberg (2015)
22. Kiltz, E.: Chosen-ciphertext security from tag-based encryption. In: Halevi, S., Rabin, T. (eds.) TCC 2006. LNCS, vol. 3876, pp. 581–600. Springer, Heidelberg (2006)
23. Krawczyk, H. (ed.): CRYPTO 1998. LNCS, vol. 1462. Springer, Heidelberg (1998)
24. Lindell, Y.: Highly-efficient universally-composable commitments based on the DDH assumption. In: Paterson, K.G. (ed.) EUROCRYPT 2011. LNCS, vol. 6632, pp. 446–466. Springer, Heidelberg (2011)
25. MacKenzie, P.D., Reiter, M.K., Yang, K.: Alternatives to non-malleability: definitions, constructions, and applications. In: Naor, M. (ed.) TCC 2004. LNCS, vol. 2951, pp. 171–190. Springer, Heidelberg (2004)
26. Nishimaki, R., Fujisaki, E., Tanaka, K.: An efficient non-interactive universally composable string-commitment scheme. IEICE Trans. 95–A(1), 167–175 (2012)
27. Okamoto, T., Pointcheval, D.: REACT: rapid enhanced-security asymmetric cryptosystem transform. In: Naccache, D. (ed.) CT-RSA 2001. LNCS, vol. 2020, pp. 159–175. Springer, Heidelberg (2001)
28. Pedersen, T.P.: Non-interactive and information-theoretic secure verifiable secret sharing. In: Feigenbaum [14], pp. 129–140

29. Rackoff, C., Simon, D.R.: Non-interactive zero-knowledge proof of knowledge and chosen ciphertext attack. In: Feigenbaum [14], pp. 434–444
30. Sarkar, P., Iwata, T. (eds.): ASIACRYPT 2014. LNCS, vol. 8874. Springer, Heidelberg (2014)
31. Shoup, V.: A proposal for an ISO standard for public key encryption. Cryptology ePrint Archive, Report 2001/112, December 2001

The Whole is Less Than the Sum of Its Parts: Constructing More Efficient Lattice-Based AKEs

Rafael del Pino[1,2,3], Vadim Lyubashevsky[4(✉)], and David Pointcheval[1,2,3]

[1] INRIA, Paris, France
[2] École Normale Supérieure, Paris, France
Rafael.Del.Pino@ens.fr
[3] CNRS, Paris, France
[4] IBM Research Zurich, Rüschlikon, Switzerland

Abstract. Authenticated Key Exchange (AKE) is the backbone of internet security protocols such as TLS and IKE. A recent announcement by standardization bodies calling for a shift to quantum-resilient crypto has resulted in several AKE proposals from the research community. Because AKE can be generically constructed by combining a digital signature scheme with public key encryption (or a KEM), most of these proposals focused on optimizing the known KEMs and left the authentication part to the generic combination with digital signatures.

In this paper, we show that by simultaneously considering the secrecy and authenticity requirements of an AKE, we can construct a scheme that is more secure and with smaller communication complexity than a scheme created by a generic combination of a KEM with a signature scheme. Our improvement uses particular properties of lattice-based encryption and signature schemes and consists of two parts – the first part increases security, whereas the second reduces communication complexity.

We first observe that parameters for lattice-based encryption schemes are always set so as to avoid decryption errors, since many observations by the adversary of such failures usually leads to him recovering the secret key. But since one of the requirements of an AKE is that it be forward-secure, the public key must change every time. The intuition is therefore that one can set the parameters of the scheme so as to not care about decryption errors and everything should still remain secure. We show that this naive solution is not quite correct, but the intuition can be made to work by a small change in the scheme. Our new AKE, which now remains secure in case of decryption errors, fails to create a shared key with probability around 2^{-30}, but adds enough security that we are able to instantiate a KEM based on the NTRU assumption with rings of smaller dimension.

Our second improvement is showing that certain hash-and-sign lattice signatures can be used in "message-recovery" mode. In this mode, the signature size is doubled but this longer signature is enough to recover

Supported by the European Horizon 2020 ICT Project SAFEcrypto (H2020/2014–2020 Grant Agreement ICT-644729 – SAFECrypto), the French FUI Project FUI AAP 17 – CRYPTOCOMP, and the SNSF ERC Transfer Grant CRETP2-166734 – FELICITY. The full version of this work appears as an eprint Report 2016/435.

© Springer International Publishing Switzerland 2016
V. Zikas and R. De Prisco (Eds.): SCN 2016, LNCS 9841, pp. 273–291, 2016.
DOI: 10.1007/978-3-319-44618-9_15

an even longer message – thus the signature is longer but the message does not need to be sent. This is advantageous when signing relatively long messages, such as the public keys and ciphertexts generated by a lattice-based KEM. We show how this technique reduces the communication complexity of the generic construction of our AKE by around 20 %. Using a lattice-based signature in message-recovery mode is quite generic (i.e. it does not depend on the structure of the message), and so it may be used in AKE constructions that use a different KEM, or even simply as a way to reduce the transmission length of a message and its digital signature.

1   Introduction

Lattice-based cryptography has matured to the point that it is seen as a viable replacement to number-theoretic cryptography. There are very efficient public-key encryption schemes (and thus Key Encapsulation Mechanisms) based on the NTRU [14,15] and Ring-LWE problems [6,22,24,30], as well as digital signature schemes that are also based on NTRU [7,8,13] and Ring-LWE [11,21].

Once we have practical protocols for digital signatures and public key encryption / key encapsulation, it is clear that one can construct an authenticated key exchange (AKE) scheme, and even a forward-secure one which guarantees the key privacy after long-term authentication means are compromised. A rough outline for a simple construction is described in Fig. 1, which uses a generic key encapsulation scheme and a digital signature scheme. The simple idea is that Party 1 picks an encapsulation/decapsulation key pair $(\mathcal{K}_e, \mathcal{K}_d)$, sends the encapsulation key in an authenticated way to Party 2, which in turn uses it to encapsulate a random seed k, in an authenticated message. Only Party 1 is then able to decapsulate the seed k derived into a session key sk. Authentication means are the signing keys, and their compromise or the compromise of any future or past encryption/decryption keys does not have any impact on the privacy of the session encrypted under key sk.

1.1   Recent Work

There has been a lot of recent work that deals with proposing optimizations of lattice-based KEMs. The works of [2,4,6,30] gave constructions (and instantiations) of a KEM derived from the Ring-LWE encryption scheme [23], while the work of [14] optimized the parameters for a particular version of the NTRU KEM. All these papers left the authentication part of the AKE to known signature schemes and the generic composition in Fig. 1. The work of Zhang et al. [32] adapted the (H)MQV [18,19] discrete log-based AKE protocol to the Ring-LWE problem. But it seems that this approach leads to schemes that have larger communication complexity (for similar security levels) than the approach

Party 1   Party 2

$\texttt{Generate}(\mathcal{K}_d, \mathcal{K}_e)$

$\sigma_1 = \texttt{Sig}(\mathcal{K}_e)$ $\quad\xrightarrow{\mathcal{K}_e, \sigma_1}\quad$ $\texttt{Ver}(\mathcal{K}_e, \sigma_1)$
$\qquad\qquad\qquad\qquad\qquad (c, k) = \texttt{Enc}(\mathcal{K}_e)$

$\texttt{Ver}(c, \sigma_2)$ $\quad\xleftarrow{c, \sigma_2}\quad$ $\sigma_2 = \texttt{Sig}(c)$
$k' = \texttt{Dec}(\mathcal{K}_d, c)$

$sk' = H(\texttt{View}, k')$ $\qquad\qquad$ $sk = H(\texttt{View}, k)$

Fig. 1. A generic AKE construction from a KEM and a digital signature

in Fig. 1. Thus, it currently appears that the most efficient way of constructing lattice-based AKE schemes is a generic composition of a KEM with a digital signature scheme.

1.2 Our Contributions

In our work, we propose two enhancements to the generic AKE construction – allowing decapsulation errors, which increases security, and using digital signatures with message recovery, which decreases the communication.

Handling Decapsulation Errors. The security of lattice-based encryption / encapsulation schemes relies on the hardness of solving linear equations in the presence of noise. The larger the noise is (with respect to the field that we are working over), the harder it is to recover the solution. On the other hand, if the noise is too large, decryption may fail. These decryption failures are not just an inconvenience – their detection usually results in the adversary being able to recover the secret key (c.f. [17]). For this reason, stand-alone encryption schemes use parameters such that decryption failures occur with only a negligible probability.

In a forward-secure AKE, however, where the encryption keys are ephemeral, there is *intuitively* no danger of decryption failures (which will result in the users not agreeing on a shared key) since the users will restart and a fresh public key will be used in the next key-agreement attempt. The cost of a restart is an increase in the expected run-time and communication complexity of the scheme. For example, if one run of the protocol uses T of some resource and has a failure probability of ϵ, then the expected amount of this resource the complete protocol will require until it completes successfully is $T/(1 - \epsilon)$. For values of ϵ that are small, this is very close to T.

A natural idea to construct such an AKE is to take a KEM that may have decapsulation failures and plug it into the prototype in Fig. 1. This solution, however, is not necessarily secure. Consider an encapsulation scheme where *invalidly* formed ciphertexts immediately lead to the recovery of the *decapsu-lated* key[1]. The Adversary's attack would then involve intercepting the cipher-text sent by Party 2 and recovering the key k' that will be the one decapsulated by Party 1 in the event of a decapsulation error (which occurs with non-negligible probability). The Adversary and Party 1 now share a session key. While a KEM in which malformed ciphertexts can be opened by the Adversary to the decap-sulated key may appear to be contrived, it does show that the protocol in Fig. 1 cannot be proven to be secure when instantiated with a generic scheme with decryption failures.

Our first contribution (Sect. 4) is a construction of a forward-secure AKE that remains secure even when instantiated with a KEM that leads to decapsulation failures. In particular, we prove that our scheme is secure as long as recovering the *encapsulated* key is a hard problem (regardless of what happens during decap-sulation) – so essentially all we need for security is for the KEM to be a one-way function. The modification of the scheme is not particularly complicated – Party 2 simply needs to apply a hash function to k and include it in his message (see the informal description in Fig. 2 and the formal one in Fig. 3)– but the proof contains several subtleties.

In order to instantiate the AKE, we show that a KEM based on NTRU (Sect. 2) very naturally fits into the requirements of our generic construction. We give a quick description of it, and leave the full details to Sect. 2. The decapsula-tion key is a polynomial $\mathbf{g}$ with small coefficients (chosen according to Table 3) in the ring $\mathbb{Z}_q[\mathbf{x}]/\langle \mathbf{x}^n + 1 \rangle$ for $q = 12289$ and $n = 512$ or 1024. The encapsula-tion key is $\mathbf{h} = \mathbf{f}/\mathbf{g}$, where $\mathbf{f}$ is another polynomial with small coefficients. The encapsulation procedure works by picking two polynomials $\mathbf{r}$ and $\mathbf{e}$ with small coefficients and computing the ciphertext/shared key pair $(2\mathbf{hr} + \mathbf{e}, \mathbf{e} \bmod 2)$. To decapsulate the ciphertext $\mathbf{c} = 2\mathbf{hr} + \mathbf{e}$ using the decapsulation key $\mathbf{g}$, one computes

$$\mathbf{cg} \bmod q \bmod 2/\mathbf{g} = (2\mathbf{fr} + \mathbf{ge} \bmod q) \bmod 2/\mathbf{g} = \mathbf{e} \bmod 2,$$

which is the shared key. Note that for the above equality to hold, it is crucial that $2\mathbf{fr} + \mathbf{ge} \bmod q \bmod 2 = 2\mathbf{fr} + \mathbf{ge} \bmod 2$, which happens exactly when the coefficients of $\mathbf{f}, \mathbf{r}, \mathbf{e}, \mathbf{g}$ are small enough that a reduction modulo q does not take place. If a reduction does take place, then we will end up with a decapsulation error.

Because in our construction decapsulation errors are no longer a security risk, we can set the parameters such that these failures occur a non-negligible number

---

[1] It is simple to construct such a scheme. Suppose we have an encapsulation scheme (without decapsulation errors) with encapsulation procedure Enc and a decapsulation procedure where $\text{Dec}(\mathcal{K}_d, 0) = 0$. We modify it to a scheme where the encapsulation procedure Enc' runs Enc to obtain (c, k) and outputs it with probability $1 - \epsilon$. With probability ϵ, it outputs $(0, k)$. Notice that this new scheme is still secure (i.e. one-way) because k is still hard to recover (and actually information-theoretically hard to recover when $(0, k)$ is the output), but with probability ϵ, the decapsulated key is the constant $\text{Dec}(\mathcal{K}_d, 0) = 0$.

Party 1	Party 2
$\text{Generate}(\mathcal{K}_d, \mathcal{K}_e)$	

$$\sigma_1 = \text{Sig}(\mathcal{K}_e) \xrightarrow{\quad \mathcal{K}_e, \sigma_1 \quad} \text{Ver}(\mathcal{K}_e, \sigma_1)$$

$$(c, k) = \text{Enc}(\mathcal{K}_e)$$
$$a = H_2(\mathcal{K}_e, \sigma_1, c, k)$$

$$\text{Ver}(c, a, \sigma_2) \xleftarrow{\quad c, a, \sigma_2 \quad} \sigma_2 = \text{Sig}(c, a)$$
$$k' = \text{Dec}(\mathcal{K}_d, c)$$
$$\text{if } a \neq H_2(\mathcal{K}_e, \sigma_1, c, k')$$
$$\text{then RESTART}$$

$$sk' = H_1(\text{View}, k') \qquad\qquad sk = H_1(\text{View}, k)$$

Fig. 2. Informal AKE construction from encapsulation and digital signatures with decapsulation errors

of times – for example with probability 2^{-30}. If a failure does occur, then the protocol can be safely restarted. We believe that 2^{-30} is a low-enough failure probability that some external, for example, networking error may have a higher probability of occurring. Table 3 shows the security gained when we instantiate our scheme such that it has decapsulation error of 2^{-30} vs. 2^{-128}. We discuss the security of our proposals later in this section.

Signatures in Message Recovery Mode. Just as for signatures based on standard number-theoretic assumptions, lattice-based signatures come in two flavors – Fiat-Shamir and hash-and-sign.[2] The improvement we present in this paper is only for hash-and-sign signature schemes – in particular for the specific parameters of the scheme presented in [8]. We now give a brief description of that scheme, which combines the pre-image sampling algorithm from [10] with a particular instantiation of an NTRU lattice [12].

The public key is a polynomial $\mathbf{h} \in \mathbb{Z}_q[\mathbf{x}]/\langle \mathbf{x}^n + 1 \rangle$ which is equal to $\mathbf{f}/\mathbf{g}$, where the coefficients of $\mathbf{f}$ and $\mathbf{g}$ are somewhat small.[3] The secret key, which is a basis of a particular lattice induced by $\mathbf{h}$, allows the signer to find polynomials $\mathbf{s}_1, \mathbf{s}_2$ with small coefficients such that $\mathbf{h}\mathbf{s}_1 + \mathbf{s}_2 = H(m)$, where m is the message and H is a hash function modeled as a random oracle that maps $\{0, 1\}^*$ to random elements in $\mathbb{Z}_q[\mathbf{x}]/\langle \mathbf{x}^n + 1 \rangle$.

The signature of a message m is $(\mathbf{s}_1, \mathbf{s}_2)$, and the verification procedure checks that $\mathbf{s}_1, \mathbf{s}_2$ have small coefficients and that $\mathbf{h}\mathbf{s}_1 + \mathbf{s}_2 = H(m)$. Note that because $\mathbf{s}_2$ is completely determined by $\mathbf{s}_1$ and m, there is no reason to send it. Thus the signature can be just $\mathbf{s}_1, m$. For ease of exposition of our improvement,

---

[2] There are also lattice signature schemes that do not use random oracles, but those are much less practical.

[3] The distribution of $\mathbf{f}$ and $\mathbf{g}$ is different from the way the secret key is constructed for the KEM. In particular, we *do not* want $\mathbf{f}$ and $\mathbf{g}$ to be too small. Full details are provided in [8].

assume that the bit-length of m is a little less than the bit-length of elements in $\mathbb{Z}_q[\mathbf{x}]/\langle \mathbf{x}^n + 1\rangle$ (e.g. $n \log q - 256$ bits). Then rather than sending $\mathbf{s}_1, m$ as the signature, we will send $\mathbf{s}_1', \mathbf{s}_2'$ that satisfy the equation $\mathbf{hs}_1' + \mathbf{s}_2' = \mathbf{t}$ where $\mathbf{t}$ is the polynomial in $\mathbb{Z}_q[\mathbf{x}]/\langle \mathbf{x}^n + 1\rangle$ whose first coefficients are $m + F(H'(m))$ and its last $256/\lfloor \log q\rfloor$ coefficients are $H'(m)$. Here H' is a random oracle mapping $\{0,1\}^*$ to $\{0,1\}^{256}$ (thus its output fits into $256/\lfloor \log q\rfloor$ coefficients) and F is another random oracle whose output range is $n \log q - 256$ bits. Notice that if we send $\mathbf{s}_1'$ and $\mathbf{s}_2'$ as the signature, the message m can be recovered by first computing $\mathbf{t} = \mathbf{as}_1' + \mathbf{s}_2'$. Then from $\mathbf{t}$, we can recover $H'(m)$, then $F(H'(m))$, and finally m. More details (in particular how one would handle messages that are longer than $n \log q$ bits) is discussed in Sect. 3.2.

The main advantage of the message recovery signature scheme is that instead of sending the message m, one can send the shorter element $\mathbf{s}_2$. Note that if the message we are signing is short, then our technique of sending $\mathbf{s}_2$ instead of a message is counterproductive and should not be used.[4] The public key and the ciphertext of a KEM, however, are polynomials that are pseudorandom over $\mathbb{Z}_q[\mathbf{x}]/\langle \mathbf{x}^n + 1\rangle$, and so require $n \log q$ bits to represent, and their signatures would benefit from the message-recovery technique. The efficacy of the message recovery technique clearly does not depend on anything except the message size, and so it may also be appropriate to use in combination with other KEMs. In Table 2, we illustrate the savings of this technique when working over the ring $\mathbb{Z}_q[\mathbf{x}]/\langle x^{1024} + 1\rangle$. When combining our signature scheme with our KEM, or with the Ring-LWE based KEM in [2], the savings are about 20 %. Note that our complete scheme has less total communication complexity due to the fact that our NTRU KEM is a little bit more compact than the Ring-LWE one.

1.3 Putting Everything Together

Table 1 shows the communication complexity of our full AKE when instantiated with $n = 512$ and $n = 1024$ (the security of these choices will be discussed later) for the case of two-sided authentication and for the case of when only the second party needs to be authenticated (as is often the case in TLS). In the full version of this paper, we also describe a modification of our protocol in which the identities of the parties are hidden from a passive adversary (this is sometimes a desirable property and is an option in the IKE protocol). This anonymity property is impossible to achieve in a 2-round scheme,[5] and so a third round is required. Additionally, since maintaining anonymity requires the splitting of the key/signature pair usually sent in the first round, we cannot use the message-recovery technique there (but it can still be used when signing the

---

[4] We point out that this is in contrast to using message-recovery mode in other hash-and-sign signatures, such as RSA. In those cases, the signature size does not increase in message-recovery mode, and so this mode is always advantageous to use.

[5] The intuition is that the player who moves first has to send his signed message in the clear because there is no encryption key (public or private) available to him at the start of the protocol. Therefore a passive adversary can simply perform a verification procedure with that player's public verification key to see if he is indeed the sender.

Table 1. Parameter sizes and communication length for our AKE. We consider the versions where both parties authenticate themselves and the version in which only the server is authenticated.

	One-way authenticated KE		Two-way authenticated KE	
Dimension n	512	1024	512	1024
Modulus	12289	12289	12289	12289
First flow size (bits)	≈ 7200	≈ 14400	≈ 9800	≈ 19300
Second flow size (bits)	≈ 10300	≈ 19600	≈ 10300	≈ 19600
Signing key size (bits)	≈ 2100	≈ 3700	≈ 2100	≈ 3700
Verification key size (bits)	7168	14336	7168	14336

ciphertext in the second flow), thus the total communication complexity will be somewhat larger than in our 2-round scheme.

The comparison of our AKE with $n = 1024$ to the one in [2] is given in Table 2. Because [2] only proposed a KEM, we combine it with the digital signature scheme that we use for our KEM in this paper. One can see that our AKE is slightly shorter than the one from [2] for essentially the same security level. Also, the message-recovery technique reduces the communication lengths of both AKEs by the same amount.

1.4 Computational Efficiency

We will now discuss the efficiency of our AKE. The KEM part of our scheme requires generation of small polynomials and arithmetic operations in the ring $\mathbb{Z}_q[\mathbf{x}]/\langle \mathbf{x}^n + 1 \rangle$. Rather than generating polynomials with each coefficient being independently chosen from some distribution, we follow the original NTRU way of generating such polynomials by prescribing exactly how many of each coefficient the polynomial should have. Such polynomials can be created using n random swaps within an integer array. We remark that while such an algorithm would be weak to timing attacks the permutation can be done in constant time using a sorting network, as in e.g. [3], this incurs a small overhead resulting in a complexity of $O(n \log^2 n)$. Addition and subtraction similarly requires $O(n)$ integer operations. Multiplication and division can be done in quasi-linear time by employing the Number Theoretic Transform (i.e. FFT over a finite field) which has very efficient implementations (e.g. [20]). The prime $q = 12289$ was chosen such that $x^n + 1$ (for $n = 512$ and $n = 1024$) splits into n linear terms and is therefore amenable to the number theory transform. We point out that this is the same ring that was used in [2,7], and those works produced schemes that were faster than number-theoretic schemes of comparable security parameters. The KEM part of our scheme is therefore very efficient.

Table 2. Comparison of our paper with [2]. For the comparison to be meaningful we consider the AKE obtained by adding a Hash-and-Sign signature (either without or with message-recovery) to the scheme in [2]. We illustrate the savings of message-recovery mode by presenting the naive generic AKE construction and one that uses the digital signature in message-recovery mode.

	New hope [2]		Our scheme	
Hash-and-Sign	Naive	Message-recovery	Naive	Message-recovery
First flow size (bits)	≈ 24000	≈ 19600	≈ 23300	≈ 18900
Second flow size (bits)	≈ 25800	≈ 21400	≈ 23600	≈ 19200
Total communication (bits)	≈ 49800	≈ 41000	≈ 46900	≈ 38100

Lattice-based signatures that use the hash-and sign approach use a technique known as lattice pre-image sampling [10, 27, 29] and this generally results in digital signatures that are longer and much less efficient to compute than those generated using the Fiat-Shamir approach [7, 11, 21]. But there has been a lot of recent work on trying to optimally (and securely) instantiate hash-and-sign signatures over polynomial rings. In [8], it was shown that hash-and-sign signatures over carefully-constructed NTRU lattices that are very similar to those in [12] may be instantiated in a way such that they have signature sizes that are somewhat smaller than the most compact Fiat-Shamir NTRU-based signature [7]. Then it was shown in [25] that for many polynomial rings, the GPV sampling algorithm [10] that is used to produce the compact signatures in [8], can actually be run in time $O(n^2)$ (and in $O(n)$ space) rather than $O(n^3)$ time required for general lattices. And very recently, it was further shown that pre-image sampling can be done in quasi-linear time over rings $\mathbb{Z}_q[\mathbf{x}]/\langle \mathbf{x}^n + 1 \rangle$ using ideas from the FFT procedure [9].

Asymptotically, therefore, hash-and-sign signatures are as efficient as the Fiat-Shamir ones. The caveat is that the lattice pre-image sampling requires the intermediate storage of a vector of a high precision approximations to real numbers.[6] This requires roughly 300–700 K bits of storage and so may not be a suitable option for constrained devices. One should therefore consider the situation in which the AKE is used before deciding whether using hash-and-sign signatures (and thus benefiting from their message-recovery mode) is appropriate. The most common scenario in which it would be appropriate is TLS where only the server (which is usually not a device with strong computational constraints) is being authenticated. On the other hand, if mutual authentication is required and one of the devices has resource limitations, then the hash-and-sign approach may not be appropriate and one may choose to forego the savings in the communication complexity.

---

[6] It was shown in [26] that one can do pre-image sampling without high-precision arithmetic, but the resulting vector (and thus the signature size) ends up being larger than when using sampling procedures such as [10].

1.5   Security

Obtaining the *exact* computational hardness of lattice-based schemes is an extremely difficult problem. In order to put our work into context and obtain an "apples-to-apples" comparison, we will use some security estimates from the recent work in [2]. The most efficient attacks against the KEM and signature scheme which comprise lattice-based AKEs are lattice reduction attacks.[7] The lattice attacks fall into two categories – sieving and enumeration.

The attacks based on sieving are asymptotically more efficient, but have a very big downside in that the space complexity is essentially equivalent to the time complexity. Moreover, all known approaches to sieving have lower bounds to the required space complexity, and it would be a huge breakthrough if an algorithm were discovered that required less space. The attacks based on enumeration are less efficient time-wise, but do not require a lot of space, and thus are the attacks that are preferred in practice. We analyze our schemes with respect to both attacks following the methodology in [2].[8] All the schemes that we propose have complexity against enumeration attacks (with quantum speedup) larger than 128 bits (see Tables 3 and 4). Furthermore, all our schemes, with the exception of the digital signature component of the AKE for $n = 512$ have security larger than 128 bits against sieving attacks as well. While the signature scheme for $n = 512$ appears to have less than 128 bits of security, we point out that the sieving complexity we state follows that from [2], which uses the asymptotic complexity while leaving out the lower order terms. Those lower-order terms are in fact quite significant in practice, and put the security of the signature scheme above 128-bits. The analysis in [2] was purposefully done to be extremely optimistic in favor of the attacker, and for that reason, that paper only proposes parameters for $n = 1024$. But they admit that there is no currently-known attack that exceeds 2^{128} for $n = 512$.

There have recently been recent attacks on NTRU encryption schemes where the modulus is much larger than the size of the secret polynomials $\mathbf{f}, \mathbf{g}$ [1,5]. But those attacks do not apply to schemes such as ours, where the size of these polynomials is not too far from the range in which their quotient will be uniformly-random in the ring [31].

1.6   Our Recommendations for Lattice-Based AKE

We presented two approaches for improving the generic construction of an AKE scheme from lattice assumptions. The first approach introduces a very small chance of protocol failure, but increases security. The second approach reduces the communication size of the flows in the AKE assuming that the public key and ciphertexts of the KEM are "large enough".

---

[7] There are also combinatorial attacks (e.g. [16]), but the dimensions considered in this paper are too high for them to be effective.

[8] The paper [2] also discussed a "distinguishing" attack, but such an attack does not seem to be relevant in our case because the security in our AKE is based on the 1-wayness of the KEM – thus on a search, rather than a decision, problem.

If one were to make a recommendation for parameter sizes to be used today, one should probably err on the side of caution and recommend that one use $n = 1024$. In this sense, we agree with the decision to only propose parameters for $n = 1024$ in the Ring-LWE based KEM of [2]. On the other hand, there are currently no attacks that make our scheme with $n = 512$ less than 128-bit secure. Nor are there really algorithmic directions that look promising enough to make a significant impact on this parameter range. Thus the main reason for recommending $n = 1024$ is to guard against completely surprising novel attacks – in other words, to guard against "unknown unknowns." But we believe that if cryptanalysis over the next several years intensifies and still does not reveal any novel attack ideas, it is definitely worth re-examining the possibility that the parameters for $n = 512$ are indeed secure enough.

As in [2], when we set $n = 1024$, the security against even the most optimistic attacks is way above the 128-bit threshold. In this case, we see little sense for using KEM parameters that increase security at the expense of having a 2^{-30} chance of decapsulation errors (i.e. those in column III of Table 3). Thus if one were to set $n = 1024$, then we recommend using parameters in column IV of Table 3 along with those in column II of Table 4 for the signature. And one should use the signature in message-recovery mode. The communication size of the resulting AKE is in Table 2.

If one were to use $n = 512$, then one could use the KEM parameters in column I of Table 3. In this case, an increase in 13 bits (compare to column II) of the security against sieve attacks may be worthwhile. One could then also use the parameters from column I of Table 4 for the signature. Note that the complexity against sieving attacks is not quite 128 bits, but we remind the reader that this does not take into account the lower order terms of the sieving attack, which are significant. Also, such an attack requires over 2^{85} space, which makes it impossible to mount. Because the enumeration complexity is still higher than 128 bits, and authentication is not as critical as secrecy,[9] we believe that using the parameters in column I gives a good trade-off between security and efficiency in all but the most sensitive applications.

As mentioned in Sect. 1.4, the hash-and-sign signatures that we propose may not be suitable if the device doing the signing is extrememly limited in computational resources. In this case, we would recommend combining our KEM with a Fiat-Shamir signature such as BLISS (perhaps adapted to $n = 1024$) [7]. And if one does not want to perform any high precision arithmetic or Gaussian sampling, then one can combine our KEM with the Fiat-Shamir scheme in [11] which only requires sampling from the uniform distribution. Also, if one uses the AKE in a way that is not completely forward-secure, i.e. the KEM public key does not change with each interaction, then our security reduction in case of decapsulation errors no longer holds. In this case, one should use our KEM with the parameters in columns II and IV of Table 3.

---

[9] If an attack on the signature scheme were discovered, the scheme could be changed. Whereas an attack on the KEM would reveal all previous secret communication.

We also mention that the modulus of the rings we use in the paper – 12289 – was chosen for efficiency purposes. It is the smallest integer q such that the polynomial $\mathbf{x}^n + 1$, for $n = 512$ or 1024, can be factored into linear factors with integer coefficients modulo q. Such a factorization, combined with the fact that n is a power of 2, allows one to perform multiplication and division operations in quasi-linear time using the Number Theory Transform. If one did not care about optimizing the efficiency of the AKE, then we could have chosen a smaller q and then performed multiplication using other techniques (e.g. Karatsuba's multiplication). The advantage of choosing a smaller modulus is that the ciphertext, which is of length $\approx n \log q$ would be shorter. Of course, if we use our schemes with a different modulus, we would have to change the distribution of all the variables in order to maintain similar security and decapsulation error. So while one cannot choose this modulus to be too small, it seems that something on the

Table 3. Parameters for the NTRU KEM

	I	II	III	IV
Polynomial	$\mathbf{x}^{512} + 1$	$\mathbf{x}^{512} + 1$	$\mathbf{x}^{1024} + 1$	$\mathbf{x}^{1024} + 1$
Modulus	12289	12289	12289	12289
±12 coeff	1	0	0	0
±11 coeff	1	0	1	0
±10 coeff	3	0	2	0
±9 coeff	5	1	4	0
±8 coeff	8	2	8	1
±7 coeff	12	4	15	3
±6 coeff	17	9	26	9
±5 coeff	24	17	42	22
±4 coeff	31	28	61	46
±3 coeff	38	41	81	80
±2 coeff	44	55	100	118
±1 coeff	48	65	113	150
0 coeff	48	68	118	166
σ	4.151	2.991	3.467	2.510
sk norm	≈ 93.21	≈ 67.17	≈ 110.42	≈ 79.54
bits (pk and ciphertext)	7168	7168	14336	14336
bits sk	2560	2560	5120	5120
failure prob	$\approx 2^{-30}$	$\approx 2^{-128}$	$\approx 2^{-30}$	$\approx 2^{-128}$
block size	487	438	1026	939
sieving complexity (log #operations)	> 128	> 115	> 269	> 246
sieving space (log bits)	> 114	> 104	> 227	> 209
enumeration complexity (log #operations)	> 185	> 157	> 645	> 503

order of 2^{11} would be possible. Compared to using the current modulus of 12289, this could result in a savings of approximately $3n$ bits in the length of the KEM public key and ciphertext. Whether this is something worth doing would depend on the scenario in which the AKE is employed. The main reason that we only use 12289 in this paper is to obtain a fair comparison to [2], whose scheme also used this modulus.

2   KEM from NTRU

In this section, we instantiate a KEM based on the hardness of the NTRU problem.

The NTRU problem deals with finding short solutions to polynomial equations over certain rings. Some of the more "popular" rings to use are $\mathbb{Z}[\mathbf{x}]/\langle \mathbf{x}^n - 1 \rangle$ where n is a prime integer and $\mathbb{Z}[\mathbf{x}]/\langle \mathbf{x}^n + 1 \rangle$ where n is a power of 2. Starting from the seminal work of [15] where the NTRU problem was first defined, there have been many different flavors of the problem mostly differing on the underlying distributions from which the keys and randomness are generated.

Elements in $\mathbb{Z}[\mathbf{x}]/\langle \mathbf{x}^n \pm 1 \rangle$ are represented as polynomials of degree at most $n-1$ and reduction modulo an odd q maps the coefficients into the range $[-(q-1)/2, (q-1)/2]$. We also define the norm of an element in $\mathbb{Z}[\mathbf{x}]/\langle \mathbf{x}^n \pm 1 \rangle$ to simply be the ℓ_2-norm of the vector formed by its coefficients. In all variants of the NTRU problem, there are some subsets D_e, D_f of $\mathbb{Z}[\mathbf{x}]/\langle \mathbf{x}^n \pm 1 \rangle$ that consist of polynomials with coefficients of small norms. Furthermore, the polynomials from the set D_f are also invertible in both $\mathbb{Z}_q[\mathbf{x}]/\langle \mathbf{x}^n \pm 1 \rangle$ and $\mathbb{Z}_2[\mathbf{x}]/\langle \mathbf{x}^n \pm 1 \rangle$.

The NTRU trap-door function intuitively rests on two assumptions. The first is that when one is given a polynomial $\mathbf{h} = \mathbf{f}/\mathbf{g} \bmod q$ where $\mathbf{f}, \mathbf{g} \leftarrow D_f$, it is hard to recover $\mathbf{f}$ and $\mathbf{g}$. The second assumption is that when one is given an $\mathbf{h}$ generated as above and $\mathbf{t} = 2\mathbf{hr} + \mathbf{e} \bmod q$ where $\mathbf{r}, \mathbf{e} \leftarrow D_e$, it is hard to recover $\mathbf{e} \bmod 2$.[10] When one has the trap-door $\mathbf{g}$, however, one can recover $\mathbf{e}$ by first computing $\mathbf{gt} \bmod q = 2\mathbf{fr} + \mathbf{ge}$. If the modulus q is large enough (i.e. $2\mathbf{fr} + \mathbf{ge}$ in $\mathbb{Z}[\mathbf{x}]/\langle \mathbf{x}^n \pm 1 \rangle$ is equal to $2\mathbf{fr} + \mathbf{ge}$ in $\mathbb{Z}_q[\mathbf{x}]/\langle \mathbf{x}^n \pm 1 \rangle$), then the preceding is equal to $\mathbf{ge}$ in the ring $\mathbb{Z}_2[\mathbf{x}]/\langle \mathbf{x}^n \pm 1 \rangle$. Since $\mathbf{g}$ has an inverse in $\mathbb{Z}_2[\mathbf{x}]/\langle \mathbf{x}^n \pm 1 \rangle$, one can then divide by $\mathbf{g}$ to recover $\mathbf{e} \bmod 2$.

Definition 1. *For some ring $R = \mathbb{Z}_q[\mathbf{x}]/\langle \mathbf{x}^n \pm 1 \rangle$ and subsets of the ring D_f and D_e, generate polynomials $\mathbf{f}, \mathbf{g} \leftarrow D_f$ and $\mathbf{e}, \mathbf{r} \leftarrow D_e$. Define $\mathbf{h} = \mathbf{f}/\mathbf{g} \bmod q$ and $\mathbf{t} = 2\mathbf{hr} + \mathbf{e} \bmod q$. The $NTRU(R, D_f, D_e)$ problem asks to find $\mathbf{e} \bmod 2$ when given $\mathbf{h}$ and $\mathbf{t}$.*

---

[10] This is somewhat different from the standard NTRU assumption in that we are going to allow the coefficients of $\mathbf{e}$ to be larger than 2, but only require $\mathbf{e} \bmod 2$ to be recovered. This is actually more related to an NTRU encryption scheme that was first introduced in [31] where the message was hidden in the lower order bits of the error. One could then think of our KEM as an encryption of a random message. But since the message itself is random, its randomness contributes to the noise making it larger.

The distributions of D_f and D_e will depend on the security and failure probability of our scheme. We direct the reader to Table 3 and Sect. 2.1. We now present a simple KEM whose one-wayness is directly based on the NTRU(R, D_f, D_e) problem in Definition 1, and whose correctness is based on the discussion preceding the definition.

$$\texttt{KEMKeyGen}\{ \ \mathbf{f}, \mathbf{g} \xleftarrow{\$} D_f, \mathbf{h} \leftarrow \mathbf{f}/\mathbf{g} \bmod q$$
$$\text{Return } (\mathcal{K}_d, \mathcal{K}_e) = (\mathbf{g}, \mathbf{h}) \qquad\qquad \}$$

$$\texttt{Enc}(\mathbf{h})\{ \ \mathbf{r}, \mathbf{e} \xleftarrow{\$} D_e, \mathbf{t} \leftarrow 2\mathbf{h}\mathbf{r} + \mathbf{e} \bmod q$$
$$\text{Return } (c, k) = (\mathbf{t}, \mathbf{e} \bmod 2) \qquad\qquad \}$$

$$\texttt{Dec}(\mathbf{g}, \mathbf{t})\{$$
$$\text{Return } k = \frac{\mathbf{g}\mathbf{t} \bmod q \bmod 2}{\mathbf{g}} \bmod 2 \qquad\qquad \}$$

2.1 KEM Parameters

Table 3 contains our proposed parameter choices for the KEM. To explain the table, we will use the first column as a running example. The polynomial ring considered in this instantiation is $\mathbb{Z}_{12289}[\mathbf{x}]/\langle \mathbf{x}^{512} + 1\rangle$ and the secret key and randomness parameters $\mathbf{f}, \mathbf{g}, \mathbf{e}$, and $\mathbf{r}$ are chosen as random permutations of degree 512 polynomials that have 1 coefficient set to ± 12 (each), 1 to ± 11, 3 to ± 10, etc. and 48 set to 0. The norm of the secret key and error elements $(\mathbf{f}, \mathbf{g})$ and $(\mathbf{r}, \mathbf{e})$ in this instance is approximately 93.21.

Note that for security, one should use a distribution that produces the largest vectors possible while not resulting in too many decryption failures. The most appropriate such distribution is the normal distribution (either the discrete normal or a rounded continuous).[11] Such an operation, though, might be somewhat more costly than simply creating a random permutation of a fixed vector. We thus fix the coefficients of our polynomials to be as close to a discrete Gaussian as possible. Concretely the number of coefficients set to an integer k is the probability that a discrete Gaussian of parameter σ outputs k multiplied by the degree of the polynomial, e.g. $512 \cdot \Pr[\mathcal{D}_{4.151} = 12] \approx 1$ so we fix the number of coefficient with value 12 to one in our first parameter set. Public keys and ciphertexts are polynomials in $\mathbb{Z}_{12289}[\mathbf{x}]/\langle \mathbf{x}^{512} + 1\rangle$ and thus need $512 \cdot \lceil \log 12289 \rceil = 7168$ bits of storage memory. On the other hand, since the coefficients of the secret key are no larger than 12 they can be stored in 5 bits, resulting in a secret key of size $512 \cdot 5 = 2560$ bits. To evaluate the failure probability of decapsulation we model

---

[11] The paper of [2] proposes to use the binomial distribution, which is a good approximation of the normal distribution and is not too difficult to generate. It should be pointed out that the distribution does not really affect the security of the scheme – of main importance is the norm of the generated vectors.

the polynomial as having Gaussian coefficients, using an error analysis similar to the one of Sect. 5.4.1 in [28], we obtain the following probability of failure:

$$\Pr\left[\|2\mathbf{fr} + \mathbf{ge}\|_\infty > \frac{q-1}{2}\right] = 1 - erf\left(\frac{q-1}{\sqrt{40n\sigma^2}}\right)$$

where erf is the Gauss error function. Though we use permutations of fixed polynomials rather than Gaussians, experiments show that the error rate is close to the expected one.

3   Digital Signatures from NTRU

After the KEM, the second component of our AKE is a digital signature scheme. As for number-theoretic schemes, there are two ways to construct (efficient) lattice-based signature schemes. The first approach is via the Fiat-Shamir transform of a sigma protocol. The currently most efficient such protocol is BLISS, which was proposed in [7]. The second approach, hash-and-sign, was proposed by Gentry et al. [10], and its most efficient instantiation is based on the hardness of finding short vectors in NTRU lattices [8].

3.1   Hash-and-sign and Message Recovery

In this section we show how to adapt the hash-and-sign scheme from [8] to create a signature scheme with message recovery. What this means is that instead of sending a signature and a message, one can simply send a larger signature which then allows for the entire message to be recovered. We first briefly outline the scheme from [8]. In the below scheme the distribution D_f is some distribution from which secret keys are drawn and the distribution D_s is the distribution of signatures. The goal of the signer is to produce polynomials according to the distribution D_s conditioned on the message that he is signing. He is able to do that using the fact that he knows the secret NTRU keys $\mathbf{f}$ and $\mathbf{g}$.

$$
\begin{aligned}
&\texttt{SigKeyGen}\{\ \mathbf{f}, \mathbf{g} \overset{\$}{\leftarrow} D_f, \mathbf{h} \leftarrow \mathbf{f}/\mathbf{g} \bmod q \\
&\qquad\qquad\quad \text{Return } (\mathcal{K}_s, \mathcal{K}_v) = ((\mathbf{f}, \mathbf{g}), \mathbf{h}) \ \ \} \\[1.5ex]
&\texttt{Sig}((\mathbf{f}, \mathbf{g}), m)\{\ \mathbf{t} \leftarrow H(m), \\
&\qquad\qquad\quad \mathbf{s}_1, \mathbf{s}_2 \overset{\$}{\leftarrow} D_s \text{ such that } \mathbf{h}\mathbf{s}_1 + \mathbf{s}_2 = \mathbf{t} \bmod q \\
&\qquad\qquad\quad \text{Return } \sigma = (\mathbf{s}_1, m) \ \ \} \\[1.5ex]
&\texttt{Ver}(\mathbf{h}, \sigma = (\mathbf{s}_1, m))\{\ \mathbf{t} \leftarrow H(m) \\
&\qquad\qquad\quad \mathbf{s}_2 \leftarrow \mathbf{t} - \mathbf{h}\mathbf{s}_1 \bmod q \\
&\qquad\qquad\quad \text{if } \|(\mathbf{s}_1, \mathbf{s}_2)\| < B \\
&\qquad\qquad\quad \text{then accept} \\
&\qquad\qquad\quad \text{else reject} \ \ \}
\end{aligned}
$$

We now give a brief intuition about the correctness of the scheme. The correctness relies on the fact that the polynomials s_1 and s_2 are drawn according to a discrete Normal distribution D_s with a small standard deviation by using the trapdoor f, g (this can be done by using e.g. [10, 25]) so for an appropriate positive value B, the probability that $\|(s_1, s_2)\| < B$ is overwhelming. The condition $s_1 h + s_2 = t$ comes directly from the way s_1 and s_2 are obtained during the sampling.

We point out that as described above, the scheme needs to be stateful in order to be secure. In particular, it needs to output the same signature for the same m, and therefore store the signatures that were output. There are two simple ways to remove this requirement. The first way is for the signer to use a pseudo-random function on the message m (with an additional secret key) in order to derive the randomness that he will use to produce the signature. The second way is for the signer to pick a random string r and compute $t \leftarrow H(m, r)$ instead of $H(m)$, and then send r along with the signature. This way, the signer is almost certainly assured that he will never sign the same (m, r) pair twice.

The security of the scheme is based on the fact that it is hard to recover f and g from h, and that forging a signature implies finding short polynomials s_1, s_2 such that $h s_1 + s_2 = 0 \bmod q$ (see [8] for more formal security statements).

Based on the way that the parameters are set, recovering f and g is harder than the corresponding problem for the KEM, and so we focus on the problem of forging signatures. However, since the polynomials s_1 and s_2 are much larger than the polynomials of our KEM (here the coefficients of s_1 and s_2 have standard deviation $1.17\sqrt{q}$ which is ≈ 50 times larger than the ones used for the KEM) the corresponding problem is no longer unique-SVP, but rather an approximate-

Table 4. Signature parameters for $n = 512$ and 1024, $q = 12289$, and message $m \in \mathbb{Z}_q[x]/\langle x^n + 1 \rangle$

	I	II
Polynomial	$x^{512} + 1$	$x^{1024} + 1$
Modulus	12289	12289
Signing key size (bits)	≈ 2100	≈ 3700
Verification key size (bits)	6956	13912
message size (bits)	6956	13912
hash-and-sign size (bits)	≈ 11600	≈ 23300
message-recovery hash-and-sign size (bits)	≈ 9600	≈ 18900
Gamma factor	1.0041	1.0022
Block size	388	906
sieving complexity (log #operations)	> 102	> 237
sieving space (log bits)	> 85	> 216
enumeration complexity (log #operations)	> 130	> 520

SVP one. To solve this problem we compute the γ factor of the associated lattice, as done in [8] (see Table 4). To solve SVP using the BKZ algorithm, one needs the vector $\mathbf{b}_1$ output by BKZ to be the shortest vector of the lattice, which corresponds to the condition $\delta \leq \gamma$ where $\delta = ((\pi\beta)^{1/\beta}\beta/2\pi e)^{1/2(\beta-1)}$. From this equation we obtain the block size β and the security analysis (see full version of the paper) gives the parameters of Table 4.

3.2 Signature with Message Recovery

Instead of sending the signature $\sigma = (\mathbf{s}_1, m)$ and then letting the verification algorithm recover $\mathbf{s}_2$, it may sometimes be intuitively useful to send the signature as $\mathbf{s}_1, \mathbf{s}_2$ and let the verifier somehow recover m. This may be advantageous because $\mathbf{s}_1$ and $\mathbf{s}_2$ are drawn according to small Gaussians, and may be compressed (see the full version of this paper), while m can be any polynomial in $\mathbb{Z}_q[\mathbf{x}]/\langle \mathbf{x}^n + 1 \rangle$ and so cannot be encoded in less than $n\log(q)$ bits. In this scenario, a better solution would thus be to modify $\mathbf{t}$ so that sending $\mathbf{s}_1$ and $\mathbf{s}_2$ would allow the verifier to recover m. Our signature with message recovery can be used to recover messages of up to $n\log q - 256$ bits, the scheme we define here can be used for messages $m = (m_1\|m_2)$ of arbitrary size but the second part of the message m_2 will not benefit from message recovery and thus needs to be output as part of the signature.

$\mathbf{Sig}((\mathbf{f},\mathbf{g}), m = (m_1\|m_2))\{\ \ \mathbf{t} = (m_1 + F(H'(m)) \bmod q\|H'(m))$

$\qquad\qquad\qquad\qquad \mathbf{s}_1, \mathbf{s}_2 \xleftarrow{\$} D_s \text{ such that } \mathbf{h}\mathbf{s}_1 + \mathbf{s}_2 = \mathbf{t} \bmod q$

$\qquad\qquad\qquad\qquad \text{Return } \sigma = (\mathbf{s}_1, \mathbf{s}_2, m_2)\ \ \}$

$\mathbf{Ver}(\mathbf{h}, \sigma = (\mathbf{s}_1, \mathbf{s}_2, m_2))\{\ \ (\mathbf{t}_1\|\mathbf{t}_2) \leftarrow \mathbf{h}\mathbf{s}_1 + \mathbf{s}_2 \bmod q$

$\qquad\qquad\qquad\qquad\qquad m_1 \leftarrow \mathbf{t}_1 - F(\mathbf{t}_2) \bmod q$

$\qquad\qquad\qquad\qquad\qquad \text{if } \|(\mathbf{s}_1, \mathbf{s}_2)\| < B \text{ and } H'(m_1\|m_2) = \mathbf{t}_2$

$\qquad\qquad\qquad\qquad\qquad \text{then accept}$

$\qquad\qquad\qquad\qquad\qquad \text{else reject}\ \ \}$

While the hash function H mapped to a random element of $\mathbb{Z}_q[\mathbf{x}]/\langle \mathbf{x}^n + 1 \rangle \simeq \mathbb{Z}_q^n$ in the previous scheme, now we want $(m_1 + F(H'(m)) \bmod q\|H'(m))$ to be a random element of $\mathbb{Z}_q[\mathbf{x}]/\langle \mathbf{x}^n + 1 \rangle$. To achieve this, we split the message m into $(m_1\|m_2)$ with $|m_1| = n\log q - 256$ bits (note that m_2 can be empty if m is small) and we set the hash function H' to output 256 bits. To prove that this scheme is secure we show that we can use an adversary that breaks this scheme to break the one from [8].

Lemma 2. *If the hash functions F and H are modeled as random oracles and an adversary can break the message-recovery hash-and-sign scheme signature unforgeability game with advantage ε, then there is an algorithm that can break the previous hash-and-sign scheme with probability close to ε.*

4 The Generic AKE Construction

In this section, we present a generic 2-round construction of a forward-secure ε-AKE that is built from an ε-KEM and a digital signature. As can be seen from the parameters in the previous section, by simply plugging in current lattice primitives into this construction, one already achieves a rather efficient concrete construction. The complete description is provided in Fig. 3, and the security claim is the following:

Theorem 3. *The authenticated key exchange $\mathcal{AKE}$ described in Fig. 3 is a forward-secure ε-AKE, when H_1 and H_2 are modeled by random oracles onto $\{0,1\}^{\ell_1}$ and $\{0,1\}^{\ell_2}$ respectively, if Σ is a secure signature scheme and $\mathcal{KEM}$ is a secure ε-KEM:*

$$Adv_{\mathcal{AKE}}^{\text{fs-ind}}(t) \leq n \times Succ_{\Sigma}^{\text{suf-cma}}(t) + 2q_s^2 q_h \times Succ_{\mathcal{KEM}}^{\text{ow}}(t) + \frac{q_s^2}{2^{\ell_2}},$$

Setup:
H_1 and H_2 are two hash function onto $\{0,1\}^{\ell_1}$ and $\{0,1\}^{\ell_2}$ respectively
Each party (i) runs the signing key generation algorithm to get its own pair of keys:
$\left(\mathcal{K}_s^{(i)}, \mathcal{K}_v^{(i)}\right) \leftarrow \text{SigKeyGen}(1^\lambda)$

Protocol:

Party 1		Party 2
$sk^{(1)} \leftarrow \bot$		$sk^{(2)} \leftarrow \bot$
$(\mathcal{K}_d, \mathcal{K}_e) \leftarrow \text{KEMKeyGen}(1^\lambda)$		
$\sigma_1 \leftarrow \text{Sig}\left(\mathcal{K}_s^{(1)}, \mathcal{K}_e\right)$	$\xrightarrow{\ \sigma_1 = \langle \mathcal{K}_e \rangle_1\ }$	if $\text{Ver}\left(\mathcal{K}_v^{(1)}, \sigma_1\right) \neq \bot$ then
		$\quad \mathcal{K}_e \leftarrow \text{Ver}\left(\mathcal{K}_v^{(1)}, \sigma_1\right)$
		$\quad (c,k) \leftarrow \text{Enc}(\mathcal{K}_e)$
		$\quad \text{Auth} \leftarrow H_2(\sigma_1, c, k)$
		$\quad \sigma_2 \leftarrow \text{Sig}\left(\mathcal{K}_s^{(2)}, (c, \text{Auth})\right)$
if $\text{Ver}\left(\mathcal{K}_v^{(2)}, \sigma_2\right) \neq \bot$ then	$\xleftarrow{\ \sigma_2 = \langle c, \text{Auth}\rangle_2\ }$	else ABORT
$\quad (c, \text{Auth}) \leftarrow \text{Ver}\left(\mathcal{K}_v^{(2)}, \sigma_2\right)$		
$\quad k' \leftarrow \text{Dec}(\mathcal{K}_d, c)$		
else ABORT		
if $\text{Auth} \stackrel{?}{=} H_2(\sigma_1, c, k')$ then		
$sk^{(1)} \leftarrow H_1(\sigma_1, \sigma_2, k')$		$sk^{(2)} \leftarrow H_1(\sigma_1, \sigma_2, k)$

Fig. 3. Generic 2-round forward-secure ε-AKE

where n is the number of players involved in the protocols, q_s the number of Send-queries, and q_h the number of hash-queries. With a checkable KEM, one gets

$$Adv_{\mathcal{AKE}}^{fs-ind}(t) \leq n \times Succ_{\Sigma}^{suf-cma}(t) + 2q_s^2 \times Succ_{\mathcal{KEM}}^{ow}(t') + \frac{q_s^2}{2^{\ell_2}},$$

where $t' \approx t + q_h \times t_{check}$, with t_{check} the expected time to check a candidate.

Acknowledgements. We thank Léo Ducas for very helpful discussions related to lattice reduction algorithms and to [2]. We also thank the committee members for their comments which helped to improve parts of the paper.

References

1. Albrecht, M., Bai, S., Ducas, L.: A subfield lattice attack on overstretched NTRU assumptions: Cryptanalysis of some FHE and graded encoding schemes. Crypto (2016)
2. Alkim, E., Ducas, L., Pöppelmann, T., Schwabe, P.: Post-quantum key exchange - a new hope. USENIX (2016)
3. Bernstein, D.J., Chuengsatiansup, C., Lange, T., van Vredendaal, C.: NTRU prime. IACR Cryptology ePrint Archive 2016/461 (2016)
4. Bos, J.W., Costello, C., Naehrig, M., Stebila, D.: Post-quantum key exchange for the TLS protocol from the ring learning with errors problem. In: 2015 IEEE Symposium on Security and Privacy, SP 2015, San Jose, CA, USA, May 17–21, 2015, pp. 553–570 (2015)
5. Cheon, J.H., Jeong, J., Lee, C.: An algorithm for NTRU problems and cryptanalysis of the GGH multilinear map without an encoding of zero. IACR Cryptology ePrint Archive (2016)
6. Ding, J., Xie, X., Lin, X.: A simple provably secure key exchange scheme based on the learning with errors problem. Cryptology ePrint Archive, Report 2012/688 (2012). http://eprint.iacr.org/
7. Ducas, L., Durmus, A., Lepoint, T., Lyubashevsky, V.: Lattice signatures and bimodal Gaussians. In: Canetti, R., Garay, J.A. (eds.) CRYPTO 2013, Part I. LNCS, vol. 8042, pp. 40–56. Springer, Heidelberg (2013)
8. Ducas, L., Lyubashevsky, V., Prest, T.: Efficient identity-based encryption over NTRU lattices. In: Sarkar, P., Iwata, T. (eds.) ASIACRYPT 2014, Part II. LNCS, vol. 8874, pp. 22–41. Springer, Heidelberg (2014)
9. Ducas, L., Prest, T.: A hybrid Gaussian sampler for lattices over rings. IACR Cryptology ePrint Archive 2015/660 (2015)
10. Gentry, C., Peikert, C., Vaikuntanathan, V.: Trapdoors for hard lattices and new cryptographic constructions. In: STOC, pp. 197–206 (2008)
11. Güneysu, T., Lyubashevsky, V., Pöppelmann, T.: Practical lattice-based cryptography: a signature scheme for embedded systems. In: Prouff, E., Schaumont, P. (eds.) CHES 2012. LNCS, vol. 7428, pp. 530–547. Springer, Heidelberg (2012)
12. Hoffstein, J., Howgrave-Graham, N., Pipher, J., Silverman, J.H., Whyte, W.: NTRUSIGN: digital signatures using the NTRU lattice. In: Joye, M. (ed.) CT-RSA 2003. LNCS, vol. 2612, pp. 122–140. Springer, Heidelberg (2003)
13. Hoffstein, J., Pipher, J., Schanck, J.M., Silverman, J.H., Whyte, W.: Transcript secure signatures based on modular lattices. In: Mosca, M. (ed.) PQCrypto 2014. LNCS, vol. 8772, pp. 142–159. Springer, Heidelberg (2014)

14. Hoffstein, J., Pipher, J., Schanck, J.M., Silverman, J.H., Whyte, W., Zhang, Z.: Choosing parameters for ntruencrypt. IACR Cryptology ePrint Archive 2015/708 (2015)
15. Hoffstein, J., Pipher, J., Silverman, J.H.: NTRU: a ring-based public key cryptosystem. In: Buhler, J.P. (ed.) ANTS 1998. LNCS, vol. 1423, pp. 267–288. Springer, Heidelberg (1998)
16. Howgrave-Graham, N.: A hybrid lattice-reduction and meet-in-the-middle attack against NTRU. In: Menezes, A. (ed.) CRYPTO 2007. LNCS, vol. 4622, pp. 150–169. Springer, Heidelberg (2007)
17. Howgrave-Graham, N., Nguyên, P.Q., Pointcheval, D., Proos, J., Silverman, J.H., Singer, A., Whyte, W.: The impact of decryption failures on the security of NTRU encryption. In: Boneh, D. (ed.) CRYPTO 2003. LNCS, vol. 2729, pp. 226–246. Springer, Heidelberg (2003)
18. Krawczyk, H.: HMQV: a high-performance secure Diffie-Hellman protocol. In: Shoup, V. (ed.) CRYPTO 2005. LNCS, vol. 3621, pp. 546–566. Springer, Heidelberg (2005)
19. Law, L., Menezes, A., Qu, M., Solinas, J.A., Vanstone, S.A.: An efficient protocol for authenticated key agreement. Des. Codes Cryptogr. $28(2)$, 119–134 (2003)
20. Longa, P., Naehrig, M.: Speeding up the number theoretic transform for faster ideal lattice-based cryptography. IACR Cryptology ePrint Archive 2016/504 (2016)
21. Lyubashevsky, V.: Lattice signatures without trapdoors. In: Pointcheval, D., Johansson, T. (eds.) EUROCRYPT 2012. LNCS, vol. 7237, pp. 738–755. Springer, Heidelberg (2012)
22. Lyubashevsky, V., Peikert, C., Regev, O.: On ideal lattices and learning with errors over rings. In: Gilbert, H. (ed.) EUROCRYPT 2010. LNCS, vol. 6110, pp. 1–23. Springer, Heidelberg (2010)
23. Lyubashevsky, V., Peikert, C., Regev, O.: On ideal lattices, learning with errors over rings. J. ACM $60(6)$, 43 (2013). Preliminary version appeared in EUROCRYPT 2010
24. Lyubashevsky, V., Peikert, C., Regev, O.: A toolkit for ring-LWE cryptography. In: Johansson, T., Nguyen, P.Q. (eds.) EUROCRYPT 2013. LNCS, vol. 7881, pp. 35–54. Springer, Heidelberg (2013)
25. Lyubashevsky, V., Prest, T.: Quadratic time, linear space algorithms for Gram-Schmidt orthogonalization and Gaussian sampling in structured lattices. In: Oswald, E., Fischlin, M. (eds.) EUROCRYPT 2015. LNCS, vol. 9056, pp. 789–815. Springer, Heidelberg (2015)
26. Lyubashevsky, V., Wichs, D.: Simple lattice trapdoor sampling from a broad class of distributions. In: Public-Key Cryptography- PKC, pp. 716–730 (2015)
27. Micciancio, D., Peikert, C.: Trapdoors for lattices: simpler, tighter, faster, smaller. In: Pointcheval, D., Johansson, T. (eds.) EUROCRYPT 2012. LNCS, vol. 7237, pp. 700–718. Springer, Heidelberg (2012)
28. Micciancio, D., Regev, O.: Lattice-based cryptography. In: Bernstein, D.J., Buchmann, J., Dahmen, E. (eds.) Chapter in Post-quantum Cryptography, pp. 147–191. Springer, Heidelberg (2008)
29. Peikert, C.: An efficient and parallel Gaussian sampler for lattices. In: Rabin, T. (ed.) CRYPTO 2010. LNCS, vol. 6223, pp. 80–97. Springer, Heidelberg (2010)
30. Peikert, C.: Lattice cryptography for the internet. In: Mosca, M. (ed.) PQCrypto 2014. LNCS, vol. 8772, pp. 197–219. Springer, Heidelberg (2014)
31. Stehlé, D., Steinfeld, R.: Making NTRU as secure as worst-case problems over ideal lattices. In: EUROCRYPT, pp. 27–47 (2011)
32. Zhang, J., Zhang, Z., Ding, J., Snook, M., Dagdelen, Ö.: Authenticated key exchange from ideal lattices. In: Oswald, E., Fischlin, M. (eds.) EUROCRYPT 2015. LNCS, vol. 9057, pp. 719–751. Springer, Heidelberg (2015)

Efficient Asynchronous Accumulators
for Distributed PKI

Leonid Reyzin and Sophia Yakoubov$^{(\boxtimes)}$

Boston University, Boston, USA
{reyzin,sonka}@bu.edu

Abstract. Cryptographic accumulators are a tool for compact set representation and secure set membership proofs. When an element is added to a set by means of an accumulator, a membership witness is generated. This witness can later be used to prove the membership of the element. Typically, the membership witness has to be synchronized with the accumulator value: it has to be updated every time another element is added to the accumulator, and it cannot be used with outdated accumulator values. However, in many distributed applications (such as blockchain-based public key infrastructures), requiring strict synchronization is prohibitive. We define *low update frequency*, which means that a witness only needs to be updated a small number of times, and *old-accumulator compatibility*, which means that a witness can be used with outdated accumulator values. Finally, we propose an accumulator that achieves both of those properties.

Keyword: Cryptographic accumulators

1 Introduction

Cryptographic accumulators, first introduced by Benaloh and de Mare [3], are compact binding (but not necessarily hiding) set commitments. Given an accumulator, an element, and a *membership witness* (or *proof*), the element's presence in the accumulated set can be verified. Membership witnesses are generated upon the addition of the element in question to the accumulator, and are typically updated as the set changes. Membership witnesses for elements not in the accumulator are computationally hard to find.

There are many applications of Cryptographic accumulators. These can be divided into *localized* applications, where a single entity is responsible for proving the membership of all the elements, and *distributed* applications, where many entities participate and each entity has interest in (or responsibility for) some small number of elements. An example of a localized application is an authenticated outsourced database, where the database owner outsources responsibility for the database to an untrusted third party. When responding to a query, that party can then use an accumulator to prove the presence of returned records in the database record set. An example of a distributed application is a credential

© Springer International Publishing Switzerland 2016
V. Zikas and R. De Prisco (Eds.): SCN 2016, LNCS 9841, pp. 292–309, 2016.
DOI: 10.1007/978-3-319-44618-9_16

system; different parties can prove the validity of their credentials by showing that they are in the accumulated set. In this paper, we focus on distributed applications, which were the original motivation for accumulators [3].

A trivial accumulator construction simply uses digital signatures. That is, when an element is added to the accumulator, it is signed by some trusted central authority, and that signature then functions as the witness for that element. The public verification key of the central authority functions as the accumulator value. However, this solution is very limited, since it requires trust in the central authority who holds the secret signing key. Many distributed applications have no central authority that can be trusted, particularly if they are executed by a number of mutually distrusting peers. In this paper, we are interested in so-called *strong* accumulators (defined formally in Sect. 2), which require no secrets.

A classic example of a strong accumulator construction is a Merkle tree [15]. A set element is a leaf of the tree, and the corresponding witness is its authenticating path (that is, the sequence of the element's ancestors' siblings). The Merkle tree root is the accumulator value. Unfortunately, like all existing strong accumulator constructions, this construction has the significant drawback of requiring strict synchronization: membership witnesses need to be updated every time a new element is added to the accumulated set, and can then only be verified against the current accumulator. If elements are added at a high rate, having to perform work linear in the number of new elements in order to retain the ability to prove membership can be prohibitively expensive for the witness holders. Additionally, because of the high update rate, the verifier might have trouble maintaining the most current accumulator to use in verifications.

To address these issues, we introduce *asynchronous accumulators*, which have two additional properties. *Low update frequency* allows witnesses to be updated only a sub-linear number of times (in the number of element additions), which in particular means that it is possible to verify a witness that is somewhat older than the current accumulator value. Conversely, *old-accumulator compatibility* allows membership verification against an old accumulator, as long as the old accumulator already contains the element whose membership is being verified.

Section 3 describes these properties in more detail.[1]

Our New Accumulator. In this work, we introduce the first strong asynchronous accumulator construction. It leverages Merkle hash trees, but maintains multiple Merkle tree roots as part of the accumulator value, not just one. Our construction has a low update frequency; it requires only a logarithmic amount of work (in the number of subsequent element additions) in order to keep a witness up to date. It is also old-accumulator compatible; unlike any prior construction, it supports the verification of an up-to-date witness against an outdated accu-

---

[1] The question of whether accumulators updates can be batched, as in our scheme, was first posed by Fazio and Nicolosi [12] in the context of dynamic accumulators, which support deletions. It was answered in the negative by Camacho [6], but only in the context of deletions, and only in the centralized case (when all witnesses are updated by the same entity).

mulator, enabling verification by parties who are offline and without access to the most current accumulator. Our construction is made even more well suited for distributed applications by the fact that it does not require knowledge of the accumulated set (or any other information linear in the number of elements) for the execution of element additions. Section 4 describes our construction in detail, and provides comparisons to prior constructions. Figure 1 describes the asynchrony of our construction.

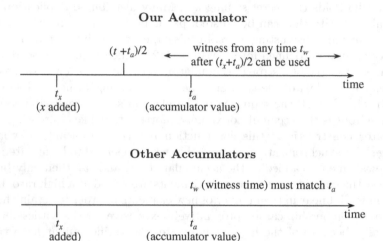

Fig. 1. A membership witness w can either be outdated, or up-to-date. Our accumulator construction is *asynchronous* because even if w is older or newer than the accumulator, verification can still work. This table illustrates the constraints on how outdated w can be. Note that in all other strong accumulator schemes, w must be perfectly synchronized with the accumulator.

1.1   Application: Distributed PKI

The original distributed application proposed by Benaloh and DeMare [3] involved a canonical common state, but did not specify how to maintain it. Public append-only bulletin boards, such as the ones implemented by Bitcoin [16] and its alternatives (altcoins, such as Namecoin [17]), provide a place for this common state. Bitcoin and altcoins implement this public bulletin board by means of blockchains; in Bitcoin they are used primarily as transaction ledgers, while altcoins extend their use to public storage of arbitrary data.

Altcoins such as Namecoin can be used for storing identity information in a publicly accessible way. For instance, they can be used to store (IP address, domain) pairs, enabling DNS authentication [21]. They can also be used to store (identity id, public key pk) pairs, providing a distributed alternative to certificate authorities for public key infrastructure (PKI) [22].

Elaborating on the PKI example, when a user Bob registers a public key pk_{Bob}, he adds the pair ("Bob", pk_{Bob}) to the bulletin board. When the bulletin board is implemented as a blockchain, it falls to the blockchain miners, who act as the conduit by means of whom content is posted, to verify the validity of this registration. They must, for instance, check that there is not already a public key registered to Bob. Details of the verification process are described by Yakoubov et al. [22]. If the registration is invalid, the miners do not post it to the bulletin board. As a result of the miners' verifications, the bulletin board does not contain any invalid entries.[2]

When Alice needs to verify Bob's public key, she can look through the bulletin board to find this pair. However, when executed naively, this procedure requires Alice to read the entire bulletin board—i.e., a linear amount of data. Bob can save Alice some work by sending her a pointer to the bulletin board location where ("Bob", pk_{Bob}) is posted, which Alice will then follow to check that it points to Bob's registration, and retrieve pk_{Bob}. However, that still requires that Alice *have access* to a linear amount of data during verification. What if Alice doesn't have access to the bulletin board at the time of verification at all, or wants to reduce latency by avoiding on-line access to the bulletin board during verification?

Adding our accumulator to the bulletin board can free Alice from the need for on-line random access to the bulletin board [22] (see also [13] for a similar use of accumulators). The accumulator would contain all of the (id, pk) pairs on the bulletin board, with responsibility for the witnesses distributed among the interested individuals. When Bob posts ("Bob", pk_{Bob}) to the bulletin board, he also adds ("Bob", pk_{Bob}) to the accumulator, and stores his witness w_{Bob}. He posts the updated accumulator to the bulletin board. The validity of this new accumulator needs to be checked, by the same parties who check the validity of Bob's registration. In the blockchain setting, this check is performed by all of the miners. Since our accumulator construction is strong (meaning trapdoor-free, as explained in Sect. 2) and deterministic, the validity of the new accumulator can be checked simply by re-adding ("Bob", pk_{Bob}) to the old accumulator and comparing the result to the new accumulator.

With our accumulator in place, Alice can simply download the latest accumulator from the end of the bulletin board at pre-determined (perhaps infrequent) intervals. When Alice wants to verify that pk_{Bob} is indeed the public key belonging to Bob, all she needs is w_{Bob} and her locally cached accumulator. As long as Bob's registration pre-dates Alice's locally cached accumulator, Alice can use that accumulator and w_{Bob} to verify that ("Bob", pk_{Bob}) has been posted to the bulletin board. She does not need to refer to any of the new bulletin board contents because our scheme is old-accumulator compatible.

Our construction also reduces the work for Bob, as compared to other accumulator constructions. In a typical accumulator construction, Bob needs to update w_{Bob} every time a new (id, pk) pair is added to the accumulator.

---

[2] Note that we do not address public key updates; see Yakoubov et al. [22] for a discussion of such updates.

However, in a large-scale PKI, the number of entries on the bulletin board and the frequency of element additions can be high. Thus, it is vital to spare Bob the need to be continuously updating his witness. Because it has a low update frequency, our accumulator reduces Bob's burden: Bob needs to update his witness only a logarithmic number of times. Moreover, Bob can update his witness on-demand—for instance, when he needs to prove membership—by looking at a logarithmic number of bulletin board entries (see Sect. 5 for details).

2 Background

As described in the introduction, informally, a cryptographic accumulator is a compact representation of a set of elements which supports proofs of membership.[3] In this section, we provide a more thorough description of accumulators, their algorithms and their security definitions. In Sect. 3, we introduce new properties for asynchronous accumulators.

2.1 Accumulator Algorithms

A basic accumulator construction consists of four polynomial-time algorithms: Gen, Add, MemWitUpOnAdd and VerMem, described below. They were first introduced in Baric and Pritzmann's [2] formalization of Benaloh and de Mare's [3] seminal work on accumulators, and a more general version was provided by Derler Hanser and Slamanig [11]. For convenience, we enumerate and explain all of the input and output parameters of the accumulator algorithms in Fig. 2.

---

k: The security parameter.

t: A discrete time / operation counter.

a_t: The accumulator at time t.

x, y: Elements which might be added to the accumulator.

w_t^x: The witness that element x is in accumulator a_t at time t.

upmsg_t: A broadcast message sent (by the accumulator manager, if one exists) at time t to all witness holders immediately after the accumulator has been updated. This message is meant to enable all witness holders to update the witnesses they hold for consistency with the new accumulator. It will often contain the new accumulator a_t, and the nature of the update itself (e.g. "x has been added and witness w_t^x has been produced"). It may also contain other information.

Fig. 2. Accumulator algorithm input and output parameters.

We separate the accumulator algorithms into (1) those performed by the accumulator manager if one exists, (2) those performed by any entity responsible

---

[3] There also exist *universal* accumulators [14] which additionally support proofs of non-membership; however, we only consider proofs of membership in this paper.

for an element and its corresponding witness (from hereon-out referred to as *witness holder*), and (3) those performed by any third party.

Algorithms Performed by the Accumulator Manager:

- $\mathsf{Gen}(1^k) \rightarrow a_0$ instantiates the accumulator a_0 (representing the empty set). In some accumulator constructions, a secret key sk and auxiliary storage m are additionally generated for the accumulator manager if these are needed to perform additions. However, this is not the case in our scheme.
- $\mathsf{Add}(a_t, x) \rightarrow (a_{t+1}, w_{t+1}^x, \mathsf{upmsg}_{t+1})$ adds the element x to the accumulator, producing the updated accumulator value a_{t+1}, and the membership witness w_{t+1}^x for x. Additionally, an update message upmsg_{t+1} is generated, which can then be used by all other witness holders to update their witnesses.

Note that accumulator constructions where Gen and Add are deterministic and publicly executable are also *strong* (as defined by Camacho et al. [7]), meaning that the accumulator manager does not need to be trusted. An execution of Gen or Add can then be carried out by an untrusted accumulator manager, and verified by any third party in possession of the inputs simply by re-executing the algorithm and checking that the outputs match. In fact, an accumulator manager is not necessary at all, since Gen and Add can be executed by the (possibly untrusted) witness holders themselves and verified as needed.

Algorithms Performed by a Witness Bolder:

- $\mathsf{MemWitUpOnAdd}(x, w_t^x, \mathsf{upmsg}_{t+1}) \rightarrow w_{t+1}^x$ updates the witness for element x after another element y is added to the accumulator. The update message upmsg_{t+1} might contain any subset of $\{w_{t+1}^y, a_t, a_{t+1}, y\}$, as well as other parameters.

Algorithms Performed by Any Third Party:

- $\mathsf{VerMem}(a_t, x, w_t^x) \rightarrow b \in \{0, 1\}$ verifies the membership of x in the accumulator using its witness.

Accumulator Size. Space-efficiency is an important benefit of using an accumulator. A trivial accumulator construction would eschew witnesses entirely, and have the accumulator consist of a list of all elements it contains. However, this is not at all space-efficient; any party performing membership verification would need to hold all of the elements in the set. Ideally, accumulators (as well as their witnesses and update messages) should remain small no matter how many items are added to them. In the construction presented in this work, the accumulator and its witnesses and updated messages grow only logarithmically.

2.2 Accumulator Security Properties

Now that we have defined the basic functionality of an accumulator, we can describe the security properties an accumulator is expected to have. Informally, the *correctness* property requires that for every element in the accumulator it should be easy to prove membership, and the *soundness* (also referred to as *security*) property requires that for every element not in the accumulator it should be infeasible to prove membership.

Definition 1 (Correctness). *A strong accumulator is* correct *if an up-to-date witness w^x corresponding to value x can always be used to verify the membership of x in an up-to-date accumulator a.*

More formally, for all security parameters k, all values x and additional sets of values $[y_1, \ldots, y_{t_x-1}], [y_{t_x+1}, \ldots, y_t]$:

$$\Pr \begin{bmatrix} a_0 \leftarrow \mathsf{Gen}(1^k); \\ (a_i, w_i^{y_i}, \mathsf{upmsg}_i) \leftarrow \mathsf{Add}(a_{i-1}, y_i) \; for \; i \in [1, \ldots, t_x - 1]; \\ (a_{t_x}, w_{t_x}^x, \mathsf{upmsg}_{t_x}) \leftarrow \mathsf{Add}(a_{t_x-1}, x); \\ (a_i, w_i^{y_i}, \mathsf{upmsg}_i) \leftarrow \mathsf{Add}(a_{i-1}, y_i) \; for \; i \in [t_x + 1, \ldots, t]; \\ w_i^x \leftarrow \mathsf{MemWitUpOnAdd}(x, w_{i-1}^x, \mathsf{upmsg}_i) \; for \; i \in [t_x + 1, \ldots, t] : \\ \mathsf{VerMem}(a_t, x, w_t^x) = 1 \end{bmatrix} = 1$$

In Sect. 3, we modify the correctness definition for asynchronous accumulators. In asynchronous accumulators, the witness w^x does not always need to be up-to-date in order for verification to work (as described in Definition 4), and the accumulator itself can be outdated (as described in Definition 6).

Definition 2 (Soundness). *A strong accumulator is* sound *(or secure) if it is hard to fabricate a witness w for a value x that has not been added to the accumulator.*

More formally, for any probabilistic polynomial-time stateful adversary $\mathcal{A}$, there exists a negligible function negl in the security parameter k such that:

$$\Pr \begin{bmatrix} a_0 \leftarrow \mathsf{Gen}(1^k); t = 1; x_1 \leftarrow \mathcal{A}(1^k, a_0); \\ while \; x_t \neq \perp \\ \quad (a_t, w_t^{x_t}, \mathsf{upmsg}_t) \leftarrow \mathsf{Add}(a_{t-1}, x_t); \\ \quad t = t + 1; \\ \quad x_t \leftarrow \mathcal{A}(a_{t-1}, w_{t-1}^{x_{t-1}}, \mathsf{upmsg}_{t-1}); \\ (x, w) \leftarrow \mathcal{A} : \\ x \notin \{x_1, \ldots, x_t\} \; and \; \mathsf{VerMem}(a_{t-1}, x, w) = 1 \end{bmatrix} \leq negl(k)$$

3 New Definitions: Asynchronous Accumulators

An accumulator is *asynchronous* if the accumulator value and the membership witnesses can be out of sync, and verification still works. An accumulator and witness can be out of sync in two ways. First, the witness can be "old" relative to the accumulator, meaning that more values have been added to the accumulator since the witness was last updated. Second, the accumulator can be "old" relative to the witness, meaning that the witness has been brought up to date relative to a newer accumulator value, but an old accumulator value is now being used for verification. We describe correctness definitions for these two scenarios in Sects. 3.1 and 3.2, respectively. The soundness definition doesn't change.

3.1 Low Update Frequency

We consider an accumulator to have a *low update frequency* if the frequency with which a witness for element x needs to be updated is sub-linear in the number of elements which are added after x. The fact that witnesses do not need to be updated with every addition naturally implies that they can be "old" relative to the accumulator, and still verify correctly. Of course, the fact that updates are needed at all implies that witnesses can't be *arbitrarily* old without verification failing.

Low update frequency requires a change in the correctness definition (but not in the soundness definition). In the new correctness definition, we introduce a function $\mathsf{UpdateTimes}(t, t_w, t_x)$ which describes when the witness needs to be updated. It returns a set T of times between t_w and t at which the witness w last updated at time t_w for an element x added at time t_x needs to be updated. Note that $\mathsf{UpdateTimes}(t_w, t_w, t_x) = \emptyset$ and $\mathsf{UpdateTimes}(t_1, t_w, t_x) \subseteq \mathsf{UpdateTimes}(t_2, t_w, t_x)$ if $t_1 < t_2$.

Definition 3 (Low Update Frequency (LUF)). *An accumulator has* low update frequency *if there exists a function* $\mathsf{UpdateTimes}(t, t_w, t_x)$ *such that (a)* $|\mathsf{UpdateTimes}(t, t_w, t_x)|$ *is sublinear in t for all fixed* t_w, t_x *s.t.* $t_w \geq t_x$, *and (b) the accumulator is* $\mathsf{UpdateTimes}(t, t_w, t_x)$-LUF-correct, *as described in Definition 4.*

Definition 4 (Low Update Frequency (LUF) Correctness). *An accumulator is* $\mathsf{UpdateTimes}(t, t_w, t_x)$-LUF-correct *if an outdated witness* w^x *from time* t_w *corresponding to value x added at time* t_x *can be used to verify the membership of x in an up-to-date accumulator a at time t as long as* $\mathsf{UpdateTimes}(t, t_w, t_x)$ *is empty.*

More formally, for all security parameters k, for all values x and additional sets of values $[y_1, \ldots, y_{t_x-1}]$, $[y_{t_x+1}, \ldots, y_t]$, *the following probability is equal to 1:*

$$\Pr\begin{bmatrix} a_0 \leftarrow \mathsf{Gen}(1^k); \\ (a_i, w_i^{y_i}, \mathsf{upmsg}_i) \leftarrow \mathsf{Add}(a_{i-1}, y_i) \, for \, i \in [1, \ldots, t_x - 1]; \\ (a_{t_x}, w_{t_x}^x, \mathsf{upmsg}_{t_x}) \leftarrow \mathsf{Add}(a_{t_x-1}, x); \\ (a_i, w_i^{y_t}, \mathsf{upmsg}_i) \leftarrow \mathsf{Add}(a_{i-1}, y_i) \, for \, i \in [t_x + 1, \ldots, t]; \\ w_i^x \leftarrow \mathsf{MemWitUpOnAdd}(x, w_{i-1}^x, \mathsf{upmsg}_i) \, for \, i \in \mathsf{UpdateTimes}(t, t_x, t_x) : \\ \mathsf{VerMem}(a_t, x, w_i^x) = 1 \, for \, i = \max(\mathsf{UpdateTimes}(t, t_x, t_x)) \end{bmatrix}$$

3.2 Old Accumulator Compatibility

We consider an accumulator to be *old accumulator compatible* if up-to-date witnesses w_t^x can be verified even against an outdated accumulator a_{t_a} where $t_a < t$, as long as x was added to the accumulator before (or at) t_a.[4] Old accumulator compatibility allows the verifier to be offline and out of sync with the latest accumulator state.

Like low update frequency, old accumulator compatibility requires a change in the correctness definition (but not in the soundness definition). Note that unlike Definition 4, Definition 6 is not parametrized by a function; we expect a witness to be compatible with an old accumulator no matter how out of sync they are, as long as the accumulator already contains the element in question.

Definition 5 (Old Accumulator Compatibility (OAC)). *An accumulator is old accumulator compatible if the accumulator is OAC-correct, as described in Definition 6.*

Definition 6 (Old Accumulator Compatiblity (OAC) Correctness). *An accumulator is OAC-correct if an up-to-date witness w^x corresponding to value x can always be used to verify the membership of x in any out-of date accumulator a which already contains x.*

More formally, for all security parameters k, all values x and additional sets of values $[y_1, \ldots, y_{t_x-1}]$, $[y_{t_x+1}, \ldots, y_t]$:

$$\Pr \begin{bmatrix} a_0 \leftarrow \mathsf{Gen}(1^k); \\ (a_i, w_i^{y_i}, \mathsf{upmsg}_i) \leftarrow \mathsf{Add}(a_{i-1}, y_i) \, for \, i \in [1, \ldots, t_x - 1]; \\ (a_{t_x}, w_{t_x}^x, \mathsf{upmsg}_{t_x}) \leftarrow \mathsf{Add}(a_{t_x-1}, x); \\ (a_i, w_i^{y_i}, \mathsf{upmsg}_i) \leftarrow \mathsf{Add}(a_{i-1}, y_i) \, for \, i \in [t_x + 1, \ldots, t]; \\ w_i^x \leftarrow \mathsf{MemWitUpOnAdd}(x, w_{i-1}^x, \mathsf{upmsg}_i) \, for \, i \in [t_x + 1, \ldots, t] : \\ \forall j \in \{t_x, \ldots, t\}, \mathsf{VerMem}(a_j, x, w_t^x) = 1 \end{bmatrix} = 1$$

4 Our New Scheme

There are several known accumulator constructions, including the RSA construction [3,8,14], the Bilinear Map construction [1,10,18], and the Merkle tree construction [7]. (Other similar Merkle tree constructions are described in [4,5].) Their properties are described in Fig. 3. None of these constructions have low update frequency or old-accumulator compatibility.

We present a different Merkle tree construction which, unlike the constructions given in [4,5,7,9], is asynchronous: that is, it has low update frequency and old-accumulator compatibility. However, unlike some of those Merkle tree constructions, it is not universal (meaning that it does not support proofs of non-membership).

---

[4] Note that this does not compromise the soundness property of the accumulator, because if x was not a member of the accumulator at t_a, w_t^x does not verify with a_{t_a}.

Accumulator Protocol Runtimes and Storage Requirements					
Accumulator	Signatures	RSA	Bilinear Map	Merkle	This Work
Add runtime	1	1	1 w/ trapdoor, n without	$\log(n)$	$\log(n)$
Add storage	1	1	1 w/ trapdoor, n without	$\log(n)$	$\log(n)$
MemWitUpOnAdd runtime	0	1	1	$\log(n)$	$\log(n)$
MemWitUpOnAdd storage	0	1	1	$\log(n)$	$\log(n)$

Accumulator Properties					
Accumulator	Signatures	RSA	Bilinear Map	Merkle	This Work
Accumulator size	1	1	1	1	$\log(n)$
Witness size	1	1	1	$\log(n)$	$\log(n)$
Strong?	no	no*	no	yes	yes
Update frequency **	0	n	n	n	$\log(n)$
Old accumulator compatibile?	yes	no	no	no	yes

Fig. 3. Various accumulator constructions and their protocol runtimes, storage requirements, and properties. For each of Add and MemWitUpOnAdd, this table gives the algorithm runtime, and the storage required for the algorithm execution. Additionally, the table describes other accumulator properties, such as accumulator size, witness size, strength, update frequency and old-accumulator compatibility. We let n denote the total number of elements in the accumulator. The RSA Construction is due to [3,8,14]. The Bilinear Map construction is due to [1,10,18]. The Merkle tree construction is due to [9], though it is not described as an accumulator construction. (Other Merkle tree constructions are given in [4,5,7].) Big-O notation is omitted from this table in the interest of brevity, but it is implicit everywhere. (*Sander [20] shows a way to make the RSA accumulator strong by choosing the RSA modulus in such a way that its factorization is never revealed. **Here n refers to the number of elements added and deleted *after* the addition of the element whose witness updates are being discussed.)

4.1 Construction

Let n be the number of elements in our accumulator, and let h be a collision-resistant hash function. When h is applied to pairs or elements, we encode the pair in such a way that it can never be confused with a single element x – e.g., a pair is prefaced with a '2', and a single element with '1'. Additionally, we encode accumulated elements in such a way that they can never be mistaken for the output of h. For instance, we might preface each element with 'elt', and the output of the hash function with 'hash'.

Our accumulator maintains a list of $D = \lceil \log(n+1) \rceil$ Merkle tree roots $r_{D-1}, \ldots, r_0$ (as opposed to just one Merkle tree root). The leaves of these Merkle trees are the accumulated elements. r_d is the root of a complete Merkle tree with 2^d leaves if and only if the dth least significant bit of the binary expansion of n is 1. Otherwise, $r_d = \bot$. Note that this accumulator is very similar to a binary counter of elements, but instead of having a 1 in the dth least significant position representing the presence of 2^d elements, the accumulator has root of the complete Merkle tree containing those elements.

A witness w^x for x is the authenticating path for x in the Merkle tree that contains x. That is, if x is in the Merkle tree with root r_d, then $w^x = ((z_1, \text{dir}_1), \ldots, (z_{d-1}, \text{dir}_{d-1}))$, where each z_i is in the range of the hash function h, and each dir is either right or left. These are the (right / left) sibling elements of all of the nodes along the path from element x to the Merkle tree root of depth d. These siblings, together with the element x, can be used to reconstruct the root of the Merkle tree. Note that, if x is in the Merkle tree of depth 0, then the witness is empty. An illustration of an accumulator a and a witness w is given in Fig. 4.

Membership Verification. Verification is done by using the authenticating path w^x and the element x in question to recompute the Merkle tree root and check that it indeed matches the accumulator root r_d, where d is the length of w^x. In more detail, this is done by recomputing the *ancestors* of the element x using the authenticating path w^x, where the ancestors are the nodes along the path from x to its root, as defined by x and by elements in w^x. If the accumulator is up to date, the last ancestor should correspond to the appropriate accumulator root r_d.

If the accumulator is outdated but still contains x, one of the recomputed ancestors should still correspond to one of the accumulator roots. This is because, as described in the full version of this paper [19], witnesses (and thus the ancestors they are used to compute) are append-only.

If the witness is outdated (that is, it is from time $t_w < t$), verification can be done at time t as long as $t < t_w + 2^d$. In Fig. 1, we lower-bound d as $\log_2(t_w - t_x)$, where t_x is the time at which the element in question was added. This results in the condition $t < 2t_w - t_x$.

Verification is described in full detail in the full version of this paper [19].

Element Addition. Element addition is done by merging Merkle trees to create deeper ones. Specifically, when the nth element x is added to $a = [r_{D-1}, \ldots, r_0]$, if $r_0 = \bot$, we set $r_0 = h(x)$. If, however, $r_0 \neq \bot$, we "carry" exactly as we would in a binary counter: we create a depth-one Merkle tree root $z = h(r_0, h(x))$, set $r_0 = \bot$, and try our luck with r_1. If $r_1 = \bot$, we can set $r_1 = z$. If $r_1 \neq \bot$, we must continue merging Merkle trees and "carrying" further up the chain. Element addition is described in full detail in the full version of this paper [19], and is illustrated in Figs. 5 and 6 of Appendix A.

Membership Witness Updates. Membership witness updates need to be performed only when the root of the Merkle tree containing the element in question is merged, or "carried", during a subsequent element addition. This occurs at most D times. Membership updates use the update message $\text{upmsg}_{t+1} = (y, w^y_{t+1})$ (where y is the element being added and w^y_{t+1} is the witness generated for y) in order to bring the witness w^x_t for the element x up to date.

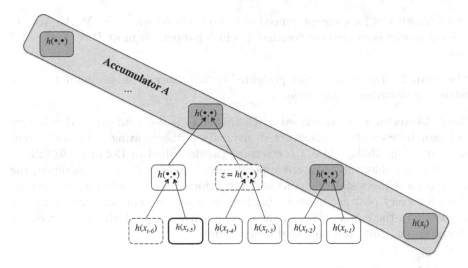

Fig. 4. An illustration of our accumulator. The accumulator itself is shaded; the unshaded elements are elements of the Merkle trees which are not actually a part of the accumulator. The elements with dashed outlines belong to the authenticating path for x_{t-5} (which itself has a bold outline). So, the witness for x_{t-5} would be $w^{x_{t-5}} = ((h(x_{t-6}), \mathsf{left}), (z, \mathsf{right}))$.

4.2   Properties

The accumulator construction presented in this paper is sound (Theorem 1), has low update frequency (Theorem 2) and is old-accumulator compatible (Theorem 3).

Theorem 1. *The construction presented in this paper is* sound *as described in Definition 2 as long as h is collision resistant.*

Proof. We prove soundness using the classical technique for Merkle trees. Say we have an adversary $\mathcal{A}_a$ who can break soundness (i.e., who can find a witness for an element that has not been added to the accumulator). We construct the accumulator Merkle forest using the elements $x_1, \dots, x_{t-1}$ that $\mathcal{A}_a$ requests be added to the accumulator. $\mathcal{A}_a$ then gives us an authenticating path for an element $x \notin \{x_1, \dots, x_{t-1}\}$, and therefore not in any of the accumulator Merkle trees. Using that path, we reconstruct the ancestors of that element. The first ancestor that actually appears in any of our accumulator Merkle trees is a collision, since we have two values that hash to it: the value or pair of values that legitimately appears in our accumulator Merkle tree, and the value or pair of values provided by the adversary.

Theorem 2. *The construction presented in this paper has* low update frequency *as described in Definition 3.*

Proof. A witness for element x need only be updated when the Merkle tree in which x resides is merged (or "carried"), which happens at most $D = \lceil \log(n+1) \rceil$ times.

Theorem 3. *The construction presented in this paper is* old-accumulator compatible *as described in Definition 5.*

Proof. Correctness (as described in Definition 1) is self-evident; a Merkle tree root can be correctly reconstructed given its authenticating path. Old accumulator compatibility (OAC) correctness (as described in Definition 6) follows from the fact that witnesses are append-only; whenever they are modified, the entire prior witness state remains and new information is tacked on at the end. Thus, for every past accumulator (as long as it already contains the element x in question), there is a subset of the current witness w_t^x which can be used for verification against that outdated accumulator.

Strength. Additionally, the construction presented in this paper is *strong*, meaning that it does not rely on a trusted accumulator manager. Since every operation is deterministic and publicly verifiable, the accumulator manager would have no more luck breaking soundness than a witness holder would. This is important for distributed use-cases, where there might not be a central trusted party to execute element additions.

Distributed Storage. The construction presented in this paper has fully distributed storage; all storage requirements are logarithmic in the number of elements. The accumulator manager does not need to store the accumulated elements, or any other additional data, to perform additions. This, too, is important for distributed use-cases, because storing a lot of data might be too burdensome for the users of the distributed system, and there might not be a central manager willing to store the necessary data.

5 Taking Advantage of Infrequent Membership Witness Updates in a Distributed PKI

We now return to the PKI application of our accumulator described in Sect. 1.1, where we have a membership witness holder who may not be able to make a witness update whenever a new element is added. As highlighted in Sect. 4.2, our accumulator scheme requires that the witness for a given element x be updated at most $D = \lceil \log(n+1) \rceil$ times, where n is the number of elements added to the accumulator after x. However, one might observe that having to *check* whether the witness needs updating each time a new element addition occurs renders this point moot, since this check itself must be done a linear number of times. We solve this problem by giving our witness holders the ability to "go back in time" to observe past accumulator updates. If they can ignore updates when they occur, and go back to the relevant ones when they need to bring their witness up to date (e.g. at when they need to show it to a verifying third party), they can avoid looking at the irrelevant ones altogether.

"Going back in time" is possible in the public bulletin board setting of our PKI application, in which our accumulator is maintained as part of a public bulletin board. The bulletin board is append-only, so it contains a history of all of the accumulator states. Along with these states, we will include the update message, and a counter indicating how many additions have taken place to date. Additionally, we will include pointers to a selection of other accumulator states, so as to allow the bulletin board user to move amongst them efficiently. The pointers from accumulator state t would be to accumulator states $t - 2^i$ for all i such that $0 < 2^i < t$ (somewhat similarly to what is done in a skip-list). These pointers can be constructed in logarithmic time: there is a logarithmic number of them, and each of them can be found in constant time by using the previous one, since $t - 2^i = t - 2^{i-1} - 2^{i-1}$. Note that storing these pointers is not a problem, since we are already storing a logarithmic amount of data in the form of the accumulator and witness.

Our witness holder can then ignore update messages altogether, performing no checks or work at all. Instead, he updates his witness only when he needs to produce a proof. When this happens, he checks the counter of the most recently posted accumulator state. The counter alone is sufficient to deduce whether his witness needs updating. If his witness does not need updating, he has merely performed a small additional constant amount of work for the verification at hand. If, as happens a logarithmic number of times, his witness does need updating, the pointers and counters allow him to locate in logarithmic time the (at most logarithmic number of) bulletin board entries he needs to access in order to bring his witness up to date, as described in Appendix C of the full version of this paper [19]. Thus, the total work performed by our witness holder will remain logarithmic in the number of future element additions.

Acknowledgements. This research is supported, in part, by US NSF grants CNS-1012910, CNS-1012798, and CNS-1422965. Leonid Reyzin gratefully acknowledges the hospitality of IST Austria and École normale supérieure, where part of this work was performed.

The authors would like to thank Dimitris Papadopoulos and Foteini Baldimtsi for their insightful feedback.

A   Element Addition

In Figs. 5 and 6, we illustrate a single element addition. Element x_{t+1} is being added to the accumulator. The depth 0 and depth 1 Merkle trees are both present in the accumulator, so two "carries" occur before x_{t+1} is successfully added into the Merkle tree of depth 2.

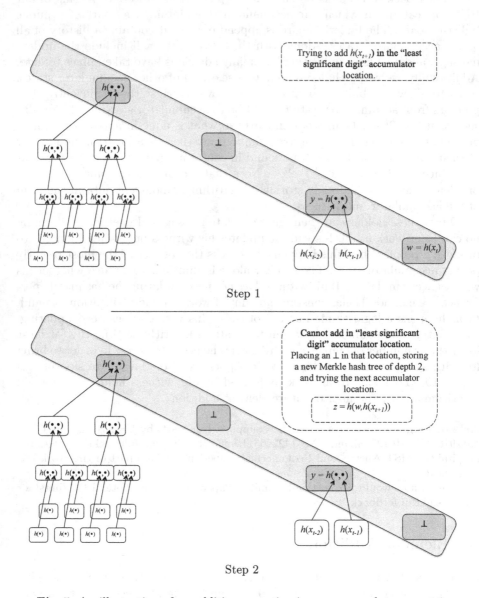

Step 1

Step 2

Fig. 5. An illustration of an addition operation in our accumulator - part 1.

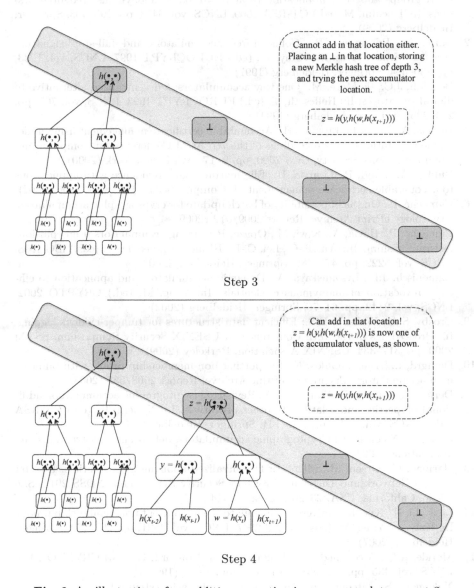

Cannot add in that location either. Placing an ⊥ in that location, storing a new Merkle hash tree of depth 3, and trying the next accumulator location.

$z = h(y,h(w,h(x_{t+1})))$

Step 3

Can add in that location! $z = h(y,h(w,h(x_{t+1})))$ is now one of the accumulator values, as shown.

$z = h(y,h(w,h(x_{t+1})))$

Step 4

Fig. 6. An illustration of an addition operation in our accumulator - part 2.

References

1. Au, M.H., Tsang, P.P., Susilo, W., Mu, Y.: Dynamic universal accumulators for DDH groups and their application to attribute-based anonymous credential systems. In: Fischlin, M. (ed.) CT-RSA 2009. LNCS, vol. 5473, pp. 295–308. Springer, Heidelberg (2009)
2. Barić, N., Pfitzmann, B.: Collision-free accumulators and fail-stop signature schemes without trees. In: Fumy, W. (ed.) EUROCRYPT 1997. LNCS, vol. 1233, pp. 480–494. Springer, Heidelberg (1997)
3. Benaloh, J.C., de Mare, M.: One-way accumulators: a decentralized alternative to digital signatures. In: Helleseth, T. (ed.) EUROCRYPT 1993. LNCS, vol. 765, pp. 274–285. Springer, Heidelberg (1994)
4. Buldas, A., Laud, P., Lipmaa, H.: Accountable certificate management using undeniable attestations. In: Proceedings of the 7th ACM Conference on Computer and Communications Security, CCS 2000, pp. 9–17. ACM, New York (2000)
5. Buldas, A., Laud, P., Lipmaa, H.: Eliminating counterevidence with applications to accountable certificate management. J. Comput. Secur. **10**(3), 273–296 (2002)
6. Camacho, P.: On the impossibility of batch update for cryptographic accumulators. Cryptology ePrint Archive, Report 2009/612 (2009)
7. Camacho, P., Hevia, A., Kiwi, M., Opazo, R.: Strong accumulators from collision-resistant hashing. In: Wu, T.-C., Lei, C.-L., Rijmen, V., Lee, D.-T. (eds.) ISC 2008. LNCS, vol. 5222, pp. 471–486. Springer, Heidelberg (2008)
8. Camenisch, J.L., Lysyanskaya, A.: Dynamic accumulators and application to efficient revocation of anonymous credentials. In: Yung, M. (ed.) CRYPTO 2002. LNCS, vol. 2442, pp. 61–76. Springer, Heidelberg (2002)
9. Crosby, S.A., Wallach, D.S.: Efficient data structures for tamper-evident logging. In: Proceedings of the 18th Conference on USENIX Security Symposium, SSYM 2009, pp. 317–334. USENIX Association, Berkeley (2009)
10. Damgrd, I., Triandopoulos, N.: Supporting non-membership proofs with bilinear-map accumulators. Cryptology ePrint Archive, Report 2008/538 (2008)
11. Derler, D., Hanser, C., Slamanig, D.: Revisiting cryptographic accumulators, additional properties and relations to other primitives. In: Nyberg, K. (ed.) CT-RSA 2015. LNCS, vol. 9048, pp. 127–144. Springer, Heidelberg (2015)
12. Fazio, N., Nicolosi, A.: Cryptographic accumulators: definitions, constructions and applications (2003)
13. Garman, C., Green, M., Miers, I.: Decentralized anonymous credentials. In: 21st Annual Network and Distributed System Security Symposium, NDSS 2014, San Diego, California, USA, 23–26 February 2014
14. Li, J., Li, N., Xue, R.: Universal accumulators with efficient nonmembership proofs. In: Katz, J., Yung, M. (eds.) ACNS 2007. LNCS, vol. 4521, pp. 253–269. Springer, Heidelberg (2007)
15. Merkle, R.C.: A certified digital signature. In: Brassard, G. (ed.) CRYPTO 1989. LNCS, vol. 435, pp. 218–238. Springer, Heidelberg (1990)
16. Nakamoto, S.: Bitcoin: a peer-to-peer electronic cash system (2008)
17. Namecoin. https://www.namecoin.org/
18. Nguyen, L.: Accumulators from bilinear pairings and applications. In: Menezes, A. (ed.) CT-RSA 2005. LNCS, vol. 3376, pp. 275–292. Springer, Heidelberg (2005)
19. Reyzin, L., Yakoubov, S.: Efficient asynchronous accumulators for distributed PKI. Cryptology ePrint Archive, Report 2015/718 (2015). http://eprint.iacr.org/

20. Sander, T.: Efficient accumulators without trapdoor extended abstract. In: Varad-harajan, V., Mu, Y. (eds.) ICICS 1999. LNCS, vol. 1726, pp. 252–262. Springer, Heidelberg (1999)
21. Slepak, G.: Dnschain + okturtles (2013). http://okturtles.com/other/dnschain_okturtles_overview.pdf
22. Yakoubov, S., Fromknecht, C., Velicanu, D.: Certcoin: a namecoin based decentralized authentication system (2014)

Outsourcing Computation

The Feasibility of Outsourced Database Search in the Plain Model

Carmit Hazay[1](✉) and Hila Zarosim[2]

[1] Faculty of Engineering, Bar-Ilan University, Ramat Gan, Israel
carmit.hazay@biu.ac.il
[2] Department of Computer Science, Bar-Ilan University, Ramat Gan, Israel
zarosih@cs.biu.ac.il

Abstract. The problem of securely outsourcing computation to an *untrusted* server gained momentum with the recent penetration of *cloud computing* services. The ultimate goal in this setting is to design efficient protocols that minimize the computational overhead of the clients and instead rely on the extended resources of the server. In this paper, we focus on the *outsourced database search* problem which is highly motivated in the context of delegatable computing since it offers storage alternatives for massive databases, that may contain confidential data. This functionality is described in two phases: (1) setup phase and (2) query phase. The main goal is to minimize the parties workload in the query phase so that it is proportional to the query size and its corresponding response.

We study whether a trusted setup or a random oracle are *necessary* for protocols with *minimal interaction* that meet the optimal communication and computation bounds in the query phase. We answer this question positively and demonstrate a lower bound on the communication or the computational overhead in this phase.

Keywords: Outsourced computation · Database search functionalities · Lower bound · Communication and computational complexities · Minimal interaction

1 Introduction

Background on Outsourced Secure Computation. The problem of securely outsourcing computation to an *untrusted* server gained momentum with the recent penetration of *cloud computing* services, where clients can lease computing services on demand rather than maintaining their own infrastructure. The ultimate

Carmit Hazay—Research partially supported by a grant from the Israel Ministry of Science and Technology (grant No. 3-10883), by the European Research Council under the ERC consolidators grant agreement n. 615172 (HIPS).

Hila Zarosim—The author is grateful to the Azrieli Foundation for the Azrieli Fellowship award.

© Springer International Publishing Switzerland 2016
V. Zikas and R. De Prisco (Eds.): SCN 2016, LNCS 9841, pp. 313–332, 2016.
DOI: 10.1007/978-3-319-44618-9_17

goal in this setting is to design efficient protocols that minimize the computational overhead of the clients and instead rely on the extended resources of the server. Of course, the amount of work invested by the client in order to verify the correctness of the computation needs to be *substantially* smaller than running the computation by itself. Another ambitious challenge of delegatable computation is to design protocols that minimize the *communication* between the cloud and the client. This becomes of particular importance with the proliferation of smartphone technology and mobile broadband internet connections, as for mobile devices communication and data connectivity is often the more severe bottleneck.

The study of delagatable computation was initiated with the study of a restricted scenario where a *single client* outsources its computation to an external server. Two main approaches are examined in this context. In the first setting there is only one phase of interaction between the client and the server such that the overall amount of work performed by the client is smaller than performing the computation on its own. Correctness in this setting is achieved by succinct zero-knowledge proofs [GLR11, BCCT12, DFH12] with the aim of minimizing the number of rounds between the client and the server. In the *amortized setting* [GGP10, AIK10] the computational complexity of the client is analyzed in an amortized sense. Namely, the client can perform some expensive preprocessing (also known as the offline phase). After this phase is completed, it is required to run very efficient computations in the online phase.

Recent results also study an extended setting with *multiple r clients* that mutually distrust each other and wish to securely outsource a joint computation on their inputs with reduced costs [KMR11, KMR12, LATV12, AJLA+12, CKKC13]. In particular, it is required that the communication between the clients and the server, as well as the communication between the clients, will be sufficiently smaller than running a secure computation in the standard setting. This more complex setting is strictly harder than the single client setting since one must handle potential corruptions of any (proper) subset of the clients, that might collude with the server. It is worth noting that in case only correctness is required then security in the multi clients setting is reduced to security in the single client setting. This is due to the fact that we can consider a protocol where $r - 1$ clients send their inputs to the rth client, that communicates with the server using all inputs. It then forwards the server's proof to the other clients who can verify its correctness. Generally speaking, outsourced secure computation in the presence of collusion between any t clients and the server implies secure computation in the standard setting with $r - t + 1$ parties. Thus, the problem of delegatable computation with multiple clients focuses on achieving privacy (with or without imposing correctness).

Modeling Outsourced Database Search. We consider an outsourced database search functionality where one client has a database, and another set of clients search the database using a sequence of queries. To simplify the presentation we denote the data owner by the sender and the other set of clients by the receiver (for simplicity, we focus on a single receiver asking for multiple queries).

The input of the sender is a database of size n.[1] The input queries of the receiver $\{q_i\}_{i \in [t]}$ are picked from a predefined set Q_n where Q_n is a set of queries that correspond to a database of size n. This functionality can be described in two phases. In the *setup phase* the sender uploads a function of its database to the server. This phase is run only once, where the sender's state after this phase is independent of n. Next, in the *query phase* the receiver picks a search query and obtains from the server the answer to this query. To restrict the number of queries, the sender must approve each query by providing a trapdoor that depends on the content of the query.

This functionality is highly motivated in the context of outsourced computation since it offers storage alternatives for massive databases that may contain confidential data (e.g., health related data about patient history). Our formalization captures a large class of search functionalities such as oblivious transfer (OT) with adaptive queries [NP99, GH11], keyword search [FIPR05], pattern matching [HT10] and the indexing problem [Goh03]. The former two functionalities are part of a class for which a query's response size is bounded by an a priori fixed length, whereas for the latter two functionalities a response is unbounded and might be $O(n)$. Consequently, secure implementations of such functionalities are more involved. Moreover, our infeasibility results are more meaningful for this class.

Security is formalized via the standard ideal/real paradigm where in the ideal setting the three parties: sender, receiver and server, communicate with an ideal functionality that first obtains the preprocessed database from the sender and later answers search queries made by the receiver, while leaking some information about the responses to the server.[2] Our modeling also captures collusion between the server and the receiver. In order to take some advantage from this modeling, we would like the setup phase to imply $O(n)$ workload, yet the overall cost of issuing a query should only *grow linearly with the size of the query's response* (which is as optimal as one can obtain). For functionalities that do not imply a fixed bound on the query responses, this optimization comes at the price of revealing some leakage about the database (for instance, in pattern matching the server learns the number of matches of some hidden query).

Another important complexity measure of secure computation that has been extensively studied in literature, is the *round-complexity* of secure protocols. In the *stand-alone* setting, Katz and Ostrovsky [KO04] determined that the exact round complexity of achieving a secure two-party computation protocol is five (and four if only one of the parties receives an output). More recently, Ostrovsky et al. [ORS15] strengthened this construction by demonstrating a five-round protocol where the underlying cryptographic primitives are used only in a "black-box" way. Both the results also provide a four-round protocol for

---

[1] We remark that the internal structure of the database is not important for our proofs.

[2] Our formalization considers the minimal leakage of the length of the queries responses, yet our proofs follow for any type of leakage as the preprocessed database is computed independently of that leakage.

single-output functionalities. In the multi-party setting, the recent work by Garg et al. [GMPP16] studies the exact round-complexity of multi-party computation (MPC) protocols in the plain model and shows that at least four rounds are necessary for realizing general functionalities.

In this work we study the feasibility of protocols with *minimal interaction* in the outsourced setting with no trusted setup, where in the setup phase the sender sends a single message to the server, whereas in the query phase the sender and the receiver exchange only two messages (one in each direction), and then one message in each direction between the receiver and the server.[3] Specifically, we focus on semi-honest security and study the *feasibility* of the outsourced database search functionality in the plain model with *minimal interaction* and using *minimal resources* of communication and computation. Security in this model implies sender's privacy against, potentially colluding, server and receiver. Whereas receiver's privacy is ensured against either corrupted sender or server. We address the following question,

Does there exist a private protocol with minimal interaction for the outsourced search functionality in the plain model, that meets the optimal communication and computation bounds in the query phase?

We prove that the answer for this question is negative and that there exists a large class of search functionalities that *cannot* be realized privately with optimal resources in the query phase.

1.1 Our Results

We prove that using a trusted setup or a random oracle is essential in order to reduce the resources of the receiver within protocols with minimal interaction, *even* if the sender's state in $o(n)$ and the number of rounds between the server and the receiver is arbitrary. This result has the consequence that for certain search functionalities (e.g., pattern matching and all its variants, and the indexing problem), either the communication complexity or the running time of the receiver must be as large as the size of the database. In this paper we examine both non-private and private channels scenarios (where in the latter setting corrupted parties do not see the communication between the honest parties), and prove that our lower bound holds in both settings, where our proof in the non-private setting relies on a weaker adversary.

More formally, let $\mathcal{ANS}_{n,q}$ denote the set of *all potential responses* for the query q when ranging over all databases T of size n, and let $H_{n,Q} = \max_{q \in Q_n} \log |\mathcal{ANS}_{n,q}|$ (intuitively, $H_{n,Q}$ is the logarithm of the number of potential query responses when ranging over all databases of size n and all queries in Q_n; see Definition 2.1). Then we prove the following theorem,

---

[3] We prove that if the order of communication between the receiver and the sender/server is swapped then our lower bounds follow more easily. We further note that our lower bounds are not restricted to a minimal interaction between the server and the receiver.

Theorem 1.1 (informal). *For any protocol with minimal interaction that securely implements the outsourced database search functionality in the presence of semi-honest adversaries, one of the following holds:*

1. *The communication complexity in the query phase is $\Omega(H_{n,Q})$.*
2. *The number of random bits used by the receiver is $\Omega(H_{n,Q})$.*

Our proof follows a similar intuition of the proof from [Nie02] when showing the impossibility of constructing non-interactive non-committing encryption schemes in the plain model. Nevertheless, the formalization is more challenging since the number of involved parties is three. One consequence that we need to take into account is the order of rounds of which the receiver interacts with the other parties. This is because for our proof in the private channels setting we need to consider an adversary that corrupts both the server and the receiver. In this case, the view of the adversary contains both the randomness of the receiver and the server, as well as the messages sent from the sender. We further must distinguish between the randomness of the receiver and that of the server and rely on the fact that the random tape of the server is uniformly independent of the receiver's view. Specifically, we need to show that when we fix a partial view of the receiver, then for almost all random tapes of the server, the receiver outputs the correct value. Note that if the receiver communicates with the server first then this independence no longer holds since the communication between the receiver and the sender may depend on the random tape of the server (as it may depend on the messages from the server). On the other hand, if the receiver communicates with the sender first then independence follows, as semi-honest adversaries cannot pick their randomness arbitrarily. This subtlety is in contrast to the proof in [Nie02] that relies on the correctness of the non-interactive decryption algorithm of the underlying encryption scheme.

We consider the two potential orders of rounds in the query phase. If the receiver *communicates with the server first*, we show that the communication complexity of the protocol must be large. This is intuitively because at the time the receiver communicates with the server, the server does not know which information to send back and essentially must send as much information as the maximal amount of information sent within any response to query q (when ranging over all databases of size n). On the other hand, if the receiver *communicates with the sender first* then recall that in the simulation of the setup phase the simulator must commit to a setup message independently of the sender's database, where this message is fixed and cannot be later changed. Then in the query phase, the simulator has to simulate the view for the corrupted parties so that it yields the correct output for the receiver. We show that this means that for every possible answer there must exist a view $(r_{\mathsf{Rec}}, \mathsf{m}_2)$ for the receiver (where r_{Rec} is the random tape of the receiver and m_2 the message from the sender to the receiver) such that with a high probability (over the random coins of the server), the receiver outputs the correct query response. This implies that the number of views (r_{Rec}, m_2) must be proportional to the number of potential query responses when ranging over all databases (and hence the length of (r_{Rec}, m_2) is linear in $H_{n,Q}$), which can be as large as the size of the database for certain search functionalities *even when the receiver's output size is small*.

It is important to note that our lower bounds hold for *any* protocol with minimal interaction. Therefore, we can always focus on a protocol that makes use of a minimal number of random coins. Saying differently, our lower bounds consider the *effective* number of bits used by the receiver and even cover scenarios where the receiver's random tape is very large, for which the receiver ignores some portion of it. The reason for this is that for every such protocol, we can consider an equivalent protocol where the receiver's random tape does not contain any unused bits and apply our lower bounds to the new protocol. This further implies a lower bound on the running time of the receiver since these random bits must be incorporated in the computation of the receiver. Moreover, our lower bounds hold *even if the receiver maintains no privacy* since they follow from the non-committing property that we require in the simulation.[4] Importantly, any attempt to replace the uniform random bits of the receiver by an output of a pseudorandom generator (PRG) in order to strengthen our lower bounds fails since it requires finding a preimage relative to the PRG; see more details in Sect. 3.3.

Finally, we note that our lower bounds also apply in the two-party setting for reactive search functionalities (with a preprocessing phase), which implies the infeasibility of private reactive pattern matching with optimal query response and minimal interaction in the plain model. This is in contrast to the non-private setting, where suffix trees [Wei73] (a data structure that solves pattern matching and related problems on unencrypted data), are useful to store the text in a way that allows fast string operations. In particular, it illustrates that private pattern matching cannot be optimized in the preprocessing setting.

1.2 Prior Work

In [FHV13], Faust et al. use novel ideas to solve pattern matching in the cloud based on a reduction to the subset sum problem, which do not rely on the hardness of the problem but rather require instances that are solvable in polynomial-time. This paper presents the first concrete protocols for this problem where the receiver wishes to learn the positions at which a pattern of length m matches the text (and nothing beyond that). Their constructions offer simulation-based security in the presence of semi-honest and malicious adversaries and limit the communication in the query phase to $O(m)$ bits plus the number of occurrences (where the semi-honest protocol is with minimal interaction). Nevertheless, Faust et al. rely heavily on the programmability property of the random oracle, and use it to equivocate a fake text. In [CS14], Chase and Shen solve outsourced

---

[4] We note that when privacy is not considered, we prove that there exists a query for which our lower bounds hold. For private protocols this implies that these lower bounds hold for all queries or else some information about the query leaks.

pattern matching by constructing a so called queryable encryption, which is an encryption scheme that supports search queries between a client and a server with three rounds of communication. Their construction is based on suffix trees.

In [CK10] Chase and Kamara informally discuss (without providing a proof) a lower bound on the token length for structured encryption scheme, that encrypts a structured data in a way that allows to privately query the data. Their intuition says that the length of the token for a given query grows with the number of potential answers when working with a simulation-based definition. Our proofs formalize this intuition for settings with multiple clients for which the data owner is a different entity than the receiver.

Another related line of works regarding symmetric searchable encryption (SSE) allows a (single) client to store data on an untrusted server and later perform keyword searches. This primitive has been widely studied recently; see [CGKO11, KPR12, KP13, JJK+13, CGPR15, ANSS16] for just few examples. The standard security definition for SSE schemes follows the ideal/real simulation paradigm and comes with two flavours of static and adaptive searches (where in the latter modeling a keyword may be determined as a function of the previous tokens/responses). We note that our results also hold for non-interactive SSE for which the tokens maintain the keyword privacy, and thus can be transferred via a 2PC protocol to a different client than the data owner (denoted by the receiver in our paper). This scenario is considered in [JJK+13] yet their security definition is weaker in the sense that the receiver cannot collude with the server.

2 Our Modeling

In this section we model the reactive database search functionality where one client has a database, and another set of clients search the database using a sequence of queries. To simplify the presentation we denote the former client by the sender and the other set of clients by the receiver. (For simplicity, we focus on a single receiver asking for multiple queries).

Inputs and Outputs. The input of the sender is a database T of size n bits. The input queries of the receiver $\{q_i\}_{i\in[t]}$ are picked from a predefined set Q_n of binary strings, where Q_n is a set of queries that correspond to a database of size n. Specifically, we let the set of queries $\{Q_n\}_{n\in\mathbb{N}}$ depend on the database size. This formalization captures search functionalities where Q_n changes with the database size, such as in oblivious transfer with adaptive queries. It further covers search functionalities where the same set of queries is used for databases of different sizes by fixing the same set of queries for all n, such as in pattern matching, (see Section [HZ14] for the formal definitions of these functionalities).

The queries made by the receiver are determined adaptively by a PPT algorithm M that takes the receiver's initial input and the outputs of prior search results. Whenever we say that the honest receiver picks a search query $q_i \in Q_n$, we assume that the receiver applies its input selection algorithm M as specified above. Queries that do not have a suitable answer in the database will be responded with a *"no match"* message whenever queried by the receiver. Finally, we assume that $|q| \leq m$ for all $q \in Q_n$ and some fixed parameter $m = m(\kappa)$. We further assume that n is polynomial in the security parameter κ.

We let T_q denote the response of the functionality on database T and query $q \in Q_n$. As above, this formalization is general enough and allows to capture different search functionalities with different output structure (for instance, when the query outcome contains a single vs. a set of records).

The Reactive Search Functionality. This functionality is described in two phases.

1. In the *setup phase* the sender sends a message $a(T)$ to the server, where $a(\cdot)$ is some polynomial-time algorithm. This phase is run only once, such that the size of the sender's state s upon completion is bounded by $\mathsf{poly}(\kappa)$.[5]
2. In the *query phase* the receiver picks a search query and obtains from the server the answer to this query. Note that this definition is meaningful only if we restrict the number of queries made by the receiver. Otherwise, no notion of privacy is guaranteed for the sender, since the receiver (or even the server) can potentially search the database for as many queries as they wish. This requirement is formalized by asking the sender's "permission" whenever a query is made, and is an important feature of payment-based search applications where the receiver pays per search. Looking ahead, we implement this restriction using a secure protocol between the sender and the receiver that allows the receiver to learn the answer to its search query while maintaining the privacy of its query.

The formal definition of outsourced database search functionality appears in Fig. 1.

Communication Model. Our result are introduced in the plain model in two different settings: (1) in the private channels case where corrupted parties do not see the communication between the honest parties. (2) In the non-private channels case. In the later setting the adversary can observe the messages between the honest parties. We note that any infeasibility result in the private setting implies the same result in the non-private setting. Nevertheless, we reprove our theorem for the latter setting as well, assuming a weaker type of adversary. Concretely, our infeasibility result in the private setting requires a collusion between the server and receiver, whereas the analogue proof relies on an adversary that corrupts only the receiver.

Complexities. In order to take some advantage from this modeling, we would like the setup phase to require $O(n)$ workload, yet the overall cost of issuing a query should only *grow linearly with the size of the query's response* (which is as optimal as one can obtain). As mentioned before, for some search functionalities,

---

[5] For this to be meaningful, we requite that the size of the sender's state is strictly less than n. This is formalized by assuming the existence of two polynomials $p_1(\cdot)$ and $p_2(\cdot)$ such that $n \leq p_1(\kappa)$, $s \leq p_2(\kappa)$ and $s \in o(n)$.

Functionality $\mathcal{F}_{\text{ODBS}}$

Let $m, t \in \mathbb{N}$ and $Q = \{Q_n\}_n$. Functionality $\mathcal{F}_{\text{ODBS}}$ sets a table $\mathcal{B}$ initially to be empty and proceeds as follows, running with sender Sen, receiver Rec, server Ser and ideal adversary $\mathcal{SIM}$.

1. Upon receiving a message (DB, T, m) from Sen, send $(\text{preprocess}, |T|, m)$ to Ser and $\mathcal{SIM}$, and record (DB, T) and $n = |T|$.
2. Upon receiving a message (query, q_i) from Rec (for $i \in [t]$), where message $(\text{DB}, \cdot)$ has been recorded, $|q_i| \leq m$ and $q_i \in Q_n$, check if the table $\mathcal{B}$ already contains an entry of the form $(q_i, \cdot)$. If not, then pick the next available identifier id from $\{0, 1\}^*$ and add (q_i, id) to $\mathcal{B}$. Send $(\text{query}, \text{Rec})$ to Sen and $\mathcal{SIM}$.
   (a) Upon receiving $(\text{approve}, \text{Rec})$ from Sen send $(\text{response}, \text{Rec}, |T_{q_i}|, \text{id})$ to server Ser. Otherwise, if no $(\text{approve}, \text{Rec})$ message has been received from Sen, send $\perp$ to Rec and abort.
   (b) Send $(\text{response}, q_i, T_{q_i}, \text{id})$ to Rec.

Fig. 1. The outsourced database search functionality

where there is no fixed bound on the query's response, this optimization comes with the price of revealing some leakage about the database. We further allow leaking the search pattern, where the server recognizes whether the same query already asked before. Finally, we require that the round complexity of any protocol implemented in this setting is minimal. I.e., in the setup phase we require a single message sent from the sender to the server, whereas in the query phase we require the receiver exchange only two messages (one in each direction) with each of the other clients.

Security Definition. Security is formalized using the standard ideal/real paradigm, considering the server as a separate entity that does not contribute any input to the computation. As in the standard two-party modeling a corrupted party is either semi-honest or malicious, where in the semi-honest setting the attacker follows the protocol's instructions but tries to gain additional information about the honest parties' inputs, whereas in the malicious setting the attacker follows an arbitrary efficient strategy. This modeling also captures collusion between some of the parties, when the adversary corrupts more than one party and the corrupted parties share a joint state. In this work we only consider collusion between the server and the receiver.[6] We say that a protocol is secure in the presence of (P_1/P_2)-*collusion* if security holds against collusion between parties P_1 and P_2 (in addition to individual corruptions). See [HZ14] for the formal definition.

---

[6] Notably, our lower bounds also apply to settings where all type of collusion are allowed since this only strengthens the model.

2.1   Useful Notations

Let n be a natural number denoting the size of the database and let $Q = \{Q_n\}_{n \in \mathbb{N}}$ be such that Q_n is a set of appropriate queries for databases of size n bits.[7] We introduce important notations next.

Definition 2.1. *For every* $q \in Q_n$, *we let* $\mathcal{ANS}_{n,q}$ *denote the set of all potential responses* T_q *for the query* q *when ranging over all databases* T *of size* n. *Formally,* $\mathcal{ANS}_{n,q} = \{T_q \mid T \in \{0,1\}^n\}$. *Furthermore, let* $H_{n,Q} = \max_{q \in Q_n} \log |\mathcal{ANS}_{n,q}|$, *which intuitively captures the maximal amount of information that a response for* any *query* $q \in Q_n$ *provides.*

For instance, consider the oblivious transfer with adaptive queries functionality where every entry in the database is of size ℓ. In this case, $\mathcal{ANS}_{n,q}$ is the set of all ℓ-length binary strings.

Definition 2.2. *We specify the following definitions:*

1. *Denote by* $\mathsf{cc}_{\mathsf{Ser}}^{n,q}(\kappa) = \mathsf{cc}_{\mathsf{Ser}}(\kappa, n, q)$ *the communication complexity of the interaction between* Rec *and* Ser *within* π_{Query} *such that the receiver's input is the query* q *and the database is of size* n. *Namely, the number of bits being transferred between the receiver and the server in the query phase with parameters* κ *and* q.
2. *Analogously, denote by* $\mathsf{cc}_{\mathsf{Sen}}^{n,q}(\kappa) = \mathsf{cc}_{\mathsf{Sen}}(\kappa, n, q)$ *the communication complexity of the interaction between the receiver and the sender within* π_{Query} *such that the receiver's input is the query* q *and the database is of size* n.
3. *Denote by* $\mathsf{cc}^{n,q}(\kappa) = \mathsf{cc}(\kappa, n, q)$ *the overall communication complexity within* π_{Query}. *Namely, the overall number of bits being transferred during the execution of* π_{Query} *such that the receiver's input is the query* q *and the database is of size* n.
4. *Finally, denote by* $\mathsf{rand}_{\mathsf{Rec}}^{n,q}(\kappa) = \mathsf{rand}_{\mathsf{Rec}}(\kappa, n, q)$ *the size of the receiver's random tape within* π_{Query} *such that the receiver's input is the query* q *and the database is of size* n.

3   Infeasibility of Outsourced Database Search in the Plain Model

In this section we introduce our infeasibility result of outsourced database search in the plain model. We introduce our lower bound in two settings: (1) In Sect. 3.1 we prove the private channels case where corrupted parties do not see the communication between the honest parties. (2) In Sect. 3.2 we prove a similar theorem in the non-private channels case. In the later proof the adversary can observe the messages between the honest parties, which implies that a corrupted receiver observes the setup message. This simplifies our proof since the simulator does not need to generate the internal state of the server. The proof in the former setting holds only for protocols secure against $(\mathsf{Ser}/\mathsf{Rec})$-collusion and is slightly more involved.

---

[7] We emphasize that the infeasibility proof holds for any database of length n (regardless of its internal structure).

3.1   The Private Channels Case

Our proof is shown in the presence of collusion between the receiver and the server and crucially relies on the assumption that the receiver communicates with the sender first. This ordering enables to split the randomness of an adversary controlling these parties into two distinct and independent sets. In Theorem 3.1 we show that this ordering in necessary, proving that if this order of rounds is modified then the communication complexity between the server and the receiver must be proportional to $H_{n,Q}$, that might be as large as the database size for some functionalities (see Lemma 3.6). Informally, this statement follows since at the time the receiver communicates with the server, the server does not know anything about the database. It therefore does not know the correct response to the receiver's query, and essentially must send as much information as the maximal amount of information sent within any response to query q (with respect to all possible databases of size n). Recall that we assume that the receiver communicates with each party only once. Formally,

Theorem 3.1. *Fix n and m, and let $\pi = (\pi_{\mathsf{Pre}}, \pi_{\mathsf{Query}})$ be a protocol with minimal interaction that securely implements $\mathcal{F}_{\mathrm{ODBS}}$ with respect to queries $Q = \{Q_n\}_n$ in the presence of $(\mathsf{Ser}/\mathsf{Rec})$-collusion and semi-honest adversaries. Then, if π_{Query} is defined such that Rec communicates with Ser first, for every n there exists $q \in Q_n$ such that it holds that $\mathrm{cc}_{\mathsf{Ser}}^{n,q}(\kappa) \geq H_{n,Q} - s$.[8]*

Proof. Fix n and assume by contradiction that $\mathrm{cc}_{\mathsf{Ser}}^{n,q'}(\kappa) < H_{n,Q} - s$ for every $q' \in Q_n$ and consider the case that only the server is corrupted. Note first whenever the receiver communicates with the server *first*, then for every query q the length of the server's response must be the same for all databases of size n. Otherwise the server can distinguish between two different databases of size n at the end of the setup phase (we recall that the server communicates with each party only once). More formally, assume that for some query q' and n, there exist two databases T_1 and T_2 of size n, such that the length of the server's response to the receiver is different for the following executions: (1) The input of the sender is T_1 and the input of the receiver is q'. (2) The input of the sender is T_2 and the input of the receiver is q'. Next, consider a corrupted server that obtains q' as part of its auxiliary input. Now, since the receiver communicates with the server first, the server can emulate this interaction by its own at the end of the setup phase and distinguish between the case where the sender's input is T_1 and the case where the sender's input is T_2 by observing the length of the emulated response to the receiver, which violates the sender's privacy. Note that this attack does not work in the case that the receiver talks to the sender first because the receiver's message to the server cannot be emulated by the server.

This implies that the *for every* fixed query $q \in Q_n$, the server must send the same number of bits for any database T. Specifically, this holds for the case that the receiver's input is the query q^*, where q^* is such that $\log |\mathcal{ANS}_{n,q^*}| = H_{n,Q}$.

---

[8] Recall that s denotes the size of the sender's state in the query phase and that $s \in o(n)$.

Now, since the number of potential answers for q^* is $|\mathcal{ANS}_{n,q^*}|$, the receiver must eventually learn $\log |\mathcal{ANS}_{n,q^*}| = H_{n,Q}$ bits. Nevertheless, since the sender can only send at most s bits to the receiver, we conclude that there exists a query q^* such that the server must send at least $H_{n,Q} - s$ bits to the receiver for all databases. ∎

We stress that for every q, $|\mathcal{ANS}_{n,q}|$ is *independent* of the actual size of T_q for a concrete T, since it counts the number of potential responses when ranging over *all databases of length* n. Thus, the above lower bound is meaningful in the sense that it shows that the communication complexity might be large even if $|T_q|$ is small for some concrete T. We are now ready to prove the following theorem.

Theorem 3.2. *Fix* n *and* m, *and let* $\pi = (\pi_{\mathsf{Pre}}, \pi_{\mathsf{Query}})$ *be a protocol with minimal interaction that securely implements* $\mathcal{F}_{\mathrm{ODBS}}$ *with respect to queries* $Q = \{Q_n\}_n$ *in the presence of* $(\mathsf{Ser}/\mathsf{Rec})$*-collusion and semi-honest adversaries in the private channels setting, such that* Rec *communicates with* Sen *first. Then one of the following holds:*

1. *For every query* $q \in Q_n$ *the communication complexity* $\mathrm{cc}_{\mathsf{Sen}}^{n,q}(\kappa) \geq \frac{H_{n,Q}-3}{2}$ *or*
2. *There exists a query* $q \in Q_n$ *such that* $\mathrm{rand}_{\mathsf{Rec}}^{n,q}(\kappa) \geq \frac{H_{n,Q}-3}{2}$.

Proof. Let $\pi = (\pi_{\mathsf{Pre}}, \pi_{\mathsf{Query}})$ be as in Theorem 3.2, let $\mathcal{A}_{\mathsf{Ser},\mathsf{Rec}}$ be a real-world semi-honest adversary controlling the server and the receiver, and let $\mathcal{SIM}_{\mathsf{Ser},\mathsf{Rec}}$ be an ideal-world adversary guaranteed to exist by the security of $\pi = (\pi_{\mathsf{Pre}}, \pi_{\mathsf{Query}})$. By definition, upon given a message $(\mathsf{preprocess}, |T|, m)$ in the setup phase $\mathcal{SIM}_{\mathsf{Ser},\mathsf{Rec}}$ outputs a string a_{Sim}. Moreover, upon given a message $(\mathsf{response}, q, T_q, \mathsf{id})$ in the query phase it outputs a valid view for $\mathcal{A}_{\mathsf{Ser},\mathsf{Rec}}$ (recall that T_q represents the correct output for query q with respect to database T). This view is a triple $(r_{\mathsf{Rec}}, \mathsf{m}_2, r_{\mathsf{Ser}})$, where r_{Rec} and r_{Ser} are the respective random tapes of Rec and Ser and m_2 is a simulated message from Sen to Rec.

For a security parameter κ and a pair of query/response (q, T_q), we denote by $\mathrm{Pr}_{\mathcal{SIM}_{\mathsf{Ser},\mathsf{Rec}}, \kappa}[a_{\mathsf{Sim}}]$ the probability distribution over the simulated message of π_{Pre} and by $\mathrm{Pr}_{\mathcal{SIM}_{\mathsf{Ser},\mathsf{Rec}}, \kappa, q, T_q}[a_{\mathsf{Sim}}, r_{\mathsf{Rec}}, \mathsf{m}_2, r_{\mathsf{Ser}}^*]$ the probability distribution on the values $(a_{\mathsf{Sim}}, r_{\mathsf{Rec}}, \mathsf{m}_2, r_{\mathsf{Ser}}^*)$ where a_{Sim} is generated by $\mathcal{SIM}_{\mathsf{Ser},\mathsf{Rec}}$ in the simulation of π_{Pre}, $(r_{\mathsf{Rec}}, \mathsf{m}_2)$ are generated by $\mathcal{SIM}_{\mathsf{Ser},\mathsf{Rec}}$ in the simulation of π_{Query} and r_{Ser}^* is a uniformly random string. Moreover, let $\mathrm{Pr}_{\pi, \mathcal{A}_{\mathsf{Ser},\mathsf{Rec}}, \kappa, T, q}[a(T), r_{\mathsf{Rec}}, \mathsf{m}_2, r_{\mathsf{Ser}}]$ denote the probability distribution on the values $(a(T), r_{\mathsf{Rec}}, \mathsf{m}_2, r_{\mathsf{Ser}})$ that are generated in a real execution of π with $\mathcal{A}_{\mathsf{Ser},\mathsf{Rec}}$, on inputs T for the sender and q of the receiver. We further denote by $\pi_{\mathsf{Output}}(a_{\mathsf{Sim}}, r_{\mathsf{Rec}}, \mathsf{m}_2, r_{\mathsf{Ser}})$ the output of the receiver in an execution of π with a message a_{Sim} from Sen to Ser in π_{Pre}, and a message m_2 from Sen to Rec in π_{Query}, where r_{Rec} and r_{Ser} denote the respective random tapes of the receiver and the server.

We begin with a claim that states that whenever $(a_{\mathsf{Sim}}, r_{\mathsf{Rec}}, \mathsf{m}_2, r_{\mathsf{Ser}}^*)$ are sampled according to the distribution $\mathrm{Pr}_{\mathcal{SIM}_{\mathsf{Ser},\mathsf{Rec}},\kappa,q,T_q}[a_{\mathsf{Sim}}, r_{\mathsf{Rec}}, \mathsf{m}_2, r_{\mathsf{Ser}}^*]$, then the receiver outputs the correct output with probability at least $3/4$. Intuitively, this claim follows by the correctness of the real protocol and the indistinguishability of the ideal and real executions. That is, by the correctness of the protocol it holds that most of the real views $(r_{\mathsf{Ser}}, \mathsf{m}_2)$ yield the correct output, when r_{Ser} is randomly chosen (recall that by the order of the rounds, r_{Ser} is independent of $(r_{\mathsf{Rec}}, \mathsf{m}_2)$ in the real protocol). By the security of the protocol this must also hold in the simulation. Therefore, the simulated views must have the property that with a high probability the receiver returns the correct output when r_{Ser}^* is picked at random.

Claim 3.3. *There exists a κ_0 such that for all $\kappa > \kappa_0$, $T \in \{0,1\}^n$ and $q \in Q_n$,*

$$\Pr_{\mathcal{SIM}_{\mathsf{Ser},\mathsf{Rec}},\kappa,q,T_q} [\pi_{\mathsf{Output}}(a_{\mathsf{Sim}}, r_{\mathsf{Rec}}, \mathsf{m}_2, r_{\mathsf{Ser}}^*) = T_q] \geq \frac{3}{4}. \tag{1}$$

Proof Sketch. Assume that for infinitely many κ's there exists $T \in \{0,1\}^n$ and $q \in Q_n$ such that

$$\Pr_{\mathcal{SIM}_{\mathsf{Ser},\mathsf{Rec}},\kappa,q,T^q} [\pi_{\mathsf{Output}}(a_{\mathsf{Sim}}, r_{\mathsf{Rec}}, \mathsf{m}_2, r_{\mathsf{Ser}}^*) = T^q] < \frac{3}{4}. \tag{2}$$

By the correctness of π, we are guaranteed that for all sufficiently large κ, every $T \in \{0,1\}^n$ and every $q \in Q_n$, there exists a negligible function $\mathsf{negl}(\cdot)$ such that

$$\Pr_{\pi,\mathcal{A}_{\mathsf{Ser},\mathsf{Rec}},\kappa,T,q} [\pi_{\mathsf{Output}}(a(T), r_{\mathsf{Rec}}, \mathsf{m}_2, r_{\mathsf{Ser}}) = T^q] > 1 - \mathsf{negl}(\kappa). \tag{3}$$

Therefore, we can construct a PPT distinguisher D that distinguishes between a real execution of π with $\mathcal{A}_{\mathsf{Ser},\mathsf{Rec}}$ and an ideal execution of $\mathcal{F}_{\mathsf{ODBS}}$ with $\mathcal{SIM}_{\mathsf{Ser},\mathsf{Rec}}$ as follows. Given input T, q and a view $(a, r_{\mathsf{Rec}}, \mathsf{m}_2, r_{\mathsf{Ser}})$ that is either generated by $\mathcal{SIM}_{\mathsf{Ser},\mathsf{Rec}}$ or by the honest parties in a real execution of π, D chooses a uniform random string r_{Ser}^* and outputs 1 if and only if $\pi_{\mathsf{Output}}(a, r_{\mathsf{Rec}}, \mathsf{m}_2, r_{\mathsf{Ser}}^*) = T^q$.

It is easy to see that if $(a_{\mathsf{Sim}}, r_{\mathsf{Rec}}, \mathsf{m}_2, r_{\mathsf{Ser}})$ were generated by $\mathcal{SIM}_{\mathsf{Ser},\mathsf{Rec}}$, then D outputs 1 with probability $\mathrm{Pr}_{\mathcal{SIM}_{\mathsf{Ser},\mathsf{Rec}},\kappa,q,T^q}[\pi_{\mathsf{Output}}(a_{\mathsf{Sim}}, r_{\mathsf{Rec}}, \mathsf{m}_2, r_{\mathsf{Ser}}^*) = T^q]$, whereas if $(a_{\mathsf{Sim}}, r_{\mathsf{Rec}}, \mathsf{m}_2, r_{\mathsf{Ser}})$ were generated in a real execution of π with $\mathcal{A}_{\mathsf{Ser},\mathsf{Rec}}$, then D outputs 1 with probability $\mathrm{Pr}_{\pi,\mathcal{A}_{\mathsf{Ser},\mathsf{Rec}},\kappa,T,q}[\pi_{\mathsf{Output}}(a(T), r_{\mathsf{Rec}}, \mathsf{m}_2, r_{\mathsf{Ser}}) = T^q]$. Hence, by Eqs. (3) and (2), D distinguishes the views with overwhelming probability. ■

To this end, we fix κ and q. Then, for every a_{Sim} and T_q let

$\mathsf{GoodView}(a_{\mathsf{Sim}}, T_q)$

$$= \left\{ (r_{\mathsf{Rec}}, \mathsf{m}_2) \Big|_{\mathcal{SIM}_{\mathsf{Ser},\mathsf{Rec}},\kappa,q,T_q} \Pr [\pi_{\mathsf{Output}}(a_{\mathsf{Sim}}, r_{\mathsf{Rec}}, \mathsf{m}_2, r_{\mathsf{Ser}}^*) = T_q \mid a_{\mathsf{Sim}}, r_{\mathsf{Rec}}, \mathsf{m}_2] > \frac{1}{2} \right\}.$$

Note that the above probability is only taken over the choice of r_{Ser}^* which is a uniformly random string. Next, for a fixed T_q we let $\mathcal{E}(T_q)$ denote the expected value of $|\mathsf{GoodView}(a_{\mathsf{Sim}}, T_q)|$ when a_{Sim} is generated by $\mathcal{SIM}_{\mathsf{Ser,Rec}}$ in the simulation of π_{Pre}. That is,

$$\mathcal{E}(T_q) = \mathbb{E}_{a_{\mathsf{Sim}}}\left[|\mathsf{GoodView}(a_{\mathsf{Sim}}, T_q)|\right] = \sum_{a_{\mathsf{Sim}}} \Pr_{\mathcal{SIM}_{\mathsf{Ser,Rec}},\kappa}[a_{\mathsf{Sim}}] \cdot |\mathsf{GoodView}(a_{\mathsf{Sim}}, T_q)|.$$

Then, we prove the following claim,

Claim 3.4. *For every T_q, it holds that $\mathcal{E}(T_q) \geq \frac{1}{4}$.*

Proof. Let T_q be such that $\mathcal{E}(T_q) < 1/4$, we show that this contradicts Claim 3.3. First, recall that $\mathcal{E}(T_q) = \mathbb{E}_{a_{\mathsf{Sim}}}\left[|\mathsf{GoodView}(a_{\mathsf{Sim}}, T_q)|\right]$. By the Markov inequality it holds that

$$\Pr_{\mathcal{SIM}_{\mathsf{Ser,Rec}},\kappa}\left[|\mathsf{GoodView}(a_{\mathsf{Sim}}, T_q)| \geq 1\right] < \frac{1}{4}. \tag{4}$$

Then, by the total probability theorem it holds that

$$\Pr_{\mathcal{SIM}_{\mathsf{Ser,Rec}},n,q,T_q}[\pi_{\mathsf{Output}}(a_{\mathsf{Sim}}, r_{\mathsf{Rec}}, \mathsf{m}_2, r_{\mathsf{Ser}}^*) = T_q]$$

$$= \Pr\left[\pi_{\mathsf{Output}}(a_{\mathsf{Sim}}, r_{\mathsf{Rec}}, \mathsf{m}_2, r_{\mathsf{Ser}}^*) = T_q \;\middle|\; |\mathsf{GoodView}(a_{\mathsf{Sim}}, T_q)| \geq 1\right] \cdot \Pr\left[|\mathsf{GoodView}(a_{\mathsf{Sim}}, T_q)| \geq 1\right]$$

$$+ \Pr\left[\pi_{\mathsf{Output}}(a_{\mathsf{Sim}}, r_{\mathsf{Rec}}, \mathsf{m}_2, r_{\mathsf{Ser}}^*) = T_q \;\middle|\; |\mathsf{GoodView}(a_{\mathsf{Sim}}, T_q)| = 0\right] \cdot \Pr\left[|\mathsf{GoodView}(a_{\mathsf{Sim}}, T_q)| = 0\right]$$

$$\leq \Pr\left[|\mathsf{GoodView}(a_{\mathsf{Sim}}, T_q)| \geq 1\right] + \Pr\left[\pi_{\mathsf{Output}}(a_{\mathsf{Sim}}, r_{\mathsf{Rec}}, \mathsf{m}_2, r_{\mathsf{Ser}}^*) = T_q \;\middle|\; |\mathsf{GoodView}(a_{\mathsf{Sim}}, T_q)| = 0\right]$$

$$< \frac{1}{4} + \frac{1}{2} = \frac{3}{4}.$$

The last inequality is due to Eq. (4) and the definition of $\mathsf{GoodView}(a_{\mathsf{Sim}}, T_q)$. This contradicts Eq. (1). $\blacksquare$

Let $X_{n,q}$ denote the sum of the expected value $\mathcal{E}(T_q)$ when ranging over all possible T_q's. Then, by Claim 3.4 it holds that $X_{n,q} \geq \frac{1}{4} \cdot |\mathcal{ANS}_{n,q}|$. Moreover, it holds that

$$X_{n,q} = \sum_{T_q \in \mathcal{ANS}_{n,q}} \mathcal{E}(T_q) = \sum_{T_q \in \mathcal{ANS}_{n,q}} \sum_{a_{\mathsf{Sim}}} \Pr_{\mathcal{SIM}_{\mathsf{Ser,Rec}}}[a_{\mathsf{Sim}}] \cdot |\mathsf{GoodView}(a_{\mathsf{Sim}}, T_q)|$$

$$= \sum_{a_{\mathsf{Sim}}} \Pr_{\mathcal{SIM}_{\mathsf{Ser,Rec}}}[a_{\mathsf{Sim}}] \cdot \sum_{T_q \in \mathcal{ANS}_{n,q}} |\mathsf{GoodView}(a_{\mathsf{Sim}}, T_q)|.$$

Note that for a fixed message a_{Sim}, every pair $(r_{\mathsf{Rec}}, \mathsf{m}_2)$ belongs to only one set $\mathsf{GoodView}(a_{\mathsf{Sim}}, T_q)$. This is due to the fact that if $(r_{\mathsf{Rec}}, \mathsf{m}_2) \in \mathsf{GoodView}(a_{\mathsf{Sim}}, T_q)$ for some T_q then by definition the following probability $\Pr[\pi_{\mathsf{Output}}(a_{\mathsf{Sim}}, r_{\mathsf{Rec}}, \mathsf{m}_2, r_{\mathsf{Ser}}^*) = T_q \mid a_{\mathsf{Sim}}, r_{\mathsf{Rec}}, \mathsf{m}_2] > \frac{1}{2}$. This implies that if a pair $(r_{\mathsf{Rec}}, \mathsf{m}_2)$ belongs to two distinct sets $T_q^0 \neq T_q^1$, then $\Pr[\pi_{\mathsf{Output}}(a_{\mathsf{Sim}}, r_{\mathsf{Rec}}, \mathsf{m}_2, r_{\mathsf{Ser}}^*) \in \{T_q^0, T_q^1\} \mid a_{\mathsf{Sim}}, r_{\mathsf{Rec}}, \mathsf{m}_2] > 1$. Therefore, for every a_{Sim} the sum $\sum_{T_q} |\mathsf{GoodView}(a_{\mathsf{Sim}}, T_q)|$ is over disjoint sets. We conclude that

$$\sum_{T_q \in \mathcal{ANS}_{n,q}} |\mathsf{GoodView}(a_{\mathsf{Sim}}, T_q)| \leq |\{(r_{\mathsf{Rec}}, \mathsf{m}_2)\}|$$

$$= \sum_{i \leq \mathsf{cc}^{n,q}_{\mathsf{Sen}}(\kappa) + \mathsf{rand}^{n,q}_{\mathsf{Rec}}(\kappa)} 2^i = 2^{\mathsf{cc}^{n,q}_{\mathsf{Sen}}(\kappa) + \mathsf{rand}^{n,q}_{\mathsf{Rec}}(\kappa) + 1} - 1$$

where the second to the last equality is implied by the fact that $\mathsf{cc}^{n,q}_{\mathsf{Sen}}(\kappa)$ is a bound on the length of m_2 and $\mathsf{rand}^{n,q}_{\mathsf{Rec}}(\kappa)$ is a bound on the length of r_{Rec}. We therefore conclude that

$$X_{n,q} \leq \sum_{a_{\mathsf{Sim}}} \Pr_{SIM_{\mathsf{Ser},\mathsf{Rec}}} [a_{\mathsf{Sim}}] \cdot \left(2^{\mathsf{cc}^{n,q}_{\mathsf{Sen}}(\kappa) + \mathsf{rand}^{n,q}_{\mathsf{Rec}}(\kappa) + 1} - 1\right) \leq 2^{\mathsf{cc}^{n,q}_{\mathsf{Sen}}(\kappa) + \mathsf{rand}^{n,q}_{\mathsf{Rec}}(\kappa) + 1} - 1.$$

Combining this with the observation that $X_{n,q} \geq \frac{1}{4} \cdot |\mathcal{ANS}_{n,q}|$, we obtain

$$2^{\mathsf{cc}^{n,q}_{\mathsf{Sen}}(\kappa) + \mathsf{rand}^{n,q}_{\mathsf{Rec}}(\kappa) + 1} - 1 \geq \frac{1}{4} \cdot |\mathcal{ANS}_{n,q}|$$

and hence for every query q,

$$\mathsf{cc}^{n,q}_{\mathsf{Sen}}(\kappa) + \mathsf{rand}^{n,q}_{\mathsf{Rec}}(\kappa) \geq \log\left(\frac{1}{4}|\mathcal{ANS}_{n,q}|\right) - 1 = \log|\mathcal{ANS}_{n,q}| - 3.$$

Therefore for every query q, it holds that $\mathsf{cc}^{n,q}_{\mathsf{Sen}}(\kappa) \geq \frac{\log|\mathcal{ANS}_{n,q}| - 3}{2}$ or $\mathsf{rand}^{n,q}_{\mathsf{Rec}}(\kappa) \geq \frac{\log|\mathcal{ANS}_{n,q}| - 3}{2}$. Recall that $H_{n,Q} = \max_{q \in Q_n} \log|\mathcal{ANS}_{n,q}|$. We conclude that there exists a query $q \in Q_n$ for which either $\mathsf{cc}^{n,q}_{\mathsf{Sen}}(\kappa) \geq \frac{H_{n,Q} - 3}{2}$ or $\mathsf{rand}^{n,q}_{\mathsf{Rec}}(\kappa) \geq \frac{H_{n,Q} - 3}{2}$. Note that if the former inequality holds, then by the security of π the communication complexity is at least $\frac{H_{n,Q} - 3}{2}$ for all queries $q \in Q_n$ (otherwise, the sender can learn the receiver's input by just looking at the length of the messages sent in π_{Query}, thus breaking privacy). This concludes the proof of Theorem 3.2. ∎

Lemma 3.6 below demonstrates that for the pattern matching functionality there exists a family of queries Q such that $H_{n,Q} = n$ for every n. Combining this with Theorems 3.1 and 3.2, the following holds,

Corollary 3.5. *There exists a family of queries $Q = \{Q_n\}_n$ such that for any protocol with minimal interaction that implements the outsourced pattern matching functionality securely with respect to Q in the private channels setting, for every n one of the following holds:*

1. *There exists $q \in Q_n$ such that the communication complexity in the query phase is at least $\frac{n-3}{2} - s$;*
2. *There exists $q \in Q_n$ such that the length of the receiver's random tape is at least $\frac{n-3}{2} - s$.*

A Bound on $H_{n,Q}$ for Pattern Matching. We prove the following simple observation relative to the pattern matching functionality; see Sect. 2.1 for the definition of this functionality.

Lemma 3.6. *For the pattern matching functionality there exists a family of queries Q such that $H_{n,Q} = n$ for every n.*

Proof. We prove the existence of a family of queries $Q = \{Q_n\}_n$ such that $H_{n,Q} = n$ for every n. Fix n and let $Q_n = \{0\}$ denote the single-bit pattern $q = 0$. In addition, recall that $H_{n,Q} = \max_{q \in Q_n} \log |\mathcal{ANS}_{n,q}|$ where $\mathcal{ANS}_{n,q} = \{T^q \mid T \in \{0,1\}^n\}$. Note that $\mathcal{ANS}_{n,q=0}$ includes all subsets of $[n]$ and thus, $|\mathcal{ANS}_{n,q=0}| = 2^n$ and $\log |\mathcal{ANS}_{n,q=0}| = n$, implying that $H_{n,Q} \geq \log |\mathcal{ANS}_{n,q=0}| = n$. ∎

3.2 The Non-private Channels Case

In this setting a corrupted party observes the communication between the honest parties. In our context this implies that a corrupted receiver sees the setup message sent from the sender to the server. Consequently, we only need to consider the corruption of the receiver where the order of communication in the query phase does not matter as in the private channels case. We continue with our main theorem for this section.

Theorem 3.7. *Fix n and m, and let $\pi = (\pi_{\mathsf{Pre}}, \pi_{\mathsf{Query}})$ be a protocol with minimal interaction that securely implements $\mathcal{F}_{\mathrm{ODBS}}$ with respect to queries $Q = \{Q_n\}_n$ in the presence of semi-honest adversaries in the non-private channels setting. Then one of the following holds:*

1. *For every query $q \in Q_n$ the communication complexity $\mathsf{cc}^{n,q} \geq \frac{H_{n,Q}-2}{2}$ or*
2. *There exists a query $q \in Q_n$ such that $\mathsf{rand}_{\mathsf{Rec}}^{n,q}(\kappa) \geq \frac{H_{n,Q}-2}{2}$.*

Proof. The proof of Theorem 3.7 is very similar to the proof of Theorem 3.2. We present the outline of the proof. Let $\pi = (\pi_{\mathsf{Pre}}, \pi_{\mathsf{Query}})$ be as in Theorem 3.7, let $\mathcal{A}_{\mathsf{Rec}}$ be a real-world semi-honest adversary controlling the receiver (note that since we do not assume private channels, $\mathcal{A}_{\mathsf{Rec}}$ sees all communication between the honest parties and in particular the message within π_{Pre}), and let $\mathcal{SIM}_{\mathsf{Rec}}$ be an ideal-world adversary guaranteed to exist by the security of $\pi = (\pi_{\mathsf{Pre}}, \pi_{\mathsf{Query}})$. By definition, upon given a message $(\mathsf{preprocess}, |T|, m)$ in the setup phase $\mathcal{SIM}_{\mathsf{Ser},\mathsf{Rec}}$ outputs a string a_{Sim}. Moreover, upon given a message $(\mathsf{response}, q, T_q, \mathsf{id})$ in the query phase it outputs a valid view for $\mathcal{A}_{\mathsf{Ser}}$ which consists of a triple $(r_{\mathsf{Rec}}, \mathsf{m}_2, \mathsf{m}_4)$, where r_{Rec} is the random tape of Rec, m_2 is a simulated message from Sen to Rec and m_4 is a simulated message from Ser to Rec.

For a security parameter κ and a pair of query/response (q, T_q), we denote by $\Pr_{\mathcal{SIM}_{\mathsf{Rec}},\kappa}[a_{\mathsf{Sim}}]$ the probability distribution over the simulated message of π_{Pre} and let $\Pr_{\mathcal{SIM}_{\mathsf{Rec}},\kappa,q,T_q}[a_{\mathsf{Sim}}, r_{\mathsf{Rec}}, \mathsf{m}_2, \mathsf{m}_4]$ denote the probability distribution on the values $(a_{\mathsf{Sim}}, r_{\mathsf{Rec}}, \mathsf{m}_2, \mathsf{m}_4)$ where a_{Sim} is generated in the simulation of π_{Pre}, and $r_{\mathsf{Rec}}, \mathsf{m}_2, \mathsf{m}_4$ are generated in the simulation of π_{Query}.

Also, let $\Pr_{\pi, \mathcal{A}_{\mathsf{Rec}}, \kappa, T, q}[a(T), r_{\mathsf{Rec}}, \mathsf{m}_2, \mathsf{m}_4]$ denote the probability distribution over the values $(a(T), r_{\mathsf{Rec}}, \mathsf{m}_2, \mathsf{m}_4)$ that are generated in a real execution of π with $\mathcal{A}_{\mathsf{Rec}}$, on inputs T for the sender and q for the receiver. We further denote by $\pi_{\mathsf{Output}}(a_{\mathsf{Sim}}, r_{\mathsf{Rec}}, \mathsf{m}_2, \mathsf{m}_4)$ the output of the receiver in an execution of π with a message a_{Sim} from Sen to Ser in π_{Pre}, a message m_2 from Sen to Rec in π_{Query} and a message m_4 from Ser to Rec, where r_{Rec} denotes the random tape of the receiver.

We continue with the following claim,

Claim 3.8. *There exists a κ_0 such that for all $\kappa > \kappa_0$ and $T \in \{0,1\}^n$, $q \in Q_n$,*

$$\Pr_{\mathcal{SIM}_{\mathsf{Rec}}, \kappa, q, T_q}[\pi_{\mathsf{Output}}(a_{\mathsf{Sim}}, r_{\mathsf{Rec}}, \mathsf{m}_2, \mathsf{m}_4) = T_q] \geq \frac{1}{2}. \tag{5}$$

Proof Sketch. Assume that for infinitely many κ's there exists $T \in \{0,1\}^n$ and $q \in Q_n$ such that

$$\Pr_{\mathcal{SIM}_{\mathsf{Rec}}, \kappa, q, T_q}[\pi_{\mathsf{Output}}(a_{\mathsf{Sim}}, r_{\mathsf{Rec}}, \mathsf{m}_2, \mathsf{m}_4) = T_q] < \frac{1}{2}.$$

By the correctness of protocol π, it is guaranteed that for all sufficiently large κ, every $T \in \{0,1\}^n$ and every $q \in Q_n$, there exists a negligible function $\mathsf{negl}(\cdot)$ such that

$$\Pr_{\pi, \mathcal{A}_{\mathsf{Rec}}, \kappa, T, q}[\pi_{\mathsf{Output}}(a(T), r_{\mathsf{Rec}}, \mathsf{m}_2, \mathsf{m}_4) = T_q] > 1 - \mathsf{negl}(\kappa)$$

Therefore we can construct a PPT distinguisher D that distinguishes a real execution of π with $\mathcal{A}_{\mathsf{Rec}}$ and an ideal execution of $\mathcal{F}_{\mathsf{ODBS}}$ with $\mathcal{SIM}_{\mathsf{Rec}}$ as follows. Given input T, q and view $a, r_{\mathsf{Rec}}, \mathsf{m}_2, \mathsf{m}_4$, output 1 if and only if the receiver's output is T_q. It is easy to verify that there is a non-negligible gap relative to the real and the simulated views, and thus D distinguishes the executions with this gap. ∎

To this end, we fix κ and q. Then, for every a_{Sim} and T_q let

$$\mathsf{GoodView}(a_{\mathsf{Sim}}, T_q) = \{(r_{\mathsf{Rec}}, \mathsf{m}_2, \mathsf{m}_4) \mid \pi_{\mathsf{Output}}(a_{\mathsf{Sim}}, r_{\mathsf{Rec}}, \mathsf{m}_2, \mathsf{m}_4) = T_q\}.$$

For a fixed T_q, we let $\mathcal{E}(T_q)$ denote the expected value of $|\mathsf{GoodView}(a_{\mathsf{Sim}}, T_q)|$ when a_{Sim} is generated by $\mathcal{SIM}_{\mathsf{Rec}}$ in the simulation of π_{Pre}. The following claim is proved similarly to the proof of Claim 3.4:

Claim 3.9. *For every T_q, it holds that $\mathcal{E}(T_q) \geq \frac{1}{2}$.*

See [HZ14] for the complete proof which follows similarly to the proof of Theorem 3.2 for the private channels case. ∎

Applying Lemma 3.6 we obtain the following corollary,

Corollary 3.10. *There exists a family of queries $Q = \{Q_n\}_n$ such that for any protocol with minimal interaction that securely implements the outsourced pattern matching functionality with respect to Q in the non-private channels setting and for every n one of the following holds:*

1. The communication complexity between the sender and the receiver in π_{Query} for any $q \in Q_n$ is at least $(n-2)/2$;
2. There exists $q \in Q_n$ such that the length of the receiver's random tape is at least $(n-2)/2$.

3.3 Difficulties with Proving a Communication Complexity Lower Bound

Recall that our infeasibility result provides a lower bound on either the communication complexity of an outsourced protocol or the size of the receiver's random tape. Clearly, it would be preferable if we could give a strict lower bound on each of these complexities separately. Towards achieving this goal, it seems very appealing to use a pseudorandom generator G that shortens the length of the receiver's random tape. Namely, replace the uniform randomness of the receiver in an outsourced protocol π by an output of a pseudorandom generator, computed on a shorter seed of length κ; thus obtaining a new protocol π' where the length of the random tape of the receiver is bounded by κ. It is simple to observe that the communication complexity of π' is exactly the same as the communication complexity of π. We can then apply our lower bound on π' in order to claim that either the random tape of Rec' in π' is large or the communication complexity of π' is large. Now, since we already know that the random tape of Rec' is of length κ, we conclude that the communication complexity of π' must be large; hence obtaining that the communication complexity of π is large as well.

Unfortunately, this intuition fails when trying to formalize it. We demonstrate why it fails as follows. Let $\pi = (\pi_{\text{Pre}}, \pi_{\text{Query}})$ be a protocol for securely computing $\mathcal{F}_{\text{ODBS}}$ in the presence of (Ser/Rec)-collusion and semi-honest adversaries, and let π' be a protocol obtained from π by having the receiver Rec' pick a random seed $s \in \{0,1\}^\kappa$ and invoke Rec with randomness $G(s)$. Our goal is to show that π' is also secure in the presence of $(\text{Ser}'/\text{Rec}')$-collusion and semi-honest adversaries by reducing its security to the security of π. Namely, we need to simulate the view of the corrupted parties in π' using the simulators constructed in the security proof of π. Consider the corruption case of the receiver Rec in π. Then, in order to construct a simulator $\mathcal{SIM}'$ for the corrupted receiver Rec' in π' we need to invoke simulator $\mathcal{SIM}$ and use its output in order to produce a simulated view for Rec'.

Recall that a valid view of Rec consists of a pair $(r_{\text{Rec}}, \text{trans})$, where r_{Rec} is a random string of length $\text{rand}_{\text{Rec}}^{n,q}(\kappa)$ and trans are the incoming messages that Rec observes during the execution of π_{Query} with randomness r_{Rec}, whereas a valid view for Rec' consists of a pair (s, trans) where s is a random seed of length κ and trans are the incoming message that Rec' observes during the execution of π_{Query} with randomness $G(s)$. Then, it is not clear how to use the output $(r_{\text{Rec}}, \text{trans})$ of $\mathcal{SIM}$ in order to construct a simulated view (s, trans) for Rec' within π'. Specifically, the difficulty is mainly because it might be that $\mathcal{SIM}$ outputs only views for which r_{Rec} is not in the range of G, and hence obtaining a corresponding s (that is part of $\mathcal{SIM}'$'s output) is not even possible.

Finally, we remark that any attempt to relax the security definition in a way that forces $\mathcal{SIM}$ to only output strings r_{Rec} that have preimages relative to G, fails as well. This is because in this case the real and the ideal ensembles that correspond to Rec''s view must consist of the seed s to the pseudorandom generator. This implies that the security argument cannot be based on the indistinguishability of $G(s)$ from a random string of the appropriate length.

References

[AIK10] Applebaum, B., Ishai, Y., Kushilevitz, E.: From secrecy to soundness: efficient verification via secure computation. In: Abramsky, S., Gavoille, C., Kirchner, C., Meyer auf der Heide, F., Spirakis, P.G. (eds.) ICALP 2010. LNCS, vol. 6198, pp. 152–163. Springer, Heidelberg (2010)

[AJLA+12] Asharov, G., Jain, A., López-Alt, A., Tromer, E., Vaikuntanathan, V., Wichs, D.: Multiparty computation with low communication, computation and interaction via threshold FHE. In: Pointcheval, D., Johansson, T. (eds.) EUROCRYPT 2012. LNCS, vol. 7237, pp. 483–501. Springer, Heidelberg (2012)

[ANSS16] Asharov, G., Naor, M., Segev, G., Shahaf, I.: Searchable symmetric encryption: optimal locality in linear space via two-dimensional balanced allocations. IACR Cryptology ePrint Archive, 2016:251 (2016)

[BCCT12] Bitansky, N., Canetti, R., Chiesa, A., Tromer, E.: From extractable collision resistance to succinct non-interactive arguments of knowledge, and back again. In: ITCS, pp. 326–349 (2012)

[CGKO11] Curtmola, R., Garay, J.A., Kamara, S., Ostrovsky, R.: Searchable symmetric encryption: improved definitions and efficient constructions. J. Comput. Secur. 19(5), 895–934 (2011)

[CGPR15] Cash, D., Grubbs, P., Perry, J., Ristenpart, T.: Leakage-abuse attacks against searchable encryption. In: CCS, pp. 668–679 (2015)

[CK10] Chase, M., Kamara, S.: Structured encryption and controlled disclosure. In: Abe, M. (ed.) ASIACRYPT 2010. LNCS, vol. 6477, pp. 577–594. Springer, Heidelberg (2010)

[CKKC13] Choi, S.G., Katz, J., Kumaresan, R., Cid, C.: Multi-client non-interactive verifiable computation. In: Sahai, A. (ed.) TCC 2013. LNCS, vol. 7785, pp. 499–518. Springer, Heidelberg (2013)

[CS14] Chase, M., Shen, E.: Pattern matching encryption. IACR Cryptology ePrint Archive, 2014:638 (2014)

[DFH12] Damgård, I., Faust, S., Hazay, C.: Secure two-party computation with low communication. In: Cramer, R. (ed.) TCC 2012. LNCS, vol. 7194, pp. 54–74. Springer, Heidelberg (2012)

[FHV13] Faust, S., Hazay, C., Venturi, D.: Outsourced pattern matching. In: Fomin, F.V., Freivalds, R., Kwiatkowska, M., Peleg, D. (eds.) ICALP 2013, Part II. LNCS, vol. 7966, pp. 545–556. Springer, Heidelberg (2013)

[FIPR05] Freedman, M.J., Ishai, Y., Pinkas, B., Reingold, O.: Keyword search and oblivious pseudorandom functions. In: Kilian, J. (ed.) TCC 2005. LNCS, vol. 3378, pp. 303–324. Springer, Heidelberg (2005)

[GGP10] Gennaro, R., Gentry, C., Parno, B.: Non-interactive verifiable computing: outsourcing computation to untrusted workers. In: Rabin, T. (ed.) CRYPTO 2010. LNCS, vol. 6223, pp. 465–482. Springer, Heidelberg (2010)

[GH11]   Green, M., Hohenberger, S.: Practical adaptive oblivious transfer from simple assumptions. In: Ishai, Y. (ed.) TCC 2011. LNCS, vol. 6597, pp. 347–363. Springer, Heidelberg (2011)

[GLR11]   Goldwasser, S., Lin, H., Rubinstein, A.: Delegation of computation without rejection problem from designated verifier CS-proofs. IACR Cryptology ePrint Archive, 2011:456 (2011)

[GMPP16]   Garg, S., Mukherjee, P., Pandey, O., Polychroniadou, A.: The exact round complexity of secure computation. In: Fischlin, M., Coron, J.-S. (eds.) EUROCRYPT 2016. LNCS, vol. 9666, pp. 448–476. Springer, Heidelberg (2016). doi:10.1007/978-3-662-49896-5_16

[Goh03]   Goh, E.-J.: Secure indexes. IACR Cryptology ePrint Archive, 2003:216 (2003)

[HT10]   Hazay, C., Toft, T.: Computationally secure pattern matching in the presence of malicious adversaries. In: Abe, M. (ed.) ASIACRYPT 2010. LNCS, vol. 6477, pp. 195–212. Springer, Heidelberg (2010)

[HZ14]   Hazay, C., Zarosim, H.: The feasibility of outsourced database search in the plain model. IACR Cryptology ePrint Archive, 2014:706 (2014)

[JJK+13]   Jarecki, S., Jutla, C.S., Krawczyk, H., Rosu, M.-C., Steiner, M.: Outsourced symmetric private information retrieval. In: CCS, pp. 875–888 (2013)

[KMR11]   Kamara, S., Mohassel, P., Raykova, M.: Outsourcing multi-party computation. IACR Cryptology ePrint Archive, 2011:272 (2011)

[KMR12]   Kamara, S., Mohassel, P., Riva, B.: Salus: a system for server-aided secure function evaluation. In: CCS, pp. 797–808 (2012)

[KO04]   Katz, J., Ostrovsky, R.: Round-optimal secure two-party computation. In: Franklin, M. (ed.) CRYPTO 2004. LNCS, vol. 3152, pp. 335–354. Springer, Heidelberg (2004)

[KP13]   Kamara, S., Papamanthou, C.: Parallel and dynamic searchable symmetric encryption. In: Sadeghi, A.-R. (ed.) FC 2013. LNCS, vol. 7859, pp. 258–274. Springer, Heidelberg (2013)

[KPR12]   Kamara, S., Papamanthou, C., Roeder, T.: Dynamic searchable symmetric encryption. In: CCS, pp. 965–976 (2012)

[LATV12]   López-Alt, A., Tromer, E., Vaikuntanathan, V.: On-the-fly multiparty computation on the cloud via multikey fully homomorphic encryption. In: STOC, pp. 1219–1234 (2012)

[Nie02]   Nielsen, J.B.: Separating random oracle proofs from complexity theoretic proofs: the non-committing encryption case. In: Yung, M. (ed.) CRYPTO 2002. LNCS, vol. 2442, pp. 111–126. Springer, Heidelberg (2002)

[NP99]   Naor, M., Pinkas, B.: Oblivious transfer with adaptive queries. In: Wiener, M. (ed.) CRYPTO 1999. LNCS, vol. 1666, pp. 573–590. Springer, Heidelberg (1999)

[ORS15]   Ostrovsky, R., Richelson, S., Scafuro, A.: Round-optimal black-box two-party computation. In: Gennaro, R., Robshaw, M. (eds.) CRYPTO 2015. LNCS, vol. 9216, pp. 339–358. Springer, Heidelberg (2015)

[Wei73]   Weiner, P.: Linear pattern matching algorithms. In: SWAT (FOCS), pp. 1–11 (1973)

Verifiable Pattern Matching
on Outsourced Texts

Dario Catalano, Mario Di Raimondo$^{(\boxtimes)}$, and Simone Faro

Dipartimento di Matematica e Informatica, Università di Catania, Catania, Italy
{catalano,diraimondo,faro}@dmi.unict.it

Abstract. In this paper we consider a scenario where a user wants to outsource her documents to the cloud, so that she can later reliably delegate (to the cloud) pattern matching operations on these documents. We propose an efficient solution to this problem that relies on the homomorphic MAC for polynomials proposed by Catalano and Fiore in [14]. Our main contribution are new methods to express pattern matching operations (both in their exact and approximate variants) as low degree polynomials, i.e. polynomials whose degree solely depends on the size of the pattern. To better assess the practicality of our schemes, we propose a concrete implementation that further optimizes the efficiency of the homomorphic MAC from [14]. Our implementation shows that the proposed protocols are extremely efficient for the client, while remaining feasible at server side.

1 Introduction

Imagine that Alice wants to store all her data on the cloud in a way such that she can later delegate, to the latter, basic computations on this data. In particular, Alice wants to be able to do this while retaining some key properties. First, the cloud should not be able to fool Alice by sending back wrong outputs. Specifically, the cloud should be able to provide a "short" (i.e. much shorter than a mere concatenation of the inputs and the output) proof that the output it computed is correct. Second, Alice should be able to check this proof without having to maintain a local copy of her data. In other words, the verification procedure should not need the original data to work correctly. An elegant solution to this problem comes from the notion of homomorphic authenticators. Informally, homomorphic authenticators are like their standard (non-homomorphic) counterparts but come equipped with a (publicly executable) evaluation algorithm that allows to obtain valid signatures on messages resulting from computing on previously signed messages. Slightly more in detail, the owner of a dataset $\{m_1, \ldots, m_\ell\}$ uses her secret key sk to produce corresponding authenticating tags $(\sigma_1, \ldots, \sigma_\ell)$ which are then stored on the cloud together with $\{m_1, \ldots, m_\ell\}$. Later, the server can (publicly) compute $m = f(m_1, \ldots, m_\ell)$ together with a succinct tag σ certifying that m is the correct output of the computation f. A nice feature of

---

A full version of this paper is available at http://www.dmi.unict.it/diraimondo/uploads/papers/vpm-full.pdf.

© Springer International Publishing Switzerland 2016
V. Zikas and R. De Prisco (Eds.): SCN 2016, LNCS 9841, pp. 333–350, 2016.
DOI: 10.1007/978-3-319-44618-9_18

homomorphic authenticators is that, as required above, the validity of this tag can be verified *without* having to know the original dataset.

Homomorphic authenticators turned out to be useful in a variety of settings and have been studied in several flavors. Examples include homomorphic signatures for linear and polynomial functions [10,11], redactable signatures [31], transitive signatures and more [36,39].

Our Contribution. In this paper we consider the setting where Alice wants to reliably delegate the cloud to perform pattern matching operations (both in their exact and approximate flavors) on outsourced text documents. While in principle this problem can be solved by combining (leveled) fully homomorphic signatures [29] and well known pattern matching algorithms (e.g. [33]), our focus here is on *efficient*, possibly practical, solutions. To achieve this, we develop new pattern matching algorithms specifically tailored to cope well with the very efficient homomorphic MAC solution from [14]. Our methods are very simple and allow to represent several text processing operations via (relatively) low degree polynomials[1]. Specifically, our supported functionalities range from counting the number of exact (or approximate) occurrences of a string in a text to finding the n-th occurrence of a pattern (and its position).

Slightly more in detail, our basic idea is to use the homomorphic MAC for polynomials from [14] to authenticate the texts one wishes to outsource, in a bit by bit fashion. Very informally this can be done as follows. If Alice wants to outsource her file **grades**, denoting with b_i the i-th bit of **grades**, she proceeds by first producing a MAC σ_i, for each b_i and then storing **grades** together with all the σ_i's on the cloud. Later, when Alice delegates a computation f to the cloud, she gets back an output z and a proof of correctness π that, by the properties of homomorphic authenticators, can be verified without having to maintain a copy of the data locally.

The catch with this solution is that, in order to be any practical, f has to be a low degree arithmetic circuit. This is because a drawback of the construction from [14] is that the size of π grows linearly with the degree d of the circuit[2].

To address this issue we observe that, when dealing with bits, relevant pattern matching functionalities can be expressed via polynomials of degree, at most, $2m$ where m is the bit-size of the pattern. To briefly illustrate the ideas underlying our techniques, let us focus on the case of exact pattern matching. There, the key observation is that checking if a pattern x, of size m, occurs in a text y, of size n, can be done via the following easy steps. First, one considers all the $(n - m + 1)$ possible substrings w of y of size m. Next, for each such w, one checks equality with x via the following simple formula

---

[1] In particular the degree of these polynomials solely depends on the size of pattern string and is independent of the size of the texts.

[2] Notice that in [14] a solution where the size of π can be made independent of d is also proposed. This solution however is computationally much less efficient as it imposes larger parameters.

$$\prod_{i=0}^{m-1} (2x_i w_i + 1 - x_i - w_i) \tag{1}$$

which is 1 if and only if all bits of x and w are equal (and 0 otherwise). Thus, x appears in y if at least one such products is non zero. This can be tested by summing the products corresponding to all possible w and checking if the result is different than zero.

Dynamic Polynomials. Notice however that, for large n, a naive application of the technique above might result in a prohibitively expensive computation for the server[3], as the latter would need to first compute and then add $\mathcal{O}(n)$ polynomials of degree $2m$.

To overcome this limitation we observe that a more careful encoding of the computation at server side, can drastically improve performances. The key point here is that, for a given pattern x, the server can reduce its costs by adapting the computation of the formula in (1) according to the bits of pattern x. Specifically, the formula (1) can be rewritten as

$$\prod_{i=0}^{m-1} (x_i w_i + (1 - x_i)(1 - w_i)) \tag{2}$$

which can be computed in m steps my using the following procedure

$$P = 1$$
$$\text{FOR } i = 0 \text{ TO } m - 1 \text{ DO}$$
$$\text{IF } (x_i = 0) \ P \leftarrow P \cdot (1 - w_i)$$
$$\text{ELSE } P \leftarrow P \cdot w_i$$
$$\text{RETURN } P$$

Thus, for each queried pattern, the computed formula is dynamically adapted to the pattern. This leads to computations which are both simpler and more efficient than those induced by (1). Our tests show that this simple observation allows to reduce the computational costs of the server by a (rough) -71% !

Evaluation over Samples and Experimental Results. As already hinted above, to better assess the efficiency of our solutions we ran extensive experiments. In order to gain better performances we further optimized our techniques as follows. First, as already suggested in [14], we adopt Fast Fourier Transform (FFT) to speed up multiplications of polynomials. Inspired by FFT, we also propose an alternative strategy, named "evaluation over samples", where the whole evaluation is performed representing the polynomials via set of samples (rather than via their coefficients). This further simplifies the implementation of polynomial multiplication and, for the case of low degree polynomials, provides

---

[3] Indeed, our first implementations show that this cost can quickly become unbearable even for texts of few thousands characters.

an additional speed up. Finally, we note that, using some basic precomputation at client side (see [8]), verification costs can be made essentially negligible.

Our experiments show that our optimized implementations are extremely fast for the client while remaining feasible for the server. In terms of concrete numbers, our tests show that it is possible to count the exact occurrences of a 4 characters pattern in a text of 10 KiB in about 4 s with a proof of 528 bytes verifiable in just 300 ms. With a bigger text of 100 KiB the evaluation time raises roughly to 38 s. The usage of large patterns sensibly slows down the evaluation process (i.e. the costs for the server). We remark that, for a fixed pattern size, the evaluation costs for the server grow linearly with n (i.e. the size of the text). This means that for very large n our protocols, while feasible, cannot be considered practical anymore.

Related Work. The problem of computing reliably on outsourced data can be solved in principle using short non interactive arguments of knowledge on authenticated data (AD-SNARKs) [7]. Such a solution would allow lower verification costs (i.e. independent from the size of the computed circuit). The main disadvantage of AD-SNARKs, with respect to our solution, is that they require much more complex machinery (thus making the costs for the server even more prohibitive). Moreover, even without considering efficiency, our homomorphic-authenticators based solution is preferable for at least two reasons. First, it requires shorter parameters: known AD-SNARKs [7] require evaluation/verification keys that grow significantly with the size of the supported circuits. Also, our solution requires only standard, falsifiable assumptions.

The questions considered in this paper share some similarities with those addressed by Verifiable Computation (VC) [26]. There, a client wants to outsource some computationally intensive task and still be able to quickly verify the correctness of the received result. Typically, VC schemes assume that the input remains available to the verifier. In our context, on the other hand, the difficulty comes from the fact that the (not necessarily complex) task involves data not locally available to the client.

The notion of homomorphic MAC was first considered (in the setting of linear functions) by [1] and later extended to more general functionalities in [8,14,15,28] In the asymmetric setting the idea of homomorphic signature was first proposed by Desmedt [23] and later refined by Johnson et al. [31]. Starting from the work of Boneh et al. [10], several other papers further studied this notion both in the standard model [4–6,18–20,25] and in the random oracle model [11,12,16,17,27]. Beyond linear functions, Boneh and Freeman in [11] proposed an homomorphic signature scheme for constant degree polynomials. This result was later improved by Catalano et al. [21] and, more recently, by Gorbunov et al. [29]. This latter construction provides the first realization of a (leveled) fully homomorphic signature scheme. See [13] for a survey on homomorphic authenticators.

Polynomial encodings have been extensively studied in past. Among others, we recall the works by Applebaum et al. [2,3] on randomized encodings.

Other Related Work. The string matching problem is one of the most fundamental problems in computer science. It consists in finding all the occurrences
of a given pattern x of length m, in a text y of length n. The worst case time
complexity of string matching problem is $\mathcal{O}(n + m)$, and was achieved for the
first time by the well known Knuth-Morris-Pratt algorithm [33]. However the
most efficient solutions to the problem in the average case have an $\mathcal{O}(nm)$ worst
case time complexity [24]. In the approximate string matching problem we allow
the presence of errors in the occurrences of the pattern in the text. Specifically
we are interested in the string matching problem with δ errors, where at most δ
substitutions of characters are allowed in order to make the pattern occur in the
text. Solution to both exact and approximate string matching problems are based
on comparisons of characters [33], deterministic finite state automata [22], simulation of non-deterministic finite state automata [9] and filtering methods [32].
In this paper we are interested in solving the string matching problem by using
polynomial functions. To our knowledge this is the first time the string matching
problem is defined in polynomial form.

In [37] Papadopoulos *et al.* propose an efficient solution for an outsourced
pattern matching scenario similar to the one considered here. Their idea combines suffix trees with cryptographic accumulators. The resulting proofs have size
comparable to ours but, thanks to an heavy pre-processing over the outsourced
texts[4], they can be generated very efficiently. We note also that this preprocessing step is not update friendly: after the text is updated it becomes necessary
to re-create the whole suffix tree. Our solution is slightly better than this as, for
the specific case of append-updates it does not require any recomputations for
the original tags.

Road Map. In Sect. 2 we recall the efficient homomorphic MAC scheme
from [14]. Our new pattern matching algorithms are presented in Sect. 3, while
the details of the proposed implementation together with relevant experimental
results are given in Sect. 4.

2   Homomorphic MACs

In this section we briefly recall the construction of homomorphic MACs from [14]
that is going to be used in our constructions. For details not discussed here we
defer the reader to the original paper. Intuitively, the constructions proposed
in [14], are given in the setting of *labeled programs* [28]. To authenticate a computation f one authenticates its inputs $m_1, \ldots m_n$ by also specifying corresponding
labels $\tau_1 \ldots \tau_n$. A label can be seen as an index of a database record or, simply,
as a name given to identify the (outsourced) input. In the application considered
in this paper a label might simply be the name of the document followed by an
indexing of its characters (bits). For example, each bit b_i of the documents **exams**
could simply be the string $\tau_i = $ **exams**$||$**i** (here $||$ denotes concatenation).

---

[4] Moreover this pre-processing has to be done by the text owner (the weak client in
our scenario) and cannot be delegated to the untrusted cloud server.

The combination of f and the labels is a labeled program $\mathcal{P}$, that is what is later executed by the cloud. For the case of pattern matching applications, labeled programs are used as follows. When outsourcing a text document T to the cloud, the client proceeds as follows. First she computes a MAC of T, by authenticating each bit b_i of T using its corresponding label τ_i. Denoting with σ_{b_i} the MAC corresponding to the i-th bit of T, the client stores $(T, \sigma_{b_1}, \ldots, \sigma_{b_{|T|}})$ on the cloud.

As in [14], we consider circuits where additive gates do not get inputs labeled by constants. We stress that adding such gates can be done easily, as one can adopt an equivalent circuit where a special variable/label for the value 1 is added. A MAC of 1 is also added to the public parameters. It is worth mentioning the fact that the construction given below does not provide succinct authenticating tags, if the number of multiplications performed is too high. This is because the size of the tag grows with the degree d of the arithmetic circuit one wants to authenticate. In our case this is not going to be a problem as (see Sect. 3) d is bounded by the size of the pattern.

The following description is taken (almost) verbatim from [14]

KeyGen(1^λ). Let p be a prime of roughly λ bits. Choose a seed K of a pseudo-random function $F_K : \{0,1\}^* \to \mathbb{Z}_p$ and a random value $x \xleftarrow{\$} \mathbb{Z}_p$. Output sk $= (K, x)$, ek $= p$ and let the message space $\mathcal{M}$ be $\mathbb{Z}_p$.

Auth(sk, τ, m). To authenticate a message $m \in \mathbb{Z}_p$ with label $\tau \in \{0,1\}^\lambda$, compute $r_\tau = F_K(\tau)$, set $y_0 = m$, $y_1 = (r_\tau - m)/x \bmod p$ and output $\sigma = (y_0, y_1)$. Thus, y_0, y_1 are the coefficients of a degree-1 polynomial $y(z)$ with the special property that it evaluates to m on the point 0 ($y(0) = m$), and it evaluates to r_τ on a hidden random point x ($y(x) = r_\tau$).

Tags σ are seen as polynomials $y \in \mathbb{Z}_p[z]$ of degree $d \geq 1$ in some (unknown) variable z, i.e., $y(z) = \sum_i y_i z^i$.

Eval(ek, f, $\boldsymbol{\sigma}$). The homomorphic evaluation algorithm takes as input the evaluation key ek $= p$, an arithmetic circuit $f : \mathbb{Z}_p^n \to \mathbb{Z}_p$, and a vector $\boldsymbol{\sigma}$ of tags $(\sigma_1, \ldots, \sigma_n)$.

Eval proceeds gate-by-gate as follows. At each gate g, given two tags σ_1, σ_2 (or a tag σ_1 and a constant $c \in \mathbb{Z}_p$), it runs the algorithm $\sigma \leftarrow$ GateEval(ek, g, σ_1, σ_2) described below that returns a new tag σ, which is in turn passed on as input to the next gate in the circuit.

When the computation reaches the last gate of the circuit f, Eval outputs the tag vector σ obtained by running GateEval on such last gate.

To complete the description of Eval we describe the subroutine GateEval.

– GateEval(ek, g, σ_1, σ_2). Let $\sigma_i = \boldsymbol{y}^{(i)} = (y_0^{(i)}, \ldots, y_{d_i}^{(i)})$ for $i = 1, 2$ and $d_i \geq 1$ (see below for the special case when one of the two inputs is a constant $c \in \mathbb{Z}_p$). If $g = +$, then:
  • let $d = \max(d_1, d_2)$. Here we assume without loss of generality that $d_1 \geq d_2$ (i.e., $d = d_1$).
  • Compute the coefficients $(y_0, \ldots, y_d)$ of the polynomial $y(z) = y^{(1)}(z) + y^{(2)}(z)$. This can be efficiently done by adding the two vectors of coefficients, $\boldsymbol{y} = \boldsymbol{y}^{(1)} + \boldsymbol{y}^{(2)}$ ($\boldsymbol{y}^{(2)}$ is eventually padded with zeroes in positions $d_1 \ldots d_2$).

If $g = \times$, then:
- let $d = d_1 + d_2$.
- Compute the coefficients $(y_0, \ldots, y_d)$ of the polynomial $y(z) = y^{(1)}(z) * y^{(2)}(z)$ using the convolution operator $*$, i.e., $\forall k = 0, \ldots, d$, define $y_k = \sum_{i=0}^{k} y_i^{(1)} \cdot y_{k-i}^{(2)}$.

If $g = \times$ and one of the two inputs, say σ_2, is a constant $c \in \mathbb{Z}_p$, then:
- let $d = d_1$.
- Compute the coefficients $(y_0, \ldots, y_d)$ of the polynomial $y(z) = c \cdot y^{(1)}(z)$.

Return $\sigma = (y_0, \ldots, y_d)$.

Notice that the size of a tag grows only after the evaluation of a multiplication gate (where both inputs are not constants). It is not hard to see that after the homomorphic evaluation of a circuit f, it holds $|\sigma| = d+1$, where d is the degree of f.

Ver($\mathsf{sk}, m, \mathcal{P}, \sigma$). Let $\mathcal{P} = (f, \tau_1, \ldots, \tau_n)$ be a labeled program, $m \in \mathbb{Z}_p$ and $\sigma = (y_0, \ldots, y_d)$ be a tag for some $d \geq 1$. Verification proceeds as follows:

- If $y_0 \neq m$, then output 0 (reject). Otherwise continue as follows.
- For every input wire of f with label τ compute $r_\tau = F_K(\tau)$.
- Next, evaluate the circuit on $r_{\tau_1}, \ldots, r_{\tau_n}$, i.e., compute $\rho \leftarrow f(r_{\tau_1}, \ldots, r_{\tau_n})$, and use x to check whether the following equation holds:

$$\rho = \sum_{k=0}^{d} y_k x^k \tag{3}$$

If this is true, then output 1. Otherwise output 0.

In [14] it is proved that the scheme above is secure under the sole assumption that pseudorandom functions exist.

3   String Matching Using Polynomial Functions

In this section we describe our new pattern matching solutions. These are specifically tailored to work nicely with the practical homomorphic MACs from [14]. We start by describing a simple methodology to count the number of exact occurrences of a pattern in a text. Next, we describe how to modify this procedure to encompass other cases.

Let X be the input pattern of length M, and let Y be the input text of length N, both over the same alphabet Σ of size σ. We use the symbol X_i to indicate the $(i + 1)$-th character of X, with $0 \leq i < m$. Moreover we use the symbol $X[i..j]$ to indicate the substring of X starting at position i and ending at position j (included), where $0 \leq i \leq j < n$. We say that X has an occurrence in Y at position j if $X = Y[j..j + m - 1]$.

Our methods performs computation using the bitwise representation of the input strings. To this purpose, observe that each character in Σ can be represented using $\log(\sigma)$ bits. For instance each character in the set of 256 elements of the ASCII table can be represented using 8 bits. Let x and y be bitwise representation of X and Y, respectively. We use m to indicate the length of x and n for the length of y, so that $m = M \log(\sigma)$ and $n = N \log(\sigma)$. Moreover $x_i, y_j \in \{0,1\}$, for each $0 \le i < m$ and $0 \le j < n$.

In the following sections we will describe string matching problems in terms of functions, where the input strings play the role of variables. Additional relevant definitions will be introduced where needed. Proofs to lemmas and theorems stated below are deferred to the full version of this paper.

3.1 Counting the Number of Exact Occurrences of a String

In this section we address the problem of counting the number of exact occurrences of a string X of size M in a string Y of size N. We recall that a string X has an exact occurrence at position j of Y if and only if $X = Y[j..j + N - 1]$. More formally the problem of counting all exact occurrences of a string can be defined as the problem of computing the cardinality of the set

$$\{j : 0 \le j < N \text{ and } X = Y[j..j + M - 1]\}$$

When both strings are defined over the binary alphabet $\Sigma = \{0,1\}$, comparisons between strings and characters can be represented as polynomials. For instance we can use the polynomial function $(2ab + 1 - a - b)$ for computing comparison between two given binary values $a, b \in \{0,1\}$.

Formally we have

$$2ab + 1 - a - b = \begin{cases} 1 & \text{if } a = b \\ 0 & \text{otherwhise} \end{cases} \tag{4}$$

Specifically we come up with the following definition for a polynomial which count the number of occurrences X in Y, using their bitwise representations, x and y. For the sake of clarity and brevity we will use in the following the symbol $y_{(i,j)}$ to indicate the character $y[j \log(\sigma) + i]$.

Definition 1 (Exact Matches Function). *Let X be a pattern of length M, and let Y be a text of length N, both over the same alphabet Σ of size σ. Let x and y be their bitwise representations, of length m and n, respectively. Then we can compute the number of exact occurrences of X in Y by using the polynomial function $\alpha(X,Y)$ defined as*

$$\alpha(X,Y) = \sum_{j=0}^{N-M} \left(\prod_{i=0}^{m-1} \left(2x_i y_{(j,i)} + 1 - x_i - y_{(j,i)} \right) \right) \tag{5}$$

The function $\alpha(X,Y)$ defined above requires $\mathcal{O}(NM \log(\sigma))$ multiplications while the resulting polynomial has degree $2m = 2M \log(\sigma)$. When computing such polynomial function we are able to retrieve the number of occurrences of X in Y, but we are not able to know the positions of such occurrences. Theorem 1 given below proves the correctness of the function given in (5). We first prove the following technical lemma which defines a method for comparing two binary strings with the same length.

Lemma 1. *Let* $x = x_0 x_1 .. x_{m-1}$ *and* $w = w_0 w_1 .. w_{m-1}$ *be two strings of length* m, *both over the binary alphabet* $\Sigma = \{0,1\}$. *Then we have that*

$$x = w \Leftrightarrow \prod_{i=0}^{m-1} (2x_i w_i + 1 - x_i - w_i) = 1 \qquad (6)$$

□

Theorem 1. *Given a pattern* X, *of length* M, *and a text* Y, *of length* N, *both over the binary alphabet* Σ *of size* σ, *let* x *and* y *their bitwise representations, of length* m *and* n, *respectively. Then the exact matches polynomial function given in Definition 1 computes correctly the number of occurrences of* X *in* Y. *Formally*

$$\alpha(X,Y) = \left| \{ j : 0 \le j \le N - M \text{ and } X = Y[j..j + M - 1] \} \right| \qquad □$$

3.2   Finding the Positions of All Occurrences

In many applications it is required to find the positions of the occurrence of the pattern X in Y. Let $\pi(X,Y,j)$ be initial position of the j-th occurrence of X in Y, with $i > 0$. We assume that $\pi(X,Y,j) = \infty$ if the number of occurrences of X in Y is less than i. The position of the first occurrence (i.e. $\pi(X,Y,1)$) can be obtained by asking the server to compute such position, say p_1, and subsequently to verify if such information is correct. Specifically we have that

$$\pi(X,Y,1) = p_1 \Leftrightarrow \alpha(X,Y[0..p_1 + M - 2]) = 0 \text{ and } \alpha(X,Y[p_1..p_1 + M - 1]) = 1$$

If $\pi(X,Y,1) = \infty$, indicating that no occurrence of X is contained in Y, we can verify such information by computing $\alpha(X,Y)$. Specifically we have

$$\pi(X,Y,1) = \infty \Leftrightarrow \alpha(X,Y) = 0$$

In general, if we are interested in computing the position of all occurrences of X in Y it is possible to iterate the above procedure along the whole text Y. Let p_j be the position of the j-th occurrence of X in Y, i.e. $\pi(X,Y,j) = p_j$, for $j > 0$, and let $k = \alpha(X,Y)$ the total number of occurrences. Thus we have that $\pi(X,Y,j) = \infty$ for all $j > k$.

It turns out that, for all $0 < j \le k$, $\pi(X,Y,j) = p_j$ if and only if we have $\alpha(X,Y[p_{j-1} + 1..p_j + M - 2]) = 0$ and $\alpha(X,Y[p_j..p_j + M - 1]) = 1$. Moreover, for $j > k$, we have that $\pi(X,Y,j) = \infty$ if and only if $\alpha(X,Y[p_k + 1..N]) = 0$.

3.3   Counting the Approximate Occurrences of a String

In our setting of the approximate string matching problem, given a pattern X of length M, a text Y of length N, and a bound $\delta < M$, we want to find all substring of the text of length M which differ from the pattern of, at most, δ characters. In literature such variant of the approximate string matching problem is referred as string matching with δ errors [35].

More formally we want to find all substrings $Y[j..j + M - 1]$, for $0 \leq j < N$, such that

$$\left| \{i : 0 \leq i < M \text{ and } X_i \neq Y_{j+i}\} \right| \leq \delta$$

We first define the following k-error constant τ_k, for a strung of length M, which will be used later. Specifically we set

$$\tau_k = \prod_{i=1}^{k} i \times \prod_{i=k-M}^{-1} i \qquad (7)$$

We next prove the following lemma which introduces a polynomial function for computing the number of mismatches between two strings of equal length. We recall that we use the symbol $y_{(j,i)}$ to indicate $y_{j \log(\sigma)+i}$.

Lemma 2 (Mismatch Function). *Let X and W two strings over a common alphabet Σ of size σ. Let x and w be their bitwise representations of length $m = M \log(\sigma)$. The mismatch function $\Psi : \Sigma^M \times \Sigma^M \to \{0, 1, .., M\}$, defined as*

$$\Psi(X, W) = \sum_{j=0}^{M-1} \left[1 - \prod_{i=0}^{\log \sigma - 1} \left(2x_{(j,i)} w_{(j,i)} + 1 - x_{(j,i)} - w_{(j,i)} \right) \right] \qquad (8)$$

counts the number of mismatches between X and W.

$\square$

Let us take into account the value $\tau_k(x, w)$, defined as the product of the differences between $Psi(x, w)$ and the values int he range $\{1..m\}$. Formally

$$\tau(X, W) = \prod_{i=0}^{M} (\Psi(X, W) - i). \qquad (9)$$

Since $0 \leq \Psi(X, W) \leq M$, it turns out that the value of $\tau(X, W)$ is always equal to 0. In fact one (and only one) of the factors in (9) is equal to zero.

We are now ready to prove the following lemma which introduces a polynomial function for detecting if X and W differs exactly of k characters.

Lemma 3 (k-Mismatch Function). *Let X and W be two strings of length M over an alphabet Σ of size σ. Moreover let k an error value in $\{0, .., M\}$. Then the k-mismatch function, $\tau_k : \Sigma^m \times \Sigma^m \to \{0, 1\}$, defined as*

$$\tau_k(X, W) = \frac{1}{\tau_k} \prod_{i=0}^{k-1} (\Psi(X, W) - i) \times \prod_{i=k+1}^{M} (\Psi(X, W) - i). \qquad (10)$$

is equal to 1 if X and W has k mismatches, otherwise it is equal to 0. $\square$

Observe that the resulting polynomial for computing $\tau(X, Y)$ has degree $2m$ while the polynomial for computing τ_k has degree $(m - 1)$.

The following corollary gives a method to compute the number of approximate occurrences of a given pattern X in a text Y with exactly k errors. It trivially follows from Lemma 3.

Corollary 1 (Count k Errors Matches Function). *Given a pattern X, of length M, a text Y, of length N, and an error value $k \leq M$, we can compute the number of occurrences of X in Y with (exactly) k errors by using the function $\beta_k(X,Y)$ defined as*

$$\beta_k(X,Y) = \sum_{i=0}^{N-M} \tau_k(X, Y[i..i+M-1])$$

Finally, the following corollary introduces the function for computing the number of approximate occurrences of X in Y assuming an error bound δ. It trivially follows from Corollary 1.

Corollary 2 (Count δ-Approximate Matches Function). *Given a pattern X, of length M, a text Y, of length N, and an error bound $\delta \leq M$, we can compute the number of occurrences of X in Y with at most δ errors by using the function $\gamma(X,Y)$ defined as*

$$\gamma(X,Y) = \sum_{k=0}^{\delta} \beta_k(X,Y) \tag{11}$$

As previously described we can also adapt such technique to find the position of the first occurrence, as the position of all occurrences of X in Y.

3.4   Using Dynamic Polynomials

In our experimental results, using the polynomials introduced above, we observed a prohibitively expensive computation for the server, especially for large texts. It turns out, in fact, that for both exact and approximate pattern matching we need to first compute and then add $\mathcal{O}(N)$ polynomials of degree $2m$.

In this section we present a method to overcome this limitation and decrease the degree of the resulting polynomials. Specifically we observe that a more careful encoding of the computation at server side can drastically improve the performances. The key point here is that, for a given pattern X, the server can reduce its costs by adapting the computation of the polynomials according to the bits of the pattern X.

Specifically, the formulas (6) and (8) can be rewritten, respectively, as

$$\prod_{i=0}^{m-1} (x_i w_i + (1 - x_i)(1 - w_i)) \tag{12}$$

$$\sum_{i=0}^{M-1} \left[1 - \prod_{i=0}^{\log \sigma - 1} \left(x_{(j,i)}(1 - w_{(j,i)}) + (1 - x_{(j,i)})w_{(j,i)} \right) \right] \tag{13}$$

EXACT-MATCHING(X, M, Y, N)
1. $F = 0$
2. FOR $j = 0$ TO $N - M$ DO
3. $P = 1$
4.   FOR $i = 0$ TO $m - 1$ DO
5.   IF $(x_i = 0)$ THEN
6. $P \leftarrow P \cdot (1 - y_{(j,i)})$
6.   ELSE $P \leftarrow P \cdot y_{(j,i)}$
7. $F \leftarrow F + P$
8. RETURN F

PRODUCT-FACTORS(X, M, Y, N)
1. FOR $j = 0$ TO $N - M$ DO
2.   FOR $i = 0$ TO $M - 1$ DO
3. $P[j, i] = 1$
4.   FOR $h = 0$ TO $\log(\sigma) - 1$ DO
5.   IF $(x_{(i,h)} = 0)$ THEN
6. $P[j, i] \leftarrow P[j, i] \cdot (1 - y_{(j,h)})$
6.   ELSE $P[j, i] \leftarrow P \cdot y_{(j,h)}$

APPROXIMATE-MATCHING(X, M, Y, N, δ)
1. PRODUCT-FACTORS(X, M, Y, N)
2. FOR $k = 0$ TO δ DO
3. $\tau_k = \prod_{i=1}^{k} i \cdot \prod_{i=k-M}^{-1} i$
4. $F = 0$
5. FOR $j = 0$ TO $n - m$ DO
6. $\Psi = 0$
7.   FOR $i = 0$ TO $M - 1$ DO
8. $\Psi \leftarrow \Psi + (1 - P[j + i, i])$
9.   FOR $k = 0$ TO δ DO
10. $\beta_k = 1$
11.   FOR $i = 0$ TO m DO
12.   IF $(i \neq k)$ THEN
13. $\beta_k \leftarrow \beta_k \cdot (\Psi - i)$
14. $\beta_k = \beta_k / \tau_k$
15. $F = F + \beta_k$
16. RETURN F

Fig. 1. Procedure EXACT-MATCHING (on the left) for computing the dynamic polynomial given in (5) and procedure APPROXIMATE-MATCHING (on the right) for computing the dynamic polynomial in (11).

Thus for instance, if all bits in x are equal to 0, i.e. $x = 0^m$, then the polynomial in (12) is equal to $\prod_{i=0}^{m-1}(1 - w_i)$, while it is equal to $\sum_{i=0}^{m-1} w_i$ when $x = 1^m$. According to such observation the number of exact and approximate occurrences of the string X in Y can be computed using the algorithms shown in Fig. 1, which construct the polynomial according to the bits contained in X.

Specifically, the algorithm EXACT-STRING-MATCHING shown in Fig. 1 (on the left) computes the dynamic polynomial correspondent to the function in (5) in $\mathcal{O}(NM \log(\sigma))$ time. The resulting polynomial has a degree equal to $m = M \log(\sigma)$. Similarly, the algorithm APPROXIMATE-STRING-MATCHING shown in Fig. 1 (on the right) computes the dynamic polynomial correspondent to the function in (11). Procedure PRODUCT-FACTORS computes a matrix P of dimension $N \times M$ where $P[j, i]$ is 1 if $Y_j = X_i$, and 0 otherwise. Such computation is performed in time $O(NM \log(\sigma))$. The overall time complexity of procedure APPROXIMATE-STRING-MATCHING is $\mathcal{O}(NM\delta \log(\sigma))$ while the resulting polynomial has a degree equal to m.

4   Implementation Details

In this section we discuss the details of our implementation together with some optimizations. These, in particular, target both server evaluation and client verification.

Optimizations. The first optimization we consider is the usage of the dynamic polynomials technique described in Sect. 3.4. Beyond reducing computational costs at server side, this technique also reduces bandwidth costs *both* when the client sends a pattern query and when the server provides back the answer. In the first case, the gain comes from the fact that the pattern can be sent unauthenticated (i.e. without authenticating it bit by bit, as the basic, non dynamic, version of our technique would require). In the second case, one gains from computing a lower degree polynomial (m instead of $2m$)[5].

The second optimization (referred as "Evaluation over Samples" in our tables) works at a lower level: the way the server evaluates tags (i.e. polynomials). Recall that in our case a MAC is a polynomial with coefficients in $\mathbb{Z}_p$ and Eval essentially performs additions and multiplications of polynomials (with multiplication being the computationally most intensive operation). A naive implementation of polynomial multiplication has time complexity $\mathcal{O}(n^2)$, when starting from polynomials of degree n. It is well known, that this can be reduced to $\mathcal{O}(n \log n)$ using FFT. Very informally, FFT allows to quickly perform multiplication by temporarily switching to a more convenient representation of the starting polynomials. In particular a set of complex points is (carefully) chosen and the polynomials are computed over such points. Multiplication can now be achieved by multiplying corresponding points and then going back to the original representation via interpolation.

Inspired by this, we notice that, since we work with low degree polynomials, we can stick to a "fast" point representation the whole time, without switching representation at each multiplication, as done in FFT. Specifically, instead of representing each polynomial f via its coefficients, we keep the points $f(i_1), \ldots, f(i_\ell)$, where $i_1, \ldots, i_\ell$ are (non complex) fixed points and ℓ is large enough to perform interpolation at the end. In particular addition (multiplication) of polynomials is obtained by adding (multiplying) the corresponding points[6]. We stress that, differently than FFT we keep this alternative representation along the whole evaluation: polynomial interpolation is applied only once, to compute the final tag that the server sends back to the client. We also remark that our technique is alternative to FFT and they cannot be used together.

Our experiments show that verification at client's side is very fast (few seconds even with the largest considered texts). Still, we could reduce these costs even further via preprocessing. This is because the homomorphic MAC from [14] allows for a two phase verification procedure. The most expensive phase is the one that involves the computation of ρ (see Sect. 2). This phase, however, can be done "offline", before knowing of the answer provided by the server (in particular it can be done while waiting for the server's response). Once receiving an answer, the client can complete the residual verification procedure with a total

---

[5] Recall that in the homomorphic MAC scheme from [14] the size of the tags grows with the degree of the arithmetic circuit.

[6] Notice that the fact that we consider low degree polynomials is crucial here. Our technique is efficient solely because ℓ does not need to be too big to be able to interpolate correctly at the end.

cost of $\mathcal{O}(d)$ multiplications, where d is the degree of the tag. Our experimental results show that this on-line phase has a negligible cost of few milliseconds.

Testing Environment and Experiment Parameters. Our code was written in C using (mainly) the GMP [30] library but also exploiting NTL [38] and gcrypt [34] codes, respectively, for a good implementation of the FFT-based polynomial multiplication and for AES (as underlying PRF). Our single-thread code was executed on a laptop equipped with a 64-bit Intel i7 6500U dual-core CPU running at 2.50 GHz speed. Given a specific experiment, the reported timing is obtained as the average value over multiple runs.

In our experiments, we first implemented the pattern matching algorithm reporting the number of exact matches of a pattern in a given text, as explained in Sect. 3. Then, we progressively applied the proposed optimizations in order to properly quantify the contribution added by each technique. We also implemented the approximate variant of our algorithm to test its performances. The algorithmic solutions of Sect. 3 producing the position of selected occurrences are clearly a mere application of previous algorithms, so no specific tests were conducted.

All the involved cryptographic tools where tuned to work with a long-term security level of 128 bits. We also implemented a (very) low security, 64 bit variant of our methods[7]. In this latter case it is possible to get an additional 20 %–30 % gain in performances.

Optimization Timings. A former set of experiments were carried on in order to estimate the single contribution of each considered optimization. The usage of (standard) FFT on the single tag multiplications was also included. The experiments involved a wide range of parameters (mainly varying text and pattern length). Here we report, the timings of a representative sample: a 1024 characters long text with a pattern of 8 characters. The time complexity of the evaluation step is clearly linear in the size of the text, so the performance on larger or smaller texts can be easily deduced.

For the chosen parameters, the timings for the server evaluation are reported in Table 1. It is interesting to note that evaluation over samples beats FFT only when used in conjunction with the dynamic polynomials optimization.

Additional Tests. Next, we considered the behaviour of our methods when considering different text sizes and pattern lengths[8].

We consider three possible pattern lengths: 4, 8 and 16 characters. These patterns are searched in texts of sizes: 1 KiB, 10 KiB and 100 KiB. As stated above, the linear complexity in the length of the text allows to easily deduce the behaviour with longer texts.

---

[7] These timings are not reported in this paper but are available upon request.

[8] We stress that we focused on our optimized techniques, as they are better than the alternative solutions discussed before in essentially all settings considered here.

Table 1. Evaluation of an 8 chars pattern on a 1024 chars text

Algorithm + optimizations	Evaluation time (s)
"count exact occurrences" algorithm	35.585
+FFT	8.572
+evaluation over sample	15.937
+dynamic polynomials	10.012
+dynamic polynomials +FFT	3.835
+dynamic polynomials +evaluation over samples	1.424

The timings and some bandwidth/memory measures using the considered settings are reported in Table 2. For a specific pattern size, the sampled evaluation and verification timings confirm the linearity in the text length. On the other side, it rapidly grows using longer patterns. The reported verification timings do not include the possible on-line/off-line optimization discussed before (in such a case the off line cost of verification becomes essentially the whole cost).

Table 2. Timings and sizes of exact pattern matching with both optimizations applied

Text (chars)	Pattern	Key gen (ms)	Text auth	Evaluation	Verification	Text tags (bytes)	Proof tag
1K	4	0.107	12	408	29	256K	528
1K	8	0.107	12	1424	59	256K	1040
1K	16	0.100	12	7685	117	256K	2064
10K	4	0.100	117	4106	307	2.5M	528
10K	8	0.100	113	15263	581	2.5M	1040
10K	16	0.100	116	81383	1176	2.5M	2064
100K	4	0.100	1430	37826	3274	25M	528
100K	8	0.133	1169	151369	6431	25M	1040
100K	16	0.133	1155	788093	11717	25M	2064

The cloud storage space for the authenticated text indicates a non-negligible fundamental factor of 1 KiB/character: it could be almost halved with a smart implementation considering that the known term of the 1-degree polynomial representing the tag is always a single bit and not a full 128 bits field element. The size of the proof reported by the server is quite small and it grows linearly with the size of the pattern.

Further experimental results on the approximate pattern matching algorithms are available in the full version of this paper.

Acknowledgements. This research was supported in part by a FIR 2014 grant by the University of Catania. Thanks to Nuno Tiago Ferreira de Carvalho for his Homomorphic MACs library (Available at https://bitbucket.org/ntfc/cf-homomorphic-mac/).

References

1. Agrawal, S., Boneh, D.: Homomorphic MACs: MAC-based integrity for network coding. In: Abdalla, M., Pointcheval, D., Fouque, P.-A., Vergnaud, D. (eds.) ACNS 2009. LNCS, vol. 5536, pp. 292–305. Springer, Heidelberg (2009)
2. Applebaum, B., Ishai, Y., Kushilevitz, E.: Computationally private randomizing polynomials and their applications. Comput. Complex. **15**(2), 115–162 (2006)
3. Applebaum, B., Ishai, Y., Kushilevitz, E.: From secrecy to soundness: efficient verification via secure computation. In: Abramsky, S., Gavoille, C., Kirchner, C., Meyer auf der Heide, F., Spirakis, P.G. (eds.) ICALP 2010. LNCS, vol. 6198, pp. 152–163. Springer, Heidelberg (2010)
4. Attrapadung, N., Libert, B.: Homomorphic network coding signatures in the standard model. In: Catalano, D., Fazio, N., Gennaro, R., Nicolosi, A. (eds.) PKC 2011. LNCS, vol. 6571, pp. 17–34. Springer, Heidelberg (2011)
5. Attrapadung, N., Libert, B., Peters, T.: Computing on authenticated data: new privacy definitions and constructions. In: Wang, X., Sako, K. (eds.) ASIACRYPT 2012. LNCS, vol. 7658, pp. 367–385. Springer, Heidelberg (2012)
6. Attrapadung, N., Libert, B., Peters, T.: Efficient completely context-hiding quotable and linearly homomorphic signatures. In: Kurosawa, K., Hanaoka, G. (eds.) PKC 2013. LNCS, vol. 7778, pp. 386–404. Springer, Heidelberg (2013)
7. Backes, M., Barbosa, M., Fiore, D., Reischuk, R.M.: ADSNARK: nearly practical and privacy-preserving proofs on authenticated data. In: 2015 IEEE Symposium on Security and Privacy, pp. 271–286. IEEE Computer Society Press (2015)
8. Backes, M., Fiore, D., Reischuk, R.M.: Verifiable delegation of computation on outsourced data. In: Sadeghi, A.-R., Gligor, V.D., Yung, M. (eds.) ACM CCS 13, pp. 863–874. ACM Press, November 2013
9. Baeza-Yates, R.A., Gonnet, G.H.: A new approach to text searching. Commun. ACM **35**(10), 74–82 (1992)
10. Boneh, D., Freeman, D., Katz, J., Waters, B.: Signing a linear subspace: signature schemes for network coding. In: Jarecki, S., Tsudik, G. (eds.) PKC 2009. LNCS, vol. 5443, pp. 68–87. Springer, Heidelberg (2009)
11. Boneh, D., Freeman, D.M.: Homomorphic signatures for polynomial functions. In: Paterson, K.G. (ed.) EUROCRYPT 2011. LNCS, vol. 6632, pp. 149–168. Springer, Heidelberg (2011)
12. Boneh, D., Freeman, D.M.: Linearly homomorphic signatures over binary fields and new tools for lattice-based signatures. In: Catalano, D., Fazio, N., Gennaro, R., Nicolosi, A. (eds.) PKC 2011. LNCS, vol. 6571, pp. 1–16. Springer, Heidelberg (2011)
13. Catalano, D.: Homomorphic signatures and message authentication codes. In: Abdalla, M., De Prisco, R. (eds.) SCN 2014. LNCS, vol. 8642, pp. 514–519. Springer, Heidelberg (2014)
14. Catalano, D., Fiore, D.: Practical homomorphic MACs for arithmetic circuits. In: Johansson, T., Nguyen, P.Q. (eds.) EUROCRYPT 2013. LNCS, vol. 7881, pp. 336–352. Springer, Heidelberg (2013)

15. Catalano, D., Fiore, D., Gennaro, R., Nizzardo, L.: Generalizing homomorphic MACs for arithmetic circuits. In: Krawczyk, H. (ed.) PKC 2014. LNCS, vol. 8383, pp. 538–555. Springer, Heidelberg (2014)

16. Catalano, D., Fiore, D., Gennaro, R., Vamvourellis, K.: Algebraic (trapdoor) one-way functions and their applications. In: Sahai, A. (ed.) TCC 2013. LNCS, vol. 7785, pp. 680–699. Springer, Heidelberg (2013)

17. Catalano, D., Fiore, D., Gennaro, R., Vamvourellis, K.: Algebraic (trapdoor) one-way functions: constructions and applications. Theoret. Comput. Sci. **592**, 143–165 (2015)

18. Catalano, D., Fiore, D., Nizzardo, L.: Programmable hash functions go private: constructions and applications to (homomorphic) signatures with shorter public keys. In: Gennaro, R., Robshaw, M. (eds.) CRYPTO 2015. LNCS, vol. 9216, pp. 254–274. Springer, Heidelberg (2015)

19. Catalano, D., Fiore, D., Warinschi, B.: Adaptive pseudo-free groups and applications. In: Paterson, K.G. (ed.) EUROCRYPT 2011. LNCS, vol. 6632, pp. 207–223. Springer, Heidelberg (2011)

20. Catalano, D., Fiore, D., Warinschi, B.: Efficient network coding signatures in the standard model. In: Fischlin, M., Buchmann, J., Manulis, M. (eds.) PKC 2012. LNCS, vol. 7293, pp. 680–696. Springer, Heidelberg (2012)

21. Catalano, D., Fiore, D., Warinschi, B.: Homomorphic signatures with efficient verification for polynomial functions. In: Garay, J.A., Gennaro, R. (eds.) CRYPTO 2014, Part I. LNCS, vol. 8616, pp. 371–389. Springer, Heidelberg (2014)

22. Crochemore, M., Rytter, W.: Text Algorithms. Oxford University Press, Oxford (1994)

23. Desmedt, Y.: Computer security by redefining what a computer is. In: NSPW (1993)

24. Faro, S., Lecroq, T.: The exact online string matching problem: a review of the most recent results. ACM Comput. Surv. **45**(2), 13 (2013)

25. Freeman, D.M.: Improved security for linearly homomorphic signatures: a generic framework. In: Fischlin, M., Buchmann, J., Manulis, M. (eds.) PKC 2012. LNCS, vol. 7293, pp. 697–714. Springer, Heidelberg (2012)

26. Gennaro, R., Gentry, C., Parno, B.: Non-interactive verifiable computing: outsourcing computation to untrusted workers. In: Rabin, T. (ed.) CRYPTO 2010. LNCS, vol. 6223, pp. 465–482. Springer, Heidelberg (2010)

27. Gennaro, R., Katz, J., Krawczyk, H., Rabin, T.: Secure network coding over the integers. In: Nguyen, P.Q., Pointcheval, D. (eds.) PKC 2010. LNCS, vol. 6056, pp. 142–160. Springer, Heidelberg (2010)

28. Gennaro, R., Wichs, D.: Fully homomorphic message authenticators. In: Sako, K., Sarkar, P. (eds.) ASIACRYPT 2013, Part II. LNCS, vol. 8270, pp. 301–320. Springer, Heidelberg (2013)

29. Gorbunov, S., Vaikuntanathan, V., Wichs, D.: Leveled fully homomorphic signatures from standard lattices. In: 47th ACM STOC, pp. 469–477. ACM Press (2015)

30. Granlund, T., GMP Development Team.: GNU MP: The GNU Multiple Precision Arithmetic Library, 6.1.0 edn (2016)

31. Johnson, R., Molnar, D., Song, D., Wagner, D.: Homomorphic signature schemes. In: Preneel, B. (ed.) CT-RSA 2002. LNCS, vol. 2271, pp. 244–262. Springer, Heidelberg (2002)

32. Kärkkäinen, J., Chae Na, J.: Faster filters for approximate string matching. In: Proceedings of the Nine Workshop on Algorithm Engineering and Experiments, ALENEX 2007, New Orleans, Louisiana, USA, January 6, 2007. SIAM (2007)

33. Knuth, D.E., Morris Jr., J.H., Pratt, V.R.: Fast pattern matching in strings. SIAM J. Comput. **6**(2), 323–350 (1977)
34. Koch, W., Libgcrypt Development Team.: Libgcrypt, 1.7.0 edn (2016)
35. Landau, G.M., Vishkin, U.: Efficient string matching with k mismatches. Theor. Comput. Sci. **43**, 239–249 (1986)
36. Micali, S., Rivest, R.L.: Transitive signature schemes. In: Preneel, B. (ed.) CT-RSA 2002. LNCS, vol. 2271, pp. 236–243. Springer, Heidelberg (2002)
37. Papadopoulos, D., Papamanthou, C., Tamassia, R., Triandopoulos, N.: Practical authenticated pattern matching with optimal proof size. Proc. VLDB Endowment **8**(7), 750–761 (2015)
38. Shoup, V.: NTL: A Library for doing Number Theory, 9.7.1 edn (2016)
39. Yi, X.: Directed transitive signature scheme. In: Abe, M. (ed.) CT-RSA 2007. LNCS, vol. 4377, pp. 129–144. Springer, Heidelberg (2006)

Digital Signatures

Virtual Smart Cards: How to Sign with a Password and a Server

Jan Camenisch[1], Anja Lehmann[1(✉)], Gregory Neven[1], and Kai Samelin[1,2]

[1] IBM Research – Zurich, Rüschlikon, Switzerland
{jca,anj,nev,ksa}@zurich.ibm.com
[2] Technische Universität Darmstadt, Darmstadt, Germany

Abstract. An important shortcoming of client-side cryptography on consumer devices is the poor protection of secret keys. Encrypting the keys under a human-memorizable password hardly offers any protection when the device is stolen. Trusted hardware tokens such as smart cards can provide strong protection of keys but are cumbersome to use. We consider the case where secret keys are used for digital signatures and propose a password-authenticated server-aided signature Pass2Sign protocol, where signatures are collaboratively generated by a device and a server, while the user authenticates to the server with a (low-entropy) password. Neither the server nor the device store enough information to create a signature by itself or to perform an offline attack on the password. The signed message remains hidden from the server. We argue that our protocol offers comparable security to trusted hardware, but without its inconveniences. We prove it secure in the universal composability (UC) framework in a very strong adaptive corruption model where, unlike standard UC, the adversary does not obtain past inputs and outputs upon corrupting a party. This is crucial to hide previously entered passwords and messages from the adversary when the device gets corrupted. The protocol itself is surprisingly simple: it is round-optimal, efficient, and relies exclusively on standard primitives such as hash functions and RSA. The security proof involves a novel random-oracle programming technique.

1 Introduction

Mobile devices such as smart phones and tablets are used more and more for security-critical tasks such as e-banking, authentication, and signing documents. However, they can be infected by malware and, due to their mobility, the devices are easily lost or stolen. Keeping cryptographic keys safe in such an environment is challenging. Typically, they are simply encrypted with a human-memorizable password. If a device is lost, stolen, or compromised by malware, the password-encrypted keys are usually easily recovered through an offline dictionary attack.

This work was supported by the European Commission through the Seventh Framework Programme under grant agreement #321310 for the PERCY grant.

© Springer International Publishing Switzerland 2016
V. Zikas and R. De Prisco (Eds.): SCN 2016, LNCS 9841, pp. 353–371, 2016.
DOI: 10.1007/978-3-319-44618-9_19

Such attacks are extremely effective on modern hardware, especially given the low entropy in human-memorizable passwords [23].

Higher-security use cases such as online banking or government-issued electronic identification (eID) therefore often resort to tamper-proof hardware such as smart cards, SIM cards or trusted platform modules (TPMs) for extra protection. The hardware tokens offer interfaces to interact with the keys, e.g., to compute digital signatures on messages provided by the host, while the signing key never leaves the confined environment. Usually, a password or PIN code is added as a second layer of protection. Offline attacks on the password or PIN are infeasible as the token blocks after too many failed attempts. In case a hardware token is compromised, it can additionally be rendered useless by revoking its public key.

The protection is not perfect though; without a dedicated display, malware on the host machine may instruct the plugged-in token to sign more or different messages than the user intended to sign. Also, side-channel attacks such as differential power analysis only become more powerful with time. In other words, what is considered tamper-proof hardware today, may not be so anymore tomorrow [29]. Additionally, trusted hardware suffers from poor usability and high deployment and maintenance costs. Users find it inconvenient to carry a hardware token for each security-sensitive application. Desktop and laptop computers rarely come with built-in smart card readers and not all consumer-grade machines have TPMs. External USB card readers are available, but supporting drivers and browser plug-ins on several platforms simultaneously requires a considerable effort. Using trusted hardware in combination with mobile devices is even more problematic, as they often lack connectivity to interact with external tokens.

So the question is, can we somehow realize similar security guarantees as hardware tokens, but avoid their practical inconveniences? Software obfuscation may come to mind, but does not help at all: leaking an obfuscated signing algorithm to an adversary is just as bad as leaking the signing key itself. As network connectivity is far more ubiquitous than trusted hardware in consumer devices, how about relying on the assistance of an online server to create signatures? A solution must protect the keys as long as at least one of the device or the server is not corrupted. Moreover, we want the user to remember at most a potentially weak password or a PIN code, while offering protection against offline password guessing attacks. Involving an online server in the signing process enables additional control of the use of the signing key, as the server can block the account or involve a second authentication factor.

Our Primitive. We introduce the notion of *password-authenticated server-aided signatures* (Pass2Sign), where the signing key is distributed over the user's device and an online server. The signing key is never reconstructed; rather, the device and the server must engage in a distributed protocol to compute signatures. For added security, the user must enter a password on the device each time a signature is generated. The server not only verifies the password, but also the identity of the device, i.e., an adversary without access to the device cannot even perform an online guessing attack. This prevents an adversary from blocking an honest user's account by swamping the server with fake login attempts: the server simply ignores signing attempts from the wrong device. If the device falls into the wrong hands, or if the device is compromised by malware, then the attacker must still perform an *online* guessing attack before it can generate signatures. When the server detects too many failed password attempts or signing requests per time period, it can take appropriate action such as blocking the account or requiring additional authentication. The server neither learns the message that is being signed, nor does it learn the user's password (or password attempts). This not only protects the user against malicious servers, but also protects the password in case the server is broken into by hackers.

Malware running on the device can of course capture both the device keys and the password, enabling the adversary to sign any messages it wants, but only by interacting with the server for each new signature. The server can therefore implement additional security measures on top of our protocol, e.g., a logic which detects abnormal signing behavior, or a secondary communication channel via which the server informs the user about his account activity. When suspicious transactions are detected, the server can block the user's account to ensure that no further signatures can be created, and revoke the user's public key.

The resulting security level is almost identical to the protection offered by trusted hardware tokens, but without their inconveniences. Only few smart card readers feature integrated trusted keypads and displays; built-in secure elements such as SIM cards or TPMs never do. Malware running on the host system can therefore also capture the user's PIN code and have different messages signed than what is shown on the screen. The main security guarantee of trusted hardware tokens is therefore that no more signatures can be generated after unplugging the token—which can actually be quite cumbersome or even impossible for SIM cards and TPMs. In the same way, our protocol prevents further signatures from being generated when the user's account is blocked by the server. When the device is lost, our solution even offers better protection than hardware: while it may be possible to extract the keys from a compromised token, the only information that an adversary can extract from a corrupted device is a useless key share.

Strong Security Notion and Corruption Model. We define the security of a Pass2Sign scheme in the universal composability (UC) framework [12]. The main goal of our protocol is to guarantee protection of the user's password and signing key in the event of device or server compromise. We therefore propose a very strong corruption model that, unlike standard corruptions as defined in the UC framework, does not hand all past inputs and outputs to the adversary when a party is corrupted. In case the device gets corrupted, these inputs include the user's password and all previously signed messages, which obviously goes directly against our security goals. Clearly, it is impossible to achieve such a strong corruption model without secure erasures: if the entered passwords are not erased, then there is no way to hide it from an adversary upon corruption.

The UC framework is well known to provide superior and more natural security guarantees for the particular case of password-based protocols than traditional game-based notions [14]. In particular, by letting the environment generate all passwords and password attempts, UC formulations correctly model arbitrary dependencies between passwords. For example, their game-based counterparts fail to provide any security guarantees when honest users make typos while entering their passwords, a rather frequent occurrence in real life. Also, by absorbing password guessing attacks inside the functionality, secure composition with other protocols is guaranteed to hold; this is much less clear for game-based notions that tolerate a non-negligible adversarial success probability.

Efficient Protocols. One might expect that meeting such stringent security standards comes at a considerable cost in efficiency. Indeed, similar protocols involve a factor 4–10 in performance penalty to protect against (standard) adaptive corruptions [9], while generic techniques to obtain adaptive security at least double the number of communication rounds [34]. Blindness for signed messages is another feature that is notoriously expensive to achieve in the UC framework [28]. It is therefore even more surprising that our protocol, in the random-oracle model, is refreshingly simple, round-optimal, and efficient. Generating a signature requires only three modular exponentiations on the device and two on the server, plus a few hash function evaluations, with only one protocol message from the device to the server and back. The resulting signature is an RSA-FDH signature on a double salted hash of the message and some session identifiers. We also describe two simpler variants of our protocol for the setting where message blindness is not required. Our first variant exposes the message only to the server, a second variant does not hide the message at all.

Proof Technique. In spite of its simplicity, the security proof of the protocol is actually quite intricate. The many cases triggered by adaptive corruptions (which are allowed even during setup and arbitrarily interleaved signing sessions) and the mixture of passwords, encryption, and signatures require very careful bookkeeping, especially of the random-oracle responses during simulation. We employ an interesting and, to the best of our knowledge, novel technique to reconcile the seemingly contradictive requirements that the simulator must be able to determine the value of each signature, but without learning the message being signed. We avoid typical blind signature techniques and the associated "one-more"-type security assumptions [4] by letting the device and the server both contribute to the randomness of the signature, and by programming the random oracle "just-in-time" at the moment that the signature is verified, not when it is created. This technique is of independent interest, and may find applications in other scenarios as well.

Implementation. We implemented our protocol on a commodity mobile device and provide a thorough performance analysis of our prototypical implementation to demonstrate the practicality of our protocol. With signature generation for a 2048-bit key requiring about 250 ms in total, our protocol is clearly efficient enough for use in practice. An overview is given in Sect. 5

Related Work. We give a short overview of related work here. Additional related work is provided in the full version. Threshold signatures [2,8,17,20,33] let a signing key be split over more than one entity. In their basic form, threshold signatures assume that all parties somehow know and agree on the message being signed, and do not specify how a signing protocol is triggered. Some protocols rely on trusted hardware [16,31], assume a non-corruptible server [6], allow the server or a threshold of servers to sign in the user's name without access to the device [26,35], or use signing keys or key shares derived from the user's password and are therefore vulnerable to offline attacks by a corrupt server [19,21,22].

The S-RSA protocol due to MacKenzie and Reiter [30] envisages many of the goals that we also pursue, such as requiring the adversary to compromise the device to perform even an online attack, avoiding offline attacks as long as the server and the device are not both compromised, and "key disabling" by blocking a user's account on the server. Their protocol is proven secure in a property-based (i.e., non-UC) notion that is weaker than ours in several respects. Foremost, it does not enjoy the many advantages of UC password-based protocols discussed earlier, such as preserving security in case of mistyped passwords and secure composition with other protocols. Also, the server in their protocol sees the message being signed, can only be corrupted between (and not during) signing sessions, and can actually perform an offline dictionary attack on the password based on the information it sees during the signing protocol (but this problem is easy to fix). Our protocol is the first to support fully adaptive corruptions of the server as well as the device in the UC model even during signing sessions. One could of course evaluate the signing algorithm using generic adaptively UC-secure MPC, but this comes at great cost: evaluating even a *single* multiplication gate is considerably more expensive than our protocol [10].

2 Preliminaries

Here we introduce the building blocks for our construction. These include RSA-FDH signatures ($\mathsf{DSIG_{RSA}}$), non-committing encryption (NCE), trapdoor one-way permutations (TDP), and three UC-functionalities.

Notation. We use $\tau \in \mathbb{N}$ as our security parameter. 1^τ is the string of τ ones. All algorithms receive 1^τ as an implicit input. $a \xleftarrow{} S$ denotes that a is assigned a random element chosen uniformly from the set S. If A is a PPT algorithm we write $y \xleftarrow{r} A(x; r)$ to denote that y is assigned the output of A with input x and external random coins r. If we drop r, the random coins are drawn internally. For deterministic algorithms, we write $y \leftarrow A(x)$. A function $\epsilon : \mathbb{N} \to \mathbb{R}$ is negligible if $\epsilon(\tau) = \tau^{-\omega(1)}$. By $|m|$ we denote the binary length of a message m. $|S|$ denotes the cardinality of the set S. If an argument is a list, we assume that the list has an injective encoding which allows embedding it into $\{0,1\}^*$.

Ideal Functionality $\mathcal{F}_{CA}$. We assume a public-key infrastructure where servers can register their public keys, modeled by the ideal functionality $\mathcal{F}_{CA}$ [13]. These keys can be retrieved by any party using the entity's identity for which the public key is requested. A formal definition of $\mathcal{F}_{CA}$ is given in the full version.

Ideal Functionality $\mathcal{F}_{RO}^{\mathcal{D} \rightarrow \mathcal{R}}$. A random oracle can be seen as an idealized hash function that consistently maps inputs from domain $\mathcal{D}$ to random values in range $\mathcal{R}$ [5]. It is adjusted for our notation, as we parametrize it with domain $\mathcal{D}$ and range $\mathcal{R}$. We sometimes use more than one random oracle with the same range $\mathcal{R}$ and domain $\mathcal{D}$ for easier analysis, i.e., more than one random oracle corresponds to $\mathcal{F}_{RO}^{\mathcal{D} \rightarrow \mathcal{R}}$. To distinguish different random oracles, we assume that each call is prefixed with a unique identifier. The formal definition of $\mathcal{F}_{RO}^{\mathcal{D} \rightarrow \mathcal{R}}$ is based on [27] and given in the full version.

Ideal Functionality $\mathcal{F}_{Auth}$. The $\mathcal{F}_{Auth}$ functionality provides authenticated (but public) channels between parties [12,13]. For our protocol, we can use the simplified version of [12], which allows to send a single authenticated message to the designated receiver. The formal definition of $\mathcal{F}_{Auth}$ is given in the full version.

One-Wayness of RSA. Let $(N, e, d, p, q) \xleftarrow{r} \mathsf{RSAGen}(1^\tau)$ be an RSA-key generator returning an RSA modulus $N = pq$, where p and q are random distinct primes, $e > 1$ an integer coprime to $\varphi(N)$, and $d \equiv e^{-1} \bmod \varphi(N)$. The RSA one-wayness problem associated to RSAGen is, given N, e, and $y \xleftarrow{r} \mathbb{Z}_N^*$, to find x such that $x^e \equiv y \bmod N$. The RSA (one-wayness) assumption now states that for every PPT adversary $\mathcal{A}$, $\Pr[(N, e, d, p, q) \xleftarrow{r} \mathsf{RSAGen}(1^\tau), y \xleftarrow{r} \mathbb{Z}_N^*, x \xleftarrow{r} \mathcal{A}(N, e, y) : x^e \equiv y \bmod N] \leq \epsilon(\tau)$ for some negligible function ϵ.

RSA-FDH Signatures. We use a RSA Full-Domain Hash (FDH) signature scheme $\mathsf{DSIG}_{RSA} = (\mathsf{SKGen}_{RSA}, \mathsf{Sign}_{RSA}, \mathsf{Verify}_{RSA})$ associated to RSA-key generator RSAGen defined as follows. The key generation algorithm $(spk, ssk) \xleftarrow{r} \mathsf{SKGen}_{RSA}(1^\tau)$ runs $(N, e, d, p, q) \xleftarrow{r} \mathsf{RSAGen}(1^\tau)$ and outputs $ssk = (d, p, q)$ and $spk = (N, e)$. It also requires a hash function $\mathcal{H}_{RSA} : \{0,1\}^* \rightarrow \mathbb{Z}_N^*$, modeled as a random oracle. To sign a message $m \in \{0,1\}^*$ with key $ssk = (d, p, q)$, Sign_{RSA} computes $\sigma \leftarrow (\mathcal{H}_{RSA}(m))^d \bmod N$. To verify if a signature σ is valid for a message $m \in \{0,1\}^*$ and $spk = (N, e)$, Verify_{RSA} outputs true if $0 < \sigma < N$ and $\mathcal{H}_{RSA}(m) = \sigma^e \bmod N$, else it outputs false. RSA-FDH signatures are strongly unforgeable against chosen message attacks in the random-oracle model if the RSA assumption holds [15].

Trapdoor One-Way Permutations. Let $(f, f^{-1}, \Sigma) \xleftarrow{r} \mathsf{TFGen}_f(1^\tau)$ be the instance generator for a function $f : \Sigma \rightarrow \Sigma$ defining a permutation over Σ, with an inversion function $f^{-1} : \Sigma \rightarrow \Sigma$, such that we have 1) for all $x \in \Sigma$, all $\tau \in \mathbb{N}$, and for all $(f, f^{-1}, \Sigma) \xleftarrow{r} \mathsf{TFGen}_f(1^\tau)$, we have $x = f^{-1}(f(x))$, and 2) for all PPT adversaries $\mathcal{A}$ we have $\Pr[(f, f^{-1}, \Sigma) \leftarrow \mathsf{TFGen}_f(1^\tau), x \xleftarrow{r} \Sigma : x = \mathcal{A}(f, f(x), \Sigma)] \leq \epsilon(\tau)$ for some negligible function ϵ. We also require that we can efficiently sample from Σ. An RSA-key generator RSAGen yields a trapdoor one-way permutation under the RSA assumption with $\Sigma = \mathbb{Z}_N^*$, $f(x) = x^e \bmod N$ and $f^{-1}(y) = y^d \bmod N$ [5].

Experiment $\mathsf{Exp}_{\mathsf{NCE},\mathcal{A},\mathsf{SIM_{NCE}}}^{\mathsf{RECV-SIM-ideal}}(\tau)$:
  $epk \xleftarrow{r} \mathsf{SIM_{NCE}}(\mathsf{publickey}, 1^\tau)$
  $\mathcal{Q} \leftarrow \emptyset$
  $state_\mathcal{A} \xleftarrow{r} \mathcal{A}^{\mathcal{O}^{\mathcal{H}(\cdot)}, \mathcal{O}^{\mathsf{Enc}(\cdot,\cdot)}, \mathcal{O}^{\mathsf{Dec}(\cdot,\cdot)}}(epk)$
  where $\mathcal{O}^{\mathsf{Enc}(\cdot,\cdot)}$ on input (m_i, ℓ_i):
    $C_i \xleftarrow{r} \mathsf{SIM_{NCE}}(\mathsf{encrypt}, |m_i|, \ell_i)$
    $\mathcal{Q} \leftarrow \mathcal{Q} \cup \{(C_i, m_i, \ell_i)\}$
    return C_i
  where $\mathcal{O}^{\mathsf{Dec}(\cdot,\cdot)}$ on input (C_j, ℓ_j):
    if $(C_j, m_j, \ell_j) \in \mathcal{Q}$, return m_j
    else, return $m_j \leftarrow \mathsf{SIM_{NCE}}(\mathsf{decrypt}, C_j, \ell_j)$
  where $\mathcal{O}^{\mathcal{H}(\cdot)}$ on input q_k:
    return $h_k \xleftarrow{r} \mathsf{SIM_{NCE}}(\mathsf{roquery}, q_k)$
  $esk \xleftarrow{r} \mathsf{SIM_{NCE}}(\mathsf{keyleak}, \mathcal{Q})$
  return $\mathcal{A}^{\mathcal{O}^{\mathcal{H}(\cdot)}}(esk, state_\mathcal{A})$

Experiment $\mathsf{Exp}_{\mathsf{NCE},\mathcal{A}}^{\mathsf{RECV-SIM-real}}(\tau)$:
  $(epk, esk) \xleftarrow{r} \mathsf{EKGen}(1^\tau)$
  $state_\mathcal{A} \xleftarrow{r} \mathcal{A}^{\mathcal{O}^{\mathcal{H}(\cdot)}, \mathcal{O}^{\mathsf{Enc}(\cdot,\cdot)}, \mathcal{O}^{\mathsf{Dec}(\cdot,\cdot)}}(epk)$
  where $\mathcal{O}^{\mathsf{Enc}(\cdot,\cdot)}$ on input (m_i, ℓ_i):
    return $C_i \xleftarrow{r} \mathsf{Enc}(epk, m_i, \ell_i)$
  where $\mathcal{O}^{\mathsf{Dec}(\cdot,\cdot)}$ on input (C_j, ℓ_j):
    return $m_j \leftarrow \mathsf{Dec}(esk, C_j, \ell_j)$
  where $\mathcal{O}^{\mathcal{H}(\cdot)}$ on input q_k:
    return $h_k \xleftarrow{r} \mathcal{H}(q_k)$
  return $\mathcal{A}^{\mathcal{O}^{\mathcal{H}(\cdot)}}(esk, state_\mathcal{A})$

Fig. 1. Experiments RECV-SIM-ideal and RECV-SIM-real for our RECV-SIM definition.

Non-committing Labeled Public-Key Encryption Scheme. To deal with adaptive corruptions, we require a non-committing encryption scheme. In the security proof, the simulator needs to be able to simulate ciphertexts without knowing the corresponding plaintexts which would be encrypted in the real protocol. However, when the adversary later corrupts the receiver of a simulated ciphertext, the simulator has to provide a state of the corrupted party such that all the ciphertexts decrypt to some concrete plaintext. This is related to the "selective de-commitment problem" [3]. The notion of non-committing encryption that we require is stronger than some that were proposed in the literature [18,25] and weaker than others [32]. To minimize the security assumptions for our protocol and open the possibility for more efficient instantiations, we introduce our own definition and provide a non-interactive construction in the random-oracle model.

A *labeled non-committing encryption scheme* $\mathsf{NCE} = (\mathsf{EKGen}, \mathsf{Enc}, \mathsf{Dec})$ consists for three algorithms: a key generation algorithm $(epk, esk) \xleftarrow{r} \mathsf{EKGen}(1^\tau)$ outputting a public and secret key, where the public key specifies a finite message space $\mathcal{M}$, an encryption algorithm $C \xleftarrow{r} \mathsf{Enc}(epk, m, \ell)$ computing a ciphertext C on input a public key epk, a message $m \in \mathcal{M}$, and a label $\ell \in \{0, 1\}^*$, and a decryption algorithm $m' \leftarrow \mathsf{Dec}(esk, C, \ell)$ that takes as input a secret key esk, a ciphertext C and a label ℓ and outputs either a message m' or $\perp$ if decryption failed. We require the usual correctness properties to hold. Sometimes we need to explicitly talk about the random choices of the encryption algorithm. To this end, let Σ be the space of these choices.

We now define the RECV-SIM security property that a labeled non-committing encryption scheme needs to satisfy in our context.

Definition 1 (RECV-SIM Security). *An encryption scheme* $\mathsf{NCE} = (\mathsf{EKGen}, \mathsf{Enc}, \mathsf{Dec})$ *is RECV-SIM-secure if for all PPT adversaries* $\mathcal{A}$ *there exists a stateful PPT simulator* $\mathsf{SIM_{NCE}}$ *such that* $\left| \Pr[\mathsf{Exp}_{\mathsf{NCE},\mathcal{A}}^{\mathsf{RECV-SIM-real}}(\tau) = 1] - \Pr[\mathsf{Exp}_{\mathsf{NCE},\mathcal{A},\mathsf{SIM_{NCE}}}^{\mathsf{RECV-SIM-ideal}}(\tau) = 1] \right| \leq \epsilon(\tau)$ *for some negligible function* ϵ *and the experiments of Fig. 1.*

This definition says an encryption scheme is RECV-SIM-secure (RECeiVer-SIMulatable), if there exists a simulator that is given control over the random oracle such that no adversary can distinguish between simulated ciphertexts (which do not contain any information) and honestly generated ones.

More precisely, the adversary must not be able to tell in which of the two experiments it is run in, even if it can adaptively query for new encryptions, decryptions, and receives the secret key at some point. The crucial difference is that in the ideal game the adversary receives simulated ciphertexts instead of real ones, which are computed by a simulator on input only the length of the plaintext. Moreover, the adversary $\mathcal{A}$ receives the secret key of the receiver at a later point of its own choice. In the ideal world, this secret key is provided by the simulator which only now learns the plaintexts to which it produced the simulated ciphertexts. The adversary expects that the ciphertexts indeed decrypt to the messages queried to the encryption oracle using the given secret key.

Compared to the definition given by Fehr et al. [18], our adversary $\mathcal{A}$ is allowed adaptive queries, and receives the secret key esk (but not the randomness used to create it) at the last step of the experiment, while the definitions given by Hazay et al. [25] only consider a single (or randomly sampled according to some distribution) message per key pair, which is not enough for our protocol. Likewise, Nielsen [32] gives a formulation of non-committing encryption—in the sense of secure message transmission—in the UC framework. However, his functionality is stronger than what we need, because it simulates all randomness, which we do not require, as our protocol relies on secure erasures anyway. In the full version, we prove that any encryption scheme that RECV-SIM security implies IND-CCA2 security.

Instantiation. We now give a concrete instantiation for an encryption scheme that achieves RECV-SIM security. We modify the CCA2-secure encryption scheme introduced in [5] to include labels and handle arbitrary-length messages. Let $\mathcal{G} : \{0,1\}^* \to \{0,1\}^\tau$ and $\mathcal{K} : \{0,1\}^* \to \{0,1\}^\tau$ denote two hash functions, modeled as random oracles. Let $\mathsf{ec} : \{0,1\}^* \to (\{0,1\}^\tau)^+$ be an injective encoding function and let $\mathsf{dc} : (\{0,1\}^\tau)^+ \to \{0,1\}^*$ denote the corresponding decoding function that returns $\perp$ if no valid pre-image exists. We require that the output length of ec only depends on the length of its input.

$\mathsf{EKGen}(1^\tau)$: Generate a random trapdoor one-way permutation, i.e., $(f, f^{-1}, \Sigma) \xleftarrow{r} \mathsf{TFGen}_f(1^\tau)$. The message space $\mathcal{M}$ is $\{0,1\}^*$. Output the public key $epk = (f, \Sigma)$, and $esk = f^{-1}$ as the secret key.

$\mathsf{Enc}(epk, m, \ell)$: Let $(m_1, m_2, \ldots, m_k) \leftarrow \mathsf{ec}(m)$. Draw $x \xleftarrow{r} \Sigma$, compute $C_1 \leftarrow f(x)$, $C_2^i \leftarrow \mathcal{G}(i, x) \oplus m_i$ for $i = 1, \ldots, k$, and $C_3 \leftarrow \mathcal{K}(x, k, m, \ell)$ and output the ciphertext $C := (C_1, (C_2^1, \ldots, C_2^k), C_3)$.

$\mathsf{Dec}(esk, C, \ell)$: Parse C as $(C_1, (C_2^1, \ldots, C_2^{k'}), C_3)$ for some $k' \geq 1$. Compute $x' \leftarrow f^{-1}(C_1)$ and $m_i' \leftarrow \mathcal{G}(i, x') \oplus C_2^i$ for $i = 1, \ldots, k'$. Let $m' \leftarrow \mathsf{dc}(m_1', \ldots, m'_{k'})$. If $m' = \perp$ or $C_3 \neq \mathcal{K}(x', k', m', \ell)$, output $\perp$. Output m'.

The above construction fulfills perfect correctness. The proof of the following theorem is given in the full version [11].

Theorem 1. *The construction above is RECV-SIM-secure, if $\mathcal{G}$ and $\mathcal{K}$ are modeled as random oracles and $\mathsf{TFGen_f}(1^\tau)$ is a secure TDP generator.*

3   Ideal Functionality

We now formally define password-authenticated server-aided signatures (Pass2Sign) by describing its ideal functionality in the universal composability (UC) framework [12].

First, recall the high-level goal of our Pass2Sign scheme: signatures on messages are derived collaboratively between two parties, a device $\mathcal{D}$ and a server $\mathcal{S}$, meaning that a valid signature can only be obtained if both parties agree to the generation. Access to the server's signing operation is protected by a user password *pwd* that is chosen at setup and needs to be provided for every signing request. The server then verifies whether the password is correct and also whether the request came from the correct device, which has the additional advantage that an attacker cannot block an honest user's account by swamping the server with false login attempts. The protocol must be secure against offline attacks on the password used during setup and on the password attempts during signing. That is, as long as at least one party remains honest, the adversary does not learn anything about the used passwords. In particular, the server learns only whether a password attempt in a signing request was correct or not, but not the actual password attempt itself. The server also does not learn the messages being signed. (If this blindness feature is not required, we discuss how it can easily be removed in the full version [11].) Security must be guaranteed for adaptive corruptions in order to protect against the main threat, namely the user losing his device. Note that we subsume the user of the device into the environment to have a more readable functionality. How this maps to real-life scenarios is discussed at the end of this section.

The detailed description of our ideal functionality $\mathcal{F}_{\mathsf{Pass2Sign}}$ for password-authenticated server-aided signatures is given in Figs. 2 and 3. When describing our functionality, we use the following conventions to reduce repetitive notation:

- For the SETUPREQ and KEYGEN interfaces, the ideal functionality only considers the first input for each *sid*. Subsequent inputs to the same interface for the same *sid* are ignored. For the SIGNREQ, DELIVER, PROCEED, SIGNATURE interfaces the functionality only considers the first input for each combination of *sid* and *qid*.
- At each invocation, the functionality checks that $sid = (\mathcal{S}, \mathcal{D}, sid')$ for some server identity $\mathcal{S}$, device identifier $\mathcal{D}$ and $sid' \in \{0,1\}^*$. Also, whenever we say that $\mathcal{F}$ receives input from or provides output to $\mathcal{S}$ or $\mathcal{D}$, we mean $\mathcal{S}$ or $\mathcal{D}$ as specified in the *sid*, respectively.
- When we say that the functionality "looks up a record", we implicitly understand that if the record is not found, the functionality ignores the input and returns control to the environment.

1. **Setup Request Device.** On input (SETUPREQ, sid, pwd) from device $\mathcal{D}$:
   - Create a record (setup-req, sid, pwd) and send (SETUPREQ, sid) to $\mathcal{A}$.
2. **Key Generation.** On input (KEYGEN, sid, pwd^*, pk) from adversary $\mathcal{A}$:
   - Look up a record (setup-req, sid, pwd).
   - If $\mathcal{D}$ (taken from sid) is corrupt, then mark this instance as key-corrupt.
   - If $\mathcal{D}$ is corrupt and $pwd^* \neq \bot$, then create a record (setup, sid, pwd^*, pk). Else, create a record (setup, sid, pwd, pk).
   - Output (SETUP, sid, pk) to $\mathcal{D}$.

---

3. **Sign Request.** On input (SIGNREQ, sid, qid, pwd', m) from device $\mathcal{D}$:
   - Look up a record (setup, sid, pwd, pk).
   - Create a record (sign-req, sid, qid, pwd', m).
   - Send (SIGNREQ, sid, qid) to $\mathcal{A}$.
4. **Sign Delivery.** On input (DELIVER, sid, qid, pwd^*, m^*) from adversary $\mathcal{A}$:
   - Look up records (setup, sid, pwd, pk) and (sign-req, sid, qid, pwd', m).
   - If $\mathcal{D}$ is corrupt and $pwd^* \neq \bot$, then set $pwd' \leftarrow pwd^*$ and $m \leftarrow m^*$.
   - If $pwd' = pwd$ then set $status \leftarrow$ pwdok, else set $status \leftarrow$ pwdwrong.
   - Create a record (sign, sid, qid, m, $status$).
   - Output (SIGNREQ, sid, qid, $status$) to $\mathcal{S}$.
5. **Server Proceed.** On input (PROCEED, sid, qid) from server $\mathcal{S}$:
   - Look up a record (sign, sid, qid, m, $status$) with $status =$ pwdok.
   - Update the record to $status \leftarrow$ proceed, and send (PROCEED, sid, qid) to $\mathcal{A}$.
6. **Signature Generation.** On input (SIGNATURE, sid, qid, σ) from $\mathcal{A}$:
   - Look up a record (sign, sid, qid, m, $status$).
   - If $\mathcal{S}$ is honest, only proceed if $status =$ proceed.
   - If there is no record (signature, pk, m, σ, false), then create a record (signature, pk, m, σ, true), and output (SIGNATURE, sid, qid, σ) to $\mathcal{D}$.

---

7. **Verify.** On input (VERIFY, sid, pk', m, σ) from a party $\mathcal{P}$:
   - Create a record (verify, sid, pk', m, σ, $\mathcal{P}$) and send (VERIFY, sid, pk', m, σ, $\mathcal{P}$) to $\mathcal{A}$.
8. **Verified.** On input (VERIFIED, sid, pk', m, σ, ϕ) from $\mathcal{A}$ with $\phi \in \{$true, false$\}$:
   - Look up, and delete afterwards, a record (verify, sid, pk', m, σ, $\mathcal{P}$).
   - Record (signature, pk', m, σ, f) and output (VERIFIED, sid, pk', m, σ, f) to $\mathcal{P}$, where f is determined as follows:
     - If a record (signature, pk', m, σ, f') for some f' exists, set $f \leftarrow f'$. *(consistency)*
     - Else, if a record (setup, sid, pwd, pk) exists with $pk = pk'$ and the instance is not marked key-corrupt, set $f \leftarrow$ false. *(strong unforgeability)*
     - Else, set $f \leftarrow \phi$.

Fig. 2. Main interfaces of our functionality $\mathcal{F}_{\mathsf{Pass2Sign}}$.

– We assume that the session (sid) and query identifiers (qid) given as input to our functionality are globally unique. In the two-party setting that we consider, this can be achieved by exchanging random nonces between both parties and including the concatenation of both in the identifiers. We also assume that

---

9. **Corruption.** On input (CORRUPT, $sid, \mathcal{P}, \Sigma$) from adversary $\mathcal{A}$:
   - Look up a record (setup, sid, pwd, pk) and initialize a list $\mathcal{L} \leftarrow \emptyset$.
   - If $\mathcal{P} = \mathcal{S}$, then assemble $\mathcal{L}$ containing (qid_i, c_i) for all existing records (sign-req, sid, qid_i, pwd'_i, m_i), where $c_i \leftarrow$ pwdok if $pwd = pwd'_i$ and $c_i \leftarrow$ pwdwrong otherwise.
   - If now both $\mathcal{D}$ and $\mathcal{S}$ are corrupt, then mark this instance as key-corrupt and complete the abandoned sign requests: For all $(qid_i, \sigma_i) \in \Sigma$, look up m_i from record (sign-req, sid, qid_i, pwd'_i, m_i). If there does not exist a record (signature, pk, m_i, σ_i, false), then create a record (signature, pk, m_i, σ_i, true).
   - Send (CORRUPT, $sid, \mathcal{P}, \mathcal{L}$) to $\mathcal{A}$.

10. **Password Guessing.** On input (PWDGUESS, sid, qid, pwd^*) from adversary $\mathcal{A}$:
    - If not both $\mathcal{D}$ and $\mathcal{S}$ are corrupt, then ignore this input.
    - If $qid = \perp$ then look up a record (setup-req, sid, pwd).
    - If $qid \neq \perp$ then look up a record (sign-req, sid, qid, pwd, m).
    - Set $c \leftarrow$ pwdok, if $pwd^* = pwd$ and $c \leftarrow$ pwdwrong otherwise.
    - Send (PWDGUESS, sid, qid, c) to $\mathcal{A}$.

Fig. 3. Interfaces of our functionality $\mathcal{F}_{\mathsf{Pass2Sign}}$.

honest parties drop any inputs with session or query identifiers to which they did not contribute.
- When we say that an instance is "marked", we mean that the specified label is associated with the instance of the functionality with the current sid. This does not affect other instances of the functionality with a different sid.

If the device is already corrupt at the time of setup, we consider the instance as key-corrupt even though the server might still be honest. A stronger security notion, requiring only slight changes to the functionality, would be achievable where the instance is only considered key-corrupt when both the device and server are corrupted. However, this would mean that in the realization, the key generation be done distributively between the server and the device. This is possible but for RSA rather inefficient [1,24] and seems to offer little added security; hence we chose not to do this. A detailed discussion of the interfaces is given in the full version.

Discussion. Let us discuss how real-world attack scenarios map to our ideal functionality. If a user loses his device, we assume that the adversary is able to extract *all* the data from the device, so the device becomes corrupted. As long as the server is not corrupted, though, the adversary controlling the device still has to make online password guesses to be able to sign, but does not obtain the (full) signing key. To protect against online password guessing, the server should implement some kind of throttling on top of our protocol, such as refusing to serve further queries after too many failed password attempts.

If the device becomes infected by malware, we also capture the worst case scenario: it may get *all* the data from the device and hence the device becomes corrupted. In contrast with the scenario above, the malware may also learn the (correct) password of the user if he's unaware of the infection and continues to use the device. This behavior is subsumed into the environment; we model this correctly by letting the environment provide the correct password to the adversary. Some protection against this kind of attack can be implemented on top of our protocol by adding intrusion detection logic on the server's side, e.g., by stopping to serve requests if they become too frequent. This situation is actually similar to that of a smart card inserted in an infected device: the device could intercept the PIN and sign any messages it wants until the card is removed.

One could consider a more gradual corruption model where the device can be semi-corrupted, e.g., if an application turns malicious, but the uncompromised operating system separates it from other applications on the device. Our model covers this as long as applications have their own protected execution space: the device in our model represents the application, while everything else is subsumed into the environment. More advanced models where applications can observe other applications (e.g., their running times) are beyond the scope of this paper.

4   Our **Pass2Sign** Protocol

The core idea of our protocol is fairly simple: an RSA secret key $d = d_{\mathcal{D}} \cdot d_{\mathcal{S}} \bmod \varphi(N)$ is split between the device and the server who then jointly perform the signing operation for each message m. To hide the message from the server, the device "blinds" it with randomness r as $h_m \leftarrow \mathcal{H}(r, m)$ and lets the server sign it as $\sigma_{\mathcal{S}} \leftarrow h_m^{d_{\mathcal{S}}}$. The device completes the signature as $\sigma \leftarrow \sigma_{\mathcal{S}}^{d_{\mathcal{D}}}$. For each signing request, the user authenticates towards the server using a salted password hash $h_p \leftarrow \mathcal{H}(k, pwd)$, where the salt k is stored on the device.

Our Corruption Model and the Need for Secure Erasures. The main challenge is to maintain this simplicity while achieving the strong security properties that we envisage. Most often, security against adaptive corruptions in the UC model comes at a considerable price in terms of computation and communication, and our corruption model is even substantially stronger. In particular, recall that we want to protect the user's password and previously signed messages in case the device is lost or stolen. The "standard corruption" model in the UC framework [12] hands all previous inputs and outputs of a party to the adversary upon corruption of that party, which in case of the device would include all previous passwords and messages. It is quite obvious that standard corruption does not suffice for our purposes, and also that our model cannot be achieved without secure erasures, as there would be no way to securely erase previous inputs. Given the usual difficulty of achieving even standard UC corruption, it is surprising that our protocol remains refreshingly simple, round-optimal, and efficient.

Achieving Blindness. Achieving blind signatures against adaptive corruptions in the UC model is notoriously hard: the only scheme is due to Kiayias and Zhou [28] and requires six rounds of communication and several zero-knowledge proofs. We decided to strike a reasonable compromise between security and efficiency by dropping the unlinkability requirement, i.e., the property that the signer cannot link a signature to a previous signing transcript, but focusing entirely on hiding the message from the signer. We describe a new "just-in-time" programming technique for the random oracle that inserts the correct entries into the oracle when signatures are verified, rather than when they are created. We thereby obtain an efficient and round-optimal construction without having to rely on one-more-type assumptions that are typical for full-domain-hash blind signatures [4,7].

In a bit more detail, to enable the simulator to open any signing transcript to any message-signature pair, the server adds another layer of randomness, i.e., he signs $h'_m \leftarrow \mathcal{H}(r', h_m)$ for some randomly chosen r'. When the simulator has to provide a signature σ to the functionality without knowing the message m, it simply signs a random value $h'_m \overset{r}{\leftarrow} \{0,1\}^\tau$. The connection to m is only established when the signature is verified, which we call "just-in-time" programming. Namely, whenever a random oracle query $\mathcal{H}(r', \mathcal{H}(r, m))$ is made where r, r' were previously used in a simulated blind signature, the simulator verifies whether (m, σ) is valid with the help of the ideal functionality. If so, the simulator programs the random oracle to map the message m it just learned to the randomly chosen h'_m that was signed as σ.

Non-committing Communication and State. As we allow corruptions *during* setup and signing sessions, we have to take special care that messages sent by the device and server do not commit the simulator to values that it might not know at that time in the proof. We achieve this by employing non-committing encryption for the passwords hashes $h_p \leftarrow \mathcal{H}(k, pwd)$ and each password attempt $h'_p \leftarrow \mathcal{H}(qid, \mathcal{H}(k, pwd'))$ that the device sends to the server. At a first glance that might seem unnecessary since we also assume secure erasures. However, secure erasures are not sufficient as an adversary can intercept the ciphertexts and later corrupt the server to learn the decryption key. He then expects all ciphertexts to open to the proper password hashes (that in the security proof might be unknown when the ciphertexts are generated). The non-committing encryption gives us exactly that flexibility. To determine the correct password hashes h_p and h'_p upon server corruption we use different random oracle programming techniques, eventually also relying on the password guessing interfaces of the ideal functionality (if both parties are corrupted).

We have to take similar care for the intermediate state records that the device keeps during interactive protocols. After sending a signing request, the device cannot store the message m, or even the randomness r and the message hash $h_m \leftarrow \mathcal{H}(r, m)$, as the simulator does not learn m upon corrupting the device. Nevertheless, the device must be able to verify whether the server's contribution is correct. Therefore, when sending the message hash h_m, the device also sends a value $t \leftarrow \mathcal{H}(\text{"MAC"}, qid, k, h_m)$ that acts as a message authentication code (MAC) for h_m. This allows the device to check that the server signed the correct message upon receiving the signature share, but without requiring state information that depends on m.

Authentication of Participants. As already mentioned earlier, the session identi-
fier *sid* contains the identities of the device $\mathcal{D}$ and the server $\mathcal{S}$. This means that
$\mathcal{D}$ and $\mathcal{S}$ have to be authenticated. We do so by employing $\mathcal{F}_{\mathsf{Auth}}$ for authenticated communication, thereby making abstraction of how the authentication
is performed. This could be through a shared secret, through digital signatures
(e.g., TLS with client authentication), or in an "offline fashion" by letting the
user use a trusted third party to register the device, such as a bank or a local
municipal office. The last option has the additional advantage that one could
also check the name or other credentials of the user, and also directly certify the
resulting public key of the user.

4.1   Protocol Description

We now present the detailed protocol for our Pass2Sign scheme. We assume
that a server has a key pair (epk, esk) for a non-committing encryption scheme
(EKGen, Enc, Dec), generated by EKGen on input the security parameter 1^τ. We
also assume a public-key infrastructure, where devices and servers can regis-
ter their public keys, modeled by the ideal functionality $\mathcal{F}_{\mathsf{CA}}$ [13], and authenticated message transmission, modeled by $\mathcal{F}_{\mathsf{Auth}}$. In the protocol description
we denote inputs to and outputs from them informally to make the protocol
more readable (e.g., we will write that $\mathcal{S}$ sends m to $\mathcal{D}$ via $\mathcal{F}_{\mathsf{Auth}}$ instead of an
explicit call to $\mathcal{F}_{\mathsf{Auth}}$ with sub-session IDs etc.). We further assume that parties
check the correctness of session and sub-session IDs in all inputs. Moreover, we
use $\mathcal{H}$ and $\mathcal{H}_{\mathsf{RSA}}$ as shorthand notations for two random-oracle functionalities
$\mathcal{F}_{\mathsf{RO}}^{\{0,1\}^* \to \{0,1\}^\tau}$ and $\mathcal{F}_{\mathsf{RO}}^{\{0,1\}^* \to \mathbb{Z}_N^*}$, respectively. Note that these are single-instance
functionalities; one can obtain a secure multi-instance implementation by pre-
fixing each call to them with *sid*. Our protocol further makes use of an RSA-key
generator RSAGen.

   As discussed earlier, secure erasures are necessary to achieve our security
guarantees. We thus assume that after each protocol step all variables are deleted
unless we explicitly state that a variable is stored.

   Finally, we assume that whenever a check performed by the server or device
fails, the checking party will abort the protocol.

Setup Protocol. The setup procedure is the following protocol that a device $\mathcal{D}$
runs on input (SETUPREQ, *sid*, *pwd*) with server $\mathcal{S}$, where $sid = (\mathcal{S}, \mathcal{D}, sid')$.

Setup – Step 1. Device generates account data:
   (a) Upon input (SETUPREQ, *sid*, *pwd*), retrieve *epk* for $\mathcal{S}$ from $\mathcal{F}_{\mathsf{CA}}$.
   (b) Generate RSA key material as $(N, e, d, p, q) \xleftarrow{r} \mathsf{RSAGen}(1^\tau)$ and share
       the secret exponent d by choosing a random $d_\mathcal{D} \xleftarrow{r} \mathbb{Z}_{\varphi(N)}^*$ and setting
       $d_\mathcal{S} \leftarrow d \cdot d_\mathcal{D}^{-1} \bmod \varphi(N)$, where $d_\mathcal{S}$ is encoded as an $|N|$-bit string.
   (c) Compute $h_p \leftarrow \mathcal{H}(k, pwd)$ for a random $k \xleftarrow{r} \{0,1\}^\tau$.
   (d) Encrypt the RSA key share $d_\mathcal{S}$ and the authentication information h_p
       under *epk* and with the label $(sid, (N, e))$. That is, compute $C \xleftarrow{r}$
       $\mathsf{Enc}(epk, (d_\mathcal{S}, h_p), (sid, (N, e)))$.

(e) Store the record (setup-temp, $sid, k, d_\mathcal{D}, (N, e)$) and send the message $m = (sid, (N, e), C)$ to the server $\mathcal{S}$ using $\mathcal{F}_{\mathsf{Auth}}$.

Setup – Step 2. Server registers account:

(a) Upon receiving $m = (sid, (N, e), C)$ from $\mathcal{D}$ via $\mathcal{F}_{\mathsf{Auth}}$, check that sid is not registered yet.

(b) Decrypt C as $(d_\mathcal{S}, h_p) \leftarrow \mathsf{Dec}(esk, C, (sid, (N, e)))$. If decryption succeeds, store (setup, $sid, h_p, d_\mathcal{S}, (N, e)$).

(c) Acknowledge the created account by sending (sid) to $\mathcal{D}$ via $\mathcal{F}_{\mathsf{Auth}}$.

Setup – Step 3. Device completes registration:

(a) Upon receiving a message (sid) from $\mathcal{S}$ via $\mathcal{F}_{\mathsf{Auth}}$, check that a record (setup-temp, $sid, k, d_\mathcal{D}, (N, e)$) for sid exists.

(b) Store (setup, $sid, k, d_\mathcal{D}, (N, e)$) and end with output $(\mathsf{SETUP}, sid, (N, e))$.

Signing Protocol. The signing protocol starts when the device $\mathcal{D}$ receives an input $(\mathsf{SIGNREQ}, sid, qid, m, pwd')$, where $sid = (\mathcal{S}, \mathcal{D}, sid')$, upon which he runs the following protocol with the server $\mathcal{S}$. Recall that we assume that both parties have previously agreed upon a common and globally unique query identifier qid. All messages sent between the device and server also contain the qid as prefix, and only those messages with the corresponding qid are further processed.

Sign – Step 1. Device sends signing request:

(a) Upon input $(\mathsf{SIGNREQ}, sid, qid, m, pwd')$, retrieve (setup, $sid, k, d_\mathcal{D}, (N, e)$).

(b) "Blind" the message by drawing $r \xleftarrow{r} [0, 1]^\tau$ and computing $h_m \leftarrow \mathcal{H}(r, m)$.

(c) Compute the (re-)authentication value $h'_p \leftarrow \mathcal{H}(qid, \mathcal{H}(k, pwd'))$.

(d) Compute a "MAC" t of h_m as $t \leftarrow \mathcal{H}(\texttt{"MAC"}, qid, k, h_m)$.

(e) Generate a non-committing encryption of h'_p, h_m, and t under the public key epk and with label (sid, qid) as $C' \xleftarrow{r} \mathsf{Enc}(epk, (h'_p, h_m, t), (sid, qid))$.

 f) Store the record (sign, sid, qid, r) and send (sid, qid, C') to $\mathcal{S}$ via $\mathcal{F}_{\mathsf{Auth}}$.

Sign – Step 2. Server verifies information:

(a) Upon receiving (sid, qid, C') from $\mathcal{D}$ via $\mathcal{F}_{\mathsf{Auth}}$, retrieve (setup, $sid, h_p, d_\mathcal{S}, (N, e)$) for sid.

(b) Decrypt C' to $(h'_p, h_m, t) \leftarrow \mathsf{Dec}(esk, C', (sid, qid))$.

(c) Check the password by verifying whether $\mathcal{H}(qid, h_p) = h'_p$ and set $c \leftarrow$ pwdok if so and $c \leftarrow$ pwdwrong otherwise.

(d) Store the record (sign, sid, qid, h_m, t, c) and output $(\mathsf{SIGNREQ}, sid, qid, c)$.

Sign – Step 3. Server creates its signature share:

(a) Upon input $(\mathsf{PROCEED}, sid, qid)$, retrieve (sign, sid, qid, h_m, t, c) for qid and abort if $c \neq$ pwdok.

(b) Compute the signature share $\sigma_\mathcal{S} \leftarrow \mathcal{H}_{\mathsf{RSA}}(sid, qid, \mathcal{H}(r', h_m))^{d_\mathcal{S}} \bmod N$ for a random $r' \xleftarrow{r} \{0, 1\}^\tau$.

(c) Send $(sid, qid, h_m, t, r', \sigma_\mathcal{S})$ to $\mathcal{D}$ via $\mathcal{F}_{\mathsf{Auth}}$.

Sign – Step 4. Device completes the signature:

(a) Upon receiving $(sid, qid, h_m, t, r', \sigma_\mathcal{S})$ from $\mathcal{S}$ via $\mathcal{F}_{\mathsf{Auth}}$, retrieve (sign, sid, qid, r) for qid and setup record (setup, $sid, k, d_\mathcal{D}, (N, e)$).

(b) Verify that $t = \mathcal{H}(\texttt{"MAC"}, qid, k, h_m)$.

(c) Complete the signature by computing $\sigma_{\mathsf{RSA}} \leftarrow (\sigma_S)^{d_D} \bmod N$. Verify that $(\sigma_{\mathsf{RSA}})^e = \mathcal{H}_{\mathsf{RSA}}(sid, qid, \mathcal{H}(r', h_m)) \bmod N$ holds, i.e., that the server's signature share was correct.

(d) Set $\sigma \leftarrow (\sigma_{\mathsf{RSA}}, qid, r, r')$ and end with output $(\mathsf{SIGNATURE}, sid, qid, \sigma)$.

Signature Verification. On input $(\mathsf{VERIFY}, sid, m, \sigma, pk)$, parse $pk = (N, e)$, $\sigma = (\sigma_{\mathsf{RSA}}, qid, r, r')$ and set $M \leftarrow (sid, qid, \mathcal{H}(r', \mathcal{H}(r, m)))$. If σ_{RSA} is a valid RSA signature on M, i.e., if $0 < \sigma_{\mathsf{RSA}} < N$ and $\mathcal{H}_{\mathsf{RSA}}(M) = \sigma_{\mathsf{RSA}}^e \bmod N$, output $(\mathsf{VERIFIED}, sid, m, \sigma, pk, \mathsf{true})$ and $(\mathsf{VERIFIED}, sid, m, \sigma, pk, \mathsf{false})$ otherwise.

4.2   Security

The detailed proof of the following theorem is given in the full version [11].

Theorem 2. *The* Pass2Sign *scheme described in Sect. 4 securely implements the ideal functionality $\mathcal{F}_{\mathsf{Pass2Sign}}$ defined in Sect. 3 in the $(\mathcal{F}_{\mathsf{CA}}, \mathcal{F}_{\mathsf{RO}}, \mathcal{F}_{\mathsf{Auth}})$-hybrid model with secure erasures if the RSA one-wayness assumption associated to* RSAGen *holds and* (EKGen, Enc, Dec) *is an RECV-SIM secure encryption scheme.*

Using the RECV-SIM secure encryption scheme proposed in Sect. 2, which is an extension of the Bellare-Rogaway CCA2 encryption scheme, and instantiated with the RSA trapdoor permutation, we get the following corollary:

Corollary 1. *The* Pass2Sign *scheme described in Sect. 4 and instantiated as described above, securely implements the ideal functionality $\mathcal{F}_{\mathsf{Pass2Sign}}$ defined in Sect. 3 in the $(\mathcal{F}_{\mathsf{CA}}, \mathcal{F}_{\mathsf{RO}}, \mathcal{F}_{\mathsf{Auth}})$-hybrid model with secure erasures if the RSA assumption associated with* RSAGen *holds.*

5   Implementation of Our Pass2Sign Scheme

In this section we give a short summary of our prototypical implementation of the Pass2Sign scheme. A more detailed description is given in the full version. We measured our protocol with three different RSA-moduli sizes, 1,024, 2,048 and 4,096 Bit to account for different security requirements. The key size is used for both the signing key and the trapdoor permutation in the non-committing encryption scheme. To instantiate the random oracles $\mathcal{K}, \mathcal{G}$, and $\mathcal{H}$ we use SHA-512 and prefix each call accordingly. The instantiation of the full-domain hash $\mathcal{H}_{\mathsf{RSA}}$ is based on the construction given in [5], and uses rejection sampling to uniformly map into $\mathbb{Z}_N^*$. Messages are sent using standard TCP-Sockets.

Our implementation uses Java 8 without any optimization. Our server is a laptop with a 2.7 GHz processor and 16 GB RAM, while the device is a Nexus 10 tablet with 1.7 GHz, 2 GB RAM and Android 5.1.1, while the identification of the participants is done using standard TLS certificates.

Table 1. Overview of our measurements. All values are in ms.

	Setup			Signing		
Key size	1,024 Bit	2,048 Bit	4,096 Bit	1,024 Bit	2,048 Bit	4,096Bit
Device						
Median	648.11	3'335.34	14'343.46	19.08	79.83	482.60
Average	855.58	3'646.27	16'202.58	19.79	83.40	574.41
Server						
Median	14.32	63.96	388.11	11.76	64.53	456.38
Average	15.20	65.69	393.27	12.31	65.50	466.73

Table 1 depicts the average time for the setup and signing protocol, split between the device and server part, based on measurements of 100 protocol runs. The table does not include network latencies, as they strongly depend on the actual location setting. However, assuming a round-trip time takes 100 ms, a full signing protocol with 2,048 Bit keys then requires roughly 250 ms in total.

References

1. Algesheimer, J., Camenisch, J., Shoup, V.: Efficient computation modulo a shared secret with application to the generation of shared safe-prime products. In: Yung, M. (ed.) CRYPTO 2002. LNCS, vol. 2442, pp. 417–432. Springer, Heidelberg (2002)
2. Almansa, J.F., Damgård, I.B., Nielsen, J.B.: Simplified threshold RSA with adaptive and proactive security. In: Vaudenay, S. (ed.) EUROCRYPT 2006. LNCS, vol. 4004, pp. 593–611. Springer, Heidelberg (2006)
3. Beaver, D., Haber, S.: Cryptographic protocols provably secure against dynamic adversaries. In: Rueppel, R.A. (ed.) EUROCRYPT 1992. LNCS, vol. 658, pp. 307–323. Springer, Heidelberg (1993)
4. Bellare, M., Namprempre, C., Pointcheval, D., Semanko, M.: The one-more-rsa-inversion problems and the security of Chaum's blind signature scheme. J. Cryptol. 16(3), 185–215 (2003)
5. Bellare, M., Rogaway, P.: Random oracles are practical: a paradigm for designing efficient protocols. In: CCS 1993, pp. 62–73 (1993)
6. Bellare, M., Sandhu, R.S.: The security of practical two-party RSA signature schemes. ePrint Report 2001/060 (2001)
7. Boldyreva, A.: Threshold signatures, multisignatures and blind signatures based on the gap-diffie-hellman-group signature scheme. In: Desmedt, Y.G. (ed.) PKC 2003. LNCS, vol. 2567, pp. 31–46. Springer, Heidelberg (2002)
8. Boyd, C.: Digital multisignatures. In: Cryptography and Coding 1989, pp. 241–246 (1989)
9. Camenisch, J., Enderlein, R.R., Neven, G.: Two-server password-authenticated secret sharing UC-secure against transient corruptions. ePrint Report 2015/006 (2015)
10. Camenisch, J., Enderlein, R.R., Shoup, V.: Practical and employable protocols for UC-secure circuit evaluation over $\mathbb{Z}_n$. In: Crampton, J., Jajodia, S., Mayes, K. (eds.) ESORICS 2013. LNCS, vol. 8134, pp. 19–37. Springer, Heidelberg (2013)

11. Camenisch, J., Lehmann, A., Neven, G., Samelin, K.: Virtual smart cards: how to sign with a password and a server. ePrint Report 2015/1101 (2015)
12. Canetti, R.: Universally composable security: a new paradigm for cryptographic protocols. ePrint Report 2000/067 (2000)
13. Canetti, R.: Universally composable signature, certification, and authentication. In: CSFW 2004, pp. 219–233 (2004)
14. Canetti, R., Halevi, S., Katz, J., Lindell, Y., MacKenzie, P.: Universally composable password-based key exchange. In: Cramer, R. (ed.) EUROCRYPT 2005. LNCS, vol. 3494, pp. 404–421. Springer, Heidelberg (2005)
15. Coron, J.-S.: On the exact security of full domain hash. In: Bellare, M. (ed.) CRYPTO 2000. LNCS, vol. 1880, pp. 229–235. Springer, Heidelberg (2000)
16. Damgård, I., Mikkelsen, G.L.: On the theory and practice of personal digital signatures. In: Jarecki, S., Tsudik, G. (eds.) PKC 2009. LNCS, vol. 5443, pp. 277–296. Springer, Heidelberg (2009)
17. Desmedt, Y.G., Frankel, Y.: Threshold cryptosystems. In: Brassard, G. (ed.) CRYPTO 1989. LNCS, vol. 435, pp. 307–315. Springer, Heidelberg (1990)
18. Fehr, S., Hofheinz, D., Kiltz, E., Wee, H.: Encryption schemes secure against chosen-ciphertext selective opening attacks. In: Gilbert, H. (ed.) EUROCRYPT 2010. LNCS, vol. 6110, pp. 381–402. Springer, Heidelberg (2010)
19. Ganesan, R.: Yaksha: augmenting kerberos with PKC. In: NDSS 1995, pp. 132–143 (1995)
20. Gennaro, R., Rabin, T., Jarecki, S., Krawczyk, H.: Robust and efficient sharing of RSA functions. J. Cryptol. 13(2), 273–300 (2000)
21. Gjøsteen, K.: Partially blind password-based signatures using elliptic curves. ePrint Report 2013/472 (2013)
22. Gjøsteen, K., Thuen, Ø.: Password-based signatures. In: Petkova-Nikova, S., Pashalidis, A., Pernul, G. (eds.) EuroPKI 2011. LNCS, vol. 7163, pp. 17–33. Springer, Heidelberg (2012)
23. Gosney, J.M.: Password cracking HPC. In: Passwords^12 Conference (2012)
24. Hazay, C., Mikkelsen, G.L., Rabin, T., Toft, T.: Efficient RSA key generation and threshold paillier in the two-party setting. In: Dunkelman, O. (ed.) CT-RSA 2012. LNCS, vol. 7178, pp. 313–331. Springer, Heidelberg (2012)
25. Hazay, C., Patra, A., Warinschi, B.: Selective opening security for receivers. ePrint Report 2015/860 (2015)
26. He, Y.-Z., Wu, C.-K., Feng, D.-G.: Server-aided digital signature protocol based on password. In: CCST 2005, pp. 89–92 (2005)
27. Hofheinz, D., Müller-Quade, J.: Universally composable commitments using random oracles. In: Naor, M. (ed.) TCC 2004. LNCS, vol. 2951, pp. 58–76. Springer, Heidelberg (2004)
28. Kiayias, A., Zhou, H.-S.: Equivocal blind signatures and adaptive UC-security. In: Canetti, R. (ed.) TCC 2008. LNCS, vol. 4948, pp. 340–355. Springer, Heidelberg (2008)
29. Kömmerling, O., Kuhn, M.G.: Design principles for tamper-resistant smartcard processors. In: WOST 1999 (1999)
30. MacKenzie, P.D., Reiter, M.K.: Networked cryptographic devices resilient to capture. Int. J. Inf. Sec. 2(1), 1–20 (2003)
31. Mannan, M., van Oorschot, P.C.: Using a personal device to strengthen password authentication from an untrusted computer. In: FC 2007, pp. 88–103 (2007)
32. Nielsen, J.B.: Separating random oracle proofs from complexity theoretic proofs: the non-committing encryption case. In: Yung, M. (ed.) CRYPTO 2002. LNCS, vol. 2442, pp. 111–126. Springer, Heidelberg (2002)

33. Rabin, T.: A simplified approach to threshold and proactive RSA. In: Krawczyk, H. (ed.) CRYPTO 1998. LNCS, vol. 1462, pp. 89–104. Springer, Heidelberg (1998)
34. Venkitasubramaniam, M.: On adaptively secure protocols. In: Abdalla, M., De Prisco, R. (eds.) SCN 2014. LNCS, vol. 8642, pp. 455–475. Springer, Heidelberg (2014)
35. Xu, S., Sandhu, R.: Two efficient and provably secure schemes for server-assisted threshold signatures. In: Joye, M. (ed.) CT-RSA 2003. LNCS, vol. 2612, pp. 355–372. Springer, Heidelberg (2003)

Signatures Resilient to Uninvertible Leakage

Yuyu Wang[1,2]([✉]), Takahiro Matsuda[2], Goichiro Hanaoka[2],
and Keisuke Tanaka[1,3]

[1] Tokyo Institute of Technology, Tokyo, Japan
wang.y.ar@m.titech.ac.jp, keisuke@is.titech.ac.jp
[2] National Institute of Advanced Industrial Science and Technology (AIST),
Tokyo, Japan
{t-matsuda,hanaoka-goichiro}@aist.go.jp
[3] JST CREST, Tokyo, Japan

Abstract. In this paper, we present a fully leakage resilient signature scheme in the selective auxiliary input model, which captures an extremely wide class of side-channel attacks that are based on physical implementations of algorithms rather than public parameters chosen. Our signature scheme keeps existential unforgeability under chosen message attacks as long as the adversary cannot completely recover the entire secret state from leakage in polynomial time with non-negligible probability. Formally speaking, the leakage is allowed to be any computable uninvertible function on input the secret state, without any additional restrictions. We instantiate such a signature scheme by exploiting a point-function obfuscator with auxiliary input (AIPO) and a differing-inputs obfuscator (diO).

As far as we know, this is the first signature scheme secure against uninvertible leakage. Furthermore, our signature scheme is public-coin, in the sense that the randomness used in the signing procedure is a part of a signature and no additional secret randomness is used.

Additionally, we provide a variant of the above signature scheme, for which leakage functions are additionally required to be injective, and the sizes of the circuits representing leakage functions are upper bounded. This scheme is resilient to uninvertible leakage that information-theoretically determines the secret information, and can be constructed based only on diO, without exploiting AIPO.

Keywords: Leakage resilient signature · Selective auxiliary input · Uninvertible leakage · Side-channel attack

1 Introduction

1.1 Background

Leakage Resilient Primitives. A cryptographic primitive is usually proved to be secure in the attack models where intermediate values, e.g., secret keys (or

---

Y. Wang—This author is supported by a JSPS Fellowship for Young Scientists.

K. Tanaka—A part of this work was supported by MEXT/JSPS KAKENHI 16H01705.

V. Zikas and R. De Prisco (Eds.): SCN 2016, LNCS 9841, pp. 372–390, 2016.
DOI: 10.1007/978-3-319-44618-9_20

signing keys in the case of signatures) and randomizers used to encrypt or sign messages, are assumed to be completely hidden. However, it is becoming more and more unrealistic to rule out the possibility that an adversary learns leakage on secret information (including secret keys and secret randomizers) from the physical implementation of algorithms by executing the side-channel attacks [29]. Motivated by this scenario, previous works put a great effort into constructing leakage resilient (LR) primitives (e.g. [1,15,19,32]). Since LR primitives remain secure even when some part of secret information is leaked, they are more reliable when implemented in the practical world, where various side-channel attacks can be easily executed with low cost, compared with traditional primitives with no leakage resilience.

The Auxiliary Input Model. Most of LR primitives are proved to be secure in the bounded leakage model [1], continual leakage model [15,19], or noisy leakage model [32], which simulate the practical environment where secret information may be leaked. Although these models are well defined, all of them assume that partial information of the secret key is information-theoretically hidden, while the leakage information-theoretically determines the secret information (including the secret key and other secret randomness) typically in the practical world [35]. Intrigued by this fact, Dodis et al. [21] initialized the research in the auxiliary input model (also called the hard-to-invert leakage model), in which, it is only assumed that it is hard to recover the secret key from the leakage, i.e., the secret key may be information-theoretically revealed by the leakage. There are several researches focusing on encryption in the auxiliary input model [14,18,26,37,38,40], while proposing signatures in such a model seemed to be hopeless. For signatures in the auxiliary input model, a leakage function could be of the form $f(\cdot) = \mathsf{Sign}(pk, \cdot, m^*; r)$, which is the signing algorithm for a challenge message m^*. It is obvious that in this case, the leakage obtained by the adversary, which is $f(sk) = \mathsf{Sign}(pk, sk, m^*; r)$, is itself a successfully forged signature on m^*. However, since signatures play a very important role in public-key cryptography and previously proposed LR signatures do not capture a large class of side channel attacks, defining and constructing signatures in the auxiliary input model have remained an important and practically-motivated problem. To avoid the aforementioned trivial attack, the followup works define the auxiliary input model for signatures by making some restrictions.

The Auxiliary Input Model for Signatures. Faust et al. [22] firstly defined LR signatures in the auxiliary input model. The restriction they made is that the leakage should be exponentially hard-to-invert instead of polynomially hard-to-invert. The signature schemes they provided were not fully leakage resilient (FLR) since they only considered leakage on signing keys, where FLR signatures [28] denote signature schemes remaining secure in the presence of leakage on not only signing keys but also randomizers used in the signing procedure.

The Selective Auxiliary Input Model for Signatures. Independently of the work of Faust et al., Yuen et al. [39] defined the selective auxiliary input model. This model avoids the aforementioned trivial attack by letting the adversary choose candidates of leakage functions before seeing the verification key. The signature scheme they gave is FLR and the leakage is allowed to be polynomially hard-to-invert.

The selective auxiliary input model is reasonably defined since it captures the implementation-based side-channel attacks which help an adversary learn leakage on the secret information independently of the public parameters chosen in the system [39] (e.g., the power analysis of the CPU). Furthermore, a signature scheme secure in this model can be typically proved to be secure in the model of [22] by making use of complexity leveraging.

However, the restriction made on the class of leakage functions in [39] is very strong. Roughly speaking, the leakage function f should satisfy $\Pr[sk \leftarrow \mathcal{A}(f(state), pk, \mathcal{S})] \approx 0$ in [39], where $\mathcal{A}$ denotes any adversary, (pk, sk) a randomly generated verification/signing key pair, $\mathcal{S}$ the set of signatures obtained from the signing oracle, and $state$ the secret state (including sk and the secret randomizers used to generate $\mathcal{S}$). Our point of view that their restriction is too strong lies in: (a) By making this restriction, *they ruled out the possibility that $\mathcal{A}$ may recover sk from the leakage in the presence of pk and $\mathcal{S}$*, which in turn makes obtaining a secure signature scheme in this model much easier. (b) Hardness of recovering the secret state should not bypass the hardness of recovering the signing key itself (i.e., it is more practical to assume that it is hard for $\mathcal{A}$ to recover $state$ rather than sk).

Signatures Secure Against Uninvertible Leakage. It is a natural question to ask if it is possible to construct a signature scheme in the selective auxiliary input model where the restriction on the class of leakage functions is extremely weak, especially when leakage functions are only required to be *uninvertible*. Note that in this case, the leakage function f is only required to satisfy $\Pr[state \leftarrow \mathcal{A}(f(state))] \approx 0$ rather than $\Pr[sk \leftarrow \mathcal{A}(f(state), pk, \mathcal{S})] \approx 0$. It is obvious that such a signature scheme is secure against much wider class of side-channel attacks, compared with the one proposed in [39].

1.2   Our Results

In this paper, we study signatures secure against uninvertible leakage in the selective auxiliary input model and obtain the following results.

- We propose an FLR signature scheme, for which the leakage is allowed to be any computable uninvertible function on input the secret information. To achieve our goal, we exploit a point-function obfuscator with auxiliary input (AIPO) and a differing-inputs obfuscator (diO) for circuits[1].

  As far as we know, this is the first FLR signature scheme secure in the presence of uninvertible leakage. It is also the first FLR signature scheme with public-coin construction, which does not make use of secret randomness in the signing procedure, as far as we know.

---

[1] In this paper, when we say an "obfuscator", we mean an obfuscator for circuits, unless we clearly state that it is an obfuscator for Turing machines or point functions.

- We propose a weak version of the above signature scheme, for which leakage functions are additionally required to be injective and the sizes of (the circuits representing) them are upper bounded[2], based on diO, without making use of AIPO. Such restriction makes sense since the leakage information-theoretically determines the secret information typically in the practical world [35] as we mentioned before, and the upper bound on the sizes of leakage functions can be set reasonably, depending on the computational ability of adversaries in the practical world.

Although our constructions are based on strong assumptions, they show that signature schemes resilient to uninvertible leakage are achievable. Furthermore, they can be treated as a solution to the open problem mentioned in [13], which is whether it is possible to achieve public-coin (or deterministic) constructions of FLR signatures[3]. Constructing signature schemes with such strong security based on standard assumptions is an open problem we hope to address in future works.

High-Level Idea. A high-level idea about how we obtain the proposed signature schemes is as follows.

It is obvious that if a leakage function f is allowed to be any computable uninvertible function and *state* contains the signing key sk and the secret randomness $\mathcal{R}$, then an adversary may trivially obtain sk by setting a leakage function f as $f(sk, \mathcal{R}) = (sk, f'(\mathcal{R}))$, where f' is uninvertible. To avoid such attack, we choose the way mentioned by Boyle et al. [13] to achieve FLR signatures, which is letting *state* contain only sk. This requires the signature scheme to be deterministic or only make use of public coins in the signing procedure.

Furthermore, since uninvertible leakage helps an adversary obtain extremely large amount of information of sk, we have to make sure that the verification key and signatures from the signing oracle reveal no information about sk other than the leakage (which do not have to be considered in [39] since they had already assumed that an adversary cannot recover sk from the leakage in the presence of the verification key and signatures, as explained above).

As the first step to achieve our goal, we define the notion of uninvertible leakage resilient (ULR) hard relations. Roughly speaking, this is a binary relation R_{HR} such that if a pair (y, x) satisfying R_{HR} is chosen randomly, then it is hard for any adversary to find x^* such that $R_{\mathsf{HR}}(y, x^*) = 1$, even given y and uninvertible leakage on x. Inspired by Brzuska and Mittelbach [16], who proposed a public key

---

[2] Note that for FLR signatures in the bounded leakage model, it is the number of total leaked bits that is upper bounded, while for FLR signatures in our model, it is the sizes of leakage functions that are upper bounded. Furthermore, the upper bound in the bounded leakage model must be smaller than the size of signing keys, or an adversary can let leakage queries (which can be any polynomially computational functions) output a whole signing key, while the upper bound in our model could be any polynomial.

[3] The only previously proposed FLR signature scheme with deterministic construction is the one proposed by Katz and Vaikuntanathan [28], which is only one-time secure, and there are no known constructions of FLR signatures with public-coin property.

encryption scheme in the auxiliary input model by making use of weak multi-bit AIPO (which is based on AIPO and indistinguishability obfuscator (iO), where iO a special case of diO), we instantiate such a relation by making use of AIPO.

Next we let $(pk, sk) = ((y, \widetilde{\textbf{Sign}}, \widetilde{\textbf{Verify}}), x)$ be the verification/signing key pair of our signature scheme, where $\widetilde{\textbf{Sign}}$ is a signing program obfuscated by diO, $\widetilde{\textbf{Verify}}$ a verification program obfuscated by iO, and (y, x) is a public/secret key pair satisfying the ULR-hard relation. When signing a message m, $\widetilde{\textbf{Sign}}$ takes as input (y, x, m) and checks if $R_{\textsf{HR}}(y, x) = 1$. If the check works out, it outputs $F(K, y||m)$, which is a Sahai-Waters style signature [34] linked with y, where F is a puncturable pseudorandom function and K is a hard-wired value in both $\widetilde{\textbf{Sign}}$ and $\widetilde{\textbf{Verify}}$[4]. Otherwise, it aborts. When verifying a message/signature pair (m, σ), $\widetilde{\textbf{Verify}}$ takes as input (y, m, σ) and checks if $\sigma = F(K, y||m)$. Since $\widetilde{\textbf{Sign}}$ and $\widetilde{\textbf{Verify}}$ are independent of (y, x) and signatures contain no information about x other than y, an adversary is not able to recover x, given pk, a set of signatures, and the leakage $f(x)$. As a result, the adversary has no "access" to K to obtain a forged signature linked with y. Since such a scheme is only selectively unforgeable (i.e., an adversary is required to determine the challenge message, on which a signature will be forged, before seeing the verification key), we extend it into an adaptively secure one by letting $\widetilde{\textbf{Sign}}$ output the Ramchen-Waters style signatures [33] instead of the Sahai-Waters style ones, linked with y.

If we generate y as an iO-obfuscated point-function that maps all inputs to 0 except for x, instead of AIPO, we obtain another primitive that we call injective uninvertible leakage resilient (IULR) hard relation, for which leakage functions are additionally required to be injective and the sizes of them are upper bounded. By substituting the ULR-hard relation with an IULR-hard relation in the signature scheme we described above, we immediately obtain a signature scheme resilient to injective uninvertible leakage, while the sizes of leakage functions are upper bounded.

Status of iO, diO, and AIPO. To achieve signatures secure against uninvertible (full) leakage, we make use of iO [23], diO [2,4,11], and AIPO [9], the existence of which is a strong assumption.

iO can be used to obfuscate circuits without changing their functionality, and two iO-obfuscated circuits are indistinguishable (in the presence of auxiliary input) if they have the same functionality. diO is a natural extension of iO. The difference is that diO provides a stronger guarantee such that two circuits are indistinguishable if it is hard to find an input that leads the underlying original circuits to different outputs, in the presence of auxiliary input. Boyle et al. [11] proved that iO can be used as diO, if the number of inputs leading the two circuits to different outputs is polynomial. AIPO focuses on obfuscating point functions that map all strings to 0 except for a single string mapped to 1, when auxiliary input is present.

---

[4] K is deleted after generating $\widetilde{\textbf{Sign}}$ and $\widetilde{\textbf{Verify}}$.

The first candidate of iO was given in the breakthrough work by Garg et al. [23] based on multilinear maps. Following their work, many multilinear map based iO schemes have been proposed. Although a lot of works demonstrate that existing multilinear maps suffer from vulnerabilities, most of them have no direct impact on the security of iO candidates, as discussed by Ananth et al. [3, Appendix A]. Furthermore, Ananth et al. [3] showed how to build iO combiners using LWE and DDH respectively. By using their combiners, we can produce an instantiation of iO from serval iO candidates, and the resulting instantiation is secure as long as one of the original candidates is secure. They also constructed a universal iO scheme, which is secure as long as any secure iO scheme exists, and noted that iO exists if $P = NP$, which give us more confidence in iO-based schemes.

Compared with iO, there are more negative results on diO. Garg et al. [24] showed that general-purpose diO for circuits does not exist if there exists some special-purpose obfuscator for Turing machine. However, the heuristic analysis they used to justify the special-purpose obfuscator is itself much stronger than assuming diO as discussed by Bellare et al. in [8]. Following this work, Boyle and Pass [12] showed some negative results on public-coin diO [27] which is a relaxed notion of diO. They proved that if extractable one-way functions w.r.t. some auxiliary input (respectively, succinct non-interactive arguments of knowledge) exist, then public-coin diO for Turing machines (respectively, for NC^1 circuits) does not exist. Recently, Bellare et al. [8] showed that sub-exponentially secure (respectively, polynomially secure) diO for Turing machines does not exist if sub-exponentially secure one-way function (respectively, sub-exponentially secure iO) exists. Although the status of diO is in flux, as far as we know, there is no negative results on diO for circuits (rather than Turing machines) based on weak or standard assumptions yet, beyond the known negative results on iO.

The notion of AIPO was firstly formalized by Bitansky and Paneth [9] while the first candidate of AIPO was proposed by Canetti [17]. Bitansky and Paneth extended the point-function obfuscator proposed by Wee [36] to a candidate of AIPO based on a novel assumption on a trapdoor permutation. The candidate by Canetti is based on the Auxiliary-Input Diffie-Hellman Inversion assumption. Lynn et al. [30] also showed that it is easy to obtain AIPO in the random oracle model. Recently, Bellare and Stepanovs [6] gave three candidates of AIPO respectively based on iO and one-way functions relative to target generators, deterministic public-key encryption, and universal computational extractors [5].

1.3   Related Work

Akavia et al. [1] introduced the bounded leakage model, in which a primitive is said to be LR if it is secure against an adversary who may learn partial information of the secret key. The leakage is denoted as $f(sk)$ where sk is the secret key, and f can be any efficiently computable function as long as the number of output bits of f is not larger than the leakage parameter ℓ. In [28], Katz and Vaikuntanathan introduced the notion of FLR, which is a stronger security against the adversary who may learn leakage on not only the secret key, but also the intermediate values during the whole lifetime of a signature scheme. It is obvious that ℓ must be smaller than the length of the secret key, or an adversary can easily break a system by letting a leakage function output the whole secret key. As an extension of the bounded leakage model, Dodis et al. [19] and Brakerski et al. [15] suggested the continual leakage model, which is the same as the bounded leakage model except that it requires the system to be able to update the secret key periodically without changing the public key. Another model called the noisy leakage model, which can be treated as a generalization of the bounded leakage model, was proposed by Naor and Segev [32]. In the noisy leakage model, there is no bound on the number of leaked bits. It is only required that the secret key keeps some min-entropy, given leakage.

Although there have been a great deal of research focusing on LR cryptographic primitives (including FLR ones) in the bounded, continual, and noisy leakage model (e.g., [13,19,20,28,31,32]), all of these models assume that partial information of the secret key is information-theoretically hidden.

In [21], Dodis et al. introduced the auxiliary input model, in which, it is only assumed that recovering the secret key from leakage is difficult. The cryptographic primitive they gave is a secret key encryption scheme, while a follow-up paper by Dodis et al. [18] focused on public key cryptosystems with auxiliary input. Goldwasser et al. [26] and Brakerski and Goldwasser [14] also considered hard-to-invert leakage when constructing their encryption schemes.

The first auxiliary input model for signatures was proposed by Faust et al. [22]. The leakage in their work is denoted as $f(pk, sk)$, which is given to the adversary along with pk at the beginning of the security game, where f is the leakage function and (pk, sk) is the verification/signing key pair. To formalize the attack model, they followed [18] to define two classes of leakage functions. For a function f in the first class, it is required that given $(pk, f(pk, sk))$, it is hard to compute sk, while in the second class, the requirement is that it is hard to compute sk given only $f(pk, sk)$. They proposed two signature schemes. The first one is unforgeable against random message attacks, which is resilient to polynomially hard-to-invert leakage w.r.t. the first class of leakage functions and exponentially hard-to-invert leakage w.r.t. the second class. The second one is existentially unforgeable against chosen message attacks (EUF-CMA), and resilient to exponentially hard-to-invert leakage w.r.t. both classes of leakage functions.

In [39], Yuen et al. defined another model called the selective auxiliary input model. The leakage functions $\{f_i\}_i$ take as input *state* instead of sk where *state* contains all the secret information. The restriction on the functions is that it is hard for an adversary to recover sk given $\{f_i(state)\}_i$, pk, and signatures obtained from the signing oracle. They require the adversary to determine the leakage functions before seeing the verification key but allow it to make leakage queries at any point.

Another signature scheme satisfying the same security was proposed by Yuen et al. [40] by exploiting the Goldreich-Levin randomness extractor [25], while this tool was also used by Yu et al. [37] to achieve a chosen-ciphertext PKE scheme secure in the presence of hard-to-invert leakage. This method is based on the well-known fact that given $f(x)$ where f is hard-to-invert, the hard-core bit string is indistinguishable from randomness. Therefore, by making use of the secret key x, intermediate values can be generated by computing the hard-core bit string $h(x)$ instead of choosing the real randomness, while $f(x)$ can be learnt by the adversary as the leakage. However, f must be exponentially hard-to-invert or restricted in other ways. What is more, the more hard-core bits are generated, the more restrictions have to be applied to f. The only known randomness extractor that can provide poly-many hardcore bits for any one-way function was proposed by Bellare et al. [7], based on iO and diO. However, since the construction of their hard-core bits generator depends on the one-way function, it cannot be used as a building block of LR primitives.

1.4   Outline of This Paper

In Sect. 2, we recall several definitions of cryptographic primitives. In Sect. 3, we define and instantiate two new LR primitives called a ULR-hard relation and an IULR-hard relation, which will be used as building blocks in our proposed signature schemes. We also show how to construct the former (respectively, the latter) from AIPO (respectively, iO). In Sect. 4, we propose an FLR signature scheme against uninvertible leakage (respectively, injective uninvertible leakage) based on a ULR-hard relation (respectively, an IULR-hard relation) and diO, which is the main result of this paper. Due to page limitation, we give the security proofs in the full paper.

2   Preliminaries

Notation. We let $x \leftarrow \mathcal{X}$ denote sampling an element x from a set $\mathcal{X}$ at random. Furthermore, when describing a program, we use characters with check marks above (e.g., $\check{x}$) to denote the inputs.

2.1   One-Way Function and Uninvertible Function

Now we recall the definitions of a one-way function and an uninvertible function.

Definition 1 (One-Way Function). *A function $f : \{0,1\}^* \to \{0,1\}^*$ is said to be* one-way *if it is efficiently computable, and for any probabilistic polynomial time (PPT) adversary $\mathcal{A}$[5], there exists a negligible function negl such that we have $\Pr[x \leftarrow \{0,1\}^k, x^* \leftarrow \mathcal{A}(1^k, f(x)) : f(x^*) = f(x)] \leq negl(k)$.*

Definition 2 (Uninvertible Function). *A function $f : \{0,1\}^* \to \{0,1\}^*$ is said to be* uninvertible *if it is efficiently computable, and for any PPT adversary $\mathcal{A}$, there exists a negligible function negl such that we have $\Pr[x \leftarrow \{0,1\}^k : x \leftarrow \mathcal{A}(1^k, f(x))] \leq negl(k)$.*

---

[5] In this paper, when we say PPT adversary, we mean a non-uniform PPT adversary.

A one-way or uninvertible function is said to be injective if it additionally satisfies that for all a and b in $\{0,1\}^*$, $f(a) = f(b)$ implies $a = b$. Note that a function is an injective one-way function iff it is injective and uninvertible.

It is not hard to see that an uninvertible function is not necessarily a one-way function while a one-way function must be uninvertible, which means that the class of uninvertible functions is larger than that of one-way functions.

2.2 Fully Leakage Resilient Signatures in the Selective Auxiliary Input Model

Now we give the definition of FLR signatures in the selective auxiliary input model. In this model, we allow an adversary to learn any uninvertible leakage on sk and learn all the randomizers used in the signing procedure. We do not consider leakage during the key generation procedure since the verification/signing key pair can be generated "off-line" [13]. The syntax, correctness, and security for signatures in the selective auxiliary input model are as follows.

Syntax. A signature scheme consists of three PPT algorithms. KeyGen is a probabilistic algorithm that takes as input 1^k, and returns a verification/signing key pair (pk, sk). Sign is a probabilistic algorithm that takes as input a verification/signing key pair (pk, sk) and a message m, and returns a signature $\sigma = \mathsf{Sign}_{pk,sk}(m; r)$ where r is the randomizer chosen in the signing procedure. Verify is a deterministic algorithm that takes as input a verification key pk, a message m, and a signature σ, and returns 1 (accept) or 0 (reject). The message space is denoted as $\mathcal{M}$ and the randomizer space is denoted as $\mathcal{R}$.

We say that a signature scheme is *public-coin* if randomizers used in the signing procedure are contained in signatures.

Correctness. A signature scheme is said to be correct if we have $\mathsf{Verify}_{pk}(m,$ $\mathsf{Sign}_{pk,sk}(m; r)) = 1$, for all security parameters k, all $(pk, sk) \leftarrow \mathsf{KeyGen}(1^k)$, all $m \in \mathcal{M}$, and all $r \in \mathcal{R}$.

Now we give the definition of EUF-CMA security in the selective auxiliary input model. In the security game, we allow the adversary to learn leakage, which is selective (i.e., independent of the verification key), on the signing key. Furthermore, we let the signing oracle return (σ_i, r_i) when answering an adaptive signing query m_i, where σ_i is a signature on m_i and r_i is the randomizer used to generate σ_i. Since r_i is public information, the secret state for the signature scheme only contains the signing key, which means that a signature scheme satisfying this security is FLR.

Definition 3 (EUF-CMA Security in the Selective Auxiliary Input Model). *Let $\mathcal{F}$ denote a polynomial-time computable function family[6]. A signature scheme* (KeyGen, Sign, Verify) *is said to be EUF-CMA in the selective auxiliary input model w.r.t. $\mathcal{F}$ if for any PPT adversary $\mathcal{A}$ and any $f \in \mathcal{F}$,*

---

[6] In this paper, when we say functions, we mean the descriptions of them, which are of the form of circuits.

there exists a negligible function negl such that we have $\Pr[\mathcal{A} \text{ wins}] \leq negl(k)$, *in the following experiment:*

1. *The challenger computes* $(pk, sk) \leftarrow \mathsf{KeyGen}(1^k)$.
2. *On input tuple* $(1^k, pk, f(sk))$, $\mathcal{A}$ *may make queries to the signing oracle, defined as follows.*
   - *Signing oracle: On receiving a query* $m_i \in \mathcal{M}$, *the signing oracle samples* $r_i \leftarrow \mathcal{R}$, *computes* $\sigma_i \leftarrow \mathsf{Sign}_{pk,sk}(m_i; r_i)$, *and returns* (σ_i, r_i).
3. *At some point,* $\mathcal{A}$ *stops and outputs* (m^*, σ^*).
4. $\mathcal{A}$ *wins in the experiment if: (a)* $\mathsf{Verify}_{pk}(m^*, \sigma^*) = 1$. *(b)* m^* *was not queried to the signing oracle.*

Now we give the definition of FLR signatures and a variant of it called weak FLR signatures, in the selective auxiliary input model. For an FLR signature scheme, leakage functions are allowed to be any computable uninvertible function, while for a weak FLR one, they are additionally required to be injective and the sizes of them are upper bounded.

Definition 4 (FLR Signatures in the Selective Auxiliary Input Model). *A signature scheme is said to be FLR in the selective auxiliary input model if it is correct and EUF-CMA secure in the selective auxiliary input model w.r.t.* $\mathcal{F}_{uf}$, *where* $\mathcal{F}_{uf}$ *denotes the family of all the (polynomial-time computable) uninvertible functions.*

Definition 5 (Weak FLR Signatures in the Selective Auxiliary Input Model). *Let* $\lambda = \lambda(k)$ *be a polynomial. A signature scheme is said to be* λ-weak FLR *in the selective auxiliary input model if it is correct and EUF-CMA secure in the selective auxiliary input model w.r.t.* $\mathcal{F}_{\lambda-iuf}$, *where* $\mathcal{F}_{\lambda-iuf}$ *denotes the family of all (polynomial-time computable) injective uninvertible functions whose sizes are less than or equal to* λ.

2.3   Obfuscations

In this subsection, we recall the definitions of diO (for circuits), iO (for circuits), and AIPO. Below, $\mathcal{C}_k$ denotes a family of circuits whose size is some polynomial of k.

Definition 6 (Same-Functionality Sampler/Differing-Inputs Sampler). *Let* Samp *be a (non-uniform) PPT algorithm that takes* 1^k *as input, and outputs two circuits* $C_0, C_1 \in \mathcal{C}_k$ *and a string* $\alpha \in \{0,1\}^*$. Samp *is said to be*

- *a same-functionality sampler for* $\{\mathcal{C}_k\}$ *if the two circuits in the output of* Samp *have the same functionality (i.e.* $C_0(x) = C_1(x)$ *for all inputs* x).
- *a differing-inputs sampler for* $\{\mathcal{C}_k\}$ *if for any PPT adversary* $\mathcal{A}$, *there exists a negligible function negl such that we have*

$$\Pr[(C_0, C_1, \alpha) \leftarrow \mathsf{Samp}(1^k), x \leftarrow \mathcal{A}(1^k, C_0, C_1, \alpha) : C_0(x) \neq C_1(x)] \leq negl(k).$$

Definition 7 (Differing-Inputs Obfuscation (diO)). *A uniform PPT algorithm $\mathcal{DIO}$ is said to be a* differing-inputs obfuscator *for circuit class $\{\mathcal{C}_k\}$, if it satisfies the* functionality preserving *property and the* differing-inputs *property.*

The functionality preserving property is satisfied if for all security parameters k, all $C \in \mathcal{C}_k$, all $C' \leftarrow \mathcal{DIO}(1^k, C)$, and all inputs x, we have $C'(x) = C(x)$.

The differing-inputs property is satisfied if for any differing-inputs sampler Samp for $\{\mathcal{C}_k\}$ and any PPT adversary $\mathcal{D}$, there exists a negligible function negl such that we have

$$| \Pr[(C_0, C_1, \alpha) \leftarrow \mathsf{Samp}(1^k) : \mathcal{D}(1^k, \mathcal{DIO}(1^k, C_0), \alpha) = 1]$$
$$- \Pr[(C_0, C_1, \alpha) \leftarrow \mathsf{Samp}(1^k) : \mathcal{D}(1^k, \mathcal{DIO}(1^k, C_1), \alpha) = 1]| \leq negl(k).$$

Definition 8 (Indistinguishability Obfuscation (iO)). *A uniform PPT algorithm $\mathcal{IO}$ is said to be an* indistinguishability obfuscator *for circuit class $\{\mathcal{C}_k\}$ if it satisfies the* functionality preserving *property and* indistinguishability *property. The former property is defined in exactly the same way as that of diO. The indistinguishability property is also defined in the same way as the differing-inputs property of diO, except that we replace "for any differing-inputs sampler" with "for any same-functionality sampler".*

Definition 9 (Point Function). *A function p_x for a value $x \in \{0,1\}^*$ is called a point-function if for any $\check{x} \in \{0,1\}^*$, we have $p_x(\check{x}) = 1$ if $\check{x} = x$, and $p_x(\check{x}) = 0$ otherwise.*

Definition 10 (Unpredictable Distribution). *A distribution ensemble $\{Z_k, X_k\}$ associated with a PPT algorithm Samp is said to be* unpredictable *if for any PPT adversary $\mathcal{A}$, there exists a negligible function negl such that we have $\Pr[(z,x) \leftarrow \mathsf{Samp}(1^k) : x \leftarrow \mathcal{A}(1^k, z)] \leq negl(k).$*

Definition 11 (Point Obfuscation with Auxiliary Input (AIPO)). *A PPT algorithm $\mathcal{AIPO}$ is said to be AIPO if on input x it outputs a polynomial-size circuit $\tilde{p}_x$ such that $\tilde{p}_x(\check{x}) = 1$ if $\check{x} = x$ and $\tilde{p}_x(\check{x}) = 0$ otherwise, and the following property is satisfied.*

For any unpredictable distribution associated with a PPT algorithm Samp over $\{0,1\}^* \times \{0,1\}^k$ and any PPT algorithm $\mathcal{D}$, there exists a negligible function negl such that we have

$$| \Pr[(z,x) \leftarrow \mathsf{Samp}(1^k), r \leftarrow \{0,1\}^k, \tilde{p} \leftarrow \mathcal{AIPO}(r) : \mathcal{D}(1^k, \tilde{p}, z) = 1]$$
$$- \Pr[(z,x) \leftarrow \mathsf{Samp}(1^k), \tilde{p} \leftarrow \mathcal{AIPO}(x) : \mathcal{D}(1^k, \tilde{p}, z) = 1]| \leq negl(k).$$

We will utilize the following simple fact about AIPO, and the formal proof of it appears in the full version of this paper.

Lemma 1. *If a PPT algorithm $\mathcal{AIPO}$ is AIPO, then $\mathcal{AIPO}$ is a probabilistic uninvertible function, i.e., the distribution of $(\mathcal{AIPO}(r), r)$ where r is randomly chosen from $\{0,1\}^k$ is unpredictable.*

2.4 Puncturable Pseudorandom Function

Now we recall the definition of a puncturable pseudorandom function (puncturable PRF) [10,34], which is a variant of PRF.

Definition 12 (Puncturable Pseudorandom Function (Puncturable PRF)). *A* puncturable PRF *consists of three algorithms* $(F, Puncture, Eval)$. $F : \mathcal{K} \times \{0,1\}^{m(k)} \to \{0,1\}^{n(k)}$ *is a PRF function that takes as input* $K \in \mathcal{K}$ *and a bit string* $x \in \{0,1\}^{m(k)}$, *and outputs a string* $y \in \{0,1\}^{n(k)}$, *where* m *and* n *are polynomial functions.* Puncture *takes as input* $K \in \mathcal{K}$ *and a bit string* $s \in \{0,1\}^{m(k)}$, *and outputs a punctured key* $K\{s\}$. Eval *takes as input a punctured key* $K\{s\}$ *and a bit string* $x \in \{0,1\}^{m(k)}$, *and outputs a string* $y \in \{0,1\}^{n(k)}$. *The puncturable PRF must satisfy two properties, which are* functionality preserved under puncturing *property and* pseudorandom at punctured point *property.*

The functionality preserved under puncturing *property is satisfied if for all security parameters* k, *all* $s, x \in \{0,1\}^{m(k)}$ *such that* $x \neq s$, *and all* $K \in \mathcal{K}$, *we have* $Eval(K\{s\}, x) = F(K, x)$ *where* $K\{s\} = Puncture(K, s)$.

The pseudorandom at punctured point *property is satisfied if for any PPT adversary* $(\mathcal{A}_1, \mathcal{A}_2)$, *there exists a negligible function* negl *such that we have*

$$| \Pr[(s, \alpha) \leftarrow \mathcal{A}_1(1^k), K \leftarrow \mathcal{K}, K\{s\} = Puncture(K, s) : \mathcal{A}_2(K\{s\}, F(K, s), \alpha) = 1]$$
$$- \Pr[(s, \alpha) \leftarrow \mathcal{A}_1(1^k), K \leftarrow \mathcal{K}, K\{s\} = Puncture(K, s), r \leftarrow \{0,1\}^{n(k)} :$$
$$\mathcal{A}_2(K\{s\}, r, \alpha) = 1]| \leq negl(k).$$

3 Uninvertible Leakage Resilient Hard Relations

We define two new primitives called a *ULR-hard relation* and an *IULR-hard relation* in Sect. 3.1, and give the constructions of them in Sect. 3.2. They will be used as building blocks to achieve our proposed signature schemes.

3.1 Definitions

Now we give the definition of a ULR-hard relation. Roughly speaking, for a randomly chosen public/secret key pair (y, x) satisfying the ULR-hard relation, it is hard for any adversary to find a valid secret key w.r.t. y, even given y and uninvertible leakage on x. The formal definition is as follows.

Definition 13 (ULR-Hard Relation). *A* ULR-hard relation *consists of two algorithms* $(\mathsf{KeyGen_{HR}}, R_{\mathsf{HR}})$. $\mathsf{KeyGen_{HR}}$ *takes as input* 1^k *and outputs a public/secret key pair* (y, x). R_{HR} *takes as input a public/secret key pair* (y, x) *and outputs either 1 ("accept") or 0 ("reject").*

A ULR-hard relation *must satisfy the* correctness *property and* security *property.*

The correctness property is satisfied if we have $R_{HR}(y, x) = 1$ for all security parameters k and all $(y, x) \leftarrow \mathsf{KeyGen}_{HR}(1^k)$.

Let $\mathcal{F}_{uf}$ denote the family of all the (polynomial-time computable) uninvertible functions. The security property is satisfied if for any PPT adversary $\mathcal{A}$ and any $f \in \mathcal{F}_{uf}$, there exists a negligible function negl such that we have $\Pr[\mathcal{A} \text{ wins}] \leq \mathsf{negl}(k)$ in the following game:

1. The challenger computes $(y, x) \leftarrow \mathsf{KeyGen}_{HR}(1^k)$.
2. On input $(1^k, y, f(x))$, $\mathcal{A}$ outputs x^* and wins if $R_{HR}(y, x^*) = 1$.

Now we give the definition of an IULR-hard relation, which is the same as that of a ULR-hard relation, except that leakage functions are required to be injective and the sizes of them are upper bounded.

Definition 14 (IULR-Hard Relation). *Let $\lambda = \lambda(k)$ be a polynomial. A pair of algorithms $(\mathsf{KeyGen}_{HR}, R_{HR})$, whose syntax is the same as that of a ULR-hard relation, is said to be a λ-IULR-hard relation if it satisfies the correctness property and security property. The correctness property is defined in exactly the same way as that of a ULR-hard relation. The security property is also defined in the same way as the that of a ULR-hard relation, except that we replace "$\mathcal{F}_{uf}$" with "$\mathcal{F}_{\lambda-iuf}$" which denotes the family of all (polynomial-time computable) injective uninvertible functions whose sizes are less than or equal to λ.*

3.2   Constructions

In this subsection, we give our constructions of a ULR-hard relation and an IULR-hard relation.

ULR-Hard Relation Based on AIPO. Let $\mathcal{AIPO}$ be AIPO. Then the construction of a ULR-hard relation is as follows.

- $\mathsf{KeyGen}_{HR}(1^k)$: Randomly select $x \leftarrow \{0, 1\}^k$, compute $y \leftarrow \mathcal{AIPO}(x)$, and output (y, x).
- $R_{HR}(y, x)$: Output $y(x)$.

Theorem 1. *The above scheme $(\mathsf{KeyGen}_{HR}, R_{HR})$ is a ULR-hard relation if $\mathcal{AIPO}$ is AIPO.*

The high-level idea of the proof of Theorem 1 is as follows.

An adversary $\mathcal{A}$ wins the security game if it outputs x^* such that $y(x^*) = 1$, which happens if and only if $x^* = x$ since y is a point function. As a result, the goal of $\mathcal{A}$ is to find x, given 1^k, y, and $f(x)$. However, according to Lemma 1, $\mathcal{A}$ cannot find x when seeing only 1^k and y, and intuitively, seeing $f(x)$ does little to help $\mathcal{A}$ since f is uninvertible. The formal proof appears in the full paper.

IULR-Hard Relation Based on iO. Let $\mathcal{IO}$ be iO, p_a a point-function for a, and $\mathbf{y}$ the program given in Fig. 1. The construction of an IULR-hard relation is as follows.

y	**y′**
Constant: x.	Constant: $f, f(x)$ where $|f| \leq \lambda$ and f is injective uninvertible.
Input: $\check{x}$.	Input: $\check{x}$.
Output $p_x(\check{x})$.	Output 1 if $f(\check{x}) = f(x)$. Output 0 otherwise.

Fig. 1. Programs **y** and **y′**. Here, **y** is padded so that its size is equal to ℓ which denotes the maximum possible size of **y′**.

- KeyGen$_{\mathsf{HR}}(1^k)$: Randomly select $x \leftarrow \{0,1\}^k$, compute $y \leftarrow \mathcal{IO}(1^k, \mathbf{y})$ where **y** is the program described in Fig. 1, and output (y, x).
- $R_{\mathsf{HR}}(y, x)$: Output $y(x)$.

Theorem 2. *Let $\{\mathcal{C}_k\}$ denote a family of circuits whose size is equal to the size of* **y**. *If $\mathcal{IO}$ is iO for $\{\mathcal{C}_k\}$, then the above scheme (KeyGen$_{\mathsf{HR}}, R_{\mathsf{HR}}$) is a λ-IULR-hard relation.*

The high-level idea of the proof of Theorem 2 is as follows.

An adversary $\mathcal{A}$ wins the security game if it outputs x^* such that $y(x^*) = 1$, which happens if and only if $x^* = x$ since y is a point function. As a result, the goal of $\mathcal{A}$ is to find x, given 1^k, y, and $f(x)$. However, since f is uninvertible, $\mathcal{A}$ cannot find x when it sees only 1^k and $f(x)$, and intuitively, y contains no more information on x than $f(x)$ due to the power of iO. The formal proof appears in the full paper.

Note that in the formal proof, we define hybrid games in which y denotes obfuscations of different but functionally equivalent circuits **y** and **y′** (see Fig. 1). In our construction and in all these hybrids, we pad the circuits so that their sizes are equal to ℓ, which denotes the maximum possible size of **y′**.

4 Fully Leakage Resilient Signatures in the Selective Auxiliary Input Model

In this section, we give our main results, which are constructions of FLR signatures in the selective auxiliary input model.

In Sect. 4.1, we give the construction of an FLR resilient signature scheme (by making use of a ULR-hard relation) while the formal security proof appears in the full paper. In Sect. 4.2, we explain that by substituting the underlying ULR-hard relation with an IULR-hard relation in our FLR signature scheme, we can immediately obtain a weak FLR signature scheme.

4.1 Fully Leakage Resilient Signature Scheme

Construction. The high-level idea of the construction of our FLR signature scheme is given in Sect. 1.2, and the concrete construction is as follows.

Let $\mathcal{DIO}$ be diO, $\mathcal{IO}$ iO, and (KeyGen$_{\mathsf{HR}}, R_{\mathsf{HR}}$) a ULR-hard relation, while the output size of KeyGen$_{\mathsf{HR}}$ is $(l + k)$-bit (where l is the size of public keys and

k the size of secret keys). Let $(F, Puncture, Eval)$, $(F_1, Puncture_1, Eval_1)$, $\cdots$, $(F_k, Puncture_k, Eval_k)$ be puncturable PRFs respectively with key spaces $\mathcal{K}, \mathcal{K}_1$, $\cdots, \mathcal{K}_k$, where $F(K, \cdot)$ maps $(l + \log k + 1 + k)$-bit inputs to k-bit outputs and $F_j(K_j, \cdot)$ maps $(l + j)$-bit inputs to k-bit outputs for $j = 1, \cdots, k$[7]. Then our signature scheme (KeyGen, Sign, Verify) with message space $\{0,1\}^k$ is as follows. In the following, for strings $m, t \in \{0,1\}^k$ we denote by $m[j]$ the jth bit of m, and by $t^{(j)}$ the first j bits of t.

- KeyGen(1^k):
    1. Compute $(y, x) \leftarrow \mathsf{KeyGen}_{\mathsf{HR}}(1^k)$.
    2. Choose $K \leftarrow \mathcal{K}$, $K_1 \leftarrow \mathcal{K}_1, \cdots, K_k \leftarrow \mathcal{K}_k$.
    3. Compute $\widetilde{\mathbf{Sign}} \leftarrow \mathcal{DIO}(1^k, \mathbf{Sign})$ and $\widetilde{\mathbf{Verify}} \leftarrow \mathcal{IO}(1^k, \mathbf{Verify})$ where $\mathbf{Sign}$ and $\mathbf{Verify}$ are the programs in Fig. 2.
    4. Output $(pk, sk) = ((y, \widetilde{\mathbf{Sign}}, \widetilde{\mathbf{Verify}}), x)$[8].
- Sign$_{pk,sk}(m)$:
    1. Randomly choose $t \leftarrow \{0,1\}^k$ and output $\sigma = \widetilde{\mathbf{Sign}}(y, x, m, t)$.
- Verify$_{pk}(m, \sigma)$:
    1. Output $\widetilde{\mathbf{Verify}}(y, m, \sigma)$.

Sign	**Verify**
Constant: $K, (K_j)_{j=1}^k$.	Constant: $K, (K_j)_{j=1}^k$.
Input: $\check{y}, \check{x}, \check{m}, \check{t}$.	Input: $\check{y}, \check{m}, \check{\sigma}$.
If $R_{\mathsf{HR}}(\check{y}, \check{x}) = 0$, output $\perp$.	Parse $\check{\sigma} = (\check{s}_1, \check{s}_2, \check{t})$.
Compute $\check{s}_1 = \oplus_{j=1}^k F(K, \check{y}\|j\|\check{m}[j]\|\check{t})$.	If $\check{s}_1 = \oplus_{j=1}^k F(K, \check{y}\|j\|\check{m}[j]\|\check{t})$
Compute $\check{s}_2 = \oplus_{j=1}^k F_j(K_j, \check{y}\|\check{t}^{(j)})$.	and $\check{s}_2 = \oplus_{j=1}^k F_j(K_j, \check{y}\|\check{t}^{(j)})$, output 1.
Output $\check{\sigma} = (\check{s}_1, \check{s}_2, \check{t})$.	Otherwise, output 0.

Fig. 2. Programs **Sign** and **Verify**. **Sign** and **Verify** are respectively padded so that their sizes are equal to the programs in the security proof that appears in the full paper.

It is obvious that our construction is public-coin, since like the Ramchen-Waters style signature scheme, we only use a randomness t, which is part of a signature, in the signing procedure.

The security of our proposed scheme is guaranteed by the following theorem.

---

[7] We do not necessarily have to let the size of messages, number of PRFs (excluding $(F, Puncture, Eval)$), and size of outputs of puncturable PRFs be k. We do this only for simplicity.

[8] $\widetilde{\mathbf{Sign}}$ and $\widetilde{\mathbf{Verify}}$ do not have to be generated in every key generation procedure since they do not depend on (y, x). Instead, they can be used as global parameters for this scheme.

Theorem 3. *Let C_k denote a family of circuits whose size is equal to the size of* **Sign** *and C'_k a family of circuits whose size is equal to the size of* **Verify**. *If* $(\mathsf{KeyGen}_{HR}, R_{HR})$ *is a ULR-hard relation, $\mathcal{DIO}$ is diO for $\{C_k\}$, $\mathcal{IO}$ is iO for $\{C'_k\}$, $(F, Puncture, Eval)$ and $\{(F_j, Puncture_j, Eval_j)\}_{j=1}^k$ are puncturable PRFs, and there exists an injective one-way function $h : \{0,1\}^k \to \{0,1\}^{*9}$, then* $(\mathsf{KeyGen}, \mathsf{Sign}, \mathsf{Verify})$ *is an FLR signature scheme in the selective auxiliary input model.*

In the security proof of Theorem 3, we define hybrid games in which $\widetilde{\mathsf{Sign}}$ (respectively, $\widetilde{\mathsf{Verify}}$) denotes obfuscations of different circuits, and we pad the underlying circuits of $\widetilde{\mathsf{Sign}}$ (respectively, $\widetilde{\mathsf{Verify}}$) in our construction and in all these hybrids so that they have the same size. Due to page limitation, we give the proof in the full paper.

4.2 Weak Fully Leakage Resilient Signature Scheme

If we substitute the ULR-hard relation with a λ-IULR-hard relation in the FLR signature scheme $(\mathsf{KeyGen}, \mathsf{Sign}, \mathsf{Verify})$ in Sect. 4.1, we immediately obtain a λ-weak FLR signature scheme in the selective auxiliary input model, as described in the following theorem.

Theorem 4. *Let C_k denote a family of circuits whose size is equal to the size of* **Sign** *and C'_k a family of circuits whose size is equal to the size of* **Verify**. *If* $(\mathsf{KeyGen}_{HR}, R_{HR})$ *is a λ-IULR-hard relation, $\mathcal{DIO}$ is diO for C_k, $\mathcal{IO}$ is iO for C'_k, $(F, Puncture, Eval)$ and $\{(F_j, Puncture_j, Eval_j)\}_{j=1}^k$ are puncturable PRFs, and there exists an injective one-way function $h : \{0,1\}^k \to \{0,1\}^*$, then* $(\mathsf{KeyGen}, \mathsf{Sign}, \mathsf{Verify})$ *is a λ-weak FLR signature scheme in the selective auxiliary input model.*

We omit the proof of Theorem 4 since it is the same as the proof of Theorem 3 except that the uninvertible (leakage) function is substituted with an injective uninvertible one, the size of which is upper bounded by λ.

Remark. We also give several extensions for our proposed signatures, such as proving the strong existential unforgeability against chosen message attacks of them and removing the use of diO by weakening the unforgeability. We refer the reader to the full paper for details.

References

1. Akavia, A., Goldwasser, S., Vaikuntanathan, V.: Simultaneous hardcore bits and cryptography against memory attacks. In: Reingold, O. (ed.) TCC 2009. LNCS, vol. 5444, pp. 474–495. Springer, Heidelberg (2009)
2. Ananth, P., Boneh, D., Garg, S., Sahai, A., Zhandry, M.: Differing-inputs obfuscation and applications. IACR Cryptology ePrint Archive 2013:689 (2013)

---

[9] h appears in the security proof.

3. Ananth, P., Jain, A., Naor, M., Sahai, A., Yogev, E.: Universal obfuscation and witness encryption: boosting correctness and combining security. Cryptology ePrint Archive, Report 2016/281 (2016)

4. Barak, B., Goldreich, O., Impagliazzo, R., Rudich, S., Sahai, A., Vadhan, S.P., Yang, K.: On the (im)possibility of obfuscating programs. In: Kilian, J. (ed.) CRYPTO 2001. LNCS, vol. 2139, pp. 1–18. Springer, Heidelberg (2001)

5. Bellare, M., Hoang, V.T., Keelveedhi, S.: Instantiating random oracles via UCEs. In: Canetti, R., Garay, J.A. (eds.) CRYPTO 2013, Part II. LNCS, vol. 8043, pp. 398–415. Springer, Heidelberg (2013)

6. Bellare, M., Stepanovs, I.: Point-function obfuscation: a framework and generic constructions. In: Kushilevitz, E., Malkin, T. (eds.) TCC 2016-A. LNCS, vol. 9563, pp. 565–594. Springer, Heidelberg (2016). doi:10.1007/978-3-662-49099-0_21

7. Bellare, M., Stepanovs, I., Tessaro, S.: Poly-many hardcore bits for any one-way function and a framework for differing-inputs obfuscation. In: Sarkar, P., Iwata, T. (eds.) ASIACRYPT 2014, Part II. LNCS, vol. 8874, pp. 102–121. Springer, Heidelberg (2014)

8. Bellare, M., Stepanovs, I., Waters, B.: New negative results on differing-inputs obfuscation. In: Fischlin, M., Coron, J.-S. (eds.) EUROCRYPT 2016. LNCS, vol. 9666, pp. 792–821. Springer, Heidelberg (2016). doi:10.1007/978-3-662-49896-5. ISBN: 978-3-662-49895-8

9. Bitansky, N., Paneth, O.: Point obfuscation and 3-round zero-knowledge. In: Cramer, R. (ed.) TCC 2012. LNCS, vol. 7194, pp. 190–208. Springer, Heidelberg (2012)

10. Boneh, D., Waters, B.: Constrained pseudorandom functions and their applications. In: Sako, K., Sarkar, P. (eds.) ASIACRYPT 2013, Part II. LNCS, vol. 8270, pp. 280–300. Springer, Heidelberg (2013)

11. Boyle, E., Chung, K.-M., Pass, R.: On extractability obfuscation. In: Lindell, Y. (ed.) TCC 2014. LNCS, vol. 8349, pp. 52–73. Springer, Heidelberg (2014)

12. Boyle, E., Pass, R.: Limits of extractability assumptions with distributional auxiliary input. In: Iwata, T., Cheon, J.H. (eds.) ASIACRYPT 2015. LNCS, vol. 9453, pp. 236–261. Springer, Heidelberg (2015). doi:10.1007/978-3-662-48800-3_10

13. Boyle, E., Segev, G., Wichs, D.: Fully leakage-resilient signatures. In: Paterson, K.G. (ed.) EUROCRYPT 2011. LNCS, vol. 6632, pp. 89–108. Springer, Heidelberg (2011)

14. Brakerski, Z., Goldwasser, S.: Circular and leakage resilient public-key encryption under subgroup indistinguishability - (or: quadratic residuosity strikes back). In: Rabin, T. (ed.) CRYPTO 2010. LNCS, vol. 6223, pp. 1–20. Springer, Heidelberg (2010)

15. Brakerski, Z., Kalai, Y.T., Katz, J., Vaikuntanathan, V.: Overcoming the hole in the bucket: public-key cryptography resilient to continual memory leakage. In: FOCS 2010, pp. 501–510 (2010)

16. Brzuska, C., Mittelbach, A.: Indistinguishability obfuscation versus multi-bit point obfuscation with auxiliary input. In: Sarkar, P., Iwata, T. (eds.) ASIACRYPT 2014, Part II. LNCS, vol. 8874, pp. 142–161. Springer, Heidelberg (2014)

17. Canetti, R.: Towards realizing random oracles: hash functions that hide all partial information. In: Kaliski Jr., B.S. (ed.) CRYPTO 1997. LNCS, vol. 1294, pp. 455–469. Springer, Heidelberg (1997)

18. Dodis, Y., Goldwasser, S., Tauman Kalai, Y., Peikert, C., Vaikuntanathan, V.: Public-key encryption schemes with auxiliary inputs. In: Micciancio, D. (ed.) TCC 2010. LNCS, vol. 5978, pp. 361–381. Springer, Heidelberg (2010)

19. Dodis, Y., Haralambiev, K., López-Alt, A., Wichs, D.: Cryptography against continuous memory attacks. In: FOCS 2010, pp. 511–520 (2010)
20. Dodis, Y., Haralambiev, K., López-Alt, A., Wichs, D.: Efficient public-key cryptography in the presence of key leakage. In: Abe, M. (ed.) ASIACRYPT 2010. LNCS, vol. 6477, pp. 613–631. Springer, Heidelberg (2010)
21. Dodis, Y., Kalai, Y.T., Lovett, S.: On cryptography with auxiliary input. In: STOC 2009, pp. 621–630 (2009)
22. Faust, S., Hazay, C., Nielsen, J.B., Nordholt, P.S., Zottarel, A.: Signature schemes secure against hard-to-invert leakage. In: Wang, X., Sako, K. (eds.) ASIACRYPT 2012. LNCS, vol. 7658, pp. 98–115. Springer, Heidelberg (2012)
23. Garg, S., Gentry, C., Halevi, S., Raykova, M., Sahai, A., Waters, B.: Candidate indistinguishability obfuscation and functional encryption for all circuits. In: FOCS 2013, pp. 40–49 (2013)
24. Garg, S., Gentry, C., Halevi, S., Wichs, D.: On the implausibility of differing-inputs obfuscation and extractable witness encryption with auxiliary input. In: Garay, J.A., Gennaro, R. (eds.) CRYPTO 2014, Part I. LNCS, vol. 8616, pp. 518–535. Springer, Heidelberg (2014)
25. Goldreich, O., Levin, L.A.: A hard-core predicate for all one-way functions. In: STOC 1989, pp. 25–32 (1989)
26. Goldwasser, S., Kalai, Y.T., Peikert, C., Vaikuntanathan, V.: Robustness of the learning with errors assumption. In: ICS 2010, pp. 230–240 (2010)
27. Ishai, Y., Pandey, O., Sahai, A.: Public-coin differing-inputs obfuscation and its applications. In: Dodis, Y., Nielsen, J.B. (eds.) TCC 2015, Part II. LNCS, vol. 9015, pp. 668–697. Springer, Heidelberg (2015)
28. Katz, J., Vaikuntanathan, V.: Signature schemes with bounded leakage resilience. In: Matsui, M. (ed.) ASIACRYPT 2009. LNCS, vol. 5912, pp. 703–720. Springer, Heidelberg (2009)
29. Kocher, P.C.: Timing attacks on implementations of Diffie-Hellman, RSA, DSS, and other systems. In: Koblitz, N. (ed.) CRYPTO 1996. LNCS, vol. 1109, pp. 104–113. Springer, Heidelberg (1996)
30. Lynn, B.Y.S., Prabhakaran, M., Sahai, A.: Positive results and techniques for obfuscation. In: Cachin, C., Camenisch, J.L. (eds.) EUROCRYPT 2004. LNCS, vol. 3027, pp. 20–39. Springer, Heidelberg (2004)
31. Malkin, T., Teranishi, I., Vahlis, Y., Yung, M.: Signatures resilient to continual leakage on memory and computation. In: Ishai, Y. (ed.) TCC 2011. LNCS, vol. 6597, pp. 89–106. Springer, Heidelberg (2011)
32. Naor, M., Segev, G.: Public-key cryptosystems resilient to key leakage. In: Halevi, S. (ed.) CRYPTO 2009. LNCS, vol. 5677, pp. 18–35. Springer, Heidelberg (2009)
33. Ramchen, K., Waters, B.: Fully secure and fast signing from obfuscation. In: ACM CCS 2014, pp. 659–673 (2014)
34. Sahai, A., Waters, B.: How to use indistinguishability obfuscation: deniable encryption, and more. In: STOC 2014, pp. 475–484 (2014)
35. Standaert, F.-X.: Leakage resilient cryptography: a practical overview. In: Invited Talk, SKEW 2011 (2011)
36. Wee, H.: On obfuscating point functions. In: STOC 2005, pp. 523–532 (2005)
37. Yu, Z., Xu, Q., Zhou, Y., Hu, C., Yang, R., Fan, G.: Weak-key leakage resilient cryptography. IACR Cryptology ePrint Archive 2014:159 (2014)
38. Yuen, T.H., Chow, S.S.M., Zhang, Y., Yiu, S.M.: Identity-based encryption resilient to continual auxiliary leakage. In: Pointcheval, D., Johansson, T. (eds.) EUROCRYPT 2012. LNCS, vol. 7237, pp. 117–134. Springer, Heidelberg (2012)

39. Yuen, T.H., Yiu, S.M., Hui, L.C.K.: Fully leakage-resilient signatures with auxiliary inputs. In: Susilo, W., Mu, Y., Seberry, J. (eds.) ACISP 2012. LNCS, vol. 7372, pp. 294–307. Springer, Heidelberg (2012)
40. Yuen, T.H., Zhang, Y., Yiu, S.: Encryption schemes with post-challenge auxiliary inputs. IACR Cryptology ePrint Archive 2013:323 (2013)

Practical Round-Optimal Blind Signatures in the Standard Model from Weaker Assumptions

Georg Fuchsbauer[1], Christian Hanser[2(✉)], Chethan Kamath[3],
and Daniel Slamanig[2]

[1] Inria, ENS, CNRS and PSL Research University, Paris, France
georg.fuchsbauer@ens.fr
[2] IAIK, Graz University of Technology, Graz, Austria
{christian.hanser,daniel.slamanig}@iaik.tugraz.at
[3] Institute of Science and Technology Austria, Klosterneuburg, Austria
ckamath@ist.ac.at

Abstract. At Crypto 2015 Fuchsbauer, Hanser and Slamanig (FHS) presented the first standard-model construction of efficient round-optimal blind signatures that does not require complexity leveraging. It is conceptually simple and builds on the primitive of structure-preserving signatures on equivalence classes (SPS-EQ). FHS prove the unforgeability of their scheme assuming EUF-CMA security of the SPS-EQ scheme and hardness of a version of the DH inversion problem. Blindness under adversarially chosen keys is proven under an interactive variant of the DDH assumption.

We propose a variant of their scheme whose blindness can be proven under a non-interactive assumption, namely a variant of the bilinear DDH assumption. We moreover prove its unforgeability assuming only unforgeability of the underlying SPS-EQ but no additional assumptions as needed for the FHS scheme.

1 Introduction

Blind signatures allow a user (or obtainer) to obtain a signature from a signer (or issuer) without the latter learning the message that is actually signed. They are an important building block for various privacy and anonymity related applications including e-cash, e-voting, anonymous credentials and ticketing. Since their invention by Chaum [18], research has led to numerous blind signature schemes in various settings and models [2,15,16,39]. The most appealing setting is that of (i) *round-optimal* schemes, i.e., schemes that require only two moves (and are thus automatically concurrently secure), that (ii) *do not require* any

C. Hanser—Supported by EU FP7 through project MATTHEW (GA No. 610436).
C. Kamath—Research supported by the European Research Council, ERC starting grant (259668-PSPC) and ERC consolidator grant (682815 - TOCNeT).
C. Hanser and D. Slamanig—Supported by EU HORIZON 2020 through project PRIS-MACLOUD (GA No. 644962).

© Springer International Publishing Switzerland 2016
V. Zikas and R. De Prisco (Eds.): SCN 2016, LNCS 9841, pp. 391–408, 2016.
DOI: 10.1007/978-3-319-44618-9_21

heuristic assumptions (such as random oracles) *nor* (*iii*) a setup assumption, such as common reference strings or honestly generated keys.

Blindness is formalized by a game between a malicious signer and a challenger who asks for two blind signatures on messages of the signer's choice, but in random order. If both signature issuings succeed, the signer is given the resulting signatures and should not be able to tell in which order they were signed. It is natural to let the malicious signer choose its own key pair (rather than having the challenger create it), in which case we speak of the *malicious-key model*.

There are well known efficient round-optimal constructions in the honest-key model with security proofs in the random oracle model [11,15,19]; and there are various constructions without random oracles and in the malicious-key model, but relying on a trusted setup, such as a common reference string (CRS). Among those are constructions using structure-preserving signatures [4] and Groth-Sahai (GS) proofs [31] instantiating the framework of Fischlin [21], as well as other approaches in the bilinear group setting [12–14,43]. There is also a very recent construction [33] without a CRS but relying on non-falsifiable "knowledge" assumptions with security in the honest-key model. Some constructions [16,30] require both a CRS and honestly generated keys.

Round-Optimal Schemes in the Plain Model. Until now, only very few schemes [26–28] were proposed that are round-optimal and require neither random oracles nor setup assumptions, that is, satisfying (*i*)–(*iii*). Due to known impossibility results, such constructions are indeed hard to find. Lindell [38] showed that concurrently secure blind signatures are impossible in the standard model when relying on simulation-based security notions. Later, Fischlin and Schröder [23] proved that black-box reductions from unforgeability to non-interactive assumptions in the standard model are impossible for blind signature schemes satisfying certain conditions.

Known constructions bypass these impossibility results in several ways: All rely on game-based security definitions [42] instead of simulation-based ones. The constructions due to Garg et al. [28] as well as Garg and Gupta [27] make use of complexity leveraging in their proofs and thus do not use black-box reductions. The first scheme [28] can only be considered a feasibility result and the second [27] is still too inefficient for practical applications. In contrast, the most recent construction by Fuchsbauer et al. [26], whose signatures consist of 5 elements from a bilinear group, can be considered practical. It is based on the recent concept of structure-preserving signature schemes on equivalence classes (SPS-EQ) [25,32], whose unforgeability is proven in the generic group model, and commitments. A drawback of the scheme is that blindness (in the malicious-key model) is proven under an interactive assumption.

The FHS Construction. Before looking at the ideas underlying the FHS construction, let us recall SPS-EQ. Defined over groups equipped with a bilinear map $e\colon \mathbb{G}_1 \times \mathbb{G}_2 \to \mathbb{G}_T$, structure-preserving signatures [4] are schemes whose verification keys, signatures and messages all consist of elements from the base groups $\mathbb{G}_1$ and $\mathbb{G}_2$ and signatures are verified by evaluating the bilinear map on these elements. In SPS-EQ the message space, typically $\mathbb{G}_1^\ell$ for some $\ell > 1$, is partitioned into equivalence classes, where all multiples of a vector belong to one class. These classes should be indistinguishable, that is, it should be hard to tell whether two messages belong to the same class or not (which follows from DDH in $\mathbb{G}_1$).

Given an SPS-EQ signature on a message, anyone can publicly *adapt* the signature to a different representative of the same class. Unforgeability is therefore defined w.r.t. equivalence classes, that is, after being given signatures on messages of its choice, no adversary should be able to compute a signature on a message from a different class. SPS-EQ moreover guarantees that after signing a message, not even the signer is able to distinguish an adaptation of the signature to another representative of the same class from a fresh signature on a completely random message.

The FHS blind-signature scheme [26] works as follows: the obtainer assembles a representative of an equivalence class as a vector containing a commitment to the message and a normalization element (the group generator). She then blinds this message by changing it to another representative and sends it to the signer. The signer signs the representative and sends the signature to the obtainer. Given this signature, the obtainer adapts it to a signature on the original representative. (Due to the normalization element, the obtainer can only switch back to the original representative.) The blind signature is then the rerandomized (unlinkable) signature for the original representative, which contains a commitment to the message, plus an opening of the commitment.

The FHS scheme uses a variant of Pedersen commitments that are perfectly hiding and computationally binding under the co-DHI$_1^*$ assumption (cf. Sect. 3.1 for a more detailed discussion). The commitment key is part of the signer's public key, which guarantees that the obtainer cannot open commitments to different messages (and thereby break unforgeability). Consequently, unforgeability relies on the co-DHI$_1^*$ assumption in addition to EUF-CMA security of the SPS-EQ scheme. To prove blindness in the malicious-key model (where the reduction has no access to the adversarially generated signing key), FHS argue that during the blindness game the adversary must always produce valid SPS-EQ signatures, as otherwise the challenger does not send any blind signatures in the end, in which case the adversary cannot win the game as all it sees are perfectly hiding commitments.

Intuitively, blindness follows, since under the DDH assumption the randomization of the representative containing the commitment during signature issuing can be replaced by a random representative of a random class. In the latter case, the order in which the messages are signed is perfectly hidden and thus the adversary cannot win. However, since the commitment key is chosen by the adversary, to actually make this replacement, FHS need an interactive assumption. Moreover, this replacement is only indistinguishable to a simulator that does not know the randomization of the representative used. This however means that the simulator cannot later adapt back the signer's SPS-EQ signatures in order to produce the blind signatures. FHS overcome this by relying on SPS-EQ security, which guarantees that adapted signatures look like fresh ones. Thus, if the reduction knew the signing key (which is the case in the honest-key model) then it could simply produce the final blind signatures by itself. In the malicious-key model, the reduction computes the fresh signatures by using the adversary as a signing oracle: it runs the adversary to obtain these signatures and then rewinds it. In the second (and actual) run, it embeds an (interactive) DDH instance and uses the signatures from the first run.

Open Questions. As the FHS scheme is the most efficient scheme having all the discussed properties, it would be desirable to base its security (or that of a related scheme) on weaker assumptions. The first question we ask is whether one can relate the unforgeability of a blind signature scheme based on SPS-EQ directly to the EUF-CMA security of the latter without necessitating any further assumptions. Even more interesting would be whether it is possible to remove the requirement for an interactive assumption for blindness. To address the first question, instead of the perfectly hiding commitment, one could use a perfectly binding one, as then each SPS-EQ signature from the signer can only be opened in one way, meaning that SPS-EQ unforgeability would directly imply blind-signature unforgeability. This however means that the commitment key cannot be chosen by the signer anymore, as knowing the underlying randomness could allow the signer to break hiding of the commitment and thus blindness of the scheme. But even if we let the user choose the commitment key, the information-theoretic argument by FHS that a signer must send valid SPS-EQ signatures does not apply anymore: even when not seeing the final blind signatures, the signer still obtains information on which message corresponds to which issuing, as the commitments are only computationally hiding.

Our Contribution. We answer the two above questions in the affirmative and reduce the strength of the required assumptions for both security notions. We construct a variant of the FHS blind signature scheme and prove unforgeability solely under the EUF-CMA security of the underlying SPS-EQ scheme. More importantly, we show that our scheme is blind in the malicious-key model under a non-interactive (and non-"q-type") assumption, namely an extension of the bilinear DDH assumption in asymmetric bilinear groups.

Our scheme replaces the perfectly hiding commitments in FHS by perfectly binding ones, which means unforgeability follows directly from SPS-EQ unforge-ability. As there are no trusted parameters, we let the user choose the commit-ment key during signature issuing and include it in the final signature. Straight-forward implementation of this approach however turns out not to result in a blind scheme. We therefore "distribute" the commitment key over several group elements, which enables us to show blindness.

Our blindness proof follows FHS's idea of rewinding the signer in order to use it as a signing oracle for signatures which the simulator cannot adapt on its own. The proof is however much more involved, since we need to consider adversaries that might return invalid SPS-EQ signatures but still break blindness. Our proof works by rewinding the blindness adversary numerous times to increase the success probability of the reduction noticeably beyond one half. We moreover show in the full version that these multiple rewinds are *necessary* by giving a counterexample for the case of only rewinding once.

Organization. Sect. 2 discusses preliminaries including signature schemes on equivalence classes (SPS-EQ). Section 3 discusses blind signatures, the FHS construction and presents our construction of round-optimal blind signatures and the extension to partially blind signatures.

2   Preliminaries

A function $\epsilon \colon \mathbb{N} \to \mathbb{R}^+$ is called negligible if for all $c > 0$ there is a k_0 such that $\epsilon(k) < 1/k^c$ for all $k > k_0$. By $a \xleftarrow{R} S$, we denote that a is chosen uniformly at random from a set S. Furthermore, we write $\mathsf{A}(a_1, \dots, a_n; r)$ if we want to make the randomness r used by a probabilistic algorithm $\mathsf{A}(a_1, \dots, a_n)$ explicit and denote by $[\mathsf{A}(a_1, \dots, a_n)]$ the set of points with positive probability of being output by A. For an (additive) group $\mathbb{G}$ we use $\mathbb{G}^*$ to denote $\mathbb{G} \setminus \{0_{\mathbb{G}}\}$.

Definition 1 (Bilinear Map). Let $\mathbb{G}_1$, $\mathbb{G}_2$ and $\mathbb{G}_T$ be cyclic groups of prime order p, where $\mathbb{G}_1$ and $\mathbb{G}_2$ are additive and $\mathbb{G}_T$ is multiplicative. Let P and $\hat{P}$ be generators of $\mathbb{G}_1$ and $\mathbb{G}_2$, resp. We call $e \colon \mathbb{G}_1 \times \mathbb{G}_2 \to \mathbb{G}_T$ a *bilinear map* or *pairing* if it is efficiently computable and it is:

Bilinear: $e(aP, b\hat{P}) = e(P, \hat{P})^{ab} = e(bP, a\hat{P}) \quad \forall\, a, b \in \mathbb{Z}_p,$
Non-degenerate: $e(P, \hat{P}) \neq 1_{\mathbb{G}_T}$, i.e., $e(P, \hat{P})$ generates $\mathbb{G}_T$.

If $\mathbb{G}_1 = \mathbb{G}_2$ then e is *symmetric* (Type-1) and *asymmetric* (Type-2 or 3) otherwise. For Type-2 pairings there is an efficiently computable isomorphism $\Psi \colon \mathbb{G}_2 \to \mathbb{G}_1$; for Type-3 pairings no such isomorphism is known. Type-3 pairings are currently the optimal choice in terms of efficiency for a given security level [17].

Definition 2 (Bilinear-Group Generator). A *bilinear-group generator* BGGen is a (possibly probabilistic[1]) polynomial-time algorithm that takes a security parameter 1^κ and outputs a bilinear group description $\mathsf{BG} = (p, \mathbb{G}_1, \mathbb{G}_2, \mathbb{G}_T, e, P, \hat{P})$ consisting of groups $\mathbb{G}_1 = \langle P \rangle$, $\mathbb{G}_2 = \langle \hat{P} \rangle$ and $\mathbb{G}_T$ of prime order p with $\log_2 p = \lceil \kappa \rceil$ and an asymmetric pairing $e \colon \mathbb{G}_1 \times \mathbb{G}_2 \to \mathbb{G}_T$.

Definition 3 (DDH). Let BGGen be a bilinear-group generator that outputs $\mathsf{BG} = (p, \mathbb{G}_1, \mathbb{G}_2, \mathbb{G}_T, e, P_1 = P, P_2 = \hat{P})$. For $i \in \{1, 2\}$ the *decisional Diffie-Hellman assumption* holds in $\mathbb{G}_i$ for BGGen if for all PPT adversaries $\mathcal{A}$ there is a negligible function $\epsilon(\cdot)$ such that

$$\Pr\left[\begin{array}{l} b \xleftarrow{R} \{0,1\}, \ \mathsf{BG} \xleftarrow{R} \mathsf{BGGen}(1^\kappa), \ r, s, t \xleftarrow{R} \mathbb{Z}_p, \\ b^* \xleftarrow{R} \mathcal{A}(\mathsf{BG}, rP_i, sP_i, ((1-b) \cdot t + b \cdot rs)P_i) \end{array} : b^* = b \right] - \frac{1}{2} \leq \epsilon(\kappa).$$

---

[1] For BN-curves [9], the most common choice for Type-3 pairings, group generation is deterministic.

The next assumption is in the spirit of the bilinear Diffie-Hellman assumption (BDDH) [35], which in *symmetric* bilinear groups states that given rP, uP, vP, the element $ruvP$ looks random. In asymmetric groups, we can additionally give uvP, $u\hat{P}$ and $v\hat{P}$. We therefore call the assumption ABDDH$^+$.

Definition 4 (ABDDH$^+$). Let BGGen be a bilinear-group generator that outputs $\mathsf{BG} = (p, \mathbb{G}_1, \mathbb{G}_2, \mathbb{G}_T, e, P_1 = P, P_2 = \hat{P})$. The ABDDH$^+$ assumption holds for BGGen if for all PPT algorithms $\mathcal{A}$ there is a negligible function $\epsilon(\cdot)$ such that

$$\Pr\left[\begin{array}{l} b \xleftarrow{R} \{0,1\}, \ \mathsf{BG} \xleftarrow{R} \mathsf{BGGen}(1^\kappa), \ r,u,v,t \xleftarrow{R} \mathbb{Z}_p \\ b^* \xleftarrow{R} \mathcal{A}(\mathsf{BG}, rP, uP, uvP, u\hat{P}, v\hat{P}, ((1-b)\cdot t + b\cdot ruv)P) \end{array} : b^* = b\right] - \frac{1}{2} \le \epsilon(\kappa).$$

In the generic group model, in order to distinguish $ruvP$ from random, one basically needs to construct this element in the target group. It is easily seen that this cannot be done from the remaining elements, which we now make formal:

Proposition 1. *The assumption in Definition 4 holds in generic groups and reaches the optimal, quadratic simulation error bound.*

We prove the above proposition in the full version. Moreover, note that given an ABDDH$^+$ instance $(\mathsf{BG}, R, U, W, \hat{U}, \hat{V}, T)$, we could use a DDH oracle to decide it: simply query (BG, R, W, T) to the oracle and return the result. We thus have:

Lemma 1. *If ABDDH$^+$ holds for a bilinear-group generator* BGGen *then DDH in $\mathbb{G}_1$ also holds for it.*

2.1 SPS on Equivalence Classes

Structure-preserving signatures (SPS) [3–8, 10, 24, 29, 37] can handle messages that are elements of a bilinear group, without requiring any prior encoding. In such a scheme public keys, messages and signatures consist only of group elements and the verification algorithm evaluates a signature by deciding group membership of signature elements and by evaluating pairing-product equations (PPEs).

The notion of SPS on equivalence classes (SPS-EQ) was introduced by Hanser and Slamanig [32]. Their initial instantiation was only secure against random-message attacks, but together with Fuchsbauer [25] they subsequently presented a scheme that they proved EUF-CMA-secure in the generic group model.

The idea is as follows. For a prime p, $\mathbb{Z}_p^\ell$ is a vector space. Thus, if $\ell > 1$ we can define a projective equivalence relation on it, which propagates to $\mathbb{G}_i^\ell$ and partitions $\mathbb{G}_i^\ell$ into equivalence classes. Let $\sim_{\mathcal{R}}$ be this relation, i.e., for $M, N \in \mathbb{G}_i^\ell$ we have $M \sim_{\mathcal{R}} N \Leftrightarrow \exists s \in \mathbb{Z}_p^* : M = sN$. An SPS-EQ scheme signs an equivalence class $[M]_{\mathcal{R}}$ for $M \in (\mathbb{G}_i^*)^\ell$ by actually signing a representative M of $[M]_{\mathcal{R}}$. It then allows to switch to other representatives of $[M]_{\mathcal{R}}$ and to update the corresponding signature without having access to the secret key. If the DDH assumption holds on the message space, then a random representative of a given class $[M]_\mathcal{R}$ is indistinguishable from a message vector outside of $[M]_\mathcal{R}$. Moreover, the malicious-key perfect adaptation property (defined in Definition 9) guarantees that updated signatures are random elements in the corresponding space of signatures. The combination of both properties implies the unlinkability of message-signature pairs (under the same pk) corresponding to the same class.

The Abstract Signature Scheme. Here, we discuss the abstract model, the security model of such a signature scheme [25,26,32] and a concrete construction, as presented in [25].

Definition 5 (SPS-EQ). A *structure-preserving signature scheme for equivalence relation* $\mathcal{R}$ over $\mathbb{G}_i$ with $i \in \{1,2\}$ is a tuple SPS-EQ of the following PPT algorithms:

$\mathsf{BGGen}_\mathcal{R}(1^\kappa)$ is a (probabilistic) bilinear-group generation algorithm which on input a security parameter 1^κ outputs a prime-order bilinear group BG.

$\mathsf{KeyGen}_\mathcal{R}(\mathsf{BG}, 1^\ell)$ is a probabilistic algorithm which on input a bilinear group BG and a vector length $\ell > 1$ (in unary) outputs a key pair (sk, pk).

$\mathsf{Sign}_\mathcal{R}(M, \mathsf{sk})$ is a probabilistic algorithm which on input a representative $M \in (\mathbb{G}_i^*)^\ell$ of an equivalence class $[M]_\mathcal{R}$ and a secret key sk outputs a signature σ for the equivalence class $[M]_\mathcal{R}$.

$\mathsf{ChgRep}_\mathcal{R}(M, \sigma, \mu, \mathsf{pk})$ is a probabilistic algorithm, which on input a representative $M \in (\mathbb{G}_i^*)^\ell$ of an equivalence class $[M]_\mathcal{R}$, a signature σ for M, a scalar μ and a public key pk returns an updated message-signature pair (M', σ'), where $M' = \mu \cdot M$ is the new representative and σ' its updated signature.

$\mathsf{Verify}_\mathcal{R}(M, \sigma, \mathsf{pk})$ is a deterministic algorithm which given a representative $M \in (\mathbb{G}_i^*)^\ell$, a signature σ and a public key pk outputs 1 if σ is valid for M

$\mathsf{VKey}_\mathcal{R}(\mathsf{sk}, \mathsf{pk})$ is a deterministic algorithm which given a secret key sk and a public key pk checks their consistency and returns 1 on success and 0 otherwise.

An SPS-EQ scheme SPS-EQ defined on message-space $\mathbb{G}_i$ is *secure* if the DDH assumption holds in $\mathbb{G}_i$, if SPS-EQ is *correct*, *EUF-CMA secure* and if it *perfectly adapts signatures*.

Definition 6 (Correctness). An SPS-EQ scheme SPS-EQ over $\mathbb{G}_i$ with $i \in \{1,2\}$ is *correct* if for all security parameters $\kappa \in \mathbb{N}$, for all $\ell > 1$, all bilinear groups $\mathsf{BG} = (p, \mathbb{G}_1, \mathbb{G}_2, \mathbb{G}_T, e, P, \hat{P}) \in [\mathsf{BGGen}_\mathcal{R}(1^\kappa)]$, all key pairs (sk, pk) $\in$ $[\mathsf{KeyGen}_\mathcal{R}(\mathsf{BG}, 1^\ell)]$, all messages $M \in (\mathbb{G}_i^*)^\ell$ and all scalars $\mu \in \mathbb{Z}_p^*$ we have:

$$\mathsf{VKey}_\mathcal{R}(\mathsf{sk}, \mathsf{pk}) = 1 \quad \text{and}$$

$$\Pr\left[\mathsf{Verify}_\mathcal{R}(M, \mathsf{Sign}_\mathcal{R}(M, \mathsf{sk}), \mathsf{pk}) = 1\right] = 1 \quad \text{and}$$

$$\Pr\left[\mathsf{Verify}_\mathcal{R}(\mathsf{ChgRep}_\mathcal{R}(M, \mathsf{Sign}_\mathcal{R}(M, \mathsf{sk}), \mu, \mathsf{pk}), \mathsf{pk}) = 1\right] = 1.$$

In contrast to the standard unforgeability definition for signatures, EUF-CMA security for SPS-EQ is defined with respect to equivalence classes, i.e., a forgery is a signature on a message from an equivalence class from which the adversary has not asked any messages to be signed.

Definition 7 (EUF-CMA). An SPS-EQ scheme SPS-EQ over $\mathbb{G}_i$ with $i \in \{1,2\}$ is *existentially unforgeable under adaptive chosen-message attacks* if for all $\ell > 1$ and all PPT algorithms $\mathcal{A}$ having access to a signing oracle $\mathsf{Sign}_{\mathcal{R}}(\cdot, \mathsf{sk})$, there is a negligible function $\epsilon(\cdot)$ such that:

$$\Pr \left[\begin{array}{l} \mathsf{BG} \xleftarrow{R} \mathsf{BGGen}_{\mathcal{R}}(1^\kappa), \\ (\mathsf{sk}, \mathsf{pk}) \xleftarrow{R} \mathsf{KeyGen}_{\mathcal{R}}(\mathsf{BG}, 1^\ell), \ : \\ (M^*, \sigma^*) \xleftarrow{R} \mathcal{A}^{\mathsf{Sign}_{\mathcal{R}}(\cdot, \mathsf{sk})}(\mathsf{pk}) \end{array} \begin{array}{l} [M^*]_{\mathcal{R}} \neq [M]_{\mathcal{R}} \ \forall M \in Q \ \wedge \\ \mathsf{Verify}_{\mathcal{R}}(M^*, \sigma^*, \mathsf{pk}) = 1 \end{array} \right] \leq \epsilon(\kappa) \ ,$$

where Q is the set of queries that $\mathcal{A}$ has issued to the signing oracle.

The next two definitions were introduced in [26]. They formalize the notion that signatures output by $\mathsf{ChgRep}_{\mathcal{R}}$ are distributed like fresh signatures on the new representative.

Definition 8 (Signature Adaptation). Let $\ell > 1$. An SPS-EQ scheme $\mathsf{SPS-EQ}$ on $(\mathbb{G}_i^*)^\ell$ with $i \in \{1,2\}$ *perfectly adapts signatures* if for all tuples $(\mathsf{sk}, \mathsf{pk}, M, \sigma, \mu)$ with

$$\mathsf{VKey}_{\mathcal{R}}(\mathsf{sk}, \mathsf{pk}) = 1 \qquad \mathsf{Verify}_{\mathcal{R}}(M, \sigma, \mathsf{pk}) = 1 \qquad M \in (\mathbb{G}_i^*)^\ell \qquad \mu \in \mathbb{Z}_p^*$$

$\mathsf{ChgRep}_{\mathcal{R}}(M, \sigma, \mu, \mathsf{pk})$ and $(\mu M, \mathsf{Sign}_{\mathcal{R}}(\mu M, \mathsf{sk}))$ are identically distributed.

The following definition demands that this even holds for maliciously generated verification keys. As for such keys there might not even exist a corresponding secret key, we require that adapted signatures are random elements in the space of valid signatures.

Definition 9 (Signature Adaptation Under Malicious Keys). Let $\ell > 1$. An SPS-EQ scheme $\mathsf{SPS-EQ}$ on $(\mathbb{G}_i^*)^\ell$ with $i \in \{1,2\}$ *perfectly adapts signatures under malicious keys* if for all tuples $(\mathsf{pk}, M, \sigma, \mu)$ with

$$\mathsf{Verify}_{\mathcal{R}}(M, \sigma, \mathsf{pk}) = 1 \qquad M \in (\mathbb{G}_i^*)^\ell \qquad \mu \in \mathbb{Z}_p^* \qquad (1)$$

we have that $\mathsf{ChgRep}_{\mathcal{R}}(M, \sigma, \mu, \mathsf{pk})$ outputs $(\mu M, \sigma')$ such that σ' is uniformly random in the space of signatures, conditioned on $\mathsf{Verify}_{\mathcal{R}}(\mu M, \sigma', \mathsf{pk}) = 1$.

In Fig. 1, we restate the SPS-EQ construction from [25]. It is EUF-CMA secure in the generic group model and satisfies Definitions 8 and 9.

3   Blind Signatures

Before we discuss the construction from [26] and then present our new blind signature construction, we give the abstract model and the security properties of blind signature schemes. These are correctness, unforgeability and blindness and were initially studied in [36,41] and later on rigorously treated in [22,42].

Definition 10 (Blind Signature Scheme). A blind signature scheme BS consists of the following PPT algorithms:

BGGen$_\mathcal{R}$(1^κ): On input a security parameter 1^κ, output BG $\overset{R}{\leftarrow}$ BGGen(1^κ).

KeyGen$_\mathcal{R}$(BG, 1^ℓ): On input a bilinear-group description BG and vector length $\ell > 1$ (in unary), choose $(x_i)_{i \in [\ell]} \overset{R}{\leftarrow} (\mathbb{Z}_p^*)^\ell$, set secret key sk $\leftarrow$ $(x_i)_{i \in [\ell]}$, compute public key pk $\leftarrow (\hat{X}_i)_{i \in [\ell]} = (x_i \hat{P})_{i \in [\ell]}$ and output (sk, pk).

Sign$_\mathcal{R}$(M, sk): On input a representative $M = (M_i)_{i \in [\ell]} \in (\mathbb{G}_1^*)^\ell$ of equivalence class $[M]_\mathcal{R}$ and a secret key sk $= (x_i)_{i \in [\ell]} \in (\mathbb{Z}_p^*)^\ell$, choose $y \overset{R}{\leftarrow} \mathbb{Z}_p^*$ and output $\sigma \leftarrow (Z, Y, \hat{Y})$ with

$$Z \leftarrow y \sum_{i \in [\ell]} x_i M_i \qquad Y \leftarrow \tfrac{1}{y} P \qquad \hat{Y} \leftarrow \tfrac{1}{y} \hat{P} .$$

Verify$_\mathcal{R}$(M, σ, pk): On input a representative $M = (M_i)_{i \in [\ell]} \in (\mathbb{G}_1^*)^\ell$ of equivalence class $[M]_\mathcal{R}$, a signature $\sigma = (Z, Y, \hat{Y}) \in \mathbb{G}_1 \times \mathbb{G}_1^* \times \mathbb{G}_2^*$ and public key pk $= (\hat{X}_i)_{i \in [\ell]} \in (\mathbb{G}_2^*)^\ell$, check whether

$$\prod_{i \in [\ell]} e(M_i, \hat{X}_i) = e(Z, \hat{Y}) \qquad \wedge \qquad e(Y, \hat{P}) = e(P, \hat{Y})$$

and if this holds output 1 and 0 otherwise.

ChgRep$_\mathcal{R}$(M, σ, μ, pk): On input a representative $M = (M_i)_{i \in [\ell]} \in (\mathbb{G}_1^*)^\ell$ of equivalence class $[M]_\mathcal{R}$, a signature $\sigma = (Z, Y, \hat{Y})$, $\mu \in \mathbb{Z}_p^*$ and public key pk, return $\perp$ if Verify$_\mathcal{R}$(M, σ, pk) $= 0$. Otherwise pick $\psi \overset{R}{\leftarrow} \mathbb{Z}_p^*$ and return $(\mu \cdot M, \sigma')$ with $\sigma' \leftarrow (\psi \mu Z, \tfrac{1}{\psi} Y, \tfrac{1}{\psi} \hat{Y})$.

VKey$_\mathcal{R}$(sk, pk): On input sk $= (x_i)_{i \in [\ell]} \in (\mathbb{Z}_p^*)^\ell$ and pk $= (\hat{X}_i)_{i \in [\ell]} \in (\mathbb{G}_2^*)^\ell$, output 1 if $x_i \hat{P} = \hat{X}_i$ $\forall i \in [\ell]$ and 0 otherwise.

Fig. 1. Scheme 1, an EUF-CMA secure SPS-EQ scheme

KeyGen$_{BS}$(1^κ), on input κ, returns a key pair (sk, pk). The security parameter κ is also an (implicit) input to the following algorithms.

($\mathcal{U}_{BS}$(m, pk), $\mathcal{S}_{BS}$(sk)) are run by a user and a signer, who interact during execution. $\mathcal{U}_{BS}$ gets input a message m and a public key pk and $\mathcal{S}_{BS}$ has input a secret key sk. At the end $\mathcal{U}_{BS}$ outputs σ, a signature on m, or $\perp$ if the interaction was not successful.

Verify$_{BS}$(m, σ, pk) is deterministic and given a message-signature pair (m, σ) and a public key pk outputs 1 if σ is valid on m under pk and 0 otherwise.

A blind signature scheme BS is *secure* if it is *correct*, *unforgeable* and *blind*.

Definition 11 (Correctness). A blind signature scheme BS is *correct* if for all security parameters $\kappa \in \mathbb{N}$, all key pairs $(\mathsf{sk}, \mathsf{pk}) \in [\mathsf{KeyGen_{BS}}(1^\kappa)]$, all messages m and all signatures $\sigma \in [(\mathcal{U}_{\mathsf{BS}}(m, \mathsf{pk}), \mathcal{S}_{\mathsf{BS}}(\mathsf{sk}))]$ it holds that $\mathsf{Verify_{BS}}(m, \sigma, \mathsf{pk}) = 1$.

Definition 12 (Unforgeability). BS is *unforgeable* if for all PPT algorithms $\mathcal{A}$ having access to a signer oracle, there is a negligible function $\epsilon(\cdot)$ such that:

$$\Pr\begin{bmatrix}(\mathsf{sk}, \mathsf{pk}) \leftarrow \mathsf{KeyGen_{BS}}(1^\kappa), & m_i^* \neq m_j^* \; \forall i, j \in [k{+}1], i \neq j \; \wedge \\ (m_i^*, \sigma_i^*)_{i=1}^{k+1} \leftarrow \mathcal{A}^{(\cdot, \mathcal{S}_{\mathsf{BS}}(\mathsf{sk}))}(\mathsf{pk}) & : \mathsf{Verify_{BS}}(m_i^*, \sigma_i^*, \mathsf{pk}) = 1 \; \forall i \in [k{+}1]\end{bmatrix} \leq \epsilon(\kappa),$$

where k is the number of completed interactions with the oracle.

There are several different kinds of blindness, where the strongest (and arguably most natural) definition is blindness in the *malicious-key* model [1,40]. In this case, the public key is generated by the adversary, whereas in the weaker *honest-key* model the key pair is initially set up by the environment, i.e., it requires a trusted setup. We use the stronger notion to prove the blindness of our construction—as also done by other existing round-optimal standard-model constructions [26–28]:

Definition 13 (Blindness). A blind signature scheme BS is called *blind* in the malicious-key model if for all PPT algorithms $\mathcal{A}$ having one-time access to two user oracles, there is a negligible function $\epsilon(\cdot)$ such that:

$$\Pr\begin{bmatrix}b \xleftarrow{R} \{0, 1\}, \; (\mathsf{pk}, m_0, m_1, \mathsf{st}) \xleftarrow{R} \mathcal{A}(1^\kappa), \\ \mathsf{st} \xleftarrow{R} \mathcal{A}^{(\mathcal{U}_{\mathsf{BS}}(m_b, \mathsf{pk}), \cdot)^1, (\mathcal{U}_{\mathsf{BS}}(m_{1-b}, \mathsf{pk}), \cdot)^1}(\mathsf{st}), \\ \text{Let } \sigma_b \text{ and } \sigma_{1-b} \text{ be the resp. outputs of } \mathcal{U}_{\mathsf{BS}}, \; : \; b^* = b \\ \text{If } \sigma_0 = \bot \text{ or } \sigma_1 = \bot \text{ then } (\sigma_0, \sigma_1) \leftarrow (\bot, \bot), \\ b^* \xleftarrow{R} \mathcal{A}(\mathsf{st}, \sigma_0, \sigma_1)\end{bmatrix} - \frac{1}{2} \leq \epsilon(\kappa).$$

3.1 The FHS Construction

The construction in [26] uses unconditionally hiding commitments to the messages and SPS-EQ to sign these commitments. The latter allows for blinding and unblinding, as it implies the ability to derive a signature for arbitrary representatives of this class (without knowing the private signing key). The construction is unforgeable under the EUF-CMA security of the SPS-EQ and an asymmetric-group variant of the Diffie-Hellman inversion assumption. It is blind under an interactive DDH variant in the malicious-key model without requiring any trusted setup. Its design principle is as follows.

A signer public key consists of an SPS-EQ verification key pk and two elements $(Q = qP, \hat{Q} = q\hat{P})$ for some random $q \in \mathbb{Z}_p^*$. When asking for a signature on a message m, the user picks $r \xleftarrow{R} \mathbb{Z}_p^*$ and creates a Pedersen commitment $C = mP + rQ$ and forms a vector (C, P), which is a representative of equivalence class $[(C, P)]_\mathcal{R}$. Then she chooses a randomizer $s \xleftarrow{R} \mathbb{Z}_p^*$ and uses it to randomize (C, P) to another representative (sC, sP), thereby blinding the vector, and sends (sC, sP) to the signer. When the signer returns an SPS-EQ signature on

(sC, sP), the user is able to derive a signature for the unblinded (original) message (C, P), using SPS-EQ's changing of representatives. Verification of the blind signature will only accept messages whose second component is P. Together with SPS-EQ unforgeability, this means that the only such message for which the user can derive a signature is (C, P).

The Pedersen commitment $C = mP + rQ$ has a tweaked opening, which is (m, rP) instead of (m, r), and which lets one check the well-formedness of C via the pairing equation $e(C - mP, \hat{P}) = e(rP, \hat{Q})$. This can be thought of as showing knowledge of the discrete logarithm r without revealing it (revealing r would lead to attacks against blindness). Under the co-DHI$_1^*$ assumption commitments with opening of this form are binding, meaning the user can open a commitment only to one message, which is required for blind-signature unforgeability. The user includes the values $T \leftarrow C - mP$ and $R \leftarrow rP$ in the blind signature to allow the verification of the opening.

Blindness intuitively follows from the fact that the message $(sC, sP) = (smP + srQ, sP)$ that the signer sees during issuing looks unrelated to the message m and the resulting blind signature (which contains rP): under DDH, given sP and rP, the element srP looks random. However, the blinding factor in the randomized commitment is not srP but srQ, with Q chosen by the signer. This is what forced FHS to introduce an interactive variant of DDH, where the adversary chooses Q and $\hat{Q}$ and then gets an instance rP, rQ, sP, tQ and needs to decide whether $t = rs$.

3.2 Construction

In previous round-optimal blind-signature schemes (using a related approach involving commitments) the commitment is done w.r.t. a commitment key contained in the CRS. Since we aim at constructing a scheme in the standard model where there is no CRS, we could add the commitment key to the signer's public key—as done in [26]. In this case the commitment must be perfectly hiding and can thus only be computationally binding. (Binding protects the signer from a user generating signatures on more messages than signatures issued by the signer.) We choose a different approach, namely to let the user choose the commitment key. To prevent forgeries, the commitment now needs to be perfectly binding, which we achieve by using an encryption scheme. We then show that, together with the properties of the used SPS-EQ scheme, computational hiding of the commitment implies blindness of our construction.

In our signing protocol the user chooses a public key Q for ElGamal encryption and then commits to the message m by encrypting mP as $(C, R) = (mP + rQ, rP)$. The user then forms a vector (C, R, Q, P), consisting of the ciphertext, the public key and the group generator P. (Note that this vector uniquely defines m.) Next, to blind the message, the user transforms this tuple to a random element of the equivalence class $[(C, R, Q, P)]_\mathcal{R}$: she picks $s \overset{R}{\leftarrow} \mathbb{Z}_p^*$, computes $M \leftarrow (sC, sR, sQ, sP)$, and sends M to the signer. When the signer returns an SPS-EQ signature on (sC, sR, sQ, sP), the user derives a signature for the unblinded (original) message (C, R, Q, P). For unforgeability, this unblinding must be unambiguous, which is why verification only accepts tuples whose last component is P.

Finally, the user needs to "open" $(C, R, Q = qP)$ to the actual message m. This could be done by publishing $Z = rQ$ and $\hat{Q} = q\hat{P}$: then for a message m we could check whether the signature is valid on $(mP + Z, R, Q, P)$ and whether Z is of the correct form, by checking $e(Q, \hat{P}) = e(P, \hat{Q})$ and

$$e(Z, \hat{P}) = e(R, \hat{Q}). \tag{2}$$

This is basically the opening that FHS use (where $\hat{Q}$ is part of the commitment key). In their scheme R is only given in the final signature; here however, the signer also sees sR, which leads to the following attack: The signer can check whether $M = (sC, sR, sQ, sP)$ received during the signing protocol corresponds to a particular m, by testing $e(M_1 - mM_4, \hat{P}) = e(M_2, \hat{Q})$, since this corresponds to the pairing equation $e(srQ, \hat{P}) = e(srP, \hat{Q})$.

To prevent this attack, we "split" the logarithm of Q and define $Q = uvP$. Instead of publishing $\hat{Q}$, we publish $X = ruP$ and $\hat{V} = v\hat{P}$ and replace the RHS of (2) with $e(X, \hat{V}) = e(r \cdot uvP, \hat{P})$. Now we additionally need to enable a check that X and $\hat{V}$ are correctly formed, which we do by publishing $U = uP$ and $\hat{U} = u\hat{P}$. As in [25,26], we assume the bilinear group generation algorithm of the SPS-EQ scheme to be deterministic and to produce one bilinear group per security parameter. We then show that assuming ABDDH[+] for such a group generation algorithm, our scheme satisfies malicious-key blindness. Our blind-signature scheme is detailed in Fig. 2.

3.3 Security

The correctness of the scheme in Fig. 2 follows by inspection.

Theorem 1. *If the underlying SPS-EQ scheme is EUF-CMA secure, then the scheme in Fig. 2 is unforgeable.*

Unforgeability of the SPS-EQ scheme guarantees that after k signing queries the adversary possesses only signatures on k tuples of the form (C_i, R_i, Q_i, P). (Since the last component fixes each equivalence class to one representative.) It remains to show that each such tuple can only be opened to one message m: let (C, R, Q, P) and σ be such a valid message-signature pair. Then we show that any choice of $(Y, U, X, \hat{U}, \hat{V})$ that satisfies verification together with (σ, Q, R) leads to the same m. Let u, v be such that $\hat{U} = u\hat{P}$ and $\hat{V} = v\hat{P}$. Then by (3.2), the 2nd equation in (3): $Q = uvP$; and (4.1) implies $U = uP$. With r s.t. $R = rP$, we have $X = ruP$ by (4.2) and $Y = ruv = rQ$ by (4.3). This means that R and Q uniquely determine Y, which together with $C = mP + Y$ uniquely determines m.

The formal proof is given in the full version. The reduction has a natural security loss determined by the number of signing queries by the adversary, since the reduction has to guess which of the $k + 1$ valid signatures is the forgery.

$\underline{\mathsf{KeyGen}_{\mathsf{BS}}}(1^\kappa)$: Given a security parameter $\kappa > 0$ (in unary), compute $\mathsf{BG} \leftarrow \mathsf{BGGen}_{\mathcal{R}}(1^\kappa)$; compute $(\mathsf{sk}, \mathsf{pk}) \xleftarrow{R} \mathsf{KeyGen}_{\mathcal{R}}(\mathsf{BG}, 1^4)$ and output $(\mathsf{sk}, \mathsf{pk})$.

$\underline{\mathcal{U}_{\mathsf{BS}}^{(1)}}(m, \mathsf{pk})$: Given pk and a message $m \in \mathbb{Z}_p$, compute $\mathsf{BG} \leftarrow \mathsf{BGGen}_{\mathcal{R}}(1^\kappa)$; choose $r, s, u, v \xleftarrow{R} \mathbb{Z}_p^*$ s.t. $m + ruv \neq 0$ and output

$$M \leftarrow (s(mP + ruvP), srP, suvP, sP) \qquad \mathsf{st} \leftarrow (\mathsf{pk}, M, r, s, u, v)$$

$\underline{\mathcal{S}_{\mathsf{BS}}}(M, \mathsf{sk})$: Given $M \in (\mathbb{G}_1^*)^4$ and a secret key sk, output $\pi \xleftarrow{R} \mathsf{Sign}_{\mathcal{R}}(M, \mathsf{sk})$.

$\underline{\mathcal{U}_{\mathsf{BS}}^{(2)}}(\mathsf{st}, \pi)$: Parse st as $(\mathsf{pk}, M, r, s, u, v)$. If $\mathsf{Verify}_{\mathcal{R}}(M, \pi, \mathsf{pk}) = 0$, return $\perp$. Else run $((mP + ruvP, rP, uvP, P), \sigma) \xleftarrow{R} \mathsf{ChgRep}_{\mathcal{R}}(M, \pi, \frac{1}{s}, \mathsf{pk})$; output $\tau \leftarrow (\sigma, Y = ruvP, Q = uvP, R = rP, U = uP, X = ruP, \hat{U} = u\hat{P}, \hat{V} = v\hat{P})$.

$\underline{\mathsf{Verify}_{\mathsf{BS}}}(m, \tau, \mathsf{pk})$: Given message $m \in \mathbb{Z}_p$, blind signature $\tau = (\sigma, Y, Q, R, U, X, \hat{U}, \hat{V})$ and public key pk, output 1 if the following holds and 0 otherwise.

$$\mathsf{Verify}_{\mathcal{R}}((mP + Y, R, Q, P), \sigma, \mathsf{pk}) = 1 \qquad e(Q, \hat{P}) = e(U, \hat{V}) \qquad (3)$$

$$e(U, \hat{P}) = e(P, \hat{U}) \qquad e(X, \hat{P}) = e(R, \hat{U}) \qquad e(Y, \hat{P}) = e(X, \hat{V}) \qquad (4)$$

Fig. 2. A blind signature scheme from SPS-EQ.

Blindness. In the full version, we first show that ABDDH$^+$ (Definition 4) implies that when given $rQ, Q, R, U, X, \hat{U}, \hat{V}$ (the elements which the signer sees in the final signature), the elements srQ (the blinding factor of the message in the issuing protocol), and sQ, srP and sP (the remaining components seen during issuing) are indistinguishable from random. This intuitively means that what the adversary sees during issuing looks unrelated to the derived blind signature.

We start with the basic idea to prove blindness. Given an instance of the decision problem just described ($\mathsf{BG}, R, S = sP, U = uP, X = uR, Q = uvP, Y = rQ, \hat{U} = u\hat{P}, \hat{V} = v\hat{P}, T, W, Z$), where either (a) $T = sR$, $W = sQ$ and $Z = sY$ or (b) T, W and Z are random, in the blindness game the challenger could compute the message sent to the signer during issuing as

$$M \leftarrow (m \cdot S + Z, T, W, S), \qquad (3)$$

which is correctly distributed in case (a) but independent of m (and the resulting blind signature) in case (b). In the blindness game, the challenger next receives an SPS-EQ signature on M, which it needs to adapt to the unblinded message in order to construct a blind signature.

Overall, we distinguish two behaviors of blindness adversaries. Type I does not return correct SPS-EQ signatures during issuing. As in this case the adversary does not obtain blind signatures at the end, the above simulation already works and we are done.

However, if the adversary returns valid signatures (Type II) then the simulator, after embedding the instance when creating M as in (3), does not know the blinding factor s, meaning the simulator cannot adapt the SPS-EQ signature to the unblinded message. By perfect adaptation however, the distribution of an adapted signature is the same as that of a fresh signature on the unblinded message. In the honest-key model, where the simulator knows the signing key, it could therefore compute a signature σ on $(m \cdot P + Z, R, Q, P)$ and return the blind signature $(\sigma, Y, Q, R, U, X, \hat{U}, \hat{V})$. Blindness follows, since during issuing the signer obtained a random quadruple; thus the game is independent of bit b.

For blindness in the malicious-key model, we do not have access to the adversarially generated signing key, meaning we cannot recompute the signature on the unblinded message. Instead, we use the adversary $\mathcal{A}$ as a signing oracle by rewinding it. (This is similar to Coron's [20] meta-reduction strategy, which was extended to randomizable signatures by Hofheinz et al. [34].) The idea is to first run the adversary to obtain a signature on $(s'(mP+Y), s'R, s'Q, s'P)$ for a known s', which we can therefore transform into a signature on $(mP+Y, R, Q, P)$. We then rewind the adversary to the point after it output the public key and the messages, and then run it again (using a new random bit b), this time setting M as in (3), thus not knowing s. In the second run we are not able to transform the signature, but we can use the signature from the first run, which is distributed identically, thanks to the property of the SPS-EQ scheme.

Making this approach actually work turns out quite tricky. In the proof in [26] it is argued that an adversary must always output two valid signatures, as otherwise the bit b is perfectly hidden due to the perfectly hiding commitments. For such adversaries if the original blindness game is won with some probability then the game that rewinds the adversary will yield valid signatures in the first run and in the second run the adversary wins with the same probability as in the original (non-rewinding) game.

This is not true anymore for our scheme, as an aborting adversary (one that returns invalid SPS-EQ signatures) can still win the game. In particular, we show in the full version that *rewinding once is not enough* by giving an example of an adversary's coin distribution (before and after the point of rewinding) that leads to the original blindness game being won with non-negligible probability, while the game with rewinding (which outputs a random bit if it receives invalid signatures in the first run) is won with probability *less than one half*.

However, if we rewind more than once then it suffices to obtain valid signatures *in at least one* of the rewinds. We therefore consider a game where we rewind the adversary λ times and abort if all runs yield invalid signatures (outputting a random bit); otherwise, we run the adversary a final time and check if it wins or not.

In the full version we show the following: suppose the adversary wins the blindness game with non-negligible advantage, that is, for some polynomial p and infinitely many security-parameter values κ, the probability of winning the blindness game is greater than $\frac{1}{2} + \frac{1}{p(\kappa)}$. Then if we rewind the adversary $\lambda = \kappa \cdot p(\kappa)$ times, the probability that at least one of the λ runs yields valid SPS-EQ signatures *and* the adversary wins the final run is greater than $\frac{1}{2} + \frac{1}{2 \cdot p(\kappa)}$ for infinitely many κ's. We make this formal in the following theorem.

Theorem 2. *If the underlying SPS-EQ scheme has perfect adaptation of signatures under malicious keys and $ABDDH^+$ holds for* BGGen *then the scheme in Fig. 2 satisfies blindness in the malicious-key model.*

Efficiency of the Construction. When instantiating our blind signature construction with the SPS-EQ scheme from [25], we obtain a public key size of $4\,\mathbb{G}_2$, a communication complexity of $6\,\mathbb{G}_1 + 1\,\mathbb{G}_2$ and a signature size of $7\,\mathbb{G}_1 + 3\,\mathbb{G}_2$ elements. We will now contrast this to the FHS construction [26] and to the DLIN construction from [27].

Instantiating the FHS construction with the SPS-EQ scheme from [25] yields a blind signature scheme having a public key size of $1\,\mathbb{G}_1 + 3\,\mathbb{G}_2$, a communication complexity of $4\,\mathbb{G}_1 + 1\,\mathbb{G}_2$ and a signature size of $4\,\mathbb{G}_1 + 1\,\mathbb{G}_2$ elements. While being more efficient, we recall that blindness of the FHS construction is based on an interactive and, thus, much stronger assumption.

Ignoring the increase of the security parameter due to complexity leveraging for the construction from [27], it has a public key size of $43\,\mathbb{G}_1$ elements, a communication complexity of $18 \log_2 q + 41\,\mathbb{G}_1$ elements (where, for instance, we have $\log_2 q = 155$ when assuming that the adversary runs in at most 2^{80} steps) and a signature size of $183\,\mathbb{G}_1$ elements.

Extension to Partially Blind Signatures. We note that analogously to the extension of the round-optimal blind signature construction in [26], it is possible to derive a partially blind signature scheme from the scheme in Fig. 2. To include a common information $\gamma \in \mathbb{Z}_p^*$, the underlying SPS-EQ scheme is set up for $\ell = 5$ (instead of $\ell = 4$) and the additional vector component is being used to include γ. In contrast to the blind signature scheme in Fig. 2, the signer on receiving $M \leftarrow (s(mP + ruvP), srP, suvP, sP)$ computes an SPS-EQ signature for vector $(s(mP + ruvP), srP, suvP, \gamma(sP), sP)$. In the verification of the partially blind signature, the SPS-EQ signature is verified on $(mP + Y, R, Q, \gamma P, P)$.

References

1. Abdalla, M., Namprempre, C., Neven, G.: On the (im)possibility of blind message authentication codes. In: Pointcheval, D. (ed.) CT-RSA 2006. LNCS, vol. 3860, pp. 262–279. Springer, Heidelberg (2006)
2. Abe, M.: A secure three-move blind signature scheme for polynomially many signatures. In: Pfitzmann, B. (ed.) EUROCRYPT 2001. LNCS, vol. 2045, pp. 136–151. Springer, Heidelberg (2001)

3. Abe, M., Chase, M., David, B., Kohlweiss, M., Nishimaki, R., Ohkubo, M.: Constant-size structure-preserving signatures: generic constructions and simple assumptions. In: Wang, X., Sako, K. (eds.) ASIACRYPT 2012. LNCS, vol. 7658, pp. 4–24. Springer, Heidelberg (2012)

4. Abe, M., Fuchsbauer, G., Groth, J., Haralambiev, K., Ohkubo, M.: Structure-preserving signatures and commitments to group elements. In: Rabin, T. (ed.) CRYPTO 2010. LNCS, vol. 6223, pp. 209–236. Springer, Heidelberg (2010)

5. Abe, M., Groth, J., Haralambiev, K., Ohkubo, M.: Optimal structure-preserving signatures in asymmetric bilinear groups. In: Rogaway, P. (ed.) CRYPTO 2011. LNCS, vol. 6841, pp. 649–666. Springer, Heidelberg (2011)

6. Abe, M., Groth, J., Ohkubo, M., Tibouchi, M.: Structure-preserving signatures from Type II pairings. In: Garay, J.A., Gennaro, R. (eds.) CRYPTO 2014, Part I. LNCS, vol. 8616, pp. 390–407. Springer, Heidelberg (2014)

7. Abe, M., Groth, J., Ohkubo, M., Tibouchi, M.: Unified, minimal and selectively randomizable structure-preserving signatures. In: Lindell, Y. (ed.) TCC 2014. LNCS, vol. 8349, pp. 688–712. Springer, Heidelberg (2014)

8. Abe, M., Haralambiev, K., Ohkubo, M.: Signing on elements in bilinear groups for modular protocol design. Cryptology ePrint Archive, Report 2010/133 (2010). http://eprint.iacr.org/2010/133

9. Barreto, P.S.L.M., Naehrig, M.: Pairing-friendly elliptic curves of prime order. In: Preneel, B., Tavares, S. (eds.) SAC 2005. LNCS, vol. 3897, pp. 319–331. Springer, Heidelberg (2006)

10. Barthe, G., Fagerholm, E., Fiore, D., Scedrov, A., Schmidt, B., Tibouchi, M.: Strongly-optimal structure preserving signatures from Type II pairings: synthesis and lower bounds. In: Katz, J. (ed.) PKC 2015. LNCS, vol. 9020, pp. 355–376. Springer, Heidelberg (2015)

11. Bellare, M., Namprempre, C., Pointcheval, D., Semanko, M.: The one-more-RSA-inversion problems and the security of Chaum's blind signature scheme. J. Cryptol. **16**(3), 185–215 (2003)

12. Blazy, O., Fuchsbauer, G., Pointcheval, D., Vergnaud, D.: Signatures on randomizable ciphertexts. In: Catalano, D., Fazio, N., Gennaro, R., Nicolosi, A. (eds.) PKC 2011. LNCS, vol. 6571, pp. 403–422. Springer, Heidelberg (2011)

13. Blazy, O., Pointcheval, D., Vergnaud, D.: Compact round-optimal partially-blind signatures. In: Visconti, I., De Prisco, R. (eds.) SCN 2012. LNCS, vol. 7485, pp. 95–112. Springer, Heidelberg (2012)

14. Blazy, O., Pointcheval, D., Vergnaud, D.: Round-optimal privacy-preserving protocols with smooth projective hash functions. In: Cramer, R. (ed.) TCC 2012. LNCS, vol. 7194, pp. 94–111. Springer, Heidelberg (2012)

15. Boldyreva, A.: Threshold signatures, multisignatures and blind signatures based on the gap-Diffie-Hellman-group signature scheme. In: Desmedt, Y.G. (ed.) PKC 2003. LNCS, vol. 2567, pp. 31–46. Springer, Heidelberg (2002)

16. Camenisch, J.L., Koprowski, M., Warinschi, B.: Efficient blind signatures without random oracles. In: Blundo, C., Cimato, S. (eds.) SCN 2004. LNCS, vol. 3352, pp. 134–148. Springer, Heidelberg (2005)

17. Chatterjee, S., Menezes, A.: On cryptographic protocols employing asymmetric pairings - the role of ψ revisited. Discret. Appl. Math. **159**(13), 1311–1322 (2011)

18. Chaum, D.: Blind signatures for untraceable payments. In: Chaum, D., Rivest, R.L., Sherman, A.T. (eds.) CRYPTO 1982, pp. 199–203. Plenum Press, New York (1982)

19. Chaum, D.: Blind signature system. In: Chaum, D. (ed.) CRYPTO 1983, p. 153. Plenum Press, New York (1984)

20. Coron, J.-S.: Optimal security proofs for PSS and other signature schemes. In: Knudsen, L.R. (ed.) EUROCRYPT 2002. LNCS, vol. 2332, pp. 272–287. Springer, Heidelberg (2002)

21. Fischlin, M.: Round-optimal composable blind signatures in the common reference string model. In: Dwork, C. (ed.) CRYPTO 2006. LNCS, vol. 4117, pp. 60–77. Springer, Heidelberg (2006)

22. Fischlin, M., Schröder, D.: Security of blind signatures under aborts. In: Jarecki, S., Tsudik, G. (eds.) PKC 2009. LNCS, vol. 5443, pp. 297–316. Springer, Heidelberg (2009)

23. Fischlin, M., Schröder, D.: On the impossibility of three-move blind signature schemes. In: Gilbert, H. (ed.) EUROCRYPT 2010. LNCS, vol. 6110, pp. 197–215. Springer, Heidelberg (2010)

24. Fuchsbauer, G.: Automorphic signatures in bilinear groups and an application to round-optimal blind signatures. Cryptology ePrint Archive, Report 2009/320 (2009). http://eprint.iacr.org/2009/320

25. Fuchsbauer, G., Hanser, C., Slamanig, D.: Structure-preserving signatures on equivalence classes and constant-size anonymous credentials. Cryptology ePrint Archive, Report 2014/944 (2014). http://eprint.iacr.org/2014/944

26. Fuchsbauer, G., Hanser, C., Slamanig, D.: Practical round-optimal blind signatures in the standard model. In: Gennaro, R., Robshaw, M. (eds.) CRYPTO 2015. LNCS, vol. 9216, pp. 233–253. Springer, Heidelberg (2015)

27. Garg, S., Gupta, D.: Efficient round optimal blind signatures. In: Nguyen, P.Q., Oswald, E. (eds.) EUROCRYPT 2014. LNCS, vol. 8441, pp. 477–495. Springer, Heidelberg (2014)

28. Garg, S., Rao, V., Sahai, A., Schröder, D., Unruh, D.: Round optimal blind signatures. In: Rogaway, P. (ed.) CRYPTO 2011. LNCS, vol. 6841, pp. 630–648. Springer, Heidelberg (2011)

29. Ghadafi, E.: Short structure-preserving signatures. In: Sako, K. (ed.) CT-RSA 2016. LNCS, vol. 9610, pp. 305–321. Springer, Heidelberg (2016)

30. Ghadafi, E., Smart, N.P.: Efficient two-move blind signatures in the common reference string model. In: Gollmann, D., Freiling, F.C. (eds.) ISC 2012. LNCS, vol. 7483, pp. 274–289. Springer, Heidelberg (2012)

31. Groth, J., Sahai, A.: Efficient non-interactive proof systems for bilinear groups. In: Smart, N.P. (ed.) EUROCRYPT 2008. LNCS, vol. 4965, pp. 415–432. Springer, Heidelberg (2008)

32. Hanser, C., Slamanig, D.: Structure-preserving signatures on equivalence classes and their application to anonymous credentials. In: Sarkar, P., Iwata, T. (eds.) ASIACRYPT 2014. LNCS, vol. 8873, pp. 491–511. Springer, Heidelberg (2014)

33. Hanzlik, L., Kluczniak, K.: A short paper on blind signatures from knowledge assumptions. FC 2016. LNCS. Springer, Heidelberg (2016)

34. Hofheinz, D., Jager, T., Knapp, E.: Waters signatures with optimal security reduction. In: Fischlin, M., Buchmann, J., Manulis, M. (eds.) PKC 2012. LNCS, vol. 7293, pp. 66–83. Springer, Heidelberg (2012)

35. Joux, A.: A one round protocol for tripartite Diffie-hellman. In: Bosma, W. (ed.) ANTS 2000. LNCS, vol. 1838, pp. 385–394. Springer, Heidelberg (2000). http://dx.doi.org/10.1007/10722028_23

36. Juels, A., Luby, M., Ostrovsky, R.: Security of blind digital signatures. In: Kaliski Jr., B.S. (ed.) CRYPTO 1997. LNCS, vol. 1294, pp. 150–164. Springer, Heidelberg (1997)

37. Kiltz, E., Pan, J., Wee, H.: Structure-preserving signatures from standard assumptions, revisited. In: Gennaro, R., Robshaw, M. (eds.) CRYPTO 2015. LNCS, vol. 9216, pp. 275–295. Springer, Heidelberg (2015)
38. Lindell, Y.: Bounded-concurrent secure two-party computation without setup assumptions. In: 35th ACM STOC, pp. 683–692. ACM Press, San Diego, 9–11 June 2003
39. Okamoto, T.: Provably secure and practical identification schemes and corresponding signature schemes. In: Brickell, E.F. (ed.) CRYPTO 1992. LNCS, vol. 740, pp. 31–53. Springer, Heidelberg (1993)
40. Okamoto, T.: Efficient blind and partially blind signatures without random oracles. In: Halevi, S., Rabin, T. (eds.) TCC 2006. LNCS, vol. 3876, pp. 80–99. Springer, Heidelberg (2006)
41. Pointcheval, D., Stern, J.: Security arguments for digital signatures and blind signatures. J. Cryptol. **13**(3), 361–396 (2000)
42. Schröder, D., Unruh, D.: Security of blind signatures revisited. In: Fischlin, M., Buchmann, J., Manulis, M. (eds.) PKC 2012. LNCS, vol. 7293, pp. 662–679. Springer, Heidelberg (2012)
43. Seo, J.H., Cheon, J.H.: Beyond the limitation of prime-order bilinear groups, and round optimal blind signatures. In: Cramer, R. (ed.) TCC 2012. LNCS, vol. 7194, pp. 133–150. Springer, Heidelberg (2012)

Cryptanalysis

How (Not) to Instantiate Ring-LWE

Chris Peikert[(✉)]

University of Michigan, Ann Arbor, USA
cpeikert@alum.mit.edu

Abstract. The *learning with errors over rings* (Ring-LWE) problem—
or more accurately, family of problems—has emerged as a promising
foundation for cryptography due to its practical efficiency, conjectured
quantum resistance, and provable *worst-case hardness*: breaking certain
instantiations of Ring-LWE is at least as hard as quantumly approximating the Shortest Vector Problem on *any* ideal lattice in the ring.

Despite this hardness guarantee, several recent works have shown that
certain instantiations of Ring-LWE can be broken by relatively simple
attacks. While the affected instantiations are not supported by worst-
case hardness theorems (and were not ever proposed for cryptographic
purposes), this state of affairs raises natural questions about what other
instantiations might be vulnerable, and in particular whether certain
classes of rings are inherently unsafe for Ring-LWE.

This work comprehensively reviews the known attacks on Ring-LWE
and vulnerable instantiations. We give a new, unified exposition which
reveals an elementary geometric reason why the attacks work, and provide rigorous analysis to explain certain phenomena that were previously
only exhibited by experiments. In all cases, the insecurity of an instantiation is due to the fact that the error distribution is insufficiently "well
spread" relative to the ring. In particular, the insecure instantiations use
the so-called *non-dual* form of Ring-LWE, together with *spherical* error
distributions that are much narrower and of a very different shape than
the ones supported by hardness proofs.

On the positive side, we show that any Ring-LWE instantiation which
satisfies (or only almost satisfies) the hypotheses of the "worst-case hardness of search" theorem is *provably immune* to broad generalizations of
the above-described attacks: the running time divided by advantage is
at least exponential in the degree of the ring. This holds for the ring of
integers in *any* number field, so the rings themselves are not the source of
insecurity in the vulnerable instantiations. Moreover, the hypotheses of
the worst-case hardness theorem are *nearly minimal* ones which provide
these immunity guarantees.

C. Peikert—This material is based upon work supported by the National Science
Foundation under CAREER Award CCF-1054495 and CNS-1606362, the Alfred
P. Sloan Foundation, and by a Google Research Award. The views expressed are
those of the authors and do not necessarily reflect the official policy or position of
the National Science Foundation, the Sloan Foundation, or Google.

V. Zikas and R. De Prisco (Eds.): SCN 2016, LNCS 9841, pp. 411–430, 2016.
DOI: 10.1007/978-3-319-44618-9_22

1   Introduction

Cryptography based on *lattices* is an exciting and fast-developing area of research, due in part to conjectured security against quantum attacks, asymptotic efficiency and parallelism, and a wide range of applications spanning from basic tasks like key exchange, to powerful objects like fully homomorphic encryption. A large fraction of lattice-based cryptographic constructions are built upon the average-case *learning with errors* (LWE) problem [25] or its more efficient variant *learning with errors over rings* (Ring-LWE) [16,17]. These are actually *families* of problems, which are instantiated by choosing a particular dimension or ring, an integer modulus, and an error distribution.

A main attraction of the (Ring-)LWE problems is their *worst-case hardness theorems*, also known as worst-case/average-case reductions. These say that breaking certain instantiations of (Ring-)LWE (or the cryptosystems based upon them) is provably at least as hard as quantumly solving *any* instance of certain lattice problems, i.e., in the worst case. For Ring-LWE, the underlying lattice problem is the approximate Shortest Vector Problem (approx-SVP) on *ideal lattices*, which are algebraically structured lattices corresponding to ideals in the ring. To date, no known quantum (or classical) algorithm for approx-SVP has significantly better worst-case performance on ideal lattices (in any concrete ring of interest) than on general lattices of the same dimension. For the polynomial approximation factors often used in cryptography, the fastest known algorithms require exponential time and space in the dimension (see, e.g., [1,2,22]).

Despite the above-described hardness guarantees, several recent works [9–11,13,14] have shown that certain *ad-hoc* instantiations of Ring-LWE are *insecure*, via relatively simple attacks. How should we interpret such results? We emphasize that the vulnerable instantiations were not previously proposed for any cryptographic application, and were specifically sought out for their insecurity.[1] In addition, the attacks do not appear to translate to any improved algorithms for ideal-lattice problems, because the vulnerable instantiations do not satisfy the hypotheses of the worst-case hardness theorems. Yet this explanation leaves several natural questions unanswered, such as:

- How "close" are these insecure instantiations to ones that do enjoy worst-case hardness?
- Do these vulnerable instantiations imply anything about what *rings* might be more or less secure for Ring-LWE?
- How can we evaluate other instantiations that may not be backed by worst-case hardness theorems?

The goals of this work are twofold: first, to shed further light on recent attacks and vulnerable Ring-LWE instantiations; and second, to articulate a general set of principles by which we can systematically evaluate the (in)security of an instantiation. Toward this end, we provide the following main contributions.

---

[1] Indeed, it is easy to design trivially insecure (Ring-)LWE instantiations for any choice of dimension or ring: just define the error distribution to always output zero. However, the vulnerable instantiations in question do involve some nontrivial error.

Review of Attacks. We comprehensively review the attacks and insecure Ring-LWE instantiations from the above-cited works. We give a new, unified exposition of the attacks in terms of the geometry of *dual* ideals, and provide formal analysis to explain certain phenomena that were previously only exhibited by experiments. In all cases, the heart of the insecurity is the use of a non-standard, *"non-dual"* form of Ring-LWE with relatively narrow spherical error, rather than the *"dual"* form that was defined and proved to have worst-case hardness in [16]. Using a simple "tweak" that allows for a direct comparison of the dual and non-dual forms, we find that the *error distributions* in the insecure instantiations are much narrower than those in the provably hard ones, which is why they are vulnerable to attacks.

In a bit more technical detail: for the instantiations from [14], we give a simpler proof of the fact, first noticed and exploited in [9], that the (discretized) errors lie in a very low-dimensional linear subspace of the ring. This means that every Ring-LWE sample reveals many errorless LWE samples, which leads to an elementary linear-algebraic attack (no ring algebra needed). We also show that the instantiations from [10,11], with slightly narrower error distributions, fall to the same kind of attack. Finally, we give formal analyses showing why the (unmodified) instantiations of [10,11] are broken by a different but closely related distinguishing attack.

Invulnerable Instantiations. On the positive side, we consider Ring-LWE instantiations that satisfy, or only "almost" satisfy, the "worst-case hardness of search" theorem from [16, Sect. 4]. We show that *any* such instantiation is *provably immune to* broad classes of attacks which include all those described above. By "immune" we mean that the attacks perform no better than known attacks (e.g., [5,6]) against *plain* LWE when instantiated to have worst-case hardness; in particular, the running time divided by advantage is at least exponential in the LWE dimension (in the typical case of modulus $q = \text{poly}(n)$).

We stress that the worst-case hardness theorem from [16, Sect. 4] works for the ring of integers (or more generally, any order) of *any* number field. Therefore, all the rings appearing in the insecure instantiations from the above-cited works do indeed admit provably hard instantiations—they just need different error distributions. In other words, the rings themselves are not the source of insecurity. For illustration, in the full version we describe and graphically depict some example hard instantiations in detail, including for prime cyclotomic rings and quadratic extensions thereof.

To be clear, in this work we do not propose *concrete* security estimates for particular (Ring-)LWE instantiations, e.g., "the mth cyclotomic with Gaussian error of width r offers at least λ bits of security" (see, e.g., [3,7,15,21] for representative works that do so). We are also not concerned with the *applicability* (or lack thereof) of instantiations for cryptographic purposes, nor with lower-level computational details or efficiency (see, e.g., [12,17] for works along these lines). Our central focus is on understanding and evaluating the fundamental (in)security of Ring-LWE instantiations, which is a necessary prerequisite to these other important goals.

Discussion. The main conclusion from this work is that for the security of Ring-LWE, *proper choice of the error distribution is essential,* especially because there is so much more freedom of choice than in plain LWE. It should not be surprising that ad-hoc instantiations of Ring-LWE can be insecure—indeed, the same goes for LWE. For example, there is a roughly n^d-time attack (using roughly n^d samples) for d-bounded errors [5]. But this does not affect LWE's conjectured $2^{\Omega(n)}$ hardness when instantiated according to its worst-case hardness theorems, which require Gaussian errors of standard deviation $\Omega(\sqrt{n})$. Indeed, it may even *increase* our confidence that this is the "right" error distribution for LWE, since the wide variety of known attack strategies all require $2^{\Omega(n)}$ time beyond this threshold.

On the positive side, the fact that worst-case-hard instantiations are immune to concrete attacks also should not be surprising, since any efficient attack would translate to a comparably efficient quantum algorithm for approx-SVP on any ideal lattice in the ring—which would be a major achievement in computational number theory. But it is instructive to understand what precisely gives the hard instantiations their immunity. In particular, some of the more peculiar aspects of Ring-LWE, like the width of the error distributions and especially the role of the "dual" ideal $R^\vee$, were adopted in order to obtain the strongest and tightest hardness theorems in general number fields. (See [16, Sect. 3.3] for discussion.) Notably, these choices also turn out to be *nearly minimal* ones that provably withstand broad classes of attacks. We believe that this provides yet another example of the importance of worst-case hardness proofs in lattice cryptography.

Organization. The remainder of the paper is organized as follows.

Section 2 recalls the relevant mathematical background, the (Ring-)LWE problems and the formal relationship between them, and their known worst-case hardness theorems.

Section 3 gives a new exposition and unified framework for the Ring-LWE attacks developed in [9–11,13,14], focusing on the essential geometric reasons why they work.

Section 4 reviews the insecure Ring-LWE instantiations through the lens of the unified attack framework, and formally proves that the attacks work against them.

Section 5 gives a sufficient condition that makes a Ring-LWE instantiation *provably immune* to the attacks in the framework, and shows that the condition is satisfied for any instantiation supported by the worst-case hardness theorem of [16, Sect. 4].

2   Preliminaries

In this section we recall the necessary mathematical background on lattices, Gaussians, and (Ring-)LWE, including its "dual" and "non-dual" forms. Due to space restrictions, standard background material on algebraic number theory is omitted; we adopt the notation and concepts from [16].

2.1   Lattices and Gaussians

In ring-based lattice cryptography, it is convenient to work in the space $H \subseteq \mathbb{R}^{s_1} \times \mathbb{C}^{2s_2}$ for some nonnegative integers s_1, s_2 with $n = s_1 + 2s_2$, defined as

$$H := \{(x_1, \ldots, x_n) \in \mathbb{R}^{s_1} \times \mathbb{C}^{2s_2} : x_{s_1+s_2+j} = \overline{x_{s_1+j}} \; \forall j \in \{1, \ldots, s_2\}\}.$$

It is easy to check that H, with the inner product $\langle \mathbf{x}, \mathbf{y} \rangle = \sum_i x_i \overline{y_i}$ of the ambient space $\mathbb{C}^n$, is an n-dimensional real inner product space, i.e., it is isomorphic to $\mathbb{R}^n$ via an appropriate rotation. Therefore, the reader may mentally replace H with $\mathbb{R}^n$ in all that follows.

For the purposes of this work, a *lattice* $\mathcal{L}$ is a discrete additive subgroup of H that is full dimensional, i.e., $\mathrm{span}_{\mathbb{R}}(\mathcal{L}) = H$. Any lattice is generated as the set of all integer linear combinations of some (non-unique) linearly independent basis vectors $\mathbf{B} = (\mathbf{b}_1, \ldots, \mathbf{b}_n)$, as

$$\mathcal{L} = \mathcal{L}(\mathbf{B}) := \Big\{ \mathbf{Bz} = \sum_i z_i \mathbf{b}_i : \mathbf{z} \in \mathbb{Z}^n \Big\}.$$

The *volume* (or determinant) of a lattice $\mathcal{L}$ is $\mathrm{vol}(\mathcal{L}) := \mathrm{vol}(H/\mathcal{L}) = |\det(\mathbf{B})|$, where $\mathbf{B}$ denotes any basis of $\mathcal{L}$. The *minimum distance* $\lambda_1(\mathcal{L})$ is the length (in the Euclidean norm) of a shortest nonzero lattice vector: $\lambda_1(\mathcal{L}) = \min_{0 \neq \mathbf{x} \in \mathcal{L}} \|\mathbf{x}\|$. The *dual lattice* $\mathcal{L}^\vee$ of $\mathcal{L}$ is defined as the set of all points in H having integer inner products with every vector of the lattice: $\mathcal{L}^\vee = \{\mathbf{w} \in H : \langle \mathbf{w}, \mathcal{L} \rangle \subseteq \mathbb{Z}\}$. It is easy to verify that $(\mathcal{L}^\vee)^\vee = \mathcal{L}$.

Gaussians and Smoothing. For $r > 0$, the Gaussian probability distribution D_r of parameter (or width) r over H is defined to have probability density function proportional to $\rho_r(\mathbf{x}) := \exp(-\pi \|\mathbf{x}\|^2 / r^2)$. A standard fact is that $\langle \mathbf{w}, D_r \rangle = D_{r\|\mathbf{w}\|}$ (over $\mathbb{R}$) for any nonzero $\mathbf{w} \in H$. In addition, a one-dimensional Gaussian D_r over $\mathbb{R}$ satisfies the tail bound $\Pr_{x \leftarrow D_r}[|x| \geq t] \leq 2 \exp(-\pi(t/r)^2)$ for any $t \geq 0$.

The *smoothing parameter* [20] is an important lattice quantity that is related to several other lattice parameters.

Definition 1. *For a lattice $\mathcal{L}$ and positive real $\varepsilon > 0$, the* smoothing parameter *$\eta_\varepsilon(\mathcal{L})$ is the smallest $r > 0$ such that $\rho_{1/r}(\mathcal{L}^\vee \backslash \{\mathbf{0}\}) \leq \varepsilon$.*

Lemma 1 [20, Lemma 3.2]. *For any n-dimensional lattice $\mathcal{L}$, we have $\eta_{2^{-2n}}(\mathcal{L}) \leq \sqrt{n}/\lambda_1(\mathcal{L}^\vee)$.*[2]

The following lemma explains the name "smoothing parameter:" it says that a Gaussian whose width exceeds the smoothing parameter is essentially uniform modulo the lattice.

Lemma 2 [20, Lemma 4.1]. *For any lattice $\mathcal{L} \subset H$, $\varepsilon > 0$, and $r \geq \eta_\varepsilon(\mathcal{L})$, the statistical distance between D_r mod $\mathcal{L}$ and the uniform distribution over $H/\mathcal{L}$ is at most $\varepsilon/2$.*

---

[2] Note that have we have $\varepsilon = 2^{-2n}$ instead of 2^{-n} as in [20], but the proof is exactly the same.

2.2   Learning with Errors (Over Rings)

In this section we review the learning with errors problem [25] and its ring-based analogue [16], describe the formal relationship between them, and recall their worst-case hardness theorems.

LWE. Informally, *learning with errors* (LWE) [25] concerns "noisy" random inner products with a secret vector. More precisely, LWE is parameterized by a dimension n, a positive integer modulus q defining the quotient ring $\mathbb{Z}_q = \mathbb{Z}/q\mathbb{Z}$, and an error distribution ψ over $\mathbb{R}$.

Definition 2 (LWE, [25]). *The* search-*LWE$_{n,q,\psi}$ problem is to recover a uniformly random secret vector* $\mathbf{s} \in \mathbb{Z}_q^n$, *given many independent samples of the form*

$$(\mathbf{a}_i, \ b_i = \langle \mathbf{s}, \mathbf{a}_i \rangle + e_i \bmod q) \in \mathbb{Z}_q^n \times \mathbb{R}/q\mathbb{Z},$$

where each $\mathbf{a}_i \leftarrow \mathbb{Z}_q^n$ *is uniformly random and each* $e_i \leftarrow \psi$ *is drawn from the error distribution. The* decision-*LWE$_{n,q,\psi}$ problem is to distinguish, with some noticeable advantage, between samples generated as above, and uniformly random samples in* $\mathbb{Z}_q^n \times (\mathbb{R}/q\mathbb{Z})$.

Sometimes the number m of available samples is also considered as an additional parameter of the LWE problems, but here we let it be arbitrarily large; this can only make the problems easier to solve, because samples can be ignored. It is often convenient to group the m samples $(\mathbf{a}_i, b_i)$ into a matrix and vector

$$\mathbf{A} = [\mathbf{a}_1 \mid \mathbf{a}_2 \mid \cdots \mid \mathbf{a}_m] \in \mathbb{Z}_q^{n \times m} \quad \text{and} \quad \mathbf{b}^t = \mathbf{s}^t \mathbf{A} + \mathbf{e}^t \in (\mathbb{R}/q\mathbb{Z})^m,$$

where $\mathbf{A}$ is uniformly random and $\mathbf{e} \in \mathbb{R}^m$ is distributed as ψ^m.

Insecure Instantiations. Certain instantiations of LWE are trivially easy to solve. For instance, if the error distribution ψ always outputs 0—i.e., no error at all— then the problem is easily solved by standard linear algebra: as long as the rows of $\mathbf{A}$ are linearly independent over $\mathbb{Z}_q$ (which holds with high probability once m is a little more than n), we can easily recover $\mathbf{s}$ given $\mathbf{A}$ and $\mathbf{b}^t = \mathbf{s}^t \mathbf{A}$.

Now suppose we allow potentially dependent errors, i.e., each group of k samples has an error vector drawn from some distribution κ over $\mathbb{R}^k$. Then this form of LWE is easy if, e.g., some (discretized) error coordinate is always zero under κ: just ignore the samples corresponding to the other coordinates.

Hard Instantiations. Certain instantiations of LWE appear computationally hard, and have strong "worst-case hardness" theorems in support of this belief. Specifically, for a Gaussian error distribution $\psi = D_r$ with $r \geq 2\sqrt{n}$, solving search-LWE$_{n,q,\psi}$ is at least as hard as *quantumly* approximating certain well-studied "short vector" problems on *any* n-dimensional lattice to within $\tilde{O}(n \cdot q/r)$ factors, i.e., there is a quantum reduction from worst-case lattice problems to search-LWE [25]. Moreover, for $q \geq 2^{n/2}$ there is a *classical* reduction from a subset of these problems, for essentially the same approximation factors [23]. Finally, under mild conditions on the modulus q and the Gaussian parameter r, the search and decision problems are equivalent, i.e., there are reductions from search to decision. See, e.g., [8,18,19,23,25].

Ring-LWE. Analogously to LWE, *learning with errors over rings* (Ring-LWE) [16,17] concerns "noisy" random *ring* products with a secret ring element. Formally, it is parameterized by a ring R, which is the ring of integers (or more generally, an order) of a number field K, a positive integer modulus q, and an error distribution ψ over $K_\mathbb{R}$. Recall that $R^\vee = \{x \in K : \mathrm{Tr}(xR) \subseteq \mathbb{Z}\}$ is the (fractional) dual ideal of R, and for any fractional ideal $\mathcal{I}$ define the quotient $\mathcal{I}_q := \mathcal{I}/q\mathcal{I}$.

Definition 3 (Ring-LWE, [16]). *The* search-R-$LWE_{q,\psi}$ *problem is to find a uniformly random secret* $s \in R_q^\vee$ *given many independent samples of the form*

$$(a_i, b_i = s \cdot a_i + e_i \bmod qR^\vee) \in R_q \times K_\mathbb{R}/qR^\vee,$$

where each $a_i \leftarrow R_q$ *is uniformly random and each* $e_i \leftarrow \psi$ *is drawn from the error distribution. (Observe that each* $s \cdot a_i \in R_q^\vee$.*) The* decision-R-$LWE_{q,\psi}$ *problem is to distinguish, with some noticeable advantage, between samples generated as above, and uniformly random samples in* $R_q \times K_\mathbb{R}/qR^\vee$.

The above definition is sometimes called the "dual" form of Ring-LWE owing to the appearance of $R^\vee$, whose role might appear somewhat mysterious. However, its importance for obtaining the "right" definition of Ring-LWE is discussed at length in [16, Sect. 3.3]. In short, the combination of $R^\vee$ and (nearly) *spherical* Gaussian error ψ (in the canonical embedding) yields both the tightest connection with worst-case problems on ideal lattices, and the best error tolerance and computational efficiency in cryptographic applications. (See [16,17] for full details.) Nevertheless, for various reasons it may be more convenient to work with a "non-dual" form of Ring-LWE, where the secret is a uniformly random $s \in R_q$ (not $R_q^\vee$), and samples are of the form

$$(a_i, b_i = s \cdot a_i + e_i \bmod qR) \in R_q \times K_\mathbb{R}/qR,$$

where each $a_i \leftarrow R_q$ is uniform and each $e_i \leftarrow \psi$.

It turns out that the dual and non-dual forms of Ring-LWE are in fact *equivalent up to the choice of error distribution* ψ—so it does not really matter which syntactic form we use, as long as long as we also use an appropriate error distribution. This is because we can always convert one form to another using an appropriate "tweak" factor, as described in the full version. (Such a "tweaked" form of Ring-LWE, which replaces $R^\vee$ by R, has been used in [4,12,24].) However, it is important to note that the transformation may in general convert spherical Gaussian error to (highly) non-spherical error.

Because R is usually much sparser than $R^\vee$ (viewed as lattices in the canonical embedding), for non-dual Ring-LWE some prior works have used a volume-normalized parameter $r_0 = r/\mathrm{vol}(R)^{1/n} = r/\delta_R$ as a rough measure of how "wide" Gaussian error D_r is relative to R. We caution, however, that this measure does not account for any lack of "well-roundedness" in R (i.e., gaps among its successive minima), so even a large value of r_0 does not necessarily mean that the error is "well-spread" relative to R.

Hard Instantiations. Much like LWE, certain instantiations of Ring-LWE are supported by worst-case hardness theorems; see [16] for formal statements, which we summarize here. For $r \geq 2 \cdot \omega(\sqrt{\log n})$, [16, Theorem 4.1] says that for *any* number field K and $R = \mathcal{O}_K$, solving search-R-LWE for all continuous Gaussian error distributions $\psi = D_\mathbf{r}$, where each $r_i \leq r$, is at least as hard as quantumly approximating certain "short vector" problems on *any* ideal lattice in K, to within $\tilde{O}(\sqrt{n} \cdot q/r)$ factors. (The distribution $D_\mathbf{r}$ over H is essentially an elliptical Gaussian with parameter r_i in the ith coordinate.) Moreover, [16, Sect. 5] shows that for any *cyclotomic* number field, and for appropriate moduli q, decision is classically at least as hard as search for any *spherical* Gaussian error distribution. (The proof immediately generalizes to any Galois number field [13].) Alternatively, decision for spherical error of parameter roughly $r \cdot n^{1/4}$ is classically at least as hard as search for the class of elliptical distributions $D_\mathbf{r}$ described above. (The conditions on q have subsequently been weakened, and hardness of decision is now known for essentially any large enough modulus, via "modulus switching" [8].)

Connection to LWE. Ring-LWE can be seen as a special case of LWE, in the following sense. For simplicity we describe a reduction for the "non-dual" form, but it easily generalizes to the dual form from Definition 3.

Fix any $\mathbb{Z}$-basis B of the ring R, which is also a $\mathbb{Z}_q$-basis of R_q and an $\mathbb{R}$-basis of $K_\mathbb{R}$. Then for any $a \in R_q$, multiplication by a corresponds to a matrix $\mathbf{A}_a \in \mathbb{Z}_q^{n \times n}$ with respect to B, i.e., for any $s \in R_q$ having coefficient vector $\mathbf{s} \in \mathbb{Z}_q^n$ w.r.t. B, the coefficient vector of $s \cdot a$ w.r.t. B is $\mathbf{s}^t \mathbf{A}_a$. Moreover, if $a \in R_q$ is uniformly random then so is every column of $\mathbf{A}_a$ (though the columns are maximally dependent).

Given a Ring-LWE sample $(a \in \mathbb{R}_q, b = s \cdot a + e \in K_\mathbb{R}/qR)$, we can transform it to n LWE samples

$$(\mathbf{A}_a \in \mathbb{Z}_q^{n \times n}, \; \mathbf{b}^t = \mathbf{s}^t \mathbf{A}_a + \mathbf{e}^t \in (\mathbb{R}/q\mathbb{Z})^n),$$

where $\mathbf{s} \in \mathbb{Z}_q^n$, $\mathbf{e} \in \mathbb{R}^n$ are respectively the coefficient vectors of s, e w.r.t. B. The distribution of $\mathbf{e}$ is $\sigma(B)^{-1} \cdot \sigma(\psi)$, which is "narrow" if ψ itself is narrow and B is chosen appropriately. Note that the columns of $\mathbf{A}_a$ are not independent, nor are the entries of $\mathbf{e}$ in general.

3   Attack Framework

In this section we give a new exposition of the Ring-LWE attacks described in [9–11,13,14], focusing on the essential geometric reasons why they work. All the attacks fall into one of two classes: reduction to *errorless* LWE, for which search is trivially solvable; and reduction modulo an *ideal divisor* $\mathfrak{q}$ of the modulus qR, for which decision can be solved under certain conditions on $\mathfrak{q}$ and the error distribution. In this section we describe a simple, unified framework that encompasses both classes of attack. Then in Sect. 4 we show how certain concrete instantiations are vulnerable to the attacks, and in Sect. 5 we show that worst-case-hard instantiations are provably immune to them.

Following the above-cited works, throughout this section we restrict our attention to the so-called "non-dual" form of Ring-LWE, which involves spherical Gaussian error relative to R (in the canonical embedding). We mainly work with *continuous* rather than discrete error, which more clearly exposes the essential ideas without the extra complication of discretization. We contend that a successful attack against an instantiation with continuous Gaussian error should be enough to reject the corresponding discrete version, since we should not rely on (nor expect) discretization itself to provide any significant security. Indeed, in the full version we consider the effect of discretization, and show that the attacks frequently work in the discrete setting as well.

3.1   Attacking Ring-LWE

The authors of [9–11,13,14] describe analogous attacks on Ring-LWE that can yield rather small search spaces for the reduced secret, even for nontrivial target moduli. (The approaches are closely related to the search-to-decision reduction for Ring-LWE from [16].) As we shall see, the attacks are all instances of the following framework.

Let $\mathfrak{q} \subseteq R$ be an ideal divisor of qR, having norm $N(\mathfrak{q}) := |R/\mathfrak{q}|$, and let ψ be a continuous error distribution over $K_{\mathbb{R}}$. Given Ring-LWE samples

$$(a_i\,,\, b_i = s \cdot a_i + e_i) \in R_q \times K_{\mathbb{R}}/qR$$

where $a_i \leftarrow R_q$ and $e_i \leftarrow \psi$, we can reduce them modulo $\mathfrak{q}$ to obtain samples

$$(a_i' = a_i \bmod \mathfrak{q}\,,\, b_i' = b_i \bmod \mathfrak{q}) \in R/\mathfrak{q} \times K_{\mathbb{R}}/\mathfrak{q}.$$

As above, we have $b_i' = s' \cdot a_i' + e_i \bmod \mathfrak{q}$ where $s' = s \bmod \mathfrak{q}$, so these are Ring-LWE samples with error distribution ψ, but now the secret lies in a space of size $N(\mathfrak{q})$. Also observe that reduction modulo $\mathfrak{q}$ maps uniform samples to uniform samples.

When $N(\mathfrak{q})$ is not too large, the preceding observations potentially yield attacks:

- If $\psi \bmod \mathfrak{q}$ is detectably non-uniform, then we immediately have a distinguishing attack against the search problem: try all candidates $\hat{s} \in R/\mathfrak{q}$ for s', and for each one test whether the $b_i' - \hat{s} \cdot a_i' \in K_{\mathbb{R}}/\mathfrak{q}$ are statistically non-uniform; accept if such an $\hat{s}$ exists, otherwise reject. In Sect. 3.1 below we describe a standard method of distinguishing reduced spherical Gaussians $D_r \bmod \mathfrak{q}$ from uniform.

– Similarly, if ψ has one or more coefficients (relative to some fixed $\mathbb{Z}$-basis of $\mathfrak{q}$) that usually do not "wrap around" modulo $\mathbb{Z}$, then we can attack search by reducing to errorless LWE. See Sect. 3.1 below for further details.
– On the positive side, if $\psi = D_r$ is a continuous Gaussian of parameter $r \geq \eta_\varepsilon(\mathfrak{q})$ for some very small ε, then neither of the attacks work, because every coefficient of the error "wraps around," and moreover, the reduced error ψ mod $\mathfrak{q}$ is statistically close to uniform. We return to these points in Sect. 5.

Distinguisher. To run the distinguishing attack, we need a way of efficiently distinguishing ψ mod $\mathfrak{q}$ from uniform over $K_\mathbb{R}/\mathfrak{q}$, for spherical Gaussian error $\psi = D_r$. A variety of statistical tests have been proposed in [10,11,13,14], but in this work it suffices to consider a standard method that uses a sufficiently short nonzero element w in the *dual ideal* $\mathfrak{q}^\vee$ of $\mathfrak{q}$, or equivalently, a short nonzero vector $\mathbf{w} = \overline{\sigma(w)}$ in the dual lattice $\mathcal{L}^\vee = \sigma(\mathfrak{q})^\vee$ of $\mathcal{L} = \sigma(\mathfrak{q})$. More generally, one can use multiple linearly independent dual vectors—e.g., to reduce the number of consumed samples, or to improve the effectiveness of the statistical test—but we do not pursue such optimizations because we will not need them (see the discussion below).

Lemma 3. *Let $\mathcal{L}$ be any lattice, $\mathbf{w} \in \mathcal{L}^\vee \setminus \{\mathbf{0}\}$ be any nonzero element of its dual lattice, and $r > 0$. Then for $\mathbf{x} \leftarrow D_r$ mod $\mathcal{L}$, the distribution of $\langle \mathbf{w}, \mathbf{x} \rangle$ mod $\mathbb{Z}$ is $D_{r\|\mathbf{w}\|}$ mod $\mathbb{Z}$, and*

$$\mathbb{E}_\mathbf{x}[\cos(2\pi\langle \mathbf{w}, \mathbf{x} \rangle)] = \exp(-\pi(r\|\mathbf{w}\|)^2).$$

In particular, if $r\|\mathbf{w}\| = O(1)$, then the expectation is $\Omega(1)$.

Proof. Because $\mathbf{w} \in \mathcal{L}^\vee$ we have $\langle \mathbf{w}, \mathcal{L} \rangle \subseteq \mathbb{Z}$, so the distribution of $\langle \mathbf{w}, D_r$ mod $\mathcal{L} \rangle$ mod $\mathbb{Z}$ is $\langle \mathbf{w}, D_r \rangle$ mod $\mathbb{Z} = D_s$ mod $\mathbb{Z}$, where $s = r\|\mathbf{w}\|$. The expectation $\mathbb{E}_{x \leftarrow D_s}[\cos(2\pi x)]$ is merely the Fourier coefficient at 1 of D_s mod $\mathbb{Z}$, which by a routine calculation is $\exp(-\pi s^2)$.

It is easy to see that for uniformly random $\mathbf{x}$ modulo $\mathcal{L}$, the inner product $\langle \mathbf{w}, \mathbf{x} \rangle$ mod $\mathbb{Z}$ is uniform, so $\mathbb{E}[\cos(2\pi\langle \mathbf{w}, \mathbf{x} \rangle)] = 0$. With Lemma 3, this immediately yields an efficient distinguisher between D_r mod $\mathcal{L}$ and uniform when $r\|\mathbf{w}\| = O(1)$: given many samples $\mathbf{x}_i$, compute the average of $\cos(2\pi\langle \mathbf{w}, \mathbf{x}_i \rangle)$ and accept if it exceeds an appropriate threshold $t = \Omega(1)$. (See, e.g., [25, Lemma 3.6] for more details.)

Relation to Prior Distinguishing Attacks. The distinguishing attacks from [10,11,13,14] are not described using dual ideals and the trace pairing, but in the full version, we show how they all can be expressed in these terms. Moreover, the trace-pairing perspective is strictly more general, because it can capture linear functions that are not ring homomorphisms.

Search Attack. We now describe the details of the attack on search, focusing on the case $\mathfrak{q} = R$ for simplicity.[3] This generalizes the attack from [9], and gives a simpler analysis with the same ultimate results (see below for a comparison, and Sect. 4 for concrete examples). Let $B = (b_j)_j$ be a fixed $\mathbb{Z}$-basis of R for which one or more coefficients of ψ do not wrap around, i.e.,

$$\Pr_{e \leftarrow \psi} [e_j \notin [-\tfrac{1}{2}, \tfrac{1}{2})] \approx 0 \tag{1}$$

for some j, where $e = \sum_j e_j \cdot b_j$ for $e_j \in \mathbb{R}$ is the unique representation of e with respect to B. Lemma 4 below shows that for spherical Gaussian error, this condition holds for the index j of any sufficiently short element of the *dual basis* of B.

To perform the attack, as described in Sect. 2.2 we transform each Ring-LWE sample $(a \in R_q, b = s \cdot a + e \in K_{\mathbb{R}}/qR)$ to n LWE samples

$$(\mathbf{A}_a \in \mathbb{Z}_q^{n \times n}, \ \mathbf{b}^t = \mathbf{s}^t \mathbf{A}_a + \mathbf{e}^t \in (\mathbb{R}/q\mathbb{Z})^n),$$

where $\mathbf{A}_a$ denotes the matrix of multiplication by a (whose columns are uniformly random but maximally dependent), and $\mathbf{s}, \mathbf{e}$ are respectively the coefficient vectors of s, e (all with respect to basis B). Now, for each index j for which Eq. (1) holds, we can with high probability obtain $e_j \in [-\tfrac{1}{2}, \tfrac{1}{2})$ as the distinguished representative of the jth entry of $\mathbf{b}$ mod $\mathbb{Z}$. This yields an errorless LWE sample for the jth column of $\mathbf{A}_a$. Given enough errorless samples, we can solve for $\mathbf{s}$ by standard linear algebra.

Lemma 4. *Let $D = (d_j)$ be the dual basis of $B = (b_j)$, i.e., $\mathbf{D} = \mathbf{B}^\vee := (\mathbf{B}^{-1})^*$ where $\mathbf{B} = \sigma(B)$, $\mathbf{D} = \sigma(D)$. Then for any $r, \varepsilon > 0$, if*

$$\|d_j\| \leq \left(2r\sqrt{\log(2/\varepsilon)/\pi}\right)^{-1}$$

then $\Pr_{e \leftarrow D_r}[e_j \in [-\tfrac{1}{2}, \tfrac{1}{2})] \geq 1 - \varepsilon$, where $e = \sum_j e_j \cdot b_j$ for $e_j \in \mathbb{R}$.

Proof. By definition, the distribution of $\mathbf{e}$, the coefficient vector of e with respect to B, is $\mathbf{B}^{-1} \cdot D_r$, where D_r is the spherical Gaussian of parameter r over H. Therefore, e_j is distributed as a Gaussian of parameter $s = r \cdot \|d_j\| \leq (2\sqrt{\log(2/\varepsilon)/\pi})^{-1}$. The claim then follows directly by the standard Gaussian tail bound $\Pr_{x \leftarrow D_s}[|x| \geq t] \leq 2\exp(-\pi(t/s)^2)$ for any $t \geq 0$.

Comparison with [9]. The authors of [9] also attack search using a reduction to errorless LWE, but use a different approach for showing that error coefficients are zero. In brief, they consider the matrix $\mathbf{B} = \sigma(B)$ of the linear transformation that maps from a basis B (e.g., the power basis $B = (1, X, \ldots, X^{n-1})$) to the canonical embedding. Using its singular value decomposition, they analyze the "skewness" of the transformation via its singular values, and the "alignment" of the basis elements with the singular vectors, to show that certain error coefficients are usually small. By contrast, the approach described above only needs to analyze the lengths of the dual vectors, i.e., the rows of $\mathbf{B}^{-1}$.

---

[3] The attack easily generalizes to arbitrary ideal divisors $\mathfrak{q}|qR$ of not-too-large norm; we omit the details, because the present form will be enough for our purposes.

4   Insecure Instantiations

In this section we show how the attack framework from Sect. 3 applies to the concrete insecure Ring-LWE instantiations defined in [10,11,13,14] (among others). In all cases, the core reason for the insecurity is that the error distributions are insufficiently "well spread" relative to the rings, viewed as lattices. (See, e.g., Fig. 2.) To prove this formally, it suffices by Lemmas 3 and 4 to demonstrate sufficiently short nonzero elements in the dual ideal $\mathfrak{q}^\vee$ of some ideal divisor $\mathfrak{q}$ of qR (possibly $\mathfrak{q} = R$ itself) whose algebraic norm $\mathrm{N}(\mathfrak{q})$ is not too large.

We stress that all these insecure instantiations—excepting [13], for which the following conclusions still apply—are for the "non-dual" version of Ring-LWE with spherical Gaussian errors relative to R (in the canonical embedding). By contrast, the definition of Ring-LWE from [16], and the instantiations having worst-case hardness, involve spherical errors relative to the *dual ideal* $R^\vee$ (see Sect. 2.2). When the insecure and hard instantiations are transformed to be directly comparable, the resulting error distributions turn out to have very different widths and shapes. We return to this point in Sect. 5, where we show that the hard instantiations are immune to the attacks from Sect. 3.

4.1   Rings $\mathbb{Z}[X]/(X^n + aX + b)$

The instantiations defined in [14] involve rings of the form $R = \mathbb{Z}[X]/(X^n + aX + b)$ for some nonnegative integers a, b, and spherical Gaussian error in the canonical embedding. The original attacks on these instantiations solved the *decision* problem for certain moduli q via (essentially) the distinguishing attack from Sect. 3.1, using 20 samples. Later work by [9] successfully attacked *search* for any modulus q by reduction to errorless LWE, obtaining a 100 % success probability using only 4–7 samples (depending on the instantiation). The analysis of [9] relied on the singular values of the embedded power basis elements, and the alignment of the singular vectors with those embedded powers. Here we use our simpler analysis in terms of the lengths of dual vectors, following the approach described in Sect. 3.1, to obtain the same conclusions; see Fig. 1.[4]

4.2   Prime Cyclotomics

Let the modulus q be a prime integer and let $R = \mathbb{Z}[\zeta_q]$ be the qth cyclotomic ring, where ζ_q denotes a primitive qth root of unity. It is well known (and easy to verify) that $qR = \mathfrak{q}^{q-1}$ and $qR^\vee = \mathfrak{q}$, where the ideal $\mathfrak{q} = (1 - \zeta_q)R + qR$ is prime and has norm $\mathrm{N}(\mathfrak{q}) = q$.

In [10, Sect. 6], the authors use (essentially) the approach from Sect. 3.1 to obtain distinguishing attacks that work in practice for the cases $q = 251, 503, 809,$

---

[4] A preliminary version of this work incorrectly concluded that for each instantiation, more than 90 % of the coordinates are errorless; this was due to a misinterpretation of the parameter w from [14, Sect. 9]. We thank an anonymous reviewer for pointing this out.

$f(X)$	r_0	r	threshold	num. short $\mathbf{d}_j$	samples
$X^{192} + 4092$	8.87	5,440	6.32×10^{-5}	29 (15.1 %)	7
$X^{256} + 8190$	8.35	8,390	4.01×10^{-5}	47 (18.3 %)	6
$X^{128} + 524288X + 524285$	8.00	45,540	7.79×10^{-6}	32 (25.0 %)	4

Fig. 1. Analysis of the instantiations from [14], for the power basis $B = (1, X, \ldots, X^{n-1})$ and its dual $D = (\mathbf{d}_j)$. "Threshold" denotes the value $(2r\sqrt{\log(4n)/\pi})^{-1}$ from Lemma 4 (for $\varepsilon = 1/(2n)$) for the lengths of the dual vectors $\mathbf{d}_j$, below which the jth error coefficient is zero with probability at least $1 - \varepsilon$. "Num. short $\mathbf{d}_j$" denotes the number (and percentage, out of n) of the dual vectors whose norms are below the threshold. "Samples" denotes the number of Ring-LWE samples that suffice to recover the secret via linear algebra on the errorless coefficients.

using $\mathfrak{q}$ as the ideal divisor of qR. Their experiments work for parameters

$$r \leq 1.53 \cdot \delta_R = 1.53\sqrt{q^{(q-2)/(q-1)}} < 1.53\sqrt{q}.$$

(Note that this corresponds to a volume-normalized parameter of $r_0 \leq 1.53$, which is considered quite small for LWE errors.) We remark that these distinguishing attacks are not known to translate to search, because no search-decision equivalence is known for this choice of parameters.

Our Analysis. The following lemma formally proves why the experiments work, and additionally implies that search can be solved via errorless LWE for slightly smaller parameters.

Lemma 5. *Let q, R, and $\mathfrak{q}$ be as above. Then $q^{-1} \cdot (1, \zeta_q, \ldots, \zeta_q^{q-2})$ is a $\mathbb{Z}$-basis of $\mathfrak{q}^\vee$, all of whose elements have length $\sqrt{q-1}/q$.*

Two immediate corollaries are that by Lemma 4, we can solve search by reducing to errorless LWE for, say, $r \leq \sqrt{q \cdot \pi/(4\log(4q))} = \Theta(\sqrt{q/\log q})$; and by Lemma 3 and the associated distinguisher, we can efficiently solve decision for any $r = O(\sqrt{q})$.

Proof. Because $qR^\vee = \mathfrak{q}$, the dual ideal of $\mathfrak{q}$ is $\mathfrak{q}^\vee = \mathfrak{q}^{-1}R^\vee = q^{-1}R$, for which $q^{-1} \cdot (1, \zeta_q, \ldots, \zeta_q^{q-2})$ is a $\mathbb{Z}$-basis. Because every complex embedding of ζ_q^j is a root of unity, we have $\|q^{-1} \cdot \zeta^j\| = \sqrt{q-1}/q$.

4.3 Quadratic Extensions of Cyclotomics

In [11], the authors consider non-dual Ring-LWE instantiations for certain quadratic extensions of cyclotomics, namely, $R = \mathbb{Z}[\zeta_p, \sqrt{d}]$ where ζ_p denotes a primitive pth root of unity for an odd prime p, and $d > 1$ is a square-free integer that is coprime to p, and is 3 modulo 4. They prove that for appropriate

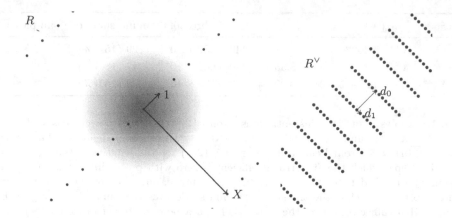

Fig. 2. On the left: the canonical embedding $\mathcal{L} = \sigma(R)$ of $R = \mathbb{Z}[\sqrt{d}]$ for $d = 31$, along with a continuous spherical Gaussian distribution of parameter $r = \sqrt{d}/2$, which corresponds to a volume normalized parameter of $r_0 := r/\det(\mathcal{L})^{1/2} = d^{1/4}/(2\sqrt{2})$. Observe that discretizing an error term to R using the power basis $P = (1, X)$ usually results in a coefficient of zero for X. On the right: the dual lattice $\mathcal{L}^\vee$ (corresponding to $R^\vee$), along with the dual basis $D = (d_0, d_1)$ of the power basis. Observe that d_1 is very short, which corresponds to the wide gap between integers multiples of X.

moduli, and for spherical Gaussian error of parameter $r \approx \sqrt{d}$, which corresponds to a volume-normalized parameter of $r_0 = r/\delta_R \approx d^{1/4}/\sqrt{p}$, one can efficiently solve search by combining a distinguishing attack with known search-decision equivalences for Galois rings. In addition, their distinguishing attacks work in practice up to larger parameters $r \approx \sqrt{p \cdot d}$ (corresponding to $r_0 \approx d^{1/4}$), though no formal analysis was provided to explain why.

Our Analysis. Here we prove that for the same class of rings, and for $r \approx \sqrt{p \cdot d/\log p}$ (i.e., $r_0 \approx d^{1/4}/\sqrt{\log p}$), we can solve search directly by reducing to errorless LWE, using the approach from Sect. 3.1. (As above, this works for any choice of modulus q.) Moreover, for any $r = O(\sqrt{p \cdot d})$ we can efficiently solve decision, and hence search, using the distinguishing attack from Sect. 3.1.

The basic reason why the attacks work on these instantiations is quite simple: $\mathbb{Z}[\sqrt{d}]$ has root discriminant $\approx d^{1/4}$, but its dual lattice has a very short vector of length $\approx 1/\sqrt{d}$. This means that error of parameter $r \approx \sqrt{d}$ (i.e., $r_0 \approx d^{1/4}$) is still so narrow relative to $\mathbb{Z}[\sqrt{d}]$ that discretizing yields a zero coefficient; see Fig. 2. The same goes for the compositum ring $\mathbb{Z}[\zeta_p, \sqrt{d}] \cong \mathbb{Z}[\zeta_p] \otimes \mathbb{Z}[\sqrt{d}]$, because $\mathbb{Z}[\zeta_p]$ has many dual elements whose lengths are essentially the inverse of the root discriminant.

Lemma 6. *For p and d as described above, let $B = (1, \zeta_p, \ldots, \zeta_p^{p-2}) \otimes (1, \sqrt{d})$, which is a $\mathbb{Z}$-basis of $R = \mathbb{Z}[\zeta_p, \sqrt{d}] \cong \mathbb{Z}[\zeta_p] \otimes \mathbb{Z}[\sqrt{d}]$. Then the dual basis $D = B^\vee$ has $p - 1$ elements of length $1/\sqrt{pd}$.*

Due to space restrictions, we defer the proof to the full version. An immediate corollary is that by Lemma 4, we can solve search via errorless LWE for, say, $r = \sqrt{p \cdot d} \cdot \pi/(4\log(8p))$. Because R has root discriminant

$$\delta_R = \delta_{\mathbb{Z}[\zeta_p]} \cdot \delta_{\mathbb{Z}[\sqrt{d}]} = \sqrt{p^{(p-2)/(p-1)} \cdot (4d)^{1/2}} \leq \sqrt{p} \cdot (4d)^{1/4},$$

this corresponds to a volume-normalized parameter $r_0 \geq (d \cdot \pi^2/64)^{1/4}/\sqrt{\log(8p)}$ $= \Theta(d^{1/4}/\sqrt{\log p})$. Another corollary is that by Lemma 3, we can solve decision for any $r = O(\sqrt{p \cdot d})$, which corresponds to $r_0 = O(d^{1/4})$.

p	d	r	r_0	$r' = 1.48\sqrt{pd}$	r_0'
31	4,967	148.5	2.38	580.7	9.30
43	4,871	168.1	2.27	677.3	9.14
61	4,643	189.8	2.15	787.6	8.94
83	4,903	222.0	2.12	944.1	8.99
103	4,951	244.4	2.08	1,056.9	8.98
109	4,919	249.6	2.06	1,083.7	8.95
151	100,447	1,296.2	4.26	5,763.9	18.94
181	100,267	1,400.0	4.20	6,304.9	18.89

Fig. 3. Instantiations of non-dual Ring-LWE for rings $R = \mathbb{Z}[\zeta_p, \sqrt{d}]$ where: (1) for spherical error of parameter $r = r_0 \cdot \delta_R$, search can be solved by reducing to errorless LWE, and (2) for spherical error of parameter $r' = r_0' \cdot \delta_R$, decision (and hence search) can be solved efficiently using the distinguishing attack. The constant factor 1.48 is chosen (somewhat arbitrarily) to ensure a Fourier coefficient of at least 10^{-3} in the distinguishing attack.

4.4   Subfields of Cyclotomics

In [10, Sect. 5], the authors consider non-dual Ring-LWE instantiations involving subfields K of cyclotomic fields $L = \mathbb{Q}(\zeta_m)$, namely, those that are fixed pointwise by the automorphisms in some subgroup of the Galois group of $L/\mathbb{Q}$. Letting $R = \mathcal{O}_K$ be the ring of integers in K, the instantiations involve spherical Gaussian error with volume-normalized parameter $r/\delta_R = r_0 = \sigma_0\sqrt{2\pi} < 3.14$ (which is considered somewhat small for LWE errors). The authors' distinguishing attacks work in practice, and they provide some heuristics as potential explanations, but no formal analysis.[5]

---

[5] We remark that the ring dimensions in these instantiations are all at most 144, which is small enough that search is reasonably easy to solve using standard basis-reduction techniques. Here we restrict our attention to the class of attacks from Sect. 3.

Our Analysis. For the sub-cyclotomic rings R considered in [10, Sect. 5], it turns out that the dual ideal $R^\vee$ contains many rather short nonzero elements, relative to the root discriminant δ_R. By Lemma 3, this implies an efficient distinguishing attack on non-dual Ring-LWE for narrow enough spherical Gaussians, which in particular includes the parameters studied in [10]. The attack works for any choice of the modulus q, at least for continuous error.

Due to space restrictions, we defer all the details to the full version.

5   Invulnerable Instantiations

In this section we give sufficient conditions that make a Ring-LWE instantiation *provably immune* to all the attacks described in Sect. 3. By "immune" we mean that the attacks perform no better than known attacks (e.g., [5,6]) against *plain* LWE when instantiated to have worst-case hardness, i.e., with Gaussian error of parameter $r \geq 2\sqrt{n}$. In particular, each attack's running time divided by its advantage is at least $2^{\Omega(n)}$, in the typical case of polynomially bounded modulus $q = \text{poly}(n)$.

We focus on instantiations that satisfy, or only "almost" satisfy, the hypotheses of the "worst-case hardness of search" theorem from [16, Sect. 4]. We show that any such instantiation, in *any* number field, satisfies the sufficient conditions, and is therefore immune to the attacks.

5.1   Class of Instantiations

Throughout the section, we consider instantiations of the "dual" Ring-LWE problem (Definition 3 and [16, Sect. 3]) for the ring of integers R in a number field K of degree n (over $\mathbb{Q}$), with a continuous, spherical Gaussian error distribution $\psi = D_r$ over $K_\mathbb{R}$ for some $r > 0$. Recall from Sect. 2.2 that in this form of Ring-LWE,

$$s \in R_q^\vee := R^\vee/qR^\vee \quad \text{and} \quad a \in R_q := R/qR,$$

so $s \cdot a \in R_q^\vee$, and we have "noisy" products $b = s \cdot a + e \in K_\mathbb{R}/qR^\vee$ where $e \leftarrow \psi$.

For showing invulnerability to attacks, using continuous rather than discrete error yields stronger results that immediately transfer to the discrete setting. This is because the attacker can always discretize continuous samples, and thereby the underlying error, on its own if it so desires.[6] We also note that all the results in this section apply (tautologically) to any equivalent form of Ring-LWE, e.g., the "tweaked" form that replaces $R^\vee$ with R. For illustration, we depict some of these forms later in the section.

---

[6] More precisely, this argument applies to any discretization $\lfloor \cdot \rceil \colon K_\mathbb{R} \to R^\vee$ for which $\lfloor z + e \rceil = z + \lfloor e \rceil$ for any $z \in R^\vee$ and $e \in K_\mathbb{R}$, which is the case for any standard method. See [17, Sect. 2.6] for further details.

Invulnerability condition. We will show that a sufficient condition for invulnerability to the attacks from Sect. 3 is

$$r \geq 2. \tag{2}$$

While at first glance this bound may appear very small, remember that it should be compared against the high "density" of $R^{\vee}$, and in this respect the error is actually quite well spread relative to $R^{\vee}$. This will become apparent in the analysis and figures below.

We remark that Condition (2) is actually a bit weaker than what is required by [16, Theorem 4.1] (worst-case hardness of search). Specifically, the theorem requires $r \geq 2 \cdot \omega(\sqrt{\log n})$, and moreover, it requires the search algorithm to work for *any* elliptical Gaussian error distribution whose parameter in each coordinate (of the canonical embedding) is bounded by r. These conditions may be artifacts of the proof technique, but in any case, they certainly require the attacker to succeed for spherical Gaussian error of some parameter $r \geq 2$, which is the case we study here.

5.2   Invulnerability to Attacks

Here we consider the two classes of attack described in Sect. 3.1: reducing to plain LWE, and reducing modulo an ideal divisor of qR. We prove that Condition (2) renders our class of instantiations invulnerable to both kinds of attack. Both analyses rely on the following standard fact about ideal lattices, which is an immediate consequence of the arithmetic mean-geometric mean inequality.

Lemma 7. *For any fractional ideal $\mathcal{I}$ in a number field K of degree n,*

$$\lambda_1(\mathcal{I}) \geq \sqrt{n} \cdot \mathrm{N}(\mathcal{I})^{1/n}.$$

Reduction to LWE. As described in Sect. 2.2, this attack simply converts each Ring-LWE sample to n plain-LWE samples, and attempts to solve the resulting LWE instance. We emphasize that the attacker may use *arbitrary* $\mathbb{Z}$-bases of R and $R^{\vee}$ to perform the transformation. More specifically, given each Ring-LWE sample

$$(a, b = s \cdot a + e) \in R_q \times K_{\mathbb{R}}/qR^{\vee}$$

where $e \leftarrow D_r$, we transform it to n LWE samples

$$(\mathbf{A}_a, \mathbf{b} = \mathbf{s}^t \mathbf{A}_a + \mathbf{e}^t),$$

where $\mathbf{b} \in (\mathbb{R}/q\mathbb{Z})^n$ and $\mathbf{e} \in \mathbb{R}^n$ are respectively the coefficient vectors of $b \in K_{\mathbb{R}}/qR^{\vee}$ and $e \in K_{\mathbb{R}}$ (with respect to the chosen basis of $R^{\vee}$), and $\mathbf{A}_a \in \mathbb{Z}_q^{n \times n}$ is the matrix of multiplication by $a \in R_q$ with any element of $R_q^{\vee}$ (with respect to the chosen bases of $R, R^{\vee}$).

The following shows that the entries of the resulting error vector $\mathbf{e}$ are Gaussians of parameter at least $2\sqrt{n}$, which is the exactly the lower bound from the worst-case hardness theorems for plain LWE [23, 25].

Theorem 1. *For any $\mathbb{Z}$-basis $B^\vee = (b_j^\vee)$ of $R^\vee$ used in the above reduction, each entry of $\mathbf{e}$ is a continuous Gaussian of parameter at least $r\sqrt{n} \geq 2\sqrt{n}$.*

Proof. Let $B = (b_j)_j = (B^\vee)^\vee$ be the ordered $\mathbb{Z}$-basis of R that is dual to $B^\vee$, i.e., $\sigma(B)^* = \sigma(B^\vee)^{-1}$. Because $\mathbf{e} \in \mathbb{R}^n$ is the coefficient vector of $e \in K_\mathbb{R}$ with respect to basis $B^\vee$, by definition we have

$$\mathbf{e} = \sigma(B^\vee)^{-1} \cdot \sigma(e) = \sigma(B)^* \cdot \sigma(e).$$

Now because $B \subseteq R$ is a $\mathbb{Z}$-basis of R, all its elements are nonzero, so $\|\sigma(b_j)\| \geq \sqrt{n}$ by Lemma 7. Because the jth row of $\sigma(B)^*$ is $\sigma(b_j)^*$, the jth entry of $\mathbf{e}$ is a continuous Gaussian of parameter $r\|\sigma(b_j)\| \geq r\sqrt{n} \geq 2\sqrt{n}$, as claimed.

We point out that while the Gaussian entries of $\mathbf{e}$ have large width, they are not necessarily *independent*. It follows from the above proof that $\mathbf{e}$ is distributed as a Gaussian with covariance matrix $r^2 \cdot \sigma(B)^* \cdot \sigma(B)/(2\pi)$. For example, when $B = (1, \zeta_p, \ldots, \zeta_p^{p-2})$ is the power basis of the pth cyclotomic for prime p, the covariance matrix of $\mathbf{e}$ is $r^2 \cdot (p\mathbf{I}_{p-1} - \mathbf{1})/(2\pi)$. Whether there are better attacks for this or other regimes that arise from reducing Ring-LWE to LWE is an interesting open question.

Reducing Modulo an Ideal. This attack uses an ideal divisor $\mathfrak{q}$ of qR to attempt to solve decision-Ring-LWE, analogously to the attack described in Sect. 3.1. More specifically, we are given independent samples $(a_i \in R_q, b_i \in K_\mathbb{R}/qR^\vee)$, which are distributed either uniformly or according to the Ring-LWE distribution with some secret $s \in R_q^\vee$. We first reduce the samples to

$$(a_i' = a_i \bmod \mathfrak{q}\,, \ b_i' = b_i \bmod \mathfrak{q}R^\vee) \in R/\mathfrak{q} \times K_\mathbb{R}/\mathfrak{q}R^\vee,$$

and for each of the $N(\mathfrak{q})$ candidate reduced secrets $s' \in R^\vee/\mathfrak{q}R^\vee$, we test whether the $b_i' - a_i' \cdot s' \in K_\mathbb{R}/\mathfrak{q}R^\vee$ are non-uniform. The exact implementation of this test is not important for our purposes, because we will show that no test can meaningfully succeed.

For the attack to work, the reduced error distribution $D_r \bmod \mathfrak{q}R^\vee$ needs to have noticeable statistical distance from uniform; otherwise, the $b_i' - a_i' \cdot s'$ are close to uniform regardless of the form of the original samples. However, the following theorem shows that for *any* ideal $\mathfrak{q}$ whose norm is not too large, and for error satisfying Condition (2), the statistical distance from uniform is exponentially small.

Theorem 2. *Let $\mathfrak{q} \subseteq R$ be any ideal of norm $N(\mathfrak{q}) \leq 2^n$, and let the error parameter $r \geq 2$ satisfy Condition (2). Then the reduced error distribution $D_r \bmod \mathfrak{q}R^\vee$ is within statistical distance 2^{-2n} of uniform over $K_\mathbb{R}/\mathfrak{q}R^\vee$.*

Proof. The dual ideal of $\mathfrak{q}R^\vee$ is $(\mathfrak{q}R^\vee)^\vee = \mathfrak{q}^{-1}$, which has norm $N(\mathfrak{q}^{-1}) = N(\mathfrak{q})^{-1} \geq 2^{-n}$. By Lemma 7, its minimum distance is

$$\lambda_1(\mathfrak{q}^{-1}) \geq \sqrt{n} \cdot N(\mathfrak{q}^{-1})^{1/n} \geq \sqrt{n}/2.$$

Then by Lemma 1, the smoothing parameter of $\mathfrak{q}R^\vee$ for $\varepsilon = 2^{-2n}$ is $\eta_\varepsilon(\mathfrak{q}R^\vee) \leq \sqrt{n}/\lambda_1(\mathfrak{q}^{-1}) \leq 2 \leq r$. The theorem then follows by Lemma 2.

In the full version, we study some example invulnerable instantiations in detail, and directly contrast them with related insecure instantiations that were studied in Sect. 4, by "tweaking" the dual form to an equivalent non-dual form. In all cases, the error distributions of the invulnerable instantiations are wider by $\Omega(\sqrt{p})$ to $\Omega(p^{3/2})$ factors in each coordinate of the canonical embedding (where p is the index of the cyclotomic used in the instantiation), and also have very different non-spherical shapes.

Acknowledgments. I thank Léo Ducas, Kristin Lauter, Vadim Lyubashevsky, Oded Regev, and Katherine Stange for many valuable discussions and comments on topics related to this work. I also thank the anonymous reviewers for helpful comments, and especially for pointing out a misinterpretation of the parameters in [14, Sect. 9].

References

1. Aggarwal, D., Dadush, D., Regev, O., Stephens-Davidowitz, N.: Solving the shortest vector problem in 2^n time using discrete Gaussian sampling. In: STOC, pp. 733–742 (2015)
2. Ajtai, M., Kumar, R., Sivakumar, D.: A sieve algorithm for the shortest lattice vector problem. In: STOC, pp. 601–610 (2001)
3. Alkim, E., Ducas, L., Pöppelmann, T., Schwabe, P.: Post-quantum key exchange - a new hope. In: USENIX Security Symposium (2016, to appear)
4. Alperin-Sheriff, J., Peikert, C.: Practical bootstrapping in quasilinear time. In: Canetti, R., Garay, J.A. (eds.) CRYPTO 2013, Part I. LNCS, vol. 8042, pp. 1–20. Springer, Heidelberg (2013)
5. Arora, S., Ge, R.: New algorithms for learning in presence of errors. In: Aceto, L., Henzinger, M., Sgall, J. (eds.) ICALP 2011, Part I. LNCS, vol. 6755, pp. 403–415. Springer, Heidelberg (2011)
6. Blum, A., Kalai, A., Wasserman, H.: Noise-tolerant learning, the parity problem, and the statistical query model. J. ACM **50**(4), 506–519 (2003)
7. Bos, J.W., Costello, C., Naehrig, M., Stebila, D.: Post-quantum key exchange for the TLS protocol from the ring learning with errors problem. In: IEEE Symposium on Security and Privacy, pp. 553–570 (2015)
8. Brakerski, Z., Langlois, A., Peikert, C., Regev, O., Stehlé, D.: Classical hardness of learning with errors. In: STOC, pp. 575–584 (2013)
9. Castryck, W., Iliashenko, I., Vercauteren, F.: Provably weak instances of Ring-LWE revisited. In: Fischlin, M., Coron, J.-S. (eds.) EUROCRYPT 2016. LNCS, vol. 9665, pp. 147–167. Springer, Heidelberg (2016). doi:10.1007/978-3-662-49890-3_6
10. Chen, H., Lauter, K., Stange, K.E.: Attacks on search RLWE. Cryptology ePrint Archive, Report 2015/971 (2015). http://eprint.iacr.org/
11. Chen, H., Lauter, K., Stange, K.E.: Vulnerable galois RLWE families and improved attacks. Cryptology ePrint Archive, Report 2016/193 (2016). http://eprint.iacr.org/
12. Crockett, E., Peikert, C.: Λ∘λ: a functional library for lattice cryptography. Cryptology ePrint Archive, Report 2015/1134 (2015). http://eprint.iacr.org/
13. Eisenträger, K., Hallgren, S., Lauter, K.: Weak instances of PLWE. In: Joux, A., Youssef, A. (eds.) SAC 2014. LNCS, vol. 8781, pp. 183–194. Springer, Heidelberg (2014)

14. Elias, Y., Lauter, K.E., Ozman, E., Stange, K.E.: Provably weak instances of Ring-LWE. In: Gennaro, R., Robshaw, M. (eds.) Advances in Cryptology – CRYPTO 2015. LNCS, vol. 9215, pp. 63–92. Springer, Heidelberg (2015)
15. Lindner, R., Peikert, C.: Better key sizes (and attacks) for LWE-based encryption. In: Kiayias, A. (ed.) CT-RSA 2011. LNCS, vol. 6558, pp. 319–339. Springer, Heidelberg (2011)
16. Lyubashevsky, V., Peikert, C., Regev, O.: On ideal lattices and learning with errors over rings. J. ACM **60**(6), 43:1–43:35 (2013). Preliminary version in Eurocrypt 2010
17. Lyubashevsky, V., Peikert, C., Regev, O.: A toolkit for Ring-LWE cryptography. In: Johansson, T., Nguyen, P.Q. (eds.) EUROCRYPT 2013. LNCS, vol. 7881, pp. 35–54. Springer, Heidelberg (2013)
18. Micciancio, D., Mol, P.: Pseudorandom knapsacks and the sample complexity of LWE search-to-decision reductions. In: Rogaway, P. (ed.) CRYPTO 2011. LNCS, vol. 6841, pp. 465–484. Springer, Heidelberg (2011)
19. Micciancio, D., Peikert, C.: Trapdoors for lattices: simpler, tighter, faster, smaller. In: Pointcheval, D., Johansson, T. (eds.) EUROCRYPT 2012. LNCS, vol. 7237, pp. 700–718. Springer, Heidelberg (2012)
20. Micciancio, D., Regev, O.: Worst-case to average-case reductions based on Gaussian measures. SIAM J. Comput. **37**(1), 267–302 (2007). Preliminary version in FOCS 2004
21. Micciancio, D., Regev, O.: Lattice-based cryptography. Post Quantum Cryptography, pp. 147–191. Springer, Heidelberg (2009)
22. Micciancio, D., Voulgaris, P.: A deterministic single exponential time algorithm for most lattice problems based on Voronoi cell computations. In: STOC, pp. 351–358 (2010)
23. Peikert, C.: Public-key cryptosystems from the worst-case shortest vector problem. In: STOC, pp. 333–342 (2009)
24. Peikert, C.: Lattice cryptography for the internet. In: Mosca, M. (ed.) PQCrypto 2014. LNCS, vol. 8772, pp. 197–219. Springer, Heidelberg (2014)
25. Regev, O.: On lattices, learning with errors, random linear codes, and cryptography. J. ACM **56**(6), 1–40 (2009). Preliminary version in STOC 2005

Pen and Paper Arguments for SIMON and SIMON-like Designs

Christof Beierle[($\boxtimes$)]

Horst Görtz Institute for IT Security, Ruhr-Universität Bochum, Bochum, Germany
christof.beierle@rub.de

Abstract. In this work, we analyze the resistance of SIMON-like ciphers against differential attacks without using computer-aided methods. In this context, we first define the notion of a SIMON-like cipher as a generalization of the SIMON design. For certain instances, we present a method for proving the resistance against differential attacks by upper bounding the probability of a differential characteristic by 2^{-2T+2} where T denotes the number of rounds. Interestingly, if $2n$ denotes the block length, our result is sufficient in order to bound the probability by 2^{-2n} for all full-round variants of SIMON and SIMECK. Thus, it guarantees security in a sense that, even having encryptions of the full codebook, one cannot expect a differential characteristic to hold. The important difference between previous works is that our proof can be verified by hand and thus contributes towards a better understanding of the design. However, it is to mention that we do not analyze the probability of multi-round differentials.

Although there are much better bounds known, especially for a high number of rounds, they are based on experimental search like using SAT/SMT solvers. While those results have already shown that SIMON can be considered resistant against differential cryptanalysis, our argument gives more insights into the design itself. As far as we know, this work presents the first non-experimental security argument for full-round versions of several SIMON-like instances.

Keywords: SIMON · SIMECK · Differential cryptanalysis · Feistel

1 Introduction

Once a new cipher is proposed, the designers are expected to provide security arguments, at least against the most important and powerful attack vectors known, that are differential [12] and linear cryptanalysis [22]. Thus, any new design itself should allow for an, if possible simple, security argument. Nowadays, a majority of block ciphers is based on Feistel- and Substitution-Permutation (SP) constructions. As the name already implies, SP designs iterate both substitution and permutation operations. While the latter is a linear function (linear layer), the substitution layer consists of highly non-linear components (e.g. S-boxes). The alternation of those layers is responsible for both offering confusion and diffusion [26].

© Springer International Publishing Switzerland 2016
V. Zikas and R. De Prisco (Eds.): SCN 2016, LNCS 9841, pp. 431–446, 2016.
DOI: 10.1007/978-3-319-44618-9_23

This separation into linear and non-linear components offers the advantage of analyzing the structure more easily. Two design principles are common, that are the wide-trail strategy [16] and the use of computer-aided methods. In the wide-trail strategy, which was introduced by Daemen and Rijmen, the idea is that the design of the linear layer is related to coding theory, as its construction is based upon a linear code over $GF(2^m)$ with high (and often optimal) minimum distance. Thereby, the parameter m defines the word size of the S-box. As the minimum distance indicates the number of active S-boxes over two consecutive rounds, it contributes to the resistance against differential and linear cryptanalysis in a provable (by pen and paper) way. A more clever choice of the linear layer even allows for arguments on four (resp. eight, sixteen,...) rounds using the so-called superbox (resp. megabox, gigabox, etc.) structure, as for example described in [8,9,17]. In fact, the Rijndael cipher [18], which was standardized as the Advanced Encryption Standard in 2000 [25], was designed according to this principle. The advantage of the wide-trail strategy is one reason why so many AES-like designs occurred in the last years. It also emphasizes that designers prefer well-understood principles. While for AES-like ciphers counting the number of active S-boxes can be somehow done independently of the choice of the S-box, some other strategies use specific properties of the non-linear components. For instance, the designers of PRESENT showed that an arbitrary five-round differential characteristic has at least 10 active S-boxes under certain assumptions [14].

The other strategy is measuring the security using computer-aided search methods. For instance, one can model the propagation of differential and linear characteristics as a mixed-integer linear programming problem [8,23,29]. Examples of a design which uses experimental arguments are KECCAK [10] and SERPENT [11]. However, the bounds obtained with this approach are not verifiable without a machine and do not contribute significantly to a better understanding of the design itself.

Basically, in both strategies, (if the non-linear component is not too weak) the design of the linear layer is the crucial step when it comes to providing security against differential and linear attacks. While a single round can often be analyzed quite easily, the analysis of the linear layer w.r.t. diffusion properties usually has to be done using a more complex argument over multiple rounds. Unfortunately, besides the wide-trail strategy, not many constructions are known that guarantee security using pen and paper arguments. Especially, almost every multi-round argument uses some sort of superbox (resp. megabox, etc.) structure. One therefore may seek for alternative design principles. Especially for lots of Feistel designs, the constructions might be less clear and less understood. However, there are some fundamental results on bounding the differential and linear behavior [24]. There are also Feistel designs which consist of SP-type round functions [27,28] combining the advantages of the Feistel construction and the simple arguments of the wide-trail strategy.

In contrast to a scientific design process, the NSA recently presented the SIMON family of lightweight block ciphers [6]. Besides its specification, no arguments on the security are provided. Especially since SIMON is an innovative

Feistel cipher, its design is harder to analyze. Besides its non-bijective round function and combining the branches after every round, the difficulties are caused by the bitwise structure. Since the design choice was left unclear, one seeks for a deeper understanding of the cipher.[1]

Related Work. The appearance of the SIMON family of block ciphers [6] in the cryptology eprint archive inspired the cryptographic community taking further investigations on the possible design rationale. Therefore, several cryptanalytic results followed. For instance, see [1–5,13,15,21,30–32] for a selection. They are mostly based on experimental search.

At CRYPTO 2015, Kölbl, Leander and Tiessen pointed out some interesting properties of SIMON-like round functions [20]. These observations were then used for a further analysis of the differential and linear behavior over multiple rounds. Although the analysis of the round function was done in a mathematical rigorous manner, the multi-round behavior was derived using a computer-aided approach. As one result, the rotation constants of SIMON turned out to be in some sense not optimally chosen. Inspired by the design, Yang et. al. proposed the SIMECK family of lightweight block ciphers at CHES 2015 [33]. It can be seen as a SIMON-like cipher using different rotation constants in its round function and a key schedule inspired by SPECK [6].

Recently, the designers of SIMON published a follow-up paper at the NIST lightweight workshop covering some implementation aspects [7]. However, the authors gave no additional insights into the design choice from a cryptanalytic point of view.

Contribution. After describing a generalization of the SIMON design by decoupling the round function into a linear and a non-linear component, we show that the structure of a SIMON-like design allows for a proof on the resistance against differential attacks under certain assumptions. The question whether the proof works depends on the interaction between these two components. If the non-linear part ρ is of the form $\rho(\mathbf{x}) = (\mathbf{x} \lll a) \wedge (\mathbf{x} \lll b)$, it can be in general formulated as a property of the linear layer. A sufficient condition is that the linear layer has a branch number of at least 11. Since this is not the case for SIMON and SIMECK, we consider these ciphers separately. In particular, for all instantiations of SIMON and SIMECK, we are able to upper bound the probability of any differential characteristic by 2^{-2n} where $2n$ denotes the block length. We show this in detail for the example of SIMON.

In clear distinction to prior work such as [20], our argument is a formal proof covering multiple rounds and can thus be verified without experimental tools. In our approach, we use the well-known property of the SIMON-like round

---

[1] As we only focus on the probabilities of differential characteristics and do not provide a full security analysis, this work should not be seen as a recommendation for using SIMON. Some design choices are still unclear. To mention is the key schedule as one example.

function that the set of possible output differences U_α defines an affine subspace depending on the input difference α and that the differential probability highly depends on the Hamming weight of α. The main idea is that we extend the analysis of the round function to the cases where α has a Hamming weight equal to 2 and consider the propagation of Hamming weights over the Feistel structure.

Figure 1 illustrates the bounds proven with our method and, as a comparison, the bounds obtained from experimental search described in [20, Sect. 5.2] for two instances of SIMON. It is to mention that, although our bounds are worse than the experimental results, they are still much better than the bounds one obtains by trivially multiplying the worst-case probabilities for every round. Moreover, since the development of the experimental bounds becomes more complex for a high number of rounds, we believe that one cannot expect to significantly improve upon our theoretical result by using a simple argument. Such an argument will likely cover lots of rounds.

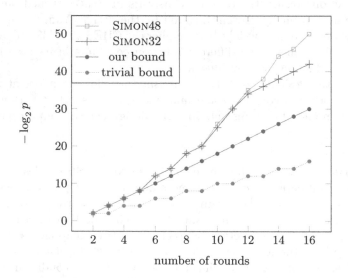

Fig. 1. Comparison of the experimental bounds for SIMON32 and SIMON48 as described in [20, Sect. 5.2] and our provable bounds.

2   Preliminaries

Elements in the vector space $\mathbb{F}_2^n$ are denoted with bold letters. The all zero vector will be denoted by $\mathbf{0}$ and the all one vector by $\mathbf{1}$, respectively. We use $\mathrm{wt}(\mathbf{x})$ to denote the Hamming weight of a vector $\mathbf{x} = (x_0, x_1, \ldots, x_{n-1})$. Moreover, a superscript notation is used for describing the index of a component. For example, the element $(0, \ldots, 0, y^{(i)}, 0, 0, \ldots, 0)$ denotes the vector $(x_0, x_1, \ldots, x_{n-1})$ with $x_i = y$ and $x_k = 0$ for all $k \neq i$. The Boolean operations, bitwise AND,

OR, NOT and bitwise XOR, are denoted by $\wedge, \vee, {}^{-}$ and $\oplus$, respectively. A cyclic rotation (with offset r) is denoted by $\lll r$, if the rotation is to the left, and by $\ggg r$, if the rotation is to the right.

Differential Cryptanalysis. In the following, we recall the basic definitions in differential cryptanalysis. We use the notion of XOR differences in this context.

Definition 1. *For a vectorial function $f : \mathbb{F}_2^n \to \mathbb{F}_2^m$, the probability of the differential $\boldsymbol{\alpha} \xrightarrow{f} \boldsymbol{\beta}$ is defined as*

$$P(\boldsymbol{\alpha} \xrightarrow{f} \boldsymbol{\beta}) := \frac{|\Delta_f(\boldsymbol{\alpha}, \boldsymbol{\beta})|}{2^n}$$

where

$$\Delta_f(\boldsymbol{\alpha}, \boldsymbol{\beta}) := \{\mathbf{x} \in \mathbb{F}_2^n \mid \boldsymbol{\beta} = f(\mathbf{x}) \oplus f(\mathbf{x} \oplus \boldsymbol{\alpha})\}.$$

If f_i denotes the i-th round function of an iterated cipher, a *valid T-round differential characteristic* $C : \boldsymbol{\alpha_0} \xrightarrow{f_1} \boldsymbol{\alpha_1} \xrightarrow{f_2} \ldots \xrightarrow{f_T} \boldsymbol{\alpha_T}$ has $|\Delta_{f_i}(\boldsymbol{\alpha_{i-1}}, \boldsymbol{\alpha_i})| \neq 0$ for all $1 \leq i \leq T$. Assuming that the probabilities of all one-round differentials are independent, we compute the probability of the characteristic C as

$$P(C) = \prod_{i=1}^{T} P(\boldsymbol{\alpha_{i-1}} \xrightarrow{f_i} \boldsymbol{\alpha_i}).$$

Note that for a key-alternating cipher, this holds under the assumption of independent round-keys. When designing a block cipher, one would like to avoid the existence of (multi-round) differentials with high probability. Since in general, computing the maximum probability of multi-round differentials is not a trivial task, one concentrates on upper bounding the probability of a characteristic instead. If n denotes the block length, a typical approach is to estimate the number of rounds T' such that $P(C) \leq 2^{-n}$ for any T'-round characteristic C and specify the number of rounds of the primitive as $T = T' + \kappa$ with a reasonable security margin κ.

A Remark on the Feistel Construction. We point out a useful property of the Feistel construction in the following. Recall that for a vectorial function $f : \mathbb{F}_2^n \to \mathbb{F}_2^n$ and $\mathbf{k} \in \mathbb{F}_2^n$, we define a *Feistel round function* as

$$F_{\mathbf{k}}^f : \mathbb{F}_2^n \times \mathbb{F}_2^n \to \mathbb{F}_2^n \times \mathbb{F}_2^n$$
$$(\mathbf{x}, \mathbf{y}) \mapsto (f(\mathbf{x}) \oplus \mathbf{y} \oplus \mathbf{k}, \mathbf{x}).$$

Thereby, f is called the *Feistel function* (or simply *f-function*) and $\mathbf{k}$ is called the *round key*. For simplicity, we will use an identical Feistel function f in every round.

A difference within the Feistel cipher is denoted as $(\boldsymbol{\gamma}, \boldsymbol{\delta})$ describing the left and the right branch, respectively. Lemma 1 presents a general observation on the Feistel construction. It states that, having upper bounds on the probability for all differential characteristics starting with $(0, \alpha)$ and ending with $(0, \beta)$, one can easily bound the probability of any characteristic.

Lemma 1. *For $t \geq 1$, let for all non-zero differences α, β, the differential probability of any t-round characteristic starting with $(0, \alpha)$ and ending with $(0, \beta)$ be upper bounded by $p(t)$.*

Let further $p(0) := 1$ and $q := \max_{\alpha \neq 0, \beta} P(\alpha \xrightarrow{f} \beta)$. Then,

$$P(C) \leq \max_{k \leq T} p(k) q^{T-k-1}$$

for any non-trivial T-round characteristics C with $T > 0$.

Proof. For a given T-round characteristic $C = (\gamma_0, \delta_0) \xrightarrow{F^f} \ldots \xrightarrow{F^f} (\gamma_T, \delta_T)$, it holds that $P(C) = \prod_{i=0}^{T-1} P(\gamma_i \xrightarrow{f} \gamma_{i+1})$ assuming independent probabilities. The proof is now split into two cases.

(i) Let's assume that there exist distinct i, j such that $\gamma_i = \gamma_j = 0$. Then one can choose w.l.o.g two distinct indices i', j' such that $\gamma_{i'} = \gamma_{j'} = 0$ and $\gamma_k \neq 0$ for all $k < i'$ and all $k > j'$. Now, by definition

$$P((\gamma_{i'}, \delta_{i'}) \xrightarrow{F^f} \ldots \xrightarrow{F^f} (\gamma_{j'}, \delta_{j'})) \leq p(j' - i').$$

Since $\gamma_{j'} = 0$ and all other $\gamma_k \neq 0$, we have

$$P(C) \leq p(j' - i') \prod_{k=0}^{i'-1} P(\gamma_k \xrightarrow{f} \gamma_{k+1}) \prod_{k=j'+1}^{T-1} P(\gamma_k \xrightarrow{f} \gamma_{k+1})$$

$$\leq p(j' - i') q^{i'} q^{T-(j'+1)} = p(j' - i') q^{T-(j'-i')-1}.$$

(ii) If $\gamma_i = 0$ for at most one i, then

$$\prod_{k<T} P(\gamma_k \xrightarrow{f} \gamma_{k+1}) \leq \prod_{k \neq i} P(\gamma_k \xrightarrow{f} \gamma_{k+1}) \leq q^{T-1} = p(0) q^{T-1}. \qquad \square$$

As Lemma 1 is a general statement for all Feistel ciphers, we give a simplified version in Sect. 3 as Corollary 1. It covers the special case of a SIMON-like round function, which will be defined next.

SIMON and SIMON-like Ciphers. We generalize the design of the SIMON block cipher to the SIMON-like structure. Figure 2 illustrates this construction. For the SIMON-like design, one requires a quadratic, rotational invariant function as the non-linear component. A vectorial function $f : \mathbb{F}_2^n \to \mathbb{F}_2^n$ is called *rotational invariant* iff $f(\mathbf{x} \lll r) = (f(\mathbf{x}) \lll r)$ for all elements $\mathbf{x} \in \mathbb{F}_2^n$ and all offsets r. This leads to the following definition.

Definition 2. *A* SIMON-*like f-function is composed of an* $\mathbb{F}_2$-*linear function* θ *and a degree-2 function* ρ *of the form* $\rho(\mathbf{x}) = \vartheta_1(\mathbf{x}) \wedge \vartheta_2(\mathbf{x})$ *with* $\mathbb{F}_2$-*linear and rotational invariant* ϑ_i *as*

$$f_S : \mathbb{F}_2^n \to \mathbb{F}_2^n, \mathbf{x} \mapsto \rho(\mathbf{x}) \oplus \theta(\mathbf{x}).$$

In this context, a SIMON-*like cipher uses such an f-function in a Feistel construction.*

Note that the rotational invariance is, in this general case, not required for the linear part θ.

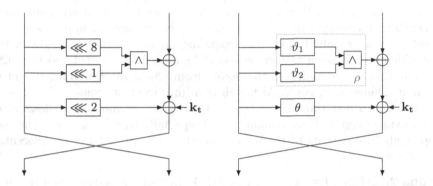

Fig. 2. Illustration of the SIMON and the generalized SIMON-like round function

3   Analysis of Differential Characteristics

In this section, we analyze the propagation characteristics of differences over several rounds under certain assumptions. We rely on the fact that a single SIMON-like round is quite well understood. Let

$$L_\alpha(\mathbf{x}) := (\vartheta_1(\mathbf{x}) \wedge \vartheta_2(\boldsymbol{\alpha})) \oplus (\vartheta_1(\boldsymbol{\alpha}) \wedge \vartheta_2(\mathbf{x})).$$

We first recall the observation that for any input difference $\boldsymbol{\alpha} \in \mathbb{F}_2^n$ into a SIMON-like round function f_S, the output difference lies in the affine subspace $U_\alpha := \operatorname{Im} L_\alpha + f_S(\boldsymbol{\alpha})$. This is formally stated in Theorem 1.

Theorem 1. (Kölbl, Leander, Tiessen [20]). *For an input difference* $\boldsymbol{\alpha} \in \mathbb{F}_2^n$ *into* f_S*, the set of possible output differences defines an affine subspace* U_α *s.t.* $P(\boldsymbol{\alpha} \xrightarrow{f_S} \boldsymbol{\beta}) \neq 0$ *if and only if* $\boldsymbol{\beta} \in U_\alpha$*. Defining* $d_\alpha := \dim \operatorname{Im} L_\alpha$ *it holds*

$$\boldsymbol{\beta} \in U_\alpha \Leftrightarrow \boldsymbol{\beta} \oplus f_S(\boldsymbol{\alpha}) \in \operatorname{Im} L_\alpha$$

and $P(\boldsymbol{\alpha} \xrightarrow{f_S} \boldsymbol{\beta}) = 2^{-d_\alpha}$ *for all valid differentials over* f_S*.*

Since the probability is the same for all output differences β in this subspace, we simply write p_α for $P(\alpha \xrightarrow{f_S} \beta)$ with $\beta \in U_\alpha$. For all output differences which are not elements in this subspace, the probability will be zero.

Because of the rotational invariance, it holds that $\operatorname{Im} L_{(\alpha \lll r)} = (\operatorname{Im} L_\alpha \lll r)$ with $p_{(\alpha \lll r)} = p_\alpha$. One can thus restrict the consideration to a single representative of this equivalence class if only one round function is analyzed.

3.1   Restriction to $\vartheta_1(x) = (x \lll A)$ and $\vartheta_2(x) = (x \lll B)$

This describes the most simple structure of a generalized SIMON-like cipher. For the θ step defined as $\theta(\mathbf{x}) = (\mathbf{x} \lll c)$, one obtains SIMON and SIMECK as a special case using $(8, 1, 2)$, resp. $(5, 0, 1)$, as a choice for the rotation constants (a, b, c). The following lemma states that we can obtain an upper bound on the differential probability over f_S depending on the Hamming weight of the input difference. While a weaker version of Lemma 2 can be deduced from [20, Theorem 3, p. 9], we improved the bound from [20] if the Hamming weight of the input difference equals 2. Although this improvement seems to be of little importance at a first glance, it is exactly this tighter bound which allows us to prove the main result. Thus, Lemma 2, and especially case (2), is one of the core components in our proof of the upper bound on the probability of differential characteristics.

Lemma 2. *Let $\vartheta_1(x) = (x \lll a)$ and $\vartheta_2(x) = (x \lll b)$. Assume that $n \geq 6$ is even and $\gcd(a - b, n) = 1$. Let α be an input difference into f_S. Then, for the differential probability over f_S it holds that*

(1) If $\operatorname{wt}(\alpha) = 1$, then $p_\alpha \leq 2^{-2}$.
(2) If $\operatorname{wt}(\alpha) = 2$, then $p_\alpha \leq 2^{-3}$.
(3) If $\operatorname{wt}(\alpha) \neq n$, then $p_\alpha \leq 2^{-\operatorname{wt}(\alpha)}$.
(4) If $\operatorname{wt}(\alpha) = n$, then $p_\alpha \leq 2^{-n+1}$.

Proof. Without loss of generality one can assume that $b = 0$ and $a < \frac{n}{2}, a \neq 0$ because of the rotational invariance and since $a - b$ and n are coprime. According to [20, Theorem 3, p. 9], it is $p_\alpha = 2^{-d_\alpha}$ with

$$d_\alpha = \begin{cases} \operatorname{wt}\left((((\alpha \lll a) \vee \alpha) \oplus (\alpha \wedge \overline{(\alpha \lll a)} \wedge (\alpha \lll 2a)))\right) & \text{iff } \operatorname{wt}(\alpha) \neq n \\ n - 1 & \text{iff } \operatorname{wt}(\alpha) = n \end{cases}.$$

Note that $d_\alpha = \dim \operatorname{Im} L_\alpha$ where

$$L_\alpha(\mathbf{x}) = ((\mathbf{x} \lll a) \wedge \alpha) \oplus ((\alpha \lll a) \wedge \mathbf{x}).$$

$(1), (3)$ and (4) follow directly from the above formula. In order to show (2), we construct three linearly independent elements in $\operatorname{Im} L_\alpha$.

Let $\operatorname{wt}(\alpha) = 2$ with $\alpha_0 = \alpha_i = 1$. Again, w.l.o.g. let $i \leq \frac{n}{2}, i \neq 0$ since every α with a Hamming weight of two is rotational equivalent to that one assumed.

Now, consider the following three elements $\mathbf{x}, \mathbf{y}, \mathbf{z}$:

$$\mathbf{x} = (0, \ldots, 0, 1^{(a)}, 0, \ldots, 0) \quad \Rightarrow L_\alpha(\mathbf{x}) = (1^{(0)}, 0, \ldots, 0, \alpha_{2a}^{(a)}, 0, \ldots, 0)$$

$$\mathbf{y} = (0, \ldots, 0, 1^{(a+i)}, 0, \ldots, 0) \quad \Rightarrow L_\alpha(\mathbf{y}) = (0, \ldots, 1^{(i)}, 0, \ldots, 0, \alpha_{i+2a}^{(i+a)}, 0, \ldots, 0)$$

$$\mathbf{z} = 1 \quad \Rightarrow L_\alpha(\mathbf{z}) = (\alpha \lll a) \oplus \alpha$$

Clearly, $L_\alpha(\mathbf{x})$ and $L_\alpha(\mathbf{y})$ are linearly independent. To show that $L_\alpha(\mathbf{z}) \notin \text{span}\{L_\alpha(\mathbf{x}), L_\alpha(\mathbf{y})\}$, consider the two cases

(i) $\alpha_{i+2a} = 0$: Then $L_\alpha(\mathbf{y})_{i+a} = 0$. Since $L_\alpha(\mathbf{z})_{n-a} = 1$ and $n - a \notin \{0, i, a\}$, the linear independence follows.

(ii) $\alpha_{i+2a} = 1$: Then $i + 2a \mod n \in \{0, i\}$ because of the construction of α. However, since $2a \neq 0 \mod n$, it follows that $i + 2a = 0 \mod n$. Hence, $2a = n - i$. Now $2a \neq i$, because otherwise $n = 4a$ which is contradictory to $\gcd(a, n) = 1$ (since $n \geq 6$). Thus $L_\alpha(\mathbf{x})_a = 0$. In addition, $i \neq a$ because otherwise $3a = 0 \mod n$ which is also contradictory to $\gcd(a, n) = 1$. Now, $L_\alpha(\mathbf{z})_{i-a \mod n} = 1$ and $i - a \notin \{0, i, i + a\}$. $\qquad\square$

In all cases, we thus have $p_\alpha \leq 2^{-2}$ if $\alpha \neq 0$ and $p_0 = 1$. The interesting property is the fact that $p_\alpha \leq 2^{-\text{wt}(\alpha)-1}$ if α has a Hamming weight of 2. This is what we make use of in the following arguments. The basic idea is to guarantee enough transitions with a probability $\leq 2^{-3}$ before a zero input difference into f_S occurs (then $p_0 = 1$). This allows us to catch up the factor 2^{-2} that we lose for the zero input difference. Otherwise, if we were not able to guarantee the tighter bound described in Lemma 2 (2), the input difference into f_S of every second round might be equal to zero in the worst case and our argument would only provide the trivial bound of 2^{-T} over T rounds. See also Fig. 1 for an illustration. For the formal proof, we give Corollary 1 at first. It is an implication of Lemma 1 for the SIMON-like f function.

Corollary 1. *Let for all non-zero differences α, β and all $t \geq 1$ the differential probability of any t-round characteristic starting with $(0, \alpha)$ and ending with $(0, \beta)$ be upper bounded by 2^{-2t}. Let further $p_\alpha \leq 2^{-2}$. Then,*

$$P(C) \leq 2^{-2T+2}$$

for any non-trivial T-round characteristics C with $T > 0$.

Proof. With the notation in Lemma 1, it is $p(t) = 2^{-2t}$ and $q = 2^{-2}$. Thus,

$$P(C) \leq \max_{k \leq T} p(k) q^{T-k-1} = \max_{k \leq T} 2^{-2k} 2^{-2T+2k+2} = 2^{-2T+2}. \qquad\square$$

Thus, in order to prove an upper bound on the probability of a differential characteristic of 2^{-2T+2} we only have to concentrate on t-round characteristics of the form $(0, \alpha) \to \cdots \to (0, \beta)$ and prove an upper bound of 2^{-2t} for all of these. We further can restrict ourselves to the shortest characteristics of this form, e.g. $\gamma_i \neq 0$ for all intermediate γ_i. The reason is that one can easily concatenate these short characteristics to longer ones for which the property holds as well.

We have to do the analysis for a specific choice of the linear mapping θ. As a more general case, Theorem 2 formulates a sufficient condition for the argument to work. For a linear mapping $\theta : \mathbb{F}_2^n \to \mathbb{F}_2^n$, the *differential branch number* is defined as the minimum number of active bits in the differential $(\alpha \xrightarrow{\theta} \theta(\alpha))$, formally

$$\mathcal{B}_\theta := \min_{\alpha \neq 0} \{ \mathrm{wt}(\alpha) + \mathrm{wt}(\theta(\alpha)) \}.$$

Theorem 2. *Let $\mathcal{B}_\theta \geq 11$. Then for any distinct a, b and any n fulfilling the properties of Lemma 2, the probability of a T-round differential characteristic is upper bounded by 2^{-2T+2}.*

Proof. Fix a t-round characteristic of the form

$$(0, \alpha) \to (\gamma_1 = \alpha, 0) \to (\gamma_2, \delta_2) \to \cdots \to (\gamma_{t-1}, \delta_{t-1}) \to (0, \beta)$$

with $\gamma_i \neq 0$ for all $i \in \{1, \ldots, t-1\}$. Thus, we have $p_{\gamma_i} \leq 2^{-2}$ for all i. Since $\gamma_1 = \alpha$ and $(0, \alpha) \xrightarrow{1} (\alpha, 0)$ holds with certainty ($p_0 = 1$), we have to show that either $p_{\gamma_i} \leq 2^{-4}$ for at least one i or that $p_{\gamma_i}, p_{\gamma_j} \leq 2^{-3}$ for at least two distinct indices i, j. In other words, one has to make sure to gain a factor of 2^{-2} within the characteristic. In order to show this, we make use of Lemma 2. If $\mathrm{wt}(\alpha) \geq 4$, we are clearly done since $p_{\gamma_1} = p_\alpha \leq 2^{-\mathrm{wt}(\alpha)}$. We thus have to distinguish 3 cases.

(i) $\mathrm{wt}(\alpha) = 1$: Because of the branch number, it is $\mathrm{wt}(\theta(\mathbf{x}) \oplus \theta(\mathbf{x} \oplus \alpha)) \geq 10$. Since further $\mathrm{wt}(\rho(\mathbf{x}) \oplus \rho(\mathbf{x} \oplus \alpha)) \leq 2$, we have $\mathrm{wt}(\gamma_2) \geq 8$ and $p_{\gamma_2} \leq 2^{-4}$.

(ii) $\mathrm{wt}(\alpha) = 2$: It is $\mathrm{wt}(\theta(\mathbf{x}) \oplus \theta(\mathbf{x} \oplus \alpha)) \geq 9$ and $\mathrm{wt}(\rho(\mathbf{x}) \oplus \rho(\mathbf{x} \oplus \alpha)) \leq 4$. Thus, $\mathrm{wt}(\gamma_2) \geq 5$ and therefore $p_{\gamma_2} \leq 2^{-4}$.

(iii) $\mathrm{wt}(\alpha) = 3$: We already have $p_\alpha \leq 2^{-3}$. Since $\mathrm{wt}(\theta(\mathbf{x}) \oplus \theta(\mathbf{x} \oplus \alpha)) \geq 8$ and $\mathrm{wt}(\rho(\mathbf{x}) \oplus \rho(\mathbf{x} \oplus \alpha)) \leq 6$, it is $\mathrm{wt}(\gamma_2) \geq 2$ and therefore $p_{\gamma_2} \leq 2^{-3}$.

See also Fig. 3 for the propagation of the differential Hamming weights.   □

We recall that θ does not have to be rotational invariant. Nevertheless, having a branch number of at least 11 is a quite restrictive property on a linear layer and in fact, for $n = 16$, there does not exist such a linear mapping. The reason is that the minimum distance d of any $[32, 16, d]$ code over $\mathbb{F}_2$ is at most 8 [19]. However, for $n \in \{24, 32, 48, 64\}$, such a linear mapping θ exists as one can also deduce from [19]. As the previous argument is more generic, we investigate the linear part of SIMON in more detail in the rest of the paper.

3.2   Obtaining the Upper Bound for SIMON and Simeck

In the following, we consider the linear layer $\theta(\mathbf{x}) = (\mathbf{x} \lll c)$ which has a branch number of only 2. Choosing $(8, 1, 2)$ for the rotation constants (a, b, c), we obtain the round function of SIMON. Theorem 3 states the same bound as above for all variants of SIMON. Note that the results are dependent on the specific choice of

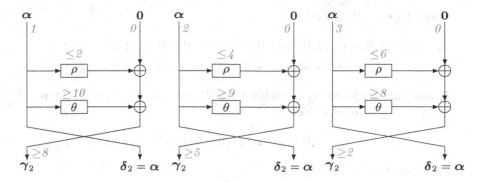

Fig. 3. Propagation of the differential Hamming weight for $\mathrm{wt}(\boldsymbol{\alpha}) \in \{1, 2, 3\}$.

the rotation constants, but can be proven for other choices in a similar way. Of course, it does not hold for all possible a, b and c. For example, if $c = a$ or $c = b$, one obtains the trivial bound of 2^{-t} since

$$\big((1, 0, \ldots, 0)\ \mathbf{0}\big) \to \big(\mathbf{0}\ (1, 0, \ldots, 0)\big) \to \big((1, 0, \ldots, 0)\ \mathbf{0}\big)$$

would be a valid two-round iterative characteristic with probability 2^{-2}.

Theorem 3 (Bounds for SIMON). *Let $n \in \{16, 24, 32, 48, 64\}$ and let $\theta(\mathbf{x}) = (\mathbf{x} \lll 2)$. For the rotation constants $a = 8, b = 1$, the probability of any T-round differential characteristic is upper bounded by 2^{-2T+2}.*

Proof Again, fix a t-round characteristic of the form

$$(\mathbf{0}, \boldsymbol{\alpha}) \to (\boldsymbol{\gamma_1} = \boldsymbol{\alpha}, \mathbf{0}) \to (\boldsymbol{\gamma_2}, \boldsymbol{\delta_2}) \to \cdots \to (\boldsymbol{\gamma_{t-1}}, \boldsymbol{\delta_{t-1}}) \to (\mathbf{0}, \boldsymbol{\beta})$$

with $\boldsymbol{\gamma_i} \neq \mathbf{0}$ for all $i \in \{1, \ldots, t-1\}$. We have to show that either $p_{\gamma_i} \leq 2^{-4}$ for at least one i or that $p_{\gamma_i}, p_{\gamma_j} \leq 2^{-3}$ for at least two distinct indices i, j. In order to show this, Lemma 2 is used several times within this proof. Again, we have to distinguish 3 cases. Note that for simplicity with indices, we assume rotations to the right in the following. We use the $*$ symbol to indicate an unknown bit.

(i) $\mathrm{wt}(\boldsymbol{\alpha}) = 1$: Considering the rotational equivalence, let w.l.o.g.

$$\boldsymbol{\alpha} = (1, 0, \ldots, 0).$$

Recall that we get $U_{\alpha} = \mathrm{Im}\, L_{\alpha} \oplus f_S(\boldsymbol{\alpha})$. Since we assume

$$f_S : \mathbf{x} \mapsto (\mathbf{x} \ggg 8) \wedge (\mathbf{x} \ggg 1) \oplus (\mathbf{x} \ggg 2),$$

we obtain

$$\boldsymbol{\gamma_2} = (0, *_1, 1, 0,\ \ 0, 0, 0, 0,\ \ *_2, 0, 0, 0,\ \ 0, 0, 0, 0\ \ \ldots) \in U_{\alpha} \oplus \mathbf{0}.$$

Case 1 ($*_2 = 0$): Then,[2]

$$\gamma_3 = (1,0,*,*, \quad 1,0,0,0, \quad 0,*,*,0, \quad 0,0,0,0 \quad \ldots) \in U_{\gamma_2} \oplus \alpha,$$
$$\gamma_4 = (0,*,*^\dagger,*, \quad *,*,1,0, \quad *,0,*,*, \quad *,0,0,0 \quad \ldots) \in U_{\gamma_3} \oplus \gamma_2.$$

If now the weight of γ_4 is higher than 1, then $p_{\gamma_3}, p_{\gamma_4} \leq 2^{-3}$. Thus, let $\text{wt}(\gamma_4) = 1$. It follows that

$$\gamma_5 = (1,0,*,*, \quad 1,0,0,*, \quad 1,*,*,0, \quad 0,0,*,0 \quad \ldots) \in U_{\gamma_4} \oplus \gamma_3$$

and thus $p_{\gamma_5} \leq 2^{-3}$.

Case 2 ($*_2 = 1$): Then $p_{\gamma_2} \leq 2^{-3}$ already holds and[3]

$$\gamma_3 = (*^\ddagger,0,*,*, \quad 1,0,0,0, \quad 0,*,*,0, \quad 0,0,0,0 \quad \ldots) \in U_{\gamma_2} \oplus \alpha.$$

Again, let w.l.o.g $\text{wt}(\gamma_3) = 1$. It follows that

$$\gamma_4 = (0,*,1,0, \quad 0,*,1,0, \quad 1,0,0,0, \quad *,0,0,0 \quad \ldots) \in U_{\gamma_3} \oplus \gamma_2$$

and thus $p_{\gamma_4} \leq 2^{-3}$.

(ii) $\text{wt}(\alpha) = 2$: Considering the rotational equivalence, let w.l.o.g.

$$\alpha = (1,0,\ldots,0,1^{(i)},0,\ldots,0)$$

with $i \leq \frac{n}{2}$. It follows that already $p_\alpha \leq 2^{-3}$.

Case 1 ($i = 1$): Then,

$$\gamma_2 = (0,*,*,1, \quad 0,0,0,0, \quad *,*,0,0, \quad 0,0,0,0 \quad \ldots) \in U_\alpha \oplus 0.$$

Again, let w.l.o.g. $\text{wt}(\gamma_2) = 1$. Then,

$$\gamma_3 = (1,1,0,0, \quad *,1,0,0, \quad 0,0,0,*, \quad 0,0,0,0 \quad \ldots) \in U_{\gamma_2} \oplus \alpha$$

and thus $p_{\gamma_3} \leq 2^{-3}$.

Case 2 ($i = 4$): Then,

$$\gamma_2 = (0,*,1,0, \quad 0,*,1,0, \quad *,0,0,0, \quad *,0,0,0 \quad \ldots) \in U_\alpha \oplus 0$$

and $p_{\gamma_2} \leq 2^{-3}$.

---

[2] $\dagger$: This bit is only unknown if the bitlength is 16 bit ($n = 16$). Therefore, w.l.o.g. we assume this bit to be unknown. In the following, we may also consider certain bits to be unknown if the actual value does not matter for the proof.

[3] $\ddagger$: Of course, this bit is already equal to 1 if the bitlength n is greater than 16.

Case 3 $(i \neq 1, i \neq 4)$: Then,

$$\gamma_2 = (*, *, 1, *, \quad *, *, *, *, \quad *, *, *, *, \quad *, *, *, * \quad \ldots) \in U_\alpha \oplus \mathbf{0}.$$

Again, let w.l.o.g. $\mathrm{wt}(\gamma_2) = 1$. Then,

$$\gamma_3 = (1, *, *, *, \quad 1, *, *, *, \quad *, *, *, *, \quad *, *, *, * \quad \ldots) \in U_{\gamma_2} \oplus \alpha$$

and thus $p_{\gamma_3} \leq 2^{-3}$.

(iii) $\mathrm{wt}(\alpha) = 3$: Let w.l.o.g. $\alpha = (1, 0, \ldots, 1^{(i)}, 0, \ldots, 1^{(j)}, 0, \ldots, 0)$ with $i \geq \frac{n}{3}$ because of the rotational invariance. Again, $p_\alpha \leq 2^{-3}$. Since $n \geq 16$, it is $i \geq 6$. We distinguish the following cases:

Case 1 $(j \neq n - 6, i \neq n - 6)$: Then,

$$\gamma_2 = (*, *, 1, *, \quad *, *, *, *, \quad \ldots \quad *, *, *, *, \quad *, *, *, *) \in U_\alpha \oplus \mathbf{0}$$

and for $\mathrm{wt}(\gamma_2) = 1$ we obtain

$$\gamma_3 = (1, 0, 0, *, \quad 1, 0, *, *, \quad \ldots \quad *, *, *, *, \quad *, *, *, *) \in U_{\gamma_2} \oplus \alpha$$

such that $p_{\gamma_3} \leq 2^{-3}$.

Case 2 $(i = n - 6)$: Then,

$$\gamma_2 = (*, *, *, *, \quad *, *, *, *, \quad \ldots \quad *, *, *, *, \quad 1, *, *, *) \in U_\alpha \oplus \mathbf{0}$$

if $j \neq n - 5$ and

$$\gamma_2 = (*, *, *, *, \quad *, *, *, *, \quad \ldots \quad *, *, *, *, \quad *, 1, *, *) \in U_\alpha \oplus \mathbf{0}$$

if $j = n - 5$. In both cases, for $\mathrm{wt}(\gamma_2) = 1$ we obtain

$$\gamma_3 = (1^{(0)}, 0, 0, 0, \quad *, *, 0, 0, \quad \ldots \quad 0, 0, 1^{(i)}, *, \quad *, *, *, *) \in U_{\gamma_2} \oplus \alpha$$

such that $p_{\gamma_3} \leq 2^{-3}$.

Case 3 $(j = n - 6)$: Now, we still have to consider the two possibilities $j - i \neq 6$ and $j - i = 6$. For the first case, one gets

$$\gamma_2 = (*, *, *, *, \quad *, *, *, *, \quad \ldots \quad *, *, *, *, \quad 1, *, *, *) \in U_\alpha \oplus \mathbf{0}$$

and for $\mathrm{wt}(\gamma_2) = 1$,

$$\gamma_3 = (1, *, *, *, \quad *, *, *, *, \quad \ldots \quad *, *, *, *, \quad *, *, 1, *) \in U_{\gamma_2} \oplus \alpha.$$

If $j - i = 6$, then,

$$\gamma_2 = (*, *, *, *, \quad \ldots \quad *, *, 1^{(i+2)}, *, \quad *, *, *, *, \quad *, *, *, *) \in U_\alpha \oplus \mathbf{0}$$

and for $\mathrm{wt}(\gamma_2) = 1$,

$$\gamma_3 = (1^{(1)}, *, *, *, \quad \ldots \quad 1^{(i)}, *, *, *, \quad 1, *, 1^{(j)}, *, \quad *, *, *, *) \in U_{\gamma_2} \oplus \alpha. \quad \square$$

Table 1. Number of rounds needed for bounding the differential probability of a characteristic by 2^{-2n} for all instances of SIMON and SIMECK. The $\star$ symbol indicates that there is an appropriate instance of SIMECK with the same number of rounds.

	Rounds	Rounds needed	Margin κ
SIMON32/64*	32	17	15
SIMON48/72	36	25	11
SIMON48/96*	36	25	11
SIMON64/96	42	33	9
SIMON64/128*	44	33	11
SIMON96/96	52	49	3
SIMON96/144	54	49	5
SIMON128/128	68	65	3
SIMON128/192	69	65	4
SIMON128/256	72	65	7

Using a similar argument, one obtains the bounds for SIMECK as the following theorem states.

Theorem 4. (Bounds for SIMECK). *Let* $n \in \{16, 24, 32\}$ *and* $\theta(\mathbf{x}) = (\mathbf{x} \lll 1)$. *For the rotation constants* $a = 5, b = 0$, *the probability of any T-round differential characteristic is upper bounded by* 2^{-2T+2}.

Interestingly, for every instance of SIMON and SIMECK, it turns out that our approach is sufficient in order to bound the probability of differential characteristics below 2^{-2n} where n denotes the bit length of one Feistel branch. For n up to 32, the security margin κ of the corresponding primitive(s) can be considered as reasonable. See Table 1 for a comparison.

4   Conclusion

We presented a more general description of SIMON-like designs by separating the round function into a linear and a non-linear component and proved upper bounds on the probability of differential characteristics for specific instances. In fact, we developed a non-experimental security argument on full-round versions of SIMON that can be verified by pen and paper. We hope that this work encourages to further research on analyzing SIMON-like designs. An open question is whether our approach can be generalized in order to obtain better bounds over multiple rounds. However, as described earlier, we believe that such an argument would be much more complex. Furthermore, it would be favorable to avoid the consideration of every special case individually. This is related to the question of how to design the linear part θ in this set-up.

Acknowledgements. The author's work was supported by DFG Research Training Group GRK 1817 Ubicrypt. Special thanks go to Gregor Leander for his valuable suggestions and comments.

References

1. Abdelraheem, M.A., Alizadeh, J., Alkhzaimi, H.A., Aref, M.R., Bagheri, N., Gauravaram, P.: Improved linear cryptanalysis of reduced-round SIMON-32 and SIMON-48. In: Biryukov, A., Goyal, V. (eds.) INDOCRYPT 2015. LNCS, vol. 9462, pp. 153–179. Springer International Publishing, Heidelberg (2015)
2. Abed, F., List, E., Lucks, S., Wenzel, J.: Differential cryptanalysis of round-reduced SIMON and SPEAK. In: Cid, C., Rechberger, C. (eds.) FSE 2014. LNCS, vol. 8540, pp. 525–545. Springer, Heidelberg (2015)
3. Alizadeh, J., Bagheri, N., Gauravaram, P., Kumar, A., Sanadhya, S.K.: Linear cryptanalysis of round reduced SIMON. Cryptology ePrint Archive, Report 2013/663 (2013). http://eprint.iacr.org/2013/663
4. Alkhzaimi, H.A., Lauridsen, M.M.: Cryptanalysis of the SIMON family of block ciphers. Cryptology ePrint Archive, Report 2013/543 (2013). http://eprint.iacr.org/2013/543
5. Ashur, T.: Improved linear trails for the block cipher Simon. Cryptology ePrint Archive, Report 2015/285 (2015). http://eprint.iacr.org/
6. Beaulieu, R., Shors, D., Smith, J., Treatman-Clark, S., Weeks, B., Wingers, L.: The SIMON and SPECK families of lightweight block ciphers. Cryptology ePrint Archive, Report 2013/404 (2013). http://eprint.iacr.org/2013/404
7. Beaulieu, R., Shors, D., Smith, J., Treatman-Clark, S., Weeks, B., Wingers, L.: SIMON and SPECK: block ciphers for the internet of things. In: NIST Lightweight Cryptography Workshop, Vol. 2015 (2015)
8. Beierle, C., Jovanovic, P., Lauridsen, M.M., Leander, G., Rechberger, C.: Analyzing permutations for AES-like ciphers: understanding ShiftRows. In: Nyberg, K. (ed.) CT-RSA 2015. LNCS, vol. 9048, pp. 37–58. Springer, Heidelberg (2015)
9. Benadjila, R., Billet, O., Gilbert, H., Macario-Rat, G., Peyrin, T., Robshaw, M., Seurin, Y.: SHA-3 Proposal: ECHO (2010). http://crypto.rd.francetelecom.com/ECHO/
10. Bertoni, G., Daemen, J., Peeters, M., Assche, G.: The Keccak reference. Submission to NIST (Round 3), 13 (2011)
11. Biham, E., Anderson, R., Knudsen, L.R.: Serpent: a new block cipher proposal. In: Vaudenay, S. (ed.) FSE 1998. LNCS, vol. 1372, p. 222. Springer, Heidelberg (1998)
12. Biham, E., Shamir, A.: Differential cryptanalysis of DES-like cryptosystems. In: Menezes, A., Vanstone, S.A. (eds.) CRYPTO 1990. LNCS, vol. 537, pp. 2–21. Springer, Heidelberg (1991)
13. Biryukov, A., Roy, A., Velichkov, V.: Differential analysis of block ciphers SIMON and SPECK. In: Cid, C., Rechberger, C. (eds.) FSE 2014. LNCS, vol. 8540, pp. 546–570. Springer, Heidelberg (2015)
14. Bogdanov, A.A., Knudsen, L.R., Leander, G., Paar, C., Poschmann, A., Robshaw, M., Seurin, Y., Vikkelsoe, C.: PRESENT: an ultra-lightweight block cipher. In: Paillier, P., Verbauwhede, I. (eds.) CHES 2007. LNCS, vol. 4727, pp. 450–466. Springer, Heidelberg (2007)
15. Chen, H., Wang, X.: Improved linear hull attack on round-reduced SIMON with dynamic key-guessing techniques. In: Peyrin, T. (ed.) FSE 2016. LNCS, vol. 9783, pp. 428–449. Springer, Heidelberg (2016). doi:10.1007/978-3-662-52993-5_22
16. Daemen, J.: Cipher and hash function design strategies based on linear and differential cryptanalysis. Ph.D. thesis, Doctoral Dissertation, KU Leuven, March 1995

17. Daemen, J., Lamberger, M., Pramstaller, N., Rijmen, V., Vercauteren, F.: Computational aspects of the expected differential probability of 4-round AES and AES-like ciphers. Computing **85**(1–2), 85–104 (2009)
18. Daemen, J., Rijmen, V.: AES Proposal: Rjindael (1998). http://csrc.nist.gov/archive/aes/rijndael/Rijndael-ammended.pdf
19. Grassl, M.: Bounds on the minimum distance of linear codes and quantum codes (2007). http://www.codetables.de. Accessed 15 Feb 2016
20. Kölbl, S., Leander, G., Tiessen, T.: Observations on the SIMON block cipher family. In: Gennaro, R., Robshaw, M. (eds.) CRYPTO 2015. LNCS, vol. 9215, pp. 161–185. Springer, Heidelberg (2015)
21. Kondo, K., Sasaki, Y., Iwata, T.: On the design rationale of SIMON block cipher: integral attacks and impossible differential attacks against SIMON variants. In: Manulis, M., Sadeghi, A.-R., Schneider, S. (eds.) ACNS 2016. LNCS, vol. 9696, pp. 518–536. Springer, Heidelberg (2016). doi:10.1007/978-3-319-39555-5_28
22. Matsui, M.: Linear cryptanalysis method for DES cipher. In: Helleseth, T. (ed.) EUROCRYPT 1993. LNCS, vol. 765, pp. 386–397. Springer, Heidelberg (1994)
23. Mouha, N., Wang, Q., Gu, D., Preneel, B.: Differential and linear cryptanalysis using mixed-integer linear programming. In: Wu, C.-K., Yung, M., Lin, D. (eds.) Inscrypt 2011. LNCS, vol. 7537, pp. 57–76. Springer, Heidelberg (2012)
24. Nyberg, K., Knudsen, L.: Provable security against a differential attack. J. Cryptol. **8**(1), 27–37 (1995)
25. PUB FIPS. 197: Advanced encryption standard (AES), National Institute of Standards and Technology (2001). http://csrc.nist.gov/publications/fips/fips197/fips-197.pdf
26. Shannon, C.E.: Communication theory of secrecy systems. Bell Syst. Tech. J. **28**(4), 656–715 (1949)
27. Shirai, T., Preneel, B.: On Feistel ciphers using optimal diffusion mappings across multiple rounds. In: Lee, P.J. (ed.) ASIACRYPT 2004. LNCS, vol. 3329, pp. 1–15. Springer, Heidelberg (2004)
28. Shirai, T., Shibutani, K.: Improving immunity of Feistel ciphers against differential cryptanalysis by using multiple MDS matrices. In: Roy, B., Meier, W. (eds.) FSE 2004. LNCS, vol. 3017, pp. 260–278. Springer, Heidelberg (2004)
29. Sun, S., Hu, L., Wang, P., Qiao, K., Ma, X., Song, L.: Automatic security evaluation and (related-key) differential characteristic search: application to SIMON, PRESENT, LBlock, DES(L) and other bit-oriented block ciphers. In: Sarkar, P., Iwata, T. (eds.) ASIACRYPT 2014. LNCS, vol. 8873, pp. 158–178. Springer, Heidelberg (2014)
30. Todo, Y., Morii, M.: Bit-based division property and application to SIMON family. In: Peyrin, T. (ed.) FSE 2016. LNCS, vol. 9783, pp. 357–377. Springer, Heidelberg (2016). doi:10.1007/978-3-662-52993-5_18
31. Wang, N., Wang, X., Jia, K., Zhao, J.: Differential attacks on reduced SIMON versions with dynamic key-guessing techniques. Cryptology ePrint Archive, Report 2014/448 (2014). http://eprint.iacr.org/2014/448
32. Wang, Q., Liu, Z., Varıcı, K., Sasaki, Y., Rijmen, V., Todo, Y.: Cryptanalysis of reduced-round SIMON32 and SIMON48. In: Meier, W., Mukhopadhyay, D. (eds.) INDOCRYPT 2014. LNCS, vol. 8885, pp. 143–160. Springer International Publishing, Heidelberg (2014)
33. Yang, G., Zhu, B., Suder, V., Aagaard, M.D., Gong, G.: The Simeck family of lightweight block ciphers. In: Güneysu, T., Handschuh, H. (eds.) CHES 2015. LNCS, vol. 9293, pp. 307–329. Springer, Heidelberg (2015)

Two-party Computation

Bounded Size-Hiding Private Set Intersection

Tatiana Bradley[✉], Sky Faber, and Gene Tsudik

University of California, Irvine, USA
tebradle@uci.edu

Abstract. Private Set Intersection (PSI) and other private set operations have many current and emerging applications. Numerous PSI techniques have been proposed that vary widely in terms of underlying cryptographic primitives, security assumptions as well as complexity. One
recent strand of PSI-related research focused on an additional privacy
property of hiding participants' input sizes. Despite some interesting
results, only one practical size-hiding PSI (SH-PSI) has been demonstrated thus far [1].

One legitimate general criticism of size-hiding private set intersection
is that the party that hides its input size can attempt to enumerate
the entire (and possibly limited) domain of set elements, thus learning
the other party's entire input set. Although this "attack" goes beyond
the honest-but-curious model, it motivates investigation of techniques
that simultaneously hide and limit a participant's input size. To this
end, this paper explores the design of *bounded size-hiding* PSI techniques
that allow one party to hide the size of its input while allowing the other
party to limit that size. Its main contribution is a reasonably efficient
(quasi-quadratic in input size) bSH-PSI protocol based on bounded keyed
accumulators. This paper also studies the relationships between several
flavors of the "Strong Diffie-Hellman" (SDH) problem.

Keywords: Private set intersection · Size hiding · Bounded input ·
Cryptographic accumulators · SDH problem

1 Introduction

Private set operations have many potential applications in secure cloud computing and storage, as well as other settings involving mutually suspicious parties
that wish to divulge to each other nothing beyond the outcome of a particular
set operation. This serves as one motivating factor for research in more efficient
and more secure techniques. The other, no less important, factor is intellectual
curiosity. There is something inherently appealing about private set operations,
perhaps because they represent an interesting and realistic-sounding application
domain for secure two-party computation.

The most natural and popular private set operation is Private Set Intersection (PSI), a cryptographic technique that allows two parties, *server* and *client*,
to interact such that one or both of them (often, *client*) computes the intersection

© Springer International Publishing Switzerland 2016
V. Zikas and R. De Prisco (Eds.): SCN 2016, LNCS 9841, pp. 449–467, 2016.
DOI: 10.1007/978-3-319-44618-9_24

$S \cap C$ over their respective input sets S and C. Typically, *server* and *client* learn nothing beyond the size of each other's set and the resulting intersection. There are multiple PSI flavors with varying privacy properties, security models, complexities and underlying cryptographic primitives [1, 8, 13–18, 22–25, 27, 28, 33].

One recent PSI research direction focused on techniques that additionally hide the input size of one participant. This property is sometimes called *one-sided input size-hiding*. This line of research is attractive because, in general, there are few cryptographic techniques that achieve non-padding-based input size-hiding. (See Sect. 2 for an overview of related work).

Meanwhile, one important criticism of size-hiding PSI (SH-PSI) is the *unlimited* nature of the size-hiding feature. In scenarios where the overall input domain is small[1], a dishonest *client* can enumerate all (or most) of the possible elements, use them as its input set and thus learn all (or most) of *server's* input set.

On the one hand, this criticism seems unfair because a *client* that enumerates, and provides as input, elements that it does not actually have, goes beyond the "honest-but-curious" (HbC) adversary model considered in, for example, [1]. On the other hand, it could be that the entire notion of input size-hiding inherently motivates a slightly different adversary model than HbC.

Consequently, the main motivation for this paper is the need to combine hiding of one party's input size with the other party's ability to upper-bound it, i.e., to limit the amount of information potentially learned by the first party. Specifically, the goal is to explore PSI techniques that allow *client* to hide its set size while assuring *server* that it does not exceed some fixed threshold t. At the first glance, it seems that this can be trivially met by modifying current SH-PSI, PSI or similar techniques.

One intuitive approach to bounded size-hiding is to amend any regular PSI protocol by having *client* always pad its (linear-size) input with dummy elements, up to the server-selected upper bound t. While this approach would meet our goals, we consider it to be undesirable, for several reasons:

- Padding by *client* always incurs $O(t)$ computation and bandwidth costs, even if $|C|$ and/or $|S|$ are small relative to t.[2]
- Representation of dummy elements must be indistinguishable from that of their genuine counterparts. This very likely entails generating a random value for every dummy element, which, depending on the underlying PRNG, can involve as little computation as a hash, or as much as a large-integer arithmetic operation.
- If $|C| < t$, a misbehaving HbC *client* can easily cheat – and learn more about S than it is entitled to – by inserting extra actual elements into its input that it could later claim are just dummies.[3]

---

[1] For example: age, blood type, birthday, country, zip code, etc.

[2] In contrast, bSH-PSI incurs only $O(|C|)$ costs, since *client* can download *server's* public key only once, ahead of time, i.e., off-line.

[3] As discussed later, although the proposed bSH-PSI has the same issue, it discourages *client's* cheating by imposing a relatively high client computational cost for each additional element in the accumulator, up to the bound.

Even if aforementioned reasons are deemed to be superficial, we still consider padding-based size-hiding techniques to be inelegant.

Another simple way to force boundedness, is to modify any PSI protocol such that *server*, acting unilaterally, uses a subset $S^* \in S$ of no more than t set elements as its PSI input. This implies that *client* would learn an intersection of at most t elements. However, *client* would also very likely learn less than it is entitled to if $|C \cap S^*| < |C \cap S| \leq t$. An equally trivial approach is for *server* to pick a random subset $C^* \in C$ of no more than t set elements (assuming $|C| > t$) of *client*'s input. This is doable since most (not size-hiding) PSI protocols involve a message from *client* to *server* that contains some linear representation of *client*'s input set. The end-result would be the same: *client* would likely learn less than $C \cap S$ even if $|C \cap S| \leq t$.

In this paper, we introduce the notion of Bounded Size-Hiding Private Set Intersection (*b*SH-PSI) and demonstrate the first provably secure and reasonably efficient[4] *b*SH-PSI protocol. In the process, we introduce two new cryptographic SDH-related assumptions and show their equivalence to more established assumptions. Finally, we discuss several *b*SH-PSI extensions and optimizations.

In a general sense, *b*SH-PSI operates as follows: before any interaction, *server* chooses a bound t. During the interaction, *client* inputs a set of size $m < t$ and *server* inputs a set of size n, which is independent of t. At the end of the interaction, *client* learns the intersection of the two sets and n, the *server*'s set size. The *server* learns nothing.

Notable features of proposed *b*SH-PSI include:

- It is particularly well-suited for scenarios where *server* needs to interact with *client* whose input set is larger than *server*'s. However, *b*SH-PSI is effective regardless of *client*'s and *server*'s relative set sizes.
- *Server* can set (and modify at will) the upper bound t on *client*'s input set size. In particular, if set elements are drawn from a small domain, this prevents *client* from enumerating all elements and determining the entirety of *server*'s set.
- It is based on a bounded cryptographic accumulator construct from [32].
- *Client* privacy is unconditional with respect to both set elements and their number, i.e., set size.
- *Server* security holds under the One-Generator [3] and Exponent [34] q-Strong Diffie-Hellman (SDH) Assumptions in the Random Oracle Model (ROM) [2].
- *Server* incurs computational complexity linear in *server*'s input size – $O(n)$ where $n = |S|$.
- *Client* incurs computational complexity of $O(m^2 log^2 m)$ in *client*'s input set size: $m = |C|$. With pre-computation, this can be lowered to $O(m^2)$.
- Overall bandwidth complexity is linear in *server*'s input size – $O(n)$.

Organization: Related work is discussed in Sect. 2. Section 3 formally defines SH-PSI, its security properties and underlying cryptographic assumptions. A concrete SH-PSI construct is presented in Sect. 4, along with its security arguments.

---

[4] The term "efficient" is used in the standard sense, i.e., efficient in the context of most cryptographic literature.

Section 5 discusses scenario-specific extensions and open problems. Next, Sect. 6 presents reductions of new cryptographic assumptions to their better-known counterparts. The paper concludes with a summary in Sect. 7. Techniques for efficient computation by *client* are discussed in the full version of this paper [5].

2   Related Work

The concept of size-hiding private set intersection (SH-PSI) was introduced by Ateniese *et al.*in [1]. It demonstrated the first SH-PSI technique using RSA accumulators, with unconditional privacy of *client*'s set size and its contents, *server* privacy based on the strong RSA assumption, and correctness in the HbC setting in the random oracle model (ROM).

D'Arco *et al.* [9] (revised in [10]) is the only other effort, to our knowledge, focused on SH-PSI. It demonstrates several results about the possibility of SH-PSI, including one that one-sided SH-PSI is possible in both the standard model and ROM. However, the proposed techniques – which are based on oblivious pseudorandom function (OPRF) evaluation and RSA, require a setup phase using a trusted third party (TTP). The revised version [10] presents a technique that avoids random oracles at the price of a commitment scheme which is unspecified; thus, the exact complexity is unclear.

There have been other efforts to define, and show feasibility of, various size-hiding two-party computation techniques. However, these results are largely theoretical.

Lindell *et al.* [30] prove some results about the feasibility of input-size hiding in two-party computation under various conditions. In particular, one-sided size-hiding is shown to be possible for every function in the HbC model without random oracles, given that the output size is upper-bounded by some function of a party's input size, which is the case in *b*SH-PSI. The concrete protocol presented in [30] is based on fully homomorphic encryption, which is not yet practical. The full version [29] shows how to modify the protocol for the case where one party hides its size and learns the outcome. Size-hiding is achieved by padding *client*'s input with random elements.

Chase *et al.* [7] present an extended definition of the real/ideal model that allows for input-size hiding in the presence of malicious players. The extended model allows one party in the ideal world to send what is called an "implicit representation" of its input (which does not necessarily reveal the input size) in lieu of the input itself. The generic protocol for two-party computation involves five rounds of communication, making use of fully homomorphic encryption. Also, the output size must be fixed, which is not the case in PSI.

Other results discuss the need for input size-hiding in secure computation, starting with Micali *et al.* [31], which introduces the notion of zero-knowledge sets – a size-hiding cryptographic primitive. The protocol allows a party to commit to a private set (with size hidden) and later prove whether a given element is a member of that set. This notion is different from PSI since the element (for which set membership is being tested) is public.

De Cristofaro *et al.* [12] focus on size- and position-hiding private substring matching in the context of genomic privacy. The proposed protocol is highly specialized, in particular, not suitable for generic PSI. Based on additively homomorphic encryption, it allows *client* to test whether a number of substrings are present in *server*'s string (genome) at pre-determined positions, while revealing neither positions nor sizes of the substrings to *server*, and precluding *client* from learning anything about *server*'s input beyond the binary result of the computation.

Ishai and Paskin [26] show that it is possible to securely evaluate branching programs while hiding the size of the program, given that the length of the program is upper-bounded by some polynomial. In this context, *size* refers the number of instructions in the program, while *length* refers to the length of the longest branch in the program. The protocol in [26] is based on strong oblivious transfer.

Goyal *et al.* [21] show that constant-round public-coin zero knowledge is possible using only black box techniques, while hiding the size of the input string. The protocol is based on a commit-and-prove scheme using extendible Merkle trees.

3 Problem Statement and Preliminaries

We now formally define bSH-PSI as well as four relevant cryptographic problems. The latter include two new assumptions: *polynomial-generalized exponent q-SDH (PG-E-SDH)* and *polynomial-generalized one-generator q-SDH (PG-OG-SDH)* as well as their better-known counterparts: *exponent q-SDH (E-SDH)* and *one-generator q-SDH (OG-SDH)*.

3.1 Bounded SH-PSI

Informally, bSH-PSI extends SH-PSI with the requirement that *client* can only input a limited number of set elements. This bound t is fixed by *server* prior to protocol execution. For ease of presentation, we define bSH-PSI directly, and refer to [4] and [1] for formal definitions of PSI and SH-PSI, respectively. In the following, $\sim$ denotes computational indistinguishability, as defined in [20].

Definition 1 (Bounded SH-PSI). *A scheme satisfying correctness, boundedness, client privacy and server privacy, (per Definitions 2, 3, 4 and 5, respectively) involving two parties: client C and server S, and two components: Setup and Interaction, where:*

- *Setup: an algorithm that selects global parameters, including t and server's public key, if any.*
- *Interaction: a protocol between S and C on respective inputs: $S = \{s_1, \ldots, s_n\}$ and $C = \{c_1, \ldots, c_m\}$.*

Definition 2 (Correctness). *If both parties are honest and $m \leq t$, then, at the end of Interaction on inputs (S, C) server outputs $\perp$, and client outputs $(n, S \cap C)$.*

Definition 3 (Boundedness). *If client's set size exceeds the bound ($|C| = m > t$), and server is honest, client only learns $n = |S|$.*

Definition 4 (Client Privacy). *For any PPT adversary S^* acting as server on input S' in execution of bSH-PSI, we say that Client Privacy holds if the views of S^* are computationally indistinguishable when interacting with any pair of client input sets: $[C^{(0)}, C^{(1)}]$. Specifically, let $Views(C)$ represent the view of S^* during protocol execution on input C. Then, Client Privacy is:*

$$\forall\, (C^{(0)}, C^{(1)}) : Views[C^{(0)}] \sim Views(C^{(1)}]$$

We note that Client Privacy implies that S^* learns no information about C, including m, i.e., Client Privacy includes privacy of *client*'s set elements and of their number.

Definition 5 (Server Privacy). *Let $View_C(C, S)$ be a random variable representing C's view during execution of bSH-PSI on inputs: C, S. We say that Server Privacy holds if there exists a PPT algorithm C^* such that:*

$$\forall\, (C, S) : C^*(C, C \cap S, n) \sim View_C(C, S).$$

In other words, for any pair of inputs $[C, S]$, C's view of the protocol can be efficiently simulated[5] by C^* on input C and $C \cap S$ alone. In particular, this means C^* does not have access to S.

Security Model. We aim to construct bSH-PSI techniques secure in the HbC model [19]. HbC assumes that, while all parties faithfully follow the protocol, they may try to infer or compute additional information from the protocol transcript(s). However, due to the unusual input-boundedness feature of bSH-PSI, we extend the HbC model for *client* by allowing it to attempt using an input set larger than the *server*-imposed bound t, while still adhering to the rest of the protocol. We refer to this as the HbC* model.[6] In particular, *client*'s messages are assumed to be well-formed. However, the HbC model for *server* is unchanged from its usual form.

3.2   q-Strong Diffie-Hellman Assumptions

As discussed later in the paper, security of the proposed bSH-PSI relies on the hardness of two non-standard cryptographic problems: *polynomial-generalized exponent q-SDH (PG-E-SDH)* and *polynomial-generalized one-generator q-SDH (PG-OG-SDH)*. These are the generalizations of well-known *exponent q-SDH (E-SDH)* and *one-generator q-SDH (OG-SDH)* problems, to allow polynomials in the group exponent. Each of these problems assumes the same public information derived

---

[5] Being simulatable means that C^* can output a computationally indistinguishable transcript.

[6] Note that because the adversarial client has more power in the HbC* model than in plain HbC, security also holds in HbC.

from the secret z. This public information is a $(q+1)$-tuple: $[g, g^z, \ldots, g^{(z^q)}]$, where all components are mod p, g is a generator of the p' order subgroup $(\mathbb{G})$ of Z_p^* and p and p' are large primes. (We omit the mod p notation from here on).

PG-E-SDH generalizes *E-SDH* to reflect the difficulty of computing g exponentiated with any polynomial in z of degree larger than q, instead of simply z^{q+1}. Similarly, *PG-OG-SDH* generalizes *OG-SDH* to the difficulty of exponentiating a base (not just g) to the power of $\frac{1}{z+c}$. Specifically, it considers base elements of the form g exponentiated to any polynomial in z of degree less than or equal to q.

We now state the problems and then discuss the assumptions on their hardness. Our definitions of the standard problems (1 and 2 below) follow the presentation in [3].

Problem 1 (One-generator q-Strong Diffie-Hellman Problem). Given a $(q+1)$-tuple $[g, g^z, \ldots, g^{(z^q)}]$ as input, the *one-generator q-SDH* problem in $\mathbb{G}$ is to output a pair: $[c, g^{\frac{1}{(z+c)}}]$ where $c \in Z_{p'}^*$. An algorithm $\mathcal{A}$ has advantage ϵ in solving *one-generator q-SDH* in $\mathbb{G}$ if:

$$\Pr\left[\mathcal{A}([g, g^z, \ldots, g^{(z^q)}]) = [c, g^{\frac{1}{z+c}}]\right] \geq \epsilon$$

where the probability is over the random choice of generator $g \in \mathbb{G}$, the random choice of $z \in Z_{p'}^*$, and random bits consumed by $\mathcal{A}$.

Problem 2 (Exponent q-Strong Diffie-Hellman Problem). Given a $(q+1)$-tuple $[g, g^z, \ldots, g^{(z^q)}]$ as input, the *exponent q-SDH* problem in $\mathbb{G}$ is to output $g^{(z^{q+1})}$. An algorithm $\mathcal{A}$ has advantage ϵ in solving *exponent q-SDH* in $\mathbb{G}$ if

$$\Pr\left[\mathcal{A}([g, g^z, \ldots, g^{(z^q)}]) = g^{(z^{q+1})}\right] \geq \epsilon$$

where the probability is over the random choice of generator $g \in \mathbb{G}$, the random choice of $z \in Z_{p'}^*$, and random bits consumed by $\mathcal{A}$.

The following are the two new problems that generalize the two above. We refer to Sect. 6 for formal reductions.

Problem 3 (Polynomial-generalized one-generator q-Strong Diffie-Hellman Problem). Given a $(q+1)$-tuple $[g, g^z, \ldots, g^{(z^q)}]$ and a polynomial $P_n(z)$ in z of degree $n \leq q$ with known coefficients in Z_p^* as input, the *polynomial-generalized one-generator q-SDH* problem in $\mathbb{G}$ is to output a pair: $[c, g^{\frac{P_n(z)}{(z+c)}}]$, where $-c$ is not a root of $P_n(z)$. An algorithm $\mathcal{A}$ has an advantage ϵ in solving *polynomial-generalized one-generator q-SDH* in $\mathbb{G}$ if:

$$\Pr\left[\mathcal{A}([g, g^z, \ldots, g^{(z^q)}], P_n(z)) = [c, g^{\frac{P_n(z)}{z+c}}]\right] \geq \epsilon$$

where the probability is over the random choice of generator $g \in \mathbb{G}$, the random choice of $z \in Z_{p'}^*$, and random bits consumed by $\mathcal{A}$.

Note 1. Note that the *polynomial-generalized one-generator q-SDH* problem described above is not hard if $(z+c)$ divides $P_n(z)$ (i.e., $-c$, the additive inverse of c, is a root) because of the restriction that $n \leq q$. If $-c$ is a root of $P_n(z)$, the problem is equivalent to computing $(c, g^{P'_{n-1}(z)})$, where $P'_{n-1}(z) = \frac{P_n(z)}{z+c}$. This is achievable by exponentiation and multiplication of elements in $[g, g^z, \ldots, g^{(z^q)}]$.

Problem 4 (Polynomial-generalized exponent q-Strong Diffie-Hellman Problem). Given as input a $(q+1)$-tuple $[g, g^z, \ldots, g^{(z^q)}]$ and $P_n(z)$, a polynomial in z of degree $n > q$ (and n being polynomial in the security parameter) with known coefficients in $\mathbb{Z}_p^*$, the *polynomial-generalized exponent q-SDH* problem in $\mathbb{G}$ is to output $g^{(P_n(z))}$. An algorithm $\mathcal{A}$ has an advantage ϵ in solving *polynomial-generalized exponent q-SDH* in $\mathbb{G}$ if:

$$\Pr\left[\mathcal{A}([g, g^z, \ldots, g^{(z^q)}]) = g^{P_n(z)} \text{ s.t. } n > q\right] \geq \epsilon$$

where the probability is over the random choice of generator $g \in \mathbb{G}$, the random choice of $z \in \mathbb{Z}_{p'}^*$, and random bits consumed by $\mathcal{A}$.

Definition 6. *For each of the four q-SDH problems described above, we say that the corresponding (q, t', ϵ)-SDH assumption holds in $\mathbb{G}$ if no t'-time algorithm has advantage at least ϵ in solving that q-SDH problem in $\mathbb{G}$.*

As discussed later, security of our bSH-PSI protocol is based on these assumptions, against polynomial time adversaries with $q = t$, and negligible advantage ϵ.

Group Selection. While there are many candidate groups, we focus on the Diffie-Hellman prime-order integer subgroups modulo a large prime. Specifically, let τ be a security parameter and let $DH.setup(\tau)$ be an algorithm that outputs a triple: (p, p', g) such that: (1) p is a prime of the form $p = 2(p')^l + 1$ for some integer l, (2) p' is a prime, and (3) g is a generator of a subgroup of $\mathbb{Z}_p^*$ of order p'. For more on our choice of group see Sect. 5.5.

4   Protocol

We now present a concrete bSH-PSI technique, followed by security arguments.

4.1   Protocol Description

We first introduce the building blocks and intuition behind this realization of bSH-PSI. The primary building blocks are: (1) a t-bounded keyed accumulator [32], (2) a keyed unpredictable function $f_{z,X}(c) = X^{\frac{1}{z+c}}$, and (3) two cryptographic hash functions $F(\cdot)$ and $H(\cdot)$ modeled as Random Oracles: $F : \{0,1\}^* \rightarrow \{0,1\}^\omega$ where ω is a security parameter[7], and $H : \{0,1\}^* \rightarrow \{0,1\}^{\log p'}$. For the time being, we assume that $\omega = \log p'$, though, in practice, ω can be smaller.

---

[7] A practical example is SHA-256 for $\omega = 256$.

Intuitively, *client* aggregates its input elements $C = \{c_1, \ldots, c_m\}$ into an accumulator of the form $X' = g^{\prod_{i=0}^{m} hc_i + z}$, where $hc_i = H(c_i)$. *Client* can compute this product using *server*'s public key $[g, g^z, \ldots, g^{(z^t)}]$ by expanding the product in the exponent into the polynomial of the form: $A(z) = a_0 + a_1 z + \ldots + a_m z^m$, where each coefficient a_k is a product-sum of a combination of *client*'s hashed inputs: $hc_1, \ldots, hc_m$.

Each a_k has a closed-form solution dependent only on *client*'s input and t. Optionally, it can be computed before protocol execution. Techniques for efficient computation of this polynomial are presented in the full paper [5]. The resulting accumulator X' is then blinded as $X = X'^r$, (using a fresh random value r) and sent to *server*. Due to this consistent random blinding *client* benefits from unconditional privacy of its input. It also obtains unconditional privacy of its input size since X is $\log p$ bits long. Furthermore, total protocol bandwidth is independent of m.

Upon receipt of X, for each hashed element hs_j, *server* computes a distinct *tag*, denoted tg_j, as the composition of F and $f_{z,X}$. That is: $tg_j = F(X^{\frac{1}{z+hs_j}})$ where $hs_j = H(s_j)$. The resulting set of tags is then sent to *client* who, in turn, uses them to determine the actual set intersection.

Note that $f_{z,X}(hs_j)$ is of the form $g^{\frac{P_m(z)}{z+hs_j}}$ for some polynomial $P_m(z)$. Also, $f_{z,X}(hs_j)$ is unpredictable given public information provided to *client*, if and only if *PG-OG-SDH* assumption holds. Applying $F(\cdot)$ converts these unpredictable values into pseudorandom values, which is essential for server privacy.

Meanwhile (either before receiving server's tags or upon receiving them), *client* computes a tag tg'_i for each hashed element hc_i in its input set. As part of computing each tg'_i *client* essentially constructs "witness" X_i for the original accumulator X, based on each hc_i, i.e., X_i is a partial accumulator, with one term missing from the product in the exponent. Specifically, each tg'_i is computed as: $F(\cdot)$ applied to a witness: g exponentiated with a product of $m-1$ binomials of the form $(hc_i + z)$ and the random value r. The product of binomials can be represented by a unique polynomial $A_i(z)$, such that: $A_i = a_{(i,0)} + a_{(i,1)} z + \ldots + a_{(i,m)} z^m$ and $a_{(i,k)}$ is a product-sum involving all of *client*'s hashed input, except hc_i. As mentioned above, *client* tags can be computed ahead of time. The intersection of: $\{tg'_i \mid 0 < i \leq m\}$ and $\{tg_j \mid 0 < j \leq n\}$, determines *client*'s output: $S \cap C$.

Figure 1 shows the *Interaction* component of this *b*SH-PSI protocol. *Setup*(z, t) returns the information extracted from the output of *DH.setup*(τ) and the public key $[g, g^z, \ldots, g^{(z^t)}]$ generated from a bound t and secret z. Before the protocol begins, *server* selects t and z and publishes the output of *Setup*.

4.2   Security Analysis

We now present proofs of security for Definitions 2, 3, 4 and 5.

Correctness. Following Definition 2, we show that when both parties are honest, *client* outputs $(n, S \cap C)$ and *server* outputs $\perp$, i.e., nothing.

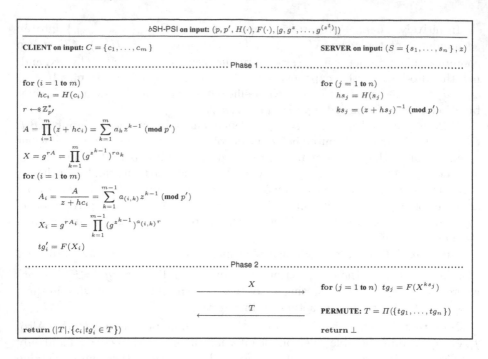

bSH-PSI on input: $(p, p', H(\cdot), F(\cdot), [g, g^z, \ldots, g^{(z^t)}])$

CLIENT on input: $C = \{c_1, \ldots, c_m\}$ **SERVER on input:** $(S = \{s_1, \ldots, s_n\}, z)$

.... Phase 1 ....

for ($i = 1$ to m)   for ($j = 1$ to n)

   $hc_i = H(c_i)$ $hs_j = H(s_j)$

$r \twoheadleftarrow \mathbb{Z}_{p'}^*$ $ks_j = (z + hs_j)^{-1} \pmod{p'}$

$A = \prod_{i=1}^{m}(z + hc_i) = \sum_{k=1}^{m} a_k z^{k-1} \pmod{p'}$

$X = g^{rA} = \prod_{k=1}^{m}(g^{z^{k-1}})^{ra_k}$

for ($i = 1$ to m)

   $A_i = \dfrac{A}{z + hc_i} = \sum_{k=1}^{m-1} a_{(i,k)} z^{k-1} \pmod{p'}$

   $X_i = g^{rA_i} = \prod_{k=1}^{m-1}(g^{z^{k-1}})^{a_{(i,k)} r}$

   $tg'_i = F(X_i)$

.... Phase 2 ....

         X $\longrightarrow$ for ($j = 1$ to n) $tg_j = F(X^{ks_j})$

         T $\longleftarrow$ **PERMUTE:** $T = \Pi(\{tg_1, \ldots, tg_n\})$

return $(|T|, \{c_i | tg'_i \in T\})$ **return** $\perp$

Fig. 1. bSH-PSI Protocol. All computation is (mod p) unless stated otherwise.

It is easy to see *client* correctly computes n. For every $s_j \in S$, HbC *server* sends exactly one tg_j to *client*. Thus, *client* needs only to count the number of tg_j's received.

To see that *client* correctly computes the intersection, let c_i be an arbitrary element in *client*'s set, such that $c_i \in S \cap C$. Then, there is some $0 < j \le n$ such that $c_i = s_j$ and $hc_i = hs_j$. Therefore, tg_j, computed by *server* and sent to *client* matches *client*'s tag tg'_i:

$$tg'_i = F(X_i) = F(g^{r(z+hc_1)\ldots(z+hc_{i-1})(z+hc_{i+1})\ldots(z+hc_m)}) =$$
$$= F(g^{\frac{r(z+hc_1)\ldots(z+hc_m)}{z+hc_i}}) = F(g^{r\frac{A}{z+hc_i}}) = F(X^{\frac{1}{z+hc_i}}) = tg_j.$$

Thus *client* concludes that c_i is in the intersection.

Now consider a *client*'s element $c_k \notin S \cap C$, i.e., there is no j such that $c_k = s_j$. Thus, there is also no j such that $hc_k = hs_j$ and $tg_j = tg'_k$ except for negligible probability, due to collisions in either $F(\cdot)$ or $H(\cdot)$, or degenerate input x such that $(H(x) + z) = 0 \bmod p'$. (If *server* ever detects such an input element, it must change its public key.) Therefore, *client* computes no match and concludes that c_k is not in the intersection.

Boundedness. As described in Definition 3, we need to show that *client* learns only *server*'s input set size if it attempts to input more than t set elements. We note that in order to extract $S \cap C$ with a set of size $m = u$, where $u > t$, *client* must aggregate u elements into X. This follows directly from our security model which requires *client* messages to be well formed. Then, we show that this is impossible under the *PG-E-SDH* assumption. Thus, if *client* is able to extract $S \cap C$ then $m \le t$.

More formally, we show by contradiction, that constructing a well-formed X, as described, is infeasible. We now assume that *client* can aggregate u elements into X. Then, *client* must have a PPT algorithm $\mathcal{A}$ which – given C, $H(\cdot)$, and $[g, g^z, \ldots, g^{(z^t)}]$ – computes:

$$ X = g^{r(z+hc_1)\ldots(z+hc_u)} = g^{(A_0+\ldots+A_{u-1}z^{u-1}+z^u)}, $$

where each A_i is a product-sum of values known to *client*: $r, hc_1, \ldots, hc_u$.

However, computing X is the same as solving the *polynomial-generalized exponent q-SDH* problem on inputs: $[g, g^z, \ldots, g^{(z^t)}]$ and $P_n(z) = A_0 + \ldots + A_{u-1}z^{u-1} + z^u$, which, based on our assumption, is infeasible since $u > t$. Hence, by contradiction, the embedding is impossible and *client* learns only n.

Client Privacy. The only message sent from *client* to *server* is:

$$ X = g^{r(z+hc_1)\ldots(z+hc_m)} \quad \mod p. $$

X is always of this form as an HbC *server* always correctly generates its public key. Since g is a generator of the cyclic subgroup $\mathbb{G} \subset \mathbb{Z}_p^*$ of order p', and no $(z+hc_i)$ is a multiple of p', except for negligible probability, we can assume that $A = g^{(z+hc_1)\ldots(z+hc_u)}$ is also a generator of $\mathbb{G}$. Since r is chosen uniformly, at random, from $\mathbb{Z}_{p'}^*$, X also has a uniform distribution in $\mathbb{G}$.

Thus with overwhelming probability[8], $\text{View}_S(C^0)$ and $\text{View}_S(C^1)$ are two uniformly distributed group elements and are thus indistinguishable. Therefore, Client Privacy holds in the presence of an HbC *server*.

By making one slight modification to the protocol, Client Privacy can be guaranteed unconditionally, regardless of the adversarial model of *server*. To mitigate the possibility of a malicious *server* presenting an invalid public key, *client* can simply verify that: $(g^{(z+hc_1)\ldots(z+hc_m)})^{p'} \mod p = 1$. If so, then g^A is a generator of $\mathbb{G}$ and $X = (g^A)^r$ is uniformly distributed in $\mathbb{G}$. Otherwise *client* aborts the protocol by sending just g^r and ignoring *server*'s response. In either case, Client Privacy is guaranteed.

Server Privacy. Following Definition 5, in order to show Server Privacy we construct an efficient simulator C^* of *client*'s view that is computationally indistinguishable from a real protocol execution. First, C^* computes the first message X from C, using $H(\cdot)$. It computes the remainder of the transcript as follows: It uses knowledge of $S \cap C$ to construct: $\{F(K_i) \mid c_i \in S \cap C\}$. Then, it adds to the set $\{F(r_j)\}$ for $0 < j \le n - |S \cap C|$, where each r_j is chosen at random. C^* then randomly permutes this set and returns the result as the second message to *server*.

---

[8] This probability is taken over the input space. Given non-degenerate inputs, these views are perfectly indistinguishable.

To arrive at a contradiction, suppose that a distinguisher D exists which can differentiate between the real protocol execution: $\text{View}_C(C, S)$ and that of the view simulated by C^*: $C^*(C, C \cap S, n)$. Then, by the hybrid argument, a PPT distinguisher D' must exist that can distinguish between random oracle outputs: $F(K_i)$ and $F(r_j)$ for some j and i, such that $s_i \notin S \cap C$. Thus, by the random oracle model, a simulator for D' can be used to construct an algorithm $\mathcal{A}$ which computes:

$$K_i = X^{\frac{1}{z+hs_i}} = g^{\frac{r(z+hc_1)...(z+hc_m)}{(z+hs_i)}}$$

where $s_i \neq c_k$, for all k. (K_i must be of this form due to boundedness and HbC behavior of *client*.)

Therefore, $(z + hs_i)$ is not a factor of $P_m(z) = r(z + hc_1)...(z + hc_m)$ and does not evenly divide it, with overwhelming probability. There are two possible events that occur with only negligible probability: (1) collisions in $H(\cdot)$, or (2) $P_m(z)/(z + hs_i)$ having a remainder that is a multiple of p'. Thus, we can use $\mathcal{A}$ to solve the *polynomial-generalized one-generator q-SDH* problem on inputs: $[g, g^z, \ldots, g^{(z^t)}]$ and $P_m(z) = r(z + hc_1)...(z + hc_m)$, which is infeasible, based on our assumption. Consequently, by contradiction, Server Privacy holds.

4.3   Computational and Communication Complexity

We now assess communication, computation and storage costs of $b\text{SH-PSI}$, as presented in Fig. 1.

Communication complexity involves: (1) a single $\log(p)$-bit group element in the first message, and (2) n outputs of $F(\cdot)$ in the second message.

We partition computation costs into *Phase 1* and *Phase 2*. Computation costs are further broken down by specific cryptographic operations: (1) invocations of random oracles: $F(\cdot)$ and $H(\cdot)$ (2) short $\log(p')$-bit multiplications, exponentiations, and inversions, and (3) and long $\log(p)$-bit multiplications and exponentiations. We analyze costs for both *server* and *client*.

Server's Phase 1 work starts with $O(t) \bmod(p)$ exponentiations to compute the public key. However, this can be done once for many interactions. It also includes $O(n)$ invocations of $H(\cdot)$, and $O(n)$ mod p' inversions. This requires *server* to know its input set S. If S is stable, this work can also be amortized for many interactions. *Server's Phase 2* work consists of $O(n)$ short $\log(p')$-bit exponentiations and $O(n)$ invocations of $F(\cdot)$.

Client's Phase 1 work is dominated by the computation of X and m witnesses: $\{X_i | 0 < i \leq m\}$. Most work is done in the expansion of the product of binomials of the form $\prod(z + hc_i)$. This can be performed as soon as *client's* input set is known. Also, as long as p' is fixed globally, *client* does not even need to know which *server* will be involved in the interaction. Coefficients of the resulting reduced polynomial in z can be computed in $O(m^2)$ time using the naïve method of repeated polynomial multiplication. Thus, we can precompute the numerator of X and each X_i in $O(m^3)$ short multiplications. This can be further reduced to $O(m^2 \log^2 m)$ by taking advantage of a more sophisticated technique (discussed in the full version [5]) leveraging an $O(d \log d)$ algorithm for d-degree polynomial multiplication.

Also, *client* must perform $O(m)$ invocations of $H(\cdot)$ and $F(\cdot)$, $O(m^2)$ long multiplications and short exponentiations, and $O(m)$ multiplications and exponentiations for each X_i in order to embed the corresponding polynomial evaluated at particular z corresponding to *server*'s public key. In more detail, given $P_t(s) = \sum_{i=0}^{m} a_i s^i$, *client* computes $\prod_{i=0}^{m} g^{s^i a_i}$, which is feasible because all g^{s^i} are known.

Client's only mandatory *Phase 2* work amounts to computing a cleartext set intersection, which is achievable with a single sort via $O((m + n) \log (m + n))$ swaps.

Storage overhead is dependent on precomputation. If all possible precomputation is performed, then *server*'s storage is dominated by $O(n) \log(p')$-bit group elements. *Client*'s storage is dominated by $O(m) \log(p)$-bit group elements and $O(m)$ outputs of $F(\cdot)$. If *client* computes Phase 1 without knowledge of *server*'s public key then storage is dominated by $O(m^2)$ short ($\log(p')$-bit) integers.

Optimizations. Choices of public parameters are essential for fast operation. In particular, bSH-PSI can operate in different groups (e.g., on some elliptic curves). We chose integers mod p due to their more efficient operation [11,12]. Practical current examples of sufficiently secure parameters are: $log(p) \approx 1024$ and $log(p') \approx 160$.

Furthermore, $H(\cdot)$ substantially influences computational complexity. If the range of H is considerably smaller than p' then $O(m^2 \log^2 m)$ short ($\log(p')$) multiplications may reduce to $O(m^2 \log^2 m)$ multiplications of $|H(\cdot)|$-bit integers, and $O(m^2)$ short multiplications (accounting for r).

5   Discussion and Open Problems

5.1   Unlinkability and Change Obliviousness

In settings where *client* and *server* interact more than once, additional privacy properties of *unlinkability* and *change obliviousness* might be desirable for either party.

Informally, *unlinkability* means that, if *client* and *server* interact twice, they should be unable to determine whether they have interacted before. *Change obliviousness* means: if one party's input changes between protocol executions, the other party should not learn this, unless: (1) input size changes, and/or (2) protocol output changes. Unlinkability subsumes change obliviousness; thus, is usually requires more effort.

The proposed bSH-PSI protocol provides both unlinkability and change obliviousness for *client*. This is due to *client*'s unconditional privacy. To attain *server* change obliviousness the protocol can be modified to use a keyed random oracle

$F'_\gamma(\cdot)$ – instead of $F(\cdot)$ – with a fresh random *server*-selected γ for every interaction. Whereas, to obtain unlinkability, *server* must also generate new secret[9] (z) and public $([g, g^z, \ldots, g^{(z^t)}])$ keys for every interaction, and communicate the latter to *client*.

These modifications require additional Phase 2 computation and storage for *client* and an extra round of communication. Specifically, γ and one-time public key $([g, g^z, \ldots, g^{(z^t)}])$ must be communicated to *client* before it can send X. *Client* must now store X_i instead of $F(X_i)$, even if the target *server* is known. If *server* unlinkability is provided, *client* must also store A and A_i and compute X and X_i during Phase 2.

5.2   Flexibility of t

At times, it may be desirable for *server* to increase the upper bound t to t'. There are at least two intuitive ways to do so. One way is for *client* and *server* to simply run the protocol $\lceil t'/t \rceil$ times. Alternatively, *server* can publish the extra elements of the public key: $[g^{z^{t+1}}, \ldots, g^{z^{t'}}]$. Either approach provides forward security for both parties. That is, no additional information can be learned from prior protocol executions, with lower bounds. Note, however, that t cannot be decreased unless an entirely new public key is generated.

5.3   Interacting with Multiple Servers

Optimizations can be made to save *client*'s resources in settings where *client* intends to interact with multiple servers using the same input set. First, if *server*'s set is not known ahead of time, or if space is a concern, *client* can compute and store A and A_i instead of X and t'_i. Of course, this is only possible if all servers use the same public key parameters: (g, p, p').

5.4   Malicious Security

While our protocol is secure in the HbC* model, it provides unconditional client privacy regardless of the behavior of *server*[10]. Security against a fully malicious server [19] would require a proof of valid computation of the random oracle $F(\cdot)$ without revealing the oracle's input. Security against a malicious *client* would require a proof that the accumulator $X = g^u$ is well-formed, for some u. We believe that such a proof is challenging since the exponent u is not known to *client*. Moreover, it is unclear how to construct a proof without revealing *client*'s input size in the process. An alternative approach is to rely on a variant of the Exponent Strong q-SDH assumption which states that: computing $(c, x^{\frac{1}{z+c}})$ is hard for all $x \in \mathbb{Z}_p$ given $[g, g^z, \ldots, g^{(z^q)}]$.

---

[9] Strictly speaking, a new z is not needed. Instead, *server* can generate a new base $\hat{g}$, compute the new $[\hat{g}, \hat{g}^z, \ldots, \hat{g}^{(z^t)}]$ and keep the same z.

[10] *Client* need only verify g^A is a generator by computing $(g^A)^{p'}$ before exponentiating with r.

5.5   Group Selection

Due to its computational efficiency of operations, we chose prime-order integer DH-groups. This efficiency is largely based on the fact that exponentiation can take advantage of the relatively small size of p'. Our protocol would work equally well in other DH-groups, such as the elliptic curve DH-group variant [6]. However, in our experience, these groups tend to be slower using existing implementations. Since computational cost (and not storage) is of primary importance, integer groups are the logical choice. We also conjecture that variants of the protocol composite groups (e.g., in the RSA setting) are easily realizable.

5.6 t-Intersection bSH-PSI

Thus far, we focused on limiting the amount of information revealed to *client* in each interaction by providing a guaranteed upper bound on *client*'s input size. An alternative approach would be limit the size of the intersection $|C \cap S|$. Although not secure against enumeration by *client*, this approach is useful in some situations. It is particularly applicable if *server*'s input set is much larger than t and the domain of set elements is large. For example, suppose that *server* owns a database and is willing to answer any query with a result set less than t. A hypothetical t-intersection bSH-PSI protocol could be realized in at least two variations (each of independent interest): (1) if $|C \cap S| > t$, *client* learns nothing, or (2) if $|C \cap S| > t$, *client* learns a random t sized subset of the intersection $C \cap S$. We defer the investigation of this topic for future work.

6   Equivalence of SDH Problems

We now show equivalence of the two new assumptions and their more established counterparts. First, we argue that *polynomial-generalized one-generator q-SDH* and *one-generator q-SDH* are equivalent. Next, we show equivalence of *polynomial-generalized exponent q-SDH* and *exponent q-SDH*. Both equivalence proofs describe two reductions (one in each direction) between respective problems.

Theorem 1. *The one-generator (q, t, ϵ)-SDH assumption holds iff the polynomial- generalized one-generator (q, t, ϵ)-SDH assumption holds.*

Proof. We show the contrapositive in each case. First, suppose that there exists an algorithm:

$$\mathcal{A}([g, g^z, \dots, g^{(z^q)}]) \to (c, g^{\frac{1}{(z+c)}})$$

that has an non-negligible advantage ϵ in solving *one-generator q-SDH*. We can then construct an algorithm:

$$\mathcal{A}'([g, g^z, \dots, g^{(z^q)}], P_n(z))) \to (c, g^{\frac{P_n(z)}{(z+c)}})$$

that has the same advantage in solving the *polynomial-generalized one-generator q-SDH* problem. First, $\mathcal{A}'$ runs $\mathcal{A}([g, g^z, \ldots, g^{(z^q)}])$. With probability at least ϵ, $\mathcal{A}$ outputs:

$$[c, g^{\frac{1}{z+c}}] \tag{1}$$

for some $c \in \mathbb{Z}_{p'}^*$. We observe that $\mathcal{A}'$ may use the polynomial division algorithm to rewrite the non-trivial part of its desired output as:

$$g^{\frac{P_n(z)}{(z+c)}} = g^{\frac{P'_n(z)+r}{z+c}} = g^{\frac{P'_n(z)}{z+c}} g^{\frac{r}{z+c}},$$

where $P'_n(z)$ is a polynomial divisible by $(z+c)$, and r is a constant in $\mathbb{Z}_{p'}^*$. Because $(z+c)$ divides $P'_n(z)$,

$$g^{\frac{P'_n(z)}{z+c}} = g^{P''_{n-1}(z)}, \tag{2}$$

where $P''_{n-1}(z)$ is a polynomial in z of degree $n-1$. Because $(n-1) < q$, $\mathcal{A}'$ may compute (2) by exponentiating and multiplying together elements from $[g, g^z, \ldots, g^{(z^q)}]$. Using (1), $\mathcal{A}'$ computes

$$(g^{\frac{1}{z+c}})^r = g^{\frac{r}{z+c}}. \tag{3}$$

Finally, $\mathcal{A}'$ multiplies (2) by (3) to obtain the value $g^{\frac{P_n(z)}{(z+c)}} = g^{\frac{P_n(z)}{z+c}}$, which is then output with the known value c. If and only if $\mathcal{A}$'s output is correct, $\mathcal{A}'$ also outputs a correct solution. Therefore, $\mathcal{A}'$ has advantage equal to ϵ in solving the *polynomial-generalized exponent q-SDH* problem.

Now, conversely, suppose that there exists an algorithm:

$$\mathcal{A}([g, g^z, \ldots, g^{(z^q)}], P_n(z)) \rightarrow (c, g^{\frac{P_n(z)}{(z+c)}})$$

that has an advantage ϵ in solving the *polynomial-generalized one-generator q-SDH* problem. Then, we can construct an algorithm:

$$\mathcal{A}'([g, g^z, \ldots, g^{(z^q)}]) \rightarrow (c, g^{\frac{1}{(z+c)}})$$

that has an advantage ϵ in solving the *one-generator q-SDH* problem with probability at least ϵ by merely running $\mathcal{A}([g, g^z, \ldots, g^{(z^q)}], 1)$ and outputting the result. If $\mathcal{A}$ yields a correct output $[c, g^{\frac{1}{(z+c)}}]$, then $\mathcal{A}'$ is also correct. Thus $\mathcal{A}'$ has advantage equal to ϵ of solving the *one-generator q-SDH* problem.

Theorem 2. *The exponent (q, t, ϵ)-SDH assumption holds iff the polynomial-generalized exponent (q, t, ϵ)-SDH assumption holds.*

Proof. We show the contrapositive for both cases. Suppose there exists an algorithm:

$$\mathcal{A}([g, g^z, \ldots, g^{(z^q)}]) \rightarrow g^{(z^{q+1})}$$

that has an advantage ϵ in solving the *exponent q-SDH* problem. We then construct another algorithm:

$$\mathcal{A}'([g, g^z, \ldots, g^{(z^q)}], P_n(z)) \rightarrow g^{(P_n(z))}$$

that has an advantage of $(\epsilon)^{poly(n)}$ in solving the *polynomial-generalized exponent q-SDH* problem. (Note that $(\epsilon)^{poly(n)}$ is non-negligible if ϵ is non-negligible). $\mathcal{A}'$ creates an $(n + 1)$-tuple of the form $[g, g^z, \ldots, g^{(z^n)}]$ as follows: for each $q < j \leq n$, it runs $\mathcal{A}([g, g^z, \ldots, g^{(z^{j-1})}])$ to obtain g^{z^j} and saves it for subsequent calls to $\mathcal{A}$. If any call fails to produce the correct output, $\mathcal{A}'$'s output will also be incorrect. We observe that $P_n(z) = a_0 + a_1 z + \ldots + a_n z^n$. Thus,

$$g^{P_n(z)} = g^{a_0} g^{a_1 z} \ldots g^{a_n z^n}.$$

Since all coefficients a_i and values $([g, g^z, \ldots, g^{(z^n)}])$ are now known to $\mathcal{A}'$, it outputs $g^{P_n(z)}$. Thus, $\mathcal{A}'$ has non-negligible advantage ϵ^{n-q} in solving the *polynomial-generalized exponent q-SDH* problem.

Now suppose there exists an algorithm:

$$\mathcal{A}([g, g^z, \ldots, g^{(z^q)}], P_n(z)) \to g^{(P_n(z))}$$

that has a non-negligible advantage ϵ in solving *polynomial-generalized exponent q-SDH*. We construct another algorithm:

$$\mathcal{A}'([g, g^z, \ldots, g^{(z^q)}]) \to g^{(z^{q+1})}$$

that has the same advantage ϵ in solving *exponent q-SDH* by simply running and outputting $\mathcal{A}([g, g^z, \ldots, g^{(z^q)}], z^{q+1})$. This call to $\mathcal{A}$ has probability at least ϵ of outputting $g^{z^{q+1}}$, and solving the *exponent q SDH* problem.

7 Conclusions

Motivated by recent advances in size-hiding secure computation and, more specifically, SH-PSI: size-hiding private set intersection techniques, this paper investigated bounded variants thereof. The main contribution of this work is the construction of the first bSH-PSI technique that allows *client* to unconditionally hide its input size while allowing *server* to limit that size. We believe that bSH-PSI can be a useful tool in the arsenal of secure computation techniques. There are at least three directions for future work: (1) alternative and/or more efficient, bSH-PSI techniques, (2) other private set operations with bounded (one-sided) size-hiding input, e.g., private set union and private set intersection cardinality, and (3) modifications of our current construct and its proofs to provide security against malicious client in the standard model, i.e., without relying on random oracles. The extended version of this paper [5] details specific techniques *client* can use to efficiently embed its input into an accumulator using *server*'s public key.

Acknowledgments. We are grateful to the anonymous reviewers for their helpful comments. We also thank Jaroslav Šeděnka for his contributions to the initial stages of this work.

References

1. Ateniese, G., De Cristofaro, E., Tsudik, G.: (If) size matters: size-hiding private set intersection. In: Catalano, D., Fazio, N., Gennaro, R., Nicolosi, A. (eds.) PKC 2011. LNCS, vol. 6571, pp. 156–173. Springer, Heidelberg (2011)
2. Bellare, M., Rogaway, P.: Random oracles are practical: a paradigm for designing efficient protocols. In: ACM Conference on Computer and Communications Security, pp. 62–73. ACM (1993)
3. Boneh, D., Boyen, X.: Short signatures without random oracles. In: Cachin, C., Camenisch, J.L. (eds.) EUROCRYPT 2004. LNCS, vol. 3027, pp. 56–73. Springer, Heidelberg (2004)
4. Boneh, D., Di Crescenzo, G., Ostrovsky, R., Persiano, G.: Public key encryption with keyword search. In: Cachin, C., Camenisch, J.L. (eds.) EUROCRYPT 2004. LNCS, vol. 3027, pp. 506–522. Springer, Heidelberg (2004)
5. Bradley, T., Faber, S., Tsudik, G.: Bounded size-hiding private set intersection. IACR Cryptology ePrint Archive, Report 2016/657 (2016). http://eprint.iacr.org/2016/657
6. Caelli, W.J., Dawson, E.P., Rea, S.A.: Pki, elliptic curve cryptography, and digital signatures. Comput. Secur. 18(1), 47–66 (1999)
7. Chase, M., Ostrovsky, R., Visconti, I.: Executable proofs, input-size hiding secure computation and a new ideal world. In: Oswald, E., Fischlin, M. (eds.) EUROCRYPT 2015. LNCS, vol. 9057, pp. 532–560. Springer, Heidelberg (2015)
8. Dachman-Soled, D., Malkin, T., Raykova, M., Yung, M.: Efficient robust private set intersection. Int. J. Appl. Cryptogr. 2(4), 289–303 (2012)
9. D'Arco, P., González Vasco, M.I., Pérez del Pozo, A.L., Soriente, C.: Size-hiding in private set intersection: existential results and constructions. In: Mitrokotsa, A., Vaudenay, S. (eds.) AFRICACRYPT 2012. LNCS, vol. 7374, pp. 378–394. Springer, Heidelberg (2012)
10. D'Arco, P., González Vasco, M.I., Pérez del Pozo, A.L., Soriente, C.: Size-hiding in private set intersection: existential results and constructions. In: Mitrokotsa, A., Vaudenay, S. (eds.) AFRICACRYPT 2012. LNCS, vol. 7374, pp. 378–394. Springer, Heidelberg (2012)
11. De Cristofaro, E., Faber, S., Gasti, P., Tsudik, G.: Genodroid: are privacy-preserving genomic tests ready for prime time? In: WPES, pp. 97–108. ACM (2012)
12. De Cristofaro, E., Faber, S., Tsudik, G.: Secure genomic testing with size- and position-hiding private substring matching. In: WPES, pp. 107–118. ACM (2013)
13. De Cristofaro, E., Gasti, P., Tsudik, G.: Fast and private computation of cardinality of set intersection and union. In: Pieprzyk, J., Sadeghi, A.-R., Manulis, M. (eds.) CANS 2012. LNCS, vol. 7712, pp. 218–231. Springer, Heidelberg (2012)
14. De Cristofaro, E., Kim, J., Tsudik, G.: Linear-complexity private set intersection protocols secure in malicious model. In: Abe, M. (ed.) ASIACRYPT 2010. LNCS, vol. 6477, pp. 213–231. Springer, Heidelberg (2010)
15. De Cristofaro, E., Tsudik, G.: Practical private set intersection protocols with linear complexity. In: Sion, R. (ed.) FC 2010. LNCS, vol. 6052, pp. 143–159. Springer, Heidelberg (2010)
16. Dong, C., Chen, L., Wen, Z.: When private set intersection meets big data: an efficient and scalable protocol. In: Proceedings of the ACM SIGSAC Conference on Computer & Communications Security, pp. 789–800. ACM (2013)
17. Faber, S., Petrlic, R., Tsudik, G.: Unlinked: private proximity-based off-line OSN interaction. In: Proceedings of the 14th ACM Workshop on Privacy in the Electronic Society, pp. 121–131. ACM (2015)

18. Freedman, M.J., Nissim, K., Pinkas, B.: Efficient private matching and set intersection. In: Cachin, C., Camenisch, J.L. (eds.) EUROCRYPT 2004. LNCS, vol. 3027, pp. 1–19. Springer, Heidelberg (2004)

19. Goldreich, O.: The Foundations of Cryptography - Volume 2, Basic Applications. Cambridge University Press, Cambridge (2004)

20. Goldwasser, S., Micali, S.: Probabilistic encryption. J. Comput. Syst. Sci. **28**(2), 270–299 (1984)

21. Goyal, V., Ostrovsky, R., Scafuro, A., Visconti, I.: Black-box non-black-box zero knowledge. In: STOC, pp. 515–524. ACM (2014)

22. Hahn, C., Hur, J.: Scalable and secure private set intersection for big data. In: International Conference on Big Data and Smart Computing, BigComp 2016, Hong Kong, China, 18–20 January 2016, pp. 285–288 (2016)

23. Hazay, C.: Oblivious polynomial evaluation and secure set-intersection from algebraic PRFs. In: Dodis, Y., Nielsen, J.B. (eds.) TCC 2015, Part II. LNCS, vol. 9015, pp. 90–120. Springer, Heidelberg (2015)

24. Hazay, C., Lindell, Y.: Efficient protocols for set intersection and pattern matching with security against malicious and covert adversaries. In: Canetti, R. (ed.) TCC 2008. LNCS, vol. 4948, pp. 155–175. Springer, Heidelberg (2008)

25. Huang, Y., Evans, D., Katz, J.: Private set intersection: are garbled circuits better than custom protocols? In: NDSS (2012)

26. Ishai, Y., Paskin, A.: Evaluating branching programs on encrypted data. In: Vadhan, S.P. (ed.) TCC 2007. LNCS, vol. 4392, pp. 575–594. Springer, Heidelberg (2007)

27. Kerschbaum, F.: Outsourced private set intersection using homomorphic encryption. In: Proceedings of the 7th ACM Symposium on Information, Computer and Communications Security, pp. 85–86. ACM (2012)

28. Kissner, L., Song, D.: Private and threshold set-intersection. Technical report, DTIC Document (2004)

29. Lindell, Y., Nissim, K., Orlandi, C.: Hiding the input-size in secure two-party computation. In: Sako, K., Sarkar, P. (eds.) ASIACRYPT 2013, Part II. LNCS, vol. 8270, pp. 421–440. Springer, Heidelberg (2013)

30. Lindell, Y., Nissim, K., Orlandi, C.: Hiding the input-size in secure two-party computation. In: Sako, K., Sarkar, P. (eds.) ASIACRYPT 2013, Part II. LNCS, vol. 8270, pp. 421–440. Springer, Heidelberg (2013)

31. Micali, S., Rabin, M.O., Kilian, J.: Zero-knowledge sets. In: FOCS, pp. 80–91. IEEE Computer Society (2003)

32. Nguyen, L.: Accumulators from bilinear pairings and applications. In: Menezes, A. (ed.) CT-RSA 2005. LNCS, vol. 3376, pp. 275–292. Springer, Heidelberg (2005)

33. Pinkas, B., Schneider, T., Zohner, M.: Faster private set intersection based on OT extension. In: 23rd USENIX Security Symposium (USENIX Security 2014), pp. 797–812 (2014)

34. Tanaka, N., Saito, T.: On the q-strong Diffie-Hellman problem. IACR Cryptology ePrint Archive, 2010:215 (2010)

On Garbling Schemes with and Without Privacy

Carsten Baum[(✉)]

Department of Computer Science, Aarhus University, Aarhus, Denmark
cbaum@cs.au.dk

Abstract. Garbling schemes allow to construct two-party function evaluation with security against cheating parties (SFE). To achieve this goal, one party (the Garbler) sends multiple encodings of a circuit (called Garbled Circuits) to the other party (the Evaluator) and opens a subset of these encodings, showing that they were generated honestly. For the remaining garbled circuits, the garbler sends encodings of the inputs. This allows the evaluator to compute the result of function, while the encoding ensures that no other information beyond the output is revealed. To achieve active security against a malicious adversary, the garbler in current protocols has to send $O(s)$ circuits (where s is the statistical security parameter).

In this work we show that, for a certain class of circuits, one can reduce this overhead. We consider circuits where sub-circuits depend only on one party's input. Intuitively, one can evaluate these sub-circuits using only one circuit and privacy-free garbling. This has applications to e.g. input validation in SFE and allows to construct more efficient SFE protocols in such cases. We additionally show how to integrate our solution with the SFE protocol of [5], thus reducing the overhead even further.

1 Introduction

Background. In actively-secure Two-party Function Evaluation (SFE) two mutually distrusting parties Alice and Bob (P_a, P_b) want to jointly evaluate a function f based on secret inputs x, y that they choose individually. This is done using an interactive protocol where both parties exchange messages such that, at the end of the protocol, they only learned the correct output $z = f(x, y)$ of the computation and no other information. This also holds if one of the parties arbitrarily deviates from the protocol. The problem was originally stated by Yao in 1982 [20], who also gave the first solution for the setting of honest, but curious parties.

Given a trusted third party $\mathcal{T}$ which both P_a, P_b have access to, one can solve the problem as follows: Both send their inputs as well as a description of

C. Baum—Supported by The Danish National Research Foundation and The National Science Foundation of China (under the grant 61061130540) for the Sino-Danish Center for the Theory of Interactive Computation, within which part of this work was performed; by the CFEM research center (supported by the Danish Strategic Research Council) within which part of this work was performed; and by the Advanced ERC grant MPCPRO.

© Springer International Publishing Switzerland 2016
V. Zikas and R. De Prisco (Eds.): SCN 2016, LNCS 9841, pp. 468–485, 2016.
DOI: 10.1007/978-3-319-44618-9_25

f which we call C_f to $\mathcal{T}$, which then does the following: We consider C_f to be a boolean circuit with dedicated input and output wires. C_f consists of gates of fan-in two. $\mathcal{T}$ represents the inputs x, y as assignments of $0, 1$ to the input wires of the circuit, and then the functions of the gates are applied (as soon as both input wires of a gate have an assignment) until all the output wires[1] of C_f are either 0 or 1. Then $\mathcal{T}$ translates the values on the output wires into z and sends it to both P_a, P_b. Yao showed in his seminal work how to replace this $\mathcal{T}$ with an interactive protocol. This technique became known as *Garbled Circuits*.

Garbled Circuits in a Nutshell. In order to obtain a garbled circuit from C_f, the garbler P_a does the following: Each gate of the circuit can be represented as a table, where for each combination of the inputs a value from $\{0, 1\}$ is assigned to the output wire. Now, the rows of this table are first shuffled and then the $0, 1$ values of the inputs and outputs are replaced by random bit strings (*keys*), such that the output key of a gate corresponds to the input key of another gate if its output is wired into the respective input in C_f and if they both correspond to the same value on the wire. One then stores information such that each output key can be derived if and only if both input keys for the corresponding row are known. Such a gate is called a *Garbled Gate* and by applying this technique recursively to all gates, P_a computes a so-called *Garbled Circuit*. One then considers the gates whose inputs are the input wires of the circuit. These keys are considered as the *input keys* of the circuit. Moreover, P_a also has to store a table of the keys that belong to the output wires of the circuit.

In the next step, P_a sends the garbled circuit and the input keys corresponding to her chosen input to the evaluator P_b. He obtains his input keys from P_a by a so-called *Oblivious Transfer*(OT) protocol, where P_a inputs all possible keys and P_b starts with his input y, such that afterwards P_b only learns the keys that correspond to his input and P_a does not learn y. P_b can now evaluate the circuit gate by gate until he obtains the output keys, which he sends to P_a. Intuitively, the security of the protocol is based on the OT hiding P_b's input while the garbling hides the input of P_a (and to some extend the computed circuit).

P_a can cheat in the above protocol in multiple ways: The circuit that is computed is hidden from P_b, so it may differ from C_f (or he obtains input keys that do not correspond to his inputs). A solution to this problem is called the *cut-and-choose* approach, where a number of circuits is garbled and sent to P_b. He then chooses a random subset to be opened completely to him and he can check that the circuit indeed computes the right function. For the other garbled instances, the above protocol is then run multiple times in parallel and the evaluator derives the result from the outputs of these instances. This may lead to new problems, see e.g. [16,17] for details.

Garbling Schemes. The garbled circuits-approach has found many applications in cryptography, such as in verifiable computation, private set intersection, zero-knowledge proofs or functional encryption with public keys (to just name

---

[1] We let $\mathcal{T}$ accept only descriptions of f where the graph representing the circuit C_f is directed and acyclic.

a few). Moreover, it has been treated on a more abstract level e.g. in [12] as *Randomized Encodings*. Kamara and Wei [14] discuss the idea of *special purpose garbled circuits* which do not yield full-fledged SFE but can on the other hand efficiently be instantiated using Structured Encryption Schemes and yield smaller overhead compared to directly using GC. Moreover, Bellare et al. [3] discussed garbling as a primitive having potentially different security notions, and studied how these are related. Using their framework one can compare different properties that a garbling scheme can have, such as *privacy, authenticity and obliviousness*. This allows to look for special schemes that may only implement a subset or different properties, which may be of use in certain contexts. As an example for such an application, one can e.g. consider the efficient *zero-knowledge protocol* due to Jawurek et al. [13] where the prover evaluates a garbled circuit in order to prove a certain statement.

Since only the evaluator in [13] has private inputs to the circuit and evaluates it on known values, no privacy of the inputs is necessary. A garbling scheme such as the one from [7] can then be used, which has lower overhead than comparable schemes with privacy.

The Problem. In this paper, we address the following question:

Can one construct Secure Function Evaluation protocols based on a combination of garbling schemes both with and without privacy, thus reducing overhead?

The question can be thought of as a generalization of [13]: Those parts of a circuit C_f that do only depend on one party's input may not need to be computed with active security. Such circuits naturally arise in the case when predicates must be computed on the inputs of each party, which includes the case when signatures must be verified or inputs in a reactive computation are checked for consistency. For such functions this separate evaluation can potentially improve the runtime of SFE, as e.g. shown by [15]. While it seems intuitive that in such a case this evaluation strategy is preferable, it is unclear how to combine those schemes while not introducing new problems. In particular, one has to make sure that the outputs of the privacy-free part correspond to the inputs of the actively-secure computation.

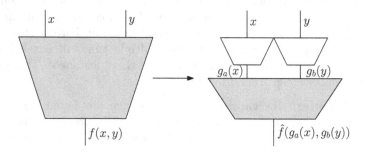

Fig. 1. A graphical depiction of the function decomposition.

Contributions. In this work, we describe a solution to the aforementioned problem. It can be applied for a certain class of functions that are decomposable as shown in Fig. 1.

On the left side of the figure, the evaluation without optimization is shown. Here the whole circuit must be evaluated using an actively secure two-party SFE scheme, while on the right side only parts of the circuit (the grey circuit) will be computed with active security. Our solution allows that the evaluation of $\hat{f}$ can be done by an arbitrary SFE scheme. To achieve this goal, we use circuit augmentation for $g_a, g_b, \hat{f}$ which in itself introduces a small overhead. We will show that this overhead can mostly be eliminated using e.g. [5] as SFE scheme.

We start with the following idea: Let P_a compute a privacy-free garbling of g_b and P_b compute a privacy-free garbling of g_a. Both parties exchange and evaluate the privacy-free garbling, whose output in turn will be the input to the evaluation of $\hat{f}$. Now we must verify that both P_a and P_b take the output of their respective functions and do not replace it before inputting it into $\hat{f}$. At the same time, the outputs of g_a, g_b are confidential and we must prevent the garbler from sending an incorrect circuit or wrong input keys. Our solution will deal with the inconsistency problem by checking that the inputs to $\hat{f}$ come indeed from g_a, g_b using a hash function whose output is properly masked. This, in turn, creates new problems since such a mask can be used to tamper with the obtained hash. Therefore, care must be taken about the timing in the protocol. Details follow in Sect. 3.

Why not Just Using Zero-Knowledge Proofs? Intuitively there is another solution to the above problem that avoids privacy-free garbling altogether: P_a commits to her inputs to $\hat{f}$ as $Com(g_a(x); r)$ and proves in zero-knowledge that this commitment indeed contains a value that lies in the image of g_a (P_b similarly uses g_b in the proof). Now all functions g_a, g_b are assumed to be binary circuits and the most efficient generic zero-knowledge proofs over $\mathbb{Z}_2$ are [9,13], where the proof-size is linear in the circuit size[2]. The crucial point is that, to the best of our knowledge, the proof itself must compute either the *Com* function or some verification function such as to tie the proof together with the SFE input. Computing public key-based primitives over $\mathbb{Z}_2$ incurs a huge blowup in the proof size. If one uses symmetric primitives like e.g. SHA-256 then our approach is still preferable, since computing such a hash function requires significantly more AND gates (see e.g. [19]) than computing the matrix multiplication that is required in our protocol.

Related Work. Our problem shares some similarity with *Verifiable Computation* [2,8]. Here, the idea is that a weak client outsources an expensive computation to a computationally stronger but possibly malicious server. This server then performs the computation and delivers a *proof* of correct computation which the client can check (in time significantly smaller than evaluating the function itself). Our setting differs, since we want that the server performs the evaluation of the

---

[2] Approaches based on SNARKs have smaller proof size but require much more work on the prover's side, which is why we do not mention them.

circuit on his own inputs and these must be kept secret. Moreover, we do only require one evaluation of the circuit.

Our solution, as already mentioned, bears resemblance with the concept of *Zero-Knowledge Proofs* [10, 11] where a prover convinces a verifier about the truth of the statement in an interactive protocol without revealing anything but the validity of this statement. In particular (in our setting), P_a proves to P_b that her input to $\hat{f}$ lies in the image of the function g_a and vice versa. In cryptographic protocols, these proofs are often used to show that certain algebraic relations among elements hold. The fact that these proofs can also be used to (efficiently) show that the prover knows a specific input to a circuit was already observed in [13]. In comparison to their work, we exploit this phenomenon in a more general sense.

In concurrent and independent work, Katz et al. [15] described a related approach to enforce input validity in SFE. Their techniques differ significantly from our work: Using a clever combination of OT and ElGamal encryption they can enforce that $\hat{f}$ and g_a, g_b have the same inputs, where g_a, g_b are predicates with public output (that validate the inputs of each party) and $\hat{f}$ is evaluated using SFE. Their approach is using the protocol of Afshar et al. [1] for the evaluation of $\hat{f}$ while we allow for a larger class of SFE schemes to be used.

2   Preliminaries

In this work, we let λ denote the computational and s denote the statistical security parameter. We use the standard definitions for a negligible function $\mathsf{negl}(\cdot)$ and polynomial function $\mathsf{poly}(\cdot)$. Two distributions of random variables are statistically indistinguishable if their distance is negligible in s. If instead distinguishing them breaks a computational assumption (parametrized by λ), then we consider them as computationally indistinguishable, which we denote as $\approx_c$. We use $\mathbb{B}$ as shorthand for $\{0, 1\}$.

Let us assume that P_a, P_b agreed to evaluate a function $f : \mathbb{B}^{2n} \to \mathbb{B}^m$, where the first n input bits are provided by P_a and the second n input bits by P_b. We assume that the function can be decomposed into $\hat{f} : \mathbb{B}^{l_a + l_b} \to \mathbb{B}^m$, $g_a : \mathbb{B}^n \to \mathbb{B}^l_a$, $g_b : \mathbb{B}^n \to \mathbb{B}^l_b$ such that

$$\forall x, y \in \mathbb{B}^n : \ \hat{f}(g_a(x), g_b(y)) = f(x, y)$$

To be more applicable in our setting, we have to look at the functions as circuits, and will do so using an approach similar to [3].

2.1   Circuits and the Split-Input Representation

Consider the tuple $\mathcal{C}_f = (n_{in}, n_{out}, n_g, L, R, G)$ where

- $n_{in} \geq 2$ is the number of input wires, $n_{out} \geq 2$ the number of output wires and $n_g \geq 1$ the number of gates. We let $n_w = n_{in} + n_g$ be the number of wires.
- we define the sets $Inputs \leftarrow \{1, ..., n_{in}\}$, $Wires \leftarrow \{1, ..., n_w\}$ as well as $Outputs \leftarrow \{n_w - n_{out} + 1, ..., n_w\}$ and $Gates \leftarrow \{n_{in} + 1, ..., n_w\}$ to identify the respective elements in the circuit.

- the function $L : Gates \mapsto Wires\backslash Outputs$ identifies the left incoming wire and $R : Gates \mapsto Wires\backslash Outputs$ identifies the right incoming wire for each gate, with the restriction that $\forall g \in Gates : L(g) < R(g) < g$.
- the mapping $G : Gates \times \mathbb{B}^2 \mapsto \mathbb{B}$ determines the function that is computed by a gate.

To obtain the outputs of the above circuit when evaluating it on an input $x = x_1...x_{n_{in}}$ one evaluates $\mathcal{C}_f$ as follows:

$eval(\mathcal{C}_f, x)$:

    (1) For $g = n_{in} + 1, ..., n_w$:
        (1.1) $l \leftarrow L(g), r \leftarrow R(g)$
        (1.2) $x_g \leftarrow G(g, x_l, x_r)$
    (2) Output $x_{n_w - n_{out} + 1}...x_{n_w}$

For a function $f : \mathbb{B}^{n_{in}} \mapsto \mathbb{B}^{n_{out}}$, we consider $\mathcal{C}_f = (n_{in}, n_{out}, n_g, L, R, G)$ as a *circuit representation of* f iff $\forall x \in \mathbb{B}^{n_{in}} : f(x) = eval(\mathcal{C}_f, x)$.

In order to be able to apply our solution, the circuit in question must be decomposable in a certain way as already outlined in Sect. 1. We will now formalize what we mean by this decomposability.

Definition 1 (Split-Input Representation (SIR)). *Let* $f : \mathbb{B}^{2n} \to \mathbb{B}^m$, $\hat{f} : \mathbb{B}^{l_a + l_b} \to \mathbb{B}^m$, $g_a : \mathbb{B}^n \to \mathbb{B}^{l_a}$, $g_b : \mathbb{B}^n \to \mathbb{B}^{l_b}$ *be functions such that*

$$\forall x, y \in \mathbb{B}^n : \quad \hat{f}(g_a(x), g_b(y)) = f(x, y)$$

Let moreover $\mathcal{C}_f, \mathcal{C}_{\hat{f}}, \mathcal{C}_{g_a}, \mathcal{C}_{g_b}$ *be their respective circuit representations. Then we call* $\mathcal{C}_{\hat{f}}, \mathcal{C}_{g_a}, \mathcal{C}_{g_b}$ *the Split-input representation of* $\mathcal{C}_f$.

For every function h with $n \geq 2$ such a decomposition always exists, but it is only of interest in our setting if (intuitively) $n_g(\mathcal{C}_{\hat{f}}) \ll n_g(\mathcal{C}_f)$.

2.2 Secure Two-Party Computation and Garbling Schemes

The notion of an SFE protocol is described by a protocol between two parties P_a, P_b that securely implements Fig. 2.

Note that $\mathcal{F}_{\text{SFE\&CommitOT}}$ moreover provides *commitments* and[3] *committed OT* [4]. Committed OT resembles OT as depicted in Fig. 3, but where the choice of the receiver is determined by a commitment.

The main reason why we need this specific functionality $\mathcal{F}_{\text{SFE\&CommitOT}}$ is that we have to ensure consistency of inputs using the commitments between the actively secure scheme and the privacy-free part, and having all of these as one functionality simplifies the proof.

---

[3] These are building blocks are used in many SFE protocols. We hence assume that they are available and cheap.

Functionality $\mathcal{F}_{\text{SFE\&CommitOT}}$

The input x to the circuit is split up into j blocks $I_1, ..., I_j$, where each block is provided by either P_a, P_b or both.

Initialization:
- On input $(\text{init}, \mathcal{C}, I_1, ..., I_j)$ from both P_a, P_b where $\mathcal{C} = (n, m, g, L, R, G)$ is a circuit, store $\mathcal{C}$. Moreover, the parties agree on a set of disjoint subsets $I_i \subseteq [n]$ such that $\bigcup I_i = [n]$.

Commit:
- Upon input (commit, id, x) from either P_a or P_b and if id was not used before, store (id, x, P_a) if the command was sent by P_a, and (id, x, P_b) otherwise. Then send (commit, id) to both parties.

Open:
- Upon input (open, id) by P_a and if (id, x, P_a) was stored, output (open, id, x) to P_b.
- Upon input (open, id) by P_b and if (id, x, P_b) was stored, output (open, id, x) to P_a.

One-sided Committed OT:
- On input (cotB, id) from P_b and $(\text{cotB}, id, \{y_0^i, y_1^i\}_{i \in [l]})$ by P_a and if there is a (id, x, P_b) stored with $x = x_1...x_l$, then output $(\text{ot}, \{y_{x_i}^i\}_{i \in [l]})$ to P_b.

Input by both parties:
- Upon input (input, id, x) by both parties and if id was not used before, store $(id, x, \sim)$.

Input of P_a:
- Upon input (inputA) from P_a where there is a $(I_i, x_i, \cdot)$ stored for each $i \in [j]$, output (inputA) to P_b.

Input of P_b:
- Upon input (inputB) from P_b where inputA was obtained, load all x_i from $(I_i, x_i, \cdot)$, compute $z \leftarrow eval(\mathcal{C}, x_1...x_j)$ and output (output, z) to P_b.

Fig. 2. SFE, commitments and committed OT for two parties.

Functionality $\mathcal{F}_{\text{OT}}$

OT for P_a:
- On input (otA, x) from P_a and $(\text{otA}, \{y_0^i, y_1^i\}_{i \in [l]})$ by P_b and if $x = x_1...x_l$, output $(\text{ot}, \{y_{x_i}^i\}_{i \in [l]})$ to P_a.

OT for P_b:
- On input (otB, x) from P_b and $(\text{otB}, \{y_0^i, y_1^i\}_{i \in [l]})$ by P_a and if $x = x_1...x_l$, output $(\text{ot}, \{y_{x_i}^i\}_{i \in [l]})$ to P_b.

Fig. 3. Functionality for OT.

Out of the framework of [3] we will now recap the notion of *projective verifiable garbling schemes*. We require the properties *correctness, authenticity and verifiability*. These intuitively ensure that the evaluated circuit shall compute the correct function, only leak the output keys that can be obtained using the provided input keys and that one can check after the fact (i.e. when obtaining all the input keys) whether the circuit in fact was a garbling of a certain function.

Let λ be a security parameter and $\mathcal{G} = (Gb, En, De, Ev, Ve)$ be a tuple of (possibly randomized) algorithms such that

$Gb(1^\lambda, \mathcal{C}_f)$: On input $1^\lambda, \mathcal{C}_f$ where $n_{in}, n_{out} = \mathsf{poly}(\lambda), n \geq \lambda$ and $|\mathcal{C}_f| = \mathsf{poly}(\lambda)$ the algorithm outputs a triple (F, e, d) where we call F the garbled circuit, e the input encoding information and d the output decoding information.

$En(e, x)$: On input e, x where $e = \{X_i^0, X_i^1\}$ is a set of keys representing the input wires, output X such that $X_i \leftarrow X_i^{x_i}$ i.e. output the 0 key for input i if $x_i = 0$ and vice versa for $x_i = 1$.

$Ev(F, X, x)$: On input (F, X, x) where F, X are outputs of the above algorithms, evaluate the garbled circuit F on the input keys X to produce output keys Z.

$De(Z, d)$: Let Z, d be input to this algorithm, where $d = \{Z_i^0, Z_i^1\}$ and Z contains l elements. The algorithm outputs a string $z \in \{0, 1, \perp\}^l$ where $z_i \leftarrow b$ if $Z_i = Z_i^b$, and $z_i \leftarrow \perp$ if $Z_i \notin \{Z_i^0, Z_i^1\}$.

$Ve(\mathcal{C}_f, F, e)$: On input $\mathcal{C}_f, F, e$ with the same semantics as above, the algorithm outputs 1 if F, e is a garbling of $\mathcal{C}_f$.

The definitions are according to [7]. Correctness is straightforward and implies that combining the above algorithms yields the expected output from evaluating f directly.

Definition 2 (Correctness). *Let $\mathcal{G}$ be a verifiable projective garbling scheme. Then $\mathcal{G}$ is correct if for all $n_{in}, n_{out} = \mathsf{poly}(\lambda), f : \mathbb{B}^{n_{in}} \to \mathbb{B}^{n_{out}}$ with circuit representation $\mathcal{C}_f$ and for all $x \in \mathbb{B}^{n_{in}}$ it holds that*

$$\Pr\left[De(Ev(F, (X_i^{x_i}), x), d) \neq f(x) \mid (F, e, d) \leftarrow Gb(1^\lambda, \mathcal{C}_f) \wedge \right.$$
$$\left. (X_i^{x_i}) \leftarrow En(e, x) \qquad\qquad \right] \leq \mathsf{negl}(\lambda)$$

Authenticity is very important for our later application. It prevents the adversary from successfully outputting other output keys than those he can derive from the input keys and the garbling.

Definition 3 (Authenticity). *Let $\mathcal{G}$ be a verifiable projective garbling scheme. Then $\mathcal{G}$ provides authenticity if for all $n_{in}, n_{out} = \mathsf{poly}(\lambda), f : \mathbb{B}^{n_{in}} \to \mathbb{B}^{n_{out}}$ with circuit representation $\mathcal{C}_f$ and for all $x \in \mathbb{B}^{n_{in}}, y \in \mathbb{B}^{n_{out}}$ with $y \neq f(x)$ it holds that*

$$\Pr\left[De(\mathcal{A}(\mathcal{C}_f, F, (X_i^{x_i}), x), d) = y \mid (F, e, d) \leftarrow Gb(1^\lambda, \mathcal{C}_f) \wedge \right.$$
$$\left. (X_i^{x_i}) \leftarrow En(e, x) \qquad\qquad \right] \leq \mathsf{negl}(\lambda)$$

for every $\mathcal{A}$ that is running in probabilistic polynomial time in λ.

In the definition of verifiability one has to consider that the Ve algorithm can also output 1 for adversarially chosen garblings F'. In such a case, we require that no information about the input is leaked if the evaluator honestly evaluates the garbled circuit.

Definition 4 (Verifiability). *Let $\mathcal{G}$ be a verifiable projective garbling scheme. Then $\mathcal{G}$ has verifiability if for all $n_{in}, n_{out} = \mathsf{poly}(\lambda)$, $f : \mathbb{B}^{n_{in}} \to \mathbb{B}^{n_{out}}$ with circuit representation $\mathcal{C}_f$ and for all $x, y \in \mathbb{B}^{n_{in}}, x \neq y, f(x) = f(y)$ it holds that*

$$\Pr\left[Ev(F, (X_i^{x_i}), x) \neq Ev(F, (X_i^{y_i}), y) \mid Ve(\mathcal{C}_f, F, \{X_i^0, X_i^1\}) = 1 \wedge \right.$$
$$\left. (F, \{X_i^0, X_i^1\}) \leftarrow \mathcal{A}(1^\lambda, \mathcal{C}_f) \quad \right] \leq \mathsf{negl}(\lambda)$$

for every probabilistic polynomial-time $\mathcal{A}$.

A garbling scheme $\mathcal{G}$ that fulfils all the above three conditions will from now on be called *privacy-free*.

2.3 Universal Hash Functions

A third ingredient that we need for our protocol are universal hash functions. For such a function two inputs will yield the same output only with small probability for as long as the function itself is randomly chosen *after the inputs are fixed*. This is a rather weak requirement in comparison to e.g. collision-resistant hash functions, but it is strong enough in our setting: If the circuits are first garbled and the inputs are fixed before the hash function is chosen, then the chance of two inputs colliding is very small (even though the universal hash function might be easily invertible).

Definition 5 (Universal Hash Function). *Let $\mathcal{H} = \{h : \mathbb{B}^m \to \mathbb{B}^s\}$, then $\mathcal{H}$ is a family of universal hash functions if*

$$\forall x, y \in \mathbb{B}^m, x \neq y \; : \; \Pr_{h \in_R \mathcal{H}}[h(x) = h(y)] \leq 2^{-s}$$

A family of universal hash functions has the uniform difference property if

$$\forall x, y \in \mathbb{B}^m, x \neq y, \forall z \in \mathbb{B}^s \; : \; \Pr_{h \in_R \mathcal{H}}[h(x) \oplus h(y) = z] \leq 2^{-s}$$

An family of functions that we will later use is defined as follows:

Definition 6. *Let $t \in \mathbb{B}^{m+s-1}$ and $M \in \mathbb{B}^{s \times m}$ such that $M_{i,j} = t_{i+j-1}$ and define $h_t : x \mapsto Mx$. Moreover, define the family $\mathbb{H}$ as $\mathbb{H} = \{h_t \mid t \in \mathbb{B}^{m+s-1}\}$.*

Remark 1. $\mathbb{H}$ is a family of universal hash functions with the uniform difference property.

Proof. See [5, Appendix E]

3 Construction

In our protocol, we use the functions defined above to protect against the adversary providing an inconsistent input to $\hat{f}$. To do so, we augment the computed circuits slightly. A graphical depiction of that can be found in Fig. 4.

The solution is tailored for protocols with one-sided committed OT (which is normally available for SFE schemes based on garbled circuits). If there is committed OT for both or none of the parties, then the protocol and function augmentation can be adjusted in a straightforward manner.

We let $f, \hat{f}, g_a, g_b$ be functions as defined before. To compute a *proof* that P_a computed g_a correctly, we will make P_a additionally compute a *digest* on the output of g_a. Therefore, we augment g_a with a universal hash function h_t drawn from $\mathbb{H}$ to which P_a then adds a random string s_a that is fixed in advance. As such, the output will not reveal any information about the computed value. On the other hand, since P_a will commit to the input before h_t is chosen, the inputs $g_a(x), s_a$ to $\hat{f}$ will differ from the output g'_a with high probability. We observe that t, g'_a can be public inputs to $\hat{f}'$.

$$g'_a : \mathbb{B}^{l_a+s-1} \times \mathbb{B}^n \times \mathbb{B}^{l_a} \to \mathbb{B}^{l_a}$$
$$(t, x, s_a) \mapsto h_t(g_a(x)) \oplus s_a$$

In the case of P_b, it is not necessary for him to compute an actual hash of $g_b(y)$. This is because only P_a can arbitrarily send differing inputs for $\hat{f}$ by choosing different values that blind her input (whereas committed OT is available for P_b to circumvent this). Nevertheless, P_b adds a one-time-pad s_b to $g_b(y)$, so that we once again can make the value g'_b a public input to $\hat{f}'$.

$$g'_b : \mathbb{B}^n \times \mathbb{B}^{l_b} \to \mathbb{B}^{l_b}$$
$$(y, s_b) \mapsto g_b(y) \oplus s_b$$

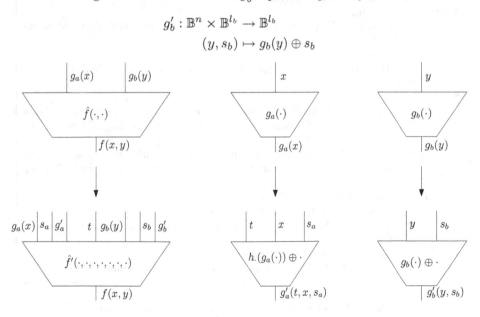

Fig. 4. The functions and how they will be augmented.

The actively secure protocol will evaluate $\hat{f}$ on the inputs $g_a(x), g_b(y)$ as before. The correct value will only be output of $\hat{f}'$ if, given the auxiliary inputs s_a, s_b and the public inputs t, g_a', g_b' it holds that $h_t(g_a(x)) \oplus s_a = g_a'$ and $g_b(y) \oplus s_b = g_b'$. Otherwise, an abort symbol $\perp$ will be delivered:

$$\hat{f}' : \begin{pmatrix} \mathbb{B}^{l_a} \times \mathbb{B}^s \times \mathbb{B}^s \times \mathbb{B}^{l_a+s-1} \times \\ \mathbb{B}^{l_b} \times \mathbb{B}^{l_b} \times \mathbb{B}^{l_b} \end{pmatrix} \to \mathbb{B}^m \cup \{\perp\}$$

$$(g_a(x), s_a, g_a', t, g_b(y), s_b, g_b') \mapsto \begin{cases} \hat{f}(g_a(x), g_b(y)) & \text{if } g_b(y) \oplus s_b = g_b' \wedge \\ & \quad h_t(g_a(x)) \oplus s_a = g_a' \\ \perp & \text{else} \end{cases}$$

Protocol Π_{SIREval} (part 1)

Both parties P_a, P_b want to evaluate a function $f : \mathbb{B}^{2n} \to \mathbb{B}^m$ and we consider its SIR $\mathcal{C}_{\hat{f}}, \mathcal{C}_{g_a}, \mathcal{C}_{g_b}$. P_a has input $x \in \mathbb{B}^n$ and P_b has input $y \in \mathbb{B}^n$.

Input phase:
(1) Let $\mathcal{C}_{\hat{f}'}, \mathcal{C}_{g_a'}, \mathcal{C}_{g_b'}$ be circuits representing $\hat{f}', g_a', g_b'$ which were defined before.
(2) Both parties send $(\text{init}, \mathcal{C}_{\hat{f}'}, "g_a(x)", "s_a", "g_a'", "h_t", "g_b(y)", "s_b", "g_b'")$ to $\mathcal{F}_{\text{SFE\&CommitOT}}$.
(3) P_a computes $g_a(x)$ locally and chooses $s_a \in_R \mathbb{B}^s$. P_b computes $g_b(y)$ locally and chooses $t \in_R \mathbb{B}^{l_a+s-1}$, $s_b \in_R \mathbb{B}^{l_b}$.
(4) P_a sends $(\text{commit}, "g_a(x)", g_a(x)), (\text{commit}, "s_a", s_a)$ to $\mathcal{F}_{\text{SFE\&CommitOT}}$. P_b sends $(\text{commit}, "y", y)$, $(\text{commit}, "g_b(y)", g_b(y)), (\text{commit}, "s_b", s_b)$, $(\text{commit}, "h_t", t)$ to $\mathcal{F}_{\text{SFE\&CommitOT}}$.

Function sampling:
(1) P_a computes $(F_b, \{y_0^i, y_1^i\}_{i \in [n]} \{s_{0,b}^i, s_{1,b}^i\}_{i \in [l_b]}, d_b) \leftarrow Gb(1^s, \mathcal{C}_{g_b'})$ and sends F_b to P_b.
(2) P_b computes $(F_a, \{t_0^i, t_1^i\}_{i \in [l_a+s-1]} \{x_0^i, x_1^i\}_{i \in [n]} \{s_{0,a}^i, s_{1,a}^i\}_{i \in [s]}, d_a) \leftarrow Gb(1^s, \mathcal{C}_{g_a'})$ and sends F_a to P_a.

Privacy-free phase:
(1) P_a sends (otA, x) and P_b sends $(\text{otA}, \{x_0^i, x_1^i\}_{i \in [n]})$ to $\mathcal{F}_{\text{OT}}$, hence P_a obtains $\{x^i\}_{i \in [n]}$. They do the same for $"s_a"$ so P_a obtains $\{s_a^i\}_{i \in [s]}$. Moreover, P_b sends $\{t^i\}_{i \in [l_a]+s-1}$ to P_a.
(2) Conversely, P_b sends $(\text{cotB}, "y")$ and P_a sends $(\text{cotB}, "y", \{y_0^i, y_1^i\}_{i \in [n]})$ to $\mathcal{F}_{\text{SFE\&CommitOT}}$, hence P_b obtains $\{y^i\}_{i \in [n]}$. They do the same for $"s_b"$ so P_b obtains $\{s_b^i\}_{i \in [l_b]}$.
(3) P_b sends $(\text{open}, "h_t")$ to $\mathcal{F}_{\text{SFE\&CommitOT}}$.
(4) P_a evaluates the privacy-free garbling as $(g_a^{i'})_{i \in [s]} \leftarrow Ev(F_a, \{t^i\}_{i \in [l_a]+s-1} \{x^i\}_{i \in [n]} \{s_a^i\}_{i \in [s]}, t x s_a)$ and then commits to $(g_a^{i'})_{i \in [s]}$.
(5) P_b evaluates the privacy-free garbling as $(g_b^{i'})_{i \in [l_b]} \leftarrow Ev(F_b, \{y^i\}_{i \in [n]} \{s_b^i\}_{i \in [l_b]}, y s_b)$ and then commits to $(g_b^{i'})_{i \in [l_b]}$.

Fig. 5. Protocol Π_{SIREval} to evaluate SIR of a function.

The protocol will be as follows:

Input Phase. Both parties P_a, P_b first locally compute $g_a(x), g_b(y)$. They then commit to the inputs $x, y, s_a, s_b, g_a(x), g_b(y)$ using $\mathcal{F}_{\text{SFE\&COMMITOT}}$.

Function Sampling. P_b samples a hash function $h_t \in \mathbb{H}$ and sends its description t to $\mathcal{F}_{\text{SFE\&COMMITOT}}$. He then sends a privacy-free garbling of $g_a'(\cdot, \cdot, \cdot)$. P_a sends a privacy-free garbling of a circuit computing $g_b'(\cdot, \cdot)$ to P_b.

Privacy-Free Phase. P_b uses committed OT to obtain the input keys that correspond to the his commitments from the input phase. P_a uses $\mathcal{F}_{\text{OT}}$. Afterwards, P_b decommits t and thereby reveals the hash function h_t. They then evaluate the privacy-free garblings locally and commit to the output keys.

Check Phase. P_a, P_b open the whole privacy-free garbling towards the other party. They each verify that the circuit was constructed correctly and afterwards open the commitments to the output keys. These values are then used as public inputs g_a', g_b' to $\hat{f}'$ in the next step.

Computation Phase. P_a and P_b evaluate $\hat{f}'$ securely using SFE. The inputs are defined by the commitments from the input phase and the opened commitments from the check phase.

The Concrete Protocol. We are now ready to present the protocol as outlined in the previous subsection. It can be found in Figs. 5 and 6.

Protocol Π_{SIREval} (part 2)

Check phase:

(1) P_a sends $(F_b, \{y_0^i, y_1^i\}_{i\in[n]} \{s_{0,b}^i, s_{1,b}^i\}_{i\in[l_b]}, d_b)$ to P_b who checks that he obtained correct input and output keys and that
$$Ve(\mathcal{C}_{g_b'}, F_b, \{y_0^i, y_1^i\}_{i\in[n]} \{s_{0,b}^i, s_{1,b}^i\}_{i\in[l_b]}) = 1.$$ If not, then P_b aborts.

(2) P_b sends $(F_a, \{t_0^i, t_1^i\}_{i\in[l_a+s-1]} \{x_0^i, x_1^i\}_{i\in[n]} \{s_{0,a}^i, s_{1,a}^i\}_{i\in[s]}, d_a)$ to P_a who checks that she obtained correct input and output keys and that
$$Ve(\mathcal{C}_{g_a'}, F_a, \{x_0^i, x_1^i\}_{i\in[n]} \{s_{0,a}^i, s_{1,a}^i\}_{i\in[s]}) = 1.$$ If not, then she aborts.

(3) P_a opens her commitments to $(g_a^{i'})_{i\in[s]}$. P_b computes $g_a' \leftarrow De((g_a^{i'})_{i\in[s]}, d_a)$ and aborts if one of the indices is $\bot$. Otherwise, both send (input, "g_a'", g_a') to $\mathcal{F}_{\text{SFE\&CommitOT}}$.

(4) P_b opens his commitments to $(g_b^{i'})_{i\in[l_b]}$. P_a computes $g_b' \leftarrow De((g_b^{i'})_{i\in[l_b]}, d_b)$ and aborts if one of the indices is $\bot$. Otherwise, both send (input, "g_b'", g_b') to $\mathcal{F}_{\text{SFE\&CommitOT}}$.

Computation phase:

(1) P_a sends (inputA) to $\mathcal{F}_{\text{SFE\&CommitOT}}$, followed by P_b sending (inputB).

(2) P_b obtains (output, z) from $\mathcal{F}_{\text{SFE\&CommitOT}}$ and outputs z.

Fig. 6. Protocol Π_{SIREVAL} to evaluate SIR of a function, continued.

4   Security

We will now prove the security of the protocol from the previous section. More formally, consider the stripped-down functionality in Fig. 7 which focuses on the SFE.

Theorem 1. *Let $\mathcal{G} = (Gb, En, De, Ev, Ve)$ be a privacy-free garbling scheme, λ its computational security parameter, and s be a statistical security parameter, then Π_{SIREVAL} securely implements $\mathcal{F}_{\text{SFE}}$ in the $\mathcal{F}_{\text{SFE\&CommitOT}}, \mathcal{F}_{\text{OT}}$-hybrid model against static, malicious adversaries corrupting either P_a or P_b.*

We split the proof into two different simulators, one for P_a being corrupt and the other one for a malicious P_b, where the second one is a simplified version of the malicious-P_a simulator. The proof works as follows: In the ideal world, the simulator runs a protocol where it intercepts all the commitments coming from P_a and simulates an honest $\tilde{P}_b$ (with some default input) for the protocol. It aborts when the committed values between the stages do not match up, or when P_a sends keys that she was not supposed to obtain. Then, a hybrid argument proves the claimed statement.

Functionality $\mathcal{F}_{\text{SFE}}$

Initialization:
- On input $(\text{init}, \mathcal{C})$ from both P_a, P_b where $\mathcal{C} = (2n, m, g, L, R, G)$ is a circuit, store $\mathcal{C}$.

Input of P_a:
- Upon input (inputA, x) from P_a where $x \in \mathbb{B}^n$ and where no input was given by P_a before, store x and send (inputA) to P_b.

Input of P_b:
- Upon input (inputB, y) from P_b where $y \in \mathbb{B}^n$ and where no input was given by P_b before and if (inputA) was obtained by P_b, compute $z \leftarrow eval(\mathcal{C}, xy)$ and output z to P_b.

Fig. 7. Secure function evaluation.

Proof. As in the protocol Π_{SIREVAL} we assume that both parties P_a, P_b want to evaluate a function $f : \mathbb{B}^{2n} \rightarrow \mathbb{B}^m$ and we consider its SIR $\mathcal{C}_{\hat{f}}, \mathcal{C}_{g_a}, \mathcal{C}_{g_b}$. P_a has input $x \in \mathbb{B}^n$ and P_b has input $y \in \mathbb{B}^n$.

Proof for Malicious P_a. We first show a simulator $\mathcal{S}_A$ to prove that from P_a's perspective, $\mathcal{F}_{\text{SFE}} \diamond \mathcal{S}_A \approx \mathcal{F}_{\text{SFE\&CommitOT}} \diamond \Pi_{\text{SIREVAL}}$.

Let $\mathcal{T}_{P_a Real}$ be the distribution of the transcripts that are obtained by executing Π_{SIREVAL} and $\mathcal{T}_{P_a Sim}$ be the distribution obtained from $\mathcal{S}_A$ (both of them only for a corrupted P_a), so the goal is to show that $\mathcal{T}_{P_a Real} \approx \mathcal{T}_{P_a Sim}$ (Fig. 8).

Define the following hybrid distributions:

Simulator $\mathcal{S}_A$

Input phase:
(1) Start a copy of $\mathcal{F}_{\text{SFE\&CommitOT}}$ with which P_a will communicate in the simulated protocol.
(2) $\tilde{P}_b$ sends $(\text{init}, \mathcal{C}_f)$ to $\mathcal{F}_{\text{SFE\&CommitOT}}$. Moreover, the simulator sends $(\text{init}, \mathcal{C}_f)$ to $\mathcal{F}_{\text{SFE}}$.
(3) $\tilde{P}_b$ follows Step $1 - 3$ of the protocol normally.
(4) In Step 4 of the simulated protocol, extract the inputs that P_a is sending to $\mathcal{F}_{\text{SFE\&CommitOT}}$. Save these values as $o_a, s_{a,1}$ locally. Moreover, let y be a default input for the $\tilde{P}_b$, which $\tilde{P}_b$ uses in Step 4 of the protocol.

Function sampling:
(1) $\tilde{P}_b$ behaves like in the protocol.

Privacy-free phase:
(1) Run Step $1 - 5$ of the protocol. During Step 1 extract the values that P_a inputs into the $\mathcal{F}_{\text{OT}}$ functionality as x and $s_{a,2}$.

Check phase:
(1) Run Step $1 - 2$ of the protocol.
(2) In Step 3 compute the keys that P_a should have obtained based on $s_{a,2}, h_t, x$. If P_a opens commitments to different keys, then abort.
(3) In Step 4 follow the protocol normally.

Computation phase:
(1) Run Step $1, 2$ of the protocol, with the following restriction:
   - If $o_a \neq g_a(x)$ where o_a, x are the extracted values above and $g_a(x)$ is the function evaluated on the extracted input, then abort. Also abort if $s_{a,1} \neq s_{a,2}$.
   - If no abort (also not from $\tilde{P}_b$) happened, then send (inputA, x) to $\mathcal{F}_{\text{SFE}}$.

Fig. 8. The simulator for a malicious P_a.

$\mathcal{T}_{P_a Hybrid1}$ which is obtained from using the simulator $\mathcal{S}_A$ with the following change: In the **Computation phase**, abort in Step 2 only if the output z of $\mathcal{F}_{\text{SFE}}$ would be $z = \bot$, i.e. if the hash function does not detect a differing input.

$\mathcal{T}_{P_a Hybrid2}$ which is obtained from using the simulator generating $\mathcal{T}_{P_a Hybrid1}$ with the following change: In the **Check phase**, do only abort if $\tilde{P}_b$ would abort instead of aborting if P_a opens commitments to wrong, but still valid keys.

Consider the distributions $\mathcal{T}_{P_a Sim}$ and $\mathcal{T}_{P_a Hybrid1}$, then the only difference lies in the outputs when P_a is cheating. In the first case, P_a will always be caught cheating whereas in the second case, she gets away with it as long as $\hat{f}'$ does not output $\bot$. There are three different events to consider:

(1) $o_a = g_a(x)$, but $s_{a,1} \neq s_{a,2}$: In this case, both $o_a, g_a(x)$ hash to the same value, hence $h_t(o_a) \oplus s_{a,1} \neq h_t(g_a(x)) \oplus s_{a,2}$ which will always be detected by $\hat{f}'$, so the success probability is 0.

(2) $o_a \neq g_a(x)$, but $s_{a,1} = s_{a,2}$: Since both $o_a, g_a(x)$ are independent of h_t and since h_t is chosen uniformly at random from the family $\mathbb{H}$, by Remark 1 they will collide with probability 2^{-s}, which is negligible in s.

(3) $o_a \neq g_a(x)$ and $s_{a,1} \neq s_{a,2}$: $\mathcal{F}_{\text{SFE\&CommitOT}}$ will not output $\bot$ iff $h_t(o_a) \oplus s_{a,1} = h_t(g_a(x)) \oplus s_{a,2}$. Hence it must hold that

$$h_t(o_a) \oplus h_t(g_a(x)) = s_{a,1} \oplus s_{a,2} = c$$

and a succeeding P_a will have to fix this c before learning h_t. By Remark 1 the success in doing so is 2^{-s} due to the uniform difference property and therefore negligible in s.

We hence conclude that $\mathcal{T}_{P_a Sim} \approx_s \mathcal{T}_{P_a Hybrid1}$. For the difference of $\mathcal{T}_{P_a Hybrid1}$ and $\mathcal{T}_{P_a Hybrid2}$, the simulator aborts in the first case if P_a commits to the wrong values, whereas it aborts in $\mathcal{T}_{P_a Hybrid2}$ if P_a provides strings that are not valid output keys of $\mathcal{G}$. By assumption, $\mathcal{G}$ provides *Correctness and Authenticity*, meaning that if P_a does not cheat, then she will obtain the correct keys and $\tilde{P}_b$ will continue. On the other hand, she can succeed in providing wrong keys only with probability $\text{negl}(\lambda)$. Therefore, we also obtain that $\mathcal{T}_{P_a Hybrid1} \approx_c \mathcal{T}_{P_a Hybrid2}$.

Now consider the distributions $\mathcal{T}_{P_a Hybrid2}, \mathcal{T}_{P_a Real}$. The output that is delivered to $\mathcal{Z}$ as the output of P_b is the same in both distributions, so we focus on the messages that P_a obtains. The only difference between those is that in the **Check phase**, Step 4 these depend on a fixed input in $\mathcal{T}_{P_a Hybrid2}$ and on the real input of P_b in $\mathcal{T}_{P_a Real}$. In both cases, these keys correspond to values that are uniformly random to P_a since they are obtained by XOR-ing a uniformly random value s_b to $g_b(x)$ if P_a sent a correct garbling. Assume that F_b was not generated by $\mathcal{G}$, but instead chosen arbitrarily by the adversary. Then the output wires may leak some information about the inputs. In Step 1 of the **Check phase** the garbling F_b was verified and by the *Verifiability* of the garbling scheme $\mathcal{G}$ the computed output keys only depend on the output of the function except with probability negligible in λ. For every fixed output g_b' of the circuit and for every y there exists at least one s_b to obtain g_b' from y, and therefore the opened keys differ only with probability $\text{negl}(\lambda)$. Hence $\mathcal{T}_{P_a Hybrid2} \approx_c \mathcal{T}_{P_a Real}$ which proves the statement for a malicious P_a.

Proof for Malicious P_b. The proof of security for a malicious P_b goes along the same lines as the proof for P_a and is included in the full version.

5   Optimizations

We will now discuss how the overhead from the protocol presented in Sect. 3 can be reduced. In particular, our construction requires more rounds of interaction and some computational overhead for securely computing the hash function and the committed OT for P_b. We will show that, by making non-trivial use of the SFE protocol by Frederiksen et al. [5] (FJN14) one can avoid parts of these extra computations. Due to the complexity of FJN14, we will just sketch this solution without a proof of security.

A Short Overview Over the FJN14 Construction

In Sect. 1 we sketched how an SFE protocol based on garbled circuits generally works. The presented pattern introduces a number of problems (as mentioned in the introduction), which are addressed in FJN14 using techniques which we will discuss now. We only focus on those techniques that are important with respect to our protocol.

Consistency of P_b's Inputs. If one uses standard OT during the above protocol, then P_b may ask for various input keys for different circuits. As an example, he could (for a subset of circuits) decide that the 5th wire shall be 1 whereas it will be 0 for the other instances. This may, depending on the computed function, leak information about P_a's input. To thwart this attack, FJN14 performs OT for longer strings, where all zero- or one-keys for a certain input wire for all circuits will be obtained in one iteration[4].

Consistency of P_a's Inputs. Similarly to P_b, also P_a can send different input keys for the instances. A solution similar to the above for P_b does not work, since P_b will then learn P_a's inputs. Instead, one lets P_a commit to her input keys ahead of time. P_b chooses a message digest function from $\mathbb{H}$ and P_a will garble the circuits such that they also compute a digest of her inputs. P_b checks during the evaluation that the hash value is the same for all evaluated circuits, and aborts if not. To prevent leakage of information about P_a's input, P_a will *mask the hash* with a fixed string[5].

Using the FJN14 Construction with Our Protocol

Using the OT of FJN14. Let P_b obtain the input keys for the privacy-free circuit *together with the input keys of the actively-secure garbling*, by also including these keys for s_b in the same OT. We therefore have to transfer an only slightly longer string for each input wire related to s_b[6].

Evaluating the Hash in the SFE for Free. In the actively secure protocol P_b will choose the hash function for the consistency check. We can let this be the same hash function that is used in our protocol with the same random padding s_a. This means that we will use a lightweight version of our suggested $\hat{f}'$ function that only checks for consistency of P_b's input, while P_a's consistency is implicitly checked during the evaluation of the actively secure protocol. Note that in the case of a cheating P_a the protocol will then be aborted before the actual output is computed by P_b. Therefore, P_a must send her input keys for

---

[4] To the best of our knowledge, a similar idea was first introduced in [17].

[5] We used the same technique, but for a different reason, in Π_{SIREval}. It was first introduced in the context of SFE with garbled circuits in [6,18].

[6] This means that we have to change the function $g'_b(\cdot, \cdot)$ slightly, due to a technique that avoids selective failure-attacks in FJN14. This change does not increase the size of the privacy-free circuit that is sent, since only XOR gates are added.

FJN14 and must have obtained her keys for the privacy-free garbling *before* h_t is revealed to her.

Public Inputs. An approach to implement public inputs is to let the SFE protocol have a *second input phase* where P_a can submit the keys for the public inputs. Like in the FJN14 protocol, the input keys will be linked to a polynomial (whose evaluations are linked to either the 0-keys or 1-keys for each wire i) which is of degree $s/2$. Before the evaluation, P_b checks that all such points for the keys lie on the same polynomial (using the already opened circuits and keys from the cut-and-choose phase as well as the newly obtained keys). Now P_b can identify to which wire the keys sent by P_a belong by taking one of the submitted keys for both the 0, 1-wires, interpolating the polynomial and checking whether all other keys belong to the polynomial that is linked to the correct bit of the publicly chosen input. We require that these public input keys, the polynomials and the links are generated by P_a during the garbling phase. They are sampled the same way as in the original protocol, and P_a is committed to the keys.

Acknowledgements. We want to thank Ivan Damgård and Tore Frederiksen for helpful discussions.

References

1. Afshar, A., Mohassel, P., Pinkas, B., Riva, B.: Non-interactive secure computation based on cut-and-choose. In: Nguyen, P.Q., Oswald, E. (eds.) EUROCRYPT 2014. LNCS, vol. 8441, pp. 387–404. Springer, Heidelberg (2014)
2. Applebaum, B., Ishai, Y., Kushilevitz, E.: From secrecy to soundness: efficient verification via secure computation. In: Gavoille, C., Kirchner, C., Meyer auf der Heide, F., Spirakis, P.G., Abramsky, S. (eds.) ICALP 2010. LNCS, vol. 6198, pp. 152–163. Springer, Heidelberg (2010)
3. Bellare, M., Hoang, V.T., Rogaway, P.: Foundations of garbled circuits. In: Proceedings of the ACM Conference on Computer and Communications Security, pp. 784–796. ACM (2012)
4. Crépeau, C., van de Graaf, J., Tapp, A.: Committed oblivious transfer and private multi-party computation. In: Coppersmith, D. (ed.) CRYPTO 1995. LNCS, vol. 963, pp. 110–123. Springer, Heidelberg (1995)
5. Frederiksen, T.K., Jakobsen, T.P., Nielsen, J.B.: Faster maliciously secure two-party computation using the GPU. In: Abdalla, M., De Prisco, R. (eds.) SCN 2014. LNCS, vol. 8642, pp. 358–379. Springer, Heidelberg (2014)
6. Frederiksen, T.K., Nielsen, J.B.: Fast and maliciously secure two-party computation using the GPU. Cryptology ePrint Archive, Report 2013/046 (2013). http://eprint.iacr.org/
7. Frederiksen, T.K., Nielsen, J.B., Orlandi, C.: Privacy-free garbled circuits with applications to efficient zero-knowledge. In: Oswald, E., Fischlin, M. (eds.) EUROCRYPT 2015. LNCS, vol. 9057, pp. 191–219. Springer, Heidelberg (2015)
8. Gennaro, R., Gentry, C., Parno, B.: Non-interactive verifiable computing: outsourcing computation to untrusted workers. In: Rabin, T. (ed.) CRYPTO 2010. LNCS, vol. 6223, pp. 465–482. Springer, Heidelberg (2010)

9. Giacomelli, I., Madsen, J., Orlandi, C.: ZKBoo: faster zero-knowledge for boolean circuits. Cryptology ePrint Archive, Report 2016/163 (2016). http://eprint.iacr.org/

10. Goldreich, O., Micali, S., Wigderson, A.: Proofs that yield nothing but their validity or all languages in NP have zero-knowledge proof systems. J. ACM (JACM) **38**(3), 690–728 (1991)

11. Goldwasser, S., Micali, S., Rackoff, C.: The knowledge complexity of interactive proof-systems. In: Proceedings of the Seventeenth Annual ACM Symposium on Theory of Computing, pp. 291–304. ACM (1985)

12. Ishai, Y., Kushilevitz, E.: Randomizing polynomials: a new representation with applications to round-efficient secure computation. In: Proceedings of 41st Annual Symposium on Foundations of Computer Science, pp. 294–304. IEEE (2000)

13. Jawurek, M., Kerschbaum, F., Orlandi, C.: Zero-knowledge using garbled circuits: how to prove non-algebraic statements efficiently. In: Proceedings of the ACM SIGSAC Conference on Computer and Communications Security, pp. 955–966. ACM (2013)

14. Kamara, S., Wei, L.: Garbled circuits via structured encryption. In: Adams, A.A., Brenner, M., Smith, M. (eds.) FC 2013. LNCS, vol. 7862, pp. 177–188. Springer, Heidelberg (2013)

15. Katz, J., Malozemoff, A.J., Wang, X.: Efficiently enforcing input validity in secure two-party computation. Cryptology ePrint Archive, Report 2016/184 (2016). http://eprint.iacr.org/2016/184

16. Lindell, Y.: Fast cut-and-choose based protocols for malicious and covert adversaries. In: Canetti, R., Garay, J.A. (eds.) CRYPTO 2013, Part II. LNCS, vol. 8043, pp. 1–17. Springer, Heidelberg (2013)

17. Lindell, Y., Pinkas, B.: An efficient protocol for secure two-party computation in the presence of malicious adversaries. In: Naor, M. (ed.) EUROCRYPT 2007. LNCS, vol. 4515, pp. 52–78. Springer, Heidelberg (2007)

18. Shen, C., Shelat, A.: Fast two-party secure computation with minimal assumptions. In: Proceedings of the ACM SIGSAC Conference on Computer and Communications Security, pp. 523–534. ACM (2013)

19. Tillich, S., Smart, N.: Circuits of basic functions suitable for MPC and FHE. https://www.cs.bris.ac.uk/Research/CryptographySecurity/MPC/. Accessed 25 June 2016

20. Yao, A.C.: Protocols for secure computations. In: 2013 IEEE 54th Annual Symposium on Foundations of Computer Science, pp. 160–164. IEEE (1982)

What Security Can We Achieve Within 4 Rounds?

Carmit Hazay[1]($\boxtimes$) and Muthuramakrishnan Venkitasubramaniam[2]

[1] Faculty of Engineering, Bar-Ilan University, Ramat Gan, Israel
carmit.hazay@biu.ac.il
[2] University of Rochester, Rochester, NY 14611, USA
muthuv@cs.rochester.edu

Abstract. Katz and Ostrovsky (Crypto 2004) proved that five rounds are necessary for stand-alone general black-box constructions of secure two-party protocols and at least four rounds are necessary if only one party needs to receive the output. Recently, Ostrovsky, Richelson and Scafuro (Crypto 2015) proved optimality of this result by showing how to realize arbitrary functionalities in four rounds where only one party receives the output via a black-box construction (and an extension to five rounds where both parties receive the output). In this paper we study the question of what security is achievable for stand-alone two-party protocols within four rounds.

We first provide a *four-round* two-party protocol for coin-tossing that achieves $1/p$-*simulation security* (i.e. simulation fails with probability at most $1/p$ + negl), in the presence of malicious corruptions. Next, we provide a four-round two-party protocol for general functionalities, where both parties receive the output, that achieves $1/p$-security in the presence of malicious adversaries corrupting one of the parties, and full security in the presence of non-aborting malicious adversaries corrupting the other party.

Next, we provide a *three-round* oblivious-transfer protocol, that achieves $1/p$-*simulation security* against arbitrary malicious senders, while simultaneously guaranteeing a meaningful notion of privacy against malicious corruptions of either party.

Finally, we show that the simulation-based security guarantees for our three-round protocols are optimal by proving that $1/p$-simulation security is impossible to achieve against both parties in three rounds or less when requiring some minimal guarantees on the privacy of their inputs.

Keywords: Secure computation · Coin-tossing · Oblivious transfer · Round complexity

C. Hazay—Research partially supported by a grant from the Israel Ministry of Science and Technology (grant No. 3-10883), by the European Research Council under the ERC consolidators grant agreement n. 615172 (HIPS), and by the BIU Center for Research in Applied Cryptography and Cyber Security in conjunction with the Israel National Cyber Bureau in the Prime Minister's Office.
M. Venkitasubramaniam—Research supported by Google Faculty Research Grant and NSF Award CNS-1526377.

© Springer International Publishing Switzerland 2016
V. Zikas and R. De Prisco (Eds.): SCN 2016, LNCS 9841, pp. 486–505, 2016.
DOI: 10.1007/978-3-319-44618-9_26

1   Introduction

Secure two-party computation enables two parties to mutually run a protocol that computes some function f on their private inputs, while preserving a number of security properties. Two of the most important properties are privacy and correctness. The former implies data confidentiality, namely, nothing leaks by the protocol execution but the computed output. The latter requirement implies that the protocol enforces the integrity of the computations made by the parties, namely, honest parties learn the correct output. Feasibility results are well established [4,12,22,30], proving that any efficient functionality can be securely computed under full simulation-based definitions (following the ideal/real paradigm). Security is typically proven with respect to two adversarial models: the semi-honest model (where the adversary follows the instructions of the protocol but tries to learn more than it should from the protocol transcript), and the malicious model (where the adversary follows an arbitrary polynomial-time strategy), and feasibility holds in the presence of both types of attacks.

An important complexity measure of secure computation that has been extensively studied in literature, is the *round-complexity* of secure protocols. In the *stand-alone* setting, Yao [30] presented the first constant-round secure two-party computation protocol in the semi-honest model. In contrast, Goldreich et al. [12] showed how to obtain protocols that tolerate malicious adversaries which requires non-constant number of rounds, followed by Lindell [19] who gave the first constant-round secure two-party protocol tolerating such attacks. In an important characterization, Katz and Ostrovsky [18] determined that the exact round complexity of achieving a (black-box) maliciously secure two-party computation protocol is five (and four if only one of the parties receives an output) where by a round of communication we mean a single message transmission from one party to another. More precisely, they constructed a five-round protocol to securely compute arbitrary functionalities and showed that there cannot exist any four-round black-box construction that securely realizes the coin-tossing functionality with black-box simulation. More recently, Ostrovsky et al. [25] strengthened this construction by demonstrating a five-round protocol where additionally the underlying cryptographic primitives are used only in a "black-box" way. Both the results also provide a four-round protocol for single-output functionalities. While these results only consider the stand-alone model, assuming some trusted-setup such as a common reference string (CRS), it is possible to construct round-optimal (i.e. two-round) secure two-party protocols; see [17] for a recent example.

Motivated by this line of works, the main question we address in this work is:

What security is achievable for stand-alone two-party computation in four rounds when both parties receive the output?

Relaxed Notions of Security. In this work, we focus on what security is achievable in the standard message model (i.e. not simultaneous message passing) in the two-party setting. More precisely, we initiate the study of what security guarantees can be achieved in round-efficient protocols. We overview the relaxed notions of security we consider in this work.

1. *1/p-security.* The first relaxation we consider is to weaken the indistinguishability requirement on the simulation. Namely, in the real/ideal paradigm definition when comparing an ideal simulated execution to the real execution, this relaxation implies that the ideal execution is defined as in the original definition yet the simulation notion is relaxed. More concretely, the two executions are now required to be distinguishable with probability at most $1/p + \mathsf{negl}$, where $p(\cdot)$ is some specified polynomial. This relaxation has been considered in the past in the context of achieving coin-tossing [7,23] and fairness for arbitrary functionalities [13]. Then, in case of malicious adversaries we require that our protocol admits $1/p$-security. We note that this notion is meaningful and sufficient for many practical scenarios and certain values of $1/p$. It is related to the notion of covert security, introduced by Aumann and Lindell in [2]. This notion models adversaries that may deviate arbitrarily from the protocol specification in an attempt to cheat, but do not wish to get caught doing so. In one of their variants, the simulator is allowed to fail, as long as it is guaranteed that the real and ideal output distributions are distinguishable with a probability that is related to the probability of detecting cheating. We note that our security notion directly implies covert security as the simulator may only fail in case the adversary aborts, which is always detected as cheating.

2. *Privacy only.* Loosely speaking, privacy is a weaker notion of simulation-based definition for which no party should be able to distinguish two views generated based on distinct set of inputs for the other party but yield the same output. Private oblivious-transfer (OT) was formalized by Halevi and Kalai in [15] that considered two separate definitions. Namely, *receiver privacy* requires that no malicious sender be able to distinguish the cases when the receiver's input is 0 or 1 (for instance, the standard OT protocol of [8] satisfies this notion). Moreover, *sender privacy* requires that for every malicious receiver and honest sender with input (s_0, s_1) there exists some input b for which the receiver cannot distinguish an execution where s_{1-b} is set to the correct value from an execution where s_{1-b} is sampled uniformly at random.

3. *Non-aborting (malicious) adversaries.* Non-aborting adversaries imply adversaries who are guaranteed to not abort in the middle of the execution. Security against non-aborting strategies implies that if an adversary deviates from the protocol it will be detected (either because of an ill-formed message or because of an abort). This notion is therefore stronger than semi-honest security where malicious behavior can go undetected. It is further useful in settings that apply external measures to ensure fairness, such as the recent work of [5] that has shown how to rely on external mechanisms, such as bitcoins to ensure fairness. Another line of works, considers "optimistic" fairness where a trusted party can be used to compensate the loss of information due to aborting adversaries [1,20]. In this setting, the trusted party is involved only

if one of the parties prematurely aborts and is not involved in the computation otherwise. In such settings it is a reasonable assumption to develop and analyze security in the presence of non-aborting adversaries.

In general, $1/p$-security and privacy are incomparable. While privacy always guarantees some form of input-indistinguishable security, $1/p$-secure protocols could lose complete security with probability $1/p$. For example, in the case of oblivious-transfer, a protocol that is $1/p$-secure against malicious receivers implies that with probability $1/p$ it could be the case that the receiver knows both the inputs of the sender. On the other hand, privacy against malicious receivers ensures that there is at least one of the two inputs that are "indistinguishable" to the receiver (this is formalized via a notion introduced by Halevi and Kalai [15]). The same intuition extends to general two-party computation where $1/p$-security implies that with probability at most $1/p$ all security is lost. It is harder to generalize the notion of privacy to two-party functionalities and it is an interesting direction for future work. In this work we design OT protocols that satisfy a combination of all these notions but explore only the possibility of $1/p$-security and security against non-aborting adversaries for general functionalities, where both parties receive the output.

Related Work. The work of Ishai et al. [17] shows how to construct a two-round secure two-party computation protocol in the so-called OT-hybrid, where the parties are assumed access to an ideal functionality implementing oblivious-transfer (OT). In essence, their work shows that improving the round complexity of secure computation is closely related to constructing round-efficient oblivious transfer protocols. When assuming setup, the work of Peikert et al. [28] shows how to construct highly efficient two-round protocols for the OT functionality in the CRS model. In the plain model, weaker security requirements for the OT functionality have been considered. In the Random Oracle model, Naor and Pinkas [24] developed a two-round OT protocol that obtains one-sided simulation (w.r.t. the sender), whereas only privacy is guaranteed against a malicious receiver. Halevi and Kalai in [15] showed how to construct two-round protocols for OT without the random-oracle where only privacy is guaranteed against both the sender and receiver. We further note that the notion of private OT is related to the notion of input-indistinguishable computation, introduced by Micali et al. in [21], which considers a weaker security notion for two-party computation. Nevertheless, we remark that private OT is more general than input indistinguishability as the latter requires that the inputs are (statistically)-bound to the transcript.[1]

Another related notion is that of super-polynomial time simulation [3,26,29] which allows the simulator to run in super-polynomial (potentially exponential) time. In the context of zero-knowledge proofs, exponential time simulation is equivalent to witness indistinguishability. However, more generally, for secure

---

[1] Formally, they require an "implicit input" function that can, from a transcript of the interaction, specify the input of a particular party. Our protocols provide statistical privacy guarantees and such a security guarantee cannot be input-indistinguishable.

computation it seems that the implication is only one-way where exponential time simulation implies privacy. Concretely, the protocols in [8,15] and some of our protocols guarantee statistical privacy against at least one party and hence cannot admit exponential time simulation. A more recent work by Garg et al. [10] studies the round-complexity of secure protocols in the simultaneous message model, where in a single round multiple parties are allowed to simultaneously transmit messages. They extend the Katz-Ostrovsky lower bound to show that four rounds are necessary to realize the coin-tossing functionality in the multiparty setting (where all parties receive the output).

In the context of (partial) fairness, Gordon and Katz [13] showed how to construct secure protocols with $1/p$-security which are fully private. The focus of their work is to achieve a meaningful notion of fairness, while the round complexity incurred by their protocols is high. More recently, Garay et al. [9] considered a utility-based security definition that is both $1/p$-secure and fully private (and in that sense, stronger than $1/p$-security). We remark that our definition of privacy is weaker than the definition of [13]. While their definition has a simulation-based flavor ours is an indistinguishability-based definition (where the combination of both guarantees is discussed above). Nevertheless, the focus of our work is not related to fairness rather to minimize the number of rounds.

1.1   Our Results

Our first result concerns with the coin-tossing functionality where we show how to achieve $1/p$-security. More precisely, we prove the following theorem:

Theorem 1.1 (Informal). *Assuming the discrete logarithm problem is hard, there exists a four-round protocol that securely realizes the coin-tossing functionality with $1/p$-security.*

We remark that if we allow our simulator to run in expected polynomial-time, we actually obtain perfect simulation against one of the parties and $1/p$-security against the other (even against aborting adversaries). On the other hand, if we require strict polynomial-time simulation, where this polynomial is independent of the adversary's running time, our protocol achieves $1/p$-security relative for both corruption cases. We further provide an abstraction for this protocol using a two-round cryptographic primitive denoted by homomorphic trapdoor commitment scheme, where the commitment transcript, as well as the trapdoor, are homomorphic. This abstraction captures a larger class of hardness assumptions such as RSA and factoring.

Next, we explore the possibility of extending this idea to realize the oblivious-transfer functionality with $1/p$-simulation security. In our first result, we construct an OT protocol that achieves $1/p$-security against arbitrary (possibly aborting) malicious senders and full simulation security against non-aborting receivers. More precisely, we prove the following theorem: More precisely, we prove the following theorem:

Theorem 1.2 (Informal). *Assuming the Decisional Diffie-Hellman problem is hard, there exists a four-round oblivious-transfer protocol where the receiver receives the output at the end of the third round which is $1/p$-secure in the presence of aborting senders and fully secure in the presence of non-aborting receivers.*[2]

We remark here that, if the receiver is required to learn the output only at the end of the fourth round, then the protocol of [25] already provides such a protocol with full simulation security against malicious (aborting) senders and receivers. Our contribution is providing a protocol where the receiver learns the output in the third round. The main advantage of this protocol is that we can combine our oblivious-transfer protocol with the two-round protocol of [17] to obtain four-round secure computation where both parties receive the output with analogous security guarantees. Specifically, the receiver in the above OT protocol obtains its input already in the third round. This allows to apply the [17] protocol within the second and third OT rounds. More precisely, we obtain the following corollary:

Theorem 1.3 (Informal). *Assuming the Decisional Diffie-Hellman problem is hard, there exists a four-round two-party secure protocol for any functionality, where both parties receive the output, that is $1/p$-secure in the presence of aborting senders and fully secure in the presence of non-aborting receivers.*

While these protocols achieve $1/p$-security against corrupted senders and full security against non-aborting receivers, it is unsatisfactory in that all security is compromised if a malicious receiver aborts (after receiving the output in the third round). Finally, in our third protocol we provide a different protocol for the oblivious-transfer functionality that guarantees $1/p$-security against malicious (possibly aborting) senders while guaranteeing privacy against malicious (possibly aborting) senders and receivers (with the later guarantee analogous to [15]), based on claw-free trapdoor permutations. More formally, we obtain the following theorem.

Theorem 1.4 (Informal). *Assuming the existence of claw-free permutations, there exists a three-round oblivious-transfer protocol that is $1/p$-secure in the presence of aborting senders and private in the presence of aborting senders and receivers.*

Comparing our two OT protocols, we note that they achieve incomparable notions of security with respect to malicious receivers. Specifically, the first protocol is fully secure in the presence of non-aborting adversaries and requires four-rounds, whereas the second protocol requires only three-rounds and achieves privacy against malicious receivers. In the full version we explore the possibility of extending the second OT protocol to functionalities that provide output to only one party and additionally provide a privacy guarantee. An interesting

---

[2] By fully secure, we mean standard simulation-based security.

future work would be to extend the notions of privacy and construct protocols in the case where there are outputs to both parties.

Lower Bounds. We complement our positive results with two lower bounds, where we show that achieving $1/p$-security against aborting receivers is impossible under black-box simulation. Our first result is:

Theorem 1.5 (Informal). *Assuming NP $\not\subseteq$ BPP, there exists no three-round secure protocol for arbitrary functionalities with black-box simulation, with $1/p$-security in the presence of malicious receivers and correctness with probability 1.*

Our proof follows by extending the [11] lower bound, to show that three-round black-box zero-knowledge proofs (or arguments) with negligible soundness and $1/p$-security exist only for languages in BPP. Indeed, it is possible to construct zero-knowledge proofs with $1/p$-soundness and $1/p$-zero-knowledge security (for instance by repeating the Blum's Hamiltonicity proof [6] $\log p$ times).

Our second lower bound is:

Theorem 1.6 (Informal). *There exists no three-round oblivious transfer protocol that achieves privacy in the presence of malicious senders and $1/p$-security in the presence of malicious receivers for $p > 2$.*

We remark that privacy against both parties is in some sense the minimal requirement of any secure computation protocol. Our lower bound shows that under this minimal requirement if we want to additionally achieve $1/p$-security in three rounds, it can be achieved *only* against a malicious sender, which matches our upper bound, thus establishing its optimality.

1.2 Our Techniques

Coin Tossing [16]. We briefly sketch the technical details of our constructions for our four-message (i.e. three message when only one party receives output) protocols, beginning with our coin tossing protocol. In this protocol we make use of an extension variant of Pedersen's trapdoor commitment scheme [27]. Basically, party P_1 generates a set of generators for P_2's commitment scheme using pairs of shares, and then reveals the discrete logarithm of half of the shares by responding to a random challenge given by P_2. Looking ahead, this allows to define a simulator that extracts a trapdoor for this commitment scheme using rewinding which, in turn, allows the equivocation of the committed message. Forcing a particular outcome when P_2 is corrupted is carried out by first observing the decommitted value of P_2 and then rewinding, where in the second execution the simulator programs its input according to the outcome it received from the trusted party. We note that Pedersen's commitment scheme is captured under our abstraction for trapdoor commitment schemes. This is shown in the full version.

4-Round 2PC Against Non-aborting Adversaries (Sect. 3). Our general approach would be to first construct an OT protocol with same guarantees and then combine it with the 2-round 2PC protocol in the OT-hybrid of [17].

In order to construct a 4-round protocol for general two-party computation where both parties receive the output, using this approach, we require that our OT protocol deliver its output to the sender at the end of the fourth round. We will therefore construct a 4-round OT protocol with the property that the receiver receives the output at the end of third round.

As a warmup, our first OT protocol employs a common paradigm for securely realizing this functionality. Namely, the receiver picks two public keys for which it knows only one of the corresponding secret keys, and sends them to the sender, that uses these keys to encrypt its OT inputs. If indeed the receiver knows only one of the secret keys, then it will not be able to decrypt both inputs. Thus, the main challenge in designing OT protocols with security in the presence of malicious adversaries is a mechanism to enforce the receiver to choose its public keys correctly. In this work we enforce that by asking the public key for the unknown secret key to take a particular form, for which the receiver does not know the trapdoor associated with it (concretely, this trapdoor is a discrete logarithm of some generator picked by the sender). Enforcing this choice is carried out by a witness-indistinguishable proof-of-knowledge (WI-PoK), that further allows to extract the bit b for which the receiver indeed knows the corresponding secret key (which implies input extraction of the receiver's input).

On a very high-level, our security guarantee against (malicious) non-aborting receivers is achieved by first obtaining a three-round protocol that is defensibly private with respect to malicious receivers [14] and then combining it with a zero-knowledge proof-of-knowledge (ZK-PoK) protocol in order to achieve full security against malicious (non-aborting) adversaries. We recall here that an OT protocol is said to be defensibly-private with respect to the receiver if no adversarial receiver can distinguish the sender's input corresponding to input $1 - b$ from a random input, while outputting a valid defense, i.e. random coins τ that are consistent with the view for input b. Given a defensibly-private OT protocol, obtaining a protocol that guarantees full security against malicious non-aborting receivers is obtained by combining it with a ZK-PoK protocol where the receiver proves the knowledge of a valid defense. (We stress that in our actual protocol, a witness-indistinguishability proof as opposed to a ZK proof will be sufficient).

On the other hand, we achieve security against non-aborting senders as follows. The sender picks two public-keys to be combined (in order to enforce a public-key for which its secret key is unknown), so that the receiver is only allowed to choose one secret key to be opened by the sender. Simulation is achieved by rewinding and extracting both the secret-keys (or trapdoors) which is possible as the sender is non-aborting.

Finally, to obtain secure computation for general functionalities, we combine our OT with the two-round protocol of [17] which is specified in the OT-hybrid. Their protocol provides an output to only one of the parties (namely, the receiver of the OT instances). Yet, we run this protocol in parallel with our OT protocol where the second and third messages of the OT protocol run in parallel with the [17] protocol. As a result, the receiver of the OT receives the output of the computation at the end of third round. Finally, to extend this protocol to have outputs delivered to both parties, we can rely on the fourth round where the receiver transmits the output the sender.

4-Round 2PC with 1/p-Security Against Aborting Senders and Full Security Against Non-aborting Receivers (Sect. 4). As with our warmup protocol, to construct a protocol for general functionalities, it will suffice to construct an OT protocol with same guarantees (where the receiver receives the output at the end of third round).

We begin with the observation that our previous OT-protocol is already $1/p$ secure for $p = 1 + \frac{1}{3}$ against malicious aborting senders. To see this, suppose that for some trapdoor the sender aborts with probability at most $\frac{1}{2}$ when it is asked to reveal it, then in expectation the simulator needs to rewind the sender just twice in order to extract that trapdoor. If both trapdoors satisfy this condition then the simulator can easily extract both of them. Now, suppose this is not the case, then it would have to be the case that the sender aborts with probability at least $\frac{1}{2}$ when it is asked to open one of the trapdoors. Then, the overall probability with which the sender aborts is $\frac{1}{4}$ (as each trapdoor is requested to be revealed with probability $\frac{1}{2}$). In order to achieve $\frac{3}{4}$ security, it suffices to output a distribution that is $\frac{3}{4}$-close to the real distribution. As the sender aborts with probability at least $\frac{1}{4}$ a simulator that simply outputs all the views on which the sender aborts already achieves $\frac{3}{4}$ security.

With this observation, we show that $1/p$-security for an arbitrary polynomial p, can be achieved by amplifying the indistinguishability argument via parallel repetition. More precisely, by repeating the basic protocol $O(\kappa p)$ times, where κ is the security parameter, we can show, using a careful application of Yao-type amplification, that if the adversary does not abort with probability at least $\Omega(1/p)$, then the simulation can extract most of the trapdoors. This idea is used in conjunction with the combiner of Ostrovsky et al. [25] to ensure that the simulator extracts the sender's inputs if and only if the receiver successfully extracts it, or in other words, prevents any form of input dependent attacks.

3-Round OT with 1/p-Security Against Aborting Senders and Privacy Against Aborting Receivers (Sect. 5). We conclude with our third OT protocol which demonstrates the feasibility of $1/p$ sender security and privacy against aborting receivers in three rounds. We begin with a basic protocol that only achieves receiver privacy and then amplify it security to get $1/p$ sender simulation. Implicit in our first OT protocol is a strategy to amplify the security of a protocol that achieves privacy against malicious senders to one that is $1/p$ secure whenever there exists a trapdoor, that given the first message of the sender can be used to generate a receiver message that will allow extraction. Our basic protocol based on claw-free trapdoor permutations is simple: The sender samples a pair of functions f_0, f_1 from a claw-free family and provides the description to the receiver. The receiver samples $y = f_b(x)$ for a random x and returns y to the sender. The sender with inputs (s_0, s_1) using the trapdoors for f_0 and f_1 obtains $x_b = f_b^{-1}(x)$ and masks s_0 with the Goldreich-Levin hard-core predicate of x_b. To prove receiver privacy, we need to show it is impossible for the receiver to distinguish both the games where the sender's input are sampled according to (s_0, U) and (U, s_1) from the real-game (where U is the uniform distribution over $\{0, 1\}$). We argue that if such a receiver exists, then using the list-decodable extractor guaranteed by the Goldreich-Levin Theorem we can extract x_0 and x_1, thus finding a claw, i.e. x_0 and x_1 such that $f_0(x_0) = f_1(x_1)$. This reduction is subtle as creating a predictor to run the list-decodable extractor requires being able to sample a view of the receiver by supplying sender's messages without knowledge of the trapdoors. Nevertheless, by using a careful averaging argument we show this is possible. Finally, we amplify this protocol to achieve $1/p$ sender simulation. As mentioned above, we just need to produce a trapdoor that will allow generating the receiver message in a way that will help to extract the sender's input. The trapdoor is simply one of the trapdoors corresponding to the functions f_0 and f_1, as with this trapdoor it is possible to sample a random claw. Our protocol can be implemented based on the RSA claw-free collection of functions. Details of this construction can be found in Sect. 5. In the full-version, we explore an extension of this protocol in conjunction with [17] to obtain a three-round protocol for general functionalities that deliver an output to only one of the parties and leave it as future work to consider functions with outputs to both parties.

2 Preliminaries

Definition 2.1. *Let* $X = \{X(a, n)\}_{a \in \{0,1\}^*, n \in \mathbb{N}}$ *and* $Y = \{Y(a, n)\}_{a \in \{0,1\}^*, n \in \mathbb{N}}$ *be two distribution ensembles. We say that* X *and* Y *are computationally* $1/p$-*indistinguishable, denoted* $X \overset{1/p}{\approx} Y$, *if for every PPT distinguisher D there exists a negligible function $\mu(\cdot)$ such that for every $a \in \{0, 1\}^*$ and all sufficiently large n*

$$\left| \Pr\left[D(X(a, n), 1^n) = 1\right] - \Pr\left[D(Y(a, n), 1^n) = 1\right] \right| < \frac{1}{p(n)} + \mu(n).$$

Private Oblivious Transfer. We consider a privacy definition in the presence of malicious receivers and senders [15]. Recall first that the OT functionality is defined by $\mathcal{F}_{\text{OT}}: (b, (s_0, s_1) \mapsto (-, s_b))$. Then, let $\langle \text{Sen}(s_0, s_1), \text{Rec}^*(b) \rangle (1^n)$ denote the random variable describing the corrupted receiver's output when interacting with Sen that is invoked on inputs (s_0, s_1), whereas $\langle \text{Sen}^*(s_0, s_1), \text{Rec}(b) \rangle (1^n)$ denote the random variable describing the corrupted sender's output when interacting with Rec that is invoked on inputs b. Then define privacy as follows,

Definition 2.2 (Sender's Privacy). *A protocol π that realizes the $\mathcal{F}_{\text{OT}}$ functionality is private with respect to the receiver if for any PPT adversary Rec^* corrupting Rec there exists a negligible function $\mathsf{negl}(\cdot)$ and a PPT distinguisher D such that for all n's large enough it holds that*

$$\left| \Pr[D(\langle \text{Sen}(s_0, s_1), \text{Rec}^*(b) \rangle (1^n)) = 1] \right.$$
$$\left. - \Pr[D(\langle \text{Sen}(s_0, \tilde{s}), \text{Rec}^*(b) \rangle (1^n)) = 1] \right| \leq \mathsf{negl}(n), \ or$$

$$|\Pr[D(\langle \mathrm{Sen}(s_0, s_1), \mathrm{Rec}^*(b)\rangle(1^n)) = 1]$$
$$- \Pr[D(\langle \mathrm{Sen}(\tilde{s}, s_1), \mathrm{Rec}^*(b)\rangle(1^n)) = 1]| \le \mathsf{negl}(n)$$

where the probability is taken over the choice of $\tilde{s}$ and the randomness of the parties.

Definition 2.3 (Receiver's Privacy). *A protocol π that realizes the $\mathcal{F}_{\mathrm{OT}}$ functionality is private with respect to the sender if for any PPT adversary Sen^* corrupting Sen there exists a negligible function $\mathsf{negl}(\cdot)$ and a PPT distinguisher D such that for all n's large enough it holds that*

$$|\Pr[D(\langle \mathrm{Sen}^*(s_0, s_1), \mathrm{Rec}(0)\rangle(1^n)) = 1]$$
$$- \Pr[D(\langle \mathrm{Sen}^*(s_0, s_1), \mathrm{Rec}(1)\rangle(1^n)) = 1]| \le \mathsf{negl}(n)$$

where the probability is taken over the randomness of the parties.

3   Warmup: 4-Round 2PC Against Non-aborting Adversaries

In this section, as a warmup, we present a four-round 2PC protocol for arbitrary functionalities, where both parties receive the output, in the presence of arbitrary adversaries that are restricted to be non-aborting. We first introduce a four-round OT protocol that securely computes functionality $\mathcal{F}_{\mathrm{OT}}$: $((s_0, s_1), b) \mapsto (-, s_b)$ in the presence of non-aborting senders and receivers, where the receiver receives the output in the third round. Next, we induce a four-round 2PC protocol with the same security guarantees by combining our OT with [17]. In the following section, we rely on this protocol as a building block to construct another OT protocol that achieves $1/p$-security against malicious (aborting) senders and full simulation-based security against non-aborting receivers.

Protocol 1 (Protocol π_{OT}).
Public parameters: *The description of a group $\mathbb{G}$ of prime order p.*
Inputs: *The sender Sen holds s_0, s_1 and the receiver Rec holds a bit b.*
The protocol:

1. **Sen $\rightarrow$ Rec:**
   (a) Sen *picks a random generator $g \leftarrow \mathbb{G}$ and computes $h_0 = g^{r_0}$ and $h_1 = g^{r_1}$ where $r_0, r_1 \leftarrow \mathbb{Z}_p$.*
   (b) Sen *sends g, h_0, h_1 to Rec.*
2. **Rec $\rightarrow$ Sen:**
   (a) Rec *generates two public-keys according to the El Gamal PKE as follows: $\mathrm{PK}_b = g^m$ and $\mathrm{PK}_{1-b} = (h_0 h_1)^{\tilde{m}}$ where $m, \tilde{m} \leftarrow \mathbb{Z}_p$. Rec sets $\mathrm{SK} = m$.*
   (b) Rec *sends $\mathrm{PK}_0, \mathrm{PK}_1$ to Sen.*
   (c) Rec *sends the first message of the WI-PoK for proving the knowledge of the discrete logarithms of either PK_0 or PK_1 with respect to $(h_0 h_1)$ (namely, Rec sends the first message with respect to $\pi_{\mathrm{DL}}^{\mathrm{WI}}$ for the compound statement with PK_0 and PK_1 being the statements).*
   (d) Rec *sends a challenge bit β.*

3. **Sen → Rec:**

  (a) Sen *computes ciphertexts* c_0, c_1 *as follows:* $c_0 = (g^{u_0}, PK_0^{u_0} \cdot s_0)$ *and* $c_1 = (g^{u_1}, PK_1^{u_1} \cdot s_1)$ *where* $u_0, u_1 \leftarrow \mathbb{Z}_p$.

  (b) Sen *sends* c_0, c_1 *to Rec*

  (c) Sen *sends the second message* e_{Sen} *for the WI-PoK protocol* π_{DL}^{WI} *given by the receiver (recall that this message is a random challenge).*

  (d) Sen *sends* $r_\beta = \log_g(h_\beta)$

4. **Rec → Sen:**

  (a) *Upon receiving the sender's ciphertexts* $c_0 = \langle c_0[1], c_0[2] \rangle$ *and* $c_1 = \langle c_1[1], c_1[2] \rangle$, *Rec computes* s_b *by decrypting* c_b *under* SK_b. *More precisely, it computes* $s_b = c_b[2]/(c_b[1])^{SK}$.

  (b) *Rec sends the last message for the WI-PoK protocol* π_{DL}^{WI}.

Theorem 3.1 (Warmup). *Assume that the Decisional Diffie-Hellman assumption holds in* $\mathbb{G}$ *and that* π_{DL}^{WI} *is as above. Then, Protocol 1 is a four-round protocol, where the receiver receives the output in the third round, that securely realizes* $\mathcal{F}_{OT}$ *in the presence of non-aborting senders and non-aborting receivers.*

See [16] for the complete proof.

Obtaining 4-Round 2PC. Due to space limitations, we defer the discussion of this section to the full version and only specify our theorem; see also Sect. 4.2.

Theorem 3.2. *Assuming the Decisional Diffie-Hellman problem is hard, there exists a four-round two-party protocol for any functionality, where both parties receive the output, that is fully secure in the presence non-aborting senders and non-aborting receivers.*

4   4-Round 2PC with 1/p Sender Security and Full Security Against Non-aborting Receivers

In this section we extend our OT protocol from Sect. 3 and demonstrate how to achieve $1/p$-simulation with respect to corrupted aborting senders while retaining the same guarantees against non-aborting receivers. Next, in Sect. 4.2, we show how to induce a general 2PC protocol with the same security guarantees. Our OT protocol is inspired by the recent result of Ostrovsky et al. [25]. Roughly speaking, the protocol in [25] provide a cut-and-choose mechanism to transform an oblivious-transfer protocol that is vulnerable to input dependent abort by a malicious sender to full security. The basic idea is to use a special kind of "verifiable" secret sharing that will allow the receiver to open a subset of the shares of both the sender inputs to verify the validity of the shares and input consistency. Only if the checks pass the receiver proceeds to obtain its real output. This extra step helps prevent input dependent abort as if the validity checks pass then with high probability we can reconstruct unique values for both inputs of the sender from the shares. In our protocol we will implicitly perform the cut-and-choose by relying on the OT protocol itself. We remark that while the issue that needed to be resolved was an input-dependent abort in [25], in our case, we use it to boost the extraction probability of sender's inputs while maintaining the privacy against the receiver. The secret sharing ensures that the receiver cannot learn more than one output and extracting a significant fraction of shares is sufficient to extract the outputs. Another advantage of relying on the OT protocol to perform the cut-and-choose is that the sender needs to use its input only in the third-round of our protocol after the receiver submits its input for the OT instance.

We begin with the following building blocks used in our construction: let (1) Commit be a statistically binding commitment scheme, (2) let (Share, Rec) be a $(M + 1)$-out-of-$2M$ Shamir secret-sharing scheme over $\mathbb{Z}_q$, together with a linear map $\phi : \mathbb{Z}_q^{2M} \to \mathbb{Z}_q^{M-1}$ such that $\phi(v) = 0$ iff v is a valid sharing of some secret. We further note that the WI-PoK $\pi_{\mathrm{DL}}^{\mathrm{WI}}$ that is given by Rec in Protocol 1, is extended here to handle the parallel case. Namely, the receiver proves the validity of one of the public keys it generates within each pair, in parallel.

The security guarantees of this protocol are $1/p$-security against malicious senders and full security against non-aborting receivers. We remark that the receiver's simulation essentially follows a similar approach as in the simulation of Protocol 1. On the other hand, the sender simulation needs to achieve $1/p$-simulation. The high-level idea is to apply techniques from the simulation in [25], given that the simulator extracts sufficiently enough shares of the sender's inputs to the parallel OTs. The core of our argument and the main technical part of this protocol is to show that if an adversarial sender does not abort before sending the third message too often (i.e. $< 1 - \frac{1}{p}$) then the simulator can extract the trapdoor by rewinding sufficiently many times.

4.1   4-Round OT with 1/p Sender Security and Full Security Against Non-aborting Receivers

We construct a four-round OT protocol with the stronger guarantee of $1/p$ security in the presence of (possibly aborting) malicious senders.

Protocol 2 (Protocol π_{OT}).
Public parameters: *The description of a group $\mathbb{G}$ of prime order $\overline{p}$.*
Inputs: *The sender Sen holds s_0, s_1 and the receiver Rec holds a bit b.*
The protocol:

1. **Sen → Rec:**
   (a) *Let $N = 3M$. Then, for $i \in [N]$, Sen picks random generator $g_i \leftarrow \mathbb{G}$ and computes $h_{i,0} = g_i^{r_{i,0}}$ and $h_{i,1} = g_i^{r_{i,1}}$ where $r_{i,0}, r_{i,1} \leftarrow \mathbb{Z}_{\overline{p}}$.*
   (b) *Sen sends the N tuples $\{g_i, h_{i,0}, h_{i,1}\}_{i \in [N]}$ to Rec.*
2. **Rec → Sen:**
   (a) *Rec samples uniformly at random $c_1, \ldots, c_M \leftarrow \{0, 1\}$. The c_i values serve as the input to the first M OT executions.*
   (b) *Rec selects a random subset $T_{1-b} \subseteq [2M]$ of size $M/2$. Define $T_b = [2M]/T_{1-b}$. For every $j \in [2M]$, Rec sets $b_j = \alpha$ if $j \in T_\alpha$. The b_j values serve as the inputs to the OT for the next $2M$ executions.*

(c) *According to its input for the 3M OT executions, Rec generates $N = 3M$ pairs of El Gamal PKE's as follows:*

- *For every $i \in [M]$, $\mathrm{PK}_{i,c_i} = g_i^{m_i}$ and $\mathrm{PK}_{i,1-c_i} = (h_{i,0}h_{i,1})^{\widetilde{m}_i}$ where $m_i, \widetilde{m}_i \leftarrow \mathbb{Z}_{\widetilde{p}}$. Rec sets $\mathrm{SK}_i = m_i$.*
- *For every $j \in [2M]$, $\mathrm{PK}_{M+j,b_j} = g_{M+j}^{m_{M+j}}$ and $\mathrm{PK}_{M+j,1-b_j} = (h_{M+j,0}h_{M+j,1})^{\widetilde{m}_{M+j}}$ where $m_{M+j}, \widetilde{m}_{M+j} \leftarrow \mathbb{Z}_{\widetilde{p}}$. Rec sets $\mathrm{SK}_{M+j} = m_{M+j}$.*

(d) *Rec sends $\{\mathrm{PK}_{i,0}, \mathrm{PK}_{i,1}\}_{i \in [N]}$ to Sen.*

(e) *Rec sends the first message of the WI-PoK for proving the knowledge for every $i \in [N]$ of the discrete logarithms of either PK_0^i or PK_1^i with respect to $(h_{i,0}h_{i,1})$.*

(f) *Rec sends a challenge string $\beta = (\beta_1, \ldots, \beta_N)$.*

(g) *Rec sends the first message for the statistically-binding commitment scheme* com.

3. **Sen $\rightarrow$ Rec:**

(a) *Sen picks two random strings $x_0, x_1 \leftarrow \mathbb{Z}_q$ and secret shares them using the Shamir's secret-sharing scheme. In particular, Sen computes $[x_b] = (x_b^1, \ldots, x_b^{2M}) \leftarrow \mathsf{Share}(x_b)$ for $b \in \{0,1\}$. Sen commits to the shares $[x_0], [x_1]$ as follows. It picks random matrices $A_0, B_0 \leftarrow \mathbb{Z}_q^{M \times 2M}$ and $A_1, B_1 \leftarrow \mathbb{Z}_q^{M \times 2M}$ such that $\forall i \in [M]$:*

$$A_0[i, \cdot] + B_0[i, \cdot] = [x_0], \quad A_1[i, \cdot] + B_1[i, \cdot] = [x_1].$$

Sen computes two matrices $Z_0, Z_1 \in \mathbb{Z}_q^{M \times M-1}$ and sends them in the clear such that:

$$Z_0[i, \cdot] = \phi(A_0[i, \cdot]), Z_1[i, \cdot] = \phi(A_1[i, \cdot]).$$

(b) *Sen sends the committed matrices $(\mathrm{com}_{A_0}, \mathrm{com}_{B_0}, \mathrm{com}_{A_1}, \mathrm{com}_{B_1})$ to Rec where each element of each matrix is individually committed using* com.

(c) *For $i \in [M]$, Sen computes ciphertexts $c_{i,0}, c_{i,1}$ where $c_{i,0}$ is an encryption of the decommitment of the rows $A_0[i, \cdot]$ and $A_1[i, \cdot]$ under public key $\mathrm{PK}_{i,0}$ and $c_{i,1}$ is an encryption of the decommitment of the rows $B_0[i, \cdot]$ and $B_1[i, \cdot]$ under public key $\mathrm{PK}_{i,1}$. Sen sends $\{c_{i,0}, c_{i,1}\}_{i \in [M]}$ to Rec.*

(d) *For $j \in [2M]$, Sen computes ciphertexts $\tilde{c}_{j,0}, \tilde{c}_{j,1}$, where $\tilde{c}_{j,b}$ is an encryption of the decommitment of the columns $A_b[\cdot, j], B_b[\cdot, j]$ under public key $\mathrm{PK}_{M+j,b}$. Sen sends $\{\tilde{c}_{j,0}, \tilde{c}_{j,1}\}_{j \in [2M]}$ to Rec.*

(e) *Sen sends the second message e_{Sen} for the WI-PoK protocol $\pi_{\mathrm{DL}}^{\mathrm{WI}}$ given by the receiver (recall that this message is a random challenge).*

(f) *Sen sends $r_{\beta_i} = \log_{g_i}(h_{i,\beta})$ for all $i \in [N]$.*

(g) *Sen sends $C_0 = s_0 \oplus x_0$ and $C_1 = s_1 \oplus x_1$ to Rec.*

4. **Rec $\rightarrow$ Sen:**

(a) **Decryption Phase:** *Upon receiving the all the sender's ciphertexts the receiver decrypts them to obtain the OT outputs. These include decommitments to $A_0[i, \cdot], A_1[i, \cdot]$ for every $i \in [M]$ when $c_i = 0$ and decommitments to $B_0[i, \cdot], B_1[i, \cdot]$ when $c_i = 1$. They also include columns $A_{b_j}[\cdot, j], B_{b_j}[\cdot, j]$ for every $j \in [2M]$.*

(b) **Shares Validity Check Phase:** *For $i = 1, \ldots, M$, if $c_i = 0$ check that $Z_0[i, \cdot] = \phi(A_0[i, \cdot])$ and $Z_1[i, \cdot] = \phi(A_1[i, \cdot])$. Otherwise, if $c_i = 1$ check that $\phi(B_0[i, \cdot]) + Z_0[i, \cdot] = 0$ and $\phi(B_1[i, \cdot]) + Z_1[i, \cdot] = 0$. If all the checks pass, the receiver proceeds to the next phase and otherwise aborts.*

(c) **Shares Consistency Check Phase:** *For each $b \in \{0,1\}$, Rec randomly chooses a set T_b for which $b_j = b$ at $M/2$ coordinates. For each $j \in T_b$, Rec checks that there exists a unique x_b^i such that $A_b[i,j] + B_b[i,j] = x_b^j$ for all $i \in [M]$. If so, x_b^j is marked as consistent. If all shares obtained in this phase are consistent, Rec proceeds to the reconstruction phase. Else it aborts.*

(d) **Reconstruction Phase:** *For $j \in [2M]/T_{1-b}$, if there exists a unique x_b^j such that $A_b[i,j] + B_b[i,j] = x_b^j$, Rec marks share j as a consistent column. If R obtains less than $M + 1$ consistent columns, it aborts. Otherwise, let $x_b^{j_1}, \ldots, x_b^{j_{M+1}}$ be any set of $M + 1$ shares obtained from consistent columns. Rec computes $x_b \leftarrow \mathsf{Reconstruct}(x_b^{j_1}, \ldots, x_b^{j_{M+1}})$ and outputs $s_b = C_b \oplus x_b$.*

(e) *Rec sends the last message for the WI-PoK protocol $\pi_{\mathrm{DL}}^{\mathrm{WI}}$.*

Theorem 4.1. *Assume that the Decisional Diffie-Hellman assumption holds in $\mathbb{G}$ and that $\pi_{\mathrm{DL}}^{\mathrm{WI}}$ is as above. Then Protocol 2 is a four-round protocol, where the receiver receives the output in the third round, that securely realizes $\mathcal{F}_{\mathrm{OT}}$ with $1/p$-security in the presence of aborting senders and with full security in the presence of non-aborting receivers.*

See [16] for the proof. As a final remark, we note that Protocol 2 can be viewed as a three-round protocol by removing the WI-PoK given by the receiver. This implies that we can remove the last round sent by the receiver. Then the security guarantee of the modified protocol is the same with respect to malicious senders, whereas security against malicious receivers is ensured in the presence of defensible private adversaries [14], where a "proof" of an honest behaviour implies privacy. Intuitively, the proof follows due to the following argument. If a malicious receiver is able to provide a valid defence, which includes an input and randomness, this implies that for each pair of keys it provides a discrete logarithm with respect to $h_{i,0}, h_{i,1}$. Then, a reduction to the privacy of El Gamal can be constructed similarly by reducing the distinguishing probability between the two views to the distinguishing probability between two ciphertexts.

4.2   4-Round 2PC Protocol

Obtaining general secure two-party computation is carried out analogous to Protocol 1 by embedding the two-round protocol of [17] within the second/third messages of our OT protocol. It follows just as before that we obtain a two-party protocol that is secure against malicious non-aborting adversaries.

Note that, in our previous protocol, to achieve simulation when the receiver is corrupted, we consider a simulator that honestly generates the sender's messages with arbitrary inputs for the functionality being computed and then extracts the receiver's inputs to the OT by rewinding the WI-PoK. By relying on precisely the same strategy, we can obtain the receiver's inputs in this protocol and then complete the simulation by relying on the simulator for the malicious receiver in [17] protocol.

To achieve simulation when the sender is corrupted, we combine two observations:

- First, using the approach from our previous protocol, it follows that whenever the simulator extracts the required trapdoor, it is possible to generate the OT part in the second message from the receiver in a way that it is identically distributed to the real receiver's message while at the same time extracting the sender's inputs to the OT. Furthermore, whenever the sender's input extraction is successful, we can rely on the simulation of [17] in the $\mathcal{F}_{\mathrm{OT}}$-hybrid to complete the rest of the simulation.
- Second, we observe that, if the sender aborts before sending the third message, no extraction is needed to be carried out since no inputs need to be feed to $\mathcal{F}_{\mathrm{OT}}$.

We can now conclude that our simulation achieves $1/p$-security against malicious senders, by using the same two cases as we considered for Protocol 2 based on the abort probability of the sender. More precisely,

Case: non-aborting probability of $\mathcal{A}$ is greater than $\frac{1}{pN}$. In this case, we know that except with probability $O(\frac{1}{p})$ the simulator extracts the required trapdoors and we achieve perfect simulation with probability at least $1-O(\frac{1}{p})$.

Case: non-aborting probability of $\mathcal{A}$ is at most $\frac{1}{pN}$. If the non-aborting probability is smaller than $\frac{1}{pN}$ then the probability mass of aborting views is at least $1 - \frac{1}{pN} > 1 - \frac{1}{p}$ and since no extraction needs to be carried out we achieve $1/p$-security.

Therefore, we have the following theorem:

Theorem 4.2. *Assuming the Decisional Diffie-Hellman problem is hard, there exists a four-round two-party secure protocol for any functionality, where both parties receive the output, that is $1/p$-secure in the presence of aborting senders and fully secure in the presence of non-aborting receivers.*

5 3-Round OT with 1/p Sender Security and Receiver Privacy

In this section, we construct a three-round protocol that achieves receiver privacy while maintaining $1/p$ security against malicious senders. We rely on claw-free (trapdoor) permutations instead of the discrete-logarithm assumption. We begin with a description of a basic protocol that only provides receiver privacy and then, relying on the techniques from Sect. 4, we discuss how to achieve $1/p$-security against aborting senders and full security against non-aborting senders.

Protocol 3 (Protocol π_{OT}).
Inputs: *The sender Sen holds s_0, s_1 and the receiver Rec holds a bit b.*
The protocol:

1. **Sen → Rec:** Sen *samples $(i, \mathsf{tk}^0, \mathsf{tk}^1) \leftarrow \mathsf{Gen}(1^n)$ and sends i to the receiver Rec.*
2. **Rec → Sen:** Rec *samples $x \leftarrow D_i$ and sends $y = f_i^b(x)$.*

3. **Sen → Rec:** *Upon receiving* y, *Sen computes* $x_\beta = (f_i^\beta)^{-1}(y)$ *for all* $\beta \in \{0,1\}$, *and sends* $(\langle x_0, r_0 \rangle \oplus s_0, r_0)$ *and* $(\langle x_1, r_1 \rangle \oplus s_1, r_1)$ *for random* r_0, r_1.[3]

Theorem 5.1 *Assume the existence of claw-free trapdoor permutations. Then, Protocol 3 is a three-round protocol that securely realizes* $\mathcal{F}_{\mathrm{OT}}$ *with privacy in the presence of aborting receivers and senders.*

See [16] for the proof. Note that Protocol 3 information theoretically hides the receiver's input from the malicious sender as y is uniformly distributed over D_i. While this guarantees perfect privacy against malicious senders, it is not simulatable. We make the observation that to achieve sender simulation, we need a mechanism to extract the sender's input while maintaining the receiver's message distribution. This can be achieved if the simulator knows tk^b for at least one value of b. With tk^b, the simulator can sample x_{1-b} at random and compute $x_b = (f_i^b)^{-1}(y)$ using tk^b where $y = f_i^{1-b}(x_{1-b})$. Now, the simulator supplies this y as the input and using both x_0 and x_1 extracts both s_0 and s_1. Since y is distributed identically as the real distribution we achieve simulation. Hence, there is a trapdoor information that allows simulation which is committed to by the sender in the first message via the function index i.

To achieve $1/p$ simulation against aborting senders, we repeat our basic protocol in parallel analogous to Protocol 2 where we rely on the OT protocol to perform the cut-and-choose checks. In slight more detail, we modify the sender's algorithm analogously to also commit to its input by appropriately secret-sharing its input. Recall that we needed $3M$ parallel invocations in the previous protocol to achieve this transformation. Here we will repeat it $6M$ times where only half of them will be used by the sender.

To argue receiver privacy, we observe that receiver privacy composes in parallel just as WI does. Privacy then holds from following an argument analogous to our previous protocol where we show that receiver can learn sufficiently many shares for only one of the two sender's inputs. Achieving $1/p$ sender simulation, on the other hand, follows using a standard cut-and-choose argument to establish that, through rewinding, a simulator can extract sufficiently many trapdoors as long as the sender does not abort too often. This protocol additionally achieves full simulation against non-aborting senders. A complete proof will be provided in the full version.

Protocol 4 (Protocol π_{OT}**).**
Inputs: *The sender* Sen *holds* s_0, s_1 *and the receiver* Rec *holds a bit* b.
The protocol:

- **Sen → Rec:** *Let* $N = 6M$. *Then, for* $j \in [N]$, *Sen samples* $(ind_j, \mathsf{tk}_j^0, \mathsf{tk}_j^1) \leftarrow \mathsf{Gen}(1^n)$ *and sends* $ind_1, \ldots, ind_N$ *to the receiver* Rec.
- **Rec → Sen:** *Rec picks a subset* $Trap \subset [N]$ *of size* $N/2$ *and sends* $Trap$ *to Sen. Let the remaining* $3M$ *indices be* $\{a_1, \ldots, a_{3M}\}$. *For these indices, the receiver proceeds as follows*
    1. *Rec samples uniformly at random* $c_1, \ldots, c_M \leftarrow \{0,1\}$. *The* c_i *values serve as the input to the first* M *OT executions.*

---

[3] We can consider some canonical representation of elements in D_i in $\{0,1\}^*$.

2. Rec *selects a random subset* $T_{1-b} \subseteq [2M]$ *of size* $M/2$. *Define* $T_b = [2M]/T_{1-b}$. *For every* $j \in [2M]$, Rec *sets* $b_j = \alpha$ *if* $j \in T_\alpha$. *The* b_j *values serve as the inputs to the OT for the next 2M executions.*

3. *According to its input for the 3M OT executions,* Rec *generates image elements as follows:*
   - *For every* $i \in [M]$, *it samples* $x_j \leftarrow D_{a_i}$, *and sends* $y_j = f^{c_i}_{a_i}(x_j)$.
   - *For every* $j \in [2M]$, *it samples* $x_{M+j} \leftarrow D_{a_{M+j}}$, *and sends* $y_{M+j} = f^{b_j}_{a_{M+j}}(x_{M+j})$.

- **Sen $\rightarrow$ Rec:**
  1. *Upon receiving* $Trap$ *and* $y_1, \ldots, y_{3M}$, Sen *sends* tk^0_j *for all* $j \in Trap$.
  2. Sen *picks two random strings* t_0, t_1 *and secret shares them using the Shamir's secret-sharing scheme. In particular,* Sen *computes* $[t_b] = (t^1_b, \ldots, t^{2M}_b) \leftarrow \mathsf{Share}(t_b)$ *for* $b \in \{0,1\}$. Sen *commits to the shares* $[t_0], [t_1]$ *as follows. It picks random matrices* $A_0, B_0 \leftarrow \mathbb{Z}^{M \times 2M}_q$ *and* $A_1, B_1 \leftarrow \mathbb{Z}^{M \times 2M}_q$ *such that* $\forall i \in [M]$:

$$A_0[i, \cdot] + B_0[i, \cdot] = [t_0], \quad A_1[i, \cdot] + B_1[i, \cdot] = [t_1].$$

  Sen *computes two matrices* $Z_0, Z_1 \in \mathbb{Z}^{M \times M-1}_q$ *and sends them in the clear such that:*

$$Z_0[i, \cdot] = \phi(A_0[i, \cdot]), Z_1[i, \cdot] = \phi(A_1[i, \cdot]).$$

  3. Sen *sends the committed matrices* $(\mathsf{com}_{A_0}, \mathsf{com}_{B_0}, \mathsf{com}_{A_1}, \mathsf{com}_{B_1})$ *to* Rec *where each element of each matrix is individually committed using* com.
  4. *For* $i \in [M]$, Sen *computes* $x^i_\beta = (f^\beta_{a_i})^{-1}(y_i)$ *for all* $\beta \in \{0,1\}$ *and sends* $(\langle x^i_0, r^i_0 \rangle \oplus t^i_0, r^i_0)$ *and* $(\langle x^i_1, r^i_1 \rangle \oplus t^i_1, r^i_1)$ *for random* r^i_0, r^i_1.
  5. *For all* $j \in [2M]$, Sen *computes* $x^{M+j}_\beta = (f^\beta_{a_{M+j}})^{-1}(y_{M+j})$ *for all* $\beta \in \{0,1\}$ *and sends the tuples* $(\langle x^{M+j}_0, r^{M+j}_0 \rangle \oplus (A_0[\cdot, j], B_0[\cdot, j]), r^{M+j}_0)$ *and* $(\langle x^{M+j}_1, r^{M+j}_1 \rangle \oplus (A_1[\cdot, j], B_1[\cdot, j]), r^{M+j}_1)$ *for random* r^{M+j}_0, r^{M+j}_1.
  6. Sen *sends* $C_0 = s_0 \oplus t_0$ *and* $C_1 = s_1 \oplus t_1$ *to* Rec.

- Rec *computes the output of the as follows:*
  1. **Decryption Phase:** *Upon receiving the senders message, the receiver computes the actual OT outputs for all parallel invocations. These include decommitments to* $A_0[i, \cdot], A_1[i, \cdot]$ *for every* $i \in [M]$ *when* $c_i = 0$ *and decommitments to* $B_0[i, \cdot], B_1[i, \cdot]$ *when* $c_i = 1$. *They also include columns* $A_{b_j}[\cdot, j], B_{b_j}[\cdot, j]$ *for every* $j \in [2M]$. *If any of the decommitments are incorrect, the receiver aborts.*
  2. **Shares Validity Check Phase:** *For* $i = 1, \ldots, M$, *if* $c_i = 0$ *check that* $Z_0[i, \cdot] = \phi(A_0[i, \cdot])$ *and* $Z_1[i, \cdot] = \phi(A_1[i, \cdot])$. *Otherwise, if* $c_i = 1$ *check that* $\phi(B_0[i, \cdot]) + Z_0[i, \cdot] = 0$ *and* $\phi(B_1[i, \cdot]) + Z_1[i, \cdot] = 0$. *If all the checks pass, the receiver proceeds to the next phase.*
  3. **Shares Consistency Check Phase:** *For each* $b \in \{0,1\}$, Rec *randomly chooses a set* T_b *for which* $b_j = b$ *at* $M/2$ *coordinates. For each* $j \in T_b$, Rec *checks that there exists a unique* x^i_b *such that* $A_b[i, j] + B_b[i, j] = x^j_b$ *for all* $i \in [M]$. *If so,* x^j_b *is marked as consistent. If all shares obtained in this phase are consistent,* Rec *proceeds to the reconstruction phase. Else it aborts.*
  4. **Reconstruction Phase:** *For* $j \in [2M]/T_{1-b}$, *if there exists a unique* x^j_b *such that* $A_b[i, j] + B_b[i, j] = x^j_b$, Rec *marks share* j *as a consistent column. If* R *obtains less than* $M + 1$ *consistent columns, it aborts. Otherwise, let* $x^{j_1}_b, \ldots, x^{j_{M+1}}_b$ *be any set of* $M + 1$ *shares obtained from consistent columns.* Rec *computes* $x_b \leftarrow \mathsf{Reconstruct}(x^{j_1}_b, \ldots, x^{j_{M+1}}_b)$ *and outputs* $s_b = C_b \oplus x_b$.

We conclude with the following theorem.

Theorem 5.2. *Assume the existence of claw-free trapdoor permutations. Then Protocol 4 is a three-round protocol that securely realizes $\mathcal{F}_{OT}$ with $1/p$-security in the presence of aborting senders and with privacy in the presence of aborting senders and receivers.*

References

1. Asokan, N., Shoup, V., Waidner, M.: Optimistic fair exchange of digital signatures. IEEE J. Sel. Areas Commun. **18**(4), 593–610 (2000)
2. Aumann, Y., Lindell, Y.: Security against covert adversaries: efficient protocols for realistic adversaries. J. Cryptol. **23**(2), 281–343 (2010)
3. Barak, B., Sahai, A.: How to play almost any mental game over the net - concurrent composition via super-polynomial simulation. IACR Cryptology ePrint Archive 2005:106 (2005)
4. Beaver, D.: Foundations of secure interactive computing. In: Feigenbaum, J. (ed.) CRYPTO 1991. LNCS, vol. 576, pp. 377–391. Springer, Heidelberg (1992)
5. Bentov, I., Kumaresan, R.: How to use bitcoin to design fair protocols. In: Garay, J.A., Gennaro, R. (eds.) CRYPTO 2014, Part II. LNCS, vol. 8617, pp. 421–439. Springer, Heidelberg (2014)
6. Blum, M.: How to prove a theorem so no one else can claim it. In: Proceedings of the International Congress of Mathematicians, USA, pp. 1444–1451
7. Cleve, R.: Limits on the security of coin flips when half the processors are faulty (extended abstract). In: STOC, pp. 364–369 (1986)
8. Even, S., Goldreich, O., Lempel, A.: A randomized protocol for signing contracts. Commun. ACM **28**(6), 637–647 (1985)
9. Garay, J.A., Katz, J., Tackmann, B., Zikas, V.: How fair is your protocol? A utility-based approach to protocol optimality. In: PODC, pp. 281–290 (2015)
10. Garg, S., Mukherjee, P., Pandey, O., Polychroniadou, A.: The exact round complexity of secure computation. In: Fischlin, M., Coron, J.-S. (eds.) EUROCRYPT 2016. LNCS, vol. 9666, pp. 448–476. Springer, Heidelberg (2016). doi:10.1007/978-3-662-49896-5_16
11. Goldreich, O., Krawczyk, H.: On the composition of zero-knowledge proof systems. SIAM J. Comput. **25**(1), 169–192 (1996)
12. Goldreich, O., Micali, S., Wigderson, A.: How to play any mental game or a completeness theorem for protocols with honest majority. In: STOC, pp. 218–229 (1987)
13. Gordon, S.D., Katz, J.: Partial fairness in secure two-party computation. In: Gilbert, H. (ed.) EUROCRYPT 2010. LNCS, vol. 6110, pp. 157–176. Springer, Heidelberg (2010)
14. Haitner, I., Ishai, Y., Kushilevitz, E., Lindell, Y., Petrank, E.: Black-box constructions of protocols for secure computation. SIAM J. Comput. **40**(2), 225–266 (2011)
15. Halevi, S., Kalai, Y.T.: Smooth projective hashing and two-message oblivious transfer. J. Cryptol. **25**(1), 158–193 (2012)
16. Hazay, C., Venkitasubramaniam, M.: What security can we achieve in 4-rounds? IACR Cryptology ePrint Arch. **2015**, 797 (2015). http://eprint.iacr.org/2015/797

17. Ishai, Y., Kushilevitz, E., Ostrovsky, R., Prabhakaran, M., Sahai, A.: Efficient non-interactive secure computation. In: Paterson, K.G. (ed.) EUROCRYPT 2011. LNCS, vol. 6632, pp. 406–425. Springer, Heidelberg (2011)
18. Katz, J., Ostrovsky, R.: Round-optimal secure two-party computation. In: Franklin, M. (ed.) CRYPTO 2004. LNCS, vol. 3152, pp. 335–354. Springer, Heidelberg (2004)
19. Lindell, Y.: Parallel coin-tossing and constant-round secure two-party computation. In: Kilian, J. (ed.) CRYPTO 2001. LNCS, vol. 2139, p. 171. Springer, Heidelberg (2001)
20. Micali, S.: Simple and fast optimistic protocols for fair electronic exchange. In: PODC, pp. 12–19 (2003)
21. Micali, S., Pass, R., Rosen, A.: Input-indistinguishable computation. In: FOCS, pp. 367–378 (2006)
22. Micali, S., Rogaway, P.: Secure computation. In: Feigenbaum, J. (ed.) CRYPTO 1991. LNCS, vol. 576, pp. 392–404. Springer, Heidelberg (1992)
23. Moran, T., Naor, M., Segev, G.: An optimally fair coin toss. In: Reingold, O. (ed.) TCC 2009. LNCS, vol. 5444, pp. 1–18. Springer, Heidelberg (2009)
24. Naor, M., Pinkas, B.: Efficient oblivious transfer protocols. In: SODA, pp. 448–457 (2001)
25. Ostrovsky, R., Richelson, S., Scafuro, A.: Round-optimal black-box two-party computation. IACR Cryptology ePrint Archive 2015:553 (2015)
26. Pass, R.: Simulation in quasi-polynomial time, and its application to protocol composition. In: Biham, E. (ed.) EUROCRYPT 2003. LNCS, vol. 2656, pp. 160–176. Springer, Heidelberg (2003)
27. Pedersen, T.P.: Non-interactive and information-theoretic secure verifiable secret sharing. In: Feigenbaum, J. (ed.) CRYPTO 1991. LNCS, vol. 576, pp. 129–140. Springer, Heidelberg (1992)
28. Peikert, C., Vaikuntanathan, V., Waters, B.: A framework for efficient and composable oblivious transfer. In: Wagner, D. (ed.) CRYPTO 2008. LNCS, vol. 5157, pp. 554–571. Springer, Heidelberg (2008)
29. Prabhakaran, M., Sahai, A.: New notions of security: achieving universal composability without trusted setup. In: STOC, pp. 242–251 (2004)
30. Yao, AC.-C.: How to generate and exchange secrets (extended abstract). In: FOCS, pp. 162–167 (1986)

Secret Sharing

Secret Sharing Schemes
for Dense Forbidden Graphs

Amos Beimel[1], Oriol Farràs[2], and Naty Peter[1(✉)]

[1] Ben Gurion University of the Negev, Be'er Sheva, Israel
amos.beimel@gmail.com, naty@post.bgu.ac.il
[2] Universitat Rovira i Virgili, Tarragona, Spain
oriol.farras@urv.cat

Abstract. A secret-sharing scheme *realizes a given graph* if every two vertices connected by an edge can reconstruct the secret and every independent set in the graph does not get any information about the secret. A secret-sharing scheme *realizes a forbidden graph* if every two vertices connected by an edge can reconstruct the secret and every two vertices which are not connected by an edge do not get any information about the secret. Similar to secret-sharing schemes for general access structures, there are gaps between the known lower bounds and upper bounds on the total share size for graphs and for forbidden graphs. Following [Beimel et al. CRYPTO 2012], our goal in this paper is to understand how the total share size increases by removing few edges from a graph that can be realized by an efficient secret-sharing scheme.

We show that if a graph with n vertices contains at least $\binom{n}{2} - n^{1+\beta}$ edges for some $0 \leq \beta < \frac{1}{2}$, i.e., it is obtained by removing few edges from the complete graph, then there is a scheme realizing its forbidden graph in which the total share size is $O(n^{7/6+2\beta/3})$. This should be compared to $O(n^{3/2})$, the best known upper bound for the total share size in general forbidden graphs. Additionally, we show that a forbidden graph access structure obtained by removing few edges from an arbitrary graph G can be realized by a secret-sharing scheme with total share size of $O(m + n^{7/6+2\beta/3})$, where m is the total size of the shares in a secret-sharing scheme realizing G and $n^{1+\beta}$ is the number of the removed edges.

We also show that for a graph obtained by removing few edges from an arbitrary graph G with n vertices, if the chromatic number of the graph that contains the removed edges is small, then there is a fairly efficient scheme realizing the resulting graph; specifically, we construct a secret-sharing scheme with total share size of $\tilde{O}(m^{2/3}n^{2/3+2\beta/3}c^{1/3})$, where m is the total size of the shares in a secret-sharing scheme realizing G, the value $n^{1+\beta}$ is an upper bound on the number of the removed

Amos Beimel–Supported by ISF grant 544/13 and by the Frankel center for computer science.
Oriol Farràs–Supported by the Spanish Government through a Juan de la Cierva grant and TIN2014-57364-C2-1-R, by the European Union through H2020-ICT-2014-1-644024, and by the Government of Catalonia through Grant 2014 SGR 537.

V. Zikas and R. De Prisco (Eds.): SCN 2016, LNCS 9841, pp. 509–528, 2016.
DOI: 10.1007/978-3-319-44618-9_27

edges, and c is the chromatic number of the graph of the removed edges. This should be compared to $O(n^2/\log(n))$, the best known upper bound for the total share size for general graphs.

Keywords: Secret sharing · Covers by graphs · Avoiding covers

1   Introduction

A secret-sharing scheme, introduced by [11,32,41], is a method in which a dealer, which holds a secret (i.e., a string of bits), can distribute shares (which are strings) to a set of participants such that only predefined subsets of the participants can reconstruct the secret from their shares, while other subsets get no information about the secret. The collection of the subsets that can reconstruct the secret is called the access structure. Secret-sharing is an important primitive for storing sensitive information, being able to give access to just some subsets of parties. For example, secret-sharing schemes can be used in access control, giving access to the secret to some subsets of parties. Furthermore, secret-sharing schemes are used in many secure protocols and applications, such as multiparty computation [8,18], threshold cryptography [24], access control [38], attribute-based encryption [31,46], and oblivious transfer [42,45]. The question whether there is a secret-sharing scheme with small share size, i.e., polynomial in the number of participants, is the main open problem in secret-sharing schemes. Clearly, secret-sharing schemes with super-polynomial share size are not usable in the above-mentioned application of secret sharing.

In this paper we will mainly consider secret-sharing schemes in which the minimal authorized sets are of size 2, and we represent such access structures by graphs, where each vertex represents a participant and each edge represents a minimal authorized set. Following [5], we will study the problem of realizing graph access structures, in particular for graphs obtained by removing few edges from an arbitrary graph, and from the complete graph. Given a scheme realizing a graph, we want to understand how the size of the shares increases when removing few edges from the graph, compared to the size of the shares in the scheme of the original graph. We consider graphs with "good" schemes, i.e., graphs with schemes in which the size of the shares is small. We present efficient constructions both for graph access structures and for forbidden graph access structures.

1.1   Related Work

Works on Arbitrary Access Structures. Secret-sharing schemes were introduced by Shamir [41] and Blakley [11] for the threshold case, and by Ito et al. [32] for the general case. Threshold access structures, in which the authorized sets are all the sets containing at least t participants (for some threshold t), can be realized by secret-sharing schemes in which the size of each share is the size of the secret [11,41]. There are other access structures that have secret-sharing schemes in which the size of the shares is small, i.e., polynomial (in the number of participants) share size [9,10,14,34]. In particular, Benaloh and Leichter [9] proved that if an access structure can be described by a small monotone formula, then it has an efficient secret-sharing scheme. Improving on this result, Karchmer and Wigderson [34] showed that if an access structure can be described by a small monotone span program, then it has an efficient secret-sharing scheme. However, the best known schemes for general access structures (e.g., [10,14,32,34]) are highly inefficient, i.e., they have share size of $2^{O(n)}$ (where n is the number of participants). The best lower bound known on the total share size of schemes realizing an access structure is $\Omega(n^2/\log(n))$ [21,22]. For linear secret-sharing schemes, which are secret-sharing schemes described by linear mappings, the best lower bound on the share size is $2^{\Omega(n^c)}$ for some constant $c < 1$ [20] (this very recent lower bound improves the results in [2,6,27,28]). Most known secret-sharing schemes are linear, and many applications require linear schemes. More information about secret sharing can be found in [3].

Graph Access Structures. A secret-sharing scheme realizes a given graph if every two vertices connected by an edge can reconstruct the secret and every independent set in the graph does not get any information on the secret. The trivial secret-sharing scheme for realizing a graph is sharing the secret independently for each edge; this results in a scheme whose total share size is $O(n^2)$ (times the length of the secret, which will be ignored in the introduction). This can be improved – every graph access structure can be realized by a linear secret-sharing scheme in which the size of the shares is $O(n^2/\log(n))$ [16,26].

Graph access structures have been studied in [5,6,12,13,15,17,23,43]. Capocelli et al. [17] proved that there exists a graph with 4 vertices such that the size of the share of at least one party is at least $3/2$ times the size of the secret. Brickell and Davenport [15] showed that a graph access structure (with n vertices) can be realized by a secret-sharing scheme in which the total size of the shares is n if and only if the graph is a complete multipartite graph. Stinson [43] showed that for a graph with average degree d, there is a secret-sharing scheme realizing its graph access structure in which the average share size of a vertex is at most $(d+1)/2$. Blundo et al. [13] presented upper and lower bounds on the size of the shares of a scheme realizing graph access structures, for multipartite graphs, connected graphs, paths, cycles, and trees. In particular, it is proven in [13] that the smallest share size of a scheme which realizes a graph access structure is the size of the secret or at least 1.5 times greater than the size of the secret. Blundo et al. [12] showed that there exists a d-regular graph such that the share size of each vertex in any scheme that realizes its graph access structure is at least $(d+1)/2$. Beimel et al. [6] proved a lower bound of $\Omega(n^{3/2})$ on the total share size of a linear schemes realizing a certain graph access structure. Csirmaz [23], extending a result of van Dijk [25], showed that there exist graphs for which the total share size in every secret-sharing scheme realizing their graph access structures is $\Omega(n\log(n))$.

Beimel et al. [5] showed that a graph with n vertices that contains $\binom{n}{2} - n^{1+\beta}$ edges for some constant $0 \le \beta < 1$ can be realized by a scheme in which the total share size is $\tilde{O}(n^{5/4+3\beta/4})$. They also showed that if $n^{1+\beta}$ edges are removed from an arbitrary graph that can be realized by a secret-sharing scheme with total share size m, then the resulting graph can be realized by a secret-sharing scheme with total share size $\tilde{O}(m^{1/2}n^{1+\beta/2})$.

Some of the results for graph access structures have been extended to general access structures, e.g., Martí-Farré and Padró [36], generalizing results of [13], showed that in every secret-sharing scheme realizing an access structure that is not a port matroid (and, hence, not ideal) the size of the shares is at least 1.5 times the size of the secret. Other results have been extended to homogenous access structures [35,39], which are access structures in which the minimal authorized sets are of the same size (in graph access structures, this size is 2), e.g., Padró and Sáez [39] showed upper bounds on the size of the shares of secret-sharing schemes realizing homogenous access structures. These results demonstrate that graph access structures can be used to understand problems about general access structures.

Forbidden Graph Access Structures. Another model we consider is the forbidden graph access structures, which was first described in [44]. A secret-sharing scheme realizes a forbidden graph access structure if every two vertices can reconstruct the secret if and only if they are connected by an edge. We do not care if sets of 3 or more vertices can reconstruct the secret (in [44], every set of 3 or more vertices can reconstruct the secret). The requirement that every set of 3 or more vertices can reconstruct the secret (as in [44]) increases slightly the total share size, since we can independently share the secret using the 3-out-of-n scheme of Shamir [41], in which the size of the share of every participant is the size of the secret (when the size of the secret is at least $\log(n)$).

The requirements for graph access structures are stronger than for forbidden graph access structures, since for graph access structures every independent set in the graph is an unauthorized subset, and in forbidden graph access structures we only require independent sets of size 2 to be unauthorized sets.

Every forbidden graph access structure can be realized by a secret-sharing scheme in which the size of the shares is $O(n^{3/2})$ [7]. Furthermore, this can be done by a linear scheme [29]. In contrast, the best *known* upper bound for graph access structures is $O(n^2/\log(n))$ [23].

Gertner et al. [30] presented conditional disclosure of secrets (CDS). In this problem, two parties want to disclose a secret to a referee if and only if their inputs (strings of N bits) satisfy some predicate (e.g., if their inputs are equal). For that, each party sends one message to the referee (this message depends only on its input and the secret), and if the predicate holds the referee can reconstruct the secret from the messages it received. This problem is interesting, since in [30] CDS is used to efficiently realize a symmetrically-private information retrieval (SPIR) schemes. Additionally, in [29] it is shown that CDS can be used for attribute-based encryption [31,40].

We can represent the CDS problem as the problem of realizing a secret-sharing scheme for a forbidden graph access structure of a bipartite graph and vice-versa: Every possible input for the first party is a vertex in the first part of the graph and every possible input for the second party is a vertex in the second part of the graph, and there is an edge between two vertices from different parts if and only if the two corresponding inputs satisfy the predicate. The size of the share of each vertex is equivalent to the size of the message sent to the referee by the party, when it holds the input associated with the vertex. We get a bipartite graph with 2^N vertices in each part (where N is the size of the input of the parties).

It was shown in [29] that for every predicate there exists a linear CDS such that the size of each of the messages sent by the two parties to the referee is $2^{N/2}$.[1] It implies that there exists a linear secret-sharing scheme in which the total size of the shares is $O(n^{3/2})$ (where n is the number of the participants) for every forbidden graph access structure.

By a generalization of a result of [37], we get a lower bound of $\Omega(n^{3/2})$ on the size of the shares of a linear scheme realizing an implicit forbidden graph access structures.

1.2   Our Results

The first problem we deal with in this paper is the construction of secret-sharing schemes realizing forbidden graph access structures for dense graphs, i.e., for graphs in which its complement graph contains few edges. Given a dense graph with n vertices and with at least $\binom{n}{2} - n^{1+\beta}$ edges, for some $0 \leq \beta < \frac{1}{2}$, we construct a secret-sharing scheme that realizes its forbidden graph access structure, in which the total size of the shares is $O(n^{7/6+2\beta/3})$. Compared to [5], which shows that graph access structures of such graphs can be realized by a scheme with total share size $\tilde{O}(n^{5/4+3\beta/4})$, our scheme for forbidden graph access structures is more efficient.

As a corollary, we show that if a graph with n vertices contains $\binom{n}{2} - \ell$ edges for some $0 < \ell < n$, then it can be realized by a secret-sharing scheme in which the total share size is $O(n + \ell^{7/6})$. For example, if $\ell = O(n^{6/7})$, then the total share size of the scheme is $O(n)$.

In addition, we show that if an arbitrary forbidden graph access structure (with n vertices) can be realized by a secret-sharing scheme in which the total size of the shares is m, and we remove $n^{1+\beta}$ edges from it (for some $0 \leq \beta < \frac{1}{2}$), then the resulting forbidden graph access structure can be realized by a secret-sharing scheme in which the total size of the shares is $O(m + n^{7/6+2\beta/3})$.

The second problem we consider is constructing secret-sharing schemes that realize graph access structures for graphs obtained when removing few edges from an arbitrary graph that has a "good" scheme, i.e., the size of the shares in this scheme is relatively small. We solve this question when the graph of the removed edges has a small chromatic number.

Namely, we consider a graph with n vertices that can be realized by a secret-sharing scheme with total share size m, and we remove a set of at most $n^{1+\beta}$ edges from the graph, for some $0 \leq \beta < 1$. Then we show that if the chromatic number

---

[1] A linear CDS is a CDS in which if the predicate holds, then the reconstruction function of the referee is linear.

c of the graph with the removed edges satisfies $c < \frac{n^{1-\beta/2}}{m^{1/2}}$, then the obtained graph has a secret-sharing scheme with total share size $\tilde{O}(m^{2/3}n^{2/3+2\beta/3}c^{1/3})$.

It should be compared to the result of Beimel et al. [5], showing that such a graph can be realized by a scheme with total share size $\tilde{O}(m^{1/2}n^{1+\beta/2})$ without any restrictions on the chromatic number of the removed edges. Thus, our scheme is better when the chromatic number is relatively small and m is not too big (it is always more efficient when $c < \frac{n^{1-\beta/2}}{m^{1/2}}$).

Remark 1.1. In particular, our result is valid for graphs obtained by removing few edges from a graph with small chromatic number, denoted by c, since in this case the graph which contains the removed edges is a subgraph of the original graph, and thus, its chromatic number is at most c.

As a corollary, we show that if a graph with n vertices can be realized by a secret-sharing scheme with total share size m, and we remove ℓ edges from it, for some $0 < \ell < n$, such that the chromatic number of the graph containing the removed edges is c, where $c < \frac{\ell}{m^{1/2}}$, then we can realize the remaining graph by a secret-sharing scheme in which the total share size is $\tilde{O}(cm + m^{2/3}\ell^{2/3}c^{1/3})$. Thus, if $\ell = \Theta(cm^{1/2})$, then the total share size of the scheme is $\tilde{O}(cm)$.

Techniques. A cover of a graph G is a collection of subgraphs of G satisfying that every edge in G appears in at least one subgraph of the collection. Covers of graphs where used to construct secret-sharing schemes (e.g., in [5,43]). The idea of the construction is to share the secret independently for each subgraph in the cover. By choosing subgraphs that have efficient secret-sharing schemes (e.g., multipartite graphs, which have an ideal scheme), it is possible to find efficient schemes for other graphs.

When realizing the graph access structure of a graph obtained by removing few edges from a general graph G, we use a new technique of *avoiding covers*. We cover a bipartite graph, which is a subgraph of G, by bipartite graphs $G_1, \ldots, G_r$ in such a way that for every bipartite graph G_i of the cover, there are no removed edges between any two vertices (in the same part or in different parts) in the graph G_i. Then, for every graph G_i of the cover, we share the secret independently using the scheme of the graph G.

Following [5], we construct a scheme realizing graph access structures of graphs obtained by removing few edges with small chromatic number from a general graph in 3 main steps. We first realize all the edges incident to vertices with high degree in the graph of the removed edges by stars, and remove these vertices and their incident edges from the graph. After this step, the degree of every vertex in the graph of the removed edges is bounded. Next, we reduce the maximum degree of a vertex in the graph of the removed edges by using the chromatic number of the graph, and in the final step we use the avoiding cover to realize the remaining graph.

Similar to graph access structures, the main scheme realizing forbidden graph access structures of dense graphs contains 3 main steps. First, we realize all the edges incident to vertices with high degree in the complement graph by two independent schemes, for the induced graph on these vertices, and for the bipartite graph between these vertices and the remaining vertices. We then remove these vertices and their incident edges from the graph. In this step, we use the scheme of [7,29] and get a more efficient scheme than the cover by stars used in [5] for graph access structures. We get a graph in which the degree of every vertex in its complement is bounded. Next, we decrease the maximum degree of a vertex in the complement graph $\log \log(n)$ times, and finally we realize the remaining graph using a *forest cover*.

2 Preliminaries

In this section we define secret-sharing schemes, secret-sharing schemes for graphs and for forbidden graphs, and some other useful definitions. Additionally, we present the graph terminology we use.

Notations. We denote the logarithmic function with base 2 and base e by log and ln, respectively. We use the $\tilde{O}$ notation, which ignores polylogarithmic factors, i.e., $O(n^\delta \log^a(n)) = \tilde{O}(n^\delta)$ for a constant a. For any two strings of bits s_1, s_2, let $s_1 \oplus s_2$ denote the bitwise exclusive-or between the strings.

Secret Sharing. We start by defining access structures, distribution schemes, and secret-sharing schemes, as described in [4,19].

Definition 2.1 (Access Structures, Distribution Schemes, and Secret Sharing). *Let $P = \{p_1, \ldots, p_n\}$ be a set of parties. A collection $\Gamma \subseteq 2^P$ is monotone if $B \in \Gamma$ and $B \subseteq C$ imply that $C \in \Gamma$. An access structure is a monotone collection $\Gamma \subseteq 2^P$ of non-empty subsets of P. Sets in Γ are called authorized, and sets not in Γ are called unauthorized. The family of minimal authorized subsets is denoted by $\min \Gamma$.*

A distribution scheme $\Sigma = \langle \Pi, \mu \rangle$ with domain of secrets K is a pair, where μ is a probability distribution on some finite set R called the set of random strings and Π is a mapping from $K \times R$ to a set of n-tuples $K_1 \times K_2 \times \cdots \times K_n$, where K_j is called the domain of shares of party p_j. A dealer distributes a secret $k \in K$ according to Σ by first sampling a random string $r \in R$ according to μ, computing a vector of shares $\Pi(k,r) = (s_1, \ldots, s_n)$, and privately communicating each share s_j to party p_j. For a set $A \subseteq P$, we denote $\Pi_A(s, r)$ as the restriction of $\Pi(s, r)$ to its A-entries. Given a distribution scheme, the size of the secret is $\log(|K|)$, the (normalized) size of the share of party p_j is $\frac{\log(|K_j|)}{\log(|K|)}$, and the (normalized) total share size of the distribution scheme is $\sum\limits_{j=1}^{n} \frac{\log(|K_j|)}{\log(|K|)}$.

Let K be a finite set of secrets, where $|K| \geq 2$. A distribution scheme $\langle \Pi, \mu \rangle$ with domain of secrets K is a secret-sharing scheme realizing an access structure Γ if the following two requirements hold:

Correctness requirement: *The secret k can be reconstructed by any authorized set of parties.*

Privacy requirement: *Every unauthorized set cannot learn anything about the secret from their shares.*

Graph Terminology. In this paper we consider graph access structures and forbidden graph access structures. In the sequence, $G = (V, E)$ is an undirected graph, where the vertices of V will also denote parties of an access structure as discussed below.

The degree of a graph is the maximum degree of a vertex in the graph. A graph $G' = (V', E')$ is a subgraph of the graph $G = (V, E)$ if $V' \subseteq V$ and $E' \subseteq E \cap (V' \times V')$. All through this paper, n is the number of the vertices in the graph $G = (V, E)$, i.e., $|V| = n$.

Definition 2.2 (The Complement Graph and Intersection of Graphs). *Given a graph $G = (V, E)$, the complement graph of G is the graph $\overline{G} = (V, \overline{E})$, where every two vertices $u, v \in V$ satisfy $(u, v) \in \overline{E}$ if and only if $(u, v) \notin E$. Given two graphs $G_1 = (V, E_1)$ and $G_2 = (V', E_2)$ such that $V' \subseteq V$, the intersection of G_1 and G_2 is $G_1 \cap G_2 = (V', E_1 \cap E_2)$.*

Next we define one of the techniques to construct a secret-sharing scheme realizing a graph that uses covers of graphs.

Definition 2.3 (λ-Covers). *Let $G = (V, E)$ be a graph. A λ-cover of G is a collection of graphs $G_1 = (V_1, E_1), \ldots, G_r = (V_r, E_r)$ such that each G_i is a subgraph of G, and each edge in E is in at least λ graphs of the collection. A cover of G is a 1-cover of G.*

Recall that a bipartite graph $G = (U, V, E)$ is a graph where the vertices are $U \cup V$ (U and V are called the parts of G) and $E \subseteq U \times V$. A bipartite graph is complete if $E = U \times V$. A complete bipartite λ-cover of G is a λ-cover of G by complete bipartite graphs. A complete bipartite cover of G is a complete bipartite 1-cover of G.

Definition 2.4 (Equivalence Graphs and Equivalence Covers) [1]. *An equivalence graph is a vertex-disjoint union of cliques. An equivalence cover of the graph $G = (V, E)$ is a cover $G_1 = (V_1, E_1), \ldots, G_r = (V_r, E_r)$ of G such that each G_i is an equivalence graph.*

Definition 2.5 (The Graph G_F and the Graph G_F^*). *Given a graph $G = (V, E)$ and a set of vertices $F \subset V$, we define the bipartite graph $G_F = (F, V \setminus F, E \cap (F \times (V \setminus F)))$, which is the bipartite graph with parts F and $V \setminus F$, restricted to the edges of G.*

For a set of vertices $F \subset V$ and a set of edges $E^* \subset E$ (which is the set of the removed edges), we define $G_F^* = (F, V \setminus F, \overline{E^*} \cap (F \times (V \setminus F)))$, i.e., G_F^* is a bipartite graph with parts F and $V \setminus F$, which contains only the edges that are not removed from G.

Forbidden Graphs and Secret Sharing. We next present the definition of forbidden graph access structures, in which we only require that sets of size 2 that are edges can reconstruct the secret, while sets of size 2 that are not edges cannot learn any information about the secret.[2]

Definition 2.6 (Forbidden Graph Access Structures). *Given a graph $G = (V, E)$, its forbidden graph access structure Γ is the access structure on V composed of all the sets in E and all the sets of 3 or more vertices. For a graph $G = (V, E)$, a secret-sharing scheme realizes its forbidden graph if the scheme realizing its forbidden graph access structure, i.e., if every edge of E and every set of size at least 3 can reconstruct the secret, and every edge of $\overline{E}$ cannot get any information about the secret.*

In our constructions for forbidden graph access structures, edges are removed from the complete graph $G = (V, E)$, where $|E| = \binom{V}{2}$. The set $E^* \subset E$ is the set of edges we remove from the graph G, i.e., the excluded edges, such that $|E^*| \leq n^{1+\beta}$ for some constant $0 \leq \beta < \frac{1}{2}$, i.e., we remove at most $n^{1+\beta}$ edges from the complete graph. We want to realize the graph $G \cap G^* = G^*$, where $G^* = (V, \overline{E^*})$, i.e., we want to find a secret-sharing scheme in which each edge in $E \setminus E^* = \overline{E^*}$ can reconstruct the secret and each edge in E^* cannot learn any information about the secret. Note that since $|E^*| \leq n^{1+\beta}$, the number of edges in the graph G^* is $|\overline{E^*}| \geq \binom{n}{2} - n^{1+\beta}$, i.e., the graph G^* is a dense graph in which its complement contains few edges. Our constructions are only useful when $0 \leq \beta < \frac{1}{2}$, since for larger values of β, the total share size of the schemes we present is larger than $n^{3/2}$ and every forbidden graph access structure can be realized by a secret-sharing scheme whose total share size is $O(n^{3/2})$.

Graphs and Secret Sharing. Next, we formally define graph access structures.

Definition 2.7 (Graph Access Structures). *Given a graph $G = (V, E)$, its graph access structure is the access structure whose set of participants is V and whose minimal authorized sets are the edges in E, that is, a set is authorized if it contains an edge, and a set is not authorized if it is an independent set in G. We say that a secret-sharing scheme realizes a graph if the scheme realizes its graph access structure, i.e., if every edge can reconstruct the secret, and every independent set in G cannot get any information about the secret.*

Remark 2.8. When we say that a secret-sharing scheme realizes a graph, we mean that the scheme realizes its graph access structure or its forbidden graph access structure, according to the context, e.g., if we discuss forbidden graph access structures, we say that a secret-sharing scheme realizing a graph if the scheme realizing its forbidden graph access structure. In Sect. 3 we consider forbidden graph access structures and in Sect. 4 we consider graph access structures.

---

[2] In [44], the access structure is specified by the complement graph, i.e., by the edges that are forbidden from learning information on the secret.

We use the following notations: the graph $G = (V, E)$ is the original graph. The set $E^* \subset E$ is the set of edges we remove from the graph G, i.e., the excluded edges, such that $|E^*| \leq n^{1+\beta}$ for some constant $0 \leq \beta < 1$. Furthermore, m is the total share size of a secret-sharing scheme realizing the graph G.

We want to find a secret-sharing scheme in which each edge in $E \setminus E^*$ (equivalently, in $E \cap \overline{E^*}$) can reconstruct the secret, and such that every set of vertices with no edge in $E \setminus E^*$ cannot learn any information on the secret. Additionally, we use the notation G^*, where $G^* = (V, \overline{E^*})$, i.e., G^* is the graph of the edges that are not removed, and $\overline{G^*} = (V, E^*)$ is the graph which contains the removed edges from G. The value $\chi(\overline{G^*})$ is the chromatic number of $\overline{G^*}$, i.e., the minimal number of colors needed to color the vertices of V such that there are no edges of E^* between any two vertices with the same color. Our construction applies only when the graph of the removed edges has a small chromatic number.

In the definition of secret-sharing schemes realizing graph access structures we require that every independent set cannot learn any information about the secret. However, in our constructions in Sect. 4 we only claim that non-edges cannot learn information on the secret. The next claim shows that, due to the selection of special covers, in our constructions the latter requirement implies the former strong requirement (as discussed in Sect. 3, this is not true for general constructions).

Claim 2.9. *Let $G = (V, E)$ be a graph, and $G_1 = (V_1, E_1), \ldots, G_r = (V_r, E_r)$ be graphs such that each G_i is a subgraph of G. If we independently realize each graph G_i using a scheme that realizes the graph access structure of G_i (i.e., every independent set in G_i does not get any information on the secret), then every independent set in G cannot learn any information on the secret.*

Remark 2.10. In our construction, we use the scheme of the graph G to realize subgraphs of G with no removed edges (i.e., with no edges from E^*). We also use the trivial scheme for some edges from $E \setminus E^*$ (i.e., sharing the secret independently for each edge). These schemes also realize subgraphs of G with no edges from E^* (each such subgraph contains only one edge). Since we use schemes that realize the graph access structures of subgraphs of G, a set of vertices can reconstruct the secret if and only if it contains an edge from the graph G. So, by Claim 2.9, to argue that every independent set of $G \cap G^*$ cannot learn any information on the secret, it is sufficient to show that every edge in $\overline{E} \cup E^*$ cannot learn any information on the secret.

3 Schemes for Forbidden Graph Access Structures

In this section, we consider forbidden graph access structures, where every edge in the graph can reconstruct the secret, and every edge not in the graph cannot reconstruct the secret. In all the schemes in this section, except for the schemes presented in Lemma 3.1 and in Theorem 3.2, the size of the secret should be at least $\log(n)$, since in these schemes we use the t-out-of-n scheme of Shamir [41]. Some of the proofs in this section are deferred to the full version of this paper.

3.1   Constructions for Arbitrary Graphs

In the first scheme we realize bipartite graphs. The following schemes are based on the construction for CDS of [29].

Lemma 3.1. *Let $H = (U, V, E)$ be a bipartite graph such that $|U| = k$ and $|V| = n$. Then, there is a secret-sharing scheme such that: (1) each edge in H can reconstruct the secret, (2) each edge not in H cannot learn any information about the secret, and (3) if $k^2 \leq n$ then the total share size of the scheme is $O(n)$. Otherwise, the total share size of the scheme is $O(n^{1/2}k)$.*

The following theorem provides a scheme realizing an arbitrary graph G. We use the scheme of Lemma 3.1 for bipartite graphs $\log(n)$ times to get a scheme for an arbitrary graph.

Theorem 3.2 ([7,29]). *Let $G = (V, E)$ be a graph such that $|V| = n$. Then, there is a secret-sharing scheme such that: (1) each edge in G can reconstruct the secret, (2) each edge not in G cannot learn any information about the secret, and (3) if the size of the secret is 1, then the total share size of the scheme is $O(n^{3/2} \log(n)) = \tilde{O}(n^{3/2})$. If the size of the secret is $\Omega(\log^2(n))$, then the total share size of the scheme is $O(n^{3/2})$.*

3.2   Constructions for Bounded Degree Excluded Graphs

The next lemma shows that given a forest, i.e., a graph that does not contain any cycle, we can realize its complement graph with a scheme in which the total share size is $O(n)$. In the sequence, we use this scheme in the following construction, to realize the complement of a bounded degree graph.

Lemma 3.3. *Let $G = (V, E)$ be a graph such that its complement graph $\overline{G} = (V, \overline{E})$ is a forest. Then, there is a secret-sharing scheme such that: (1) each edge in G can reconstruct the secret, (2) each edge not in G cannot learn any information about the secret, and (3) the total share size of the scheme is at most $3n$.*

Proof Sketch. Denote $V = \{v_1, \ldots, v_n\}$. Since $\overline{G}$ is a forest, it is composed of trees. Let $T_1 = (V_1, E_1), \ldots, T_k = (V_k, E_k)$ be the trees in the graph $\overline{G}$ containing all the vertices in G (isolated vertices in $\overline{G}$ are trees with one vertex). First, we share the secret by generating $n + k$ shares $r_1, \ldots, r_{n+k}$ using the 4-out-of-$(n + k)$ scheme of Shamir [41]. For every $1 \leq i \leq k$, we give shares to the vertices in the tree T_i as follows: For the tree $T_i = (V_i, E_i)$, denote $|V_i| = t$ and $V_i = \{v_{i_1}, \ldots, v_{i_t}\}$. We consider the tree as a rooted tree, with a root v_{i_1}, and for every vertex v in T_i, we denote the parent of v by $\pi(v)$. The root vertex v_{i_1} gets the shares r_{n+i}, r_{i_1}, and for every $2 \leq j \leq t$, vertex $v_{i_j} \in V_i$ gets the shares r_p, r_{i_j}, where $\pi(v_{i_j}) = v_p$.

Additionally, we denote the maximum distance of a vertex from the root by D_i. For every $1 \leq \ell \leq D_i$, define $F_{i,\ell} = \{v \in V_i : \text{The distance of } v$

from the root in the tree T_i is ℓ}. For every $F_{i,\ell}$, we independently share the secret by generating $|F_{i,\ell}|$ shares $t_1, \ldots, t_{|F_{i,\ell}|}$ using the 2-out-of-$|F_{i,\ell}|$ scheme of Shamir, and giving the jth vertex in $F_{i,\ell}$ the share t_j. It can be verified that the above scheme is correct, private, and has shares of size $3n$.   □

Definition 3.4 (Covers by Forests). *Let $H = (V, E)$ be a graph. A forest cover of H is a cover $G_1 = (V, E_1), \ldots, G_r = (V, E_r)$ of H such that each G_i is a forest.*

The next lemma shows that every graph with degree d can be covered by a forest cover of size d.

Lemma 3.5. *Let $H = (V, E)$ be a graph such that the degree of each vertex in H is bounded by d. Then, there is a cover of H by d forests $G_1 = (V, E_1), \ldots, G_d = (V, E_d)$ such that every edge $e \in E$ appears in exactly one graph of the cover.*

The forest cover is used below to construct a scheme for the complement of a bounded degree graph. The secret-sharing scheme we present saves a factor of $\Theta(\log(n))$ compared to the scheme of [5], which realizes graph access structures of bounded degree graphs (we only realize forbidden graph access structures).

Theorem 3.6. *Let $G = (V, E)$ be a graph such that the degree of every vertex in its complement graph $\overline{G} = (V, \overline{E})$ is bounded by d. Then, there is a secret-sharing scheme realizing the forbidden graph access structure of G such that the total share size of the scheme is at most $3dn$.*

Definition 3.7. (The Bipartite Complement). *Let $H = (U, V, E)$ be a bipartite graph. The bipartite complement of H is the bipartite graph $\overline{H} = (U, V, \overline{E})$, where every $u \in U$ and $v \in V$ satisfy $(u, v) \in \overline{E}$ if and only if $(u, v) \notin E$.*

First, we show how to construct a scheme realizing a bipartite graph such that the degree of every vertex in one part in its bipartite complement is bounded.

Lemma 3.8. *Let $H = (U, V, E)$ be a bipartite graph with $|V| = n$ and $|U| = k \le n$ satisfying that the degree of every vertex in V in the bipartite complement graph $\overline{H} = (U, V, \overline{E})$ is at most d. Then, there is a secret-sharing scheme such that: (1) each edge in H can reconstruct the secret, (2) each edge not in H (including edges between vertices in the same part in the bipartite graph H) cannot learn any information about the secret, and (3) the total share size of the scheme is at most $8dn$.*

Proof. To share a secret s, we choose random strings s_1, s_2, s_3 such that $s = s_1 \oplus s_2 \oplus s_3$. We give s_1 to each vertex in U and give s_2 to each vertex in V. The total share size for these shares is at most $2n$. By Lemma 3.5, there is a cover of $\overline{H}$ by d forests such that every edge in $\overline{H}$ appears in exactly one graph of the cover. Next, consider the graph $G = (U \cup V, E \cup (U \times U) \cup (V \times V))$. Notice that G is the complement graph of the graph $\overline{H}$. We share s_3 to the graph G using the forest cover of $\overline{H}$ by the scheme from Theorem 3.6 such that each edge in G

can reconstruct the secret and each edge in $\overline{H}$ cannot learn any information on the secret, and the total share size of the scheme is at most $3d(|U|+|V|) \leq 6dn$. Thus, the total share of the resulting scheme is at most $8dn$.

For an edge $(u,v) \in E$ such that $u \in U$ and $v \in V$, the edge (u,v) is in G, and thus, the edge (u,v) can reconstruct s_3. Moreover, since $u \in U$, the vertex u holds s_1 and since $v \in V$, the vertex v holds s_2, and, hence, the edge (u,v) can reconstruct the secret s by performing bitwise exclusive-or between the strings s_1, s_2, s_3.

For an edge $(u,v) \notin E$ such that $u, v \in U$, vertices u, v do not hold the string s_2, and, hence, cannot learn any information on the secret. For an edge $(u,v) \notin E$ such that $u, v \in V$, the vertices u, v do not hold the string s_1, and, hence, cannot learn any information on the secret. For an edge $(u,v) \notin E$ such that $u \in U$ and $v \in V$, the edge (u,v) is in $\overline{H}$, and thus, the edge (u,v) cannot learn any information on s_3, and cannot learn any information about the secret. $\square$

We use a different construction to realize a bipartite graph such that one part is much smaller than the other and the degree of every vertex in its bipartite complement is bounded.

Lemma 3.9. *Let $H = (U, V, E)$ be a bipartite graph with $|V| = n$ and $|U| = k \leq n$ satisfying that the degree of every vertex in $U \cup V$ in the bipartite complement graph $\overline{H} = (U, V, \overline{E})$ is at most d, where $d < k$. Then, there is a secret-sharing scheme realizing the forbidden graph access structure of H such that the total share size of the scheme is $O(n + d^{2/3}k^{4/3})$.*

Proof. Define $D_1 = \{v \in V : \text{There exists } u \in U \text{ such that } (u,v) \in \overline{H}\}$. Since the degree of every vertex of U in $\overline{H}$ is at most d, the size of D_1 is at most dk. Furthermore, the complete bipartite graph $H_1 = (U, V \setminus D_1, U \times (V \setminus D_1))$ is a subgraph of H. We realize H_1 by an ideal scheme in which the total share size is at most $|U| + |V| = O(n)$ (see Fig. 1).

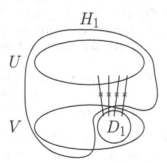

Fig. 1. The bipartite graph H_1. Edges in $\overline{E}$ are marked with blue crosses.

Next, define $D_2 = \{v \in D_1 : \text{The degree of } v \text{ in } \overline{H} \text{ is at least } (\frac{k}{d})^{\frac{1}{3}}\}$. Because the graph $\overline{H}$ contains at most dk edges, we get that $|D_2| \leq dk/(\frac{k}{d})^{\frac{1}{3}} = d^{4/3}k^{2/3}$.

Let $H_2 = (U, D_2, E \cap (U \times D_2))$. Since $d < k$, we get that $|U|^2 = k^2 = k^{4/3}k^{2/3} > d^{4/3}k^{2/3} \geq |D_2|$, and, hence, by Lemma 3.1, we can realize the graph H_2 such that each edge in H_2 can reconstruct the secret, each edge not in H_2 cannot learn any information about the secret, and the total share size of the scheme is $O(|D_2|^{\frac{1}{2}} \cdot |U|) = O((d^{4/3}k^{2/3})^{\frac{1}{2}}k) = O(d^{2/3}k^{4/3})$.

Finally, let $D_3 = D_1 \setminus D_2$ and $H_3 = (U, D_3, E \cap (U \times D_3))$. The degree of each vertex of D_3 in the graph $\overline{H_3}$ is at most $(\frac{k}{d})^{\frac{1}{3}}$. By Lemma 3.6, we can realize the graph H_3 by a scheme in which the total share size is $O((\frac{k}{d})^{\frac{1}{3}}dk) = O(d^{2/3}k^{4/3})$.

As H_1, H_2, and H_3 cover H, we constructed a scheme realizing H such that each edge in H can reconstruct the secret, each edge not in H cannot learn any information about the secret, and the total share size of the scheme is $O(n + d^{2/3}k^{4/3})$.   □

3.3   Constructions for Excluded Graphs with Few Edges

Given a graph, the following construction shows how to realize the edges incident to vertices with high degree in its complement. Recall that $\overline{G^*}$ is the graph which contains the removed edges.

Lemma 3.10. Let $G = (V, E)$ be the complete graph and $E^* \subset E$ such that $|E^*| \leq n^{1+\beta}$, where $0 \leq \beta < \frac{1}{2}$. Then, for every $d = n^{\beta+\varepsilon}$ for some constant $0 < \varepsilon \leq \frac{1}{2}$, we can remove a set of vertices and all their incident edges from the graph G^* and obtain the graph G_d^* such that the degree of every vertex in $\overline{G_d^*}$ is at most d, the graph $\overline{G_d^*}$ contains at most $n^{1+\beta}$ edges, and the total share size for the removed edges from G^* is $O(\frac{n^{3/2+\beta}}{d})$.[3]

Proof Sketch. To prove the above lemma, note that there are at most $O(n^{1+\beta}/d)$ vertices whose degree in the graph of excluded edges is greater than d. We use Lemma 3.1 to realize the bipartite graph, where one part contains the vertices of degree greater than d and the other part are all other vertices. The share size in the above scheme is $O((n^{1+\beta}/d) \cdot n^{1/2}) = O(n^{3/2+\beta}/d)$. We also use the the scheme of Theorem 3.2 to realize the graph containing the edges between the vertices of degree at least d; the share size of this secret-sharing scheme is smaller than $O(n^{3/2+\beta}/d)$.   □

For a graph such that the degree of every vertex in its complement is bounded, we show how to decrease the maximum degree of a vertex in its complement by removing few vertices from the graph and realize all the removed edges from it.

Lemma 3.11. Let $0 < \alpha' < \alpha \leq 1$ such that $\alpha \geq \frac{1}{6}$ and let $G = (V, E)$ be the complete graph. Furthermore, let $E^* \subset E$ such that $|E^*| = \ell$, and assume that the degree of each vertex in $\overline{G^*}$ is at most n^α. Then, we can remove a set of vertices and all their incident edges from the graph G^* and obtain the graph

---

[3] We intend to the total share size of the scheme realizing the graph of the edges we removed from G^* in Lemma 3.10 and are contained in $E \setminus E^*$. The same is also valid for Lemma 3.11.

$G^*_{\alpha'}$, such that the degree of every vertex in $\overline{G^*_{\alpha'}}$ is at most $n^{\alpha'}$, the graph $\overline{G^*_{\alpha'}}$ contains $\ell - \ell'$ edges for some $\ell' > 0$, and the total share size for the removed edges from G^* is $O(\ell' n^{1/4+\alpha/2-\alpha'})$.

Proof. Define $d = n^\alpha$ and $d' = n^{\alpha'}$ (notice that $d' < d$). Additionally, let

$$D = \{v \in V : \text{The degree of } v \text{ in } \overline{G^*} \text{ is at least } d'\}.$$

We remove the vertices of D in steps, where in each step we choose a set F of $k = \frac{n^{3/4}}{d^{1/2}} > 1$ (since $d \leq n$) vertices, and remove F and all the edges incident to the vertices of F (if the number of the remaining vertices with degree at least d' in $\overline{G^*}$ is smaller than k, then we take the remaining vertices with degree at least d' and put them in F).

First, consider all the edges between two vertices in F. By Theorem 3.2, we can realize the graph $G^*[F] = (F, \overline{E^*} \cap (F \times F))$ by a scheme such that every edge in $G^*[F]$ can reconstruct the secret and every edge not in $G^*[F]$ cannot learn any information about the secret, in which the total share size is $O(k^{\frac{3}{2}}) = O((\frac{n^{3/4}}{d^{1/2}})^{\frac{3}{2}}) = O(\frac{n^{9/8}}{d^{3/4}}) = O(n)$ (since $d \geq n^{1/6}$).

Next, consider the bipartite graph $G^*_F = (F, V \setminus F, \overline{E^*} \cap (F \times (V \setminus F)))$. Because the degree of every vertex in $\overline{G^*}$ is at most d, the degree of every vertex in the bipartite complement graph $\overline{G^*_F}$ is at most d. Hence, by Lemma 3.9, we can realize the graph G^*_F such that: (1) every edge in G^*_F can reconstruct the secret, (2) every edge not in G^*_F cannot learn any information about the secret, and (3) the total share size of the scheme is $O(n)$. Thus, we can remove the vertices of F and all the edges incident to them from the graph G^*, and the total share size of the scheme for this step is $O(n)$.

We continue in the same manner until the degree of all the vertices in the graph $\overline{G^*}$ is at most d' and obtain the graph $G^*_{\alpha'}$ after removing all the vertices with degree greater than d' in the graph $\overline{G^*}$ and the edges incident to them from G^*. Let ℓ' be the total number of edges we removed from $\overline{G^*}$ in these steps until the degree of every vertex in $\overline{G^*}$ is at most d'. The graph $\overline{G^*_{\alpha'}}$ contains $\ell - \ell'$ edges and the degree of every vertex in $\overline{G^*_{\alpha'}}$ is at most d'. Additionally, in every iteration, except for the last, we remove at least kd' edges. Thus, there are at most $1 + \frac{\ell'}{d'k} = O(\frac{\ell' d^{1/2}}{d' n^{3/4}})$ iterations in this process, and the total share size for the removed edges from G^* is $O(\frac{\ell' d^{1/2}}{d' n^{3/4}} \cdot n) = O(\ell' n^{1/4+\alpha/2-\alpha'})$.   □

The next scheme realizes dense graphs using three main steps as described in the beginning of this section. We apply the degree reduction of the second step $\log\log(n)$ times, to get a scheme with smaller total share size.

Theorem 3.12. *Let $G = (V, E)$ be the complete graph and $E^* \subset E$ such that $|E^*| \leq n^{1+\beta}$, where $0 \leq \beta < \frac{1}{2}$. Then, there is a secret-sharing scheme such that: (1) each edge in $E \setminus E^*$ can reconstruct the secret, (2) each edge in E^* cannot learn any information about the secret, and (3) the total share size of the scheme is $O(n^{7/6+2\beta/3})$.*

3.4   Constructions for Arbitrary Graphs When Removing Few Edges

In the following theorem, we realize the graph obtained from an arbitrary graph G when removing few edges from it. We first share the secret using the 2-out-of-2 scheme. We share the first share using the scheme of the graph G and share the second share using the scheme of the graph G^*, which is the complement of the graph of the removed edges.

Theorem 3.13. *Let $G = (V, E)$ be a graph and $E^* \subset E$ such that $|E^*| \leq n^{1+\beta}$, where $0 \leq \beta < \frac{1}{2}$. Furthermore, assume that the forbidden graph access structure of G can be realized by a scheme in which the total share size is m. Then, there is a secret-sharing scheme such that: (1) each edge in $G \cap G^* = (V, E \setminus E^*)$ can reconstruct the secret, (2) each edge in $\overline{E} \cup E^*$ cannot learn any information about the secret, and (3) the total share size of the scheme is $O(m + n^{7/6+2\beta/3})$.*

Proof. Let s be the secret, and let s_1, s_2 be random strings such that $s = s_1 \oplus s_2$ (i.e., s_1 is chosen with uniform distribution and $s_2 = s_1 \oplus s$). We independently share s_1 using the scheme of the graph G with total share size m.

The graph $G^* = (V, \overline{E^*})$ is a dense graph, in which the number of edges in its complement is $|E^*| \leq n^{1+\beta}$, where $0 \leq \beta < \frac{1}{2}$. Hence, by Theorem 3.12, we can realize the graph G^* such that: (1) every edge not in E^* can reconstruct the secret, (2) every edge in E^* cannot learn any information about the secret, and (3) the total share size of the scheme is $O(n^{7/6+2\beta/3})$. We share s_2 using the scheme of the graph G^* with total share size $O(n^{7/6+2\beta/3})$. Combining, the total share size of the scheme is $O(m + n^{7/6+2\beta/3})$.

For an edge $e \in E \setminus E^* = E \cap \overline{E^*}$, since $e \in E$, the edge e can reconstruct s_1 from the scheme of G, and since $e \in \overline{E^*}$, the edge e can reconstruct s_2 from the scheme of G^*, and, hence, the edge e can reconstruct the secret s by performing bitwise-xor between the strings s_1 and s_2.

For an edge $e \in \overline{E} \cup E^*$, if $e \in \overline{E}$, the edge e cannot learn any information on s_1 from the scheme of G, and cannot reconstruct the secret s. Otherwise $e \in E^*$, and the edge e cannot learn any information on s_2 from the scheme of G^*. Hence, the edge e cannot learn any information on the secret s.   □

Remark 3.14. The last scheme does not realize graph access structures. Indeed, every independent set in $G \cap G^*$ which contains an edge e_1 from E^* and an edge e_2 from $\overline{E}$ can reconstruct the secret, because the edge e_1 can reconstruct s_1 and the edge e_2 can reconstruct s_2, and together they can reconstruct the secret s.

Additionally, any improvement of the total share size of the scheme presented in Theorem 3.12 will lead to an improvement of the total share size of the scheme for a general graph G when removing few edges from it, for $m = o(n^{7/6+2\beta/3})$, where m is the total share size of a scheme in which each edge in G can reconstruct the secret, and each edge not in G cannot learn any information about the secret.

4   Using Avoiding Covers to Realize Graph Access Structures

In this section, we define avoiding covers and show how to use them to realize graphs obtained by removing few edges from an arbitrary graph, such that the degree of the graph which contains the removed edges is bounded. Avoiding covers are a special kind of covers by complete bipartite graphs that are used to reach the following goal. We want to realize a graph obtained by removing few edges from an arbitrary graph G. For that, we want to use a cover by complete bipartite graphs of the complete graph without the removed edges from the graph G (i.e., every edge between the parts in each graph in the cover is not a removed edge).

We would like to realize every graph in the cover by the scheme of the graph G restricted to the vertices of the graph. Notice that the graph G might contain edges between vertices in the same part; such edges would be able to reconstruct the secret. However, if one of the graphs in the cover contains removed edges between vertices in the same part, then they can reconstruct the secret although these edges are unauthorized sets and should not learn any information about the secret.

Thus, for a graph $G = (V, E)$ and a set $F \subset V$, we want to find a cover of the bipartite graph G_F (defined in Definition 2.5) by complete bipartite graphs such that there are no edges of $\overline{G}$ between any two vertices in the same part of each complete bipartite graph in the cover. We next define avoiding covers, which have this property.

Definition 4.1 (Avoiding λ-Covers by Complete Bipartite Graphs). *Let $G = (V, E)$ be a graph and $F \subset V$. A complete bipartite λ-cover $G_1 = (U_1, V_1, E_1), \ldots, G_r = (U_r, V_r, E_r)$ of G_F avoids $\overline{E}$ if $\overline{E} \cap ((U_i \times U_i) \cup (V_i \times V_i)) = \emptyset$ for every $1 \leq i \leq r$, that is, there are no edges of $\overline{G}$ between any two vertices in the same part of any G_i. A complete bipartite $\overline{E}$-avoiding cover of G_F is a complete bipartite $\overline{E}$-avoiding 1-cover of G_F.*

We show in the following claim the use of avoiding covers in our constructions.

Claim 4.2. *Let $G = (V, E)$ be a graph that can be realized by a scheme in which the total share size is m, and let $E^* \subset E$. Let $F \subset V$ be a set satisfying that there is an E^*-avoiding cover of G_F^* by complete bipartite graphs such that each vertex $v \in V$ is in at most μ graphs of the cover. Then, there is a secret-sharing scheme such that: (1) each edge in $G \cap G_F^*$ can reconstruct the secret, (2) every independent set in $G \cap G^*$ cannot learn any information on the secret (we do not care if the edges in $E \setminus E^*$ and not in G_F^* can learn information on the secret), and (3) the total share size is at most μm.*

For a graph G and a set of vertices F, the next lemma proves the existence of a small avoiding cover of the bipartite graph G_F when the degree of every vertex in its complement $\overline{G}$ is bounded by d. In this cover the number of graphs is $O(d^2 \log(n))$, compared to $O(d \ln(n))$ graphs of the complete bipartite cover presented in [33]. However, each vertex in the cover we construct appears in $O(d \log(n))$ graphs of the cover. This makes this cover equivalent to the complete bipartite cover when comparing the total share size of the secret-sharing scheme in which we share the secret independently for each graph of the cover.

Lemma 4.3. *Let $G = (V, E)$ be a graph such that the degree of each vertex in $\overline{G}$ is bounded by $d > 1$ and $F \subset V$. Then, there is a $\log(n)$-cover of size $r = O(d^2 \log(n))$ of G_F by complete bipartite graphs that avoids $\overline{E}$ such that every vertex $v \in V$ appears in $O(d \log(n))$ graphs of the cover.*

Theorem 4.4. *Let $G = (V, E)$ be a graph that can be realized by a scheme with total share size m, and let $E^* \subset E$. If the degree of each vertex in $\overline{G^*}$ is bounded by d, then $G \cap G^*$ can be realized by a scheme in which the total share size is $\tilde{O}(dm)$.*

Remark 4.5. The degree in $\overline{G^*}$ is bounded by d, so by [5, Lemma 5.2] there exists an equivalence $\ln(n)$-cover, and in particular an equivalence cover of G^* with $O(d \ln(n))$ equivalence graphs. For every equivalence graph in the cover, and for every clique in it, we can share the secret among the vertices in the clique using the scheme of the graph G with total share size m. The edges that can reconstruct the secret are the edges of $E \setminus E^*$, and every independent set in $G \cap G^*$ cannot learn any information on the secret. The total share size of realizing each graph of the equivalence cover is m and the total share of the resulting scheme (realizing all the graphs of the cover) is $O(dm \ln(n)) = \tilde{O}(dm)$, slightly better than the above theorem. Using Stinson's technique [43], if the secret size is $\Omega(\log^2(n))$, then the total share size of the scheme realizing $G \cap G^*$ from Theorem 4.4 is $O(dm)$, which improves the total share size of the scheme from [5].

In the full version of this paper, we prove the following theorem, using avoiding covers and adapting techniques from [5].

Theorem 4.6. *Let $G = (V, E)$ be a graph that can be realized by a scheme with total share size m, let $E^* \subset E$ with $|E^*| \leq n^{1+\beta}$ and $0 \leq \beta < 1$, and let $c = \chi(\overline{G^*})$. If $c < \frac{n^{1-\beta/2}}{m^{1/2}}$, then $G \cap G^*$ can be realized by a scheme in which the total share size is $\tilde{O}(m^{2/3} n^{2/3 + 2\beta/3} c^{1/3})$.*

References

1. Alon, N.: Covering graphs by the minimum number of equivalence relations. Combinatorica **6**(3), 201–206 (1986)
2. Babai, L., Gál, A., Wigderson, A.: Superpolynomial lower bounds for monotone span programs. Combinatorica **19**(3), 301–319 (1999)
3. Beimel, A.: Secret-sharing schemes: a survey. In: Chee, Y.M., Guo, Z., Ling, S., Shao, F., Tang, Y., Wang, H., Xing, C. (eds.) IWCC 2011. LNCS, vol. 6639, pp. 11–46. Springer, Heidelberg (2011)

4. Beimel, A., Chor, B.: Universally ideal secret-sharing schemes. IEEE Trans. Inf. Theor. **40**(3), 786–794 (1994)
5. Beimel, A., Farràs, O., Mintz, Y.: Secret-sharing schemes for very dense graphs. J. Cryptol. **29**(2), 336–362 (2016)
6. Beimel, A., Gál, A., Paterson, M.: Lower bounds for monotone span programs. Comput. Complex. **6**(1), 29–45 (1997)
7. Beimel, A., Ishai, Y., Kumaresan, R., Kushilevitz, E.: On the cryptographic complexity of the worst functions. In: Lindell, Y. (ed.) TCC 2014. LNCS, vol. 8349, pp. 317–342. Springer, Heidelberg (2014)
8. Ben-Or, M., Goldwasser, S., Wigderson, A.: Completeness theorems for noncryptographic fault-tolerant distributed computations. In: Proceedings of the 20th ACM Symposium on the Theory of Computing, pp. 1–10 (1988)
9. Benaloh, J.C., Leichter, J.: Generalized secret sharing and monotone functions. In: Goldwasser, S. (ed.) CRYPTO 1988. LNCS, vol. 403, pp. 27–35. Springer, Heidelberg (1990)
10. Bertilsson, M., Ingemarsson, I.: A construction of practical secret sharing schemes using linear block codes. In: Zheng, Y., Seberry, J. (eds.) AUSCRYPT 1992. LNCS, vol. 718, pp. 67–79. Springer, Heidelberg (1993)
11. Blakley, G.R.: Safeguarding cryptographic keys. In: Proceedings of the 1979 AFIPS National Computer Conference, AFIPS Conference proceedings, vol. 48, pp. 313–317. AFIPS Press (1979)
12. Blundo, C., De Santis, A., de Simone, R., Vaccaro, U.: Tight bounds on the information rate of secret sharing schemes. Des. Codes Crypt. **11**(2), 107–122 (1997)
13. Blundo, C., De Santis, A., Stinson, D.R., Vaccaro, U.: Graph decomposition and secret sharing schemes. J. Cryptol. **8**(1), 39–64 (1995)
14. Brickell, E.F.: Some ideal secret sharing schemes. J. Combin. Math. Combin. Comput. **6**, 105–113 (1989)
15. Brickell, E.F., Davenport, D.M.: On the classification of ideal secret sharing schemes. J. Cryptol. **4**(73), 123–134 (1991)
16. Bublitz, S.: Decomposition of graphs and monotone formula size of homogeneous functions. Acta Inf. **23**(6), 689–696 (1986)
17. Capocelli, R.M., De Santis, A., Gargano, L., Vaccaro, U.: On the size of shares for secret sharing schemes. J. Cryptol. **6**(3), 157–168 (1993)
18. Chaum, D., Crépeau, C., Damgård, I.: Multiparty unconditionally secure protocols. In: Proceedings of the 20th ACM Symposium on the Theory of Computing, pp. 11–19 (1988)
19. Chor, B., Kushilevitz, E.: Secret sharing over infinite domains. J. Cryptol. **6**(2), 87–96 (1993)
20. Cook, S.A., Pitassi, T., Robere, R., Rossman, B.: Exponential lower bounds for monotone span programs. Electron. Colloq. Comput. Complex. **23**, 64 (2016). www.eccc.uni-trier.de/eccc/
21. Csirmaz, L.: The dealer's random bits in perfect secret sharing schemes. Studia Sci. Math. Hungar. **32**(3–4), 429–437 (1996)
22. Csirmaz, L.: The size of a share must be large. J. Cryptol. **10**(4), 223–231 (1997)
23. Csirmaz, L.: Secret sharing schemes on graphs. Technical report 2005/059, Cryptology ePrint Archive (2005). eprint.iacr.org/
24. Desmedt, Y.G., Frankel, Y.: Shared generation of authenticators and signatures. In: Feigenbaum, J. (ed.) CRYPTO 1991. LNCS, vol. 576, pp. 457–469. Springer, Heidelberg (1992)
25. van Dijk, M.: On the information rate of perfect secret sharing schemes. Des. Codes Crypt. **6**(2), 143–169 (1995)

26. Erdös, P., Pyber, L.: Covering a graph by complete bipartite graphs. Discrete Math. **170**(1–3), 249–251 (1997)
27. Gál, A.: A characterization of span program size and improved lower bounds for monotone span programs. In: Proceedings of the 30th ACM Symposium on the Theory of Computing, pp. 429–437 (1998)
28. Gál, A., Pudlák, P.: Monotone complexity and the rank of matrices. Inform. Process. Lett. **87**, 321–326 (2003)
29. Gay, R., Kerenidis, I., Wee, H.: Communication complexity of conditional disclosure of secrets and attribute-based encryption. In: Gennaro, R., Robshaw, M. (eds.) CRYPTO 2015. LNCS, vol. 9216, pp. 485–502. Springer, Heidelberg (2015)
30. Gertner, Y., Ishai, Y., Kushilevitz, E., Malkin, T.: Protecting data privacy in private information retrieval schemes. J. Comput. Syst. Sci. **60**(3), 592–629 (2000)
31. Goyal, V., Pandey, O., Sahai, A., Waters, B.: Attribute-based encryption for fine-grained access control of encrypted data. In: Proceedings of the 13th ACM conference on Computer and Communications Security, pp. 89–98 (2006)
32. Ito, M., Saito, A., Nishizeki, T.: Secret sharing schemes realizing general access structure. In: Proceedings of the IEEE Global Telecommunication Conference, Globecom, vol. 87, pp. 99–102 (1987). Journal version: Multiple assignment scheme for sharing secret. J. Cryptol. **6**(1), 15–20 (1993)
33. Jukna, S.: On set intersection representations of graphs. J. Graph Theor. **61**(1), 55–75 (2009)
34. Karchmer, M., Wigderson, A.: On span programs. In: Proceedings of the 8th IEEE Structure in Complexity Theory, pp. 102–111 (1993)
35. Martí-Farré, J., Padró, C.: Secret sharing schemes on sparse homogeneous access structures with rank three. Electr. J. Comb. **11**(1) (2004). http://www.combinatorics.org/ojs/index.php/eljc/article/view/v11i1r72/
36. Martí-Farré, J., Padró, C.: On secret sharing schemes, matroids and polymatroids. J. Math. Cryptol. **4**(2), 95–120 (2010)
37. Mintz, Y.: Information ratios of graph secret-sharing schemes. Master's thesis, Department of Computer Science, Ben Gurion University (2012)
38. Naor, M., Wool, A.: Access control and signatures via quorum secret sharing. In: 3rd ACM Conference on Computer and Communications Security, pp. 157–167 (1996)
39. Padró, C., Sáez, G.: Lower bounds on the information rate of secret sharing schemes with homogeneous access structure. Inform. Process. Lett. **83**(6), 345–351 (2002)
40. Sahai, A., Waters, B.: Fuzzy identity-based encryption. In: Cramer, R. (ed.) EUROCRYPT 2005. LNCS, vol. 3494, pp. 457–473. Springer, Heidelberg (2005)
41. Shamir, A.: How to share a secret. Commun. ACM **22**, 612–613 (1979)
42. Shankar, B., Srinathan, K., Rangan, C.P.: Alternative protocols for generalized oblivious transfer. In: Rao, S., Chatterjee, M., Jayanti, P., Murthy, C.S.R., Saha, S.K. (eds.) ICDCN 2008. LNCS, vol. 4904, pp. 304–309. Springer, Heidelberg (2008)
43. Stinson, D.R.: Decomposition construction for secret sharing schemes. IEEE Trans. Inf. Theor. **40**(1), 118–125 (1994)
44. Sun, H., Shieh, S.: Secret sharing in graph-based prohibited structures. In: Proceedings IEEE INFOCOM 1997, pp. 718–724 (1997)
45. Tassa, T.: Generalized oblivious transfer by secret sharing. Des. Codes Crypt. **58**(1), 11–21 (2011)
46. Waters, B.: Ciphertext-policy attribute-based encryption: an expressive, efficient, and provably secure realization. In: Catalano, D., Fazio, N., Gennaro, R., Nicolosi, A. (eds.) PKC 2011. LNCS, vol. 6571, pp. 53–70. Springer, Heidelberg (2011)

Proactive Secret Sharing with a Dishonest Majority

Shlomi Dolev[1], Karim ElDefrawy[2(✉)], Joshua Lampkins[2], Rafail Ostrovsky[3], and Moti Yung[4]

[1] Department of Computer Science, Ben-Gurion University, Beersheba, Israel
[2] Information and Systems Sciences Laboratory, HRL Laboratories, Malibu, USA
eldefrawy@gmail.com
[3] Department of Computer Science and Department of Mathematics, UCLA, Los Angeles, USA
[4] Snapchat and Department of Computer Science, Columbia University, New York, USA

Abstract. In standard Secret Sharing (SS) a dealer shares a secret s among n parties such that an adversary corrupting no more than t parties does not learn s, while any $t + 1$ parties can efficiently recover s. Over a long period of time all parties may be corrupted and the threshold t may be violated, which is accounted for in *Proactive Secret Sharing (PSS)*. PSS retains confidentiality even when a *mobile adversary* corrupts *all parties* over the lifetime of the secret, but no more than a threshold t during a certain window of time, called the refresh period. Existing PSS schemes only guarantee secrecy in the presence of an honest majority with at most $n/2 - 1$ total corruptions during such a refresh period; an adversary that corrupts a single additional party beyond the $n/2 - 1$ threshold, even if only passively and only temporarily, obtains the secret. We develop *the first PSS scheme secure in the presence of a dishonest majority*. Our PSS scheme is robust and secure against $t < n - 2$ passive adversaries when there are no active corruptions, and secure but non-robust (but with identifiable aborts) against $t < n/2 - 1$ active adversaries when there are no additional passive corruptions. The scheme is also secure (with identifiable aborts) against mixed adversaries controlling a combination of passively and actively corrupted parties such that if there are k active corruptions there are less than $n - k - 2$ total corruptions. Our scheme achieves these high thresholds with $O(n^4)$ communication when sharing a single secret. We also observe that communication may be reduced to $O(n^3)$ when sharing $O(n)$ secrets in batches. Our work is the first result demonstrating that PSS tolerating such high thresholds and mixed adversaries is possible.

1 Introduction

Secret sharing is a cornerstone primitive often utilized in constructing secure distributed systems and protocols [CH94, HJKY95, FGMY97, CL02, BCS03, DGGK09] [DGGK11, DGG+15], and especially in secure multiparty computation (MPC) [GMW87, CCD88, RB89, OY91, DIK+08, BTH08, DIK10, BFO12,

© Springer International Publishing Switzerland 2016
V. Zikas and R. De Prisco (Eds.): SCN 2016, LNCS 9841, pp. 529–548, 2016.
DOI: 10.1007/978-3-319-44618-9_28

HML13, BELO14]. In standard (linear) secret sharing [Sha79, Bla79] a dealer shares a secret (s) among n parties such that an adversary that corrupts no more than a threshold (t) of the parties does not learn s, while any $t + 1$ parties can efficiently recover it. In reality, over a long period of time all parties may be corrupted and the threshold may be violated, even if sometimes only for short duration. An approach to deal with an adversary's ability to move around and eventually corrupt all parties is the so-called *proactive security model* introduced in [OY91]. The *proactive security model* puts forward the notion of a *mobile adversary* motivated by the persistent corruption of parties in a protocol, or nodes/servers in a distributed system. A mobile adversary is one that moves around and can corrupt all parties in a protocol during the execution but with the following limitations: (1) only a constant fraction of parties can be corrupted during any round of the protocol; (2) parties are periodically rebooted (reset) to a pristine predictable initial state, guaranteeing small fraction of corrupted parties, assuming that the corruption rate is not more than the reboot rate. The model assumes that the process of rebooting to a clean state includes global computation information, e.g., identities of other parties, access to secure point-to-point channels and to a broadcast channel; the model also assumes that parties can erase information from their memory and that such information cannot be recovered by adversaries.

Long-term Confidentiality via Proactive Security: It is common these days to see news of massive breaches that expose private information of millions of individuals. A notable example is the 2015 breach [Tim16] of the health insurance company Anthem which affected 80 million patient and employee records. The breach occurred over several weeks, beginning in December 2014. While storing encrypted data, and regularly re-encrypting it improves security, it does not protect against determined capable attackers that exfiltrate encrypted data by compromising servers storing it, and by obtaining encryption keys through other means. The situation becomes more challenging when insiders are involved in such attacks, or when the confidentiality of the data has to be guaranteed for tens of years, e.g., for sequenced genomes of individuals, or other sensitive personal, corporate or government information. Utilizing proactive secret sharing to distribute the data among several storage servers, and periodically rerandomize (also called refresh) shares in a distributed manner can significantly increase the security guarantees for such data. A high level of security ensures that as long as *a single server remains uncorrupted during the period between two refreshes* (and thus deletes its old shares when refreshed), and as long as different servers are uncorrupted at different periods, then the secret shared data is never revealed; this should be the case even if all the data (shares) on all other servers is obtained when they are corrupted. To achieve this requires (ideally) tolerating a passive corruption threshold of up to $n - 1$ in the face of mobile adversaries. Realizing a high security level *close to the one described above* is the main goal of this paper. While we do not achieve secrecy against $n - 1$ passive corruptions, we achieve it against less than $n - 2$ passive corruptions with no active ones, and with ability to recover shares of a single rebooted party at each instant (and less than $n - c - 1$ when c parties are to be rebooted in parallel). In addition, our PSS scheme tolerates mixed adversaries that combine both passive and active corruptions and may add up to a dishonest majority (more details below).

Contributions: We develop *the first PSS scheme secure in the presence of a dishonest majority.* Our new scheme is secure and robust against $t < n - 2$ passive adversaries when there are no active corruptions, and secure but non-robust (with identifiable aborts) against $t < n/2 - 1$ active adversaries when there are no additional passive corruptions. The scheme is also secure (but non-robust with identifiable aborts) against mixed adversaries that control a combination of passively and actively corrupted parties such that if there are k active corruptions there are less than $n - k - 2$ total corruptions. Existing PSS schemes *cannot handle* a dishonest passive majority, and mixed adversaries that may form a majority as described above. Existing PSS schemes can only guarantee secrecy in the presence of an honest majority with at most $n/2 - 1$ total compromises; an adversary that compromises a single additional party beyond the $n/2 - 1$ threshold, even if only passively and only for a short period of time, obtains the secret. While we also discuss techniques to reduce communication in our protocols, we do not achieve optimal communication. To construct our PSS scheme requires designing new protocols for refreshing and recovering shares, this is achieved using a combination of information-theoretic, e.g., additive sharing, and cryptographic commitments to protect against active adversaries.

Outline: The rest of the paper is organized as follows, Sect. 2 provides an overview of existing PSS schemes and why they are insecure in the face of a passively dishonest majority or mixed adversaries that also exceed a majority. Section 3 contains definitions and preliminaries required for the rest of the paper, and Sect. 4 contains the technical details of our new PSS scheme. We conclude with a discussion of open problems and possible follow up work in Sect. 5.

2 Related Work and Roadblocks

Existing Proactive Secret Sharing (PSS) schemes, summarized in Table 1, are insecure when a majority of the parties are compromised, even if the compromise is only passive. Such schemes [OY91, HJKY95, WWW02, ZSvR05, Sch07, BELO14] typically store the secret as the free term in a polynomial of degree $t < n/2$; once an adversary compromises a majority of the parties (even if only passively) it will obtain more than $t + 1$ shares, and it will be able to reconstruct the polynomial and recover the secret. PSS schemes with optimal-communication [BELO14, BELO15] also use a similar technique but instead of storing the secret in the free term, they store a batch of $b = O(n)$ secrets at different points in the polynomial; similar to the single secret case, even when secrets are stored as multiple points on a polynomial, once the adversary compromises a majority of the parties, it can reconstruct the polynomial and recover the stored secrets.

The most relevant related work in (non-proactive) secret sharing is [HML13], it develops a gradual secret sharing scheme for mixed adversaries, and utilizes it

Table 1. Comparison of Proactive Secret Sharing (PSS) schemes. Threshold is for each reboot/refresh phase. Communication complexity is amortized per bit. Note that in the above table none of the previous schemes could tolerate the combination of the active threshold plus one or more passively compromised parties.

Scheme	Threshold passive (active)	Security	Network type	Comm. complexity
[WWW02]	$t < n/2$ $(n/2)$	Crypto	Synch.	$\exp(n)$
[ZSvR05]	$t < n/3$ $(n/3)$	Crypto	Asynch.	$\exp(n)$
[CKLS02]	$t < n/3$ $(n/3)$	Crypto	Asynch.	$O(n^4)$
[Sch07]	$t < n/3$ $(n/3)$	Crypto	Asynch.	$O(n^4)$
[HJKY95]	$t < n/2$ $(n/2)$	Crypto	Synch.	$O(n^2)$
[BELO14]	$t < n/3 - \epsilon$ $(n/3 - \epsilon)$	Perfect	Synch.	$O(1)$ (amortized)
[BELO14]	$t < n/2 - \epsilon$ $(n/2 - \epsilon)$	Statistical	Synch.	$O(1)$ (amortized)
This paper	$t < n - 2$ (passive only)	Crypto	Synch	$O(n^4) for$
	$t < n/2 - 1$ (active only)			Single secret
	& mixed passive/active adversaries			$O(n^3) for$
	Where with k active corruptions			Batch of n secrets
	$< n - k - 2$ total corruptions exist			

to build MPC protocols for such adversaries. Our work essentially proactivizes the gradual secret sharing scheme of [HML13]. We stress that if the adversary is static, i.e., non-mobile, then our protocols reduce to those in [HML13], no refreshing or recovering of shares is needed against static adversaries.

3   Definitions and Preliminaries

This section provides required definitions and preliminaries. We build on previous definitions of Verifiable Secret Sharing (VSS) for mixed adversaries from [HML13], and Proactive Secret Sharing (PSS) from [BELO14,BELO15]; we combine and extend these two to define PSS for mixed adversaries in Sect. 3.3.

3.1   System and Network Model

We consider a set of n parties, $\mathcal{P} = \{P_i\}_{i=1}^n$, connected via a synchronous network, and an authenticated broadcast channel. Each pair of parties also share a secure authenticated communication channel which can be instantiated via appropriate encryption and digital signature schemes.

Time Periods and Refresh Phases: We assume that all parties are synchronized via a global clock. Time is divided into *time periods or epochs*; at the beginning of each period (e.g., an hour, a day or a week) all parties engage in an interactive refresh protocol (also called refresh phase). At the end of the refresh phase all parties hold new shares for the same secret, and delete their old shares. We note that honest parties *must* delete their old shares so that if they get compromised in future periods, the adversary *cannot* recover their shares from old periods. The parties may additionally engage in a recovery protocol to allow parties that have lost their shares due to corruption or rebooting to recover new shares for the same secret. In Sect. 3.3 we provide a detailed definition of PSS and the refresh and recovery phases and protocols.

3.2   Adversary Model

To model a *mixed mobile adversary*, we adopt a characterization similar to the one for static mixed adversaries in [HML13], and extend it to the mobile case, i.e., the protocol has phases and as long as the corruption thresholds are not violated in each phase, the properties and security of a PSS scheme (defined below) are guaranteed. We assume the existence of an adversary with (polynomially) bounded computing power who moves around and passively corrupts a set of parties ($\mathcal{P}^*$) and only reads their internal state; the adversary may also actively corrupt some of these parties ($\mathcal{A}^*$) and makes them misbehave arbitrarily, i.e., they do not follow the steps of the protocol, and may inject, modify, or delete messages, among other actions. To simplify the notation we assume that $\mathcal{A}^* \subseteq \mathcal{P}^*$. Note that $\mathcal{A}^*$ may also be empty. We believe that this mixed mobile adversary model captures the situation in practice, where sometimes the same attacker may be able to compromise different components of a distributed system with various degrees of success, e.g., escalation of privileges leading to a complete compromise may only work on some components, while on some other components all the adversary is able to achieve is reading portions of the memory or some files without being able to modify or control the software.

We note that the thresholds of $t < n-2$ and $t < n/2-1$ given in Table 1 apply to the cases of $\mathcal{A}^* = \emptyset$ and $\mathcal{A}^* = \mathcal{P}^*$, respectively. When discussing mixed adversaries, we use the symbol t_a to denote the threshold of active corruptions and t_p to denote the threshold of passive corruptions. That is, $|\mathcal{A}^*| \leq t_a$ and $|\mathcal{P}^*| \leq t_p$. The inequalities in Table 1 can then be written $t_p < n - 2$ and $t_a < n/2 - 1$. Combinations of active and passive corruptions can be obtained by "swapping" active and passive corruptions such that each active corruption is "worth" two passive corruptions. More formally, in addition to satisfying $t_p < n - 2$ and $t_a < n/2 - 1$, the corruptions must also satisfy $t_a + t_p < n - 2$. Note that since each active corruption is also a passive corruption, each active corruption is counted twice in the preceding inequality. To simplify the illustration, we assume that if a party does not receive an expected message (or gets an invalid one), a default one is used instead. Finally, in the rest of the paper *honest parties* are the uncorrupted parties, while non-actively corrupted parties are called *correct parties*. To model security guarantees against incomparable maximal adversaries, we consider multiple pairs of thresholds similar to [HML13]. We use multi-thresholds $T = \{(t_{a,1}, t_{p,1}), \ldots, (t_{a,k}, t_{p,k})\}$, i.e., sets of pairs of thresholds (t_a, t_p). In this model, security is guaranteed if $(\mathcal{A}^*, \mathcal{P}^*) \leq (t_a, t_p)$ for some $(t_a, t_p) \in T$, denoted by $(\mathcal{A}^*, \mathcal{P}^*) \leq T$, where $(\mathcal{A}^*, \mathcal{P}^*) \leq (t_a, t_p)$ is a shorthand $|\mathcal{A}^*| \leq t_a$ and $|\mathcal{P}^*| \leq t_p$. Similar to [HML13], the level of security (correctness, secrecy, robustness) depends on the number $(\mathcal{A}^*, \mathcal{P}^*)$ of actually corrupted parties. We consider three multi-thresholds T^c, T^s, T^r.

Correctness (with agreement on abort, and identification of misbehaving parties) is guaranteed for $(\mathcal{A}^*, \mathcal{P}^*) \leq T^c$, secrecy is guaranteed for $(\mathcal{A}^*, \mathcal{P}^*) \leq T^s$, while robustness is guaranteed for $(\mathcal{A}^*, \mathcal{P}^*) \leq T^r$. We note that $T^r \leq T^c$ and $T^s \leq T^c$, as secrecy and robustness are not well defined without correctness.

3.3   Definition of Proactive Secret Sharing (PSS)

A Secret Sharing (SS) scheme consists of two protocols, **Share** and **Reconstruct**. **Share** allows a dealer to share a secret, s, among n parties such that the secret remains secure against an adversary that controls up to t_a parties and reads the state/informtion of up to t_p parties, while allowing any group of $n - t_a$ or more uncorrupted parties to reconstruct the secrets via **Reconstruct** if it is a robust scheme against t_a. If the SS scheme is non-robust against t_a then the remaining honest parties may not be able to reconstruct the secret, but if the protocol provides identifiable aborts against t_a (e.g., similar to [HML13]) then corrupted parties are identified on abort. A Verifiable Secret Sharing (VSS) scheme allows parties to verify that a dealer has correctly shared a secret. The definition of a Proactive Secret Sharing (PSS) scheme is similar to that of a standard SS scheme, but operates in phases, where between consecutive phases refreshing of shares (and recovery of shares of rebooted parties) is performed. PSS requires the addition of two new protocols to perform **Refresh** and **Recovery** for securing the secret against a mobile adversary that can corrupt all n parties over a long period of time, but no more than a specific threshold during any phase. The **Refresh** protocol refreshes shares to prevent a mobile adversary from collecting (over a long period) a large number of shares that could exceed the reconstruction threshold and thus reveal the secret. The **Recovery** protocol allows de-corrupted (or rebooted) parties to recover their shares, preventing the adversary from destroying the secrets that are shared. As our definitions of SS and VSS are standard, we refer to their previous formal definitions in [HML13]; we provide a definition of PSS below. We start by first defining the refresh and recovery phases.

Definition 1. *Refresh and Recovery Phases Execution of PSS proceeds in phases. A refresh phase (resp. recovery phase) is the period of time between two consecutive executions of the* **Refresh** *(resp.* **Recovery***) protocol. Furthermore, the period between* **Share** *and the first* **Refresh** *(resp.* **Recovery***) is a phase, and the period between the last* **Refresh** *(resp.* **Recovery***) and* **Reconstruct** *is a phase. Any* **Refresh** *(resp.* **Recovery***) protocol is considered to be in both adjacent phases, i.e., their execution occurs between phases number w and $w + 1$.*

Definition 2. *Proactive Secret Sharing (PSS) for Mixed Adversaries A (T^s, T^r, T^c)-secure PSS scheme consists of four protocols,* **Share**, **Refresh**, **Recover**, *and* **Reconstruct**. **Share** *allows a dealer to share a secret, s, among a group of n parties.* **Refresh** *is executed between two consecutive phases, phases w and $w + 1$, and generates new shares for phase $w + 1$ that encode the same secret as shares of phase w.* **Recover** *allows parties that lost their shares to obtain new* *shares encoding the same secret s with the help of the other honest parties. Recover allows parties to recover a value s'. These four protocols are (T^s, T^r, T^c)-secure if the following holds:*

1. **Termination:** *All honest parties will complete each execution of* **Share,** *Refresh, Recover, and Reconstruct.*
2. **Correctness:** *Upon completing* **Share,** *the dealer is bound to a value s', where s' = s if the dealer is correct. If $(\mathcal{A}^*, \mathcal{P}^*) \leq T^c$ and upon completing* **Refresh** *and/or* **Recover,** *either the shares held by the parties encode s', or all (correct) parties abort. In* **Reconstruct,** *either each (correct) party outputs s' or all (correct) parties abort.*
3. **Secrecy:** *If $(\mathcal{A}^*, \mathcal{P}^*) \leq T^s$, then in* **Share** *the adversary obtains no information about s. If $(\mathcal{A}^*, \mathcal{P}^*) \leq T^s$ in both phase w and in phase w + 1, and if* **Refresh** *and* **Recover** *are run between phases w and w+1, then the adversary obtains no information about s.*
4. **Robustness:** *The adversary cannot abort* **Share.** *If $(\mathcal{A}^*, \mathcal{P}^*) \leq T^r$, then the adversary cannot abort* **Refresh, Recover,** *and* **Reconstruct.**

3.4   Batched Secret Sharing

One of the main techniques to achieve efficient amortized communication complexity is batched (or packed) secret sharing, it is a generalization of the polynomials based linear secret sharing scheme. The idea, introduced in [FY92], is to encode a "batch" of multiple secrets as distinct points on a single polynomial, and then distribute shares to each party as in standard linear secret sharing [Sha79]. The number of secrets stored in the polynomial (the "batch size") is $O(n)$. This allows parties to share $O(n)$ secrets with $O(n)$ communication complexity which results in an amortized complexity of $O(1)$ per secret.

3.5   Homomorphic Commitments and Verifiable Secret Sharing

A commitment scheme is a protocol between two parties, P_1 and P_2, that allows P_1 to commit to a secret message m by sending to P_2 the value of the commitment to m computed with some randomness r, i.e., $Comm(m, r)$. Later P_1 may open the commitment and reveal to P_2 that she committed to m, typically by revealing the randomness that was used. Commitment schemes must be binding and hiding. The binding property ensures that P_1 cannot change her mind, a commitment can only be opened to a single message m; the hiding property ensures that P_2 does not learn the message that P_1 committed to. An (additively) homomorphic commitment scheme, allows P_2 to compute the commitment to the sum of m_1 and m_2 under the sum of r_1 and r_2 using $Comm(m_1, r_1)$ and $Comm(m_2, r_2)$ as follows: $Comm(m_1 + m_2, r_1 + r_2) = Comm(m_1, r_1) \boxplus Comm(m_2, r_2)$, where $\boxplus$ indicates the homomorphic operator of the group the commitment is typically defined over.

A problem with standard secret sharing, e.g., Shamir's scheme or a batched version thereof, is that a dishonest dealer may deal inconsistent shares from which $t + 1$ or more parties may not be able to reconstruct the secret. This malicious behavior can be prevented by augmenting the secret sharing scheme with homomorphic commitments, this is essentially what a VSS scheme does. (In the full version we utilize Feldman's VSS [Fel87], where security is based on the hardness of computing discrete logarithms over $\mathbb{Z}_p$ for a large prime p.)

4   Proactive Secret Sharing for a Dishonest Majority

This section starts with notation required to describe our PSS scheme, it then provides an overview and then the details of the four protocols constituting the PSS scheme. We note that protocols for sharing and reconstructing a secret are similar to those in [HML13] but with a minor difference in the number of summands and the highest degree of the sharing polynomials used.

4.1   Notation and Preliminaries

Field operations occur over a finite field $\mathbb{Z}_p$ for some prime p. Let α be a generator of $\mathbb{Z}_p^*$ and let $\beta = \alpha^{-1}$. In the case of multiple secrets, secrets will be stored at locations that are multiple values of β, i.e., if $f(x)$ is a sharing polynomials then $f(\beta_1)$ and $f(\beta_2)$ will evaluate to secret 1 and 2 respectively, while shares will be computed as the evaluation of $f(x)$ at different values of α, i.e., $f(\alpha_1)$ and $f(\alpha_2)$ are the shares of party 1 and 2 respectively, the α_i for party P_i is public information. We note that in the case of sharing a single secret, only one β is needed, and in that case it will not be the inverse of α, traditionally it has been the case that for single secrets $\beta = 0$, thus the secret s is stored at the free term of the sharing polynomial, i.e., $f(0) = s$. The shares can be evaluations of $f(x)$ at indices of the parties, i.e. $f(1), f(2) \ldots f(n)$. (We defer more details on handling multiple secrets to the full version.)

4.2   Intuition and Overview of Operation

To simplify the illustration we assume in this subsection when describing the intuition of the share, reconstruct and refresh protocols, that adversaries only compromise parties temporarily, so only refreshing of shares is needed. If recovery of shares of rebooted parties is required, the tolerated threshold of those protocols has to be decreased by the maximum number of parties that are rebooted in parallel and can loose their shares at the same time. If parties are rebooted serially such that only a single share needs to be recovered at any instant, then the tolerated thresholds are only decreased by 1. Specifically, if no recovery of shares is needed then the protocols can withstand $< n/2$ active only corruptions, and $< n$ passive only corruptions, and combinations of passive and active corruptions that may exceed half the parties but where with k active corruptions there are less than $n - k$ total corruptions; when recovery of a single share is needed then the thresholds become $< n/2 - 1$ active only corruptions, and $< n - 2$ passive only corruptions, and combinations of passive and active corruptions that may exceed half the parties but where with k active corruptions there are less than $n - k - 2$ total corruptions (when c shares should be recovered at once then the condition becomes $< n/2 - c$ active only corruptions, and $< n - (c+1)$ passive only corruptions, and with k active corruptions there are $< n - k - (c+1)$ total corruptions).

As mentioned in the related work and roadblocks section (Sect. 2), in order to tolerate a dishonest majority it is not enough to directly store secrets in the free term, or as other points on a polynomial. What is needed is to encode the secret in a different form resistant to a dishonest majority of say up to $n - 2$ parties. This can be achieved by first additively sharing the secret into $d = n - 2$ random summands (this provides security against $t < n - 1$ passive adversaries), then those random additive summands may be shared and proactively refreshed using methods that can tolerate $t < n/2$ active adversaries with aborts, i.e., if less than $n/2$ of the parties are actively corrupted their misbehavior will be detected and flagged by the other $n/2 + 1$ or more parties while ensuring confidentiality of the shared secret. This is the blueprint that we follow, specifically, we start from the gradual secret sharing schemes from [HML13] which can tolerate up to $n - 1$ passive adversaries with no active corruptions, or up to $n/2 - 1$ active corruptions such that when there are k active corruptions there no more than $n - k - 1$ total corruptions in total. We develop two new protocols to verifiably generate refreshing polynomials with the required properties, i.e., they have a random free term that encodes random additive shares that add up to zero. To recover shares with the above security guarantees, we observe that it is enough that the recovery protocol ensures security against $t < n/2 - 1$ active adversaries, as passive adversaries only generate random polynomials and send them to the recovering party, i.e., if they respect the polynomials generation process, and as long as one honest party generates a random polynomial, the rest of the $n - 3$ potentially passively corrupted parties will only see random polynomials with the appropriate degrees.

4.3   Sharing and Reconstruction for Dishonest Majorities

To simplify the presentation and due to space constraints we describe our protocols in this section using a generic homomorphic commitment scheme and in terms of a single secret[1]. For completeness, we provide below the protocols for gradual sharing of a secret (DM-Share), and gradual reconstruction of the same secret (DM-Reconstruct) which are secure against a dishonest majority, both similar to those in [HML13]. The gradual secret sharing scheme in [HML13] is secure against $t < n$ passive adversaries, and $t < n/2$ active adversaries, and *mixed adversaries* that control a combination of passively and actively corrupted parties that add up to more than $n/2$, but such that if there are k active corruptions there no more than $n - k - 1$ total corruptions. Sections 4.4 and 4.5

---

[1] In the full version we generalize the protocols to handle multiple secrets to increase communication and storage efficiency, and provide an instantiation using commitments based on hardness of discrete logarithms using Feldman's VSS [Fel87].

contain our new refresh and recovery protocols that together with DM-Share and DM-Reconstruct constitute a PSS scheme secure against a dishonest majority of parties. Our PSS scheme provides security against $< n/2 - 1$ active corruptions only with no additional passive ones, and $< n - 2$ passive only corruptions with no active ones, and combinations of passive and active corruptions that may exceed half the parties but where with k active corruptions there are less than $n - k - 2$ total corruptions.

Sharing a Secret with a Dishonest Majority. The protocol DM-Share shares a secret s in two phases, first an additive sharing phase (Step 1 in DM-Share) by splitting s into d random summands; in our case to achieve the maximum secrecy thresholds we use $d = n - 3$, where as in [HML13] the protocol is described in terms of the variable $d < n$, and thus called gradual d-sharing (see Definition 3 in [HML13]). This first sharing phase provides protection against less than $n - 2$ passive adversaries only. In the second phase (Steps 2.1 to 2.4 of the loop in step 2 in DM-Share) one performs linear secret sharing of each of the additive shares from the first phase by using polynomials of increasing degrees, from 1 to d. We stress that the above value of $d = n - 3$ assumes that recovery of shares of a single node will be needed; if this is not the case and only refreshing of shares is needed, then only $d = n - 1$ is needed. Note also that other lower values of d can be chosen but they would result in lower thresholds.

Secret Sharing for Dishonest Majorities (DM-Share) [HML13]

A dealing party (P_D) sharing a secret s performs the following:

1. P_D chooses d random summands $s_1, ..., s_d$ which add up to s, $\Sigma_{i=1}^{d} s_i = s$.

2. For $i \in \{1, \ldots, d\}$ P_D does the following:

   2.1 P_D generates a random polynomial $f_i(x)$ of degree i with the free term equal to the i-th summand, $f_i(0) = s_i$.

   2.2 P_D then computes and broadcasts to each of the other $n - 1$ receiving parties, P_r, (homomorphic) commitments of the coefficients of $f_i(x)$.

   2.3 For each share $sh_{i,r} = f_i(\alpha_r)$, each receiving party, P_r, locally computes a commitment $c_{i,r}$; this is possible based on the homomorphism of the commitment scheme. P_D sends the corresponding opening information $o_{i,r}$ to party P_r. P_r broadcasts a complaint bit, indicating whether $o_{i,r}$ correctly opens $c_{i,r}$ to some value $sh'_{i,r}$.

   2.4 For each share $sh_{i,j}$ for which an inconsistency was reported, P_D broadcasts the opening information $o_{i,j}$, and if $o_{i,j}$ opens $c_{i,j}$, P_r accepts $o_{i,j}$. Otherwise, P_D is disqualified (and a default sharing of a default value is used).

3. Each receiving party P_r outputs its d shares $(sh_{1,r}, o_{1,r}), ..., (sh_{d,r}, o_{d,r})$ and all commitments.

DM-Share requires $O(n^2)$ communication to share a single secret s, s is first split into $O(n)$ summands, then each one is split into $O(n)$ shares because $d = O(n)$.

Reconstructing a Secret with a Dishonest Majority. Assuming that a secret s is shared using DM-Share with the number of summands and the highest degree of sharing polynomials being d, the protocol DM-Reconstruct gradually reconstructs the d (again, $d = n - 3$ for highest secrecy threshold) summands by requiring parties to broadcast their shares of each of the $i = \{d, \ldots 1\}$ polynomials of decreasing degrees i. Each polynomial can be interpolated from the shares that are broadcast if at least $i + 1$ parties are honest.

Secret Reconstruction for Dishonest Majorities (DM-Reconstruct) [HML13]

Given a sharing of a secret s using DM-Share, parties can reconstruct s as follows:

1. For $i \in \{d, \ldots, 1\}$ do:

    1.1   Each party P_j broadcasts openings of the commitments to its shares $sh_{i,j}$ corresponding to the sharing polynomial $f_i(x)$. Remember that the i-th summand of s is stored in the free term of that polynomial, i.e., $f_i(0) = s_i$.

    1.2   If $i + 1$ or more parties correctly opened their commitments to their respective shares, each party locally interpolates $f_i(x)$ and computes the i-th summand as the free term of the recovered $f_i(x)$, $s_i = f_i(0)$.

    1.3   If only i parties or less opened correctly, then abort and each party outputs the set B of parties that did not broadcast correct openings to their commitments.

2. Each party outputs the secret as the sum of the reconstructed summands, $s = s_1 + s_2 + \cdots + s_d$.

DM-Reconstruct requires $O(n^2)$ communication to reconstruct a single secret, as $d = O(n)$, $O(n)$ shares are broadcast for each of the $O(n)$ summands.

4.4   Refreshing Shares with a Dishonest Majority

In the DM-Refresh protocol below, each party generates d (again, $d = n - 3$ for highest secrecy threshold) random refreshing polynomials with the appropriate degrees, i.e., from 1 to d. Each party then verifiably shares these refreshing polynomials with the other $n-1$ parties by committing to the coefficients of these generated refreshing polynomials. These refreshing polynomials should satisfy the following condition: they have random constant coefficients (when a single secret is shared in the free term) that add up to 0, this can be enforced by checking that the polynomials shared by each party have this property. This condition ensures that the shared secret remains unchanged when its shares are refreshed by adding the shares generated from the new polynomials to the old shares. Once each party receives all the shares generated by other parties, they add them to their local shares, and delete the shares that resulted from the previous execution of DM-Refresh.

Refreshing Shares for Dishonest Majorities (DM-Refresh)

---

1. Each party P_j generates an additive random sharing (of d randomization summands) which add up to 0, i.e., $\Sigma_{i=1}^d r_{j,i} = 0$.

2. For $i \in \{1, \ldots, d\}$ do:

    2.1   Each party P_j generates a random polynomial $g_{j,i}(x)$ of degree i with the free term equal to its i-th randomization summand, i.e., $g_{j,i}(0) = r_{j,i}$.

    2.2   Each party verifiably shares its generated randomization summands by sharing the random polynomial $g_{j,i}(x)$ with the other $n-1$ parties as follows: P_j computes and broadcasts to each of the other $n-1$ receiving parties, P_r, (homomorphic) commitments of the coefficients of $g_{j,i}(x)$ and sends to each P_r each share $sh_{j,i}^r = g_{j,i}(\alpha_r)$ over a private channel.

    2.3   For each share $sh_{j,i}^r$, each receiving party P_r, locally computes a commitment $c_{j,i}^r$; this is possible based on the homomorphism of the commitment scheme. P_j sends the opening information $o_{j,i}^r$ corresponding to each of the $c_{j,i}^r$ commitments to party P_r. P_r broadcasts a complaint bit, indicating if $o_{j,i}^r$ correctly opens $c_{j,i}^r$ to some value $z_{j,i}^r$.

    2.4   For each share $sh_{j,i}^r$ for which an inconsistency was reported, P_j broadcasts the opening information $o_{j,i}$, and if $o_{j,i}$ opens $c_{j,i}$, P_r accepts $o_{j,i}$. Otherwise, P_j is disqualified, and P_j is added to the set B of parties that did not share correctly and did not broadcast correct openings to their commitments.

3. Each party P_j broadcasts an opening to the commitment to $\Sigma_{i=1}^d g_{j,i}(0) = \Sigma_{i=1}^d r_{j,i}$, and each receiving party P_r checks that the free terms of the d sharing polynomials used by each other party P_j add up to 0 by combining the commitments to the free terms and using the broadcast opening information. This can be checked based on the homomorphic properties of the commitment scheme. If P_j does not broadcast correct commitments it is added to the set B of parties that did not share correctly and did not broadcast correct openings to their commitments.

4. For $i \in \{1, \ldots, d\}$ each receiving party P_r adds up the shares it receives from the other $n-1$ parties P_j at the current time period (denoted $sh_{j,i}^r$ where $j \neq r$), and its shares of the randomization polynomials it generated at p_{w+1} (denoted $sh_{r,i}^r$), to its existing share at the previous time period p_w (denoted $sh_i^{p_w,r}$); the result is the final refreshed shares at the end of the current time period p_{w+1} (denoted $sh_i^{p_{w+1},r}$), i.e., $sh_i^{p_{w+1},r} = sh_i^{p_w,r} + \Sigma_{j=1}^n sh_{j,i}^r$.

5. Each honest party must delete all old shares it had from period p_w ($sh_{j,i}^{p_w,r}$) after executing the above steps.

There are $O(n)$ parties, and each one will generate $O(n)$ shares (step 2.1 to 2.4) for each of the $O(n)$ ($d = O(n)$) refreshing polynomials, hence a total of $O(n^3)$ communication.

4.5 Recovering Shares with a Dishonest Majority

When recovery of shares of a single rebooted party has to be performed, then the other $n - 1$ parties can recover the shares of that rebooted party using the protocol DM-Recover below. Remember that in each refresh period there are d ($d = n - 3$ for maximum secrecy threshold) current sharing polynomials with degrees ranging from d to 1, and each party has a share for each of these polynomials. When a party P_{rc} is rebooted and needs to recover its shares, i.e., the evaluation of each of the current sharing polynomials at P_{rc}'s evaluation point α_{rc}, what the other parties need to perform is generate and verifiably share d random polynomials that evaluate to the same values as the current sharing polynomials at α_{rc}. To achieve this, parties generate and verifiably share d random recovery polynomials that evaluate to 0 at α_{rc}. All parties add their local shares of the current sharing polynomials to the shares of these random recovery polynomials, this results in d shared random recovery polynomials that have only the point at α_{rc} in common with the current sharing polynomials. All parties then send their shares of these d shared random recovery polynomials to P_{rc}, and P_{rc} can then interpolate these polynomials without learning anything about the secret or the actual sharing polynomials of the current period. We note that passively corrupted parties in the recovery will execute the protocol correctly, and actively corrupted parties are limited to $t < n/2 - 1$; we mainly need a recovery protocol secure against $t < n/2 - 1$ active adversaries because only the recovering party receives information. Every other party generates random polynomials and shares it with the rest of the parties, so there is no information related to the secret that is revealed to any party. As long as there is a single honest party, the random recovery polynomials that such an honest party generates ensures randomness of overall recovery polynomials; this ensures that the only thing P_{rc} learns are its d shares at α_{rc}.

Recovering Shares for Dishonest Majorities (DM-Recover)

---

1. Assume that party P_{rc} is the one that needs recovery and that its shares are the evaluation of the sharing polynomials ($f_i(x)$ for $i \in \{1, \ldots, d\}$) at α_{rc}.
2. For $i \in \{1, \ldots, d\}$ do:
    2.1 Each party P_j generates a random polynomial $g_{j,i}(x)$ of degree i with $g_{j,i}(\alpha_{rc}) = 0$.
    2.2 Each party verifiably shares its generated polynomial with the other $n - 2$ parties (which do not include P_{rc}) as follows: P_j computes and sends to each of the other $n - 2$ receiving parties P_r the value

$g_{j,i}(\alpha_r)$, and broadcasts (homomorphic) commitments of the coefficients of $g_{j,i}(x)$ to all parties.

2.3   For each share $sh_{j,i}^r = g_{j,i}(\alpha_r)$, each receiving party P_r, locally computes a commitment $c_{j,i}^r$, each party also ensures that the polynomials corresponding to its received share evaluates to 0 at α_{rc}, i.e., $g_{j,i}(\alpha_{rc}) = 0$. Both checks are possible based on the homomorphism of the commitment scheme. P_j sends the opening information $o_{j,i}^r$ corresponding to each of the $c_{j,i}^r$ commitments to party P_r. P_r broadcasts a complaint bit, indicating if $o_{j,i}^r$ correctly opens $c_{j,i}^r$ to some value $z_{j,i}^r$.

2.4   For each share $sh_{j,i}^r$ for which an inconsistency was reported, P_j broadcasts the opening information $o_{j,i}$, and if $o_{j,i}$ opens $c_{j,i}$, P_r accepts $o_{j,i}$. Otherwise, P_j is disqualified and is added to the set B of parties that did not share correctly and did not broadcast correct openings to their commitments.

2.5   Each party P_r adds all the shares it received from the other $n - 2$ parties for the random recovery polynomials $g_{j,i}(\alpha_r)$ to its share of f_i, i.e., $z_i^r = f_i(\alpha_r) + \Sigma_{j=1}^{n-2} sh_{i,j}^r = f_i(\alpha_r) + \Sigma_{j=1}^{n-2} g_{j,i}(\alpha_r)$.

2.6   Each party P_r sends z_i^r to P_{rc}; P_{rc} then interpolates the random recovery polynomial z_i and obtain its current share as $z_i(\alpha_{rc}) = f_i(\alpha_{rc})$

Since $O(n)$ parties may need recovery in series at each period, for each recovering party $O(n)$ parties will need to share $O(n)$ polynomials, with each resulting in $O(n)$ shares, the total will be $O(n^4)$ communication.

4.6   Security and Correctness of the PSS Scheme

Recall that d, the degree of gradual secret sharing adopted from [HML13], is the crucial parameter in the PSS scheme. d determines in DM-Share the number of summands in the additive sharing phase, the number of polynomials used to linearly share those summands, and the maximum degree of those polynomials. A similar set of polynomials of similar degrees is used for refreshing shares of, recovering shares of, and reconstructing those summands in DM-Refresh, DM-Recover, and DM-Reconstruct. d should be less than $n - c - 1$ (where c is the maximum number of parties that will be recovering in parallel, $c = 1$ when only a single party at a time is recovered), and for the maximum secrecy threshold with a single recovering party $d = n - 3$. We stress the maximum secrecy threshold because this is typically the main motivation for proactive secret sharing of data, i.e., to ensure long-term confidentiality against a mobile adversary.

Theorem 1. *Given a gradual secret sharing parameter $d < n - 2$ the four protocols* DM-Share, DM-Reconstruct, DM-Refresh *and* DM-Recover *form a computationally secure (T^s, T^r, T^c)-secure PSS scheme, utilizing a computationally secure homomorphic commitment scheme, according to Definition 2 of PSS for* *mixed adversaries characterized by* $(\mathcal{A}^*, \mathcal{P}^*)$ *where* $\mathcal{A}^* \subseteq \mathcal{P}^*$. *The PSS scheme ensures secrecy if* $|\mathcal{P}^*| \leq d$, *is robust against* $|\mathcal{A}^*| \leq k$ *if* $d < n - k - 1$ *and* $|\mathcal{P}^*| \leq d$, *and is correct with agreement on aborts if* $|\mathcal{P}^*| \leq d \wedge |\mathcal{P}^*| + |\mathcal{A}^*| \leq n-2$.

Proof. Termination, correctness, secrecy, and robustness for DM-Share and DM-Reconstruct are similar to the proofs of [HML13]. We prove those properties for DM-Refresh and DM-Recover via the Lemmas below.

Similar to [HML13] we provide below proof sketches in a property-based security model; this enables us to simplify the security arguments and present them in an intuitive and understandable manner. All statement could be made formal in simulation-based model using standard techniques; because the focus on this paper is on secret sharing, as opposed to MPC, we do not utilize simulation-based proofs, we also do not make claims about composability in this paper. Extending our work to MPC, and proving composability, is an interesting direction but outside the scope of this paper.

Proof Sketches for DM-Refresh

Lemma 1. *Termination of DM-Refresh: The protocol will always terminate after* $O(n^3)$ *steps.*

Proof. There are $O(n)$ parties, and each one will generate $O(n)$ shares (step 2.1 to 2.4) for each of the $O(n)$ $(d = O(n))$ summands, hence a total of $O(n^3)$ steps.

Lemma 2. *Correctness of DM-Refresh: If* $|\mathcal{P}^*| \leq d \wedge |\mathcal{P}^*| + |\mathcal{A}^*| \leq n - 2$, *when the protocol terminates, either all parties will receive new shares (in phase* $w + 1$) *encoding the same secret as those old shares (in phase* w) *they had before executing the protocol, or the parties will refuse incorrect shares generated by a subset of the parties and abort while identifying such misbehaving parties.*

Proof. In Steps 2.1 and 2.2, any well-formed commitments broadcasted by any party are correct, otherwise by security of the commitment scheme inconsistencies will be detected and reported, the protocol will then abort and the responsible misbehaving party will be identified. In Step 2.3, commitments to all shares are computed locally by each receiving party directly from the commitments to the coefficients broadcasted in Step 2.2. All non-actively corrupted parties (that are passively corrupted, called correct, and are honest) have a consistent view with correct commitments. When $|\mathcal{P}^*| \leq d$ then $|\mathcal{A}^*| \leq n - d - 2$, there will always be at least $n - |\mathcal{A}^*| = n - n + d + 2 = d + 2$ parties (or $d + 1$ if a party is rebooted) either honest or behaving correctly (while passively corrupted), so there are enough shares among those parties to uniquely define all polynomials (of maximum degree d). In Steps 2.3 and 2.4, due to the binding property of the commitments, the adversary cannot distribute inconsistent opening information without being detected, and causing an abort and identification of misbehaving parties. Step 3 demonstrates to parties that the shared summands all add up to 0 to preserve the additively shared secret, this can also be guarnteed via the homomorphic property of the commitment scheme; essentially parties ensure that the commitments to the free terms of the d refresh polynomials from each party, when summed up are commitments to 0 to make sure the new shares still encode the same old d summands. Hence, the new sharing is a correct one and the secret is preserved.

Lemma 3. *Secrecy of* DM-Refresh: *When the protocol terminates, all parties will receive new random shares (in phase $w + 1$) encoding the same secret as those old shares (in phase w) they had before executing the refresh protocol. The new shares are independent of the old ones, and the protocol does not reveal any information about the secret when the number of summands $d < n - 2$, and when up to d parties are passively corrupted, $|\mathcal{P}^*| \le d$.*

Proof. The commitments are computationally hiding, therefore, the adversary obtains no information in Step 2.2 of DM-Refresh. Furthermore, the randomization summands generated by each party $r_{j,i}$ are chosen independent of the shared secret, and are shared with a degree i polynomial (where $i \le d$). In Step 2.3, if no more than d parties are passively corrupted, the adversary obtains no information about one of the shared summand s_i (because there will be an i for which $i + 1 > d$ and it takes $i + 1$ points to interpolate a polynomial of degree i and learn the free term in it), and therefore learns no information about s. Also, if there's at least a single honest party it will generate a random polynomial with a free term equals to 0, adding shares of this polynomial to those of the polynomials of other (possibly passively corrupted parties) will ensure that the final resulting refreshing polynomials is a random one, and thus new shares of all parties are random. In Steps 2.3 and 2.4, whenever a value is broadcast, the adversary knew this value already beforehand if it arose due to a dispute, otherwise the broadcast information does not reveal anything about the secret.

Lemma 4. *Robustness of* DM-Refresh: *The protocol is robust and the secret is never lost when shares are refreshed if $|\mathcal{A}^*| \le k$ when $d < n - k - 1$ and $|\mathcal{P}^*| \le d$.*

Proof. When a secret is shared with DM-Share, and refreshed with DM-Refresh, and to be able to withstand active corruptions $|\mathcal{A}^*| \le k$ there will be $d = n - k - 2$ additive summands shared with polynomials of degrees i from 1 to $n - k - 2$. The shares of the $n - k - 2$ polynomials need to be refreshed with random polynomials of the corresponding degrees with 0 as their free terms. A polynomial of degree i can be interpolated with $i + 1$ points. To interpolate the polynomial with the highest degree of $n - k - 2$ one needs $n - k - 1$ points. Given that out of n parties, one party may be rebooted and recovering and thus has no shares, and if $|\mathcal{A}^*| \le k$, there will always be $n - k - 1$ correct parties that will be able to participate in DM-Refresh and generate correct polynomials to refresh (and maintain) $n - k - 1$ shares, which are enough to preserve, refresh, and recover a secret, that was shared with $d = n - k - 2$, at any later point in time.

Note that the maximum secrecy threshold corresponds to $k = 1$, in that case $d = n - 3$ as specified in the description of the protocols above.

Proof Sketches for DM-Recover

Lemma 5. *Termination of DM-Recover: The protocol will always terminate after $O(n^3)$ steps.*

Proof. A single recovering party has to recover d ($d = O(n)$) shares (Step 2), one for each of the d sharing polynomials. Each of the $O(n)$ parties will generate $O(n)$ shares (Step 2.1 to 2.5) for each of the shares to be recovered, a maximum total of $O(n^3)$ steps are executed.

Lemma 6. *Correctness of DM-Recover: If $|\mathcal{P}^*| \leq d \ \wedge \ |\mathcal{P}^*| + |\mathcal{A}^*| \leq n - 2$, either the protocol aborts, or a recovering party, P_{rc}, will receive at least d new shares $z_i(\alpha_{rc})$, encoding the same values of the current sharing polynomials at the party's evaluation point α_{rc}, i.e., $z_i(\alpha_{rc}) = f_i(\alpha_{rc})$ for $i \in \{1, \ldots, d\}$.*

Proof. In Step 2.3, any well-formed commitments broadcasted by the a party are correct, otherwise by security of the commitment scheme inconsistencies will be detected and reported. In Step 2.3, commitments to all shares are computed locally by each receiving party directly from the commitments to the coefficients broadcasted in Step 2.2. Hence, all correct (passively corrupted and honest parties) parties have a consistent view with correct commitments. In Step 2.3, a commitment to 0 can also be computed from commitments to the coefficients of the polynomials. When $|\mathcal{P}^*| \leq d$ then $|\mathcal{A}^*| \leq n - d - 2$, there will always be at least $n - |\mathcal{A}^*| = n - n + d + 2 - 1 = d + 1$ parties (as one party is rebooted and recovering) either honest or behaving correctly (while passively corrupted), so there are enough shares among those parties to uniquely define all polynomials (of maximum degree d). In Step 2.5 the shares of the final d random recovery polynomials are computed as $z_i^r = f_i(\alpha_r) + \Sigma_{j=1}^{d+1} sh_{ij}^r = f_i(\alpha_r) + \Sigma_{j=1}^{d+1} g_{ji}(\alpha_r)$ and given that $\Sigma_{j=1}^{d+1} g_{ji}(\alpha_{rc}) = 0$, P_{rc} in steps 2.6 recovers its d shares after interpolating the polynomials $z_i(x)$ as: $z_i(\alpha_{rc}) = f_i(\alpha_{rc}) + \Sigma_{j=1}^{d+1} g_{ji}(\alpha_{rc}) = f_i(\alpha_{rc})$ as required.

Lemma 7. *Secrecy of DM-Recover: When number of summands is $d < n - 2$, and when up to d parties are passively corrupted, $|\mathcal{P}^*| \leq d$, either the protocol aborts identifying misbehaving parties, or a recovering party, P_{rc}, receives shares encoding the same secret as old shares it should have had, and the protocol does not reveal any information about the secret or shares of other parties.*

Proof. In step 2.1 each party generates random polynomials evaluating to 0 at the evaluation point of the recovering party α_{rc}, these polynomials are independent of the shared secret and of the shares of other parties. The commitments to the coefficients of these polynomials are computationally hiding, and thus do not reveal anything about the polynomials, therefore, the adversary obtains no information in Step 2.2 of DM-Recover. If a single honest party exists (always the case if $d < n - 2$ and $|\mathcal{P}^*| \leq d$, and because $\mathcal{A}^* \subseteq \mathcal{P}^*$), then the polynomial it will generate will be random, and the polynomials resulting from adding all the shares of all the polynomials to the old shares will result in new random polynomials that share the same values as the current sharing polynomials at α_{rc}, otherwise the values of the new recovery polynomials are random. In step 2.6, P_{rc} receives shares of these random recovery polynomials and when interpolating, the only relevant information learned is the evaluations at α_{rc} which are its required shares.

Lemma 8. *Robustness of* DM-Recover: *The protocol is robust and the secret is never lost when shares are recovered for c parties if* $|\mathcal{A}^*| \leq k$ *when* $d < n - k - c$ *and* $|\mathcal{P}^*| \leq d$.

Proof. A similar argument to that made for the robustness of DM-Refresh can be made here, the only difference is that instead of assuming a single recovering party, we now assume c recovering parties and adjust d to be $d < n - k - c$. In that case the highest polynomial will have degree $d = n - k - c - 1$, and if there are k actively corrupt parties, and c recovering parties, the remaining $n - k - c$ parties will have among themselves enough shares to generate random polynomials with the correct degrees and the correct values as the shares of the recovering parties at their public evaluation point.

4.7   Reducing the Required Communication

To reduce communication by $O(n)$, one can construct generalizations of the four protocols in the PSS scheme and that operate using a batch of $b = O(n)$ secrets instead of a single secret. The batched versions of DM-Share and DM-Reconstruct would require $O(n^2)$ communication to share and reconstruct $O(n)$ secrets, effectively reducing their communication to $O(n)$, while DM-Refresh and DM-Recover would require $O(n^3)$ and $O(n^4)$ communication to refresh and recover $O(n)$ secrets, and thus effectively reducing their communication to $O(n^2)$ and $O(n^3)$. (Due to space constraints we defer the full specification of the batched versions of the protocols to a full version of this paper.)

5   Conclusion and Open Questions

We present the *first Proactive Secret Sharing (PSS) scheme for a dishonest majority*. Our PSS scheme is robust and secure against $t < n - 2$ passive adversaries with no active corruptions, and secure but non-robust (but with identifiable aborts) against $t < n/2 - 1$ active adversaries when there are no additional passive corruptions. The scheme is also secure, and non-robust but with identifiable aborts, against mixed adversaries that control a combination of passively and actively corrupted parties such that with k active corruptions there are less than $n - k - 2$ total corruptions. The following issues remain open: (i) It is unclear what the lowest communication required for a PSS scheme secure against a dishonest majority is; we achieve $O(n^3)$ for batches of $O(n)$ secrets, and it remains open if this can be further reduced. We conjecture that $O(n)$ is the lower bound for our blueprint which first shares the secret via an additive scheme as such an additive step does not seem to be amenable to batching using standard techniques for batching the linear sharing step. (ii) There are currently no PSS schemes secure against dishonest majorities and operate over asynchronous networks. Our scheme assumes a synchronous network.

Acknowledgments. We thank Jeremiah Blocki for helpful comments and discussions on an earlier version of this paper. We also thank the anonymous reviewers for their useful feedback. Part of this work was carried out while visiting The Simmons Institute for Theory of Computation.

References

[BCS03] Backes, M., Cachin, C., Strobl, R.: Proactive secure message transmission in asynchronous networks. In: Proceedings of the Twenty-Second ACM Symposium on Principles of Distributed Computing, PODC, Boston, Massachusetts, USA, 13–16 July 2003, pp. 223–232 (2003)

[BELO14] Baron, J., ElDefrawy, K., Lampkins, J., Ostrovsky, R.: How to withstand mobile virus attacks, revisited. In: Proceedings of the ACM Symposium on Principles of Distributed Computing, PODC 2014, pp. 293–302. ACM, New York (2014)

[BELO15] Baron, J., Defrawy, K.E., Lampkins, J., Ostrovsky, R.: Communication-optimal proactive secret sharing for dynamic groups. In: Malkin, T., et al. (eds.) ACNS 2015. LNCS, vol. 9092, pp. 23–41. Springer, Heidelberg (2015). doi:10.1007/978-3-319-28166-7_2

[BFO12] Ben-Sasson, E., Fehr, S., Ostrovsky, R.: Near-linear unconditionally-secure multiparty computation with a dishonest minority. In: Safavi-Naini, R., Canetti, R. (eds.) CRYPTO 2012. LNCS, vol. 7417, pp. 663–680. Springer, Heidelberg (2012)

[Bla79] Blakley, G.R.: Safeguarding cryptographic keys. In: Proceedings of AFIPS National Computer Conference vol. 48, pp. 313–317 (1979)

[BTH08] Beerliová-Trubíniová, Z., Hirt, M.: Perfectly-secure MPC with linear communication complexity. In: Canetti, R. (ed.) TCC 2008. LNCS, vol. 4948, pp. 213–230. Springer, Heidelberg (2008)

[CCD88] Chaum, D., Crépeau, C., Damgard, I.: Multiparty unconditionally secure protocols. In: Proceedings of the Twentieth Annual ACM Symposium on Theory of Computing, STOC 1988, pp. 11–19. ACM, New York (1988)

[CH94] Canetti, R., Herzberg, A.: Maintaining security in the presence of transient faults. In: Desmedt, Y.G. (ed.) CRYPTO 1994. LNCS, vol. 839, pp. 425–438. Springer, Heidelberg (1994)

[CKLS02] Cachin, C., Kursawe, K., Lysyanskaya, A., Strobl, R.: Asynchronous verifiable secret sharing and proactive cryptosystems. In: ACM Conference on Computer and Communications Security, pp. 88–97 (2002)

[CL02] Castro, M., Liskov, B.: Practical Byzantine fault tolerance and proactive recovery. ACM Trans. Comput. Syst. **20**(4), 398–461 (2002)

[DGG+15] Dolev, S., Garay, J.A., Gilboa, N., Kolesnikov, V., Yuditsky, Y.: Towards efficient private distributed computation on unbounded input streams. J. Math. Cryptol. **9**(2), 79–94 (2015)

[DGGK09] Dolev, S., Garay, J., Gilboa, N., Kolesnikov, V.: Swarming secrets. In: 47th Annual Allerton Conference on Communication, Control, and Computing, Allerton, pp. 1438–1445, September 2009

[DGGK11] Dolev, S., Garay, J.A., Gilboa, N., Kolesnikov, V.: Secret sharing Krohn-Rhodes: private and perennial distributed computation. In: Proceedings of the Innovations in Computer Science, ICS, 7–9 January 2011, pp. 32–44. Tsinghua University, Beijing (2010)

[DIK+08] Damgård, I., Ishai, Y., Krøigaard, M., Nielsen, J.B., Smith, A.: Scalable multiparty computation with nearly optimal work and resilience. In: Wagner, D. (ed.) CRYPTO 2008. LNCS, vol. 5157, pp. 241–261. Springer, Heidelberg (2008)

[DIK10] Damgård, I., Ishai, Y., Krøigaard, M.: Perfectly secure multiparty computation and the computational overhead of cryptography. In: Gilbert, H. (ed.) EUROCRYPT 2010. LNCS, vol. 6110, pp. 445–465. Springer, Heidelberg (2010)

[Fel87] Feldman, P.: A practical scheme for non-interactive verifiable secret sharing. In: Proceedings of the 28th Annual Symposium on Foundations of Computer Science, SFCS 1987, pp. 427–438. IEEE Computer Society, Washington, DC (1987)

[FGMY97] Frankel, Y., Gemmell, P.S., MacKenzie, P.D., Yung, M.: Proactive RSA. In: Kaliski Jr., B.S. (ed.) CRYPTO 1997. LNCS, vol. 1294, pp. 440–454. Springer, Heidelberg (1997)

[FY92] Franklin, M.K., Yung, M.: Communication complexity of secure computation (extended abstract). In: STOC, pp. 699–710 (1992)

[GMW87] Goldreich, O., Micali, S., Wigderson, A.: How to play any mental game. In: Proceedings of the Nineteenth Annual ACM Symposium on Theory of Computing, STOC 1987, pp. 218–229. ACM, New York (1987)

[HJKY95] Herzberg, A., Jarecki, S., Krawczyk, H., Yung, M.: Proactive secret sharing or: how to cope with perpetual leakage. In: Coppersmith, D. (ed.) CRYPTO 1995. LNCS, vol. 963, pp. 339–352. Springer, Heidelberg (1995)

[HML13] Hirt, M., Lucas, C., Maurer, U.: A dynamic tradeoff between active and passive corruptions in secure multi-party computation. In: Canetti, R., Garay, J.A. (eds.) CRYPTO 2013, Part II. LNCS, vol. 8043, pp. 203–219. Springer, Heidelberg (2013)

[OY91] Ostrovsky, R., Yung, M.: How to withstand mobile virus attacks (extended abstract). In: PODC, pp. 51–59 (1991)

[RB89] Rabin, T., Ben-Or, M.: Verifiable secret sharing and multiparty protocols with honest majority. In: Proceedings of the Twenty-First Annual ACM Symposium on Theory of Computing, STOC 1989, pp. 73–85. ACM, New York (1989)

[Sch07] Schultz, D.: Mobile proactive secret sharing. Ph.D. thesis, Massachusetts Institute of Technology (2007)

[Sha79] Shamir, A.: How to share a secret. Commun. ACM **22**(11), 612–613 (1979)

[Tim16] Los Angeles Times. Anthem is warning consumers about its huge data breach. Here's a translation (2016). http://www.latimes.com/business/hiltzik/la-fi-mh-anthem-is-warning-consumers-20150306-column.html. Accessed 10 Feb 2015

[WWW02] Wong, T.M., Wang, C., Wing, J.M.: Verifiable secret redistribution for archive system. In: IEEE Security in Storage Workshop, pp. 94–106 (2002)

[ZSvR05] Zhou, L., Schneider, F.B., van Renesse, R.: APSS: proactive secret sharing in asynchronous systems. ACM Trans. Inf. Syst. Secur. **8**(3), 259–286 (2005)

Obfuscation

Shorter Circuit Obfuscation in Challenging Security Models

Zvika Brakerski$^{(\boxtimes)}$ and Or Dagmi

Weizmann Institute of Science, Rehovot, Israel
{zvika.brakerski,or.dagmi}@weizmann.ac.il

Abstract. The study of program obfuscation is seeing great progress in recent years, which is crucially attributed to the introduction of graded encoding schemes by Garg, Gentry and Halevi [20]. In such schemes, elements of a ring can be encoded such that the content of the encoding is hidden, but restricted algebraic manipulations, followed by zero-testing, can be performed publicly. This primitive currently underlies all known constructions of general-purpose obfuscators.

However, the security properties of the current candidate graded encoding schemes are not well understood, and new attacks frequently introduced. It is therefore important to assume as little as possible about the security of the graded encoding scheme, and use as conservative security models as possible. This often comes at a cost of reducing the efficiency or the functionality of the obfuscator.

In this work, we present a candidate obfuscator, based on composite-order graded encoding schemes, which obfuscates circuits directly a la Zimmerman [34] and Applebaum-Brakerski [2]. Our construction requires a graded encoding scheme with only 3 "plaintext slots" (= subrings of the underlying ring), which is directly related to the size and complexity of the obfuscated program. We prove that our obfuscator is superior to previous works in two different security models.

1. We prove that our obfuscator is indistinguishability-secure (iO) in the *Unique Representation Generic Graded Encoding* model. Previous works either required a composite-order scheme with polynomially many slots, or were provable in a milder security model. This immediately translates to a polynomial improvement in efficiency, and shows that improved security does not come at the cost of efficiency in this case.

2. Following Badrinarayanan et al. [3], we consider a model where finding any "non-trivial" encoding of zero breaks the security of the encoding scheme. We show that, perhaps surprisingly, secure obfuscation is possible in this model even for some classes of *non-evasive functions* (for example, any class of conjunctions). We define the property required of the function class, formulate an appropriate (generic) security model, and prove that our aforementioned obfuscator is virtual-black-box (VBB) secure in this model.

Research supported by the Israel Science Foundation (Grant No. 468/14), the Alon Young Faculty Fellowship, Binational Science Foundation (Grant No. 712307) and Google Faculty Research Award.

V. Zikas and R. De Prisco (Eds.): SCN 2016, LNCS 9841, pp. 551–570, 2016.
DOI: 10.1007/978-3-319-44618-9_29

1   Introduction

A program obfuscator is a compiler that takes a program as input, and outputs a functionally equivalent program that is hard to reverse engineer. Early works by Hada [24] and Barak et al. [6] provided rigorous definitional treatment of obfuscation, but also showed the impossibility of achieving strong security notions for general circuits. In particular Virtual Black-Box (VBB) security, where interaction with the obfuscated program can be simulated using only black-box access to the obfuscated program, was proven impossible in general.

Constructing secure obfuscators, even heuristically, is a very challenging task. Indeed, until recently, candidate obfuscators were only known to exist for a few simple function classes. The game changer in this field had been the introduction of *graded encoding schemes* (GES) by Garg, Gentry and Halevi [20] and follow-up constructions by Coron, Lepoint and Tibouchi [18,19]. GES allow to encode ring elements (from some underlying ring) in a way that hides the identity of the ring element, but still allows algebraic manipulation on the encoding (addition and multiplication). Each encoding is associated with a *level*, which is a positive integer (or more generally an integer vector). Addition is only allowed within a level, and in multiplication the level of the output is the sum of the levels of the inputs. A GES allows to test if the contents of an encoding is the zero element, but only at a predetermined "zero-test level", and not beyond. Thus GES allows arithmetic operations of bounded degree.

Garg et al. [21] presented a candidate obfuscator for general circuits based on GES. They conjectured, with some supporting evidence, that their obfuscator is a secure *indistinguishability obfuscator* (iO). Indistinguishability obfuscation is a weak security notion and it first glance it may seem useless. However, Sahai and Waters [32] showed that iO is actually sufficient for a wide variety of applications. Numerous follow-up works showed how to use iO to construct many desirable cryptographic primitives, thus establishing iO itself as one of the most important cryptographic primitives. The goal of formally establishing the security of obfuscation candidates had since been central in cryptographic research.

Brakerski and Rothblum [12] presented a similar obfuscator candidate, and proved its security in the *generic GES model*. This model addresses adversaries that are restricted to algebraic attacks on the encoding scheme, i.e. generate encodings, perform algebraic manipulations and test for zero, while being oblivious to the representation of the element. This is modeled by representing the encodings using random strings, thus making them completely opaque. The algebraic functionality is provided as oracle. Other candidate obfuscators with generic proofs followed [1,5,28]. Pass, Seth and Telang [31] replaced the generic model with a strong notion of "uber-assumption".

The constructions mentioned so far were all based on converting the obfuscated program into a branching program, thus having computational cost which scaled with the *formula size* of the program to be obfuscated.[1] This was improved

---

[1] An additional "bootstrapping" step established that obfuscating polynomial-size formulae is sufficient in order to obfuscate general circuits.

by newer constructions that used *composite order* GES (where the underlying ring is isomorphic to $\mathbb{Z}_N$ for a composite N). In a nutshell, composite order rings allow for "slotted" representation of elements via the Chinese Remainder Theorem, so that each ring element is viewed as a tuple of slots, and algebraic operations are performed slot-wise. In particular, Zimmerman [34] and Applebaum and Brakerski [2] presented obfuscators whose overhead relates to the *circuit size* of the program and not its formula size. However, using known candidate GES, the underlying encodings again incorporated overhead that depends on the formula size. Nonetheless, these constructions carry the promise that given more efficient GES candidates, the dependence on the formula size can be completely removed. Proofs in generic models were provided.

Since the generic model restricts the adversary beyond its actual attack capabilities, such proofs should be taken only as evidence in lieu of standard model proofs. In order for the evidence to carry more weight, we should be prudent and use models that pose as few restrictions as possible on the adversary.

For example, [2,5,34] consider a model where one assumes that not only encodings of different elements appear to the adversary as independent uniform strings, but also if the same element is computed in two different ways then it will have two independent-looking representations. This is a fairly strong assumption and in particular one that does not hold in cryptographic multilinear-maps, if such exist [7]. It is shown in [2] that the suggested obfuscation scheme actually breaks if one is allowed to even test for zero at levels below the zero-test level. They therefore proposed a more robust obfuscator that is secure in the unique representation model of [10–12], in which each ring element has a unique representation. Unfortunately, this added security came at a cost of reducing efficiency, specifically the number of "input slots" goes up from 2 to $n + 2$ (where n is the input length). This directly translates to an efficiency loss in the construction.[2] Boneh, Wu and Zimmerman [8] proposed a way to immunize GES so that zero encodings cannot be created below the zero-test level.

A notable progress in the study of secure obfuscation had been made recently by Gentry, Lewko, Sahai and Waters [22]. They showed an obfuscator whose security is based on an assumption in the *standard model*. It is yet unclear whether their hardness assumption holds true in known candidate GES (recent attacks [16,30] suggest it might not). It should further be noted that this construction again requires a large number of input slots (essentially proportional to the formula size of the obfuscated circuit).[3]

We see that the attempts to come up with a more realistic security model comes at the cost of increasing the number of required slots, and therefore reducing the efficiency. It is not clear whether this trade-off is necessary.

Does a stronger security model come at the cost of efficiency?

---

[2] Miles, Sahai and Weiss [28] suggested constraining the model in a different, orthogonal manner. Their model is less relevant for this work.

[3] They also suggest a construction using a single-slot GES, however the efficiency cost was even greater.

In this work, we show that at least in the generic model, one does not need to pay in efficiency to achieve better security.

We proceed to consider an even more conservative security model, one where even finding a non-trivial encoding of the zero element is assumed to obliterate security completely.[4] This model is motivated by new attacks on the security of *all known* proposed GES candidates [15–17,20,25,30], showing that having access to encodings of the ring's zero element results, in some cases, in a complete security breach. Indeed, current attacks do not work with just *any* non-trivial zero encoding, however they do raise concern that having an adversary access an encoding of zero might be a vulnerability. This concern had been significantly heightened recently as Miles, Sahai and Zhandry [29] presented an attack on obfuscators that are based on the [20] GES candidate. This new attack again makes crucial use of top-level encodings of zero (but does not require "low-level" zero encodings like some prior attacks).

To hedge against these risks, Badrinarayanan, Miles, Sahai and Zhandry [3] proposed to avoid zeros completely. Namely, to construct an obfuscator in such a way that the adversary is unable to generate such encodings altogether. However, this seems to defeat the purpose, since zero-testing is the way to extract information out of an encoding for functionality purposes. They get around this barrier in a creative way, by only obfuscating *evasive functions*, where finding an accepting input using oracle access is (unconditionally) hard.[5] Classes of evasive functions have played an important role in the study of obfuscation, since many classes that are desirable to obfuscate are evasive (e.g. various variants of point functions, starting with the work of Canetti [14]) and one could hope that they can even be obfuscatable in the strong VBB setting. (See [4] for more information and the state of the art about evasive functions.) Badrinarayanan et al. show that when their obfuscator is applied to an evasive function, the adversary is unable to find an encoding of zero. The proof here is in the generic model as well. The restriction to evasive functions, however, excludes interesting function classes such as conjunctions [10,13]. We therefore address the following question.

Can we obfuscate non-evasive functions in the zero-sensitive model?

Perhaps surprisingly, we answer this question in the affirmative, and show that our obfuscator (the same as above) is secure in a zero-sensitive model, even for some non-evasive function classes, and in particular for worst-case conjunctions.

1.1   Our Results

A More Efficient Circuit Obfuscator. We present a new direct circuit obfuscator, i.e. one that does not go through branching programs. Our construction is inspired

---

[4] A "trivial" zero is, for example, the result of subtracting an encoding from itself, or of similar computations that nullify based on the syntax of the equation rather than the encoded values.

[5] We note that if the [3] obfuscator is applied to non evasive functions, and top-level zeros can occur, then the [29] attack applies. This highlights the significance of completely avoiding zeros.

by the "robust obfuscator" RobustObf of [2]. However, whereas RobustObf works over a composite order graded encoding scheme with $(n + 2)$ message slots, our obfuscator only requires 3 slots. Our obfuscator provides equivalent level of security to RobustObf in the unique representation generic GES model (see details below). This improvement translates directly to a factor n improvement in the size of the encodings, and a $poly(n)$-factor improvement in the computational complexity of generating and evaluating the obfuscated program.[6] We therefore show that at least in the generic model, there is no real efficiency gain to working in a less secure model. We hope that our techniques can be translated to reduce the number of required slots in the non-generic setting as well, in particular in the [22] scheme.

We prove that the resulting obfuscator is indistinguishability secure in the unique representation graded encoding model. The proof outline is similar in spirit to that of the robust obfuscator of [2], while incorporating some proof techniques from [34]. In particular, we rely on the sub-exponential hardness of factoring the order of the underlying ring, in addition to the security of the generic model. In contrast, [2] work in a model where the order of the ring is hidden so that factoring it is *information theoretically* hard.

We note that one can consider many variants of the generic model: known modulus, unknown modulus and information theoretic hardness, computational hardness. Furthermore, [34] also shows how to prove VBB security at the cost of increasing the size of the obfuscator by additional n^2 encodings. Our improvement can be applied to all of these variants, transforming them to the unique representation model while preserving the number of slots as constant. For the sake of concreteness, we chose to prove in a setting that we found interesting.

The Zero-Sensitive Oracle and All-or-Nothing Functions. We show that the [3] approach discussed above can be extended even beyond evasive functions. This may come as a surprise since applying our obfuscator to non-evasive functions gives the adversary access to zero encodings. As a motivating example, consider the class of conjunctions that had been studied in [10]. One can think of a conjunction as string-matching with wildcards. Namely, the function is defined by a string $v \in \{0, 1, \star\}^n$, and $f_v(x) = 1$ if and only if for all i, either $v[i] = x[i]$ or $v[i] = \star$. Indeed, some distributions on this class of functions are evasive, but what if we want to obfuscate it *in the worst case*?

Naturally, in the worst case there could be an adversary that can find an accepting input (more generally, no function class is evasive in the worst case except the zero function). However, the critical observation is that this does not necessarily hinder security, since given an accepting input, one can *learn the entire function*. In the case of conjunctions this is easy to do by taking an accepting x and flipping each of its bits in turn to see if this bit is a wildcard (and switching it back afterwards). Therefore, if we find an accepting input, we should not expect the obfuscator to hide anything anyway!

---

[6] See e.g. [23, Appendix B] for suggested trade-offs between the number of input slots and the size of the encoding.

We generalize this property and define *All-or-Nothing* (AoN) function classes to be ones where if an adversary finds an accepting input, then it can recover the function in its entirety (a formal definition is provided). We would like to show that indeed such function classes can be securely obfuscated even in a setting where a non-trivial zero encoding implies that the GES is insecure.

In the proof of [3] for evasive functions, proving security was split into two tasks: presenting a simulator, and showing that the adversary cannot compute encodings of zero. Our notion of security, however, requires additional definitional treatment, since we would like successful simulation even in the case where an accepting input had been found, and we cannot tell in advance whether such an input will be found or not. We therefore define a new generic model where the GES oracle keeps track of the encodings that the adversary generates, and if one of those is a non-trivial zero, then the adversary gets access to a *decoding oracle* that allows to decode any given encoding to obtain the plaintext. This is how we model the risk in non-trivial zeros.

Finally, we prove that our obfuscator is indeed a secure VBB obfuscator for AoN functions in our new zero-sensitive model. Interestingly, we don't need to use complexity leveraging here and we can prove VBB security without increasing the number of encodings. We view this as evidence that AoN functions may be strictly easier to obfuscate than general functions, and are perhaps a good candidate for VBB obfuscation in the standard model.

What GES Candidate To Use? We stress that our work is completely abstract and not directly related to any specific GES candidate, but naturally it would be more convincing if it could be instantiated with one. To date, the only candidate composite order GES is that of [18,19], and indeed this candidate can be used with our scheme. We stress that the only known attacks on this candidate uses encodings of zero, and there are no known attacks in the zero evading model (this is also true for the [20] candidate). In fact, even in the "standard" model, the attacks of [17,29] do not seem to apply to our obfuscator when instantiated with [18,19]. However, these attacks suggest that obfuscators such as ours might be vulnerable to future attacks. The goal of finding secure instantiations of composite order candidate GES is a very important one, but orthogonal to the contributions of this paper.

1.2   Our Techniques

Our Obfuscator. Our building block is a graded encoding scheme whose plaintexts are elements in a composite order ring. We denote the encoding of the element a by $[a]$. Encodings can be added, subtracted, multiplied and tested for zero (subject to constraints imposed by the levels, which we will ignore in this outline since they are similar to previous works). We think of a itself as a tuple of elements via the Chinese Remainder Theorem. Each sub-ring is of high cardinality and it is assumed that "isolating" the components of an encoded element is computationally hard (in the generic model this relates to the hardness of factoring the order of the ring). The [2] obfuscator (following [10–12]) adds an additional layer on top of this encoding and rather than encoding $[a]$ itself, it produces a pair of encodings $[r]$ and $[r \cdot a]$, for a random r, i.e. the plaintext value is the ratio between the values in the two encodings. This "rational encoding" plays an important role in both functionality and security. For the purpose of this outline only, we use $[a]^{\diamond}$ as shorthand notation for the pair $[r], [r \cdot a]$. It can be shown that rational encodings can be added and multiplied, subject to constraints as in previous works.

The starting point of our construction is the "robust obfuscator" from [2]. This obfuscator, in turn, is derived from a simpler solution [2,34] that applies in a more forgiving generic model. In the "simple obfuscator", for each input bit i, two encodings are given as a part of the obfuscator. These encodings are of the form $[(y_i, b)]^{\diamond}$, for $b \in \{0, 1\}$, where y_i is a random value that is the same whether $b = 0$ or 1. The weakness of this scheme stems from the ability to subtract the two encodings that correspond to the same i, and cancel out the y_i value to obtain an encoding of the form $[(0, 1)]^{\diamond}$, which in turn allows to test whether the second slot of a given encoding is zero or not (via multiplying by $[(0, 1)]^{\diamond}$ and zero-testing). In the less restrictive multiple representation generic model, this attack is prevented by disallowing to test for zero in some situations. However, this cannot be avoided in a model where each element has a unique representation since one can always test for zero by comparing to a known encoding of zero.

The robust obfuscator from [2] prevents this problem by adding n additional slots to the encodings, and publishing, for each input bit of the obfuscated function, the values $[w_{i,b}]^{\diamond}$, for $b \in \{0, 1\}$, where $w_{i,b} = (y_i, b, \rho_{1,b}, \ldots, \rho_{n,b})$. The ρ values are uniform and independent, and therefore subtracting $[w_{i,1}]^{\diamond} - [w_{i,0}]^{\diamond}$ here will not cancel out the ρ values. The ρ values should be eliminated in the end of the computation, and this is done by providing additional encodings of a special form $\hat{w}_{i,b} = (\hat{y}_i, \beta_{i,b}, \hat{\rho}_{1,b}, \ldots, \hat{\rho}_{i-1,b}, 0, \hat{\rho}_{i+1,b}, \ldots, \hat{\rho}_{n,b})$. Namely, encodings that zero out the ith ρ value. In the evaluation, the value $\prod_i \hat{w}_{i,x_i}$ is computed and multiplied with the result of the computation so far, thus zeroing out the last n slots. Note that even though the ρ values can be zeroed out, this does not enable the previous attack. This is due to the level constraints that impose structural limitations. In particular, $[\hat{w}_{i,0}]^{\diamond}$ and $[w_{i,1}]^{\diamond}$ cannot be used in the same computation, which is in contrast to $[w_{i,0}]^{\diamond}$ and $[w_{i,1}]^{\diamond}$ that cannot be prevented from interacting (at a high level, this is because each input bit can be used many times in the circuit, but the $\hat{w}$ values are designed to only be used once).

Our modification to this scheme is quite simple. We observe that the use of n different ρ slots is only due to the cancellation step via $\hat{w}$, where we need to enforce that an adversary must use a $[\hat{w}_{i,b}]^{\diamond}$ value *for each and every* i. The reason is that this use prevents the dangerous mix-and-match of $[w_{i,0}]^{\diamond}$ and $[w_{i,1}]^{\diamond}$. We notice, however, that since rational encodings can be added and not just multiplied, one could enforce that an $\hat{w}_{i,b}$ is used for every i using a sum rather than a product. We set $\hat{w}_{i,b} = (\hat{y}_i, \beta_{i,b}, \hat{\rho}_i)$, thus reducing the number of sub-rings to only 3. We choose the $\hat{\rho}_i$ values at random, subject to the constraint that $\sum_i \hat{\rho}_i = 0$. This means that in order to zero-out the $\hat{\rho}$ coordinate, an adversary needs to use a $[\hat{w}_{i,b}]^{\diamond}$ element for every i. As before, we must prevent $[\hat{w}_{i,0}]^{\diamond}$ and $[\hat{w}_{i,1}]^{\diamond}$ from interacting, since taking their difference zeros out the

$\hat{\rho}$ coordinate and is therefore dangerous, but this is done in the same way as previous works.

Proving Security. As has been shown in a number of previous works, in the generic model, the adversary is limited to applying arithmetic circuits over the encodings received as input, and testing the output for zero. The simulator, therefore, generates a collection of random strings to play the role of the encodings in the obfuscated program, and then to answer queries of the form of an arithmetic circuit, determining whether applying this circuit to the encodings at hand evaluates to zero.[7] The problem is that the simulator needs to do this with only oracle access to the obfuscated circuit. Namely, it does not fully know what is the plaintext in the encoding that it generated.

We use a proof practice that started with [10]. They notice that if we use rational encoding as described above, then the polynomial computed by an arithmetic circuit can be decomposed into a sum of terms that we call *semi-monomials*. A semi-monomial is a polynomial of the form $M(\vec{r})Q(\vec{w})$, where $M(\vec{r})$ is a product of "randomizing" variables, and $Q(\vec{w})$ is a polynomial in the "content" variables. Since the randomizer variables are random and independent, the task of testing the polynomial for zero is identical to the task of finding whether there exists a non-zero semi-monomial.

We distinguish between semi-monomials that are "valid", in the sense that they represent a legal evaluation of the circuit on an input, and ones that are "invalid". We show how to test if a semi-monomial is valid or not, and that an invalid semi-monomial cannot zero-out, regardless which circuit had been obfuscated, assuming the hardness of factoring the ring order. We show that "valid" monomials zero-out if and only if the obfuscated circuit accepts their associated input x.

Therefore, our proof strategy is straightforward. We extract semi-monomials from the circuit one after the other.[8] For each semi-monomial, we check whether it is invalid, in which case we can immediately return that the arithmetic circuit computes a non-zero. If the semi-monomial is valid for some input x, we query the obfuscated circuit oracle on x. If it rejects, then the answer is again non-zero, but if it accepts, then the answer is still undetermined and we need to proceed to the next semi-monomial.

This process takes 2^n time in the worst case, since there can be at most 2^n valid semi-monomials. Thus the running time of our iO simulator is exponential in the input length. However, in the case of AoN functions, the situation is much simpler and in fact only *one* semi-monomial needs to be inspected. The reason is that if the extracted x is an accepting input for the circuit, then we don't need to proceed at all, since for AoN functions, we can efficiently learn the code of the circuit, which allows us to continue the simulation trivially by just assigning the right values to the $\vec{w}$ variables. This completes the proof.

---

[7] It may seem that the simulator needs to do much more than that, but it can be shown that all other functionalities reduce to this problem.

[8] In fact, our extraction procedure might output terms with a few semi-monomials, but in such case one of them must be invalid, which will be detected in the next step.

1.3 Paper Organization

In Sect. 2 we present our new generic model as well as our new zero-sensitive model, which is a new contribution. Section 3 features the specifics of our obfuscator, and security is proven in Sect. 4, where we also define the class of AoN functions. Due to space constraints, much of the technical content is deferred to the full version [9].

2 The Generic GES Model and Our New Zero-Sensitive Variant

We would like to prove the security of our construction against *generic adversaries*. To this end, we will use the *generic graded encoding scheme* model, adapted from [5,10–12], which is analogous to the *generic group model* (see Shoup [33] and Maurer [27]).

There are various flavors of generic models suggested in the literature. In this work, we follow [2,10] and use the *unique-representation* model, where each element in the underlying ring, at each level, has a unique representation. This is in contrast to the *multiple-representation* model [2,5,34] which (roughly) states that if the same element is being computed via different computational paths, then each path will lead to a different and independent representation of that element. While the latter model makes the task of proving security easier, it is inadequate in some situations, as we described in the introduction. We note that a proof in the unique representation model immediately carries over to the multiple representation model, but not the other way around. We provide a definition of this model in Sect. 2.1 below.

We then introduce our zero-sensitive model. This model is motivated by recent attacks that leverage non-trivial encodings of zero. In this model we treat a non-trivial encoding of zero at any level as perilous. In particular, once such an encoding had been generated, the GES oracle will no longer keep any secret, and surrender the plaintexts of all encodings to the adversary. As we explained above, we can prove security of all-or-nothing functions in this model. See Sect. 2.2 for details.

Lastly, in Sect. 2.3, we define indistinguishability and virtual black-box obfuscation in the presence of our oracles.

2.1 The Ideal GES Oracle

We present the "online" variant of the unique representation model. As shown in previous works, this variant is equivalent to the "offline" variant up to negligible statistical distance. See [2,10] for more details. We model the GES using an oracle $\mathcal{RG}$ which implements the functionality of a GES in which the representations of elements are uniform and independent random strings.

The Online $\mathcal{RG}$ Oracle. The online $\mathcal{RG}$ oracle is implemented by an *online poly-nomial time process*, which samples representations for ring elements on-the-fly. Specifically, the oracle will maintain a table of entries of the form $(\mathbf{v}, a, \mathsf{label}_{\mathbf{v},a})$, where $\mathsf{label}_{\mathbf{v},a} \in \{0,1\}^t$ is the representation of $[a]_{\mathbf{v}}$ in $\mathcal{RG}$, and F is either a for-mal variable or an arithmetic circuit over formal variables. The table is initially empty and is filled as described below.

- Whenever a sampling query is made, $\mathcal{RG}$ generates an element a from $\mathcal{R}$ (or the appropriate sub-ring), and a uniform length t label. It then stores the tuple $(\mathbf{0}, a, \mathsf{label}_{\mathbf{0},a})$ in its table.
- For encoding and arithmetic operations, the oracle takes the input labels and finds appropriate entries in the table that correspond to these labels. If such don't exist then $\bot$ is returned. Otherwise, the oracle retrieves the appropriate $(\mathbf{v}, a)$ values to perform the operation. It then checks that the level values are appropriate (e.g. encRand can only be applied to level zero encodings, addition can only take two operands of the same level), and computes the output of the operation. It then performs the computation on the ring elements. Finally, the oracle needs to return an encoding of an element of the form $(\mathbf{v}', a')$. To do this, the oracle checks whether $(\mathbf{v}', a')$ is already in the table, and if so returns the appropriate $\mathsf{label}_{\mathbf{v}',a'}$. Otherwise it samples a new uniform label, and inserts a new entry into the table. Otherwise it samples a new uniform label, and inserts a new entry into the table.
- Extraction is trivial in our representation, one can just use $\mathsf{label}_{\mathbf{v}',a'}$ as the extracted value for $[a]_{\mathbf{v}}$.
- Zero testing is performed by finding the appropriate entry in the table and checking whether the respective ring element is indeed 0.

2.2   The Zero-Sensitive Generic Model

We propose a new generic model that incorporates the zero-evading requirement of [3] into the generic GES model. Whereas our oracle is a modification of the unique representation generic model presented above, similar modifications can be made to other generic models in the literature.

We propose a generic model with an additional *decoding* functionality which will allow the adversary to retrieve the plaintext of any encoding of its choosing, once an encoding of zero had been generated. Some care needs to be taken, since it is easy to produce "syntactic zeros" which are harmless. E.g. subtracting an encoding from itself will produce such a zero encoding, or less trivially, computing an expression of the form $(A + B) * C - (C * A + C * B)$. These expressions will evaluate to zero regardless of the values that are actually encoded in A, B, C and we refer to them as "trivial" or "syntactic" zeros. Such encodings of zero are unavoidable, but they are not dangerous. (Indeed, in known instantiations of GES [18–20], syntactic zeros are always encoded by the all-zero string and thus provide no meaningful information.) We design an oracle that whenever a non-syntactic zero is created (or rather, when it could potentially be created), enables the decoding feature.

We consider the encodings that are generated by the encRand function as atomic variables, and for every encoding generated by the adversary throughout the computation, we maintain its representation as an algebraic circuit over these variables. Whenever two syntactically different such arithmetic circuits evaluate to the same value, we enable the decoding feature. Details follow.

The $\mathcal{RG}_{\mathcal{Z}}$ Oracle. The new oracle is based on the functionality of the oracle $\mathcal{RG}$ defined in Sect. 2.1. It will maintain a table similarly to $\mathcal{RG}$, but in addition each entry in the table will contain an additional value in the form of an arithmetic circuit over the formal variables $X_1, X_2, \ldots$. Elements encoded at level $\mathbf{0}$ will not have a circuit associated with them, but whenever encRand is executed, the resulting element will be stored in the table together with a new variable X_i. It will also maintain a global binary state decode which is initialized to false.

When the arithmetic functionality of $\mathcal{RG}_{\mathcal{Z}}$ is called, say on operands A_1, A_2 whose table entries are $(\mathbf{v}_1, a_1, A_1, C_1)$, $(\mathbf{v}_1, a_2, A_2, C_2)$, it performs exactly as $\mathcal{RG}$ and computes the values $(\mathbf{v}', a')$ corresponding to the level and value of the result. In addition $\mathcal{RG}_{\mathcal{Z}}$ also defines $C' = C_1 \mathrm{op} C_2$, where op is the arithmetic operation to be performed (e.g. $C' = C_1 + C_2$ or $C' = C_1 \times C_2$). Then, just like in $\mathcal{RG}$, we search the table to find whether $(\mathbf{v}', a')$ already appears. If it does not, then a new label A' is generated, $(\mathbf{v}', a', A', C')$ is stored in the table, and A' is returned. However, if there already exists $(\mathbf{v}', a', A'', C'')$ in the table, then there is potential for a non-trivial zero in the case where $C' \not\equiv C''$. This equivalence is easy to check (even in polynomial time using Schwartz-Zippel). If the circuits are equivalent: $C' \equiv C''$, then there is no risk, the table entry does not change and A'' is returned. However, if indeed $C' \not\equiv C''$, then the adversary can create a non trivial zero (since he generated the element a' in two syntactically different ways). Therefore, in this event, $\mathcal{RG}_{\mathcal{Z}}$ sets decode = true.

As explained above, $\mathcal{RG}_{\mathcal{Z}}$ also provides an additional decoding functionality: Decode(A). This function, upon receiving an encoding A as input, first checks the decode variable. If decode = false then it returns $\perp$. Otherwise, it searches the table for and entry whose label is A, and returns the corresponding "plaintext" value a.

Non-trivial Zeros in the Unique Representation Model. Our zero evading model has unique representations, in the sense that the oracle assigns a single string to each ring element. This state of affairs may be confusing, since if there is only one representation for each element (in particular, the zero element), it may seem that the distinction between trivial and non-trivial zeros is meaningless. While this intuition is true in the standard model, in a generic model the $\mathcal{RG}$ oracle can judge whether an encoding of zero is trivial or not even though they are represented by the same string, since it can keep track of the path the adversary took in generating said encoding. In fact, security in our model is *stronger* than in a model that allows multiple representations. Details follow.

We note that unique representation GES (call it uGES for short) is effectively equivalent to multiple representations GES (mGES) in which zero-testing can be performed anywhere below level $\mathbf{v}_{zt}$ and not just at $\mathbf{v}_{zt}$ itself. This is because the adversary can always think about the first representation of a specific element as the "real" one. Whenever it sees a new encoding, it can subtract it from all previous ones that it saw in the same level, and test for zero, thus discovering if two different encodings in fact refer to the same element. Therefore, by using uGES we only give the adversary extra power. Another advantage of using uGES is that the extraction procedure becomes trivially defined and does not need additional machinery. One can thus think of our use of uGES as a formalism that allows us to seamlessly handle cases such as mGES with low-level zero-testing (and extraction).

2.3 Obfuscation in the Generic GES Model

These definitions are fairly standard and originate from [10]. We start with correctness, which should hold with respect to an arbitrary GES implementation.

Definition 2.1 (Preserving Functionality). *A GES-based obfuscation scheme* (Obf, Eval) *for $\mathcal{C}$ is* functionality preserving *if for every instantiation $\mathcal{G}$ of GES, every $n \in \mathbb{N}$, every $C_K \in \mathcal{C}$ where $K \in \{0,1\}^{m(n)}$, and every $x \in \{0,1\}^n$, with all but $\mathsf{negl}(\lambda)$ probability over the coins of Obf, Eval and the GES oracle $\mathcal{G}$ it holds that:*

$$\mathsf{Eval}^{\mathcal{G}}(1^n, 1^\lambda, \hat{C}, x) = C_K(x), \qquad where \; \hat{C} \xleftarrow{\$} \mathsf{Obf}^{\mathcal{G}}(1^n, 1^\lambda, K).$$

We define Indistinguishability Obfuscator with respect to some (possibly inefficient) GES instantiation. Our definition is formulated in terms of unbounded simulation which is equivalent to the more standard indistinguishability-based definition (cf. [12]).

Definition 2.2 (Indistinguishability/VBB Security [6]). *A GES-based obfuscation scheme* (Obf, Eval) *for $\mathcal{C}$ is called an* Indistinguishability Obfuscator *(iO) with respect to some GES instantiation $\mathcal{G}$ (which possibly contains a decode function) if for every polynomial size adversary $\mathcal{A}$, there exists a (computationally unbounded) simulator $\mathcal{S}$, such that for every $n \in \mathbb{N}$ and for every $C_K \in \mathcal{C}$ where $K \in \{0,1\}^{m(n)}$:*

$$\left| \Pr[\mathcal{A}^{\mathcal{G}}(1^\lambda, \hat{C}) = 1] - \Pr[\mathcal{S}^{C_K}(1^{|K|}, 1^n, 1^\lambda) = 1] \right| = \mathsf{negl}(\lambda),$$

where $\hat{C} \xleftarrow{\$} \mathsf{Obf}^{\mathcal{G}}(1^n, 1^\lambda, K)$. If the simulator can be implemented by polynomial size circuits than the obfuscator is Virtually Black-Box *(VBB) secure.*

3   Description of Our Obfuscator and Its Correctness

3.1   Setting and Definitions

We define $\mathcal{C} = \{\mathcal{C}_K\}_{K \in \{0,1\}^*}$ to be a family of efficiently computable functions with n-bit inputs, representation size $m = m(n)$ and universal evaluator $\mathcal{U}$.

And we let $\hat{\mathcal{U}}$ be the arithmetized version of $\mathcal{U}$. That is, an arithmetic circuits with $\{+, \times\}$ gates such that for any field $\mathbb{F}$ if $(x, K) \in \{0,1\}^{n+m} \subseteq \mathbb{F}^{n+m}$, then $\hat{\mathcal{U}}(x, K) = C_K(x)$. We also denote by $D_{\hat{\mathcal{U}}}$ the degree of the polynomial computed by $\hat{\mathcal{U}}$.

We define the *multiplicity* of input wire i as follows. We consider an enumeration of the wires of $\hat{\mathcal{U}}$ in topological order, such that the first $n+m$ wires refer to the wires of the x, C inputs. For each wire i we define a vector $\mathbf{s}_i \in \mathbb{Z}^{n+m}$ as follows. If $i \le n+m$, then $\mathbf{s}_i = \mathbf{e}_i$ (the ith indicator vector). For a wire i which is the output wire of a gate whose input wires are j_1, j_2, we define $\mathbf{s}_i = \mathbf{s}_{j_1} + \mathbf{s}_{j_2}$. The *multiplicity* is defined to be $M_i = \mathbf{s}_{\text{out}}[i]$, where "out" is the output wire of $\hat{\mathcal{U}}$.

3.2 The Obfuscator Obf

For all $i \in [n]$, $b \in \{0,1\}$ we define $\mathbf{v}_{i,b} \in \mathbb{Z}^{(n+m+1)\times 4}$ as $\mathbf{v}_{i,b} = \mathbf{e}_i \otimes [b, 1, 1-b, 0]$. We further define $\hat{\mathbf{v}}_{i,b} = \mathbf{e}_i \otimes [(1-b)\cdot M[i], 0, b \cdot M[i], 1]$.

For all $i \in \{n+1, \ldots, n+m\}$ we define $\mathbf{v}_i = e_i \otimes [1,1,1,0]$. We define $\mathbf{v}_0 = \mathbf{e}_{n+m+1} \otimes [1,1,1,0]$ and $\mathbf{v}^* = \mathbf{e}_{n+m+1} \otimes [0,0,0,1]$. Lastly, we define: $\mathbf{v}_{\text{zt}} = (\mathbf{s}_{\text{out}} + \mathbf{e}_{n+m+1}) \otimes [1,1,1,0] + \left(\sum_{i=1}^{n+m} \mathbf{e}_i\right) \otimes [0,0,0,1] + D \cdot \mathbf{v}^* \in \mathbb{Z}^{(n+m+1)\times 4}$, where $D = D_{\hat{\mathcal{U}}} + n$. We note that for all $x \in \{0,1\}^n$ it holds that $\mathbf{v}_{\text{zt}} = \mathbf{v}_0 + \sum_{i=1}^{n} (M[i] \cdot \mathbf{v}_{i,x_i} + \hat{\mathbf{v}}_{i,x_i}) + \sum_{i=n+1}^{n+m} M[i] \cdot \mathbf{v}_i + D \cdot \mathbf{v}^*$. We illustrate the various level vectors in Fig. 1.

$$\mathbf{v}_{i,0} = \left[\begin{array}{ccccc|c} 0 & \cdots & 0 & \cdots & 0 & 0 \\ 0 & \cdots & 1 & \cdots & 0 & 0 \\ 0 & \cdots & 1 & \cdots & 0 & 0 \\ \hline 0 & \cdots & 0 & \cdots & 0 & 0 \end{array}\right], \quad \mathbf{v}_{i,1} = \left[\begin{array}{ccccc|c} 0 & \cdots & 1 & \cdots & 0 & 0 \\ 0 & \cdots & 1 & \cdots & 0 & 0 \\ 0 & \cdots & 0 & \cdots & 0 & 0 \\ \hline 0 & \cdots & 0 & \cdots & 0 & 0 \end{array}\right], \quad \mathbf{v}_{i} = \left[\begin{array}{ccccc|c} 0 & \cdots & 1 & \cdots & 0 & 0 \\ 0 & \cdots & 1 & \cdots & 0 & 0 \\ 0 & \cdots & 1 & \cdots & 0 & 0 \\ \hline 0 & \cdots & 0 & \cdots & 0 & 0 \end{array}\right]$$

$$\hat{\mathbf{v}}_{i,0} = \left[\begin{array}{ccccc|c} 0 & \cdots & M[i] & \cdots & 0 & 0 \\ 0 & \cdots & 0 & \cdots & 0 & 0 \\ 0 & \cdots & 0 & \cdots & 0 & 0 \\ \hline 0 & \cdots & 1 & \cdots & 0 & 0 \end{array}\right], \quad \hat{\mathbf{v}}_{i,1} = \left[\begin{array}{ccccc|c} 0 & \cdots & 0 & \cdots & 0 & 0 \\ 0 & \cdots & 0 & \cdots & 0 & 0 \\ 0 & \cdots & M[i] & \cdots & 0 & 0 \\ \hline 0 & \cdots & 1 & \cdots & 0 & 0 \end{array}\right], \quad \mathbf{v}_0 = \left[\begin{array}{ccc|c} 0 & \cdots & 0 & 1 \\ 0 & \cdots & 0 & 1 \\ 0 & \cdots & 0 & 1 \\ \hline 0 & \cdots & 0 & 0 \end{array}\right], \quad \mathbf{v}^* = \left[\begin{array}{ccc|c} 0 & \cdots & 0 & 0 \\ 0 & \cdots & 0 & 0 \\ 0 & \cdots & 0 & 0 \\ \hline 0 & \cdots & 0 & 1 \end{array}\right]$$

$$\mathbf{v}_{\text{zt}} = \left[\begin{array}{cccccc|c} M[1] & \cdots & M[n] & M[n+1] & \cdots & M[n+m] & 1 \\ M[1] & \cdots & M[n] & M[n+1] & \cdots & M[n+m] & 1 \\ M[1] & \cdots & M[n] & M[n+1] & \cdots & M[n+m] & 1 \\ \hline 1 & \cdots & 1 & 0 & \cdots & 0 & D \end{array}\right]$$

Fig. 1. The level vectors for the obfuscator.

The Obfuscator Obf*:*

- **Input:** Circuit identifier $K \in \{0,1\}^m$ where $C_K \in \mathcal{C}$ and a security parameter λ.
- **Output:** Obfuscated program with the same functionality as C_K.
- **Algorithm:**

1. Instantiate a 3-composite graded encoding scheme

$$(params, evparams) = \text{InstGen}(1^{\lambda + \log \|\mathbf{v}_{zt}\|_1}, 1^3, \mathbf{v}_{zt}).$$

2. For all $i \in [n]$, compute random encodings $R_{i,b} = [r_{i,b}]_{\mathbf{v}_{i,b}}$ as well as encodings of $Z_{i,b} = [r_{i,b} \cdot w_{i,b}]_{\mathbf{v}_{i,b}+\mathbf{v}^*}$, where $w_{i,b} = (y_i, b, \rho_{i,b})$ and $y_i, \rho_{i,b}$ are uniform.

3. For all $i \in [i]$, compute random encodings: $\hat{R}_{i,b} = [\hat{r}_{i,b}]_{\hat{\mathbf{v}}_{i,b}}$ as well as encodings of $\hat{Z}_{i,b} = [\hat{r}_{i,b} \cdot \hat{w}_{i,b}]_{\hat{\mathbf{v}}_{i,b}+\mathbf{v}^*}$, where $\hat{w}_i = (\hat{y}_i, \hat{\beta}_i, \hat{\rho}_i)$, where $\hat{y}_i, \hat{\beta}_i, \{\hat{\rho}_i\}_{i \neq n}$ are all uniform but $\hat{\rho}_n = -\sum_{i=1}^{n-1} \hat{\rho}_i$.

4. For all $i \in \{n+1, \ldots, n+m\}$, compute random encodings $R_i = [r_i]_{\mathbf{v}_i}$ as well as encodings of $Z_i = [r_i \cdot w_i]_{\mathbf{v}_i+\mathbf{v}^*}$, where $w_i = (y_i, K_{i-n}, \rho_i)$, where K_i is the ith bit of the circuit description and y_j, ρ_i are uniform.

5. Compute random encoding $R_0 = [r_0]_{\mathbf{v}_0}$ and $Z_0 = [r_0 \cdot w_0]_{\mathbf{v}_0+D\mathbf{v}^*}$, where $w_0 = \left(\sum_{i \in [n]} \hat{w}_i\right) \cdot (y_0, 1, 0)$ and $y_0 = \hat{\mathcal{U}}(y_1, \ldots, y_{n+m})$.

6. The obfuscated program will contain the following:
   - The evaluation parameters $evparams$.
   - For all $i \in [n], b \in \{0, 1\}$ the elements $R_{i,b}, Z_{i,b}, \hat{R}_{i,b}, \hat{Z}_{i,b}$.
   - For all $i \in \{n+1, \ldots, n+m\}$ the elements R_i, Z_i.
   - The elements R_0, Z_0.

We denote by $\mathcal{D}_\lambda(n, K)$ the distribution over the encoded ring elements the obfuscator outputs according to the construction. Evaluating an obfuscated program is done in a straightforward manner, similarly to previous works. See full version [9] for details.

4   Security

This section contains security proofs for Obf for all-or-nothing functions (defined in Sect. 4.1) in the zero-sensitive $\mathcal{RG}_{\mathcal{Z}}$ model (Sect. 4.2).

Due to space limitations we are only able to present the outline of the security analysis. The proof in the classical generic model follows fairly similar lines and is outline in the end of Sect. 4.2. Many details are missing in this high level presentation and we encourage the reader who wishes to see the entire analysis in context to refer to the full version [9].

4.1   All-or-Nothing (AoN) Functions

We define a category of "all or nothing" functions. These are functions such that are either evasive or perfectly learnable, namely, finding an accepting input for a function in the class implies that the code of the function can be retrieved. This class is an extension of the class of evasive functions. For simplicity we provide the definition in the standalone setting, but it can be extended to the auxiliary input setting as well.

Definition 4.1. *An ensemble of functions* $\mathcal{C} = \{\mathcal{C}_n\}$ *is* AoN *if for any* PPT *algorithm* $\mathcal{A}$*, there exists a* PPT *algorithm* $\mathcal{B}$ *such that for all* $C \in \mathcal{C}_n$,

$$\Pr_r \left[\left(C\left(\mathcal{A}^C\left(1^n; r\right)\right) = 1\right) \wedge \left(\mathcal{B}^C(1^n; r) \neq C\right)\right] = \mathsf{negl}(\lambda) \ ,$$

that is $\mathcal{A}, \mathcal{B}$ *use the same random tape* r.

We can also define an average-case analogue:

Definition 4.2. *An ensemble of functions* $\mathcal{C} = \{\mathcal{C}_n\}$ *together with distributions* $\{\mathcal{D}_n\}$ *over* $\mathcal{C}$ *is average-case* AoN *if for any* PPT *algorithm* $\mathcal{A}$*, there exists a* PPT *algorithm* $\mathcal{B}$ *such that:*

$$\Pr_{r, \, C \leftarrow \mathcal{D}_n} \left[\left(C\left(\mathcal{A}^C\left(1^n; r\right)\right) = 1\right) \wedge \left(\mathcal{B}^C(1^n; r) \neq C\right)\right] = \mathsf{negl}(\lambda) \ ,$$

- *that is* $\mathcal{A}, \mathcal{B}$ *use the same random tape* r.

Note that we ask that $\mathcal{B}$ outputs the exact code of C, given only black box access. Therefore, AoN function classes which are not evasive need to have programs with unique representations. This indeed holds for classes such as conjunctions.

4.2 Zero-Sensitive Security for All-or-Nothing Functions

The following theorem states the VBB security of Obf for any class of AoN functions. We note that while we provide a proof for worst-case AoN, the average case setting follows by a similar proof (note that there could exist function classes that are average case AoN but not worst case AoN).

Theorem 4.3. *Assuming factoring is hard then if* $\mathcal{C}$ *is a family of* AoN *functions, then* Obf *is VBB-secure with respect to the oracle* $\mathcal{RG}_{\mathcal{Z}}$.

Proof. In order to prove VBB security, we want to define an efficient simulator $\mathcal{S}$ that will simulate the view of the adversary using only an oracle access to C_K.

Similarly to the definition of the $\mathcal{RG}_{\mathcal{Z}}$ oracle in Sect. 2.2, the simulator $\mathcal{S}$ will need to act differently when a non-trivial encoding of zero is encountered (that is, simulate the performance of $\mathcal{RG}_{\mathcal{Z}}$ when decode = true). The simulator will maintain a variable decode that upon initialization will be set to false and only when we encounter a non-trivial encoding of zero it will be set to true. As long as decode = false, we use the hardness of factorization in order to show that finding non-trivial zero using invalid monomials is unlikely, therefore up to the point where such encoding is found, the simulator will not use the factorization of the ring at all. The factorization will only be used afterwards in order to continue the simulation after decode was set to true.

Initialization: The simulator generate a number N which it knows how to factor into three factors p_1, p_2, p_3 (which have $\gcd(p_i, p_j) = 1$ for $i \neq j$, but does not have to be primes). In similar with the $\mathcal{RG}_\mathcal{Z}$ oracle, the simulator will also create a table $\mathcal{L}$. For each encoding the obfuscator outputs, $\mathcal{S}$ will create a row in the table associating random label string with the formal variable represented by the encoding and the appropriate level of the encoding. $\mathcal{S}$, just like the obfuscator, will output a list of label strings for each of the obfuscated encodings and give them to the adversary. The only difference between the simulator and the oracle here is that the ring element is not stored in the table at this point.

$\mathcal{S}$.Add($\mathsf{enc}_1, \mathsf{enc}_2$), $\mathcal{S}$.Mult($\mathsf{enc}_1, \mathsf{enc}_2$), $\mathcal{S}$.Negate(enc): Given an arithmetic operation (Add, Mult, Negate), the simulator will construct an arithmetic-circuit $A_{\mathrm{res}} = A_{\mathsf{enc}_1}$ op A_{enc_2} (where A_{enc_1} and A_{enc_2} are the arithmetic-circuits associated with enc_1 and enc_2 respectively) and check if it is equivalent to one of the other elements in the table with the same level. It can easily be done by subtracting A_{res} from the arithmetic-circuit in the table and using isZero procedure. If they are equivalent, the simulator will response with the same label. Otherwise, the simulator will create a new row in $\mathcal{L}$ containing a new label, A_{res} and the new level. Outputs the label to the adversary.

$\mathcal{S}$.isZero(enc): The isZero algorithm works differently when decode is set to true or false.

The Case Where decode = false: The simulator will check if enc is in $\mathcal{L}$. If not it will output $\perp$, otherwise the simulator use the following algorithm:

1. Use the AoNZero algorithm from Lemma 4.5 on the arithmetic-circuit associated with enc in order to determine whether it evaluates to zero or in order to find an accepting input. If the algorithm output a decision regarding the evaluation of the arithmetic-circuit output it.
2. Otherwise, we note that the adversary together with the simulator up to this point is an efficient algorithm that finds an accepting input. From the definition of the function class (Definition 4.1) we can use the $\mathcal{B}$ algorithm associated with this combined algorithm in order to find the code of the obfuscated circuit C.
3. Generate values to all the formal variables given in the initialization step using the known factorization of the ring. And store the values for future use. We note that when we choose random variables, we could have broken consistency with previous queries, as it could have been that using these values previous isZero calls would have response with true. But note that such inconsistency can only occur with negligible probability.
4. Set decode = true and run $\mathcal{S}$.isZero(enc) again.

Remark 4.4. The isZero algorithm this case can only return that the value is indeed "zero" if the encoded element is a trivial zero. In any other case we either output "non-zero" or we change to the case where decode = true.

The Case Where decode = true: In this case, the simulator has already assigned values to each of the formal variables in the table $\mathcal{L}$, and therefore it can easily evaluate the result of the arithmetic-circuit associated with enc and reply to the isZero accordingly.

S.Decode(enc): If decode = false simply return $\perp$ as this is what the simulator will do. We note that in every arithmetic operation that the adversary does, we initiate isZero on all the elements at the same level. Therefore, if the adversary succeeded in finding a non-trivial zero or received the same element in two different ways, the simulator will change decode to be true. Thus in that case, the simulator has already assigned values to all the formal variables used in the arithmetic-circuit associated with enc. By substituting those variables into this arithmetic-circuit results the decoded value of enc which we can output to the adversary.

Correctness: We want to show the correctness of the S.isZero procedure in both cases. We note that if decode = true, the simulator already knows the function evaluated and it have assignments to all the formal variables that are in use, therefore, it is clear that substituting this values in the arithmetic-circuit associated with the encoding the adversary wish to zero test will yield a correct answer.

On the other hand, while decode = false, the correctness is immediate from the correctness of Lemma 4.5 together with the definition of the AoN class and the hardness of factoring. But using the hardness of factoring is delicate since S knows factors of N, therefore we cannot simply solve factoring using the simulator, because in order to construct the simulator those factors are needed to be known in advanced. We note that once decode = true the hardness of factoring doesn't play a role in the correctness of the simulator.

Because we only care when decode = false, we can construct a new simulator S_1 that will abort when decode = true. It is clear that if AoNZero in S broke factoring while decode = false so it must during S_1. Now, we introduce the simulator S_2 which is similar to S_1 only that S_2 does not know any proper factors of N. We notice that those factors are only being used when we set decode = true, and since S_1 aborts when decode is set to true the behavior of S_1 and S_2 is the same, and therefore the behavior of S_2 and S is the same as long as decode = false.

Now, we want to bound the probability that AoNZero, when being used in the S during the time decode = true, will output a factor or fail (which occurs only in negligible probability as explained in Lemma 4.5). We note that in simulator S_2 the probability to either of those event is negligible since factoring is hard. Thus, because the behavior of S and S_2 is the same as long as decode = false, the probability will have to be negligible in S.

Lemma 4.5. *Let C be from a family of AoN functions. There exists an algorithm AoNZero^C that when given an arithmetic circuit A either determines whether it evaluates to zero, outputs an accepting input for C or output a non-trivial factor of N.*

4.3   Indistinguishability Obfuscation in the Classic Generic Model

In a nutshell, the proof in the classic generic model is simpler since the detection of non-trivial zeros and the decode oracle are not required. However, we cannot rely on recovering the code of the circuit when an accepting input is encountered. Therefore, we have to go over all semi-monomials, and only if all of them are valid and correspond to an accepting input, we declare that the result is zero. This requires computation that scales with 2^n and therefore we must take are parameters large enough to make factoring hard even for such algorithms. See details in the full version [9].

References

1. Ananth, P.V., Gupta, D., Ishai, Y., Sahai, A.: Optimizing obfuscation: avoiding Barrington's theorem. In: Proceedings of the ACM SIGSAC Conference on Computer and Communications Security, Scottsdale, AZ, USA, 3–7 November 2014, pp. 646–658 (2014)
2. Applebaum, B., Brakerski, Z.: Obfuscating circuits via composite-order graded encoding. In: Dodis, Y., Nielsen, J.B. (eds.) TCC 2015, Part II. LNCS, vol. 9015, pp. 528–556. Springer, Heidelberg (2015)
3. Badrinarayanan, S., Miles, E., Sahai, A., Zhandry, M.: Post-zeroizing obfuscation: new mathematical tools, and the case of evasive circuits. IACR Cryptology ePrint Archive, 2015:167 (2015). To appear in Eurocryppt 2016
4. Barak, B., Bitansky, N., Canetti, R., Kalai, Y.T., Paneth, O., Sahai, A.: Obfuscation for evasive functions. In: Lindell [26], pp. 26–51
5. Barak, B., Garg, S., Kalai, Y.T., Paneth, O., Sahai, A.: Protecting obfuscation against algebraic attacks. In: Nguyen, P.Q., Oswald, E. (eds.) EUROCRYPT 2014. LNCS, vol. 8441, pp. 221–238. Springer, Heidelberg (2014)
6. Barak, B., Goldreich, O., Impagliazzo, R., Rudich, S., Sahai, A., Vadhan, S.P., Yang, K.: On the (im)possibility of obfuscating programs. In: Kilian, J. (ed.) CRYPTO 2001. LNCS, vol. 2139, pp. 1–18. Springer, Heidelberg (2001)
7. Boneh, D., Silverberg, A.: Applications of multilinear forms to cryptography. IACR Cryptology ePrint Archive, 2002:80 (2002)
8. Boneh, D., Wu, D.J., Zimmerman, J.: Immunizing multilinear maps against zeroizing attacks. IACR Cryptology ePrint Archive, 2014:930 (2014)
9. Brakerski, Z., Dagmi, O.: Shorter circuit obfuscation in challenging security models (full version of this work). Cryptology ePrint Archive, Report 2016/418 (2016). http://eprint.iacr.org/2016/418
10. Brakerski, Z., Rothblum, G.N.: Obfuscating conjunctions. In: Canetti, R., Garay, J.A. (eds.) CRYPTO 2013, Part II. LNCS, vol. 8043, pp. 416–434. Springer, Heidelberg (2013)
11. Brakerski, Z., Rothblum, G.N.: Black-box obfuscation for d-cnfs. In: Naor, M. (ed.) Innovations in Theoretical Computer Science, ITCS 2014, Princeton, NJ, USA, 12–14 January 2014, pp. 235–250. ACM (2014)
12. Brakerski, Z., Rothblum, G.N.: Virtual black-box obfuscation for all circuits via generic graded encoding. In: Lindell [26], pp. 1–25
13. Brakerski, Z., Vaikuntanathan, V., Wee, H., Wichs, D.: Obfuscating conjunctions under entropic ring LWE. In: Sudan, M. (ed.) Proceedings of the ACM Conference on Innovations in Theoretical Computer Science, Cambridge, MA, USA, 14–16 January 2016, pp. 147–156. ACM (2016)

14. Canetti, R.: Towards realizing random oracles: hash functions that hide all partial information. In: Kaliski Jr., B.S. (ed.) CRYPTO 1997. LNCS, vol. 1294, pp. 455–469. Springer, Heidelberg (1997)
15. Cheon, J.H., Han, K., Lee, C., Ryu, H., Stehlé, D.: Cryptanalysis of the multilinear map over the integers. In: Oswald, E., Fischlin, M. (eds.) EUROCRYPT 2015. LNCS, vol. 9056, pp. 3–12. Springer, Heidelberg (2015)
16. Cheon, J.H., Lee, C., Ryu, H.: Cryptanalysis of the new CLT multilinear maps. Cryptology ePrint Archive, Report 2015/934 (2015). http://eprint.iacr.org/
17. Coron, J., et al.: Zeroizing without low-level zeroes: new MMAP attacks and their limitations. In: Gennaro, R., Robshaw, M. (eds.) CRYPTO 2015, Part I. LNCS, vol. 9215, pp. 247–266. Springer, Heidelberg (2015)
18. Coron, J.-S., Lepoint, T., Tibouchi, M.: Practical multilinear maps over the integers. In: Canetti, R., Garay, J.A. (eds.) CRYPTO 2013, Part I. LNCS, vol. 8042, pp. 476–493. Springer, Heidelberg (2013)
19. Coron, J., Lepoint, T., Tibouchi, M.: New multilinear maps over the integers. IACR Cryptology ePrint Archive, 2015:162 (2015)
20. Garg, S., Gentry, C., Halevi, S.: Candidate multilinear maps from ideal lattices. In: Johansson, T., Nguyen, P.Q. (eds.) EUROCRYPT 2013. LNCS, vol. 7881, pp. 1–17. Springer, Heidelberg (2013)
21. Garg, S., Gentry, C., Halevi, S., Raykova, M., Sahai, A., Waters, B.: Candidate indistinguishability obfuscation and functional encryption for all circuits. In: 54th Annual IEEE Symposium on Foundations of Computer Science, FOCS 2013, Berkeley, CA, USA, 26–29 October 2013, pp. 40–49 (2013)
22. Gentry, C., Lewko, A., Sahai, A., Waters, B.: Indistinguishability obfuscation from the multilinear subgroup elimination assumption. Cryptology ePrint Archive, Report 2014/309 (2014). To appear in FOCS 2015
23. Gentry, C., Lewko, A., Waters, B.: Witness encryption from instance independent assumptions. In: Garay, J.A., Gennaro, R. (eds.) CRYPTO 2014, Part I. LNCS, vol. 8616, pp. 426–443. Springer, Heidelberg (2014)
24. Hada, S.: Zero-knowledge and code obfuscation. In: Okamoto, T. (ed.) ASIACRYPT 2000. LNCS, vol. 1976, pp. 443–457. Springer, Heidelberg (2000)
25. Hu, Y., Jia, H.: Cryptanalysis of GGH map. Cryptology ePrint Archive, Report 2015/301 (2015). http://eprint.iacr.org/
26. Lindell, Y. (ed.): TCC 2014. LNCS, vol. 8349. Springer, Heidelberg (2014)
27. Maurer, U.M.: Abstract models of computation in cryptography. In: Smart, N.P. (ed.) Cryptography and Coding 2005. LNCS, vol. 3796, pp. 1–12. Springer, Heidelberg (2005)
28. Miles, E., Sahai, A., Weiss, M.: Protecting obfuscation against arithmetic attacks. IACR Cryptology ePrint Archive, 2014:878 (2014)
29. Miles, E., Sahai, A., Zhandry, M.: Annihilation attacks for multilinear maps: cryptanalysis of indistinguishability obfuscation over GGH13. Cryptology ePrint Archive, Report 2016/147 (2016). http://eprint.iacr.org/
30. Minaud, B., Fouque, P.-A.: Cryptanalysis of the new multilinear map over the integers. Cryptology ePrint Archive, Report 2015/941 (2015). http://eprint.iacr.org/
31. Pass, R., Seth, K., Telang, S.: Indistinguishability obfuscation from semantically-secure multilinear encodings. In: Garay, J.A., Gennaro, R. (eds.) CRYPTO 2014, Part I. LNCS, vol. 8616, pp. 500–517. Springer, Heidelberg (2014)

32. Sahai, A., Waters, B.: How to use indistinguishability obfuscation: deniable encryption, and more. In: Shmoys, D.B. (ed.) Symposium on Theory of Computing, STOC, New York, NY, USA, 31 May–03 June 2014, pp. 475–484. ACM (2014)
33. Shoup, V.: Lower bounds for discrete logarithms and related problems. In: Fumy, W. (ed.) EUROCRYPT 1997. LNCS, vol. 1233, pp. 256–266. Springer, Heidelberg (1997)
34. Zimmerman, J.: How to obfuscate programs directly. In: Oswald, E., Fischlin, M. (eds.) EUROCRYPT 2015. LNCS, vol. 9057, pp. 439–467. Springer, Heidelberg (2015)

Bounded KDM Security from iO and OWF

Antonio Marcedone[1]([✉]), Rafael Pass[1], and Abhi Shelat[2]

[1] Cornell University, Ithaca, USA
{marcedone,rafael}@cs.cornell.edu
[2] Northeastern University, Boston, USA
abhi@neu.edu

Abstract. To date, all constructions in the standard model (i.e., without random oracles) of Bounded Key-Dependent Message (KDM) secure (or even just circularly-secure) encryption schemes rely on specific assumptions (LWE, DDH, QR or DCR); all of these assumptions are known to imply the existence of collision-resistant hash functions. In this work, we demonstrate the existence of bounded KDM secure encryption assuming indistinguishability obfuscation for *P/poly* and just one-way functions. Relying on the recent result of Asharov and Segev (STOC'15), this yields the first construction of a Bounded KDM secure (or even circularly secure) encryption scheme from an assumption that provably does not imply collision-resistant hash functions w.r.t. black-box constructions. Combining this with prior constructions, we show how to augment this Bounded KDM scheme into a Bounded CCA2-KDM scheme.

1 Introduction

The notion of Key Dependent Message (KDM) security, introduced by Black et al. [BRS02], requires an encryption scheme to remain secure even if the attacker can request encryptions of functions of the secret key, and more generally encryptions of different secret keys in use by different players. This notion generalizes *circular security* introduced by Camenish and Lysyanskaya [CL01] in which the adversary can request encryptions of the form $\mathsf{Enc}_{pk_i}(sk_{i+1 \bmod N})$. Both circularly-secure and KDM-secure encryption schemes have various applications, such as anonymous credential schemes, the "bootstrapping" technique used to construct fully homomorphic encryption, and disk encryption in the cases where the key itself might be encrypted.

The original works of Black et al. [BRS02] and of Camenish and Lysyanskaya [CL01] provided construction of circularly-secure encryption and even "full" KDM security (where there is no bound on the class of functions) in the Random Oracle model. Subsequent results provided constructions in the standard model (i.e., without random oracles), which is the focus of this paper.

R. Pass—Supported in part by NSF Award CNS-1217821, AFOSR Award FA9550-15-1-0262, a Microsoft Faculty Fellowship, and a Google Faculty Research Award.
A. Shelat—Supported in part by NSF grants CNS-0845811, TC-1111781, TC-0939718, a Microsoft Faculty Fellowship, an SAIC Faculty Award, and a Google Faculty Research Award.

© Springer International Publishing Switzerland 2016
V. Zikas and R. De Prisco (Eds.): SCN 2016, LNCS 9841, pp. 571–586, 2016.
DOI: 10.1007/978-3-319-44618-9_30

Circular Security and KDM for Simple Functions. In a breakthrough result, Boneh et al. [BHHO08], provided the first construction of circular-secure encryption in the standard model (without a random oracle); their construction is based on the DDH assumption. Subsequently, schemes which expanded the class of permissible KDM queries and which were based on different assumptions were presented: Applebaum et al. [ACPS09] obtain KDM security for affine functions under the Learning With Error (LWE) assumption; Brakerski et al. [BGK09] give a transformation to convert a KDM scheme (with some additional properties) into one that is secure w.r.t. a richer class of functions: applying such transformation to the [BHHO08, ACPS09] gives a scheme secure w.r.t. the class to functions that can be expressed as polynomials of bounded degree, and a second one where the class consists of functions expressed as Turing machines of logarithmic size description. Malkin et al. [MTY11] achieves KDM security w.r.t. modular arithmetic circuits of bounded degree but (unbounded) polynomial size, based on the Decisional Composite Residuosity assumption (DCR). Wee [Wee16] explains [BHHO08, BGK09, BG10] as instantiations of a common framework based on smooth projective hashing, but known constructions of such hashing are based on the DDH, QR and DCR assumptions.

Bounded KDM Security. Barak et al. [BHHI10] significantly expand the class of permissible functions by showing how to realize KDM secure encryption for any set of circuits of a-priori bounded size; this notion is referred to as Bounded KDM security. Roughly speaking, their construction shows how to utilize schemes that satisfy KDM-security w.r.t. affine functions (and additional properties, which are satisfied by the known constructions) to get KDM security w.r.t. *any* circuit of bounded size. Their constructions can be instantiated from schemes relying on either DDH or LWE. Applebaum [App14] also show how to use randomized encodings to amplify KDM security against a small class of functions to Bounded KDM security[1].

Our Results. Summarizing, all known constructions in the standard model (i.e., without random oracles) of Bounded KDM secure, and even just circularly-secure encryption rely on specific assumptions (LWE, DDH, QR or DCR). This gives rise to the following natural question:

Can Bounded KDM encryption be based on general assumptions?

In fact, all assumptions under which Bounded KDM schemes can be constructed imply the existence of collision-resistant hash functions. An orthogonal, but related, question is thus:

---

[1] Both [App14, BHHI10] discuss how to strengthen their schemes to achieve a notion called length-dependent KDM security, which is slightly stronger than Bounded KDM security in the sense that the functions queried by the adversary can have circuit size which grows polynomially in the length of their inputs and outputs. We choose to state our result using Bounded KDM security for simplicity of exposition, but our construction can be similarly adapted to achieve this stronger notion by padding the obfuscated circuits appropriately.

Can Bounded KDM encryption be constructed from an assumption that does not imply collision-resistant hash functions?

In this work we address both of these questions *assuming the existence of indistinguishability obfuscation* (iO). Roughly speaking, program obfuscation is a class of cryptographic primitives aimed at making programs "intelligible" while preserving their functionality: in particular, iO guarantees that the obfuscations of two circuits of the size that compute the same function (although potentially very different) are computationally indistinguishable. Our key result shows:

Theorem 1 (Informally Stated). *Assume there exists an indistinguishability obfuscator for $P/poly$, and a family of one way functions, then there exists a Bounded KDM secure public key encryption scheme.*

Interpreting Our Results. Although iO is seemingly stronger than all assumptions from which KDM security could previously be based, our construction relies on assumption of qualitatively different and more general nature (we make no number-theoretic or lattice-based assumptions).

By the recent beautiful result by Asharov and Segev [AS15], it is known that black-box construction of CRH from iO and OWF is not possible[2], and as such, the assumption we use are separated (at least w.r.t. oracle-aided black-box constructions) from the assumptions previously used. As such, our work also addresses the second italicized question[3]. Notably, by embedding (in the security reduction) the code of the functions that the adversary asks as queries inside obfuscated circuits, our construction circumvents the impossibility result of [HH09], which shows that KDM security is impossible to get from any hardness assumption, as long as the reduction's proof of security treats both the adversary and functions queried as black boxes.

CCA2-KDM Security. Camenisch et al. [CCS09] construct a CCA2-KDM secure encryption scheme by using a KDM-secure scheme for the function family, an NIZK proof system, a CCA2-secure encryption scheme, a strongly secure one time signature scheme, and applying the Naor-Yung construction [NY90]. By combining our Bounded-KDM construction with the known constructions of CCA2 encryption and NIZK from sub-exponentially secure iO, one-way functions and signatures, we construct bounded CCA2-KDM secure encryption.

---

[2] They show that a CRHF cannot be constructed in a blackbox-manner from a one-way permutation and an indistinguishability obfuscator for all polynomial-sized *oracle-aided* circuits without exponential-loss in security. Such oracle-aided circuits can model most common uses of iO in cryptographic constructions such as puncturing in which the circuits that are obfuscated make oracle calls to the one-way permutation.

[3] In fact, combining our result with [AS15] directly rules black-box constructions of CRH from single-key BKDM security. On the other hand, it is not directly clear whether our final construction of multi-key BKDM falls into the class of oracle-aided circuits.

IND-CPA Security and Circular Security. The dual problem of separating IND-CPA security from n-circular (and therefore KDM) security for $n > 1$ has also been open for a long time, and was solved assuming indistinguishability obfuscation and one way functions in [MO14, KRW15], and more recently relying on LWE in [KW16, AP16].

1.1   Proof Overview

Informally, the (N, L)-Bounded KDM security definition[4] states that no efficient adversary has non-negligible advantage in the following game:

1. The challenger generates a random bit b and N key pairs $(sk_1, PK_1), \ldots,$ (sk_N, PK_N) (where the secret keys have length k) and runs the adversary $\mathcal{A}$ on input the public keys.
2. $\mathcal{A}$ can adaptively make queries of the form (h, i), where $i \in \{1, \ldots, N\}$ and h is a circuit of size at most L, input size kN and output size k (representing a function from N secret keys to a k bit message). If $b = 1$, $\mathcal{A}$ receives an encryption $\mathsf{Enc}_{PK_i}(h(sk_1, \ldots, sk_n))$, and otherwise receives $\mathsf{Enc}_{PK_i}(0^k)$.
3. $\mathcal{A}$ halts and outputs a bit b'. $\mathcal{A}$ wins if $b = b'$.

The Single-Key Case. We start by giving an high level overview of our Bounded KDM secure scheme in the simpler case where $N = 1$. The secret key of our construction is just a string $s \in \{0, 1\}^k$, while the public key consists of (p, K), where K is the key for an injective[5] one way function and $p = \mathrm{OWF}_K(s)$. To encrypt a message m, the ciphertext consists of the obfuscation of a program that on input x returns m if $\mathrm{OWF}_K(x) = p$ and $\bot$ otherwise. Decryption consists of running the obfuscated ciphertext program on input the secret key.

Informally, such a scheme should be IND-CPA secure because, if we treat the obfuscation as a black box, the only way to extract the message from a ciphertext (i.e. an obfuscated circuit) is to run the circuit on input the secret key, which is a sufficiently long uniformly random string. To argue the IND-CPA security of the scheme relying on an indistinguishability obfuscator, one can instead leverage a theorem from [BCP14]: informally, any adversary that distinguishes obfuscations of two circuits that differ on polynomially many inputs can be turned into an adversary that computes one input on which the two circuits differ. Therefore, an adversary distinguishing between encryptions of two different messages, i.e. only having different output on input an x such that $\mathrm{OWF}_K(x) = p$, can be turned into an adversary that computes such an x, effectively inverting the one way function.

---

[4] For simplicity, in this paper we assume that the message and key space of the encryption scheme are both $\{0, 1\}^k$, where k is the security parameter.

[5] [BPW16] shows how to construct a family of one way functions where randomly sampled functions are injective with overwhelming probability. Their construction requires $i\mathcal{O}$, one way functions and q-wise independent hashing, as detailed in Sect. 2.

To prove that the scheme is also KDM secure, the simulator needs to answer queries about a function h of a secret key s it does not know: this can be achieved by obfuscating a program that on input x, first checks whether $\mathrm{OWF}_K(x) = p$, and then returns either $h(x)$ if the check passes or $\bot$ otherwise. Since this new program is functionally equivalent to an honest encryption of $h(s)$ (as the one way function is injective[6] and therefore there is only one input s that passes the equality test, namely the secret key), indistinguishability obfuscation guarantees that no adversary will notice the difference. Moreover, since such a simulation does not require the secret key, we can later switch (in a standard hybrid argument) to a game where the public key is a pair (p, K) on which the simulator wants to invert the one way function, and prove security as in the IND-CPA case. This proof outline omits several subtle corner cases which complicate the formal proof.

The Multi-key Case. We can extend the idea of computing $h(s)$ "on the fly" inside the ciphertext program when the correct secret key is given as input to the case where multiple secret keys are involved. The challenge is that the new ciphertext program is given as input only one of the secret keys and has to compute a function possibly depending on other independently generated keys[7].

We circumvent the problem by embedding in the simulated ciphertexts the relationship between secret keys $s_1, \ldots, s_n$ in the form a vector $r = (s_1 \oplus s_1, s_2 \oplus s_1, \ldots, s_n \oplus s_1)$. Note that the vector itself is uniformly distributed (since the secret keys are, except for the first component $0^k = s_1 \oplus s_1$ which is left there for convenience of notation) and it allows the (simulated) ciphertext program, given one of the secret keys, to compute on the fly all the other secret keys (and therefore functions of them).

To reduce the security of the encryption scheme to the hardness of inverting the one way function, we have one last problem: the simulator has to compute the vector r without knowing the secret keys. Equivalently, we use the vector r to define the secret keys: the simulator will get a tuple (p_1, K_1) for which it has to find a preimage and sample a random r, thus implicitly defining each secret key s_i as the string that satisfies $\mathrm{OWF}_{K_1}(s_i \oplus r_i) = p_1$. Note that this change does not modify the distribution of the secret keys and that the ciphertext programs will still be functionally equivalent to the ones in the real experiment. However, the simulator now cannot compute as public keys values (p_i, K_i) consistent with $p_i = \mathrm{OWF}_{K_i}(s_i)$. We therefore modify the original encryption scheme so that the public keys are also released in obfuscated form: the modified encryption scheme will have as public keys obfuscations of programs that have (p_i, K_i) embedded and on input x output 1 if $p_i \overset{?}{=} \mathrm{OWF}_{K_i}(x)$ and $\bot$ otherwise.

---

[6] To be more precise, the function is only injective with overwhelming probability. We will deal with this and other subtleties in the formal proof.

[7] Note that [BHHI10] solves the problem by embedding in their ciphertexts an encryption of the other secret keys under the appropriate public key, which is why circular security is required as an additional assumption for their underlying encryption scheme.

The ciphertexts will be modified accordingly as obfuscations of programs that have the obfuscated public key PK embedded and on input x return the message if $PK(x) \overset{?}{=} 1$ and $\bot$ otherwise. In the simulation, these public key programs will be substituted with (functionally equivalent) obfuscated programs that output 1 iff $p_1 = \mathrm{OWF}_{K_1}(x \oplus r_i)$. This last modification allows the simulation to be completed without knowledge of any of the secret keys.

Lastly, as before, the same lemma from [BCP14] allows us to switch to a hybrid in which all the ciphertexts returned to the adversary are encryptions of 0; this implies the KDM security of the scheme.

2   Preliminaries

Notation and Conventions. If S is a finite set $s \leftarrow S$ is a uniformly random sample from S. If A is a randomized algorithm, $x \leftarrow A$ is the output of A on a uniformly random input tape.

Definition 1 (Injective OWF Family (as Stated in [BPW16])). *Let l be a polynomially-bounded length function. An efficiently computable family of functions*

$$\mathcal{OWF} = \{\mathrm{OWF}_K : \{0,1\}^k \rightarrow \{0,1\}^* : K \in \{0,1\}^{l(k)}, k \in \mathbb{N}\}$$

associated with an efficient (probabilistic) key sampler $\mathcal{K}_{\mathcal{OWF}}$ is said to be an injective OWF family if it satisfies:

1. **Injectiveness:** *With overwhelming probability over the choice of $K \leftarrow \mathcal{K}_{\mathcal{OWF}}(1^k)$, the function OWF_K is injective*
2. **One-wayness:** *For any polysize inverter Adv there exists a negligible function $\mathrm{negl}(\cdot)$, such that for all $k \in \mathbb{N}$,*

$$\Pr\left[x \leftarrow \{0,1\}^k, K \leftarrow \mathcal{K}_{\mathcal{OWF}}(1^k) : \mathsf{Adv}(K, \mathrm{OWF}_K(x)) \overset{?}{=} x\right] \leq \mathrm{negl}(k)$$

[BPW16] shows how to construct injective one way functions assuming one way functions and indistinguishability obfuscation.

2.1   Bounded Key Dependent Message Security

Definition 2 (KDM Security w.r.t. $\mathcal{H}$). *Let $\mathsf{PKE} = (\mathsf{Gen}, \mathsf{Enc}, \mathsf{Dec})$ be a public key encryption scheme with message space $\mathcal{M}$ and secret key space $\mathcal{K}$, where for simplicity we assume $\mathcal{M} = \mathcal{K} = \{0,1\}^k$. Fix a positive integer valued function $N = N(k) > 0$. Consider the following probabilistic experiment (i.e. a random variable) between a challenger and an adversary $\mathcal{A}$, parametrized by a bit b:*

$\mathbf{KDM}_{N,\mathcal{A}}^b(k)$:

– *The challenger runs $N = N(k)$ times $\mathsf{Gen}(1^k)$ to get $(pk_1, sk_1), \ldots,$ (pk_N, sk_N) and runs the adversary $\mathcal{A}$ on input $\mathbf{pk} = (pk_1, \ldots, pk_N)$.*

– *The adversary can adaptively submit queries of the form* (h, i), *where* $h :$ $\mathcal{K}^N \rightarrow \mathcal{M}$ *is a function (encoded as a circuit) and* $i \in 1, \ldots, N$. *If* $b = 1$, *the challenger answers these queries with* $Enc(pk_i, h(\mathbf{sk}))$, *otherwise with* $Enc(pk_i, 0^k)$, *where* $\mathbf{sk} = (sk_1, \ldots, sk_N)$.
– *The adversary stops and outputs a bit* b', *which is defined as the output of the game (i.e. the value of the random variable).*

The KDM advantage of $\mathcal{A}$ *is defined as*

$$\mathsf{Adv}^{KDM}_{PKE,N,\mathcal{A}}(k) \stackrel{\text{def}}{=} |\Pr[\mathbf{KDM}^1_{N,\mathcal{A}}(k) = 1] - \Pr[\mathbf{KDM}^0_{N,\mathcal{A}}(k) = 1]|$$

We say that PKE *is KDM secure with respect to a function class* $\mathcal{H} = \{\mathcal{H}_k\}$ *iff for every polynomial* N *and every PPT* A *that in the above game only queries the challenger with functions* $h \in \mathcal{H}_k$, *the advantage function* $\mathsf{Adv}^{KDM}_{PKE,N,\mathcal{A}}(k)$ *is negligible in* k.

Definition 3 (Bounded KDM Security). *A public key encryption scheme* PKE *is said to be* (N, L)-*Bounded KDM secure if it is KDM secure with respect to the class* $\mathcal{H} = \{\mathcal{H}_k\}$, *where* $\mathcal{H}_k$ *consists of all functions* $h : \mathcal{K}^{N(k)} \rightarrow \mathcal{M}$ *that can be encoded as circuits[8] of size bounded by the polynomial function* $L(k)$.

Note that, for simplicity, we have denoted with $N(k)$ both the arity of the functions in $\mathcal{H}$ and the number of key pairs generated in the security experiment above. In general, the number of keys in the experiment might be higher than the arity of the functions in $\mathcal{H}$, and it is easy to extend our proofs to hold even in this case.

2.2 Indistinguishability Obfuscation

Definition 4 (Indistinguishability Obfuscation [GGH+13]). *Given a circuit class* $\{\mathcal{C}_k\}$, *a (uniform) PPT machine* $i\mathcal{O}$ *is called an indistinguishability obfuscator (iO) for* $\{\mathcal{C}_k\}$ *if it satisfies:*

Preserving Functionality: *For every* $k \in \mathbb{N}$ *and* $C \in \mathcal{C}_k$,

$$\Pr[C'(x) = C(x)|C' \leftarrow i\mathcal{O}(k, C)] = 1 \quad \forall x$$

Indistinguishability: *For any (not necessarily uniform) polynomial-size distinguisher* $\mathcal{D}$, *all security parameters* k *and all couples* $C_0, C_1 \in \mathcal{C}_k$ *such that* $C_0(x) = C_1(x)$ *for all inputs* x, *we have that*

$$\left| \Pr[D(i\mathcal{O}(k, C_0)) = 1] - \Pr[D(i\mathcal{O}(k, C_1)) = 1] \right| \leq \mathrm{negl}(k)$$

---

[8] Recall that we assume for simplicity $\mathcal{M} = \mathcal{K} = \{0,1\}^k$.

2.3 Extractability Obfuscation

Definition 5 (Weak Extractability Obfuscation [BCP14]). *A uniform transformation $\mathcal{O}$ is a weak extractability obfuscator for a class of circuits $\mathcal{C} = \{\mathcal{C}_k\}$ if the following holds. For every PPT adversary $\mathcal{A}$ and polynomial $p(k)$, there exists a PPT algorithm E and polynomials $p_E(k), t_E(k)$ for which the following holds. For every polynomial $d(k)$, for all sufficiently large k, and every pair of circuits $C_0, C_1 \in \mathcal{C}_k$ differing on at most $d(k)$ inputs, and every auxiliary input z,*

$$\Pr[b \leftarrow \{0,1\}; \tilde{C} \leftarrow \mathcal{O}(1^k, C_b) : \mathcal{A}(1^k, \tilde{C}, C_0, C_1, z) = b] \geq \frac{1}{2} + \frac{1}{p(k)}$$

$$\Rightarrow \Pr[x \leftarrow E(1^k, C_0, C_1, z) : C_0(x) \neq C_1(x)] \geq \frac{1}{p_E(k)},$$

and the runtime of E is $t_E(k, d(k))$.

Lemma 1 ([BCP14]). *Let $i\mathcal{O}$ be an indistinguishability obfuscator for $P/poly$. Then $i\mathcal{O}$ is also a weak extractability obfuscator for $P/poly$.*

3 (1,L)-Bounded KDM Construction

The scheme is parametrized over a polynomial function $L(k)$ (which is a bound on the size of the circuits for which we can prove the Bounded KDM security of the scheme).

Π_L :

Key Generation: The algorithm $\mathsf{Gen}(1^k)$ generates a random secret key $s \leftarrow \{0,1\}^k$ and a key for an injective one way function $K \leftarrow \mathcal{K}_{\mathcal{OWF}}(1^k)$. It outputs s as the secret key and the couple (p, K) where $p \leftarrow \mathsf{OWF}_K(s)$ as the public key.

Encryption: The algorithm $\mathsf{Enc}((p, K), m)$ on input a public key (p, K) and a message $m \in \{0,1\}^k$ outputs an obfuscated circuit $C \leftarrow i\mathcal{O}(G_{p,K,m}(\cdot))$ (the circuit $G_{p,K,m}$ is described in Fig. 1).

Decryption: The algorithm $\mathsf{Dec}(s, \overline{C})$ on input a secret key $s \in \{0,1\}^k$ and a ciphertext $\overline{C} \in \mathcal{P}$ outputs $m' = \overline{C}(s)$.

It can be verified that correctness of the Obfuscator implies correctness of the encryption scheme. The following theorem argues that the scheme achieves Bounded KDM Security.

Theorem 2. *If $i\mathcal{O}$ is an indistinguishability obfuscator for $P/poly$ and $\mathcal{OWF}$ is a family of injective one way functions, then for any polynomial function $L(\cdot)$ the encryption scheme $\Pi_L = (\mathsf{Gen}, \mathsf{Enc}, \mathsf{Dec})$ described above is $(1, L)$-Bounded KDM secure.*

$G_{p,K,m}$:
Constants: $p \in \{0,1\}^*, m \in \{0,1\}^k, K \in \{0,1\}^{l(k)}$
Inputs: $x \in \{0,1\}^k$

1. If $(\text{OWF}_K(x) \stackrel{?}{=} p)$, then output m; else output $\perp$.

$G'_{p,K,h}$:
Constants: $p \in \{0,1\}^*, h \in \{0,1\}^L, K \in \{0,1\}^{l(k)}$
Inputs: $x \in \{0,1\}^k$

1. If $(\text{OWF}_K(x) \stackrel{?}{=} p)$, then output $h(x)$; else output $\perp$.

All the circuits are padded to a specific length $\ell(k, L)$ which will be specified in the proof.

Fig. 1. Circuits used in the encryption of the (1-L)-Bounded KDM scheme

Proof. The proof proceeds by a hybrid argument. Assume by contradiction that there exists an adversary $\mathcal{A}$ such that $\text{Adv}^{KDM}_{\Pi_L,1,\mathcal{A}}(k)$ is non negligible in k, i.e. there exists a polynomial p such that $\text{Adv}^{KDM}_{\Pi_L,1,\mathcal{A}}(k) > \frac{1}{p(k)}$ for infinitely many k. We define the random variable $\textbf{KDM}^{Hyb}_{1,\mathcal{A}}(k)$ exactly as $\textbf{KDM}^1_{1,\mathcal{A}}(k)$, but where queries $(h, 1)$ by the adversary[9] are answered by returning as the ciphertext an obfuscation $i\mathcal{O}(G'_{p,K,h})$, where (p, K) is the public key generated in the first step of the game and G' is described in Fig. 1. Since $\mathcal{A}$ has non negligible advantage, it must be that either $|\Pr[\textbf{KDM}^1_{1,\mathcal{A}}(k) = 1] - \Pr[\textbf{KDM}^{Hyb}_{1,\mathcal{A}}(k) = 1]|$ or $|\Pr[\textbf{KDM}^{Hyb}_{1,\mathcal{A}}(k) = 1] - \Pr[\textbf{KDM}^0_{1,\mathcal{A}}(k) = 1]|$ are non negligible. However, the next two lemmas will prove that both these quantities are negligible, which is a contradiction and therefore proves the claim. In the following, for brevity, we will denote $\textbf{KDM}^b_{1,\mathcal{A}}(k)$ for $b = 0, 1, Hyb$ as Z_b.

To make sure we can rely on the security of the $i\mathcal{O}$ in the lemmas below, we set $\ell(k, L)$ to be an upper bound on the size of the circuits $G_{p,K,m}$ and $G'_{p,K,h}$ of Fig. 1. $\qquad\qquad\square$

Lemma 2.
$$|\Pr[Z_1 = 1] - \Pr[Z_{Hyb} = 1]| < \text{negl}(k)$$

The proof of the above lemma relies on the security of the $i\mathcal{O}$ obfuscator. For lack of space, it is deferred to the full version of the paper.

Lemma 3.
$$|\Pr[Z_{Hyb} = 1] - \Pr[Z_0 = 1]| < \text{negl}(k)$$

Proof. The proof is by contradiction of the one-wayness property of the function family leveraging Lemma 1. Let $q(k)$ be a (polynomial) upper bound on the

---

[9] Since there is only one public key, in the rest of the theorem we will just refer to the query for a function h and implicitly assume $i = 1$.

number of queries that $\mathcal{A}$ makes. We consider a series of hybrid games: for $j = 0, \ldots, q(k)$ define the random variable H_j as an interactive experiment where the first and third step (i.e. the key generation phase and the output of the game) are defined as in $\mathbf{KDM}^0_{1,\mathcal{A}}(k)$, while the queries are handled as follows. The first $q(k) - j$ queries made by $\mathcal{A}$ are answered with $i\mathcal{O}(G'_{p,K,h})$ (where h is the function the adversary queried), i.e. according to what would happen in game Z_{Hyb}; instead, the last j queries are answered with $i\mathcal{O}(G_{p,K,0^k})$ (i.e. according to Z_0). Since H_0 has the same distribution as Z_{Hyb} and $H_{q(k)}$ has the same distribution as Z_0, to prove the claim it is enough to show that for all j, $|\Pr[H_j = 1] - \Pr[H_{j+1} = 1]| < \mathrm{negl}(k)$.

Assume by contradiction that there exist a specific index j and an adversary $\mathcal{A}$ that can distinguish between H_j and H_{j+1} with non negligible probability $a(k)$. Note that, as in the previous lemma, the view of the adversary in games H_j and H_{j+1} has the same distribution up to the point where $\mathcal{A}$ makes the $(q(k) - j)^{th}$ query. We will use such an adversary to build an adversary B that breaks the one wayness of $\mathcal{OWF}$. B takes as input randomly chosen function key $K \leftarrow \mathcal{K}_{\mathcal{OWF}}$ and the image p of the function on a random input, and has to compute a preimage x such that $\mathrm{OWF}_K(x) = p$.

By Lemma 1, the existence of an adversary C that distinguishes (with non negligible probability) between obfuscations of two circuits that differ on only one input implies the existence of a polynomial time algorithm E that computes the input on which they are different with overwhelming probability. B proceeds in two stages: first, it simulates for $\mathcal{A}$ an experiment similar to H_{j+1}, using its own input (p, K) as the public key and up to the point where the $(q(k)-j)^{th}$ query for a function $\bar{h}$ is asked. Let t be the state of the adversary $\mathcal{A}$ (including its view) at this point in the simulation. Note that this simulation is possible because knowledge of the preimage x is not necessary to compute obfuscations of the programs $G'_{p,K,h}$ that are returned as answers to the queries. As a second step, B can run the algorithm E (given by Lemma 1) on input $(1^k, G'_{p,K,\bar{h}}, G_{p,K,0^k}, t)$, which runs in polynomial time, and return its output.

We now analyze the success of B in two steps: we define a property of the states t sampled by B (a state satisfying the property will be called a "good" state), and show that B samples a good state with non negligible probability. Second, we show there exists an algorithm E that succeeds with noticeable probability conditioned on the fact that t is good.

Denote with T the distribution on the states of $\mathcal{A}$ obtained by running H_{j+1} up to the point where the $(q(k) - j)^{th}$ query for a function $\bar{h}$ is asked. A state $t \leftarrow T$ (containing the public key (p, K) and the $(q(k) - j)^{th}$ query $\bar{h}$) is said to be "good" if all the following holds:

1. K denotes an injective function
2. $\bar{h}$ is such that $\forall x, OWF_K(x) = p \Rightarrow \bar{h}(x) \neq 0^k$
3. $\left| \Pr[H_j = 1|t] - \Pr[H_{j+1} = 1|t] \right| > \frac{a(k)}{2}$. Here $\Pr[H_j = 1|t]$ denotes the probability that the value of the random variable H_j is 1 given that after the $(q(k) - j)^{th}$ query is asked $\mathcal{A}$ is in state t.

Denote with T_g the set of good states, with T_1 the set of states that do not satisfy condition 1, with T_2 the states that satisfy condition 1 but not condition 2, and with T_3 the states that satisfy conditions 1 and 2 but not 3. Note that T_g, T_1, T_2, T_3 are a partition of T. First, although $\mathcal{B}$ executes $\mathcal{A}$ using its own input (p, K) as the public key, when this input is randomly sampled $(x \leftarrow \{0,1\}^k; K \leftarrow \mathcal{K}_{\mathcal{OWF}}(1^k); p \leftarrow \mathrm{OWF}_K(x))$ the distribution of t obtained by $\mathcal{B}$ is exactly T. To argue that $t \leftarrow T$ is good with non negligible probability, assume by contradiction it was not. We have that, by a union bound

$$a(k) = \left| \Pr[H_j = 1 \mid t \in T_g] - \Pr[H_{j+1} = 1 \mid t \in T_g] \right| \Pr[t \in T_g] +$$

$$\sum_{i=1}^{3} \left| \Pr[H_j = 1 \mid t \in T_i] - \Pr[H_{j+1} = 1 \mid t \in T_i] \right| \Pr[t \in T_i] \leq (*)$$

We note that $\Pr[t \in T_1]$ is negligible because the $\mathcal{OWF}$ is injective. Moreover, it is not hard to prove that $\left| \Pr[H_j = 1 \mid t \in T_2] - \Pr[H_{j+1} = 1 \mid t \in T_2] \right|$ is negligible as well: in fact, if $\bar{h}(x) = 0^k$ then $G'_{p,K,\bar{h}}$ and $G_{p,K,0^k}$ would be functionally equivalent, and therefore their obfuscations computationally indistinguishable (because of the security of $i\mathcal{O}$), so $\mathcal{A}$ in an execution from state t would only be able to distinguish between them (and therefore between H_j and H_{j+1}) with negligible probability. Moreover, since for $t \in T_3$ condition 3 is not satisfied, $\left| \Pr[H_j = 1 \mid t \in T_3] - \Pr[H_{j+1} = 1 \mid t \in T_3] \right| \leq a(k)/2$ from which

$$(*) \leq \left| \Pr[H_j = 1 \mid t \in T_g] - \Pr[H_{j+1} = 1 \mid t \in T_g] \right| \Pr[t \in T_g] + \frac{a(k)}{2} + negl(k)$$

Therefore, if $\Pr[t \in T_g]$ was negligible, then $a(k)$ would be bounded by a negligible function, which is a contradiction.

For the second step we prove that, conditioned on $t \in T_g$, $\mathcal{B}$ inverts with non negligible probability. Note that, on good states, there is exactly one x such that $OWF_K(x) = p$, and moreover it holds that $\bar{h}(x) \neq 0^k$. Therefore $G'_{p,K,\bar{h}}$ and $G_{p,K,0^k}$ will differ on input x and have the same output on all others. Under this condition, $\mathcal{B}$ inverts the function iff algorithm E (given by Lemma 1) is successful, which happens with overwhelming probability as long as we can prove that as long as we can prove that there is an adversary C such that for each $t \in T_g$, C distinguishes obfuscations of $G'_{p,K,\bar{h}}$ and $G_{p,K,0^k}$ with non negligible probability. Consider the following adversary $C(O, G'_{p,K,\bar{h}}, G_{p,K,0^k}, t))$:

1. Resume running $\mathcal{A}$ from the saved state t, answering its first (i.e. $(q(k) - j)^{th}$) query with O.
2. Answer all subsequent queries with obfuscations of $G_{p,K,0^k}$.
3. When $\mathcal{A}$ halts outputs a bit b', halt and output the same bit.

Note that when $O \leftarrow i\mathcal{O}(G'_{p,K,h})$, the output of C has the same distribution as $H_j | t$, while if instead C is run on an obfuscation $O \leftarrow i\mathcal{O}(G'_{p,K,0^k})$, the view of $\mathcal{A}$ is consistent with $H_{j+1} | t$.

Therefore, if $t \in T_g$, the advantage of C in distinguishing obfuscations of the two circuits is equal to $\left| \Pr[H_j = 1 \mid t] - \Pr[H_{j+1} = 1 \mid t] \right| > \frac{a(k)}{2}$ which is non negligible. This proves that algorithm E exists and has overwhelming success probability on good states. Since we have also proven that $\mathcal{B}$ samples good states with non negligible probability, we can conclude that it has non negligible probability of inverting the $\mathcal{OWF}$, which contradicts its one-wayness.   □

4   (N,L)-Bounded KDM Construction

The scheme is parametrized over polynomial functions $L(k), N(k)$ (which are bounds on the size of the circuits and number of keys for which we can prove the Bounded KDM security of the scheme).

$F_{p,K}$:
Constants: $p \in \{0,1\}^*, K \in \{0,1\}^{l(k)}$
Inputs: $x \in \{0,1\}^k$

1. if $(\mathrm{OWF}_K(x) \stackrel{?}{=} p)$, then output 1; else output $\bot$.

$F'_{p,r,K}$:
Constants: $p \in \{0,1\}^*, r \in \{0,1\}^k, K \in \{0,1\}^{l(k)}$
Inputs: $x \in \{0,1\}^k$

1. if $(\mathrm{OWF}_K(x \oplus r) \stackrel{?}{=} p)$, then output 1; else output $\bot$.

All the circuits are padded to a specific length $\ell_{PK}(k, N, L)$ which will be specified in the proof.

Fig. 2. Circuits used in the key generation of the (N-L)-Bounded KDM scheme

Π_L :
Key Generation: The algorithm $\mathsf{Gen}(1^k)$ samples a random secret key $s \leftarrow \{0,1\}^k$ and a key for an injective one way function $K \leftarrow \mathcal{K}_{\mathcal{OWF}}(1^k)$. Then it computes $p \leftarrow \mathrm{OWF}_K(s)$. It outputs s as the secret key, and the program $PK(\cdot) \leftarrow i\mathcal{O}(F_{p,K}(\cdot))$ as the public key (the circuit $F_{p,K}$ is described in Fig. 2).
Encryption: The algorithm $\mathsf{Enc}(PK, m)$ on input a public key PK (which is interpreted as an obfuscated program) and a message $m \in \{0,1\}^k$ outputs an obfuscated circuit $C \leftarrow i\mathcal{O}(G_{PK,m}(\cdot))$ (the circuit $G_{PK,m}$ is described in Fig. 3).
Decryption: The algorithm $\mathsf{Dec}(s, \overline{C})$ on input a secret key $s \in \{0,1\}^k$ and a ciphertext $\overline{C} \in \mathcal{P}$ outputs $m' = \overline{C}(s)$.

$G_{PK,m}$:
Constants: $PK \in \{0,1\}^{\ell'_{PK}(k,N,L,iO)}, m \in \{0,1\}^k$
Inputs: $x \in \{0,1\}^k$

1. If $(PK(x) \stackrel{?}{=} 1)$, then output m; else output $\bot$.

$G'_{PK,r,h,i}$:
Constants: $PK \in \{0,1\}^{\ell'_{PK}(k,N,L,iO)}, \mathbf{r} = (r_1,\ldots,r_N) \in \{0,1\}^{k \cdot N}, h \in \mathcal{H}, i \in \{1,\ldots,N\}$
Inputs: $x \in \{0,1\}^k$

1. If $(PK(x \oplus r_i) \stackrel{?}{=} 1)$, then output $h(x \oplus r_i \oplus r_1, \ x \oplus r_i \oplus r_2, \ \ldots, \ x \oplus r_i \oplus r_N)$; else output $\bot$.

All the circuits are padded to a specific length $\ell_{\mathsf{Enc}}(k, N, L, iO)$ which will be specified in the proof.

Fig. 3. Circuits used in the encryption of the (N-L)-Bounded KDM scheme

It can be easily verified that correctness of the Obfuscator implies correctness of the encryption scheme. The following theorem argues that the scheme achieves Bounded KDM Security.

Theorem 3. *If iO is an indistinguishability obfuscator for P/poly and there exists a family of injective $\mathcal{OWF}$, then for any polynomial function L and any $N \in \mathbb{N}$ the encryption scheme $\Pi_{N,L} = (\mathsf{Gen}, \mathsf{Enc}, \mathsf{Dec})$ described above is (N, L)-Bounded KDM secure.*

Proof. The proofs proceeds by an hybrid argument, with a very similar structure to Theorem 2. Given any adversary $\mathcal{A}$ define the following random variables:

Z_1: this is the same as $\mathbf{KDM}^1_{\Pi_{N,L},N,\mathcal{A}}(k)$.
Z_2: this is the same as the previous one, but the public keys are generated as follows: the challenger samples $s_1, \ldots, s_N \leftarrow \{0,1\}^k$ and $K \leftarrow \mathcal{K}_{OWF}$; then it computes $p \leftarrow \mathrm{OWF}_K(s_1)$, $\mathbf{r} \leftarrow (0^k, s_1 \oplus s_2, s_1 \oplus s_3, \ldots, s_1 \oplus s_n)$ and sets $PK_i \leftarrow iO(F'_{p,r_i,K})$ for all i.
Z_{Hyb}: this is the same as the previous one, but queries (h, i) by the adversary are answered by returning as the ciphertext an obfuscation $iO(G'_{PK_1,r,h,i})$. (Note that knowing the secret keys is not needed to simulate this step).
Z_3: this is the same as Z_0, but the public keys are generated (as in Z_2) as follows: the challenger samples $s_1, \ldots, s_N \leftarrow \{0,1\}^k$ and $K \leftarrow \mathcal{K}_{OWF}$; then it computes $p \leftarrow \mathrm{OWF}_K(s_1)$, $\mathbf{r} \leftarrow (0^k, s_1 \oplus s_2, s_1 \oplus s_3, \ldots, s_1 \oplus s_n)$ and sets $PK_i \leftarrow iO(F'_{p,r_i,K})$ for all i.
Z_0: this is the same as $\mathbf{KDM}^0_{\Pi_{N,L},N,\mathcal{A}}(k)$.

Arguing that each couple of consecutive hybrids is indistinguishable is analogous to what was done in the proof of 2. For lack of space, we defer the details to the full version of this paper.

To make sure we can rely on the security of the $i\mathcal{O}$ in all the above hybrids, we first set $\ell_{PK}(k, N, L)$ to be an upper bound on the maximum size of the circuits $F_{p,K}$ and $F'_{p,r,K}$ of Fig. 2 (which depends on k, N, L). Then we can define $\ell'_{PK}(k, N, L, i\mathcal{O})$ (which in turns determines the size of $G_{PK,m}$ and $G'_{PK,r,h,i}$) to be a bound on the size of the output of $i\mathcal{O}$ on input a circuit of length $\ell_{PK}(k, N, L)$. At last, we set $\ell_{\mathsf{Enc}}(k, N, L, i\mathcal{O})$ to be an upper bound on the size of circuits $G_{PK,m}$ and $G'_{PK,r,h,i}$. Notice that all these functions are polynomially bounded. □

Combining the above theorem with the construction of a family of one way permutations by Bitansky et al. [BPW16] gives the following corollary:

Corollary 1. *If there exists an indistinguishability obfuscator for P/poly, and a family of one way functions, then for any polynomial function L and any $N \in \mathbb{N}$ there exists a (N, L)-Bounded KDM secure public key encryption scheme.*

Avoiding Reliance on a Specific OWF. As an additional interesting result, we note that the scheme can be further simplified so that its security does not depend on a specific (injective) one way function, but rather on the existence of an (injective) one way functions which can be computed by a circuit whose size is below an explicitly specified bound. The idea behind this construction is the fact that in our encryption scheme the public key is just an obfuscation of a point function, and therefore an obfuscated public key is indistinguishable from the obfuscation of a program (padded to an appropriate size) which directly checks if its input x is equal to the secret s (as opposed to checking whether $\mathrm{OWF}_K(x) = s$) and therefore does not have to internally compute the one way function.

We can leverage this fact and design a new encryption scheme where the key generation algorithm chooses a secret key s uniformly at random and outputs as the public key the obfuscation of a program that returns 1 iff its input $x \overset{?}{=} s$ (encryption and decryption algorithms are unchanged). To prove security, we argue that the public keys of this new scheme are indistinguishable from the ones of $\Pi_{N,L,i\mathcal{O}}$ (when instantiated with a secure OWF) and therefore reduce to the latter's Bounded KDM security.

Bounded KDM-CCA2 Security. Our construction can also be used to construct Bounded KDM-CCA2 security in which, informally, the KDM adversary may also ask CCA2 queries on any ciphertexts except for the ones received as answers to KDM queries (see [CCS09] for a formal definition). Camenish et al. [CCS09] show a generic transformation for any KDM secure encryption scheme into a KDM-CCA2 secure one (w.r.t. the same family of functions) by applying the Naor-Yung paradigm [NY90]. Their transformation thus requires an NIZK proof system and a CCA2-secure (normal) encryption scheme and a strongly secure one time signature. Combining our construction with their Theorem 1, and the construction of NIZK, CCA2 and signatures from sub-exponentially secure iO and one-way functions from [SW14], we get the following corollary:

Corollary 2. *If there exists a sub-exponentially secure indistinguishability obfuscator for P/poly, and a family of one way functions, then for any polynomial function L and any $N \in \mathbb{N}$ there exists a (N, L)-Bounded KDM-CCA2 secure public key encryption scheme.*

References

[ACPS09] Applebaum, B., Cash, D., Peikert, C., Sahai, A.: Fast cryptographic primitives and circular-secure encryption based on hard learning problems. In: Halevi, S. (ed.) CRYPTO 2009. LNCS, vol. 5677, pp. 595–618. Springer, Heidelberg (2009)

[AP16] Alamati, N., Peikert, C.: Three's compromised too: circular insecurity for any cycle length from (ring-) LWE. Technical report, Cryptology ePrint Archive, Report /110 (2016)

[App14] Applebaum, B.: Key-dependent message security: generic amplification and completeness. J. Cryptology 27(3), 429–451 (2014)

[AS15] Asharov, G., Segev, G.: Limits on the power of indistinguishability obfuscation and functional encryption. In: FOCS 2015. IEEE (2015)

[BCP14] Boyle, E., Chung, K.-M., Pass, R.: On extractability obfuscation. In: Lindell, Y. (ed.) TCC 2014. LNCS, vol. 8349, pp. 52–73. Springer, Heidelberg (2014)

[BG10] Brakerski, Z., Goldwasser, S.: Circular and leakage resilient public-key encryption under subgroup indistinguishability. In: Rabin, T. (ed.) CRYPTO 2010. LNCS, vol. 6223, pp. 1–20. Springer, Heidelberg (2010)

[BGK09] Brakerski, Z., Goldwasser, S., Kalai, Y.: Circular-secure encryption beyond affine functions. Technical report, Citeseer (2009)

[BHHI10] Barak, B., Haitner, I., Hofheinz, D., Ishai, Y.: Bounded key-dependent message security. In: Gilbert, H. (ed.) EUROCRYPT 2010. LNCS, vol. 6110, pp. 423–444. Springer, Heidelberg (2010)

[BHHO08] Boneh, D., Halevi, S., Hamburg, M., Ostrovsky, R.: Circular-secure encryption from decision Diffie-Hellman. In: Wagner, D. (ed.) CRYPTO 2008. LNCS, vol. 5157, pp. 108–125. Springer, Heidelberg (2008)

[BPW16] Bitansky, N., Paneth, O., Wichs, D.: Perfect structure on the edge of chaos. In: Kushilevitz, E., et al. (eds.) TCC 2016-A. LNCS, vol. 9562, pp. 474–502. Springer, Heidelberg (2016)

[BRS02] Black, J., Rogaway, P., Shrimpton, T.: Encryption-scheme security in the presence of key-dependent messages. In: Nyberg, K., Heys, H.M. (eds.) SAC 2002. LNCS, vol. 2595, pp. 62–75. Springer, Heidelberg (2003)

[CCS09] Camenisch, J., Chandran, N., Shoup, V.: A public key encryption scheme secure against key dependent chosen plaintext and adaptive chosen ciphertext attacks. In: Joux, A. (ed.) EUROCRYPT 2009. LNCS, vol. 5479, pp. 351–368. Springer, Heidelberg (2009)

[CL01] Camenisch, J.L., Lysyanskaya, A.: An efficient system for non-transferable anonymous credentials with optional anonymity revocation. In: Pfitzmann, B. (ed.) EUROCRYPT 2001. LNCS, vol. 2045, pp. 93–118. Springer, Heidelberg (2001)

[GGH+13] Garg, S., Gentry, C., Halevi, S., Raykova, M., Sahai, A., Waters, B.: Candidate indistinguishability obfuscation and functional encryption for all circuits. In: FOCS 2013. IEEE (2013)

[HH09] Haitner, I., Holenstein, T.: On the (im)possibility of key dependent encryption. In: Reingold, O. (ed.) TCC 2009. LNCS, vol. 5444, pp. 202–219. Springer, Heidelberg (2009)

[KRW15] Koppula, V., Ramchen, K., Waters, B.: Separations in circular security for arbitrary length key cycles. In: Dodis, Y., Nielsen, J.B. (eds.) TCC 2015, Part II. LNCS, vol. 9015, pp. 378–400. Springer, Heidelberg (2015)

[KW16] Koppula, V., Waters, B.: Circular security counterexamples for arbitrary length cycles from LWE. Technical report, Cryptology ePrint Archive, Report /117 (2016)

[MO14] Marcedone, A., Orlandi, C.: Obfuscation $\rightarrow$ (IND-CPA security $\nrightarrow$ circular security). In: Abdalla, M., De Prisco, R. (eds.) SCN 2014. LNCS, vol. 8642, pp. 77–90. Springer, Heidelberg (2014)

[MTY11] Malkin, T., Teranishi, I., Yung, M.: Efficient circuit-size independent public key encryption with KDM security. In: Paterson, K.G. (ed.) EUROCRYPT 2011. LNCS, vol. 6632, pp. 507–526. Springer, Heidelberg (2011)

[NY90] Naor, M., Yung, M.: Public-key cryptosystems provably secure against chosen ciphertext attacks. In: STOC 1990. ACM (1990)

[SW14] Sahai, A., Waters, B.: How to use indistinguishability obfuscation: deniable encryption, and more. In: STOC 2014. ACM (2014)

[Wee16] Wee, H.: KDM-security via homomorphic smooth projective hashing. In: Cheng, C.-M., et al. (eds.) PKC 2016. LNCS, vol. 9615, pp. 159–179. Springer, Heidelberg (2016)

A Unified Approach to Idealized Model Separations via Indistinguishability Obfuscation

Matthew D. Green[1], Jonathan Katz[2], Alex J. Malozemoff[2],
and Hong-Sheng Zhou[3]([⊠])

[1] Johns Hopkins University, Baltimore, USA
mgreen@cs.jhu.edu
[2] University of Maryland, College Park, USA
{jkatz,amaloz}@cs.umd.edu
[3] Virginia Commonwealth University, Richmond, USA
hszhou@vcu.edu

Abstract. It is well known that the random-oracle (RO) model is not sound in the sense that there are schemes that are secure in the RO model but are insecure when instantiated by any family of hash functions. However, existing separation results do not hold for *all* cryptographic schemes in the RO model (e.g., bit encryption), leaving open the possibility that such schemes can be soundly instantiated.

In this work we refute this possibility, assuming the existence of indistinguishability obfuscation. First, we present a separation for bit encryption; namely, we show that there exists a bit-encryption protocol secure in the RO model but is insecure when the random oracle is instantiated by any concrete function. Second, we show how to adapt this separation to work for most natural simulation-based and game-based definitions. Our techniques can easily be adapted to other idealized models, and thus we present a *unified approach* to showing separations for many protocols of interest in various idealized models.

1 Introduction

A common technique in cryptography is the use of *idealized models*, where one assumes oracle access to some (ideal) process. Idealized models provide powerful mechanisms for constructing elegant and simple protocols while still being able

Full version available at http://eprint.iacr.org/2014/863.

M.D. Green—Work supported in part by the Defense Advanced Research Projects Agency (DARPA) and the Air Force Research Laboratory (AFRL) under contract FA8750-11-2-0211 and the Office of Naval Research under contract N00014-14-1-0333.

J. Katz—Work supported in part by NSF award #1223623.

A.J. Malozemoff—Work supported in part by NSF award #1223623 and with Government support through the National Defense Science and Engineering Graduate (NDSEG) Fellowship, 32 CFG 168a, awarded by DoD, Air Force Office of Scientific Research.

© Springer International Publishing Switzerland 2016
V. Zikas and R. De Prisco (Eds.): SCN 2016, LNCS 9841, pp. 587–603, 2016.
DOI: 10.1007/978-3-319-44618-9_31

to provide some provable guarantees. Some common examples of such models are the random oracle model [5], the generic group model [28], and more recently, the generic graded encoding model [1,7], among others.

Over the past several years, there has been significant interest in understanding the implications of using these models when developing cryptographic protocols. Indeed, it is well-known that such models do not match "reality" in the sense that there exist secure schemes in generic models which are not secure when concretely instantiated. The first work to present such a result was that of Canetti, Goldreich, and Halevi [10], who showed such a separation for the random oracle model. Following this result, Dent showed a similar separation for the generic group model [15]. Likewise, a separation for the generic graded encoding model has been demonstrated by Brakerski and Rothblum and Barak et al. [1,7], who each construct virtual black-box obfuscators in the generic graded encoding model even though it is known that virtual black-box obfuscation is impossible in the standard model [2].

However, each of the above separation results employs different techniques and only covers a subset of cryptographic schemes. For example, the random oracle separation presented by Canetti et al. [10] does not apply to CPA-secure bit-encryption [16]. Thus, the existing results have left open the possibility that certain protocol classes (such as bit-encryption) are not subject to the counterexamples described in prior work. We note that this omission may have practical implications due to the renewed interest in fully-homomorphic bit-encryption systems secure in the random oracle model [13,19]. More fundamentally, it leaves us with critical gaps in our theoretical understanding of the security of cryptosystems analyzed in idealized models. Might these exceptions provide a "loophole" through which certain protocols could be safely instantiated?

Our Results. In this work, we refute this notion, assuming the existence of indistinguishability obfuscation ($i\mathcal{O}$). Specifically, we show that if there exists a secure $i\mathcal{O}$ scheme (in the standard model), then for a large class of cryptographic tasks there exists a variant of said protocol which is secure in a given idealized model but completely insecure when concretely instantiated.

The core of our technique is using $i\mathcal{O}$ to obfuscate a circuit which hides some secret information needed to break security. Finding the proper input to reveal this secret information in the idealized model is hard, whereas as soon as the idealized model is instantiated by some concrete function, it is easy to construct a proper input. Our specific results are as follows:

1. *A counterexample for bit-encryption in the random oracle model.* Our first result is to show a separation for bit-encryption in the random oracle model (Sect. 3). In presenting our counterexample we solve a longstanding open problem raised by Dent [15]. Simultaneously, we demonstrate the generality of our technique by observing that the same result cannot be derived using the original Canetti et al. [10] or Maurer et al. [26] approaches, since these do not work for bit-encryption.

   Specifically, our result shows that if an $i\mathcal{O}$ scheme exists in the standard model, then for any length ℓ, there exists an IND-CPA secure bit-encryption scheme that is provably secure when a hash function h is instantiated using a random oracle, but becomes *insecure* when h is instantiated using any concrete function which can be represented in $\leq \ell$ bits. To achieve this result we employ the obfuscation of a universal circuit, and show how an adversary with knowledge of the description of h can win the IND-CPA game with non-negligible probability.[1] As in previous counterexamples, the proposed scheme breaks *catastrophically* when instantiated using a concrete function by revealing the secret key for the scheme.

2. *A generic approach to constructing idealized model separations for cryptographic tasks.* Next, we generalize our initial result to show random oracle model separations for most natural protocols secure under simulation-based or game-based definitions (Sect. 4). These results can be easily adapted to apply to other idealized models, including the generic group model, the random permutation model, etc. Thus, we present a unified approach to constructing separations for most cryptographic tasks of interest in most idealized models of interest.

These results deepen our understanding of how to define "secure" protocols and help us to understand the implications of these idealized models. They also provide additional justification for the ongoing effort to develop new and *instantiable* assumptions/models in which we may analyze these protocols (e.g., the UCE framework [4]).

1.1 Related Work

The random oracle model was first introduced formally by Bellare and Rogaway [5]; this was also the first work to put forward the notion of an "idealized model" as a way to simplify both cryptographic constructions and proofs. However, soon after Canetti et al. [10] demonstrated that the random oracle model is not *sound* in the sense that there exist schemes secure in the random oracle model but completely insecure when instantiated in the standard model. This separation spawned a large body of work showing separations for both new classes of protocols [3,11,17,20,24,25,27] as well as other idealized models [15].

In a separate line of work, since the breakthrough result of Garg et al. [18] demonstrating a candidate indistinguishability obfuscation ($i\mathcal{O}$) scheme, several works have studied the implications of $i\mathcal{O}$; here, we discuss those most relevant to our work. Bitansky et al. [6] showed that virtual-black-box obfuscation cannot exist for super-polynomial pseudo-entropic functions assuming $i\mathcal{O}$ exists. Their techniques are similar in spirit to ours, in that they utilize the "uncompressability" of certain classes of functions to derive their separation, similar to how we utilize the "uncompressability" of the random oracle.

Concurrently and independently, Brzuska, Farshim, and Mittelbach [8] show that some cryptographic transformations based on random oracles are uninstantiable in the standard model. Their underlying technique is very similar to ours

---

[1] Note that using $i\mathcal{O}$ for *circuit* obfuscation only gives a separation for hash functions of *a priori* fixed length.

at a high level, in that they obfuscate a universal circuit taking as input the description of a hash function; the technical details, however, differ. Besides the similarity in the underlying technique, both works are in some sense orthogonal, as Brzuska et al. [8] show separations for cryptographic *transformations* whereas we show separations for cryptographic *constructions*.

Finally, a recent line of work constructs schemes which use *both* $i\mathcal{O}$ and the random oracle model [14,21,22]. Our results serve as a warning sign that combining these two approaches may lead to insecure schemes when the random oracle is instantiated in the standard model.

2   Preliminaries

Let n denote the security parameter. For a polynomial-time function f, we let $\langle f \rangle$ denote the (binary) *description* of an algorithm computing f. We use the notation $x \leftarrow_{\$} S$ to denote that x is chosen uniformly at random from the set S, and use PPT to mean "probabilistic polynomial time". As our main results show separations in the random oracle model (although our results can be extended to other idealized models), we review this idealized model and how to instatiate it in the standard model using *function ensembles* [10].

Random Oracle Model. Let $\ell_{\text{out}} : \mathbb{N} \to \mathbb{N}$ be a length function. The random oracle model is defined by a (stateful) function $\mathcal{O} : \{0,1\}^* \to \{0,1\}^{\ell_{\text{out}}(n)}$ available to all parties which works as follows: $\mathcal{O}$ maintains an internal table T which stores inputs and their associated outputs. If $x \in T$, let $T(x)$ denote the associated output. On input x, If $x \in T$, then $\mathcal{O}$ outputs $T(x)$; otherwise, $\mathcal{O}$ chooses $y \leftarrow_{\$} \{0,1\}^{\ell_{\text{out}}(n)}$, adds (x, y) to T, and outputs y.

Initialization: Security parameter 1^n, length function $\ell_{\text{out}} : \mathbb{N} \to \mathbb{N}$, list of parties $P_1, \dots, P_m$, and adversary $\mathcal{A}$.

1. $\mathcal{F}_{\text{RO}}$ maintains a table T which stores inputs and their associated outputs; if $x \in T$, let $T(x)$ denote the associated output.
2. On receiving value $x \in \{0,1\}^*$ from party P_i or $\mathcal{A}$, $\mathcal{F}_{\text{RO}}$ does the following:
   - If $x \in T$, output $T(x)$ to the appropriate party.
   - Otherwise, choose $y \leftarrow_{\$} \{0,1\}^{\ell_{\text{out}}(n)}$, add (x, y) to T, and output y to the appropriate party.

Fig. 1. Functionality $\mathcal{F}_{\text{RO}}$.

We define ideal functionalities $\mathcal{F}_{\text{RO}}$ (for a random oracle [23]) and $\mathcal{F}_{\text{GG}}$ (for a generic group) in Figs. 1 and 2, respectively.

Function Ensembles. We use the notion of *function ensembles* introduced by Canetti et al. [10], and we reproduce it here mostly verbatim. The idea

---

Initialization: Security parameter 1^n, length function $\ell_{\text{out}} : \mathbb{N} \to \mathbb{N}$, n-bit prime p, set $S = \{0,1\}^{\ell_{\text{out}}(n)}$, list of parties $P_1, \ldots, P_m$, and adversary $\mathcal{A}$.

1. $\mathcal{F}_{\text{GG}}$ maintains a table T which stores inputs and their associated outputs; if $x \in T$, let $T(x)$ denote the associated output.
2. On receiving tuple (enc, x) from party P_i or $\mathcal{A}$, $\mathcal{F}_{\text{GG}}$ does the following:
   - If $x \notin \mathbb{Z}_p$, output $\perp$ to the appropriate party.
   - If $x \in T$, output $T(x)$ to the appropriate party.
   - Otherwise, choose $y \leftarrow_{\$} S$ conditioned on y not appearing as an output in T, add (x, y) to T, and output y to the appropriate party.
3. On receiving tuple (add, y, y', b) from party P_i or $\mathcal{A}$, $\mathcal{F}_{\text{GG}}$ does the following:
   - If $y \notin S$ or $y' \notin S$ or $b \notin \{0,1\}$, output $\perp$ to the appropriate party.
   - If there does not exist an x (resp., x') such that (x, y) (resp., (x', y')) is in T, output $\perp$ to the appropriate party.
   - Otherwise, compute $x'' = x + (-1)^b x'$, store x'' in T, and output the associated output y'' to the appropriate party.

Fig. 2. Functionality $\mathcal{F}_{\text{GG}}$.

of a function ensemble is to capture the intuitive notion of what it means to "instantiate" a random oracle.

Let $\ell_{\text{out}} : \mathbb{N} \to \mathbb{N}$ be a length function. An ℓ_{out}-*ensemble* is a sequence $\mathcal{F} = \{F_n\}_{n \in \mathbb{N}}$ of families of functions $F_n = \{f_s : \{0,1\}^* \to \{0,1\}^{\ell_{\text{out}}(n)}\}_{s \in \{0,1\}^n}$ such that the following condition holds:

1. There exists a polynomial-time algorithm Eval such that for every $s \in \{0,1\}^n$ and $x \in \{0,1\}^*$ it holds that $\mathsf{Eval}(s, x) = f_s(x)$.

Let $\ell_{\text{eval}}(n)$ be the length of the bitstring representation of Eval for function family F_n; we have that $\ell_{\text{eval}}(n) \leq p(n)$, where $p(\cdot)$ is a polynomial.

Let an $(\ell_{\text{out}}, \ell_{\text{eval}})$-ensemble be an ℓ_{out}-ensemble such that the bitstring representation of Eval is less than or equal to ℓ_{eval}. In what follows, we in general do not care what the output length of the function is, as long as it is polynomial in the security parameter. We denote this class of ensembles as (poly, ℓ)-ensembles; that is, the class of ℓ'-ensembles such that $\ell' < p(n)$, where $p(\cdot)$ is some polynomial, and the bitstring representation of Eval is less than or equal to ℓ.

Indistinguishability Obfuscation. All our constructions use *indistinguishability obfuscation* $(i\mathcal{O})$, defined as follows. Let $\{\mathcal{C}_\lambda\}$ be the class of circuits of size at most λ, where $\lambda \leq p(n)$ for some polynomial $p(\cdot)$. We utilize the notion of *family-indistinguishability obfuscators* [2,18], and we reproduce it here mostly verbatim.

A uniform PPT algorithm $i\mathcal{O}$ is a *family-indistinguishability obfuscator for a circuit class* $\{\mathcal{C}_\lambda\}$ if the following two conditions hold:

1. For all $\lambda \in \mathbb{N}$ and for all $C \in \mathcal{C}_\lambda$, it holds that

$$\Pr\left[\forall x, C'(x) = C(x) : C' \leftarrow i\mathcal{O}(1^\lambda, C)\right] = 1.$$

2. For all PPT adversaries Samp and $\mathcal{A}$, there exists a negligible function $\mathsf{negl}(\cdot)$ such that if

$$\Pr\left[\forall x, C_0(x) = C_1(x) : (C_0, C_1, \sigma) \leftarrow \mathsf{Samp}(1^\lambda)\right] > 1 - \mathsf{negl}(\lambda)$$

then

$$\left| \Pr[\mathcal{A}(\sigma, i\mathcal{O}(1^\lambda, C_0)) = 1 : (C_0, C_1, \sigma) \leftarrow \mathsf{Samp}(1^\lambda)] \right.$$
$$\left. - \Pr[\mathcal{A}(\sigma, i\mathcal{O}(1^\lambda, C_1)) = 1 : (C_0, C_1, \sigma) \leftarrow \mathsf{Samp}(1^\lambda)] \right| \leq \mathsf{negl}(\lambda).$$

3   Random Oracle Separation for Bit-Encryption

As our first result, we present a random oracle separation for the case of (public-key) bit-encryption. Note that most existing techniques for showing idealized model separations work by having the adversary send some specially-crafted message to an oracle; the oracle, given this message, leaks the secret key and thus the adversary can easily break security. However, in the case of bit-encryption, the only values an adversary can send are bits, and thus these approaches do not work in this setting.

Consider the security game $\mathsf{PubK}_{\mathcal{A},\Pi}$ between a challenger $\mathcal{C}$ and an adversary $\mathcal{A}$ for a public-key bit-encryption scheme $\Pi = (\mathsf{Gen}, \mathsf{Enc}, \mathsf{Dec})$:

1. $\mathcal{C}$ runs $(\mathsf{pk}, \mathsf{sk}) \leftarrow \mathsf{Gen}(1^n)$, chooses $b \leftarrow_\$ \{0,1\}$, computes $c \leftarrow \mathsf{Enc}_{\mathsf{pk}}(b)$, and sends (pk, c) to $\mathcal{A}$.
2. $\mathcal{A}$ outputs a bit b' and succeeds if $b = b'$.

Definition 3.1 (IND-CPA Security). *A public-key bit-encryption scheme Π is IND-CPA -secure if for all PPT adversaries $\mathcal{A}$ there exists a negligible function negl such that* $\Pr\left[\mathsf{PubK}_{\mathcal{A},\Pi}(n) = 1\right] \leq \frac{1}{2} + \mathsf{negl}(n)$.

Theorem 3.2. *Assume there exists an IND-CPA-secure public-key bit-encryption scheme and an indistinguishability obfuscator secure in the standard model. Let $p(\cdot)$ be a polynomial. Then for all $\ell < p(n)$, there exists a public-key bit-encryption scheme that is IND-CPA-secure in the random oracle model but insecure when the random oracle is instantiated using any (poly, ℓ)-ensemble.*

Proof. Our construction, at a high level, works as follows. Taking an existing bit-encryption scheme, we modify it by appending an obfuscated circuit to the public-key. The obfuscated circuit is built as follows. We choose ℓn random values x_i and compute $y_i \leftarrow H(x_i)$, where H is either a random oracle or a function ensemble, depending on whether we are operating in the random oracle or standard model. The circuit hardcodes the values x_i and y_i, along with the secret key to the original bit-encryption scheme. On input a description of a hash function h, the circuit outputs the secret key if and only if $y_i = h(x_i)$ for all i. In the random oracle model it is unlikely that such a hash function can be found to satisfy $y_i = h(x_i)$ for all i, whereas in the standard model this is easily satisfied (since h is public).

Constants: $x_1, \ldots, x_{\ell n}, y_1, \ldots, y_{\ell n}$, sk.
Input: a description $\langle h \rangle \in \{0,1\}^{\ell}$ of a function h.

1. For $i \in \{1, \ldots, \ell n\}$, compute $\widehat{y}_i := h(x_i)$.
2. If for $i \in \{1, \ldots, \ell n\}$ it holds that $\widehat{y}_i = y_i$, then output sk; otherwise, output $\bot$.

Fig. 3. Program C.

Constants: $x_1, \ldots, x_{\ell n}, y_1, \ldots, y_{\ell n}$, sk.
Input: a description $\langle h \rangle \in \{0,1\}^{\ell}$ of a function h.

1. Output $\bot$.

Fig. 4. Program C'.

Note that this approach is similar to that given by Maurer et al. [26], who provide an alternate proof of the separation result given by Canetti et al. [10]. The main difference is our use of indistinguishability obfuscation, which allows the adversary to break security in the standard model *without* needing to send messages to the challenger. Next, we present the proof details.

Let $i\mathcal{O}$ be an indistinguishability obfuscator, let $\Pi' = (\mathsf{Gen}', \mathsf{Enc}', \mathsf{Dec}')$ be an existing IND-CPA-secure public-key bit-encryption scheme, and let $\mathcal{O}$ be a random oracle. Fix some polynomial $p(\cdot)$ and value $\ell < p(n)$. The scheme $\Pi = (\mathsf{Gen}, \mathsf{Enc}, \mathsf{Dec})$ is constructed as follows. Note that all algorithms are provided oracle access to $\mathcal{O}$.

- Gen: On input 1^n, proceed as follows. For $i \in \{1, \ldots, \ell n\}$, choose $x_i \leftarrow_{\$} \{0,1\}^n$ and compute $y_i \leftarrow \mathcal{O}(x_i)$. Next, run $(\mathsf{pk}', \mathsf{sk}') \leftarrow \mathsf{Gen}'(1^n)$, and set $\mathsf{sk} := \mathsf{sk}'$. Then, create an obfuscation $i\mathcal{O}(C)$ of the program C as described in Fig. 3. Finally, let $\mathsf{pk} := (\mathsf{pk}', i\mathcal{O}(C))$ and output $(\mathsf{pk}, \mathsf{sk})$.
- Enc: On input pk and bit b, parse pk as $(\mathsf{pk}', i\mathcal{O}(C))$ and compute $c \leftarrow \mathsf{Enc}'_{\mathsf{pk}'}(b)$. Output c.
- Dec: On input private key $\mathsf{sk} = \mathsf{sk}'$ and ciphertext c, compute $m := \mathsf{Dec}'_{\mathsf{sk}'}(c)$. Output m.

Lemma 3.3. *Assume that Π' is an IND-CPA-secure public-key bit-encryption scheme and that $i\mathcal{O}$ is an indistinguishability obfuscator. Then, for any choice of $\ell < p(n)$ the construction Π is an IND-CPA-secure bit-encryption scheme in the random oracle model.*

Proof. Consider the following two hybrids.

Hybrid H_0: This is the IND-CPA game for scheme Π.

HybridH$_1$: This hybrid is the same as **H$_0$** except that now we change program C into program C' as in Fig. 4.

Claim. *If $i\mathcal{O}$ is an indistinguishability obfuscator in the standard model, then with high probability over the choices of the random oracle the two hybrids* **H$_0$** *and* **H$_1$** *are computationally indistinguishable.*

Proof. The proof is by a reduction to the security of the indistinguishability obfuscator. The proof relies on the fact that with high probability there is no "small representation" of a random oracle. That is, the probability that there exists a description $\langle h \rangle \in \{0, 1\}^\ell$ of a function h such that for $i \in \{1, \ldots, \ell n\}$ it holds that $y_i = h(x_i)$ is negligible. Thus, with high probability over the choices of the random oracle, programs C and C' are equivalent, and thus we can reduce security to that of indistinguishability obfuscation.

More formally, let $\mathsf{Func}_{\ell_{\mathrm{out}}(n)}$ be the class of all functions mapping $x_1, \ldots, x_{\ell n}$ to $\ell_{\mathrm{out}}(n)$-bit outputs; there are $2^{\ell n \ell_{\mathrm{out}}(n)}$ such functions. Also note that there exist $\leq 2^\ell$ functions capable of being represented by ℓ bits. Thus, the probability that a random function from $\mathsf{Func}_{\ell_{\mathrm{out}}(n)}$ can be represented in ℓ bits is $\leq 2^\ell / 2^{\ell n \ell_{\mathrm{out}}(n)} = \mathsf{negl}(n)$. Thus, with all but negligible probability over the choices of the random oracle, programs C and C' are equivalent. Therefore, if there is a difference in advantage, we can create an algorithm $\mathcal{B}$ that breaks the security of indistinguishability obfuscation.

Algorithm $\mathcal{B}$ runs as the challenger in the IND-CPA game. When it is time to create the obfuscated program it submits both programs $C_0 = C$ and $C_1 = C'$ to an indistinguishability obfuscation challenger. If the challenger chooses the first then we are in **H$_0$**; if it chooses the second then we are in **H$_1$**. Thus, any adversary with non-negligible advantage in the two hybrids leads to $\mathcal{B}$ as an attacker on the security of the indistinguishability obfuscator.   □

We now show that an adversary who can successfully attack hybrid **H$_1$** can be used to construct an adversary attacking the underlying IND-CPA scheme.

Claim. $\Pr\left[\mathsf{PubK}_{\mathcal{A},\mathbf{H_1}}(n) = 1\right] \leq \Pr\left[\mathsf{PubK}_{\mathcal{B},\Pi'}(n) = 1\right]$ *where $\mathcal{A}$ is the adversary in* **H$_1$** *and $\mathcal{B}$ is the IND-CPA adversary against the underlying encryption scheme Π'.*

Proof. The adversary $\mathcal{B}$ runs $\mathcal{A}$. When $\mathcal{B}$ receives pk', it generates $i\mathcal{O}(C')$ as in **H$_1$** and provides $\mathsf{pk} := (\mathsf{pk}', i\mathcal{O}(C'))$ to $\mathcal{A}$. When $\mathcal{B}$ receives a challenge ciphertext c, it forwards c to $\mathcal{A}$. Finally, $\mathcal{B}$ outputs the bit b' output by $\mathcal{A}$.

Clearly, if $\mathcal{A}$ can win the **H$_1$** game with probability ϵ then $\mathcal{B}$ can win the IND-CPA game with at least ϵ.   □

Together, these claims show $\Pr\left[\mathsf{PubK}_{\mathcal{A},\Pi}(n) = 1\right] \leq \Pr\left[\mathsf{PubK}_{\mathcal{B},\Pi'}(n) = 1\right]$, where $\mathcal{A}$ is the IND-CPA adversary against Π and $\mathcal{B}$ is the IND-CPA adversary against the underlying encryption scheme Π'. Since the underlying Π' is IND-CPA-secure, we have that $\Pr\left[\mathsf{PubK}_{\mathcal{B},\Pi'}(n) = 1\right] \leq \frac{1}{2} + \mathsf{negl}(n)$. Therefore we obtain $\Pr\left[\mathsf{PubK}_{\mathcal{A},\Pi}(n) = 1\right] \leq \frac{1}{2} + \mathsf{negl}(n)$, which completes the proof.   ∎

Lemma 3.4. *For all $\ell < p(n)$, there exists a public-key bit-encryption scheme secure in the random oracle model but insecure when implemented with any efficiently computable* (poly, ℓ)-*ensemble.*

Proof. Fix some $\ell < p(n)$. We modify the scheme Π described above to use (poly, ℓ)-ensemble $\mathcal{F}$ to implement the random oracle, thus obtaining the scheme $\widetilde{\Pi} = (\widetilde{\mathsf{Gen}}, \widetilde{\mathsf{Enc}}, \widetilde{\mathsf{Dec}})$:

- $\widetilde{\mathsf{Gen}}$: On input 1^n, choose $s \leftarrow_\$ \{0,1\}^n$, run (pk, sk) $\leftarrow_\$ \mathsf{Gen}^{f_s}(1^n)$, and output $((\mathsf{pk}, s), (\mathsf{sk}, s))$.
- $\widetilde{\mathsf{Enc}}$: Output $\mathsf{Enc}_{\mathsf{pk}}(b)$.
- $\widetilde{\mathsf{Dec}}$: Output $\mathsf{Dec}_{\mathsf{sk}}(c)$.

Now the seed s is part of the public key, and it is known to the adversary. Thus, the adversary can simply parse pk into $(\mathsf{pk}', i\mathcal{O}(C))$, and provide as input to $i\mathcal{O}(C)$ the description of Eval [2], thus learning sk.   ∎

4 Extensions

Our approach used in Sect. 3 can be applied to more than just bit-encryption. Here we show how to extend our result to provide separations for protocols satisfying most "natural" simulation- or game-based definitions. In Sect. 4.1, we show how to adapt our separation to work for a large class of protocols secure under simulation-based definitions. Likewise, in Sect. 4.2, we adapt our separation to work for a class of protocols secure under game-based definitions. Although the theorem statements below provide separations in the random oracle model, the same approach can be applied to other idealized models (e.g., the generic-group model).

4.1 Separations for Simulation-Based Definitions

Here we focus on the universal composability (UC) framework [9]; we believe the separation detailed below can be easily adapted to other simulation-based models. In what follows, we assume the reader is familiar with the UC framework.

We consider well-formed functionalities [12]. We call an ideal functionality f *trivial* if it can be realized by an "all revealing" protocol π as described in the following:

Definition 4.1. *Let f be an ideal functionality in the UC framework, and let π be a protocol where, upon initialization, all parties broadcast their initial randomness and inputs. Then f is* trivial *if for all environments $\mathcal{E}$ and for all adversaries $\mathcal{A}$, there exists a simulator S such that $\Pr[\mathrm{EXEC}_{f,S,\mathcal{E}} = \mathrm{EXEC}_{\pi,\mathcal{A},\mathcal{E}}] = 1$.*

We now prove the following.

---

[2] Recall that Eval is the algorithm such that $\mathsf{Eval}(s, x) = f_s(x)$ for all $s \in \{0,1\}^n$ and $x \in \{0,1\}^*$.

Theorem 4.2. *Consider a non-trivial ideal functionality f in the UC framework, and let π be a protocol which UC-realizes f in the $\mathcal{F}$-hybrid world. Then for all choices of $\ell \in \text{poly}(n)$, there exists some protocol π' which UC-realizes f in the $(\mathcal{F}, \mathcal{F}_{RO})$-hybrid world[3] but is not UC-realizable when instantiated with a (poly, ℓ)-ensemble.*

Proof. Fix some non-trivial ideal functionality f for some set of parties $\mathcal{P} = \{P_1, \ldots, P_m\}$, and let π be a t-round protocol which UC-realizes f. On protocol initialization, each party P_i is initialized with randomness r_i and given input x_i. Let $M_{i,j}^k$ denote the message sent from party P_i to party P_j in round k; without loss of generality, we assume that for all parties P_i and P_j and for all rounds $1 \leq k \leq t$, message $M_{i,j}^k$ exists[4].

Now fix some $\ell \in \text{poly}(n)$. We construct a protocol π' as follows. Protocol π' runs exactly as π except for the first round of the protocol. In this round, each party P_i proceeds as follows. For $j \in \{1, \ldots, \ell n\}$, P_i chooses $z_j \leftarrow_\$ \{0,1\}^n$ and computes $y_j \leftarrow \mathcal{O}(z_j)$. Then, based on input x_i, randomness r_i, as well as $\{z_j, y_j\}_j$, party P_i creates an obfuscation of the program C_i as defined in Fig. 5 and sends $i\mathcal{O}(C_i)$ over the standard channel, in addition to sending message $M_{i,j}^1$ as normal (i.e., this message may be sent using some hybrid functionality).

Constants: $z_1, \ldots, z_{\ell n}, y_1, \ldots, y_{\ell n}, r_i, x_i$.
Input: a description $\langle h \rangle \in \{0,1\}^\ell$ of a function h.

1. For $i \in \{1, \ldots, \ell n\}$, compute $\widehat{y}_i := h(z_i)$.
2. If for $i \in \{1, \ldots, \ell n\}$ it holds that $\widehat{y}_i = y_i$, then output r_i and x_i; otherwise, output $\perp$.

Fig. 5. Program C_i.

Lemma 4.3. *Assume that $i\mathcal{O}$ is an indistinguishability obfuscator. Then for any choice of $\ell \in \text{poly}(n)$ the construction π' UC-realizes f in the $(\mathcal{F}, \mathcal{F}_{RO})$-hybrid world.*

Proof (Sketch). This follows directly from the fact that with high probability there is no "small representation" of a random oracle, and the argument is very similar to that shown in Lemma 3.3. We thus only give the high-level idea below.

Let $\mathcal{A}'$ be an adversary attacking protocol π'; we construct a simulator $\mathcal{S}'$ as follows. The simulator $\mathcal{S}'$ simply runs the simulator $\mathcal{S}$ for protocol π and outputs whatever $\mathcal{S}$ outputs. Intuitively, the output of $\mathcal{S}'$ is indistinguishable from that of $\mathcal{A}'$ because π' is exactly the same as π except for the sending of $i\mathcal{O}(C_i)$ by

---

[3] $\mathcal{F}_{RO}$ is defined in Fig. 1.
[4] This is without loss of generality because $M_{i,j}^k$ can always be the empty message.

party P_i. However, with high probability over the choices of the random oracle (cf. Lemma 3.3), this obfuscation is identical to the obfuscation of the zero circuit, and thus $\mathcal{A}'$ gains no advantage from this additional information. $\qquad\square$

Lemma 4.4. *Assume that $i\mathcal{O}$ is an indistinguishability obfuscator. Then for any choice of $\ell \in \mathsf{poly}(n)$ the construction π' is completely insecure in the $\mathcal{F}$-hybrid world (i.e., when the random oracle is instantiated by any efficiently computable (poly, ℓ)-ensemble).*

Proof (Sketch). Let $\mathcal{A}$ be an adversary attacking π'. Adversary $\mathcal{A}$ reads the messages sent by all parties, and thus receives $i\mathcal{O}(C_i)$ from all parties P_i (recall that $i\mathcal{O}(C_i)$ is sent over the standard channel). Thus, $\mathcal{A}$ can extract P_i's randomness and input by providing the instantiation of the random oracle as input to $i\mathcal{O}(C_i)$, and can thus reproduce the internal state and inputs of all parties.

Now suppose towards a contradiction that π' UC-realizes f. This implies that there exists some simulator $\mathcal{S}$ which when interacting with f produces a similar transcript to that produced by $\mathcal{A}$; namely, $\mathcal{S}$ must be able to reproduce the internal state and inputs of all honest parties given only access to f. However, this implies that f is trivial, a contradiction. $\qquad\square$

This completes the proof. $\qquad\blacksquare$

Theorem 4.2 can be easily adapted to other idealized models besides the random oracle model, such as the generic group model, the random permutation model, etc. Thus, assuming $i\mathcal{O}$, we are able to show idealized model separations for most protocols secure in the UC framework.

4.2 Separations for Game-Based Definitions

We first give a general framework for what we mean by a "game-based" definition. We consider only single-stage games, where an adversary $\mathcal{A}$ interacts with some challenger $\mathcal{C}$. A *game-based definition* $\mathcal{G}$ is defined by a tuple $(\mathcal{C}, \mathcal{O}_1, \ldots, \mathcal{O}_k, \mathcal{O}_{k+1}, \ldots \mathcal{O}_m, k, f, T)$, where $\mathcal{C}$ denotes a PPT algorithm (i.e., the challenger's code), $\mathcal{O}_1, \ldots, \mathcal{O}_k$ denote oracles available to both $\mathcal{A}$ and $\mathcal{C}$, $\mathcal{O}_{k+1}, \ldots, \mathcal{O}_m$ denote oracles available to *only* $\mathcal{C}$, f denotes a predicate function, and T denotes a threshold function. Each oracle $\mathcal{O}_i$ outputs tuples of strings. The randomness of all the oracles is initialized by $\mathcal{C}$. A scheme/protocol Π *implements* $\mathcal{G}$ if it implements the oracles $\mathcal{O}_1, \ldots, \mathcal{O}_m$.

For definition $\mathcal{G}$ and scheme Π which implements $\mathcal{G}$, let $z \leftarrow \mathcal{A}^{\mathcal{O}_1, \ldots, \mathcal{O}_k}$ denote the output of the adversary after interacting with $\mathcal{C}$, where all the oracle calls are "routed through" $\mathcal{C}$. That is, each oracle available to $\mathcal{A}$ is first initialized by $\mathcal{C}$, where the initialization fixes both the oracle's randomness and (optionally) some of the oracle's inputs; all queries by $\mathcal{A}$ to oracle $\mathcal{O}_i$ go through this (fixed) oracle. For example, if $\mathcal{O}_i$ is an encryption oracle, $\mathcal{C}$ fixes both the initial randomness as well as the public key; any queries by $\mathcal{A}$ will thus be encrypted under the fixed public key using the fixed initial randomness. The predicate f takes as input the initial randomness of $\mathcal{C}$ and the output of $\mathcal{A}$, and outputs a bit.

We define $\mathcal{A}$'s success probability against scheme Π in $\mathcal{G}$ as

$$\mathsf{Succ}^{\mathcal{A}}[\mathcal{G}, \Pi] \overset{\text{def}}{=} \Pr_{r,r_1,\ldots,r_k} \left[z \leftarrow \mathcal{A}^{\mathcal{O}_1,\ldots,\mathcal{O}_k} : f(r,z) = 1 \right].$$

That is, $\mathcal{A}$'s success probability is the probability it can make the predicate f output 1, where the probability is over the choices of $\mathcal{C}$'s and the oracles' randomness. We say that a scheme Π *securely implements* $\mathcal{G}$, or is *secure*, if it holds that $\mathsf{Succ}^{\mathcal{A}}[\mathcal{G}, \Pi] \leq T(n) + \mathsf{negl}(n)$; otherwise the scheme is called *insecure*.

As an example, consider the definition for bit-encryption as presented in Sect. 3. This is captured in our framework as follows. We define three oracles, $\mathcal{O}_1 = \mathsf{Enc}$, $\mathcal{O}_2 = \mathsf{Gen}$, and $\mathcal{O}_3 = \mathsf{Dec}$, corresponding to the three algorithms required for bit-encryption. Since $\mathcal{A}$ only has access to the encryption oracle, we set $k = 1$. The challenger $\mathcal{C}$ is defined as in Sect. 3. The predicate $f(r,z)$ runs $\mathcal{C}(r)$ until $\mathcal{C}$ computes b, and outputs whether or not b equals z (where z is the value output by $\mathcal{A}$). The threshold function is set to $T(n) = 1/2$.

We call a game-based definition $\mathcal{G}$ *trivially secure* if for all secure schemes Π it holds that

$$\mathsf{Succ}^{\mathcal{A}}[\mathcal{G}, \Pi] = \Pr_{r,r_1,\ldots,r_k} \left[z \leftarrow \mathcal{A}^{\mathcal{O}_1,\ldots,\mathcal{O}_k}(r) : f(r,z) = 1 \right].$$

That is, a definition is trivially secure if a scheme satisfying the definition is as secure as the setting where the adversary is given all the initial randomness to $\mathcal{C}$. As an example, note that bit encryption is *not* trivially secure, as if $\mathcal{A}$ was given the randomness r of $\mathcal{C}$, it could simply run $\mathcal{C}$ internally and extract the secret key sk, thus succeeding with probability 1, whereas without r we have that $\mathcal{A}$ succeeds with probability $1/2 + \mathsf{negl}(n)$ (assuming some underlying hard problem, of course). However, consider a game where $\mathcal{C}$ chooses a random x, computes $y := H(x)$ for some cryptographic hash function H, and sends y to $\mathcal{A}$; security holds if $\mathcal{A}$ cannot find an $x' \neq x$ such that $H(x') = y$. In this setting, whether $\mathcal{A}$ has x or not does not necessarily help it break security, and thus this definition may be trivially secure for certain instantiations of H.

Note that we can easily integrate idealized models, such as the random oracle model, into this framework by including an additional oracle which implements the desired idealized functionality to both $\mathcal{A}$ and $\mathcal{C}$.

Now we want to show that for all game-based definitions $\mathcal{G}$, for all protocols Π which securely implement $\mathcal{G}$ in the random oracle model, and for all choices of $\ell \in \mathsf{poly}(n)$, there exists some protocol Π' secure in the random oracle model but insecure in the standard model when instantiated with a (poly, ℓ)-ensemble.

However, it turns out that the notion of a game-based definition defined above is too strong to prove this result. This is because we place no restrictions on the challenger $\mathcal{C}$. As an example, consider a modified bit-encryption game where the challenger acts exactly as before, except it refuses to send any bits to $\mathcal{A}$ that "look like" an obfuscated circuit. This simple modification to the challenger prevents our attack from working for particular implementations of $i\mathcal{O}$, e.g., ones that prepend each obfuscated circuit with the string "this is an obfuscated circuit".

We thus consider a restriction on the above framework, and in particular, a restriction on the actions of $\mathcal{C}$. Consider a challenger which, on input randomness r, runs with oracle access to $\mathcal{O}_1, \ldots, \mathcal{O}_m$ as before. When $\mathcal{C}$ queries an oracle, it receives back a tuple $(s_1, \ldots)$. We call a challenger *weakened* if all messages sent to $\mathcal{A}$ are values within the tuples output by the oracle queries. For example, if $\mathcal{C}$ queries an oracle which implements key generation for some public-key cryptosystem, it receives back the tuple $(\mathsf{pk}, \mathsf{sk})$. If the challenger is weakened, it can send pk, sk, both or neither to $\mathcal{A}$, but it cannot send $f(\mathsf{pk})$ for some arbitrary function f, and likewise it cannot send some value x not output by an oracle. Note that most game-based definitions use this weakened challenger notion.

We call $\mathcal{G}$ a *weak game-based definition* if it is a game-based definition as defined above, except with the requirement that $\mathcal{C}$ be a weakened challenger. We are now ready to prove the following theorem.

Theorem 4.5. *Consider a non-trivially secure weak game-based definition $\mathcal{G}$, and let Π be a protocol which securely implements $\mathcal{G}$. Then for all choices of $\ell \in \mathsf{poly}(n)$, there exists some protocol Π' secure in the random oracle model but insecure when instantiated with a (poly, ℓ)-ensemble.*

Proof. Fix some non-trivially secure weak game-based definition $\mathcal{G}$, and let Π be a protocol which securely implements $\mathcal{G}$ (Π need not be in the random oracle model). Fix some $\ell \in \mathsf{poly}(n)$. We construct a protocol Π' as follows. Protocol Π' runs exactly as Π except for the first message sent from $\mathcal{C}$ to $\mathcal{A}$. Let M be this message. In protocol Π', $\mathcal{C}$ proceeds as follows. Let r be the initial randomness of $\mathcal{C}$. For $i \in \{1, \ldots, \ell n\}$, $\mathcal{C}$ chooses $x_i \leftarrow_{\$} \{0,1\}^n$ and computes $y_i \leftarrow \mathcal{O}(x_i)$. Then, $\mathcal{C}$ creates an obfuscation $i\mathcal{O}(C)$ of the program C defined in Fig. 6 and sends $\widehat{M}$ to $\mathcal{A}$, where $\widehat{M} = (M, i\mathcal{O}(C))$.

Constants: $x_1, \ldots, x_{\ell n}, y_1, \ldots, y_{\ell n}, r$.
Input: a description $\langle h \rangle \in \{0,1\}^{\ell}$ of a function h.

1. For $i \in \{1, \ldots, \ell n\}$, compute $\widehat{y}_i := h(x_i)$.
2. If for $i \in \{1, \ldots, \ell n\}$ it holds that $\widehat{y}_i = y_i$, then output r; otherwise, output $\perp$.

Fig. 6. Program C.

Lemma 4.6. *Assume that $i\mathcal{O}$ is an indistinguishability obfuscator. Then for any choice of $\ell \in \mathsf{poly}(n)$ the construction Π' securely implements $\mathcal{G}$ in the random oracle model.*

Proof (Sketch). This follows exactly as in Lemma 4.3.   □

Lemma 4.7. *Assume that $i\mathcal{O}$ is an indistinguishability obfuscator. Then for any choice of $\ell \in \mathsf{poly}(n)$ the construction Π' is insecure when the random oracle is instantiated by any efficiently computable (poly, ℓ)-ensemble.*

Proof (Sketch). We apply the same idea as in Lemma 4.4. Let $\mathcal{A}$ be the adversary. Upon receiving the first message from $\mathcal{C}$, $\mathcal{A}$ can extract $\mathcal{C}$'s initial randomness r and thus reproduce the internal state of $\mathcal{C}$. By our assumption that $\mathcal{G}$ is not trivially secure, Π' is thus insecure.   □

This completes the proof.   ∎

   Note that as in the simulation-based case, we can easily adapt Theorem 4.5 to other idealized models and thus achieve idealized model separations for most game-based protocols, assuming indistinguishability obfuscation.

5   Extensions to the Generic Group Model

To demonstrate how to adapt Theorems 4.2 and 4.5 to other idealized models, we provide here an adaptation to the generic group model. We first define the generic group model and how this model is instantiated using *encoding ensembles* [15] (which can be thought of as analogous to the *function ensembles* used for instantiating the random oracle model).

Generic Group Model. Let $\ell_{\mathsf{out}} : \mathbb{N} \to \mathbb{N}$ be a length function with $\ell_{\mathsf{out}}(n) \geq n$, and define the set $S = \{0,1\}^{\ell_{\mathsf{out}}(n)}$. Let p be an n-bit prime. The generic group model is defined by two oracles, $\mathcal{O}_{\mathsf{enc}}$ and $\mathcal{O}_{\mathsf{add}}$, available to all parties, where $\mathcal{O}_{\mathsf{enc}} : \mathbb{Z}_p \to S$ such that $\mathcal{O}_{\mathsf{enc}}(x) = \mathcal{O}_{\mathsf{enc}}(y)$ iff $x = y$ and $\mathcal{O}_{\mathsf{add}} : S \times S \times \mathbb{Z}_2 \to S$ such that $\mathcal{O}_{\mathsf{add}}(\mathcal{O}_{\mathsf{enc}}(x), \mathcal{O}_{\mathsf{enc}}(y), b) = \mathcal{O}_{\mathsf{enc}}(x + (-1)^b y)$.[5]

Encoding Ensembles. Let $\ell_{\mathsf{out}} : \mathbb{N} \to \mathbb{N}$ be a length function with $\ell_{\mathsf{out}}(n) \geq n$. An ℓ_{out}-*encoding-ensemble* is a sequence $\mathcal{F} = \{F_n\}_{n \in \mathbb{N}}$ of families of functions $F_n = \{f_s : \mathbb{Z}_p \to \{0,1\}^{\ell_{\mathsf{out}}(n)}\}_{s \in \{0,1\}^n}$ such that the following conditions hold:

1. There exists a polynomial-time algorithm Eval such that for every $s \in \{0,1\}^n$ and $x \in \mathbb{Z}_p$ it holds that $\mathsf{Eval}(s, x) = f_s(x)$.
2. There exists a polynomial-time algorithm Add such that $\mathsf{Add}(s, f_s(x), f_s(y), b) = f_s(x + (-1)^b y)$.

As in the function ensemble case, let $\ell_{\mathsf{eval}}(n)$ be the length of the bitstring representation of Eval. Let a (poly, ℓ)-encoding-ensemble be a class of ℓ'-encoding-ensembles such that $\ell' \in \mathsf{poly}(n)$ (with the restriction that $\ell' \geq n$) and the bitstring representation of Eval is $\leq \ell$.

   Let $\mathcal{F}_{\mathsf{GG}}$ denote the "natural" adaptation of the generic group model to the UC framework (see Fig. 2). We can now prove the following theorem.

---

[5] Note that we only need $\mathcal{O}_{\mathsf{enc}}$ to prove our separations results.

Theorem 5.1. *Consider a non-trivial ideal functionality f in the UC framework, and let π be a protocol which UC-realizes f in the $\mathcal{F}$-hybrid world. Then for all choices of $\ell \in \text{poly}(n)$, there exists some protocol π' which UC-realizes f in the $(\mathcal{F}, \mathcal{F}_{GG})$-hybrid world[6] but is not UC-realizable when instantiated with a (poly, ℓ)-encoding-ensemble.*

Proof. The proof structure follows exactly that shown in Theorem 4.2. The only difference is that instead of each party querying the random oracle when constructing the obfuscated circuit, they instead query $\mathcal{O}_{enc}$. The proof follows immediately from the fact that with high probability there is no "small representation" of $\mathcal{O}_{enc}$, whereas when $\mathcal{O}_{enc}$ is instantiated with a concrete function, the adversary can easily extract the hidden information to break security. ∎

The adaptation of Theorem 4.5 is similar, and thus we only present the theorem statement.

Theorem 5.2. *Consider a non-trivially secure weak game-based definition $\mathcal{G}$, and let Π be a protocol which securely implements $\mathcal{G}$. Then for all choices of $\ell \in \text{poly}(n)$, there exists some protocol Π' secure in the generic group model but insecure when instantiated with a (poly, ℓ)-encoding-ensemble.*

Acknowledgments. The authors would like to thank Brent Waters and Susan Hohenberger for helpful conversations during the course of this work.

References

1. Barak, B., Garg, S., Kalai, Y.T., Paneth, O., Sahai, A.: Protecting obfuscation against algebraic attacks. In: Nguyen, P.Q., Oswald, E. (eds.) EUROCRYPT 2014. LNCS, vol. 8441, pp. 221–238. Springer, Heidelberg (2014)
2. Barak, B., Goldreich, O., Impagliazzo, R., Rudich, S., Sahai, A., Vadhan, S.P., Yang, K.: On the (Im)possibility of obfuscating programs. J. ACM **59**(2), 6 (2012)
3. Bellare, M., Boldyreva, A., Palacio, A.: An uninstantiable random-oracle-model scheme for a hybrid-encryption problem. In: Cachin, C., Camenisch, J.L. (eds.) EUROCRYPT 2004. LNCS, vol. 3027, pp. 171–188. Springer, Heidelberg (2004)
4. Bellare, M., Hoang, V.T., Keelveedhi, S.: Instantiating random oracles via UCEs. In: Canetti, R., Garay, J.A. (eds.) CRYPTO 2013, Part II. LNCS, vol. 8043, pp. 398–415. Springer, Heidelberg (2013)
5. Bellare, M., Rogaway, P.: Random oracles are practical: a paradigm for designing efficient protocols. In: Ashby, V. (ed.) ACM CCS 1993, pp. 62–73. ACM Press (1993)
6. Bitansky, N., Canetti, R., Cohn, H., Goldwasser, S., Kalai, Y.T., Paneth, O., Rosen, A.: The impossibility of obfuscation with auxiliary input or a universal simulator. In: Garay, J.A., Gennaro, R. (eds.) CRYPTO 2014, Part II. LNCS, vol. 8617, pp. 71–89. Springer, Heidelberg (2014)
7. Brakerski, Z., Rothblum, G.N.: Virtual black-box obfuscation for all circuits via generic graded encoding. In: Lindell, Y. (ed.) TCC 2014. LNCS, vol. 8349, pp. 1–25. Springer, Heidelberg (2014)

---

[6] $\mathcal{F}_{GG}$ is defined in Fig. 2.

8. Brzuska, C., Farshim, P., Mittelbach, A.: Random-oracle uninstantiability from indistinguishability obfuscation. In: Dodis, Y., Nielsen, J.B. (eds.) TCC 2015, Part II. LNCS, vol. 9015, pp. 428–455. Springer, Heidelberg (2015)
9. Canetti, R.: Universally composable security: a new paradigm for cryptographic protocols. In: 42nd FOCS, pp. 136–145. IEEE Computer Society Press (2001)
10. Canetti, R., Goldreich, O., Halevi, S.: The random oracle methodology, revisited. J. ACM **51**(4), 557–594 (2004)
11. Canetti, R., Goldreich, O., Halevi, S.: On the random-oracle methodology as applied to length-restricted signature schemes. In: Naor, M. (ed.) TCC 2004. LNCS, vol. 2951, pp. 40–57. Springer, Heidelberg (2004)
12. Canetti, R., Lindell, Y., Ostrovsky, R., Sahai, A.: Universally composable two-party and multi-party secure computation. In: 34th STOC, pp. 494–503. ACM Press (2002)
13. Coron, J.-S., Naccache, D., Tibouchi, M.: Public key compression and modulus switching for fully homomorphic encryption over the integers. In: Pointcheval, D., Johansson, T. (eds.) EUROCRYPT 2012. LNCS, vol. 7237, pp. 446–464. Springer, Heidelberg (2012)
14. De Caro, A., Iovino, V., Jain, A., O'Neill, A., Paneth, O., Persiano, G.: On the achievability of simulation-based security for functional encryption. In: Canetti, R., Garay, J.A. (eds.) CRYPTO 2013, Part II. LNCS, vol. 8043, pp. 519–535. Springer, Heidelberg (2013)
15. Dent, A.W.: Adapting the weaknesses of the random oracle model to the generic group model. In: Zheng, Y. (ed.) ASIACRYPT 2002. LNCS, vol. 2501, pp. 100–109. Springer, Heidelberg (2002)
16. Dent, A.W.: Fundamental problems in provable security and cryptography. Philos. Trans. R. So. A **364**, 3215–3230 (2006)
17. Dodis, Y., Oliveira, R., Pietrzak, K.: On the generic insecurity of the full domain hash. In: Shoup, V. (ed.) CRYPTO 2005. LNCS, vol. 3621, pp. 449–466. Springer, Heidelberg (2005)
18. Garg, S., Gentry, C., Halevi, S., Raykova, M., Sahai, A., Waters, B.: Candidate indistinguishability obfuscation and functional encryption for all circuits. In: FOCS (2013)
19. Gentry, C.: A fully homomorphic encryption scheme. Ph.D. thesis, Stanford University (2008)
20. Goldwasser, S., Kalai, Y.T.: On the (in)security of the Fiat-Shamir paradigm. In: 44th FOCS, pp. 102–115. IEEE Computer Society Press (2003)
21. Hofheinz, D., Jager, T., Khurana, D., Sahai, A., Waters, B., Zhandry, M.: How to generate and use universal samplers. Cryptology ePrint Archive, Report 2014/507 (2014). http://eprint.iacr.org/2014/507
22. Hofheinz, D., Kamath, A., Koppula, V., Waters, B.: Adaptively secure constrained pseudorandom functions. Cryptology ePrint Archive, Report 2014/720 (2014). http://eprint.iacr.org/2014/720
23. Hofheinz, D., Müller-Quade, J.: Universally composable commitments using random oracles. In: Naor, M. (ed.) TCC 2004. LNCS, vol. 2951, pp. 58–76. Springer, Heidelberg (2004)
24. Kiltz, E., Pietrzak, K.: On the security of padding-based encryption schemes – or – why we cannot prove OAEP secure in the standard model. In: Joux, A. (ed.) EUROCRYPT 2009. LNCS, vol. 5479, pp. 389–406. Springer, Heidelberg (2009)

25. Leurent, G., Nguyen, P.Q.: How risky is the random-oracle model? In: Halevi, S. (ed.) CRYPTO 2009. LNCS, vol. 5677, pp. 445–464. Springer, Heidelberg (2009)
26. Maurer, U.M., Renner, R.S., Holenstein, C.: Indifferentiability, impossibility results on reductions, and applications to the random oracle methodology. In: Naor, M. (ed.) TCC 2004. LNCS, vol. 2951, pp. 21–39. Springer, Heidelberg (2004)
27. Nielsen, J.B.: Separating random oracle proofs from complexity theoretic proofs: the non-committing encryption case. In: Yung, M. (ed.) CRYPTO 2002. LNCS, vol. 2442, p. 111. Springer, Heidelberg (2002)
28. Shoup, V.: Lower bounds for discrete logarithms and related problems. In: Fumy, W. (ed.) EUROCRYPT 1997. LNCS, vol. 1233, pp. 256–266. Springer, Heidelberg (1997)

Author Index

Printed in the United States
By Bookmasters